Mac OS X UNLEASHED

John Ray
William C. Ray

201 West 103rd Street, Indianapolis, IN 46290

Mac OS X Unleashed

International Standard Book Number: 0672322293

Library of Congress Catalog Card Number: 2001089383

Printed in the United States of America

First Printing: November 2001

04 03 02 6 5

Trademarks

All terms mentioned in this book that are known to be trademarks or service marks have been appropriately capitalized. Sams cannot attest to the accuracy of this information. Use of a term in this book should not be regarded as affecting the validity of any trademark or service mark.

Warning and Disclaimer

Every effort has been made to make this book as complete and as accurate as possible, but no warranty or fitness is implied. The information provided is on an "as is" basis. The author(s) and the publisher shall have neither liability nor responsibility to any person or entity with respect to any loss or damages arising from the information contained in this book.

Executive Editor
Jeff Schultz

Acquisitions Editor
Jeff Schultz

Development Editor
Susan Hobbs

Managing Editor
Charlotte Clapp

Project Editor
Heather McNeill

Production Editor
Michael Henry

Indexer
Larry Sweazy

Proofreader
Bob LaRoche

Technical Editor
Anne Groves

Team Coordinator
Amy Patton

Interior Designer
Gary Adair

Cover Designer
Aren Howell

Page Layout
Ayanna Lacey

Contents at a Glance

Contents

Appendixes

About the Author

John Ray is an award-winning developer and security consultant with more than 16 years of programming and administration experience. He has worked on projects for the FCC, the National Regulatory Research Institute, The Ohio State University, Xerox, and the State of Florida, as well as serving as IT Director for Blue Cosmos Design, Inc. He has written or contributed to more than 10 titles currently in print, including *Special Edition Using TCP/IP*, *Sams Teach Yourself Dreamweaver UltraDev 4 in 21 Days*, and *Maximum Linux Security*. He bought his first Macintosh in 1984, and remains a strong proponent for the computer and operating system that revolutionized the industry.

Dr. William C. Ray is a mathematician turned computer scientist turned biophysicist who has gravitated to the field of bioinformatics for its interesting synergy of logic, hard science, and human-computer-interface issues. A long-time Macintosh and Unix enthusiast, he has owned Macs since 1985, and has worked with Unix since 1987. Prior to switching his professional focus to the biological sciences, Ray spent 5 years as a Unix programmer developing experimental interfaces to online database systems. Shortly after migrating to biophysics, he developed a Macintosh- and Unix-based computational biology/graphics laboratory and training center for The Ohio State University's College of Biological Sciences. At the facility, which he managed for five years, he introduced hundreds of students and faculty to Unix, and provided training and assistance in the development of productive computing skills on the paired Macintosh and Unix platforms.

Ray is currently a researcher at the Wexner Research Institute of Children's Hospital in Columbus, Ohio, where he is developing Web-based database tools and working to build a core computational research and training facility.

Dedication

Diane Burkholder—Thank you for your neverending support and encouragement. Troy Burkholder—Thank you for having such a wonderful wife. Robyn Ness—Thank you for putting up with me and my friends, including Diane Burkholder. My Parents—Thank you for raising me and providing the means for me to meet Diane Burkholder. Maddy the Dog—Thank you for befriending (and not biting) Diane Burkholder.

Acknowledgments

Many thanks to the wonderful people at and involved with Sams Publishing, including Susan Hobbs and Jeff Schultz. I'd also like to express my gratitude to Anne Groves and George Ruzek, the tech editor, for checking and double-checking each example and URL, and for making the text as accurate as possible. Without the help of these individuals, this book would not have been possible.

Tell Us What You Think!

As the reader of this book, *you* are our most important critic and commentator. We value your opinion and want to know what we're doing right, what we could do better, what areas you'd like to see us publish in, and any other words of wisdom you're willing to pass our way.

You can fax, e-mail, or write me directly to let me know what you did or didn't like about this book—as well as what we can do to make our books stronger.

Please note that I cannot help you with technical problems related to the topic of this book, and that due to the high volume of mail I receive, I might not be able to reply to every message.

When you write, please be sure to include this book's title and author as well as your name and phone or fax number. I will carefully review your comments and share them with the author and editors who worked on the book.

Fax: 317-581-4770

E-mail: `networking@samspublishing.com`

Mail: Mark Taber
Associate Publisher
Sams Publishing
201 West 103rd Street
Indianapolis, IN 46290 USA

Introduction

May 1998. After hours of driving, I arrived at the conference hall just in time to see the World Wide Developer conference keynote speech by Apple CEO Steve Jobs. We, the Apple faithful, had been waiting years for this event. Within minutes, we'd know when the new modern revision of Mac OS would ship. In late 1996, Apple Computer purchased NeXT Computer in order to gain access to its advanced OpenStep operating system. At the developer conference in 1997, we saw the first signs of life when OpenStep booted on Macintosh hardware for the first time. Now, in mid 1998, we fully expected Apple to proclaim that the operating system was rapidly approaching a release date. Instead, we heard an announcement that would shock everyone: The operating system codenamed Rhapsody was not destined for the Mac desktop. Instead, a new "similar" system named Mac OS X (pronounced "ten") would become the first *modern* consumer Mac operating system.

Panic

Within minutes of the keynote ending, developers and users alike were in a panicked state. To paraphrase a friend who had been working on porting software to Rhapsody: "I went back to my hotel room and became ill." Apple had, once again, changed its operating system direction and shattered the hopes of those who found themselves increasingly required to turn to other operating systems for speed and stability.

To fully comprehend the situation, you need to understand the corner that Apple had painted itself into. The Macintosh OS was being rapidly overtaken by competing operating systems and Apple's plans to modernize the existing Mac OS had failed.

- **1991**—Apple introduces System 7.0. System 7.0 provides the first seamless multitasking environment for the Macintosh. At the time, System 7.0 provides better stability and a far better user experience than Windows.
- **1994/1995**—Apple updates to System 7.5. System 7.5 provides new features above the earlier Mac OS release, but is still based on the same system as 7.0 and carries many of the same problems. After five years, the base OS is still very much the same. To address the need for better stability and speed, Apple announces Copland—the next generation operating system that would be numbered Mac OS 8.
- **1995**—Microsoft introduces Windows 95. Windows 95 provides many of the features of Mac OS, as well as pre-emptive multitasking and an early form of memory protection. Windows 95 proves to be more responsive and stable than Mac OS.

- **1995/1996**—Microsoft Windows NT takes hold. Featuring the Windows 95 interface, Microsoft's Windows NT operating system offers vastly increased speed and stability over Windows 95. Capable of running weeks without a crash, Windows NT is heralded as the next big thing.
- **1996**—Apple scraps Copland. A few short weeks after the 1996 developer conference, Apple announces that it is abandoning the Copland project. BeOS and OpenStep become candidates for replacement. In late 1996, Apple acquires NeXT.
- **1997**—Apple introduces System 8.0, and Microsoft introduces Windows 98. Using pieces of the Copland project, Apple builds Mac OS 8. Unfortunately, the basis of the operating system is rapidly approaching ancient in industry terms. To replace the dying Mac OS, Apple introduces Rhapsody at the 1997 Developer conference. Based on OpenStep, Rhapsody is proclaimed to be the future of Mac OS.

Now, a year later, with the failure of Copland firmly ingrained in the public's memory, it appeared that Apple was making the same mistake again by scrapping the Rhapsody project. In reality, the situation was not nearly as dismal as it seemed.

Resolution

As the dust cleared, it became obvious that the operating system known as Rhapsody *was*, in fact, the basis for Mac OS X. The difference was a key component known as Carbon. Apple had wisely chosen to delay the new operating system because there weren't any available applications. The reason for the lack of developer support was the new system architecture. Based on a completely object-oriented design, Rhapsody did not make it easy to port existing software to the new platform. Top developers such as Microsoft and Adobe made no promises to support Rhapsody, and, without developer support, the operating system would be stillborn. Carbon was to be the savior that would make the platform viable for both new and existing developers.

Based on the traditional Macintosh toolbox, Carbon allowed existing programs to be easily revised to run under the new OS as well as earlier versions. With Mac OS X, new programmers could use the rapid application design capabilities of the object-oriented foundation, and existing Mac developers could leverage their years of experience and existing code to bring software to the platform quickly. In addition, Apple announced that Mac OS X would even be able to run existing non-Carbonized software using a compatibility layer called Classic. Apple had finally covered all the bases for its new OS; now all we had to do was wait.

1999 saw the first developer release of Mac OS X. It bore little resemblance to the existing desktop Mac operating system. Instead, it seemed almost identical to the original

Rhapsody project, which had started shipping under the name Mac OS X Server. Several months later, it was followed up with the second developer release. This time, it was apparent that Apple was on to something. The Macintosh user experience had returned, and the excitement mounted.

This excitement reached fever pitch when, in January of 2000, Apple dropped another bombshell at the MacWorld expo tradeshow. The traditional Mac platinum look and feel was being replaced by a brand-new interface, known as Aqua. The Aqua interface demo featured windows with drop shadows, a dynamically shrinking and expanding program launcher, and some of the most impressive graphics ever seen on a computer monitor. Mac OS X continued to be developed, released (in both developer versions and a public beta), and refined for the next year. Finally, one year after demonstrating Aqua to the world, Steve Jobs announced the shipping date: Saturday, March 24, 2001. After almost five years of delays, false starts, and public unrest, Apple rolled out Mac OS X. The new operating system keeps the promises that Apple made during its introduction: It provides a revolutionary user experience, modern foundation, easy development, and backward compatibility.

The Release

By its very design, Mac OS X accomplishes two seemingly contradictory goals. It creates an extremely easy-to-use system that is crash-resistant and very resilient to user error. First-time users can sit down in front of the system, find the tools they need, and immediately start working. At the same time, advanced users have complete access to an underlying Unix subsystem, advanced networking capabilities, and a wealth of Open Source technologies including the Apache Web server, Perl, Sendmail, and many other powerful applications.

Much of the difficulty in creating a Mac OS X book was deciding which portions of the system should be detailed and which should be left to other, more in-depth resources. For example, for the first time ever, Apple is shipping a full, world-class development environment with every single copy of Mac OS X. Documenting this environment alone could take an entire volume. Additionally, literally thousands of command-line applications make up the BSD subsystem under the Aqua interface. We've worked to create a text that provides focused information on those topics most likely to provide the most benefit to the reader.

This book gives you the knowledge to use Mac OS X to its fullest—both from the perspective of a traditional Mac user and that of a seasoned Unix administrator. The book is arranged so that you can quickly find the topics that interest you without reading through tons of extraneous information. As your familiarity with the operating system grows, you'll find the tips and tricks you need to perform everything from interface customization to shell scripting and creating a fully capable Internet server system.

Mac OS X is likely to grow and update rapidly as Apple continues its efforts to optimize the OS X system performance and user experience. In fact, during the first week of writing this book, Apple released the first Mac OS X software update, which added new features and bug fixes to the operating system. Now, with 10.1 shipping (and filling the gaps in the initial release), the operating system has truly arrived. Rapid updates are likely to continue throughout the early years, building OS X into a truly powerful and unique environment.

As we work to create this resource, we will make every attempt to provide the latest and most accurate Mac OS X information available. By working closely with the Apple Developer Connection, we hope to provide the best possible reference.

Comments, suggestions, and questions, are always welcomed.

Sincerely,

John Ray (`jray@macosxunleashed.com`)

William Ray (`wray@macosxunleashed.com`)

Introduction to Mac OS X

PART I

IN THIS PART

CHAPTER 1

Mac OS X Component Architecture

In This Chapter

Mac OS X Overview

Mac OS X has had a very long and rocky birth process. In late 1996, Apple purchased NeXT Computer, Inc. with the thought of using its OpenStep operating system as the basis for the next-generation Mac OS. Developed initially under the moniker Rhapsody, this new operating system was little more than a graphic makeover for OpenStep. Mac OS users were left without support for existing software, and developers were left without support for existing code. Steve Jobs touted the component model of the new operating system as being the future of the Macintosh, but people weren't buying it.

Thankfully, Apple listened to the feedback of its users and developers, and slowly but surely molded the architecture of the new system to create a powerful *and* compatible system. With each successive conference or trade show, it seemed that modules of the architecture would be added, removed, or undergo a name change. Finally, at MacWorld Expo in January 2000, the final model, shown in Figure 1.1, was unveiled.

Each layer represents an independent component of the Mac OS X operating system. The lower levels (such as Darwin and QuickTime) provide the foundation of technologies on higher levels.

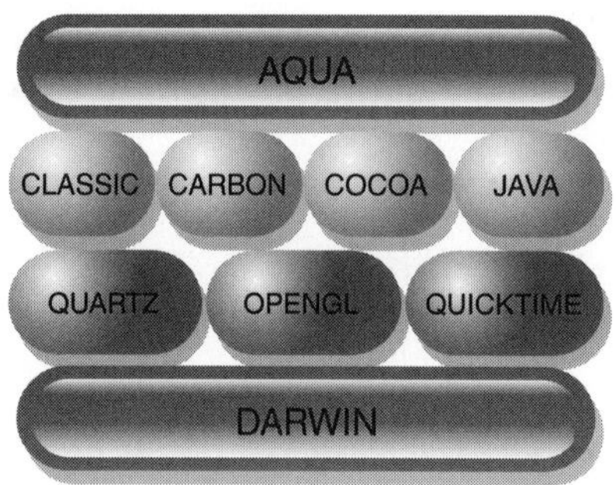

FIGURE 1.1
The Mac OS X architecture can be represented using a layered, component-based model.

The Mac OS X architecture comprises nine components (as represented in Figure 1.1):

- **Darwin**—The open source core operating system. Darwin includes a full BSD implementation (more on that later in the chapter).
- **QuickTime**—Apple's award-winning multimedia technologies are built in to the graphics foundation of Mac OS X.
- **OpenGL**—OpenGL is the SGI-created industry standard for 3D graphics. Although OpenGL is heavily challenged by Direct3D on the Microsoft platform, even Microsoft grudgingly supports the standard.

- **Quartz**—Apple's new 2D imaging framework and window server based on the PDF format. Quartz breaks new ground in handling the onscreen interface.
- **Classic**—The Classic environment (originally called Blue Box in the Rhapsody implementation) enables existing Mac OS applications to run under Mac OS X.
- **Carbon**—An API (application programming interface) to ease the transition to Mac OS X for traditional Mac programmers. This is based on the original Mac OS API, and can be used to create programs that run on Mac OS 8/9 as well as Mac OS X.
- **Cocoa**—Cocoa (originally called Yellow Box in Rhapsody) is the robust modern API that enables applications to be built from scratch in a fraction of the time it would take traditionally.
- **Java**—For the first time ever, the Mac OS is a player in the Java development and deployment arena. Java 2SE v1.3 is a first-class citizen and distributed with each copy of Mac OS X.
- **Aqua**—Aqua uses the Quartz imaging engine to create the most astounding user interface available on any platform. Applications written in Cocoa, Carbon, or Java can access the capabilities of the Aqua GUI.

Note

If you're interested in the Mac OS X architecture from a developer's viewpoint, you can download an overview from `http://developer.apple.com/macosx/architecture/`.

What Is an API?

An API, or *Application Programming Interface*, is a collection of procedures and functions that a programmer can use when writing software. APIs are usually specific to a particular task; for example, the QuickTime API can be employed to add multimedia to applications. The system-level API for traditional Macintosh programming is called the Macintosh Toolbox. In Mac OS X, the Carbon API has replaced the Toolbox.

Let's examine each of these technologies and how it will affect the total end-user experience. Much of what will be covered here will be unfamiliar territory even for the most seasoned Mac fanatic. I highly recommend that you read through these sections to gain an overview of the information that you'll encounter later in the book—it could be quite jarring if you don't know what to expect.

Darwin

In the standard OS X architecture model, Darwin is represented by a single layer. In reality, Darwin itself is composed of two layers: the Mach kernel and the BSD subsystem. This distinction is important to Mac users because this represents the first time that the consumer Mac OS has been kernel based.

Mach Kernel

A *kernel* is a small piece of controlling code that abstracts the hardware of a computer from the software that runs on it. The kernel serves as a gatekeeper for all other processes and programs. In a kernel-based system, only the kernel can directly access hardware (I/O systems, memory, and peripherals). By only allowing a single piece of software to perform critical activities, individual applications can no longer crash or corrupt the system. As any user of earlier Mac OS revisions knows, this is *not* how the Macintosh has worked in the past.

Darwin uses the Mach v.3 kernel, which is highly optimized and stress tested. By ensuring that the base kernel is as stable as possible, stability cascades up to the rest of the OS X architecture. If a program crashes in one of the layers above the Darwin core, the system remains operational. In the traditional Mac operating system, *any* program can directly access system memory if it so desires. Creating an application that crashes Mac OS 8 or 9 is trivial. This is not the case with Mac OS X.

In addition to stability, the Darwin kernel also provides some unexpected benefits to the rest of the operating system. By implementing new technologies at a kernel level, the benefits are made available to the rest of the system without the need for updating end-user applications. Here are just a few of the technologies that the kernel makes available to the rest of the Mac OS X operating system transparently:

- **Protected Memory**—In the traditional Mac OS, each application could request memory from the system and it was up to that application to not write to memory outside of the available space. The system, however, couldn't prevent this from happening. In Mac OS X, each application runs in its own memory space. It may not access the memory space of the system or of other running applications (unless running with advanced permissions). The use of protected memory also means that one can use the "force quit" option of the operating system without the need to reboot to regain system stability.

- **Virtual Memory**—The mach kernel handles all memory access and can dynamically allocate virtual memory as needed. This replaces the user-defined swap file of earlier Mac operating systems. Memory management is now handled automatically with no interaction needed.
- **Pre-emptive Multitasking**—Under Mac OS X, applications cannot lock up your computer by taking up all the computer's processing time. Long-time Mac users will appreciate this feature because we've all waited minutes for our systems to come back when Netscape hits a complex page. In Mac OS X, when even a single application is chugging away or has become unresponsive, you can switch to another program and keep on working.
- **Symmetric Multiprocessing**—SMP turns the Macintosh into a highly scalable computing platform. Several models of the Macintosh have included multiple processors, but only applications that have been explicitly programmed for the Mac OS multiprocessing API could take advantage of them. In Mac OS X, SMP is handled at the kernel level, allowing basic tasks at all levels of the operating system to take advantage of multiple processors.
- **Network Kernel Extensions**—The advanced networking model of the Darwin kernel allows protocol stacks to be loaded and unloaded dynamically, as well as real-time monitoring and modification of network traffic. This allows complex network applications such as firewalls to be built easily under Mac OS X.
- **Multiple File System Support**—The default file system under earlier Mac OS versions and Mac OS X is HFS+. Additional file systems can be added as modules to the kernel. After they're added, these file systems are available to all applications running on the system, regardless of whether the program understands the foreign file structure.

Although some of these features might seem complex and not something that you would want to deal with, the good news is that you don't have to. The Darwin kernel abstracts all the technical details from the end user. While developers can create new modules that operate at the kernel level, end users need do nothing more than sit back and reap the benefits.

There is one potential benefit of a kernel-based system that has not yet been exploited by Apple, but it might very well change the face of the Macintosh forever.

Since its inception, the Macintosh has been tied to the Motorola processor. First, the Motorola 68000-series CPU provided the computing power through the early 1990s. In 1994, Apple moved to the PowerPC platform, which is still in use today. The PowerPC platform, which uses a RISC architecture, offers some speed advantages over the traditional CISC (Pentium) design. Unfortunately, it also means that Apple is dependent on

IBM and Motorola (the PowerPC development partners) for the advancement of the Macintosh platform.

In the early 2000s, the megahertz wars started to make a dent in Apple's apparent speed advantage. Intel and AMD pushed their processors above 1GHz, while the PowerPC *finally* reached 733MHz in early 2001. Although it's faster for some tasks, the PowerPC cannot keep up with AMD's latest offerings overall.

All of this might soon change if Apple decides to exploit the kernel-based nature of its operating system by porting it to other processing platforms. The Darwin kernel has already been ported to the Intel platform. With minor work, it's very possible that Mac OS X could be deployed on Intel or AMD-based systems. In fact, up until the very final release of Mac OS X Server, the Rhapsody Developer releases also ran on the Intel platform! Even though there is no official word from Cupertino, many speculate that Apple is secretly maintaining an Intel-based version of Mac OS X somewhere in its development labs.

The BSD Subsystem

Above the Darwin kernel lays the BSD (Berkeley Software Distribution) subsystem. This portion of the Mac OS X operating system was designed never to be visible to end users unless they wanted to use it. We, the authors of *Mac OS X Unleashed*, hope that with the help of this book, you will be able to fully exploit the BSD portion of Mac OS X to accomplish tasks that were never before possible on the Mac platform.

So, what is BSD? The simple answer is that BSD is a collection of software that makes up a Unix-like operating system. Unfortunately, this leads to the question, what is Unix? This is a little bit more difficult to answer.

Unix is a multi-tasking multi-user operating system developed at Bell Labs during the 1970s. It was created to be a stable and powerful development platform for programmers. Today, Unix is largely regarded as a highly cryptic operating system that sends today's coddled point-and-click Windows NT administrators running in fear of actually having to think. Unix is composed of hundreds of different programs that work together to provide access to files and other standard operating system functions.

There are two primary distributions of Unix. The first is the Berkeley Software Distribution (BSD), which (obviously) was developed at Berkeley. The second distribution is System V, which was developed as a commercial Unix by AT&T. Although many of the functional differences are minor, the philosophies behind the two distributions are much different. BSD is preferred by academic institutions and hobbyists, whereas System V is used in commercial Unix distributions.

Many people have asked why Apple didn't choose to base its new OS on the very popular Linux operating system. What those people fail to understand is that Linux is actually a kernel, not a complete operating system. The Linux kernel, although interesting, is extremely unstable in terms of development. Linux users grow accustomed to updating their systems several times a year. This is fine for power users, but it isn't appropriate for production environments or home users. The Mach kernel is time-tested and provides a stable operating environment.

Linux users, however, will find themselves at home on Mac OS X, because the software that runs on top of the kernel is largely the same as popular Linux distributions. The same programs and scripts that run on Linux can be easily configured to operate on Mac OS X.

Under BSD, tasks such as listing the files in a directory (folder) work a bit differently than in the standard Mac OS. Let's take a look at a few examples of exactly what the BSD subsystem looks like. This marks the first time that the Mac OS has had a true command line, so brace yourself!

> **Note**
>
> Some Mac users might argue that AppleScript forms the basis of a command line in Mac OS X. AppleScript, however, runs at a much higher level than the BSD subsystem in X. The command line in OS X can control all aspects of the base operating system. AppleScript, on the other hand, was added well after the Mac OS reached maturity and can control only portions of the system that have been explicitly built to support it.

First, let's take a look at the actions needed to view a directory listing of files. Under traditional Mac operating systems, you simply double-click a folder, switch to List view, and look at your files, as seen in Figure 1.2.

Under the BSD subsystem, you can use the `ls` command to generate a file listing. For example, the following is a list of the top level of a Mac OS X hard drive:

```
[localhost:/] jray% ls -al
ls: Music: Permission denied
total 18216
drwxr-xr-x  36 root  admin     1180 Apr  1 10:52 .
drwxr-xr-x  36 root  admin     1180 Apr  1 10:52 ..
-rw-rw-rw-   1 root  admin     8220 Mar 31 16:28 .DS_Store
d-wx-wx-wx   3 root  admin      264 Mar 30 18:45 .Trashes
-r--r--r--   1 root  wheel      142 Feb 25 03:05 .hidden
dr--r--r--   2 root  wheel       96 Apr  1 10:51 .vol
```

```
-rwxrwxrwx   1 root  wheel    688128 Mar 31 10:16 AppleShare PDS
drwxrwxr-x  26 root  admin       840 Mar 30 18:45 Applications
drwxrwxrwx  12 root  wheel       364 Mar 27 22:34 Applications (Mac OS 9)
-rw-r--r--   1 root  admin    688128 Mar 31 00:09 Desktop DB
-rw-r--r--   1 root  admin   3170274 Mar 31 14:50 Desktop DF
drwxrwxrwx   9 root  staff       264 Mar 30 18:30 Desktop Folder
drwxrwxr-x  13 root  admin       398 Mar 10 00:05 Developer
-rw-r--r--   1 jray  admin         0 Mar 26 22:55 Icon?
drwxrwxr-x  21 root  admin       670 Mar 24 00:35 Library
drwxrwxrwx  19 root  wheel       602 Mar 20 23:36 Mac OS 9
drwxr-xr-x   7 root  wheel       264 Mar 24 00:35 Network
drwxr-xr-x   3 root  wheel        58 Mar 23 10:02 System
drwxrwxrwx   3 root  wheel       264 Mar 31 15:06 Temporary Items
drwxrwxrwx   4 root  wheel       264 Mar  9 21:03 TheVolumeSettingsFolder
drwxrwxrwx   5 root  wheel       264 Mar 31 10:16 Trash
drwxr-xr-x   5 root  wheel       126 Mar 26 20:35 Users
drwxrwxrwt   2 root  wheel       264 Mar 31 15:49 Volumes
drwxr-xr-x  33 root  wheel      1078 Mar  1 21:03 bin
lrwxr-xr-x   1 root  admin        13 Apr  1 10:52 cores -> private/cores
dr-xr-xr-x   2 root  wheel       512 Apr  1 10:51 dev
lrwxr-xr-x   1 root  admin        11 Apr  1 10:52 etc -> private/etc
lrwxr-xr-x   1 root  admin         9 Apr  1 10:52 mach -> /mach.sym
-r--r--r--   1 root  admin    652056 Apr  1 10:52 mach.sym
-rw-r--r--   1 root  wheel   4039448 Mar  1 09:58 mach_kernel
drwxr-xr-x   7 root  wheel       264 Apr  1 10:52 private
drwxr-xr-x  56 root  wheel      1860 Mar  1 21:01 sbin
lrwxr-xr-x   1 root  admin        11 Apr  1 10:52 tmp -> private/tmp
drwxr-xr-x  11 root  wheel       330 Mar 26 14:31 usr
lrwxr-xr-x   1 root  admin        11 Apr  1 10:52 var -> private/var
```

FIGURE 1.2
Viewing a file list in Mac OS is as easy as double-clicking a folder icon.

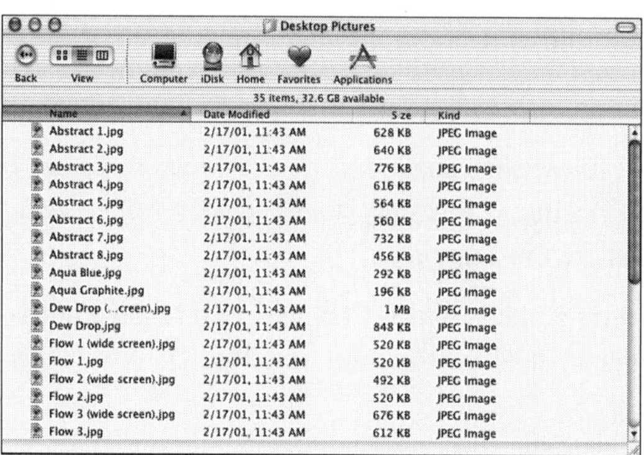

Instead of a graphical representation of the files, their sizes, and their modification dates, information is presented in a text format. In this particular example, a variety of files and directories are foreign to the Macintosh community: Desktop DB, mach.kernel, usr, var, etc, and so on. These elements are hidden from the Mac OS X end user, and do not need to be modified unless you are interested in tweaking the system from the BSD level. Information for performing file listings and other common tasks will be introduced in Chapter 12, "Introducing BSD."

Caution

Unlike previous versions of the Mac OS, Mac OS X does not store all the operating system–critical files in a single system folder. Although (as seen in the listing) there is a System folder that does contain important portions of the operating system, it does not contain the BSD subsystem. The BSD portion of the operating system is hidden in the private, sbin, var, usr, tmp, bin, and dev directories. Although they are not normally visible, if the names or locations of these directories are changed, Mac OS X is likely to become inoperable.

Let's take a look at another common task on Mac OS—viewing the applications that are currently running on the system. Under versions of Mac OS earlier than X, the running programs are shown in the Application Switcher menu or tear-off palette, displayed in Figure 1.3.

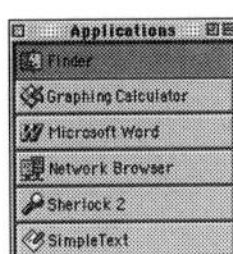

FIGURE 1.3
Mac users are used to seeing lists of running tasks represented graphically within the Application Switcher.

In Mac OS X, the active applications are moved from the task manager menu/palette to the Dock, which offers another visual representation of current processes. To view the active processes under the BSD subsystem, however, one would use `ps` to list the active processes. For example, I can view all the processes on my Mac OS X computer by typing `ps axg` at a command-line prompt:

```
[localhost:~] jray% ps axg
  PID  TT  STAT      TIME COMMAND
    1  ??  SLs    0:00.03 /sbin/init
    2  ??  SL     0:01.10 /sbin/mach_init
   38  ??  Ss     0:01.58 kextd
   56  ??  Ss     0:04.14 /System/Library/Frameworks/ApplicationServices.framew
   58  ??  Ss     1:43.61 /System/Library/CoreServices/WindowServer
   60  ??  Ss     0:01.96 update
   63  ??  Ss     0:00.00 dynamic_pager -H 40000000 -L 160000000 -S 80000000 -F
   85  ??  Ss     0:00.41 autodiskmount -v -a
```

```
104  ??  Ss     0:01.39 configd
113  ??  Ss     0:00.03 ipconfigd
149  ??  Ss     0:00.14 syslogd
160  ??  S<s    0:00.67 /usr/local/sharity/sbin/sharityd -f /usr/local/sharit
188  ??  Ss     0:00.02 portmap
191  ??  Ss     0:00.04 nibindd
192  ??  S      0:00.22 netinfod local (master)
199  ??  Ss     0:01.15 lookupd
208  ??  S<s    0:01.33 ntpd -f /var/run/ntp.drift -p /var/run/ntpd.pid
213  ??  Ss     0:00.02 DesktopDB
218  ??  Ss     0:00.00 inetd
228  ??  S      0:00.00 nfsiod -n 4
229  ??  S      0:00.00 nfsiod -n 4
230  ??  S      0:00.00 nfsiod -n 4
231  ??  S      0:00.00 nfsiod -n 4
240  ??  Ss     0:00.00 automount -m /Network/Servers -fstab
252  ??  Ss     0:00.29 /System/Library/CoreServices/SecurityServer
276  ??  Ss     0:00.49 /usr/sbin/sshd
279  ??  Ss     0:00.01 cron
282  ??  Ss     0:06.68 /System/Library/CoreServices/loginwindow.app/loginwin
285  ??  S      0:02.67 /System/Library/CoreServices/pbs -psn_0_262145
286  ??  S      0:03.51 /System/Library/CoreServices/Finder.app/Contents/MacO
287  ??  S      0:05.09 /System/Library/CoreServices/Dock.app/Contents/MacOS/
288  ??  S      0:50.01 /Applications/Mail.app/Contents/MacOS/Mail -psn_0_655
289  ??  S      0:04.33 /System/Library/CoreServices/DocklingServer.app/Conte
290  ??  S      0:23.27 /Applications/Network Stuff/Fire.app/Contents/MacOS/F
291  ??  Ss     0:00.56 /System/Library/Services/AppleSpell.service/AppleSpel
292  ??  S      5:14.81 /Applications/Network Stuff/OmniWeb.app/Contents/MacO
308  ??  S      0:09.61 /Applications/Utilities/Terminal.app/Contents/MacOS/T
334  ??  S      0:04.08 /Applications/System Preferences.app/Contents/MacOS/S
335  ??  Ss     0:00.65 /System/Library/PrivateFrameworks/Admin.framework/Res
381  ??  Ss     9:40.62 /System/Library/Frameworks/ScreenSaver.framework/Vers
386  ??  S      0:00.05 /usr/sbin/sshd
309  p1  Ss+    0:00.25 -tcsh (tcsh)
```

A close inspection of the process listing shows a few understandable lines that contain Mail.app (the Mac OS X e-mail application), Terminal.app (the application used to access the command line), and a few other goodies; largely, it is filled with seemingly meaningless entries.

These processes, such as nibindd and lookupd, are integral parts of the Mac OS X operating system. Unix and Mac OS X were designed so that multiple small programs would work together to provide robust services system-wide. When using the Mac OS X user interface, they do not appear in the Dock, but they are running nonetheless.

Next, let's take a look at the use of Sherlock to find files on the system. In Mac OS X and earlier, you can simply invoke the Sherlock application by pressing Command+F. To find a file, just type its name and press Enter. Figure 1.4 shows a Sherlock window with a search for filenames that contain the word Java.

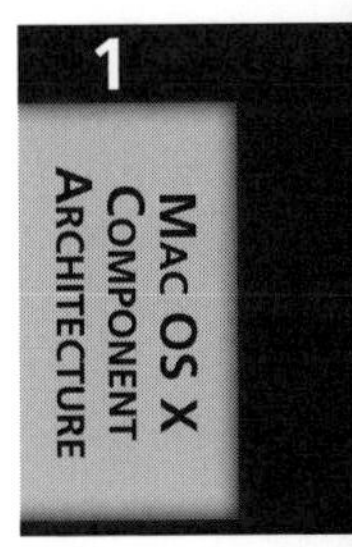

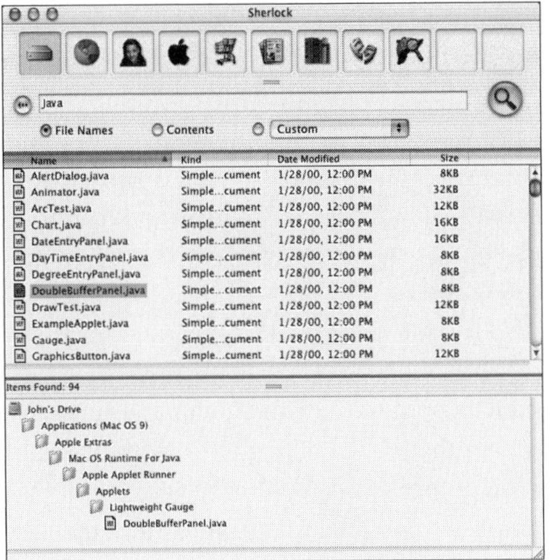

FIGURE 1.4
Sherlock provides a fast way to locate files, but the `locate` command is faster.

The BSD system has an equivalent feature that is actually *faster* at locating files than Sherlock. Appropriately enough, the command is `locate`.

```
[localhost:~] jray% locate Java
/Trash/Rescued items from Picasso 1/QTJava.zip
/usr/lib/java/libAdminJava.A.dylib
/usr/lib/java/libAdminJava.dylib
/usr/lib/java/libAppKitJava.B.dylib
/usr/lib/java/libAppKitJava.dylib
/usr/lib/java/libFoundationJava.B.dylib
/usr/lib/java/libFoundationJava.dylib
/usr/lib/java/libNIAccessJava.B.dylib
/usr/lib/java/libNIAccessJava.dylib
/usr/lib/java/libNIInterfaceJava.B.dylib
/usr/lib/java/libNIInterfaceJava.dylib
/usr/lib/java/libObjCJava.A.dylib
/usr/lib/java/libObjCJava.dylib
/usr/lib/java/libPreferencesJava.A.dylib
/usr/lib/java/libPreferencesJava.dylib
/usr/lib/java/libPureAppKitJava.B.dylib
/usr/lib/java/libPureAppKitJava.dylib
```

Within one or two seconds of issuing a `locate` command, all the files matching the supplied command-line string are printed. In the case of Java, more than 3,000 files were found that include Java in the pathname. The example shown here has been trimmed quite a bit; otherwise, the rest of the chapter would consist of nothing more than a very long file listing.

Note

If you've jumped ahead and started playing with Terminal.app, you might notice that `locate` does not work out of the box. The `locate` command uses a database to conduct its blindingly fast searches. To construct this database, you must first issue the command `/usr/libexec/locate.updatedb`. This takes a few minutes to execute, but needs to be run only when changes occur to the file system.

Finally, there is one very unique benefit to the Unix command-line environment: the ability to use two commands together that have nothing to do with one another. This is accomplished by redirecting the output of one command into the input of another. For example, in the previous example, I stated that there were more than 3,000 entries that matched *Java* in the pathname. No, I wasn't crazy enough to actually count all the files. Instead, I used the `wc` command to count the number of lines in the output of the `locate` command:

```
[localhost:~] jray% locate Java | wc -l
    3196
```

The `locate` command sends its output to `wc -l`, which counts the number of text lines that are handed off to it. The `|` (pipe) symbol is used to connect the output of `locate` to the input of `wc`.

Using similar techniques, you can create very complex utilities that can connect to remote hosts, download information, and process that information without ever writing a line of code yourself.

The command line provides a very powerful resource for advanced users and adds an entirely new dimension to the Macintosh operating system.

Note

Again, this section of the text is provided as an introduction to the capabilities and differences that come from the Darwin portion of the operating system. You will find extensive documentation of many of the available command-line utilities starting in Chapter 12.

Darwin's Open Source Innards

One of the most intriguing aspects of Darwin is that it is open source software. The Open Source software movement has been the driving force behind such powerhouses as the Apache Web server and the Linux distributions.

Open source software takes a different approach to the development of applications. Rather than confining the programming to an internal team of developers, open source projects can be accessed by *anyone*. Changes to the application are submitted back into the source code tree and integrated into the final product. This empowers people who are interested in improving the Mac OS to work on the Darwin source code and create a more powerful operating system for everyone.

The Open Source movement enables users to inspect the code that is running on their computer. This is in direct contrast to proprietary systems such as Microsoft Windows, where the user can only assume that the parent company is making the appropriate decisions on how the software should operate. The success of open source software relies on the people, not a particular company.

> **Note**
>
> In early 2001, Microsoft CEO Steve Ballmer compared Linux and the free software movement to communism. As more and more operating systems open up portions of their code to the public, it can only be assumed that Microsoft is starting to feel the heat from competition that it can't buy. For more information, check out `http://www.theregister.co.uk/content/1/12266.html`.

Apple is the first major computer manufacturer to embrace the Open Source movement by placing several key components of its software library under the Apple Public Source License. Both Darwin and the QuickTime Streaming Server are APSL projects and have been warmly received by the developer community. In fact, Darwin has been ported to the Intel platform and QuickTime Streaming Server is available for Linux and NT—courtesy of open source developers. Projects are underway to bring additional driver support to Darwin, which, in turn, will bring the same support to the commercial version of Mac OS X.

Note

Apple's APSL has not been without criticism from the open source community itself. Most open source software falls under the GNU General Public License (`http://www.gnu.org/copyleft/gpl.html`). Apple's APSL, however, exerts ownership of any code submitted to the project and does not require that Apple's own modifications fall under the license. At this time, this has not proven to be an issue with any of the projects, but it is still a cause for alarm among some open source proponents. Learn more about Apple's open source projects at `http://www.opensource.apple.com`.

Interestingly enough, Darwin is a complete operating system in and of itself. Interested users can download the Darwin installation and have a full working operating system without paying a dime for admission. Apple has not placed any of the other Mac OS X components under the APSL, so components such as Carbon, Cocoa, and Quartz remain proprietary software. Regardless, this represents a big step forward for the computer industry and is likely to be repeated industry-wide for many other popular applications.

Darwin is an extremely important component of the total Mac OS X operating system and will be the focus for several chapters of this book. In many respects, Mac OS X is a composite of two operating systems. The BSD system is a completely functional environment in its own right. Mac OS X, however, is known to its users as a lush graphical environment with a cutting-edge interface and advanced Mac-like operation. Together they combine to form a system that is as appropriate in an elementary school classroom as it is in a server room.

QuickTime

The second layer of the OS X foundation is the imaging layer—these are the tools that higher-level operating system applications (like those you use daily in Mac OS 8 or 9) can call on to create multimedia presentations or render three-dimensional images.

The first of these tools is the QuickTime API. For many people, QuickTime is nothing more than a brushed aluminum window that occasionally plays a movie or song.

QuickTime, however, is far more than a movie or MP3 player. It forms the heart of all multimedia operations in Mac OS X. Any application using QuickTime can transparently support reading or writing dozens of image file formats, including:

PICT—(the native Mac OS 7/8/9 picture format)

TIFF—Tagged Image File Format (Mac OS X native)

JPEG—Joint Photographic Experts Group

GIF—Graphics Interchange Format

BMP—Bitmap graphics format (Windows native)

PNG—Portable Network Graphics

Targa—Targa file format

In addition, QuickTime also supports audio and video standards such as

MPEG 1—Moving Picture Experts Group

AVI—Audio Video Interleave (Windows standard)

DV—Digital Video (the standard supported by most digital video cameras)

MP3—MPEG Layer 3 (a popular music compression and distribution format)

WAV—WAVE sound File (Windows native)

AIFF—Audio Interchange File Format (Mac OS X Native)

By employing QuickTime in applications such as the Finder, suddenly an entirely new capability is added to the system. Figure 1.5 shows the new OS X Finder's Info window. Unlike previous versions of the Mac OS, file information now includes a full preview of any media that QuickTime supports—from still images to music and video.

Tip

You can learn more about the supported QuickTime formats by visiting Apple's QuickTime spec page, located at `http://www.apple.com/quicktime/specifications.html`.

FIGURE 1.5
Showing the information of a file now includes a preview of QuickTime-supported content.

Although best known for its capability to handle movie and audio formats seamlessly in the operating system, QuickTime also includes features such as QuickTime VR. QuickTime VR allows the creation of three-dimensional panoramic models that can be linked together to create entire 3D worlds. If you're already using Mac OS X, you can view several sample QuickTime 5.0 VR movies at `http://www.apple.com/quicktime/preview/gallery/`.

From the perspective of the Internet service provider, QuickTime supplies a robust and scalable streaming media platform. Capable of adjusting to the user's available bandwidth, QuickTime streaming server can offer thousands of instant-access video streams from a single workstation. Because the QuickTime Streaming Server is distributed under Apple's open source license, it can be installed directly onto OS X, even though the software, by default, comes loaded only on Mac OS X Server.

OpenGL: Open Graphics Language

For many years, Apple stayed in its own little world and created the technology it needed for its operating system. Sadly, some pieces of technology were not adopted by the computing industry and Apple had to adapt or be left behind. An example of this is QuickTime 3D. QuickTime 3D was a fully cross-platform 3D API. Unfortunately, it was not widely used by developers, and its very existence hindered the development of 3D applications on the Macintosh.

As Apple continued to build and refine QuickTime 3D, the industry took another direction. Building on a standard developed by SGI, most developers were increasingly turning to OpenGL to create both games and productivity applications.

The best description of OpenGL is found in SGI's OpenGL FAQ `http://www.sgi.com/software/opengl/faq.html`, quoted here:

> The OpenGL API is the most widely adopted 3D graphics API in the industry, bringing thousands of applications to a wide variety of computer platforms. The API is not tied to any one operating system and reflects the thinking and talents of software developers from diverse graphics backgrounds. As a highly versatile 2D and 3D graphics API, the OpenGL API enables developers of software for PC, workstation, and supercomputing hardware to create high-performance, visually compelling graphics software applications. The OpenGL API is a rendering-only, vendor-neutral API providing 2D and 3D graphics functions, including modeling, transformations, color, lighting, and smooth shading, as well as advanced features such as texture mapping, NURBS, fog, alpha blending, and motion blur. The OpenGL API works in both immediate and retained (display list) graphics modes.
>
> The OpenGL API is window-system and operating-system independent. The OpenGL API has been integrated with Microsoft Windows and with the X Window

> System under Unix. Also, the OpenGL API is network-transparent. A defined common extension to the X Window System allows an OpenGL client on one vendor's platform to run across a network to another vendor's OpenGL server. The OpenGL functions described on the data-sheet are available in every OpenGL implementation to make applications written with OpenGL easily portable between platforms. All licensed OpenGL implementations are required to pass the conformance tests and come from a single specification and language-binding document.

Although the FAQ mentions only Windows and X Window System directly, it is also available (obviously) on Mac OS X and Mac OS 8 and 9. OpenGL has been available on the Macintosh platform only since the late 1990s, but already the Mac is seeing a surge in the production of game software. Game creators such as id Software, which refused to create Mac OS 8/9 games inhouse, are returning to develop for Mac OS X. In early 2001, Apple became the envy of the gaming community when id Software demonstrated an early version of the new DOOM game, running on the nVidia GeForce 3 card, which was announced as being available on the Macintosh platform before the Windows counterpart. Mac OS X 10.1 is fully optimized to take advantage of the GeForce 3—bringing high-end workstation 3D capabilities to a stable and robust platform.

Quartz

The final piece of Apple's imaging framework is Quartz. Announced only a year before Mac OS X's final release (a year is not a long time in the development of an operating system), Quartz provides a graphics model unlike anything seen before—with the possible exception of the NeXT computer.

In all previous versions of the Mac operating system, the graphics toolbox was called QuickDraw. QuickDraw was composed of a large number of routines for drawing and manipulating graphics primitives. Over the years, QuickDraw expanded to include new technologies such as color, but for the most part, it stayed the same. Windows computers quickly caught up with the Macintosh and offered programmers features similar to the QuickDraw toolbox. When Apple created Mac OS X, it decided to go all the way and create an entirely new imaging model that was far more advanced than the competition.

The original NeXTSTEP (and later the OpenStep) operating system was based on Display PostScript. PostScript is a page description language from Adobe used to create resolution-independent output (usually on printers). NeXTSTEP extended that technology to the operating system's display API. For the first time ever, the user could *truly* get a WYSIWYG display because both the output printer and the display device were using the same language to generate their images. Additionally, NeXTSTEP offered the capability to work with remote displays; that is, to display the output of a program on a computer other than that which was running the software.

The first release of Mac OS X Server used the same Display PostScript standard found in OpenStep and NeXTSTEP. Licensing issues and the availability of more modern standards meant that a change needed to take place before the consumer version of OS X appeared. Instead of PostScript, Apple based its new Quartz 2D imaging model on another Adobe standard: PDF, the Portable Document Format, which combines PostScript with several additional features.

Quartz offers the capability to create dramatic effects within applications with only a minimal amount of work. For example, it automatically handles tasks such as

- Anti-aliasing graphics and text
- Image scaling and rotation
- Image compositing with translucency
- Buffered windows

These might seem like operations reserved for graphics applications, but in fact they are available across the entire Mac OS X system. Figure 1.6 shows the Mac OS X Terminal window on top of the iTunes application. As iTunes creates its dynamic visualizations, they are visible *through* the partially translucent Terminal window.

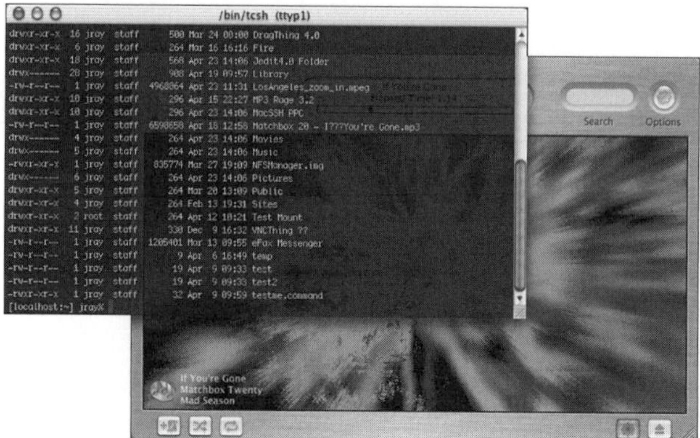

FIGURE 1.6
Quartz's advanced features allow real-time compositing of graphics.

What is truly remarkable is that the terminal remains fully responsive and usable. Quartz handles the compositing of the two windows without the need for either of the applications to know anything about one another. Although it is not responsible for the look and feel of the system, Quartz is the driving force behind the incredible effects that make up the Mac OS X interface. Speaking personally, I'd be surprised to find a Mac fan out there who did not brush away a tear when Steve Jobs demonstrated the Dock and Genie effects for the first time. Quartz is the engine that makes it all possible.

Classic

The next step in the OS X layered model is the APIs that can be used to create applications. Classic, although lumped into this group, is truly an amazing piece of engineering. When Apple released Mac OS X, the company knew that it would be several months before native applications started to appear. Many developers, burned in the past, wanted to see a real shipping product before they committed to porting their applications to Mac OS X. So, how could Apple ship an OS that didn't have any native applications? By creating an environment that would allow any existing Mac OS application to run transparently under Mac OS X.

What makes this truly astounding is that in no way is Mac OS X's foundation even remotely similar to the traditional Mac operating system. Luckily, Apple has a bit of experience with similar situations. In 1994, when Apple made the transition to the PowerPC processor, it knew that none of the existing software could run on the system—including portions of the operating system itself! To get around this, Apple built a dynamic recompiling emulator that, on the fly, would turn existing Motorola 68000-series code into native PowerPC code. It worked flawlessly. When faced with a similar problem in Mac OS X, Apple worked another miracle and created a transparent environment capable of running early Mac OS software.

When Mac OS X Server first shipped in 1998, it included the Mac OS Blue Box. This compatibility environment took over the Macintosh's screen and literally booted a copy of Mac OS 8 within a process of Mac OS X Server. The Blue Box required the user to be in either the server or classic OS environments at any given time—they did not share the same screen space. Although it was fine for occasionally using a piece of software, this arrangement would never fly with Mac enthusiasts. Maintaining two desktops and constantly jumping between environments was far from seamless, and often very confusing.

During the two and half years between the release of Mac OS X Server and Mac OS X, Apple refined the Blue Box, turning it into a Transparent Blue Box, and finally renamed it Classic. Like Blue Box, Classic requires that the system boot a full working version of Mac OS 9.2. After the system boots, what happens next is almost magic.

Upon starting, the Classic application vanishes and the system returns to an idle state. From that point on (until the user logs out), existing applications may be started and run as they would on a pre-X system. Windows from Classic applications intermingle with OS X–native windows, and the OS X Dock updates appropriately with the loaded Classic application.

Aside from a few cosmetic differences, the user cannot tell that Mac OS X is running a complete copy of another operating system just to run his legacy application. In addition to the close integration, applications in Classic also gain access to the OS X I/O system and virtual memory. In many cases, this results in increased application speed and stability. Apple has done such an amazing job of integrating the environments that software that uses video acceleration (such as games) continues to run as normal.

Unfortunately, not all of OS X's advantages are passed on to the Classic environment. Even though many USB/FireWire devices are supported under Classic, there is a large amount of hardware that simply will not work without booting directly into Mac OS 9.2. Additionally, the added stability and performance of features such as protected memory and symmetric multiprocessing are not available in Classic. If a Classic application crashes, it might take down the entire Classic subsystem. Luckily, the rest of Mac OS X will be unaffected, and Classic can easily be restarted.

Although it's only my opinion, there is little doubt in my mind that Apple sees Classic as a necessary evil, but an evil that will eventually go away. After all major applications are ported to native OS X code, Classic will have little to no purpose on the Mac platform. At the present time, it is very much the limiting factor in moving Mac OS X to alternative hardware platforms.

Note

Most applications run fine in the Classic environment, but you might want to check Apple's compatibility list first. You can find it here: `http://www.apple.com/macosx/applications/`.

Carbon

Steve Jobs announced the addition of Carbon to the list of OS X technologies by stating that "all life is based on Carbon." As I've mentioned elsewhere in this chapter, Mac OS X was originally planned to be nothing more than a made-over version of the OpenStep operating system. When developers refused to bite at the new programming interface, it became obvious that there needed to be an easier transition for existing Mac developers.

Carbon is a rewriting of the existing Macintosh toolbox to take advantage of the new technologies in Mac OS X. It also removes routines that were rarely used and incompatible with an advanced operating system environment (such as direct access to system memory).

When an application is written in Carbon, it can run on both Mac OS X and on Mac OS 8/9 (with a free piece of software called CarbonLib installed). With a minimum amount of effort, a developer can take a piece of software that was written for early versions of Mac OS, update it to use Carbon, and end up with an application that runs natively in both OS X and Mac OS 8/9.

Figure 1.7 shows a popular development environment called RealBasic running on System 9.2. The same application is shown in Figure 1.8 under Mac OS X. Aside from the interface differences, they function identically and run from the same binary file.

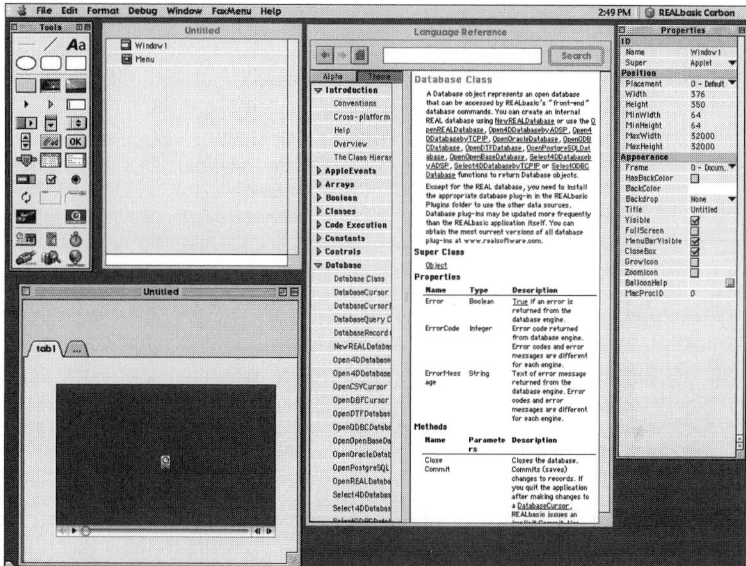

FIGURE 1.7
This is RealBasic, running on Mac OS 9.2…

Note

If you're interested in programming basic GUI applications for Mac OS X, you might want to look into RealBasic. Using a straightforward syntax, RealBasic can create standalone applications that, using CarbonLib, can run on Mac OS 8/9 and Mac OS X.

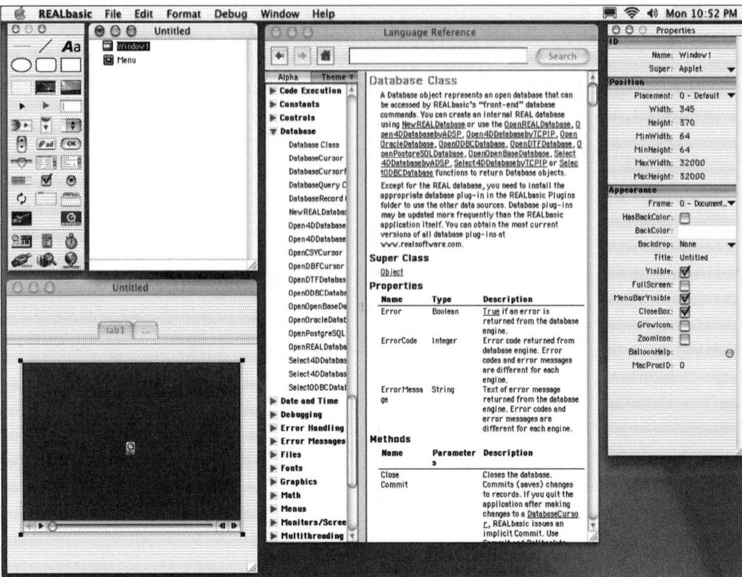

FIGURE 1.8
...and on Mac OS X!

As Steve Jobs hinted, Carbon is the basis for all *current* life on the Macintosh platform. Almost all existing applications can be ported to OS X using Carbon. This is not, however, the only way to build applications. OS X offers two other APIs: Cocoa and Java.

Cocoa

Cocoa has been through several name changes during its life. Cocoa, for all intents and purposes, *is* OpenStep. Originally designed to be a highly portable API accessed through the Objective-C programming language, Cocoa's first Mac implementation was called Yellow Box and was included in Mac OS X Server. In addition to the Mac, Yellow Box could also run on several versions of Unix as well as Windows NT. To understand why this is possible, you must first understand the WebObjects project.

One of NeXT's crown jewels was the Web application development environment called WebObjects. Inextricably entwined with the OpenStep/Yellow Box implementation, NeXT pushed WebObjects to as many platforms as possible, including its own OpenStep BSD-based system, as well as Windows NT, HPUX, and Solaris. Apple's original plan was to use the Yellow Box implementation on NT to allow developers to create software that ran on both Mac OS X and on Windows. Unfortunately, this project seemed to stall and has apparently been dropped by Apple for the time being. It wouldn't be surprising to see this reincarnated at some time in the future. It was a promising cross-platform technology, but hardware speed, space limitations, and licensing of the PostScript engine made it impractical for all but commercial developers.

Even without the NT component, Cocoa offers a compelling development environment for Mac OS X. Cocoa is a highly object-oriented environment that is similar in some ways to Java, and considered by many to be vastly superior. Programmed primarily using the Objective-C language, Cocoa is finally starting to catch on with new developers. Compared to traditional programming methods, Cocoa offers advanced rapid design tools, real-time prototyping, and the ability for a single programmer to create full-scale applications in a fraction of the time of other approaches.

Unfortunately, the Cocoa learning curve remains relatively high and the Objective-C language can bewilder those who are skilled in C++. Apple has taken steps to eliminate this problem by including developer tools with each copy of OS X sold. (Previously, the NeXT developer tools cost thousands of dollars.)

Java 2

The final programming environment included in Mac OS X is Java 2, Standard Edition v1.3. This marks the first time that the Macintosh has had a current version of Java available, and the first version of Java 2 available for *any* Macintosh operating system.

If you've kept up on computer technologies, chances are that you've heard of Java. Developed by Sun Microsystems and available for different operating systems, Java implements a true cross-platform "write once, run anywhere" development environment.

Java consists of two primary components:

- **The Java Virtual Machine**—The virtual machine acts as an entirely self-contained processing unit that can execute Java programs. The JVM reads Java bytecode (a Java application), translates it into API calls that are appropriate for the OS hosting the JVM, and then executes it.
- **A Java compiler**—The Java compiler creates Java byte code, given raw Java source code. This is similar to a traditional compiler, but it does not create an executable that can be run directly on the computer. Instead, it outputs a Java byte code file that can then be run on the JVM.

Java also includes a component called SWING that can be used to create applications that appear as native applications within whatever operating system they are running. SWING-based Java applications look like native Windows applications when running on Windows and native OS X applications when running on OS X. Figure 1.9 shows a SWING Java application running under Mac OS X. As you can see, it takes on the appearance of a native Mac OS X application.

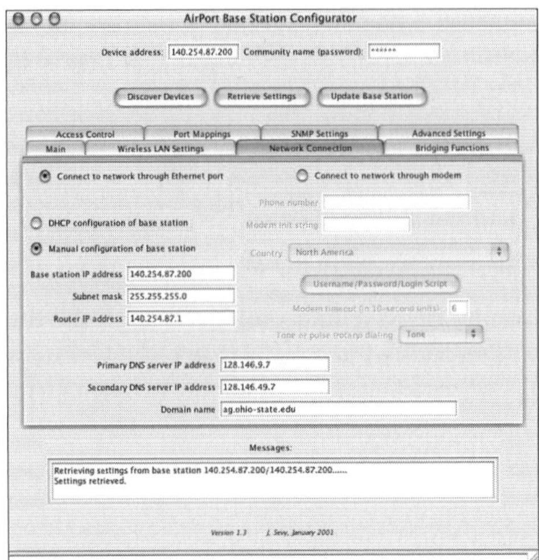

FIGURE 1.9
Java software can be created that runs anywhere, but looks like native OS X applications.

Besides the standard Java API, Apple has also opened up the entire Cocoa API to the Java programming language. This means that programmers can access the entire advanced Cocoa functionality, including Quartz, all from within the comfortable familiarity of Java.

Since the introduction of OS X, there have been several pieces of software released or announced for the operating system that have never been available on Mac OS before. Applications such as real-time stock trading are now becoming available thanks to the robust Java 2 implementation. It's likely that the trend will continue as enterprise developers realize the potential for increasing their market across the Macintosh platform.

Aqua

The final layer, Aqua, provides the user interface to the Mac OS X operating system. Based on translucent colors, transparent windows, and graphics that morph in and out of position, Aqua is a sight to behold. Mac users have had only six years to get accustomed to the Platinum appearance introduced in Mac OS 8, and now they are transported into the land of candy colors and pulsating buttons, as shown in Figure 1.10.

All the standard Mac OS user interface elements have been replaced within Aqua. Scroll bars, buttons, window shapes, and every other control are now represented using the Aqua translucent theme. In early developer releases of Mac OS X, designers complained that the bright colors were distracting. To address this complaint, Apple created a second Aqua theme, called Graphite, which replaces the interface with a more toned-down grayscale representation.

FIGURE 1.10
Aqua makes up the new Mac OS X interface.

The only true way to understand Aqua is to use it. You'll have plenty of opportunity to do just that after installing the system, which is covered in Chapter 2, "Installing Mac OS X."

Migration Issues

There are two primary types of users who will be interested in Mac OS X initially: traditional Mac users and die-hard Unix fans. Before jumping into the Mac OS X installation, I'd like to give users a heads up about what to expect as they make the transition from Mac OS 9 or Linux to Mac OS X.

Mac OS users are going to find a number of interface elements missing or changed. Table 1.1 shows what changes Mac OS users can expect.

TABLE 1.1 Interface Element Changes

Element	*Change*
Pop-up folders	Removed.
Springloaded folders	Removed.
Finder Font customization	Removed.
Apple menu	Mostly replaced by the Dock.

TABLE 1.1 continued

Element	*Change*
Control panels	Replaced by a central preference area (similar to Mac OS 6.0).
Window shades	Window shading has been replaced by minimized windows.
Trash can	Moved to the Dock.
Zoom rectangles	Windows appear instantly; zoom rectangles are gone.
Screen savers	Integrated into Mac OS X.
Large icons	Previously limited to 32×32 pixels, icons can now be as large as 128×128.
Process menu	Replaced by the Dock process manager.
Menu organization	The OS X menu organization has changed. Systemwide options are now located under the Apple menu.
Control strip	Replaced by the Dock and Menu Extras, but missing much of the functionality.
Contextual menus	Much functionality is removed.
Hardware support	Limited support in the initial Mac OS X release for scanners, printers, and video devices.

Although several of these changes might seem like a step backward, many of these features will return to future versions of the operating system. For the most part, your Macintosh computing experience will translate directly into the OS X environment. There are many other differences in the operation of the system. This list was intended to give you an idea of what GUI features will be missing when you start the system. Don't fret, the advantages gained by running Mac OS X outweigh the negatives.

Note

Apple has set an aggressive upgrade schedule for Mac OS X. It is likely that many shortcomings will be addressed within the first year of release. The 10.1 upgrade, for example, doubled the speed over the initial Mac OS X release, and included support for CD burning and DVD playback.

Linux and BSD users are going to find themselves right at home within the command-line environment. The addition of the XFree86 X Windows implementation can turn OS X into a full-featured Unix workstation. Unfortunately, OS X is lacking many of the graphical configuration tools that Linux users have grown accustomed to. Linuxconf, for

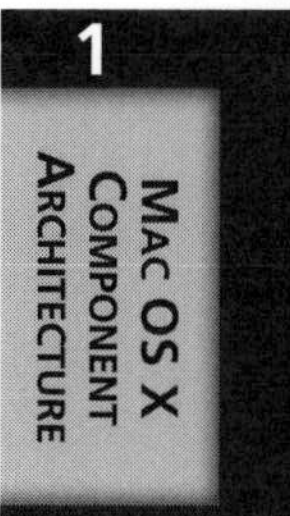

example, allows easy configuration of features ranging from e-mail and DNS servers to user accounts.

If you're looking for an easy-to-configure Unix server, consider purchasing Mac OS X Server 2.X instead. OS X Server offers GUI configuration of e-mail, DNS, DHCP, AppleShare, andmany other services. If you're a more adventurous sort, this book will provide all the information you need to run the same sort of services as Mac OS X Server, but without a simple GUI.

Note

Strangely enough, Windows users might find themselves right at home under OS X. The rearranged window controls, process Dock, and Finder navigation are much closer to their Windows counterparts than to previous versions of Mac OS!

Overall, Mac OS X is a pleasant user experience, but it is *not* Mac OS 9. Given a few months to grow and stabilize, it will easily replace traditional Mac OS. If you find it difficult to use or lacking features you need, *tell Apple!* Above all, don't be afraid to decide to wait before installing Mac OS X. All operating systems are a bit shaky on their legs following their birth, and Mac OS X is no exception.

Summary

Mac OS X represents a radical departure from the traditions set by Mac OS 8 and 9. Users will experience greater stability and flexibility than ever before. The OS X foundation is built on industry-standard APIs that enable advanced imaging and rapid application development using a wide variety of methods. On top of everything lies the beautiful Aqua user interface, which must be seen to be believed. Although it is an excellent start, Mac OS X still has a few rough edges that will be overcome with time. If your favorite application does not yet run natively under OS X, or does not function within Classic, you may want to wait before upgrading to Mac OS X as your full-time operating system.

Installing Mac OS X

IN THIS CHAPTER

Before you can start using Apple's new operating system, you must first install it. For almost 20 years, Mac users have had the easiest operating system installation of any personal computing platform (aside from those with the OS in ROM). Mac OS X is no different, but it can be slightly awkward even for those who are used to installing and upgrading on the Macintosh. This chapter will discuss the installation process and what makes it different from other Mac OS installations.

Pre-Installation Considerations and Tips

In the early days, to be able to install the Mac operating system, all you needed to do was to copy a folder called System Folder to whatever device you wanted to be bootable—that was about as complicated as things could get. In fact, although the Mac OS has its own installation program, you can copy your OS 8 or 9 System Folder to another disk if you want to make it bootable. In OS X, the operating system occupies far more space than just a System Folder. Although they are not viewable in the Mac OS X file listing, there are several directories that are tied to the BSD Unix subsystem and cannot be directly moved or copied to other disks in a user-friendly manner. A few of these directories are listed here:

- **bin**—Most basic system applications and command-line tools
- **dev**—Devices
- **private**—Houses directories used for temporary files, logs, configuration files, and so on
- **sbin**—Administrative tools and servers

If these directories are removed from the system, Mac OS X will refuse to boot. Interestingly enough, the actual file that Mac OS X uses to boot the computer (the kernel) is named `mach_kernel` and is located outside of what appears to be the OS X equivalent of the System Folder.

To be able to successfully install Mac OS X, you *must* run the included installation program. Attempting to install by copying the files directly from an OS X install CD or from an existing installation will very likely fail.

Evaluating Your Hardware

Because of the additional applications required to support Mac OS X, the system requirements are greater than previous versions of the Mac OS. We're no longer talking about

120MB of hard drive space and 32MB of RAM—instead, Mac OS X requires 128MB of RAM and 1.5GB of available storage.

Note

If you're not interested in using the Classic environment, you *can* run OS X with only 64MB of RAM; Classic will be inoperable. I recommend upgrading as soon as possible, but the system will boot and be functional.

In fact, the Mac OS X hardware requirements might be steeper than Apple states. According to Apple, Mac OS X 10.1 runs on the following computers:

- All original G4 computers
- All iMac desktops, including the Bondi 233
- All PowerBooks, excluding the original PowerBook G3
- All iBooks
- All beige desktop G3s

Unfortunately, although the operating system might "run" on these computers, it is misleading to say that it is usable on all but the most recent Macs. Users of original iMacs and iBooks might want or to stick with an earlier version of Mac OS.

Note

Owners of earlier 604-based Macintoshes (7300, 7500, 7600, 8500, 8600, 9500, 9600) and 604-based Macintosh clones from Umax and Motorola are in luck! An application called Unsupported UtilityX will enable you to install Mac OS X on your hardware. Although you should not expect outstanding performance, it does provide an upgrade path for older Macs.
`http://eshop.macsales.com/OSXCenter/framework.cfm?page=UnsupportedUtilityX.html.`

The general consensus is that a 350MHz G3 is the lowest-end computer under which Mac OS X runs comfortably. If you're using a slower computer, you're likely to experience extreme sluggishness in launching applications, slow startups, and poor multimedia performance. If you're a non-Mac user and your first OS X encounter is on an original iMac, you're likely to swear off using a Mac ever again.

Tip

Although some might disagree with this stance, it seems only fair to point out that Mac OS X *is* a far greater resource hog than Mac OS 8 or 9. I think that users should stick with the operating system that offers the best overall experience, rather than upgrading for the sake of having the latest version.

Mac OS X is optimized for the G4 processor with Altivec, so G3 users might experience delays in heavy graphic operations such as anti-aliasing and image transformations. The best possible system on which to use Mac OS X is a G4-based multiprocessor workstation; and, if reports coming from Apple are correct, there will be many more such systems to choose from in the near future.

Additional Hardware Support

Although OS X supports the base model machines that are listed on the hardware page, there are a number of issues that might affect the usefulness of *any* machine. In the shipping version of Mac OS X, there are only a few supported devices ranging from printers Some issues you might experience with OS X 10.1 are documented here.

- **Sound Output**
    - The beige G3 series is listed as a supported model, but those users who have a DVD Personality card in their machine will be without sound until Apple issues an update.
    - Users of 233, 266, and 333MHz iMacs must use the headphone jack for sound output.
    - Classic-based MIDI software will not function.
- **Disk Support**
    - USB devices are not supported for booting.
    - FireWire devices are not supported for booting.
    - Adaptec OS X drivers *are* available.
- **CDRW Support**
    - Apple and some third-party CDRW drives are supported in 10.1 but not the initial release,except via Roxio's Toast package.
    - Classic-based CD-authoring applications will not function under Mac OS X.

- **DVD Support**
  - DVD authoring is supported in 10.1 via iDVD2.
  - DVD playback is available in Mac OS X 10.1.
- **Digital Images**
  - Scanner OEM support is limited to Classic-based applications. Although developers such as HP and Afga are working on third-party solutions, many film and flatbed scanners can be used with VueScan—a third-party scan utility. Download VueScan from `http://www.hamrick.com/`.
  - Although Apple includes an image capture application with OS X, it does not support many popular cameras, including several Kodak models.

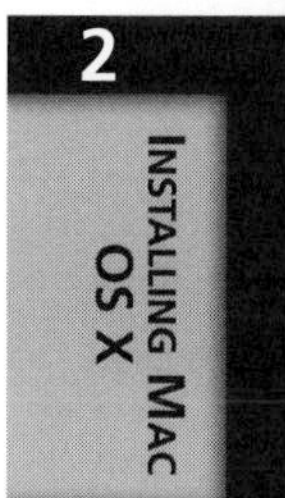

- **Video**
  - Analog video inputs are not supported except through analog to DV conversion units, such as the Formac Studio and Sony Media Converter.
  - Digital video input is not supported in Classic.
  - Third-party digital video input cards are not supported.
  - Apple, ATI, nVidia, and Radeon video cards are the only supported video output devices.
- **Modem Support**
  - Some internal modems do not make a sound while connecting.
  - No fax support at time of shipping. Third-party support is expected to fill this void by the time this book is printed.
- **Networking**
  - The AirPort (`http://gicl.mcs.drexel.edu/people/sevy/airport/`) base-station feature is not available on 10.1. Use of the BSD nat utility can restore this functionality.
  - Orinoco/WaveLAN support missing. Although present in the Apple drivers in Mac OS 8 and 9, the shipping version of OS X does not support the Lucent-branded cards. An open source version of the drivers has been created and is available for download at `http://homepage.mac.com/yuriwho`.
  - Many third-party network cards do not function. (Some Asanté, Farallon, and Stallion cards do have drivers available.)
- **Printing**
  - PostScript LPR/EtherTalk printers are supported out of the box.
  - Most popular Epson, Canon, and HP printers are supported out of the box. Many manufactures are promising support, but have yet to deliver.
  - LocalTalk-based printers are not supported.

- **CPU Upgrades**
  - Apple does not support any CPU upgrades on the shipping version of OS X. Many users have reported success with their upgrades, but you should check with your manufacturer before you attempt to install.

As you can see, the hardware support at shipping is less than stellar. You should check with your hardware manufacturer to make sure that the critical components of your system will still be functioning after an upgrade.

Evaluating Your Needs

Evaluating whether or not you actually *need* OS X is probably the hardest step to make before upgrading. For many users, the desire to upgrade is based on the supposition that "if it's newer, it's better." For Mac OS X, that is not necessarily the case. It is my goal to make it clear that Mac OS X might *not* be for everyone at the current time. This doesn't mean that you should never consider upgrading, or that Mac OS X is a bad product, just that it might not be ready to suit your needs.

Apple has created a completely amazing operating system that is getting rave reviews throughout the industry. I was taken aback recently when I picked up one of the half-dozen "enterprise computing" weeklies that arrive at my house, only to see a Mac OS X cover story. It has been years since the Mac has received positive press—especially from sources that usually focus on the Windows platform.

What does this mean for the typical Mac user? Not much! Many of the industry reports are coming from reviewers with a background in NT or Unix. They're running Mac OS X on the latest (and fastest) hardware and are impressed with its capabilities. Remember, these are the people who use less-than-perfect interfaces and the command line everyday. Most Mac users, however, are interested in the quality of the user experience coupled with the power of the operating system.

So, it isn't a question of whether you're ready for Mac OS X. It's a matter of Mac OS X being ready for you. Before deciding to go any further, ask yourself these questions:

Is my system new enough to handle OS X comfortably? (G3 400MHz or better)

Are the applications I need available under OS X?

Do my legacy applications work correctly under Classic?

Is the hardware I use supported?

Am I happy with my current Mac OS setup?

If you answer *no* to any of the first four questions, or *yes* to the last, upgrading might not be right for you at this time. There is no shame in continuing to run Mac OS 9 until Mac OS X matures to the point where the applications and services match your needs.

Note

Due to the rather strange positioning of OS X as both a high-end Unix system and an easy-to-use consumer operating system, I see OS X as most appealing to two types of users: beginners and power users.

Beginners will appreciate the easy navigation and file launching. If the primary use of a computer is e-mail and Web browsing, OS X provides all the tools and none of the computer-maintenance headaches.

Likewise, power users will appreciate the command line and Unix backend. Mac OS X can easily be integrated into existing Unix clusters and use many of the existing tools.

The people most likely to feel growing pains are those who fall in the middle. These are the users who rely on their Macs to do a wide variety of tasks, have an extensive existing software collection, and have customized their computer with various extensions and control panels. For these people, moving to Mac OS X will result in no small amount of culture shock.

OS X Features on Mac OS 9

A possibility for those not wanting to upgrade immediately is to manipulate their system in a way that will prepare them for OS X in the future, but let them stay within Mac OS 9 for the time being. Obviously, you can't expect to get all the benefits of Mac OS X without upgrading, but you can make your system closely resemble the OS X environment with only a few minor additions.

Mac OS 9.x

Mac OS X rearranges the basic Macintosh file system to include an Applications (Mac OS 9) folder for Mac OS 9–based programs, as well as Documents and System Folder. This streamlined layout is similar (minus a few folders) to the default OS X folder arrangement. By default, OS X keeps the root level of your hard drive static. Normal users cannot add folders at this level—only at lower levels. Although Mac OS 9.x *will* let you rearrange this structure, it does prepare you for the inevitable changes coming in OS X.

Additionally, Mac OS 9.x includes a Window menu that lets you quickly access open Finder windows. Mac OS X introduces a system-wide Window menu that lets users quickly navigate an application's open windows. Although this is not universal under OS 9.x, it's a step closer.

Application Switcher (AKA "the Dock")

Many people are unaware that the application switcher in Mac OS 8.5/9 can very closely emulate the Mac OS X Dock. By running a simple AppleScript, you can create a Dock-like list palette of icons that shows the applications that are running on your computer. Figure 2.1 shows the application switcher configured to rest near the lower-right portion of the screen.

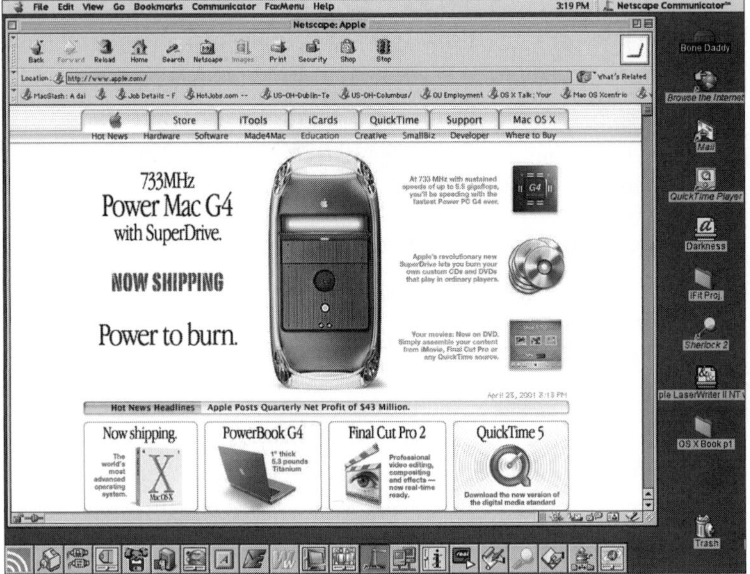

FIGURE 2.1
Mac OS 8.5/9 support reconfiguring the application switcher to be similar to the Mac OS X Dock.

To create this effect on your computer, you must first click and drag the application switcher until it "tears" off from the menu bar. Next, you need to create a simple AppleScript to reconfigure its appearance. Open the Script Editor application and enter the following:

```
tell application "Application Switcher"
    set icon size of palette to large
    set names visible of palette to false
    set anchor point of palette to lower right
    set orientation of palette to horizontal
    set position of palette to lower left
    set frame visible of palette to false
end tell
```

You can then either save the script as a double-clickable executable, or click the Run button to see the change immediately.

Tip

If you'd prefer not to mess with the AppleScript yourself, there are a number of pre-built tools for changing the appearance and behavior of the switcher. The most widely recommended is Prestissimo, located at `http://www.polymorph.net/prestissimo.html`. If you'd like to look at other solutions, perform a search for "application switcher" on `http://www.versiontracker.com`.

Several third-party application switchers offer features beyond those built into Mac OS 9. In fact, some of these even offer full OS X compatibility. If you choose one of the following solutions, and then upgrade to OS X, you'll be able to maintain your existing setup:

DragThing 4.0—The DragThing application supports multiple levels of application and file Docks as well as an interactive process listing. Built as a Carbon application, it runs on both Mac OS 9 and Mac OS X, and can display OS X large-format icons under the older operating system. Download DragThing at `http://www.dragthing.com/`.

Drop Drawers—Like DragThing, Drop Drawers offers multiple levels of Docks accessible through a tabbed interface. The tabs, however, open hidden pop-up windows that are similar in appearance to the traditional Mac OS pop-up folders. These drawers can hold files, applications, sounds, pictures, text clippings, and even movies. It is also a Carbon-based application and runs on both Mac OS 9 and OS X. Download Drop Drawers from `http://www.sigsoftware.com/dropdrawers/`.

A-Dock—Although it is not OS X–compatible, A-Dock comes the closest of all the available task-switchers to the real Mac OS X Dock. All the features of the OS X Dock are present, except the fancy icon scaling. To make your OS 9 computer look like OS X, A-Dock is the way to go. You can find A-Dock at `http://jerome.foucher.free.fr/ADock.html`.

Windows/Menu Translucency

Some of the biggest "gee-whiz" features of the Mac OS X user experience are the translucent menus and the ability to drag the windows around with the contents intact. This capability is also available under Mac OS 9 through the use of Power Windows.

Power Windows enables Mac OS 9 users to choose the level of translucency applied as they drag their windows around the screen. It even allows background tasks to proceed as windows are being moved, moving users one step closer to a true pre-emptive multitasking system like Mac OS X. Finally, Power Windows also offers menu translucency and does an excellent job of emulating the menu fade out effect found in Mac OS X. Figure 2.2 shows the Power Windows control panel.

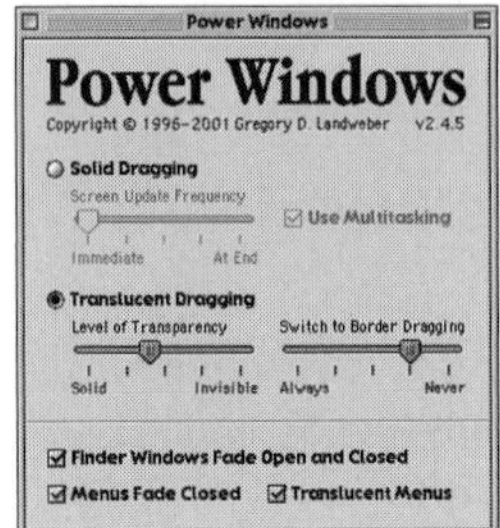

FIGURE 2.2
Power Windows creates translucent windows and menus on a Mac OS 9 system.

Power Windows is mostly about appearance, so if your biggest envy of Mac OS X users is the look and feel, Power Windows is a great place to start.

Aqua Themes

There are several freely downloadable Mac OS themes that can transform your existing computer into a Mac OS X look-alike. Although they lack the pulsing push buttons and warping windows (alliteration!) of the real OS X, they provide a quick makeover for anyone sticking to Mac OS 9 for the time being. Figure 2.3 shows a Mac OS 9.x system running an Aqua theme.

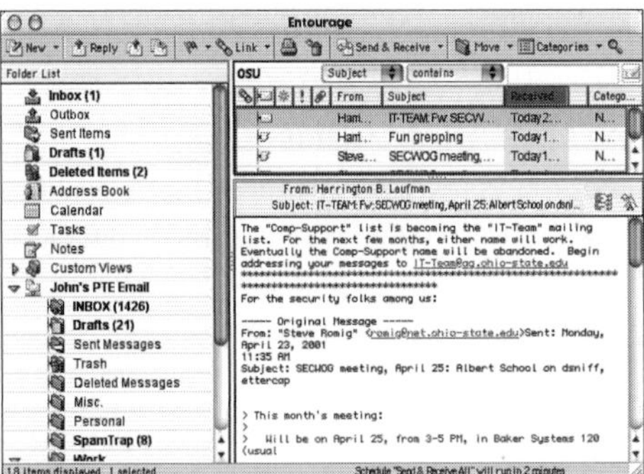

FIGURE 2.3
The Mac OS X appearance within Mac OS 9.

You can download the theme shown here from http://www.macosr.com/ (search for *Liquid* or *Aqua*). After downloading the theme file, drop it on your System Folder, let Mac OS 9.x automatically place it in the Appropriate location, and then switch to it from the Appearance tab of the Appearance control panel.

Unfortunately, Apple has pushed to keep Aqua themes from reaching the public. Even though the link provided here has been online for more than a year, at some point you might find it necessary to download from an alternative location. A Google search for *Mac OS Aqua Themes* will almost certainly turn up a few download locations.

Tip

If you're a stickler for appearance and plan to upgrade to OS X, you might want to consider downloading and installing an Aqua theme on your existing Mac OS 9.x system. Although themes aren't compatible with OS X natively, they do work within the Classic environment.

Mac OS 9.x, when running under Mac OS X, keeps the default Platinum appearance. By using an Aqua theme under Mac OS 9.x, you can create a more seamless Classic/Carbon/Cocoa environment.

An alternative to Apple's built-in theme technology is the shareware product Kaleidoscope. Kaleidoscope offers more variation and a larger variety of themes, and an OS X native version is currently planned. You can download Kaleidoscope from http://www.kaleidoscope.net.

Folder Backgrounds

Another new built-in feature introduced in Mac OS X is the ability to set a different background pattern or color for each window in the finder. If you tend to keep large numbers of windows open simultaneously, this can help you quickly differentiate between them based on their appearances. For Mac OS 8/9 users, this feature has been available for years in the form of a shareware product called Window Monkey. Figure 2.4 shows a Finder window that has a background pattern added, courtesy of Window Monkey.

Window Monkey also provides a system-wide Window menu to jump easily between windows in open applications. Superior to the Mac OS 9.x Window menu, this provides similar functionality but can run on Mac OS 8 as well. Download Window Monkey from http://www.tigertech.com.

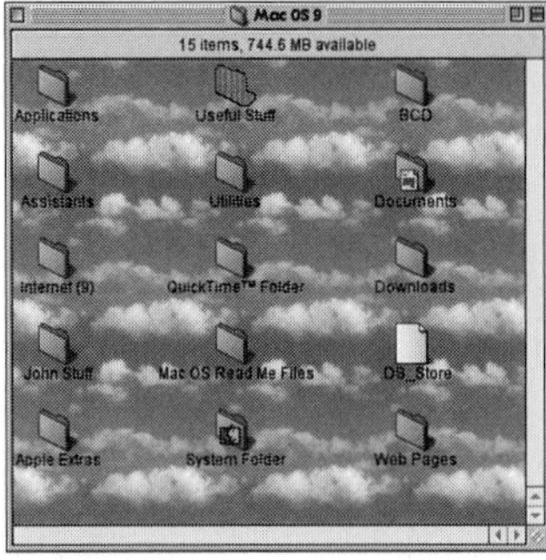

FIGURE 2.4
Window Monkey can alter the appearance of your Finder windows to include background patterns.

File Navigation

The final program we'll look at for creating a Mac OS X–like experience under Mac OS 9.x is Greg's Browser. Mac OS X provides an entirely new way to navigate the file system. NeXT users will recognize the Mac OS X Finder's multipane view that allows easier navigation into and out of folders.

Greg's Browser emulates the original NeXT file browsing experience and adds additional features such as the ability to change file types and quickly delete selected files. Figure 2.5 shows Greg's Browser running under 9.x.

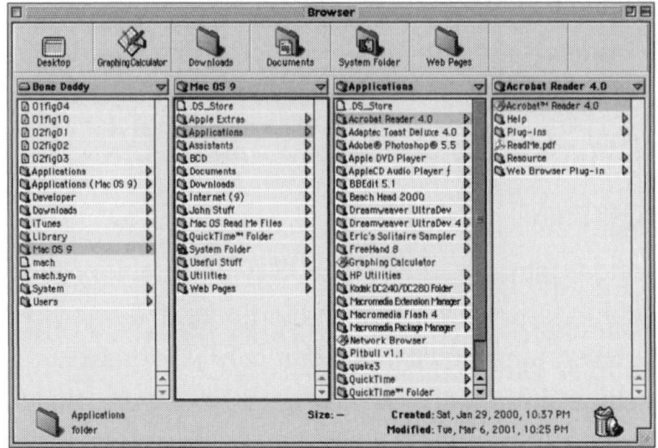

FIGURE 2.5
Greg's Browser emulates the new features found in the Mac OS X Finder.

Mac OS X's Finder and Greg's Browser make it easy to move through large directory trees and are likely to quickly become your preferred method of working with files. You can download Greg's Browser at `http://www.kaleidoscope.net/`.

Preparing Your Drive for Mac OS X

If you've made the decision to move forward with the installation of Mac OS X, you'll need to prepare your hard drive for installation. Mac OS X is very flexible in the possible system configurations allowed, and supports multiple partitions and both UFS and HFS+ out of the box.

Simple Upgrade from Mac OS 9.x

Determining the best configuration depends entirely on your needs. The simplest path to Mac OS X, while maintaining your current system software setup, is to upgrade to Mac OS 9.x9.x, and then perform the OS X installation. Apple recommends this approach only if you have existing data and cannot start from scratch.

If you are using Mac OS 8.5 or earlier, you will need to purchase the full Mac OS 9 CD and perform the upgrade like you normally would. Mac OS 9.x is a free update to 9.0 and is available for download from Apple's Web site (`http://www.apple.com/`).

Note

Systems earlier than 9.x, as long as they are running on a Mac OS Extended file system (HFS+), can have Mac OS X installed, and upgraded to 9.x at a later date. You will not be able to run Classic applications, but you will be able to access all the data files on your drive. If you are running *any* system using the base HFS file system, you will have to reinitialize your system as HFS+ or use a utility such as Alsoft's PlusMaker (`http://www.alsoft.com/PlusMaker/support.html`) to convert your existing data.

Any system that has been upgraded to Mac OS 9.x is ready to run the OS X installation, with a few minor exceptions. Due to differences in the drive controllers, the following machines might require special preparations:

PowerBook G3 Series

Power Macintosh G3 Desktop

Power Macintosh G3 Mini Tower

Power Macintosh G3 All-in-One

Macintosh Server G3

iMac 233MHz (Rev. A & B)

iMac 266MHz (Rev. C)

iMac 333MHz (Rev. D)

If you are using one of these machines, you might find that Mac OS X does not allow you to select your boot drive during the installation procedure. If this is the case, and you have the prerequisite 1.5GB of available space, the problem lies with your disk partition layout, not the install program.

What Is Partitioning?

Mac users don't usually have to worry about partitions, and might not be familiar with the term. A *partition* is a logical division on a piece of storage medium—usually a hard disk. To the computer, these divisions appear to be separate disks and each can be formatted with a different file system. In reality, they are all located on the device.

Computers that have the Mac OS pre-installed are usually configured with a single partition with the Mac OS Extended (HFS+) file system.

When installing on one of the listed computers, Mac OS X must reside within the first 8GB of the drive. There are two likely scenarios that would prevent the installation from continuing:

- If your computer has a hard drive greater than 8GB, which is mounted as a single volume, the OS X installation will not be allowed. The only option in this case is to partition your drive.
- If you have a large hard drive in your computer and it is split into partitions that exceed 8GB, none of the partitions will be available for installation. You must delete and re-create the first partition so that the first portion of it is less than 8GB.

Unfortunately, the Macintosh does not support partitioning without destroying the data on your drives. If your computer is one of the affected models and your drive requires partitioning, the only option is to back up your computer, repartition, and then continue with the installation. We'll look at the process of partitioning in the "Partitioning Your Drive" section later in this chapter. Assuming that issues with drive partitioning do not affect your machine, you can proceed directly to the Mac OS X installation guide.

Tip

The Mac OS X installation procedure will not optimize your drive during installation. If you're upgrading from a system that has been running Mac OS 8 or 9 for quite a while, I recommend that you run a commercial optimization program such as TechTool Pro or Norton Utilities on the existing system before you continue the installation.

Performing a Clean Installation

Although upgrading an existing 9.x installation is acceptable, it might not lead to the best possible system performance. Many users have found that Mac OS X's Classic environment is incompatible with various system extensions that they were using at the time of the upgrade. The process of finding the incompatible extensions while running Mac OS X is time-consuming and nonintuitive. Personally, I recommend starting from scratch with Mac OS X. Apple has done an admirable job of allowing OS X to install on top of the older OS; however, if a problem does occur, it might not be easy to track down.

Another consideration is drive partitioning. If you've decided to go with a clean install, you might want to think about partitioning your existing drive into separate volumes for Mac OS 9 and Mac OS X.

Tip

Some users might not have the option of whether to partition their drives. Please glance through the "Simple Upgrade from 9.x" section earlier in this chapter to see if your machine is affected.

Partitioning Your Drive

Partitioning creates one or more logical volumes contained within the single hard disk. This process is often used to separate system-critical files from user files. Standard Unix implementations usually have multiple partitions for the operating system, user directories, applications, and application support files. Mac OS X breaks this tradition by using a single primary partition for all data.

For the time being, it's easier to follow the OS X all-in-one model than it is to fight it. Multiple partitions are visible under Mac OS X, but to use them with the base operating system as anything other than additional file storage, you'll need to work directly with the command line. Because Apple is pushing its auto-update application, making changes to the base configuration of the operating system by hand is not advisable.

Note

Users coming from more conventional Unix/Linux distributions will likely take issue with the Mac OS X partition setup. It is important to keep in mind that the system was designed from the perspective of a traditional Mac user.

continues

Under earlier versions of Mac OS, all storage media is mounted in the same location and accessible to the user as independent volumes. Unix users are more accustomed to being able to mount storage media *anywhere* in their file system. For example, suppose that a user has a My Documents directory somewhere on her system and would like to dedicate an entire drive to that. On Mac OS, the drive would be forced to sit on the desktop, just like the main boot volume. Under Unix, the new drive could be mounted directly at the level of the My Documents folder. This becomes what is called a *mount point*. Although this is possible on Mac OS X, it is not easily accomplished with the included GUI tools.

So, if Apple isn't making drive partitioning a necessity, why bother doing it at all? There are a few reasons why a partitioned drive might be beneficial to your system:

- **Compatibility with existing Unix systems**—Mac OS X supports both HFS+ and UFS (Unix File System). This allows it to easily interoperate with other Unix-based operating systems, including the original version of Mac OS X Server. Creating a UFS-based partition on a drive would allow the drive to be mounted and used under other operating systems, and then moved to Mac OS X. Very few operating systems other than Mac OS support the native file system type of HFS+.

What Is the Difference Between a Partition and a File System?

A partition is a logical division of the storage medium into subvolumes. A partition does not define the contents of the subvolume, just the position on the disk and amount of space consumed.

Before a partition can be used, it must have a file system installed. A *file system* defines the way data will be stored on a given partition. The terms *partition* and *file system* are intimately related, and can often be used interchangeably, but they operate at two different levels on the hard drive.

- **Separating critical resources**—Although Mac OS X partitions are mounted as individual volumes, that doesn't prevent you from taking advantage of the separation of resources. Partitions are based on a single hard drive, but are independent of one another. For example, if you have three partitions on a single drive, unless there is an actual *physical* problem with the drive or a low-level error in the driver software, the contents of the three partitions cannot affect one another in any way.

Drive errors typically come in the form of file system corruption, rather than a true crash of the disk hardware. If you've ever been forced to boot from a CD after a system crash, only to see the message "This disk cannot be read, erase?" you've experienced file system corruption. By dividing critical data, you can lessen the risk of file corruption occurring to a given volume. A partition created solely for the purposes of storing documents is unlikely to be affected by a serious system crash. Although you might need to reinstall your operating system, your data will probably still be safe.

Unfortunately, even though partitions limit damage from everyday use, physical problems can still occur on a hard disk itself that might result in data loss across all partitions. Backup options are covered in Chapter 32, "Maintenance and Troubleshooting."

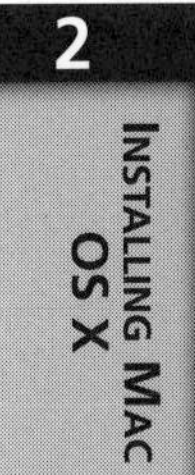

- **Disk fragmentation**—Disk fragmentation is similar to file system corruption. For Mac users, disk fragmentation is a way of life. The Macintosh operating system makes it too easy to install, remove, and move files, while doing a poor job of allocating storage for these files. Over the course of time, disk accesses can slow significantly.

  If you're using both Mac OS 9.x and OS X running from the same volume, your interactions when booted into 9.x can have the same detrimental effect on the file system. Keeping Mac OS 9.x and Mac OS X in separate partitions results in a cleaner environment that is less susceptible to fragmentation.

  For the sample installation shown in this chapter, I will use one partition for Mac OS 9.x, and a second partition for Mac OS X.9.x.

- **Boot Options**—By using separate partitions for Mac OS X and Mac OS 9, you can use the Open Firmware startup selection to choose the boot volume. This provides an excellent means of starting the computer if Mac OS X (or 9) fails.

Creating the Partitions

The first step in partitioning your drives is to choose the type of file system that will be installed on the partition.

As mentioned earlier, two types of file systems are supported within Mac OS X:

- UFS—Unix File System
- HFS+—Hierarchical File System Plus

The recommended file system for Mac OS X installations is HFS+. HFS+ has been the Macintosh file system since the late 1990s, and is compatible with your existing Mac drives. UFS, on the other hand, exists for compatibility in Unix environments. If you're using OS X on its own, or with other Macs, choose HFS+.

There is one *very* important difference between HFS+ and UFS that might cause nervous breakdowns for those used to working within a Unix environment: The Macintosh file system has been, and continues to be, case insensitive.

This means that a file named John.doc is identical to one named john.doc. Case insensitivity is one of the ease-of-use features of the Macintosh that does not translate well into the Unix environment. Programmers who have written scripts that use differences in case to differentiate between files will have to rework the applications to function in a case-insensitive environment.

The case issue can cause problems if a Mac OS X installation is required to provide complete compatibility with existing Unix software. If you're using OS X as a migration platform from Linux or another Unix system, you might want to consider using UFS rather than having to review all the code that is currently in place.

Caution

Amusingly enough, one of the first companies to be bitten by the case sensitivity issue is Apple. Although Mac OS X will install and operate correctly on the UFS file system, the AirPort wireless driver package makes the assumption that it is on a case-insensitive system. When it attempts to load components of the driver, it fails because the files could not be located. If you're using UFS as your installation partition type, you will not be able to use your wireless network.

You can read more about this almost-amusing bug in Apple's Tech Info Library (TIL) reference: `http://til.info.apple.com/techinfo.nsf/artnum/n106252`.

Apple's Tech Info Library is the source for updated information, problems, and solutions related to Mac OS X and other Apple products. Before calling technical support or turning to a user group, always check the TIL!

Assuming that you're going with the HFS+ file system, you'll need to choose the size and number of partitions to be created. In the original HFS implementation, file allocation block size was determined by dividing the total drive storage by 65,536. As drive space grew, storage efficiency plummeted. The HFS+ file system uses 4KB blocks no matter what the size of the containing partition. Because of this, partitioning is no longer necessary to maintain drive efficiency. Other than the reasons already discussed, your partition sizes are up to you.

What Is a File Allocation Block?

Instead of allowing every file to take advantage of every bit of available space, file systems allocate blocks of space that are used one at a time. The total amount of space that a file takes up must be a multiple of the block size, regardless of whether all the space is used.

In the original Mac OS HFS implementation, on a 1GB drive, a single file allocation block takes up 16KB (1024*1024/65536). This means that a file whose size is 1KB will actually consume 16KB on the drive. On HFS+ (the default file system of Mac OS X), the block size is 4KB, so the same 1KB file will take up only 4KB.

Extrapolate this to today's high-capacity hard drives, and you'll see that if HFS were used on an 80GB drive, a 1KB file would occupy more than 1MB of total drive space!

Running Drive Setup

When you're ready to partition your drive, boot your Macintosh from the 9.x CD that is included in your Mac OS X package. To boot from the CD, start the computer with the CD-ROM in the drive while holding down the C key. It is important that you use the Apple-supplied 9.x CD rather than an earlier version of the operating system. Version 1.8.1 of the HD Setup tool creates UFS partitions that are incompatible with Mac OS X.

Tip

The Mac OS 9.x CD that is included with the first release of Mac OS X does not boot all of the computers that were available at the time of release. If you are using a PowerBook G4, PowerMac G4 (digital audio), or a 2001 iMac, you will need to use the Mac OS 9.x CD that came with your computer. See `http://til.info.apple.com/techinfo.nsf/artnum/n106236` for information.

On booting your Macintosh from Mac OS 9.x, start the Drive Setup application located in the Utilities folder. The program should show a list of the available hard drives, as shown in Figure 2.6. On a system with a single drive, there will be two entries: one for the CD that booted the system and one for the hard drive.

To begin the process of partitioning, choose the disk in the list that matches the drive you want to use for your Mac OS X installation. EIDE drives are listed under the type ATA, whereas SCSI disks are of the type SCSI. After making your selection, click the Initialize button.

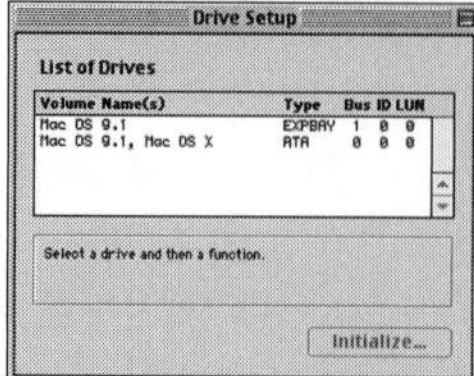

FIGURE 2.6
Choose the hard drive that you want to set up.

Choosing a Partition Scheme

Drive Setup will warn you, as demonstrated by the dialog box in Figure 2.7, that all the data on your drive is about to be deleted. It will also give you the option to create a custom setup. This is where you can choose the partition scheme you'd like, or choose between the HFS+ and UFS file systems.

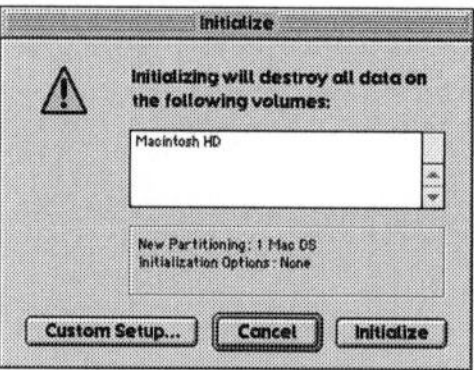

FIGURE 2.7
Click Custom Setup to create a new partition scheme.

The Custom Setup dialog box makes it easy to create multiple partitions on a drive. The left portion of the window shows a visual representation of the hard drive and the subvolumes (partitions) that have been created. A black border surrounds each partition. This border can be dragged to change the amount of space allocated to that partition.

To the right of the highlighted partition is displayed the name, type, and size (in megabytes) of the selected item. You can change these values to change the type and size of the partition. To create a partition scheme, choose the number of partitions that you want to use from the Partitioning Scheme pop-up menu located at the top of the dialog box. Figure 2.8 shows a dual partition schema with two Mac OS Extended (HFS+) partitions.

FIGURE 2.8
Create your partition scheme.

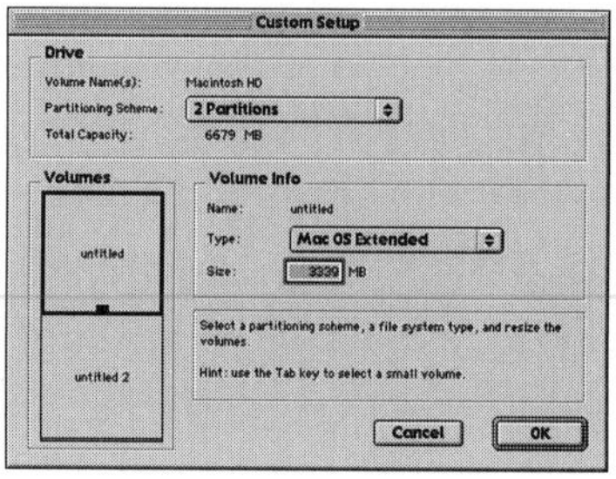

If you want to delete partitions, select them and press the Delete key on your keyboard, or choose a new schema from the pop-up menu and start again. By default, the partitions that you create will use the Mac OS Extended file system. Unless you plan to use UFS, no changes should need to be made to the partition type.

Tip

Remember that if you are using one of the older iMacs or G3s listed earlier, the first partition (located at the top of the volume layout) must fall within the first 8GB of drive space.

Caution

There are quite a few partition types listed in the Type menu (as well as some predefined schema in the Partitioning Scheme menu) that do not apply to either Mac OS X or Mac OS 9.x. Be sure not to choose any of the A/UX, Linux, or Mac OS X Server partition types. These will not function correctly under Mac OS X.

After choosing the partition layout, click the OK button to go back to the warning screen that cautions about all data being destroyed. If you're sure that there's nothing you want on the disk, click Initialize.

Drive Setup will take approximately 10 seconds per partition to initialize your new drive structure. After initialization is completed, the drives will be mounted on your Mac OS 9.x desktop.

You should take this opportunity to name the two drives. The first partition (named "untitled") will typically be the Mac OS X partition. Again, if you're using one of the older iMacs/G3s, the first partition might *have* to be the Mac OS X partition. The subsequent partitions will be named untitled2, untitled3, and so on. Assuming that you've created a two-partition configuration, the second partition can be named Mac OS 9.x. Although this isn't necessary for Mac OS X to be installed correctly, it will help you identify the appropriate drives to choose during your Mac OS X installation.

You're now ready to install Mac OS 9.x.

Note

If you prefer to partition your drive with native Mac OS X tools, you can access the OS X Disk Utility from the File menu of the Installer application. Disk Utility is documented in Chapter 6.

Installing Mac OS 9.x

The Mac OS 9.x install procedure will be documented very briefly here. This procedure should be pretty familiar for most Mac users and is quite simple. If you already have Mac OS 9.x installed, jump ahead to "Installing Mac OS X."

If you've just partitioned your drive, you're probably already booted from the Mac OS 9.x CD. If not, boot from the CD now by holding the C key while turning on your computer with the CD inserted.

Double-click the Mac OS Install application. The Mac OS 9.x installation is like most wizard-based tools. The initial welcome screen is shown in Figure 2.9.

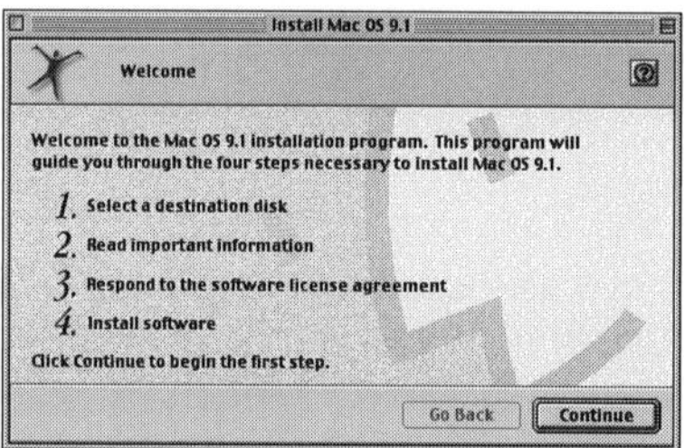

FIGURE 2.9
The Mac OS 9.x installer should be completed with only minimal interaction.

Click the Continue button on the welcome screen to continue with the installation. Next, the Select Destination window will prompt for the drive that will contain Mac OS 9.x. If you're going with a multi-partition setup, hopefully you've named the drive that will receive OS 9. If you're on a single-partition setup, only one choice is available. Figure 2.10 displays the destination selection screen.

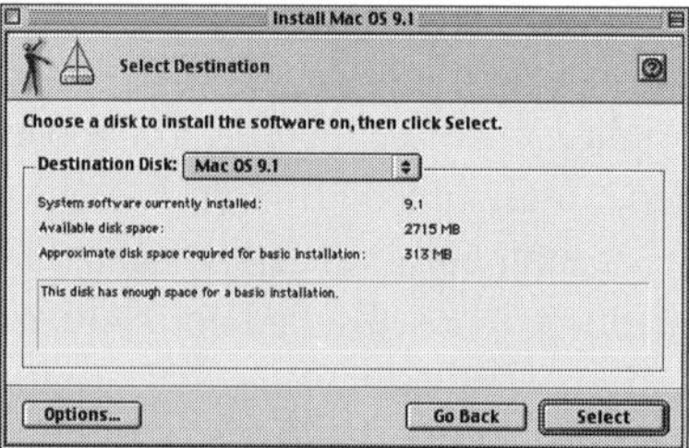

FIGURE 2.10
Choose the drive to receive Mac OS 9.x.

Click Select to continue.

The installation software will display some important information about Mac OS 9.x. In particular, it lists these concerns (not all will apply if this installation is on a fresh partition and you've followed the instructions so far):

- Turn off security software
- Make sure that your PowerBook is plugged in
- Be sure that the computer is booted from the 9.x CD

Click the Continue button to proceed.

The Apple installer displays the software license agreement. Be sure to read this thoroughly, you'll be tested on it later during the Mac OS X installation (just kidding).

Click Continue to continue. If you agree with the software license, click Agree in the dialog box that appears. If you don't, you're not going to get any further!

At long last, you're ready to start the actual installation. The Install Software window is displayed in Figure 2.11. The installer is prepared to begin copying files.

FIGURE 2.11
Click Start to begin copying files.

Tip

Even if you're a well-versed Mac user, it's best not to use any of the customization options that are available during the installation procedure. Mac OS X will make modifications to the OS 9.x installation so that the Classic environment can be used. It expects certain components to be present in order to work correctly.

Click Start to begin the installation. The entire process will take about 15 minutes on a reasonably fast G3, and under 10 minutes on most G4s. At completion, you'll be prompted to reboot your machine.

Finishing Up the 9.x Install

If you've installed Mac OS 8 or 9, you know what comes next. When Mac OS 9.x boots for the first time, you'll be taken through a series of assistants that will help configure file sharing. Luckily, there is no need to go through with this process if you're installing

Mac OS X. When Mac OS X updates the 9.x installation, it will install additional software that inherits your settings from the parent OS X environment. You can choose Quit from the File menu to exit out of the assistant.

If you plan to boot directly into Mac OS 9.x occasionally, you might want to go ahead and complete the setup assistant process. The assistant asks for a piece of information related to the system setup, and then makes the appropriate changes to the configuration files. You can navigate between the assistant screens by clicking the left and right arrows near the lower-right portion of the window.

The steps are self explanatory, and are documented briefly in Table 2.1.

TABLE 2.1 Using the Setup Assistant Process

Information	*Change*
Standards for keyboard layout, time, currency, and so on	Choose the country's settings that best match your location.
Name and organization	Enter your name and, if applicable, your company, school, and so on.
Time and Date	Select whether you are observing daylight saving time and choose the current day and time.
Location	To set your time zone, click the location closest to you.
Simple Finder Preferences	If necessary, you can simplify the Finder's menu system.
Computer Name and Password	A name for your computer, and a password you can use to log in to it on the network.
Folder Sharing	If you'd like to share files with other computers on your network, you can turn on file sharing and create a shared folder.
Internet Setup	Choose the method of connection to the Internet and a name for the configuration.
Network/Modem Settings	Choose the network or modem settings that are appropriate for your installation.

You're now ready to install Mac OS X. If you'd like to continue at a later time, shut down your computer. Otherwise, insert the Mac OS X installation disk now.

> **Note**
>
> Apple mentions in the installation instructions that the most recent firmware upgrades should be installed before installing Mac OS X. According to the documentation, these updates are located on the Mac OS X CD. However, my CD does not include any firmware updates. I recommend checking future revisions of the OS X CD as well as Apple's Web site.

Installing Mac OS X

Installing Mac OS X is much like installing 9.x. The process has changed slightly with the new version because it takes place under Apple's Mac OS X Installer program, booted from a "lite" version of Mac OS X on the Install CD. The entire process will take roughly 20 minutes on a G4 system, or 30–45 minutes on a slower G3.

If you're running Mac OS 9.x and have inserted the Mac OS X 10.0 CD, double-click the Install Mac OS X icon. Your computer will display a welcome message and then restart after a few moments and begin to boot from the CD. If you are starting the installation from a power-off state, make sure that the CD is in your drive, and then start the computer while holding down the C key.

While the installer boots, you'll see a Mac OS X loading screen. It is normal for this screen to stay visible for a few minutes. The installation procedure begins immediately after the operating system is loaded.

> **Note**
>
> During the installation, there are a few non-install actions you can choose from the Installer menu at the top of the screen:
>
> Reset Password is useful if you are locked out of your computer. This will be discussed in Chapter 29.
>
> The Open Disk Utility selection will open the Mac OS X native version of the Drive Setup utility that you used to partition your drives. In addition, this application contains the combined functionality of Disk First Aid, making it easy to repair your disks when booted from the Installer CD. Learn more about using this tool in Chapter 6, "Native Utilities and Applications."

Choosing a Language

Mac OS X includes built-in support for many languages including English, Japanese, French, Dutch, Spanish, Italian, and German.

Previous versions of the operating system required localized system and application software. In OS X, a single application can contain all the resources necessary to choose the appropriate display language for the person using the software.

The language selection screen is the first option that will appear during the installation process, as shown in Figure 2.12.

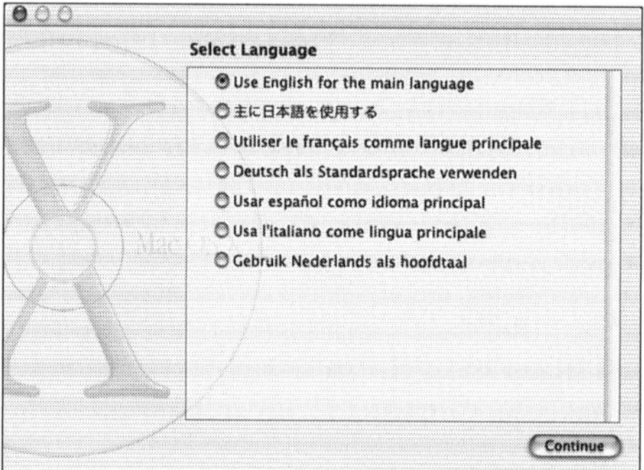

FIGURE 2.12
Choose the language you want to use on your computer.

Click the radio button in front of the language you'd like to use. Be aware that this sets the language for the *entire* operating system, not just the installer! If you choose Japanese, you'll boot into an operating system that is fully localized for Japan! (If that's what you intend, by all means, proceed!)

Click Continue to move on.

Welcome, Read Me, License

The installer will now take you through a sequence of three screens: the introductory Welcome message, a Read Me file that contains information about the version of Mac OS X you are installing, and finally, a License Agreement similar to the one within Mac OS 9.x. The license agreement is shown in Figure 2.13. If you'd like to view the license in another language, simply choose from the pop-up menu at the top of the agreement.

You can use the Continue and Go Back buttons at the bottom of the installer window to navigate forward and backward between the screens. After clicking Continue on the license page, a license agreement dialog will be shown. You must click Agree to continue the installation.

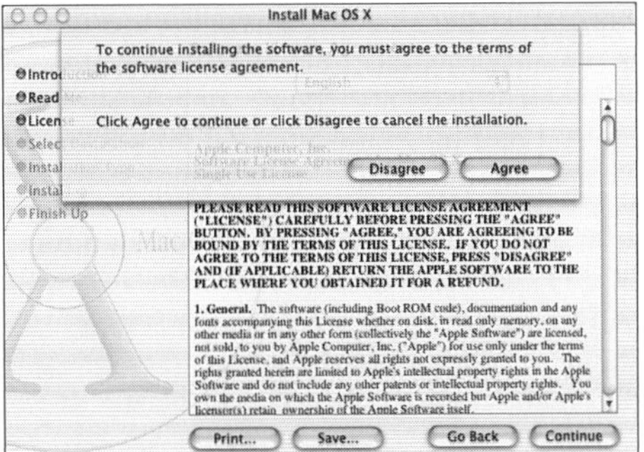

FIGURE 2.13
Click Agree to proceed with the installation.

Tip

Your first reaction might be to skim through the Read Me file, or ignore it altogether. I highly recommend that you take the time to read this information; it might contain errata not printed in the installation guide that came with your computer. One of the more common frustrations with installing Mac OS X on older computers (the 8GB partition limit) is documented in the Read Me screen of the installer. It wasn't until Apple posted an additional TIL article on its Web site that people realized what the problem was.

Select a Destination

The installation is about to begin: There are only two more steps before you can take a breather and let the installer do its thing. You must now choose the drive that will receive the OS X installation. Click on the icon of the drive that corresponds to the volume you've prepared for Mac OS X, as shown in Figure 2.14.

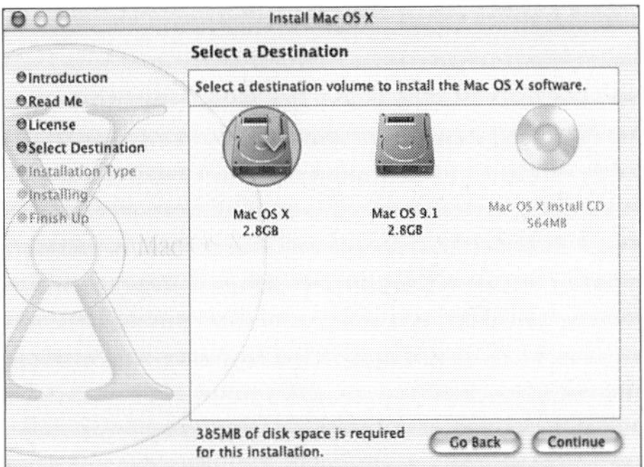

FIGURE 2.14
Choose the drive that will contain Mac OS X.

A gray circle and arrow will form over the selected drive. Figure 2.14 shows a system with a single dual-partition drive, and the Mac OS X destination volume selected.

If you'd like to erase the volume as part of the installation process, you can click the Erase Destination and Format as check box and choose a type of partition (Mac OS Extended [HFS+], or UNIX File System [UFS]) from the pop-up menu.

> **Caution**
>
> If you're a traditional Mac user and have installed Mac OS before, the Erase Destination option appears in roughly the same spot as Mac OS 8/9's Perform Clean Installation. It should be noted that this is *entirely* different from the older OS's clean install.
>
> In Mac OS 8/9, a clean install will disable your current system folder and install a new folder. All existing applications will be untouched. On Mac OS X, the Erase Destination selection will completely remove any information that is stored on the volume. All existing data will be lost.

When you're satisfied that you've chosen the correct volume, click Continue to move on to the final step.

Installation Type

The final step of the installation process is choosing the *type* of the install. For most users, the recommended option is to click the Install button. This will copy all the standard Mac OS X components to your computer. If this is the first time you've used Mac OS X, this is the best course of action to take. If, however, you're feeling adventurous, click the Customize button to display the individual components that can be added/removed from the system. Figure 2.15 shows the custom installation options.

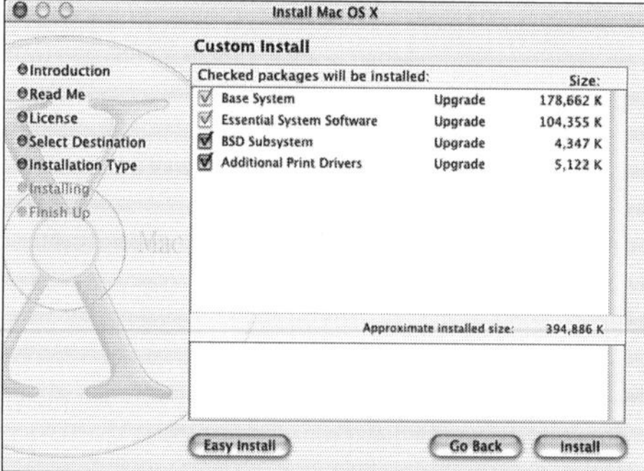

FIGURE 2.15
If you want to, you can customize your installation options.

There are four components to the basic Mac OS X 10.0 installation:

- **Base System**—The Base operating system contains everything that is needed to boot, such as the Mach kernel and system libraries. The component cannot be deselected.
- **Essential System Software**—This package contains the standard assortment of Mac OS X applications and utilities. Like the Base System, the Essential System Software option cannot be removed.
- **BSD Subsystem**—The command-line BSD environment tools are contained in the BSD Subsystem. This will be necessary to access many of the advanced features of the operating system, so I suggest that you include this option.
- **Additional Print Drivers**—The Additional Print Drivers package includes drivers for many Canon, Epson, and HP printers. If you do not plan to print from your computer or are using a LaserWriter/LaserWriter-compatible printer, there is no need for this optional component.
- **Additional Languages**—By default, all available language packs are installed. Pick and choose what you need on your computer.

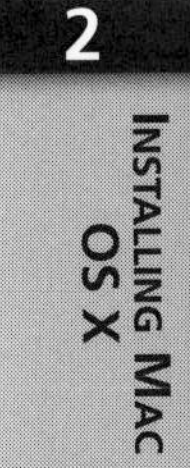

To add or remove a component, click the check box in front of the item. Checked items are installed, unchecked items are not.

Finally, click the Install button to start the installation. The process of copying and installing files will take around 15–30 minutes, depending on the speed of your machine. After the installation is complete, your system will reboot and start Mac OS X for the first time.

Note

If you'd like to keep a close watch on the Mac OS X installation procedure, choose Show Log from the Installer's File menu. The log will display extensive information about your system configuration and what the installer application is doing.

The Mac OS X Setup Assistant

The first time Mac OS X boots, it will run an installer assistant that helps set up the basic features of your new operating system. This installation process is actually much more streamlined than Mac OS 8 or 9, and should take only a few minutes. During the procedure, your network settings will be configured and registration details will be sent back to Apple. If you do not have the necessary information present, you should collect it before proceeding.

Note

When Mac OS X boots for the first time, it will prepare several system files. This takes two or three minutes longer than normal. Don't worry, this happens only once!

Country

The first step of the setup process is setting your country. By default, the Mac OS X installation shows only the countries specific to the distribution area of the software. Even though OS X supports multiple languages out of the box, the packaging and other materials are localized. If your country is not listed, click the Show All button, as shown in Figure 2.16.

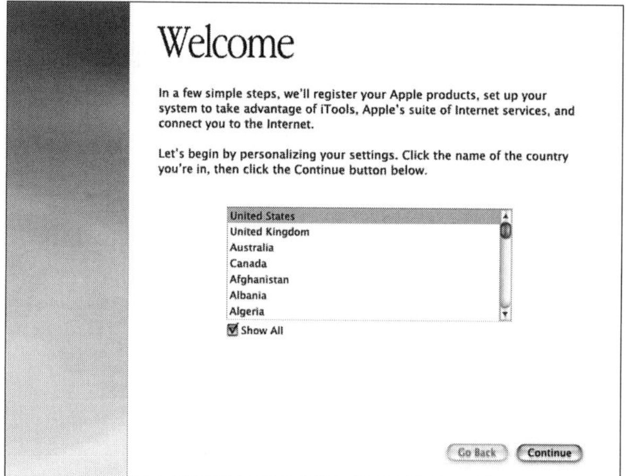

FIGURE 2.16
Select your country then click continue to move on. If your country isn't listed, click the Show All check box.

Click the country name in the list to highlight and select it. After making your choice, click the Continue button to move on.

Keyboard Layout

The second step of the installation is almost identical to the first: You choose the keyboard layout that Mac OS X will use, based on country. The same rules from the last step apply here. If you don't see your country in the default list, click the Show All check box to display all the available layouts. Figure 2.17 shows the layout selection screen.

FIGURE 2.17
Now, choose your keyboard layout.

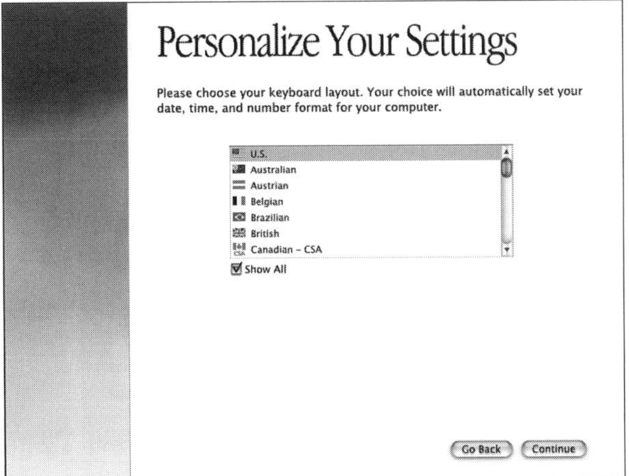

Again, click the name of your choice to select it, and then click Continue to move to the next step.

> **Note**
>
> These settings can be changed at any time in the future, so don't worry if you make a mistake. If you realize you clicked the wrong thing during this setup process, you can fix it immediately by clicking the Go Back button to retrace your steps.

Registration Information

Now, you'll need to do some typing. This step requires the completion of a registration form that will be sent back to Apple and serve to register your Mac OS X purchase. Of the fields shown on the form (displayed in Figure 2.18), only the e-mail address and company/school fields are optional. All other data must be completed in order to proceed. If you're concerned about how Apple will use your data later on, click the Privacy button for Apple's full information disclosure policy.

Click Continue to move to the next part of the registration.

The second page of the registration process asks for a few pieces of user information—where you will use your computer and what profession you are in. This is, again, required information.

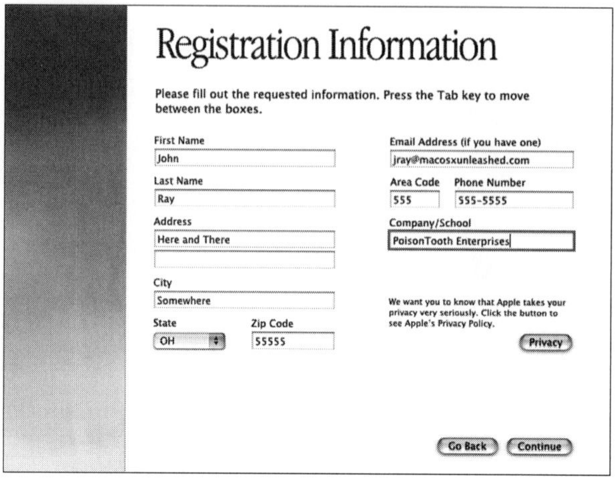

FIGURE 2.18
Enter your personal information to register the Mac OS X software with Apple.

Clicking Continue after filling out this final registration form will greet you with a Thank You screen. Don't get excited; there are still quite a few steps to complete!

Create Your Account

Mac OS X is different from previous versions of the Macintosh operating system in that it is a true multiuser OS. While Mac OS 9 offered the capability to let different users log in to the system, the base OS didn't really understand the difference between users. Multiple users couldn't be running processes simultaneously, nor could multiple people access the system simultaneously.

Mac OS X *requires* multiple users in order to operate. Each user has a private password that is used to access the operating system. This helps to keep programs from interfering with each other and creates the stable environment that you're going to love. If you're thinking to yourself, "I live in an apartment by myself (except for a small fluffy Pomeranian). Why would I want to password-protect my machine? I just want to sit down and use it!" Don't fret—Mac OS X can be configured so that you start your computer and begin working immediately, the same way you have since 1984. You'll learn more about user accounts and their purpose in Chapter 11, "Additional System Components" and Chapter 24, "User Management."

In step 4 of the setup process, you will configure your first user account. This information will be used to control your access to the system and to prevent unauthorized changes from being made to your software. The account creation screen can be seen in Figure 2.19.

FIGURE 2.19
Create the account you'll use to access your Mac OS X system.

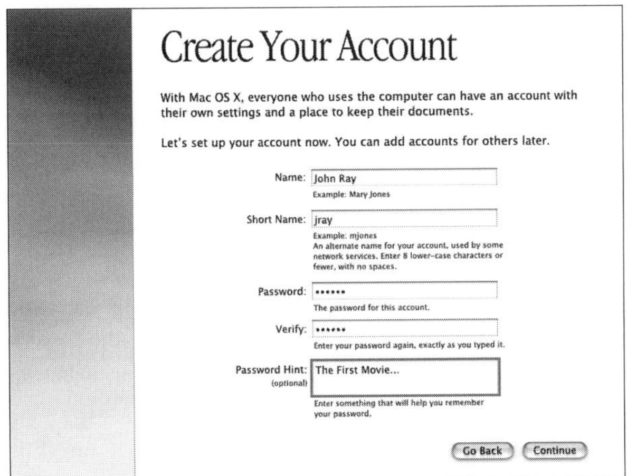

Because this is likely to be new territory for many Mac users, the account setup fields are explained here:

Name—Your full name. This can be used to log in to the system and will be used by Mac OS X to identify you while you are using your computer (software registrations, and so on).

Short Name—The short name is the name of your account. This identifies you to the underlying Unix operating system and should be comprised of *eight* or fewer lowercase letters or numbers. Spaces and punctuation are not allowed. If this is confusing, just think of your e-mail address. If you've registered with your ISP, you've given it your full name (like you did in the previous field) and you picked a username that is used for logging in to the system and accessing e-mail. This is the same idea. Mac OS X will pick a default value for you, but you're welcome to change it to anything you'd like.

Password—The Password field is used to set a secret word or string of characters that Mac OS X will use to verify that you are who you say you are. Passwords should normally be easy to remember, but should contain a mixture of uppercase and lowercase characters as well as numbers or symbols.

Verify—Type the same string you entered into the Password field into the Verify field. This is used to make sure that the password you typed is actually what you intended.

Password Hint—The password hint is exactly what it implies: something that will remind you of your password. If you attempt to log in to your system three times without success, the hint is displayed. For machines that are used in public computing labs, it's best to keep this something very general, or not supply a hint at all. It won't take someone long to figure out a hint such as "My password is my last name and my first name reversed."

Click Continue to proceed to the fifth stage of the Mac OS X installation: Internet setup.

Note

If more than one person will be logging in to the system, you will need to create multiple user accounts. This process is documented in Chapter 11 and Chapter 24.

Internet Setup

After creating your Mac OS X account, Mac OS X will prompt you regarding your Internet configuration. There are four possible options: sign up for EarthLink with promotional code, sign up with EarthLink without promotional code, skip Internet setup, or use an existing Internet connection. These choices can be seen in Figure 2.20.

If you choose either of the EarthLink options, you'll be guided through the process of signing up for Apple's preferred ISP. This involves providing contact and billing information. For more information on EarthLink, please check out `http://www.earthlink.net/`.

If you already have Internet access, but don't have all the information required to connect to your network or dial in to your ISP, I suggest skipping this step for now—you can jump ahead to "Selecting a Time Zone."

If you do know how your Internet access should be configured, select the I'll Use My Existing Internet Service radio button, and then click Continue to begin setup.

FIGURE 2.20
Choose to set up an EarthLink account, use an existing ISP, or forego any network configuration.

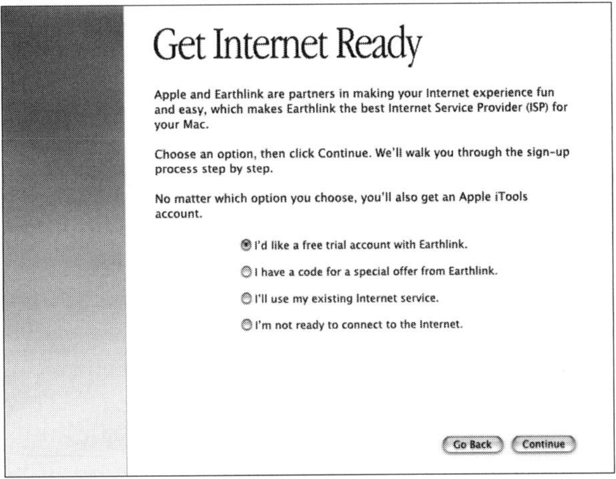

Choosing a Connection Method

Mac OS X will now display ascreen where you can choose the method by which you connect to the Internet. Figure 2.21 shows the five potential choices for setup:

Telephone Modem—Choose this if you use your computer's modem to dial in to an ISP.

Local Area Network (LAN)—A local area network configuration assumes that you are connected to a network directly. This is usually the appropriate option for businesses or educational institutions.

Cable Modem—Cable modems provide high-speed broadband Internet access to the home. You can obtain speeds similar to dedicated T1 lines for a fraction of the price.

DSL (Digital Subscriber Line)—DSL service tends to be a bit pricier than cable modem access, but is also more stable and has the potential of offering higher bidirectional transfers than a cable modem.

AirPort Wireless—The AirPort selection should be used if you are part of an AirPort or other 802.11b-based network. If you do not have an AirPort card installed, this option will be grayed.

Choose the option that best represents your method of accessing the Internet, and then click Continue.

Tip

The LAN, Cable Modem, and DSL selections are identical. In fact, if you change the settings for one, go back and choose another, your configuration choices are maintained. If your ISP requires PPPoE or other more advanced settings, you'll have to set them up later.

FIGURE 2.21
Choose your Internet connection method.

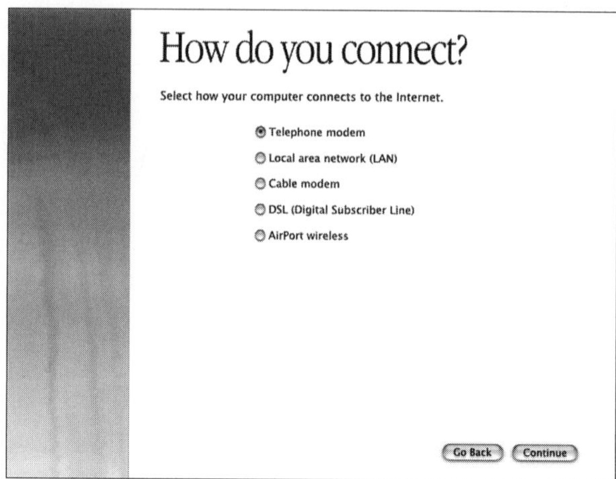

Modem Configuration

If you chose to configure your system to connect with your Mac's modem, you should make sure that you have your account information handy.

Here you will need to enter several pieces of information that help your computer dial and log in to your ISP:

User Name—This is the username given to you by your ISP. It is *not* the username you picked while creating your Mac OS X account.

Password—Again, this is the password for your ISP's dial-in account. It is *not* related to the password you set for your Mac OS X account.

ISP Phone Number—The phone number used to access your ISP.

Outside Access Numbers—Typically needed for company or hotel connections, if you need to dial additional digits to access an outside line, place them here.

Do You Have Call Waiting—If you choose Yes for this question, Mac OS X will attempt to disable call waiting before calling the ISP.

Click Continue to move to the second screen of your dial-in configuration.

The final step of setting up your modem is telling the system what type of modem is connected to your computer and how it is hooked up. The second screen of the modem configuration has only two settings:

How is your modem connected to the computer?—Choose the type of connection between your computer and modem. Users can choose Internal Modem or USB Modem if the modem is an external model.

What kind of modem do you have?—There are well over 100 modems supported within Mac OS X. Choose your model from the pop-up menu. Most systems will have an Apple Internal Modem installed.

When finished, click Continue to move to the iTools account setup.

LAN/Cable/DSL

Because the setup of these three connection types is identical, they will be covered here under a single section. It is assumed that the reader already has the information that is needed to configure their network settings. Although a short description is given here, you can learn more about TCP/IP networking in Chapter 9, "Network Setup."

If you've chosen one of the three LAN/Cable/DSL options, you should see a screen like that of Figure 2.22.

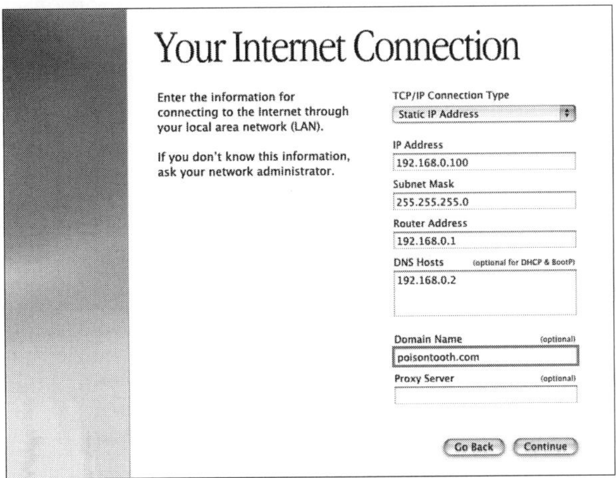

FIGURE 2.22
Your LAN/DSL/Cable configuration screen should look like this.

Connection Type—The first step for your network configuration is to choose the connection type. There are three options: Static IP Address, BootP Server, and DHCP Server. If you're using a cable or DSL modem, the proper choice is likely DHCP Server, but your ISP should know for certain. LAN users might need either DHCP or a static IP address—ask your system administrator to be safe. BootP is no longer widely used.

IP Address—The IP address identifies your computer on the network. For DHCP/BootP users, this value is set automatically. Other users can ask their network administrator for the appropriate address.

Subnet Mask—A subnet mask resembles an IP address but is used to tell your system what part of its IP address identifies the network it is attached to. For DHCP/BootP users, this value is set automatically. Other users can ask their network administrator for the appropriate mask.

Router Address—The router address is another IP address that tells your computer where to send information that should leave your local network. For DHCP/BootP users, this value is set automatically. Other users can ask their network administrator for the appropriate address.

DNS Hosts—A DNS (domain name server) translates between number IP addresses and the names you see on the Internet (such as `www.apple.com`). Your ISP will usually supply at least two DNS entries for your use. Most DHCP/BootP users will have this configured automatically, but also can supply values manually. Contact your network administrator or ISP for the appropriate settings.

Domain Name—If you're part of a LAN, you're most likely part of an existing domain. For example, machines on my local subnet are part of the poisontooth.com domain. This information is optional.

Proxy Server—If your LAN requires the use of a proxy server to access outside resources, enter the address of the proxy here. Your network administrator can provide this information. This configuration is for a *Web* proxy.

After setting up your information, click Continue to move on to the iTools account setup.

AirPort Configuration

There are two parts to setting up your computer to use an AirPort network: choosing the AirPort network and configuring TCP/IP. The AirPort wireless network is just an access method; it doesn't necessarily automate the process of configuring your computer's network settings.

Figure 2.23 shows the AirPort network selection screen.

Select the AirPort network to use for your connection and then fill in the appropriate information. Use the LAN/Cable/DSL section as a reference—the settings will be identical. Click Continue to enter the information to identify your computer on the AirPort network.

Click Continue to proceed with iTools setup.

FIGURE 2.23
Choose the AirPort network to connect to.

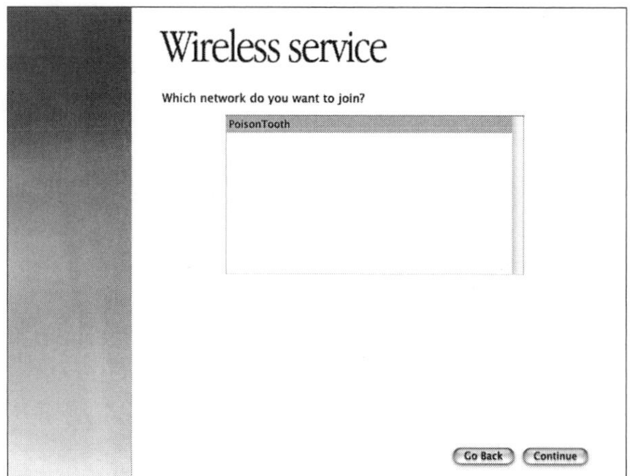

iTools Setup

Mac OS X integrates Apple's iTools with the operating system. If you don't have iTools, get it! Through Apple's iTools service, you gain access to a free e-mail account, 20MB of personal storage, personalized electronic greeting cards, and more!

Mac OS X does not require that you have an iTools account to set up the system. In fact, it will create an account for you, use an existing account, or let you skip iTools for the time being and set it up later. The first screen of the iTools configuration presents you with these three options.

If you already have an iTools account, click the radio button in front of "I'm already using iTools," and then enter your username and password in the supplied fields. These are *not* necessarily the same as the username and password you used when you set up your Mac OS X user account.

If you'd rather not use iTools at the present time, choose "I'm not ready for iTools."

Finally, if you want to set up an iTools account right now, click the "I'd like to create my iTools account" radio button.

Tip

If you want to learn more about iTools before signing up, click the iTools button on the iTools Setup page. You'll be presented with information about the iTools service and what it can do for you.

Click Continue to finish configuring your computer.

Creating an iTools Account

If you've selected the option to create an iTools account immediately, you should see a registration form similar to that of Figure 2.24.

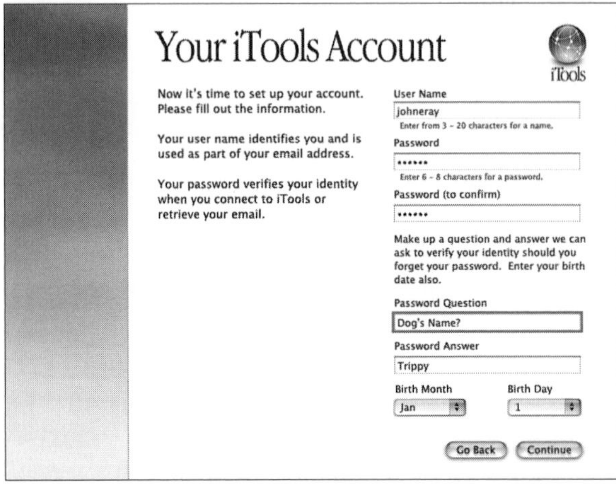

FIGURE 2.24
Register with iTools during the Mac OS X setup.

You'll need to fill out all the fields in the registration form. Apple requires that all the information be present to establish an account. This information will be stored in your account, but you should make a note of it in case of you need to re-enter it at some point.

User Name—A 3–20 character name (no spaces) that will be used to uniquely identify your iTools account. This is unrelated to your Mac OS X username.

Password—This is 6–8 characters to protect your account. The password you choose protects all information stored on your iDisk and all your iTools e-mail. Choose a password that mixes uppercase and lowercase letters and numbers.

Password (to Confirm)—Enter the same password as in the previous field. This will be used to verify that you typed what you think you typed!

Password Question—Provide a straightforward question that only you can answer. This will be used to retrieve your password in case you forget it.

Password Answer—The answer to your password question. You must type this exactly in order to access an account you've lost the password for.

Birth Month—The month in which you were born. This, along with your Birth Day and Password answers, will help recover lost passwords.

Birth Day—The day on which you were born.

Click Continue to save your network settings and connect to the Internet. Your computer will then attempt to contact Apple and send the registration information you've entered. If the registration information can't be sent, you'll be prompted either to try again or click Continue. As with everything during the setup steps, this can happen later, so don't worry if the connection fails.

E-mail Setup

There are only a few more steps before you can start playing with OS X. The remaining settings help configure your environment so that your system is ready to use when you log in for the first time.

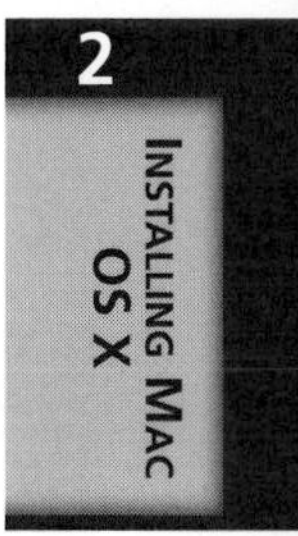

Mac OS X includes its own e-mail client that supports advanced features and a look and feel that matches the OS X environment perfectly. In the Set Up Mail screen, shown in Figure 2.25, you can enter the data needed to access your iTools e-mail or another account.

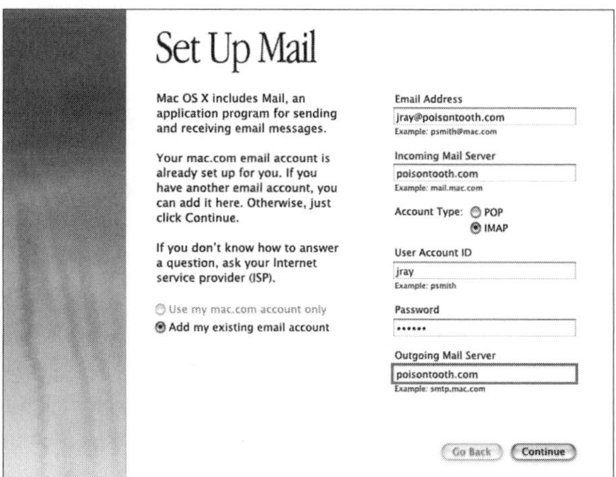

FIGURE 2.25
Set up your e-mail accounts for use within the Mac OS X mail program.

You can choose between your iTools (Mac.com) e-mail account and another account by clicking the radio buttons beside Use my mac.com account only or Add my existing e-mail account. You can always add accounts from directly in the application at a later time.

Tip

By default, if you choose Use my mac.com account only, the Mac OS X installer will fill in all the appropriate information. Unfortunately, it doesn't allow you to alter these settings—IMAP support is a great option offered by Apple, but you can't use it directly. A simple way around this is to write down the existing mac.com information, select the Add my existing email account option, and re-enter the information as you'd like it to appear.

Email Address—The e-mail address to use with your Mail software (such as `yourname@mac.com`).

Incoming Mail Server—The server that holds your messages until you retrieve or delete them. The iTools mail server is mail.mac.com. Your ISP or network administrator should be able to supply this information.

Account Type—The Mail application supports two types of access: POP and IMAP. POP service downloads mail directly to your computer each time it logs in. IMAP, in contrast, keeps the mail on the server until you delete it—this allows you to access the same messages from multiple computers. iTools e-mail supports both types. Most ISPs support only POP-based mail. Check with your network administrator or ISP to be sure.

User Account ID—The username used with your e-mail account. This is the part of your e-mail address to the left of the @ symbol. This is *not* necessarily the same username used when setting up Mac OS X.

Password—The password used to access your e-mail account. Again, this is not necessarily (unless you chose to make it so) the same password used when setting up Mac OS X.

Outgoing Mail Server—The mail server used to deliver messages to the Internet. The iTools outgoing mail server is `smtp.mac.com`. Your ISP or network administrator should be able to supply this information.

Click Continue to move on to the next step—setting a time zone.

Selecting a Time Zone

Finally, a few simple steps! One of the last setup steps is configuring the time zone your computer is located in. Setting a time zone is important for applications that receive information from outside of the local area—such as e-mail. Without the time zone properly configured, e-mail software cannot display the correct time on incoming messages from other zones. Mac OS X will display a small world map, shown in Figure 2.26.

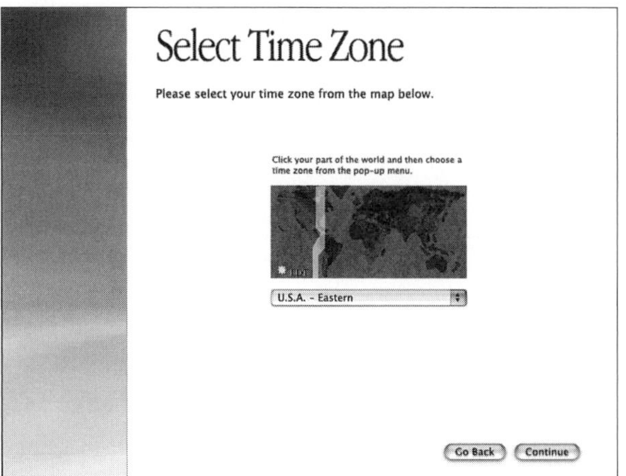

FIGURE 2.26
Choose a time zone for your computer.

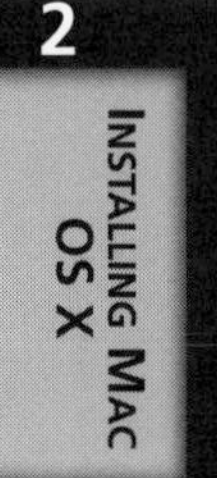

To choose a time zone, first click your location on the map. The highlight will move to where you clicked and the name of the most commonly used zone (EST, PST, and so on) will be displayed in the lower-left corner of the map.

Next, click the pop-up menu to change to the appropriate zone within the highlighted region. For example, I live in Ohio, so I click on the Eastern United States, and then choose U.S.A. - Eastern from the pop-up menu.

Click Continue when you've chosen the appropriate zone.

Setting Date and Time

We've arrived at the last step in the Mac OS X setup process—setting the day and time. This step requires little explanation. A screenshot of the configuration window is shown in Figure 2.27.

The date and time are configured by interacting with the clock and calendar displayed on the setup screen. To set a date, you can use the arrows near the top of the calendar to navigate through years and months, and then click the day on the calendar graphic to choose a specific date.

Dragging the minute hand on the clock can be used to set the time; this is slow, but it works just like setting an analog wristwatch. Click the AM or PM in the lower-right corner of the clock graphic to alternate between AM and PM. Alternatively, you can click the hour, minute, or second position in the digital clock display, and then use the arrows to the right to change the current setting. If you'd rather not use the arrows, you can simply type in a value after choosing the component of the time you want to adjust.

When the clock is set, click Continue.

FIGURE 2.27
Set the date and time.

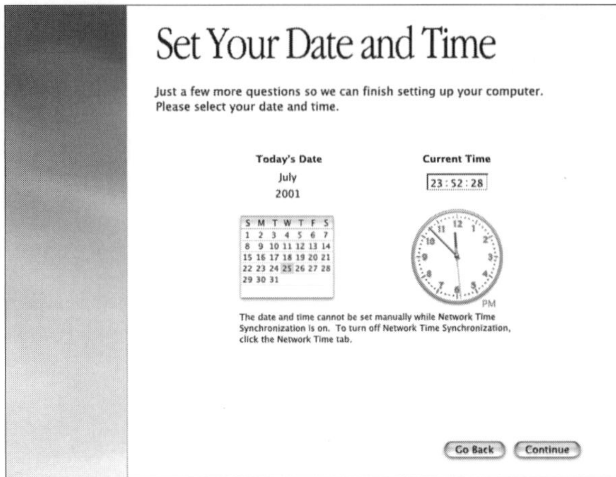

Wrap Up

You've just reached the last step of the configuration process. When prompted, click Done and Mac OS X will take you to the familiar desktop that you've seen in so many demonstrations.

There are far more options that can be used to personalize your system, and we'll get to them in the upcoming chapters. If you need to change something you set during the install, or feel you've made a mistake, check the book's index for information on the particular setting you'd like to change.

Assuming you're ready to go, Chapter 3 will provide a tour through the operating system so that you can start playing immediately.

Summary

Mac OS X is best installed on a dual partition system, with one partition dedicated to Mac OS 9.x, and the other to Mac OS X. If you are using a single partition 9.x system, you can install on the same partition without losing any information. Before installing, it's best to read all the related Apple TIL articles. In the first two weeks of release, more than fifty articles were released. As time passes, this number will only grow.

Although Mac OS X is a fantastic system, you should not install Mac OS X if you are using a G3 system running at less than 400MHz. Some users are best advised to stay in Mac OS 9.x until more hardware support and optimizations are added to the system.

CHAPTER 3

Mac OS X Basics

In This Chapter

After installing Mac OS X and completing the included installer assistant, you'll be transported to the Mac OS X desktop. Unfortunately, many users will find themselves staring at a completely unfamiliar desktop. This chapter will approach Mac OS X from the perspective of a user who has just logged in, and will look at some of the features that make Mac OS X a powerful system and unique user experience. The more complex components shown here will be discussed in depth elsewhere, so don't worry if all your questions aren't answered immediately.

Welcome to Mac OS X

The Mac OS X desktop, seen in Figure 3.1, looks simple enough. Many of the visual cues that Mac users have come to rely on are present, along with a few new elements.

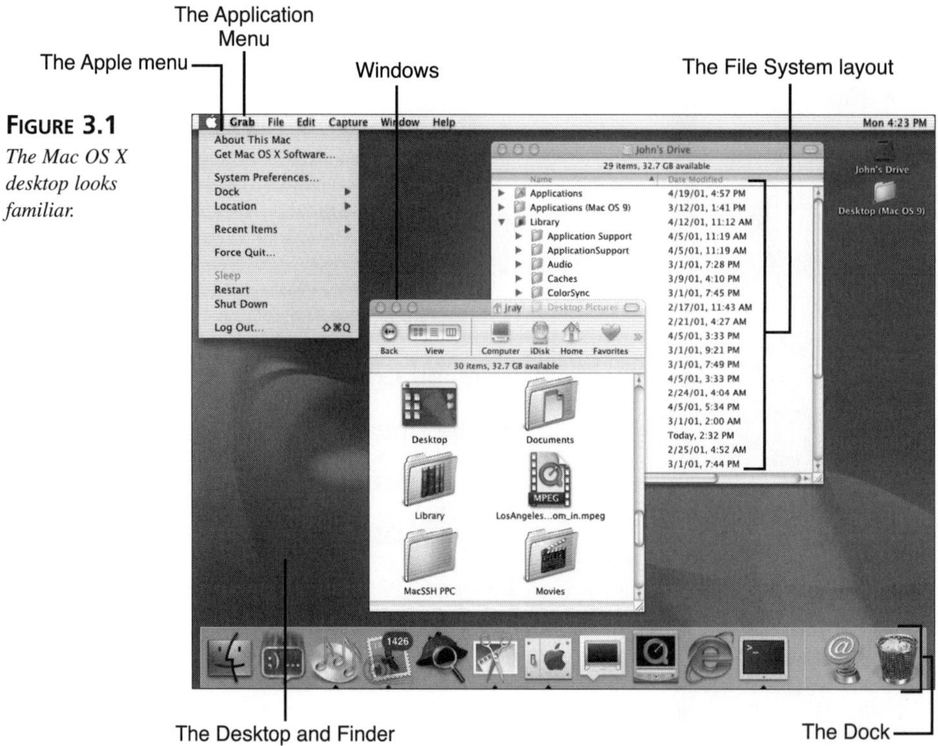

FIGURE 3.1
The Mac OS X desktop looks familiar.

Let's take a look at many of the Mac OS X system components and how they compare to their Mac OS 9.x counterparts.

- **The file system layout**—Where did everything go? Mac OS X imposes a strict structure on the file system. Learn where you can find your files and applications.

- **The Apple menu**—The Apple menu provides access to recent applications and common system-wide function. Gone are desk accessories and access to individual control panels.
- **Windows**—The new Mac OS X look extends to the windows themselves, which sport new features as well.
- **The Application menu**—Previous versions of the Mac operating system started program-specific menus with File. In Mac OS X, each application has its own self-named menu that contains functions common to any program.
- **The desktop and Finder**—The primary playground of many a Mac user, the desktop and Finder still operate in much the same way as under earlier versions of Mac OS.
- **The Dock**—Taking the place of the task menu located on the right of the Mac menu bar in earlier versions of the operating system, the Dock also includes components from the traditional Mac desktop and Apple menu.
- **Menu Extras**—Mac OS X 10.1 introduces Menu Extras—replacing much of the functionality lost when the Control Strip was removed. Many of the system preference panels (Sound, Date and Time, Network, and so on) offer the capability of adding a menu extra to the menu bar for quick access to settings.

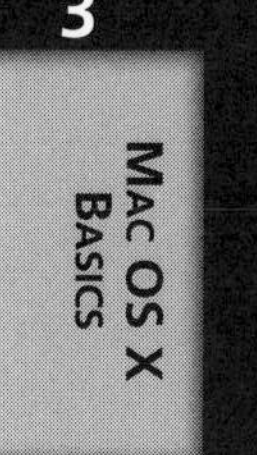

Let's take a look at each of these elements of the OS X environment, its basic use, and what problems/differences you might encounter as you work with it.

The File System—Where Did Everything Go?

Mac OS X radically changes the way that Mac users interact with their files by imposing structure on a system that previously allowed a user to delete just about every file and folder on his hard drive before complaining. For those of you who have been using the Mac OS for 15 years, this change might come as an unwelcome surprise. Interestingly, Windows 2000/XP and Linux users are likely to be more accustomed to these restrictions already.

The goal of the OS X project is to provide system stability and ease of use to as wide a range of users as possible. To do this, Apple created sets of directories that *must* exist on each Mac OS X installation. This produces consistency across different copies of the operating system, and makes it simple for application installers to choose the appropriate place for storing files. Users cannot modify the system-level directories or move them out of their default location. Anyone with experience using Mac OS 8 or 9 will, at one point in time, have installed a piece of software only to ask "Where in the world did that file just go?" Under Mac OS X, you'll know.

The "Computer Level" of the File System Hierarchy

Like the My Computer icon in Windows, Mac OS X provides a topmost view of the storage devices accessible to the machine. You can still see your drives mounted on the desktop, but you can also access them by looking at the Computer view of your system. Figure 3.2 shows a Finder window that is viewing the top level of the system.

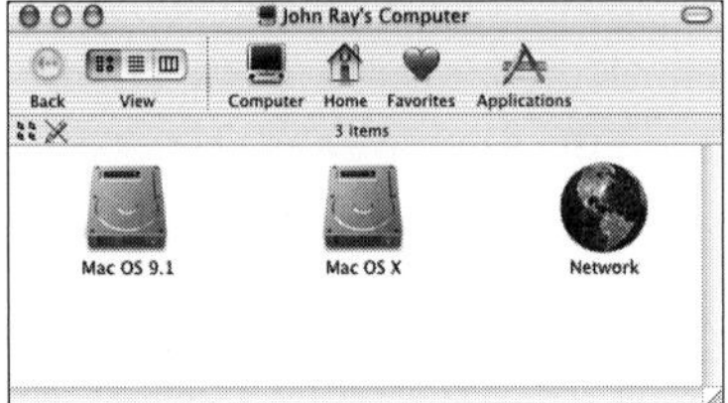

FIGURE 3.2
Mac OS X provides access to your drives and network within a Finder window, as well as on the desktop.

In Figure 3.2, there are three icons visible: Network, Mac OS X, and Mac OS 9.x. Within these three locations are all the files that are located on my system. Any additional FireWire or USB drives that are plugged into the system will appear in this location, as well as being mounted directly on the desktop.

The purpose of the hard drive icons should be obvious: to navigate the file system just as you would in Mac OS 8/9 or Windows. The Network icon, however, might require a bit of explanation.

Network Icon

The Network icon will be used on clustered Mac OS X installations to provide a central point of access to multiple servers, shared applications, and other network resources. In its current incarnation, it serves little purpose but to confuse the user. Mounted AppleShare volumes *cannot* be found within the Network directory, nor can you browse the available servers from this location. Later in the book you'll learn about a Windows-compatible file sharing tool called Sharity, which allows browsing of Windows shares within Network, but until this feature is better fleshed out by Apple, its practicality for the home user is debatable.

> **Note**
>
> Linux and Unix users might recognize the Computer level of the file system as being the same as the root level of a Unix file system. In reality, the root level starts with the Mac OS X boot disk—all other volumes use mount points below that volume (under the `/Volumes` directory). The Computer view of the file system is an artificial construct created by Apple to provide a top-level view of all resources available on the computer—similar to My Computer on Windows.

The Top-Level Mac OS X File System

When you open your Mac OS X boot drive, you should see a collection of permanent folders, similar to those in Figure 3.3. These directories contain all the preinstalled applications, utilities, and configuration files for your system. This will be your starting point of accessing most of the functions of your system.

FIGURE 3.3
The Mac OS X top-level file system contains several permanent folders.

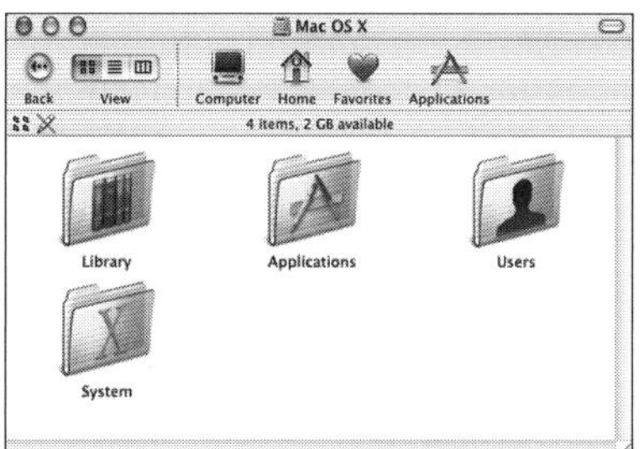

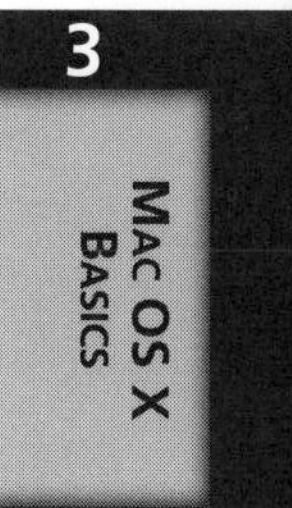

As a normal Mac OS X user, you cannot modify these folders by moving, renaming, or deleting them. In addition, you cannot create new folders at this level of the drive. Don't worry too much about this. If you *really* want to create a new folder, there are ways to do it by using the `root` user account. You can also create folders and files *within* these locations if necessary.

Applications

The Applications folder contains all the preinstalled Mac OS X applications, such as TextEdit, Mail, QuickTime Player, and many others. Any application located within this folder will be accessible to any user on the system. If you're installing an application that should be accessed by only a single person, it might make more sense to store the application within the user's home directory (home directories will be covered shortly).

Perhaps more interesting than the applications in the Applications folder is the Utilities folder also located within. The Utilities folder contains tools necessary to set up your printers, calibrate your display, and other important tasks.

Caution

The Utilities folder *can* be modified by the default Mac OS X user. You can move, rename, or delete the folder if you'd like, but problems might arise. For reasons beyond explanation, Apple hardcoded the location of the Print Center into the system. When you attempt to print from Mac OS X, if Print Center cannot be located in the Utilities folder, it will not be launched. If you *must* rename your Utilities folder, you can manually start Print Center to complete any pending print jobs. This problem is fully described in Apple's TIL: `http://til.info.apple.com/techinfo.nsf/artnum/n106265`.

This problem might affect other applications automatically launched from the Utilities folder as well.

Library

The Library is a new addition to the Mac OS file system, and demonstrates the modular construction of the OS X system. Although is does not have a strict definition, you can think of the Library as a storage location for system-wide application preferences, application libraries, and information that should be accessible to any user. Figure 3.4 shows the contents of the Library folder on a clean Mac OS X installation.

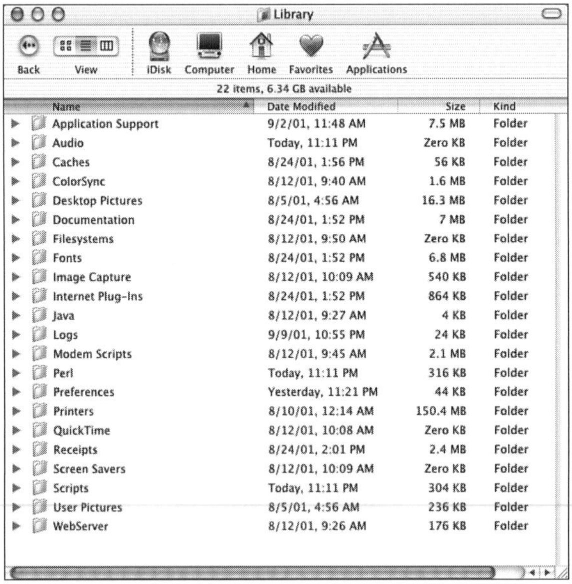

Library

Back View iDisk Computer Home Favorites Applications

22 items, 6.34 GB available

Name	Date Modified	Size	Kind
Application Support	9/2/01, 11:48 AM	7.5 MB	Folder
Audio	Today, 11:11 PM	Zero KB	Folder
Caches	8/24/01, 1:56 PM	56 KB	Folder
ColorSync	8/12/01, 9:40 AM	1.6 MB	Folder
Desktop Pictures	8/5/01, 4:56 AM	16.3 MB	Folder
Documentation	8/24/01, 1:52 PM	7 MB	Folder
Filesystems	8/12/01, 9:50 AM	Zero KB	Folder
Fonts	8/24/01, 1:52 PM	6.8 MB	Folder
Image Capture	8/12/01, 10:09 AM	540 KB	Folder
Internet Plug-Ins	8/24/01, 1:52 PM	864 KB	Folder
Java	8/12/01, 9:27 AM	4 KB	Folder
Logs	9/9/01, 10:55 PM	24 KB	Folder
Modem Scripts	8/12/01, 9:45 AM	2.1 MB	Folder
Perl	Today, 11:11 PM	316 KB	Folder
Preferences	Yesterday, 11:21 PM	44 KB	Folder
Printers	8/10/01, 12:14 AM	150.4 MB	Folder
QuickTime	8/12/01, 10:08 AM	Zero KB	Folder
Receipts	8/24/01, 2:01 PM	2.4 MB	Folder
Screen Savers	8/12/01, 10:09 AM	Zero KB	Folder
Scripts	Today, 11:11 PM	304 KB	Folder
User Pictures	8/5/01, 4:56 AM	236 KB	Folder
WebServer	8/12/01, 9:26 AM	176 KB	Folder

FIGURE 3.4
The Library provides applications with a system-wide information storage area.

Some of these folders are used by applications to data such as preferences, whereas others hold printer drivers or other system additions made by the user. The default Library folders you'll find upon installation include:

- **Application Support**—Contains files that are used by, but are not necessarily part of, an application. For example, the StuffIt engine is used globally by several compression utilities. Rather than having multiple copies of the engine for each program, a single copy of the engine is located in the Application Support folder.
- **Audio**—Contains application or user-added sounds and plug-ins for the Mac OS X audio system.
- **Caches**—Stores cached network information.
- **ColorSync**—Stores ColorSync output device profiles as well as scripts to work with ColorSync information. Mac OS X includes a large number of AppleScripts that can be used immediately, including the ability to mimic the color settings of a typical PC monitor.
- **Desktop Pictures**—Although desktop pictures can be loaded from any picture file, the Desktop Pictures directory provides a central storage area for all users to access picture files.
- **Documentation**—If a third-party application installs documentation beyond traditional program helps, it should automatically be added to this folder.
- **Fonts**—User-installed fonts can be added to the Fonts folder.
- **Image Capture**—Mac OS X includes an extensible utility for retrieving images from digital cameras and other forms of digital media. This folder contains scripts that can automatically crop images or create Web page galleries.
- **Internet Plug-Ins**—Rather than multiple browsers needing multiple copies of the same plug-in, or multiple users each needing a copy, the Internet Plug-Ins directory stores a single copy, accessible by any program that needs them.
- **Java**—Java is an integral portion of Mac OS X. If there are Java class libraries that should be available to anyone using the system, they can be stored in the Java folder.
- **Logs**—Log files generated by user-level services, such as file sharing are stored here.
- **Modem Scripts**—The scripts necessary to initialize all the Mac OS X–supported modems are stored here. These scripts are simple text files that can easily be modified to work with unlisted modems.
- **Perl**—Perl module information is stored within the Perl directory. Users should never need to manually update the contents of this folder.

- **Preferences**—System-wide preference files. Because Mac OS X supports multiple users, each user should have his own preference file (located in his home directory). This folder contains preferences that are global; that is, across all users.
- **Printers**—Drivers and utility software to manage third-party printers. Printer page description files can also be found here.
- **Receipts**—When an application uses the Apple installer to copy files to the system, it leaves behind a .pkg (package) file that contains a complete list of all the files that were installed on the system and where they are located. This list can be read by opening the Installer application (double-click the .pkg file) and choosing Show Files from the Edit menu.
- **Screen Savers**—Mac OS X includes its own screen saver engine. Within two weeks of the OS X release, more than 30 new screensaver modules were written. To add a new screen saver, just download the module and place it in this folder. It will be accessible by all user accounts on the system.
- **Scripts**—A number of useful AppleScripts are stored in the `Scripts` folder. Everything from Finder to e-mail automation is included.
- **StartupItems**—If a StartupItems folder doesn't exist on your system, you can create one. Any properly configured services will be executed from this location automatically. Note: This is *not* to be used in the same manner as the Startup folder on Mac OS 9. Applications placed here will not start when the computer is booted.
- **User Pictures**—In Mac OS X 10.1, Apple returned to a graphical login screen, similar to the multiuser interface in OS 9.x. To add custom pictures for all users to choose from, place them here.
- **WebServer**—CGIs (executable programs designed to work with a Web browser), and HTML documents are stored here. These can be used to build an industrial-strength Web server.

Keep in mind that if you plan to run a system with multiple user accounts, these folders affect all users on the system. For example, if you purchase a screen saver module for yourself, putting it in the Screen Savers folder gives access to all users. To restrict access to a single account, you'll have to install directly into your home directory, discussed shortly.

> **Tip**
>
> If your computer is being used as a personal workstation, it's best to leave the Mac OS X installation as "untainted" as possible. Almost all the items contained in the Library folder can also exist within your home directory. As you'll soon learn, your home directory is yours to configure however you see fit. Keeping system-wide configuration as simple as possible helps to make backing up and restoring a system very straightforward.

System

Next up on the list is the Mac OS X System folder. By default, the System folder contains one other folder, called Library. This is a more specific version of the same Library folder that contains the Fonts folder and other resources. Within the System's Library folder are contained the components that make up the core of the Mac OS X experience. Even though it is possible to perform some interesting hacks to the operating system, these files and folders should not be changed unless you are aware that any modifications you make could result in your computer becoming unbootable.

Users

The Users directory is probably the most interesting and important addition to the Macintosh file system. Although it is present in Mac OS 9, the multiuser capability pales in comparison to what is available under Mac OS X.

Mac OS X is based on an underlying Unix operating system. Within Unix, each file and folder belongs to a specific user and group. The *owner* of a file is exactly what it sounds like—the person to whom that file belongs. If you create a file, you own it. As the owner, you have the right to decide whether you want other people to be able to view it or edit it. A file or directory's *group* is similar to the owner, but whereas an owner is a single person, a group can consist of many different people.

For example, assume that you (Joe) are working with team members on an annual budget report. The members of the team who should be able to read the file are Betty, Bob, and Sue. Because there can be only one owner, Betty, Bob, and Sue can be given access to the file by assigning them to a group, such as ReportReaders, and then allowing ReportReaders the ability to read the files.

In Mac OS X, there is a default group named Staff that is shared between all accounts on the system. This makes it very easy to share a file between all the accounts on the system. If you'd like tighter control for limiting access to smaller groups of people, you can do that as well—with a little bit of work. Chapter 24, "User Management," discusses the use of user and group permissions from the BSD command line and using Mac OS X's graphical tools.

There is another possibility for allowing multiple people to have access to a single file: granting access to the "world." In the event that *everyone* should be able to read a file, you can also grant access to anyone. This is the typical mode of operation for the traditional Mac operating system—everyone has access to everything.

These three attributes for allowing access to a file (owner, group, and world) are controlled via three sets of permissions:

- **Owner Permissions**— Also called user permissions, these control whether a file's owner can read, write, or execute a file or application.
- **Group Permissions**—Group permissions control read, write, and execute access for members of the group that is assigned to the file. If only the owner should have access to the file, the group permissions can be set to "none."
- **World Permissions**—Permissions that affect everyone else; that is, those not in the file's group and not the owner. If a file has world read/write/execute access turned on, anyone with access to the system will be able to edit or delete the file.

Note

The owner of a file can always change the permissions that are associated with that file—even if they've turned off read or write access for themselves. Why would a file's owner want to shut off the ability to read or write his or her own file? Have you ever accidentally deleted a file on your system? If so, you already know why.

Of the three permissions that can be set for the owner, group, or world, the read and write attributes should be obvious. They control the capability to read from files and write to them. The execute attribute controls whether a file should be capable of being launched by someone on the system. Some applications should be accessible by only certain users, and this attribute provides a means of selectively enabling a program to execute in the same way you can enable reading or writing.

Note

As mentioned earlier, Mac OS X does not allow normal user accounts the capability to modify the folders at the top level of the hard drive. This is because those folders are owned by an account called the root or super-user account. Although it's tempting to use the root account to gain complete control over the system, it's also highly dangerous. For this very reason, Apple has disabled the root account in Mac OS X. Enabling the account will be covered, but isn't recommended unless you're comfortable making changes that could affect your system's ability to boot.

The Home Directory

So, the system allows users to own their own files and provides a means of controlling other users' access to these files—what does that have to do with the Users directory that we're discussing? The Users directory contains the home directories of all of the users on the machine. A user's home directory can be considered that user's workplace. It is hers, and hers alone. Files and folders that are stored within a user's home directory are protected from other users.

If you've been a Mac user for a long time, you should start to think of your home directory as the place where you can make all your modifications to the folder arrangement and structure. Your home directory is the *start* of your personal area on Mac OS X. You can add documents, applications, fonts, screen savers—just about anything you can think of. Best of all, no one can mess with your configuration; conversely, you can't mess with anyone else's!

Within the Users directory are directories for each of the users on the system—these are the home directories themselves. Your directory will be named using the short name that you chose when you created your Mac OS X user account. Apple has created several default folders in your home directory, as shown in Figure 3.5.

FIGURE 3.5
The home directory is filled with several default folders.

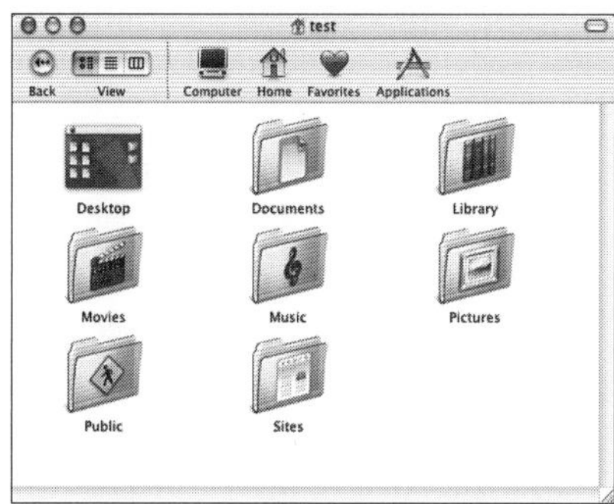

Desktop—The Desktop folder is much like what it always has been: a folder that contains everything that shows up on your desktop. In older versions of the Mac OS, this folder is invisible unless you are connecting to a remote Macintosh AppleShare server, in which case you could see the remote machine's Desktop folder. In Mac OS X, the Desktop folder is always visible in your home directory.

Documents—A generic store-all location for any documents that you create. This is just a recommended storage location to help organize your files.

Library—The Library folder is the same as the top-level Library folder and the Library folder within the System folder. Within the directories *in* this directory, you can store fonts, screen savers, and many other extensions to the operating system.

Movies—This is another generic storage location where you can keep your iMovies and other media.

Music—A generic location for storing your MP3s and various audio files.

Pictures—A generic location for storing pictures. As with the other storage location, these are just suggestions for you to use. Some software might default to the appropriate location for the file type it is creating, but there's nothing stopping you from storing your files elsewhere.

Public—If you plan to share your files over the network, you can do so by placing them in the Public folder and activating file sharing within the Sharing System Preferences panel. This will be discussed in Chapter 9, "Network Setup." Inside the Public folder is another folder called Drop Box. Other users can place items inside your drop box, but they cannot open the Drop Box folder itself. A small down arrow is located at the lower-right corner of the Drop Box icon to identify it visually.

Sites—The Sites folder contains your personal Web site. Unlike Mac OS 8/9, which allows a personal site to be located anywhere, Mac OS X uses the Sites folder. This small sacrifice in flexibility is easily overlooked when you consider that each user's personal Web site can be served simultaneously.

Tip

The top-level Library folder, the System folder's Library folder, and the Library folder in the user's home directory are all similar. Each can hold components that are used by other parts of the operating system.

The operating system evaluates these in the order of System Library, top-level Library, and then the Library in each user's folder. To keep files as consolidated as possible, it's best to store components in your home Library folder. If there are items that should be accessible to all of the operating system's users, place these within the top-level Library.

You should never need to change the contents of the System folder.

Even though Apple has been kind enough to include specific folders for different file types, feel free to do anything you'd like with your home directory. The only folders that should not be modified are the Desktop and Library folders. These are critical to system operation and must be maintained.

Note

By default, a user can access only the Public and Sites folders within another user's home directory. Other folders appear with a red minus symbol in the lower-right corner. This indicates that no access is available to that location.

The Apple Menu

In 1984, Apple introduced what many MS Windows users now call the Start menu. The Apple menu has provided an access point for small applications and system controls. Originally, the Mac OS allowed only special applications called Desk Accessories to exist in the Apple menu. Later, the menu became a simple folder that a user could place an application or folder in, and then access that item from within any application, at any time.

Unfortunately, the Apple menu also became the dumping point for just about anything. Applications that could best be described as control panels (because they configured system-wide functionality) started to show up under the Apple menu. The more complex the menu became, the less user friendly was the result. Under Mac OS X, this has been corrected by restricting the Apple menu to system-wide tasks that are helpful to anyone using the operating system. The Mac OS X Apple menu is seen in Figure 3.6.

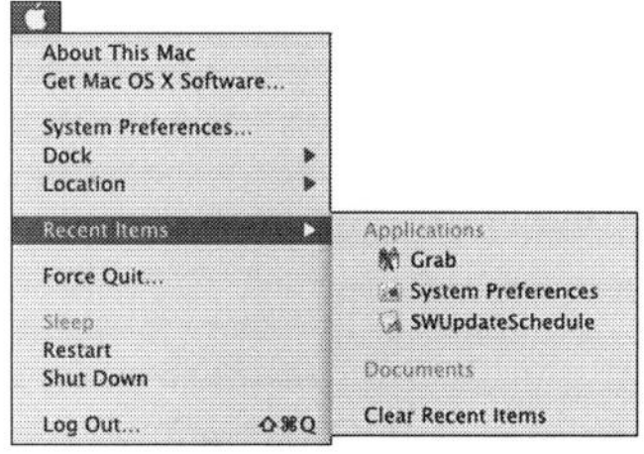

FIGURE 3.6
The Mac OS X menu can be used to access common system-wide functions.

The choices that are now available from the Apple menu are

- **About This Mac**—Displays information about the computer. This shows the current version of the operating system, the amount of available memory, and the type of processor that the system is using.

- **Get Mac OS X Software…**—Launches the user's preferred Web browser and loads the URL `http://www.apple.com/downloads/macosx/`. There, you can download third-party applications from Apple's list of available OS X software.
- **System Preferences…**—The equivalent of the traditional control panels, the System Preferences… selection launches the application used to control almost all aspects of the Mac OS X configuration.
- **Dock**—The Mac OS X Dock is one of the most visible additions to the new operating system—it is also one of the most controversial. This submenu provides quick access to common functions, such as the ability to hide the Dock. These functions, as you might expect, are also located in System Preferences.
- **Location**—The Location submenu allows you to quickly reconfigure the Mac OS X network settings. This is the equivalent of the Location Manager Control Strip module. Unfortunately, Mac OS X can only alter network settings based on location, severely limiting the versatility provided in earlier versions of the Mac OS. Locations are configured within System Preferences. Future versions of Mac OS X might bring back Location Manager functionality, but for now, this will have to suffice.
- **Recent Items**—Displays the most recently launched applications and documents. This submenu is visible in Figure 3.6.
- **Force Quit…**—Causes the currently active application to quit, regardless of its current state. This is the equivalent of pressing Command+Option+Escape to force an application that has hung to exit. Unlike Mac OS 8 or 9, forcing an application to quit in Mac OS X does not disrupt operating system stability.
- **Sleep**—Places your computer in a sleep state that requires very little power and can be started in a matter of seconds without the need for a full reboot. PowerBook/iBook users might want to shut down completely rather than put their computers to sleep. The power drain for these machines is higher than in Mac OS 8/9. It works, but you might find that your battery life has decreased from what you are accustomed.
- **Restart**—Closes all applications, prompts the user to save open files, and gracefully reboots the computer.
- **Shut Down**—Closes all applications, prompts the user to save open files, and shuts down the computer.
- **Log Out…**—Closes all applications, prompts the user to save open files, and then returns to the Mac OS X login screen. If Mac OS X has not been configured to display a login screen (the default state), the system will simply shut down all open applications and return to the initial power-on state.

Tip

Three of the eleven Apple menu items can be accessed by pressing Command+Eject on the new Apple keyboards. This keystroke will display a dialog box with Restart, Shutdown, and Sleep options.

If you're the lucky owner of a machine with a power button on the keyboard, pressing the power button will have the same effect. Pressing the power button on an Apple monitor or computer will put the machine to sleep.

What's Changed?

For the most part, the Apple menu should seem familiar to Mac users, but is likely to leave some wondering where a few of the features have gone. The best phrase to keep repeating to yourself is, with all due respect to the late Douglas Adams, "Don't Panic!" Most of the features you are looking for are still present, they've just moved around. Here are the common Apple menu items, and where they've gone:

- **AirPort**—The AirPort functionality is now moved to the Menu Extras as well as the System Preferences. Chapter 9 will provide information about the Mac OS X AirPort monitoring and configuration tools.
- **System Profiler**—An OS X native version of the Apple System Profiler is located in the system Utilities folder.
- **Calculator**—A Mac OS X calculator is located in the system Applications folder.
- **Chooser**—After 15 years of existence, the Mac OS loses the Chooser! Mac OS X moves the functionality of mounting network volumes directly into the Finder, within the Go menu. Printer selection is handled by the Print Center application. Network connections will be covered at length in Chapter 9, whereas Print Center is documented in Chapter 10, "Printer and Font Configuration."
- **Recent Applications/Recent Documents**—These menu items have moved to a single submenu, Recent Items. Mac OS X also adds a Recent Folders menu to the Finder so that you can quickly return to your most frequently visited locations.
- **Favorites**—The Favorites menu has become integrated with the various network and file system features of Mac OS X.
- **Key Caps**—A Mac OS X Key Caps program is located in the system Utilities folder.
- **Sherlock**—Access to the Sherlock search utility is now consolidated to the Finder's Find command, located in the File menu. By default, Sherlock is also found directly in the Dock and can always be launched as an application from the system Applications folder.

- **Speakable Items**—Although it is no longer accessible under the Apple menu, the Speakable Items folder still exists. You can have the system open it automatically for you from within the Speech panel of System Preferences. You can also find it by going to your home directory, opening the Library folder, and then opening the Speech folder inside of that (`~/Library/Speech/Speakable Items/` from the Finder's Go To Folder…" option under Go).
- **Stickies**—The Stickies application has been rewritten with new features for OS X. It can be found in the system Applications folder.

The remainder of the Mac OS Apple menu items have either gone the way of the dodo, or have become directly integrated into the Finder. The good news is that the functionality is still present. The bad news is that you're going to have to do some clicking to find it.

Windows

There's no getting around it—the Aqua interface is beautiful. One of the most obvious places that you'll deal with the interface is through onscreen windows, demonstrated in Figure 3.7. There are a number of changes between the Mac OS X operating system and previous versions. Let's take a look at a Finder window and see what's different.

FIGURE 3.7
Mac OS X windows are familiar, but the position of common elements has changed and a few new ones have been added.

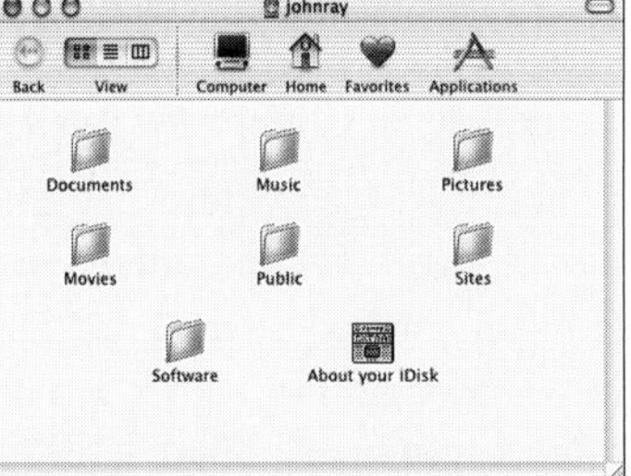

Close/Minimize/Maximize

In the upper-left corner of each window is located the Close (red X), Minimize (yellow -), and Maximize (green +) buttons. Differentiated only by color and position, the corresponding character symbol appears in each bubble button when the mouse cursor nears.

Clicking the Close button will close the open window. The OS X Minimize button takes the place of the windowshade function in early versions of the Mac OS. Instead of reducing the window to its title bar only, this shrinks the window into an icon view that is contained within the Dock. This icon is a full representation of the original contents of the window, and sometimes might even update its appearance as the parent application generates new output. Clicking the icon in the dock will restore the window to its original position and size on the screen.

Tip

Double-clicking the title bar of a window has the same effect as clicking the Minimize button.

The Maximize button does *not* perform in the way to which most Windows users are accustomed. Rather than filling the entire screen (which has always bothered me no end), Maximize opens the window to the size necessary to display the available information. If there are three icons that need to be shown, you don't need to waste your entire screen showing them.

Tip

Holding down Option while clicking the Minimize or Close button will result in all the windows in the current application being minimized or closed.

Hide/Show Toolbar

In the upper-right corner of certain windows (such as the Finder and Mail windows) is an elongated button that can be used to quickly show or hide toolbars in applications. Apple has stressed ease of use within Mac OS X, and is advocating customizable toolbars within applications. Although only a few packages have toolbars, that number will only increase as more applications become adapted to the Mac OS X interface.

Tip

In some applications (the Finder excluded), you can hold down the Command key and click the toolbar button to cycle through different available toolbar states, such as text-only, icon-only, and text/icon. Strangely enough, this trick seems to work only if there is already a toolbar visible.

There are also shortcuts to customizing the toolbar by holding down a combination of modifier keys while clicking the toolbar button. For example, within the Finder, hold Shift while clicking the button, or use `Command+Option` within Mail.

Because developers must implement the functionality of the toolbar button, you shouldn't expect all applications that have toolbars to include the toolbar button. If you have a favorite application that could benefit from this user interface feature, be sure to provide feedback directly to the developer.

Window Moving and Resizing

A noticeable new window feature, or lack thereof, is the borderless content area. As seen in Figure 3.8, the display in most OS X application windows goes directly up to the edge of the content window.

FIGURE 3.8
The content in a window goes right up to the edge.

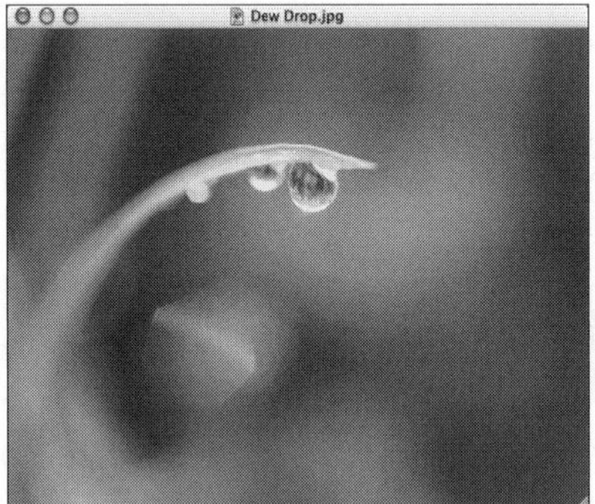

Although this creates a more attractive and more integrated feeling, you can no longer drag windows using the familiar border in Mac OS 8/9. Luckily, Apple has prevented users from completely dragging the title bar of a window off the screen. Title bars will not extend past the menu bar; several pixels of the edge of the window remain if you attempt to push a window off the edge of the screen.

Resizing windows works as you're accustomed: Click and drag on the resize icon in the lower-right corner of each window. Many applications in Mac OS X take advantage of *live resizing;* that is, as you resize the window, the contents of the window change. Unless you have a fast machine, live resizing is, sadly, painfully slow. One can only hope that this is addressed in a future release of the operating system.

Tip

There are a few new tricks that you can use when working with Mac OS X windows. In previous versions of the OS, the only way to move a window was if it was the frontmost window on the display. In Mac OS X, if you hold down the Command key, you can drag non-active windows that are located behind other windows. If fact, holding down Command enables you to click buttons and move scrollbars in many background applications.

Another fun trick is to hold down the Option key while clicking on an inactive application's window. This will hide the frontmost application and bring the clicked application to the front.

Finally, rather than switching to another window to close, minimize, or maximize it, positioning your cursor over the appropriate window controls will highlight them—allowing you to get rid of obtrusive windows without leaving your current workspace.

Apple's new window design has brought much criticism from those accustomed to the Mac's platinum appearance. With Mac OS X, the window controls have taken on much of the appearance of their Windows counterparts. Creating an environment that is comfortable for *all* users, regardless of what they've used before, is an important part of Apple's strategy to attract new users.

Window Widgets

There are other portions of the interface that have changed along with the addition of the Aqua interface. Both Mac and Windows users should be accustomed to these elements, even though they have a slightly different OS X appearance. Samples of many of the OS X Aqua interface elements are shown in Figure 3.9.

Aqua interface elements include:

- **Push buttons**—Push buttons are rendered as translucent white or aqua-colored ovals with the appropriate label text. These are typically used to activate a choice or to respond to a question posed by the operating system or application. The default choice, activated by pressing the Return key, pulses for easy visual confirmation.
- **Check boxes/Radio buttons**—These elements perform identically to their OS 8/9 counterparts aside from an update in coloring. Check boxes are used to choose multiple attributes (AND), whereas radio buttons are used to choose between attributes (OR).

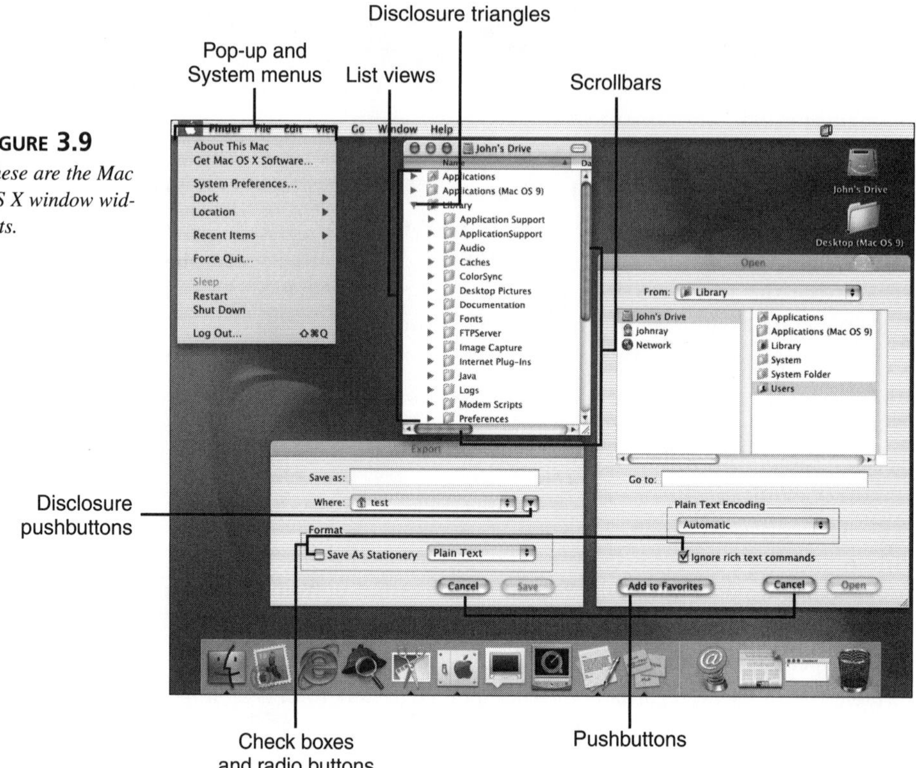

FIGURE 3.9
These are the Mac OS X window widgets.

- **List views**—List views are also very similar to early Mac OS implementations. Clicking a category sorts by that selection. Clicking again reverses the direction of the sort (ascending to descending, or vice versa). Category headings can be resized by clicking the edge of the heading and dragging in the direction you want to shrink or expand the column.
- **Pop-up menus/System menus**—Menus remain largely unchanged in Mac OS X. Single-clicking a menu will drop the menu down until a selection is made. Unlike Mac OS 8/9, the menu will *stay* down indefinitely. Previous versions of the system would halt all processes until a selection was made, so the system would automatically deselect a menu after several seconds. With Mac OS X's multitasking system, other applications can continue to work while the menu is down.
- **Disclosure triangles**—Disclosure triangles continue to work as they always have. Click the triangle to reveal addition information about an object.

- **Disclosure push buttons**—Like disclosure triangles, these push buttons are used to reveal all possible options (a full, complex view), or reduce a window to a simplified representation. This is used in the new File Save dialog boxes. This is new to Mac OS X.
- **Scrollbars**—Scrollbars have lost the option of having arrows on one end, but now visually represent the amount of data within the current document by changing the size of the scrollbar handle in relation to the data to display. The larger the handle, the less data there is to scroll through. The smaller the handle, the more information to display.

Sheet Windows and Window Trays

Two other unique interface elements are introduced in Mac OS X: sheet windows and window trays. The sheet-style windows are used in place of traditional dialog boxes. Normally, when a computer wants to get your attention, it displays a dialog box containing a question, such as "Do you want to save this document?". If you have ten open documents on your system, how do you know which one needs to be saved?

Sheet-style windows appear directly from the title bar of an open window. Rather than being "application-centric" or "system-centric," sheet windows are "document-centric." Figure 3.10 demonstrates a sheet-style window used to confirm saving the contents of a text document.

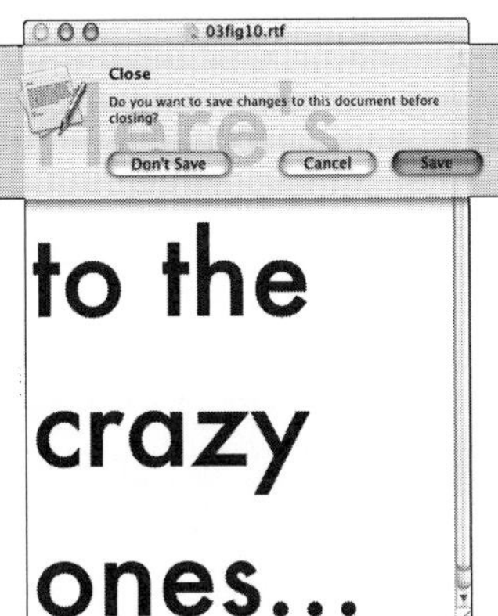

FIGURE 3.10
The sheet-style window appears to drop from an open window's title bar.

Sheet windows are used just like any other window, except they are attached to a document. Unlike many dialog boxes, which keep you from interacting with the system until you interact with *them*, sheet dialog boxes only limit access to the window that it is related to.

Apple has included a few gee-whiz features in the implementation of these new styled dialog boxes. If a window is too close to the edge of the screen or too small to hold the entire dialog sheet that appears, it will spring from the edge of the screen or scale the sheet appropriately so that it fits. This is just a visual effect, but quite amusing in action.

The second interface element introduced in Mac OS X is the window tray. Various interpretations of this element exist in programs on Mac OS 8/9 and Windows—such as Internet Explorer and Netscape 6.0, which use a form of a tray for holding bookmarks. In Mac OS X, the tray is a native interface element and can be used by developers in new and ported applications. The tray is used to store commonly used settings and options that might need to be accessed while a program is running. The OS X Mail application's tray, holding a list of active mailboxes, is shown in Figure 3.11.

FIGURE 3.11
The tray elements hold options that are often needed during a program's execution.

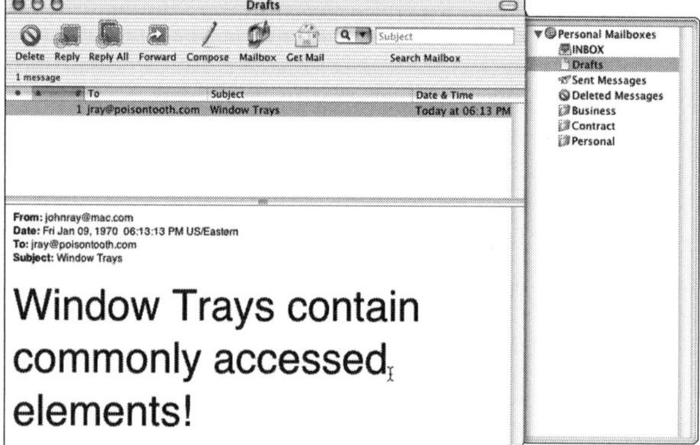

Applications supporting the use of a tray typically activate it by clicking a button in the toolbar. After a tray is open, the tray's edge can be dragged to change the size of the open tray.

Tip

Although only a few applications make use of the OS X tray feature, there are already two standards in how it operates. By default, the tray slides out from the right of the main window after clicking a button to activate it. If the window is too close to the side of the screen, the tray either will be forced out of the other side of the window, or will push the main window over to make room.

If you're using an application in which the tray can appear from either side, you might be able to force the side that the tray will use in the future. For example, in the Mail application, if you position the window near the right side of the screen and then display the mailbox tray, it will appear from the left side of the window. This position change will be remembered for future activations of the tray.

The Application Menu

When an application launches in Mac OS X, it creates an application menu based on its own name, and places it in the first position after Apple on the menu bar. For example, if you start an application named TextEdit, the first menu item after Apple will be TextEdit.

This menu contains items that act on the entire application rather than on its files. For example, traditionally, you would quit an application by choosing Quit from the File menu. Even though we're all familiar with this, it doesn't really make sense. Quitting an application has nothing to do with a File—it affects the running application. Because of this, the application menu was created to consolidate all the application-specific menus into one location. Figure 3.12 displays the application menu for Mail—an included application.

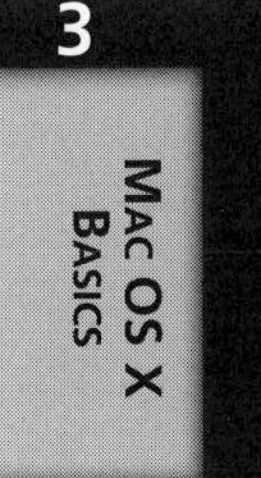

FIGURE 3.12
Application menus contain the functions, which act upon an entire application.

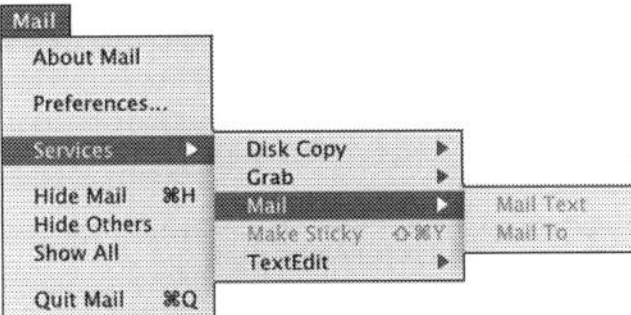

Seven default items make up the application menu:

- **About**—The About menu, which reveals information about the running program, used to be located under the Apple menu. The Apple menu is now reserved for system-wide options, so About has been placed within the application menu.
- **Preferences...**—For many years, preferences haven't really had a home. Some applications placed the option under the File menu, others under the Edit menu. The application menu provides a convenient location for preferences because they apply to the entire application.

- **Services**—Services are one of the more interesting, but rarely advertised, features of Mac OS X. A service is installed by an application and can act on a selected item on the system. For example, if you want to e-mail some text from a Web page, you could select it, and then choose Mail Text from the Mail service menu. This would launch the Mail application and start a new message containing your text.
- **Hide**—Hides the current application. This command hides all the frontmost application windows. This was previously located within the application switcher menu—in the upper-right corner of Mac OS 8 or 9. Command+H is a shortcut for Hide.
- **Hide Others**—Hides all applications other than the frontmost application. This effectively clears the screen except for the program you're currently using. In earlier versions of the operating system, this was also located in the application switcher menu.
- **Show All**—Shows all hidden applications.
- **Quit**—Quits the current application. Command+Q is the universal Quit shortcut.

The application menu is a wise addition to the Apple menu, but does take a while to get used to. I still find myself hunting through the menus looking for preferences, even when I *know* where I should be looking. Unfortunately, just because there is a place for a preferences menu, it doesn't mean that developers will fully use it. If applications are not modified to take advantage of this new menu, you might have to continue searching through your software's menu bar to find the real location of your preference menu item.

Menu Extras

Mac OS X 10.1 introduces replacements for many of the features of the long-gone Control Strip: Menu Extras. The Menu Extras are provided to give users quick access to common system settings. A number of Menu Extras can be seen in Figure 3.13.

FIGURE 3.13
Menu Extras provide quick access to system settings.

Each Extra is added to the menu bar through System Preference panels that correspond to the item's function. A few of the extras provided in 10.1 include

Displays—Adjust the resolution and color depth from the menubar.

Volume—Change the sound volume.

AirPort—Monitor AirPort signal strength and quickly adjust network settings.

Date and Time—The traditional menu bar time and date display is now a Menu Extra and can be displayed graphically as a miniature clock or using the standard text format.

Battery—Keep track of battery usage and recharge time through an all-new Battery item.

Clicking a Menu Extra opens a pop-up menu that displays additional information and settings. Items such as Battery and Date/Time can be modified to show textual information rather than a simple icon status representation. In addition, users can alter the position of Menu Extras by holding down the Option key and dragging the icons to the desired position.

The Finder

The biggest changes to Mac OS X user experience come in the shape of the new Finder. These changes are not trivial, so the next chapter will focus on working within the Finder. For now, let's just take a look at a general overview of the Finder and its capabilities.

Missing Features

The Finder is still your workbench for navigating your hard drive, launching applications, and moving and modifying files. It keeps many of the same features you've grown accustomed to but, sadly, has lost a few that you might have relied on:

- **Pop-up Windows**—The dock can simulate pop-up folders, but for the time being, pop-up windows are a thing of the past.
- **Spring Loaded Folders**—In Mac OS 8 and 9, you could drag an item over a folder, wait a few seconds, and the folder would open, allowing you to continue dragging. This is entirely absent from Mac OS X. Likewise, the capability to examine the contents of a folder by single-clicking, and then click-holding, does not work.
- **Finder Labels**—In a seeming oversight, Apple has included the capability to *display* labels within the list view of the initial 10.0, but there was no way to *set* labels in the new system. This feature has been dropped in 10.1.
- **Put Away**—The Put Away command could previously be used to return a file that you've temporarily moved back to its original destination. The Undo menu largely replaces this, but unlike the older command, Undo will work only if you haven't moved any other files or folders after moving the original file.

- **Preferences**—Everyone let out a collective sigh. The Finder has lost many of the preferences that we've relied on to create a truly personalized and usable work environment. No longer can you change list fonts, icon fonts, grid spacing, or other necessities. Although I'm sure that it's just a matter of time before these features return, if you've ever used them in Mac OS 8 or 9, you *will* miss them!
- **Desktop Trash**—The trash can still works much the same way it always has, but it is no longer located on the desktop. No more dragging it wherever you'd like. It is now firmly fixed in the Mac OS X Dock. It's possible, however, to create a desktop link to the trash can by using BSD commands.
- **Desktop Printers**—Desktop printers are completely gone and show no signs of coming back. Much of the same functionality is available in the Print Center utility, but this does not offer the same convenience as the desktop printer implementation.
- **Limited Contextual Menus**—Contextual menus still exist, but they have very little functionality under Mac OS X.

The good news is that although there are things missing, a great deal of functionality has been added to the Finder. As I've already mentioned, much of the next chapter will be devoted to working with the Finder and the Dock, so we'll get down to details later.

Modes of Operation

Mac OS X introduces two modes of operation within the Finder. You'll recognize the first mode immediately. Shown in Figure 3.14, the toolbar-less Finder works just the way you've grown accustomed to.

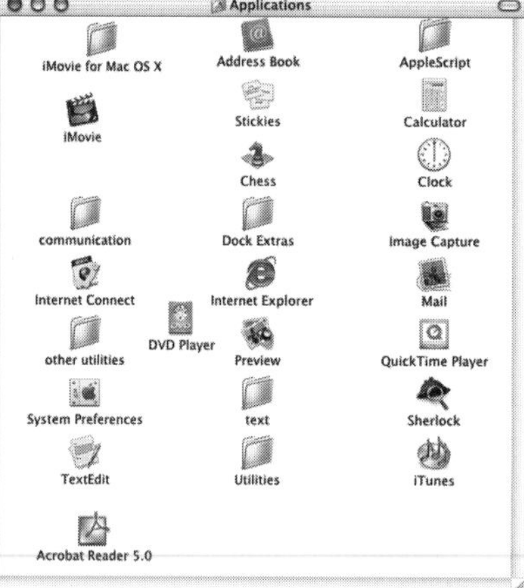

FIGURE 3.14
The toolbar-less mode works in the same fashion as older versions of the Mac operating system.

From here, you can double-click folders to open them or applications and documents to launch them. You can drag icons to customize the arrangement of the windows, and so on. For all intents and purposes, aside from the laundry list of missing features, this mode of Finder use is identical to its earlier incarnations.

One minor change, which you won't notice unless you look for it, is that unlike the previous Finder, you don't have to double-click a folder or a disk icon to make a new file navigation window. Using the key combination Command+N, you can create a new Finder window at any time. This window starts at the Computer level of the file navigation tree, and shows all available mounted media. Additionally, the Finder window that is created will default to the toolbar mode of operation, which works a bit differently from what you're accustomed to.

Note

As you sit pounding your keyboard trying to make a new folder by pressing Command+N, you'll notice that your screen is quickly filling up with new Finder windows—not new folders. In Mac OS X, creating a new folder is accomplished by pressing Shift+Command+N.

It boggles my mind to think that Apple believes I need more windows on my screen more often than I need a new folder. Maybe it's just me, but this is one of the more annoying changes you'll need to get used to. Of course, because other applications use Command+N to create a new document, maybe this is just me.

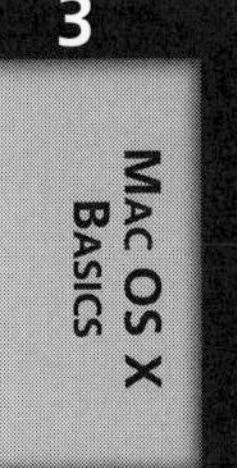

A toolbar version of the Finder window, displayed in Figure 3.15, can be created either by using Command+N within the finder, or by using the toolbar button in the upper-right corner of the Finder window. This button will allow you to quickly toggle between the toolbar and toolbar-less modes.

Although it might seem that the addition of a toolbar is only a visual change, the Finder also modifies how you navigate from folder to folder within this style of window.

Normally, you click on a folder and it opens a new window. This is how the Macintosh operating system has worked since 1984. If you have an application that is buried ten folders deep, you'll probably end up with ten open folders on your screen before you can launch it. The toolbar mode of the Finder changes that.

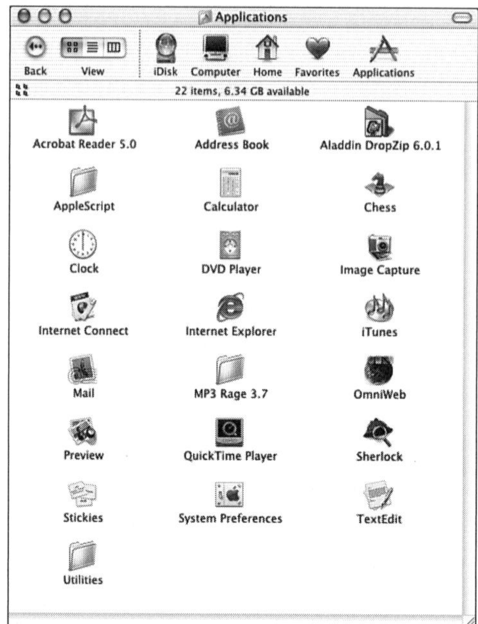

FIGURE 3.15
The toolbar version of the Finder window offers some surprises.

When the toolbar is present, double-clicking a folder will *not* open a new window. Instead, it will refresh the current window with the item you just clicked. In the upper-right corner of the toolbar is a back arrow—click it to return to the folder you just came from. Using this technique, you can dig many levels deep into the file system, and then quickly back out by using the arrow.

An obvious problem with this method of navigation is that you don't have access to multiple levels of the file system at once. This is where the toolbar can come in handy to eliminate the need for multiple open windows. You can add commonly used folders and applications to the toolbar itself and instantly drag documents from the current Finder window into them.

Note

Although the toolbar mode of the Finder window, by default, has only one window open at a time, you can use the Finder preferences to force a new window to be created each time a folder is double-clicked. The toolbar loses some of its functionality in this mode because the bar's Back button is no longer active.

Note

In another seemingly bizarre choice, Apple allows the single-window mode to operate only when the toolbar is visible (thus, my references to them as toolbar and toolbar-less modes). It certainly seems that having a single window mode would be useful within the toolbar-less mode, but alas, it is not to be.

The toolbar, single-window mode of operation is definitely unusual to most Mac users, but Windows and Linux (KDE/GNOME) already have similar features in their operating systems. If you don't like this new style of navigation, you can continue to work with files in the same way as always. Toggling between these two Finder styles is as simple as clicking a button.

Tip

To quickly toggle from toolbar mode to toolbar-less mode, hold down Command while double-clicking a folder to open it.

Delayed Reaction

There is a problem in the Mac OS X operating system that warrants its own subheading: delayed updates in the Finder. Users expect that when they start to download a file or decompress an archive, it will immediately appear in the location where it was stored. In Mac OS X, this is occasionally not the case. Both the desktop and Finder windows can take several seconds (or minutes!) to show items that have been created by programs other than the Finder.

Often this can be solved just by closing and opening the window where the item should appear, or by clicking on the desktop background. In some cases, it might require logging in and out before the items show up. Mac OS X 10.1 has largely resolved this issue, but you might still experience delays at times.

The Dock

The most striking user experience element that we'll be looking at today is the Dock. This is the gorgeous piece of software that you've seen in all the Apple demonstrations. The Dock, shown in its default state in Figure 3.16, has several functions, including providing a resting place for the trash can, replacing the application switcher menu, and acting as substitutes for the control strip and the Apple menu. Although displayed in horizontal orientation in Figure 3.16, the Dock preferences also allow it to be placed vertically on either side of the screen.

FIGURE 3.16
The Dock wears many hats...

Docked Windows, Files, and Folders

There are two parts of the Dock, separated by a vertical divider line in the middle. On the right side (or bottom, in vertical orientation) of the dock are static documents, folders, and application windows. You can drag commonly used documents into this area of the Dock, and a link to them will be stored for later use. Clicking a file that you've put in the Dock has the same result as double-clicking a file in the Finder.

Folders that are dragged into this area can be used to a reasonable facsimile of the Apple menu. Single-clicking a docked folder will open the folder on the desktop. Click-holding (or right-clicking) on a docked folder will display a menu of the contents of the folder, and the contents of the folders within that folder. Figure 3.17 shows the hierarchical file listing in action.

FIGURE 3.17
The Dock can be a replacement for the Apple menu.

Windows that have been minimized are displayed in this portion of the Dock as well. Several Mac OS X applications update their windows in real-time (QuickTime, Terminal), which makes it possible to watch the output of an application without having to view the entire window.

Located on the far-right side of the Dock (or very bottom, in vertical orientation) is the trash can. This operates just like the old trash can located on the desktop. You can drag files and folders to this icon to place them in the trash.

Tip

Disks and CDs can be ejected by dragging their icons onto the trash can. During the drag process, the trash icon will change into the eject symbol.

Docked Applications

Applications can be dragged to the left side (or top in vertical orientation) of the Dock to create a quick launching point, no matter where the software is located on your hard drive. In addition, applications that are already running place their icon in this area of the Dock. Running applications are represented by a small triangle directly under the icon. This can be seen in Figure 3.18.

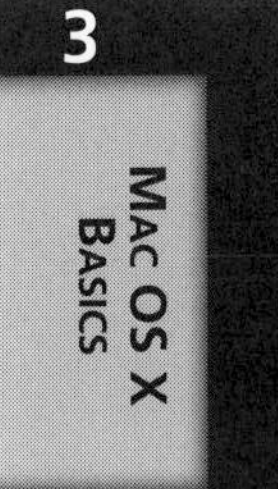

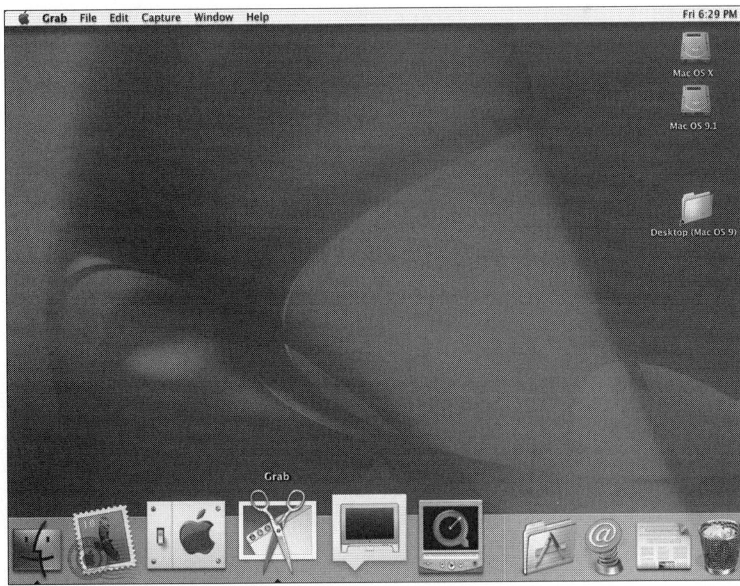

FIGURE 3.18
Triangles under Dock icons indicate active applications.

After an application is active, you can click and hold on the icon to pop up a menu that allows you to add the running application to the dock (if it isn't stored there already), quit the application, switch between the application's open windows, or access other special functions of the application.

To switch between applications, just click the icon in the Dock that you want to become the frontmost application.

Tip

You can also switch between open applications by pressing Command+Tab anywhere in the system.

Docklings

The final type of Dock item is the Dockling. This is an application that allows you to adjust system settings, control a system service, or display information, without ever physically launching an application. To activate a Dockling, all you need to do is click your mouse on the icon—no waiting for loading or working with windows. Although several Docklings were included in the initial release of Mac OS X, they have been removed from 10.1. This functionality has been replaced by the new Menu Extras. There are a number of free Docklings available, including news and weather monitors. Check out `http://www.versiontracker.com/` to find Docklings for your system.

Figure 3.19 shows the Calindock Dockling being used to view a monthly calendar.

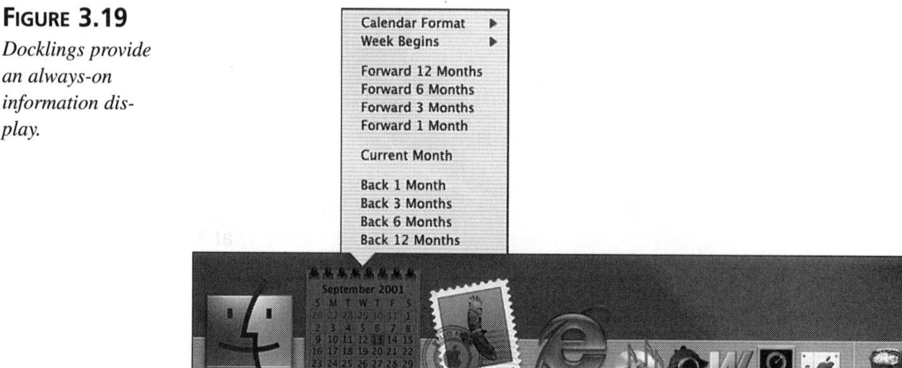

FIGURE 3.19
Docklings provide an always-on information display.

Dock Miscellany

There will be more discussion of the Dock in Chapter 4, "The Finder: Working with Files and Applications." Because I'm sure that you're eager to get started, here are a few more things you should know about the Dock before you begin:

- As you add more documents to the Dock, it will grow until it reaches the edge of the screen. When it must grow beyond this point, the Dock will automatically shrink the icons to fit the available space.
- Clicking and dragging on the white divider line in the Dock provides an easy means of resizing the icons manually.
- To show the name of an item in the Dock, position your mouse cursor over it. The name will be displayed.
- Items can be removed from the Dock by dragging the icon out of the Dock onto the desktop or dragging them to the trash icon.
- Control-clicking the divider line provides quick access to all of the Dock's settings, including screen position.

Because the Finder and the Dock are inseparable parts of the operating system experience, you can think of them collectively as the new Mac OS X implementation of the traditional Mac OS Finder. Even though they are technically separate applications, each plays an important role in the user interaction with the operating system.

Other OS Components

There are a few other OS components that don't quite fit into the categories we've looked at. To provide a simple point of reference, they'll be included here:

Open/Save Dialogs—Choosing a document to open, and where to save a file, have changed drastically in Mac OS X.

Color Picker—The Mac OS X Color Picker is intuitive, simple, and available globally. Unfortunately, it has a clone that offers slightly different functionality in different applications.

Font Panel—Applications can now take advantage of a global Mac OS X font panel. This eliminates the myriad of font-choosing devices (menus, windows, and so on) previously employed in the OS.

Volume and Brightness—Although available to portable users under Mac OS 8/9 for several years, Mac OS X 10.1 now extends global display controls to all Macintosh systems.

Apple's embracement of OS-wide component technologies bodes well for the operating system from the perspective of both a user and a developer.

Open/Save Dialog Boxes

Open and Save dialog boxes now feature the Mac OS X column display, which is also used in one of the Finder's new window views. In addition, these dialogs also make much better use of the Favorites feature that was introduced and never really promoted in earlier versions of the Mac OS.

Favorites are preferred folders that are added to quick navigation menus in the Finder and in the Open/Save dialog boxes. You'll learn more about how to add to your Favorites in Chapter 4.

Open

When opening a document from within an application, you'll see a window similar to the one in Figure 3.20.

FIGURE 3.20
The default Open dialog box is shown here.

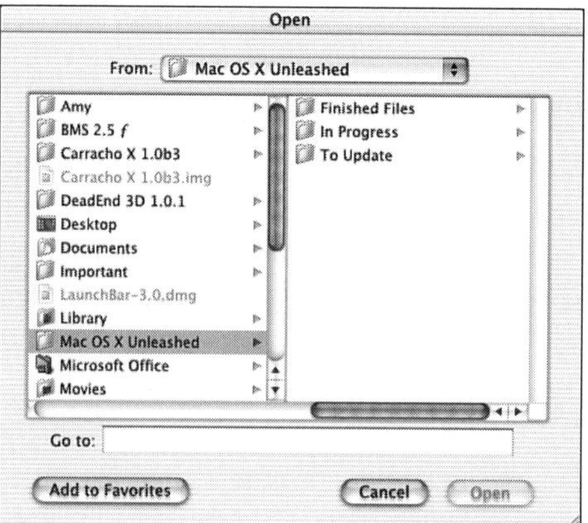

At the top of the window is a pop-up menu labeled From. This menu lists all your Favorite folders, recently visited folders, as well as the Desktop, Home directory, and iDisk folders. If you choose something from your iDisk, your system might pause briefly while the iDisk is automatically mounted.

The center of the window contains the column file navigation view. Clicking on a folder or disk in one of the columns will reveal the contents of that object in the column to the right. If the folder you're choosing is in the rightmost column already, it will be shifted to the left. A scrollbar at the bottom of the window lets you quickly move back through the path you chose to reach your file. If your folders or disks have custom icons, you can easily differentiate between them and normal files by the right-pointing arrow following each object you can move into.

Alternatively, you can type a path to locate your file into the Go to: field. Common pathnames are covered in Table 4.1. Another convenient shortcut is to drag a file from a finder window into the Open dialog box. The file will immediately be highlighted in the window. To open the selected file, click Open or double-click the filename in the window.

When navigating the file system, you can add the current folder to your favorite folder list by clicking the Add To Favorites button.

Tip

The Open and Save dialog boxes are now resizable. When resized, additional columns will be added to the column navigation view, making navigation even easier.

Save

The new style of file system navigation also carries over to the Save dialog box, which, as seen in Figure 3.21, has changed even more.

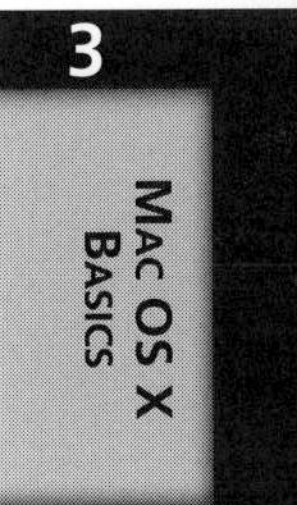

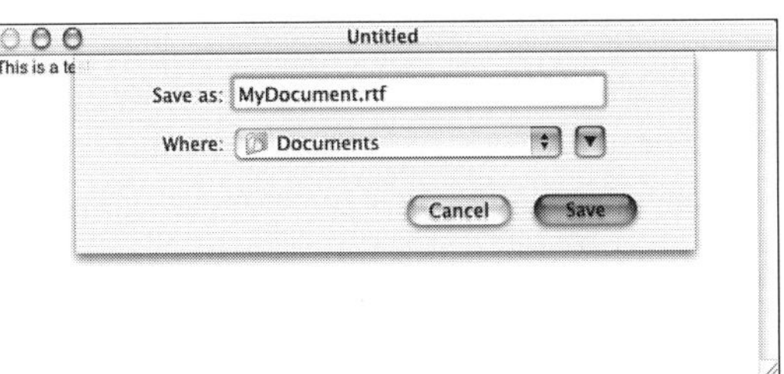

FIGURE 3.21
The default save window is teensy.

In its default minimal state, the Save dialog sheet contains only a Save as field for a filename and a Where pop-up menu that shows common folders (the same as the pop-up list in the Open dialog box). If you want to save the document in one of your recently visited or favorite folders, you're saved the task of navigating your drive.

If the location to which you want to save your files isn't in the pop-up menu, you can click the disclosure push button to the right of the pop-up menu. The dialog box will expand to a full-sized save box, shown in Figure 3.22.

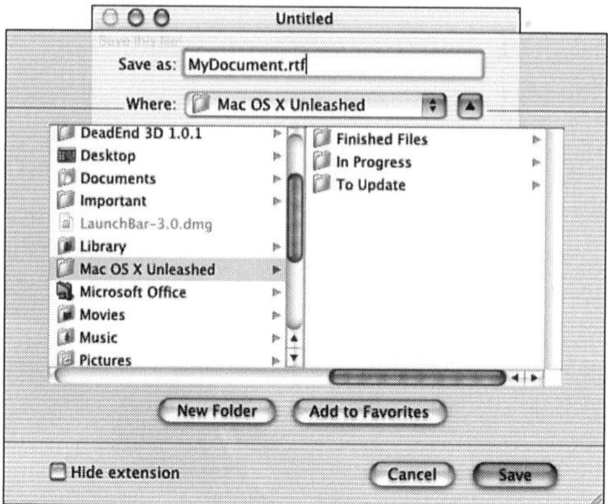

FIGURE 3.22
The Save dialog has an expanded view as well.

The file navigation within the Save dialog box works identically to the Open dialog. You can add the current folder to your Favorites list by clicking the Add to Favorites button. Clicking New Folder creates a new folder in the current folder.

When you've located the folder in which you want to save your file and entered a name in the Save as field, click the Save button to save the file.

One interesting new feature here is the Hide Extension check box. Clicking this will display the file without an added file extension. In the case of Figure 3.22, it would remove the `.rtf` from the end of the filename. This is the way Macintosh users are used to seeing files, and might make some people more comfortable in the new operating system. If you prefer to see the entire filename, including the extension, leave this box unchecked.

Color Picker

Mac OS X has two different color choosing devices: one that works with Cocoa applications and another that works with Carbon. Presumably these will merge over time, but for now, they represent two vastly different methods of picking colors.

Cocoa Colors

The Cocoa color picker is shown in Figure 3.23. This appears in applications such as TextEdit and Stickies—both written using the Cocoa API.

FIGURE 3.23
The Cocoa color chooser is shown here.

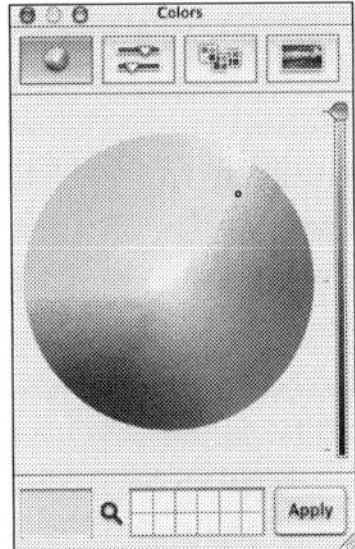

Along the top of the window are various color selection methods. These range from RGB sliders to a spectrum selection window. There are three features common to all the color selection methods:

- **Color Well**—At the bottom left of the window is a color well. Some applications support dragging colors directly from this rectangle to the object that should take on the color.
- **Magnifying Glass**—The magnifying glass can be used to choose a color from any window or location on the screen, even the menu bar.
- **Favorite Colors**—To the right of the magnifying glass is a favorite colors palette that you can use to store commonly used colors. Drag them from the color well into any of the palette squares to store them.

After choosing the color you want to use, click the Apply button. The color chooser will not close after applying—you will need to click the window's close button.

Carbon Colors

The Carbon application color chooser functions similarly to the Cocoa version, but has a vastly different appearance. A sample of the Carbon color picker is displayed in Figure 3.24.

FIGURE 3.24
The Carbon color chooser is similar, but is laid out differently from the Cocoa version.

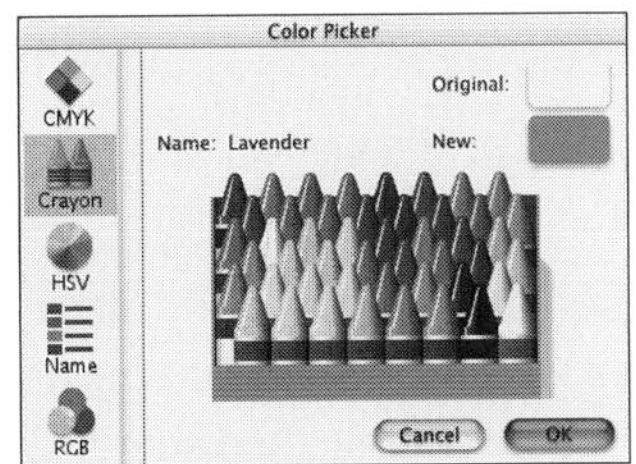

Instead of placing the selection methods along the top, the available selectors are shown down the left side of the window. Each selector includes two color wells: one that displays the original color before changes were made, and the new color, showing your current color choice. You can quickly revert to the original color by clicking in the original color well.

To choose a color from anywhere on the screen, hold down Option while moving your cursor across the screen. The mouse pointer will change to an eyedropper and function much like the magnifying glass in the Cocoa chooser.

Click Okay after you have found the color you want to use.

> **Tip**
>
> Try using the eyedropper within the Crayon color picker. If you position the eyedropper near the edges of the crayons, the system will show you "-ish" versions of the colors. Not terrifically useful, but definitely amusing.

Font Panel

The Mac OS X Font panel is a new method of choosing and organizing fonts on your system. Gone is the need for third-party utilities such as Suitcase. Unfortunately, just because the font panel exists, that doesn't mean that applications use it.

The font panel will be covered in detail in Chapter 10. For now, let's take a look a few of its modes of operation. By default, the Font Panel appears looking similar to that of Figure 3.25.

FIGURE 3.25
The font panel displays available font families, typefaces, and sizes in a single floating window.

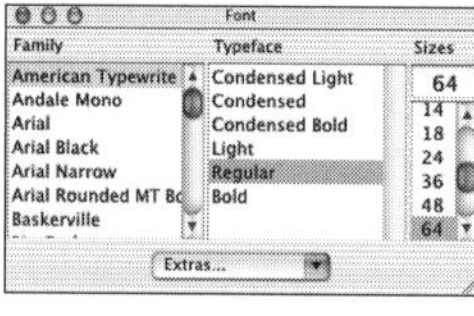

You can easily see the available font families, the typefaces, and sizes. Much like the Finder's column navigation, you start at the left and work your way to the right. Each choice in a column limits the choices in the next column, and so on. If you want more control over the fonts, just drag the bottom-right color of the window to expand it. A new column, Collections, will appear. Collections are user-customizable font sets that help you keep track of the hundreds of available system fonts.

If, on the other hand, the font panel is too bulky for your tastes, resize the window into its smallest possible form. It will take on a new look, seen in Figure 3.26. Each of the columns is reduced to a single pop-up menu, conveying a maximum amount of information in a minimum amount of space.

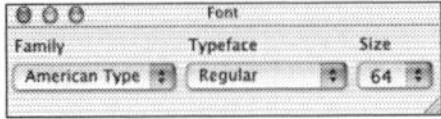

FIGURE 3.26
When resized, the font panel adjusts its appearance accordingly.

Again, there are many other new features of the font panel. If you're interested in learning more now, turn to Chapter 11, "Additional System Components."

Volume and Brightness

Finally, those volume controls on your Apple keyboard are useful! Mac OS X 10.1 includes support for adjusting screen brightness and system volume. Although this is not overly exciting in and of itself, Apple's implementation is beyond elegant.

Pushing the sound keys on your keyboard will display a transparent overlay of the current sound level on your screen, as seen in Figure 3.27.

FIGURE 3.27
Users can now adjust volume and brightness from their keyboard.

The keyboard brightness controls work in much the same way—providing instant access to your screen settings. Although these keys are not labeled on desktop keyboards, the dim/brighten controls are accessible by pressing F14 and F15, respectively.

This is an excellent example of the attention to detail given to Mac OS X 10.1. Even though the operating system is still in its infancy, Apple is now adding features above and beyond what we've ever had in Mac OS before.

Summary

This chapter provided the basic information you need to find your way around the Mac OS X operating system. It is not meant to explain every possible feature, but to provide an overview of what features have been added to, and removed from, Mac OS X.

If you are reading the chapters in this book sequentially, this would be a good time to try working your way around the operating system. Subsequent chapters will assume that you've familiarized yourself with the pointing and clicking aspects of using the system and will focus on all the features that are available. Specific questions about the Dock and the Finder will be answered in Chapter 4, "The Finder: Working with Files and Applications."

The Finder: Working with Files and Applications

In This Chapter

We're now ready to take an inside look at Mac OS X and its operation. This chapter will cover the Finder and Dock, how these two features interoperate, all the possible file and application operations, and how to customize the Finder's tools to suit your tastes. Although much of this chapter will cover a tool that many users are already familiar with (the Finder), I urge you to read through the text nonetheless. The Mac OS X Finder has many tricks that were not present in previous versions.

Using the Finder

The Finder is the application that Mac OS X and earlier versions of the operating system use to launch and manipulate files and applications. The Finder handles all common tasks such as creating, deleting, moving, and copying files and folders. It is, in effect, the window into the Mac OS X operating system.

Unlike other tools and utilities, the Finder is always active and is automatically launched immediately after logging in to the system. Much of the Macintosh's legendary ease of use is attributed to the Finder and its intuitive interface to the file system.

The Mac OS X Finder is completely rewritten for the new operating system. Although many users will find that it functions in *mostly* the same way as Mac OS 8/9, there are many new features and changes. This section will provide an in-depth look at these new capabilities and how the Finder is used to navigate through Mac OS X.

Finder Views and Navigation

The Finder offers many ways to navigate through your data using windows, menus, and the keyboard. All navigation takes place inside of a Finder window. To be able to open a new Finder window, you must first double-click a folder or disk icon that is on your desktop. Alternatively, you can use the New Finder Window selection from the Finder's File menu (Command+N).

Icon View

The first time you log in, the Finder will be in toolbar mode (see Chapter 3, "Mac OS X Basics," for a description of the Finder's toolbar mode) and using the Icon view. If you have already been using the Finder and are no longer in Icon view, you can quickly switch to Icon view by choosing As Icons from the View menu, or by clicking the first icon in the View area of the toolbar. Figure 4.1 shows a Finder window in Icon view.

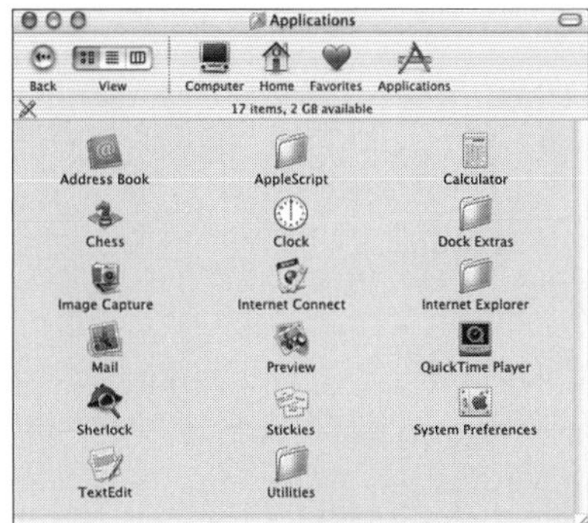

FIGURE 4.1
The default view mode is the Icon view.

Within the Icon view mode, you can navigate through the folders on your drive by double-clicking them. If you prefer to use the keyboard, you can move between the icons in the frontmost Finder window by pressing the arrow keys or by pressing the letter key that starts the name of the folder/file you want to select. To open a selected item, press Command+O on the keyboard.

Remember, by default, if the toolbar is displayed in the window, moving from folder to folder will refresh the current window. You can switch to a multi-window view by clicking the toolbar button in the upper-right corner of the Finder window or by using the Finder Preferences. You can disable the toolbar from the View menu by choosing Hide Toolbar, or by pressing Command+B to toggle between toolbar states.

One final method navigating your drive is to Command-click the icon or text in the center of the Finder window's title bar. Seen in Figure 4.2, this pop-up menu displays a bottom-to-top hierarchy of the folder path required to reach the current directory. You can choose any of the folders in the list to quickly jump to that folder.

Note

The one catch to the rule of navigating the Mac OS X file system occurs when a new Finder window is created, or the Computer button is clicked within the Finder toolbar. The Finder will display Disks and Network storage icons. Although these aren't *folders* per se, you can still open them to get to the files and folders within.

If, instead, you'd prefer to move to your home directory when a new Finder window is created, this option is available within the Finder preferences.

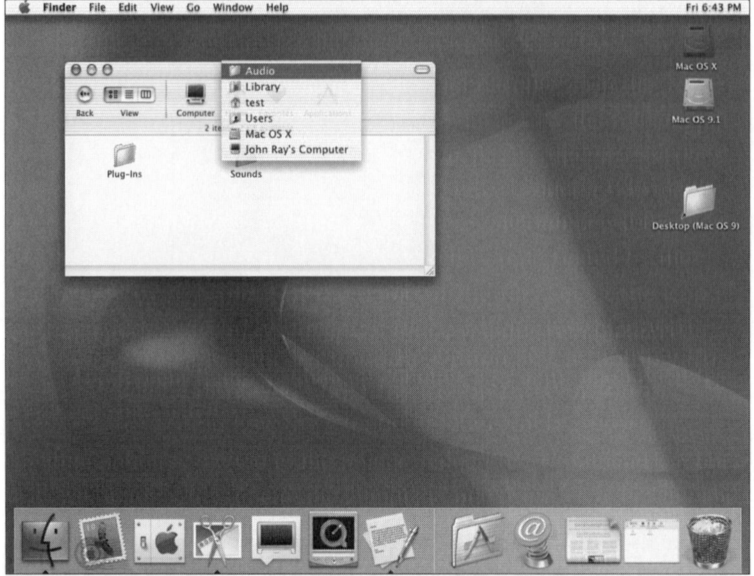

FIGURE 4.2
The pop-up folder list gives quick access to folders above the currently open directory.

Why Are All My Filenames Cut Off?

At long last, the Mac OS supports long filenames (well, 255 character names within HFS+). The Finder, however, displays only 2 lines of each name, abbreviating the middle with an ellipsis (...).

Thankfully, there is a way to view more of the name of the file. Select the icon and leave your mouse cursor over an abbreviated title, or hold down Option while moving your mouse over the title. Without the Option key, a tooltip with the full name of the file will be displayed under the icon in three or four seconds. If you hold down the Option key, the expanded label will be shown instantly.

Icon View Options

You can customize the Icon view by dragging the icons around to suit your tastes. This is the most basic form of customization offered. To add more dramatic effects to a window in Icon view, choose Show View Options from the View menu, or press Command+J. The View Options window for the Icon view is displayed in Figure 4.3.

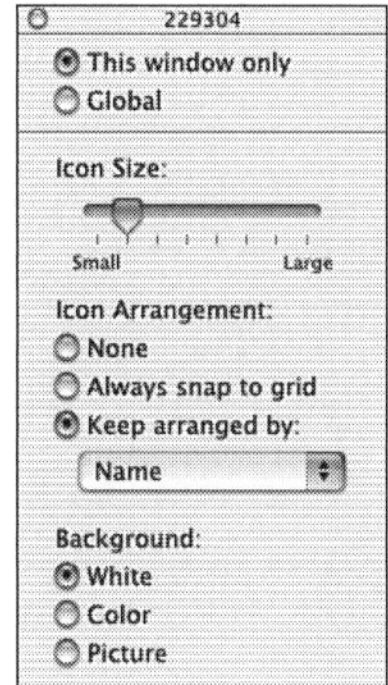

FIGURE 4.3
The Icon View options let you create a different look for the Finder window.

The first decision you must make when adjusting view options is whether or not to inherit global settings, or apply the changes to the current window. At the top of the View Options window are two choices: This Window Only and Global. Choosing the first setting tells Mac OS X that the changes you make to the view are specific to that window—no other windows will be changed. For example, using This Window Only, you can set your home directory and each of the directories within it to their own style independently of one another. On the other hand, picking Global applies a system-wide view option to the window, and indicates that any changes made to the view options will affect any other windows set to inherit the Global settings. This is a great way to create a common look and feel across multiple folders without having to maintain separate settings for each.

> **Tip**
>
> If you are setting the attributes for multiple Finder windows, you can speed up the process by opening all of the windows to adjust and then opening the View Options window. As you click between the different Finder windows, the contents of the View Options window change to reflect the settings of the current window. There is no need to close View Options after setting up a window—just click the next Finder window to work with, adjust its settings, and so on.

There are three primary settings for the view, the first being icon size. Mac OS X supports icon sizes from 16×16 pixels all the way up to 128×128 (the standard Mac size was previously 32×32). The large icons are very impressive and are far more detailed than any icons you've ever seen before. You can scale the icons from their smallest size to the largest size by dragging the Icon Size slider from the left to the right. Figure 4.4 shows the Applications folder of the Mac OS X drive using the largest icon size.

FIGURE 4.4
The largest icon size allows for extremely detailed, photo-realistic icons.

Tip

Not only is the smallest icon size tiny, but placing the system in this mode also moves the icon's label to the right of the small icon, rather than underneath it. This is a far more effective use of space and works much like the small icon view in Mac OS 8/9.

The next setting is Icon Arrangement, which controls how the icons are listed on the screen. By default, the arrangement is set to None. This allows you to move the icons anywhere you'd like within a folder.

Note

If you take advantage of the Icon view with no preset arrangement, you might find that your icons get a bit messy after awhile. To quickly align your icons to the Finder's grid, choose Clean Up from the View menu.

To keep your icons straight and neat all the time, choose "Always snap to grid" as the icon arrangement. Mac OS X maintains an invisible grid within Finder windows that is used to keep icons evenly aligned with one another. Unfortunately, there are no provisions for changing the spacing on the grid. As a result, Mac OS X icons that are aligned to the grid might seem more loosely spaced than you'd like. Until a hack is found or Apple updates the Finder, there is no workaround for this problem.

A final form of icon arrangement is to keep the icons arranged by attributes of the files that they represent. Click the Keep Arranged By radio button, and then choose from the list of available options:

- **Name**—Sort the icons by the alphabetical order of their names.
- **Date Modified**—Sort the icons by the day and time they were last modified. Newly modified files and folders appear at the bottom of the list.
- **Date Created**—Sort the icons by the date and time they were created. The first time a file is saved, the created and modified times are identical.
- **Size**—Sort by the size of the files or the size of the files contained within folders.
- **Kind**—Sort the files by their type (that is, folders, applications, images, and so on).

Tip

To quickly arrange icons in a Finder window by Name, use Arrange by Name from the View menu. This rearranges the current position of the icons into alphabetical order. It's a quick way to add some order to your life without opening View Options.

Finally, the Folder Background option is a brand-new feature of the Mac OS X Finder that offers you the capability to choose a background color or picture on a per-folder basis. This enables you to create a very visually impressive system and can also provide quick cues for your current location within the operating system.

The default folder background is None. This uses a standard white background for all windows. To choose an alternative color, just click the Color radio button. A small square will appear to the right of the button. Click this square to launch the Mac OS X Color Picker. You can learn more about the Color Picker in Chapter 3. Figure 4.5 shows a Finder window with a tinted background.

An even more impressive effect is to use a background picture for the window rather than just a color. Background images can be based on any of the QuickTime-supported formats (GIF, JPEG, TIFF, and so on). Click the Picture radio button, and then click the Select button that appears. You will be prompted to open an image file from the system. Using the Open and Save dialogs is covered in Chapter 3.

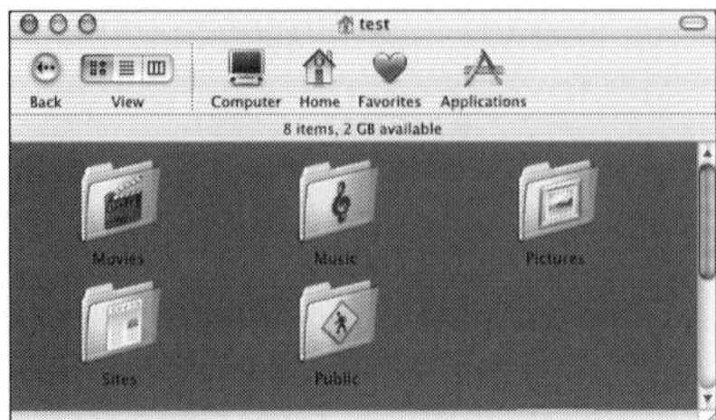

FIGURE 4.5
You can use the OS X Color Picker to choose your window background color.

After you choose a picture, a thumbnail of your choice will be shown in the small square (image well) to the left of the Select... button. Your Finder window will refresh with the chosen image in the background. Figure 4.6 shows a Finder window with an image in the background.

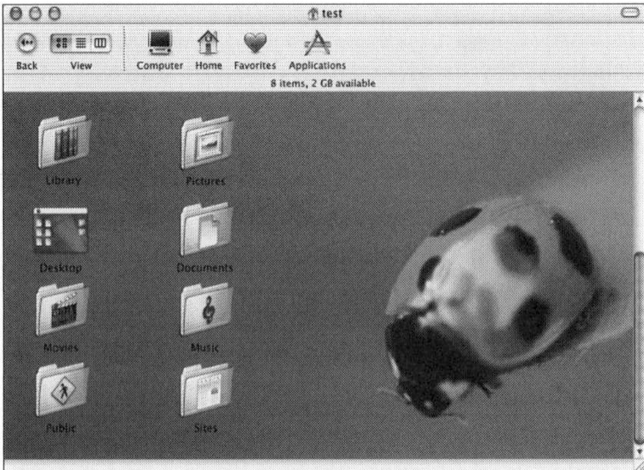

FIGURE 4.6
Any image can be used as a background in a Finder window.

In the current 10.1 release of Mac OS X, pictures cannot be scaled to match the size of a window. Instead, Finder background pictures are tiled, much like a repeating background on a Web page.

> **Note**
>
> The Icon view is presently the only view that supports background colors or images.

List View

The next view to explore is the Finder's List view. You can switch to List view by clicking the middle icon in the Finder's View toolbar, or, if the toolbar isn't present, by choosing As List from the Finder's View menu. Demonstrated in Figure 4.7, the List view is a straightforward means of displaying all available information about a file or folder on a multi-columned screen.

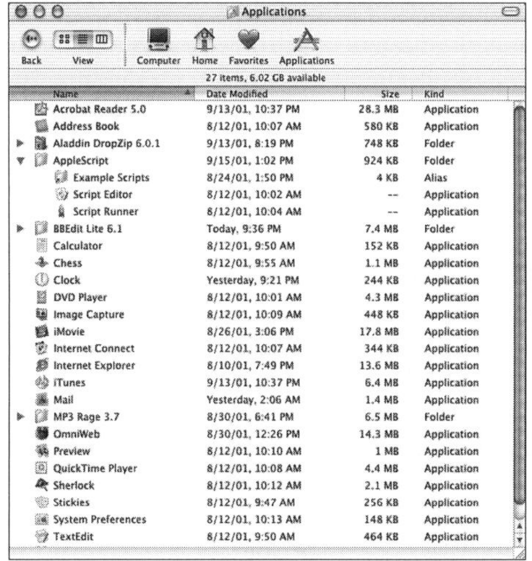

FIGURE 4.7
List view packs a lot of information into a small amount of space.

The columns in the List view represent the attributes for each file. You can contract or expand the columns by placing the mouse cursor at the edge of the column and click-dragging to the left or right. Clicking a column highlights it and sorts the file listing based on that column's values. By default, the column values are listed in descending order. Clicking a column again will toggle the sorting order. An arrow pointing up or down at the right of each column represents the current sort order.

You can reposition the columns by clicking and dragging them into the order you'd like. However, the first column, Name, cannot be repositioned.

When a folder appears in the file listing, a small disclosure arrow precedes its name. Clicking this arrow will reveal the file hierarchy within that folder. You can drill down even further if you'd like, revealing multiple levels of files. Figure 4.8 shows three levels of files displayed simultaneously. Windows users might find a level of comfort in this view because it is similar to the Windows Explorer.

FIGURE 4.8
The List view can show multiple levels of the file system within a single window.

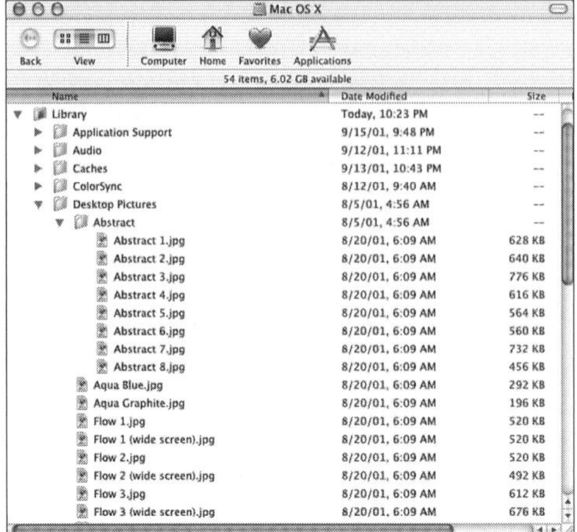

As with the Icon view, double-clicking a folder anywhere within this view will either open a new window (toolbar-less mode) or refresh the contents of the existing window with the new location.

Tip

The default view for all windows is the Icon view. If you are in toolbar-mode, it can get annoying to double-click a folder only to find yourself back in Icon view. To automatically keep the same view as you traverse the file system, you can use the Finder preferences (under the Finder menu) and enable "Keep a window's view the same when opening other folders in the window" option. This lends a bit more continuity to the file browsing experience.

If keyboard navigation is your thing, the same rules as the Icon view apply. You can navigate up and down through the listing using the up-arrow key and down-arrow key. In addition, you can use the left-arrow key and right-arrow key to move in and out of folders in the hierarchy. Holding down Command+Option along with the right-arrow key or left-arrow key will expand or collapse all folders inside the currently selected folder. Pressing the first character of an object's name will highlight that object in the listing. You can then use Command+O to open it.

Finally, Command-clicking on the title of the window will reveal the same pop-up list of folders as the Icon view. Choose one of the items in the list to jump to it.

List View Options

Like the Icon view, there are a number of options that you can use to customize the appearance and functionality of the List view. To alter the options for a window, make sure that it is the frontmost Finder window, and then choose Show View Options (Command+J) from the View menu. The List View Option window is shown in Figure 4.9.

FIGURE 4.9
The list view also can be customized.

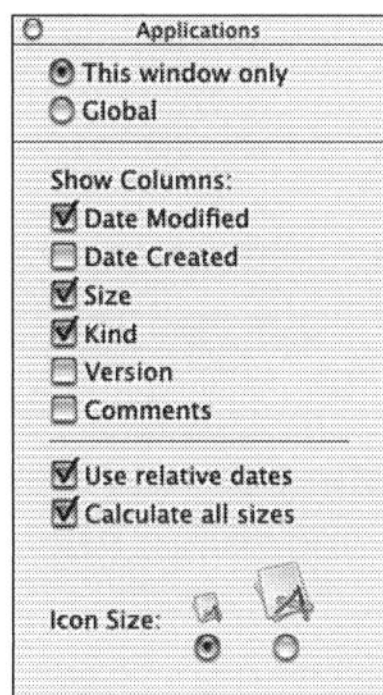

The Show Columns option offers seven different attributes that can be displayed in each list view:

- **Date Modified**—The date that a file or folder was last changed.
- **Date Created**—The date that a file or folder was created.
- **Size**—The size of a file on the system.
- **Kind**—An abstract representation of a file (image, application, and so on).
- **Version**—Displays the version of an application. Not always available in Mac OS X.
- **Comments**—Shows any comments set for the file or folder. Comments are set from the Show Info (Command+I) window.

By checking or unchecking the box in front of each option, you can add or remove the corresponding column to the List view.

Tip

To determine a file's type from the command line, use `file <filename>`:

```
% file jeans1024x768.jpg
jeans1024x768.jpg: JPEG image data, JFIF standard
```

For more information about the command line, see Chapter 12, "Introducing the BSD Subsystem."

There are two additional settings that affect the display of these columns:

- **Use relative dates**—Relative dates are a way of representing dates *relative* to the current day. For example, items modified during the current day are listed as Today, whereas files modified a day earlier are Yesterday. Clicking the "Use relative dates" check box will display the Created and Modified columns using these conventions.
- **Calculate all sizes**—By default, folder sizes are not calculated and displayed in the file listing. Checking this box will enable folder sizes to be displayed in the file listing.

Caution

Calculating folder sizes might seem like a good idea, but it can bog down your system tremendously. If you have multiple file listing windows open, and each is calculating folder sizes, it can slow down Finder operations and application responsiveness.

A quick way to display the usage of each directory is the du command from the command line:

```
% du -s *
40      Addresses
0       Assistants
0       Audio
4096    Caches
0       ColorPickers
8       Documentation
16      Favorites
2520    Fire
```

You can learn more about the command line and its uses starting in Chapter 12.

The Icon Size option offers a choice of two icon sizes: small or large. To change the size of the icon that precedes every line in the list, click the radio button below the size that you prefer.

Column View

The final type of window view is the Column view. This will be recognized by NeXT-heads as almost identical to the original File Browser used on the NeXT system. There are two primary advantages of this view: ease of navigation and file identification. You can switch to the Column view style by choosing As Columns from the View menu, or by clicking the third icon in the View area of the toolbar. Figure 4.10 shows a Finder window in Column view.

FIGURE 4.10
The Column view uses...well... columns.

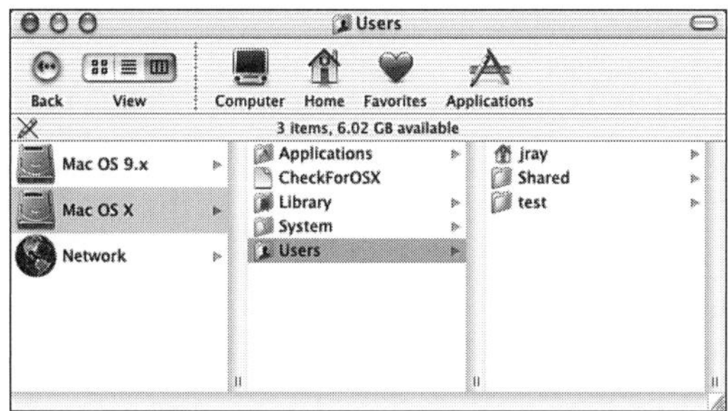

Note

The Column view is also used in the Open/Save dialog boxes discussed in Chapter 3. If you're already familiar with the concept, you might want to skip this section—it is largely the same.

The key feature of the Column view is its navigation. Unlike the other views, which can either overwhelm you with information or require multiple windows to move easily from point to point, the Column view is designed with one thing in mind: ease of navigation.

The concept is very simple: Click an item in the first column, and its contents will be shown in the next column. This would be less than useful if the programmers stopped at this point, so they didn't. You can continue to drill down further into the file system by choosing a folder that was within your original folder. The display will then do one of two things: If your window is open wide enough, it will display the contents of the second folder in yet another column. If no other columns are available, the columns will slide to the left, and a scroll bar will appear at the bottom of the window. Using this scroll bar, you can quickly trace the steps you've taken to reach a file. If you'd like to adjust the width of the columns, grab the handle (represented by two vertical lines) and drag it—all the columns will resize accordingly. Holding down Option while dragging the handle will resize only the columns to the left or right of the divider line. Figure 4.11 shows a multi-column display that reaches down several levels.

Tip

If you use the horizontal scroll bar to move back along a path, the folders you've chosen will remain highlighted in the columns. You can, at any time, choose a different folder from any of the columns. This will refresh the column to the right of your choice. There is no need to start from the beginning every time you want to change your location.

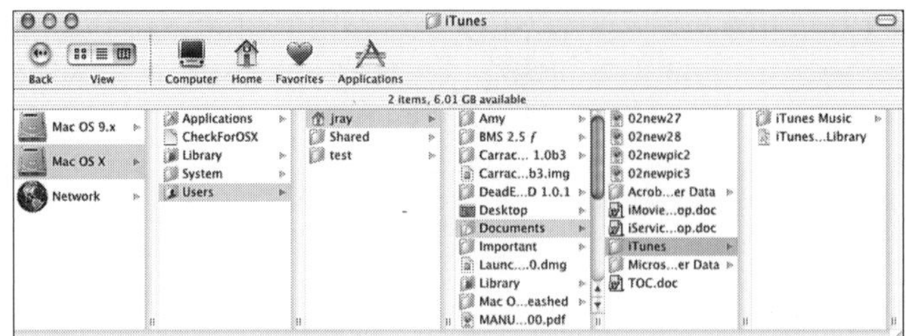

FIGURE 4.11
Using the Column view, you can easily drill down through the folders on your hard drive.

If at first glance this seems too complicated or awkward, I urge you to try it. The Column mode is a very fast and efficient means of finding what you're looking for.

Finally, Command-clicking on the title of the window will reveal the same pop-up list of folders as the Icon view. Choose one of the items in the list to jump to it.

There is one other *big* bonus of using the Column view: the ability to instantly see the contents of a file without opening it. You already know that as you choose folders, their contents appear in the column to the right, but what happens if you choose a file or application instead?

The answer is that a preview or description of the selected item will appear in the column to the right. For an example, take a look at Figure 4.12, where the front page of a PDF file is displayed.

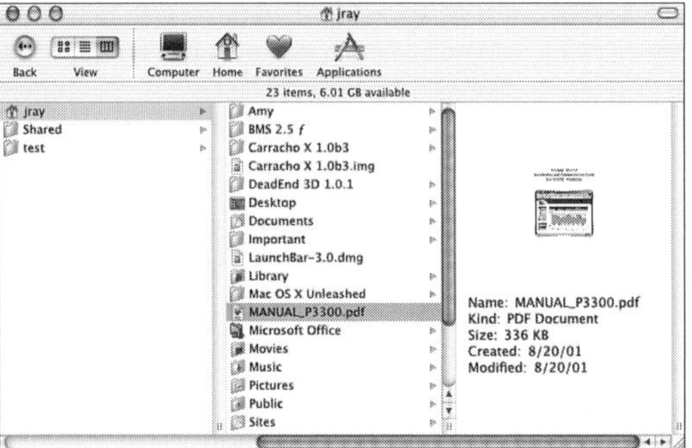

FIGURE 4.12
When a file is selected, a preview is shown in the rightmost column.

This is a convenient way of viewing pictures and other forms of supported QuickTime media. When an application or a file that cannot be previewed is chosen, information about the file will be displayed, such as the creation/modification dates, size, and version.

Tip

Do not underestimate the power of this feature. Not only can you view pictures, you can also view QuickTime movies and other media using this same technique.

In fact, if you have a large collection of MP3s (legally obtained, of course) and you're using the Column view mode, you can actually listen to your MP3s without launching an MP3 player application. Unfortunately, the MP3 does not continue to play if you switch off the selected file, but that's hardly worth mentioning considering the added functionality.

Column View Options

Unlike the other Finder views, the Column view does not have any available options. Despite this fact, the Finder still allows you to choose Show View Options from the View menu. It just doesn't do anything.

The Column view obviously has its advantages, such as file previews and an easy way to reach files deep in the file system. But it is lacking in one respect in which the other, more traditional, views excel: jumping between and viewing multiple folders simultaneously.

The Icon view, for example, appeals to Mac users who are accustomed to having many windows open simultaneously. Moving between windows has been the key to successfully operating the Mac for many years. The List view allows a single window to display the contents of multiple folders simultaneously, which also makes it a breeze to navigate.

So, why is the Column mode more difficult? Because it was designed to be used with the Mac OS X Finder's toolbar. The original NeXT version of what we call the Finder had a feature similar to the toolbar that allowed frequently used items to be stored in it. Similarly, the toolbar can be used to store common folders and applications, allowing the users of the Column view (and any other view) to move files without having to navigate up the directory path. Later this chapter will look at the toolbar and its various customizations.

The Go Menu

If you'd like to navigate quickly from any view, you can use the folder shortcuts contained in the Go menu. This menu is introduced in Mac OS X and enables the user to jump the Finder to one of several predefined locations, or to manually enter the name of a directory to browse. Let's take a look at these potential options:

- **Computer**—Jump to the Computer level of the file hierarchy. At the Computer level, you can browse connected storage devices and network volumes (Option+Command+C).
- **Home**—Go to your home directory (Option+Command+H).
- **iDisk**—The iDisk selection is one of the more interesting options. If you have signed up for an account (see Chapter 2, "Installing Mac OS X"), choosing this option will mount your iDisk on your desktop. If this selection fails, be sure that you have entered your iDisk username and password into the Internet System Preferences panel (Option+Command+I) and make sure you are online!
- **Favorites**—Favorite folders are determined by *you*. First introduced in the save/open panels discussed in Chapter 3, Favorites let you specify the folders that you'd like to access quickly. In addition to using the Open Save dialogs, you can also add Favorites using the Add to Favorites... option in the Finder's File menu (Command+T). Select the folder you want to be a Favorite, and then use the menu to add it. If you do not have a folder selected, the directory represented by the frontmost Finder window will be used.
- **Applications**—Jump to the System Applications folder (Option+Command+A).
- **Recent Folders**—The Recent Folders submenu contains a system-maintained list of the last ten folders you visited.

The final quick-navigation option is the Go to the Folder dialog box (Command+`). For now, this is as close as we're going to come to the command line. Mac users beware and Windows/Linux users rejoice. You're about to tell the Finder where you want to be, based on a pathname you enter! Figure 4.13 shows the Go to the Folder dialog box.

FIGURE 4.13
Go to the Folder lets you enter your destination by hand!

You can type any folder pathname into the Go to the folder field. Folder names are separated by the / character. Think of it as being similar to a Web URL. Table 4.1 shows a few shortcuts you can use to navigate your drive.

TABLE 4.1 These Shortcuts Can Help You Navigate Your System

Path	*Purpose*
`/`	The root (top) level of your hard drive.
`~/`	Your home directory.
`~<username>`	Replace `<username>` with the name of another user to jump to that user's home directory.
`/<directory>`	Move to a directory relative to the root of the file system.
`<directory>`	Move to a directory relative to the directory you're currently in.

As you type in your pathname, Mac OS X will watch what you're typing and attempt to auto-complete the name of the directory. Click Go or press Return when you've finished typing the directory you want to visit.

Note

This function is provided mostly for those users who are comfortable dealing with pathnames. Unfortunately, Linux users hoping to navigate the BSD subsystem will be disheartened to learn that very few of the Unix directories can be specified at the command line. Although some (such as `/etc/httpd`) work, the vast majority currently fail.

If you'd like to make all of the BSD subsystem viewable within the Finder, you can do so by entering the following command in a terminal window: `defaults write com.apple.Finder AppleShowAllFiles YES`. To turn off the feature, use the same command with `NO` at the end. You can learn more about the Mac OS X Defaults system in Chapter 20, "Command-Line Configuration and Administration," and more about the command line in Chapter 12.

Tip

The Mac and Unix systems make strange bedfellows. The Mac has traditionally used a : (colon) to separate folder names in a path; therefore, it didn't allow : within filenames. Unix, on the other hand, doesn't allow / within filenames, but it does allow : (colon).

In the Mac OS X Finder, the : character still isn't allowed (it is replaced with a - (hyphen) if you try to use it in a file or directory name), but / *can* be used in a name. Unfortunately, the Go to the Folder dialog cannot deal with directories that include the / because *it* is thinking in terms of Unix directories. The moral of the story is, "Don't name your directories with a / and expect to be able to navigate to them using the Go to the Folder dialog box."

Finder Status Bar

Not quite the toolbar but useful nonetheless, the status bar has long supplied Mac users with important information about their system. The Finder's status bar shows the number of items contained in a folder and the amount of space available on the drive. The status bar can be toggled on and off using the Show/Hide Status Bar item in the View menu of the Finder. Figure 4.14 shows a window with the status bar turned on and the toolbar off.

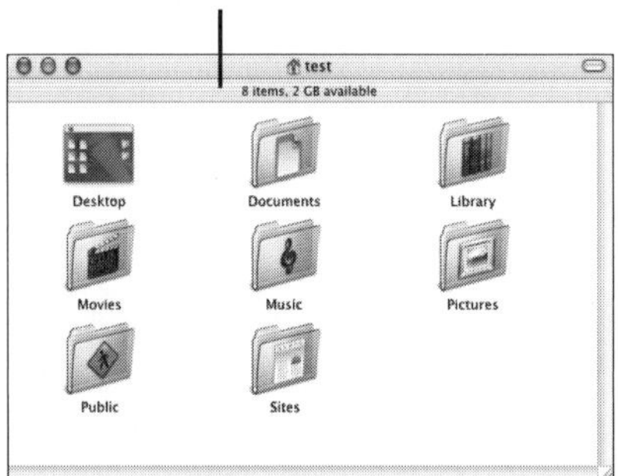

FIGURE 4.14
The status bar is standard fare in earlier versions of the Mac OS—it's optional in Mac OS X.

> **Caution**
>
> Even if you add up the sizes of all the folders that you use, you're probably going to come up short. There are many hidden Unix directories that also count when calculating the amount of available space. Unfortunately, to an end user, it's going to appear as if he's lost several hundred megabytes on his hard drive.

In addition to the disk space available and number of items in a folder, the status bar also can contain one of two icons in the left corner of the bar:

- **Grid Pattern**—If a small grid pattern appears, the view is set to snap to grid, allowing minimal flexibility in the movement of icons.
- **Slash Pencil**—A pencil with a line through it means that you can read the items in the directory, but not store files within it (so, the directory is read only).

Finder Toolbar

You've seen the toolbar by now, and were given a brief introduction to its features in Chapter 3. The toolbar holds useful functions that you might want to access from wherever you are in the Finder. There are two ways to customize the Mac OS X toolbar: by using the supplied shortcuts and by adding your own applications and folders.

Predefined Shortcuts

To customize your Finder windows with any of the predefined Mac OS X shortcuts, choose Customize Toolbar from the View menu, or hold down Shift and click the toolbar button in the upper-right corner of your Finder window. A drop-down sheet containing all the available shortcuts will appear, as shown in Figure 4.15.

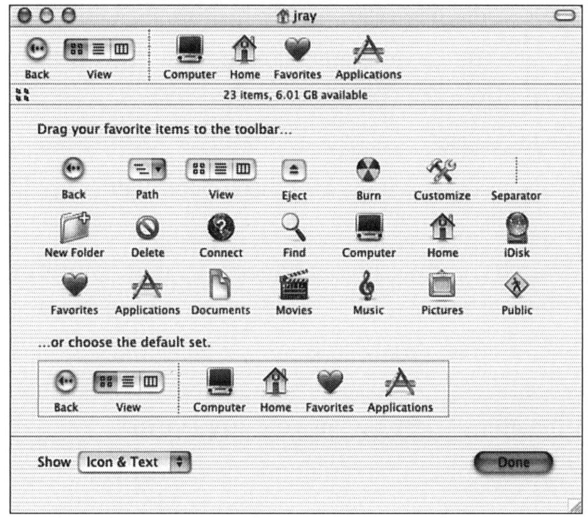

FIGURE 4.15
Finder shortcuts give single-click access to applications, folders, and special features.

To add one of these shortcuts to the toolbar, simply drag it from the window to wherever you'd like it to appear in the toolbar. If the number of shortcuts in the toolbar exceeds the size of the window, the shortcuts that can't be displayed appear in a pop-up menu at the right side of the toolbar. These shortcuts include the following:

- **Back**—Return to the previously visited folder. This is part of the default toolbar set.
- **Path**—Path adds a pop-up menu to the toolbar that contains all the folders in the current path. Choose an item from the menu to jump to that folder. This is virtually identical to holding down the Command key while clicking on the title of a Finder window, but doesn't require a modifier key.
- **View**—Quickly toggle between the three available Finder views. This is part of the default Finder toolbar.
- **Eject**—Eject drive media (CDs, DVDs, and so on). If you have a modern Apple keyboard, you already have an Eject key, so this added button really won't be necessary. This is the same as pressing Command+E or dragging a disk icon to the Dock's trash can.
- **Burn**—Burn the currently active CD—if available. CD burning will be covered later in this chapter.

- **Customize**—The Customize shortcut takes you to the shortcut menu.
- **Separator**—Serves to separate icons in the Finder's toolbar. Does not have a true function. A separator is included after the View element in the default toolbar.
- **New Folder**—Creates a new folder within the current Finder window. This is the same as pressing Shift+Command+N.
- **Delete**—Moves the currently selected Window item (or items) to the trash. This command does not *empty* the trash.
- **Connect**—Opens the file server connection window. This is the same as choosing Connect To Server... from the Go menu.
- **Find**—Launches Sherlock.
- **Computer**—Jumps to the top level of the computer hierarchy. This is a default toolbar element.
- **Home**—Jump from the current Finder window to your home directory. This is a default toolbar element.
- **iDisk**—If you've set up an iTools account and given the system your username and password (either during installation or in the Internet System Preferences panel), this shortcut will automatically mount your Apple iDisk.
- **Favorites**—Opens the folder containing the items that you've designated as your favorites. The folder contains aliases (shortcuts) to all the items you've added. If you manually add a shortcut to this location, it will appear in your Favorites menu. This is a default toolbar icon.
- **Applications**—Jumps to the system application folder. This is a default toolbar icon.
- **Documents**—Jumps to the Documents folder in your home directory.
- **Movies**—Jumps to the Movies folder in your home directory.
- **Music**—Jumps to the Music folder in your home directory.
- **Pictures**—Jumps to the Pictures folder in your home directory.
- **Public**—Jumps to the Public folder in your home directory.
- **Default Set**—Replaces the existing toolbar icons with the default set (Back, View, Separator, Computer, Home, Favorites, Applications).

At the bottom of the toolbar customization panel, you can choose how you want the toolbar displayed using the Show pop-up menu. You can pick Icon Only, Text Only, or Icon & Text if you prefer both. The default selection is Icon & Text.

As you are editing your toolbar, you might want to reorder the existing icons or remove them entirely. Just drag the toolbar elements into the order you'd like—they will automatically move to adjust to the new ordering. To remove an element, drag it outside the current toolbar and it will disappear. Click Done when you're satisfied with the results.

Note

The toolbar icons can be rearranged or removed only while you're in Customize Toolbar mode unless you are working with a user-defined shortcut such as an application or a folder.

User-Defined Shortcuts

In addition to the many predefined customizations, the toolbar also supports user-defined shortcuts. Users can drag common applications, documents, or folders to any place in the toolbar. Like the predefined customizations, the existing toolbar icons will rearrange themselves to accommodate what you are adding.

When folders and applications are added to the toolbar, a single click on the icons will open or launch the respective element. Users can also drag documents onto toolbar application and folder icons to open the file using the application or to move the file into a folder.

Tip

Storing your common folders in the toolbar is a great way to make moving files a cinch, especially in the Column view of the Finder. Rather than dragging an icon from folder to folder, just place your most frequently used folder in the toolbar and drag your files directly from the Finder window onto the folder in the toolbar.

Figure 4.16 shows a Finder window with several user-defined shortcuts added.

Note

Toolbar customization is done on a per-Finder, per-user basis. When you modify your toolbar, it is modified for all Finder windows in your workspace, not just the currently open folder. These changes also happen on a per-user basis, meaning that the changes you make to your toolbar will not affect other users.

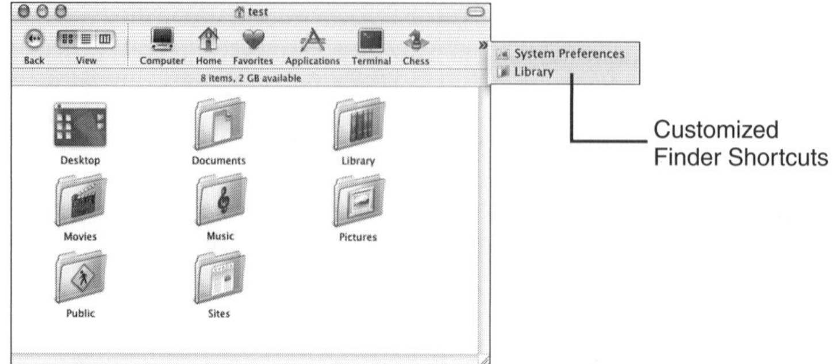

FIGURE 4.16
User-defined shortcuts let you add whatever you want to your Finder toolbar.

Finder File Operations

Because you're reading an *Unleashed* title, you probably already know the basics of most graphical operating systems: click and drag files to move them, double-click applications to launch them. Mac OS X doesn't break any new ground in the handling of files. Everyone who has used Windows, KDE/GNOME, or an earlier version of Mac OS will be able to carry their existing knowledge over to the new operating system. To be thorough, this portion of the chapter will serve as a quick reference to standard file and application operations.

Moving Files and Folders

Moving a file changes its location, but does not alter the contents of the file or its creation and modification dates. To move a file on Mac OS X, drag its icon to the folder or location where you want it to reside. If you are dragging within a Finder window, the window will automatically scroll as your cursor reaches the border, allowing you to move around within the view without having to drop the icon and manually scroll the window. Sadly, this does *not* hold true for the Column view.

If you are attempting to move a file from one device (such as a disk) to another, the file will be *copied* instead of moved. The original file will stay in its current location, and a new version will be created on the other storage media. You must delete the original copy of the file if you do not want to keep multiple versions of the file.

Tip

Finder (and some application) windows include a proxy icon in the title bar. If you click and hold this miniature icon for a few seconds, it becomes draggable. The icon represents the currently open folder or document and can be used just like dragging the item's icon within the Finder window.

Copying Files and Folders

Copying a file creates an exact duplicate of an original file. The new file sports a new creation and modification date, although the contents are identical to the original. There are a number of ways to create a copy on Mac OS X.

Drag a file to a different disk—Dragging a file to a disk other than the one it is currently stored on will result in a copy of the file being created at the destination. The copy will have the same name as the original.

Drag a file while holding down Option—If you drag a file to a folder on the same disk it is currently located on while holding down the Option key, a duplicate of that file will be created in the new location. If the Option key is not held down, this will normally just move the file. The copy will have the same name as the original.

Choose Duplicate from contextual/Finder menu—If you want to create an exact duplicate of a file within the same folder, highlight the file to copy, and then choose Duplicate from the Finder's File menu (Command+D). Or, alternatively, Control-click the icon and choose Duplicate from the pop-up contextual menu. A new file will be created with the word *copy* appended to the name.

Use the Finder Contextual Menus—Control-click on a Finder icon (or selection of multiple icons); then choose Copy. Next, locate where you'd like to copy the files to and then choose Paste from the Edit menu. Windows users will recognize this immediately.

Tip

Mac OS X recognizes many two-button mice and automatically maps the second button to the Control-click command. Additionally, many mice that include scroll-wheel functionality will automatically work in Cocoa-based applications.

As the file copies, the Finder will display a window, like that in Figure 4.17, where you can see the progress of the copy operation. If multiple copies are taking place at the same time, the status of each operation will be shown stacked on one another in the copy status window. There are two copies taking place in Figure 4.17. If you'd like to collapse the copy to show only summary information about the copy (time remaining), click the disclosure triangle at the left of the copy status.

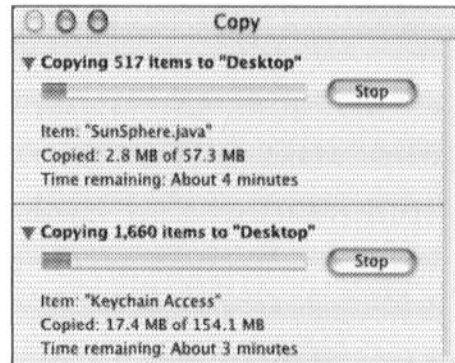

FIGURE 4.17
A single window contains all the status information for multiple copy operations.

If you attempt to copy over existing files, the Finder will prompt you whether you want to replace them. Remember that under Mac OS X, you *cannot* alter certain system files and directories or another user's files. If you attempt to replace existing files to which you do not have access, the copy operation will fail.

Deleting Files and Folders

Deleting files and folders permanently removes them from your system. Although the Mac OS X Finder has a new Undo menu, it cannot undo the effects of erasing a file from your system. Like copying a file, there are a number of ways to delete one:

Drag to Dock trash—Dragging an icon from a Finder window into the Dock's trash can is one of the most obvious and easy ways to get rid of a file.

Move To Trash contextual/Finder menu—You can move a selected item to the trash by Control-clicking the icon and choosing Move To Trash from the contextual menu, or choosing the option of the same name from the Finder's File menu.

Finder Toolbar—A Delete shortcut can be added to the Finder's toolbar. Any items selected can be quickly moved to the trash by clicking the Delete shortcut. Delete is *not* one of the default toolbar icons.

Moving an item to the trash does not delete it permanently from your drive. Instead, it places the item inside an invisible folder called `.Trash`—you cannot see or access this folder directly from the Mac OS X GUI. If you're interested in getting to the contents of the folder, check out the discussion of command-line navigation, starting in Chapter 12. The Trash Can icon in the Dock fills with crumpled paper when it contains items waiting to be deleted.

Although Mac OS X doesn't give you a true representation of the `.Trash` folder, it does let you view the contents of the trash by clicking the Trash Can icon. The Trash window works identically to other Finder windows. If you want to rescue a file you've accidentally sent to the trash, you can drag the file's icon out of the trash.

To completely remove a file from your system, choose Empty Trash from the Finder's application menu, or press Shift+Command+Delete. Alternatively, you can Control-click or click and hold on the trash can, and choose Empty Trash from the resulting pop-up menu.

Emptying the trash might take a few moments if you are deleting a large number of files. During this time, the Finder will bring up a dialog box very similar to the Copy dialog box. You can click Stop to cancel the trash operation, sparing the files that haven't yet been erased.

Creating Aliases

An *alias* is a representation of a file that, for all intents and purposes, *appears to be* the file. Windows users will recognize it as being similar to a shortcut.

Suppose that you have a document called My Diary buried deep in your drive, but you want to leave a copy of the icon on your desktop. Rather than duplicating the file and maintaining two copies, you can create an alias of the original file, and then place the alias wherever you'd like. Accessing the alias is the same as accessing the real file. The Finder uses aliases for things like Recent Folders and Favorites. Rather than having to move the real directories, it can just create aliases of them. You can tell an alias from the original by the arrow in the lower-left corner of the icon. Figure 4.18 shows the Favorites folder, filled with aliases to other folders.

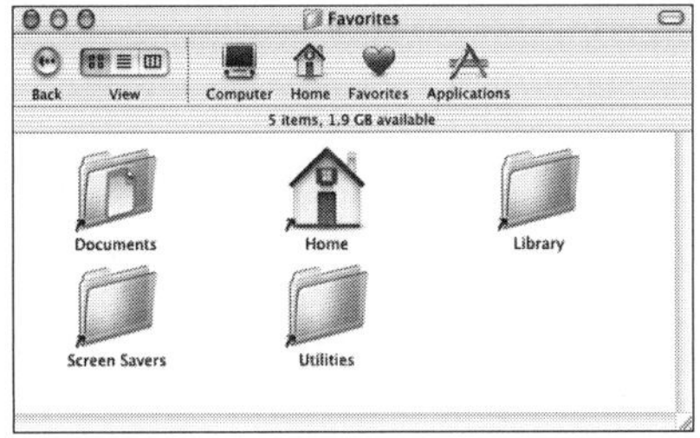

FIGURE 4.18
Aliases represent real files on your system.

There are two ways to create aliases:

- **Drag a file while holding down Option+Command**—If you drag a file to a folder while holding down the Option+Command keys, an alias of that file will be created in the new location.
- **Choose Make Alias from contextual/Finder menu**—If you want to create an alias of a file within the same folder, highlight the file to alias, and then choose Make Alias from the Finder's File menu (Command+L), or Control-click the icon and choose Make Alias from the pop-up contextual menu. A new file will be created with the word *alias* appended to the name.

Although aliases can be used to represent the original file, throwing them away does *not* delete the original file. Alternatively, deleting the original file doesn't delete the alias. If the original file is erased, the alias simply becomes broken. Double-clicking a broken alias will display a dialog similar to the one in Figure 4.19.

FIGURE 4.19
Broken aliases can be deleted or fixed.

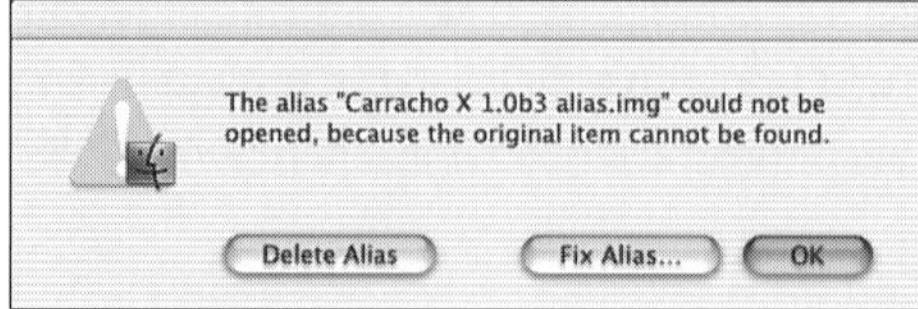

If you'd just like to get rid of a broken alias, click the Delete Alias button. If you want to point the alias to a different file, choose Fix Alias, locate the file you want to use, and the alias will be reattached. To leave things the way they are, click OK.

Note

Aliases aren't quite the same as symbolic links in Linux. The Mac file system assigns a unique identifier to each file. Aliases reference that identifier and can be used to locate a file wherever it is on your drive. If the original is moved, the ID does not change, and the alias continues to work.

Show Original

To locate the file to which an alias points, select the alias and choose Show Original (Command+R) from the Finder's File menu. The original file will be highlighted in the Finder.

Launching Applications/Documents

We're saving the easiest for last. Launching an application is a matter of double-clicking its icon, or dragging a document on top of the application's icon. In the latter case, the application will start and load or process the document that was dropped on it.

You can also launch an application by selecting it, and then choosing Open from the Finder's File menu or from the application's contextual menu.

Note

If you use a contextual menu to open an application, you might notice a Show Package Contents selection in the menu as well. Only available on certain applications, this will effectively open the application as if it were a folder, showing the various resources (images, sounds, and so on) that the application uses. You'll find out more about this in Chapter 11, "Additional System Components."

While an application is launching, its icon will bounce in the Dock. With 10.1, your software will be running in seconds. If you're stuck with the initial release of Mac OS X, applications can take 10–20 bounces to load—even on fast machines!

Unrecognized Files

If you attempt to double-click a document that the system does not recognize, Mac OS X will warn you that there is "no application available to open the document" you've tried to access, as demonstrated in Figure 4.20. If you're sure that a program on your system is capable of viewing the file, select the Choose Application.... You will be prompted to choose the application that will open the file. If the system does not allow you to pick the appropriate application, change the selection in the Show pop-up menu to read All Applications rather than Recommended Applications. By default, the system tries to guess the best app for the job—sometimes it fails miserably.

FIGURE 4.20
If a file can't be opened, you can choose an application to open it with.

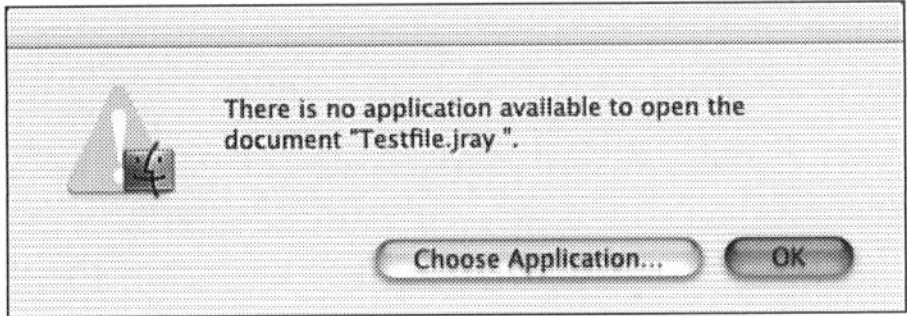

You can also fix unrecognized files by setting the application to open them through the Show Info Finder command, discussed later in this chapter.

Renaming Files

To rename a file in the Finder, click once to select the file, and then click a second time on the file's name. The filename will become editable in a few seconds. If you're the impatient sort, just press Return after selecting an icon; you'll immediately find yourself in edit mode.

Alternatively, you can use the Show Info option in the Finder File menu to edit the name in a larger field.

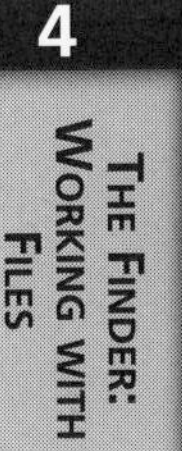

The Edit Menu

The Edit menu is used universally in almost every application that you'll run under Mac OS X. It has been duplicated on Linux, Windows, and just about every other GUI-based OS on the planet. The Edit menu allows a user to quickly select, copy, and cut information from one place in the system and paste it somewhere else. While the information is waiting to be added to another document, it is temporarily housed in what is called the *Clipboard*.

Mac OS X has six basic features available from the Finder's Edit menu:

Undo/Redo—The Undo command was introduced with Mac OS X. It allows you to reverse just about any action you've taken in the Finder, aside from emptying the trash. If you've moved a file or created a copy you don't need, just undo it. If you find that you've undone something you didn't mean to, the Undo menu will change to Redo—effectively enabling you to undo your undo. Although useful, this command has little in common with the other Edit menu options (Command+Z).

Cut—Cuts a piece of information (text, graphic, sound, and so on) from a document. The information is removed from the current file and placed in the Clipboard for reuse (Command+X).

Copy—Like Cut, but leaves the information in the original document and creates a copy of the data within the system Clipboard. If Copy is chosen when a Finder icon is selected, that file is prepared for duplication. The process is completed by choosing Paste (Command+C).

Paste—Pastes the contents of the clipboard back into the frontmost document or field. If the receiving element cannot handle the type of data you are attempting to paste (pasting a sound into a text field, for example), the Paste operation will fail. If you've previously used Copy while a Finder file icon was selected, the file will be copied to the location represented by the currently active Finder window (Command+V).

Select All—Highlights all selectable items within a window or document (Command+A).

Show Clipboard—Choosing Show Clipboard will display a small Finder window with the data that has been cut or copied from an application. Restarting your computer or logging out will lose the contents of the Clipboard.

Note

The Edit menu works to cut and copy information between native Mac OS X applications and applications running in the Classic environment. Unfortunately, the integration between these two effectively separate operating systems is such that you might need to wait a second or two between a cut/copy and a paste for the information to find its way to the appropriate destination.

Getting File Information

The Mac OS has always returned a wealth of information about a file via the Get Info option from the Finder's File menu. In Mac OS X, this is no different, although the menu is now named Show Info (Command+I). Unlike Mac OS 8/9, the Mac OS X Info window can display a great deal more information about your files and folders, such as graphical previews and user permissions.

Let's take a look at each one of the possible views, the information it contains, and what it means to you.

General Information

The default Show Info window can be displayed by selecting the file you want to examine within the Finder, and then choosing Show Info (Command+I) from the File menu. As shown in Figure 4.21, the initial information window provides basic facts about the selected resource. The Show Info window can display additional information about a selected resource by switching to different panels within that window. Although there doesn't seem to be an official word to describe different views of information contained within a single window, *panel* and *pane* are a frequently used terms.

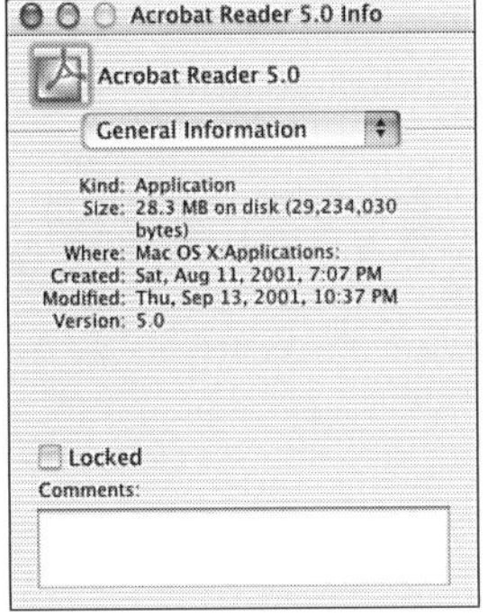

FIGURE 4.21
The General Information panel provides basic size/location/type information about a file.

Selecting a file and choosing Show Info displays data about that file, and has several options for revealing additional information:

- **Show**—This pop-up menu sets the type of information being shown. Use this to toggle between the different Show Info display panels. Not all types are available for all files (you can't, for example, show a preview of an application).
- **Kind**—The type of file being examined (application, movie, and so on).
- **Size**—The size of the file or folder.
- **Where**—The full path to the selected resource.
- **Created**—The day and time the item was created.
- **Modified**—The day and time the item was last modified.
- **Version**—The version of the document. Usually available only on application files.

- **Stationery Pad**—Available for document files only. If the Stationery Pad check box is checked, the file can be used to create new files, but cannot be modified itself. This is used to create template files for common documents.
- **Locked**—If this option is checked, the file cannot be modified or deleted until it is unlocked. For Linux/Unix users, this is equivalent to setting the immutable flag for the file.
- **Comments**—Enter any comments you want to make about a file in the Comments field. This enables the user to annotate files in the file system.

If the file you are viewing is an alias file, the General Information panel will also show the location of the original file along with a Select New Original button that lets you pick a new file to attach the alias to.

Changing Icons

If you're unhappy with the icon of the resource you're examining, you can click the object's icon within the General Information panel, and then use the Copy and Paste options in the Edit menu to move icons or images from other files onto the selected item.

Tip

An excellent source for high-quality Mac OS X icons is Iconfactory at `http://www.iconfactory.com` or Xicons, located at `http://www.xicons.com`.

Name & Extension

Mac OS X shares something with Windows: file extensions. Although it is still possible for files to have the traditional Macintosh file types and creators, it is no longer the norm. To shield users from the shock of seeing extensions to the names of their files, Apple introduced the ability to hide file extensions in Mac OS X 10.1. Users can turn off this option on a file-by-file basis by accessing the Name & Extension portion of the Show Info panel, as seen in Figure 4.22.

To edit the filename itself (including the extension) make modifications within the File system name field. Turn on (or off) file extensions by clicking the Hide Extension check box.

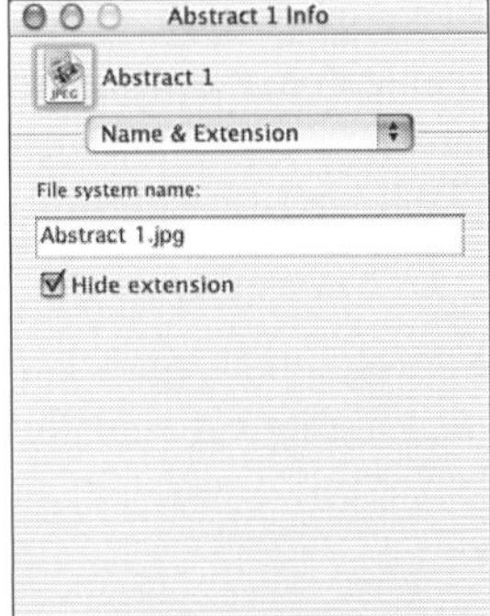

FIGURE 4.22
The Name & Extension panel can hide or reveal file extensions.

Note

Mac OS X will function identically whether or not file extensions are visible. This is simply a change in appearance, not functionality.

Open with Application

If you have selected a document icon (not an application or a folder), you should be able to access the Application panel within the Show Info window. This is used to configure the applications that open certain types of documents on the system. Unlike previous versions of Mac OS, which relied on a hidden creator and file type, Mac OS X can also use file extensions *or* creator/file-type resources. If you download a file from a non-Mac OS X system, your computer might not realize what it needs to do to open the file. The Open with application panel, shown in Figure 4.23, lets you configure how the system reacts. To use the panel, select a file, open the Show Info window, and choose Open with application from the window's pop-up menu.

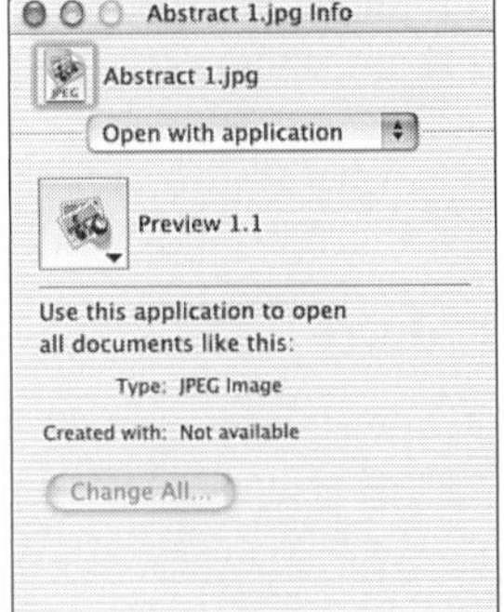

FIGURE 4.23
The Open with application panel lets you choose what application will read a particular file or type of file.

The default application name is shown alongside a pop-up menu containing alternative application choices. Click and hold the application icon in the window to display options and make a selection. If the application you want to use isn't shown, choose Other, and then use the standard Mac OS X file dialog to browse to the application you want to use.

If you have a group of files that you'd like to open with a given application, you can select the entire group, and then click Change All to set the application for all of them at once. This beats selecting each file and making the setting individually.

Languages

If you have an application selected, you might be able to choose Languages from the Show Info pop-up menu. Applications can have multiple internal resources that adjust the application to the appropriate system conditions—the Language panel allows you to adjust the language resources used by an application.

In early versions of the Mac OS, resources were contained within a file's resource fork. Unfortunately, resource forks are unique to the Mac file system. To store Mac files and applications on a non-Mac file system, various contortions had to be made. Typically, the data portion of an application would be stored like a normal file, while the resource fork would be converted to a second invisible file that was stored elsewhere.

Although this has worked for many years, it requires computers that interact with Mac files to understand the unusual quality of Mac files. In Mac OS X, files can still have resources, but they have been bundled in an entirely new way. First introduced in Mac OS 9, the Mac OS now supports a new concept called a package. A *package* is nothing more than a folder structure that appears to the user to be a single file. In reality, a package is a folder that contains individual files for all the resources it might need. Other operating systems need not understand the specifics of the Mac file system to store package files. The Languages panel, shown in Figure 4.24, displays the language resources available for each application, allowing a user to immediately localize software with the appropriately packaged resources. The Add and Remove buttons can be used to add additional language resources to the software.

FIGURE 4.24
Language resources can be examined in this view.

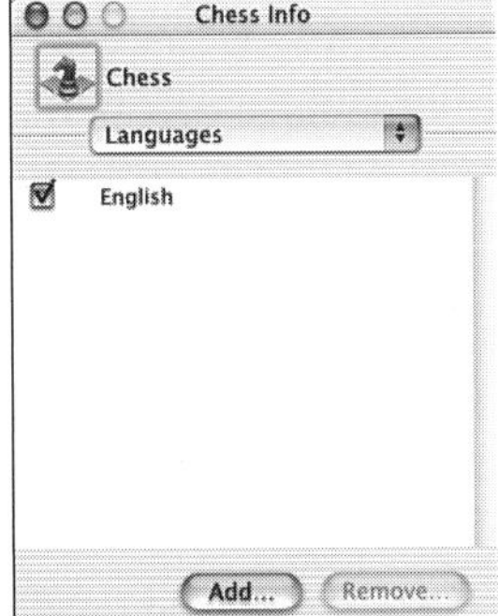

> **Note**
>
> Although only language resources are shown in the current version of Mac OS X, you might find interesting things appearing in the future. When NeXT Computer was shipping OpenStep, the operating system could run on multiple CPU architectures, such as x86, Motorola 68000, and Sparc. Applications for OpenStep could contain resources for each of the different CPUs, allowing a single application file to run unchanged on multiple different computers.
>
> Even though Intel support for Mac OS X is currently only a dream, it is possible that Apple might reintroduce this feature in the future.

Privileges

Mac OS X enables you to take control over who can view your files. Without your password (or the system administrator [root] password), other users can be completely restricted from accessing your folders and files. Choose the Privileges panel of the Show Info window after selecting the file or folder you want to adjust. Your screen should look similar to Figure 4.25.

FIGURE 4.25
File and folder permissions can be set in the Privileges panel.

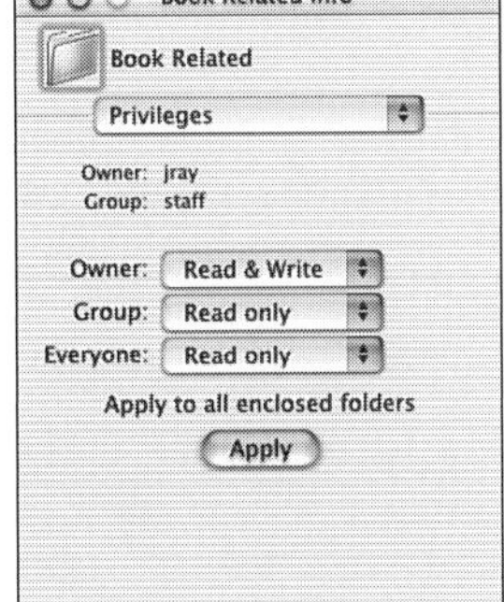

As discussed in Chapter 3, there are three levels of access you can adjust:

- **Owner**—The person who owns a file. Most files on a default Mac OS X installation are owned by a system user. You own files that you create.
- **Group** —The default OS X group is Staff, and all members of the operating system are part of the Staff group. Chapter 24, "User Management," discusses the creation of additional groups.
- **Everybody** —Users who are not the owner and not part of the default group. Because all Mac OS X users are part of the Staff group, you shouldn't have to enable access to everybody else unless you are creating a customized, multi-group system.

For each of these levels of access, there are multiple user rights. Adjusting these rights controls *what* the owner, group, and everyone else can do to a file or folder:

- **Read Only**—The file or folder can be read but not modified in any way.
- **Write Only (Drop Box)**—Available only as an option for folders, write only access allows users to add files to a folder, but not to read what is inside the folder.
- **Read & Write**—The file or folder can be read, written to, or deleted.
- **None**—The file or folder may not be read, written to, deleted, or modified in any way.

When viewing the file information for a folder, the Privileges window will also show a Copy button that will copy all the access rights on the folder to the files underneath. Just because a folder does not have read permissions doesn't mean the files inside the folder can't be read or modified unless they have the same permissions.

A final setting exists for storage volumes. If a disk is selected while viewing privilege information, an "ignore privileges on this volume" check box will appear. Clicking this box will cause the volume to appear as wide open to the operating system. Users can modify anything on the drive—just as in previous versions of the Mac OS. Activating this setting is *not* recommended.

Preview

If a QuickTime-recognized document is selected, there will be another available Show Info option: Preview. Preview lets you quickly examine the contents of a wide variety of media files including MP3s, CD audio tracks (aiff), JPEGs, GIFs, TIFFs, PDFs, and many, many more.

If you are previewing a video or audio track, the QuickTime player control will appear and enable you to play the contents of the file. This is a great way to play your CDs or listen to MP3s without starting up a copy of iTunes. Figure 4.26 shows a CD audio track being played in the Preview panel.

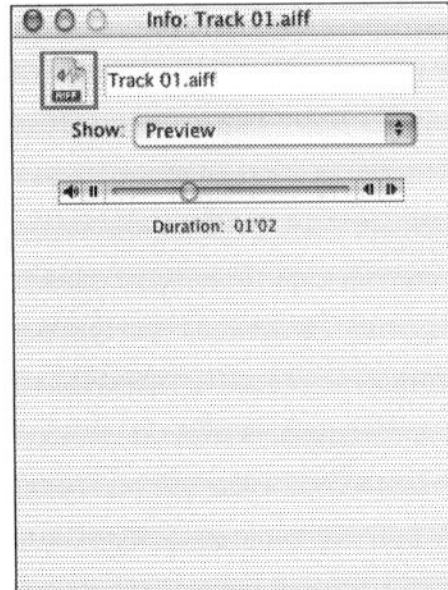

FIGURE 4.26
Play your CD tracks using the Finder's Show Info Preview panel.

Tip

As with the Finder's View window, the Show Info window adjusts to the current selected object. You can leave a single Info window open and click between different Finder icons; the information will update as you move from file to file.

The Desktop and Finder Preferences

The desktop is, for all intents and purposes, a global Finder window that sits behind all the other windows on the system. You can copy files to the desktop, create aliases on the desktop, and so on. The primary difference is that the desktop is only available in the Icon view mode.

Tip

The contents of the desktop are also accessible from the Desktop folder contained within your home directory (Path: `~/Desktop`).

Like other Finder windows, the Desktop layout is controlled by the View Options located in the View menu. Use the Icon Size slider and arrangement settings exactly as you would adjust any other window within Icon View mode.

Desktop: System Preference Panel

A more visually exciting change that you can perform on your Finder Desktop is changing the background image. To do this, you must access the Desktop panel within the System Preferences application (Path: `/Applications/System Preferences`).

To open the System Preferences, you have a number of options:

- Click the System Preferences icon in the Dock. (By default, this is the sixth item from the left side of the Dock and features a gray Apple in the icon.)
- Choose System Preferences from the Apple menu.
- Launch System Preferences manually. It is located in the system's Applications folder (Path: `/Applications/System Preferences`).

After System Preferences is running, click the Desktop icon, located within the Personal category of the Preferences window. The Desktop preference panel is displayed in Figure 4.27.

FIGURE 4.27
Set your background image using the Desktop System Preference Panel.

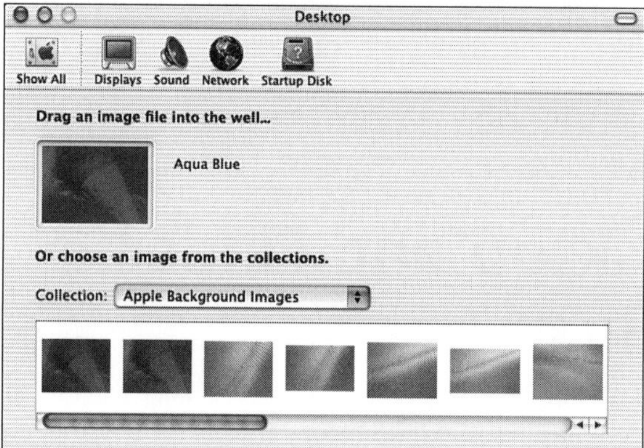

To change the current background, drag an image file from the Finder into the image-well within the panel. Alternatively, you can browse Collections of images by choosing from the Collection pop-up menu then using the horizontal scrollbar to move through the available files. A collection is nothing more than a folder of images. There are five preset collections: Apple backgrounds, Nature, Abstract, Solid Colors, and Pictures. The Pictures option selects your personal `~/Pictures` folder. To browse an arbitrary folder, pick the Choose Folder item, and then select the folder you want to use.

Note

The Apple image collections are located within `/Library/Desktop Pictures`, and can be added to or modified by any administrative user on the system.

Tip

By default, desktop icon titles are drawn in white. Depending on your background picture, this might be a problem. To set the icon text to black, just open a terminal window and type the following at a command line: `defaults write com.apple.finder Desktop.HasDarkBackground 0` and press Return. To undo the change, use `defaults write com.apple.finder Desktop.HasDarkBackground 1`. You must restart to see the change take effect.

Finder Preferences

The Finder Preferences can be used to adjust a few more settings that control how you will interact with your desktop and icons. Open these settings by choosing Preferences from the Finder's application menu. The available options are shown in Figure 4.28.

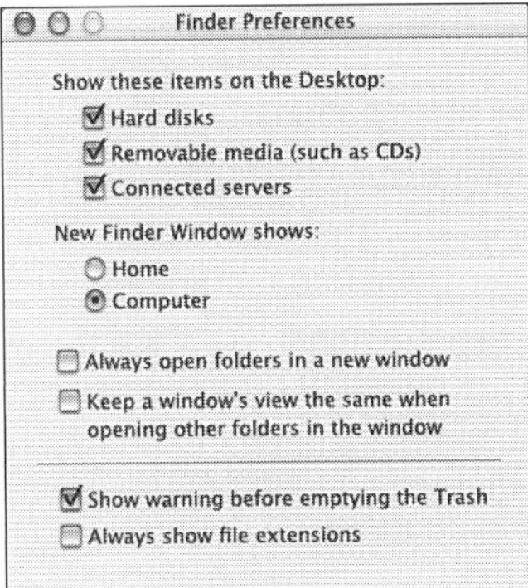

FIGURE 4.28
Finder Preferences control file extensions, Trash warnings, and more.

Use the Finder Preferences to configure these elements:

- **Show these items on the Desktop**—Choose whether or not different storage devices will be mounted automatically on the desktop. Use the check boxes beside Hard disks, Removable media, and Connected servers to display the associated devices on the desktop. If an item is *not* mounted on the desktop, it will be accessible by moving to the Computer level of the file system hierarchy.

- **New Finder Window shows**—Determine what location a new Finder window will open in. Choose Computer to open a window displaying all mounted storage devices or Home to start in your home directory.
- **Always open folders in a new window**—Clicking this option will force a new window to open each time a folder is double-clicked. This is the only way to make the toolbar-mode Finder windows behave like the traditional Finder.
- **Keep a window's view the same...**—This, as explained earlier in the chapter, will prevent the Finder from switching to different views as you move from folder to folder in the file system. For example, if you're using List view and double-click a folder, the Finder will switch to the standard Icon view by default. This behavior can be awkward and confusing, but is easily overridden with this setting.
- **Show warning before emptying the Trash**—When emptying the trash can, Mac OS X will display a warning message. To bypass this dialog, deselect this check box. Alternatively, hold down Option when choosing Empty Trash to temporarily bypass the warning.
- **Always show file extensions**—Turn this setting on to force all file extensions to be shown in the Finder and other windows. Most Mac users won't want to do this.

Close the Finder Preferences window when you're satisfied with your settings.

Burning CDs

Burning CD-Rs or CD-RWs within the Mac OS X Finder is extremely easy and very similar to working with any other storage device. To make the process as transparent as possible, Mac OS X creates a hidden CD-sized temporary storage area on your hard drive. Applications, files, and folders that are added to a CD are actually copied to this location until the user tells the system to burn the CD. Only after the burn starts are files actually transferred to the CD media.

To write your own CD, first insert media into the CD writer. The Mac OS X Finder will prompt you to prepare the CD, as seen in Figure 4.29. Again, this doesn't actually write anything to the CD just yet, but it tells the computer what your intentions are for the disk.

Enter a name for the CD you are writing—it will appear with this name on the Desktop. Next, choose a format. There are three formats provided:

Standard—An HFS+/ISO 9660 disk for storing Macintosh data and files.

MP3 CD—A strict ISO 9660 volume, useful for cross-platform data and writing MP3s.

iTunes Audio—A standard music CD to be used with consumer CD players.

FIGURE 4.29
Before you can start using a CD, you must tell Mac OS X what type of CD it will be.

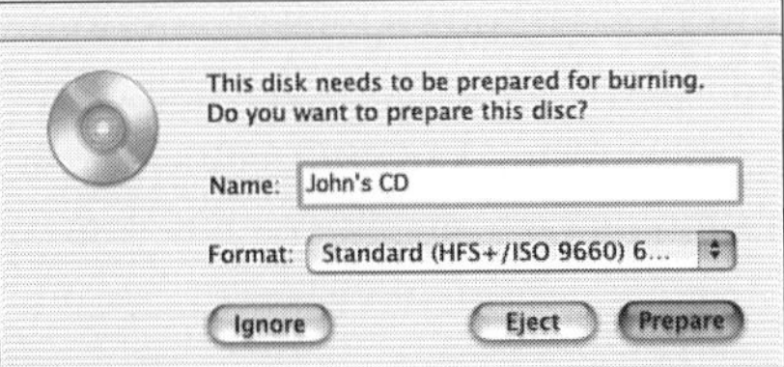

Finally, click Prepare to start using the CD on your system. If you'd like to leave the CD in the drive but *not* prepare it (for use in another application, such as Roxio's Toast), click Ignore.

After a few seconds, an icon representing the CD will appear on your desktop. You can interact with this virtual volume as you would any other under Mac OS X. Copy files to it, delete files, and so on.

When you've created the CD layout that you like, you can start the burn process by choosing Burn Disc from the File menu, or by clicking the Burn toolbar shortcut. In addition, dragging the CD to the trash will also prompt for burning to begin. Mac OS X will display the dialog shown in Figure 4.30.

Note

To choose Burn Disc from the File menu, the frontmost Finder window must be the CD's window. If the CD is not the active window, the menu item will be disabled.

FIGURE 4.30
Choose Burn to write the CD.

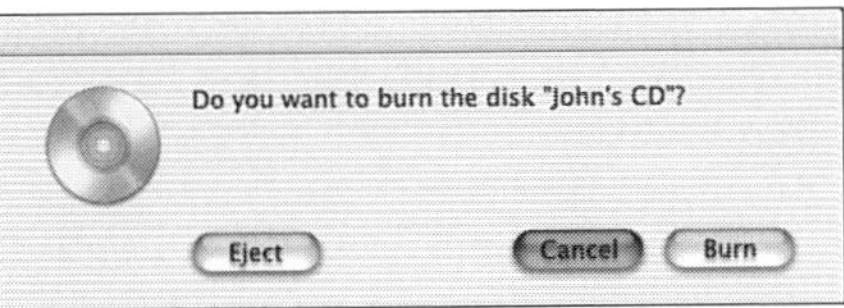

Click the Burn button to start the process of writing the CD. This will take a few minutes, and will be tracked by the Finder must like a normal copy operation. If you've decided against writing the CD, click Eject to remove the media and erase the CD layout you've created.

Using the Dock

In Chapter 3, you learned how the basic features of the Dock work. In this chapter, we'll recap those features and provide additional information on how you can customize the Dock to suit your desktop.

Application Switcher and Launcher

Commonly used applications can be added to the Dock, much like a Finder toolbar, by dragging them to the position you want on the left side (or top in vertical mode) of the Dock divider bar. This half of the bar contains all docked and currently running applications. A running application is denoted by a small triangle under its icon.

To switch between the active programs, just click the icon of the application that you want to bring to the front. Holding down Option as you click on an application will bring the application to the front and hide the previously active process. Simultaneously holding down both Option+Command while clicking will bring the clicked application to the front and hide *all* other applications.

To switch between open programs from the keyboard, use Command+Tab—this should seem very familiar to Windows users.

Finally, if you have placed an application on the Dock, you can launch it by single-clicking the icon. The application icon will begin bouncing (unless configured not to), and will continue to do so until the software is ready for user interaction.

Tip

To add an application that is currently running to a permanent spot in the Dock, just click and hold (or Control-click) the icon, and then choose Keep in Dock from the pop-up menu.

Interacting with Running Applications

Common functions, such as quitting an application or jumping to one of its open windows, can be accessed by clicking and holding a running application's Dock icon or by Control-clicking on the icon. Some applications, such as iTunes, even allow basic controls (playback controls, in the case of iTunes) to be accessed through the Dock pop-up menu. After the menu has appeared, you can press the Option key to reveal hidden menu options; this particular key/mouse combination will change a Dock icon's Quit select to Force Quit when used.

Application icons also serve as proxy drop points for documents. As with the traditional Mac operating system, you can drag documents on top of an application icon to open them in that application. In Mac OS X, you can use the application's Dock icon, rather than having to locate the real application file on your hard drive.

Tip

Dragging a document to a running application or to the trash is a bit of a pain in Mac OS X. In an effort to accommodate the icon you're dragging with the assumption that you're adding it to the Dock, the other icons will move out of its way. For a user, this means that the icon she's headed for might not hold still long enough for a traditional drag-and-drop. To keep the Dock icons from sliding, hold down the Command key during the drag.

Tip

To force a docked application to accept a dropped document that it doesn't recognize, hold down Command+Option when holding the document over the application icon. The icon will immediately highlight, allowing you to perform your drag-and-drop action.

File and Folder Shortcuts

Shortcuts to files and folders that are used frequently can be stored to the right (or bottom in vertical mode) of the Dock separator bar. When a folder is added to the Dock, it can be single-clicked to open a Finder window containing the contents of that folder. Clicking and holding (or Control-clicking) a folder in the Dock will create a pop-up hierarchical menu displaying the contents of the folder. Any elements added to the folder will be immediately visible in the pop-up menu.

Note

Moving an icon to the Dock does not change the location of the original file or folder. The icon within the Dock is just a shortcut to the real file. Unfortunately, the Dock's icon is not the same as an alias. If a docked application is moved, the Dock will no longer be able to launch that application.

In a similar but unrelated note, it is not possible to add aliases of folders to the Dock. Dragging an alias is the same as dragging the original folder. It will be added to the Dock, but if the original item is moved, the Dock alias will still break.

Tip

To locate an application, file, or folder that you've dragged to the Dock, hold down Command and click the Dock icon, or choose Show in Finder while Control-Clicking or click-holding the icon. The Finder will open a window and highlight the original file or folder.

Docklings

Docklings are small, always-on applications that provide instant-access features from within the Dock. Unlike other applications, a Dockling lives its whole life within the Dock and does not have a user interface that extends beyond the Dock icon and a pop-up menu. Unlike other Dock elements, Docklings can be positioned anywhere on the Dock, except after the trash can. To activate a Dockling's configuration menu, either click-and-hold or Control-click the icon.

The Trash Can

The Mac OS trash can has been given a makeover and moved to the far-right side of the Dock. You can drag files and folders directly from the Finder into the Dock's trash can. If you want to remove an item from the trash, click the Trash Can icon and a window appears containing all the items waiting to be deleted. You can drag files from this window just as you can in any other Finder window.

To empty the trash, use the Finder's application menu and choose Empty Trash (Shift+Command+Enter); or click-and-hold or Control-click the Trash can icon, and choose Empty Trash from the pop-up menu. Holding down Option while emptying the trash will bypass any system warning messages. The Finder preferences can permanently disable the Empty Trash warning.

Ejecting Media

There are a number of ways to eject disks under Mac OS X. Control-clicking on a mounted volume will open a contextual menu with an Eject option. Alternatively, you can highlight the resource to remove and choose Eject (Command+E) from the Finder's File menu or press the Eject key on some models of the Apple USB keyboard.

The final method of ejecting a disk might seem a bit unusual to some users, but it has been a standard on the Macintosh for many years. Disks can be safely unmounted and ejected by dragging them to the trash can. To get around the obvious "Hey, isn't that going to erase my disk?" reaction that many have, Mac OS X now conveniently changes the Trash Can icon into an eject symbol during a drag operation that includes a storage volume.

Windows

Windows that are minimized are placed in a thumbnail view beside the trash can. Depending on the application, these iconified windows might continue to update as their respective applications attempt to display new information. The QuickTime player, for example, can continue to play miniaturized movies in the Dock.

> **Tip**
>
> There are three built-in minimizing effects for Mac OS X, two of which (Genie and Scale) are accessible in the Dock System Preference Panel. You can switch between the three effects manually by using the following commands within the Terminal window:
>
> - The standard Genie effect: `defaults write com.apple.Dock mineffect genie`
> - An aptly named suck effect: `defaults write com.apple.Dock mineffect suck`
> - A simple window scaling: `defaults write com.apple.Dock mineffect scale`

Customizing the Dock

After the initial "gee whiz, that's pretty" reaction to the Dock wears off, you'll probably want to customize the Dock to better suit your Finder settings. Depending on your screen size, you might be looking at a Dock that, by default, eats up about 1/3 of the available desktop space on your machine. Don't worry, there are ways to rectify the situation.

Instant Resizing

The easiest and fastest way to resize the Dock is to click and hold on the divider line that separates the right and left sides of the Dock. With your mouse held down, drag up and down. The Dock will dynamically resize as you move your mouse. Let go of the mouse button when the Dock has reached the size you want.

Tip

As the Dock grows or shrinks, the icons will change size with it and the divider line will shift to the left or right as needed. After the resize has started, you do not need to keep your mouse cursor centered over the divider line—the resize will continue until the mouse button is released, regardless of your pointer position.

After playing with different Dock sizes, you might notice that some sizes look better than others. This is because Mac OS X must interpolate between several different native icon graphics in order to scale the images. To choose only native icon sizes, hold down the Option key while using the separator bar to resize.

Dock: System Preferences Panel

For more fine-tuning of the Dock, you must turn to the System Preferences application. The Dock has a settings panel within System Preferences that can adjust its size, its icon magnification, and make it disappear when not in use. Users of Apple's Titanium Powerbooks or Cinema-aspect displays will be pleased to find that the Dock can even move into a vertical mode, occupying space along the sides of the screen.

Open System Preferences, then click the Dock icon within System Preferences. Your screen should now resemble Figure 4.31.

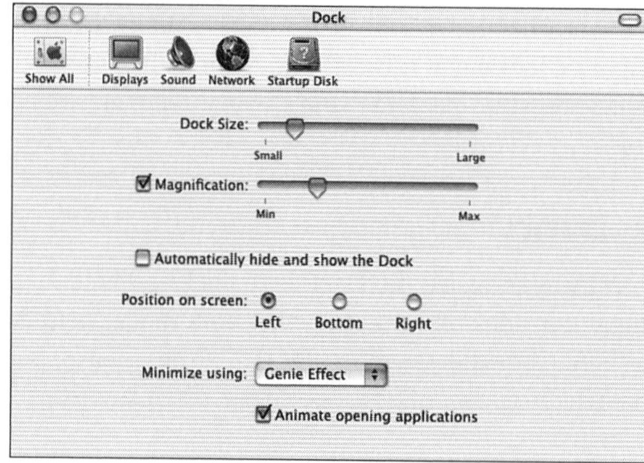

FIGURE 4.31
Customize the Dock's appearance from the System Preferences application.

Within this panel, you can choose how you'd like the Dock to look and act on your computer. There are four settings:

- **Dock Size**—This sets the size of the Dock icons. Moving this slider from left to right will increase the size of the default Dock icon and is identical to dragging the separator bar that was discussed earlier in "Instant Resizing." Keep in mind that the Dock will not expand beyond the edges of the screen and will shrink automatically to make room for additional icons.
- **Magnification**—If you activate Dock magnification by clicking the check box, the Dock icons will automatically scale as you move your cursor over them. You can use the magnification slider to adjust the maximum size that a magnified icon will take. Although this is useful if you have an extremely small Dock, its main purpose seems to be eye candy. If you haven't seen this effect demonstrated, turn it on—you're in for a treat.

Note

Although it is possible to set a magnification size *lower* than the normal icon size in the Dock, the icons will not shrink as you move your pointer over them. This potential configuration is meaningless to the system.

- **Automatically hide and show the dock**—If this check box is set, the Dock will automatically disappear when you move your mouse out of it. To make the Dock reappear, just move your cursor to the bottom of the screen—it will grow back into the original position. You can toggle this at any time from the Finder by pressing Option+Command+D.
- **Position on screen**—Use these radio buttons (Left, Bottom, Right) to control where the Dock will appear on your Desktop. The default position is at the bottom of the screen, but many users may find that a vertical orientation (left or right) is more useful and appealing.
- **Minimize using**—Audiences were wowed when they first saw the Dock's Genie effect for minimizing windows. Although nifty, it isn't exactly the fastest thing on the planet. In Mac OS X 10.1, Apple included a second minimization effect: Scale. This effect is much less dramatic, but also much faster. Use the Minumize using pop-up menu to choose your minimization style.
- **Animate opening applications**—By default, when an application is starting, the Dock will bounce the application's icon up and down. This provides visual feedback that the system hasn't stalled. Shutting off this feature might result in a small

speed increase, but is likely to be a bit frustrating when you can no longer tell whether the system is starting the application you selected.

When you've completed your Dock configuration, choose Quit (Command+Q) from the System Preferences application menu.

Note

Unlike control panels in Mac OS 8/9, the system preferences do not automatically quit if you close their window. To Quit, choose Quit (Command+Q) from the application menu.

Easy access to several of the Dock's configuration options is also available through the Dock submenu in the Apple menu

Process Manager: Force Quitting Applications

The final topic in this chapter is the force quit feature. The Macintosh has never had an effective and reliable method of quitting a "hung" application before the release of Mac OS X. Windows users are accustomed to pressing Control+Alt+Del to force an application to exit, but Mac users were stuck pressing Option+Command+Escape and hoping for the best. If a force quit worked without completely crashing Mac OS, it usually made the system unstable and forced a reboot within minutes.

With Mac OS X, the Option+Command+Escape keystroke still works, but now it brings up a process manager with a list of running applications, as shown in Figure 4.32.

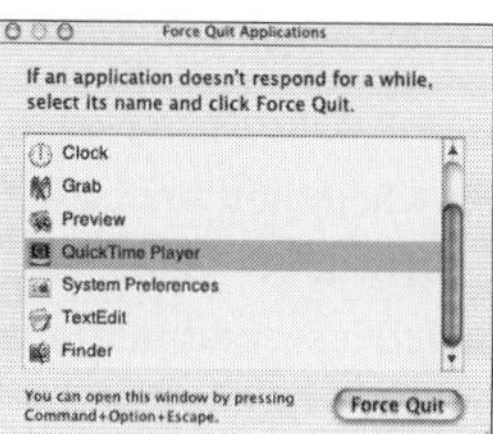

FIGURE 4.32
Choose an application to kill, and then click Force Quit.

To force an application to exit, just choose it from the list and click Force Quit. This will terminate the application without reducing your system stability. If the Finder seems to be misbehaving, you can choose it from the application list and the Force Quit button will become Relaunch, allowing you to quit and restart the Finder without logging out.

You can also access the Force Quit feature from the Apple menu, or by opening the pop-up Dock menu for a running application and pressing the Option key to toggle the standard Quit selection to Force Quit.

Note

Forcing an application to quit does not save any open documents. Be sure that the application is truly stalled, not just busy, before you use this feature.

Tip

Forcing an application to quit is the same as using the command-line function `kill`. Learn more about the command line starting in Chapter 12, "Introducing the BSD Subsystem."

Mac OS X offers another utility that can also force applications, including system processes, to quit. This program, ProcessViewer, will be discussed in Chapter 6, "Native Utilities and Applications."

Summary

The Mac OS X Finder represents a brand-new start for the Macintosh operating system. The Finder toolbar and Column view open up new possibilities in file system navigation, but lose several traditional features such as pop-up windows and many customization options. For now, the Finder is still an open area of exploration. Each day that this chapter was in development brought new tips and tricks that uncover additional new features. We will continue to add new features until publication to be able to bring you the most information-rich text available.

CHAPTER 5

Running Classic Mac OS Applications

If you've never had a Mac or are a NeXT user who's happy to have finally found a home, Mac OS X probably has more than enough available software and functionality to make you happy. Those of us who have been using the Mac operating system regularly for years, however, are likely to already have a software library that we rely on. To accommodate this need, Apple included the Classic environment. Classic provides a runtime layer for older, non-Carbonized Mac applications. It even allows certain pieces of hardware to be accessible, such as USB scanners and cameras. It is not a perfect solution, but it does allow for a high degree of compatibility with legacy hardware and software from within Mac OS X.

This chapter looks at the Classic environment, how it works, how it can be configured, and what to do if you absolutely must boot into Mac OS 9.x.

The Classic Environment

As defined in Chapter 1, "Mac OS X Component Architecture," the Classic environment is a complete implementation of Mac OS 9.x on top of Mac OS X. To Mac OS X, Classic is nothing but another application; to a user, however, Classic is a gateway to his older software programs.

> **Tip**
>
> You *must* have at least 128MB of memory to use Classic, and a 400MHz G3 (or faster) is recommended. When it comes to Classic, more is definitely better.
>
> Classic is a process *under* Mac OS X. Mac OS X must be running for Classic to work. In essence, you're booting two operating systems simultaneously.

When using the Classic environment, the 9.x operating system must access all hardware through the Mac OS X kernel. This means software that accesses hardware directly will fail. Users of 3Dfx video cards, hardware DVD playback, video capture cards, and even CD writers will find that their hardware no longer functions correctly.

On the other hand, Classic brings the benefit of Mac OS X's virtual memory underpinnings to legacy applications. Each Mac OS 9.x application can be configured for a much larger memory partition than was possible previously. To the Classic environment, the virtual memory appears to be real memory. Programs have much more breathing room in which to function.

Working with the Classic environment is a somewhat unusual experience. Depending on the application running, there can be graphic anomalies and confusing file system navigation. This chapter will show what you'll see and what to do when things don't seem to work right.

Launching Classic

The Classic environment is typically launched once during a Mac OS X login session—either manually or automatically. After it is running, Classic remains active until you log out or manually force it to shut down.

> **Note**
>
> Classic does *not* gain all the stability features of Mac OS X, such as protected memory. If an application crashes in Classic, it can bring down all applications running in Classic. The Mac OS X system will be unaffected, but you might need to manually restart the Classic environment.

There are two ways to launch the Classic environment: by double-clicking a Classic application and through the Classic panel within System Preferences.

Classic applications appear to the Mac OS X Finder just like any other application. To verify that a piece of software is indeed a Classic application, you can select the icon and select Show Info (Command+I) from the Finder's File menu. Or Control-click on the icon and choose Show Info from the context menu. Figure 5.1 shows the General Information panel for the Graphing Calculator, a Classic application.

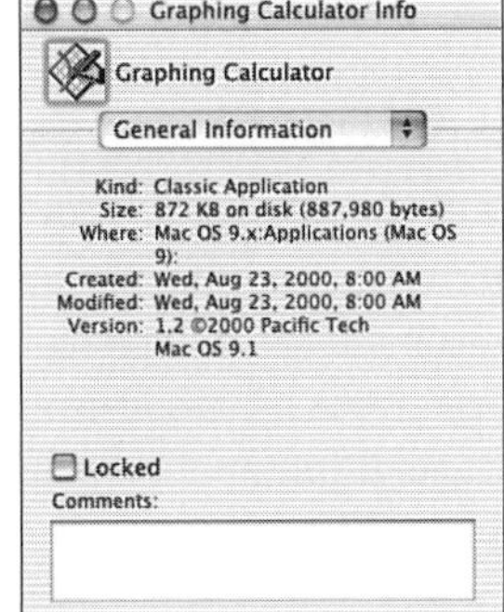

FIGURE 5.1
The General Information panel will identify Classic applications.

Memory Settings

Classic applications, because they still use the Mac OS 9.x Memory Manager, require a preferred and minimum memory size to be set. Because you have no direct access to the 9.1 Finder under OS X, Classic applications have an additional Show Info panel called Memory. This is shown in Figure 5.2.

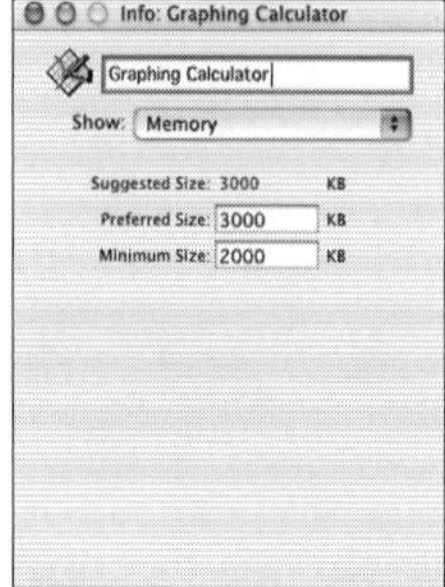

FIGURE 5.2
Classic applications allow memory limits to be set.

Two limits can be set:

Preferred Size—The amount of memory that you want the application to have. This is the upper limit of the memory partition that will be requested from Mac OS 9.x.

Minimum Size—The minimum amount of memory that an application must have in order to run. The Mac OS 9.x environment will prohibit the application from launching unless the minimum memory size can be met.

To take advantage of the new Mac OS X memory architecture, set these values higher than you would in older versions of the Mac OS. If you do, be aware that your settings here will carry over if you boot directly into Mac OS 9.x, where you might not have as much real or virtual memory available.

Forcing Carbon Apps into Classic

Carbon applications are a special case of Mac OS X application. They are capable of running natively on Mac OS X, and on Mac OS 9.x through the use of CarbonLib. If you'd like to use the Classic environment to launch a Carbon application, there is a setting within the General Information panel that can force a Carbon-compliant package to launch through Classic. Figure 5.3 shows the General Information panel for a Carbon application.

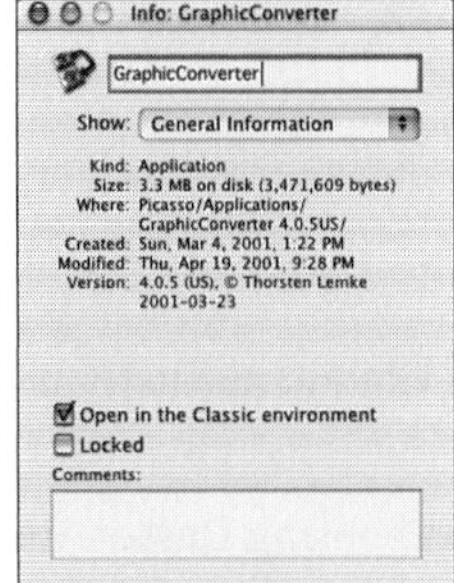

FIGURE 5.3
Carbon applications can be forced to launch in the Classic environment.

To launch a Carbon application in Classic, check the "Open in the Classic environment" check box, and then close the info panel. Double-clicking the application will launch it in Classic rather than in Mac OS X.

Manually Starting and Configuring Classic

If you have multiple Mac OS 9.x installations, or want to manually start or stop the Classic environment, you can do so from the Classic System Preferences panel. First, open System Preferences (path: `/Applications/System Preferences`), and then click the Classic icon.

The basic Classic controls are shown in Figure 5.4.

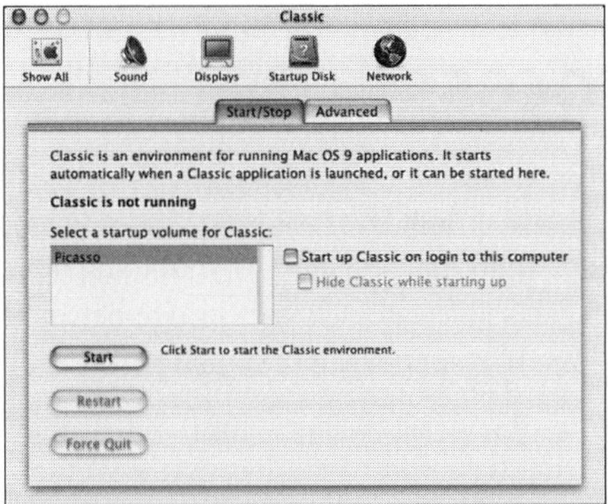

FIGURE 5.4
The Classic System Preferences panel configures the startup volume and allows manual startup and shutdown.

The Classic Preferences panel can control how and when Classic boots. The following options are found in the Start/Stop tab of the Classic panel:

- **Select a startup volume for Classic**—Mac OS X can start the Classic environment by booting any available Mac OS 9.x system. It is recommended that you use a separate drive or partition for Mac OS 9.x. Refer to Chapter 2, "Installing Mac OS X," for more information.

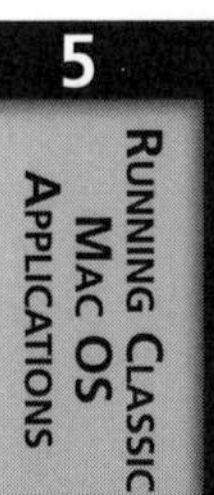

- **Start up Classic on login to this computer**—If you'd like Classic to start up immediately after you log in to your computer (or immediately at startup, if you're using Mac OS X as a single-user system), click this button. Be warned, the Classic environment takes a few minutes to start and your system performance will be degraded during this time.
- **Start/Stop**—Click the Start button to launch Classic manually or Stop to shut it down.
- **Restart**—The Restart button is equivalent to choosing Restart from the Mac OS 9.x Finder. Open applications will prompt you to save open documents, and then exit. The Classic environment will reboot.
- **Force Quit**—If Classic becomes unresponsive (that is, it crashes), the only option is to force it to quit. Open documents are lost, exactly as if Mac OS 9.x crashed (as it tends to do from time to time). You can also use the Control+Option+Escape keystroke to force it to quit.

Note

The Classic System Preferences panel also shows the status of the Classic environment—whether it is running or not. Because Classic does not appear as an active task in the Dock, this is one way to check its status.

The Boot Process

Mac OS X requires 9.1 or later to be installed in order to boot Classic. If you are running an earlier version, you must upgrade it first.The first time that Mac OS X boots the Classic environment, it must add additional software to your computer to be able to operate, demonstrated in Figure 5.5. This software acts as a bridge between the Mac OS X process monitors and I/O systems. If you choose not to add these components when prompted, Classic will exit.

Note

If you have a Mac OS X compatible version of Mac OS 9.x that is not the most current release, Mac OS X might give you a warning with instructions on how to update the earlier operating system.

Although Mac OS 9.2 is the preferred Classic OS for Mac OS X 10.1, users with 9.1 will still be able to boot into Classic and upgrade at their leisure.

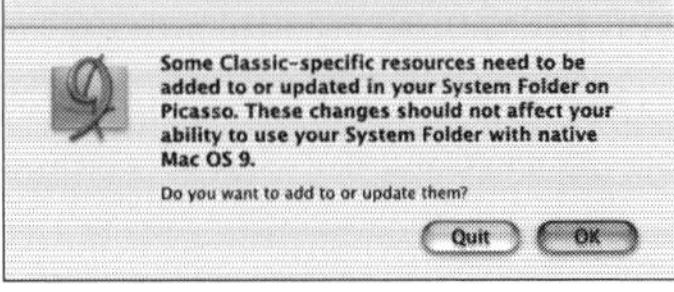

FIGURE 5.5
The first time Classic is run, Mac OS X will modify your 9.x installation.

As Classic boots, it will load all the extensions and control panels that you had previously installed on your Mac OS 9.x installation, as shown in Figure 5.6. If you installed Mac OS X from scratch, you should be in good shape. If you're upgrading an older system, you might find that some extensions cause Classic to crash.

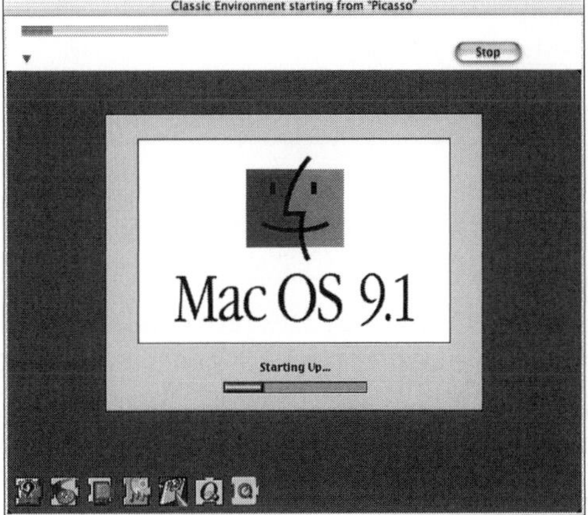

FIGURE 5.6
Classic loads your extensions as it boots.

Resolving Conflicts

Extensions or control panels that access hardware and those that patch the Mac OS system routines are most likely to cause problems. MIDI software has been reported to be extremely efficient at crashing the initial Mac OS X release. Other drivers might have similar effects, but your mileage will likely vary. In the initial beta releases of Mac OS X, my Canon scanner failed to operate under Classic, but it now works without fail under the release version.

So, what do you do when Classic won't boot?

There are two avenues for resolving a problem with Classic. The first is to use the Mac OS X Classic System Preferences panel to disable extensions during startup. Although your first reaction might be to hold down the Shift key while Classic starts, this will not work. The Classic boot window does not pass keystrokes directly to the booting Mac OS 9.x system.

Instead, you can use the advanced startup options to provide some control over the boot sequence. Open the System Preferences and choose the Classic panel. Click the Advanced tab to see the advanced startup options. Figure 5.7 shows this panel.

FIGURE 5.7
The Classic advanced options provide some control over the startup sequence.

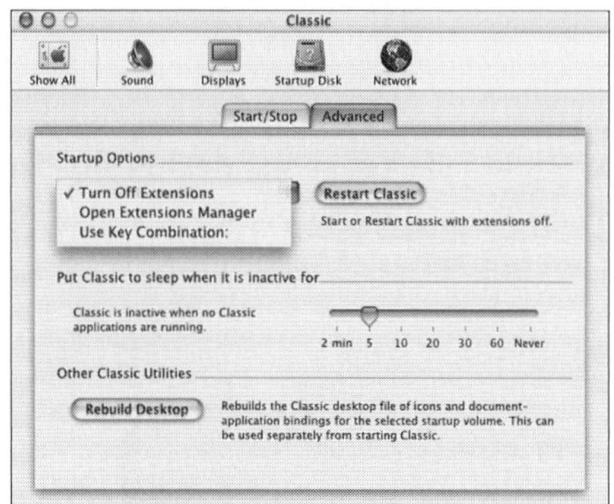

You can make three modifications to the startup process:

Turn Off Extensions—Turning off the extensions is the equivalent of pressing Shift while booting into Mac OS 8 or 9. This prohibits additional control panels and extensions—beyond those needed by the 9.1 operating system—from loading.

Open Extensions Manager—This opens the Mac OS 9.x Extensions Manager control panel during the boot process, allowing you to disable extensions that appear to be causing system instability. The Mac OS 9.x Extensions Manager will be discussed shortly.

Use Key Combination—The Key Combination option is unusual; it enables the user to choose up to five keys that will be kept in pressed state while Classic boots. Some extensions can be individually disabled by certain keystrokes—this feature lets you target those processes.

After choosing your startup options, click the Start or Restart button to implement the selection.

Mac OS 9.x Extensions Manager

If you have no idea what is causing your system problems, your best choice is to open the Extensions Manager. This will let you start with a base set of extensions and build them back up into a working system.

A few seconds into the boot process, the Extensions Manager will appear in the OS X Classic boot screen. The Extensions Manager is shown in Figure 5.8.

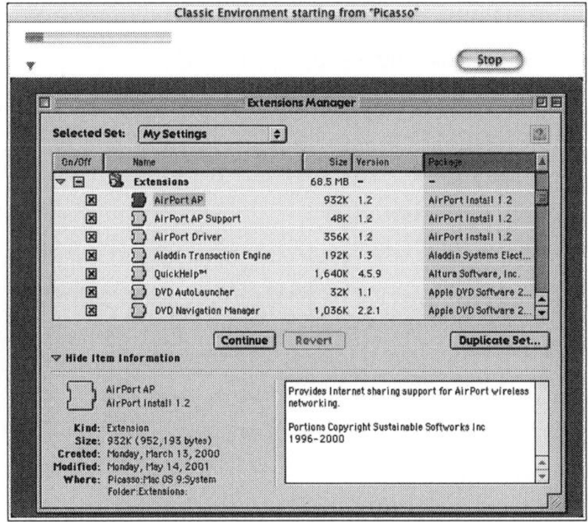

FIGURE 5.8
The Extensions Manager helps you find a base set of extensions that will let Classic boot successfully.

The Extensions Manager consists of a window that lists all the extensions, control panels, and startup items on the computer. To disable an item, toggle the On/Off check box to the Off state. Many extensions contain packaging information (what program installed them), as well as a description of their purpose.

Click the Show/Hide Item Information disclosure arrow to display extended information about any selected item.

Choosing a Base Extension Set

The easiest way to get yourself to a working 9.1 installation is to use one of the two built-in sets from the Selected Set menu at the top of the window:

Mac OS 9.x Base—The Base set includes only the basic components needed to boot 9.1. Components such as speech synthesis are not enabled.

Mac OS 9.x All—All the extensions included in Mac OS 9.x are active.

After selecting a base set, quit out of the Extensions Manager and allow the Classic environment to boot. Within a few minutes, Classic should be active. If you have no need for the extensions you've disabled, you're done. On the other hand, many applications rely on extensions to be able to function. Most Mac users are adept at fixing extension conflicts, but in case you're new to the task, the process goes a bit like this:

1. Starting with a *working* base set, add all extensions related to a package back to the system. You will be prompted to create a new extension set if you're using one of the built-in sets.
2. Restart the system with the new set.

3. If the startup fails, the fault lies in the recently added extensions. Disable them, add the remaining extensions back to the system, and restart.
4. If the startup succeeds, go to step 1 and repeat.

Seasoned users might find that this process is faster if they simply remove the extensions from the Mac OS 9.x System Folder manually.

Caution

Just because you start with a working system does not mean that Classic software added after installation will not break something. Mac OS X cannot control access to the OS 9.x System Folder.

If Classic doesn't boot even if you are using a base extension set, there might be problems with the system disk itself. You can learn how to repair common disk problems using the Mac OS X Disk Utility in Chapter 6, "Native Utilities and Applications."

Running Classic Applications

The first time that you launch a Classic application, you'll notice that several interesting things happen. Things don't quite match, as you can see in Figure 5.9. The Netscape window is shown using the Classic platinum appearance, and the Apple menu is back…but the rest of the screen contains Mac OS X elements such as windows and the Dock!

Visually, Classic applications (such as Netscape Communicator is seen in Figure 5.9) look just as they would under Mac OS 8 and 9. The Aqua appearance does not carry over to the windows, buttons, and other interface elements.

The Dock and process manager both recognize Classic applications. The Dock will show the older applications' icons, just as if they were native Mac OS X applications. Figure 5.10 shows the process manager (Command+Option+Escape) with several Classic applications listed.

Tip

A glaring visual difference when running most Classic applications is the quality of the icons in the Dock. You'll be pleased to know that you can paste high-quality OS X icons onto Classic apps. Chapter 4, "The Finder: Working with Files and Applications," covers this process.

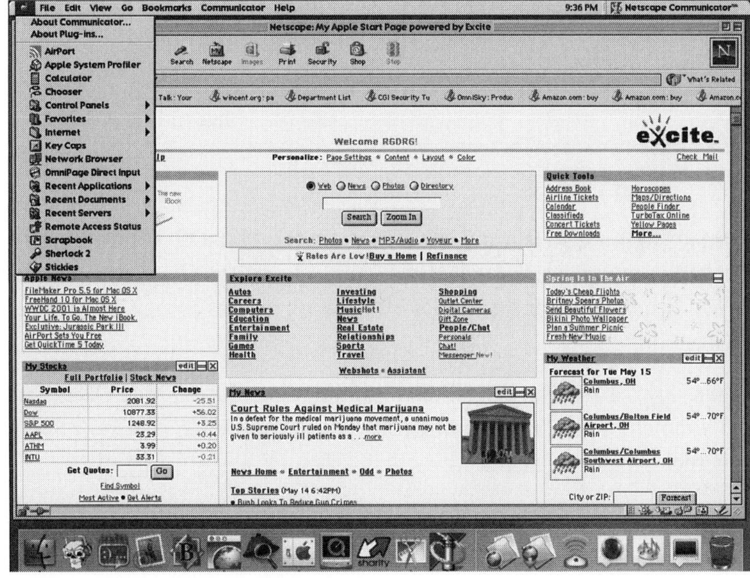

FIGURE 5.9
Classic looks a little weird.

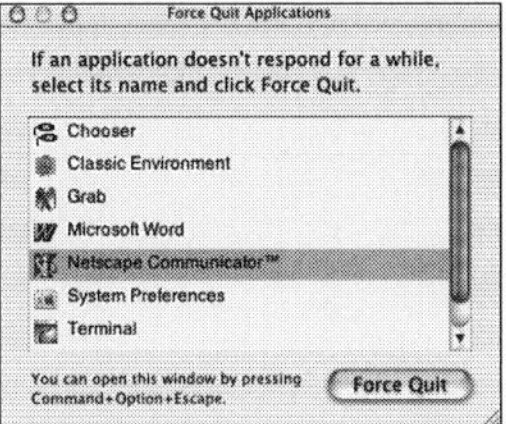

FIGURE 5.10
The Force Quit process manager lists Classic applications along with native apps.

If you use the process manager to force quit a Classic application, you should follow up immediately by saving your open documents (within Classic apps) and restarting the environment. This is another area in which Classic has not benefited from the advanced features of Mac OS X. A force quit within Classic is identical to a force quit in Mac OS 8 and 9. At best, it will work and leave your Classic system usable and slightly less stable. At worst, it will immediately crash all running Classic software.

Messing Up Classic

When running Classic, you'll notice that the Mac OS X menu bar is replaced by the Mac OS 9.x menu. Using this menu, you can access all of the earlier system's control panels and associated functionality. Settings such as appearance and sound are harmless enough, but it is possible to accidentally disrupt your network connections by working with the TCP/IP and AppleTalk control panels.

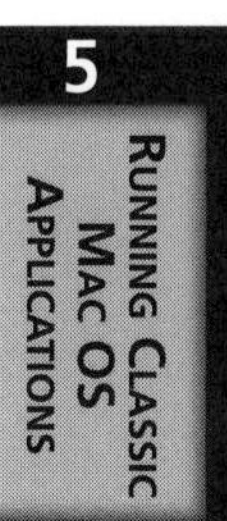

Under Mac OS 8 and 9, network connections are made via four primary methods:

- Remote access dial-in connections
- Ethernet
- IrDA
- AirPort wireless

In Mac OS X, there is a single connection: the Mac OS X network driver. Rather than implementing two separate network connections, the Classic environment uses a special OS X–installed driver that routes all network traffic through OS X's kernel-level network connection.

Figure 5.11 shows the TCP/IP configuration panel from Mac OS 9.x within the Classic environment. The corresponding Mac OS X connection is set to a static IP address over Ethernet.

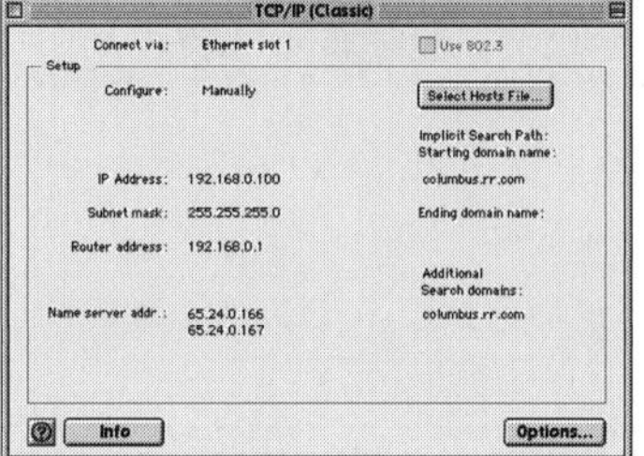

FIGURE 5.11
Mac OS X provides a special OS 9.x driver to pass Classic network traffic to the new kernel.

The Classic environment relies on a special TCP/IP configuration called Classic—do not attempt to rename or remove this configuration. If these settings are modified, you will lose the capability to connect to the network from within Classic.

Caution

Dozens of hacks have been posted on the Internet since the release of Mac OS X. Some enable the Finder from Mac OS 9.x to work within Classic, or provide access to another System 9 feature. It is tempting to try to "live the Classic life," but it can be disorienting and damaging to your system. Mac OS X *is* the future of the Mac operating system. If you're unhappy with the features it provides, let Apple know.

Usability Issues and Anomalies

Classic is largely usable without any need for knowledge of how it interacts with Mac OS X. You continue to use programs in a manner that is identical to System 9.x. There are, however, a few exceptions that might be confusing for you:

- **Copy and Paste/Drag and Drop**—Two of the most common means of moving data within Mac OS suffer when working between native and Classic applications. Data copied from one environment can take several seconds before it is available for pasting within another. Dragging and dropping text and images between native and Classic applications fails altogether.
- **Desktop Pictures and Patterns**—Mac OS X has its desktop background, but that doesn't mean Classic won't load its own. You will encounter instances when the screen does not refresh correctly and there are "holes" in the Mac OS X desktop that reveal the 9.x background image underneath. This is not a serious problem and can be ignored. If the visual defects are unbearable, you can use the 9.x Appearance control panel to set the same background image in Classic as is set in Mac OS X.
- **Favorites**—Although Favorites are available in the OS 9.x environment, they do not transfer between Classic and Mac OS X.
- **Mac OS 9 Desktop**—A Mac OS 9 Desktop folder alias is one of the default icons on the Mac OS X desktop. This alias is specific to Mac OS 9 when it is booted directly. It does *not* apply to the Classic environment. When using Classic, items that are saved to the Desktop will appear, as expected, in the Mac OS X desktop.
- **Open/Save Dialog Boxes**—Mac OS X applications are aware of the special folders and files used by the system and take care to hide them. The same cannot be said for Classic apps. The Open and Save dialog boxes clearly show the invisible items. Although it's harmless, this is probably not the best way for a new user to be introduced to Macintosh software.
- **Printing**—Printing services from Mac OS X are not extended to Mac OS 9.x. If you intend to print from within the Classic environment, you must configure your printer through the Chooser. Unfortunately, the only working printers are EtherTalk-based network printers. Workarounds will be discussed later in this chapter.

Users who are expecting a completely seamless work environment might be disappointed by these shortcomings, but many of them can be overcome through additional software or by working within the BSD subsystem, described in Chapter 12.

Workarounds

The following information should be used only if you are comfortable with potentially disrupting the functionality of your computer. Even though these tips are not expected to cause any problems with the shipping version of Mac OS X, Apple might make future changes that eliminate the usefulness of this information or introduce system errors.

Shared Folders

For the cases of both the Desktop folder and the Favorites folder, it is possible to create unified shared folders that store the same data, no matter where you are in the operating system. As with many modifications to the base Mac OS installation, there are drawbacks to doing this, so proceed at your own risk.

To create a shared folder, you must use the Unix equivalent of the Mac OS alias command; that is, `ln -s`. The `ln` or link command creates a link between a filename and a real file on your system. For example, if you have a directory named My Data that you also want to be able to access from the folder named My Files, you could use the following command within the Terminal application (path: `/Applications/Utilities`):

```
ln -s "My Data" "My Files"
```

There are two ways that this can be applied within Mac OS X. You can link files from Mac OS 9.x to Mac OS X, or in the reverse direction. Unfortunately, Mac OS 9 does not understand Mac OS X links unless they are being used in the Classic environment. This provides some limitations on how complex you can be with your links.

> **Tip**
>
> These instructions do not require an understanding of the command line, but some readers might prefer to refer to "Introduction to BSD" in Chapter 12 before continuing.

Mac OS 9 to Mac OS X Linking

To create a desktop that is shared between Mac OS 9.x (when running directly) and Mac OS X, you can link the 9.1 Desktop folder into the Desktop folder in your home directory. Any files you store on your desktop in 9.1 will automatically be a part of the Mac OS X environment as well, and vice versa. After creating this link, you can completely do away with the Desktop (Mac OS 9) alias that is placed on your OS X desktop.

You must first make sure that your Mac OS X desktop is empty. Drag any files within the desktop to your home directory. Next, determine the path of your OS 9.x Desktop folder. If you've installed on a two-partition system, the folder will be something similar to `/Volumes/Mac OS 9.x/Desktop Folder`; single-partition systems will always be `/Desktop Folder`. A quick way to check the desktop folder's path is to use the Finder's Show Info command while the Desktop (Mac OS 9) alias is selected.

From within a terminal window, use the following commands to set up the link (replacing the appropriate portions with the path you've determined):

1. `cd ~/` First, change to your home directory.
2. `rmdir Desktop` Next, remove the existing Mac OS X desktop. If your Desktop folder is not empty, this command will fail. To remove the Desktop folder and its contents, use `rm -r Desktop` instead.
3. `ln -s` *`<Path to your 9.1 Desktop Folder>`* `Desktop` Finally, create the link from your Mac OS 9.x Desktop folder to the Desktop folder in your home directory.

This same procedure can be used to link other folders, such as the Favorites folder, to your Mac OS X Favorites (`~/Library/Favorites`). Unfortunately, if multiple users are using the system, they'll all end up with the same desktop and the same Favorites folder. Obviously, this isn't the most desirable effect.

Tip

The link command works on any file (not just directories/folders), but it can often be replaced simply by using Finder aliases. For example, if you'd like to use the same bookmark file in Mac OS X's Internet Explorer as within IE on 9.1, you can create an alias from the bookmarks in 9.1 to their location in OS X (`~/Library/Preferences/Explorer`). Test both the `ln` and alias approaches. Each uses a different method to locate the original file, but both generally work.

Mac OS X to Mac OS 9 Linking

To turn the tables around a bit, instead of altering the Mac OS X file system, you can change Classic's Mac OS 9.x. This requires the use of `ln` to link folders from Mac OS X back into your OS 9 installation each time you log in. Doing so enables such nifty tricks as creating a Favorites folder that is unique for every user on the Mac OS X system.

Because Mac OS X links are recognized by System 9.x only when it is running within Classic, this technique might produce undesirable results when booting directly into Mac OS 9.x. If your only exposure to Mac OS 9 is from within Classic, this produces the most seamless link between the environments.

What we're attempting to do now is slightly more complex than creating a single link. Our example will focus on the Favorites folder. To make a link work on a per-user basis, we need to create a simple script that:

- Starts up when a user logs in
- Deletes the current link to Favorites within Classic's 9.x installation
- Establishes a new link from the current user's Favorites folder to Classic

To do this, a shell script must be created and then set to launch via the Login System Preferences panel. Shell scripts provide a means of controlling the BSD subsystem that lies beneath Mac OS X. You'll learn how to create your own shell scripts in Chapter 18.

To create linked Favorites script, you'll need to navigate your Mac OS 9.x installation (from within Mac OS X), and determine the path to the Favorites folder (it should be directly inside the Mac OS 9.x folder).

Next, open a text editor such as TextEdit (path: `/Applications/TextEdit`) and enter the following lines (without the line numbers):

```
1: #!/bin/sh

2: FAVORITES="/Volumes/Mac OS 9.x/System Folder/Favorites"
3: rm -r $FAVORITES
4: ln -s ~/Library/Favorites $FAVORITES
```

There are only four lines in this simple script. Line 1 provides the path to the shell that will be used to interpret the script. This essentially tells the system what application can run the little program we've written. Line 2 sets a variable to the location of the Favorites folder within Mac OS 9.x. The sample script assumes a dual volume/partition setup; you might have to adjust this path accordingly.

Line 3 removes the existing Favorites link within the Classic System folder. Finally, line 4 re-creates a new link from the current user's folder to the Classic System Folder.

Save the file anywhere you'd like with the name setfavorites.command. If you want all users to have access to the script, save it outside your home directory. Because the script does not hard-code a particular user's name, any user can use it to link her Favorites folder to Classic.

> **Note**
>
> It is assumed that you are using a standalone Mac OS X installation. If you are using a clustered configuration or are not the administrator of the machine, you will need to check with the system administrator before continuing.

Saving the script with the filename extension .command enables Mac OS X to determine that the file isn't just another text file; rather, it is a shell script. When a .command file is double-clicked, it automatically launches the Terminal applications, which then executes the file.

If you attempt to run the file manually, the Terminal launches, but the execution will fail, as shown in Figure 5.12.

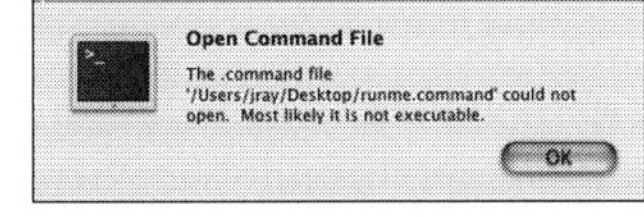

FIGURE 5.12
The script will fail unless execute permissions are set.

One final step is needed to turn the script you entered into a runnable program: setting execution permission. You will need to open a Terminal window manually for this step and enter the following command (using the appropriate path, of course):

```
chmod +x <Path to the .command file you created>
```

Any user who runs the command file will instantly have his OS X and OS 9.x Favorites folders linked together. We're not quite done yet. Forcing a user to run an application each time he logs in is usually possible. Creating a truly seamless environment requires that the system automatically run the script file each time a user logs in to the system. The Login System Preferences panel can automate this process for you.

Automating Scripts Using the Login Panel

To set a script (or any double-clickable application or document) to launch when you first log in to Mac OS X, open the System Preferences application and click the Login icon. Choose the Login Items tab. The panel shown in Figure 5.13 will appear.

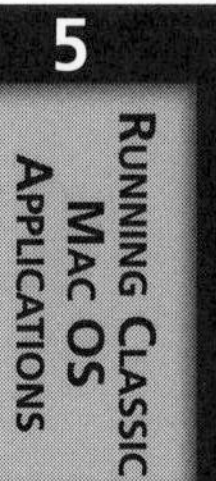

FIGURE 5.13
Automate script startup using the Login System Preferences panel.

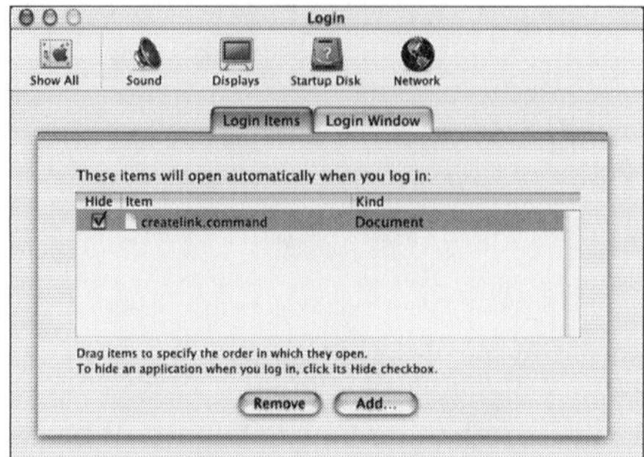

The Login Items window contains a list of applications that are automatically executed when you log in. To add to the list, use the Add button to browse the file system and choose an item. Alternatively, you can drag the file to launch from a Finder window directly into the list. Remove entries in the list by highlighting them and clicking the Remove button.

If there are multiple applications that must start, you can change the order in which they execute by dragging the lines up and down within the listing. The command files that you create should be located near the top of the list.

Finally, click the Hide check box in front of the .command script file so that it is hidden as it executes. Your system is now set up to automatically link the Favorites folders at login time.

Note

This process is almost completely transparent, except for starting and hiding the Terminal application. When the script is finished executing, the terminal remains active. One simple way to get around this is to *kill* the terminal at the end of the script. Although the specifics won't be covered until later in the book, you can include the following line at the end of any script to be able to quit the Terminal application after a script has finished executing:

```
kill -9 `ps aucx` | grep Terminal | cut -d ' ' -f 4-5`
```

PDF Printing

If you find yourself in the position of having a working printer under Mac OS X, but no print solution from within Classic, there is a reasonably simple way to transfer your print jobs from Classic into OS X.

Mac OS X uses the Portable Document Format (PDF) as its display language. Without any additional software, OS X can read, create, and print PDF files. This capability can be exploited by the Mac OS 9.x Classic environment and provides a convenient and efficient way to transfer documents between the two environments.

If you're lucky enough to have a copy of Adobe Acrobat, you can use the included PDF printer software to create high-quality PDF files that are readable on Mac OS X. If your budget is limited, the standalone product PrintToPDF performs the same function at a fraction of the price ($20). You can download PrintToPDF from `http://www.jwwalker.com/pages/pdf.html`.

After downloading, drag the PrintToPDF icon into Mac OS 9.x's System Extensions folder. This will add a new item to the Classic Chooser. You will need to open the Chooser and select the PrintToPDF icon to activate the new driver, as shown in Figure 5.14.

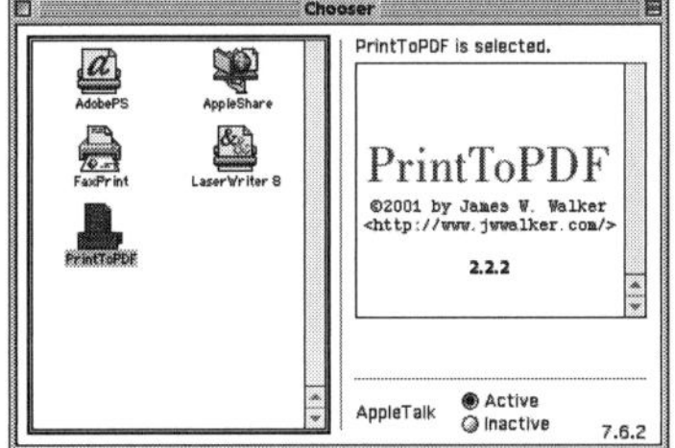

FIGURE 5.14
PrintToPDF creates documents that Mac OS X can easily open and print.

With PrintToPDF selected in the Chooser, Classic applications will prompt you for a filename when you print from them, allowing you to save a full PDF of your print job. To finish printing, you need only launch the Mac OS X Preview application (path: `/Applications/Preview`), open the PDF produced by Classic, and use Print as you normally would. Chapter 10, "Printer and Font Management," covers Mac OS X printer configuration.

Tip

You might find yourself in the opposite situation: Printing *works* under Classic, but not directly within Mac OS X. If this is the case, you can reverse the process by producing PDFs in Mac OS X and printing them in Classic. Creating PDFs is covered in Chapter 10. You will also need to download Acrobat Reader (free) from Adobe (`http://www.adobe.com`).

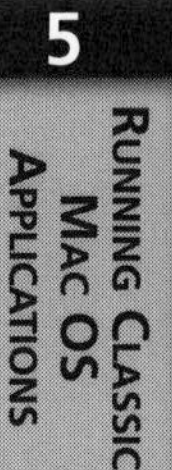

Over time, fixes such as these should become less necessary as the Mac OS X software library grows. If at all possible, you should strive to build a native-only computer. You'll find that application interoperability and reliability are much higher.

Classic Options

Maintaining a healthy Classic environment is the same as maintaining a healthy Mac OS 9.x installation. If you use Classic on your OS X computer, you're essentially charged with keeping two operating systems up and running.

Apple has kindly included two features in Mac OS X that help fix a common problem and speed up overall system functions. Figure 5.15 shows the Advanced tab of the Classic System Preferences panel.

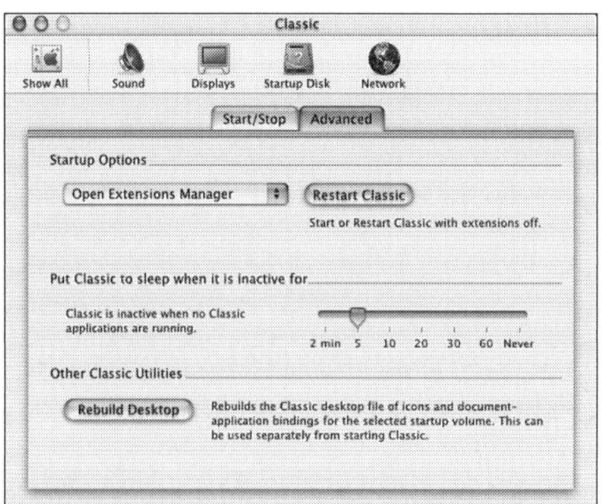

FIGURE 5.15
Choose to rebuild your OS 9.x desktop or put the system to sleep.

Options such as putting Classic to sleep and rebuilding the desktop are available within the Advanced tab. Use the following advanced settings to gain greater control of Classic:

- **Put Classic to sleep when it is inactive for**—When Classic is running, it is using your system resources. The Classic environment continues to use CPU time even if you aren't running a Classic application. This is because Mac OS 9.x must keep up the basic system maintenance and monitoring processes that happen behind the scenes. If you choose to put Classic to sleep, it will stop using these resources after the length of time you choose.

Caution

Putting Classic to sleep works well—most of the time. The drawback is an increased amount of time for Classic apps to launch and wake up the pseudo-sleeping computer. In addition, waking up *does* fail from time to time in early releases of Mac OS X, forcing you to restart Classic. Make sure that you are using the latest version of Mac OS X for the best possible Classic support.

- **Rebuild Desktop**—Rebuilding the Mac OS 9.x desktop can help solve "generic icon" problems (as demonstrated in Figure 5.16), as well as issues with documents that can't find the appropriate Classic application to open them. If your Classic environment starts to act unusual, rebuilding the desktop is a good place to start.

FIGURE 5.16
Generic icons are a good indicator of a desktop that needs rebuilt.

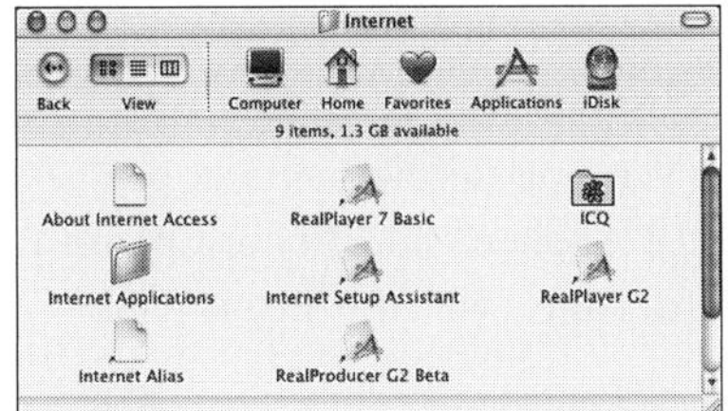

Classic functions best when it is used as a means of accessing legacy applications and data. You should maintain as minimal a system software installation as possible. Extensions and control panels that are not needed should be removed. If possible, choose one of the base extension sets from within the Extensions Manager and stick with it.

Shut off any extraneous features of Mac OS 9.x, such as the Finder soundtrack (within the Appearance control panel) and talking alerts. These slow down system performance and can cause hiccups within Mac OS X.

If you have complex needs that Classic cannot fulfill, you can also boot directly into Mac OS 9.x. In many cases, this can save you from the headaches of dealing with the inconsistencies and incompatibilities of Classic, and provide greater speed and ease of use.

Direct Booting Mac OS 9.x

To directly boot into Mac OS 9.x, use the Startup Disk System Preferences panel, shown in Figure 5.17.

After searching the mounted disks (this can take awhile) for viable systems, each of the accessible system folders is listed in the Startup Disk panel. Each icon lists the OS version and volume name. To select one, click the icon; a status message will appear at the bottom of the screen describing your choice.

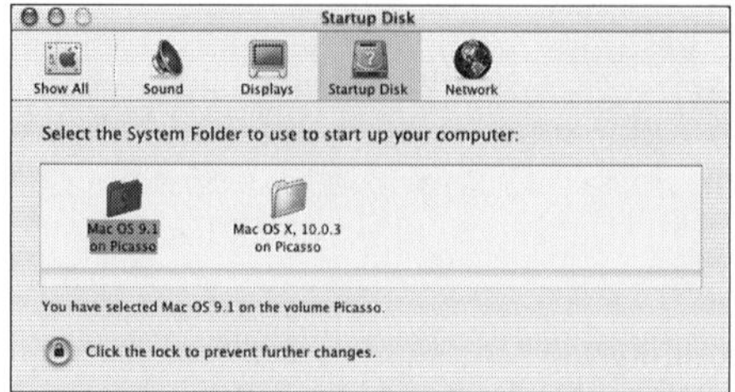

FIGURE 5.17
Boot directly into Mac OS 9.x using the Startup Disk panel.

Quit the System Preferences application when you're finished. The next time you restart your computer, it will boot into the operating system you selected.

Booting into OS X

To switch back to OS X after running 9.1, you follow a similar process as switching from Mac OS X to Mac OS 9. From the Apple menu, choose Control Panels, and then select and open the Startup Disk control panel, which is displayed in Figure 5.18.

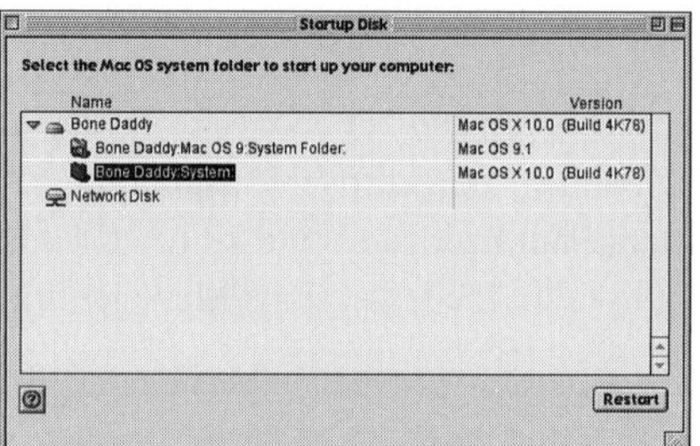

FIGURE 5.18
The Mac OS 9.x Startup Disk control panel works the same way as the Mac OS X Startup Disk panel.

Each mounted disk is displayed on a line in the control panel. Disks that include a bootable system folder have a disclosure arrow directly in front of them. Clicking the disclosure arrow displays the operating systems located on that disk, along with their path and version.

To boot into OS X, highlight the OS X installation within the list, and then click the Restart button in the lower-right corner. If you don't want to restart immediately, close the control panel. The next time the system restarts, it will boot into the selected system.

Summary

The Classic environment is a feat of software engineering. It allows legacy software to run unchanged within Mac OS X. Unfortunately, it is impossible to completely integrate two completely dissimilar operating systems, so users are likely to notice both visual and operational oddities. Some of the more annoying problems can be easily worked around, but a hybrid OS X/OS 9.x system is not likely to appeal to first-time or casual users. Try to adapt to working completely within the OS X environment with native software. If that isn't yet possible, remember that you can always boot directly into Mac OS 9.x *or* OS X.

Inside Mac OS X

Part II

In This Part

CHAPTER 6

Native Utilities and Applications

IN THIS CHAPTER

The Mac OS X installation includes a number of utilities and applications that enable you to start working as soon as your Mac is up and running. The included software ranges from disk utilities to games and simple desk accessories. This chapter will look at many of these applications and provide a synopsis of their uses, purposes, and any special features that might not be immediately obvious.

The information provided will be divided into related sections —Desk Accessories, Disk Utilities, System Monitors, and Other Applications. If you don't see information on the program that you're looking for, you might find some software that best fits in other chapters and is covered elsewhere.

With Mac OS X 10.1, Apple has included the iMovie video editing software. Because iMovie is applicable only to a limited audience, and would take much more than a few pages to document, it will not be covered here. I recommend another title, such as *The Complete Idiot's Guide to iMovie 2* for a full reference.

Desk Accessories

Desk accessories were once a special type of application that lived only under the Apple menu. In Mac OS X, however, the Apple menu doesn't contain any applications at all (aside from the Recent items). Nevertheless, a number of included applications fill the role previously played by the now-extinct desk accessory, such as Calculator, Clock, Key Caps, and Stickies.

> **Note**
>
> Don't expect to see Sherlock in this list, because you won't find it. Sherlock is covered in Chapter 7, "Internet Communications."

Calculator

The Mac's system Calculator has remained the same for almost fifteen years. Mac OS X puts a new face on the old standby. The Calculator application (Path: `/Applications/Calculator`) is shown in Figure 6.1.

The Calculator can be operated by clicking the buttons in the window or by using your numeric keypad. The number keys directly map to the calculator counterparts with the Enter key equivalent to Equal.

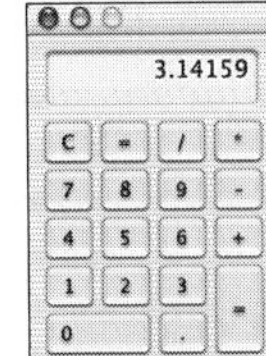

FIGURE 6.1
The Calculator finally gets a facelift.

> **Tip**
>
> If you need a scientific calculator, you might want to check out some of the third-party options:
>
> Calculator+—`http://tiran.netfirms.com/`
>
> Calc X—`http://homepage.mac.com/starman/calcx.html`
>
> More Calculator— `http://www.pixits.com/morecalculator.htm`
>
> MooseCalc— `http://www.wundermoosen.com/wmXMooseCalc.htm`

Clock

The Clock (Path: `/Applications/Clock`) is a digital/analog timepiece designed to fit into the Mac OS X dock or float on the desktop as a shaped window. Starting the Clock application will, by default, place a small analog clock in the Dock, as shown in Figure 6.2.

FIGURE 6.2
The Clock adds a digital or analog watch face to the Dock or Desktop.

Preferences

To configure the Clock application's time display, choose Preferences from the application menu. The Preference panel is displayed in Figure 6.3.

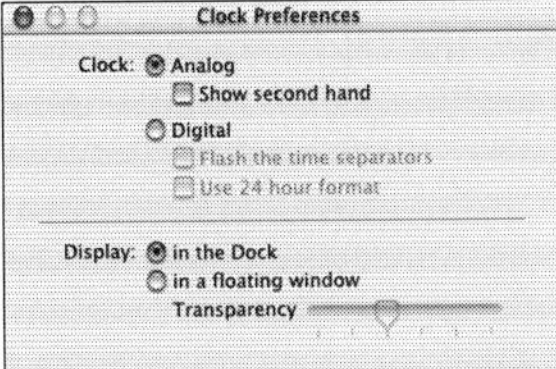

FIGURE 6.3
Configure the clock's display.

Choose your clock settings based on a combination of analog, digital, and window types:

Analog—The default view of the clock is the analog wall-clock style. If desired, click the Show second hand check box to display the Clock's second hand in addition to the minute and hour hands.

Digital—The digital Clock display resembles a tear-off calendar page. Both the date and time can be seen in this view. The digital display offers the option of flashing the time separators each second (:), or displaying the time in 24-hour mode.

Display—Finally, the Clock can be shown as either an icon contained in the Dock (its default mode), or in a shaped-floating window with variable transparency. If you choose the floating window, drag the transparency slider from left to right to decrease the transparency of the window.

After you make your choices, close the preference window and the changes will take effect immediately. To automatically launch the Clock at startup, use the Login System Preferences panel.

Advanced Clock Customization

Many Mac OS X applications can easily be customized by editing the application resources. Unlike earlier versions of the operating system, OS X typically stores pictures, sounds, and even interface description files as user-editable items within an application's folder structure.

In the case of the Clock, the images for the digital and analog faces are stored as TIFF files and can be edited with any TIFF-compatible graphics software, such as Photoshop, or Graphic Converter (see Chapter 8, "Installing Third-Party Applications").

Follow these instructions to open the existing interface files:

1. Navigate to the Clock application using the Finder (path: `/Applications/Clock`).
2. Press Control and click the Clock application icon.
3. Choose Show Package Contents from the pop-up contextual menu.
4. Open the Contents folder, then the Resources folder.
5. The editable TIFF files are `background.tiff`, `ClockTitle.tiff`, and `Clock02.tiff`.

After editing the TIFF files, quit and then restart the Clock application. Your changes should take effect upon launch.

Caution

Always make a backup of the original application and its resources before making any changes. It's unlikely that minor changes will harm the application, but it's best to be safe. Besides, you might find that you like the original look and feel of the clock after a few days with your magnificent fluorescent-orange creation.

Key Caps

Key Caps (Path: `/Applications/Utilities/Key Caps`) is a very simple application that displays your keyboard mapping and enables you to determine what special characters are available for a given font, and how to type them.

Key Caps displays an onscreen view of your keyboard layout when it's launched. The Apple Extended USB keyboard is shown in Figure 6.4.

FIGURE 6.4
Key Caps shows your keyboard layout and available characters.

Note

If Mac OS X does not have a matching keyboard layout for your system, Key Caps will display a text entry field, but no keyboard.

The field at the top of the Key Caps window can be used to test typing (either using the real keys or onscreen keyboard). Pressing the Shift, Option, Control, and Command keys (and combinations thereof) will show the special characters that can be generated. You can change the font used in the display by choosing from the Font menu.

Tip

If you don't want to remember key combinations, you can type your special characters within Key Caps; then copy and paste them from the text field into your documents.

Stickies

Stickies (Path: `/Applications/Stickies`) is a reimplementation of the original Mac OS post-it note desk accessory. The new Stickies uses the Cocoa API to provide the functionality of the original program, but with several additional features—such as multiple fonts, colors, and embedded images.

Stickies is a digital version of a Post-It notepad. You can store quick notes, graphics, or anything you might want to access later. This takes the place of both the notepad and the scrapbook. The screen displayed in Figure 6.5 is covered with Stickies.

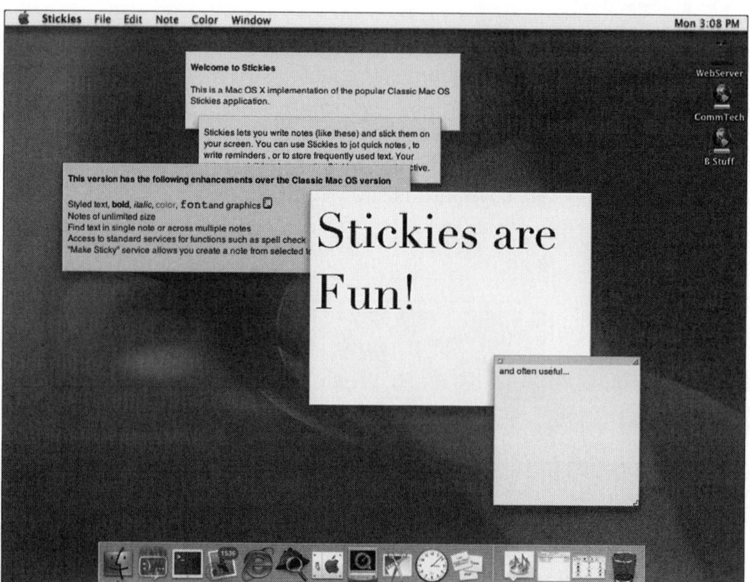

Figure 6.5
Stickies can contain any information you want.

Stickies does not use the standard Mac OS X windows. Instead, each window appears as a colored-borderless rectangle when not selected. When active, three controls appear:

- **Close Box**—The close box, in the upper-left corner of the Stickie, closes the active note. Closing a note erases it.
- **Maximize/Minimize**—In the upper-right corner is a second box that changes the shape of the current note to best fit the text. Clicking the box toggles between two sizes for the current note.
- **Grow Box**—Dragging the grow box, located in the lower-right corner, shrinks or expands the window dynamically.

In addition to the three visible controls, Mac OS X Stickies also support windowshading, just like in Mac OS 8 and 9. Double-clicking the title bar of an active window will shrink it to the size of the title bar. Double-clicking again will return the window to its previous size. When in Windowshaded mode, the Stickie displays the top line of text from its contents directly in the title bar of the collapsed window.

Note

Strangely enough, you cannot minimize Stickies into the Dock. Choosing Miniaturize from the Window menu will Windowshade the active note.

The Stickies application has very little configuration—using the Preferences located under the Application menu, you can disable confirmation of window closing. The rest of the menus enable you to customize the Stickies that you currently have opened.

Menus

Stickies are not, as you might think, individual documents. All the notes are contained in a single file written to your Library folder. The File menu enables you to create new notes, export individual notes to text files, and print the contents of notes:

New Note—Creates a new blank note. (Command+N)

Close—Closes the active Stickie note. (Command+W)

Save All—Saves changes to all notes. (Command+S)

Import Classic Stickies—Imports note files from Mac OS 8/9.

Import Text—Imports a text file into a new note. Text can be in plain-text format, or rich-text. Font style information is retained.

Export Text—Exports the frontmost note to a text file.

Page Setup—Configures printer page setup.

Print Active Note—Prints the frontmost note. (Command+P)

Print All Notes—Prints all notes.

Although the Edit menu does contain your standard items such as undo, redo, copy, cut, paste, and so on, it also has advanced features inherited from the OS X Cocoa API. In addition to the normal Edit menu items are two components you might not expect within a simple post-it application: find/replace and spell checking. These are excellent examples of the advanced features easily implemented in Cocoa-based applications. Because you'll be seeing these features frequently, we'll take a closer look in a few minutes.

The Note menu offers control over the formatting of the text in each note. Take some time to play with these settings—you might find more control in Stickies than in some word processors!

Font Panel—Opens the Mac OS X Font panel for font and size selection. The Font panel is introduced in Chapter 3, and covered at length in Chapter 10. (Command+T)

Bold—Bolds the currently highlighted text, or toggles the typing mode to between plain and bold. (Command+B)

Italic—Italicizes the currently highlighted text, or toggles the typing mode to between plain and italic. (Command+I)

Copy Font—This unusual selection copies the font style from the current text selection (size, font face, color, and so on) so that you can easily apply it elsewhere. (Command+3)

Paste Font—Pastes a copied font into note. If text is selected, it takes on the attributes of the copied font. If no text is selected, the style is applied for all subsequent typing. (Command+4)

Use as Default—Sets the current font settings as the default for new notes.

Text Colors—Opens the Mac OS X color picker (refer to Chapter 3 for details) and enables any color to be applied to the font being used.

Note Info—Because Stickies aren't actual files, you can't look at their creation dates in the Finder. Use the Note Info option to display the creation and modification dates for the frontmost note. (Shift+Command+I)

What would a Stickie note be without a bright-colored background? The color menu contains the common post-it colors for your enjoyment (yellow, blue, green, pink, purple, and gray).

Find and Replace Dialog Boxes

Using the Find submenu within the Edit menu, you can perform a full-text search of all the open notes. You can search and replace any or all the notes, as well as choose to perform case-sensitive or whole-word searches, as shown in Figure 6.6.

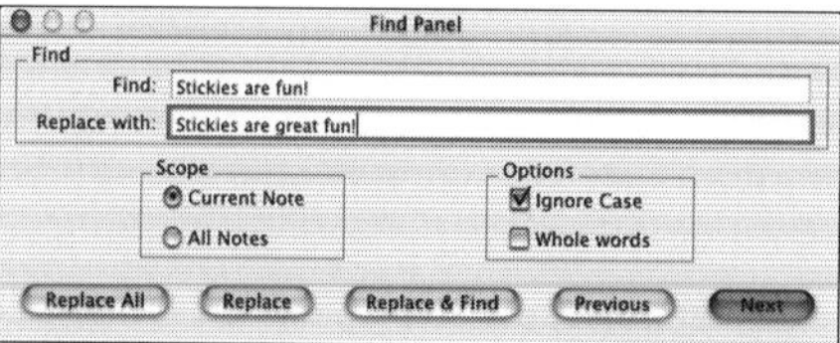

FIGURE 6.6
Have 1,000 Stickies and can't find the right one? No problem, use Find!

The Find Panel has two fields: Find and Replace with. Enter the text you want to locate in the first, and what, if anything, you want to replace it with in the second.

You can also control the breadth of the search using the scope feature. Use Current Note to confine the search to the frontmost window, or All Notes for everything. To ignore the case of characters while searching, click the Ignore Case check box. If you only want to match entire words (not pieces from the middle of words), check Whole Words. When the search is defined, use one of the five buttons at the bottom of the panel to start an action:

Replace All—Replaces all occurrences of the text with the supplied string. You will not be prompted for each replacement.

Replace—Replaces the currently found item with the replacement string.

Replace & Find—Replaces the currently found item, then finds and highlights the next occurrence.

Previous—Jumps backward to a previously matched string.

Next—Finds and highlights the next matched string in the document.

After starting a search (Command+F), you can use the shortcuts: Find Next (Command+G) and Find Previous (Command+G) to continue searching without the Find panel open.

Note

Using the Find submenu, you can also quickly enter a new search term without opening the search dialog box. Use Enter Selection or Command+E, to make the currently selected string the search term. Additionally, if you resize your window and lose the selected text, use Scroll To Selection, Command+J to find your place.

Spell Checking

As with find and replace, spell checking is another very common activity that is implemented in many Cocoa Applications.

From the Edit menu, choose Spelling. This will open a basic spell-checking panel, as shown in Figure 6.7.

FIGURE 6.7
The Spelling panel can locate and correct common missspellings in your work (yes, I meant that).

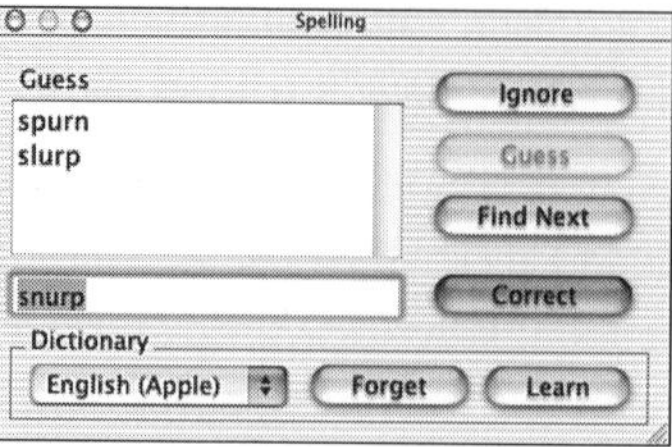

You can use the panel by itself by entering words that you want to correct into the field by the Correct button and then choosing Correct. Alternatively, navigate through the potential spelling errors using the buttons in the Spell Check window:

Ignore—Click Ignore to skip a word that you don't want to fix.

Guess—Finds other words similar to the misspelled word.

Find Next—Skips from word to (misspelled) word in your note.

Correct—Fixes the error. If multiple possibilities are shown, choose the correct word from the list on the left, and then choose Correct.

Learn—Adds the currently selected word to the Mac OS X dictionary. Switches default dictionaries using the Dictionary pop-up menu.

Forget—Removes the currently selected word from the dictionary.

Dictionary—Chooses from multiple installed dictionary files. The Default Mac OS X installation includes a single dictionary.

The Stickies application includes another way to visually check your spelling skills—the Check Spelling option under the Edit menu. This highlights misspelled words with a red underline and is used heavily throughout Mac OS X. OmniWeb, a popular Web browser, even checks your spelling as you type into Web page fields!

Note

No, we're not going to cover the find and spell check panels in each program that uses them, if you're wondering.

Note

Stickies also installs a service that is accessible from the Application menu's Services item (Shift+Command+Y). Using the Stickies service, you can quickly turn selected text in any application into a Stickie note.

Disk Utilities

Mac OS X includes two utilities that you'll commonly use when working with disks: Disk Utility and Disk Copy. The Disk Utility application combines the features of Disk First Aid and Drive Setup from Mac OS 9. Disk Copy is used to mount virtual disks—a popular way to distribute software under Mac OS X.

Disk Copy

Disk Copy (Path: `/Applications/Utilities/Disk Copy`) works in much the same way as the Disk Copy program used by Apple in OS 8/9. In recent years, Disk Copy has become a common and convenient way to distribute software. Rather than creating an archived folder, developers write their applications to a virtual disk that is loaded into memory when used. This disk appears to the computer as a *real* disk, and can be manipulated like any other disk. For the end user it is a simple way to work with new applications. A single disk image file can contain applications, support files, and any other data a program might need—and it never needs to be decompressed. In fact, many applications can actually run directly from disk images, without needing to be copied to your hard drive at all. Disk Copy even has built-in CD burning capabilities to make turning a disk image into a real CD a matter of a few clicks.

To launch the Disk Copy application, double-click it, double-click a disk image file (usually `.dmg`), or drag an image file onto its icon. The idle state of the Disk Image application is shown in Figure 6.8.

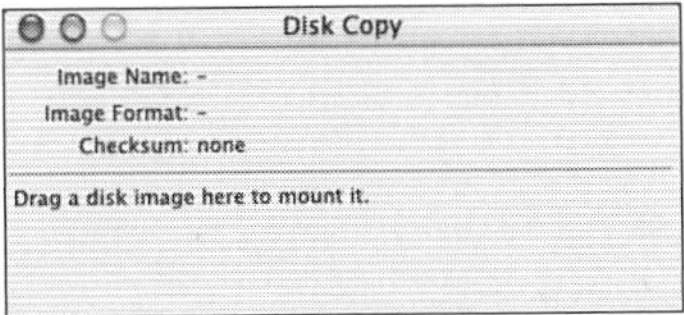

FIGURE 6.8
Disk Copy is waiting for a disk image...

To mount an image, either use Mount Image from the File menu or drag a disk image onto the Disk Copy window. The application will check the validity of the image (its checksum), and then it will appear as a white drive icon on your desktop, or at the computer level of the Finder, as shown in Figure 6.9.

If you launched Disk Copy by dragging an image file to its icon, or double-clicking an image file, the image will be automatically mounted.

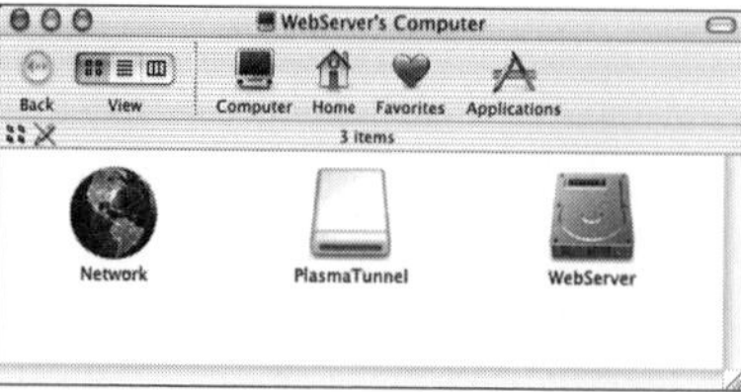

FIGURE 6.9
Mounted images appear just like any other disk.

From this point, you can copy files from the disk to wherever you'd like, or use them directly from the mounted image.

Creating Disk Images

With Mac OS X 10.1, Disk Copy can now create images as well as mount them. This is useful for creating an exact duplicate of software you don't want to lose, or for making a master image for distributing software over a network. For each image you create, you must have the appropriate amount of free space on your hard drive. For example, to create a CD image, you'll need approximately 650MB free. Apple's currently shipping computers come with at least 10GB drives, so this really shouldn't be an issue.

There are two ways to generate an image: by copying an existing volume/partition, or by creating an empty image file, mounting it, and then copying files to it. To create an empty image file, choose New Blank Image (`Command+N`) from the Image menu. The dialog box is shown in Figure 6.10.

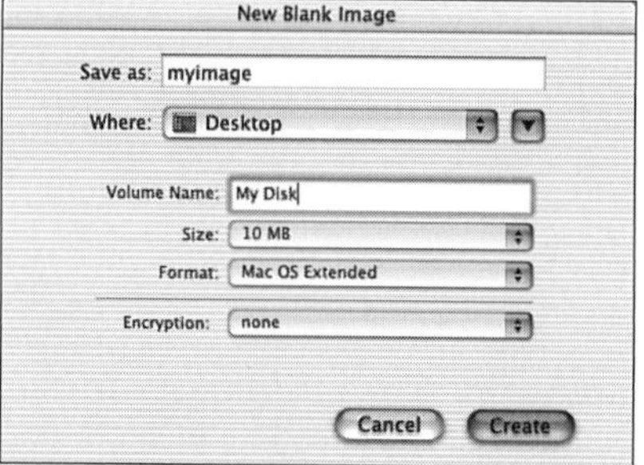

FIGURE 6.10
Generate a new image blank image; then copy files to it.

Fill in the Save as field as you normally would—this is the name of the image file, not the volume that is going to be created. Set the name of the volume within the Volume Name field. Choose a size for the image from the Size pop-up menu. There are a variety of preset sizes for common media—such as Zip disks, CDs, and DVDs—and a Custom setting for arbitrary sizes.

Next, choose a volume format with the Format pop-up menu. In addition to the HFS, HFS+, and UFS options supported as native Mac OS X file systems, you can also choose MS-DOS to create a Windows-compatible title.

Finally, if you'd like to encrypt the disk image, choose AES-128 from the Encryption pop-up menu, and then click Create. The new disk image will be created and can be used immediately.

Creating an image from an existing drive is even easier. Choose New Image From Device (`Shift+Command+I`) from the Image menu. Disk Copy will display a list of all active devices, as shown in Figure 6.11. Click the disclosure arrow in front of each device to display the individual partitions.

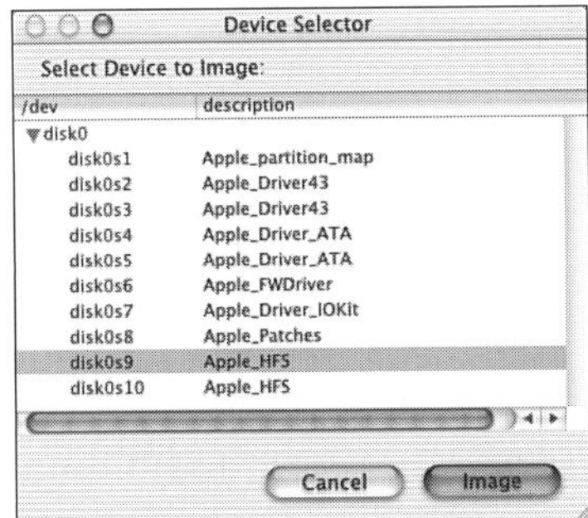

FIGURE 6.11
Choose the device and partition to use as a source.

Select the drive or partition to image, and then click the Image button. You will be prompted for the location to save the image. Using the Image Format pop-up menu, choose the type of image to create: read-only, read-write, compressed, or CD/DVD master. Apply encryption to the image file by choosing AES-128 from the Encryption pop-up menu.

> **Tip**
>
> Read-only images are a good way to distribute software because they do not allow any changes to be made to the image. This results in an image that cannot be modified or tainted, and can always be assumed to be a working master copy.

Finally, click Image to copy an image of the device onto your hard drive.

Burning CDs

To burn a CD from within CD Copy, you must have your CD writer connected and powered on. Check Apple's Web site for supported writers. Because Mac OS X provides an API for CD writing, the iTunes Web page should be a good gauge for what will and won't work with your system (`http://www.apple.com/itunes`).

Select Burn Image from the Image menu, and choose a disk image file when prompted. If the image is suitable for CD burning, Disk Copy will display the dialog shown in Figure 6.12.

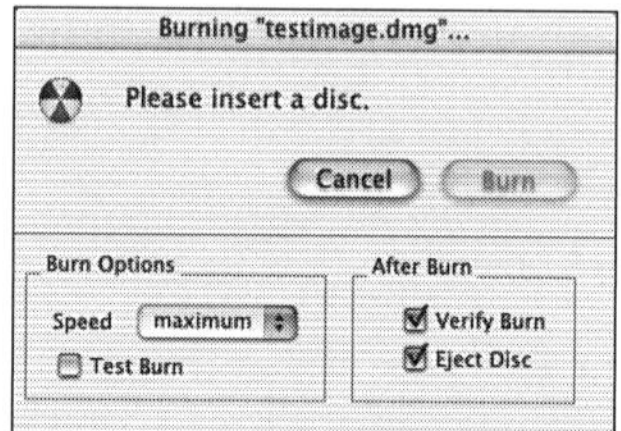

Figure 6.12
Insert a CD and click Burn.

Choose the maximum speed you want to use during the burn process, along with whether you'd like to verify and eject the disk after it has finished. If you prefer to test everything before risking a CD, click the Test Burn check box, and no data will actually be written to the disk.

When you're satisfied with your settings, click the Burn button, and Disk Copy will begin writing the CD.

Preferences

The Disk Copy Preferences window consists of five individual panels: Verifying, Creating, Imaging, Burning, and General. By default, the Verifying pane will be displayed when you first open Preferences, as shown in Figure 6.13.

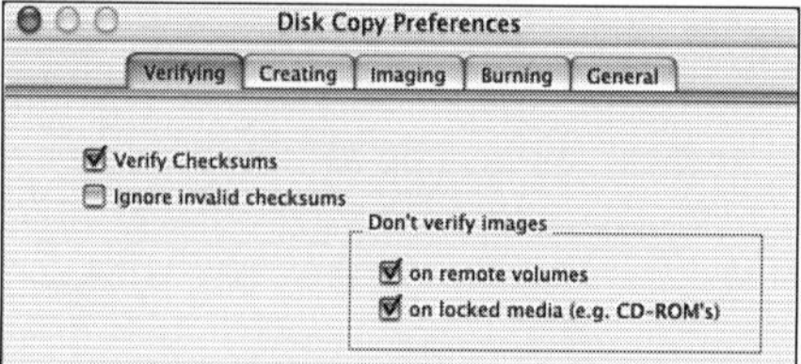

Figure 6.13
Use verifying options to disable image verification.

When an image is mounted, Disk Copy verifies the checksum on the each drive. If you'd prefer to forego the verification of checksums, deselect Verify Checksums. In addition, clicking the Ignore invalid checksums box will allow images that do not verify correctly to be mounted. This could be useful for recovering data from corrupt images.

Disk Copy does not check images on file servers, nor on locked media. To force checking on all types of storage media, uncheck both the on remote volumes and on locked media check boxes.

To adjust the default disk image settings, use the Creating preference panel, shown in Figure 6.14.

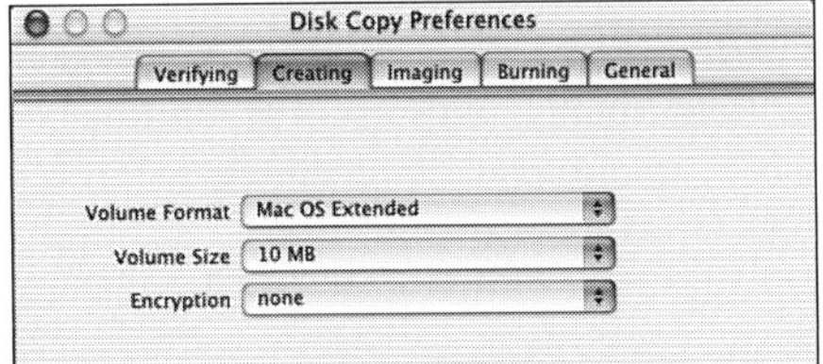

FIGURE 6.14
Choose the default volume format for new images.

Here, you can configure the defaults for new images that are created. The Volume Format, Volume Size, and Encryption settings are identical to those discussed earlier.

Similar to the Creating panel is the Imaging preference window panel. These options, displayed in Figure 6.15, configure how the image file is saved to your drive.

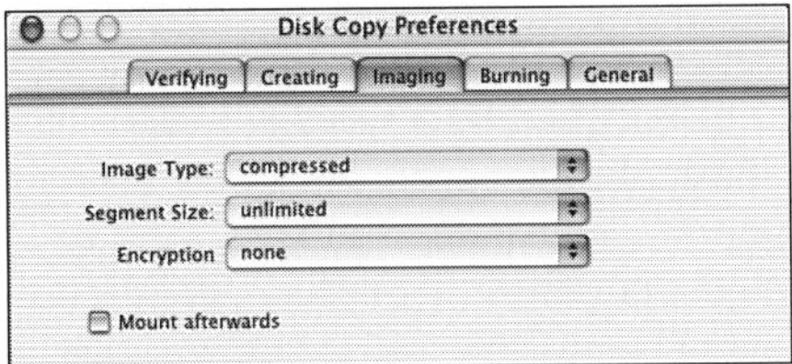

FIGURE 6.15
Pick image segment size, type, and more.

Again, the same Image Type and Encryption options are presented as were mentioned previously. A Segment Size pop-up menu is also provided to divide up a maximum disk image file size when creating a new image. If the image exceeds this size, it is divided into multiple file segments.

Click the Mount afterwards check box to automatically mount an image after it is created.

Switch to the Burning panel to set up how Disk Copy will interact with your CD burner when writing an image. These options are demonstrated in Figure 6.16.

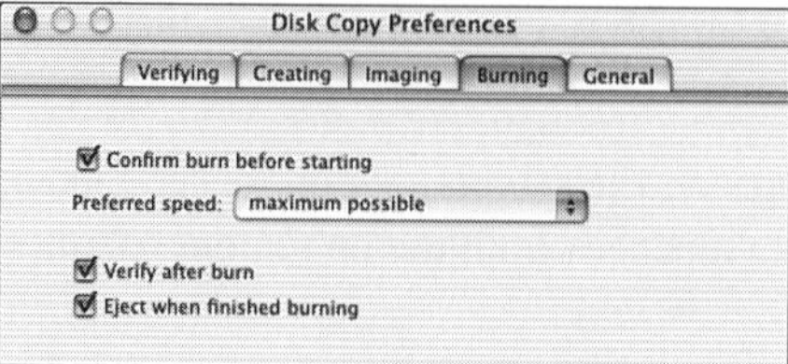

FIGURE 6.16
Burning options control interaction with the CD burner.

By default, CD burning will start by prompting the user. To disable these messages, uncheck the Confirm burn check box. Use the Preferred Speed pop-up menu to pick the speed at which your CD will be written. The Verify after burn setting forces a CD to be checked for errors after being written. Finally, click Eject when finished burning to have your computer automatically eject each completed and verified CD.

The final setting panel, General, determines how the Disk Copy program will act after it is running, as seen in Figure 6.17.

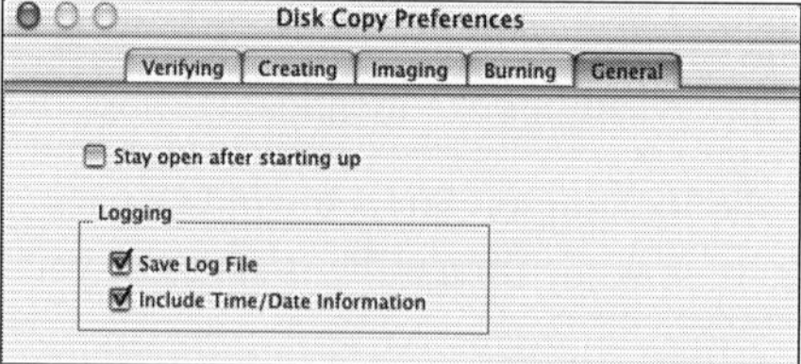

FIGURE 6.17
Choose how Disk Copy will react after starting.

By default, if you double-click an image file, Disk Copy will start, mount the image, and then quit. If you prefer to keep the application open, click Stay open after starting up. To log activity within Disk Copy, use the two logging check boxes to generate a usage log with time and date information.

> **Note**
>
> Disk Copy provides a system-wide Mount Image Service within the Application menu.

Menus

The Disk Copy menus are straightforward. The File menu contains the standard set of options, but also includes the ability to display and clear the Disk Copy log files.

Using the Image menu, users can create, verify, and convert image files:

New Blank Image (Command+N)—Creates a new blank image file which can later be written to like a Mac OS X disk.

New Image from Device (Shift+Command+I)—Creates an image file by making a direct copy from a storage device or partition.

Convert Image (Command+K)—Converts an existing image file to a new format.

Burn Image (Command+B)—Burns a CD from an existing image file.

The Utilities menu offers two options: the ability to calculate (Option+Command+=) and verify (Command+-) device checksums. After calculating a checksum for your drive image, you can provide the information to users who download or receive your image files. This, in turn, can be used to verify that an image file is indeed the original.

Disk Utility

Disk Utility (Path: `/Applications/Utilities/Disk Utility`) combines disk repair with disk formatting and partitioning. As with Mac OS 9, you cannot use either of these functions on your startup partition. If you only intend to work with a secondary disk or partition, launch Disk Utility from the Finder. To use Disk Utility to work on your primary disk, follow these steps:

1. Insert your Mac OS X Install CD into your computer.
2. Start (or restart) your Macintosh while holding down the C key.
3. Wait for the Installer to boot.
4. Choose Open Disk Utility from the Installer application menu.

After launching Disk Utility, the application will open to the first of five different panels: Information, First Aid, Erase, Partition, and RAID. Each panel performs a different function within the application, as you might guess from each panel's name.

Along the right side of the window are the available storage devices on the system, including mounted disk images. If a device has a disclosure arrow located to the right of its icon, it can be expanded to display available partitions.

Choose the disk or partition that you want to work with, and then click the tab to move to the appropriate panel. We'll start with the Information panel.

Information

Shown in Figure 6.18, the Information panel displays data about the currently selected resource, but does not perform any operations on the device.

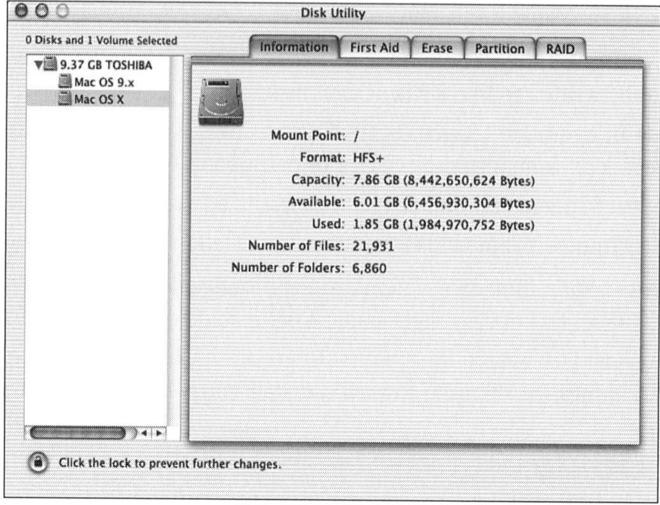

FIGURE 6.18
The Information panel supplies data about the selected resource.

If a storage device is chosen, the information display reflects the physical statistics of the hardware—such as manufacturer, capacity, and how it is connected (ATA, SCSI, Firewire, and so on).

Choosing a partition within a storage device reveals even more data, including the mount point (usually `/Volumes/<partition name>`), format, capacity, available space, used space, and the total number of files and folders.

First Aid

The First Aid panel, shown in Figure 6.19, can perform basic repair operations on a drive. It functions on UFS, HFS+, *and* HFS volumes—meaning that you can repair both types of Mac OS X partitions and both types of Mac OS 8/9 partitions. Unfortunately, Disk First Aid is not capable of repairing extensive disk damage, so third-party utilities such as Micromat's Drive 10 and TechTool Pro (`http://www.micromat.com/`) are still important parts of every software library.

To check or verify a disk, select the disk and partition from the volume list at the right of the window. Next, click the appropriate action button:

Verify—Displays any errors found in your disk, but does not attempt to repair them.

Repair—Performs the same tests as Verify, but automatically fixes any errors it might find.

Stop—Halts the current action (Verify or Repair).

FIGURE 6.19
Use Disk First Aid to repair damaged volumes.

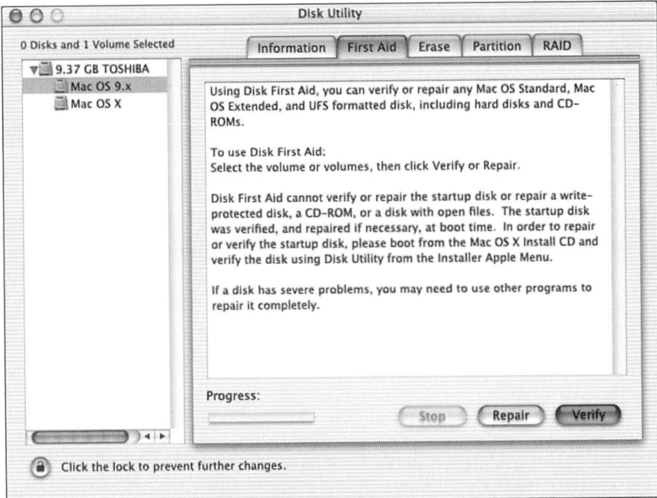

If errors are found, they will be reported. Several things are checked during this process:

Extents Overflow File—The Extents file keeps track of file information that could not be placed contiguously on a disk. As files become fragmented, the locations of the fragments are stored here.

Multi-Linked Files—Files that are incorrectly linked to the same allocation blocks on the disk.

Catalog—Contains the information that forms the structure (files, folders) of the disk.

Bitmap—A binary picture of the disk, which records which blocks are allocated to files and which are free space.

> **Tip**
>
> More information about the Disk First Aid tests and their purpose can be found at `http://www8.ewebcity.com/maconnection/dfa.htm`.

If errors cannot be repaired, Disk Utility will warn you that it is incapable of fixing your system. If this happens, try rerunning the repair—Disk First Aid often requires two passes to work correctly. If the repair does *not* work, Apple's suggested course of action is to back up the drive, erase it, and then restore your files. I'd recommend trying another disk repair tool before resorting to such desperate measures.

Note

You can batch-repair multiple volumes by selecting several disks from the volume list. Just press Command and click the icons to add to the selected list.

Note

Volumes are repaired from the command line by using the `fsck` tool, as discussed in Chapter 32.

Erase

The next panel, Erase, does exactly what you would think it should: It erases drives and partitions. This is essentially a quick-and-dirty partitioning and initialization tool; it creates a single empty partition on the selected device and erases anything that was previously there. The Erase panel is shown in Figure 6.20.

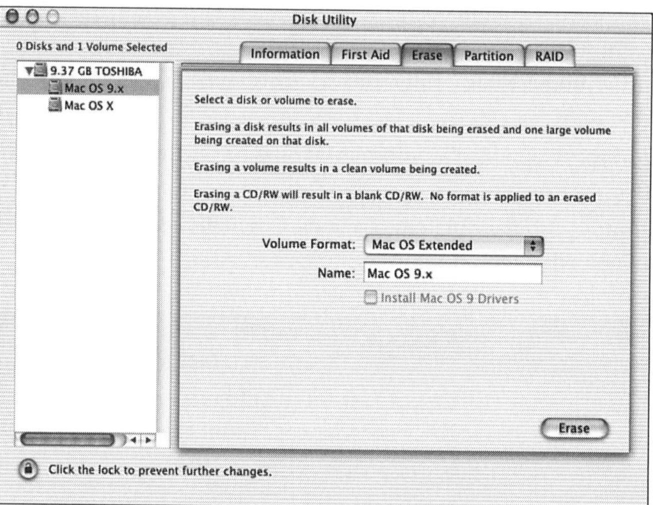

FIGURE 6.20
The Erase panel is used to quickly erase volumes and create a single empty partition.

Use the Volume Format pop-up menu to choose between HFS+ (Mac OS Extended) and HFS (Mac OS Standard) partition types. If you intend to use the volume within Mac OS X, you should use the Mac OS Extended format.

Next, enter a name for the new volume. This will appear as your disk label on the desktop. If the drive will be used with Mac OS 9 directly (not through the Classic environment), you can install Mac OS 9 drivers by clicking the Install Mac OS 9 Drivers check box.

Finally, click Erase to remove all existing information from the device and install the selected file system.

Partition

To create a more complex drive layout, use the Partition panel. If you used Drive Setup in Mac OS 8 or 9, the Partition panel will look familiar. Shown in Figure 6.21, this is the control center for working with your drive. More information on partitions, and what they are can be found in Chapter 2, "Installing Mac OS X." Be warned, changes here will erase any information on the target drive!

FIGURE 6.21
Partitioning your drive will erase any existing information.

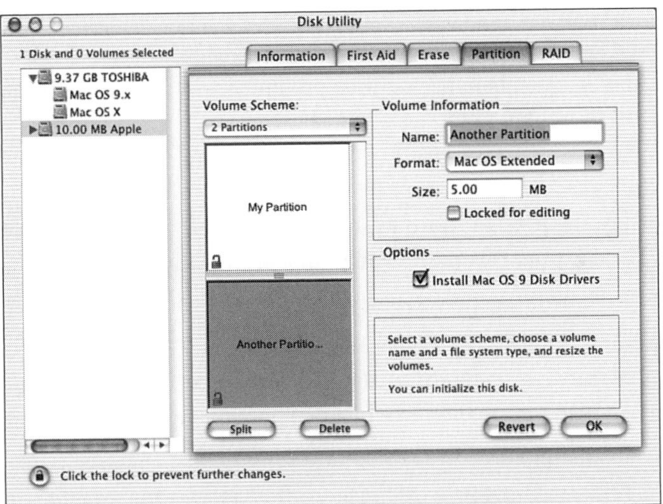

The Volume Scheme section of the Partition panel contains a visual representation of the partitions on the system. Each box is a partition. The highlighted box is the active partition.

You can change a partition's size by dragging the dividers between the partitions up and down to shrink or grow the available space. As you drag the bar, the size field on the right portion of the panel will change to show the current settings.

In addition to working with the visual view of the partition, you can use the various pop-up menus, fields, and buttons to set other parameters:

Scheme—Quickly divides your drive into 1–8 equally sized partitions.

Name—Sets the name of the highlighted partition.

Format—Sets the highlighted partition to be either HFS, HFS+, UFS, or free space.

Size—Manually enter a new size for the selected partition.

Locked for editing—When checked, the Locked for editing setting freezes the current partition's settings. You can continue to work with other partitions, but not one that is locked. Clicking the lock icon in the visual view of the partitions also toggles the lock.

Split—Splits the current partition into two equally sized partitions.

Delete—Removes the active partition.

Revert—Returns the partition map to its original state.

Partition—Commits the partition table design to the drive. This destroys all current data on the device.

Clicking the Partition button is the final step to designing your volume's layout. After you click the Partition button, you'll be prompted with a final confirmation, and then the changes will be written to the disk.

RAID

Unfortunately, the RAID feature was not yet complete in the version of Mac OS X reviewed for this title. By adding RAID support directly within the Mac OS X system, Apple is setting a new standard for high-end server and user applications.

RAID, or Redundant Array of Independent Disks, is a collection of multiple drives that function together as a single drive. By using drives performing in parallel, the computer can write and read information from the RAID set at a much higher rate than a single drive. There are four common types of RAID available:

Level 0 – Disk striping—This increases I/O speed by reading and writing to multiple drives simultaneously. It offers no fault tolerance.

Level 1 – Disk mirroring—Creates a fault-tolerant system by creating an exact mirror of one drive on another drive.

Level 3 – Disk striping with error correction—This RAID type uses three drives: two operating identically to level 0, a third containing error correction information for fault tolerance.

Level 5 – Striped data and error correction—RAID level 5 offers the best balance between performance and fault tolerance.

The Mac OS X RAID capabilities are easy to configure if you have multiple drives within a machine. The setup screen is shown in Figure 6.22.

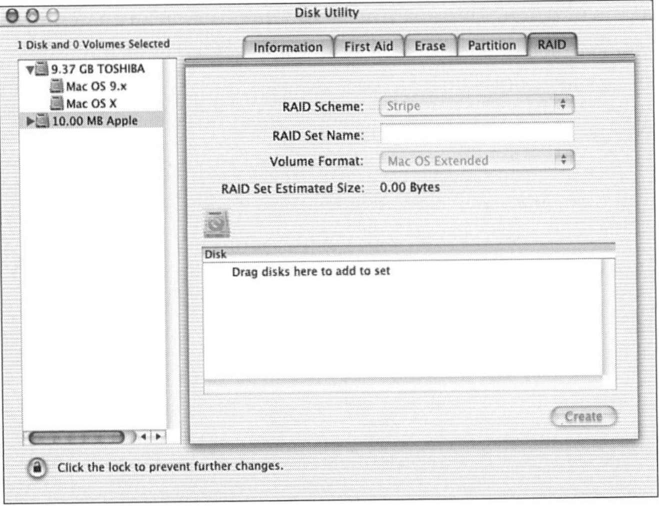

FIGURE 6.22
RAID support greatly enhances the credibility of Mac OS X as a serious platform.

To set up a RAID set, drag the icons of the drives to add to a set from the volume list to the RAID panel's disk listing. Using the RAID scheme, choose what type of RAID support will be enabled for the disks, and provide a name for the resulting virtual drive that will represent the combination of devices.

Finally, choose a volume format for the RAID set—this is identical to the choosing a format for any volume—and click the Create button to generate the RAID set.

The new volume will be mounted on the desktop.

Menus

The Options menu contains the only additional features for the Disk Utility application. After selecting a disk from the list, you can choose to Mount (Command+M), Unmount (Command+U), or Eject (Command+E) the volume.

Apple System Profiler

The Apple System Profiler (Path: `/Applications/Utilities/Apple System Profiler`) is a tool for browsing the hierarchy of components in your computer, connected to your computer, and installed on your computer. A typical use of this utility (which is also included in Mac OS 9) is to provide detailed configuration information for error reports to hardware and software manufacturers. Other uses include surveying the applications that are installed, along with their version information ad checking the status of USB or FireWire devices that are plugged into your machine.

The profiler will collect information about your computer when initially launched. This can take some time, so be patient. The initial display is a summary of your system configuration, as shown in Figure 6.23.

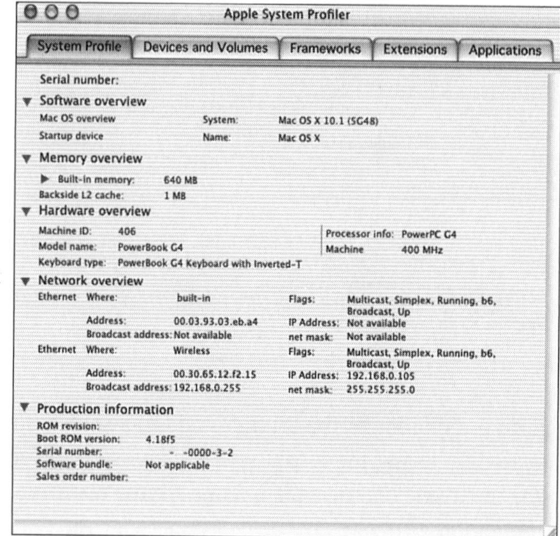

FIGURE 6.23
The System Profiler collects and displays your system's hardware and software configuration.

Each of the categories can be expanded or collapsed by clicking the disclosure arrow in front of the topic. Disclosure arrows are used extensively throughout the application, so be sure to click around—you'll be surprised at the total amount of available information.

A total of five categories of information are available: System Profile, Devices and Volumes, Frameworks, Extensions, and Applications. Click the appropriately labeled tab to move between the topics.

To generate a report of all the information generated by Apple System Profiler, choose New Report (Command+N) from the File menu.

System Profile

The System Profile panel, which was displayed in Figure 6.23, contains a summary of the base computer and operating system. By expanding each of the subtopics, you can find everything from the amount of built-in memory and your current network configuration to the serial and sales order number that was assigned when your machine was first built.

> **Tip**
>
> The information in the Profiler application is designed to be moved and pasted easily into other applications. You can click and drag within an information section to select all the data in that region and copy it to another application. You can quickly copy pertinent information into an e-mail application or any other piece of software using this technique.

Devices and Volumes

To see the devices that are connected to your computer (including the internal disks and storage devices), click the Devices and Volumes tab. An example of this screen is displayed in Figure 6.24.

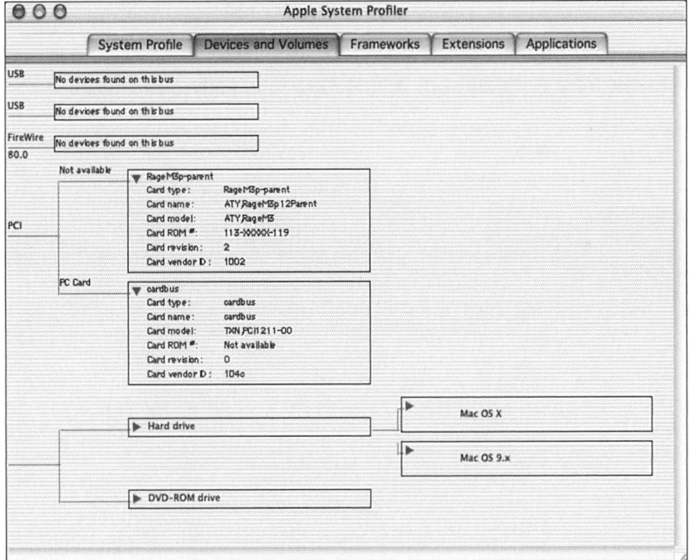

FIGURE 6.24
Devices and Volumes shows a tree of the devices on your system busses.

The Devices and Volumes display is unique—instead of a linear view of the connected devices, it presents the data as multiple trees, with each of your system busses at the base:

USB—Universal Serial Bus, a slow (12Mbps) bus used for connecting external peripherals such as low-speed storage, scanners, printers, cameras, mice, and keyboards.

FireWire—An Apple-developed bus technology that supports speeds of 400Mbps, hot swappable devices such as high-speed storage and digital-video cameras. The FireWire bus is also known by its IEEE name 1394 and Sony's iLink.

PCI—Peripheral Component Interconnect. The PCI bus was developed by Intel (yes, that Intel), and is the standard for connecting internal video cards, sound cards, and so on.

EIDE—Enhanced Integrated Drive Electronics. The EIDE standard was developed by Western Digital and is used for internal CD-ROM and disk storage.

SCSI—Small Computer System Interface. An extremely fast bus for high-speed storage devices, typically used on server-class computers.

By following the tree from the base, you can examine the devices that are connected, the manufacturer of the device, and the drivers that are installed.

Frameworks

Selecting the Frameworks tab displays a list of libraries that are installed on your computer, along with the version, and whether the Framework is an Apple creation. A sample of this screen from a default OS X installation is shown in Figure 6.25.

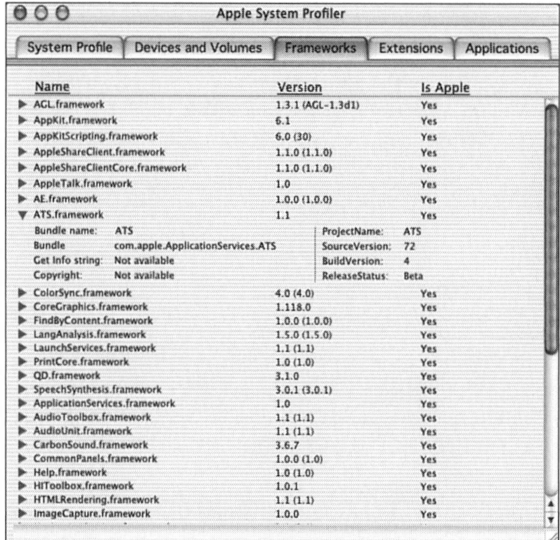

FIGURE 6.25
Frameworks provide functionality for various portions of the operating system.

There are dozens of frameworks in the base installation of Mac OS X—ranging from AppleShare to Speech Recognition. Similar to the other panels, you can click the disclosure arrow in front of the framework to show the name of the library, general information, copyright, and version. Again, this data is really just useful for debugging purposes. If a framework has accidentally been replaced with an older version, it is likely to cause problems with the system. The Frameworks panel can be used to quickly view the version numbers for comparison.

What Is a Framework?

A framework is a shared object library. Rather than each application reimplementing code, the operating system can provide commonly used functions in the form of a shared library. In Mac OS X, this library is called a *framework*. In the Windows world, this is the equivalent of a `.DLL` file.

Extensions

Extensions, like frameworks, provide functionality to the operating system. Unlike frameworks, they work directly with the hardware to enable the operating system to access devices such as network cards, sound cards, and other components. Mac users are familiar with Extensions. In Mac OS 8 and 9, extensions had similar capabilities but often made the operating system unstable. In Mac OS X, the traditional extension is replaced by a `.kext` (kernel extension). These plug-ins for the mach-kernel cannot be installed by unprivileged users and are no longer appropriate or useful for creating cool (but crash-causing) additions to the system.

The layout of the Extensions view is identical to that of the Frameworks. Each extension is displayed, along with its version, and an identifier to determine if it is Apple software. Similar to the other views, you can click the disclosure arrow to display detailed information about each kernel extension.

Applications

Finally, the Applications panel scans your drive to display all the installed applications (the BSD subsystem utilities are not taken into account). Like the Extensions and Frameworks views, you can use the basic list to determine the version and creator of an application—or expand an object to show full program information such as copyright and build status.

What Is a Bundle Identifier?

When viewing the expanded information, you might see a reference to bundle identifiers. A *bundle identifier* is Apple's way of uniquely identifying the binary files and is similar to the approach used by Java class files. Each bundle is based on the domain name of the creator along with the name of the binary. The identifier is written from most general to most specific. For example, the Calculator application, written by Apple.com, is identified as `com.apple.calculator`.

Preferences

The Apple System Profiler can create extensive reports based on the information gathered from the system. The output format and contents of the default report are configured from the Preferences panel in the Application menu. The default preferences are shown in Figure 6.26.

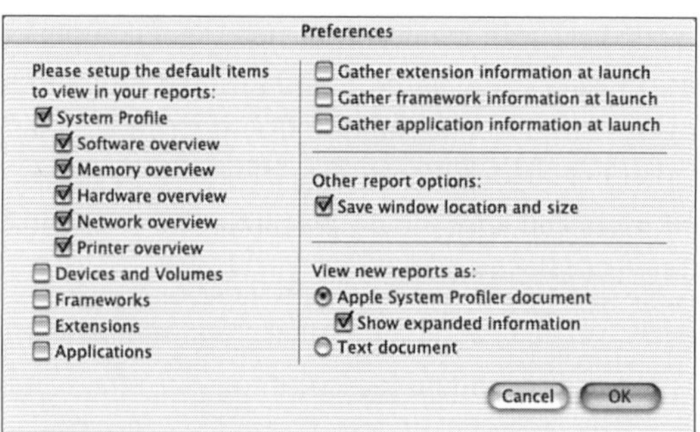

FIGURE 6.26
The Preferences set up the default reporting style for Apple System Profiler.

Using the System Profiler preferences, you can enable reporting on these portions of your system:

System Profile—By default, only the basic System Profile is enabled. You can deactivate the entire profile or individual components (Software, Memory, Hardware, Network, Production, and so on) by clicking the check boxes in the list.

Device and Volumes—Click to toggle generation of the Device and Volumes information.

Frameworks—Click to toggle generation of the Frameworks report information.

Extensions—Click to toggle generation of the Extensions report information.

Applications—Click to toggle generation of the Applications information.

Gather Extension/Framework/Application information at launch—If checked, the Profiler will search your drives at launch for the installed components. This process can take several minutes.

Save window location and size—If checked, saves the Profile window's settings between uses.

View reports as Apple System Profile document—If selected, the reports are generated using the same graphic layout as the Profiler itself. This is not useful if the report needs to be sent as plain text.

Show expanded information—Shows *all* information for each object in the Profiler report.

View reports as Text document—Saves the report in a text-only format, suitable for e-mailing or pasting into other applications.

Click OK to apply and save your settings.

Menus

Two menus that provide some additional functionality beyond what can be accessed directly in the profiler window are the File and Commands menus.

The File menu operates on reports that are generated from the Profiler's data. You can use the regular Open command to open existing report files, Save to save and open the report window, and the Print function to print and open the report window.

The Commands menu controls the Profiler's scanning of your drive information. Scanning can often take quite awhile, and, if stopped, must be resumed to get an accurate report. This menu enables the user to control the scanning process.

Gather remaining information (Command+G)—Performs all necessary scanning for frameworks, extensions, and applications.

Update all information (Command+U)—Rescans all portions of the profile for updated information.

Update Frameworks/Extensions/Applications (Command+R)—Rescans the system components for updates.

Search options(Command+F)—Configures the drive scanning options, shown in Figure 6.22.

System Profile (Command+1)—Switches to the System Profile panel.

Devices and Volumes (Command+2)—Switches to the Devices and Volumes panel.

Frameworks (Command+3)—Switches to the Frameworks panel.

Extensions (Command+4)—Switches to the Extensions panel.

Applications (Command+5)—Switches to the Applications panel.

Choosing the Search options selection enables you to limit the drives and partitions that are included when scanning your computer. Figure 6.27 shows the Search options configuration.

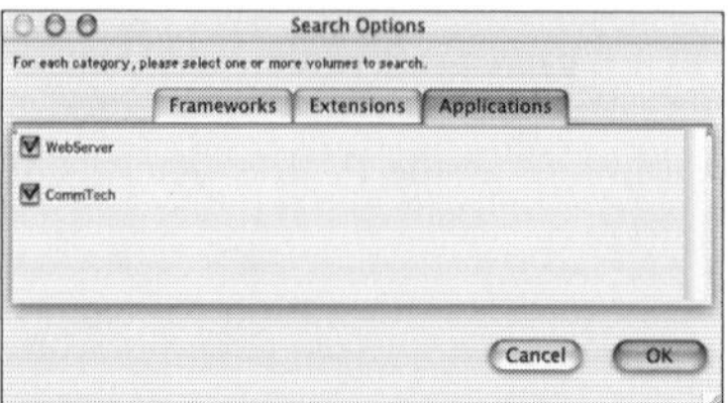

FIGURE 6.27
Search options set the devices that will be scanned when profiling your system.

Click through each of the three tabs (Frameworks, Extensions, and Applications) and click the check box beside each drive or partition that you want to scan. If a box is checked, the drive will be scanned. Scanning large volumes can be very time-intensive, so limit the scans to only the volumes that are used for applications and the operating system. Click OK to apply your choices.

The System Profiler provides an overwhelming amount of information and is rarely needed on a regular basis. In the event that a peripheral is not recognized, it can provide an easy means of identifying whether the problem is related to a missing driver, an inappropriate version of the support software, or perhaps a complete lack of communication on the peripheral's bus.

Console

The Console application (Path: `/Applications/Utilities/Console`) is literally a window into the other side of Mac OS X. While the system is running, the GUI hides a tremendous amount of information from the user. Important information is sent to what is called the Unix Console device (`/dev/console`). On many Unix systems, the console actually *is* a separate device, such as a VT100 terminal display that displays any data sent to it. This exists as a virtual device on Mac OS X and is responsible for reporting information as it arrives.

The Console application enables you to watch error and status messages as they appear. If your computer appears to be stalled or is acting in an unusual manner, the Console might be producing information that can help debug the problem. A screenshot of the Console application is shown in Figure 6.28.

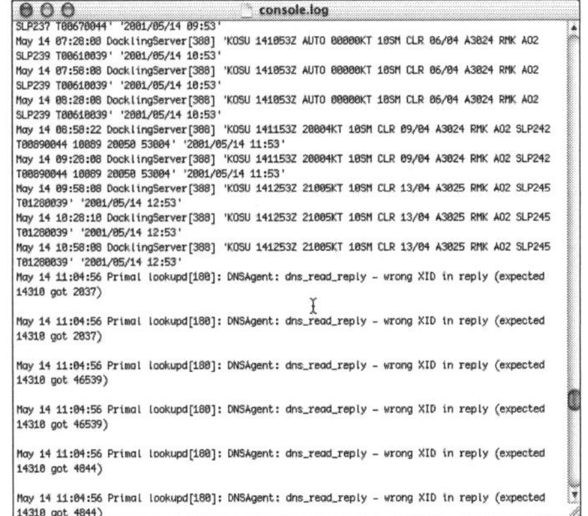

FIGURE 6.28
The Console shows internal system error and status messages as they appear.

Even on a properly working Mac OS X system, the Console will generate messages. You'll usually see a large amount of information related to the `lookupd` process. `lookupd` is a system process that handles network DNS service, user information lookups, and anything else that accesses the Mac OS X NetInfo database. Each request for information from `lookupd` is given a time-to-live. If that time is exceeded, the request fails and is logged to the console. In a networked environment, such failures are commonplace and the system will simply repeat the action until it succeeds.

Tip

You can issue a command such as `slogin thishostnamedoesntexistandnever-will.com` from the command line to see an example of a `lookupd` failure. The attempt to resolve the remote host's name will fail and be logged.

What Is NetInfo?

NetInfo is a database system that stores most of the functional information about the Mac OS X's base configuration. This database can be set up to distribute information across a Mac OS X network—enabling a single user to access his resources from anywhere on the network. Windows users will find a similarity between NetInfo and the Windows registry. NetInfo, however, is easier to work with and existed many years before the registry (NeXTStep). More information on NetInfo is provided later in this book.

In addition to `lookupd`, the Mac OS X `WindowServer` is another process you're likely to see popping up in the console. The `WindowServer` provides the base windowing and event model for Mac OS X. As I mentioned earlier, even on a working system, you're likely to see a number of error messages logged by these two processes. This does not mean that your system is incorrectly configured.

The Mac OS X System maintains a great deal of log information in addition to what is sent directly to the console. The Console application can display the contents of any log that you'd like. As you read through the book, you'll find that many of the BSD services create their own log files.

Preferences

The Console application preferences window contains two panels: Logs and Crashes. The Logs panel is shown in Figure 6.29.

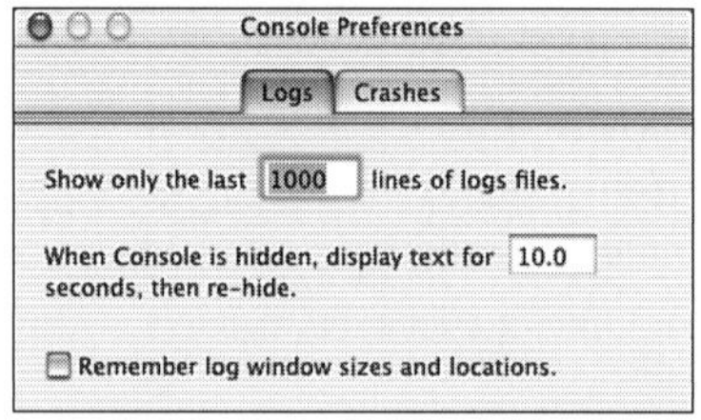

FIGURE 6.29
The Console can automatically appear and disappear as information arrives.

Here you can choose the number of lines (from the end of the log file) that will be displayed. You can also pick a delay that will be used for displaying log information as it comes in. If the console application is running but hidden when incoming information is received, the application will appear and display the new information. The Display text for xx seconds, then re-hide field is used to set the length of the delay before the Console application will hide itself.

Click the Remember log window sizes and locations check box to have the Console application remember exactly where you left it between executions.

The second Console panel, Crashes, is used to log information about system and application crashes. By default, logging is *disabled.* Click the Log crash information check box to begin collecting the log data. To automatically show the Console application when a crash occurs, be sure to check the Automatically display crash logs option.

Menus

The Console application's menus can be used to load windows with additional log file data, or change the formatting of an existing window. You won't be too surprised by some unusual elements in the menus, if you've read the earlier information on Stickies.

The File menu opens and manipulates log files. It can be used to reload or print the contents of an open window. The File menu options include

Open Log (Command+O)—Opens a log file on your Mac OS X System. By default, the application moves to the `/var/log` directory, which contains most of the system logs.

Open Console (Shift+Command+O)—Opens the Console window.

Reload (Command+R)—Reloads the contents of the currently active window.

Clean (Command+K)—Clears the contents of the currently active window.

Print (Command+P)—Prints the contents of the currently active window.

The Format menu provides control over the way text lines are displayed in the console and log windows. In fact, because of the nature of the Mac OS X operating system, you might find greater control over the output than in word processors and page layout applications. The following options can be found in the Format menu:

Font—The font submenu is, frankly, amazing. It provides access to the entire Mac OS X Font system (discussed in Chapter 10, "Printer and Font Management") including features such as kerning and ligature. Your log files never looked so… pretty.

Wrap Lines (Shift+Command+W)—Wraps lines that exceed the length of the window. If deselected, the log output will be easier to read, but you'll most likely need the horizontal scrollbar to see it all.

Note

In addition to the seemingly out-of-place Font menu, the Edit menu contains a Find feature similar to the one discussed in the Stickies application. Although this might indeed be useful, I challenge anyone reading this to find a use for the Check Spelling feature *also* accessible in the Edit menu. Properly spelled log files aren't usually the first priority of most computer users! (Of course, because this functionality can be added for free to most Cocoa applications, why not include it?)

CPU Monitor

With the multitasking capabilities of Mac OS X, users might want to check just how much of their computer's processor time is being used. In Mac OS 8 or 9, if your computer was unresponsive for a few minutes (or hours), you were pretty sure that it was busy. Mac OS X's pre-emptive multitasking is a bit more difficult to gauge. Running software like `Seti@Home` might take up large amounts of your CPU, but the system still remains snappy.

The CPU Monitor (Path: `/Applications/Utilities/CPU Monitor`) can graphically display the usage of your CPU on a simple graph from 0 to 100%. If you have multiple processors, a graph will be displayed for each CPU in your machine.

Note

Macs with multiple processors have been available for a number of years. They've come and gone with limited appeal to average users because of their reliance on specific proprietary APIs to provide multiprocessing capability to the system. Applications such as Photoshop and Premiere benefited from the use of multiple processors, but the system as a whole did not. Under Mac OS X, applications can be built to take advantage of multiple processors without the need for these APIs, and, if you're the owner of a multiprocessor machine, you'll feel a significant difference in normal day-to-day use.

The CPU Monitor supports three different types of graphs that can be displayed in a number of different ways (configurable through the Preference panel and Processes menu).

Most users will be comfortable with the Standard view. In this mode, the CPU monitor displays a window with a vertical graph of the CPU activity. If you prefer to keep the monitor visible at all times, choose the Floating Window view, which creates just the graph itself as a floating image that can be positioned anywhere on the screen—including the menu bar! An alternative to the floating window is the Icon view. This view takes advantage of the Dock's ability to display dynamic information in its icons. The CPU activity is graphed within the CPU Monitor's Dock icon, rather than taking up additional screen space (see Figure 6.30).

Advanced users might want to choose the Expanded Window view. When using the expanded mode, the graph displays information about user, system, and nice processes.

This is usually necessary only for those making use of the BSD subsystem and/or background server processes.

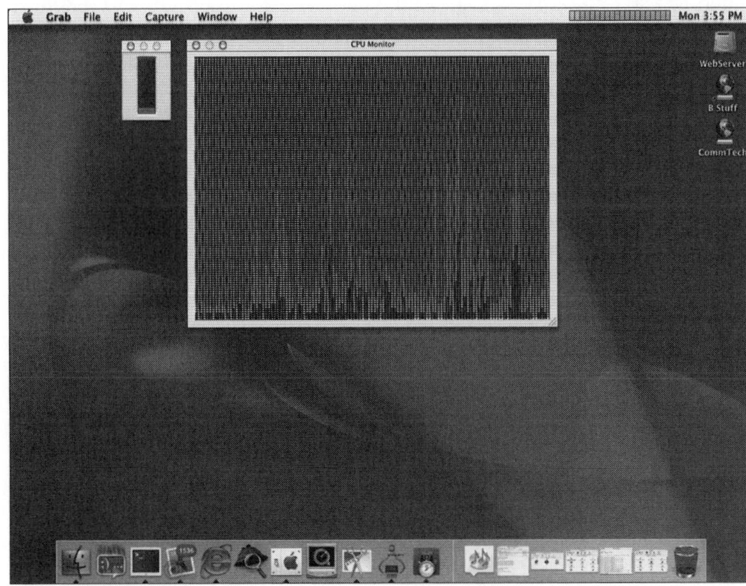

FIGURE 6.30
The CPU Monitor can display usage in a number of ways and places.

The Standard and Floating views use an average of the overall system activity in their graph. The Expanded view differentiates between three different types of activity:

- **System**—Processor usage by the system processes, such as the `WindowServer` and other components of the operating system. The System CPU time often correlates directly to the user activity. Dragging objects within an application, for example, places a load on the application and on the Mac OS X graphics and event-processing subsystem.
- **User**—CPU time that is used by user-started processes and applications.
- **Nice**—CPU time used by processes running with an altered scheduling priority. All user processes start with the same priority of execution. This priority can be adjusted with the `nice` and `renice` commands to provide them with more or less access to CPU time.

You can control the windows displayed, their orientation, and appearance through a combination of Preference settings and the use of the Processes menu.

CPUMonitor Preferences

The CPUMonitor Preferences can set appearance attributes for the floating and expanded views of the CPU Monitor, as well as configure the monitor to display with the Dock icon, as opposed to a separate window. The Preferences window is shown in Figure 6.31.

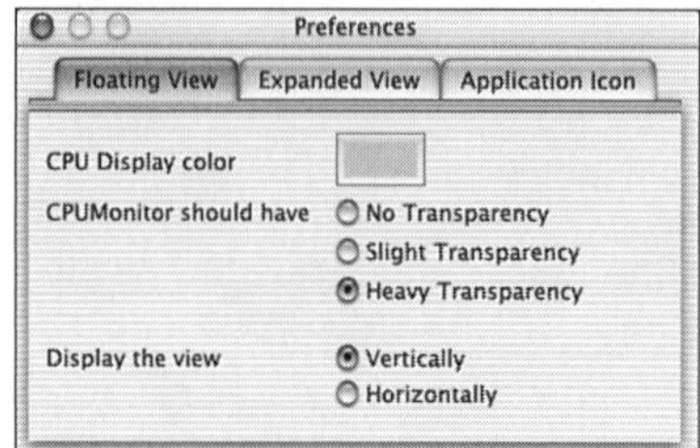

FIGURE 6.31
The CPUMonitor Preferences control the appearance of the CPU graphs.

The CPUMonitor Preferences panel has three separate panels. The first, the Floating View, includes

- **CPU Display color**—Click the color well to choose a color for the Floating monitor's graph.
- **CPUMonitor Transparency**—Use the radio buttons to set the floating view to No Transparency, Slight Transparency, or Heavy Transparency.
- **Display view**—The floating CPU monitor can display as a vertical (default) or horizontal graph based on these radio buttons.

The second section of the CPUMonitor Preferences, the Expanded View settings, enables the user to configure the colors that she wants displayed for background of the view window and the three types of CPU activity. Click each color well to open the OS X Cocoa color picker and choose a new color.

The final tab, Application Icon, chooses which CPU Monitor graph will be drawn within the Dock; choose either Display the Standard view in the icon or Display the Extended view in the icon. The corresponding graph will be drawn directly in the CPU Monitor's Dock icon. Choosing Don't display in the icon will revert to the default static Dock icon.

Tip

An interesting alternative to Apple's supplied load monitor is an application called Flame, written by Matthew Drayton. Flame draws an animated flame in a floating window or Dock icon to show the current system load. You can download Flame from `http://www.cs.newcastle.edu.au/~mdrayton/flame/flame.html`.

Menus

The Process menu provides access to the remaining CPU Monitor options. Here you can toggle the different monitor modes as well as launch related programs.

Display Standard Window (Command+S)—Displays the standard (single color) CPU Monitor graph.

Toggle Floating Window (Command+F)—Toggles the floating graphic on and off.

Display Expanded Window (Command+E)—Displays the expanded (four-color) CPU Monitor graph.

Clear Expanded Window (Command+K)—Clears the activity shown in the expanded window.

Open Process Viewer (Command+P)—Launches the Process Viewer application (see the next topic in this chapter).

Open Top (Command+T)—Launches the Terminal application running the command-line utility `top`, which monitors system processes and activity.

The CPU Monitor can give you new insight into your computer's internal processes. If the system *seems* slow, the CPU Monitor can reveal whether or not the CPU is being taxed, or if the problem lies elsewhere.

Process Viewer

In Chapter 4, "The Finder: Working with Files and Applications," you learned how pressing Option+Command+Escape opens a process list and enables you to force-quit open applications on the system. The Process Viewer application is similar, but contains information on *all* the system's processes, not just the GUI software that is running. Figure 6.32 shows the default Process Viewer display.

Using the controls in the Process Listing screen, you can configure the type of output and amount of the information displayed.

The Find and Show features help limit the amount of data that is shown within the process listing. Typing into the Find field filters processes, which match the given string. For example, typing `Internet` would limit the displayed processes to those that have the word *Internet* in their name, such as Internet Explorer. The Show pop-up menu filters processes based on the owner. You can change the setting to show only processes owned by your account (User Processes), the system (Administrator Processes), or NetBoot. (NetBoot processes are not likely to be of value on most Mac OS X non-server installations.)

FIGURE 6.32
The Process Viewer can show you everything that is running on your computer.

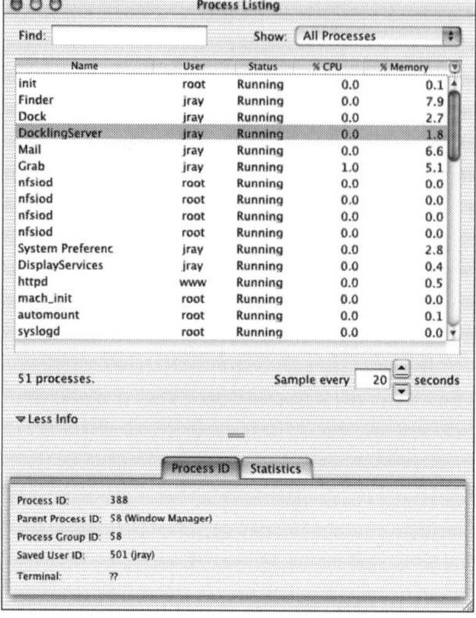

The Process Listing is not, as you might first think, a real-time view of the programs running on the system. The process information is very dynamic and is always changing. To avoid overwhelming the user with a list that jumps all over the place, the process list is only updated every few seconds. Using the Sample every X seconds option, you can change the rate at which the list is refreshed. The larger the number, the longer you must wait for updates.

Processes are listed based on five columns: Name, User, Status, % CPU, and % Memory. Each column can be sorted by clicking on the column heading. Click the small triangle in the upper-right corner of the process list to reverse the sorting order. Click its name within the listing to select a process. The Process ID and Statistics panels in the Extended view show information about the selected process. Using the basic listing, you can glean the following information about a process:

Name—The name of the process or application.

User—The user account which launched the process.

Status—The status of the process. Most should be running, although users who access the command line can also suspend processes.

% CPU—The percentage of available CPU time being used by the process.

% Memory—The percentage of available memory being used by the process.

If you'd like even more information about a process, you can click it within the listing, use the More Info disclosure triangle in the lower right of the window to reveal the Process ID and Statistics tabs. The Process ID tab displays the following information:

Process ID—Each process on a Unix system is given a unique identifier called the Process ID (PID); this number can be used to interact with or terminate the process.

Parent Process ID—The process that *started* the selected process. For example, if a user starts a program from the command line (the "shell"), the ID of the shell is listed as the program's parent process ID. Processes started at boot time list the parent process ID of 1 (init).

Process Group ID—The group ID that was used to launch the process.

Saved User ID—The user ID that launched the process.

Terminal—The controlling terminal. If the program was launched from a login session or terminal prompt, it will have a controlling terminal that is used for I/O with the process.

Clicking the Statistics tab shows data on how the process has been behaving on your system. Information about CPU usage and memory usage is readily available:

Total CPU Time—The total amount of CPU time used by the process—measured in minutes, seconds, and hundredths of a second. Because a process does not get 100% of the CPU 100% of the time, this is *not* an indication of when the program started. It is the cumulative amount of time used over the entire lifetime of the process, which could span seconds, days, or months, and still hardly make a dent in used CPU time!

Virtual Memory Size—The amount of virtual memory being used by the selected process.

Resident Memory Size—The amount of real memory being used.

Tip

When selecting a process to view information, you might want to slow down the sampling rate; otherwise, your selection might be invalidated as soon as you make it.

Menus

The Process Viewer's menus provide a bit more control over the application, such as exporting the current process list to an XML file and sorting the output list.

Use the File menu options to print or export the list of processes. These options can be useful for creating a record of normal system activity to refer to if you think your system is misbehaving:

Export (Command+E)—Exports the current list of processes as an XML file that can be viewed with Apple's XML editor (included with the Developer tools). Learn more about XML's role in Mac OS X in Chapter 16, "Command-Line Software Installation."

Print (Command+P)—Prints the process list. Only the processes in the visible portion of the window are printed!

Quit Process (Shift+Command+Q)—Quits the selected process or processes. If you are not the owner of the process, the system will forbid you from quitting. In addition, quitting some processes will log you out of the system. This is identical to using the Unix `kill` command.

Tip

You can also force-quit processes by double-clicking their name in the Process Listing window.

The Edit menu contains several options, but almost all are grayed out. The Show All Columns (Shift+Command+A) selection has little use other than enlarging the columns to fit the screen if they are accidentally resized. The Sort on Column (Shift+Command+S) function will sort the current column. This is identical to clicking the column heading, but can be useful for resorting with a key press after a new process-listing sample is taken.

Note

The Process Viewer is a nice way to introduce users to the system support processes and give them an idea of what is actually running behind the scenes on their OS X box. Unfortunately, it is lacking much of the functionality of command-line utilities such as `top`. Learn more about the command line beginning in Chapter 12, "Introducing the BSD Subsystem."

Graphic Utilities

The Mac OS X operating system comes with a few utilities for working with and creating graphics files, but, unfortunately, nothing that can enable you to create a work of art from scratch. If that's the type of application you're looking for, check out Chapter 8. The four included applications (DigitalColor Meter, Grab, Image Capture, and Preview) can help you identify onscreen colors, take screenshots, download digital photos, and view and manipulate graphics.

DigitalColor Meter

The DigitalColor Meter (Path: `/Applications/Utilities/DigitalColor Meter`) is a small application that measures and reports the color of an onscreen pixel, or the average color of a group of pixels. Graphic artists will find this useful for color matching, and Web designers can use it to quickly sample an onscreen color for use in a Web page.

When launched, the DigitalColor Meter application opens the display shown in Figure 6.33.

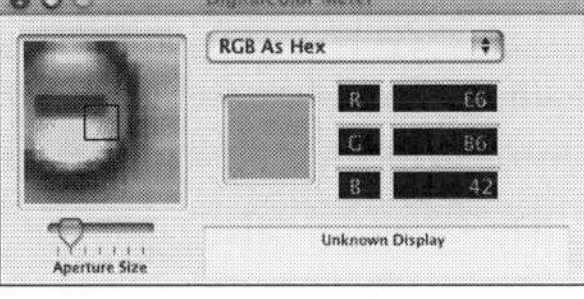

FIGURE 6.33
Use the DigitalColor meter to match onscreen colors to color palettes.

The panel at the right of the window displays an enlarged view of whatever is currently under the Mac OS X cursor. Moving the cursor across the screen results in real-time feedback. Immediately to the right of the enlarged view is a color well that contains the sampled color. By default, the displayed color is the average of several pixels (the aperture) of the enlarged image. Adjusting the Aperture Size slider controls the number of pixels sampled from one (for a true 1:1 color sample) at the minimum to a 16×16 block at the maximum.

To the right of the color well is a numeric representation of the currently selected color. The pop-up menu at the top of the window determines the color model being used:

RGB As Percentage—Displays red, green, and blue as a percentage. 100% RGB = white; 0% RGB = black.

RGB As Actual Value—Displays RGB values as a range from 0–65535.

RGB As Hex—Represents the RGB values in the range of `0x00` to `0xFF`. It's useful for Web designers to sample for HTML colors.

CIE 1931—A tristimulus color system adopted by the CIE (Commission International de l'E´clairage) in 1931.

CIE 1976—A tristimulus color system adopted by the CIE in 1976.

CIE L*a*b*—A color space usually used for working with subtractive color mixtures (paint and print) as opposed to additive mixtures (light), adopted by the CIE in 1976.

Tristimulus—Three primary color values required to match a given shade.

> **Note**
>
> For information on color systems, how they work, and the CIE systems in general, check out `http://colour.derby.ac.uk/colour/info/glossary/c/`.

Depending on the color profile of your monitor, the DigitalColor Meter application might not be able to map a given color into the chosen color space. If this is the case, you'll be warned in a message at the bottom of the window, and the tristimulus values will not change.

Menus

The Color menu has two options to help make it easier to grab a color for use elsewhere. Hold Color (Shift+Command+H) freezes on the current color. Obviously, this is best used as a keyboard shortcut; otherwise, the color will change as you select the menu item! Copy Color (Command+C) copies the color values into a pasteable string. An RGB hex value is copied as a quoted hex string (such as `"#FFAABB"`), and is ready for pasting into an HTML document.

That's it for DigitalColor Meter. It has its place, but it isn't very useful in everyday system operations.

Grab

Mac OS X 10.1 reintroduces the ability to capture a screenshot at any time by pressing Shift+Command+3 for a full-screen shot, or Shift+Command+4 for partial screens. Even with this capability, there is still room for improvement. The Grab application (Path: `/Applications/Utilities/Grab`), can do things that are not possible using the built-in screenshot function. Grab can capture screen information in three different ways:

- **Selection** (Shift+Command+A)—Captures a portion of the screen, determined by a user-drawn rectangle.
- **Screen** (Shift+Command+Z)—Captures the entire screen.
- **Timed Screen** (Shift+Command+Z)—Captures the screen with a ten-second delay. This gives you time to position your windows, pull down (or pop up) a menu, and so on. You can take screenshots with menus in the down position in Mac OS X!

Note

A fourth possibility, Window, is listed in the Grab Capture menu, but is disabled in the current version of Mac OS X.

To start a screen capture, choose the appropriate method to take the shot from the Capture menu, or press the Command key equivalent.

Grab will display a window with short instructions on how to proceed. This window is *not* included in the final screenshot, despite always being onscreen.

If you choose Selection, you must click and drag over the portion of the screen that you want to capture. A screen capture requires you to click outside of the instruction window. Finally, to use a Timed Screen capture, click the Start Timer button. The system will wait ten seconds before taking the picture and will sound a warning beep three seconds before the capture. You can position windows and prepare the screen as necessary during this time frame. Figure 6.34 shows the Timed Screen message window as the system counts down.

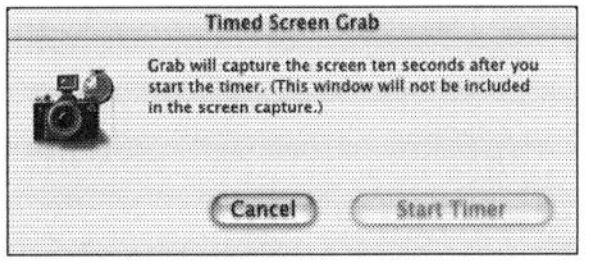

FIGURE 6.34
The Timed Screenshot gives you ten seconds to prepare your screen.

After it is taken, the screenshot will appear in a new window within the Capture application. To get information on its size and bit depth, choose the Inspector (Command+1) from the Edit menu. You can save or print the screenshot from the File menu. The default format for Mac OS X screenshots is the Tagged Image File Format (TIFF).

Preferences

When taking a screenshot, you can choose to superimpose a cursor of your choice over the screen. The default is no cursor at all. Use the Grab Preferences, under the Application menu, to change the cursor that will be used. The preferences are shown in Figure 6.35.

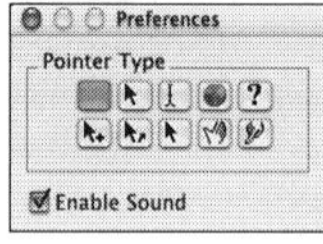

Figure 6.35
Grab can superimpose a cursor of your choice over the screen capture.

Within the Pointer Type section, click the button of the mouse pointer that you want to use.

The preferences can also toggle the camera shutter noise that is played when an image is captured. Check or uncheck the Enable Sound button as you see fit.

Note

The Grab utility does not appear to sync itself with a vertical refresh of the Macintosh screen. If you use programs with fast-moving graphics such as iTunes, you might notice image tearing as Grab captures two frames of animation in one shot.

Image Capture

Have a digital camera? What about a digital media reader? The need for extra software for viewing and manipulating images might be over. The Mac OS X Image Capture application (Path: `/Applications/Image Capture`) enables you to connect a digital camera or media reader (USB/FireWire) to your computer and instantly import pictures—even turn them into a Web page.

Apple has posted a list of the Image Capture compatible applications at http:// docs.info.apple.com/article.html?artnum=106523. Because the supported devices are updated frequently, the easiest way to see if yours will work is to plug it into the system and see what happens! Check with your camera or media reader's support page to see if additional software is available.

Tip

If your camera doesn't work with Image Capture, I recommend investing in a digital media reader. These devices cost between $20–$35, are well supported in Mac OS X, and transfer much faster than most computer to camera connections.

To use the Image Capture application, plug your camera or media reader into the computer; then place the device in Connect mode. Mac OS X will automatically launch Image Capture in a few seconds if it is recognized. Figure 6.36 shows the Image Capture application after launching.

FIGURE 6.36
The Image Capture application will automatically launch when it senses a camera or digital media reader.

All functions of the Image Capture application are carried out through this window—even closing the application is just a matter of closing the window.

Camera

The type of camera or media reader and number of available pictures are shown at the top of the window. If multiple devices are connected, choose the one you want to work with from the Camera pop-up menu.

Download To

The default location for picture downloads is the Pictures folder in the current user's home directory. To change the directory, use the Download To popup menu to choose Other, and then select the directory to hold the files.

Automatic Task

After a Hot-Plug action is executed, Mac OS X can automatically use one of eight different AppleScripts to format and arrange your photos. The AppleScripts are located in the `/Library/Image Capture/Scripts` folder and can be modified (or added to). You can learn more about AppleScript in Chapter 21, "AppleScript."

The five available scripts, by default, are

Build Web page—Builds a complete Web page, with thumbnails, for the downloaded images. The Web page is stored in a folder named `Index` in the same location as the images used.

Format 3×5—Builds multiple Web pages (`3x5index##.html`) that contain scaled versions of the images, along with a `3x5 tips.html` page with printing instructions.

Format 4×6—Builds multiple Web pages (`4x6index##.html`) that contain scaled versions of the images, along with a `4x6 tips.html` page with printing instructions.

Format 5×7—Builds multiple Web pages (`5x7index##.html`) that contain scaled versions of the images, along with a `5x7 tips.html` page with printing instructions.

Format 8×10—Builds multiple Web pages (`8x10index##.html`) that contain scaled versions of the images, along with an `8x10 tips.html` page with printing instructions.

To choose another script or application, use the Other selection to browse the file system and select an alternative.

Tip

The original image capture application, which shipped with 10.0, included three other AppleScripts to help scale downloaded images. These scripts relied on a buried faceless application called Image Capture Extension (path: `/System/Library/Frameworks/Carbon.framework/Versions/A/Frameworks/ImageCapture.framework/Versions/A/Image Capture Extension`).

Although these scripts are no longer included with Mac OS X 10.1, the Image Capture Extension *is*.

This application is accessible only through AppleScript, and can be used to scale and rotate images on your system. This tool could easily be employed to manipulate images for Web sites in real-time.

Hot-Plug Action

When the OS X system detects that media is available for downloading, you can instruct it to do one of three things:

- **Image Capture Application**—Automatically starts the Image Capture software (default).
- **None**—Does nothing. If this is selected, you'll have to open Image Capture manually to access your photographs.
- **Other**—Allows the user to choose his own application or script to run.

Downloading

When you're ready to download images, you can choose all the pictures, or select from thumbnails of the images stored on the camera. If you choose Download All, Image Capture will download the files from your camera. This process is illustrated in Figure 6.37.

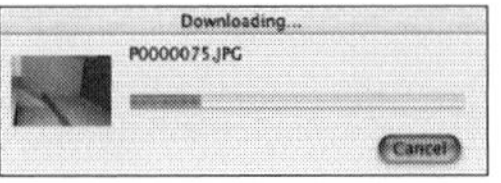

FIGURE 6.37
The process of downloading images can take quite awhile.

After the download is complete, Image Capture will launch your selected Automatic Task AppleScript, if any.

To download only certain images from your device, click the Download Some button. After a brief delay, the List View of thumbnails will appear, along with the image names and file sizes. Click to select or deselect an image for download. Use the list and icon buttons in the upper-left corner of the window to control your viewing style. The Icon view operates in the same fashion, but does not display image numbers or sizes. The Icon view can be seen in Figure 6.38.

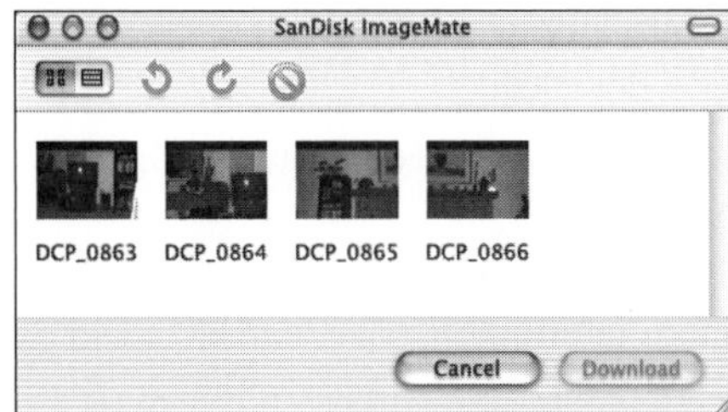

FIGURE 6.38
Choose the images that you want to download from the device.

Click Download to start the download process. When completed, the Automatic Task script, if any, will be started.

Preferences

The Image Capture application preferences control what happens when images are downloaded from a camera or media reader, and how they appear within the image file browser. There are two panels within the preferences: Download Options and View Options.

The Download Options panel, shown in Figure 6.39, customizes the image download process.

Figure 6.39
Download options are used to fine-tune image transfers.

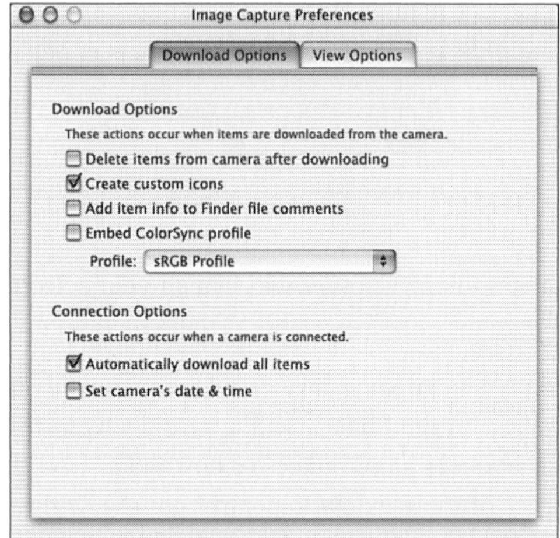

Choose from these available settings:

Delete items from camera after downloading—Removes all image files from the camera or media reader upon download.

Create custom icons—Automatically generates custom thumbnail icons for each of the downloaded images.

Add item info to Finder file comments—Uses the Finder's comment field (accessible from Show Info) to store information (size, name, and so on) about each camera file.

Embed ColorSync profile—Add a ColorSync profile to each image file to ensure consistency across output devices. Do not check this box unless you are absolutely positive of the outcome; it can drastically reduce perceived image quality in some cases.

Automatically download all items—Automatically start the download process as soon as a camera or media reader is connected.

Set camera's date and time—Synchronize the camera's time to the time of the Mac OS X host computer.

The second panel, View Options, is shown in Figure 6.40. In this panel, a user can configure how the image listing will appear within the Image Capture application.

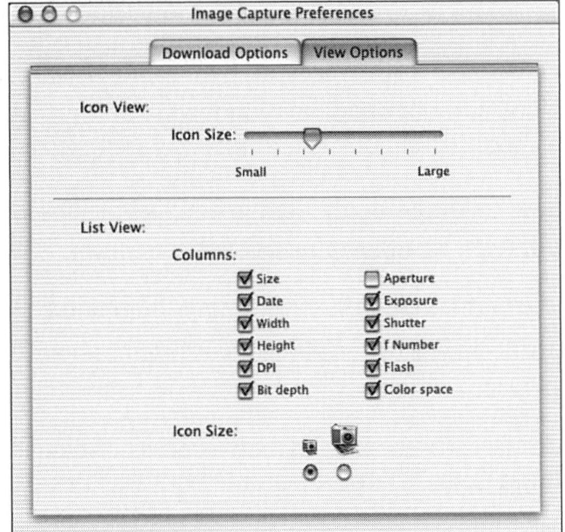

FIGURE 6.40
Customize the image listing within Image Capture.

These settings are similar to those of the Finder views:

Icon Size—Use the slider to control the size of the preview icons when viewing images in Icon View mode.

Columns—Pick and choose the columns to display within the image List View. Not all the available options are supported by all cameras, so don't be surprised if some fields are left blank.

Icon Size—There are two sizes for the icons shown within the List View. Pick your size here.

Menus

The Image Capture menus offer no options beyond what you've already seen in the Image Capture window.

Preview

Preview (Path: `/Applications/Preview`) is Apple's modern replacement for the Image Preview QuickTime component. Offering the capability to view a wide range of image formats, it also has native support for PDF. Although not as full-featured as Adobe's Acrobat Reader software (also included with the system), it *is* capable of reading PDFs without any additions to the operating system. Considering that many application distributions currently arrive with electronic documentation in PDF format, this can only be seen as a good (or possibly great) thing.

Launching

Preview can be launched in a number of ways. First, by double-clicking the application file. This will load Preview, but will not open any windows. You must then use Open from the file menu to choose a file to view.

Second, you can open Preview by dragging the image or PDF files onto its icon in the Finder or Dock. The files will each be opened in separate windows.

Third, Preview is integrated into the Mac OS X printing system and can be started by clicking Preview from any Print dialog box. You can learn more about the print system in Chapter 10.

There is a small difference in the window display between basic images and PDFs. A PDF window is shown in Figure 6.41.

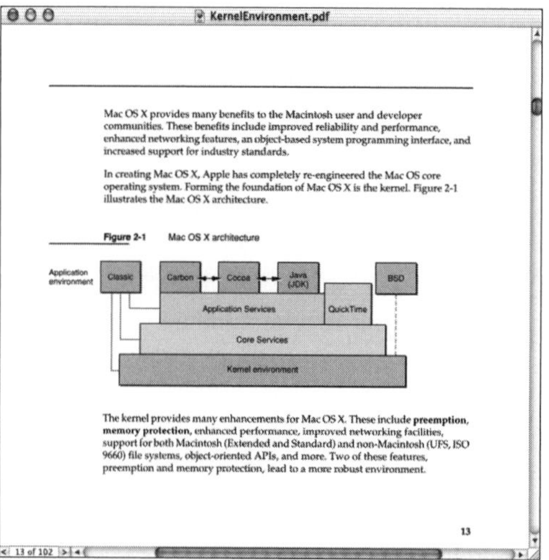

Figure 6.41
PDF Windows include page navigation controls at the bottom.

Images are displayed in a borderless window (unless resized such that scrollbars are necessary). PDFs, however, have a small arrow controller in the lower-left corner. Clicking the left arrow moves the previous page, whereas clicking the right arrow moves to the next. Click and hold on an arrow to quickly page through the document.

> **Tip**
>
> To jump to a specific page, click inside the text area between the two arrows (usually reads (`"# of #"`) and type in a number, and then press Return. Preview will jump to that page number.

Menus

The Preview menus enable you to perform some simple image conversions and transformations. Depending on whether you are working with a PDF or a simple image, some of the options might change.

The File menu can be used to open images or to convert open files into different formats.

Open (Command+O)—Opens a file.

Open Recent—Opens a recently accessed file.

Close (Command+W)—Closes the frontmost window.

Save As (Shift+Command+W)—Saves the current file under a new name.

Save As PDF(PDFs/Print Previews only)—Saves the current document as a PDF.

Export(Images only)—Exports the current image to a new file format, specified in the Format pop-up menu of the Save dialog. You can set image options (compression and so on) by clicking the Options button in the Save dialog.

Page Setup (Shift+Command+P)—Sets up the page layout of the current printer.

Print (Command+P)—Prints the frontmost window.

To zoom in or out on your image, rotate it, or otherwise affect its appearance, use the Display menu. Similar to the File menu, some options are restricted to PDFs or images.

Page Forward (Command+Right-Arrow)—(PDF Only)—Moves to the next page in a PDF.

Page Backward (Command+Left-Arrow)—(PDF Only)—Moves to the previous page in a PDF.

Actual Size (Command+A)—Resizes the frontmost document so it is displayed in its actual (printed) size.

Zoom In (Command+Up-Arrow)—Zooms in on the current window.

Zoom Out (Command+Down-Arrow)—Zooms out of the current window.

Zoom To Fit (Command+=)—Resizes the current document to fit within the window without scrollbars.

Rotate Left (Command+L) (Image Only)—Rotates an image 90 degrees to the left.

Rotate Right (Command+R) (Image Only)—Rotates an image 90 degrees to the right.

Flip Horizontal (Image only)—Flips an image along an imaginary vertical axis running through its center.

Flip Vertical (Image only)—Flips an image along an imaginary horizontal axis running through its center.

AntiAliasing (PDF only)—If checked, the PDF text and graphics will be automatically smoothed (antialiased).

Continuous Scrolling (PDF only)—If checked, the vertical scrollbar on PDF windows will smoothly move from page to page, like a word processor. If not selected (the default), each page will snap into view.

Preview's simple image handling capabilities do not provide any editing functionality. To edit or create original graphics, you'll need an application such as Graphic Converter—described in Chapter 8.

Other Applications

Three more applications will be discussed briefly in this chapter. They don't quite fit anywhere else in the book, so if you're looking for logic to this grouping, that's about as far as you're going to get! This grab bag of miscellaneous applications consists of Applet Launcher, Text Edit, Chess, and DVD player.

Applet Launcher

Most of the time, you'll start Java within Mac OS X either by visiting a Web page in your browser, or by double-clicking a Mac OS X–packaged Java application. In the event that you want to launch Java applications outside of a Web browser, or from a non-natively packaged Java application, you'll need some additional tools.

The Applet Launcher (Path: `/Applications/Utilities/Applet Launcher`) provides a simple method of launching an applet that is located at a Web (`http://`) or file (`file://`) URL.

The Launcher opens windows with a URL field at startup. This is shown in Figure 6.42. To launch an Applet, enter a URL to the containing HTML page within the field, and then click the Launch button. For local applets, click the Open button, or choose Open (Command+O) from the File menu.

FIGURE 6.42
Enter a URL and click Launch to start an applet.

The pop-up menu button at the right of the URL field contains a list of recently visited URLs. You can choose one from the list to quickly jump to it.

Menus and Preferences

The Applet Launcher is a port of the Mac OS 9 Applet Launcher utility and has not been cleanly ported to Mac OS X. Although it works, you'll notice a variety of visual anomalies, including the Preferences panel located under the Edit menu.

Very little configuration can be performed on Applet Launcher. If you want to clear the pop-up history of recent Applets, use the Clear History button in the Preferences panel (under Edit).

The Applets menu contains shortcuts to several simple demonstration applets. Choosing an item from the list will launch it within the Applet Viewer.

Quitting the Applet Viewer quits all open applets.

Java Applications

Java applications are a breed apart from applets. Applications do not rely on an HMTL file for launching information, nor can they be started from the Applet Launcher.

To run a Java application that is stored as a `.class` or `.jar` file, you must open the Terminal application to a command prompt. Chapter 12 will begin your introduction to the Unix underpinnings in OS X.

To execute a Java application based on a class filename use the following command:

```
java <theclassfile>
```

Alternatively, to launch a Java application that has been packaged as a `.jar` file, you must alter the command slightly:

```
java -jar <jarfilename>
```

To run most Java applications, you will need to be comfortable using the command line and might have to alter configuration files manually depending on the installation instructions. The information provided here is just a starting point.

TextEdit

Who among us hasn't searched our drives at one point in time and found 20 or 30 copies of SimpleText laying around on the system? For years, the Mac OS didn't automatically install a text editor or reader with the system. Application installers took it upon themselves to install SimpleText, Apple's simple styled-text editor. Over time, you could amass quite a collection of different (and identical) versions of the little editor.

In Mac OS X, Apple introduces TextEdit(Path: `/Applications/TextEdit`), the modern replacement for SimpleText. TextEdit works in a similar way as SimpleText, but saves files using the RTF (Rich Text Format) standard, and handles Unicode editing as well. RTF files can be opened in popular word-processing programs, such as Microsoft Word, and display all formatting information.

What Is Unicode?

Unicode is a character-encoding format that uses 16 bits (as opposed to the traditional eight) for storing each character. This allows for more than 65,000 characters to be represented, which is necessary for some languages such as Japanese and Greek. Unicode is expected to eventually replace ASCII encoding (which can only represent a total of 255 characters) entirely.

Like the Stickies application covered at the beginning of this chapter, TextEdit uses many of the built-in OS X features to provide advanced control over text and fonts. For more information about the individual font controls, see Chapter 10.

When started, TextEdit will open a new `Untitled.rtf` document for you to begin working. If you'd like to open an existing document, choose Open (Command+O) from the File menu.

TextEdit's Open dialog box will enable you to select any type of file, including binary files such as images. To read a file, however, it must be a supported document type such as plain text, HTML, or RTF. By default, TextEdit will open HTML documents and display the styled information similar to a Web browser. Figure 6.43 demonstrates TextEdit's rich text editing capabilities. To open an HTML file and edit the source code, you will need to adjust the preferences.

For the most part, you should be able to open TextEdit and start creating and editing text documents. However, a number of preferences and features exist that you can use to customize its appearance and functionality.

Preferences

The TextEdit Preferences panel, shown in Figure 6.44, controls the default application preferences. Most of these options can be chosen from the menu bar and stored on a per-document basis, as well as for the entire application.

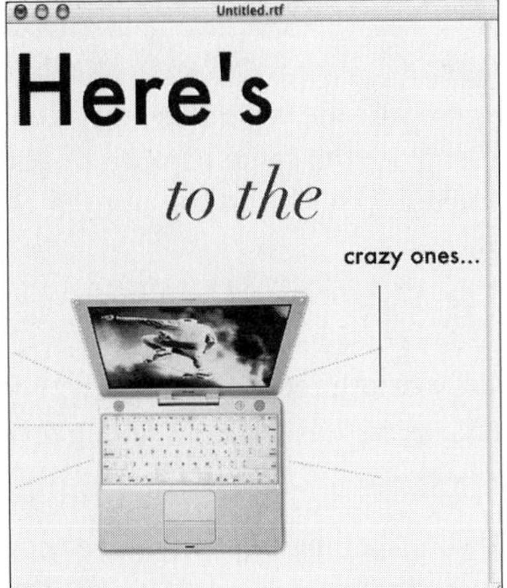

FIGURE 6.43
TextEdit can edit styled text documents stored in HTML or RTF.

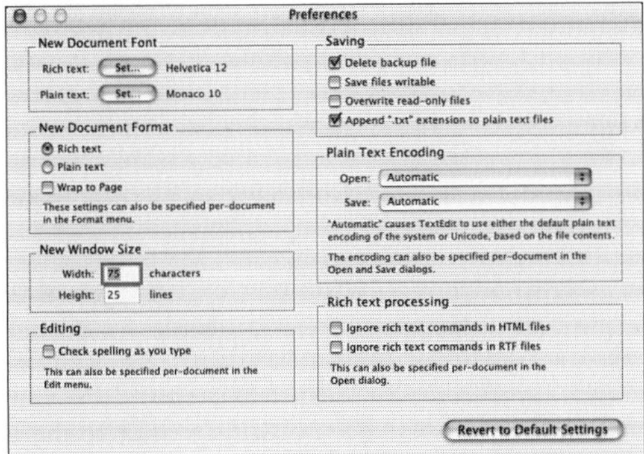

FIGURE 6.44
The TextEdit preferences can control a range of features.

Use the Set buttons in the Preferences panel to choose new default fonts for rich text and plain text documents. The default fonts are Helvetica 12 and Monaco 10, respectively.

The New Document Format section of the panel includes options for

Rich Text—This creates documents that store style information along with the text.

Plain Text—If you need to use the resulting file with a Web editor, or other plain-text application, click the Plain Text button to default to text-only mode.

Wrap to Page—TextEdit, by default, wraps typed text at the edit of the window. Choose this to wrap to a static page width.

Note

An interesting side effect of wrapping to the window width is that when printing, it will adjust the font sizes such that the same amount of text that fits in a line in the TextEdit window also takes up a line on the printer. This can result in some bizarre font scaling effects.

The New Window Size section includes a Width setting option, where you can specify the width of new windows in characters, as well as a Height setting option where you can set the height of new windows in lines.

To have TextEdit automatically check your spelling as you type, select the Check spelling as you type check box within the Editing section. Misspelled words will be underlined in red. Press Ctrl and click the misspelled word to open a contextual menu that enables you to choose from a list of corrections, ignore the word, or add it (learn) to the OS X dictionary.

The Savings options include

Delete backup file— Removes the TextEdit backup file after a document is successfully saved.

Save Files writable—Saves files with write permissions turned on.

Overwrite read-only files—Overwrites files, even if their permissions are set to read-only. (Obviously, this works only on files that you own.)

Append `.txt` extension to plain text files—Adds a `.txt` to the end of plain text files.

When opening or saving a document, TextEdit gives you the opportunity to override automatic detection of the appropriate file encoding type to use. To choose an alternative encoding, such as Unicode, use the pop-up menus.

Allowing automatic detection enables TextEdit to open files created on alternative operating systems, such as Windows, and transparently translate end-of-line characters.

By default, TextEdit attempts to read style information in whatever files it is opening. To disable rich text commands in HTML or RTF files, click the corresponding check box. Ignoring the style information opens the document as a plain text file, showing all the control codes and tags used to embed the original styles. This is required for editing HTML tags within a Web page.

To save your settings, close the Preferences window. To revert to the original configuration, click Revert to Default Settings.

Caution

We have had inconsistent results when changes are applied either after closing the Preferences window, or after restarting TextEdit. We recommend exiting TextEdit and relaunching to ensure that your settings become active.

Menus

The TextEdit menus provide control over fonts and other document-specific information. Most of the application preferences can be overridden on a per-document basis from the menu system.

Open, save, and print documents using the File menu, which includes the following options:

New (Command+N)—Starts a new document using the defaults set in the application preferences.

Open—Opens an existing document.

Open Recent—Opens a document recently accessed on the system.

Close (Command+W)—Closes the current document.

Save (Command+S)—Saves any changes to the current document.

Save As (Shift+Command+S)—Saves the active document in a new location or using a new name.

Save All—Saves changes to all open documents.

Revert to Saved—Discards changes in the current document, reverting to the last saved version.

Page Setup (Shift+Command+P)—Configures the printer's page settings.

Print (Command+P)—Prints the active document.

The Edit menu contains the basic copy and paste functions, along with the find and replace and spell-checking features introduced in Stickies.

The Format menu enables you to control your font settings, and text alignment. In addition, you can toggle wrapping modes, as well as rich and plain text, and hyphenation.

Font—Configures the font being used (size, kerning, color, and so on). If any of these options are confusing, check out Chapter 10, where the font system will be fully explained.

Text—Controls text alignment in the current paragraph. In addition, this submenu toggles the display of the TextEdit ruler, and enables the ruler settings to be copied and pasted between documents or paragraphs.

Make Plain/Rich Text (Shift+Command+T)—Toggles between plain text and rich text modes. Note: After a rich text document is converted to plain text, all styling information is lost.

Wrap to Page/Window—Toggles between wrapping the current window's text to the window size, or to a static page.

Allow/Disallow Hyphenation—Allowing hyphenation enables TextEdit to wrap long words using hyphens. If this option is not allowed (the default), lines are wrapped only when a space occurs.

Rulers

At the beginning of the chapter, you saw the Find/Replace and Spell Checking objects that are common in Mac OS X. The Ruler object, accessed from the Text subheading of the Format menu, is another common component.

Figure 6.45 shows a TextEdit window that includes the ruler—another common Cocoa object. Using the ruler, you can visually adjust tabs and other layout features of the active document.

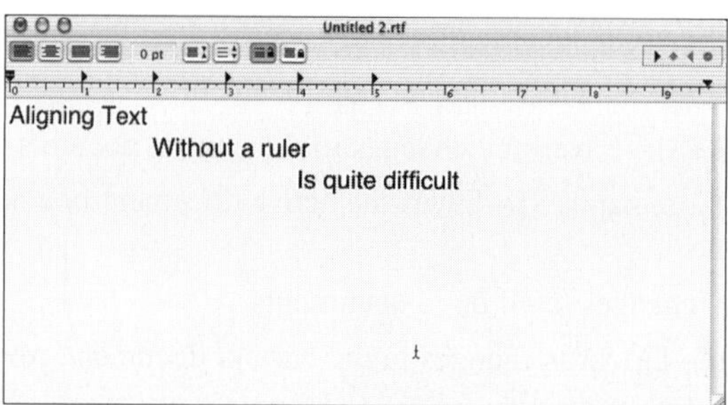

FIGURE 6.45
The ruler enables you control text alignment within the active document window.

The formatting and placement of text can be adjusted on the fly when the TextEdit ruler is active. Using the ruler, you can easily and visually change these settings:

Justification—Choose between left, center, fully justified, or right-justified text.

Line spacing—Decreases, increases, locks, or unlocks line spacing using these icons. To quickly change line spacing, click the text field to the right of the buttons and manually enter a number.

Tabs—Drags the available tabs from the tab palette to the desired location on the ruler. A readout of the current position will be shown as the object is moved.

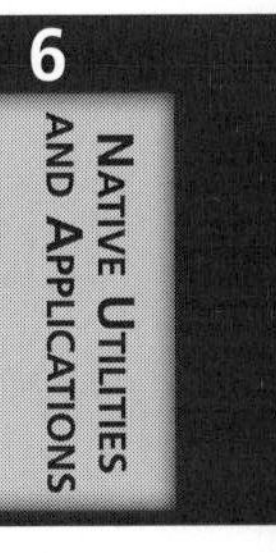

Paragraph start—Controls the cursor position when a new paragraph is started (by pressing Return).

Wrapped start—Controls the cursor position at the start of a wrapped line.

End of Line—Sets the right margin.

TextEdit is an intuitive replacement to SimpleText, but the new font configuration and Unicode text entry systems can be a bit confusing. Chapter 10's font information should shed some light on how to truly take advantage of these features.

Chess

Now for the entertainment. The first fun application is Chess (Path: `/Applications/Chess`). Microsoft includes various card games on its systems, but Apple decided to package something a bit more suited to the intellectual needs of its customers—a full-featured Chess game. Originally shipped with NeXTSTEP, Chess has been updated to work with Mac OS X and even includes support for speech recognition.

In all honesty, the underlying chess engine isn't Apple's, but that of the GNUChess, a free Chess application that has existed for the Unix platform since the mid-1980s. Apple's interface for the application, shown in Figure 6.46, is simply beautiful.

FIGURE 6.46
Chess is a GUI front end to GNUChess.

When Chess is first started, it will display a new board ready for play. Move the pieces by dragging them from their original position to the desired location. If a move is invalid, Mac OS X will play the system beep, refuse the move, and display a message in the window's title bar.

Preferences

To control the game's difficulty, or change to a computer-computer or human-human game, open the Application Preferences panel. The Chess preferences are shown in Figure 6.47.

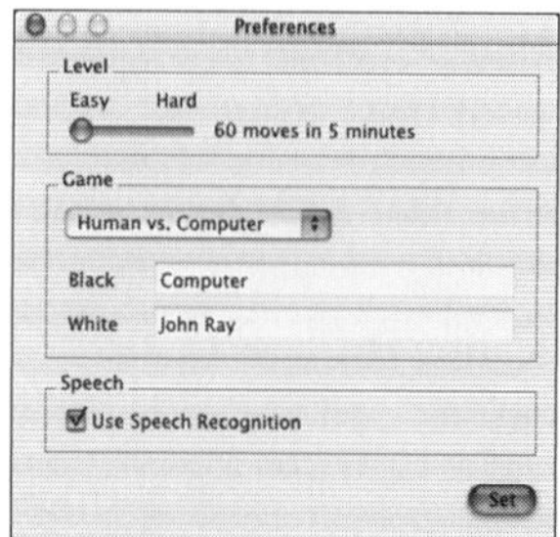

FIGURE 6.47
Control how badly you will lose using the Preferences panel.

Use Chess's preferences to control how difficult the game will be, who is playing, and whether speech recognition should be used:

Level—Use the slider to control the playing level of the computer. The harder the game, the more computation time the computer will take when making a move.

Game—Choose between human versus computer, computer versus computer, or human versus human games in the pop-up menu. You can name the players by typing their names in the black-and-white fields.

Speech—When enabled, you can use the speech recognition system built in to OS X to move your players.

Click Set to start a new game using the preferences you've chosen.

> **Note**
>
> If you're using speech recognition, be aware that Chess recognizes only a few patterns to control your pieces:
>
> `<Piece> <Square> to/takes <Square>`
>
> `Castle kingside`
>
> `Castle queenside`
>
> `Take back move`
>
> For example, `pawn b2 to b4` is a valid opening move.

A few additional preferences can be accessed by choosing the Controls option, from the File menu. Within the Controls panel, each player is represented by a chess piece and her name, as shown in Figure 6.48.

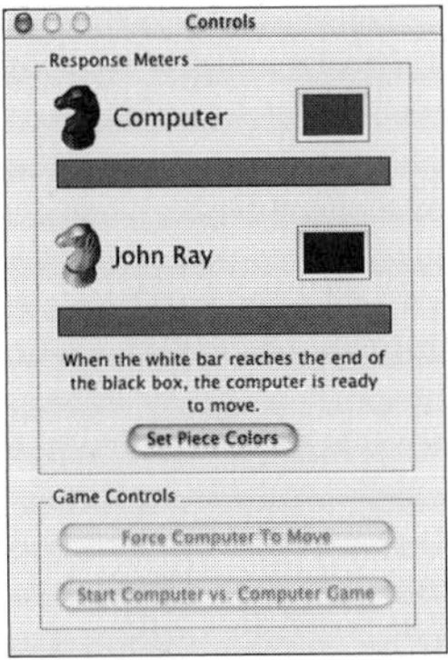

FIGURE 6.48
The Controls set some additional game preferences.

Clicking the color well to the right of the player name sets the color for that player's pieces. The color is not applied until Set Piece Color is clicked.

> **Note**
>
> The Mac OS X 10.0 and 10.1 versions of Chess do change piece colors, but not to the color you select. To pick your color, you will have to choose by trial and error until your selection appears correctly on the pieces.

Beneath each player's settings is a white progress bar. When the computer is thinking about a move, the graph will draw in (from left to right), to indicate how close the computer is to making a move. To force the computer to move before it has finished, click the Force Computer To Move button.

Finally, if you've selected a computer vs. computer game in the preferences, the game won't start until you click Start Computer vs. Computer Game in this panel.

Menus

The File menu can save or open stored games and control player colors. Options available in the File menu include

New (Command+N)—Starts a new game. The current game is discarded.

Open (Command+O)—Opens a saved game file and resumes playing.

Save (Command+S)—Saves the current game.

Save As (Shift+Command+S)—Saves the current game with a new name or in a new location.

List—Saves a text file containing a list of all moves made.

Controls—Opens a panel for setting player colors and controlling computer moves.

Print—Prints a screenshot of the current chess board.

The Move menu is used to ask for a hint, and replay or take back the last move. In a sense, the Move menu lets you cheat. The three options to choose from are

Hint (Shift+Command+H)—Shows an animated hint as to what the computer considers your best move to be.

Show Last Move (Shift+Command+M)—Shows the last move made. Useful for replaying the computer's last move while you were sleeping.

Take Back Move (Command+Z)—Takes back your last move. This can be used repeatedly to retrace your steps back to the beginning of the game.

Use the View menu to toggle between a grayscale two-dimensional representation of the board (Shift+Command+A) and the default 3D board (Shift+Command+B)

DVD Player

If you initially purchased Mac OS X with the hope of having a modern operating system that would never crash and still let you use all your hardware, you were probably slightly disappointed. One of the most visible missing features was a DVD player. The only way to play DVDs was to boot into Mac OS 9.x. Apple has fixed this shortcoming with the release of Mac OS X 10.1. Included in this new version of the operating system is DVD Player (Path: `/Applications/DVD Player`), a very-much improved version of Apple's previous DVD player application.

To start the DVD Player, simply insert a video DVD into your system, or double-click the application icon. By default, Mac OS X will launch the DVD Player automatically when it detects a new disk has been mounted. On startup, a video window and playback controller will appear onscreen. The playback controller is shown in Figure 6.49. Although I would have loved to provide a screenshot of the video window, this is not permitted with the current DVD Player application.

Use the controller window as you would a standard DVD remote. Basic playback buttons are provided, along with a selection control in the middle, and volume slider on the bottom.

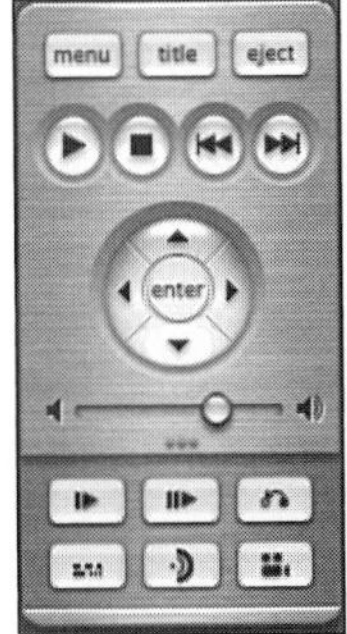

FIGURE 6.49
The DVD Player returns in Mac OS X 10.1.

Six additional advanced controls are accessible by clicking the three dots at the edge of the controller window. This opens a drawer containing Slow, Step, Return, Subtitle, Audio, and Angle buttons. In Figure 6.49, the controller window is shown with the drawer exposed. If you'd prefer a horizontally oriented player control, choose Horizontal (Shift+Command+H) from the Controller Type submenu of the Controls menu. You can switch back to the vertical layout at any time by using the Vertical (Shift+Command+V) option in the same menu.

To navigate onscreen selections without the use of the controller, you can simply point and click at a DVD menu item to select it. To navigate with the keyboard, use the arrow keys and Return key.

Preferences

The DVD Player application preferences offer a few minor modifications to the playback process and the controller. There are two panels within the preferences window: Player and Disc.

The Player panel is shown in Figure 6.50.

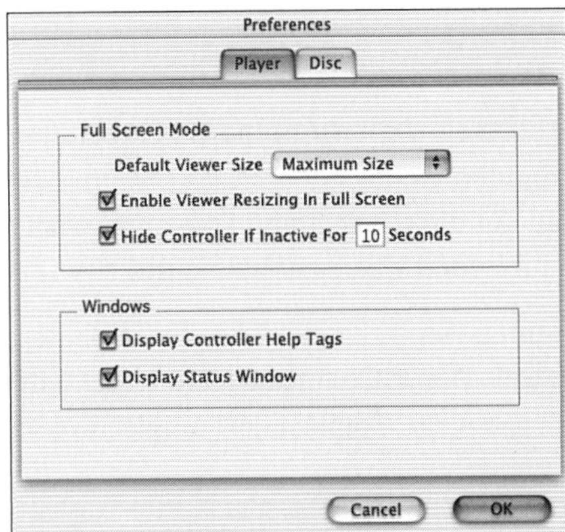

FIGURE 6.50
Adjust how the video and controller appear onscreen.

Using the pop-up menu within the Player panel, you can choose the default size of the playback area when in full-screen mode. You can also choose to enable resizing of the viewer and have the application automatically hide the DVD controller when it hasn't been used for a specified amount of time.

The Disc panel, shown in Figure 6.51, sets options that apply to the DVD itself.

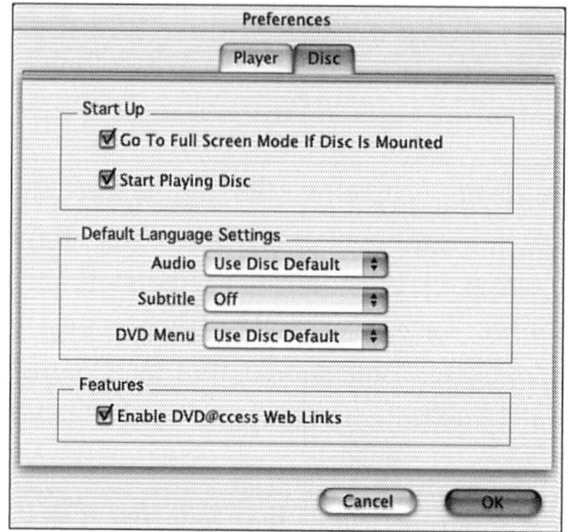

FIGURE 6.51
The Disc panel controls basic playback options.

By default, the DVD Player will start when a DVD is inserted. To control whether the computer will go into full-screen mode and immediately start playing the movie, use the Start Up options in this panel. The Language settings control the default language used for audio, subtitles, and menus. Not all languages are available for all disks, so don't assume any of the choices given is always valid.

Finally, some DVDs include DVD@ccess Web links. These are embedded hot spots that link to Internet web sites. To enable the DVD Player to recognize and react to these links, check the Enable DVD@ccess Web Links check box.

Menus

The DVD Player menus feature controls for most of the DVD features. Although many of these functions are found within the graphical controller, the menu offers the advantage of having keyboard shortcuts for almost anything you could want to do. This, coupled with a remote control, can turn your Macintosh into a true DVD playback system.

The Video menu shifts between three video sizes and toggles in and out of full-screen mode. Use Command+1, Command+2, and Command+3 to select half size, normal, and maximum size viewing areas, respectively. Command+0 toggles in and out of full-screen mode.

Tip

Moving the cursor to the top of the screen when in full-screen mode will reveal the hidden menu bar.

The Controls menu is used to start, stop, and navigate during playback. The following options are available:

Controller Type—Choose horizontal (Shift+Command+H) or vertical (Shift+Command+V) orientation.

Scan Rate—When fast forwarding or rewinding, the view is displayed at an accelerated rate. Use this menu to set the speed from two to eight times faster than normal.

Play/Pause (Spacebar)—Play or pause the video.

Fast Forward— (Command+Right arrow) Speed through the video playback.

Rewind (Command+Left arrow)—Move backwards through the video playback.

Previous Chapter (Right-arrow)—Skip to the next chapter on the DVD.

Next Chapter (Left arrow)—Skip to the previous chapter on the DVD.

DVD Menu (Command+`)—Stop playback and load the menu for the active DVD.

Volume Up (Command+Up arrow)—Increase the volume.

Volume Down (Command+Down arrow)—Decrease the volume.

Mute (Command+K)—Mute the sound.

Eject (Command+E)—Eject the current DVD.

The Window menu offers the ability to hide each of the DVD Player windows individually as well as display information (Control+I) about the disk, time remaining, and so on.

Help Center

As you've probably noticed by now, many applications include built-in documentation under a Help menu. The Mac OS X Help Viewer provides a simple browser-like interface that any application can use. For example, the basic Finder Help is shown in Figure 6.52.

To locate specific information, type a few keywords, such as `displaying PDFs` into the field at the top of the window, and then click Ask. A few seconds later, the Help Center application will display all matching documents that it found, along with a relevance rating and the guide that it was in.

FIGURE 6.52
The Help system works exactly like a Web browser.

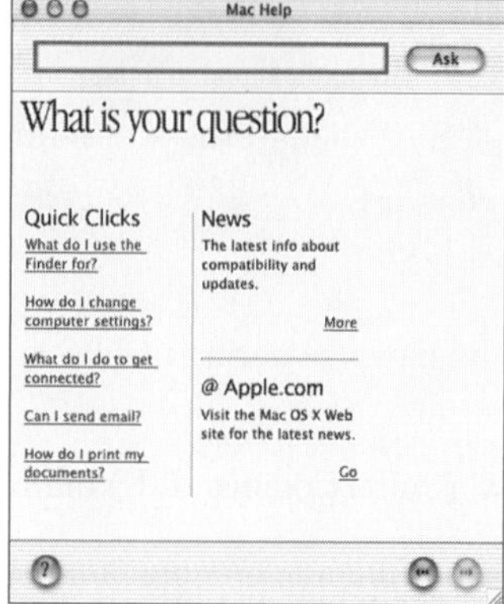

Click the blue hyperlinks in the Help Window to open the corresponding documents. The forward and back arrows at the bottom of the window move you forward and backward through the pages you've viewed.

Note

The forward arrow does not move you to the next page—it operates only on the history of pages you've seen. Look for a next hyperlink or graphic to move to another page within a help document.

Click the ? button in the lower-left corner of the window to view all the Help guides that are currently installed. This will display an index of installed guides.

Tip

The guide index is generated by aliases to individual applications HTML help folders that are placed in `~/Library/Documentation/Help`. You can copy these aliases to the system-wide `/Library/Documentation/Help` directory to make them available to all users, or delete them if you don't want the help guide to appear in the list.

Unfortunately, the Mac OS X Help system is extremely sparse. This can only improve with time, but currently the Help system is implemented in only certain applications and often doesn't include detailed usage instructions. That's why you need this book!

Summary

Mac OS X includes a wealth of applications and utilities ranging from the simple (but not so simple!) Stickies to a full-featured, voice-controlled Chess application. Similar to the original Mac OS, the experience of using one application applies to the next, and so on. The OS X system-level spell checking and font controls lend a familiar look and feel to any application that uses them.

Although much of the available software was covered in this chapter, there is still more to go. Chapter 7 takes a look at the Internet applications that make OS X an excellent e-mail and Web surfing platform.

CHAPTER 7

Internet Communications

In This Chapter

The Mac OS has long been the leader in network connectivity among desktop operating systems. The Macintosh was using MacTCP and Open Transport while Windows 3.1 struggled to get online using third-party TCP stacks and DOS-based network card drivers. Although the playing field has mostly leveled, it's little surprise that Mac OS X includes a wide variety of Internet-related tools. Users who are interested in getting online, finding old friends, listening to Internet radio, viewing streaming video, sending e-mail, and surfing the Internet will be happy to find a large number of applications to get them online in a matter of minutes.

Internet Software

Mac OS X comes with a number of network-enabled programs. This chapter covers six applications that work specifically with the Internet to gather information, messages, and make your online life easier:

Mail—(Path: `/Applications/Mail`)—Apple's first e-mail offering since the delightful (and deceased) Cyberdog project (unless you count Claris Emailer). This e-mail application features IMAP/POP3 support, HTML/RTF e-mail, dynamic filtering, and a frightfully modern interface.

Address Book—(Path: `/Applications/Address Book`)—A companion application to Mail, the Address Book stores contact data, including images. Address Book can also query LDAP servers to locate addresses.

Sherlock—(Path: `/Applications/Sherlock`)—Sherlock allows both local (disk) searches as well as multi-search engine queries on popular e-commerce, news, and entertainment sites.

QuickTime Player—(Path: `/Applications/QuickTime Player`)—The QuickTime Player provides access to digital media, either on your local drives or streamed via the Internet. QuickTime is more than just movies—it's MP3 files, WAV files, images, and interactive applications.

iTunes—(Path: `/Applications/iTunes`)—Introduced in early 2000, iTunes can tune hundreds of Internet radio stations. For those with MP3 collections, iTunes can be used to rip songs from CDs, connect to MP3 players, and burn your own music CDs.

Keychain Access—(Path: `/Applications/Utilities/Keychain Access`)—Keychain Access is both an application and an API that users and programmers can employ to store system passwords and other information. Keychain Access encrypts all stored data within a file called a keychain and provides easy global access to it by unlocking the keychain when needed.

> **Note**
>
> The iTunes application does not ship with the original Mac OS X 10.0 CD distribution. If you are using 10.0, you can download iTunes from Apple's Web site, or through the Software Update System Preference Panel.
>
> In addition, be sure to update to at least Mac OS X 10.02 to gain access to the CD burning capabilities of iTunes.
>
> Mac OS X 10.1 includes both of these features built-in. Upgrade if you haven't already!

As with the previous chapters, the applications in this chapter will be presented with basic use information, followed by configuration and menu options. The goal is to provide information for beginners as well as useful reference for advanced users.

Mail

During the Mac OS X setup procedure (see Chapter 2, "Installing Mac OS X"), the installer prompts for a default e-mail account. Although this creates a single account for a single person, additional users and multiple accounts must be configured with Mail itself. For many people, the first task will be setting up a new account—this provides a perfect place to start.

Setup

Using Mail for the first time on a new user account opens a setup window to configure a new e-mail account, as shown in Figure 7.1.

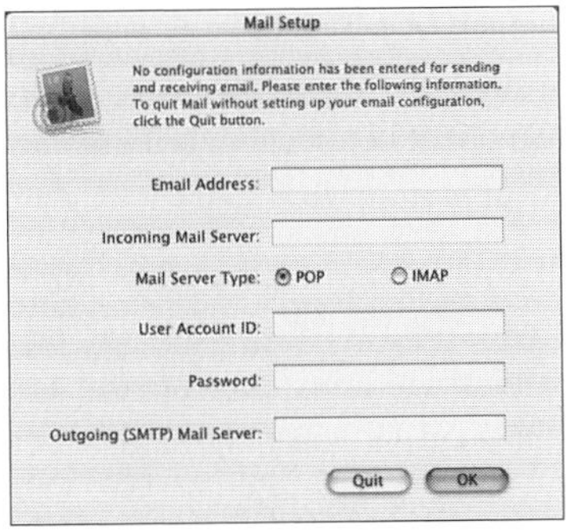

FIGURE 7.1
The first time Mail is run, it forces an e-mail account to be configured.

There are six pieces of information required to set up an e-mail account:

- **Email Address**—Your e-mail address (for example, `johnray@mac.com`).
- **Incoming Mail Server**—The server that stores your e-mail. If you're using an iTools account, use `mail.mac.com`.
- **Mail Server Type**—Most ISPs support the POP3 protocol for accessing e-mail. Apple's iTools servers include support for IMAP. Read further for more information on both protocols and their differences.
- **User Account ID**—The username used to access an e-mail account. This is typically the text that comes before the `@` in your e-mail address (that is, `johnray` is the account ID for `johnray@mac.com`).
- **Password**—The password required to retrieve mail. Leaving this field blank will prompt the user to enter the password when needed.
- **Outgoing (SMTP) Mail Server**—The server required to send messages. Users of iTools e-mail accounts can use `smtp.mac.com`.

If you are unsure of *any* of these fields, you should contact your ISP or network administrator. *Do not* attempt to use the `mac.com` hostnames unless you are using an iTools e-mail address—these are members-only servers and will deny access to those without an account.

POP3 Versus IMAP

If your e-mail provider supports both the POP3 and IMAP protocols, you're in luck! The POP3 protocol, although extremely popular, is not practical for people with multiple computers. I access the same e-mail account from a number of different computers—one at work, one at home, and another while on the road. Keeping all these machines in sync is virtually impossible with POP3.

POP3 (Post Office Protocol v.3) works much like it sounds: E-mail is "popped" from a remote server. Incoming messages are stored on the remote server, which in turn waits for a connection from a POP3 client. The client connects only long enough to download all the messages and save them to the local hard drive.

In this scenario, the server stores e-mail temporarily and handles short-lived connections—the burden of long-term storage and filing rests squarely on the shoulders of the client application. Unfortunately, after a message transfers from the server, it's gone. If you go to another computer to check your mail, it won't be there.

The more computers you use, the more fragmented your messages become. Some provisions exist for keeping messages on the server, but in reality it's a hassle and rarely works as planned. Although the same message can be downloaded to multiple machines, deleting it from one machine won't delete it from the others. The end result is, quite frankly, a mess!

IMAP takes a different approach. Rather than relying on the client for message storage, IMAP servers keep everything on the server. Messages and mail folders remain on the server unless explicitly deleted by the client. When new messages arrive, the IMAP client application downloads either the message body or header from the server, but the server contents remain the same. If multiple computers are configured to access the same e-mail account, the e-mail will appear identical between the machines—the same folders, messages, and message flags are maintained. In addition, the IMAP protocol supports shared folders between different user accounts and server-based content searches.

The drawback to IMAP lies mostly on the e-mail provider—supporting the additional features of IMAP and the added storage costs is often uneconomical on a large scale. If your ISP does not support IMAP, sign up for an iTools account. Apple's POP and IMAP service is fast, reliable, and free.

Adding Multiple Accounts

Mail supports multiple e-mail accounts for a single user. After setting up the initial account, you can add other e-mail accounts through the Accounts pane of the Application Preferences panel. Choose Preferences from the application menu; then click the Accounts icon. Figure 7.2 shows the Accounts pane of the Preference panel. Existing e-mail accounts are listed on the left.

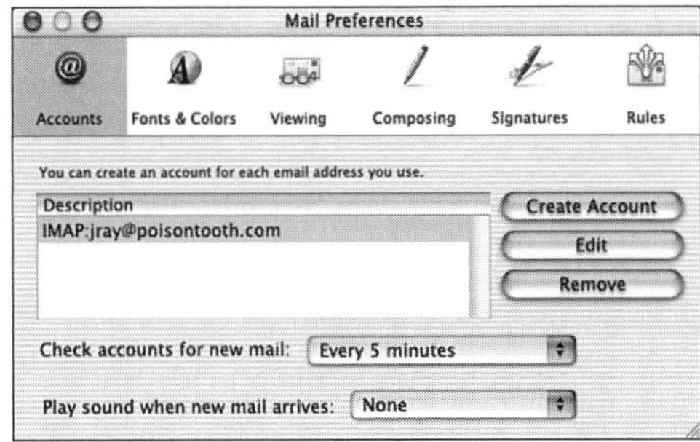

FIGURE 7.2
Multiple e-mail accounts can be added through the application preferences.

The options available in the Accounts pane of the Mail Preferences panel include

- **Create Account**—Add a new e-mail account.
- **Edit**—Edit the selected account.

- **Remove**—Delete the selected account.
- **Check accounts for new mail**—Change the frequency with which *all* the e-mail accounts will be polled.
- **Play sound when new mail arrives**—Select a sound that will be played when new messages arrive on the server. Pick Other to choose a sound file (AIFF) from your drive.

To add a new account to the list, click the Create Account button. An account information sheet will appear. This information sheet is divided into two tabs: Account Information and Account Options. The general Account Information tab can be seen in Figure 7.3.

FIGURE 7.3
Enter the new e-mail account information into this panel.

Use the Account-Type pop-up menu to set the account type; then fill in the fields as you did when creating the initial account during the install process. Instead of just IMAP or POP accounts, there are four options:

Mac.com Account—Configures a Mac.com IMAP account with the appropriate Apple defaults.

POP Account—Creates a basic POP3 account.

IMAP Account—Creates a basic IMAP account.

Unix Account—Assumes that the host computer (your Mac OS X machine) will be acting as a mail server and mail will be retrieved from a local mail spool field rather than over the Internet.

Note

If you are using Unix Account as your account type, many of the server lines will be disabled. Because this option assumes that your e-mail is located on the same computer as the e-mail reader, the reasons for this should be obvious.

To learn how to set up your own e-mail server, check out Chapter 29, "Creating a Mail Server."

Tip

If you have multiple e-mail return addresses and you want to be able to choose which address shows up in the From field on the final message, enter multiple addresses in the Email Address field on the Account Information panel. This will add a pop-up menu to the message composition window where you can choose from the listed addresses.

Near the bottom of the Account Information display are options for setting up Authenticated SMTP services. To connect using authenticated SMTP, click the Use authentication when sending mail check box, and then fill out the SMTP user and password fields.

What Is Authenticated SMTP?

The original SMTP protocol requires no authentication to send a message. Anyone could use any SMTP server to send any message (the origin of spam). Over time, servers developed advanced techniques to prohibit unauthorized use of the SMTP protocol, such as blocking by subnet or allowing users who have successfully checked mail to send mail from their IP address for a certain length of time.

This works, but it places some unreasonable restrictions on the user. Luckily, extensions have been made to the SMTP protocol that allow a username and password to be transmitted to the SMTP server when a connection is made. The server can then authenticate the user and allow unfettered access regardless of where or how the user is connecting.

Click the Account Options tab to fine-tune your account settings. Depending on the account type that you've chosen, the available options will change. Figure 7.4 displays the option panel for IMAP (or Mac.com) accounts.

Figure 7.4
Each type of e-mail account has different available options.

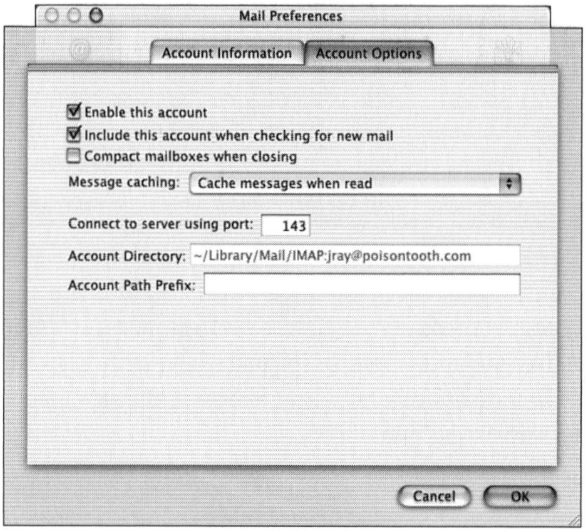

Each of the different mail account types has different available options under Account Options. Choices available on the Account Options tab when using IMAP include:

Enable this account—Includes the account in the available account listing. If not enabled, it is ignored.

Include this account when checking for new mail—If selected, the account will be polled for new messages at the interval set on the Preferences' Account panel. If not, the account will be polled only when the user manually checks his mail.

Compact mailboxes when closing—Cleans up the local mailbox files when exiting Mail. The benefit of using this is very slight and it can slow down the system when dealing with very large mailbox files.

Message caching—After a message is received on the server, the IMAP client has the option of immediately caching the text of the message on the local machine (cache all messages locally), caching read messages (cache messages when read), or never caching messages on the local drive (don't cache any messages).

Connect to server using port—The default IMAP port is `143`. If your server uses a different access port, enter it here.

Account Directory—The local directory where the Mail application stores your messages.

Account Path Prefix—The IMAP prefix required to access your mailbox. This field is normally left blank unless a value is specified by your mail server administrator.

Note

The default account directories are stored in `~/Library/Mail`. Unfortunately, the messages are not stored in a flat Unix mbox format, so command-line applications like Mail will not be able to read downloaded messages.

If you are using a POP account, you can control how messages are retrieved and when they are deleted from your account, among other things:

Enable this account—Include the account in the available account listing. If not enabled, it is ignored.

Include this account when checking for new mail—If selected, the account will be polled for new messages at the interval set on the Mail Preferences Account pane. If not, the account will be polled only when the user manually checks his mail.

Delete messages on server after downloading—When checked, the messages will be removed from the server. This is the default behavior for POP3 clients. Uncheck to leave e-mail on the server.

Show this account separately in mailboxes drawer—Rather than downloading into a user determined mailbox folder, a separate account entry and Inbox will be added to the Mail account drawer. (Remember, you can always edit these options if you don't like this arrangement.)

Download messages from this account into folder—Alternatively, Mail can download messages into a personal mailbox located at the top level of your Mail account drawer. Choose the folder from the pop-up menu list.

Prompt me to skip messages over # KB—Automatically skips messages that are over a set number of kilobytes. This is useful for keeping attachments from being downloaded.

Connect to server using port—The default POP server port is `110`. If your server uses a different port, enter it here.

Account Directory—The local directory where the Mail application stores your messages.

Tip

When using the "Download messages from this account into folder" option, you can choose from network-based IMAP folders as well. Using this technique, you can transparently transfer POP-based messages into a networked IMAP account.

Finally, users who are configuring a Unix-style mailbox can choose from these available settings:

Enable this account—Includes the account in the available account listing. If not enabled, it is ignored.

Include this account when checking for new mail—If selected, the account will be polled for new messages at the interval set on the Mail Preferences Account pane. If not, the account will be polled only when the user manually checks his mail.

Incoming mail directory—The directory where the Mac OS X mail server is storing messages. The default directory is `/var/mail`.

Account Directory—The local directory where the Mail application stores your messages.

After setting your account information and options, click OK to start using Mail.

The Mail Interface

Mail uses the special Mac OS X interface elements to create a unique and streamlined user experience. Figure 7.5 shows the Mail application, ready for action.

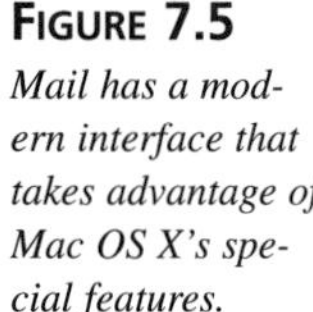

FIGURE 7.5
Mail has a modern interface that takes advantage of Mac OS X's special features.

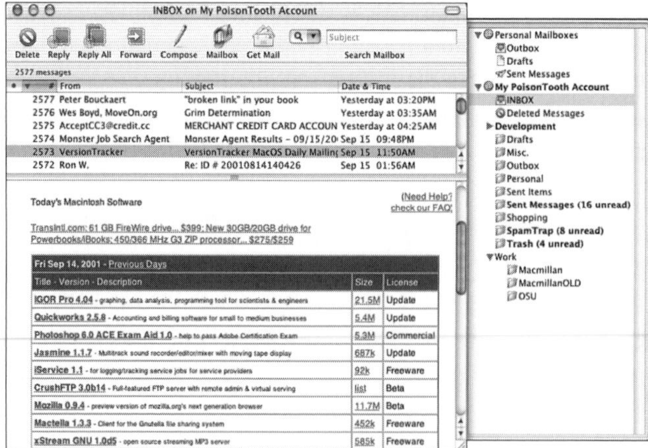

Note

If Mail opens to a screen asking for keychain access, click Allow Once, to continue. The keychain stores multiple passwords under a single master password. This allows you to unlock many resources just by remembering a single password.

This message might appear on recently upgraded systems, or if changes are made to the Mail application. It is not an error.

If you've used an e-mail program such as Eudora or Outlook Express, you'll be completely comfortable with Mail's interface. The toolbar at the top of the window holds commonly used functions for creating, responding to, and searching for messages.

Reading and Filing

In the center of the window is a list of the active messages in each mailbox. The list columns (from left to right) display read/unread status, the number of the message received, sender, subject, and day/time sent. As with most list views, the columns can be sorted by clicking their headings.

Tip

Sorting by the message number is the best way to keep track of new messages as they come in. If a client includes incorrect time or time zone information when sending a message, it will likely be sorted incorrectly when you use Date and Time as the sort field.

If a message in the list is highlighted, the bottom of the window contains a condensed view of the message headers along with the message content. To open a message in a separate window, double-click its list entry.

To display the accounts and mail folders that have been added to the system, click the Mailbox toolbar button, or choose Show Mailboxes (Shift+Command+M) from the View menu. The mailbox drawer slides out from the side of the mail window. You can use the disclosure arrows to collapse and expand the hierarchy of mail folders. The number of unread messages is displayed in parentheses to the right of each mailbox.

Note

The Mail icon displays the total number of unread messages in all the Inbox folders. Unfortunately, there is currently no way to change the mailboxes it monitors for the unread count.

To file a message, click and drag it from the list view to the folder into which you want to transfer the message. If the mailbox drawer isn't open, it will automatically pop open as the mouse approaches the edge of the window. Alternatively, you can use the Transfer option from the Message menu. Control-clicking or right-clicking a line in the message opens a contextual menu from which Transfer can also be accessed.

Pressing the Delete key, or choosing Delete from the Message menu, will remove the active message or selected group of messages from the listing. Deleted messages are not immediately removed from the system; they are transferred to a Trash folder. What happens from there can be configured from the Viewing pane of the Mail Preferences panel.

Toolbar Options

Like the Finder, the Mail application supports toolbar customization. The customization process is identical, For more information, see Chapter 4, "The Finder: Working with Fields and Applications." Open the customization sheet by choosing Customize Toolbar from the View menu. Figure 7.6 shows the available customizations.

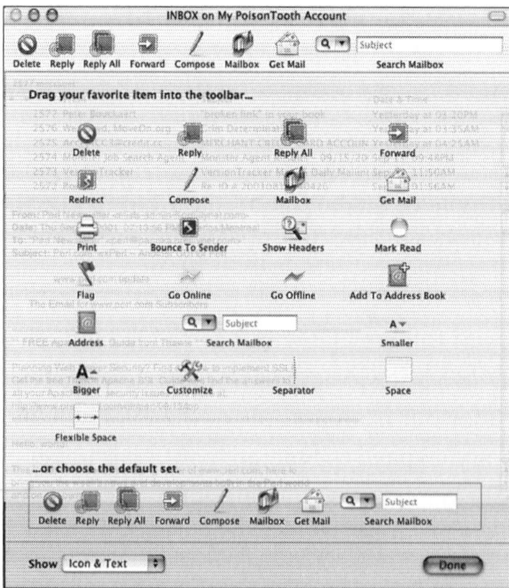

FIGURE 7.6
Customize the mail toolbar with your favorite shortcuts.

From the top left to bottom right, the available shortcuts are:

Delete—Delete the selected message(s).

Reply—Reply to the author of the current message.

Reply All—Reply to all recipients of the current message.

Forward—Forward the current message (and its attachments) to additional recipients.

Redirect—Redirect the selected message; does not quote the original message's text.

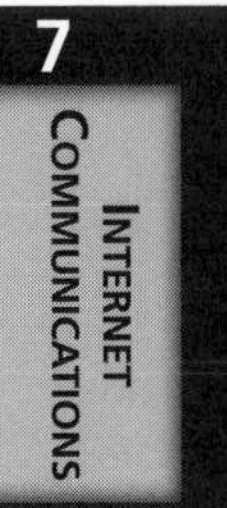

Compose—Type a new message.

Mailbox—Open the Mailbox panel.

Get Mail—Retrieve new messages from available accounts.

Print—Send the active message to the printer.

Bounce To Sender—Bounce the selected message. To the original sender, it appears that the message never reached you! Useful for getting rid of spam. The original message is automatically removed after bouncing.

Show Headers—Display all the message headers, including the relay path in the message body.

Mark Read—Toggle the read/unread state on a message.

Flag—Toggle the flagged/unflagged state message.

Go Online—Take the active e-mail account offline. No further attempts to connect to the server will be made while in this mode.

Go Offline—Take an offline e-mail account back online.

Add To Address Book—Add the sender of the selected message to the Address Book application.

Address—Open the Address Book application.

Search Mailbox—Search the open mailbox's To, From, or Subject field by choosing it from the pop-up menu, and then entering the search text in the field.

Smaller—Shrink the text size in the open message.

Bigger—Enlarge the text in the open message.

Customize—Customize the toolbar.

Separator—Add a vertical separator bar to the toolbar. This is for visual purposes only.

Space—Add an icon-sized space to the toolbar.

Flexible Space—Add a space to the toolbar that grows and shrinks with the size of the window.

Default Set—Reset to the default set of toolbar icons.

Show—Use this pop-up menu to choose between Icon, Text & Icon, or Text-only toolbar modes. Command+clicking the toolbar button cycles through these modes.

Click Done to save the changes to the toolbar.

> **Tip**
>
> When a message is opened in its own window by double-clicking in the message list, that toolbar can also be customized. The only difference is that shortcuts related to the message list and mailboxes are not included in the toolbar customization choices.

Composing Messages

To write an e-mail, click the Compose button or choose New Compose Window (Command+N) from the File menu. To reply to an existing message, select that message in the list view; then click Reply to start a new message or choose Reply to Sender (Command+R) from the Message menu. The composition window appears, as in Figure 7.7.

FIGURE 7.7 *Mail supports styled messages and drag-and-drop attachments.*

Three fields are provided for addressing the message. Use the To line for single or multiple addresses that serve as the primary recipients of the message. A comma should separate multiple addresses. The CC: line adds additional recipients who are not part of the main list. The primary recipients will be able to see these addresses. The Subject line is used to show the subject or the title of the e-mail.

Additional fields are accessible from the Message menu. Choose Add Bcc Header (Shift+Command+B) to add a Bcc header, or Add Reply-To Header (Option+Command+R) to add an alternative reply address. A Bcc (Blind Carbon Copy) works like a normal carbon copy, but does not allow the recipients to view each other's e-mail address or name. The Reply-To header is used to provide an alternative address for replying. For example, if I'm sending e-mail from my `jray@poisontooth.com` account and want replies to go to `johnray@mac.com` instead, I'd enter the Mac.com address in the Reply-To Header field.

To access a list of addresses, click the Address button in the toolbar and the Address Book application will launch. From the Address Book window, you can drag individual addresses, or multiple addresses, to the To/Cc/Bcc fields in the message composition window. Alternatively, highlight the desired addresses in the Address Book listing, and then click the Address Book's Send Mail button to open a new message addressed to the selected individuals. You'll learn more about the Address Book in the next section of this chapter.

To create the message itself, input the text into the content area of the window. The toolbar can be used to attach files or pick fonts and colors. You can also drag images and files directly into the message. Depending on the type of file, it will be added to the message as an icon (application, archive, and so on) or shown within the body (picture, movie).

Be aware that to receive rich-text e-mail, the remote user must have a modern e-mail program such as Outlook Express (or, better yet, Mail!). To create a message that anyone can receive, compose the content in Plain Text mode, selectable in the Format menu.

To send, click Send in the toolbar, or choose Send Message (Shift+Command+D) from the Message menu.

Toolbar Options

The message composition window can be customized just like the main mailbox view. When writing a message, choose Customize Toolbar from the View menu. The customizations are shown in Figure 7.8.

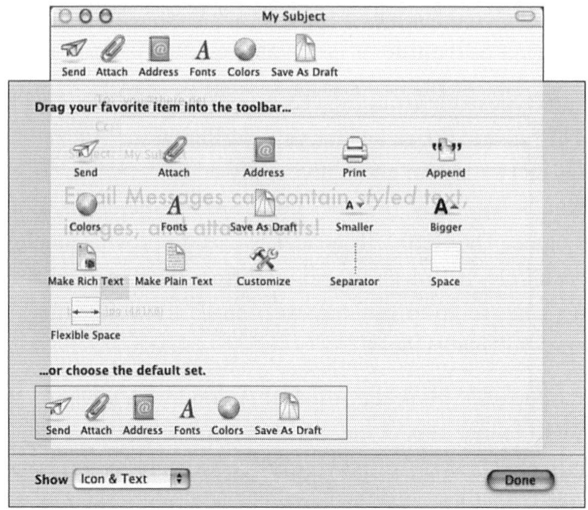

FIGURE 7.8
Customize the Compose toolbar with your favorite shortcuts.

From the top left to bottom right, the available shortcuts are:

Send—Send the current message.

Attach—Choose a file to attach to the current message.

Address—Open the Address Book application.

Print—Print the open window.

Append—Append the messages selected in the mailbox view to the contents of the current message.

Colors—Open the Colors panel.

Fonts—Open the Fonts panel.

Save As Draft—Save the message to the `Drafts` folder; it is *not* sent.

Smaller—Shrink the text size in the open message.

Bigger—Enlarge the text in the open message.

Make Rich Text—Toggle the current message to rich text mode.

Make Plain Text—Toggle the current message to plain text mode. Note that doing this removes all message formatting.

Customize—Customize the toolbar.

Separator—Add a vertical separator bar to the toolbar. This is for visual purposes only.

Space—Add an icon-sized space to the toolbar.

Flexible Space—Add a space to the toolbar that grows and shrinks with the size of the window.

Default Set—Reset to the default set of toolbar icons.

Show—Use this pop-up menu to choose between Icon, Text & Icon, or Text-only toolbar modes. Command+clicking the toolbar button cycles through these modes.

Click Done to save the changes to the toolbar.

Preferences

Mail's preference panels contain many of the hidden features of the program—including signatures and mailbox filters. Open the preference panel by choosing Preferences from the Application menu. The Accounts panel was covered earlier and will not be repeated here.

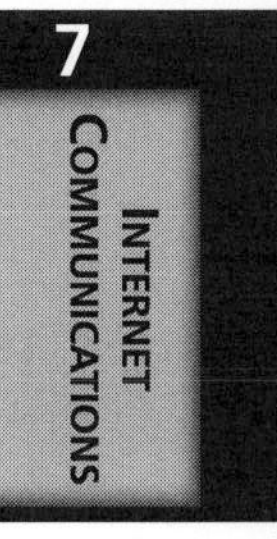

Fonts and Colors

The Fonts & Colors panel controls the default fonts that are used in the message list and message bodies. This panel is shown in Figure 7.9.

FIGURE 7.9
Choose the default message fonts and quote colors.

Options in the Font & Colors panel include

Message list font—Choose the Font and Size used in the listing of active messages.

Message font—Choose the Font and Size used in the body of messages.

Used fixed-width font for plain text messages—If checked, the system will use a monospaced ("typewriter") font for unstyled messages.

Plain text font—The font to use for plain text messages.

Color quoted text—Text included when replying is automatically quoted. If there are multiple levels of replies, each level can be set to a different color.

Tip

Using a fixed-width font is recommended for plain text messages. Many plain text messages are formatted using spaces for positioning elements—using a proportional font will result in a skewed or sometimes unreadable display.

Viewing

The Viewing preferences control what happens to deleted messages, the amount of header detail that should be displayed, and the downloading of attachments. The Viewing preference panel is shown in Figure 7.10.

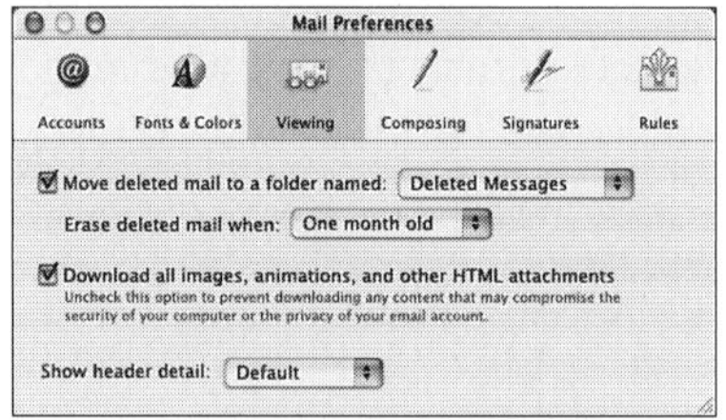

FIGURE 7.10
Control where deleted messages go before they die.

Options in the Viewing panel include

Move deleted mail to a folder—If checked (default), deleted messages are moved to a folder, chosen from the pop-up menu.

Erase deleted mail when—Choose the frequency with which deleted messages are removed from the system.

Download all images, animations, and other HTML attachments—If checked, HTML messages will download all embedded images, JavaScript, and so on, which can present a security risk.

Show header detail—By default, only a few headers (From, Date, To, Subject) are shown. Using this pop-up menu, you can choose to hide all headers, show everything, or create a custom list of headers.

Although not obvious in the settings, the deleted message folder, if using an IMAP account, *is* stored in a network folder. You can undelete a message while it is in this folder by dragging it to another folder, or choosing Undelete (Shift+Command+U) from the Message menu.

Composing

Choose where your message drafts and sent mail are saved. The Composing preference panel includes a variety of esoteric settings, displayed in Figure 7.11.

FIGURE 7.11
Choose the location for draft messages, spell checking, network address lookup, and reply options.

Options in the Composing panel include

Save unsent mail in—Choose a folder (local or network based) to store message drafts.

Save sent mail in—Choose a folder (local or network based) to store mail that has been already sent.

Default message format—Select between Rich Text and Plain Text as the default new message format. If you are communicating with a wide variety of people on unknown operating systems, it's best to stick to plain text.

Check spelling as I type—When checked, misspelled words will be underlined in red in the message composition window. Control-click (or right-click) the word to display a list of suggestions.

List private group members individually—If including a group from the Address Book application and this option is checked, the members of the group will be listed in the message header separately.

Lookup addresses in network directories—LDAP directories are supported directly within the mail application; use the Edit Server List to add an LDAP server.

Use the same format as original message—When replying to messages, use the same format (rich/plain) in the reply.

Always CC myself—If checked, you will receive a copy of any reply you send.

Include the original message—When replying, include the contents of the original message in the reply. The original message will be quoted.

Although the Address Book sports a fancy LDAP search interface, you can perform basic searches from within Mail. Clicking the Edit Server List button will open the LDAP server entry sheet, shown in Figure 7.12.

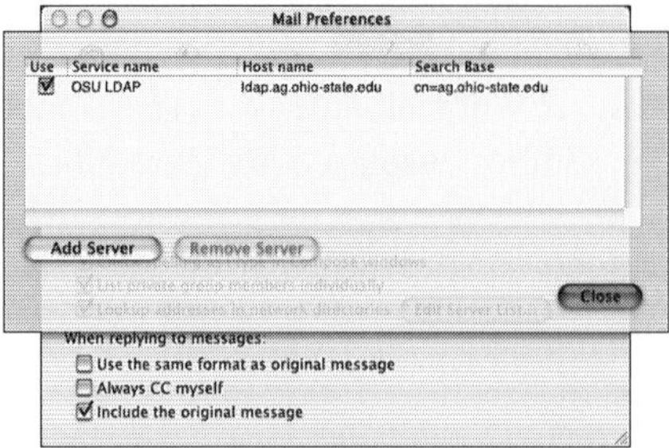

FIGURE 7.12
LDAP servers allow searching directly from the Mail application.

Click Add Server to add a new server to the list. Fill in the service name, host name, and search base for the server. To activate the server, make sure that there is a check mark in the Use check box.

Note

You can learn more about LDAP in the Address Book discussion later in this chapter.

Signatures

Everyone needs a signature—something to identify them as individuals or at least to tell others who you are! The Mail application handles multiple different signatures with ease. The Signatures panel is shown in Figure 7.13. The available signatures are listed on the left side of the panel.

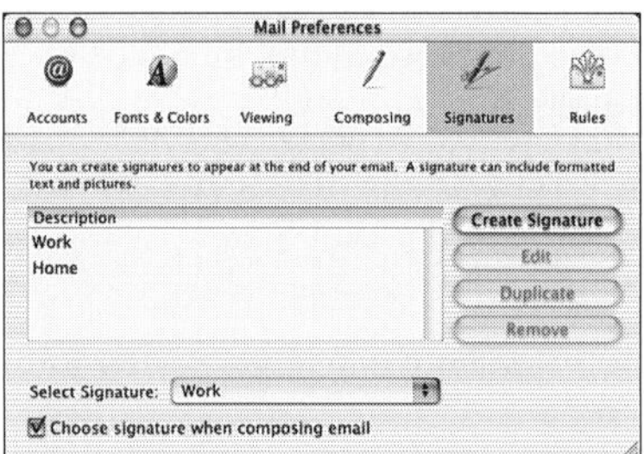

FIGURE 7.13
Create multiple signatures within the Mail application.

Options in the Signatures panel include

Create Signature—Create a new signature file. A text-entry panel will appear to type or paste a new signature. If you paste in a rich-text clipping, click the Make Plain Text button to convert it to plain text.

Edit—Edit an existing signature.

Duplicate—Duplicate an existing signature.

Remove—Delete a signature.

Select Signature—Choose the signature you want to use by default.

Choose signature when composing email—If checked, a Signature pop-up menu is added to the message composition window. From this pop-up, you can add all of the stored signatures.

Rules

Rules (filters) can perform actions on incoming messages, such as highlighting them in the message listing, moving them to other folders, or playing special sounds. The rules panel is shown in Figure 7.14.

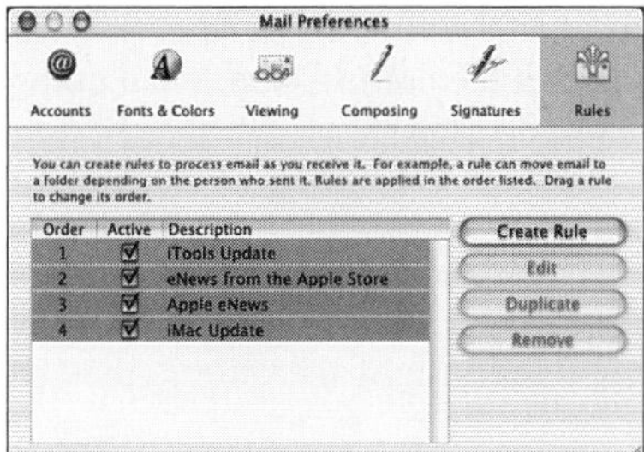

FIGURE 7.14
Rules can automate the process of going through your messages.

Each rule in the list is evaluated once per incoming message (unless the Active box is unchecked). In fact, multiple rules can act on a single message. To change the order in which the rules are applied, drag rule entries in the list to the order you want.

> **Note**
>
> Apple includes four default rules for dealing with Apple mailings. If you aren't subscribed to any Apple lists (or if you *are* and don't want them to be highlighted), you can delete these rules.

There are four options for manipulating the rule list: Create Rule, Edit, Duplicate, and Remove. The function of each option is self-explanatory.

Rule creation is simple. Each rule is a single step that looks at portions of the incoming message to determine how to react. Figure 7.15 demonstrates the rule creation process.

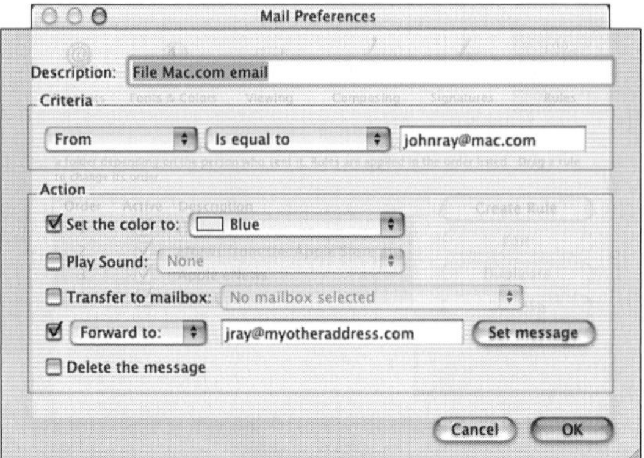

Figure 7.15
Unlike other e-mail programs, Mail's rules are simple to create.

When creating a new rule, first enter a description—this will be used to identify the rule in the listing. Next, decide on the criteria that must match the incoming message. The search criteria are the header field to use in the comparison, what comparison to use (contains, begins with, and so on), and the text to look for.

For example, to match a message from my mac.com account, I'd use From, Is equal to, and `johnray@mac.com`.

To finish the rule, set the action(s) that should run if the criteria match:

Set the color—Set the highlight color for the message.

Play Sound—Play a system (or custom AIFF) beep sound.

Transfer to mailbox—Transfer the message into one of your system mailboxes.

Forward/Redirect/Reply message to—Send the message to another e-mail address. Click the Set Message button to enter text that will be included with the message being sent.

Delete the message—Delete the message. Useful for automatically getting rid of common spam messages.

Click OK to set and activate the rule.

Menus

Wrapping up our Mail application overview, we'll look at the menu options. Most of these options have already been covered somewhere in the chapter, but there are a few obscure options you may be interested in.

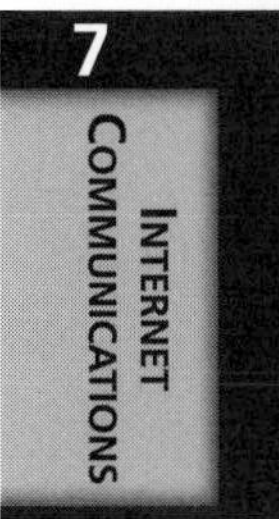

File

The File menu is used to create a new message, or multiple "views" into your mailboxes. It can also be used to save a message as a draft before sending.

New Message (Command+N)—Create a new message.

New Viewer Window (Option+Command+N)—Open another mailbox viewer. The main Mail window is called the Viewer window.

Close—Close the frontmost window.

Save As (Shift+Command+S)—Save the current message in an external file.

Save As Draft (Command+S)—Save the current message as a draft.

Restore From Draft—Restore a message from the saved draft.

Import Mailboxes—Launch an assistant to import mailbox files from Outlook Express, Netscape, Emailer, or other applications.

Page Setup (Shift+Command+P)—Configure the printer.

Print (Command+P)—Print the frontmost document.

Edit

The Edit menu performs as one would expect. Besides the usual Paste selection, it also offers the ability to Paste as Quotation, automatically quoting the text in the clipboard. The menu also includes spell checking and search-and-replace options. Please see Chapter 6's review of Stickies for more information on these common features.

View

The View menu changes the way in which messages are listed in the mail program. Users can sort, display message sizes, and display messages marked for deletion.

Sort—Choose the column by which the mailbox viewer window is open.

Show Deleted Messages (Command+L)—Show messages that are marked as deleted. When not using a Trash folder, messages are hidden from view after being marked as deleted.

Show Mailboxes (Shift+Command+M)—Show the mailbox tray.

Hide/Show Number Column —Hide message numbers in the mailbox list.

Hide/Show Flags Column—Show or hide the message flags in the listing.

Hide/Show Contents Column—Show or hide information about each message's attachments.

Hide/Show Message Sizes—Show the size of messages in the viewer listing.

Focus On Selected Messages/Show All Messages—Focus hides all messages except those selected in the mailbox viewer. To restore the view of *all* messages, choose Show All Messages.

Hide Toolbar—Hide the toolbar in the active window.

Customize Toolbar—Customize the toolbar for the frontmost window type.

Hide/Show Status Bar (Option+Command+S)—Toggle the message count status line on and off.

Mailbox

The Mailbox menu is used to create or modify local or IMAP-based mailboxes. Mac OS X will automatically switch between local and remote mailboxes depending on your account configuration.

Go Offline/Online—Log off all e-mail accounts and do not attempt to check for mail.

Take *<account name>* Offline—Log out of a specific e-mail account.

Get New Mail (Shift+Command+N)—Check for new mail in all accounts.

Get New Mail In Account—Get new messages from a specific account.

New Mailbox—Create a new mailbox. If an IMAP account is selected, the mailbox is created on the server.

Rename Mailbox—Rename the selected mailbox.

Delete Mailbox—Delete the selected mailbox.

Empty Deleted Messages (Command+K)—Empty the trash. Removes all deleted messages.

Rebuild Mailbox—Reloads the current mailbox. Occasionally, Mail will get out of sync and the message list will be displayed incorrectly. Choose this option to fix the problem.

Message

Use the Message menu to operate on the message currently highlighted or being displayed. This menu can be used to clean up replies by removing attachments or appending additional messages.

Send Message (Shift+Command+D)—Send the current message.

Reply To Sender (Command+R)—Reply to the current message. If you have text selected when choosing this option, *only* that text will be quoted.

Reply To All Recipients (Shift+Command+R)—Reply to everyone who received the original message.

Forward Message (Shift+Command+F)—Forward an existing message to another address.

Redirect Message (Shift+Command+E)—Redirect an existing message to another address. Similar to Forward Message, but does not quote the original message.

Bounce To Sender (Option+Command+B)—Bounce the message to the sender and remove it from the mailbox.

Add Sender To Address Book (Command+Y)—Add the sender to the Address Book application.

Mark As Read/Unread (Option+Command+M)—Flag a message as read or unread.

Mark As Flagged/Unflagged (Option+Command+G)—Toggle message flag status.

Delete (Delete)—Delete the selected message(s).

Undelete (Shift+Command+U)—Undelete the selected message(s). You must first use Show Deleted Messages from the Edit menu to use this option.

Show All Headers (Shift+Command+H)—Show all the message headers in the content view.

Show—Show the message in one of several different formats, including Raw Source.

Add Bcc Header (Shift+Command+B)—Add a Blind Carbon Copy field to the composition window.

Add Reply-To Header (Option+Command+R)—Add a Reply-To field to the composition window.

Transfer—Transfer the message to another mailbox.

Transfer again (Option+Command+T)—Transfer a message to the last mailbox accessed.

Apply Rules To Selection (Option+Command+L)—Manually force the rules (filters) to be applied to the selected messages.

Attach File (Shift+Command+A)—Attach a file to the message in the composition window.

Remove Attachments—Remove any attachments in the message being composed.

Append Selected Messages (Shift+Command+I)—Add selected messages to the end of the message being written.

Format

The Format menu is used to change to the text style within a message you are composing. The following options are available for your use:

Font—Choose a font and other style information for message composition.

Text—Set the text alignment (left, right, center) for the active message.

Text Encodings—Change the encoding style used for the message; used for international/cross-platform communication.

Make Plain/Rich Text (Shift+Command+T)—Toggle between plain and rich text modes. Remember, toggling a rich text message to plain text mode removes all formatting information.

Increase Quote Level (Command+')—Add a level of quotes (>) to the selection.

Decrease Quote level (Option+Command+')—Remove one level of quoting (>) from the selection.

Window

The Window menu operates as it does in other applications—providing quick access to open windows. In addition, it provides an Addresses selection for quick access to the Address Book application (Option+Command+A), as well as an Activity Viewer (Option+Command+V). Seen in Figure 7.16, the Activity Viewer shows what Mail is doing. Each account access is shown, along with a description of each action that is taking place. To cancel or stop an action, click the Stop button.

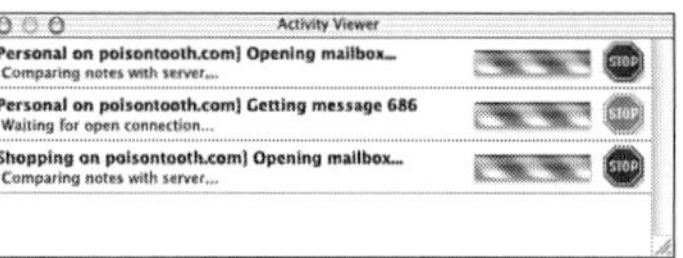

FIGURE 7.16
The Activity Viewer provides information on Mail's network tasks.

Using Mail should be painless for most users, but the application is not without its drawbacks. There are some incompatibilities in the message encoding (MIME/Base64) that result in messages being irretrievable on certain systems (Groupwise servers, for example). In addition, the integration with the Address Book application is awkward at times. If you're interested in alternatives to Mail, take a look at Eudora (`http://www.eudora.com`), Mulberry (`http://www.cyrusoft.com`), and PowerMail (`http://www.powermailtech.com`).

Address Book

The Address Book application is a network-based directory search system and contact information manager. Using the LDAP protocol (Lightweight Directory Access Protocol) and vCard 2.1 Personal Data Interchange format, it is based entirely on open standards and can be used in a cross-platform environment.

vCards

The most common way to send contact information with an e-mail is by adding a signature. Unfortunately, there is no standard for signatures, so picking up contact information from one is an exercise in futility. The vCard (.vcf) format attempts to change this by defining a simple cross-platform MIME standard for an electronic business card. vCards can be used on PDAs such as the Palm Pilot, and then copied to your system and used directly within the Address Book application.

Mac OS X uses version 2.1 of the vCard standard, developed by the Internet Mail Consortium and documented in RFC2426 (http://www.imc.org/rfc2426). A sample vCard, generated by Michael Heydasch's vCard CGI (http://www.vicintl.com/vcf/) is shown here.

```
BEGIN:VCARD
   FN:Mr. John P. Smith, Jr.
   TITLE:General Manager
   ORG:XYZ Corp.;North American Division;Manufacturing
   ADR;POSTAL;WORK:;;P.O. Box 10010;AnyCity;AnyState;00000;U.S.A.
   LABEL;POSTAL;WORK;ENCODING=QUOTED-PRINTABLE:P.O. Box 10010=0D=0A=
    Anywhere, TN  37849=0D=0A=
    U.S.A.
   ADR;PARCEL;WORK:;133 Anywhere St.;Suite 360;AnyCity;AnyState;00000;U.S.A.
   LABEL;POSTAL;WORK;ENCODING=QUOTED-PRINTABLE:133 Anywhere St.=0D=0A=
    Anywhere, TN  37849=0D=0A=
    U.S.A.
   TEL;Work;VOICE;MESG;PREF:+1-234-456-7891 x56473
   TEL;Home:+1-234-456-7891
   TEL;Pager:+1-234-456-7891
   TEL;Cell:+1-234-456-7891
   TEL;Modem;FAX:+1-234-456-7891,,*3
   EMAIL;Internet:webmaster@anywhere.com
   URL:http://www.anywhere.com/mrh.vcf
   UID:http://www.anywhere.com/mrh.vcf
   TZ:-0500
   BDAY:1997-11-29
   REV:20010510T104344
   VERSION:2.1
END:VCARD
```

The vCard defines a person object based on X.520 and X.521 directory services standards—implemented on a large scale in enterprise directory systems. Even encoded images can be included in vCards!

After a vCard is generated, it can be attached to e-mail messages for easy importing into remote address books. In the case of Mac OS X, you can simply drag the vCard from a message window into the Address Book, and it will be added to your contact list.

LDAP

The Lightweight Directory Access Protocol defines a means of querying remote directory systems. LDAP servers are typically used to hold personnel account data, but can be used to serve any hierarchy of data. Linux, Windows, and Mac OS X computers all have the ability to poll LDAP servers for account information, such as login and password.

The Address Book makes use of LDAP server connectivity to retrieve contact information from the network. There are three public LDAP servers already included in the application—Bigfoot (`http://www.bigfoot.com`), Four11 (`http://people.yahoo.com`), and WhoWhere (`http://www.whowhere.com`).

These public servers collect user information from the Internet (news postings and so on) and make it available in a searchable LDAP directory. In addition, you can add your own LDAP server to the mix as long as you know the name or IP address of the server, and the search base.

The *search base* defines a starting point in the LDAP hierarchy to begin looking for information. Companies might have their LDAP directories built based on a per-department schema or other arrangement. Unless you are the LDAP administrator, it is impossible to guess the appropriate search base. Your best bet is not to use a search base, or to contact your network administrator for the correct value. Bases are specified in the format:

```
<key name>=<base string>
```

For example, the search base for many users of Bigfoot's LDAP server is `c=US`. This simply limits the search to the United States hierarchy.

Using Address Book

Address Book is, unlike Mail, a small application. The main Window, seen in Figure 7.17, provides access to all the main features from a single location.

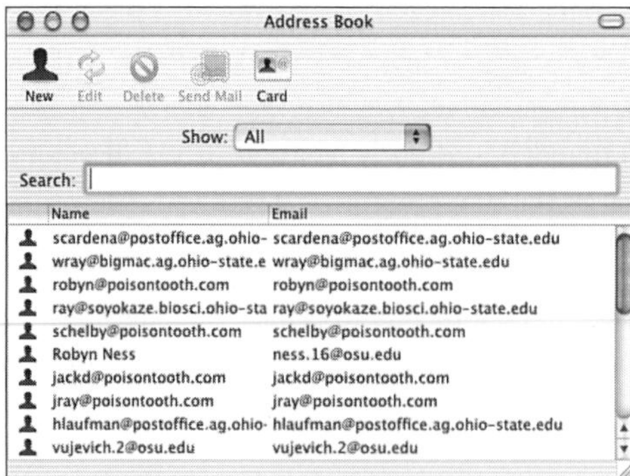

FIGURE 7.17
Address Book keeps track of your contact information with a simple uncluttered interface.

The toolbar, like Mail, contains the common application actions, such as creating new contacts or searching the contact database.

Directly below the toolbar are the Show menu and Search field. These limit the addresses that are shown in the contact listing. Typing into the Search field will display only those contact items that contain the typed string. The Show pop-up menu chooses a category of contacts to display. By default, there are seven categories (All, Buddy, Home, Favorite, Temporary, Work, Groups), three of which are special:

All—All contacts in the Address book.

Groups—Only contact groups are shown, not individuals.

Temporary Cards—When sending or replying to a message, a temporary card is created. You can reassign a temporary card to a permanent category by editing the card. This is a very easy way to populate your Address Book.

New categories can be created when editing contacts or groups of contacts. There is currently no way to add a category directly.

Contacts are listed in the center of the window. Each head icon represents an individual. Dragging that icon to another application will paste the e-mail address into the drag location (such as the Mail application's To: field). Dragging the icon to the Finder will save an exported vCard (`.vcf`) to your drive. Double-clicking a line in the listing edits the contact data.

In addition to individual contacts, you can create groups of contacts, which are represented by a two-headed icon. Groups can be used to send e-mail to a common collection of people, such as friends and family. The simplest way to create a group is to select multiple people in the contact list, and then choose the New Group From Selection from the File menu.

Finally, you (the owner of the Address Book) can designate a listed contact to be "you". A single head icon with a blue background highlights this contact. Set the owner contact by highlighting an entry in the list and choosing This is me from the Edit menu.

At the bottom of the Address Book window is a styled view of the selected contact's business card. This is provided as a way to quickly preview the contact's vCard.

Adding and Editing Contacts and Categories

To add a contact to the Address Book, click the New toolbar icon or choose New (Command+N) from the File menu.

The Contact creation screen is shown (in expanded mode) in Figure 7.18.

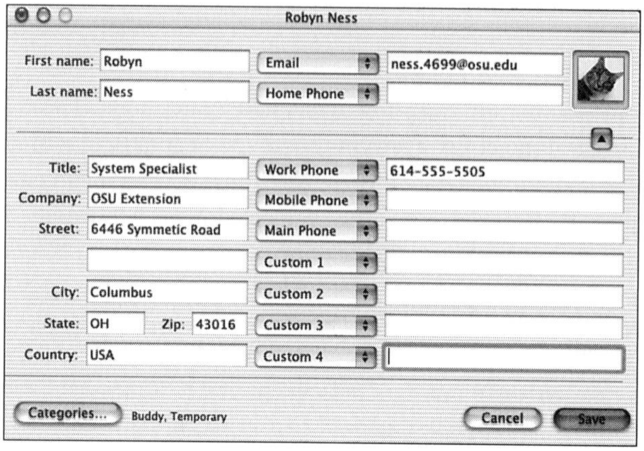

FIGURE 7.18
Enter as much (or as little) information for the contact as you'd like, including pictures.

You can add as much or as little information as you'd like within the contact window. An e-mail address is required if you plan to use the contact with Mail. By default, only a small amount of information (name, e-mail, and phone number) is collected when creating a contact. To enter more data, click the disclosure push button on the right side of the window.

This will open an expanded version of the contact entry form. The fields down the right side of the window are variable—you can choose from one of nine different types of information. In the event that there are additional data fields to store, the pop-up menus at the bottom of the window can be set to customized field names by choosing Edit from the menu.

In the upper-right corner of the contact edit screen is an image well. To add a picture to the contact, drag an image file from the Finder into the image well.

Finally, each contact can be part of a category. To assign a category, click the Categories button in the lower-left corner of the window. A category sheet, similar to that in Figure 7.19, will appear.

Click the check box in front of the category name to add the contact being edited to that category. You can add one item to multiple categories by checking multiple boxes.

To add a new category to the list, click the + button; then enter a name for the new category. To remove an existing category, highlight its name in the listing, and then click the - button. Click OK to exit the category editor.

When finished editing the contact information, click Save to save the contact within your Address Book.

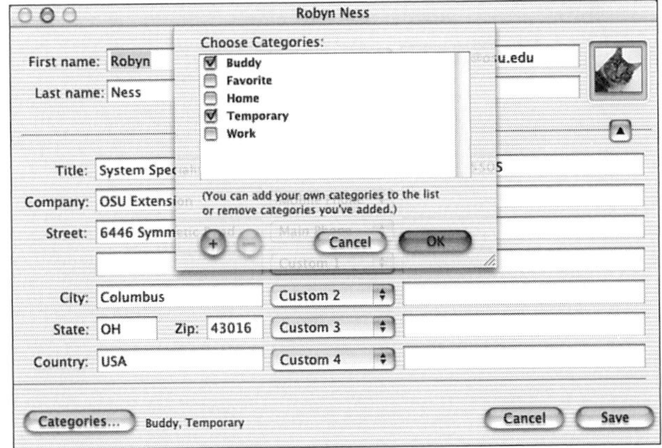

FIGURE 7.19
Use the category sheet to add or remove categories and assign the current object to one or more categories.

> **Tip**
>
> Contacts can be added from existing `.vcf` files by dragging the file from the Finder into the Address Book's contact listing, or by using the Import (Command+I) File menu item.

Adding/Editing Groups

Groups provide a means of addressing multiple related people simultaneously. To create an Address Book group, choose New Group (Shift+Command+N) from the File menu. To jump-start the process, select one or more contacts to add to the group, and then choose New Group From Selection to create a new group containing the selected contacts.

Regardless of the approach you take to creating the group, the group setup window should appear, as shown in Figure 7.20.

Create a name and a description for your group by filling in the corresponding fields. These will be displayed in the main listing. Click the Categories button to file the group under one of the existing categories or add a new category to Address Book (see the previous section for details).

To add a contact to the group, type or paste an e-mail address or contact into the Add Address: field. Click the "+" button to add it. If the contact already exists in the Address Book or within a Directory Search window, you can add it by dragging its card icon (little head-shaped thing) into the group list. You can remove entries by highlighting them in the list, and then clicking the - button.

Click Save to save the group information.

FIGURE 7.20
Groups can hold multiple contacts.

Customizing the Toolbar

The Address Book's toolbar can be customized for easy access to these functions by choosing Customize Toolbar from the View menu, or by Option+Command-clicking the toolbar button. The available shortcuts are displayed in Figure 7.21.

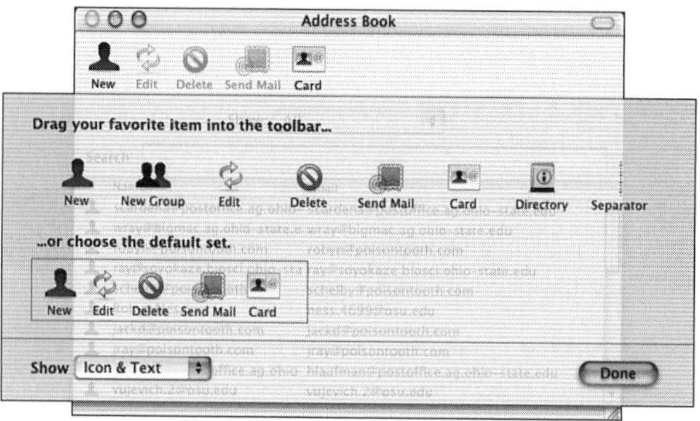

FIGURE 7.21
Even Address Book's toolbar can be customized.

From the top left to bottom right, the available shortcuts are

New —Add a new contact to the address book.

New Group—Create a new (empty) group.

Edit—Edit the selected contact's information.

Delete—Delete the selected contact's data.

Send Email—Send an e-mail to the selected person or group.

Card—Toggle a graphical display of the vCard for the selected contact.

Directory —Search an LDAP server.

Separator—Add a separator bar to the Address Book toolbar.

Default Set—Restore the default set of toolbar shortcuts.

Show—Choose the toolbar style (text, icon and text, or icon only). You can cycle through these options by Command+clicking the toolbar button.

Searching for Contacts

To query LDAP servers for contact information, click the Directory toolbar icon, choose LDAP Directory Search from the Window menu, or Search Directory from the View menu. Figure 7.22 shows the LDAP search window.

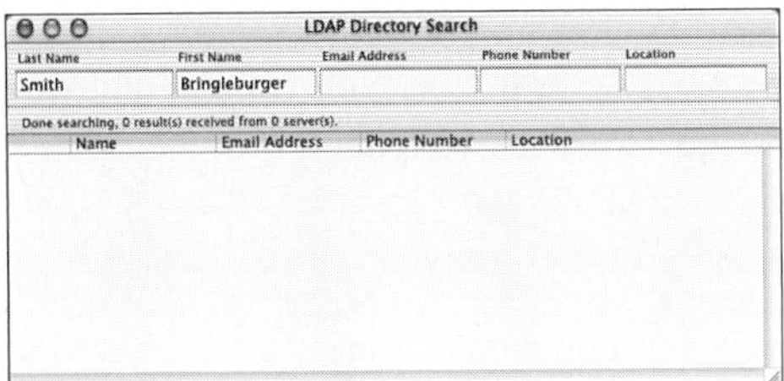

FIGURE 7.22
Search for friends and associates using the built-in LDAP capabilities of Address Book.

To search, fill in as many (or as few) fields as you'd like. The more search criteria you give, the greater the chance that the LDAP server will locate a specific person. Searching for a last name of Smith, for example, is likely to return thousands of results. Searching for Smith with the location of Bringleburger will generate a much narrower result set.

To start the search, press Enter from within any of the search criteria fields. After a few seconds, the results will be shown. The name of each queried LDAP server starts the listing generated from that machine. You can collapse a server's result list by clicking the disclosure arrow in front of its name.

If you find the contact you are looking for, you can add it to the address book by dragging the contact (using the card icon in front of the list item) to the Address Book window. It will be added to whatever category is currently selected in the Show pop-up. After the contact is in the address book, it acts like any other address book entry.

Preferences

Address Book's Preference panel is used to set the available LDAP servers. There are no other application-wide preferences.

The Preferences panel can be seen in Figure 7.23.

FIGURE 7.23
Add new LDAP servers by opening Address Book Preferences panel.

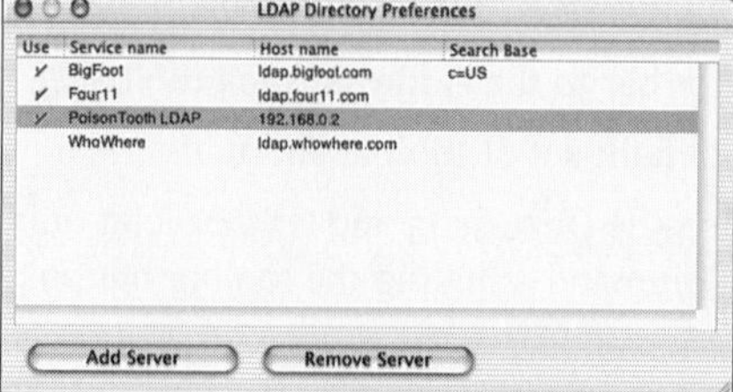

Each field in the panel is editable by double-clicking the text in the field. The Use field determines which servers are used in a query. To disable a server, click in the Use field to toggle the check mark on and off. Checked servers are queried; unchecked servers are skipped.

To add a new server, click the Add Server button. Similarly, to remove an existing LDAP server, select it in the list, and then click Remove Server.

Menus

The File, Edit, and View menus don't hold any surprises. They have the same options we've already looked at, with the addition of the Import and Save To features to the File menu.

File

The File menu is used to create new contacts and groups, as well as search the existing directory. Of the available options, one of the more useful is the ability to import VCF data, which makes it easy to enter contact data from other systems.

New (Command+N)—Create a new contact.

New Group (Shift+Command+N)—Create a new group of contacts.

New Group From Selection—Use the highlighted contacts to seed a new group.

Open (Command+O)—Open a contact file (`.vcf`) for editing.

Import (Command+I)—Import data from an existing `.vcf` file.

Close (Command+W)—Close the frontmost window.

Save (Command+S)—Save the address book.

Save To—When editing contact information, this selection will save the contact to a `.vcf` file.

Revert—Revert information to its last saved form.

Edit

Using the options in the Edit menu, you can choose who you are, as well as start a new message to your chosen contact:

Edit (Command+E)—Edit the selected contact card.

Add To Favorites (Command+F)—Add the contact to the Favorites category, allowing it to be accessed from Mail's Favorites tray.

This is Me—Designate the selected contact as the Address Book owner (you).

Compose Mail (Shift+Command+M)—Send a new e-mail message to the selected contacts.

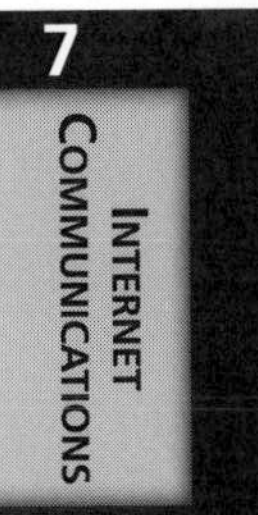

View

Use the View menu to modify the columns that can be seen in the main Address Book list. Use the Available Fields option to toggle columns on or off within the view. Choose Search Directory to open the LDAP search options. Finally, the Show Card (Command+T) option will toggle the display of a graphical representation of a person's vCard.

Address Book is a great companion to Mail. Using LDAP and `.vcf` files, you can easily search directory listings no matter where they are located. The Windows 2000 Active Directory system even offers LDAP support, making integration into the Windows world a reality.

So far, both Mail and Address Book have supported LDAP searches. If you think we're done, guess again. The Sherlock search tool also supports LDAP searches, but can extend its reach far beyond directory servers to anywhere on the World Wide Web.

Sherlock

When Sherlock was introduced in System 8.5, it signaled the beginning of Apple's integration of operating system functions with the Internet. Sherlock provides a universal Find feature that can search for files, text within files, and even Web sites. Some people might find it hard to get excited about a search tool, but it's difficult to understand the power of Sherlock until you try it. A friend of mine who recently moved to the Macintosh platform cites Sherlock as the feature that made her take the plunge. For anyone who needs instant access to information, no matter where it is stored, nothing comes close.

Sherlock Interface

Sherlock is not one tool, but three. Its most basic operation is as a file search utility. Type in a few characters from the filename you're looking for and let Sherlock go. In addition, Sherlock is a file indexer. When not actively searching, Sherlock compiles a database of the text contents of files on your drive. After the database is built, searching for a word or phrase takes a matter of seconds. Finally, Sherlock is an extensible Internet search tool that can perform Web searches on dozens of search engines simultaneously. Results are ranked and displayed with a summary of found pages. A single click launches the preferred Mac OS X Web browser to view the Web site.

Despite its advanced functionality, Sherlock works from within the extremely simple interface shown in Figure 7.24.

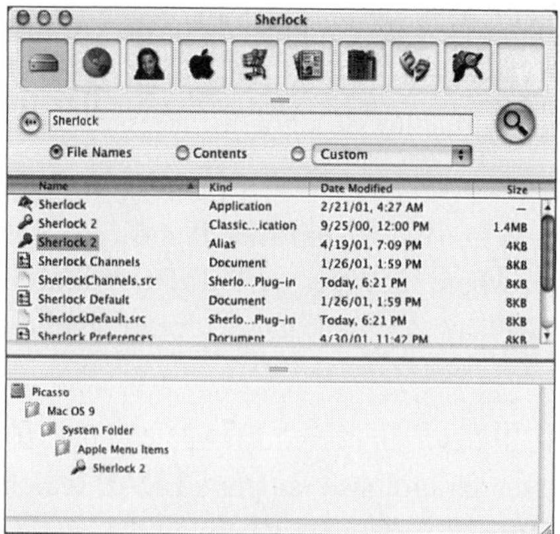

Figure 7.24
All Sherlock's features are accessed from this simple interface.

The Sherlock window is divided into three panes, which can be resized using equal-sign handles. The top pane contains collections, or channels, of searches. There are eight default channels, from left to right:

Files and File Contents—Search local drives for information.

Internet—General information Web sites.

People—LDAP searches for people.

Apple—Search through Apple's information library. Useful for locating tech notes and errata.

Shopping—E-commerce and auction Web sites.

News—CNN and other news sources.

Reference—Reference material, such as Dictionary.com and Encyclopedia.com.

Entertainment—Movie, TV, and music Web sites.

Clicking a channel icon switches to that search collection. If you don't like the ordering of the icons, you can drag them to any available icon well in the top pane. You can also create new channels based on your own favorite search engines or new search plug-ins that you've downloaded from the Internet.

In the center of the Sherlock window are the search criteria and results. Before searching, the pane includes the available objects to search. After the search, the pane shows only the results. Clicking the back arrow returns to the search objects. The results shown in this pane are interactive. You can launch programs and applications by double-clicking their icons. Dragging a Web site URL to the Finder creates a shortcut to that URL. Dragging a file or folder moves that object to a new location. This is understood by trying it; so, don't worry if it doesn't quite make sense yet.

The lower portion of the window is the detail pane. After searching, if a result is selected, the details about that item are displayed. For file and content searches, it displays the path to that file. Content searches show a text snippet surrounding the located string. In Web searches, the URL and summary text are provided.

Now, let's see how this thing actually works.

Performing File and Content Searches

To perform a file search, select the first icon in the channel tray or choose Files (Command+F) from the Channels menu. The file search screen is shown in Figure 7.25.

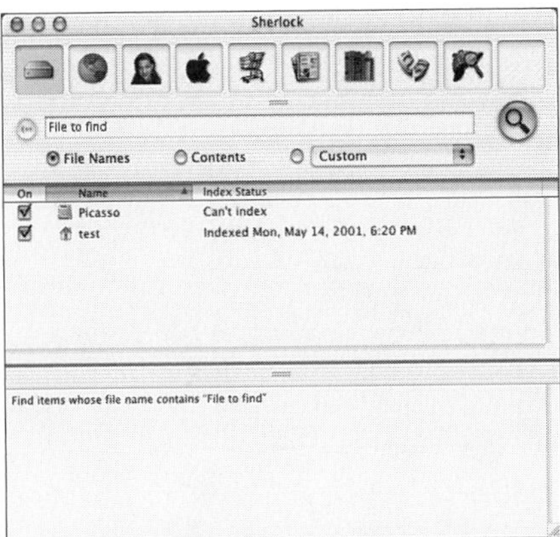

FIGURE 7.25
Use the file search screen to locate files by their name.

Each of the available search objects (hard drives, CD-ROMs, network volumes, folders, and so on) is listed. By default, only the mounted hard drives and your home directory are available. You can drag additional folders into the list to create additional search objects. This lets you limit your searches to only a portion of a hard drive. Click the check box in front of the objects you want to include in the search.

If you want to search the contents of files (rather than the filenames), you must first *index* the files. By default, Sherlock will try to index the search volumes automatically. To force a volume to be indexed, choose Index Now from the File menu when the desired search volume is selected. The indexing process might take a few minutes or a few hours to complete, depending on the amount of data to be scanned.

Note

Unlike Mac OS 9, the entire Mac OS X startup volume *cannot* be indexed. You do not have permission to read all the directories on the system. Because you should be storing your documents within your home directory (which *can* be indexed), this should not prove to be a limitation.

To search for a file by name, click the File Names radio button, and enter your search text in the field. Press Enter or click the Search button (shaped like a magnifying glass) to start the search.

In a few moments, the search results will be displayed. To stop the search in progress, click the Search button again. Figure 7.26 shows a completed search for *Java*. For each result, Sherlock lists the filename, kind of file, date it was modified, and its size. One of the files has been highlighted, and the path is shown in the details pane.

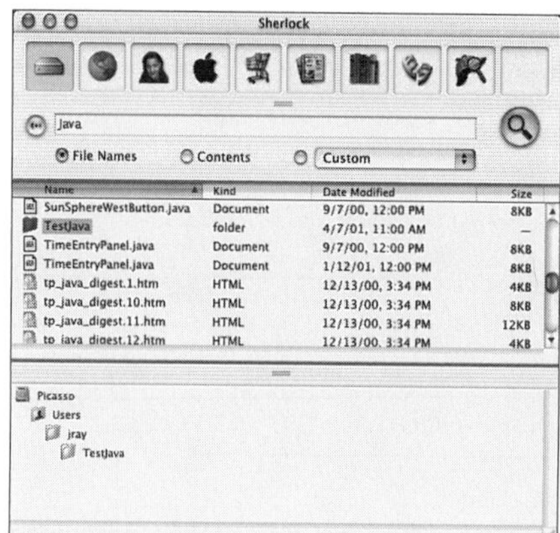

FIGURE 7.26
Choose the objects to search and then click the Search (magnifying glass) button.

Searching for file contents is exactly the same. Just click the Contents radio button, select the search volumes, enter the search text, and go. Unlike the filename search, the content search includes a relevance field in the result listing. This ranks how closely Sherlock matched your search text to the document. The larger the relevance bar, the better the match is.

Because filename and contents are only a few of the possible criteria you might want to search for, Apple included a custom search feature to create new types of searches. To use a custom search, click the Custom radio button, and then choose from the pop-up menu. Four default custom searches are available from the Custom menu: Applications, files larger than 1MB, files modified today, and files modified yesterday.

In addition to the four custom options, you can use the Edit selection in the Custom menu to add your own search type. Sherlock will open the More Search Options window to create your own search types. Click the Advanced Options disclosure push button to see even *more* available search criteria. Figure 7.27 shows the expanded search options window.

FIGURE 7.27
Don't see the search you want? Add your own.

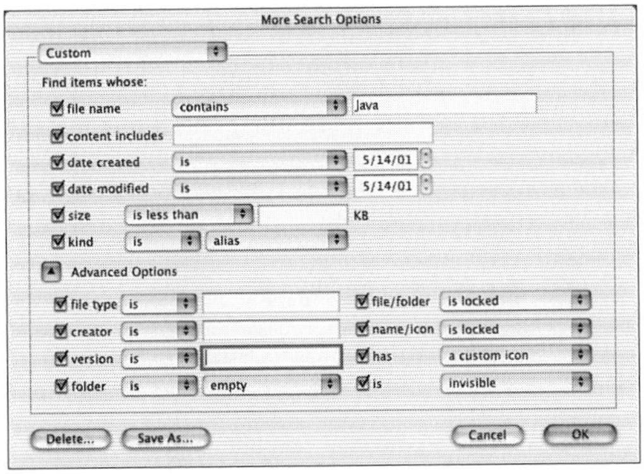

Choose from any (or all) of these available options:

File name—Match based on the filename. Use the pop-up menu to choose *how* the filename matches the given string.

Content includes—Match only files that contain a particular string in their content (this does not require file indexing).

Date created—Select based on the file's creation date.

Date modified—Select based on the file's last modification date.

Size—Match files depending on their size. This is useful for finding those pesky archives that eat up tons of disk space.

Kind—Search for a particular type of file, such as an application, folder, or alias.

File type—Choose files based on their four-character file type.

Creator—Choose files based on their four-character creator type.

Version—Select files and applications based on stored version information.

Folder—Find folders based on certain criteria, such as being empty or mounted from a server.

File/folder (locked)—Find files and folders based on their lock status.

Name/icon (locked)—Find files based on name or icon lock status.

Has (icon)—Select files and folders based on whether they have custom icons.

Is (visible)—File files or folders based on whether they are visible in the finder.

After you set your custom options, click OK to use the custom search. If you've created a search that you might want to use repeatedly, click Save As to enter a name; your new search will now appear under the Custom pop-up menu. Finally, if you happen to be editing a search and want to delete it, click Delete to remove the custom search.

Performing Internet Searches

To search the Internet, choose one of the available Internet search channels. In the center pane of the Sherlock window, you'll see the available search sites to choose from, as demonstrated in Figure 7.28.

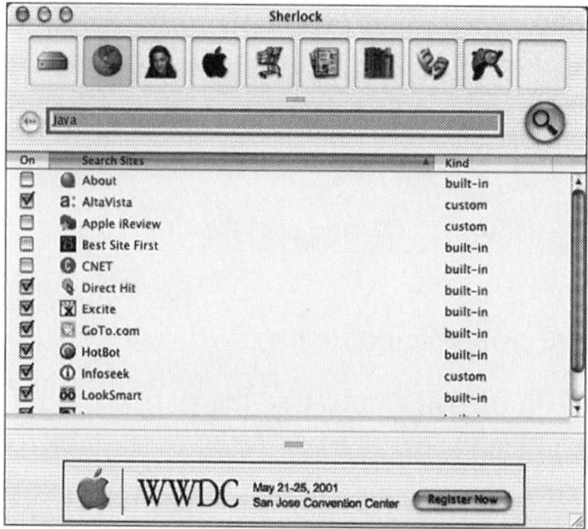

Figure 7.28
Click the search sites that you want to query.

> **Note**
>
> Sherlock search plug-ins include information on how to update themselves if the site they are querying changes. If you are warned while searching that a

new version of a search site plug-in is available, download it. Sherlock will automatically install and activate the plug-in for subsequent searches.

Choose the search engines that you want to use by clicking the check box in front of their names. To quickly toggle between all off and all on, use Turn Off/On All (Command+T) from the Edit menu. This function will also toggle highlighted items in the list between their on and off states.

Finally, enter your search text into the search field and click the magnifying glass button. Within a few seconds, the search results will be displayed. Figure 7.29 shows an Internet search for the word *Java*.

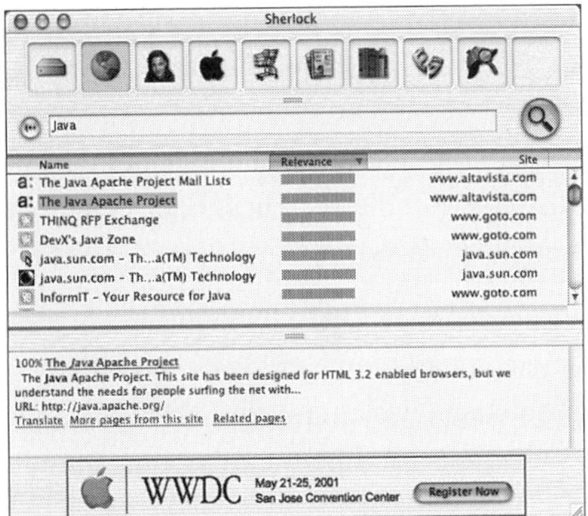

FIGURE 7.29
Each search engine is queried, and then a combined list of the results is displayed.

Depending on the type of search you're running, you might see a variety of fields in the results. The generic Internet search displays the name of the located page, the relevance, and the site it is located on. People searches, on the other hand, include phone numbers and e-mail addresses (if available). Shopping searches display the availability of a product and its cost (allowing for quick sorts based on price). Double-click any line in the search results list to open the URL in your Web browser.

Note

If a field is missing from the search results, it doesn't mean that Sherlock has malfunctioned. For example, many sites do not report a relevance ranking. In these cases, the content of the field is left blank.

To display addition information about one of the located items, select it in the search results pane. The details will be displayed at the bottom of the window. Lines highlighted in blue are hyperlinks and can be clicked to open the link in your preferred Web browser.

Customizing Channels

To organize your favorite Internet searches, you can make your own Sherlock channels. To create a new channel, choose New Channel from the Channels menu. The New Channel dialog box shown in Figure 7.30 will be displayed.

FIGURE 7.30
Create new channels with your favorite search engines.

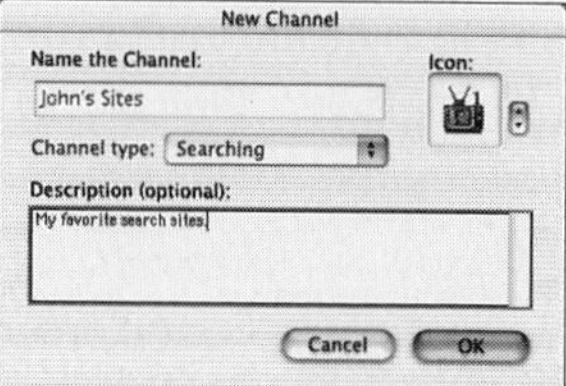

To set up your channel, you must name it and provide a channel type. The channel type determines what fields will be displayed in the searches. Four channel types are available: Searching, People, Shopping, and News.

The basic Searching channel retrieves a page URL, its relevance in a search, and the name of the site. Using the People channel, you can locate individual's e-mail addresses and phone numbers. The Shopping channel includes availability and price fields for comparison shopping. Finally, News channels are like the basic Searching channels, but include a date field.

In addition to setting the channel type, you can also choose an icon for your channel by clicking the up and down arrows by the icon well. Finally, enter a description of the channel if you're afraid you won't remember what it's for.

Click OK to create the new channel. The icon chosen for the channel will be added to the top of the Sherlock window. You can drag the icon around to position it in any of the icon wells. Dragging on top of an existing channel will delete that channel (unless it is a built-in channel).

To edit or delete a channel, select its icon and then use the appropriate menu option from the Channels menu.

Adding Search Sites

What good is a channel if it doesn't have any search sites? To add existing search sites to a channel, follow these steps:

1. Open a new Sherlock window (Command+N).
2. Choose the channel with the existing search site you want to move or copy.
3. Drag the search site's icon to the search pane of the new channel.

Tip

This procedure will *move* a search plug-in from one channel to another. To copy the search site plug-in, hold down the Option key while dragging the icon.

Chances are that you're less than thrilled with having only the option to rearrange the built-in search site plug-ins. Thankfully, Apple built Sherlock's plug-in architecture so that developers could easily create new plug-ins based on simple rules. There are hundreds of available search site plug-ins that you can download and add to your custom channels.

The Sherlock plug-in architecture relies on search Web pages to be laid out in a logical and repeating fashion. To a Web search engine, Sherlock is just another browser sending a search request. When the results are returned, Sherlock searches through them for recognizable elements.

For example, many search engines return their results in the form of a table, like this:

```
<TABLE>
<TR><TD>Result 1</TD><TD>Description</TD></TR>
<TR><TD>Result 2</TD><TD>Description</TD></TR>
<TR><TD>Result 3</TD><TD>Description</TD></TR>
<TR><TD>Result 4</TD><TD>Description</TD></TR>
...and so on...
</TABLE>
```

Here, each result is displayed within a table row—one after another. The search site plug-ins take advantage of this repeating nature to identify which text in the resulting HTML belongs in the Sherlock result fields. To learn more about this process and authoring your own Sherlock plug-ins, read Apple's developer documentation at `http://developer.apple.com/technotes/tn/tn1141.html`.

The easiest way to find prebuilt plug-ins is to visit the Sherlock Plug-ins for Power Searchers Web site, located at `http://pwsearcher.users1.50megs.com/sherlock/srccoms.html`. See Chapter 8 for information on downloading and uncompressing applications and files.

A downloaded plug-in can be recognized by its `.src` extension. To install a plug-in, drag its icon from the Finder into the search pane of the Sherlock window. It will be immediately added to the current channel. You can also choose Add Search Site from the Channels menu, and then locate the `.src` file on your drive.

Sherlock continues to gain new plug-ins on a daily basis. A Google search for *Sherlock plug-in* yields an incredible number of results.

If you can find it on the web, there's a Sherlock plug-in to help you find it faster.

Configuration

Sherlock has a single Preferences panel, shown in Figure 7.31.

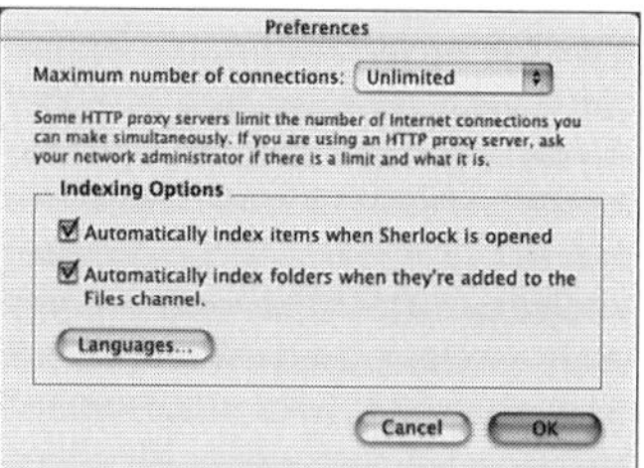

Figure 7.31
Set the number of simultaneous Web requests Sherlock can make as well as the options for indexing the drive.

There are four options you can set. These can greatly affect Sherlock's performance, so you might want to adjust the settings to suit your environment.

The first option, Maximum number of connections, determines how Sherlock uses your network. Sherlock typically performs many Web searches in parallel. The maximum number of connections is, by default, unlimited. For dial-in users, creating a large number of simultaneous connections might actually take longer than making a few connections at a time. The overhead required to manage the connections suddenly becomes a significant portion of the bandwidth. Try choosing a lower number if you are using many search engines and the results are taking a *long* time to return.

Next, the Automatically index items when Sherlock is opened option is used to trigger automatic indexing. When checked, Sherlock will start indexing your search volumes as soon as it is started. This can slow down overall system performance and is unnecessary unless you are performing content searches. If the Automatically index folders when they're added setting is checked, a folder that is dragged to the Files channel will be indexed immediately.

By default, Sherlock indexes a large number of languages besides English! You can speed up the indexing process by clicking the Languages button and choosing only the languages that you use.

Click OK to save the Sherlock preferences.

Advanced Configuration

When you add Sherlock search plug-ins, they're moved to an area where all users can access them. Unlike other components, this isn't in the `Library` folder. Instead, Sherlock stores the plug-ins *inside* the Sherlock application. If you're interested in getting to the plug-in source directly, you can access it through this path: `/Applications/Sherlock.app/Contents/Resources/English.lproj`. Similarly, the channel definitions are stored at `/Applications/Sherlock.app/Contents/Resources/Channels`.

In addition, the Content indexing system has a few files that you might want to take a look at. Open the folder `/System/Library/Find`. There are five files that control how the indexer works for English documents:

English Stopwords—A list of common words that should not be indexed.

English Substitutions—Common equivalent words for close matches.

SkipFolders—A list of folders that will be skipped during indexing (includes the standard Unix directories).

StopExts—A list of file extensions for documents that shouldn't be indexed.

StopTypes—File types that should not be indexed (for files that have Macintosh creator/file types).

Changing any of these files is an at-your-own-risk operation, but it does offer a greater level of control over the indexing process than through the Sherlock interface.

Menus

Sherlock's menus provide access to common operations for working with files. The keyboard shortcuts can help turn Sherlock into one of the easiest ways of navigating your drive, launching applications, and opening files.

File

Use the options in the file menu to operate on URLs or files and folders that have been found, as well as perform standard window operations:

New Window (Command+N)—Open a new Sherlock window.

Open Item (Command+O)—Open a selected file or application.

Open Enclosing Folder (Command+E)—Open the folder (in the Finder) that contains the selected file.

Open in New Browser Window (Command+B)—Open the selected URL in a new Web browser window.

Print Item (Command+P)—Open and print the selected file.

Move to Trash (Command+Delete)—Move the selected file or folder to the trash.

Close Window (Command+W)—Close the frontmost window.

Show Original (Command+R)—Show the original item, if the selected file is an alias.

Save Search Criteria (Command+S)—Save the current search so it can be repeated later.

Open Search Criteria—Open a saved search.

Edit

The Edit menu contains the usual cut/paste tools, along with the additional Turn Off/On toggle selection (Command+T).

Find

The Find menu can be used to control Sherlock's file indexing and custom searching. One item of interest is the Find Similar Files selection, which can be used to locate files with similar qualities to a single given file.

Add Folder—Add a folder to the available volumes for searching and indexing.

Remove Folder—Remove the selected folder from the volume list.

Index Now—Index the selected folder or volume.

Stop Indexing—Stop indexing the highlighted volume.

Delete Index—Delete the index for the highlighted volume.

Find Similar Files—Find files with similar characteristics to the selected file.

More Options—Display the custom search dialog.

Channels

The Sherlock Channels menu gives you the ability to customize your own channels with your favorite plug-ins. Custom channels are really useful only for users with large collections of plug-ins.

New Channel—Create a new search channel.

Edit Channel—Edit the selected search channel.

Delete Channel—Remove the selected channel.

Add Search Site—Add a search site plug-in to the current channel.

Files (Command+F)—Switch to the Files channel.

Internet (Command+K)—Switch to the Internet channel.

People (Command+J)—Switch to the people channel.

Apple—Switch to the Apple channel.

Shopping—Switch to the Shopping channel. (This is better than QVC, by the way.)

News—Switch to the News channel.

Reference—Switch to the Reference channel.

Entertainment—Switch to the Entertainment channel.

QuickTime 5

What would an Internet experience be like without streaming sound and video? If you have a dial-up connection, the answer is *enjoyable*—but for those of us lucky enough to have broadband access, streaming media is reasonably feasible through the use of the QuickTime Player provided with Mac OS X. QuickTime is Apple's digital media engine that processes everything from MIDI to movies and still images. For more information about the QuickTime API, see Chapter 1, "Mac OS X Component Architecture."

In this chapter, we're interested in QuickTime's streaming capabilities. QuickTime uses the Internet standard, RTSP (Real Time Streaming Protocol), to deliver high-quality streams based on any of the QuickTime codecs. In addition, QuickTime can use traditional protocols such as FTP and HTTP.

The difference between FTP/HTTP streaming and RTSP is the TCP/IP transport used to deliver the data. FTP and HTTP are known as *reliable* protocols. When a server transmits using HTTP or FTP, it must carry on a conversation with the remove client. For each piece (packet) of information that is sent, the remote machine must reply with an acknowledgement (ACK). If the client does *not* reply, the server resends the data, or, after enough time passes, closes the connection.

RTSP, on the other hand, uses the UDP protocol (a different component of the TCP/IP protocol suite) to deliver unreliable data streams. Although the term unreliable might not sound appealing, in the case of streamed video, it is. RTSP (via UDP) sends data out as quickly as it can. If there is a glitch in the connection, it doesn't have to wait for the remote computer to respond, and it doesn't have to resend data—it just keeps going. The result is a video feed that can recover from errors and doesn't slow down. When watching live video presentations, UDP is the only way to go.

Unfortunately, UDP tends to break behind firewalls or masqueraded connections. To get around this, Apple has provided the capability to stream over HTTP. RTSP is recommended when possible, but HTTPD provides a very comparable streaming experience, although it is susceptible to more hiccups than the UDP-based protocol.

Setting Up QuickTime

There are two places you're most likely to run into QuickTime media—through the QuickTime player and via a Web browser. Before you can use either, you must first configure QuickTime through its System Preference panel. Failing to do so will display the lowest-quality stream. Open System Preferences (Path: `/Applications/System Preferences`) and click the QuickTime icon to configure your QuickTime settings.

> **Note**
>
> QuickTime settings are made on a per-user basis. This *includes* registration. Each user of the system will need to license QuickTime Pro separately if he wants to access its advanced features.

Plug-In

The Plug-In preference panel is shown in Figure 7.32. At the bottom of each QuickTime preference pane are the About QuickTime and Registration buttons. Clicking the About QuickTime button displays information on the version of QuickTime installed, and provides a link to Apple's QuickTime Web site. Choosing Registration allows you to enter registration information for QuickTime Pro. The QuickTime Pro software adds additional features to the Player application—we'll take a look at these a little later.

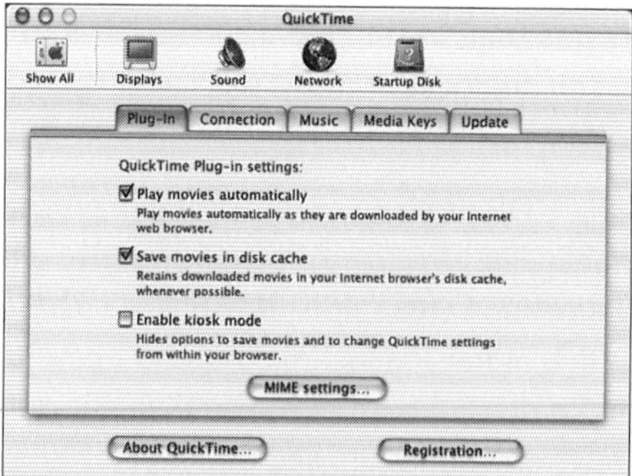

FIGURE 7.32
The Plug-In pane controls how the QuickTime browser plug-in works.

The QuickTime plug-in is used when movies are viewed in a browser. There are four configurable options: Play movies automatically, Save movies in disk cache, Enable kiosk mode, and MIME settings.

If you've checked Play movies automatically, QuickTime will start playing a movie after enough of it has been buffered. This applies to *nonstreamed* movies. If this option is not selected, you must click the Play button to start viewing a movie. If you'd like to save movies that have played in your browser, click the Save movies in disk cache check box. This will speed up commonly accessed movies and is great for those days when you keep pulling up the one funny video clip repeatedly to show your co-workers.

Users who are interested in using QuickTime in kiosks can limit the end user's access to QuickTime controls by clicking the Enable kiosk mode check box. This isn't needed for normal use.

The final available preference, the MIME settings button, opens a list of all the MIME types that QuickTime can handle, and everything it is currently configured to display. Some items are intentionally disabled (such as Flash) because they are better handled by other browser plug-ins.

Connection

The Connection pane, shown in Figure 7.33, configures the type of network access QuickTime can expect your computer to have.

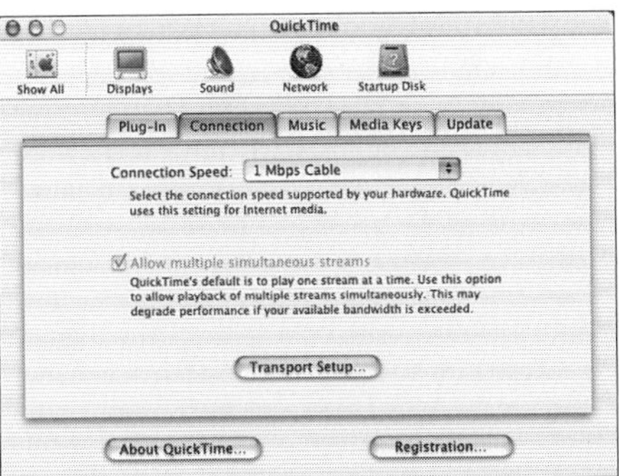

FIGURE 7.33
Choose your connection speed and transport type for best movie quality.

Choose your network speed from the Connection Speed pop-up menu. This is not the speed you *wish* you had, but the actual speed of your line. This choice helps QuickTime choose the appropriate type of media to display depending on how fast it can be received.

Click the Transport Setup button to choose the protocol used for streaming. By default, QuickTime will attempt to choose the best transport based on your network topology. It's best not to change these settings unless you know your network supports them. Users behind a firewall can choose the ports used for either HTTP or UDP transports. It's best to talk to your network administrator before changing anything.

Note

If your computer is connected directly to the Internet via a DSL/cable modem or you are on a network without a firewall, either of the transports should work fine for you. Try each to see which displays faster and cleaner streams on your system.

By default, QuickTime allows only a single media stream. If your bandwidth allows, click the Allow Multiple Simultaneous Streams option to stream many sources at once. This option is automatically selected when selecting a high-speed network.

Music

QuickTime supports multiple plug-in synthesizers when playing MIDI music. By default, it uses the QuickTime Music Synthesizer, as shown in Figure 7.34.

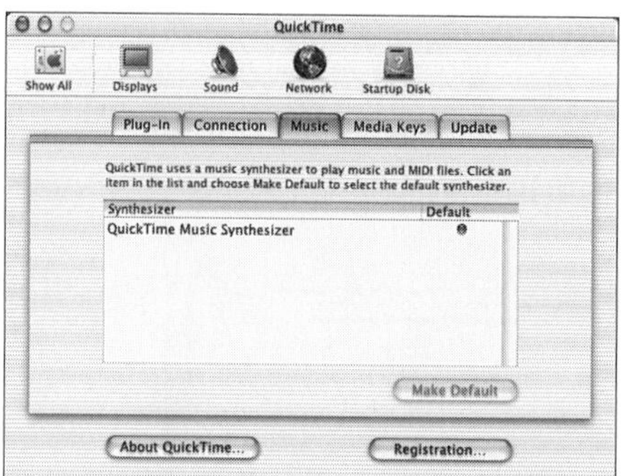

FIGURE 7.34 *Set the default QuickTime synthesizer.*

If you install software that offers another synthesizer plug-in, you can select it from the list in this preference pane. Highlight the item you want to use by default and click Make Default. This will set it as the default synthesizer used by any application playing QuickTime MIDI files.

Media Keys

Some media files may be secured with an access key. The Media Keys pane allows you to enter keys directly into the QuickTime preferences so that the files can be accessed transparently at any time. Figure 7.35 displays the Media Keys pane in the QuickTime System Preference panel. Use the Delete, Edit, and Add buttons to modify your access keys.

FIGURE 7.35
Add keys to access protected QuickTime media.

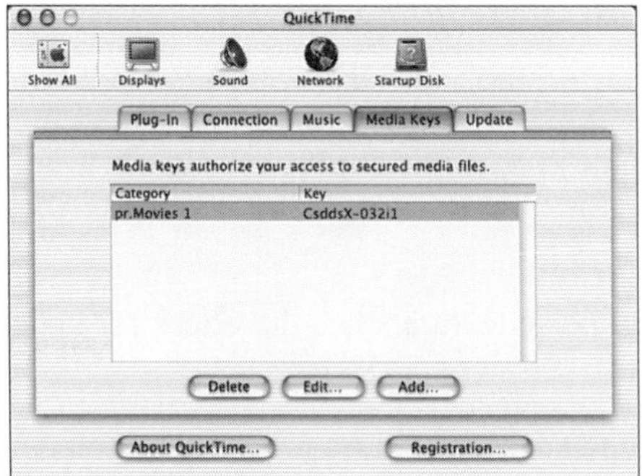

Update

QuickTime supports automatic updating in much the same way as the Mac OS X operating system (see Chapter 29 for more information). Unlike the operating system, however, QuickTime checks for updates outside of the normal system updater context. When you're using QuickTime, it will occasionally scan for updates and additions that can be downloaded.

The Update pane, pictured in Figure 7.36, allows you to force an update of QuickTime software at any time.

FIGURE 7.36
Force a QuickTime software update.

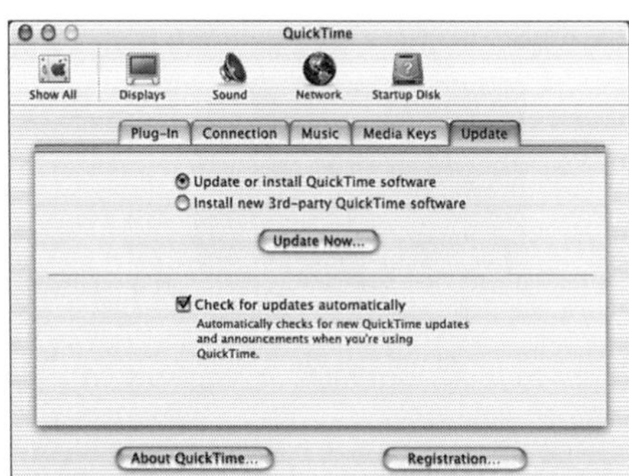

The QuickTime updater can also be used to add third-party software, such as new codecs, to the system.

Click the Update or install QuickTime software or Install new 3rd-party QuickTime software radio buttons, and then click Update Now to start. Follow the onscreen instructions to complete the installation.

Note

The actual installation is performed using the Software Update utility built in to the system, although the process is controlled by QuickTime's own update application. For more information on Software Update, see Chapter 29.

To toggle the QuickTime auto-update feature, click the Check for updates automatically check box.

When you're finished setting up QuickTime, close the System Preferences application.

Browser Plug-in

Many QuickTime movies play from within your browser window. This is probably the most common place you'll view streaming media, so let's take a look at the controls of the QuickTime browser plug-in. Figure 7.37 shows a QuickTime movie playing in the Internet Explorer browser.

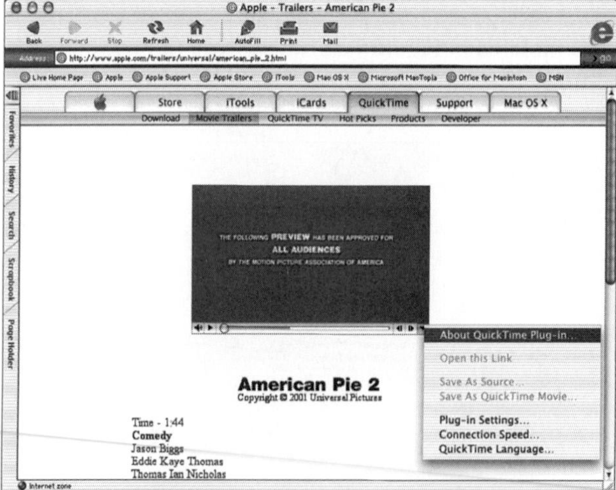

FIGURE 7.37
Most users will experience QuickTime through their browser.

The movie controls are located across the bottom of the video. If you've used a VCR or other media player, you've certainly seen these before. There are, however, a few shortcuts you might want to know.

The volume control, for example, can be instantly muted by clicking the speaker icon. You can also control the volume level using the up-arrow and down-arrow keys on the keyboard. To increase the volume beyond its normal limit, hold down the Shift key while dragging the volume control.

Playback controls can be activated from the keyboard, saving the need to mouse around on your screen. To toggle between playing and pausing, press the space bar. To rewind or fast forward, use the left-arrow and right-arrow keys, respectively.

At the lower far-right of the control bar area is the QuickTime menu. This provides quick access to QuickTime settings. QuickTime Pro users can use this menu to save movies to their hard drive. (Note: Saving a streaming movie saves a *reference* to the movie, not the actual contents of the movie.)

If the movie being played is streaming from the remote server, some of these controls might not be available. For example, live streams can't be fast-forwarded or rewound, but streamed files can be. The available controls depend entirely on the movie you're viewing.

The QuickTime Player

The QuickTime Player application (Path: `/Applications/QuickTime Player`) provides another means of viewing movies and streams. In fact, many users might be surprised to find that they can use the player application to tune in a variety of interesting streams—ranging from news to entertainment, without the need for a Web browser.

Apple has been working with entertainment and news outlets for the past few years to develop QuickTime TV. The stations that comprise QuickTime TV provide streaming media 24 hours a day. Don't have a good source for NPR in your neighborhood? Use QuickTime TV to play a high-quality NPR stream, anytime, anywhere.

QuickTime TV

To start using the QuickTime player, open it from its default home in the Dock, or from the System Applications folder. The QuickTime window should open directly to the QuickTime TV view, as seen in Figure 7.38.

FIGURE 7.38
QuickTime Player opens to the QuickTime TV view.

A button in the window represents each of the QuickTime TV stations. Clicking a station might load streaming video, a Web page, or a menu to choose between different possible subchoices. For example, clicking HBO shows the current HBO offerings, as demonstrated in Figure 7.39.

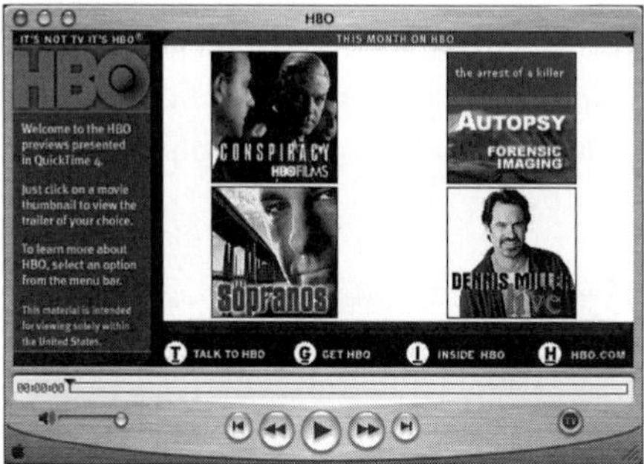

FIGURE 7.39
Clicking a station may load a menu with additional choices.

When QuickTime starts to load a streaming video clip, it will go through four steps before displaying the video:

- **Connecting**—Connection is made to the streaming server.
- **Requested Data**—Waits for acknowledgement from remote server.
- **Getting Info**—Retrieves information about the QuickTime movie.
- **Buffering**—QuickTime buffers several seconds of video to eliminate stuttering from the playback.

If the player stalls during any of these steps, it might be a problem with the remote server or your transport setting. Try another streaming source, and if it still fails, use the QuickTime Preference panel to select an alternative transport.

Other QuickTime Sources

You can use the QuickTime Player to play information from other sources in addition to QuickTime TV. You can open local movie files by choosing Open Movie from the File menu (Command+O) or by dragging a movie file onto the QuickTime Dock icon. If you have a streaming server URL, you can select Open URL (Command+U) from the File menu to directly open the stream.

QuickTime refers to *any* media type as a movie. For example, you can open and play CD audio tracks and MP3s using the Open Movie command. Even though there aren't any visuals, these media types are still referred to as *movies* in QuickTime's vocabulary.

Tip

An interesting example of QuickTime Streaming in action is the Race Rocks Web site. Race Rocks is an inside view of an ecological preserve being transmitted 24 hours a day using Macintosh and AirPort technology: `http://www.racerocks.com/`. To immediately view streaming video from the Race Rocks island, enter the URL `http://stream.qtv.apple.com/channels/ali/sdp/racerocks/camera1_ref.mov` into the QuickTime Player application.

QuickTime Player Controls

The QuickTime Player, shown in Figure 7.40, works much like a VCR. The top of the window holds the video pane. Directly below the video is a status bar to display the progress of the player and any feedback it needs to provide to the user.

FIGURE 7.40
If you've used a VCR, you can control the QuickTime Player.

There are three components to the status bar: the elapsed time, the playback progress, and a miniature frequency monitor. Dragging the arrow above the progress bar quickly moves the current position in the movie (except in the cases of live streams, for reasons that should be obvious).

Tip

QuickTime Pro users might notice that directly below the progress bar are two selection triangles. Use these triangles to select start and end points for the video clip. The selection can then be copied or pasted into other movies.

Although the frequency monitor is of little value as-is, clicking it will toggle the status bar to and from basic sound controls—balance, bass, and treble control. Use the + and - buttons to adjust the values of these settings.

Below the status bar are the main playback controls, that provide the basic control over movie playback. In addition, you'll find a TV button that quickly opens the QuickTime TV stations.

Because many video clips are small, the QuickTime Player window can be resized by using the window resize handle in the lower-right corner. By default, QuickTime Player resizes the window to maintain the same aspect ratio. To squeeze or stretch the window, hold down Shift while resizing. To switch between common sizes, use the Movie menu to select from Half Size (Command+0), Normal Size (Command+1), Double Size (Command+2), and Fill Screen (Command+3).

Tip

Minimizing a QuickTime Player movie *while* it is playing will add a live icon to the Dock. The movie (with sound) will continue to play in the minimized Dock icon. Even if you don't have a use for this, give it a try—it's extremely cool!

Note

QuickTime Pro users have an additional option to present the movie on the screen. This clears all other information from the monitor and plays the full-screen video.

QuickTime Favorites

To keep track of your favorite movies (either local files or streaming), you can use the QuickTime Favorites panel. Open the Favorites panel by clicking the QuickTime TV button, and then selecting the heart tab. The Favorites panel is shown in Figure 7.41. You can also choose Show Favorites from the QTV menu and Favorites submenu.

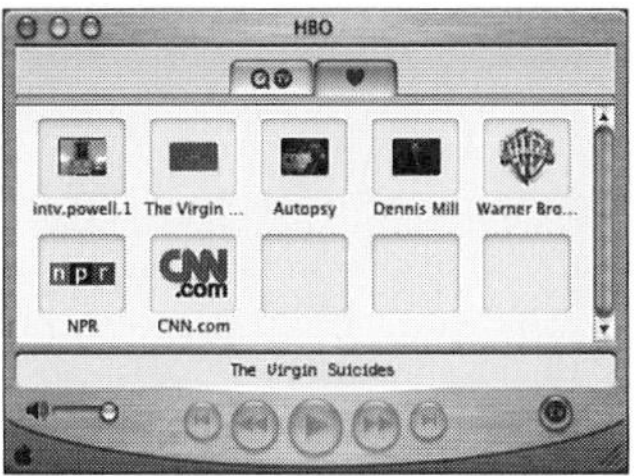

FIGURE 7.41
QuickTime Favorites can store commonly accessed media files.

To add movies to your list of favorites, drag them from the Finder into one of the available spaces in the Favorite view. Alternatively, use Add Movie As Favorite (Command+D) from the QTV menu's Favorites submenu.

Within the Favorites view, you can rearrange movies by dragging their icons from icon well to icon well. To delete a movie reference altogether, drag its icon to the trashcan. To display the movie name under each icon, choose Show Labels from the QTV Favorites menu.

Tip

The icon added to the Favorites panel is, by default, the first frame of the video. This is called the *poster frame*. QuickTime Pro users can set the poster frame for a given file. Normal users cannot.

When adding a streaming movie, the current frame of the movie when it is added is used as the Favorites icon.

If you'd rather use the Finder to launch your favorite QuickTime clips, you can create a Finder shortcut by dragging the icon to a Finder window. Finally, to delete from the Favorites panel, drag the icon to remove into the trashcan.

Getting Movie Information

There are two ways to get extended information about a movie, including the codecs used, FPS, duration, and other useful tidbits. For a summary of information, choose Show Movie Info (Command+I) from the Window menu.

The collapsed Movie Info window displays only the title and copyright information. Click the disclosure arrow to display additional data. The expanded Movie Info window can be seen in Figure 7.42.

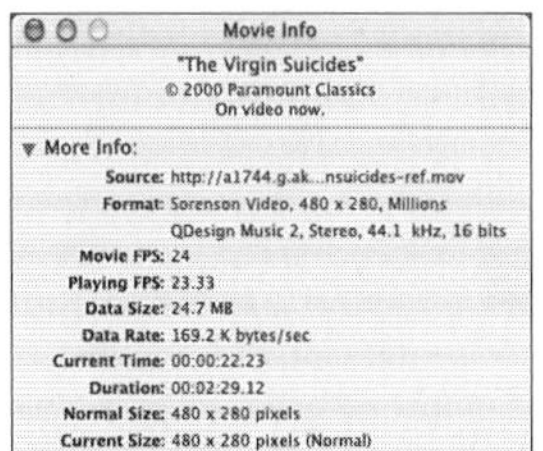

Figure 7.42
The expanded Movie Info window contains summary data on the currently playing file.

The type of information shown is dependent on the type of movie being played. Streaming video, for example, includes network data such as bit rate and quality.

To view even more detailed information, choose Get Movie Properties (Command+J) from the Movie menu.

Movie properties can be used to view information about every component of a video file or stream. Figure 7.43 displays a graph of the bit rate data for a streaming video.

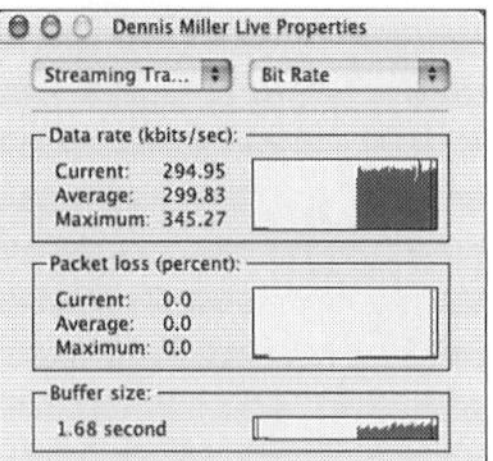

Figure 7.43
Use movie properties to view detailed information about the components of a QuickTime movie.

At the top of the Properties window are two pop-up menus. The menu on the left selects the object to examine—video tracks, audio tracks, or the movie as a whole. The pop-up menu on the right selects between the different properties that can be viewed. Common properties include Annotations, such as author, title and copyright, Movie Format, Size, and Bit Rate (streaming transmission rate).

Note

QuickTime Pro users can view a much larger number of movie properties as well as set information about a movie, such as its color palette, graphics mode, and mask.

QuickTime Preferences

The application Preferences menu actually contains three different choices: Player Preferences, QuickTime Preferences, and Registration.

The Player Preferences set preferences for the Player application itself, whereas the QuickTime Preferences refer to the QuickTime System Preferences panel discussed earlier. If you're interested in registering QuickTime (which we highly suggest), the Registration option provides an input area for entering your registration code.

The Player preferences are shown in Figure 7.44.

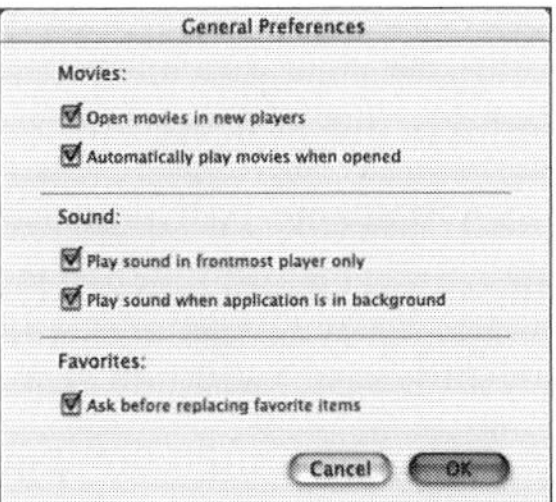

FIGURE 7.44
Choose how QuickTime Player reacts to opening and playing movies.

Use the following options in the Player Preferences to control how the application handles multiple movies and playback:

Open movies in new players—By default, QuickTime Player reuses existing windows when opening new movies. To open new movies in new windows, check this option.

Automatically play movies when opened—Does what it says! When checked, the player will start playing a movie immediately after it is opened.

Play sound in frontmost player only—By default, sound is only played in the frontmost player window. To hear sound from all playing movies simultaneously, uncheck this option.

Play sound when application is in background—If checked, sound will continue to play even when QuickTime Player isn't the frontmost application.

Ask before replacing favorite items—When manipulating Favorites items, dragging an icon on top of another will replace that favorite. Uncheck this check box if you'd rather not be warned before replacing an item.

Click OK to save the application preferences.

Menus

As always, we end our look at the QuickTime Player with an overview of the menus and their available options.

File

The File menu is used to open new Player windows (Command+N), movie files (Command+O), or URLs for online streaming sites (Command+U). Nothing out of the ordinary can be found here.

Movie

Using the Movie menu, a user can control how the movie is presented on his screen. These options are useful for presentations and making small or short movies more easily visible:

Loop (Command+L)—Play the current movie continuously in Loop mode.

Half Size (Command+0)—Display the movie at one-half its normal size.

Normal Size (Command+1)—Display the movie at its native size.

Double Size (Command+2)—Display the movie at twice its size.

Fill Screen (Command+3)—Enlarge the movie to fill the computer screen.

Show Sound Controls—Display the balance, bass, and treble controls.

Get Movie Properties (Command+J)—Show the properties (track information, bit rate data, and so on) for the current movie.

QTV

The QTV menu provides quick access to QuickTime TV and the Favorites panel. Because it's easier to just click the TV button on the Player window, it's unlikely you'll need this menu.

Window

The Window menu provides access to the open Player windows. The Show Movie Info (Command+I) option displays a summary of the currently playing movie.

QuickTime Pro Features

For most users, the standard version of QuickTime is probably more than enough to handle their media needs. If you're interested in creating or editing digital movies, you can upgrade to QuickTime Pro and gain access to some interesting new features. There isn't anything additional to install, just a registration code to enter—so it's very easy to get up and running with QuickTime Pro.

Upgrading gives you access to a number of video editing functions, such as copying and pasting portions of video tracks, applying effects filters, and altering video codecs. Users can extract and covert audio and video tracks—even export video tracks as image sequences.

Basic playback features are also improved. Users can present a movie on the entire screen, rather than just a window, as well as control contrast, tint, and brightness on a per-movie basis. If you've ever played a movie with improper gamma settings (way too dark), you'll greatly appreciate these features.

If you're solely interested in QuickTime Pro for its added playback capabilities, you might want to look into one of these free players:

inMotion—
`http://homepage.mac.com/edotsoftware/prods/inMotion/inMotion.html`

DrDJ Free—`http://studwww.rug.ac.be/~lbdkeyse/softs/`

Pix Lite— `http://www.swssoftware.com/products/piclitex.html`

Although QuickTime can play streaming audio, it isn't necessarily the best tool for the job. For that, iTunes is a more appropriate choice.

iTunes

iTunes is Apple's contribution to the digital audio playing field. It can serve as your CD player, MP3 ripper, song organizer, jukebox, eye candy, and CD burner. And, amazingly, it's simple enough to use that even if you've never burned a CD, ripped an MP3, or listened to Internet radio, you can be doing all three within five minutes—tops.

Although iTunes didn't ship with the original release of Mac OS X, you can download the latest version from `http://www.apple.com/itunes/`, or use the Software Update System Preference panel. (See Chapter 29 for more information on the automatic software updating feature of Mac OS X.) If you're using Mac OS X 10.1, iTunes was installed with the operating system.

First Run Setup

The first time you launch iTunes, it will run through a setup assistant to locate MP3s and configure Internet playback. The welcome screen is shown in Figure 7.45.

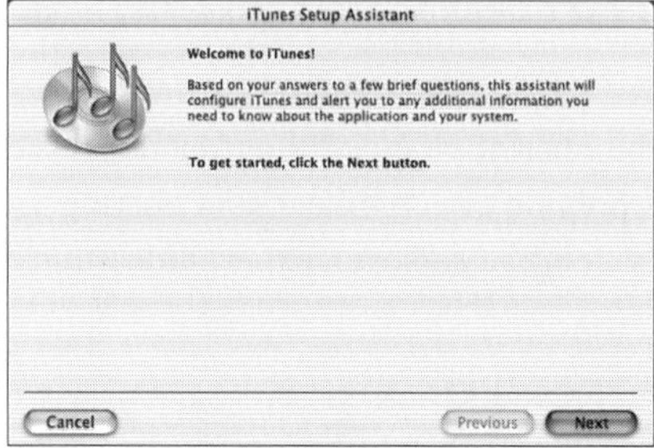

FIGURE 7.45 *Setting up iTunes requires a few clicks; then you're in digital music paradise.*

During the setup procedure, click Next to go to the next step, or Previous to return to the last screen. Clicking Cancel exits the setup utility and starts iTunes.

The second step of the setup process, displayed in Figure 7.46, allows you to set Internet access options.

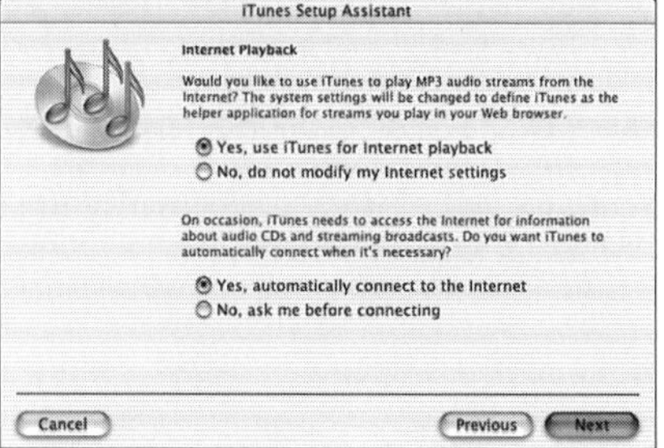

FIGURE 7.46 *Choose how iTunes works with your Internet applications.*

iTunes is perfectly suited for handling streaming MP3s. By default, the Use iTunes for Internet playback radio button will be selected. If you have another application (such as Panic Software's Audion `http://www.panic.com/`) you'd rather use for streaming, choose Do not modify my Internet settings instead.

When extracting CDs, iTunes can look up information about the CD, such as the artist and song title. The Automatically connect to the Internet radio button, set by default, enables this feature. To force iTunes to prompt before connecting to the Internet, click Ask me before connecting.

Click Next when you're satisfied with your responses.

During the final step of the configuration, shown in Figure 7.47, you are prompted on how iTunes will find MP3s.

FIGURE 7.47
iTunes can search your drive for MP3s, if desired.

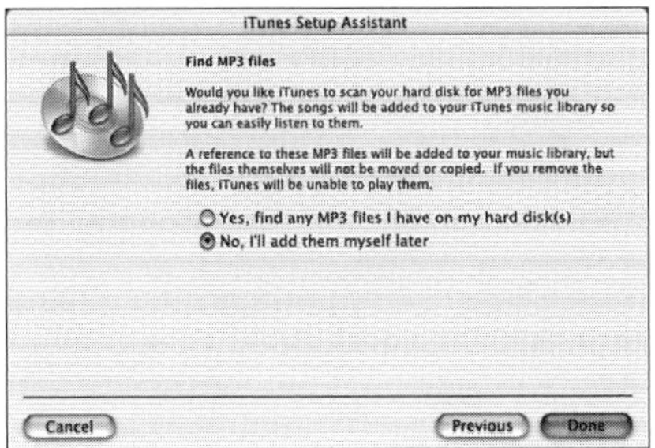

By default, iTunes will locate all of the files on your drive. To disable this feature, click I'll add them myself later. The process of searching the drive for MP3 files can take awhile, so I prefer to add MP3s when I want to.

Click Done to begin using iTunes.

> **Note**
>
> Regardless of the settings made in the iTunes setup assistant, you can always use the Application Preferences panel to modify them later.

The iTunes Interface

Everything you need to do anything (well, almost anything) in iTunes is found in the main window, pictured in Figure 7.48. The main control areas are listed here.

Player Controls—The player controls move between different songs, play, pause, and adjust the output volume of the current playing track. Clicking directly on the sound slider moves the volume adjustment immediately to that level.

Status Information—Displays information about the currently playing song. Clicking each of the status lines toggles between different types of information. The top line displays the artist and can be toggled to the name of the song with a single click. Likewise, the Elapsed Time line can be toggled to display remaining time and total time.

FIGURE 7.48
A single iTunes window provides access to almost all application functions.

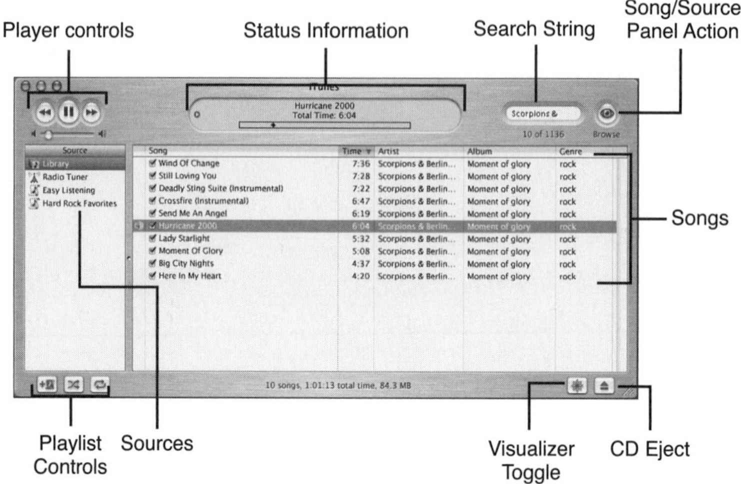

The progress bar shows how far along the playback of the current song has progressed. Dragging the progress bar handle can move the playback back or forward in the audio track.

Finally, a stereo frequency monitor can be displayed by clicking the arrow on the right of the status display.

Search String—Typing a few letters into the iTunes Search field will immediately display all audio tracks within the current playlist or library that match the string in *any* way (artist, song, album).

Song/Source Panel Action—The action button performs a different function depending on what source is currently being viewed. As you work in different areas of the program, this button changes to an appropriate action for that area:

> **Library**—When viewing the main song library, the action button toggles between two different browse modes. The first mode is similar to the Finder's List view. Each audio track is listed on its own line. The second mode uses a paradigm similar to the Column Finder view. A first column lists the artist, the second column shows the albums for that artist. Finally, a lower pane shows a list of the song tracks for that artist and album.
>
> **Radio Tuner**—The Radio Tuner's action button is Refresh—this reloads all available stations from the iTunes Internet Radio station browser.
>
> **Playlist**—A playlist is your own personal list of music that you've compiled from the main library. Playlists are the starting point for creating a CD. When viewing a playlist, the action button is Burn CD.

CD—When a CD is inserted, iTunes prepares to import the tracks to MP3 files. The action button is Import when a CD is selected as the source.

Visual Effects—No matter what source is selected, iTunes can always be toggled into Visualizer mode to display dazzling onscreen graphics. When the visual effects are active, the action button becomes Options for controlling the visual effects.

Sources—The Source pane lists the available MP3 sources. Attached MP3 players, CDs, playlists, the central music Library, and Radio Tuner make up the available sources.

> **Tip**
>
> Double-clicking a source icon opens a new window with *only* the contents of that source. This is a nice way to create a cleaner view of your audio files.

Songs—A list of the songs on the currently selected source. When in the main library view, you can click the action button to toggle this list between a simple list and column-based browser. Double-clicking a song in the list will start playing from the selected source. To change the visible fields in the list, choose View Options from the Edit menu.

Playlist Controls—Three playlist controls are available: Create Playlist, Randomize Order, and Loop. As their names suggest, these can be used to create new playlists and control the order in which the audio tracks are played back.

Visualizer Toggle—Turns the visualization effects ("music for the eyes") on and off.

CD Eject—Ejects the currently inserted CD.

So, now that you know what the controls are for, let's take a look at putting iTunes through its paces.

Encoding MP3s

Encoding, or ripping, CDs lets you take the tracks from a CD and save them in the MP3 (MPEG Layer 3) format. MP3s are a highly compressed audio format that has been made very popular due in part to controversial services such as Napster (`http://www.napster.com`) and Gnutella. These free file-sharing protocols allow users worldwide to trade audio files—much to the dismay of the recording industry.

Upon inserting a CD, iTunes will query the Gracenote's CDDB (CD Database). If you've chosen to manually query the CDDB, you can force a query by choosing Get CD Track Names from the Advanced menu. An iTunes window is shown with a CD inserted in Figure 7.49.

FIGURE 7.49
iTunes locates CD and track information for an inserted CD.

The CDDB Internet database contains information on hundreds of thousands of CDs. If a match is found, the CD will be displayed by name in the Source listing. If a CD is not located, it will be listed as Untitled.

Click the CD name in the Source pane to view the tracks. You're now ready to start importing. Select the tracks you want to encode. If *no* tracks are selected, the entire CD will be imported. Click the Import action button to encode the selected tracks.

By default, the encoded MP3s will be stored in `~/Documents/iTunes/iTunes Music`. You can adjust this location through the Application Preferences. An entire CD can take from 5–74 minutes, depending on the speed of your CD-ROM drive. To pass the time, you can continue to use iTunes while the tracks are imported. When the import is finished, the MP3s will be available under the Library source listing.

Editing Track Information

If your CD's track information is *not* shown, you can edit the CD tracks by slowly double-clicking the track name. Type in the correct name, and then press Return to save it. You'll want to take this step *before* creating MP3s.

Each MP3 file contains ID3 tags; these tags are saved with each file and identify the artist and song title. Without this information, iTunes is unable to catalog the MP3 correctly.

To fully edit the encoded information for each track, choose Get Info (Command+I) from the File menu. The track info window enables you to change titles, artists, and genres for a given song. There are three panels within the Song Information window. The top of each panel is the song name in an editable field. At the bottom are Prev Song and Next Song buttons to move forward and backward through the song tracks without exiting the Info window.

The Info panel is shown in Figure 7.50. This panel displays a summary of information on the selected track.

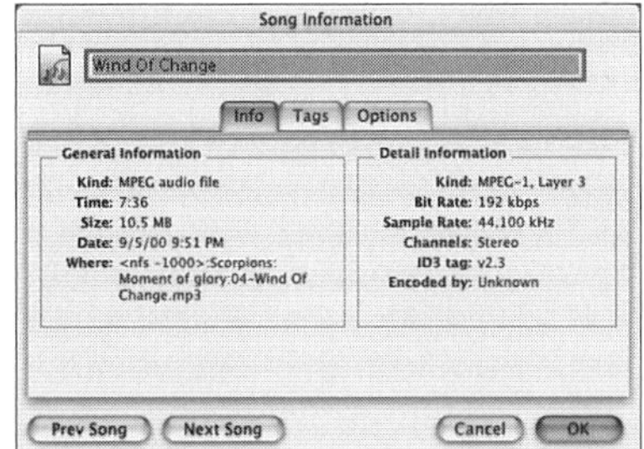

FIGURE 7.50
The Info panel shows a summary of information about the selected track.

Next, the Tags panel can be used to set each of the possible ID3 tags. Although they are not necessary to play the song, each field aids in the cataloging process. When you have several thousand songs, you'll appreciate *any* information you can get! The Tags panel can be seen in Figure 7.51.

FIGURE 7.51
ID3 tags are used when iTunes catalogs your music.

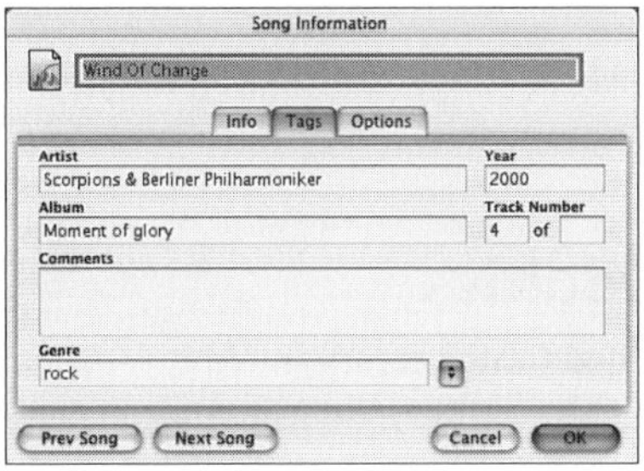

Be careful to use the exact same album titles and artist names for each track of the same album. If the strings vary by even a single space, they'll be listed as different albums or artists.

Finally, the Options panel can set a per-track audio adjustment to quiet those really loud songs during playback. In addition, a start and stop time can be set for a track. These settings will not affect the file itself. Figure 7.52 shows the Options panel.

Make your settings (if any) and click OK to exit the Song Information window. If you'd like to send CDDB your updated CD information for inclusion in its database, choose Submit CD Track Names from the Advanced menu.

Tip

The Get Info option works on MP3 files that have already been created, not only CD tracks.

Figure 7.52
Control volume on a per-track basis, or set alternative start and stop points in a song.

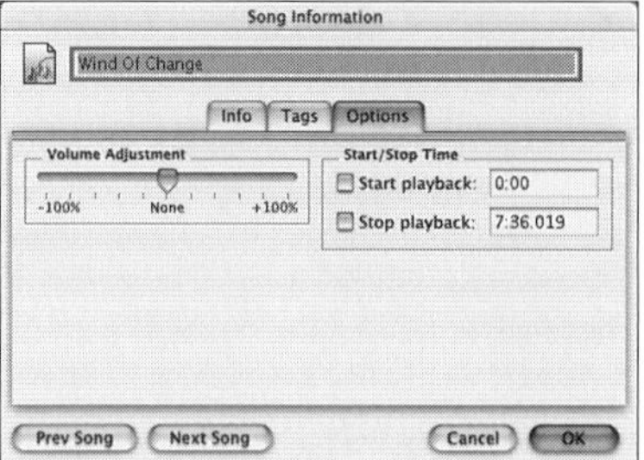

Adding MP3s to iTunes

If you're working with an existing Library of MP3s rather than a CD, you can easily add them to your MP3 library. Use the Add To Library option from the File menu to choose a folder that contains MP3s. Alternatively, you can simply drag a folder of MP3s from the Finder into the Library song list.

The process of importing MP3s takes time. Each MP3 is examined for ID3 tags and is cataloged in the iTunes database. If you're adding iTunes from a network drive, be prepared to take a quick lunch break.

iTunes Music Library Oddities

iTunes will *not* copy files that are added to its Library into the `~/Library/iTunes/iTunes Music` folder. Although the songs will work during the current execution of iTunes, subsequent program executions will *not* be able to find songs that aren't stored in the `iTunes Music folder`. You must manually copy songs to this location or reassign the iTunes music directory (using the application Preferences).

> **Note**
>
> To make matters worse, it's easy to create double listings of songs in the master Library by adding MP3s to the Library more than once.
>
> To solve the double-listing problem, select all songs in the Library and drag the listing to the Trash, or press the Delete key to erase them. This will not physically move any of the files; it will remove their Library listing.
>
> After they're removed, add the MP3s to your Library again.

Creating and Working with Playlists

The key to many of the remaining iTunes features lies in creating a playlist. A *playlist* is nothing more than a list of songs from your Library. To create a new playlist, click the

Add Playlist button in the lower-left corner of the iTunes window or choose New Playlist (Command+N) from the File menu. The new playlist ("untitled playlist") will be added to the Source pane. Use a slow double-click to rename the playlist.

The next step is to add songs to the playlist. To add songs, follow these steps:

1. Select the Library source.
2. Verify that the song you want is in the main MP3 Library. If it *isn't*, you must first add it to the Library.
3. Select one or more songs in the song list.
4. Drag the selection to the playlist in the Source pane.

The selected songs will be added to your playlist. Click the playlist to display the songs. You can drag the tracks within the playlist window to choose their order.

Burning CDs and Exporting to MP3 Players

After a playlist has been built, you can drag its name in the source listing to any listed MP3 player source. The files will automatically be copied to the connected player. If the player does not have enough available space, you will need to remove files from your playlist or select the external player and remove tracks from its memory.

If you have a Mac with a supported CD burner, you can use a playlist to burn an audio CD laid out exactly like the playlist. Click the Burn CD action button in the upper-right corner of the iTunes window, and then follow the onscreen instructions, inserting a recordable CD when prompted.

> **Note**
>
> These features are (obviously) very dependent on the hardware you have connected to or installed in your Macintosh. The original iTunes release for Mac OS X did not support CD burning. Subsequent updates have improved support for many available burners.
>
> Apple maintains an up-to-date list of supported MP3 players and CD burners on its iTunes Web site at `http://www.apple.com/iTunes/`.

Internet Radio

Before iTunes, I had only a few experiences with streaming MP3s—extremely poor experiences. As a user, I'm uninterested in the mechanics of the connection—I want to see a simple listing of radio stations, choose one, and listen. This is the approach Apple took when creating iTunes.

To display a list of the available streaming stations, click the Radio Tuner source. After a few seconds querying a station server, a list of available music genres is displayed. Each genre can be expanded to show the stations within that group by clicking its disclosure arrow. Stations are listed with a Stream (station) Name, Bit Rate, and Comment (description). The Bit Rate determines the quality of the streamed audio—the higher the bit rate, the higher the quality—*and* the higher the bandwidth requirements.

Figure 7.53 shows a list of hard rock stations (is there any other type of music?).

FIGURE 7.53
Stations are grouped by genre. Expand each genre to reveal hundreds of available stations.

Double-click a station to begin playing, or select it and then click the Play button. iTunes will buffer a few seconds of audio, and then start playing the streaming audio. If iTunes stutters while playing, look for a similar station using a lower bit rate.

Tip

Conversely to what seems logical, you can drag stations from the Radio Tuner source and play them in a playlist. The playlist will play as it normally would, but will start playing streaming audio when it gets to the added Internet Radio Station.

You cannot burn a radio station to a CD or store it on an external MP3 device.

Playing Audio

As I'm sure you've discovered by now, the iTunes push button player controls work on whatever source you currently have selected. After a song plays, iTunes moves to the next song. You can also control the playing via keyboard or from the Controls menu:

Play/Stop—Space bar

Next Song—Command+Right-arrow key

Previous Song—Command+Left-arrow key

Volume Up—Command+Up-arrow key

Volume Down—Command+Down-arrow key

Mute—Command+M

> **Tip**
>
> These functions are also available from the iTunes Dock icon. Click and hold the Dock icon to provide a shortcut for moving between the tracks in the current audio source.

To randomize the play order for the selected source, click the Shuffle button (second from the left) in the lower left of the iTunes window. If you want to repeat the tracks, use the Repeat button to toggle between Repeat Off, Repeat Once, and Repeat All.

> **Note**
>
> Although only playlists can be burned to a CD or written to an MP3 player, the Library and CD sources can use all the same options as the playlists with the exception of not being able to rearrange the track order on a CD or main library listing.

iTunes Window Modes

iTunes' window is a bit large to conveniently leave onscreen during playback. Luckily, there are two other window modes that take up far less space. Quite unintuitively, you access these small modes by clicking the window's Maximize button.

After clicking Maximize, the window is reduced to the player controls and status window. Figure 7.54 shows the "maximized" iTunes window.

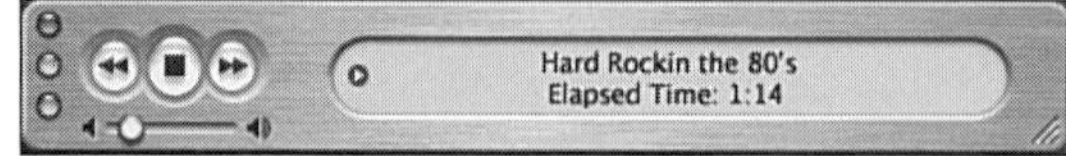

FIGURE 7.54
Click the Maximize button to collapse the iTunes window.

Even this window is a bit large for some monitors. To collapse it even more, use the resize handle in the lower-right corner of the window. A fully collapsed iTunes window can be seen in Figure 7.55.

FIGURE 7.55
The fully collapsed iTunes window includes only the basic playback controls.

To restore iTunes to its original state, click the Maximize button again.

Visualizer

The iTunes Visualizer creates a graphical visualization of your music as it plays. While playing a song, click the Visualizer button (second from the right) in the lower-left corner of the iTunes window. Use Turn Visualizer On (Command+T) to activate the display from the Visuals menu. Figure 7.56 shows the Visualizer in action.

FIGURE 7.56
The Visualizer displays images to match your music.

The Visualizer is simply a plug-in. You can download other plug-ins to add new graphics to the system. Plug-ins are stored in the `~/Library/iTunes/iTunes Plug-ins/` folder. Choose among the installed plug-ins by choosing their name from the Visuals menu.

Tip

Some plug-ins, including the standard Visualizer plug-in, can be controlled via the keyboard while they are running. Press the ? key to display a text menu of available Visualizer options.

The Visuals menu can control the size of the generated graphics as well as toggle between full-screen (Command+F) and window modes. To exit full-screen mode, press Escape.

Visualizer Options

While the windowed Visualizer display is active, the Options action button in the upper-right corner of the window will become active. The Visual Options window is displayed in Figure 7.57.

FIGURE 7.57
Visual options alter the Visualizer display.

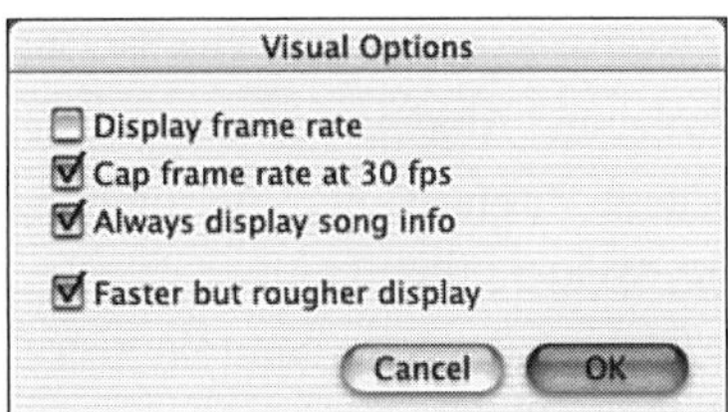

If you're interested in how quickly your computer is generating visualization images, choose Display framerate—this will add a frames-per-second counter to the display. To conserve CPU time on extremely fast machines, use the Cap framerate setting to limit the display to 30 frames per second. This is the rate at which standard movie footage is displayed. On the opposite side of the coin, some machines might not display visualizations fast enough. For these machines, click the Faster but rougher display check box to double the size of the pixels, but greatly speed up the rate of display.

The final option, Always display sound info, adds an information display to the visualization window that contains artist and song info. Typically this data is displayed only when a song begins playing.

Click OK to set your options.

iTunes Preferences

The iTunes Preferences control everything from the appearance of the iTunes listings to MP3 encoding rates and CD burner behavior. There are three panels—General, Importing, and Advanced.

The General panel, shown in Figure 7.58, controls the appearance of song listings, connections to the Internet, and what to do when a CD is inserted.

FIGURE 7.58
Use the General preferences to set appearance and other miscellaneous options.

Source Text—Choose the size of the text labels for the Source listing.

Song Text—Choose the size of the text in the main song listings.

Show Genre When Browsing—When viewing the songs in column mode, include a Genre column in addition to Artist and Album.

Connect to Internet When Needed—If checked, iTunes will automatically connect to the Internet for CDDB access and other data.

Use iTunes for Internet Music Playback—Click Set to register iTunes with the system for all Internet streaming audio playback.

CD Insert—Choose how iTunes reacts when a CD is inserted. Your options include Begin Playing, Show Songs, Import Songs, and Import Songs and Eject.

Battery Saver—If checked, and you are using a PowerBook or iBook, iTunes will use 20% of the available memory to cache songs—thus allowing your hard drive to spin down and conserve power.

The Importing panel configures how CD tracks are imported into the song library. Choose between different bit rates to create CD quality or highly compact MP3 files. Figure 7.59 displays the Importing panel.

There are three available import engines that can be used when a CD is inserted: WAV, AIFF, and MP3.

FIGURE 7.59
Choose the import encoder and sound quality.

The WAV format is native to the Windows platform, and will result in extremely large file sizes. Similarly, AIFF files are the Mac OS X default audio format. Like the WAV, an AIFF encoding of a typical CD track will be huge: 50–60MB.

The best option for building your song library is the MP3 format. MP3s are lightweight, cross platform, and the whole purpose for iTunes' existence!

After setting an import method, use the Configuration pop-up menu to choose a recording rate. The higher the bit rate, the higher quality the recording will be. Audiophiles can create their own custom configuration with even higher bit rates by choosing Custom from the pop-up menu.

To listen to songs as they are imported, make sure that Play Songs While Importing is selected.

Advanced options set the location of the iTunes music library and the parameters used when burning CDs. The Advanced panel is shown in Figure 7.60.

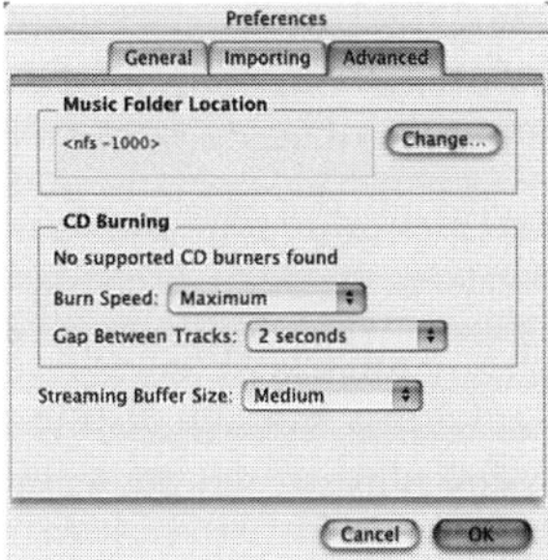

FIGURE 7.60
Advanced preferences control the location of the music library and CD burning preferences.

The Music Folder Location is where iTunes looks for your MP3 files. By default, the music folder is set to `~/Library/iTunes/iTunes Music`. You can adjust this to a more global location, such as `/Library/iTunes/iTunes Music`, so that files are shared among all users on the machine.

The options for controlling CD burning are the Burn Speed and Gap settings. The Burn Speed option controls the speed with which your CD burning will store songs. Occasionally, using the highest speed results in audible pops during playback. If this occurs, lower the burn speed and try again. To increase the amount of time between audio tracks on your CDs, adjust the Gap Between Tracks setting appropriately.

The final setting, Streaming Buffer Size, sets the size of the memory buffer for streaming music stations. If your playback is prone to stuttering, choose a larger buffer size.

Click OK to set and activate your preferences.

Menus

I've used iTunes for months without ever touching the menus. If you're interested in keyboard commands or a few obscure options, be sure to read through these listings.

File

Use the options within the File menu to create playlists, add songs, and retrieve information about selected audio tracks.

New Playlist (Command+N)—Create a new playlist.

New Playlist from Selection (Shift+Command+N)—Create a new playlist using the currently selected audio tracks.

Add to Library—Choose an MP3 folder or volume that contains MP3s. They will be cataloged and added to the Library source.

Close (Command+W)—Close the frontmost window.

Get Info (Command+I)—Get information and set ID3 tags for the selected item.

Show Song File (Command+R)—Reveal a track's file location within the Finder.

Shop for iTunes Products—Launch a Web browser to browse the Apple store for audio-related products.

Edit

The Edit menu provides the standard selection of options, along with the ability to Select none—effectively deselecting all tracks in the playlist. You can also use the Show current song option to jump the playlist to the song being played, and the View options to control what fields are seen in the listing.

Controls

The Controls menu does what its name suggests: controls playback of tracks. There are keyboard shortcuts for everything you could want to do, making iTunes an effective music entertainment system.

Play/Stop (space)—Play or stop playing the current song.

Next Song (Command+Right arrow)—Move to the next song.

Previous Song (Command+Left arrow)—Move to the previous song.

Shuffle—Shuffle the play order for the selected source,

Repeat Off—Do not repeat the playlist.

Repeat All—Repeat playing the source songs.

Repeat One—Repeat playing through the source songs once.

Volume Up (Command+Up arrow)—Turn up the volume.

Volume Down (Command+Down arrow)—Turn down the volume.

Mute/Un-Mute (Option+Commamd+Down arrow)—Disable iTunes' sound output temporarily.

Eject CD (Command+E)—Eject the currently inserted CD.

Visuals

The Visuals menu can be used to control the Visualizer, as well as choose from additional Visualizer plug-ins, if installed.

Turn Visual On/Off (Command+T)—Toggle the visuals on and off.

Small—Use small visuals (good for slow computers).

Medium—Use medium-sized visuals.

Large—Use the entire window (or screen) for displaying visuals.

Full Screen (Command+F)—Clear the screen and display *only* the Visualizer onscreen.

Note

If you have installed multiple visual plug-ins, they'll be listed at the bottom of the Visuals menu. Choose which plug-in you want to use by selecting it from the menu. The built-in visual engine is listed as iTunes Visualizer.

Advanced

The Advanced menu has several interesting features, including the capability to export text listings of your song libraries and submit information back to the CDDB. If you find a CD that isn't automatically recognized by the CDDB system, this is a great way to help CDDB find your music.

Open Stream (Command+U)—Open an MP3 stream directly by entering its URL.

Convert to MP3—Select a sound file (including CD tracks) to convert to MP3 format.

Export Song List—Save a text list of the current source. The output file includes all fields visible in the song listing.

Get CD Track Names—Force iTunes to retrieve the CD track data from the CDDB.

Submit CD Track Names—Submit edited track names back to the CDDB for future inclusion in the online music database.

Convert ID3 Tags—Convert ID3 tags to version 1.0 through version 2.3. This is necessary for some older MP3 players to recognize the tags.

iTunes is a fantastic tool for anyone interested in any type of digital audio. It provides the first glimpse at Steve Jobs' "digital hub" future, in which a single computer serves as the control point for many other devices. If you have an MP3 player and a CD burner, iTunes is your one-stop shop for everything audio.

Keychain Access

Using the Internet is a neverending struggle to keep track of passwords for e-mail servers, file servers, Web sites, and other private information. Since Mac OS 9.x, Apple has included a security application and API, called the Keychain, to make accessing your collection of passwords much easier.

The Keychain Access software (Path: `/Applications/Utilities/Keychain Access`) automatically stores passwords from Keychain-aware applications such as Mail and iTools. Users can also manually add their own passwords to the keychain. Later, the keychain can be unlocked to reveal the original cleartext password. By default, all users have their own keychain named the same as their username. Additional keychains can be created to store specific information, such as credit card numbers, PINs, and so on. Think of the keychain as a database of your most sensitive information, all accessible through your Mac OS X account password.

Caution

The default keychain is unlocked by your account password. Extremely sensitive information is best placed in a secondary keychain with a different password; otherwise a single compromise of your account will unlock access to all your information.

Automated Access

Launching Keychain Access displays the contents of your default keychain. For my account, named `jray`, this is a keychain named `jray`. For an account that has set up e-mail and iTools services, the Keychain Access window should look similar to that in Figure 7.61. There are three items listed: two for my e-mail account and its associated servers, and one for iTools.

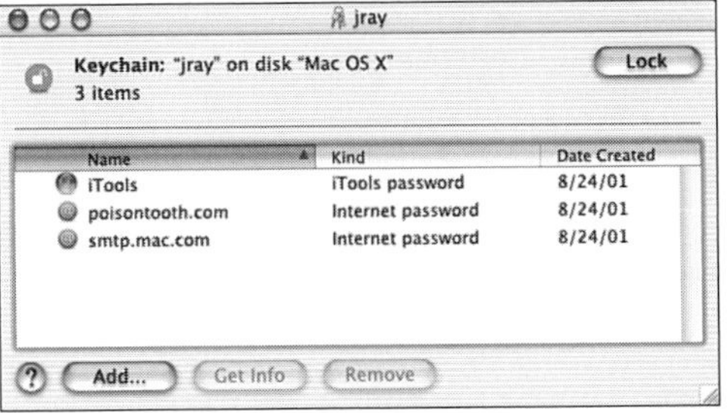

FIGURE 7.61
The Keychain Access window displays a list of stored passwords and other information.

The obvious question is, "How did these items get here?" They were added by Mac OS X applications. Typically, when an application wants to store something in the keychain, you'll be given the option of storing it. For example, when accessing a site that requires HTTP authentication, the OmniWeb browser presents a dialog box as seen in Figure 7.62. Choosing the Remember name and password option automatically adds the entered password to the default keychain. Over time, your keychain could become populated with hundreds of items and you might not ever know it!

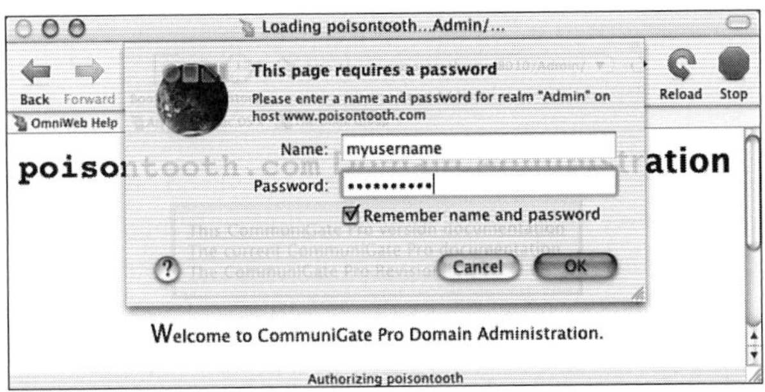

FIGURE 7.62
Applications can automatically add information to the default keychain.

When an application wants to access information from your keychain, it must first make sure that the keychain is unlocked. Your default Mac OS X keychain is automatically unlocked when you log in to your account, making its passwords accessible to the applications that stored them. To manually lock or unlock a keychain, click the Lock button in the upper-right corner of the Keychain Access window. The Keychain Access window, along with its Dock icon, will change to reflect its security status. If an application attempts to access information on a locked keychain, it will display a dialog, as shown in Figure 7.63. Entering the correct password (your account password for the default keychain) will unlock the keychain that your application is attempting to access.

FIGURE 7.63
If an application attempts to access data in a locked keychain, you will be prompted for the keychain's passphrase.

Even after a keychain is unlocked, an application might still need a bit more help before it can retrieve the information it needs from the keychain. Each stored piece of information can be controlled in a way that makes it accessible to only very specific applications. Mail passwords, for example, are only accessible by the Mail application. If a program you just downloaded off the Internet attempts to unlock your Web or e-mail passwords, you'll know something nefarious is afoot. Sometimes, usually after a system upgrade, you will have to re-educate your Mac OS X computer about what applications can access what passwords. This is an extremely simple process.

When the keychain notices an unauthorized application attempting to access a piece of information, it will prompt the user with an window similar to the one shown in Figure 7.64. Users can choose to deny the access, allow it only once (Allow Once), or allow the application to access the information whenever it wants (Always Allow). Before making a choice, you should always click the Details disclosure triangle to view which keychain is being accessed and which application wants the data. If you don't recognize the application, click Deny to disallow access.

Manual Access

Users who want to access stored data, or manually add new information to a keychain, can do so through the Keychain Access program. Each item listed in the keychain window can be opened by selecting it, and then clicking the Get Info button, or simply by double-clicking the entry. Much as the Finder's Show Info window displays information about a file, the Get Info function of the keychain shows information about the stored data.

FIGURE 7.64
Each application must be authorized to access a specific piece of information.

General Information

There are two panels of information for each keychain entry: General Information and Access control. These are selectable from the Show pop-up menu. General Information, as its name suggests, provides the basic information about the stored information. For example, Figure 7.65 shows the General Information for an IMAP password in my default keychain. The Kind field identifies the type of information, Where shows the resource that stored the information, Account displays the creating user account, and the Created/Modified fields display when the entry was added and last edited. Users can add any additional comments about the item by typing in the Comments field. Click the View Password button to display the password in cleartext. If you are viewing an entry that includes a URL, a Go There button is included in the display to take you to the remote resource.

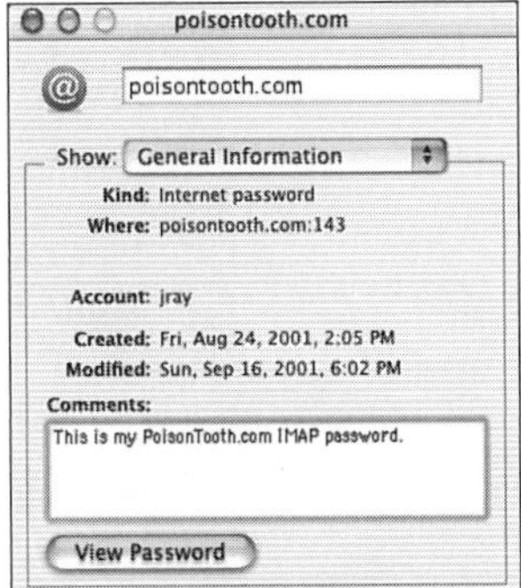

FIGURE 7.65
The General Information panel displays what type of data is stored, and when it was added to the keychain.

> **Note**
>
> When you click View Password, you often will be prompted to allow Keychain Access to retrieve the data. Although this might seem strange, it is because Keychain Access itself must obey the same rules as the rest of the system. Because Keychain Access isn't listed as having unlimited access to stored items, it will ask each time it needs to retrieve the information.

Access Control

The Access Control panel of the Get Info function enables the user to pick and choose which applications can access a given piece of information in the keychain. Shown in Figure 7.66, the controls of this panel are very straightforward. Click Allow Access to this Item Without Warning to allow applications to transparently access the resource with no user interaction. You can further specify individual applications by clicking the Allow Access Only by These Applications and then using the Add and Remove buttons to add and remove applications from the list. If you prefer to allow any program to access the resource, click the Allow Access by Any Application radio button. Those who are truly security conscious can uncheck the Allow Access to This Item Without Warning check box to force all applications to first ask permission before retrieving a password.

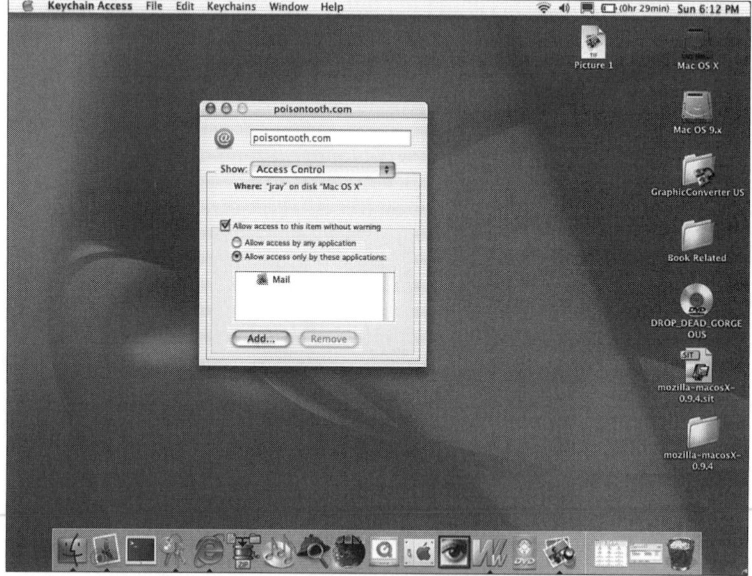

FIGURE 7.66
Use the Access Control information panel to enable or disable an application's ability to retrieve information transparently from the keychain.

Adding New Entries

New pieces of information can be added to the keychain by clicking the Add button in the main Keychain window or choosing New Password Item from the File menu. This action will open a new window, shown in Figure 7.67, for entering the data to be stored. Enter the name or URL of the stored item in the Name field, the account name associated with the data in the Account field, and, finally, the sensitive data in the Password field. By default, the password is hidden as you type. To display the password as it is typed, click the Show Typing check box. Click Add when finished.

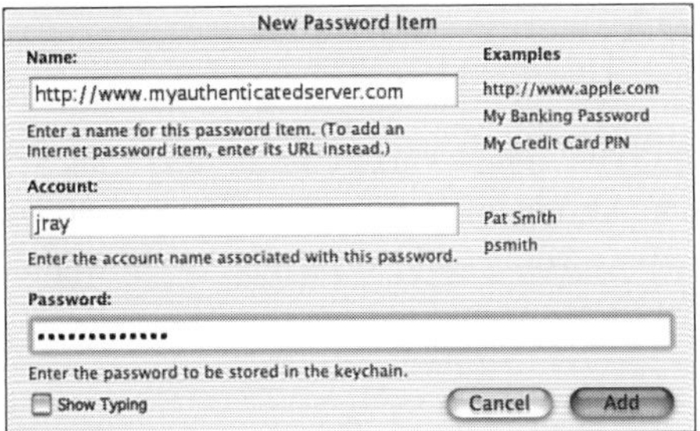

FIGURE 7.67
New items can easily be added manually to an existing keychain.

To remove any item from the keychain (either automatically or manually entered), select its name in the list, and then click the Remove button.

Managing Keychains

Each user account can have as many keychains as is needed. Choose Keychain List from the Edit menu to manage the keychain stored in your user account, the window shown in Figure 7.68 will appear.

FIGURE 7.68
Use the Keychain List to manage your available keychains.

As mentioned earlier, there is a single default keychain generated for each user account. New keychains can be created by clicking the New button in the keychain list window. You will be prompted for a name and save location for the keychain (the default is

~/Library/Keychains). Next, you will need to enter a passphrase that will unlock the new keychain. It's best to choose something different from your account password to prevent people who might gain access to your account from seeing your most sensitive information. If you'd like to add an existing keychain file (perhaps from your account on another Mac OS X machine), click Add, and then choose the keychain file on your drive.

When the new keychain is added or created within an account, you can switch to it by choosing its name from the Keychain menu. To remove a keychain from the system, highlight its name in the list, and then click Remove.

Keychain Settings

The Keychain Access application has no preferences, but it does allow some control over each keychain file, such as modifying the password that unlocks the keychain. To open the settings, open the appropriate keychain from the Keychain menu and then choose the Settings option from the Edit menu. You should see a new window, much like the one shown in Figure 7.69.

Figure 7.69
Set your keychains to lock after a certain length of time.

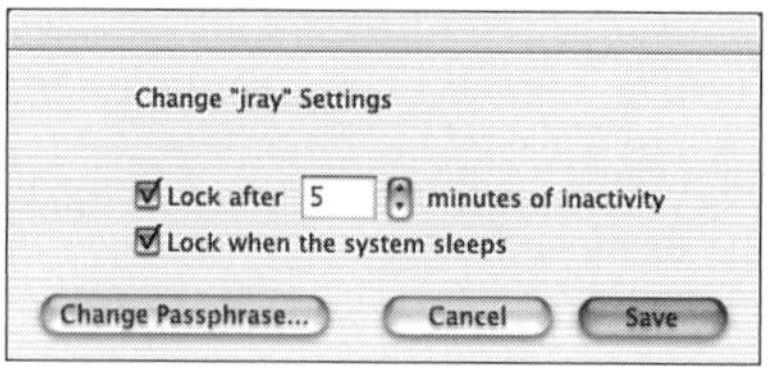

Within the settings window, you can use Lock after XX minutes of inactivity setting to force Mac OS X to lock a keychain if it isn't used for a certain length of time. Clicking Lock when the system sleeps will cause the keychain to be locked if the computer goes to sleep. Finally, click Change Passphrase to edit the password that unlocks the keychain. Press the Save button to save the settings for the keychain.

Note

If you change the password on your default keychain to something other than your Mac OS X account password, it will not be automatically unlocked when you first login.

At this time, many applications don't yet take advantage of the keychain, but Apple is aggressively promoting this technology and it is slowly creeping into applications. I highly recommend that you take advantage of this application to help keep your passwords safe and easily accessible.

Menus

Keychain Access's menus give users the ability to switch between different keychains, and export keychains to other files. They provide the quickest means of accessing and managing additional keychains beyond the Mac OS X default chain.

File

Use the File menu to create new keychains and add new entries to them. The following options are available:

New Keychain (Command+N)—Create a new keychain file. You will be prompted for a passphrase to protect the keychain.

New Password Item—Enter a new password (or other piece of data) into the currently active keychain.

Lock (Command+L)—Lock the currently active keychain.

Lock All Keychains—Lock all of the open keychains.

Close Window (Command+W)—Close the active keychain window.

Get Info (Command+I)—Show the information about the selected keychain entry.

Export—Export the keychain data to another file.

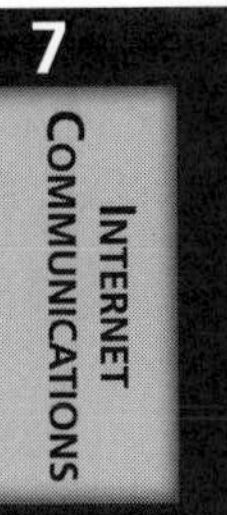

Edit

The Edit menu contains two important entries in addition to the usual cut and paste: Keychain List and Settings. The Keychain List option opens a management window with all available keychains listed. The Settings option allows the user to change when the active keychain locks and what its passphrase is.

Keychains

Use the Keychains menu to toggle between the different available keychains on the system. If you'd like to switch to a different default keychain (rather than the Mac OS X account default), this can be accomplished here as well.

Third-Party Utilities

Apple has included two other third-party applications to make your Internet browsing a bit more enjoyable. First, Java Web Start (Path: `/Applications/Utilities/Java Web Start`) is a Java application written by Sun Microsystems to provide a quick and easy way to launch and store other online Java applications. One of the biggest problems with Java applications is the lack of a standard installation and execution procedure. With Java Web Start, users can click on a Java Web Start enabled app within a Web page and transparently download, install, and execute it. For more information and demo software, visit Sun's page at `http://java.sun.com/products/javawebstart/`.

In addition, Adobe Acrobat Reader (Path: `/Applications/Adobe Acrobat Reader`) is included for those who need functionality beyond what Apple's Preview application can provide. The Reader software can search PDF documents, display PDFs within a Web browser, and, arguably, does a better job of rendering some PDFs that Apple's offering. For more information on Acrobat Reader, check out `http://www.adobe.com/`.

Summary

This chapter covered a great deal of ground—everything from searching the Internet with Sherlock , viewing movies, and listening to streaming music to managing your account passwords. The applications provided with Mac OS X can get anyone up and running with these advanced technologies in a matter of minutes.

The best way to fully understand many of these applications is to use them. At the time of this writing, Mac OS X is more than two months old. Even so, users are still finding additional shortcuts and hidden features by the dozens. Explore your system—you never know what might turn up!

CHAPTER

Installing Third-Party Applications

In This Chapter

Mac OS X comes with enough software and tools to keep an avid e-mail reader or Web browser happy for quite awhile. For the rest of us, however, it is lacking in many of the creative tools that have made the Macintosh platform so appealing. This chapter will attempt to rectify the situation by pointing out several stand-out applications that are available for the new operating system. Many of these will be unfamiliar because they come from a NeXT/OpenStep heritage—not traditional Macintosh developers. In addition, we'll take a look at how these applications are typically installed.

This chapter serves as a point of demarcation within the contents of this book. It effectively ends the coverage of using Mac OS X and begins more advanced configuration topics. I recommend reading through this chapter and spending some time getting to know your system before continuing.

Software Sources and Formats

Before you can use software, you must first download and unarchive it. The process of downloading software with Internet Explorer is not covered here because it is (I hope) a commonplace activity, although there will be a few additional applications introduced to make downloads easier.

Tip

For those with a fast connection, try accessing your iDisk from Mac OS X. Apple has done a good job of keeping an up-to-date software library on the network disks, making installs as easy as a drag-and-drop.

There are a number of good online libraries of Mac OS X software. The following sites are the best places to look for the latest and greatest downloads:

VersionTracker—`www.versiontracker.com/vt_mac_osx.shtml`—Updated continuously throughout the day, VersionTracker's Web site is often the first to carry new Mac OS X software.

Mac OS X Apps—`www.macosxapps.com/`—This site features in-depth discussions on new software and uses a Slashdot-like interface for posting and discussion.

Apple's Mac OS X Downloads—`www.apple.com/downloads/macosx/`—Although not always updated as quickly as the other two sites, Apple's collection is well documented and easily navigated.

Distribution Formats

For almost as long as the Macintosh has been able to connect to other networks and devices, it has used BinHex and MacBinary software distribution methods.

BinHex is similar to the output of the Unix `uuencode` command—it enables the transfer of binary files using a 7-bit text encoding. BinHex files can be recognized by the `.hqx` suffix. Because of its platform and transfer method independence, most Macintosh software you download will be encoded using the BinHex specification.

MacBinary is another encoding type that takes into account the Macintosh-specific features of the HFS file system. Although the Mac OS supports the notion of data and resource forks, it is impossible to store files with a resource fork on operating systems such as Microsoft's NTFS or FAT32 without some type of encoding. The MacBinary specification provides a method of representing both the data and resource fork within a single binary data stream. MacBinary files can be identified by the `.bin` suffix.

Archive Formats

Neither MacBinary nor BinHex is an archive format—they are common Macintosh file encodings, but are not capable of packaging software for installation. There are three archive methods common to Mac OS X software distributions:

> `.dmg`—Apple's preferred distribution format, the Disk Image is a double-clickable file that will mount a virtual disk image on your desktop. The `.dmg` file format is often combined with one of the other two archive types.
>
> `.sit`—The StuffIt archive is the most popular format for Carbon and Classic applications. Mac OS X ships with StuffIt Expander, an application capable of unarchiving `.sit` files and decoding `.hqx`/`.bin`-encoded distributions.
>
> `.tar.gz`—Gzipped Tarfile. This is actually a combination of the `gzip` (compression) and `tar` (archiving) utilities of the BSD subsystem. These files can be unarchived from the command line using `tar zxf` *<archive name>* or using StuffIt Expander.

In addition to `.sit` and `.tar.gz` files, StuffIt Expander can handle almost any archive format you give it. The version of StuffIt Expander included with Mac OS X 10.0.0, however, has a few bugs and should be upgraded to the latest version as quickly as possible.

Tip

After installing the latest version of StuffIt, which is a Carbonized application, remove the version installed with Mac OS 9.x. A single application can now serve both Mac OS X and Mac OS 9 environments.

Mac OS X also seems to have a bit of difficulty launching the *correct* version of StuffIt if there is more than one instance installed on your drive at a time. By using a single Carbon application, the trouble is eliminated.

Many people have replaced StuffIt Expander with the OpenUp software written by Scott Anguish. Scott's OpenUp application is better suited to handle Unix archive and encoding formats, and has the source code available for your viewing pleasure. I've had no trouble with StuffIt for most archives, but OpenUp is a powerful alternative for those who would like something a bit less commercial. Download OpenUp from `www.stepwise.com/Software/OpenUp`.

Using StuffIt Expander

The quick-and-dirty instructions for using StuffIt Expander (path: `Applications/Utilities/StuffIt Expander`) are as follows: Drag your archive file(s) (`.hqx`, `.bin`, `.sit`, `.tar.gz`, and so on) on top of the StuffIt Expander archive. StuffIt will launch and unarchive the selections.

Alternatively, start the Expander application; then use Expand (Command+E) from the File menu to choose the files to expand.

Tip

I recommend adding StuffIt Expander to the Finder window's toolbar for access from any folder. Alternatively, add the icon to the Dock for system-wide accessibility.

There are a number of settings that can fine-tune how StuffIt expander deals with archive files after they have been extracted, and the text files within. If you use StuffIt archives in a cross-platform environment, these options can help reformat files for better viewing on the Macintosh. Improper use can also corrupt source code files.

Preferences

Open the StuffIt Expander preferences from the application menu. There are eight categories of options that can be set. Switch between each area by clicking the appropriate icon on the left side of the preference window.

Expanding

The Expanding preferences, displayed in Figure 8.1, control what happens to archives as they are being extracted and after the extraction has completed.

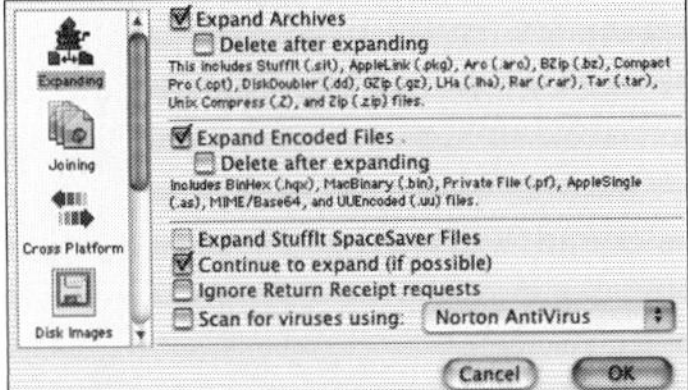

FIGURE 8.1
The Expanding panel controls the unarchiving process.

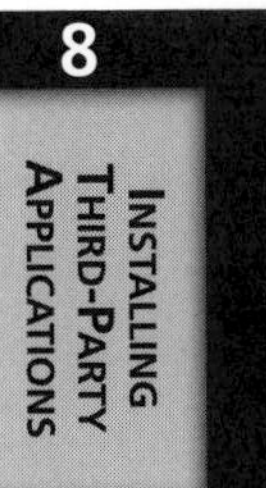

You can fine-tune the process of expanding archives with the following settings:

Expand Archives—Checked by default. If deselected, StuffIt Expander will not decompress archived files. Click the Delete After Expanding check box to automatically remote archives after successfully expanding.

Expanded Encoded Files—Selected by default, this setting ensures that StuffIt will decode MacBinary, BinHex, and other encoded files. The Delete After Expanding check box enables automatic removal of encoded files as they've been decoded.

Expand StuffIt SpaceSaver Files—Rarely used, StuffIt SpaceSaver files are created by the commercial StuffIt application. When checked, Expander will automatically decompress these archives.

Continue to Expand—If checked, StuffIt will attempt to expand archives it finds inside of a given archive.

Ignore Return Receipt Requests—Some StuffIt archives may request that a notification be sent upon expanding the file. Selecting this check box will ignore the notification requests.

Scan for Viruses Using—Use this setting and the associated pop-up menu to choose a virus-scan utility to automatically check files that are processed by StuffIt Expander.

Joining

The Joining panel, shown in Figure 8.2, controls how split archives are handled. By default, StuffIt Expander will attempt to join segmented files, and then automatically expand the completed archive. Use the check boxes on this screen to alter these settings or configure StuffIt Expander to automatically remove individual segment files after they are joined (the complete file will remain).

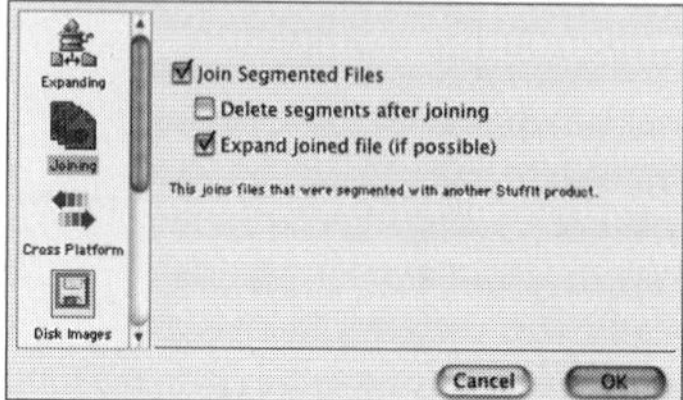

FIGURE 8.2
Joining segmented archives is controlled by the Joining panel.

Cross Platform

The Cross Platform settings, shown in Figure 8.3, determine how StuffIt will deal with text files that it finds within an archive. A user can choose to convert text files to Macintosh format when StuffIt detects text, or to never convert files.

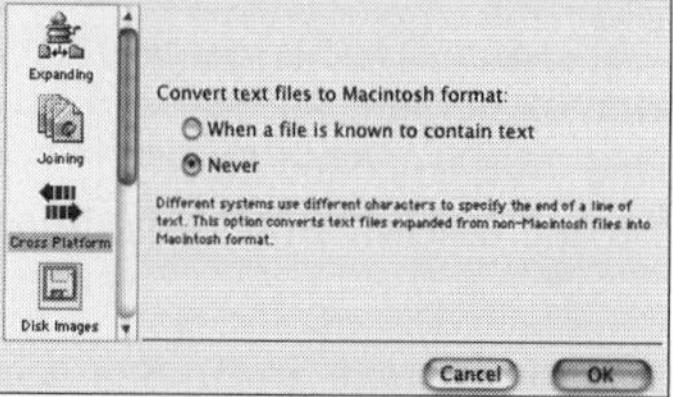

FIGURE 8.3
Configure the Cross Platform panel to automatically convert text files for readability on the Macintosh.

Caution

Be careful with this setting. StuffIt Expander does not always make the appropriate choice about whether a file contains text. If you find that files within your archive are corrupt after expanding, change this option to Never.

Disk Images

The Disk Images panel controls what StuffIt will do when it encounters a disk (ShrinkWrap) image. This feature is currently unavailable in Expander for Mac OS X.

Destination

As the panel name suggests, Destination sets the location where unarchived files will be stored. Figure 8.4 demonstrates the Destination configuration panel.

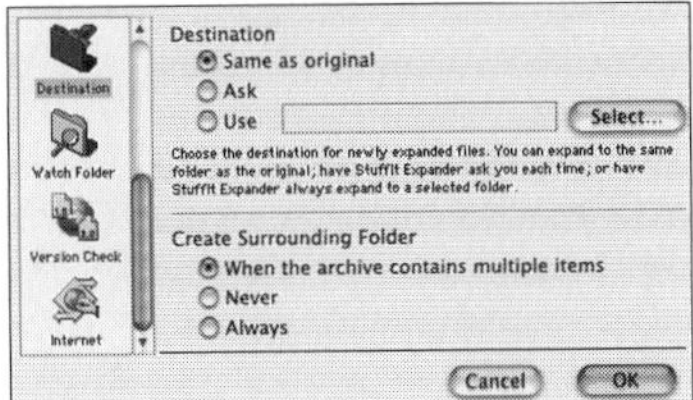

FIGURE 8.4
Choose the destination for expanded files.

The following options are available under the Destination panel:

Destination—Set the destination where the unarchived files and folders are saved. The default setting, Same as original, creates expanded items in the same volume/folder as the archive itself. Choose Ask to prompt for a destination each time the expansion begins, or click Use to pick a specific path for all unarchived files.

Create Surrounding Folder—When an archive is expanded, it usually results in one or more files and folders. Create Surrounding Folder will place these items into a single folder depending on the chosen condition: When the archive contains multiple items, Never, or Always.

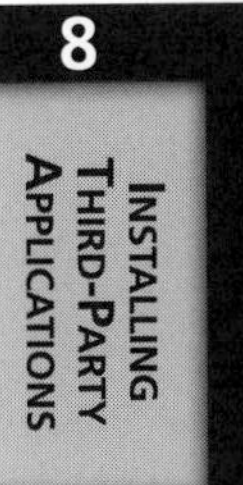

Watch Folder

Setting up a Watch Folder can be useful if you've created a drop box for other users or simply want a place to put files and have them automatically expanded as they arrive. The Watch Folder panel is shown in Figure 8.5.

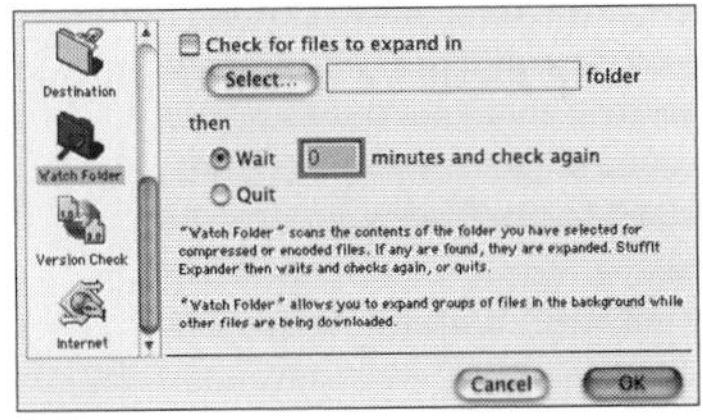

FIGURE 8.5
Set up a Watch Folder to look for incoming archives.

Control the functionality of your Watch Folder with these settings:

Check for Files to Expand In—When checked, StuffIt Expander will monitor the selected folder for new archives or encoded files.

Wait—Choose the length of time (in minutes) Expander will wait before rechecking the folder.

Quit—Choose Quit if StuffIt exits after expanding files the first time.

Note

StuffIt Expander does not install a system-level service—the Expander application itself must remain active for the Watch Folder feature to work.

Version Check

Use the check box on the Version Check panel to enable StuffIt Expander to check online for new versions. This feature is on by default and is not at all intrusive. Uncheck the feature to prevent your system from contacting Aladdin Systems. Figure 8.6 displays the Version Check panel.

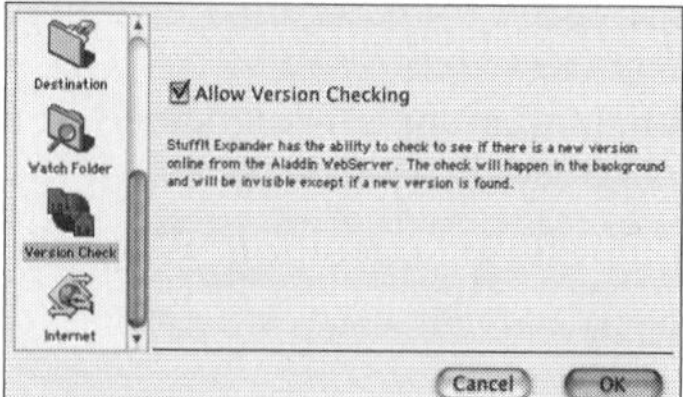

FIGURE 8.6
Version checking will automatically look for new StuffIt Expander updates.

Internet

The final configuration panel, Internet, is used to set the file types that StuffIt Expander is registered to handle on the Mac OS X system. As shown in Figure 8.7, you can mix and match among the 18 available archive and encoding types. Click the Use StuffIt Expander for all available types button as a shortcut for clicking all the check boxes.

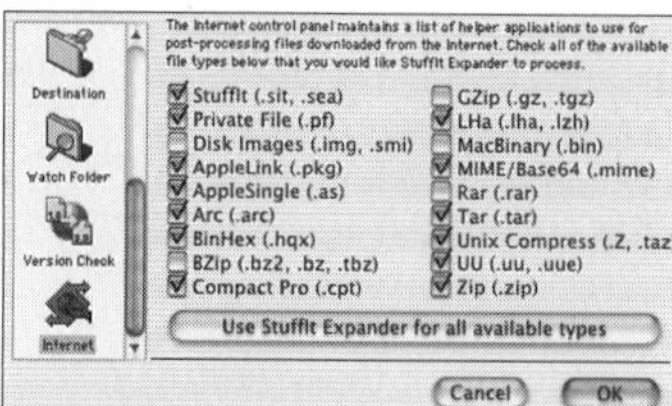

FIGURE 8.7
The Internet panel registers the file types that StuffIt Expander will handle.

Installing Software

Although there is no definitive installation technique used by all software on Mac OS X, there are two common methods that you will use repeatedly. Obviously, for any software, you should read the documentation that comes with it; but for those who are anxious to double-click, it's good to know what to expect.

Keep in mind when installing applications that other users on the computer do not implicitly have access to your home directory. If you install a large application in your home directory, it will be accessible only by you. This can lead to multiple users installing copies of the same application throughout the system. To best utilize disk space and resource sharing, applications should be installed in the `Applications` directory or within a subdirectory of `Applications`.

> **Caution**
>
> Be sure to read your software license agreements regarding operation by multiple users. If an application is only licensed for a single user (rather than a single computer), it should not be placed in `Applications` where any Mac OS X user can have access. If placed there, you should have its ownership and permissions adjusted appropriately.

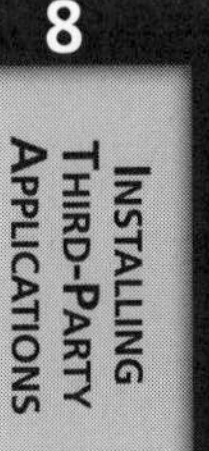

Disk Images

The vast majority of Mac OS X applications are appearing using the `.dmg` file format and a simple drag-and-drop installation. Double-clicking a disk image will launch the Disk Utility application (see Chapter 6, "Native Utilities and Applications") and mount the virtual disk on your computer. Some disk images contain a double-clickable installer, but most enable the user to drag the application from the image directly to the location where the user wants to store it.

> **Note**
>
> Unlike earlier versions of the Mac OS, you cannot drag the mounted disk icon directly to another drive. This will result in a permissions error. Instead, create a new folder on the Mac OS X drive, select all the items within the disk image, and drag them to the folder.

Apple's Installer (.mpkg/.pkg Files)

The Apple installer provides a simple step-by-step installation system for installing package and multi-package files (.pkg/.mpkg)—in fact, it is the same installation application used to set up the Mac OS X operating system itself. The Installer application does not offer an uninstall option, but does save a Bill of Materials (BOM) that can be used to determine what files were modified during installation. Unfortunately, the Installer application has a bug that might cause serious errors to occur depending on your system configuration and type of package being installed.

Although using the Installer is sometimes unavoidable, users should be sure to read the installation instructions for warnings and make sure that critical data is backed up first.

> **Note**
>
> A discussion on the Installer's problems and the conditions under which they occur can be found at `www.stepwise.com/Articles/Technical/Packages/InstallerOnX.html`.

Other Distribution Methods

There are a number of developer packages for creating software installers under Mac OS X. The operation of these applications is virtually identical to Mac OS 8 or 9, so most users will be able to keep on working exactly as they have been.

If you encounter `.tar`, `.Z`, or `.gz` files that do not unarchive correctly with StuffIt Expander or do not contain a GUI installer, turn to Chapter 12, "Introducing the BSD Subsystem," for information on working with Unix applications within the BSD subsystem.

Internet Software

For the remainder of the chapter, we'll take a look at some of the more interesting applications currently available for Mac OS X. These packages have been selected based on their unique features and immediate availability (either in full or demo form) over the Internet.

First up are Internet applications. Although Mac OS X provides a great suite of connectivity apps, it doesn't have the tools necessary to make everyone happy. The following applications can be downloaded to expand your library and Internet arsenal.

OmniWeb

OmniWeb, by the Omni Group (www.omnigroup.com/), is an excellent alternative Web browser that has been around since the days of the original NeXT. This browser sports some amazing features, such as a setting to limit JavaScript's capability to open dozens of new windows while browsing. In addition, the top-notch rendering engine produces pages that have a book-like appearance, and is an excellent choice for demonstrating online-public presentations. Figure 8.8 displays the OmniWeb browser in action.

FIGURE 8.8
OmniWeb's rendering engine is second to none!

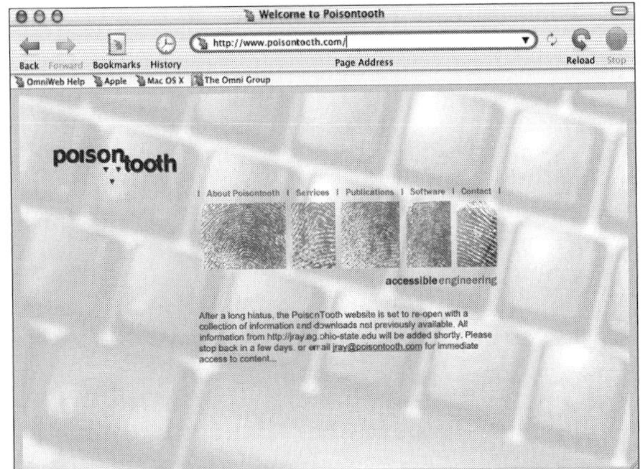

Alternatives

Even more alternatives to IE are available on the OS X platform. Although OmniWeb is by far the most stable and stunning browser available *anywhere*, the competition is quickly heating up.

iCab—A small, fast, Mac-only browser, iCab has gained a cult following in the past year and looks to offer many of the features of OmniWeb and IE within a tiny package. www.icab.de/download.html.

Opera—*The* most popular alternative browser solution on Windows comes to Mac OS X. Opera is possibly the fastest HTML-rendering engine available and at around 2MB in size, definitely worth trying. www.opera.com/download.

Netscape—Although some users might be disappointed that Netscape 4.7x isn't available, the latest release—6.1—is. Give it a try; the latest release is much better than the initial 6.0 offering. www.netscape.com.

Fire

Written by a single developer, Fire (www.epicware.com/fire.html) is the Mac OS X answer to the instant messaging battle. Rather than keeping a separate application for each service you use, Fire provides a unified interface to AIM, ICQ, IRC, JABBEER, MSN, and Yahoo! chat services. Although several of the services have attempted to alter their protocols slightly to keep out unauthorized clients, the author of Fire has been diligent in making certain that Mac OS X users have uninterrupted access to these services. Figure 8.9 displays Fire in use.

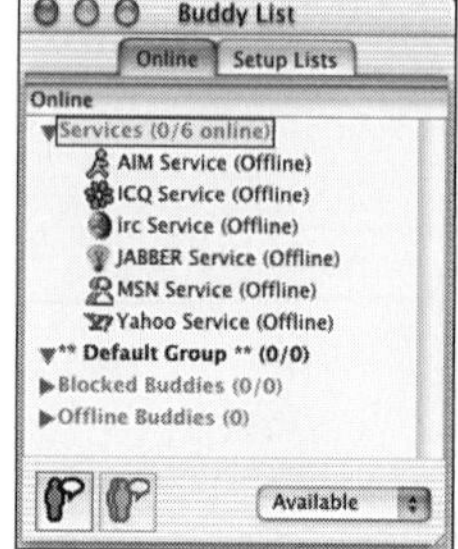

FIGURE 8.9
Fire is capable of interacting with all the popular instant messaging services.

Alternatives

If you'd rather stick with the original, several vendors have released their official IM clients on the Mac OS X platform.

AOL Instant Messenger—`www.aol.com/aim/macosx.html`

ICQ—`www.icq.com/mac/alpha`

RBrowser

Mac OS X does not come with an FTP client beyond IE's capabilities and the command-line tools. RBrowser (`www.rbrowser.com/`) rectifies the situation with a unique FTP solution. Based on a piece of software originally developed for OpenStep, RBrowser uses a column mode, similar to the Mac OS X Finder to navigate the file system. In addition, it supports SSH file transfers for complete system security. Figure 8.10 demonstrates the RBrowser display.

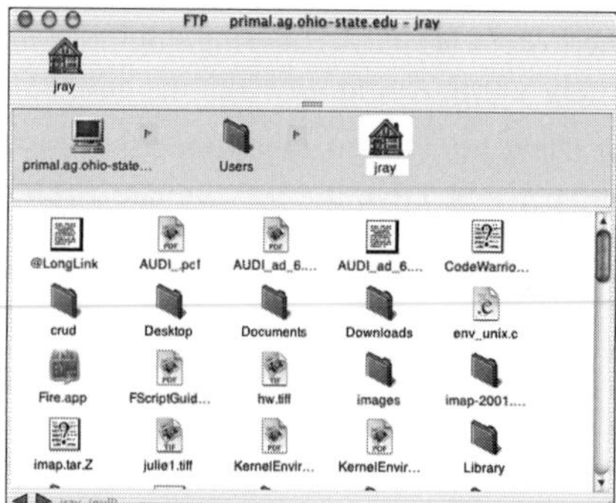

FIGURE 8.10
RBrowser uses a Mac OS X Finder-like interface for accessing FTP sites.

Alternatives

There are a *large* number of FTP clients already released or in development for Mac OS X. Although the RBrowser user experience is unique, some might find themselves more at ease with an alternative solution.

Fetch—A popular FTP client for almost as long as the Macintosh has been on the Internet, Fetch has been updated for use on Mac OS X. `fetchsoftworks.com/`.

NetFinder—With an extremely attractive and intuitive interface, NetFinder users will recognize obvious similarities between the application and the Mac OS Finder. For an attractive and intuitive FTP solution, NetFinder is king. `members.ozemail.com.au/~pli/netfinder/`.

Transmit—Transmit is an extremely simplistic FTP client that focuses on functionality and ease-of-use. A single-window control transfers to and from remote hosts. `www.panic.com/transmit/download.html`.

MP3 Rage

Ahhh, what kind of day would it be without downloading an MP3 or two? Obviously, you should download only songs that you own, and what better way to do it then over a Napster or Gnutella server. Unlike other clients for these file-sharing networks, MP3 Rage tracks alternative Napster-like servers, just in case Napster no longer carries the songs you own. This single application can search and download from both of the leading file sharing networks. Download MP3 Rage from `www.chaoticsoftware.com/ChaoticSoftware/ProductPages/MP3Rage.html`. Figure 8.11 displays the MP3 Rage application in action.

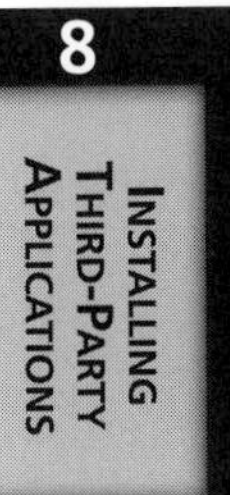

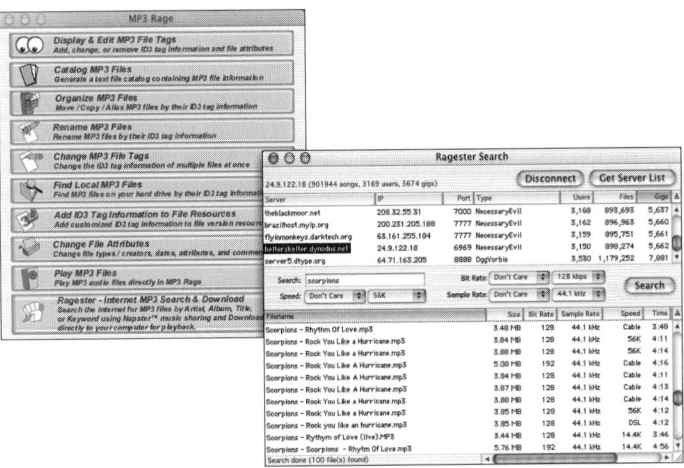

FIGURE 8.11
MP3 Rage connects you to the best music-sharing servers available.

Alternatives

There are a number of MP3-related applications available, although none has the same features as MP3 Rage. If you'd like to expand your music software collection, take a look at these:

Audion—Audion, by Panic software, is the most attractive (interface-wise) MP3 player available. Although the playback features are comparable to iTunes, the beautiful skin collection blows iTunes away. `panic.com/audion/`.

Napster—The official client—enough said. `www.napster.com/mac/download/`.

Mint Audio—Small and skinnable, this MP3 player uses very little screen space, yet offers a large number of commands. `mint.unsanity.com/`.

Applications and Utilities

Occasionally we all need to do some work. There are a growing number of productivity applications you can choose from. These are some of the highlights currently available.

Amadeus II

Amadeus II (`www.unige.ch/math/folks/hairer/martin/Amad2.html`) is a full-featured sound recording and editing application for Mac OS X. Sick of the built-in system sounds? Create your own using Amadeus. Laptop owners can use Amadeus's built-in direct-to-MP3 recording capabilities for dictation and other high-compression storage needs. Amadeus supports a wide variety of sound formats and advanced editing options for removing noise from sampled recordings. Figure 8.12 displays the Amadeus II application in use.

Alternatives

Music and sound editing software for Mac OS X is currently very limited, partially because of a lack of important APIs for technologies such as MIDI output. The following applications offer features similar to Amadeus:

Sound Studio—Sound Studio is an easy-to-use editor with straightforward controls and an attractive interface. `www.felttip.com/products/soundstudio/`.

SoundHack—Designed for digitally processing sounds to obtain unique results, SoundHack is both fun for hobbyists and useful for musicians. It's definitely worth a download. `www.soundhack.com/`.

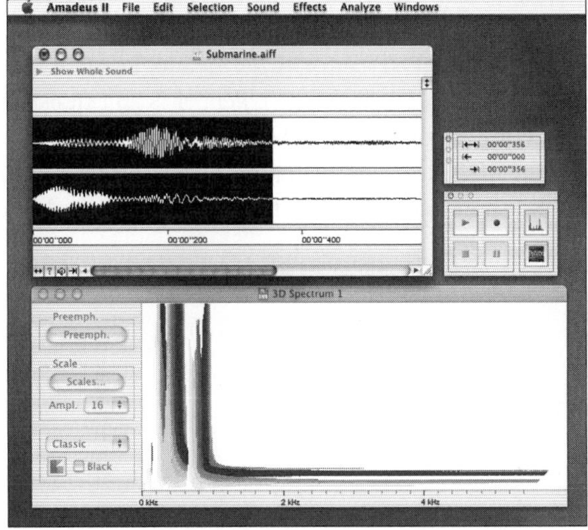

FIGURE 8.12
Use Amadeus II to record and edit sounds.

REALbasic

Nothing beats sitting down in front of your computer and creating your own applications. With REALbasic (`www.realbasic.com/`) and Mac OS X, anyone can compile standalone applications within 15 minutes of starting the development system. The REALbasic environment, pictured in Figure 8.13, uses an object-oriented model and graphical interface design tools to get up and running in no time. Users can create software ranging from games to client/server applications.

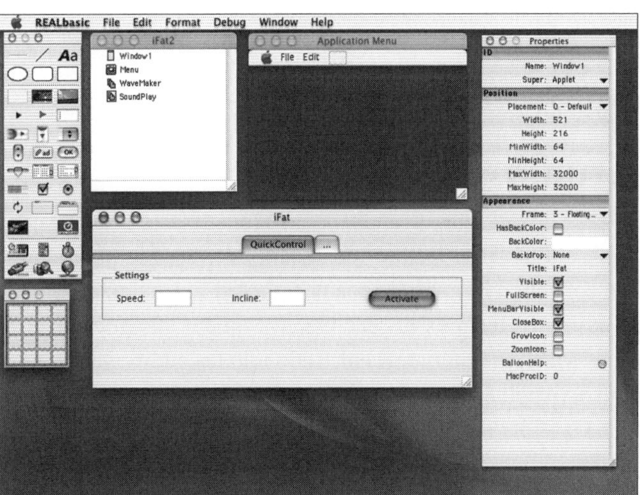

FIGURE 8.13
Build your own Mac OS X software in REALbasic.

Pepper

Need a good HTML text editor? PHP editor? C/Perl editor? Get all these by downloading Pepper (`www.hekkelman.com/pepper.html`). Pepper is an extensible text editor for many popular programming languages. Distributed as shareware, it offers features found only in other commercial offerings at a fraction of the price. The Pepper interface is unique among Mac OS X applications and is definitely worth a look. Figure 8.14 shows Pepper in action.

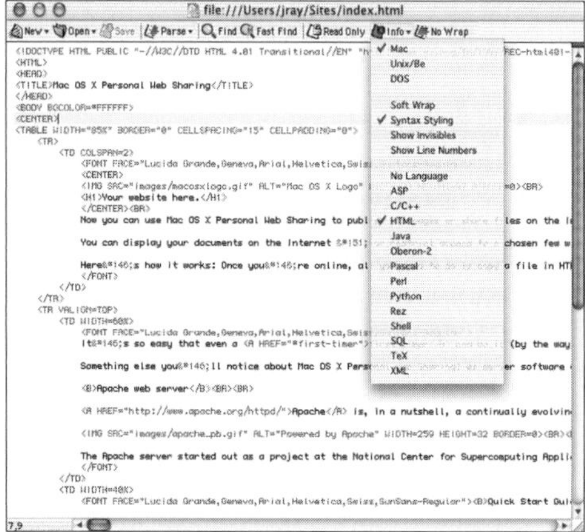

FIGURE 8.14
Pepper is an excellent text and programming editor.

Alternatives

The only real alternative to Pepper (or vice versa) is BBEdit. Available in a free Lite version, BBEdit is a fantastic program in its own right, but is feature-rich almost to the point of being excessive. Download BBEdit from `www.barebones.com/bbedit_for_X.html`.

StoneStudio

StoneStudio (`www.stone.com/StoneStudio/StoneStudio.html`), seen in Figure 8.15, is a suite of applications developed for designers interested in publishing to paper and to the Web. The collection of applications is authored in Cocoa, giving you full access to many of the advanced features of Mac OS X. StoneStudio goes head-to-head with applications such as Macromedia FreeHand, and includes additional features such as animated GIF creation and AppleScripting.

FIGURE 8.15
The StoneStudio application suite is powerful, stable, and easy to use.

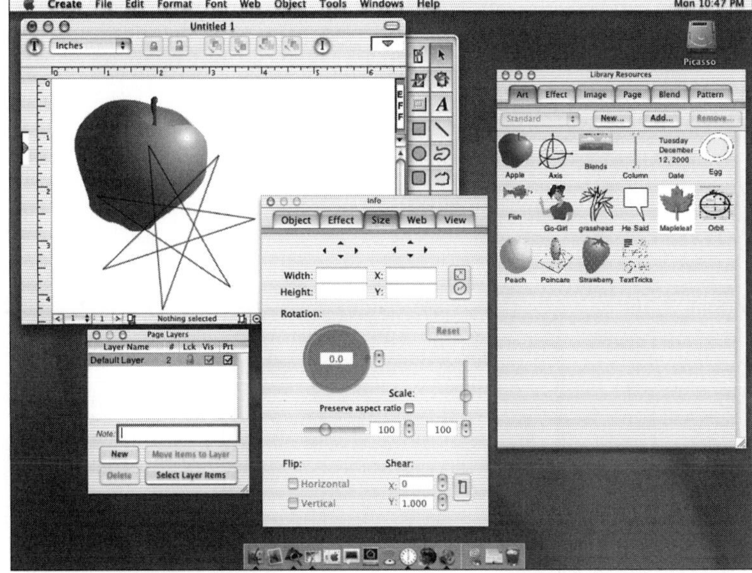

Tiffany

Going head-to-head with another mainstream photo-editing application (such as Adobe Photoshop), Tiffany (`www.caffeinesoft.com/`) offers many of the same features as its better-known counterpart and extends some of the core capabilities beyond what is currently possible. Advanced layer management and control, scriptable actions, and masking controls make this a standout among the Mac OS X graphics applications currently available. Figure 8.16 demonstrates Tiffany in action.

Like StoneStudio, Tiffany is a Cocoa application originally developed for the OpenStep platform. As such, it tightly integrates the advanced features of Mac OS X into its core.

Alternatives

Mac OS X is host to other image editing software. These applications are a great addition to any Mac OS X software library—especially for users with a digital camera.

GIMP (X Window System)—The GNU Image Manipulation Program is now available for Mac OS X. With a strong Linux following and very active development, this application gets better by the day. `ftp://gnu-darwin.sourceforge.net/pub/gnu-darwin/`.

GIMP (Cocoa)—Although not completed at the time of this writing, an early version of a Cocoa-native GIMP is available for download. Unlike the X Window

System version, which must install a number of X Window Systems–related support libraries, GIMP for Cocoa runs entirely native within the Mac OS X user interface. ftp://gnu-darwin.sourceforge.net/pub/gnu-darwin/.

GraphicConverter—Although the name implies that this software package is good at converting between image formats (and it is), it also has the capability to manipulate photos. Despite its small size, the base feature set of GraphicConverter should be enough for most common image editing functions. www.graphic-converter.net.

FIGURE 8.16
Tiffany takes many Photoshop features to the next level.

OmniGraffle

Another great application from the folks at the Omni Group (www.omnigroup.com), OmniGraffle is difficult to explain without seeing it in front of you. Part object-oriented drawing application and part flow charter, OmniGraffle can make any charting project a breeze. By enabling the user to create palettes of common objects (and including a variety of prebuilt palettes), OmniGraffle can be extended to work with customized charts and graphs. One of the more amazing features of the software is its capability to determine the best layout for a connected system based on the objects you have defined. Figure 8.17 shows the OmniGraffle application in use.

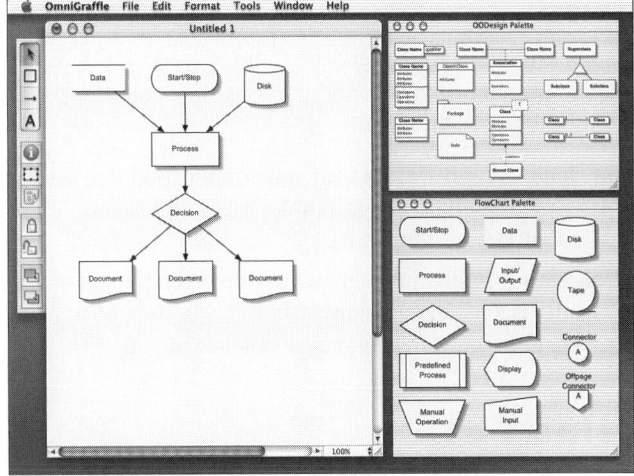

FIGURE 8.17
OmniGraffle can automatically organize your charts using its built-in best-fit algorithms.

DesktopCalendar

This simple application overlays a transparent calendar atop your current desktop background. Although useful only if you happen to need an easy-to-access view of a calendar, it serves to illustrate the unique features offered by the Quartz graphics subsystem. Figure 8.18 displays a Mac OS X desktop with the live DesktopCalendar included. `www.lisai.net/~hamada/Acti/MacOSX/DesktopCalendar/index.html`.

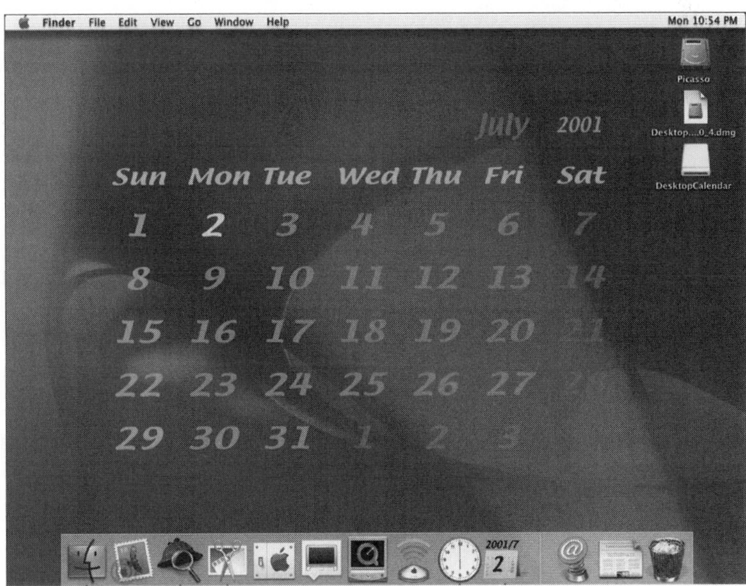

FIGURE 8.18
DesktopCalendar overlays a live calendar on top of the Mac OS X Desktop picture.

Alternatives

There are a number of alternative calendar solutions for Mac OS X, include a Dockling that will be mentioned later. If you're not interested in a calendar overlay, one of these alternatives might work best for you.

Calendar 2000—A full-featured calendar application that tracks special events as well as offering the Julian, Gregorian, Jewish, and Islamic views. `www.wunder-moosen.com/wmCalendar2000.htm`.

PandoCalendar—A small attractive desktop calendar and note keeper. PandoCalendar is simple, and entirely free. `www.PandaCorner.com/PandaSystems/PandoCalendar.html`.

Screensavers

The built-in Mac OS X screensavers are pretty, but get old rather quickly. To add some spice to your system, try downloading one of (or all) these excellent replacements. Remember, to install a screensaver, simply place it within the `Library/Screensavers` or `~/Library/Screensavers` depending on whether you want public or private access to the saver.

Mac OS X Screensavers 3.0—A collection of 22 savers, including 17 OpenGL screensavers. This package, although primarily a port of X Window System–based screensavers, is still a must-have on any system. `www.epicware.com/macosxsavers.html`.

Neko.saver—Based on the original Neko animated kitten, the Neko screensaver turns one or more cats loose on your desktop. They play, sleep, and scamper across your screen. What more could you want? `www.lisai.net/~hamada/Acti/MacOSX/Nekoware/index.html`.

Plasma Tunnel—An original Mac OS X screensaver creation, this beauty clears your screen with a pulsing, twisting, and turning OpenGL-generated 3D tunnel. `www.fruitz-of-dojo.de/php/download.php4`.

Paint Effects—The Paint Effects saver is a demonstration of the power of Maya 3D. Regardless of your interest in 3D modeling, download this screensaver. You're guaranteed to spend numerous hours gawking at the scenes it creates. `ftp://ftp.aliaswavefront.com/pub/ScreenSaver/MayaScreenSaverforOSX.dmg.sit`.

The Terrain Project—Watch your Macintosh generate a 3D-fractal landscape and then fly through it. Try not to get motion sickness. `www.macboy.org/#terrainproject`.

Dock Additions

The default sets of Mac OS X Docklings are useful, but don't really exploit the features of the Dock. Third-party developers have been hard at work creating their own additions to the Dock, and the results are great. The following is a list of a few available Docklings and the features they add to your computer:

Calindock—My personal favorite, this Dockling adds a live calendar to the Dock. Rather than just a date, Calindock displays a wall-style calendar view with the current day highlighted. `www.criticalmatter.com/calindock/`.

Network Statistics—Interested in seeing the amount of network traffic entering and exiting your Mac OS X box in real time? This Dock item will graph your network statistics in real-time. `homepage.mac.com/iclements/NetworkStatistics.html`.

Weatherling—Click the Dockling, see the current weather updated automatically from the National Weather Service. `www.versiontracker.com/moreinfo.fcgi?id=10767`.

Space.dock—Adds the notion of virtual workspaces to Mac OS X. Enables the user to attach different windows to different workspaces, and then switch instantly between them, effectively increasing the available desktop space. `space.sourceforge.net/`.

Prefling—Rather than starting the System Preferences application then choosing the desired preference panel, you can use this Dockling to select and open any preference panel from the Dock. `http://homepage.mac.com/asagoo/prefling/index.html`.

EightBall—Stupid, pointless, and indispensable. This Dockling simulates a Magic Eight Ball and provides words of wisdom for any question you ask. Try it for fun, keep it for the pretty icon. `www.inferiis.com/mac/eightball.html`.

Summary

Mac OS X uses the same compression and encoding methods that have been widespread on the Macintosh system for the last decade. In addition, it also supports Unix standards such as `.tar` and `.gz`. The included StuffIt Expander application can deal with most common archive types, and makes it simple for even the first-time user to start downloading software for his library.

Although a new operating system, Mac OS X already has many applications that utilize its cutting-edge graphics capabilities in ways never seen before on a desktop computer. Although this chapter contains a list of interesting software, it should serve only as a starting point for exploring the possibilities of the operating system.

User-Level OS X Configuration

PART III

IN THIS PART

CHAPTER 9

Network Setup

In This Chapter

Unix, as a rule, is happiest when it gets to run as an always-on, always-network-connected operating system. Unix machines tend to run continuously (talking to other machines via the network) for months or years at a time, and the underpinnings of the networking system are designed for this mode of operation. Surprisingly, Apple has managed to pin a reasonable facsimile of the Mac OS as-needed picture of networking at the user level, onto the Unix networking framework. You already learned how to set up basic networking functions during the install process. In later chapters, you'll learn how this was accomplished at the Unix level, and how to perform even more sophisticated network tricks at the command line. Here, we'll cover some of the networking technologies available, the GUI network controls, and, as a bit of network troubleshooting, we'll use the Network Utility tool.

TCP/IP

TCP/IP, the acronym that has become a de facto name for a network communication protocol, stands for Transmission Control Protocol/Internet Protocol. TCP/IP has become so ubiquitous that many think of it, not just as a communications protocol, but as the *only* network communications protocol. Although not the *only* protocol out there (AppleTalk, covered later in this chapter is one of the others), TCP/IP has proven flexible enough to support different types of data with a large range of requirements for delivery, timing, and reliability.

Basically, the TCP/IP protocol can be thought of as specifying the manner in which pieces of data should be transferred between two machines. This protocol includes the notion that the transmission of data can be broken down into a number of separate and abstract layers. Figure 9.1 shows the TCP/IP protocol stack, the conceptual breakdown of the protocol into layers. This is commonly referred to as the OSI (Open Systems Interconnect) model of networking. As the functions of the layers are conceptually separate, the manner that the function of any layer is accomplished does not matter, as long as it cooperates with the layers above and below it in the manners that they expect.

FIGURE 9.1
The OSI network model, on which the TCP/IP stack is built.

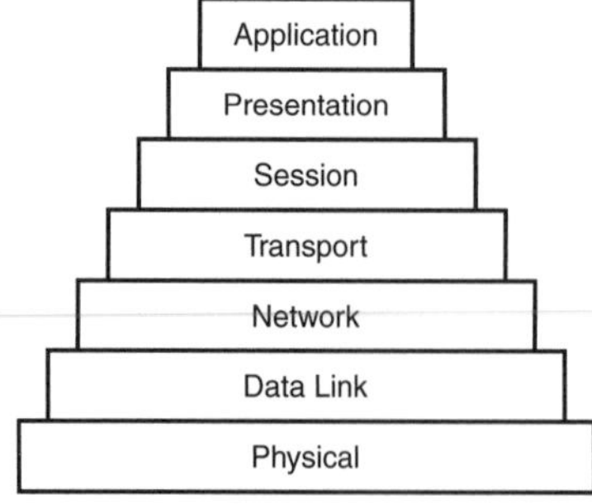

For example, it doesn't matter whether the physical layer is carried by twisted-pair Ethernet cabling, radio waves, or even with data written on slips of paper and handed back-and-forth between people sitting at terminals. As long as the data transmitted by the Physical layer gets retrieved from or inserted into data structures correctly at the Data Link layer, the rest of the TCP/IP stack will function identically.

This separation of functionality into independent and abstract pieces is typical of Unix technologies, and allows the TCP/IP protocol to handle the transmission of a wide range of data types. Whether the data is equipment control where real-time transmission is critically important, or financial transactions where security and error-free transmissions are more important than speed, it is likely that the data can be fit into the TCP/IP model.

Going forward in the chapter, there are several TCP/IP-related terms you should be familiar with. These items define your connection to the Internet:

IP Address—The address that uniquely identifies your computer on the Internet. An IP address is typically represented in the form `###.###.###.###`, such as `192.168.0.1`. An IP address is assigned either by your network administrator, or automatically via a DHCP or BOOTP server.

Hostname—Typically, a hostname simply refers to the network name of your computer. Some people might use the term *hostname* to refer to the FQDN (fully qualified domain name) as well. This is the entire Internet name of your machine as registered with a DNS server, such as `www.poisontooth.com`.

Subnet Mask—Similar in appearance to an IP address, a subnet mask tells your computer which part of the IP address identifies the network it is on, and which is the individual computer. Most users will be part of a class C network with the subnet mask `255.255.255.0`. The last segment of the IP address identifies the computer, whereas the first three segments identify the network.

Gateway/Router Address—The gateway address is an IP address of a network device that connects your local network to the rest of the Internet. A gateway handles any necessary translation between different types of networking media.

DNS—Domain name servers are Internet servers that provide translation between IP addresses and fully qualified domain names. Each request for a machine using its FQDN requires an interaction with a DNS before a connection can take place.

Network Interface—The device that connects your computer to the network. This can be an Ethernet port, AirPort card, and so on. Some computers might have multiple network interfaces. Mac OS X names its interfaces sequentially. The `en0` interface is built-in Ethernet, and `en1` is typically AirPort.

Using these pieces of information, you can configure your computer to access the Internet. Although most dial-in accounts automatically set these parameters for you, users connecting directly to a network via Ethernet or AirPort will need to know the appropriate settings for their network in order to continue.

If you'd like more information on the TCP/IP protocol and its use, I recommend *Special Edition Using TCP/IP* (ISBN: 0789718979).

The Network Control Pane

The Network control pane, already introduced during the installation, is the GUI brain center of the OS X interface to TCP/IP. This control pane, in actuality, just provides a series of hints to the underlying Unix TCP/IP control software, but it does so in a much more elegant fashion than twiddling configuration parameters at the command line. The primary control with which you should familiarize yourself is the Configuration menu. In previous versions of Mac OS, various portions of the networking software were configured by separate control panels, and each panel was controlled by its own independent saved configuration setting. Mac OS X has instead placed all network configurations under a single parent control pane, with an umbrella configuration setting that covers TCP/IP, modem control, AppleTalk, and location settings. By default, under the Configurations menu you have options for PPP (dialup), Ethernet, AirPort (if your machine has an AirPort), and Advanced.

The Advanced Subpane

The available selections in the Configure menu switch between a number of subpane groups for the Network control pane. The Advanced subpane, doesn't provide advanced network configuration, but allows you to enable and disable already existing configurations, and create new configuration sets. Figure 9.2 shows the Advanced subpane of the Network control pane. OS X, to make network configuration as easy as possible, attempts to automatically detect and select the correct network configuration for any given situation. This convenience comes at a slight cost in startup time, so unless you actually intend to use all the available configurations, we don't recommend leaving all the configurations enabled as shown in the figure.

If you've already experimented enough to find the location settings, the capability to save additional configurations might seem redundant. It becomes useful, however, in situations where you have multiple IP addresses at the same location, on a single network interface. Without iterating through different location settings, setting up several different configurations would allow the system to automatically search through each until it found a working set of parameters. This might occur if you have multiple in-building networks with different IP ranges on each, but with each connected to share resources.

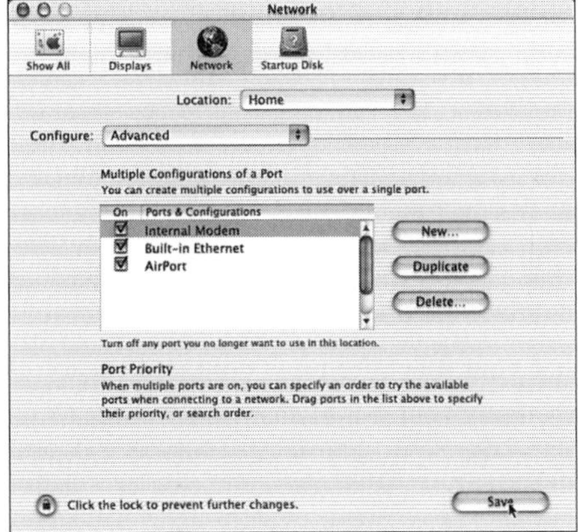

FIGURE 9.2
The Advanced subpane of the Network control pane.

Another possible use is if you have a number of different dialup service providers, and want your machine to try each until it finds an open one.

Modem

Under the Modem Configuration menu option, you can configure the settings required to establish a dialup connection. The subpanes available enable the configuration of how TCP/IP gets its settings, the PPP (Point to Point Protocol, carried over a dialup connection) configuration parameters, modem settings, and network proxy server settings.

Under the TCP/IP subpane, shown in Figure 9.3, you can configure how your TCP/IP stack gets its control and configuration information. The manual configuration settings, shown in the figure, allow you to configure individual options by hand, but it would be unusual if an ISP (Internet Service Provider) did not provide the information for these settings automatically, using PPP.

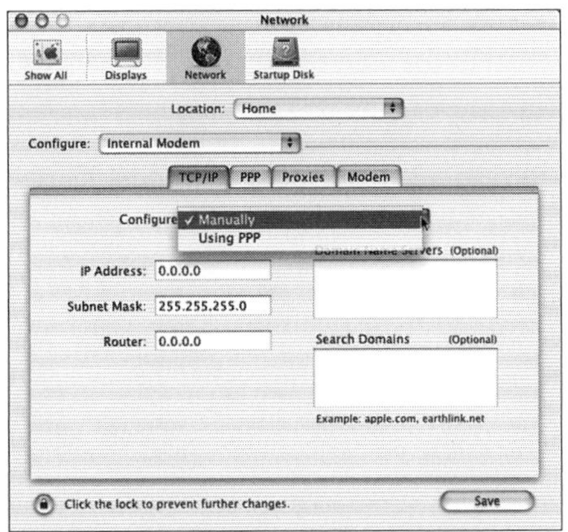

FIGURE 9.3
The TCP/IP subpane, showing available options for the dialup (Modem) configuration set.

If you need to provide manual configuration information, you will need to know and fill in the following information—you should be able to get this information from your network administrator:

- **IP Address**—Your computer's IP address. This should be four sets of digits, separated by periods, like `192.168.1.21`.
- **Subnet Mask**—This should be four sets of numbers separated by periods, as well. Most likely it will be `255.255.255.0`, or `255.255.0.0`.
- **Router**—The machine that your machine must contact to reach the outside network world. This will frequently (but not always) be similar to your IP address, only with the final number replaced by a `1`. Your network administrator might also call this machine a *gateway*.
- **Domain Name Servers**—The IP addresses of machines that will translate between IP addresses and fully qualified domain names (FQDNs) such as `www.apple.com`.
- **Search Domains**—Partial domain names to append to machine names, if you give less than an FQDN. For example, you might frequently work with machines on the domains `osxunleashed.com` and `apple.com`. If you want your machine to try to connect to `info.osxunleashed.com` or `info.apple.com` whenever you ask it to connect to info, you can enter the domains here. Your machine will try them both when it discovers that you've asked for a name that does not resolve as an FQDN.

Under the PPP subpane, shown in Figure 9.4, you can configure how to connect to your ISP. Almost all ISPs use PPP to provide TCP/IP over dialup connections. If yours does not, you will need to follow its instructions, which will probably include installation of some custom software.

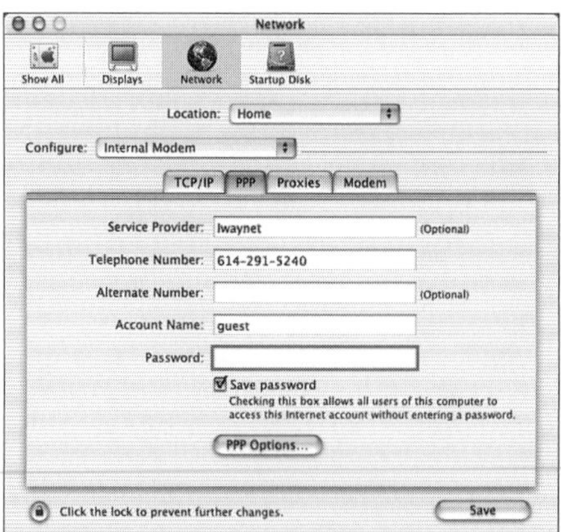

FIGURE 9.4
The PPP subpane of the Modem configuration allows you to specify your dialup account information.

The PPP subpane has the following fields:

- **Service Provider**—An optional field where you can specify a name for the service provider. This option will be useful if you have multiple providers that your machine needs to dial, and you need a better way to keep track of them than just by phone number.
- **Telephone Number**—The telephone number to dial.
- **Alternate Number**—An alternative number to dial for the same service provider. If your ISP doesn't have alternative dial-in numbers, leave this blank.
- **Account Name**—The username or account name that you have with this ISP.
- **Password**—The password for this account and ISP.
- **Save Password**—If your machine is going to be used by multiple users, and you don't want them to be able to connect to the Internet using your account information and password, don't check this box.

The PPP panel also has a PPP Options button and corresponding drop-down pane that enables you to configure several other options with respect to the dialup connection, as shown in Figure 9.5.

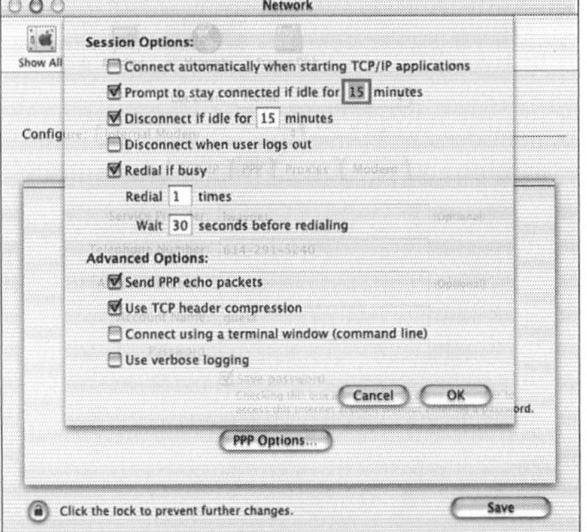

FIGURE 9.5
The Session and Advanced dialup options drop-down pane for dialup connections.

The pane enables you to configure

- Whether to automatically dial and make a connection when an application starts that needs TCP/IP services.
- Whether, and how frequently, to prompt you to stay connected, if there hasn't been any recent network activity.
- How long to wait before disconnecting when there's no network activity.

- Whether to disconnect when there's no user logged in on the console.
- Whether to, how many times to, and how rapidly to redial the phone if the ISP is busy.
- Whether to send PPP echo packets. Some ISPs periodically send little "are you really there?" messages to connected computers to make sure that everything is working properly—this option controls whether to respond. Unless you have been told by your ISP to do otherwise, leave this option checked.
- Whether to compress TCP header information. TCP/IP information is carried in packets, with a significant amount of meta-information about the contents of the packet. Compressing this information can speed your network connection, but requires processor power. On a fast machine, you'll probably get a network speedup from compressing headers, unless your ISP is using some ancient hardware that takes more time to perform the compression/decompression than the savings in transmission time.
- Whether to use a manual terminal window for connection. If your ISP doesn't use a standard PPP server, you might need to carry on some textual dialog with the server during connection. Selecting this option will open a terminal for you to interact with the host during connection.
- The verbose logging option will increase the amount of information regarding dialup connections stored in the system logs.

The Modem subpane, shown in Figure 9.6, allows you to select your modem, configure the dialing type, and determine whether you want to hear your connections as they progress.

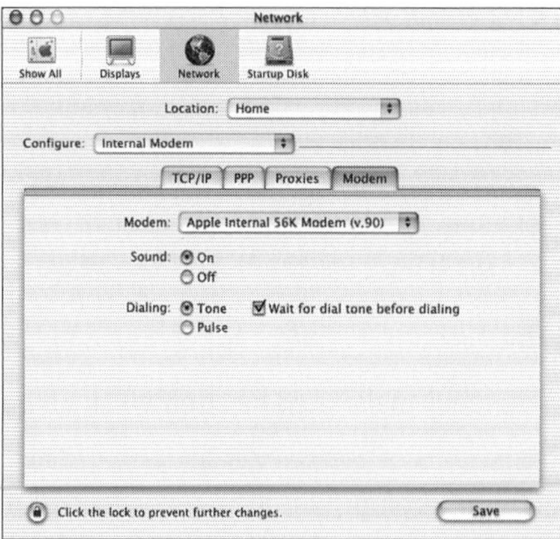

FIGURE 9.6
The Modem subpane of the Modem configuration.

If you're on a network segment where you must connect to proxy servers instead of directly to outside services such as FTP and Web servers, the Proxies subpane is the place to tell the system about the proxies. Shown in Figure 9.7, the Proxies subpane allows you to select what is needed and how to contact the proxy types.

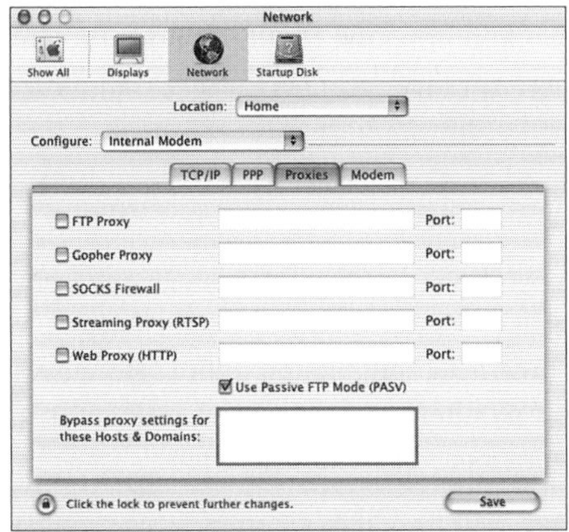

FIGURE 9.7
The Proxies subpane of the Modem configuration option. This pane is identical to Modem, Ethernet, and AirPort configuration sets.

The Proxies submenu proxy types are

- **FTP Proxy**—If you need to contact a proxy to use FTP, enter its IP address and the proxy port here.
- **Gopher Proxy**—Gopher was an early browser-based way of serving data around the Internet, and has been all but completely supplanted by Web servers. If you've found one of the worlds' few remaining Gopher servers and need to access it through a proxy, this is where you tell the system about it.
- **SOCKS Firewall**—The SOCKS firewall system can be used to proxy for a number of different network services. If your network uses a SOCKS-type firewall, enter its information here.
- **Streaming Proxy (RTSP)**—Most types of proxy setups are designed to prevent a remote host from having any chance of connecting back to your machine. This makes it difficult for streaming services that need to send a lot of data as quickly as possible; hence, a specific proxy type for streaming data. If you're behind a firewall, you probably need to configure this—if your network services allow streaming data through at all.
- **Web Proxy (HTTP)**—Configure this if you need to go through a proxy to access the Web. There are occasions where you might want to use a Web proxy even if you don't have to. For example, if you want to make your server connections anonymous by going through one of the Web's anonymous proxy servers.

You can also configure your machine to use PASV (passive) FTP mode for transferring data, an option that will probably be required if you are behind a firewall, or on a NAT (network address translation) private local network.

Finally, you can configure hosts and domains in which the proxy settings should be ignored. If you contact servers both inside and outside your local firewall, you might want to provide your local network information for this option. Therefore, your machine doesn't need to contact the proxy, and then reconnect inside your local network for interior connections.

Ethernet

If you are connected to your network via an Ethernet connection (a physical chunk of wire, typically twisted pair, which looks like a bulky phone cable), you'll need to configure your connection under the Ethernet configuration option. Because switching from one physical transport to another requires only changing a little bit in a few protocol layers, it's similar to dialup configurations you've already seen.

Again, under the TCP/IP subpane, you have the option of providing manual configuration settings or of getting your configuration parameters from a server. If you have a static IP address and configuration that you must supply manually, the options are identical to those discussed under the Modem configuration. In addition, you have the option of selecting from DHCP configuration of all options, DHCP configuration of all options except the IP address, and BootP configuration of all options.

Tip

Note that although there are essentially identical TCP/IP and other subpanes available under this and other configurations, the settings entered in each are specific to the interface configuration set in which they are entered. Information entered in one interface configuration set does not automatically become the default information for any other interface. Therefore, you might need to enter such things as proxies, for example, in more than one place, depending on how your network is set up.

As mentioned earlier, TCP/IP is just one of a number of communication protocols. It's actually possible to run multiple communication protocols over the same piece of wire at the same time. In a clever use of this capability, it's possible to establish a PPP connection via Ethernet wiring, instead of a phone line. If your service provider gives you this option, you can configure it with the subpane shown in Figure 9.9.

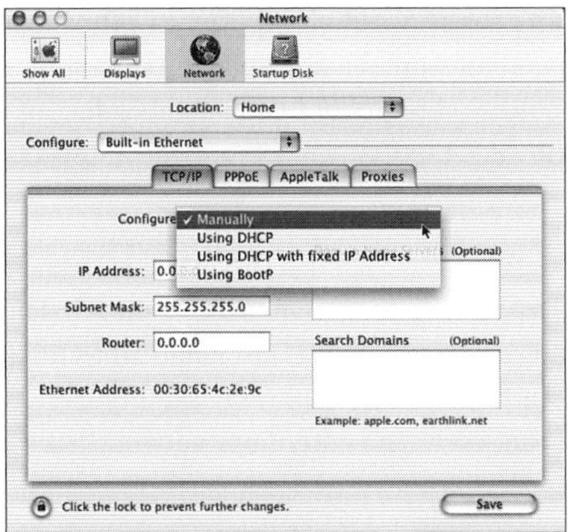

FIGURE 9.8
The TCP/IP options for the Ethernet configuration are essentially identical to those for the Modem configuration.

FIGURE 9.9
The PPPoE subpane of the Ethernet configuration set. The options available here are exactly analogous to the options under the dial-in PPP configuration.

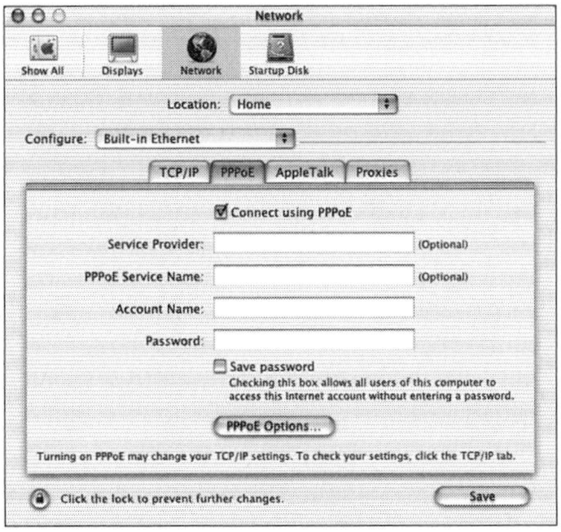

In this subpane, you have the following fields to fill in:

- **Service Provider**—An informational field similar to the service provider field for a dial-in connection.
- **PPPoE Service Name**—Another informational field.
- **Account Name**—The user or account name for your PPPoE ISP.
- **Password**—The password for your account.
- **Save Password**—Again, if you want this account to function automatically without needing to specify a password at each network connection, select this option.

The PPPoE subpane (like the PPP pane) has settings similar to the Dial-in/PPP configuration, in which you can specify options, such as how long to wait before disconnection. Click the PPPoE Options button to display the drop-down pane.

The Ethernet configuration setting set also includes a Proxies subpane identical to that under the Dialup configuration and an AppleTalk subpane. As mentioned previously, AppleTalk is a different communication protocol that is independent of TCP/IP, so this pane will be covered in a section dedicated to AppleTalk later in this chapter.

AirPort

The final default configuration type is the AirPort configuration set. This configuration has TCP/IP and Proxies subpanes with options that are identical to the Ethernet configuration settings. It also includes an AirPort subpane, shown in Figure 9.10, wherein you can choose your default AirPort network, and enter your network password if required.

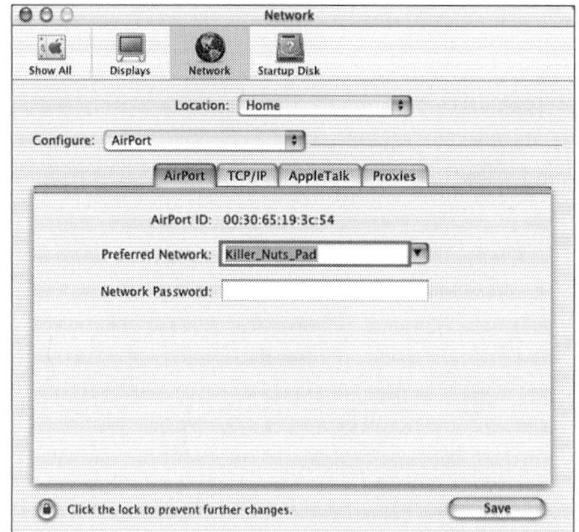

FIGURE 9.10 *The AirPort subpane of the AirPort configuration set.*

If you have an AirPort card, an AirPort Dockling will appear in your dock. The AirPort Dockling provides a continuous display of your signal strength, and access to basic AirPort functionality such as disabling the card and choosing the network to connect to.

AppleTalk

AppleTalk is a communication protocol pioneered by Apple in the era of the Macintosh Plus. This protocol was designed for networking small collections of computers on relatively small networks. Because it was designed to facilitate network-building by people with no interest in being network designers or administrators, AppleTalk is a rather chatty and inefficient protocol. Because of its ease of use, it has survived the transition to a mostly Ethernet-based world, and prospered in environments where its inefficiencies do not impair other network services.

Because of its intimate association with Apple's printing and file sharing software, AppleTalk is sometimes thought of as actually being disk services and print services. In reality, it's a communication protocol, over which disk, print, and other services can be delivered. Because of this, like TCP/IP, AppleTalk connectivity is configured from the Network control pane and services that need to use AppleTalk are configured elsewhere.

Setting Up

AppleTalk is enabled and configured from the AppleTalk subpanes of the Ethernet and AirPort configuration sets.

> **Tip**
>
> Remember that these subpanes, although they contain identical options, are configurations for two different interfaces. You can configure different parameters for each, to be used with each of the interfaces as appropriate.

Figure 9.11 shows the AppleTalk subpane for the AirPort configuration (the Ethernet version looks identical).

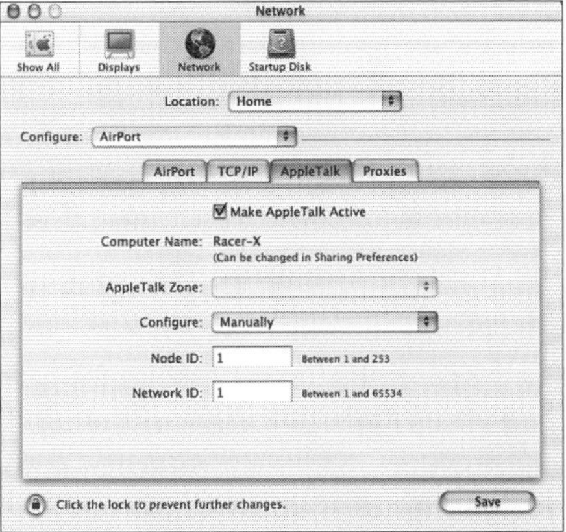

FIGURE 9.11
The AppleTalk subpane of the Network control pane. The AppleTalk settings configured here are specific for the interface configuration set that you're editing.

The AppleTalk subpane is where the following options can be configured:

- **Make AppleTalk Active**—Activate AppleTalk for this interface.
- **AppleTalk Zone**—If your AppleTalk network has multiple zones, you can select the zone you want your computer to join from this menu. If you're on a network with multiple zones, your network administrator should be able to tell you what the proper setting is for your computer.

- **Configure**—Gives you the option of manually configuring your AppleTalk network parameters, or automatically determining the information. The AppleTalk Network ID and Node ID are similar to a TCP/IP subnet and IP address. This difference is AppleTalk is designed so that the computers in a network can cooperatively and automatically work out this information for themselves, without needing it to be specified by the users or administrators. There are very few instances in which you should need to set the system up for manual configuration.
- **Node ID**—If your network administrator tells you that you need to configure your machine for fixed, rather than automatically determined AppleTalk network information, the node ID goes here.
- **Network ID**—If your network administrator tells you that you need to configure your machine for fixed AppleTalk network information, the Network ID goes here. If your network administrator gives you the network ID as ###.###, instead of a number between 1 and 65534, multiply the first by 256 and add the second to it. If you are given the number as ##.##.##, multiply the first by 256, the second by 16, and then add the those two results with the third number.

Sharing Files

With OS X, Apple has made some significant changes to the way AppleTalk works both when sharing and mounting disks and folders. Some of these changes make good sense—for example, the Unix-side file ownerships control what can be accessed from remote—no more sharing settings for drives and folders, if you have permission to use it locally, you have permission to access it remotely. On the other hand, the new model of browsing the AppleTalk network feels a little like exploring an alien planet, compared to the comfortable and convenient network-world view we've come to expect from the Chooser.

To share files under AppleTalk in OS X, you have to do only one thing—turn on AppleTalk file sharing in the Sharing panel. Figure 9.12 shows the panel with the sharing option turned on. Turning this on enables AppleTalk sharing of all the machine's resources. Instead of enabling and disabling sharing for particular drives or folders, the new model shares everything. The user ID, with which remote machines connect, controls which volumes or folders appear to be available. Regardless of other permissions, the contents of each user's Public folder are shared with guest-read permission to the world.

FIGURE 9.12
The Sharing panel with AppleTalk file sharing enabled.

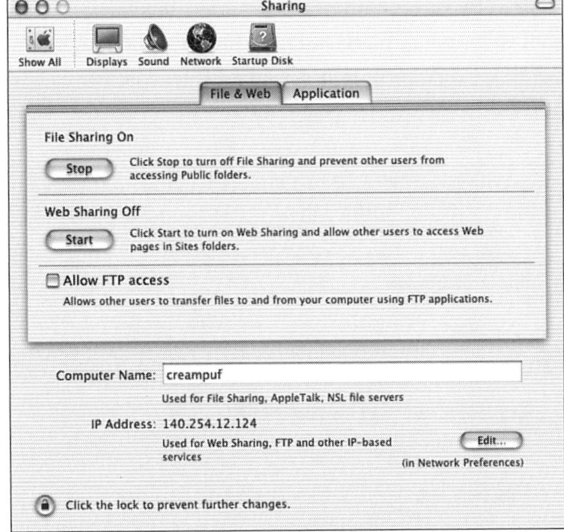

Connecting to Remote Servers

The venerable Apple Chooser is gone, long live the Chooser! Want to mount a file system shared from a remote AppleShare server? Look under the Apple menu for the…nope, it's not there—it's under the Finder's Go menu, Connect to Server. When you choose the Connect to Server menu item, you're presented with a network-browsing dialog, like the one shown in Figure 9.13, with significant similarities to the Finder list view. This dialog provides you with a list of individual machines and machines that are collected into domains. When a domain is selected in a pane, it expands to show the members of that domain in the pane to its right. In Figure 9.13, the Local Network domain has been selected; it shows two individual machines and a domain that are available under the Local Network domain.

FIGURE 9.13
The Connect to Server dialog box browsing the Local Network domain.

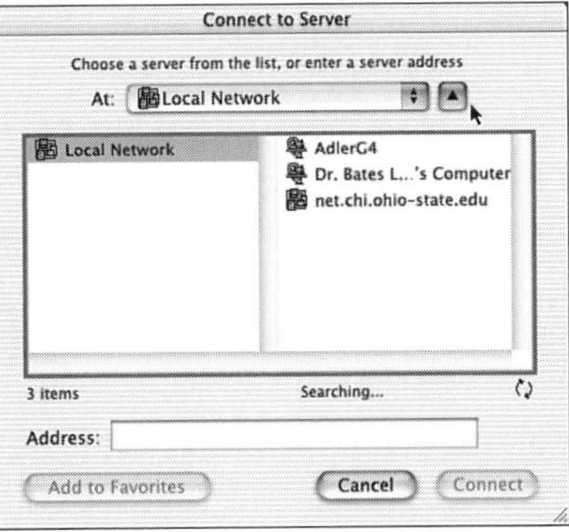

In Figure 9.14, the hierarchy of machines and domains has been moved left, and one of the machines has been selected. An URL-like address for the machine appears in the Address box of the dialog (indicating that it's an AFP [Apple Filing Protocol] server) along with its IP address.

FIGURE 9.14
The Connect to Server dialog box with a machine in the Local Network domain selected.

In Figure 9.15, the `net.chi.ohio-state.edu` subdomain of the Local Network domain was selected instead. This domain again expands into the pane to the right of it, again showing the machines that are members of the domain.

FIGURE 9.15
The Connect to Server dialog box with a subdomain selected.

To actually mount a file system or folder from a machine, browse to the machine that you're interested in, and select it from one of the panes of the Connect to Server dialog. If you want, you can add this machine to your favorites list. If a machine is selected, as shown in Figure 9.16, and the Connect button is clicked, a connection dialog box such as Figure 9.17 will appear.

FIGURE 9.16
Selecting a machine from the Connect to Server dialog box to mount a disk from it.

FIGURE 9.17
When connecting to a remote server, you must do so either as a guest, for access to Public folders, or as a user to access files that require read permission.

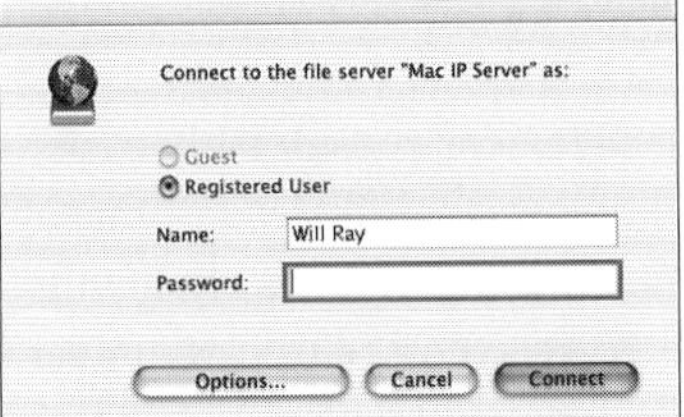

You can connect as a guest, if you want to access just the Public folders on the remote machine. Otherwise, connect with your user ID and password to access the folders and file systems on the remote machine that the user ID has read permission.

The Options button opens the dialog box shown in Figure 9.18, where you can elect to add the user ID and password information to a keychain. The Options dialog will also enable you to send your password in clear text; that is, unprotected and visible to anyone watching your network. We strongly recommend that you not enable the Clear Text option.

Disks and folders that you mount via AppleTalk will appear on your desktop if you have the option to show disks enabled on the desktop. They will also appear at the top level of the Finder hierarchy, with the other drive resources.

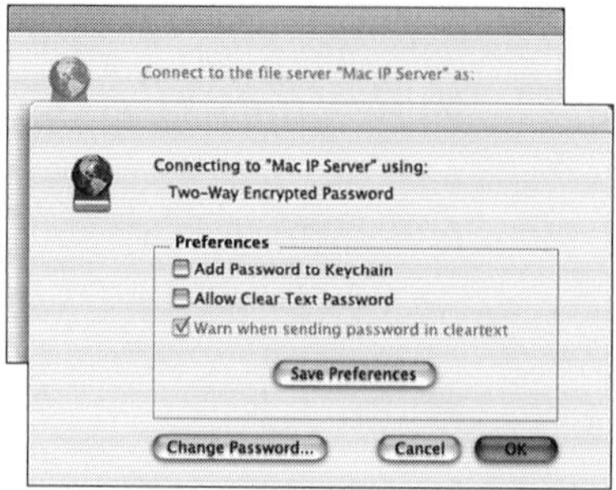

FIGURE 9.18
The options available when connecting to an AppleShare server. Please do not enable clear text passwords unless you have a very good reason to do so, and are secure against the significant risks.

Managing Locations

With OS X, Apple has made location management considerably easier than it was with previous versions of the Macintosh operating system. Instead of managing configurations for each protocol in its own panel, and then managing the switch with the location manager tool, interface configurations in OS X are accessed directly under the location setting. Figure 9.19 shows the entirety of the location management interface in OS X. From this menu, locations can be chosen, duplicated, and edited.

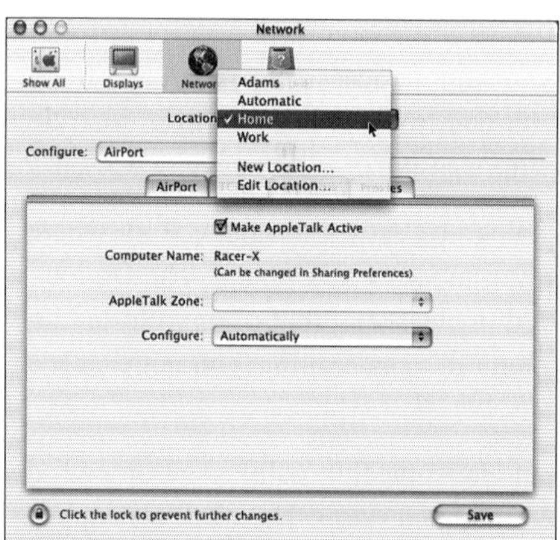

FIGURE 9.19
The location management menu in the Network control pane. Selecting a location from this menu switches between location-specific settings in the subpanes below it.

Each location in the Locations menu carries with it settings for the Configure menu and the subpanes that it switches through. That is, when you are entering information into the specific interface configuration panes, it is assigned to the currently displayed location. If you switch to a new location, you get new information and configurations in the interface configuration panels.

If you set the location setting to Automatic, the system will attempt to guess the correct location information and switch between locations, based on what it can determine regarding its network environment.

Testing Network Settings

Being inherently networked operating systems from the original design, Unix-based operating systems have a rather complete suite of network diagnostic software that comes with the basic operating system by default. We'll cover interaction with the command-line versions of these tools in several chapters to come. Apple has also provided a convenient GUI tool that functions as a front end to many of the diagnostics that the command-line tools can perform. Although it doesn't provide access to the complete range of options for each of the commands, the Network Utility application (path: `/Applications/Network Utility`) is convenient for those who don't care to remember the syntax of command-line tools. The drawback is, it tends to be considerably slower than the underlying commands that it invokes (30-plus seconds in the GUI, compared to less than a second at the command line). The Network Utility application provides access to the following network diagnostics:

Info

The Interface Information (command-line command `ifconfig`) diagnostic gives you configuration information about your network interface. Shown in Figure 9.20, this diagnostic provides information regarding the traffic and error rate of the interface, as well as speed, hardware address, and vendor information.

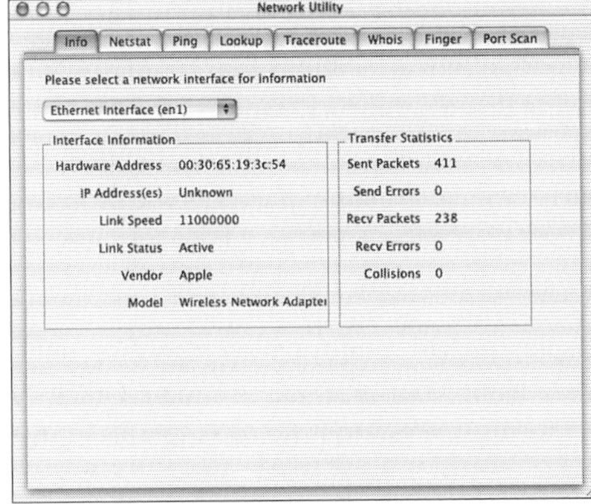

FIGURE 9.20
The Info pane of the Network utility provides information regarding the network interface and its performance.

Netstat

The Network statistics (command-line command `netstat`) diagnostic gives you statistical information regarding your network. It can provide three types of network information—routing tables, by-protocol comprehensive statistics, and multicast statistics. The information that's provided is extremely terse and dense, but with experience, it can prove invaluable in diagnosing network problems. The routing information display is shown in Figure 9.21.

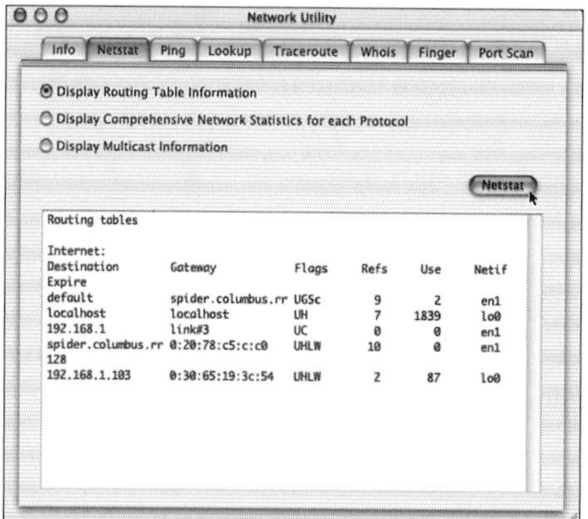

FIGURE 9.21
Click the Netstat button to look up connection information, but don't be surprised if you have to wait a while.

To get this information takes the GUI client some time, and you might have to wait for several minutes before the utility responds. The routing information specifies what your computer knows about how to get information to remote locations. The information displayed in Figure 9.21 indicates that the machine knows how to send information to two machines (`spider.columbus.rr.com` and `192.168.1.103`) directly, to an entire (`192.168.1`) by one route, and to all other locations (`default`), by going through `spider.columbus.rr.com`, which is this machine's default router. The comprehensive network statistics display includes considerably more information than fits in the display in Figure 9.22. Included is a fairly complete listing of every type of network connection and traffic that your machine has engaged in, and any problems or abnormalities that have been observed with the data transmissions for that traffic.

The multicast information display provides information regarding multicast broadcast network information. If you are using your machine to stream QuickTime video, or for other multicast applications, this display might provide you with useful information. Otherwise, you should expect it to remain essentially empty, as shown in Figure 9.23.

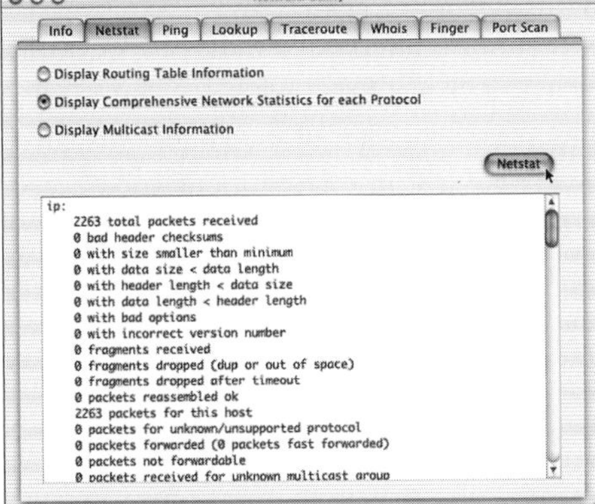

FIGURE 9.22
A portion of the comprehensive network statistics display of the Network Utility.

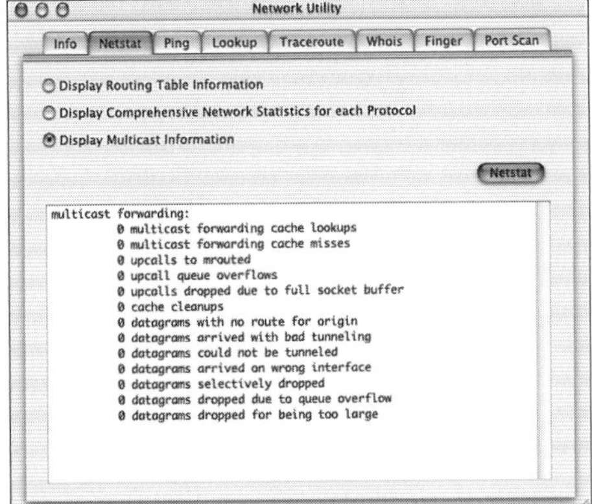

FIGURE 9.23
The multicast information display of the Network Utility. If you do not use multicast services, expect this display to remain essentially empty.

Ping

The Ping panel, provides network connection/traffic testing (command-line program `ping`), as shown in Figure 9.24. It enables you to ping a remote machine to determine whether it, and the network between your machine and it, is alive. The `ping` program injects packets destined for a remote machine into the network, destined for a mandatory service that echoes the ping back to the originating machine. Usually, 10 packets are injected into the network at one-second intervals, and the round-trip time, as well as information regarding any packets that don't complete the trip is reported back. You have the option of continuously sending packets to the remote host, but unless you have permission and a good reason to do so, this is usually considered, at the minimum, to be rude. The `icmp_seq` value increases by one for every packet sent, so if you see a gap in the values displayed, you know that one (or more) packets did not complete their round-trips. Also displayed is a TTL (Time To Live) value, which starts at 255, and decreases for every machine that reroutes the packet. Usually, all these values will be the same, but if network trouble causes packets to take alternative routes between the machines, differing TTL values might be reflected. To keep errant packets from circling the Internet forever, each packet is restricted to a finite number of machines—usually 255—that can touch it before it dies. Packets that get lost in routing loops and never make it to their destination quickly run out of TTL counts and are discarded. Finally, the time each packet took to traverse the network is displayed in milliseconds (thousandths of a second).

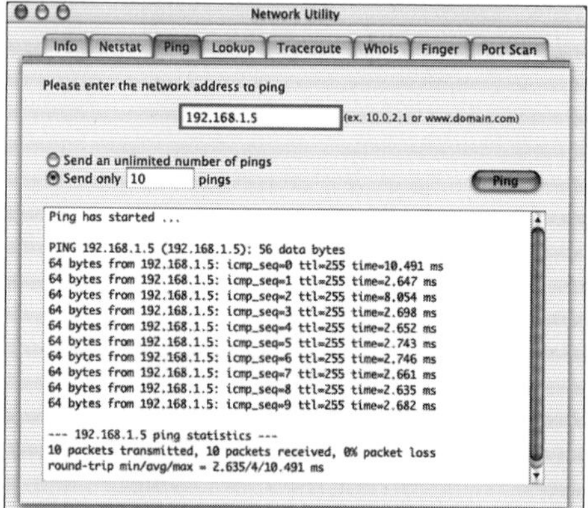

FIGURE 9.24
The Ping panel of the Network Utility allows you to determine whether a remote host can be reached, and how the network between the machines is performing.

Lookup

The Lookup (command-line command `nslookup` or `dig`) diagnostic enables you to query the DNS (Domain Name Service) information for a machine. This includes information that maps the fully qualified domain name (like `www.killernuts.org`) to an IP address, and considerable additional information as well. The default operation of the diagnostic is to look up IP addresses for an FQDN, as shown in Figure 9.25.

The diagnostic can also look up other types of information out of the DNS, such as what machine handles the e-mail for a host, and the canonical names (aliases) by which it might be known. Figure 9.26 shows the range of options for the lookup diagnostic. We recommend the use of the `dig` version because `nslookup` is deprecated, and can't be guaranteed to return complete information in the future.

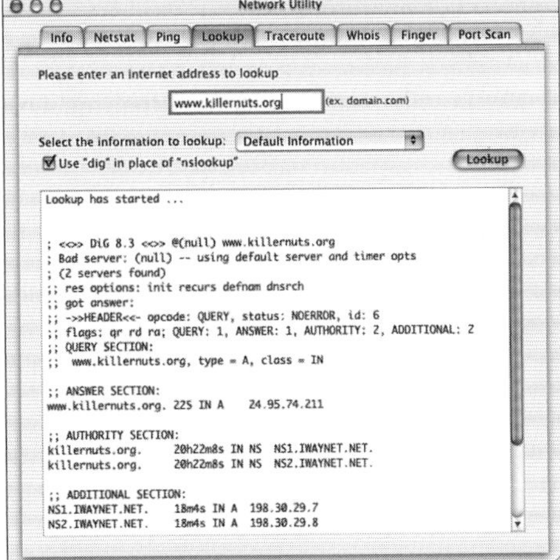

FIGURE 9.25
The results of a default search for `www.killernuts.org` *with the Lookup tool of the Network Utility application....*

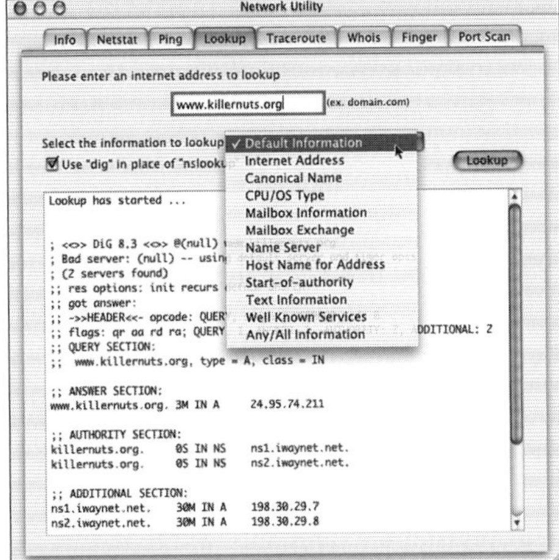

FIGURE 9.26
The Lookup type options for the Lookup tool of the Network Utility application set the amount of data that will be queried from the remote server.

The information that the Lookup tool can provide include

- **Default Information**—The default information returned by the DNS server in response to a query. Typically, the IP address to hostname mapping, the Start of Authority (SOA) record holders for the domain name, and the authoritative DNS servers for the domain.
- **Internet Address**—The IP address associated with a host name.
- **Canonical Name**—An IP address can have both a proper name, and potentially multiple alias names that point to it. The canonical name lookup provides information on the proper name that is equivalent to an alias.

- **CPU/OS Type**—Attempts to get operating system and CPU information for a remote host, but this is not a mandatory item for the host to provide to the world.
- **Mailbox Information**—Mailbox or mailing list information. There is no requirement that this information be maintained correctly on the DNS host, so the results of a query for this information should not be considered definitive.
- **Mailbox Exchange**—MX (Mail Exchanger) record information. It is frequently impractical to have every host in a domain manage its own incoming e-mail. For this reason, a DNS record might specify that mail appearing to be destined for one particular host be routed instead to an alternative destination. This allows, for example, mail to `ray@calvin.biosci.ohio-state.edu`, `ray@suzie.biosci.ohio-state.edu`, and `ray@waashu.biosci.ohio-state.edu` to all be routed to, and received by the mail server machine `ryoko.biosci.ohio-state.edu`.
- **Name Server**—Returns the list of authoritative name servers for a domain.
- **Host Name for Address**—Reverse lookup of an FQDN for a particular IP address.
- **Start-of-Authority**—A particular DNS server must be specified as the authoritative server for a particular IP-to-domain name mapping. There is an additional piece of information, known as the *Start of Authority (SOA) record*, that specifies a host that is authoritative for other information, such as contact information for problems with the domain. Frequently these are the same, but it is possible that DNS information may be delegated to servers that do not have all the same information stored as the SOA records. For example, when DNS information is maintained internally by a domain but a parent organization keeps administrative control. In this case, the SOA records should be consulted for all information other than IP-to-hostname mapping.
- **Text Information**—Any optionally registered textual information regarding the queried host. Few domains register anything interesting in this field.
- **Well Known Services**—Return information regarding well-known service types that the host might be providing. This is intended to give information regarding such things as whether the host is running FTP services, or HTTPD services, and so on. This is not a required piece of information for a host to provide to its DNS server, so few bother to provide correct or interesting information here.
- **Any/All Information**—Investigate and return all known information regarding the host. The actual information returned depends on the configuration of the server queried and the information it contains. Typically, a query for All information returns something similar to the default information.

Traceroute

The Traceroute diagnostic provides information on the route that a packet must travel between your machine and a remote machine. When the network is working properly, this information will usually be of little interest to you. If you can't reach a remote machine, however, it is sometimes useful to see to be able to tell whether the problem is with only a segment of the network, or if it's with the remote machine itself. Figure 9.27 shows the result of a successful traceroute to the host `www.tcp.com`. Each line of the output indicates a machine through which the traffic to `www.tcp.com` had to be routed, and the time it took for that particular router to respond. The trace ends at the host `www.tcp.com`, indicating that the network is successful at transmitting data between the querying host, and `www.tcp.com`.

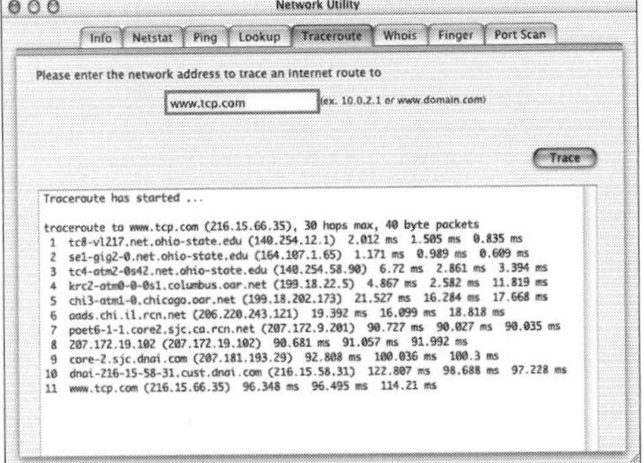

FIGURE 9.27
The Traceroute output includes diagnostic information regarding each router that the packet needed to traverse to reach the remote host.

Figure 9.28 shows the result of an attempt to trace the route to a host that is down, on the same subnet as `www.tcp.com`. The traffic in this case manages to make it almost all the way to its final destination, but cannot reach the requested final host. If we know that the host is not, in fact, the next machine along the network, we can infer that the problem is actually a network problem. Therefore, the routing of traffic between your machine and the remote machine is currently defective.

If a transient failure were occurring in the Internet and the trace stopped well before reaching the target host's subnet, we could determine that the problem reaching the host was because of something other than the host itself being down.

Whois

The Whois (command-line program `whois`) program actually has a more flexible use than is presented by this tool. It is designed to talk to remote servers that provide a sort of phone directory function. Apple has pointed the Whois tool of the Network Utility application to a subset of `whois` servers that provide directory information regarding the ownership and management of hostnames and domains. Figure 9.29 shows the results of trying to use the Whois tool to look up `www.killernuts.org`. The `whois.internic.net` machine knows only that another server, `whois.networksolutions.com`, should know the complete information for this host.

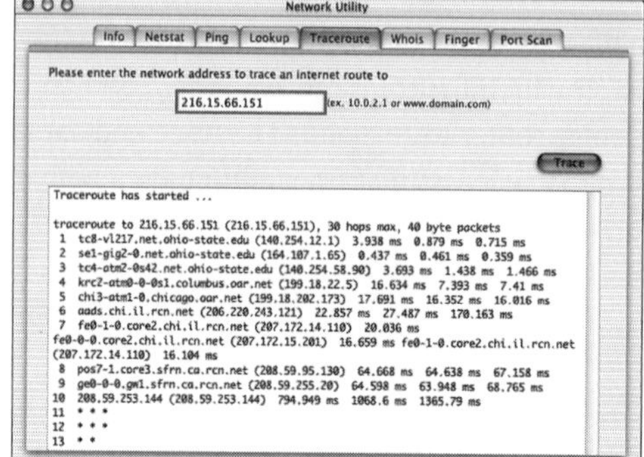

FIGURE 9.28 *The output from a Traceroute showing an unsuccessful attempt to reach a remote host on the same subnet as* `www.tcp.com`.

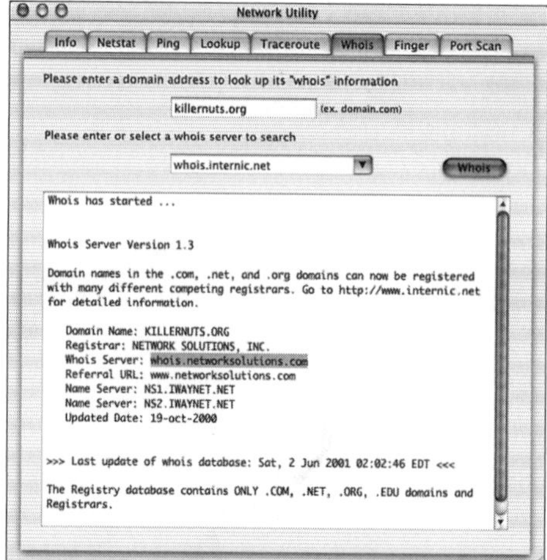

FIGURE 9.29 *The output from* `whois` *for* `www.killernuts.org` *at* `whois.internic.net`.

The information shown in Figure 9.29 indicates that the `whois` server selected, `whois.internic.net`, knows only that the complete information should be available from another server, `whois.networksolutions.com`. Figure 9.30 shows a portion of the results of selecting `whois.networksolutions.com` and reissuing the `whois` query for `www.killernuts.org`.

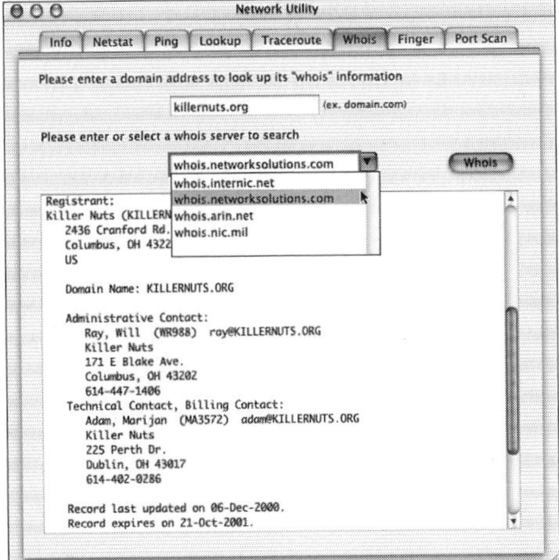

FIGURE 9.30
The output from `whois` *for* `www.killernuts.org` *at* `whois.networksolutions.com`. *This server knows considerably more about the host.*

If you're willing to ignore the sample text in Apple's dialog box, you can also use the Whois tool from the Network Utility application to query other `whois` servers. For example, if you point the host at `ohio-state.edu`, you can find out everyone who has ray in their name by searching for `ray` in the domain address box. Figure 9.31 shows a portion of the results of this search. This particular Whois server will also enable you to get more specific information regarding the people identified, and gives instructions at the bottom of the listing of names. Other `whois` servers can be contacted similarly, and can be used to obtain a range of types of information.

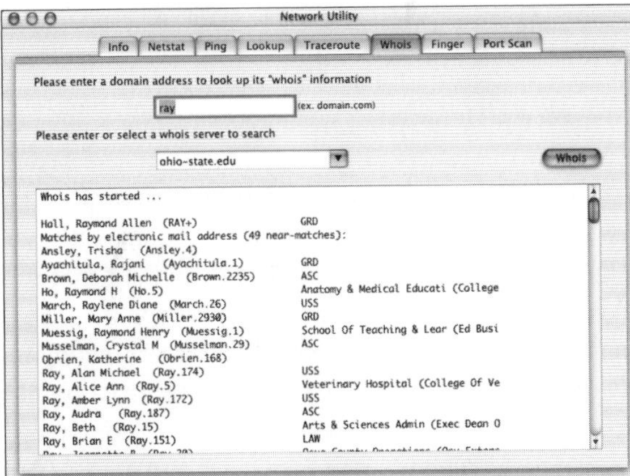

FIGURE 9.31
The output from a misuse of the Whois tool of the Network Utility application to query a `whois` *server that doesn't provide domain name information.*

Finger

The Finger (command-line program `finger`) tool of the Network Utility application gives you the ability to query the `finger` server of a host. This server, if enabled, will provide information regarding who a user is (full name, and so on), and when the user was most recently logged in. It is generally considered to be a minor security risk to run the `finger` server, because it lets crackers know whether it's safe to break into a system. But, if you know of a machine that has the service enabled, you can use this tool to access it. Figure 9.32 shows the results of using the `finger` tool to finger `ray@rosalyn.biosci.ohio-state.edu`. Notice that the server returns information about all known users with `ray` in their names. Different `finger` servers will return different information about users. This one is rather sparse, leaving out most of the users' personal information, but still indicates whether the users are logged in or not.

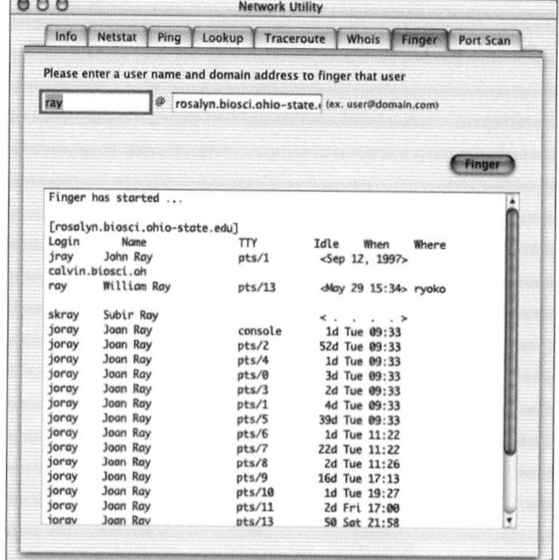

FIGURE 9.32
The output of a Finger tool lookup of `ray@rosalyn.biosci.ohio-state.edu`.

Port Scan (various command-line programs) establishes connections between logical constructs, known as *ports*, that are created by the networking software of each machine. These ports can be thought of as analogous to a series of numbered sockets into which a network connection can be plugged. The network connection must be plugged into one socket on each communicating machine; hence, it has an originating port and a destination port. Some network services always exist at particular fixed ports, and are connected to by existing at these known locations. Other applications attempt to generate a small level of security by opening a randomly numbered port and not advertising its presence. Connections then require that a connecting machine know where to look to find them. This isn't a particularly useful way of establishing security, but it does turn out to be a reasonably decent way for a cracker to hide the fact that he or she has broken into your machine. Once compromised, many crackers will install a backdoor on an unknown port, so they can come and go undetected, instead of connecting to the normal known ports, and thereby incurring a noticeable connection to a known service.

The Port Scan tool of the Network Utility application causes your machine to examine all the ports on a remote machine, and tell you which of them appear to have software listening to them. If the monitored ports don't correspond to known services, it's possible that there's been a network break in. Unfortunately, the Port Scan tool in 10.0.2 does not appear to give complete and reliable information. The machine shown in Figure 9.33 is running Sendmail, an FTP server, and an HTTPD server that exists on known ports 21, 25, and 80. None of these show up in the scan, and only some of the ports that do can be accounted for with known processes. All in all, we're not too happy about the current performance of the Port Scan tool. There are better ways of examining your own machine (`netstat`, at the command line for one), and it doesn't appear that the Port Scan tool provides reliable information. Additionally, it is considered to be excruciatingly bad form to portscan someone else's computer. This is exactly the methodology that crackers use to examine a machine for known vulnerabilities. We'd go so far as to say that it is a bit irresponsible of Apple to have put this tool in a user-level GUI application, and we recommend that you not use it, except on your own devices. Scanning a host without permission can be considered an attempted break-in, and could result in legal action against you.

FIGURE 9.33
The (incorrect in this case) output of the Port Scan tool of the Network Utility application.

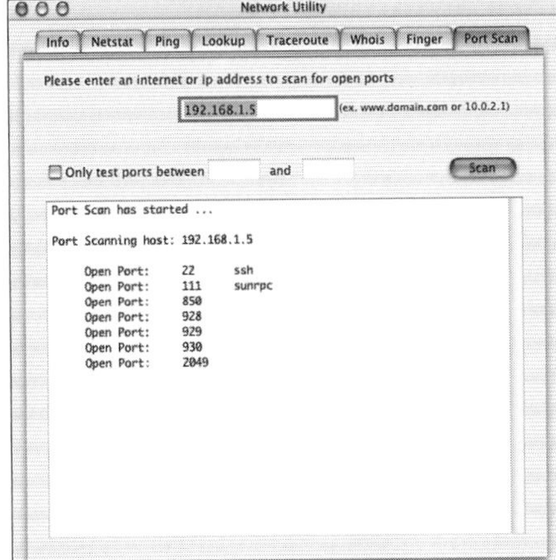

Summary

Linux and Unix operating systems have a history of being difficult to configure for online use. Users must often understand the complexities of TCP/IP to correctly set up their devices. Mac OS X puts a clean, user-friendly interface on network setup and enables the user to get online without ever seeing a command line.

This chapter covered the Mac OS X network configuration utilities, and how they can be used to create a connection through modem, Ethernet, and wireless interfaces. Macintosh users are accustomed to quickly and easily finding and connecting to network resources. Although the interface has changed, the process is just as easy.

In addition to network setup, we took an in-depth look at the Mac OS X Network Utility, which provides a suite of diagnostic tools for a Mac user to test his connections. Macintosh networking has never had a more solid and stable base than it does in Mac OS X.

CHAPTER

Printer and Font Management

In This Chapter

In this chapter, we will look at basic printer and font management in OS X. First, you will see how to add a local or network printer. Then you will learn more about your printer and its queue, as well as selecting settings for your print job and sending it to a printer. After a brief examination of the printer, we will look at font management. You will see how to manage your font collections, add a new font, and manipulate the keyboard inputs that are available in OS X.

Print Center

OS X (as of this writing) does not support Mac OS–style desktop printers. Additionally, the familiar Chooser is not a part of OS X. Instead, the heart of the OS X GUI environment printing system is the Print Center. The Print Center is the utility used for adding and deleting printers, setting the default printer, and interacting with the queues. The Print Center combines the printer tasks it once took both the Chooser and a desktop printer to accomplish. The rest of the familiar printing activities are available under the File menu of each application. The Print Center is located in `/Applications/Utilities`.

Note that just adding a printer in the Print Center is not sufficient to be able to print directly from the command line. In Chapter 23, "File and Resource Sharing," we will look at an example of adding a printer that we can use directly at the command line. However, adding a printer to the Print Center is sufficient to be able to print from the terminal application, as you would any other typical OS X application.

Local USB Printer

Because the new Macintosh hardware comes with USB ports, a local USB printer is assumed to be the default printer. OS X comes with some third-party USB printer drivers. If the drivers that come with OS X work with your printer, you should be ready to print.

When you open the Print Center, if no Printer List appears under the Printers menu, you can select View Printer List to check for your USB printer. If you still don't see your printer listed, if it is listed as unsupported, or if you can't find your local printer, check the software CD that came with your printer for OS X drivers. If it does not have any, check the manufacturer's Web site for the latest drivers and instructions. After the drivers are properly installed, your local USB printer should be available for printing. Select the USB connection and click Add Printer. Your USB printer then appears in the Printer List. At this time, OS X does not enable you to share your USB printer.

Network Printers

If you do not have a local USB printer, or if there are also network printers available, you might want to add a network printer to your Printer List.

To add a network printer to your system:

1. Select Add Printer under the Printers menu, or click the Add Printer directly from the Printer List.
2. Select the connection type. Available connection types for network printers include LPR Printers using IP and AppleTalk. LPR printers are printers shared using a traditional Unix printer-sharing scheme. The Print Center can provide connectivity for the GUI side of OS X to this well-established printing resource. In Chapter 23, we will look at adding a network printer via the Directory Services connection, for supporting printing from the command line.

Figure 10.1 shows the LPR Printers using IP window. In the window you specify

- The IP address or name of the printer or host.
- The queue. The default is to use the default printer queue. An alternate queue name can be specified instead.
- The printer model. Here you can select a specific LaserWriter model, a generic PostScript printer, or a specific PPD for your printer model.

FIGURE 10.1
Fill in information at the LPR Printer's Address using IP window to select that connection type.

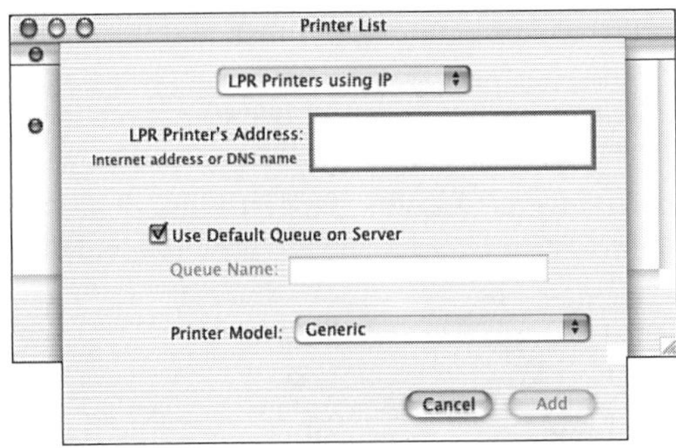

Selecting an AppleTalk printer should be much like selecting an AppleTalk printer in the Chooser. You should see a selection of familiar AppleTalk printers. Make sure that you have turned on AppleTalk in the Network pane.

3. Click Add. The printer should now be listed in the Printer List.

Examining Printers

The Printer List in the Print Center is the place to examine the printers. Each entry in the Printer List lists the printer name, the kind of printer, and its status, if appropriate. Figure 10.2 shows a sample Printer List. In this Printer List, three printers are shown. Two are LaserWriters connected via AppleTalk. One of the LaserWriters is currently printing, according to the status. A third printer, named lp, is a remote PostScript printer served by another Unix host. The Printer List describes lp as a NetInfo host. This means that the NetInfo database contains information about this printer. The NetInfo database, which we will discuss in detail in Chapter 23, is a hierarchical database that stores information on your machine's configuration and resources.

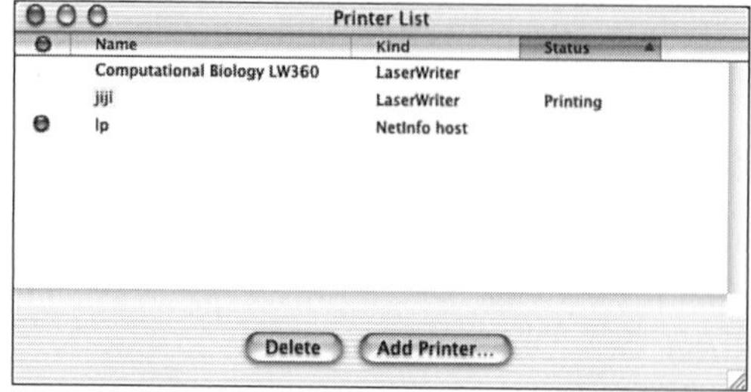

FIGURE 10.2
This Printer List shows three printers.

Printer lp has a blue dot beside it, denoting that it is the default printer. Each time you add a printer, the newly added one automatically becomes the default. To make a specific printer your default, select the printer in the Printer List, and then choose Make Default under the Printers menu. To delete a printer, select it in the Printer List and click Delete.

To see a printer's queue, select Show Queue under the Printers menu. Figure 10.3 shows a sample print queue that has experienced an error, according to the status entry. You could either delete the job, or retry it by selecting the print job and clicking the appropriate button.

FIGURE 10.3
The print queue for printer jiji shows that current print job has encountered an error. You could choose to delete the job or retry it.

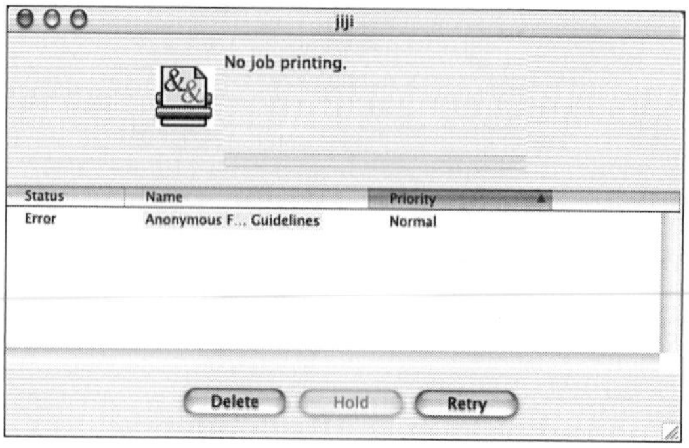

When a print job is proceeding normally, the Retry button becomes a Resume button, making the accessible buttons in the status window Delete, Hold, and Resume. While a successful job is printing, the status bar, which is grayed in Figure 10.3, is blue and alternately flashes Processing job and Preparing data for the duration of the print time. The buttons at the bottom of the status window are grayed out while the print job is processing, unless you select the print job. A sample status window for a normal print job is shown in Figure 10.4. The status entry for a printer that is printing becomes Printing, and during this time the Print Center appears in the Dock, where you could also click to get this information. In some versions of OS X, the Print Center icon shows pages remaining to be printed, and has a pop-up menu with queues and active/waiting jobs.

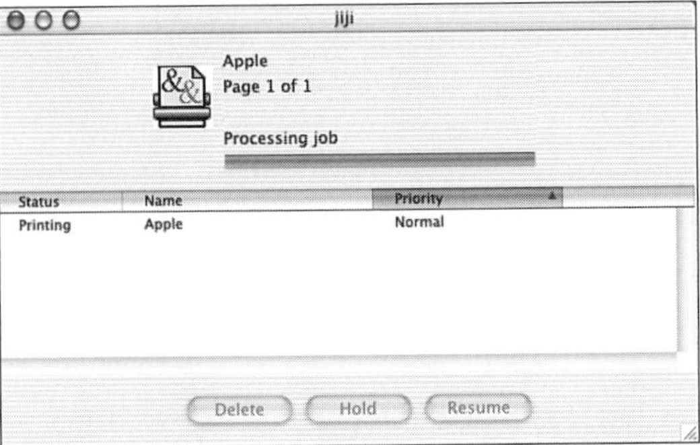

FIGURE 10.4

The print queue for printer jiji shows that the current print job is proceeding normally.

Under the Queue menu, you can choose to stop a queue. When you do that, the status entry for the printer in the Printer List reflects that the queue has stopped by listing the status as Stopped. After you have stopped a queue, the option under the Queue menu becomes Start Queue. Under the Queue menu, you can also Hold, Resume, or Delete a print job.

Printing

Sending a job to the printer from an application in OS X works as it did in previous versions of the operating system. Page Setup under the File menu is where you set basic page settings. Print under the File menu is still used to send your job to the printer and specify additional characteristics for the print job.

If you installed separate printer drivers from your manufacturer, we would expect that you have some additional available options not covered here.

Page Setup

Under the File menu of an application, choose Page Setup to set the basic settings that you are used to setting up in Page Setup. Figure 10.5 shows what Page Setup looks like in OS X. Page Setup appears as either a sheet or a window, depending on the application. Sometimes it can be accessed only from the File menu, or with Shift+Command+P. The Settings option has the major choices of Page Attributes and Summary. At the bottom of Page Setup, there is a button for direct access to the Help Center, as well as buttons for Cancel and OK. We will break our examination of Page Setup according to the Settings choices.

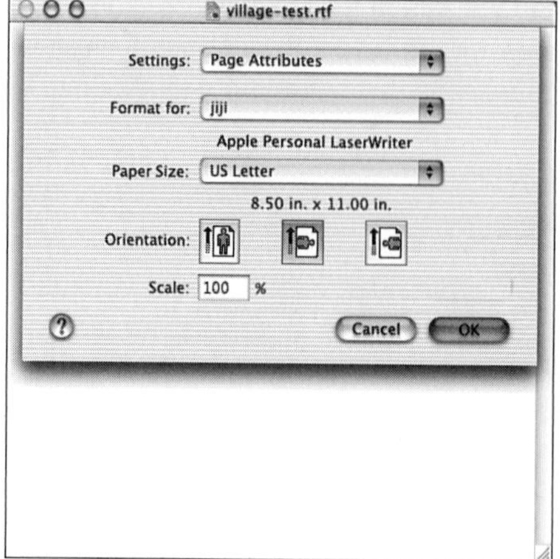

FIGURE 10.5
Page Setup can still be found under the File menu in OS X. The page settings are almost identical to previous versions of the operating system.

Page Attributes

The Settings option is set to Page Attributes by default. The Page Attributes that can be specified are the printer, the page size, orientation, and scale.

Format For

Under the Page Attributes section of Page Setup, you can select which printer to format for. The available printer choices are Any Printer and whatever printers are included as part of your Printer List. Page Setup formats for Any Printer by default, and Any Printer has an additional description of Generic Printer. When you select a printer that is in your Printer List, a more specific description appears. Note that in our example, the Page Setup describes printer jiji as an Apple Personal LaserWriter.

Paper Size

Page size is also specified in Page Setup. The available paper sizes vary with the selected printer. The default page sizes available for Any Printer are US Letter, US Legal, A4, B5, JB5 and #10 envelope. Whenever you select a paper size, its dimensions appear as an additional description. For Any Printer, US Letter, 8.5"×11", is the default paper size.

Orientation

There is a slight change in what is available for orientation. Portrait is available as well as two forms of landscape. For landscape, you can specify whether the top of the printout should be at the right or left side of the paper. Simply select the appropriate icon to suit your needs. Portrait is the default orientation.

Scale

Scale is a box where you can input the desired scaling. The default is 100%.

Summary

The Summary option of Page Setup displays a summary of the settings you have selected for all the Page Attributes categories. Figure 10.6 shows a sample summary.

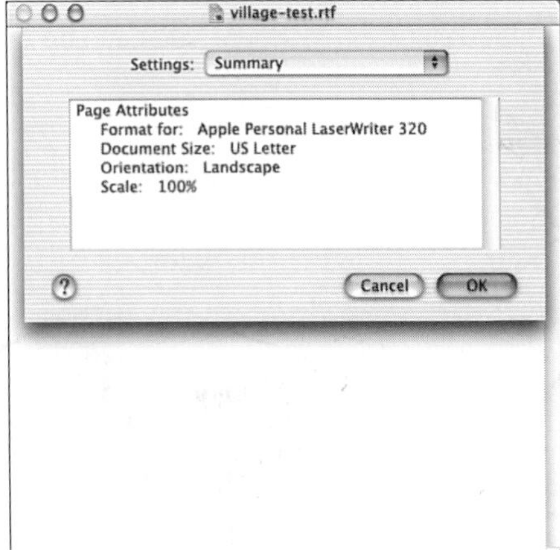

FIGURE 10.6
The Summary section of Page Setup summarizes the Page Attributes you have selected.

Print

You can still choose Print under the File menu (Command+P) to print a file, as in earlier versions of the operating system. Choosing Print opens the Print dialog box, as shown in Figure 10.7. Depending on the application, the Print dialog box appears either as a sheet or as a separate, movable window. In this section, you can choose the default printer, select another one, or even edit the Printer List to add another printer. The following can also be set or done in the Print dialog box: Copies & Pages, Layout, Output Options, Paper Feed, Error Handling, Summary, and Save Custom Setting. The bottom of the Print dialog box has a button for direct access to the Help Center as well as buttons for Preview, Cancel, and Print. Preview is sometimes available under the File menu of an application, but it always appears as a button in the Print dialog box.

Please note that the Print dialog box that is used by the Terminal application varies from the more traditional Print dialog box described in this section.

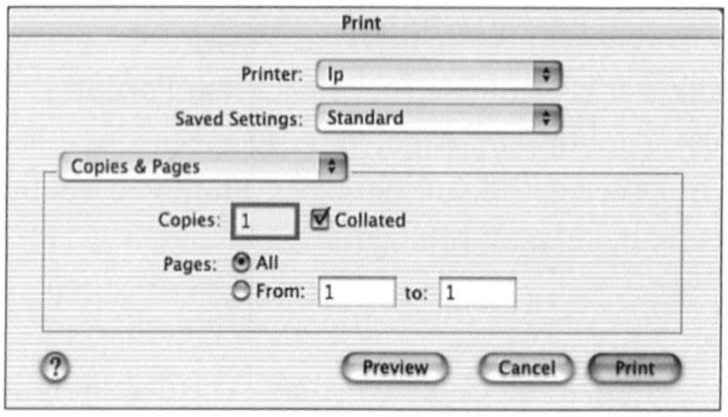

FIGURE 10.7
Choosing Print under the File menu opens the Print dialog box, where you can select a printer and various options for your print job.

Printer

By default, whichever printer is listed in your Printer List as your default printer is listed here as the default printer. You can also select from any of the other printers available in your Printer List, or you can choose Edit Printer List to edit your Printer List. This option immediately takes you to the Print Center, where you can add or delete printers.

Saved Settings

Saved Settings appears as Standard by default. After you have saved a customized setting, you will be able to select Standard or Custom.

Copies & Pages

Copies & Pages, the first item in a pop-up menu of many items, is the default settings category. Here you specify the number of copies you want to print, whether the pages should be collated, and a page range. For the page range, you can select either All or specify an actual range of page numbers.

Layout

Layout, shown in Figure 10.8, is where you select layout settings. The first available option is Pages Per Sheet, where you can select 1, 2, 4, 6, 9, or 16 pages per sheet. The next option is Layout direction. There are four layout direction options: horizontally from left to right, horizontally from right to left, vertically from left to right, and vertically from right to left. The available layout directions are indicated with helpful icons. The final layout option is Border. Available options for Border are None, Single hairline, Single thin line, Double hairline, and Double thin line.

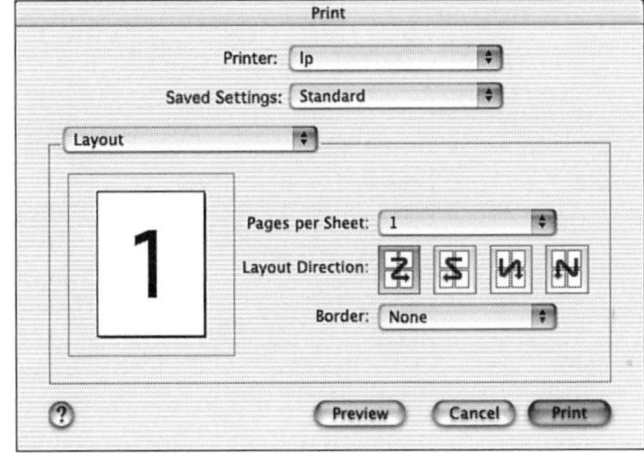

FIGURE 10.8
The Layout section of Print is where you specify the number of pages per sheet, layout direction, and border.

Output Options

Output Options allows you to save your print job to a file instead. Currently the available output options are PDF and PostScript. The Print button becomes a Save button, allowing you to select a location where your file should be saved.

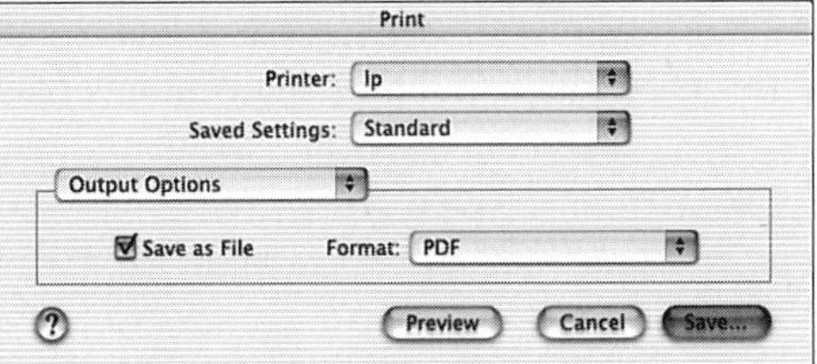

FIGURE 10.9
In the Output Options section of the Print dialog box, you can save your Print job as a PDF file or PostScript file.

Paper Feed

The Paper Feed section, shown in Figure 10.10, is where you set any special paper feed options. You can either choose to specify that all your pages come from a particular paper feed option, or that the first one come from one location and the remaining pages from a different location. This could be useful, for example, if you have a tray dedicated to letterhead. The actual paper feed choices for the different categories vary with the printer.

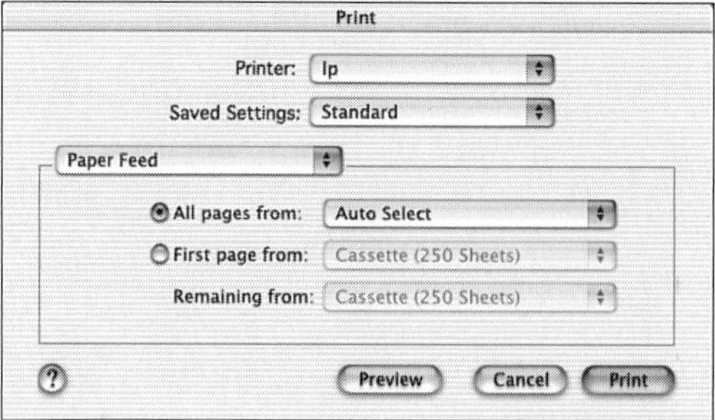

FIGURE 10.10
Special paper feed options can be set in the Paper Feed section of the Print dialog box.

Error Handling

Figure 10.11 shows the default Error Handling options for a PostScript printer that can have multiple trays. The Error Handling options that appear for this printer are for PostScript Errors and Tray Switching. The PostScript error choices are to either have No Special Reporting, which is the default, or to Print Detailed Report. The Tray Switching error options are Use Printers default, which is the default, Switch to another cassette with same paper size, or Display Alert. Unfortunately, because we have only PostScript printers readily available, we do not know if another error handling option might appear in place of the PostScript Errors option, or if that option is simply grayed out for non-PostScript printers.

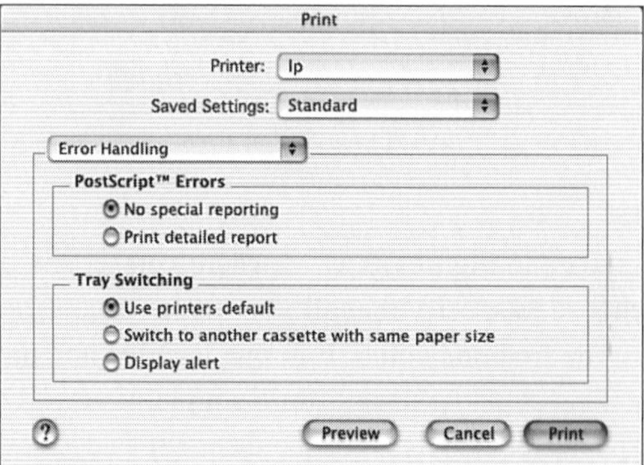

FIGURE 10.11
Error handling options can be set in the Error Handling section of the Print dialog box.

Application

Sometimes an application will have a category for additional special options unique to it. This is always a good place to check if you find that your print results are a bit unexpected. For example, if you are printing something created in color to a color printer, but it prints in grayscale, you would check here for additional options for your particular application.

Summary

The Summary option displays a summary of all the settings that you specified with Print. A sample Summary is shown in Figure 10.12.

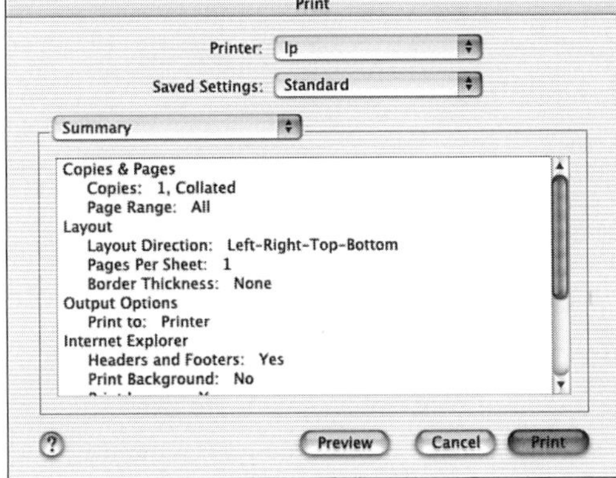

FIGURE 10.12
The Summary section of the Print dialog box displays a summary of the settings for the current print job.

Save Custom Setting

Save Custom Setting enables you to save custom print settings. When you have done this, your available choices in Saved Settings become Standard or Custom. So far, we have not observed a way to remove a custom setting if you accidentally saved one. Also, it does not appear that you can customize the name of your custom setting. After you have made a custom setting in an application, this same custom setting becomes available in your other applications. In a different application, you can change that custom setting by selecting Save Custom Setting. Although the name appears as Custom, the settings associated with it will be different for the two applications. Unfortunately, it does not appear to be possible to have more than one custom setting per application. Figure 10.13 shows a sample custom setting. In the sample, only the Layout has been customized.

Preview

The behavior of the Preview button of the Print dialog box varies with the application. In some applications, the Preview button calls the Preview application. From the Preview application itself, you can then choose such options as Save as PDF, Page Setup, or Print. In other applications, the Preview button launches a customized Preview option, where you can also choose Page Setup or Print. In either case, it is expected that you should be able to print directly from the Preview option, no matter how Preview is handled.

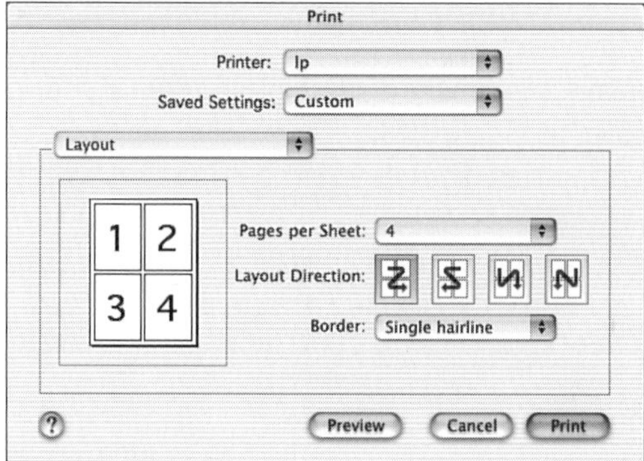

FIGURE 10.13
This is a sample custom setting.

Managing Fonts

OS X has introduced a new type of font suitcase with the extension `.dfont`. The new font suitcase stores a file's resource fork in the data fork. In addition to the new font format, OS X supports these Windows font formats: TrueType fonts with extension `.ttf`, TrueType collections with extension `.ttc`, and OpenType fonts with extension `.otf`. OS X supports PostScript Type 1, legacy bitmap fonts, and Unicode. Unicode is a universal character-encoding standard for multilingual text support across multiple platforms. Supporting Unicode enhances OS X's multilingual support. OS X's multilingual support is most clearly seen in the available keyboards in the International pane. At this point, though, you might wonder if your old collection of fonts will work in OS X. Fortunately, OS X also supports older font suitcases used in earlier versions of the operating system without any conversion.

Installing a New Font

Installing a new font on your system is not difficult. For example, to install the Pushkin handwriting font from the ParaType free fonts page (`http://www.paratype.com/shop/`), download the following file to your drive:

```
http://www.fontstock.com/softdl/PushkinTT.zip
```

This is actually a Windows TrueType font, but as we know, OS X conveniently understands these, as well as many traditional Mac OS font types. You can uncompress it at the command line by using

```
unzip PushkinTT.zip

     Archive:  PushkinTT.zip
       inflating: Pushkin.ttf
```

The first line shown here is the command you type. The next two lines are lines of output that the command produces as it unzips the file. Of course, you can also uncompress it in the GUI interface, as you are used to doing in Mac OS.

If you want this font to be available to all users on your machine, our recommended configuration, copy it either to the `/Library/Fonts/` or `/System/Library/Fonts` directories, but not both. The `/System` directories are usually reserved for Apple's usage, but *will* work if you want to place fonts in a protected area. If you want the font to be available for your use only, copy it to your `~/Library/Fonts/` directory. If you want to use the command line to copy the file, use the following syntax:

```
cp Pushkin.ttf /Library/Fonts/
```

Note

You will most likely find that even as an administrator, you do not have permission to copy to the `/System/Library/Fonts/` directory. You might need to be `root`, or use `sudo`, to copy the file to this location. However, as an administrator, you should be able to copy the font to the `/Library/Fonts/` location. The reason for this is that technically, the `/System` folder is intended for Apple usage, whereas the `/Library` folder is intended to be an area where you can add accessible system-wide files. For system-wide availability, adding the font to your `/Library/Fonts` folder is better form, as well as easier.

That's it. You'll need to restart any applications that you want to be able to use the font, but you shouldn't need to restart your machine, or even log out. Figure 10.14 shows what the terminal looks like in the Pushkin handwriting font.

Macintosh suitcases and PostScript fonts need to be copied into the `/System/Library/Fonts/` or `/Library/Fonts/` directory by dragging and dropping from the Finder because they are resource fork–type fonts, and don't always copy cleanly from the command line.

Using the Font Panel

You can access your fonts in the Font panel, which is available in many of the typical OS X applications. The location of the Font panel varies with the application. For example, some applications include Font as a menu bar item, and you select Font panel under that. Other applications include the Font panel as an option, although it might be a nested option, under another menu bar category, such as Format. The Font panel has divisions for Collections, Family, Typeface, and Sizes. Because the default collection is All Fonts, you can indeed see your entire collection of available fonts with ease. However, the Font panel also provides the capability for you to group your fonts together. It comes with some groups already created. You can modify those collections as well as create, modify, and remove your own collections. The Font panel is shown in Figure 10.15.

FIGURE 10.14
Here is a terminal window set to use the Pushkin handwriting font. Although this is an amusing change for a terminal, it is perhaps not the best font choice for regular terminal usage.

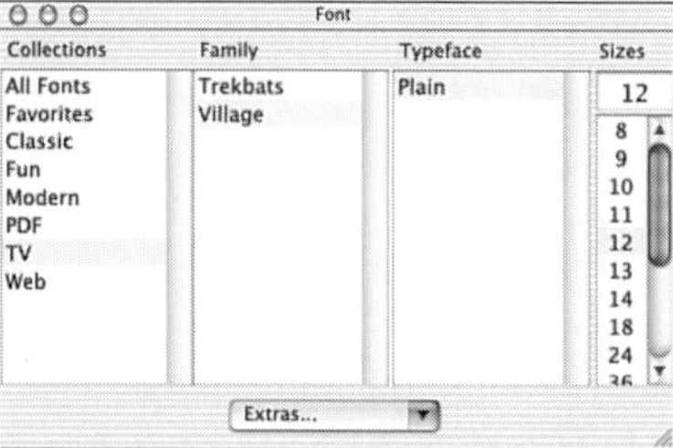

FIGURE 10.15
The Font panel is your interface to using and managing your fonts.

To switch between collections, just click the desired collection in the Collections column. Although this is rather obvious, it is not as obvious if you do not see the Collections column. If your view of the Font panel starts with the Family column, widen the panel by dragging it at the bottom right.

The Edit Collections option, which is available under the Extras option of the Font panel, is the option you use if you want to modify the collections. Figure 10.16 shows what the panel looks like when you are in the mode for editing collections. When the Font - Collections window appears, name your new collection. To add a font to the collection, select a font in the All Families column, and then click the << button. To remove a font from the collection, select the font in the Family column, and then click the >> button. The options at the bottom left, +, –, and Rename, control the collections. Keep in mind that – removes a collection. If you plan to remove a collection, make sure that you are selecting the right collection to be deleted. When you are finished editing your collections, click Done. Your edits are now available in the Font panel of any application that uses the Font panel.

The Add to Favorites option under the Extras menu enables you to add fonts directly to the Favorites collection. It opens a window that enables you to delete fonts from your Favorites collection.

FIGURE 10.16
The Font – Collections window, which appears when you select Edit Collections under the Extras section in the Font panel, is where you edit your font collections.

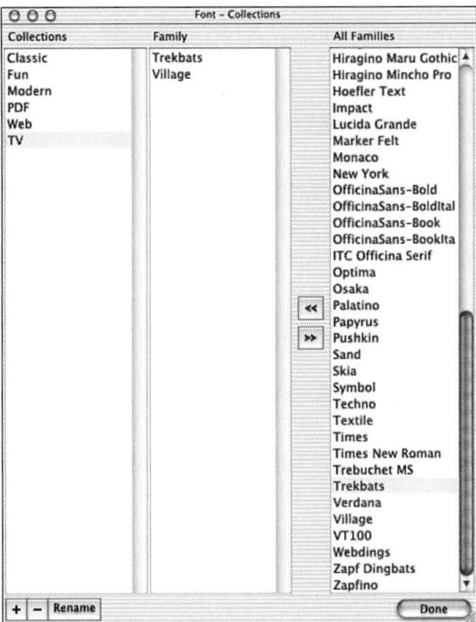

The Edit Sizes option under the Extras section of the Font panel enables you to choose whether you would like to see font sizes listed as fixed sizes or on a slider instead. It also enables you to edit the available sizes. For a fixed view, you can add or delete a specific size from the fixed list. For a sliding scale, you can edit the minimum and maximum font sizes. Figure 10.17 shows the Font - Sizes window that first appears for editing sizes. It changes slightly to enable you to adjust the minimum and maximum available font sizes on the slider.

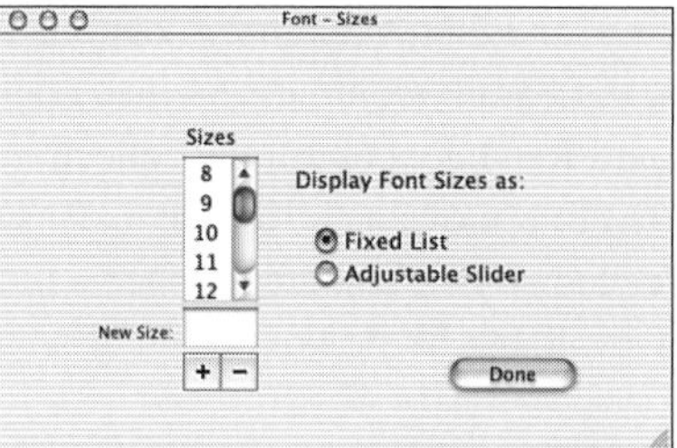

FIGURE 10.17
The Font – Sizes window, which appears when you select Edit Sizes under the Extras section in the Font panel, is where you select how the font sizes options will be displayed.

The default slider sizes are from 8-point to 72-point. Figure 10.18 shows the Font panel with the slider in the Sizes column. Selecting the Adjustable Slider option, shown in Figure 10.17, accesses this version of the panel, rather than the default fixed listing.

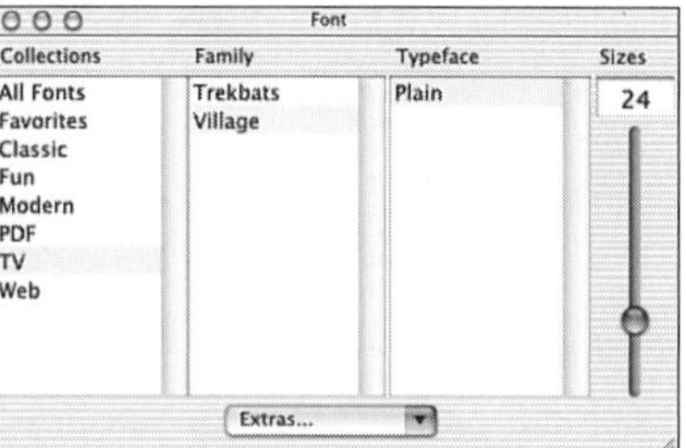

FIGURE 10.18
Here the Font panel is shown with the slider for indicating size.

The Color option under the Extras section opens a standard color browser where you can specify, by a wheel, spectrum, color scales, and so on, a color for the font you are using. Just click Apply after you have selected the color you want.

The Extras section also has a Get Fonts option that takes you to `http://www.apple.com/fonts/buy/`, which is a site where Apple is planning to sell more fonts for OS X.

If you have some preferred settings in the Font panel, you can shrink its size so that it shows your preferred defaults in a pop-up menu, as shown in Figure 10.19. This enables you to conveniently leave the Font panel showing while you are working, rather than having to minimize it. If you prefer, the Font panel can be minimized. When you quit the application associated with a particular Font panel, that Font panel also quits.

As for actually using a font in your application, select the font you want to use from the Font panel and start typing. If the font switches to a font other than what you selected, select the text you just typed, and select the desired font again. The font will switch to what you want, and you can continue typing. If you want to see what different fonts look like, you can type something, select it, and then select a font for it. Continue selecting a font until you have seen the ones you wanted to see. If you would like to see the Font panel in action, check the QuickTime movie at `http://www.apple.com/macosx/theater/fontpanel.html`.

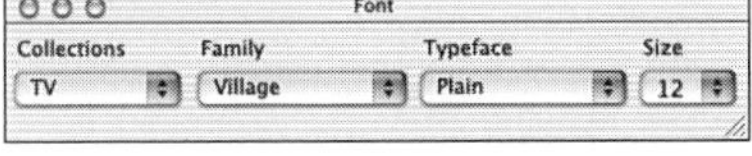

FIGURE 10.19
Here the Font panel has been shrunk so that the options are included in pop-up menus instead.

Using the Keyboard Menu and Alternative Input Scripts

Apple has, for several generations of Mac OS, made a very clever feature available as an optional part of the operating system. This software, WorldScript and the various language kits it supported, was a way of putting a layer of abstraction between what you type on the keyboard, and what is actually entered into a document that you are working with. The system was modeled on the notion that a computer might have only one physical keyboard, but a knowledge of the language and locale in which the user is working would enable a translation between what keys are physically pressed and contextually correct data output. This functionality is now a default part of OS X, and is embodied in a two-part system comprised of key-mapping tables called *keyboards*, and locale-sensitive processing software known as *input scripts*.

Keyboard mapping tables are used to map between a particular key that is pressed, and an output symbol that is generated. For example, you might have heard of the Dvorak keyboard, a more efficient alternative to the QWERTY keyboard that you are probably already familiar with. A keyboard mapping might be used to re-map the keys on your QWERTY keyboard, so that they function as though your keyboard was a Dvorak keyboard instead. A keyboard mapping can also be used to do things such as change the currency indicator to the appropriate currency for the locale—British pounds for U.K. English and American dollars for American English, for example.

Input scripts, on the other hand, can perform more sophisticated, context-sensitive alterations of data as it is entered. This modification can be anything from changing the font used to display all or certain characters, to providing phonetic ways of entering symbols that are not directly available from the keyboard.

These two pieces of functionality, accessed jointly though the Keyboard menu and the International pane of the system controls, give you the ability to enter data in character sets appropriate for other languages, whether they are English-like languages or languages with completely different symbol sets and entry needs.

The use and utility of this is probably not immediately apparent from just a description, but working through the following example should give you an idea of just how powerful the keyboard tables and input scripts can be.

The first place to examine when configuring or customizing your input environment is the International pane. Figure 10.20 shows the Languages tab of the International pane. In the bottom portion, there is an option to select the default behavior of scripts. The fine print in the tab tells us that what we select here affects sort order, case conversion, and word definitions. From the perspective of a user with an American English keyboard, nothing obvious happens, even if I switch to one of the other choices in the Roman script. This is because the Roman script is used for Roman-like language input styles. Most European languages use an alphabet, character ordering, and display styles that have significant similarities. The number of characters is roughly the same, text flows from left to right on the page, there are uppercase and lowercase letters, and so on. On the other hand, languages such as Arabic, Hebrew, Chinese, and Japanese have very different symbol sets, character ordering, and display styles that are unlike each other and the majority of European languages. By convention, therefore, languages with Roman-like characteristics use the Roman input script.

Other languages might use their own particular input scripts, which can provide language-specific input functionality, or they might use the Unicode input script. Unicode is an internationally standardized way of providing input in a number of symbol sets that cannot be conveniently represented on a standard keyboard. The Unicode input script cannot provide customized input processing in a language-contextual manner, but does provide for a standardized way to input a great number of characters from a keyboard with only a limited number of keys. To use Unicode, therefore, you need to have a mapping between keyboard sequences and output symbols. As a demonstration of the power available in other input scripts, we'll take a look at the Japanese input script, and how it maps from phonetic keyboard input in romanji, into natural Japanese Katakana, Hiragana, and Kanji.

When looking through the International panel's Language tab, browse the choices under Roman and Japanese. You will note that Roman has many choices, whereas Japanese has only Japanese. Now pick an appropriate default for yourself. Please note that the available selection on your machine might differ from what is shown here.

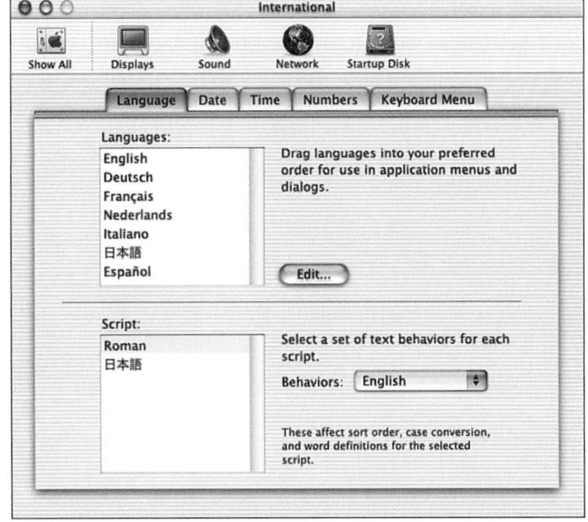

FIGURE 10.20
The Language tab of the International panel is where you select a default script.

Figure 10.21 shows the more interesting tab for our purposes, the Keyboard Menu tab. The Keyboard Menu tab enables you to pick various types of keyboard layouts. Browse through the keyboard layout options in this section. Note that there are several in the Roman script, a few that use the Unicode script, and one in the Japanese script. Select a few that use the Roman script, and select the Japanese layout.

FIGURE 10.21
You can select any keyboard layouts that might be of interest to you in the Keyboard Menu tab of the International panel.

When you select more than one keyboard, a flag icon of the country you've chosen appears in the menu bar of the Finder, as shown in Figure 10.22. This is the Keyboard menu, which shows which keyboard layouts are available, and which is chosen. The Customize Menu option takes you to the Keyboard Menu tab of the International pane. The most obvious way to switch between keyboard layouts is to select the one you want from the Keyboard menu itself. However, if you check the Options section of the Keyboard Menu tab of the International pane, you will see that you can also use Command+Option+Space to rotate to the next keyboard in the active script. In other words, if you are in a keyboard that uses the Roman script interface, the key combination rotates to the next Roman keyboard in your menu. You can use Command+Space to rotate to the default keyboard of the next script.

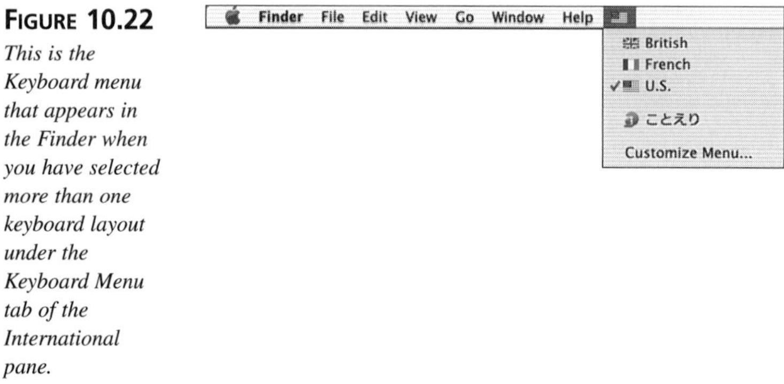

FIGURE 10.22 *This is the Keyboard menu that appears in the Finder when you have selected more than one keyboard layout under the Keyboard Menu tab of the International pane.*

Take a couple moments to play with the Roman script keyboard layouts in an application such as TextEdit. A simple example to check is the British keyboard. If you switch to it and type #, you will discover that you get £. Switch to the French keyboard and start pressing the number keys. You get many characters with accents instead. Press a number key while holding down the Shift key to get a number instead.

Hopefully, you have gotten used to the idea of the script interpreting your input as appropriate for the keyboard layout you have selected. Although these modifications of your input might seem relatively simple, this is because you've been working in your already-familiar Roman input script.

Now, let's take a look at a more interesting keyboard layout and input script—the one for Japanese. As you go through the example, notice where the input script is interpreting the input that you type, and attempting to produce contextually correct output for you. Apple has traditionally produced language kits for a large number of non-Roman script languages, and this is exactly the sort of input functionality and conversion that you should expect in any of these languages that you might need to work in.

Figure 10.23 shows a Japanese phrase. For those who don't read Japanese, the pronunciation is (as close as we can represent in English) Kazenotaninonaushika, which translates as "Nausicaä of the Valley of the Wind," the title of a popular Japanese children's film.

Without the functionality available in the language kit, typesetting this phrase from the keyboard would be very difficult. It contains characters from three different Japanese alphabets—one of which contains thousands of characters. Entering this without a language kit would entail finding the right keys to produce the characters from the two small phonetic alphabets, all the while switching between fonts and picking from a huge list of characters in the thousand-plus character alphabet. With the Japanese kit, typesetting this is only a little more complex than typing the word as it is pronounced in English.

FIGURE 10.23
The Japanese phrase Kaze no tani no Nausicaä, will serve as our example of using the input system.

Using TextEdit and the Japanese language kit, we can easily reproduce the text shown in Figure 10.23. Although this example is in Japanese, the same steps can be used for any language you use. From within the application that you want to use an alternative input script, choose the keyboard layout from the keyboard menu. The input script for that keyboard will take over the input for the application.

Figure 10.24 shows how TextEdit looks while running under the influence of an input script. A new menu created by the Japanese input script, and containing functions pertinent to operations in the language, has appeared. The menu for the Japanese input script is, of course, in Japanese. Other input scripts will provide their own menus with similar functionality, presented in a language appropriate for their intended users.

The Operation Palette that has appeared lower on the screen, is helpful for working with the Japanese keyboard layout. If you lose it, it is the second item in that Japanese menu shown in Figure 10.24.

FIGURE 10.24
After you have switched to the Japanese keyboard, another menu item appears to the right of the symbol for the Japanese keyboard. This menu is in Japanese.

The Operations Palette, which might vary depending on the language kit you are using, indicates and sets the current input method via the top row of buttons. The first button selects hiragana phonetic input, the second selects the katakana-input method, and the third and fourth enable entry in kanji and other character systems via Unicode, and entry in our normal Latin alphabet, respectively. The button with the green rectangular icon gives you an interface, in the appropriate language, to some features of the operating system. Additionally, the question mark opens the language-specific Help system. If the language kit you want to use requires complex interaction with a number of alphabetic systems, you can expect that you will be provided with similar functionality under OS X.

Now, to reproduce the Japanese phrase seen earlier, all we need is to make sure that the Operations Palette is phonetic mode, and that we know how to say (phonetically) what we want to type.

For the sample phrase, the characters we are looking for break up, partly as words, and partly as phonetics (words for the pictogram-based parts of the phrase, and phonetics for the phonetic character parts), as follows

```
kaze no tani no na u shi ka
```

In the Font panel, pick a fairly large size for the font so that you can easily read what you are typing. Then type the letter `k`. So far, nothing unexpected happens. Type the letter `a`. As soon as you type this, the input script recognizes that you have entered a phoneme, and replaces it with the appropriate phonetic character for the selected alphabet. The character for the sound `ka` has appeared, and replaced the `k` and `a` characters. Type the letter `z`. Now you have a hiragana character and the letter `z`, as shown in Figure 10.25. Now type the letter `e`. Again, the input script recognizes a phoneme. The character for the `ze` sound has appeared. Note the characters have an underscore. This means that the input script recognizes that there are other possible representations in the language that could also be appropriate, and is prompting that we might want to change the current representation.

To select from possible representations that the input can take, press the spacebar. The input system will select a character for you. If the character is not correct, press the space bar again. This opens a little window, as shown in Figure 10.26, from which you can manually select a character.

FIGURE 10.25
The Japanese character for ka *followed by the letter* z *are showing after typing* ka, *and then* z. *The underscore means that we have not picked any final representations yet.*

FIGURE 10.26
Press the space bar twice to get a menu that enables us to choose another character.

If the scrolling list of alternative representations doesn't provide what you're looking for, you can also bring up the Character Palette. In the Japanese language kit, this is accessed from the left-most button on the second row of the Operations Palette. The Character Palette provides a large selection of kanji characters, and is shown in Figure 10.27.

FIGURE 10.27
The Character Palette provides a large selection of characters to choose from.

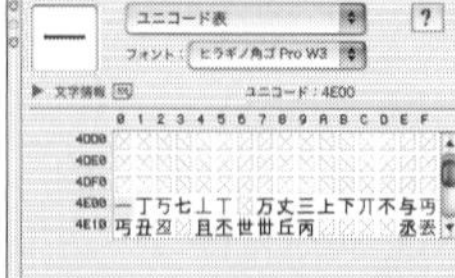

> **Note**
>
> The kanji items in the Character Palette appear to mostly be listed by radical (base character), in increasing stroke order. These characteristics are specific to a traditional method of characterizing Japanese kanji characters. If your language kit uses a similar method of characterizing pictogram or other characters, you can expect a similar presentation in the Character Palette. Otherwise, you should expect the ordering to be as the characters would be traditionally alphabetized in the language.

To select an item from the Character Palette, select the desired character in the grid. When it appears as the character in the large square, drag it to your text. The Character Palette, also available as the third menu item in the Japanese menu, has more than just kanji items, so you might be interested in playing with it more at a later date. These currently include Cyrillic, Greek, and a number of pictorial symbols such as boxes and lines.

Continue through the rest of the phrase, picking and choosing characters as you go. The final part of the title we're working on, Nausicaä is written in the other Japanese phonetic alphabet, katakana. To work in this character system, select the katakana symbol (second from the left in the top row) from the Operation Palette. Now type `na` and press Enter. Next, type `u` and press Enter. Then type `shi` and press Enter. Finally, type `ka` and press Enter. Pressing Enter after each indicates to the input script that you're done entering a phonetic equivalent, and that you want to accept the symbol that it has chosen.

Now you have finished typing the title. What you have typed should match what is shown in Figure 10.28.

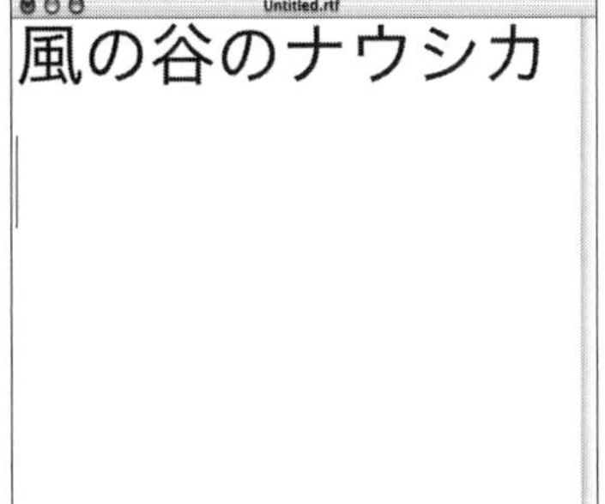

FIGURE 10.28 *Now we have successfully converted* `kazeno-taninonaushika` *into correctly written Japanese.*

This particular title was a convenient example for you to try because it uses characters from all three Japanese alphabets, giving you the opportunity to see examples of each of the input script methods, and the way they interact. Even if you're interested in working in a different language kit, we hope you find this information useful—if you understand the functionality we've presented here, you should be able to find similar functions in the language kit of your choice.

> **Note**
>
> After having spent the time to type the Japanese for the Nausicaä title, you might be interested in learning more about the animated film. Check `http://www.nausicaa.net/` to learn more about this and other films by the same studio.

Finally, Figure 10.29 shows just a small sampling of the types of characters available in the Character Palette, with some of these entered into the TextEdit application. This palette provides you with a significant resource for picking and choosing characters appropriate to different languages, even if you don't know how to pronounce the symbol phonetically.

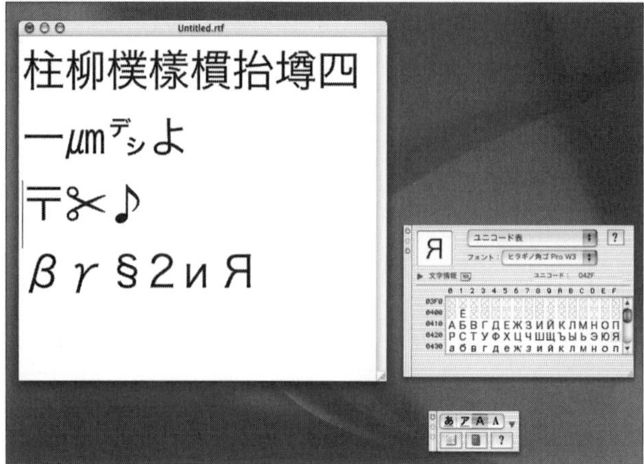

FIGURE 10.29
The Character Palette under the Japanese menu of the Japanese keyboard provides many additional characters.

Hopefully, this section has provided a fun way to learn about the available keyboard inputs offered in OS X, particularly the most complex of those installed on our system, Japanese. After you have selected multiple keyboards, a Keyboard menu appears in the menu bar. You can easily select a desired keyboard by selecting it from the Keyboard menu. For keyboards that belong to the Roman script input, the changes in the behavior of your keyboard might be subtle. With the Japanese script input keyboard, however, the input method is far more interactive than the Roman script input keyboards. Other input scripts and keyboards will undoubtedly be available in the future, and you will be able to use the techniques outlined here to work in any that you need.

Font Web Sites

There are many places that you can download fonts, including free fonts. Just do a search on your favorite Web search site, and you should be pleased with the results, perhaps even overwhelmed. Table 10.1 includes a few sites here to get you started. However, for your reference, we include sites other than ones with just downloadable fonts.

TABLE 10.1 Font-Related Web Sites

Web Site	*URL*	*Content*
iFree Top Font Sites	`http://www.ifree.com.au/top/fonts/index.html`	Lists a lot of links to font sites.
WebFontList	`http://www.webfontlist.com/`	Lists a lot of links to font sites, both free and shareware.

TABLE 10.1 continued

Web Site	*URL*	*Content*
Karen's Koncepts Free Fonts Resources	`http://www.netmegs.com/koncepts/freefont.htm.`	Lists a lot of links to sites with fonts, both free and shareware.
MyFonts.com	`http://www.myfonts.com/`	A site through which you can buy fonts through participating foundries. Provides some font utilities to help you find the right font. Has links to other font sites and font utility sites.
MyFonts.com: WhatTheFont	`http://www.myfonts.com/WhatTheFont/`	The direct link to MyFonts.com's WhatTheFont utility. This interesting utility can be used to try to identify a font from a scanned image.
Identifont—identify fonts and typefaces	`http://www.identifont.com/identify.html`	A site that helps you identify a font by asking a series of questions about the font.
Apple—Fonts/Tools	`http://fonts.apple.com/`	Apple's technical site on fonts and font development.
TrueType Typography: info about TTF fonts & technology	`http://www.truetype.demon.co.uk/index.htm`	An informative site on TrueType typography. Includes history and specification.
Adobe Solutions Network: OpenType Specification	`http://partners.adobe.com/asn/developer/opentype/`	Lists the OpenType specification.
Free Fonts, TrueType, OpenType, ClearType—Microsoft Typography	`http://www.microsoft.com/typography/default.asp`	Microsoft's Typography site. Includes technical information as well as a link to Microsoft's free fonts.
Microsoft Typography—Fonts and products	`http://www.microsoft.com/typography/fonts/default.asp`	Provides a listing of what fonts come in what Microsoft products. Does not include images of the fonts.
Unicode Home Page	`http://www.unicode.org/`	Includes information on Unicode and the Unicode standard.

Summary

In this chapter, you learned a variety of basics involving printer and font management. You learned about the Print Center, which enables you to add and delete printers, select a default printer, and work with the print queues. You learned that printing from an application works the same as in traditional Mac OS. Under the File menu, Page Setup enables you to set the attributes for your page or view a summary of the attributes. Also under the File menu, Print enables you to send a job to the printer. You can also specify further options about your printout, including an output option to print to a PDF file. After learning basics about the printer, you learned how to manage fonts. You learned how to install a new font and how to use the Font panel, including using it to manage font collections. Finally, you enhanced your fonts experience by learning about input methods that make use of multilingual characters. You experimented with switching between various Roman script inputs as well as the Japanese script input.

Additional System Components

CHAPTER 11

IN THIS CHAPTER

Mac users wouldn't be happy without the ability to customize their system. Although Mac OS X is a secure multi-user operating system, it allows individuals a great deal of freedom in customizing their settings. Users can install and choose between different desktop backgrounds, screen savers, color profiles, and even set up speech recognition. Although the notion of control panels has given way to the Mac OS X System Preferences panel, the idea is still very much the same. Using the System Preferences, users can choose an individual panel to change a series of related configuration options.

This chapter covers the available System Preferences panels, how they work, and what they will change on your system. If there are any areas of the operating system that you'd like to fine-tune, this is the place to look.

User Account Creation

In this section, we will touch on some of the basics involved in user account creation. We will look at some ways we can customize user account creation in Chapter 23, "File and Resource Sharing," and we will look at user management in detail in Chapter 24, "User Management."

Introduction to Multi-User Systems

OS X is a Unix-based operating system. As such, it is a multi-user operating system; that is, everyone who uses the machine may do so by having an account on the machine. A user can use his account on the machine either at the console or via remote access—if you should choose to enable remote access, which we will discuss in further detail in Chapter 26, "Remote Access and Administration."

A particularly nice feature of a multi-user system is that multiple users can use the machine at the same time. While each user is using the system, it seems to each user as if he is the only user on the system.

Each user has a home directory, where he stores his files. In OS X, the users' home directories are located in the `/Users` directory. Figure 11.1 shows the `/Users` directory on a sample OS X client.

Note

Although the text of this book often shows directories using their full pathname (such as `/Users`), the Mac OS X Finder shows only the name of the directory at the end of the path. In the case of `/Users`, this would simply be `Users`. The shortening of pathnames isn't critical, but to successfully interact with the system, it's important to understand how the Mac OS X directory structure looks and works.

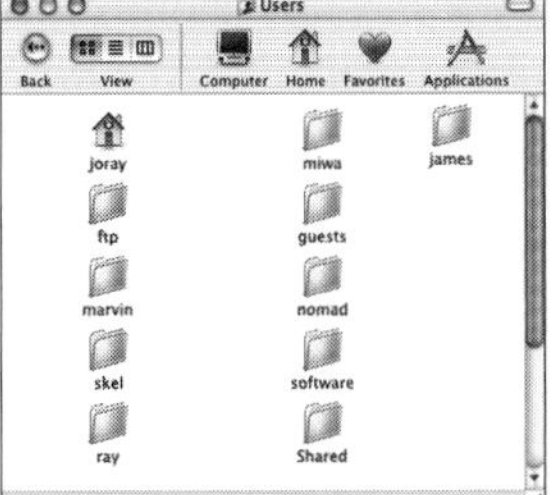

FIGURE 11.1
You can get to the `/Users` *directory by double-clicking your OS X drive and opening the* `Users` *folder.*

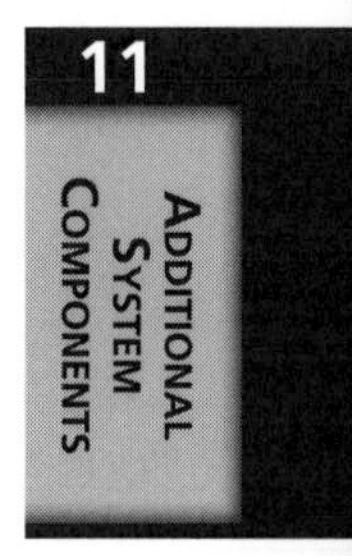

When a user logs in to the system, the default area where he is logged in is his home directory. Hence, the use of the house as an icon in the Finder window toolbar. Additionally, you see the same icon in Figure 11.1 among the user directories. Users can still see most areas on the machine, although they might not necessarily be able to see all of another user's files. In a multi-user system, users can set permissions on their files to allow different types of access. Even if other users can see your files, they can't modify them unless you have set permissions to allow them to do so. For example, Figure 11.2 shows how the home directory for user `miwa` looks to another user. A number of folders have a white minus in a red circle on them. Directories so marked are not viewable by this user. The other files and directories, however, can be viewed by this user.

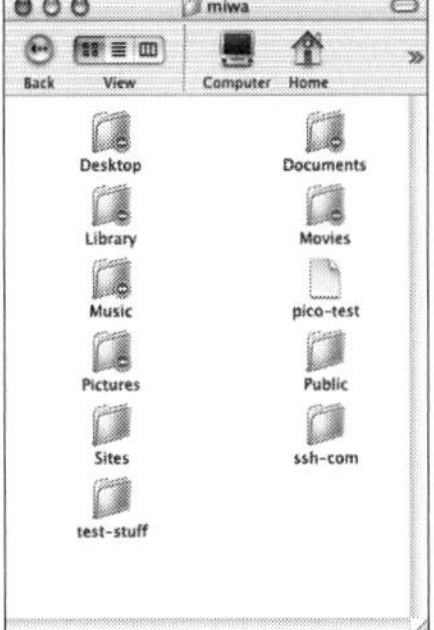

FIGURE 11.2
Depending on how the owner grants permissions on his files and directories, other users might not be able to view them at all.

Adding a New User

When you installed OS X, you were asked to provide your name and a short name that could be used as your login name. During the installation process, you created an account. Specifically, you created an administrator account. Adding another user account is much like creating the original administrator account that you created at installation time.

Because it can be used to modify the machine settings or install software, the administrator account is actually a rather powerful account. When you add a new user, you have the choice of adding a regular user or adding one with administrator capabilities. Although it is helpful to have more than one user with administrator capabilities, do not give administrator access to every user account that you create. Otherwise, every user on the machine will be able to modify your system.

You create a new user account using the Users pane in the System section of the System Preferences as follows:

1. Open the Users pane in the System Preferences.
2. Click on the make changes lock icon, if it is set not to allow changes, and enter your administrator username and password. Click on New User, which brings up a New User window. The New User window has an Identity tab, and a Password tab with fields that you complete.

FIGURE 11.3
Complete the fields under the Identity tab when creating a new Mac OS X user account.

The Identity tab of the New Users window, shown in Figure 11.3, has the following fields:

- **Name**—This is where you enter your user's name. In OS X, this is a name that the user can use to log in to the machine.
- **Short Name**—The short name is the username; that is, the name of the account. This is also a name that the user can use to log in to the machine. This name can be up to eight characters in length, must have no spaces, and be in lowercase. This name is used by some of the network services.

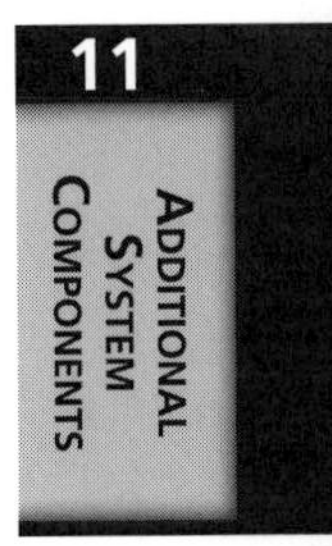

- **Login Picture**—Select a picture that can be displayed with this user's name in the user listing at login time. Either select one from the available selection in the Identity tab, or choose a custom picture elsewhere on your machine.

FIGURE 11.4
Also complete the fields under the Password tab when creating a new Mac OS X user account.

The Password tab of the New Users window, shown in Figure 11.4, has the following fields:

- **Password**—The password should be at least four characters. Many systems recommend at least six characters, with a variety of character types included in the password.
- **Verify**—This is where you re-enter the password for verification purposes.
- **Password Hint**—This is an optional field. The password hint is displayed if the user enters an incorrect password three times. If you include a hint, make sure the hint is not so obvious that other users can guess the password.
- **Allow user to administer this machine**—This is the box you check to grant a user administrative privileges. Check this box only for a trustworthy user who you feel should be allowed to have administrative privileges. It is not checked by default as a security precaution.

3. Click on Save.

You are returned to the Users pane, which now lists your new user by name. You have created a new user. In Chapter 23, you will see how to create a specific user called `software`, with a specific user ID and group ID.

You can also edit user information, such as the password, by using the Users pane of System Preferences. Just select the user account that needs to be edited, and click Edit User, which brings up an already completed window identical to that for a new user.

To delete a user account, simply select the account to be deleted, and click the Delete User button. A sheet then appears, asking you to confirm the action and to select an administrator account that should store the old user account data. The Users pane does not allow you to delete the original administrator user account.

Enabling the root Account

As mentioned earlier, the administrator account is a powerful account. But the most powerful account on a Unix machine is the account called `root`. People also refer to `root` as the super user, but the account name itself is `root`. On most Unix systems, the first available account is the `root` account. In OS X, however, the `root` account is disabled by default as a security precaution.

At some time, however, you might find it necessary to enable the `root` account. The `root` account can modify system settings, modify files it does not own, modify files that are not writable by default, modify a user's password, install software, become another user without having to know the password of that account, and so on. In other words, `root` can do anything anywhere, making the power of `root` immense. Because `root` has so much power, the only users who can become `root` are users with administrative privileges. Because a user with administrative privileges can become the `root` user, you should assign these capabilities to only completely trusted individuals.

If you choose to enable the `root` account, please remember to use it with caution. Although the `root` account might provide some extra utility, you could accidentally wipe out your system if you do not pay careful attention to what you type. In addition, the `root` password you choose should be difficult to guess. Finally, become the `root` user only as long as necessary to complete the task at hand.

With the presence of an administrative user, it might be a long time, if ever, before you discover a need for enabling the `root` user. There are many approaches that you can take for dealing with the `root` user, from ways to use `root` without enabling the `root` account to actually enabling the `root` account.

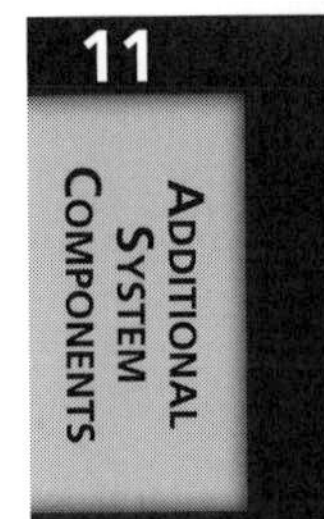

Let's take a look at four different ways to gain root access to your system. Although you can choose whichever method you like, it's useful to understand that even though some of these methods appear to work magic, they all accomplish very much the same thing.

The `root` user is disabled because it does not have a valid password set. Because there are a number of ways to set a password, there are also several ways to enable `root`, including one method (the first we'll look at), that was designed specifically for assigning the `root` account password and *only* the `root` password. In addition, you'll see how the `sudo` command can provide `root`-level access even when the `root` password is disabled. We recommend that users access the `root` account only when absolutely necessary.

Using the NetInfo Manager Utility

There are a couple of graphical ways to enable the `root` account using the NetInfo Manager utility. Do not worry if you do not understand what the NetInfo Manager utility is at this time. We will take an in-depth look at the NetInfo Manager utility in Chapter 23.

NetInfo Manager: Method One

1. Click on Applications in the Finder window toolbar. Open the `Utilities` folder and then open the NetInfo Manager utility.
2. If nothing appears automatically when you open the NetInfo Manager, under the Domain menu, select Open; then select the default domain, which will be `/`.
3. Click on the lock button in the bottom-left side of the window to enable a mode that allows making changes. Enter the name and password of an administrative user; then click OK.
4. Under the Domain menu, select Security. Then choose Enable Root User from the submenu. Unless you have previously set a `root` password, a message appears with a NetInfo Error, indicating that the password is blank. Click OK.
5. Enter the `root` password you want to use, and then click Set. Remember that the `root` password should not be easily guessable.

6. Enter the password again for verification, and then click Verify.
7. Under the Domain menu, select Save. A request to Confirm Modification appears. Click on Update this copy.
8. Under the Options menu, select Restart All NetInfo Domains on Local Host. An alert asking whether you really want to restart the machine's NetInfo servers appears. Click Yes.
9. Click on the lock button again to prevent any further changes. Then close the NetInfo Manager.

You might find it sufficient just to click on the lock button again to save your changes. Figure 11.5 shows an example of what an enabled root account looks like in the NetInfo Manager. Note that the password field no longer has an * in it.

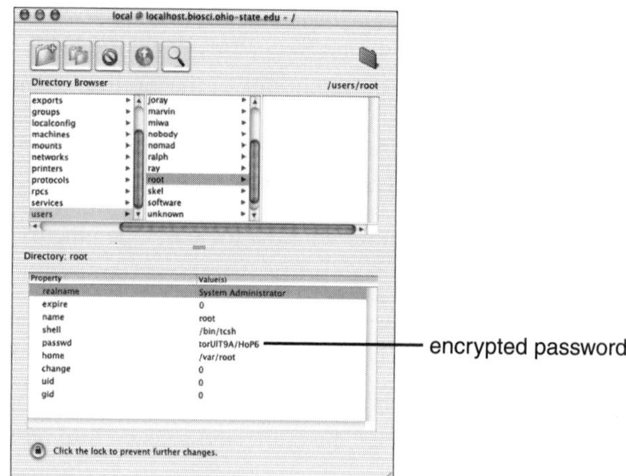

FIGURE 11.5
The `root` *account has been enabled on this machine. Note the * that was in the password field has been replaced with an encrypted password.*

NetInfo Manager: Method Two

You could try this alternative NetInfo Manager utility method if the first one does not work for you. The danger to this method is that it copies the password of another user to the `root` user.

1. Click on Applications in the Finder window toolbar. Open the Utilities folder; then open the NetInfo Manager utility. If nothing appears automatically when you first open the NetInfo Manager, from the Domain menu, select Open and then select the default domain, which will be `/`.

2. Click on the lock button in the bottom-left side of the window to enable a mode that allows making changes. Enter the name and password of an administrative user. Then click OK.
3. Click on `Users` in the second list, and then click on a user you created whose password you know.
4. Double-click on the value across from `passwd` in the bottom section of the window and copy it. What you are looking at is an encoded copy of the user's password.
5. Click on `root` in the users list. Note that the default value for the password for `root` is `*`, which means that no one can log in as `root` right now. Using `*` in the `passwd` field is a way to lock a user from the machine.
6. Double-click in the field with the `*`; then paste in the encoded password from the previous user to replace the `*`. The `*` should no longer be present when you are done.
7. Select Save from the Domain menu. A request to Confirm Modification appears. Click Update This Copy.
8. Select Restart All NetInfo Domains on Local Host under the Options menu. An alert asking whether you really want to restart the machine's NetInfo servers appears. Click Yes.
9. Click the lock button again to prevent any further changes; then close the NetInfo Manager.

Again, note that you might find it sufficient to just click on the lock button again to save your changes.

Using the OS X Installation CD

Because the OS X installation CD comes with an option to reset a user's password, you could use the installation CD itself to enable the `root` user.

To enable the `root` account using the OS X installation CD, do the following:

1. Insert the OS X CD.
2. With the CD in the CD-ROM drive, reboot the machine. Hold the C key while the machine reboots.
3. Wait for the Installer to appear and then select the Reset Password option under the Installer menu.
4. Select the OS X disk that contains the `root` account you want to enable. If you notice a spinning CD icon appear after you have chosen the Reset Password option, don't wait for the spinning to end to select your OS X disk.

The System Administrator (`root`) user appears as the default user.

5. Enter a new password and then re-enter the password for verification. Click Save. Click OK when the Password Saved box appears.
6. Quit the Password Reset application, quit the Installer, and click Restart.

Using sudo at the Command Line

Although we won't start looking at the command-line utilities in depth until Chapter 15, "Command-Line Applications," we take this opportunity to demonstrate some ways to accomplish tasks that `root` might do by using the `sudo` command-line utility. It is all right if you do not feel comfortable with trying anything you see in this section at this time. When you are more familiar with working with the command line, you can return to this section. If you do want to try anything in this section, you can run the commands in a terminal window. Just open the Terminal application in the Utilities folder in the Applications folder.

Using sudo to Run Commands as root

`sudo` is a command-line utility that allows use of the `root` account without necessarily enabling `root`.

For example, in a terminal window, you could use `sudo` to reboot the machine now:

```
[localhost:~] joray% sudo shutdown -r now
```

The most common way to use `sudo` is to preface each command that you want `root` to do with the `sudo` utility. If you are asked for a password, use the password of the user who is executing the `sudo` command. If the user is not eligible to execute `sudo`, the command is not executed.

If you need to execute a few commands in a row as `root`, you could try a couple alternative uses of `sudo`. When you are done with the tasks for `root`, type `exit` at the end of your session.

In this example, your shell is elevated to that of `root` until you `exit` the session:

```
[localhost:~] joray% sudo -s

     We trust you have received the usual lecture from the local System
     Administrator. It usually boils down to these two things:

             #1) Respect the privacy of others.
             #2) Think before you type.

     Password:

[localhost:~] root#
```

Notice that the prompt changes to include `root#`, as a reminder that you now have the power of `root`.

In this example, `sudo` is used to run `su` to become `root` until you `exit` the session. When `root` is enabled, `su` can be used to switch to the `root` user. When using `su` by itself, the password you enter to become `root` is that of `root`, rather than yours, as you do with `sudo`.

```
[localhost:~] joray% sudo su
    Password:
[localhost:/Users/joray] root#
```

Notice that in this example, the prompt also includes `root#` as a reminder of your power as `root`. Remember, to return to the status of a regular user, type `exit` when you are done with your `root` session.

Using sudo to Enable the root Account

Recall that the `sudo` command is used to execute a command that `root` might execute. A way to enable the `root` account is to use `sudo` to execute `passwd`, which is a command used to change passwords.

Here is an example:

```
[localhost:~] joray% sudo passwd root
    Password:
    Changing password for root.
    New password:
    Retype new password:
[localhost:~] joray%
```

The password that you initially enter is your password. Then you supply a password for `root`, and re-enter it for verification. If you mistype the password, you will be prompted again, as shown in this example:

```
[localhost:~] joray% sudo passwd root
    Password:
    Changing password for root.
    New password:
    Retype new password:
    Mismatch; try again, EOF to quit.
    New password:
    Retype new password:
[localhost:~] joray%
```

Groups

As mentioned earlier, a multi-user environment allows there to be many users logged on to the same machine at the same time. The users' files, as well as the rest of the files in the system, have associated permissions. These permissions are specified for the owner of the file, the group to which the user belongs, and all users. It is the group concept that we would like to look at briefly now. In later chapters, we will look at working with groups.

A group can have a group password, although use of a group password is uncommon. Additionally, a group has a group ID number, name, and members. As you saw when we created a user, the default group ID for a user created by using the User pane is `20`, which is the `staff` group. If you look at the `staff` group, however, you do not necessarily see all those who belong to the group actually listed in the group.

A user can belong to more than one group. This could be useful for a specific project, for example. Where you immediately see its usefulness, however, is with administrative privileges. The users who have administrative privileges also belong to the group called `wheel`, which has group ID `0`. This is a special group on certain flavors of Unix, including OS X. The `root` user also belongs to the group `wheel`. Although being in this group gives an administrative user a lot of power, `root` is still the most powerful user. Figure 11.6 shows how a typical administrative user might appear in the NetInfo Manager. Note that the administrative user's primary group ID is listed as being group `20 (staff)`. Chapter 24 covers the creation and modification of users and groups in depth, so don't worry if you still have questions.

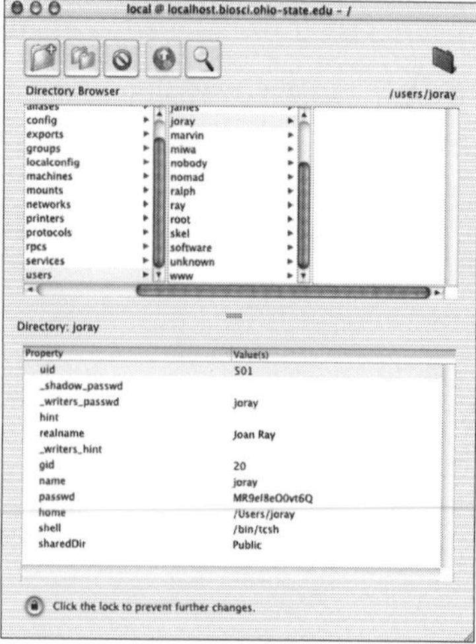

FIGURE 11.6
A typical administrative user, as shown in the NetInfo Manager.

In Figure 11.7, however, you see that our sample administrative user, `joray`, also belongs to group `wheel`, which is indeed group ID `0`, the same as what you saw for `root` in Figure 11.5. If you look at the group `admin`, you will see that administrative users also belong to that group.

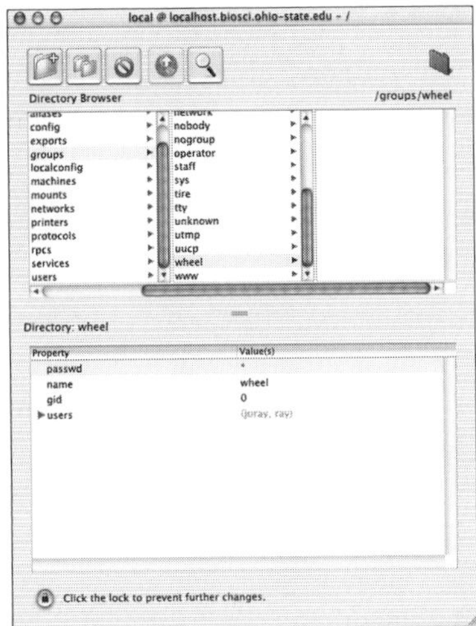

FIGURE 11.7
Administrative users belong to the group `wheel` *in OS X. As you see here, there are two administrative users on this system.*

To see permissions on a file in the Finder, under the File menu, select Show Info (Command+I). In the window that pops up, in the Show section, select Privileges. Permissions can also be changed in this same window. Figure 11.8 shows the permissions on the `/System/Library/Fonts/` directory. As you can see, users in group `wheel` have only `read` permission, which is why you have to become `root` to copy fonts into that directory. If you are interested in more permissions controls in a GUI application, check `http://www.gideonsoftworks.com/` for an application called Get Info. It allows you to change many attributes of a file, including permissions, ownership, and group.

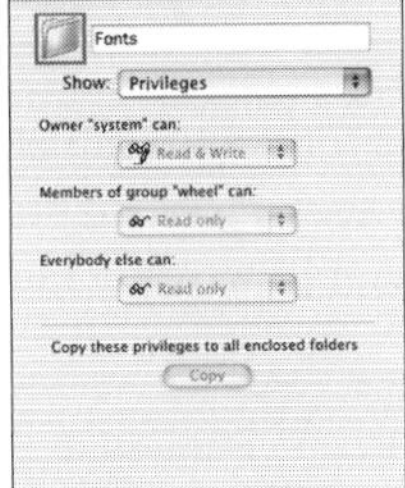

FIGURE 11.8
The permissions on the `/System/Library/Fonts/` *directory show that members of group* `wheel` *have only read permission. Therefore, even an administrative user cannot copy anything to that directory.*

If you look at the permissions on the `/Library/Fonts/` directory, you will see that users in `admin` have permission to read and write. That is why an administrative user can copy fonts to that directory.

System Preferences: Personal

The Personal section of the System Preferences panel includes panes for customizing your personal desktop experience. With the controls in this section, you can customize such settings as desktop backgrounds, highlight color, and language preferences. In this section, we specifically look at the General, International, Login, Screen Saver and Universal Access panes.

General

The General pane, shown in Figure 11.9, allows you to set some general behaviors, which can be grouped as appearance, scroll behavior, number of recent items, and font smoothing.

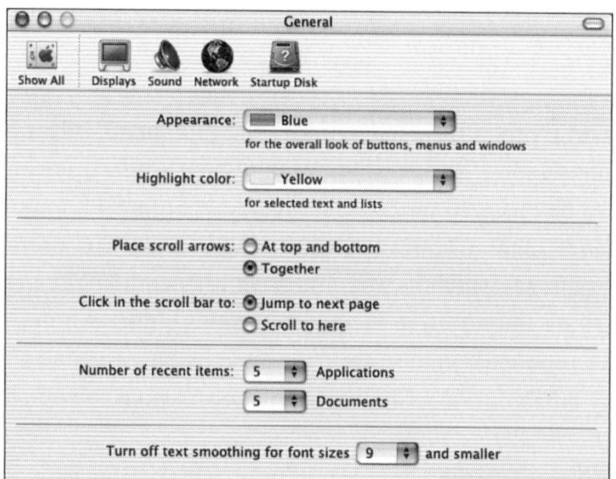

FIGURE 11.9
The General pane controls settings for overall appearance, highlight color, scroll bar behavior, and font smoothing.

In the first section of the pane, a general color scheme for the overall appearance of the menus, buttons, and windows is set. The choice is between blue and graphite. In addition, you can set the highlight color for selected text and lists. A few more choices are

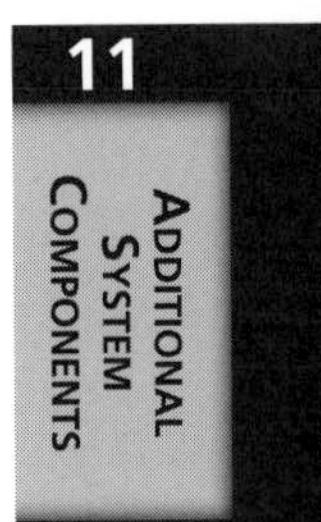

available for highlight color: graphite, silver, blue, yellow, orange, green, purple, or other, which brings up a standard color browser, where you can select any color you want.

In the next section, you can select where scroll arrows are placed and the resulting behavior of clicking in the scroll bar. Scroll arrows can be placed either at the top and bottom or together. The resulting behavior of clicking in the scroll bar can be set either to jump to the next page or to scroll to here.

The next section is where you set the number of recent items for applications and documents. For both types, the choices are 5, 10, 15, 20, 30, or 50.

In the final section of the pane, you can turn off smoothing for fonts smaller than size 9, 10, or 12.

International

Settings involving language, date format, keyboard layouts, and so on are set in the International pane.

Language

Figure 11.10 shows the Language tab. This is where you set your preferred language order use for application menus and dialogs. Just drag the languages around until you have achieved the desired order. If not all the languages you would like to rank are shown, click the Edit button to edit the language listing. Select the languages of interest, and then rank their order.

In the bottom portion of the Language tab, you select a default set of behaviors for scripts. The behaviors affect sort order, case conversion, and word definition. The Roman script has many options available to choose as the default.

Date

The long date format can be set in the Date tab. The short date format defaults to certain settings, according to the region selected. You can, however, make custom settings, if the region settings are not to your liking. You can set such items as the date separator, whether to use a leading zero, and the preferred order of month, day, and year. Figure 11.11 shows the Date tab for the German region

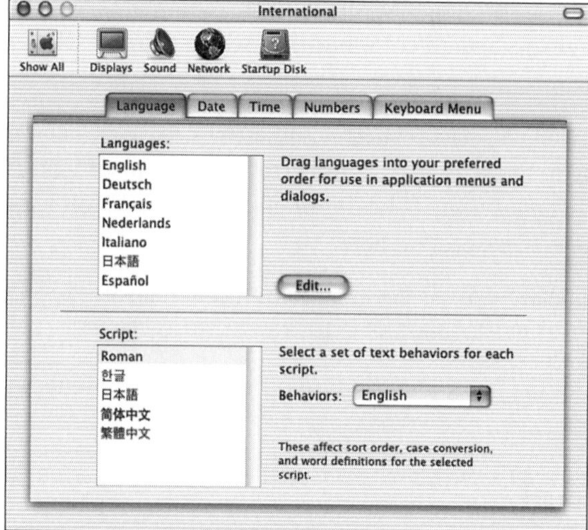

FIGURE 11.10
The preferred language order for application menus and dialogs is set in the Language tab of the International pane.

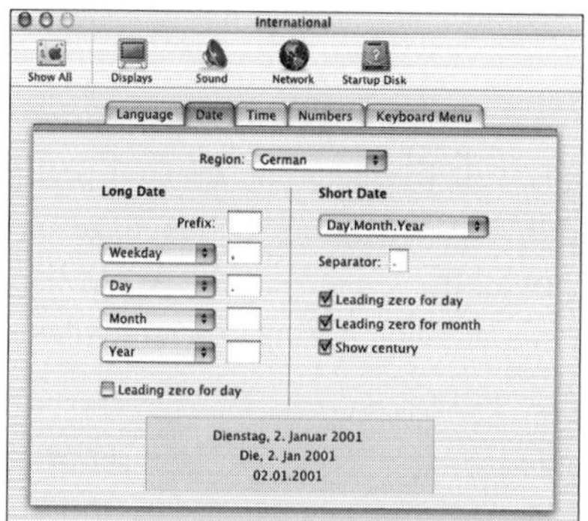

FIGURE 11.11
Long and short date formats are set in the Date tab of the International pane.

Time

The Time tab, shown in Figure 11.12, is where you specify how you want the time to be displayed. You can select whether to use a 24-hour clock or a 12-hour clock. If you select a 12-hour clock, you can specify how noon and midnight should be written, and what indicator to use for before noon and after noon. Like the Date tab, the Time tab sets certain defaults based on the region, but you can customize the settings.

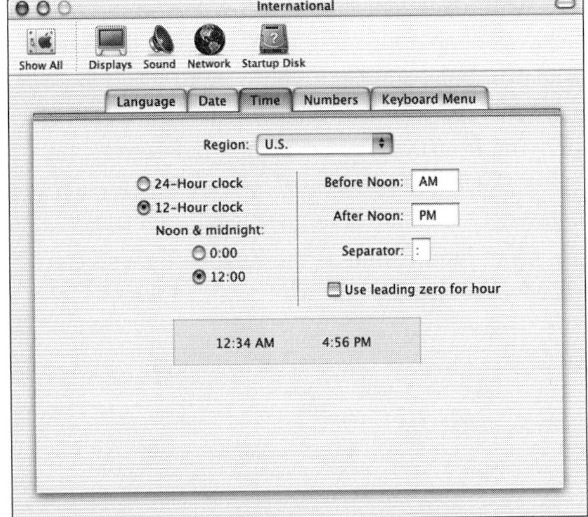

FIGURE 11.12
The time format is set in the Time tab of the International pane.

Numbers

The Numbers tab, shown in Figure 11.13, sets the symbol used for currency and where the symbol is placed, as well as what character is used for the decimal and thousands separators.

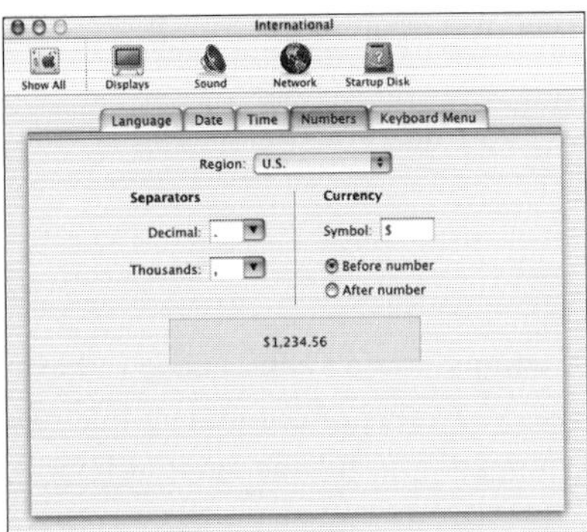

FIGURE 11.13
The currency symbol and its placement, as well as the separator characters for decimal and thousands, are specified in the Numbers tab of the International pane.

Keyboard Menu

In the Keyboard Menu tab shown in Figure 11.14, you can turn on multiple keyboard layouts. When more than one keyboard layout is selected, they appear in a Keyboard menu, and you can rotate through the choices. OS X has an interface layer that attempts to map input to an equivalent appropriate to the script. For the Roman script, many keyboard layouts are available. For example, if you were to select the U.S. keyboard, British keyboard, and French keyboard, you would see slightly different behaviors in the interpretation of the underlying Roman script for them. For example, the pound sign (#) is interpreted on the British keyboard layout as £ instead. The French keyboard layout interprets many numbers as lowercase accented characters. To get numbers in that layout, you use the Shift key. More information on the Keyboard menu can be found in Chapter 10, "Printer and Font Management."

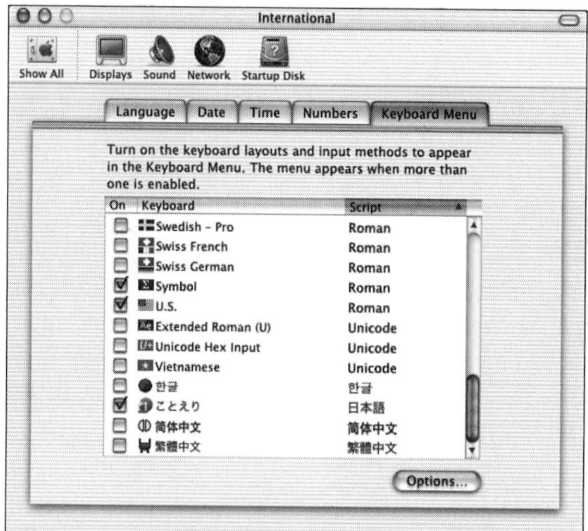

FIGURE 11.14
Multiple keyboard layouts can be specified in the Keyboard Menu tab of the International pane.

Login

When you log in to your Mac OS X computer, you can choose to have it start applications for you automatically. Additionally, owners of computers that have only a single user can choose to be automatically logged in to that account at boot time, rather than manually logging in.

Login Items

The Login Items tab, shown in Figure 11.15, is where you indicate what items, if any, you would like to start automatically when you log in.

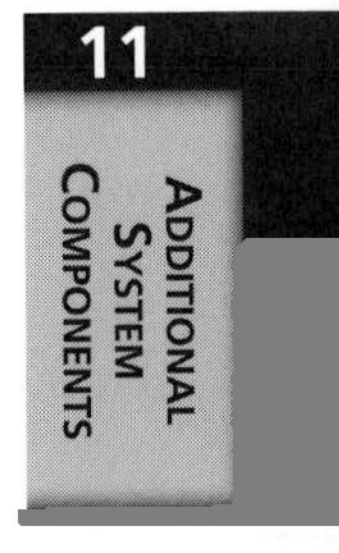

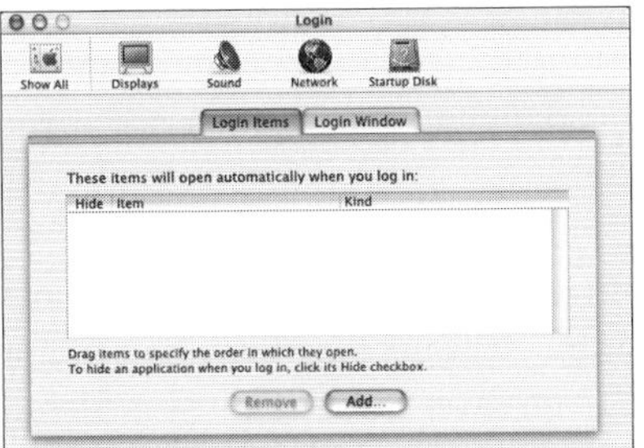

FIGURE 11.15
In the Login Items tab of the Login pane, you can select items that automatically start up when you log in.

Login Window

Characteristics about the login window are set in the Login Window tab, shown in Figure 11.16. Here you can indicate how you would like the login window to look, either as providing fields for username and password or as a list of usernames with an associated picture. Additionally, you can choose to include Other User as a choice in the list. You can also disable the Restart and Shut Down buttons of the login window here, and set whether to show the password hint after three tries. If your machine is actually being used as a multi-user machine with multiple users who might log in at the console, or if your machine is located in a public area, we recommend that you disable the Restart and Shut Down buttons. This reduces the chances of the machine accidentally being shut down.

You can also set a particular user to be logged in automatically. OS X has initially set up the machine to automatically log in the first created administrative user, to give you the Mac OS feel that you are used to. After you have added an additional user, we recommend that you disable the automatic login to get a login window instead. If you don't make that modification, your account can be modified by whoever sits at the machine.

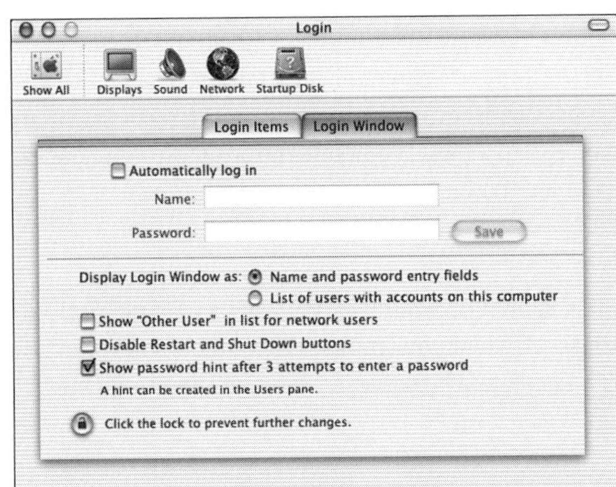

FIGURE 11.16
You can configure the behavior of the login window in the Login Window tab of the Login pane.

Screen Saver

The Screen Saver pane is where you configure your screen saver, if you want to use one.

Screen Savers

In the Screen Savers tab, shown in Figure 11.17, you can select one of the default screen savers, set up your own screen saver by choosing the Slide Show option, or choose to have the machine randomly select screen saver modules for you. Here you can test the screen savers. However, if you find that you seem to be getting the same approximate pattern for each screen saver, select one that you think you might like, and let the screen saver start naturally. It should work properly on its own.

FIGURE 11.17
Select a screen saver in the Screen Savers tab of the Screen Saver pane.

Activation

You can set when the screen saver starts in the Activation tab, shown in Figure 11.18. Set a time that is appropriate for your situation. In addition, you can specify whether the system should request a password to unlock the screen. We recommend that you select this option. This option essentially locks your screen for you if you happen to leave your machine while you are logged in.

Hot Corners

In the Hot Corners tab, shown in Figure 11.19, you can enable or disable screen corners to activate the screen saver when your mouse enters the corner. Click in the desired box until a minus appears to create a "disable" corner, or click to make a check mark to set an "activate" corner.

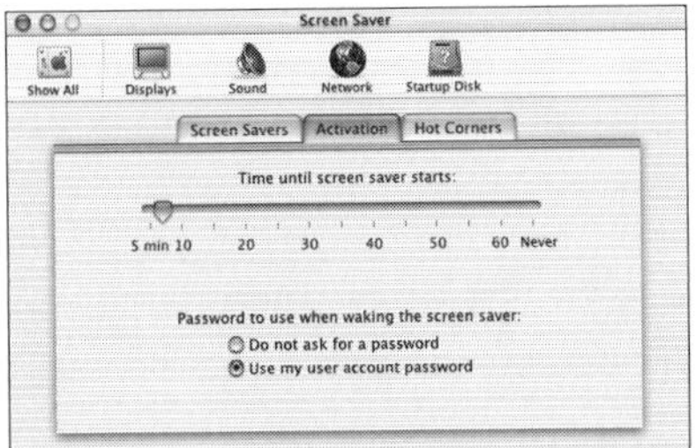

FIGURE 11.18 *Set the activation parameters in the Activation tab of the Screen Saver pane.*

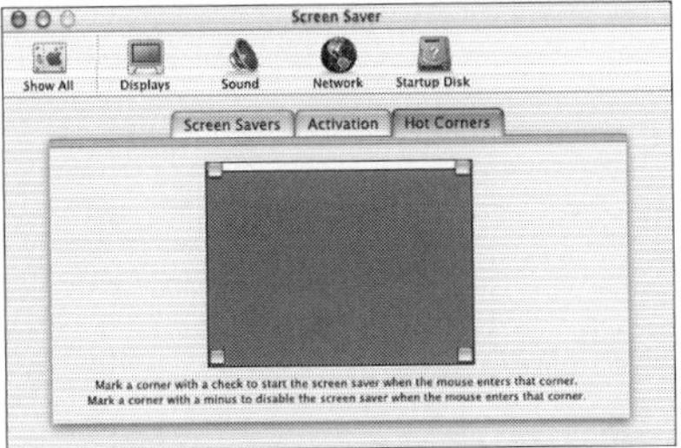

FIGURE 11.19 *Activate the screen corners in the Hot Corners tab of the Screen Saver pane.*

Universal Access

The Universal Access pane is where you can customize some keyboard and mouse behaviors, if you are having difficulties with the keyboard or the mouse itself.

Keyboard

In the Keyboard tab, shown in Figure 11.20, you can set the Sticky Keys on or off. If you set the Sticky Keys on, you can also choose to have the machine beep when a modifier key is set and to show pressed keys on screen. The Sticky Keys option is useful if you have trouble executing multiple key combinations, such as Command+I. Note that you can also toggle on and off the Sticky Keys behavior by pressing the Shift key five times.

From the Keyboard tab, you can also adjust key repeat timing. The Keyboard tab brings up the Keyboard pane to accomplish this task.

Mouse

If you have difficulties using the mouse, you can set Mouse Keys on in the Mouse tab, shown in Figure 11.21. When you turn Mouse Keys on, the numeric key pad is what you use to move the cursor around. The Mouse tab also allows you to customize mouse pointer movement by setting a preferred initial delay and maximum speed using slider controls. Note that you can also toggle on and off the Mouse Keys by pressing the Option key five times.

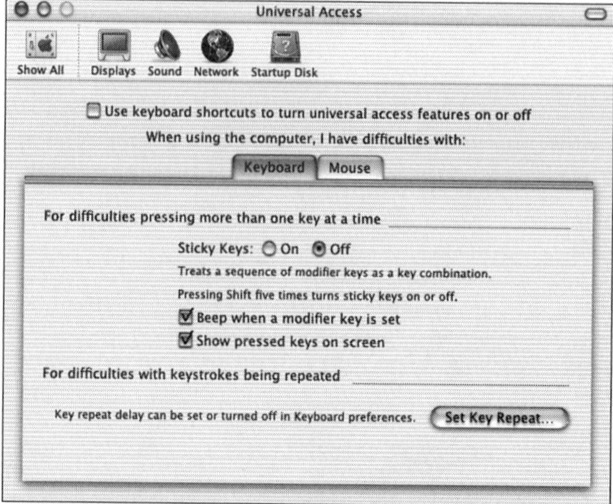

FIGURE 11.20
Set the Sticky Keys on in the Keyboard tab of the Universal Access pane if you have difficulties executing multiple key sequences at once.

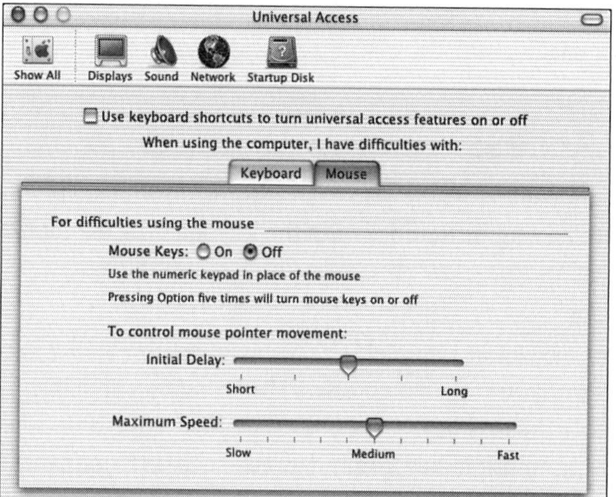

FIGURE 11.21
Set the Mouse Keys on in the Mouse tab of the Universal Access pane if you have difficulties with the mouse.

System Preferences: Hardware

The Hardware section of the System Preferences panel includes panes for customizing hardware settings. With the controls in this section, you can customize such items as color profiles, display settings, and sound settings. In this section, we look specifically at the ColorSync, Displays, Energy Saver, Keyboard, Mouse, and Sound panes.

ColorSync

The ColorSync pane works much like the ColorSync control panel of the traditional Mac OS. The ColorSync pane allows you to specify color profiles for different types of workflows. For detailed information on ColorSync, the color matching technology, see Apple's Web site at `http://www.apple.com/colorsync/`. Additionally, check this URL for a ColorSync white paper: `http://www.apple.com/creative/resources/`.

In addition to settings under the different tabs of the ColorSync pane, for each tab, you can import preferences from a ColorSync workflow document, or export preferences as a ColorSync workflow document.

Device Profiles

The Device Profiles tab, shown in Figure 11.22, is where you specify profiles for standard devices. For standard devices you can specify an input profile, display profile, output profile, and proof profile. If you calibrated your display either in the Displays pane or by running the Display Calibrator manually, and you would like that profile to be available in the ColorSync profile, copy it to `/System/Library/ColorSync/Profiles/` or `/Library/ColorSync/Profiles/`. The profile you created is automatically stored in your own `~/Library/ColorSync/Profiles/` directory.

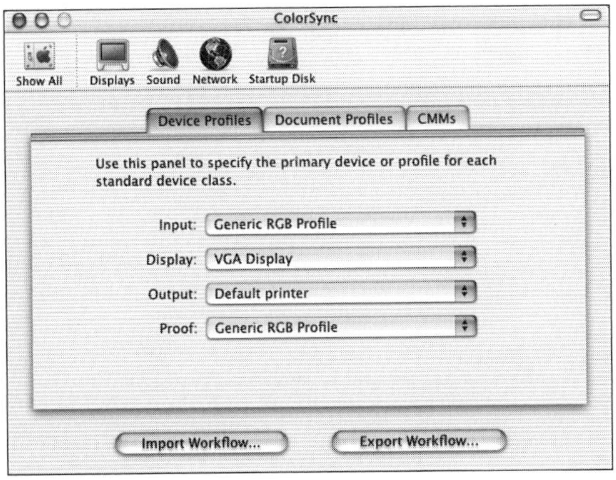

FIGURE 11.22
The Device Profiles tab of the ColorSync pane.

Document Profiles

The Document Profiles tab, shown in Figure 11.23, is where you specify profiles for documents. For documents you can specify profiles for RGB default, CMYK default, gray default, and lab default.

FIGURE 11.23
The Document Profiles tab of the ColorSync pane.

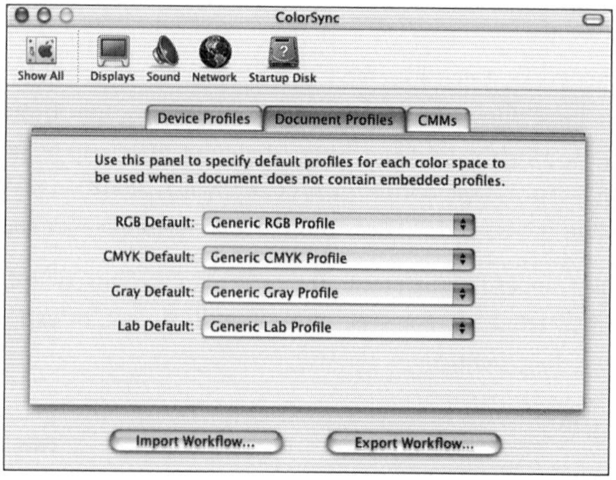

CMMs

As in the ColorSync control panel of traditional Mac OS, the ColorSync pane has a CMMs tab, where you specify the color matching method or technology to be used. The choices are Automatic and Apple CMM. The CMMs tab is shown in Figure 11.24.

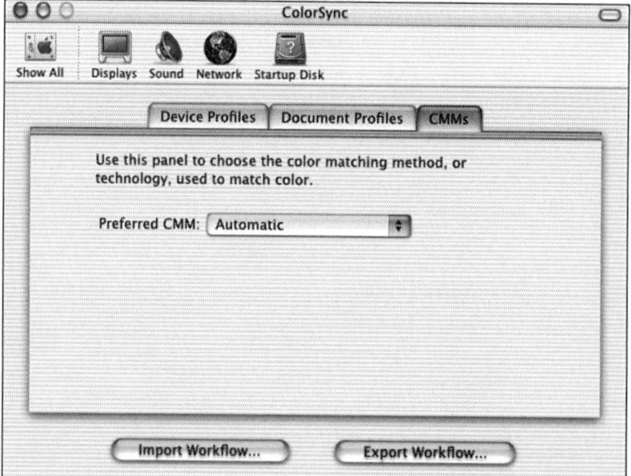

FIGURE 11.24
The CMMs tab of the ColorSync pane.

Displays

The Displays pane in System Preferences functions in a way similar to the Monitors control panel or the Monitors portion of the Monitors & Sound control panel. As you might have noticed, Displays is also located in the System Preferences toolbar. In some versions of OS X, there is also a Displays Dockling.

Display

As expected, in the Display tab, shown in Figure 11.25, you can set the resolution, the number of colors displayed, and the refresh rate. There is an option to make the Displays information available in the menu bar. There is also an option available to ask the pane to list only modes that the display recommends. You probably will see some of the options grayed out upon checking the box. Apple recommends that 256-color mode and 640×480 resolution be used, alone or in combination, in Classic applications only.

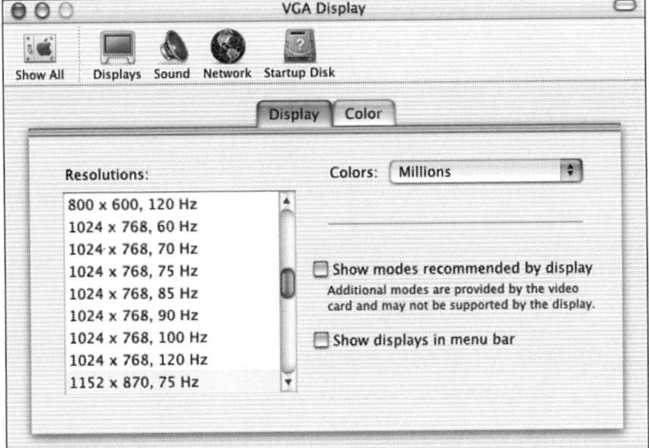

FIGURE 11.25 *The Display tab of the Displays pane is where you set resolution and color depth.*

Color

In the Color tab, shown in Figure 11.26, you select a color profile for your monitor. If no ColorSync profile is available for your monitor, you can create a custom profile by clicking the Calibrate option. The Calibrate option starts the Display Calibrator utility, which will guide you through calibrating your monitor.

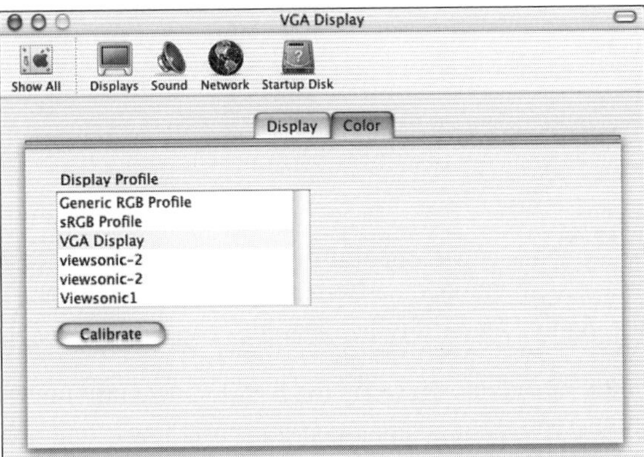

FIGURE 11.26 *The Color tab of the Displays pane is where you select a color profile for your monitor.*

Arrange

When multiple monitors are attached, the main monitor has an extra tab called Arrange, shown in Figure 11.27.

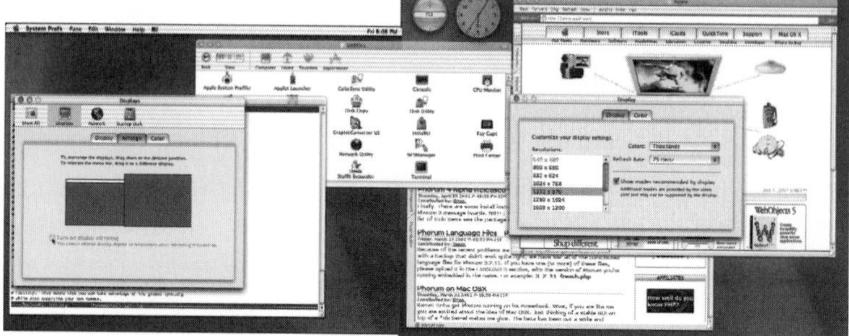

FIGURE 11.27 *When you select the Displays pane while multiple monitors are attached, the Displays pane of the main monitor includes an Arrange tab.*

When you open the Displays pane while multiple monitors are attached, the controlling monitor has the extra Arrange tab. At the same time, the other monitors display the normal Displays pane, with only the Display and Color tabs. In this area of the Displays pane, you can select how the monitors are arranged.

Figure 11.28 shows the two monitors without the added distraction of the Displays panes.

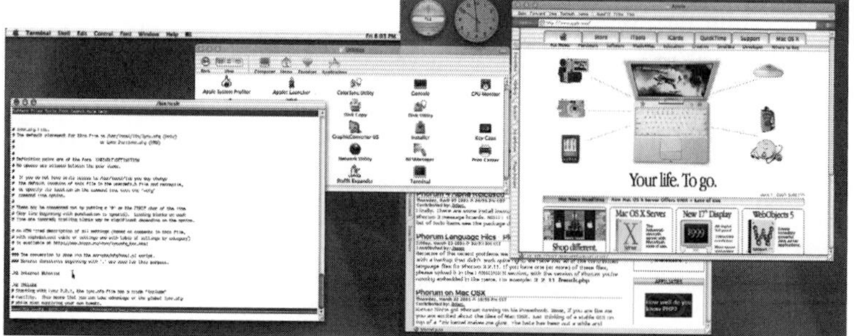

FIGURE 11.28 *Here you can see the multiple monitors without the distraction of the Displays panes.*

Display Calibrator

The Display Calibrator, as mentioned earlier, is the utility that creates a ColorSync profile specific to your monitor. The utility is located in `/Applications/Utilities`.

Figure 11.29 shows the introductory screen for the Display Calibrator. As you can see, the calibrator will guide you through adjusting your brightness and contrast, gamma, display color, and white point. The calibrator has an expert mode available, but you can turn that off by deselecting the check mark, if you so choose. The normal and expert modes are similar. Expert mode does not provide any extra steps, only more options with some of the steps.

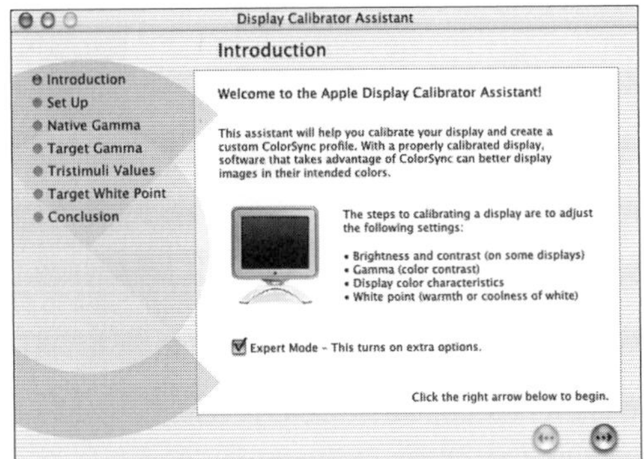

FIGURE 11.29
The introductory screen of the Display Calibrator. Here you can choose whether to be in expert mode.

Note

Depending on your monitor and the settings you've normally worked with, you might be pleasantly surprised, or surprisingly dismayed at the results of putting together a calibration for your monitor. Calibrating your monitor allows you to see image files and online contents as they was intended, assuming that the person creating the original file had their display calibrated as well. Unfortunately, many users don't have their monitors calibrated, and although the monitors provided by Apple have historically been well-behaved with respect to their color response curves, this is by no means a universal constant among all monitor manufacturers. The end result is that if you calibrate your monitor, you'll see all the errors in everyone else's monitor calibrations in the files they create. Carefully created content will look wonderful, and less carefully created content will look, well...we'll leave that to you to judge.

Overall, we recommend using a carefully and correctly calibrated monitor so that content that you create will be correct, even though much of the web content created on inexpensive hardware might look better if browsed with an incorrect setting.

The first set of adjustments you make are done in the Set Up step, shown in Figure 11.30, where you adjust your display's contrast and brightness. The Display Calibrator utility instructs you to set your contrast to the highest setting, and adjust your brightness so that the oval in the dark square is barely visible. This step is the same in the expert and normal modes.

FIGURE 11.30
In the Set Up step, you adjust the contrast and brightness of your display.

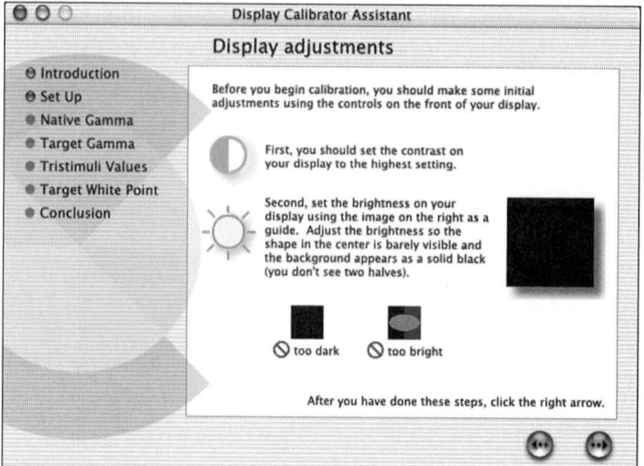

The next step is the Native Gamma step, where you determine the your display's native gamma. Figure 11.31 shows this step in expert mode. In this mode, you adjust the sliders for each of three squares—red, green, and blue—so that the apple shape in the center of each square blends as closely as possible with the background of the square. The utility suggests that it might be helpful to squint or stand back from the display to accomplish this task. In the normal mode, you adjust only one item: a gray square.

FIGURE 11.31
In the Native Gamma step, shown here in expert mode, you determine the native gamma of your display.

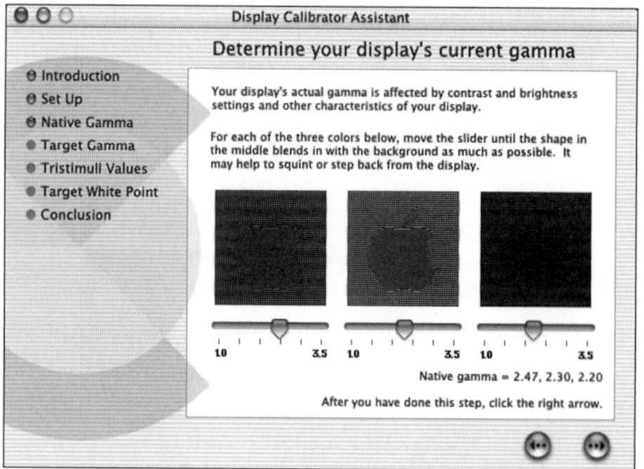

The next step is the Target Gamma step, in which you select a target gamma for your display. Figure 11.32 shows this step in normal mode. In this mode, you select from standard Macintosh gamma, standard PC gamma, or native gamma. The target gamma is selected in expert mode on a slider, which has the Macintosh and PC gammas marked. You'll find that your monitor displays a broader and smoother color palette if you choose the Macintosh default gamma of 1.8. If you do a lot of image creation for the Web, you might find it useful to create two ColorSync profiles: one for a standard Macintosh display and one for a standard PC display. Two such profiles would give you the ability to see approximately how your images will appear on each of these common display types.

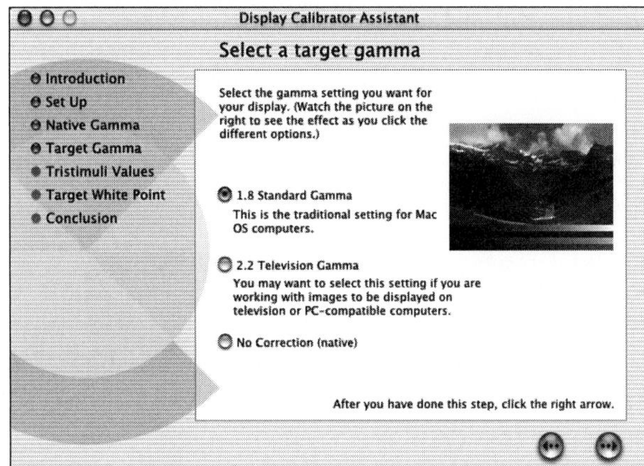

FIGURE 11.32
In the Target Gamma step, shown here in normal mode, you select the target gamma of your display.

The next step, the Tristimuli Values step, is shown in Figure 11.33. Because the color range varies with the physical characteristics of each display, this step allows you to select a color range for your display by selecting a description for your display model. This step is the same for both modes.

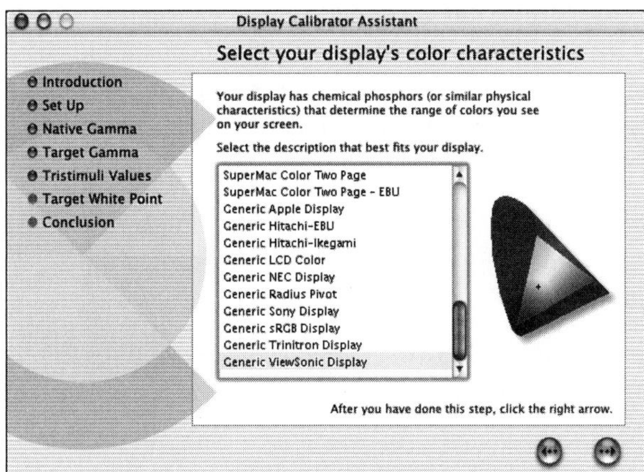

FIGURE 11.33
In the Tristimuli Values step, select a color range for your display by selecting an appropriate description for your display model.

In the next step, the Target White Point step, you select a target white point setting for your display. Figure 11.34 shows this step for the normal mode, which provides three basic choices with comments on the choices, as well as a choice for no white point correction. The expert mode provides a slider interface for these choices, but no comments on possibly pertinent choices. D65, equivalent to midday sunlight, is the default choice in both modes.

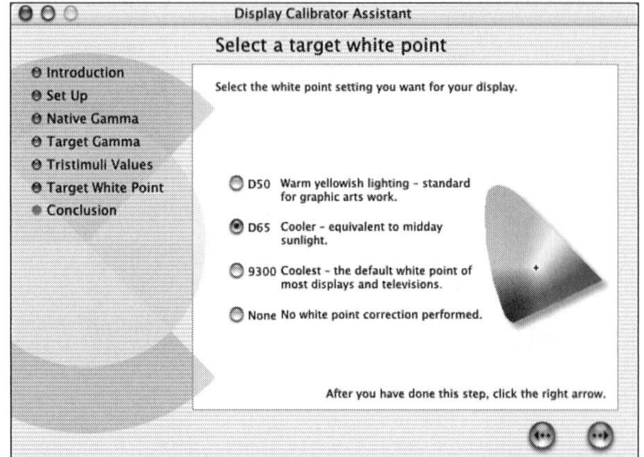

FIGURE 11.34
Select a target white point setting for your display in the Target White Point step.

In the final step, shown in expert mode in Figure 11.35, you provide a name for your new profile. In expert mode, a summary of the profile is included, but in normal mode, you simply provide a name. As mentioned earlier, this ColorSync profile is saved in your own `~/Library/ColorSync/Profiles/` directory. It then appears as an option in the Color tab of the Displays pane. Additionally, it appears either directly listed or as an Other Profile option for all the profile categories under the Device Profiles tab of the ColorSync pane, plus as an RGB Default choice under ColorSync's Document Profiles tab.

If you decide you do not like the profile you created, simply delete it.

Energy Saver

The Energy Saver pane is where you set sleep and wake options for your machine, as well as whether it should automatically restart after a power failure.

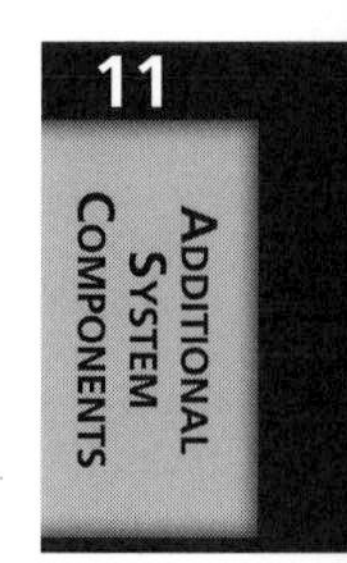

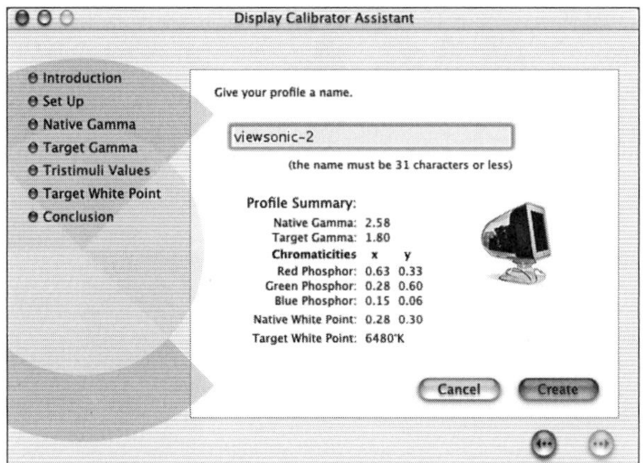

FIGURE 11.35
In the final step, you save your newly created ColorSync profile.

Sleep

The Sleep tab of the Energy Saver pane, shown in Figure 11.36, is where you set the sleep options for your machine. Sleep is a low-power mode for the machine, and is especially useful for laptops. Using a slider, you specify how long your machine should be inactive before it sleeps. Apple recommends that you set this option to Never whenever you are burning CDs in iTunes. The Energy Saver pane further allows you to specify separate sleep timing for the display and the hard disk.

On a note related to energy, in some versions of OS X, the PowerBook has a Dockling that looks like a battery and indicates the charge level of the battery. This Dockling is located in the `/Applications/Dock Extras` folder. In other versions, you can find this in the menu bar.

Options

The Options tab of the Energy Saver pane, shown in Figure 11.37, is where you set the wake options for your machine. You can set the machine to wake when the modem detects a ring, or to wake for network administrative access. Additionally, you can set your machine to automatically restart after a power failure.

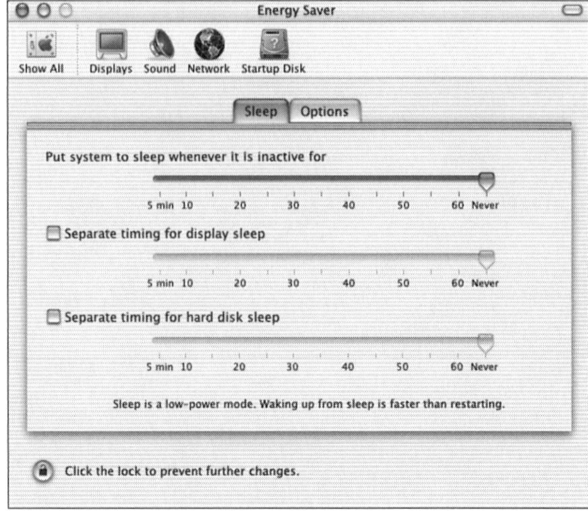

FIGURE 11.36
Sleep time and sleep timing options are specified in the Sleep tab of the Energy Saver pane.

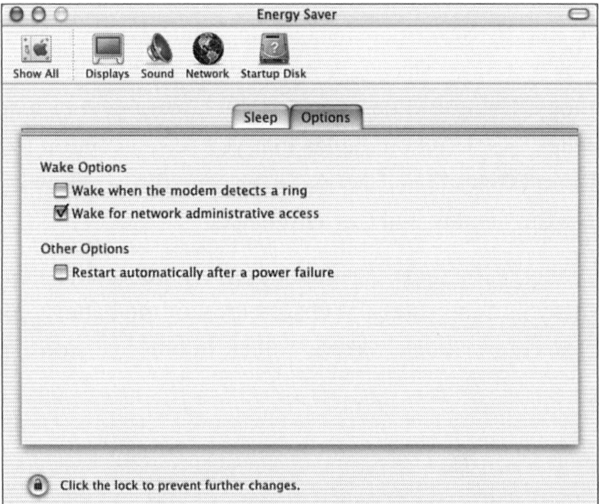

FIGURE 11.37
Wake options and whether the machine should automatically restart after a power failure are specified in the Options tab of the Energy Saver pane.

Keyboard

The Keyboard pane is where you set the repeat rate of the keyboard as well as keyboard shortcut settings.

Repeat Rate

The Repeat Rate tab of the Keyboard pane, shown in Figure 11.38, controls the key repeat rate and the amount of delay until repeat. You can test the rate and delay in a test

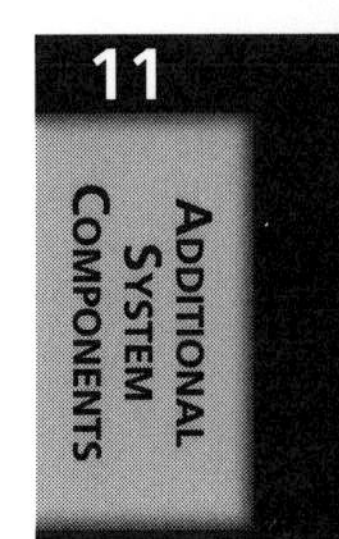

space within the pane itself. If it takes your fingers some time to release the keys as you are typing, you might want to try some longer settings here. In this day of word processing, rather than typing at the typewriter, these controls might not seem important. At the very least, we can reduce Mr. Kitty's typing speed.

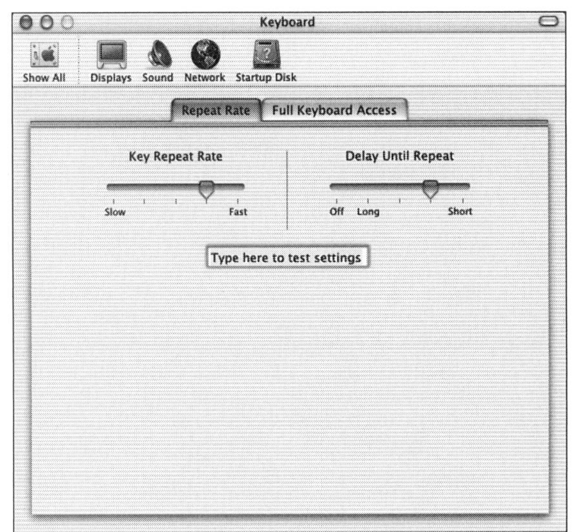

FIGURE 11.38
The key repeat rate and the delay until repeat are set in the Repeat Rate tab of the Keyboard pane.

Full Keyboard Access

The Full Keyboard Access tab of the Keyboard pane, shown in Figure 11.39, is where you can enable full keyboard access. With full keyboard access on, you can use keyboard controls in conjunction with typical navigation methods. In this tab, you can control key keyboard focus with function keys, letters, or custom key controls.

Mouse

Controls for the mouse are set in the Mouse pane, shown in Figure 11.40. Here you can control tracking speed and the double-click speed. The pane itself has a space in which you can test the double-click speed.

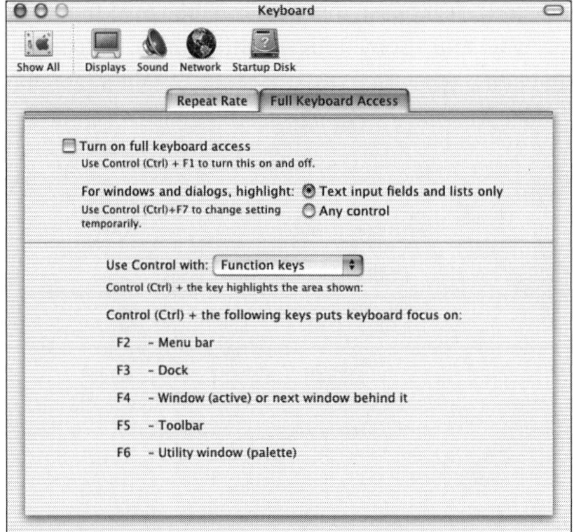

FIGURE 11.39
Full keyboard access can be enabled in the Full Keyboard Access tab of the Keyboard pane.

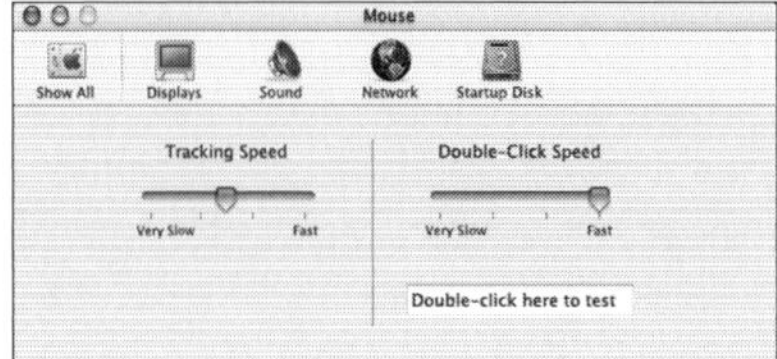

FIGURE 11.40
Tracking speed and double-click speed are set in the Mouse pane.

Sound

The Sound pane is where you set the desired sound and volume for alerts, main system sound, and a sound output device. From each tab under the Sound pane, main volume controls are accessible as well as the control for making volume control accessible from the menu bar. You can set the main volume or mute the main sound. Access to the Sound pane is readily available in the bar at the top of System Preferences, and by default in the menu bar. Additionally, you can adjust main sound from the keyboard sound controls. Apple expects that you will want to play with your sound frequently.

Alerts

The Alerts tab of the Sound pane, shown in Figure 11.41, is where you can select an alert sound, set a preferred alert volume, and select an output device for alert sounds. To listen to a particular alert sound, simply select the sound, and it will automatically play.

FIGURE 11.41
Settings involving the sound for your alerts are set in the Alerts tab of the Sound pane.

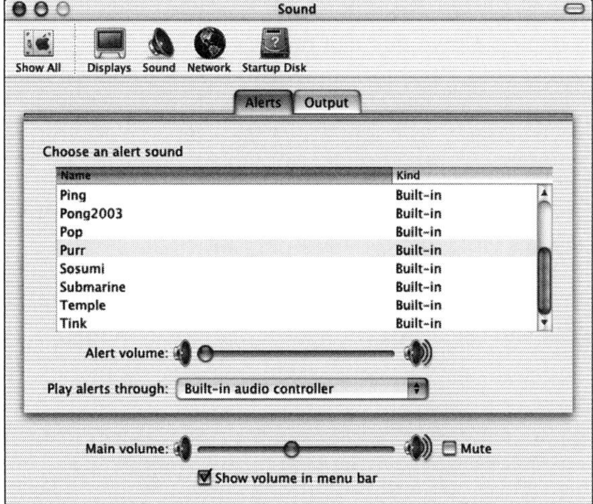

Output

The Output tab of the Sound pane, shown in Figure 11.42, is where you select an output device for sound and set the system balance.

FIGURE 11.42
Settings involving the output device for sound are set in the Output tab of the Sound pane.

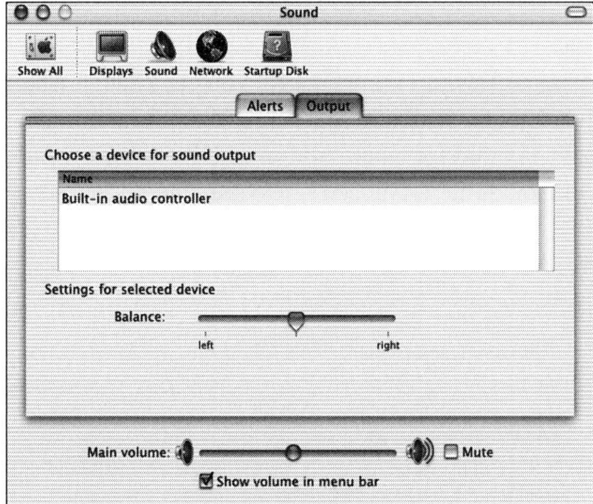

Adding a Sound to the System

After trying all the alert sounds, you might decide that you would prefer to add one of your own. Or you might already have a sound from another machine that you would like to add to the OS X machine. OS X supports AIFF (Audio Interchange File Format) sounds. Any sounds that you have that can be converted to AIFF can be used on your OS X machine.

The OS X machine even comes with a package that can convert your sounds for you, iTunes. The iTunes package can import sounds and convert them to AIFF, WAV, or MP3. You can use iTunes to convert AIFC, audio CD, MP3, System 7 Sound, uLaw (AU), WAV, Qdesign, and QuickTime audio (audio-only movies).

To use iTunes to convert a sound file to an AIFF sound file, in the iTunes Preferences, click the Importing tab and select AIFF Encoder, as shown in Figure 11.43.

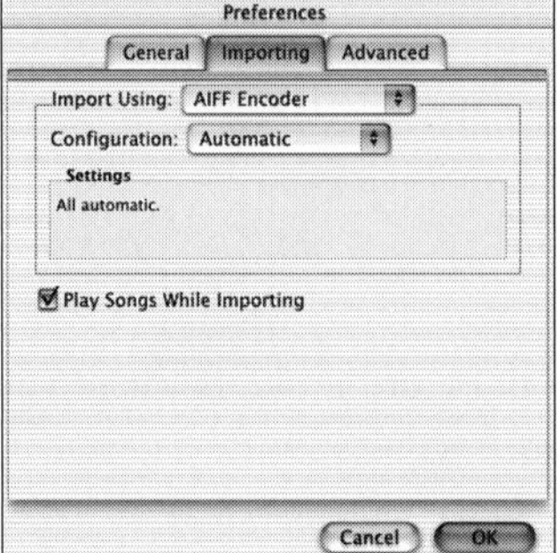

FIGURE 11.43
In the iTunes Preferences, under the Importing tab, select AIFF Encoder to convert a sound to AIFF.

Under the Advanced tab, shown in Figure 11.44, you can change where iTunes saves the file. Look at the Music Folder Location section for the information. Even if you don't have any special place in mind for where you would like to save your converted file, at least take the time to look at the Advanced tab to see where iTunes will store the file.

FIGURE 11.44
In the iTunes Preferences, under the Advanced tab, you can specify in the Music Folder Location where the converted sound file will be stored.

After you have set your preferences, from the Advanced menu, select Convert to AIFF to convert the sound. The converted sound file is saved to the folder specified in the Music Folder Location. In the graphical interface, however, the converted sound might not appear right away. However, you will be able to immediately see the converted file from the command line. iTunes saves the converted AIFF file with the `.aif` extension. Unfortunately, the Sound pane recognizes only sound files with the extension `.aiff`. Make sure that you rename the converted sound file to have the `.aiff` extension instead.

Based on your experience with fonts, you can probably guess where to place your converted sound file. As with fonts, we recommend that you make available to all users any new sounds you add. To do so, you can copy the new sound to the `/System/Library/Sounds/` directory. As with fonts, you might have to be `root` or use `sudo` to accomplish this. Alternatively, you can place the file in `/Library/Sounds/`. Please note that there is already a `/Library/Audio/Sounds/` directory; however, placing sounds in that directory has no effect. So, you will have to create a `Sounds` folder in the `Library` directory. Look at the permissions on the directory you have created. It probably belongs to group `admin`. Make sure that the privileges are read and write for the owner, read and write for the group `admin`, and read for everybody else.

You can copy the converted sound file to either `/System/Library/Sounds/` or your newly created `/Library/Sounds/` directory via the command line. If you prefer, you can drag-and-drop via the GUI interface as well. If the converted sound is not yet available in the GUI interface, log out and log back in. As with fonts, you can choose to make the sound available for your use only, and instead copy it to your own `~/Library/Sounds/` directory.

Note

Apple has requested that users and third parties do not place files in the `/System` directory, but use the `/Library` folder instead. Unfortunately, this rule has already been violated numerous times by developers. Although we recommend following Apple's guidelines, you shouldn't experience any problems either way.

The new sound file becomes available in the Sound pane after you log out and log back in. Figure 11.45 shows our sample Sound pane with a new sound called `train`. The file is actually named `train.aiff`, but appears in the Sound pane as `train`. The new `train` sound was originally a WAV file, but has been converted to AIFF.

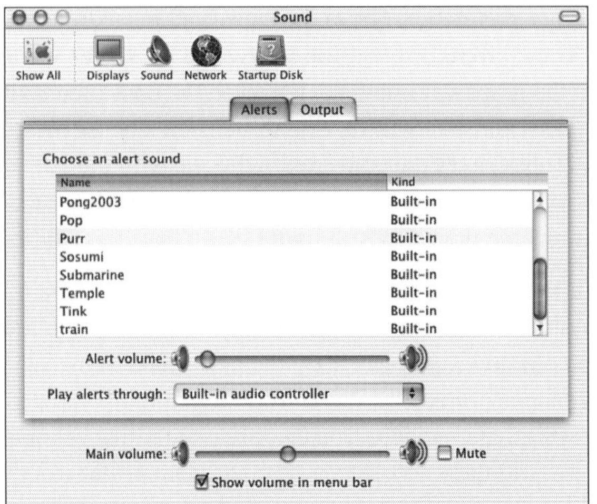

FIGURE 11.45
Our new sound, called `train`*, is now available in the Sound pane. We copied it to* `/Library/Sounds/`*, logged out, and logged back in.*

System Preferences: Internet & Network

The Internet & Network section of the System Preferences panel includes panes for customizing your Internet and network settings. With the controls in this section, you can customize settings for your network connection, Internet use, QuickTime, and remote access to your machine. In this section, however, we look at only the Internet pane because the other panes included in this part of the System Preferences are discussed in other chapters of the book.

Internet

You can specify various Internet-related settings in the Internet pane. The settings are for iTools, E-mail, Web, and News.

iTools

In the iTools tab, shown in Figure 11.46, you enter information about your iTools account. The iTools services were first introduced with Mac OS 9. The iTools Apple provides include an e-mail account, disk storage, and a Web server to serve your Web pages. If you are new to iTools, definitely check `http://www.apple.com/itools/` for more information. Because the basic iTools are free, be especially considerate in your usage of the services.

With the e-mail account that comes as part of iTools, you can store up to 5MB of e-mail, or you can choose to have the e-mail forwarded to another e-mail account. The e-mail account has the form `<membername>@mac.com`. You have up to 20MB of free storage space available on your iDisk. The iDisk appears as a volume on your desktop, which allows you to conveniently use it to store files. The iDisk icon is also a part of the Finder toolbar, readily allowing you access to your iDisk. In addition, the iDisk uses the WebDAV protocol built into OSX. WebDAV speaks the same language as a Web browser. Consequently, you are connected to your iDisk only as needed. Be sure to check your iDisk from time to time because Apple leaves software there for you. If you become addicted to this service, you can purchase up to 1GB additional storage space. Your iDisk space is also where you store your Web site, if you choose to create one. Your URL has the form `http://homepage.mac.com/<membername>/`. The size of your Web site is restricted to only the amount of iDisk storage space you have.

Under the iTools tab, you enter your iTools member name and password. If you do not have an iTools account, you can sign up for one by clicking the Sign Up button.

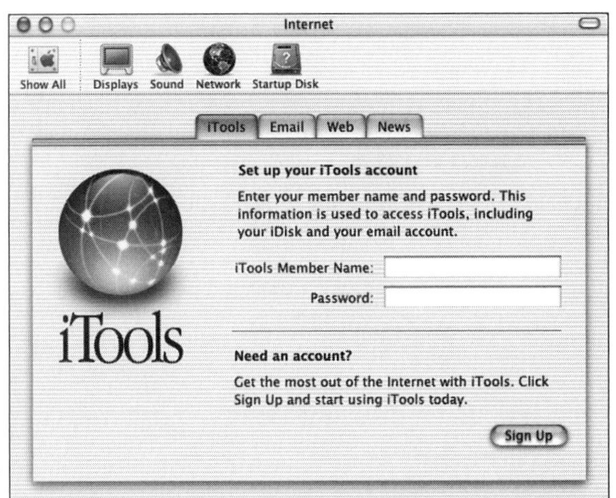

FIGURE 11.46
Enter your iTools member name and password under the iTools tab of the Internet pane. If you do not have an iTools account, you can sign up for one here.

Email

The Email tab, shown in Figure 11.47, is where you can configure information about an e-mail account. The Email tab allows you to configure the default e-mail reader. You can select from Mail or Outlook Express, or you can specify another reader. The Email tab provides a box that you can check to tell it to use your iTools account. It then automatically fills in the rest of the tab for you, based on the information you entered in the iTools tab.

If you do not want to have iTools information entered here, you can choose to enter information for another e-mail account instead.

Check your ISP for the correct information that you should provide. The information you enter here is

- **Email Address.**
- **Incoming Mail Server.**
- **Account Type.** Select either POP or IMAP. With a POP account, your mail is permanently removed from the server after you have downloaded it. With an IMAP account, your mail remains available on the server after you have downloaded it.
- **User Account ID.**
- **Password.**
- **Outgoing Mail Server.**

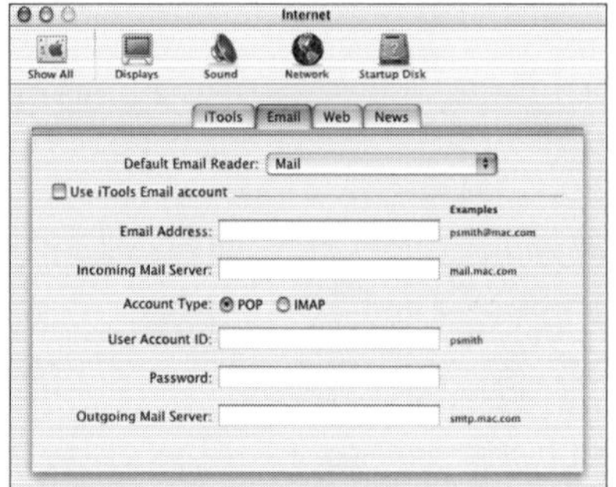

FIGURE 11.47 *You can enter e-mail account information under the Email tab of the Internet pane. If you want to use your iTools account information here, the information is automatically filled out, based on the iTools information provided under the iTools tab.*

Web

The Web tab, shown in Figure 11.48, is where you specify some important settings for your default Web browser. You specify the following fields:

- **Default Web Browser**—Either select Internet Explorer or specify another browser.
- **Home Page**—This is the home page that your default browser loads on opening. Leave this field blank if you don't want it to load any page.

- **Search Page**—This setting has no obvious effect in Internet Explorer.
- **Download Files To**—This is where files you download are stored.

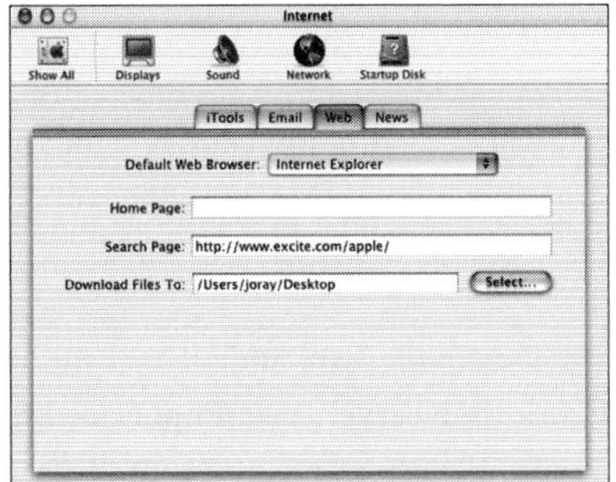

FIGURE 11.48
Enter settings for your default Web browser under the Web tab of the Internet pane.

News

Preferences for your news reader are specified in the News tab, shown in Figure 11.49. The following settings can be specified:

- **Default News Reader**—Either select Outlook Express or specify something else
- **News Server**
- **Connect As**—Select either registered user or guest
- **User Account ID**
- **Password**

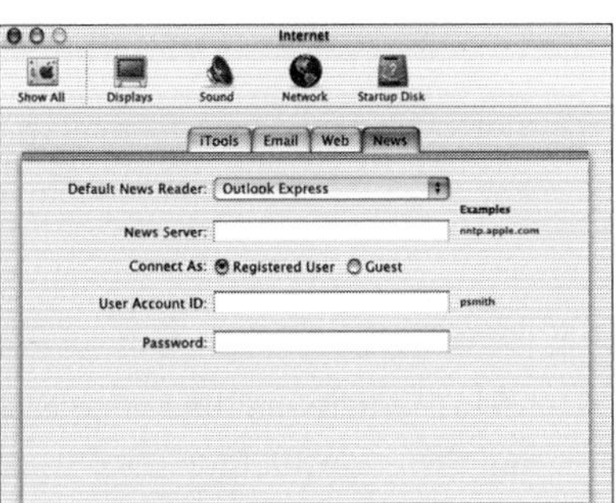

FIGURE 11.49
Enter settings for your default news reader under the News tab of the Internet pane.

System Preferences: System

The System section of the System Preferences panel includes panes for customizing system settings. With the controls in this section, you can customize such settings as the date and time display, the startup disk, and a software update schedule. The Users pane, which we looked at earlier in this chapter, is in this section of the System Preferences. In this section, we will look at the Date & Time, Software Update, and Speech panes.

Date & Time

Various aspects of the date and time are specified in the Date & Time pane of System Preferences.

Date & Time

In the Date & Time tab of the Date & Time pane, you actually set the date and time. If your computer gets time from a network time server, you do not need to set anything. Figure 11.50 shows the Date & Time tab. Please note that if you do receive your time setting from a network time server, you might have trouble when your machine boots up if it can't find the network time server.

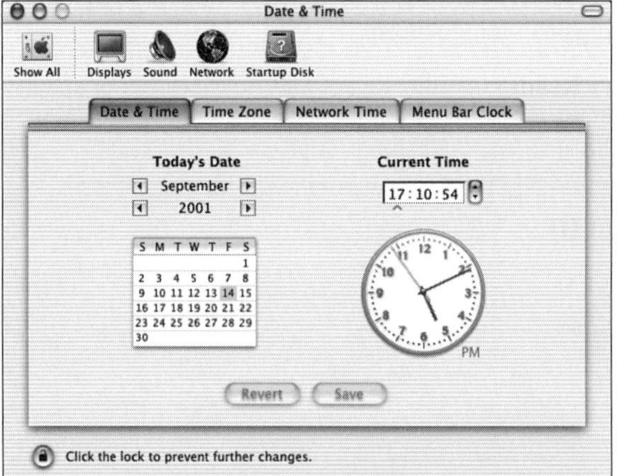

FIGURE 11.50 *The current date and time are set in the Date & Time tab of the Date & Time pane.*

Time Zone

The Time Zone tab, shown in Figure 11.51, is where the time zone is set. You just click on your approximate area on the map, and then select a time zone from the pop-up window.

FIGURE 11.51
Select your time zone in the Time Zone tab of the Date & Time pane.

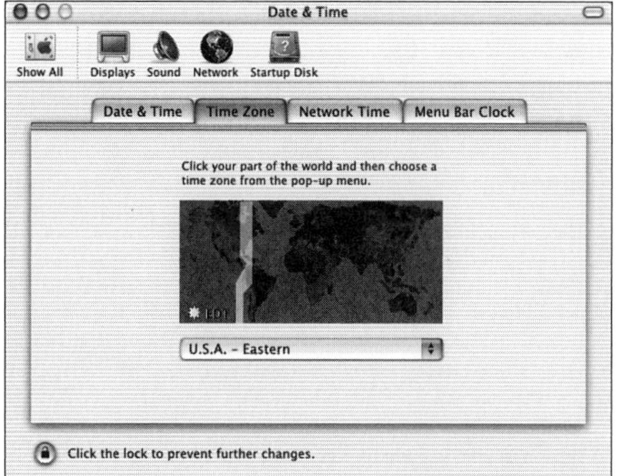

Network Time

Figure 11.52 shows the Network Time tab, where you can indicate that the machine should use a network time server, and provide an address for the network time server.

FIGURE 11.52
You can set your machine to use a network time server and provide the address of the server in the Network Time tab of the Date & Time pane.

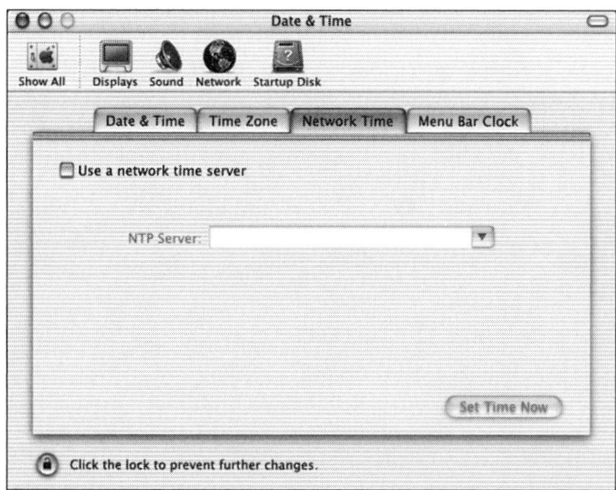

Menu Bar Clock

The menu bar clock is turned on in the Menu Bar Clock tab, shown in Figure 11.53. The menu bar clock is turned on by default, but you can turn it off here. If you choose to keep it on, you can set how it is displayed in this tab.

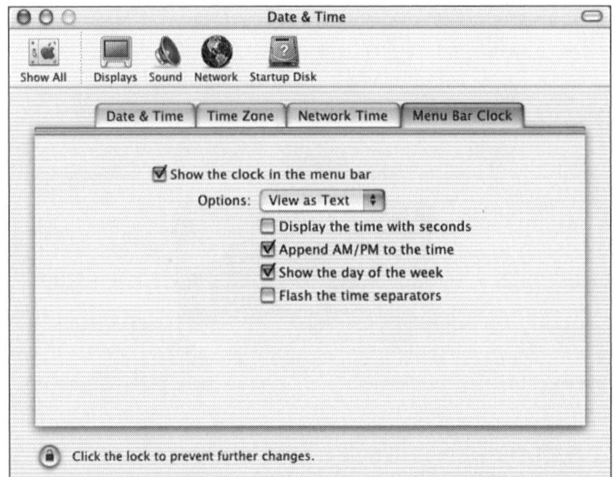

FIGURE 11.53
The menu bar clock can be turned on or off in the Menu Bar Clock tab of the Date & Time pane. Here you can also set how the clock is displayed.

Software Update

From the Software Update pane, shown in Figure 11.54, you can update your system software. This is the easiest way to keep your version of OS X current. You can choose to run the software update manually, or you can set Software Update to run on a regular schedule. This does not update any third-party software you have installed. If you would like to see what packages Software Update has updated, click on the Show Log button. Chapter 32, "Maintenance and Troubleshooting," covers the update process in depth.

FIGURE 11.54
Software updates keep your machine running with the latest applications and security patches.

Speech

The Speech pane under System Preferences controls speech recognition and text-to-speech conversion.

Speech Recognition

The Speech Recognition portion of the Speech pane has On/Off, shown in Figure 11.55, and Listening tabs, shown in Figure 11.56, for the Apple Speakable Items recognition system. The Apple Speakable Items recognition system is the system that allows you to interact with the computer by speaking certain commands to it.

FIGURE 11.55
The On/Off tab of the Speech Recognition tab of the Speech pane.

In the On/Off section, you can

- Turn speech recognition on or off.
- View some helpful hints on getting started with speech recognition.
- View the Speakable Items folder.
- Choose to open Speakable Items at log in.
- Select a sound that the computer plays when it understands your spoken command. If you added a new sound to the system, the sound appears here as one of your choices.
- Select whether the Speak text feedback check box is enabled. It is selected by default. So far, we have not observed any difference whether or not this box is checked.

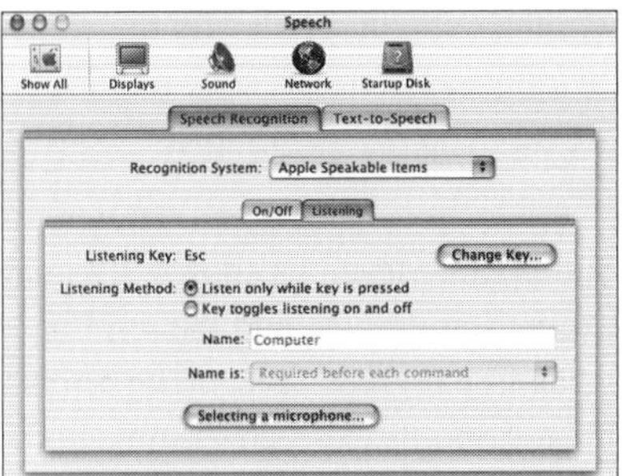

FIGURE 11.56
The Listening tab of the Speech Recognition tab of the Speech pane.

In the Listening section, you can

- Set which key is used as the listening key. The default is the Escape key.
- Set the listening method. The default is to have the machine listen when the listening key is pressed. The listening key can be set to toggle listening on and off. You can then preface a command, if you so choose, with whatever name you list here. I had so hoped to be able to preface my spoken commands with "Hello Computer," but I never got this option to work. The Speakable Items system always failed when I tried the option. Consequently, we recommend that you choose the default method.
- See information on microphone selection. The information on selecting a microphone indicates that when more than one microphone is detected, the system automatically chooses one in this order: external USB microphone, external analog microphone, built-in microphone.

Text-to-Speech

In the Text-to-Speech tab of the Speech pane, shown in Figure 11.57, you set the voice that is used by applications that speak. You can select the voice and rate of speech.

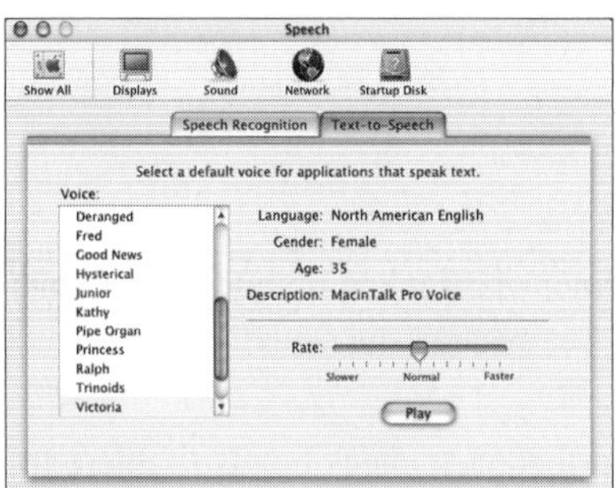

Figure 11.57
The Text-to-Speech tab of the Speech pane.

Speech Feedback

When you turn on speech recognition, the computer tells you that "Speakable Items is starting," and the Speech Feedback window appears, as shown in Figure 11.58. The Speech Feedback window, a small round window, shows microphone level.

When you are speaking, the microphone image changes and the horizontal lines, which start as just gray lines, display the microphone level, as shown in Figure 11.59. The bottom line is a blue color. The next two lines are green, and the top line is red. The Helpful Hints recommends that you try to speak in the green levels. The arrow at the bottom of the window has links to the Speech panel and the Speech Commands window. You can open the Speech Commands window by either saying "Open Speech Commands

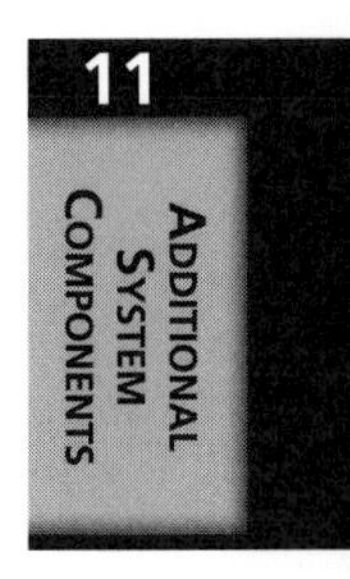

window," or clicking on the arrow. The Speech Commands window shows the commands that you may speak to the computer.

FIGURE 11.58
The Speech Feedback window, as it is shown when speech recognition is first turned on.

FIGURE 11.59
The Speech Commands window, as it appears when you are speaking to the computer.

Unfortunately, it might take you a while to get the Speech Recognition system working. When it does work for you, it will be quite exciting. Figure 11.60 shows what to expect when Speech Recognition finally works for you. The Speech Commands window shows not only which commands you may speak to the computer, but also which commands you have spoken thus far. Apple suggests that you might use the Chess application to familiarize yourself with the Speech Recognition system.

FIGURE 11.60
Here Speakable Items was used to open and control Internet Explorer. Note that the Speech Commands window shows which commands have been spoken thus far.

Summary

This chapter rounded out the user configuration options for Mac OS X. The Apple-supplied System Preferences panels give user-friendly control over a wide variety of system functions. These panels can be thought of as analogous to the older control panels of Mac OS 9.*x*. This chapter covered the System Preferences panels that control each user's desktop environment.

There are additional panels, and additional coverage is provided in other chapters where appropriate. If you did not find the information you were looking for here, it is likely covered in greater detail elsewhere. We apologize that all system preferences couldn't be covered completely in one area, but the size and complexity of Mac OS X results in trade-offs of where to place content. We chose to keep like topics together. Because of this, the QuickTime panel is covered with the QuickTime Player in Chapter 7, "Internet Communications"; Software Update is discussed in Chapter 32, "System Maintenance"; and network configuration is found in Chapter 9, "Network Setup."

Introduction to BSD Applications

Part IV

In This Part

Introducing the BSD Subsystem

In This Chapter

In this chapter, we finally reach the point for which some readers have been waiting years, and some have been dreading since they heard about the underpinnings of OS X. We now start conversing directly with the BSD-4.4-derived Unix implementation that underlies Mac OS X. BSD (Berkeley Software Distribution) is one of the two major philosophical variants of Unix. If you're a longtime Unix user, you'll probably find much of the rest of this book familiar, and you should consider it a reference to those places where the Apple implementation differs from what you're already familiar with. If, on the other hand, you're new to Unix, you'll soon have to decide whether you're satisfied with Mac OS X as simply a more stable, more powerful flavor of the Mac OS you've grown to know and love, or whether you want to learn even more. In this chapter, we'll cover the primary concepts that you'll need to understand to make use of the BSD subsystem, and introduce some of the most important command-line programs.

Unix-Based Mac OS

If you're not familiar with Unix, you've probably heard and read enough to have developed any number of preconceptions regarding what using it will be like. Almost all of them are probably at least a bit intimidating. You've probably heard that Unix commands are cryptic and that the learning curve is steep. Even worse, it uses a command-line interface—you've actually got to *type* at the thing to tell it what to do, and we all know how archaic that mode of controlling a machine is.

It might be archaic, but that does not mean that there's anything wrong with it or that it's not the best way to accomplish certain tasks. We know, many of you have been poking fun at that *other* OS for years because its unfortunate users had to type to make it work—don't worry, we've laughed, too. You're just going to have to screw up your courage and admit that you've used the keyboard in the Mac OS Finder to do things such as jump a Finder window to a file with a particular name. The mouse is a wonderful tool for doing things where the brain's visual processing machinery can come into play. The keyboard is also a powerful tool for other types of interaction, and it would be silly to intentionally restrict yourself to only one type of interface when you have other complementary interfaces available. In many ways, what Apple has given you is analogous to being provided with a high-end sports car, and a fully equipped machine shop and garage to work on it. If buzzing around in the fancy car is your pleasure, you are free to do so without ever opening the hood. On the other hand, if you feel like working on the engine, all the tools are there for you to allow you to further customize and enhance your ride to your heart's content.

Regardless of what you've heard, the idea that learning and using Unix will be fun and rewarding is likely to be farthest from your mind. We hope that in this and upcoming chapters, we'll be able to convince you differently. If we can't, don't worry. There's nothing about Mac OS X that requires you to learn and use anything other than the graphical interface that we've already covered. You can live with your Mac OS X machine, use it for the same type of applications you always have, and love it in all its "nontypishness," without ever having to learn any of this Unix stuff. However, if you want to learn how to make your machine even more powerful, make yourself more productive, customize everything to an exquisite extent, give this command line stuff a try.

Caution

Having just told you that we think you'll like the Unix side of your machine if you give it a fair chance, and encouraged you to try it out, we'll turn around and caution you about its use. **Unix is not for everyone**. Although we'd love to see every Macintosh user graduate to the power available in the BSD subsystem, we can't avoid the reality that Unix is more complicated and powerful than some users will ever want to use. Just as some of us are safer not owning superfast sports cars, some are less a threat to ourselves and others if we don't have a big box of firecrackers, and some would be better off if we couldn't buy donuts by the dozen, Unix is just too much for some people. It might be too much power, or too much flexibility, or too much information to remember, but Unix seems specially designed to create a user who epitomizes the phrase *knows just enough to be dangerous*.

Evaluate your needs honestly. We're firmly convinced that everyone can learn Unix, and everyone can use it safely, but the reality is that not everyone will. If you're hesitant about trying out the Unix side of your new OS because you think it might be too difficult, we suggest that you give it a try because we think we can convince you that it's not as tough as you think. If you're not sure that Unix is a good match for what you do, you might be right: It might be better if you use OS X as the super stable, more flexible OS on which to run your GUI-based programs, and leave the BSD subsystem alone.

BSD Philosophy

One of the complaints you might have heard from people regarding Apple's new OS is that it is based on immensely old operating system technology. They're right! The roots of Unix lie almost in the roots of modern computing itself. The thing that they're wrong about is their claim that this is a Bad Thing. Unix development started more than three decades ago, and the operating system that you can use today is the product of thousands upon thousands of developers work and improvements. Along the way, Unix has picked up some very powerful design concepts and some wonderful solutions to problems common in the computing world. Much of the "Unix way" is based on the idea of abstracting interfaces into the simplest possible terms. Initially, this was simply because the OS was experimental, and the simplest possible interface—one that wouldn't need fiddled with later—was the most expedient to construct. Over time, this "do it the easy way" methodology has evolved into a very powerful design concept: abstraction. This concept will be mentioned time and again as it makes its appearance in different topics throughout the book. As an initial explanation, though, an example will provide immediate understanding. Among many other concepts, Unix abstracts the notion of things that can be read from, or written to, as files. To Unix, everything from which data can be read is treated as though it were a file, and everything to which data can be written is treated as though it were also a file. Why? Because after you've developed an in-OS methodology to control reading and writing to files, it's a nuisance to have to implement almost identical methodologies for reading and writing to the network, or writing data to printers, or reading data from the keyboard. Instead, it's considerably easier to write an abstraction layer that talks to the particular device, and makes it appear to the OS as just another file. If you make your printer look like a file, printing is simply "writing to a file" for any application. If you make your keyboard input look like it's coming from a file, any application can automagically accept input from either the keyboard or an actual on-disk file, without knowing the difference.

What starts as a time-saving implementation turns into a powerful interface feature, allowing the addition of arbitrary devices, without needing to implement new OS features—just write something that makes the device "look like a file," and suddenly the OS can use it. This notion of abstraction ends up being very powerful for the end user, and similar abstractions will be pointed out in the sections to come.

More information on Unix and its role in computing can be found at `http://www.macosxunleashed.com/unixhistory.html`.

Using `Terminal.app`

The Terminal program, found in the `utilities` subfolder of the `Applications` folder, is the primary method for communicating with the BSD subsystem of the OS X installation, via the Unix command line. Some tricks and nifty applications are already appearing to insulate you from the need to work with the command line for some applications. We will cover these as well, but the terminal itself will probably be your primary mode of interaction.

Simply put, `Terminal.app` is the "terminal" by which you can type commands to your machine. It's the software version of what used to be implemented as a dedicated hardware device that understood how to display data and put it in specific positions on a screen. A terminal itself isn't particularly interesting, but provides the mechanism for communication between you and programs that are more interesting to talk to.

Terminal Preferences

As with most OS X GUI tools, a number of things about `Terminal.app` can be customized. Because you're probably familiar with configuring GUI apps by now, we'll just hit the highlights and give you an overview of what is configured where.

Across the top of the preferences panel, you have a number of panes from which to choose. These include

- The General pane, shown in Figure 12.1, enables you to configure the font and the number of character rows and columns shown in the terminal. It also allows configuration of the behavior of the terminal window when the shell or application running in it exits.

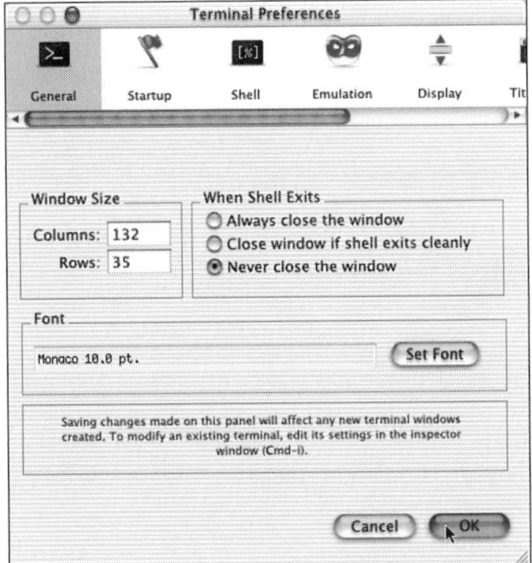

FIGURE 12.1
The General pane of the preferences panel for `Terminal.app`.

- The Startup pane, shown in Figure 12.2, allows you to configure the behavior of `Terminal.app` on startup. Most interestingly, you can configure a file to be executed when the terminal starts. Unfortunately, we don't discuss what sort of things might be put into a startup file until Chapter 18, "Advanced Unix Shell Use: Configuration and Programming (Shell Scripting)."

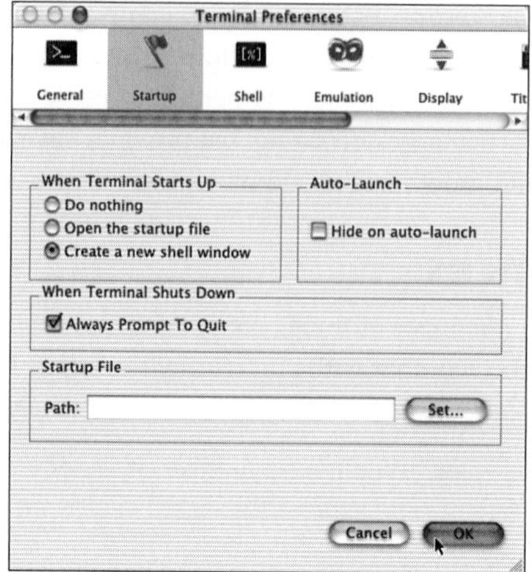

FIGURE 12.2
The Startup pane of the preferences panel for `Terminal.app`.

- The Shell pane, shown in Figure 12.3, lets you configure the shell to use for interaction in the terminal. Because everything we show in this book is in `tcsh`, we recommend that you leave the Shell field set to `tcsh`. Leaving the shell configured to read the login script is probably a good idea as well. This will control whether each terminal executes the `/etc/csh.login` script and your home directory `~/.login` script.

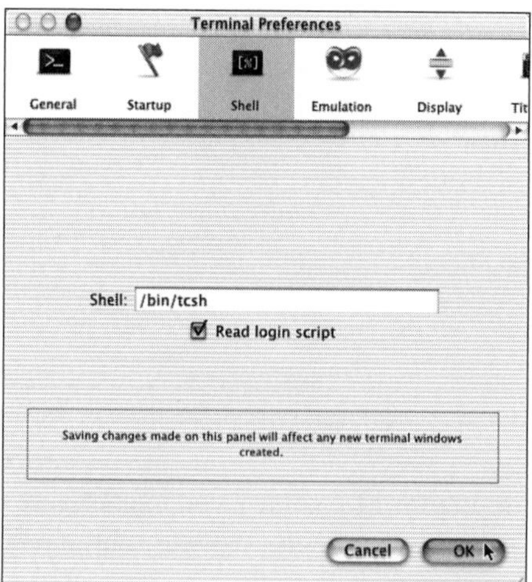

FIGURE 12.3
The Shell pane of the preferences panel for `Terminal.app`.

- The Emulation pane, shown in Figure 12.4, lets you configure whether to translate newlines to carriage returns for pasted text; in other words, to convert from Mac-like text into Unix-like text. In addition, you can configure whether to generate

VT100 keycodes from the numeric keypad. You can control the behavior of the Alt key, but because Unix doesn't frequently make use of any of the three features suggested, the best setting for this will depend on the applications you choose to run in your terminals. Text editors, in particular, might like you to have VT100 keycodes enabled so that you can use the numeric keypad to move around in your document.

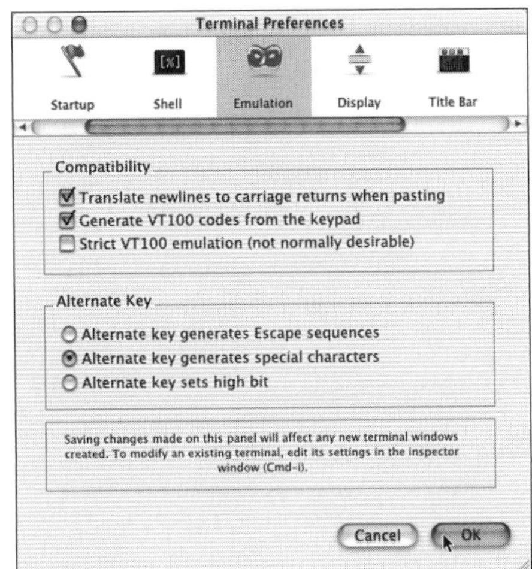

FIGURE 12.4
The Emulation pane of the preferences panel for `Terminal.app`.

- The Display pane, shown in Figure 12.5, lets you enable the scrollback buffer (do it!), and set how many lines to keep. We suggest you use many, many lines! We couldn't live with less than a 3000-line scrollback buffer. As memory and disk space become cheaper every day, you'll probably find that you want, and can use, even more. Whether to wrap and rewrap lines is your choice, as is whether you want the terminal to scroll to the bottom when you enter data into it.
- The Title Bar pane, shown in Figure 12.6, lets you control the information that appears in the title bar. For your convenience, it shows you a picture of what your title bar will look like with the selected options.
- The Colors pane, shown in Figure 12.7, lets you configure the colors and characteristics of many features of the terminal. The most obvious are the window background and the selection color. Next, you can configure how text should look, the type of cursor you want, and whether the cursor blinks. Conveniently, the pane shows you the effect of your choices before you okay them by displaying the label text for each option in the style selected for it.

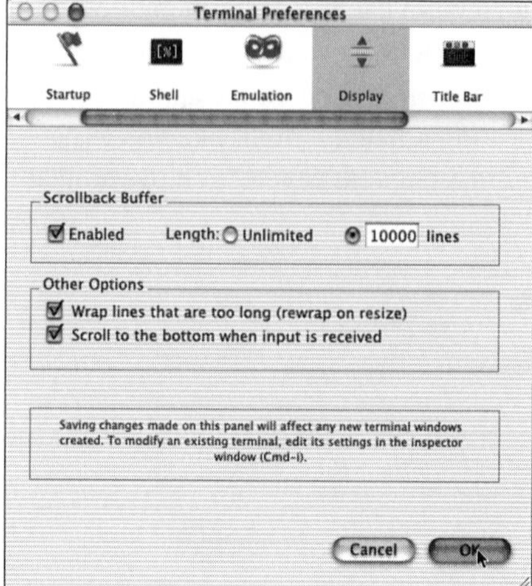

FIGURE 12.5
The Display pane of the preferences panel for `Terminal.app`.

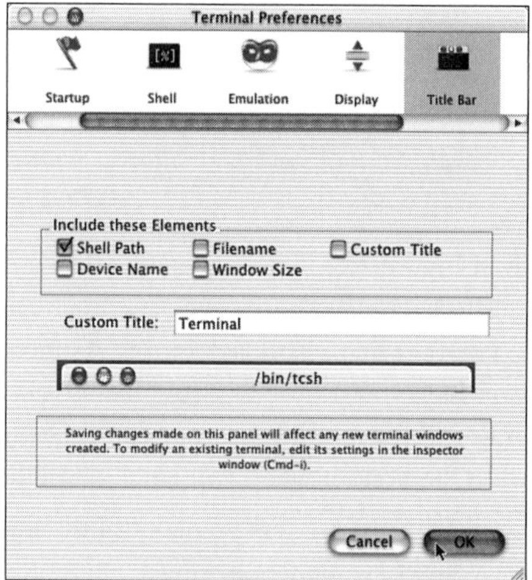

FIGURE 12.6
The Title Bar pane of the preferences panel for `Terminal.app`.

- The Activity pane, shown in Figure 12.8, has the least obvious function. As you'll learn in this chapter, Unix commands run "in" terminals, so closing a terminal when the application running "in" it is still active can have undesirable results. If you enable activity monitoring, the terminal will try to monitor whether there are any applications running in the terminal, and warn you if closing the terminal will kill any applications. If you enable the "Clean" background processes check box, the terminal will attempt to guess whether processes that are running without an obvious interface can safely continue without the terminal. It's not clear how well this works at this point in time.

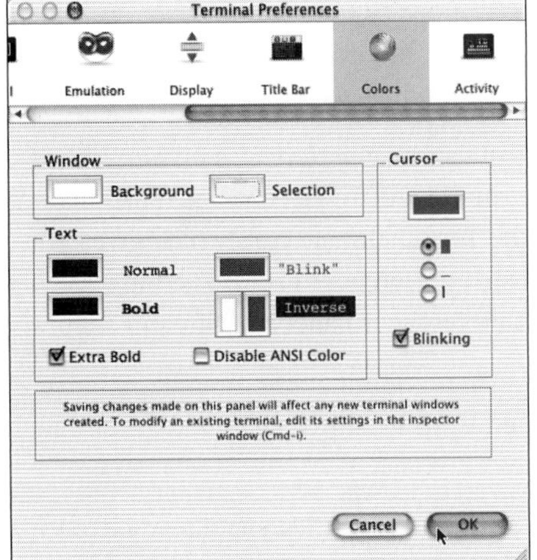

FIGURE 12.7
The Colors pane of the preferences panel for `Terminal.app`.

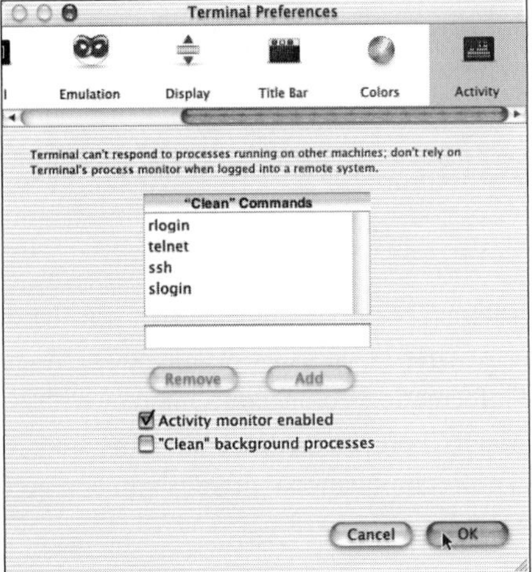

FIGURE 12.8
The Activity pane of the preferences panel for `Terminal.app`.

The Save and Save As items are accessible from the Shell menu. These allow you to save the setup and preferences of a `Terminal.app` window or window set.

Also accessible are the Save Text As and Save Selected Text As items. These allow you to save the complete text buffer of the terminal, or whatever text you have selected in the terminal. The Run Command option of the Shell menu produces the dialog box in which you can enter a command to run in a new terminal window.

If the command doesn't produce an interactive environment, the new window will just tell you that the command ran, which isn't very useful. If the command is an interactive one such as `emacs` (`emacs` is a very powerful text editor that you'll learn about in Chapter 15, "Command-Line Applications and Application Suites"), it will produce a new window and run the specified command in that window.

The Shell menu item Set Title seems like a preferences option. In fact, if you select it, you get yet another way to control the window's behavior. This menu item and the Inspector menu item bring up the Terminal Inspector, which gives you access to most of the same preferences options as the preferences panel. The biggest difference seems to be that the Terminal Inspector and Preferences panel are different shapes.

Most of the items in the Edit menu are familiar. The Find item, however, leads to an option to bring up the Find panel, from which you can search for data in the Terminal's buffer.

The Font and Windows menus have the properties you already expect, and the Control menu shows you the options you have for cursor control in the window. Additionally, this menu includes the option to send a Break signal to the terminal, which can be invaluable for stopping a program that has gone awry without taking the drastic step of closing the terminal.

Interacting with Unix: Basic Unix Commands

You've already learned how to interact with Unix using OS X's Aqua interface and the GUI tools discussed throughout the first 11 chapters of this book. Much of the rest of the book will provide you with the information you need to interact with Unix textually, through the command line. Although there are no sharp dividing lines between Unix commands, Unix programs, and Unix applications, there is some benefit in making at least a fuzzy semantic distinction between them.

The Unix design philosophy drives programs that are used in day-to-day interaction with a Unix machine to be small, single-purpose, and nonoverlapping in functionality. The presence of a vast array of these single-purpose programs, designed so that they can be combined in near-infinite combinations, allows the user to construct customized solutions for most any problem. The necessity for some programs to provide more complicated functionality, requires them to be less-single purpose, and to allow somewhat more overlap. Finally, just as in other operating systems that you're used to, there are programs that are large, multifunctional, and monolithic. Typically, Unix users think of the small, single-purpose programs as *commands*, and the large, multifunctional programs as *applications*. Although they're all programs, the term *program* is frequently reserved for a program that doesn't fit the description of a command or an application. This somewhat muddy semantic distinction between types of programs might seem confusing at first, but as you become more comfortable using Unix, it will make more sense to you. As an example to get you started, you can think of a Unix command as a small program with a single function such as listing files. A Unix application is typically a much larger program, perhaps something like a word processor or a Web browser. Moreover, although both are programs, the term *program* itself is infrequently used to describe anything that falls into either of these categories.

Thankfully for the beginning Unix user, making complete sense of the semantic distinctions isn't necessary for anything other than conversing with other Unix users. Unix commands, programs, and applications are all run by typing their names at the command line. The remainder of this chapter will cover what you need to know to start interacting with the command line, and the most basic Unix commands needed for day-to-day use.

Introduction to the Unix Shell

As mentioned previously, a terminal alone isn't sufficient to allow you to interact with your machine. The terminal needs something to talk to, and that thing is usually a program called a *shell*. Unix shells provide text-based interaction between the user and the rest of the operating system. For those who have experience with the DOS environment, you can think of a Unix shell as similar to a very, very, very powerful version of COMMAND.COM. Please don't let that put you off. COMMAND.COM does not approach being a fair comparison for a shell, but both do let you type commands to the computer.

Although it is text-based, you can think of a shell running in a terminal as sharing a few conceptual similarities with a Finder window.

Any running shell can be thought of as "being in a place" in the file system, just like a Finder window is open to a certain folder in the system. This place is the *current working directory*.

Each shell can navigate through the file system by moving to parent or higher-level directories, or by moving to child or lower-level directories. Again, this is much like the functionality provided by the folder menu in each Finder window and the folders displayed in the window.

Unlike a Finder window, a shell in a terminal is not restricted to running a command that is present in the same directory that the terminal is "at"—it can run commands that are located anywhere on the machine.

Also unlike Finder windows, shell commands that you execute in terminal windows (usually) run within the terminal window, and they (usually) consume the resources of the shell such that the shell becomes "preoccupied" and can't run another command until the current one finishes.

Most flavors of Unix come with a number of different shells from which the user can choose, and the BSD version underlying OS X is no exception. With OS X, you can choose from the following three shells, or possibly more, if Apple or another source makes them available.

- `sh`—The Bourne shell. The Bourne shell is ubiquitously available on Unix, but does not have syntax or features that are particularly friendly to the user. It is most frequently used for writing shell scripts (programs written to run using the shell; how to write them will be covered in Chapter 18) that are expected to run on any version of Unix. Sometimes it is used for the login shell of particularly important accounts, such as `root`.
- `csh`—The C shell (yes, it's pronounced *seashell*). The `csh` shell is a more user-friendly shell that takes its name from the C programming language. `csh` syntax is similar to the C language, and it provides significant power for both shell programming and for users. `csh` is almost as omnipresent as `sh`.
- `tcsh`—Enhanced C shell. Many people considered `csh` to have been a botched implementation in a number of ways, and wanted something with similar syntax, but less broken. `tcsh` was born to fix the bugs, and extend the functionality, of `csh` and includes nice features such as automatic command completion and a command history.
- `bash`—The Bourne again shell (and yes, Unix programmers frequently have a twisted sense of humor). The Bourne again shell is a modern shell that takes the enhancements that make `csh` and `tcsh` more useful for user interaction, and implements them in a shell with the `sh` syntax.
- `zsh`—`zsh` is designed to be an interactive user shell that incorporates powerful programming features. The intent in its creation seems to have been to build an amalgam of the most powerful features of the other shells, and to introduce a number of new features as well. The shell has been described as suffering from "feeping creaturism" (see the Jargon File, sometimes called the "Hacker's Dictionary"—available at `http://www.eps.mcgill.ca/jargon/jargon.html`, among a plethora of other locations), and of having a few more features than even the author knows about.

Shell preference is just that: a matter of personal preference, although you'll find references and diatribes on the Internet that make the issue seem to take on almost biblical significance. Apple has chosen to make `tcsh` the standard shell for OS X, and this will satisfy a great many users because many do not like the syntax of `sh`. On the other hand, being able to perform day-to-day work in the same shell language that you'll need to use for the most ubiquitous distribution is a strong plus for `bash`.

Examples in this book will be shown using the default `tcsh` shell, but regardless of what shell you choose, interaction with each is similar. To issue a command to the computer using a shell, you type the name of the command and press the Enter key. In general, the command you requested will be executed by the shell, and will occupy the shell until it finishes, at which time you'll be returned to the shell prompt. If the command requires additional information, it might be required on the command line in the form of flags or arguments. *Flags* are usually individual letters or words preceded by a dash (`-`) that indicate the turning on or off of an option; *arguments* are words or data provided on the command line for the command to process. Some commands also require that data be provided at internal prompts or data entry areas created by the command when it is run. As mentioned previously, we'll discuss more complex programs and applications in following chapters.

Note

When documenting commands throughout the book, we will use the following syntax:

```
commandname <required options> [optional options] <arg1> <arg2>
```

and

```
commandname <required> [optional] <arg1> <arg2> ...
```

These mean that you type *`commandname`* at the prompt, must choose one or more entries from the *`<required options>`* and may choose one or more options from the `[`*`optional options`*`]`. In the first invocation form, two additional required arguments are expected on the command line; in the second, the command accepts a variable number of arguments. In general, single-letter options, usually preceded by a `-` (minus) sign, when enclosed in <> brackets are required, and when enclosed in `[]` brackets are optional. The brackets shown in the syntax examples are not actually entered on the command line—they are shown only to distinguish required and optional options. Arguments are required if shown, and an alternative form of the command will be displayed with no options if this is also an allowable syntax. Options separated by a vertical bar, |, are exclusive; you must, or may, pick one or the other (depending on whether they're required or optional), but you cannot specify both.

For example, the fictitious command documentation shown in Table 12.1 indicates that a command named `silly` can be invoked as `silly`, `silly -L`, and `silly -P`. Invoked as `silly`, it does the same thing as `silly -L`; that is, it makes a silly laugh. Invoked as `silly -P`, it makes a silly picture. Each form also can be called with an arbitrary number of filenames following the command, in which case `silly` will place its output in the specified files.

TABLE 12.1 Command Documentation Table for the Fictitious `silly` Command

`silly`	Does something silly, optionally into files
`silly [-L|P] <filename> <filename2> ...`	
`silly [-L|P]`	
`-L`	Default: Makes a silly laugh.
`-P`	Makes a silly picture.

Shell Rules and Conventions

In dealing with the shell, there are a few rules that it will help to remember. The first rule you'll need to know is things that you type in Unix are case sensitive. This includes commands. Unlike Mac OS and Windows, you cannot mix case and still have a command function. You must type the name exactly as it is stored on the system. Mac OS X has the option (the default) of using HFS+, which isn't case sensitive, but this creates some odd behavior. There are classical Unix commands included in the BSD subsystem that have names that differ only by capitalization, and that normally do different things. Because there's no obligation for OS X to be running on HFS+, and it's quite possible that you will be mounting drives from other machines that aren't running OS X at all, you really should treat everything in the BSD subsystem as though it were case sensitive, even if your installation actually isn't.

Next, when you type at the command line, characters that you type become part of the command. Most alphanumeric characters, as well as underlines and hyphens, are valid parts of commands. Most symbols aren't valid parts of commands, and some have special meanings to the command line. Table 12.2 shows some of the symbols with special meaning to the command line.

TABLE 12.2 Command-Line Symbols

Symbol	*Meaning*
`*`	When used as part of a filename, the `*` character will substitute for zero or more characters in a filename. This is called a wildcard. For example, specifying a filename of `*.gif` as an

TABLE 12.2 continued

Symbol	*Meaning*
	argument to a command-line program will tell the shell to search the current directory for all files that have names ending in `.gif`, and substitute all these filenames on the command line at this point in the command.
?	A single character wildcard. Functions like `*`, except that it substitutes for a single character in filenames, instead of any number of characters.
Tab	If you press the Tab key at the command line, the shell will attempt to complete the command for you. If the portion of the command or filename that you've typed is unique, the shell will fill in the rest of the information for you. For example, if you're in your home directory, and you want to specify the `Documents` directory on the command line, typing `Docu`[Tab-key] will most likely fill out the command line to include the full `Documents` name.
space	Unix interprets a space between words on the command line as a separator between parts of the command. This is not always what you want because Macintosh filenames can have spaces. The Unix command line will usually interpret the space in a Mac filename such as `My File` as indicating two different files: one named `My` and one named `File`.
\	The shell escape character. If you need to insert a character into a Unix command or filename that is usually interpreted by the shell (like a space or `*` character), you can place the \ character before the character that would usually be interpreted by the shell. This is called *escaping* the special character. You will frequently see this on the command line to specify Mac filenames such as `My File`, which in Unix must be specified as `My\ File`.

Most useful shells provide a history mechanism, whereby previous commands can be recalled and reused. Previous commands may be recalled to the command line by use of the up-arrow key. If you need the last command you typed, just press the up-arrow key, and it will be recalled to the command line. You can rotate through the command history with the up-arrow and down-arrow keys to pick the command you need.

The command line also provides editing capabilities. You can use the left-arrow and right-arrow keys to move around in the command line currently displayed, and edit it by typing new characters or deleting existing characters with the Delete key. This also applies to commands that you've recalled via the command history with the arrow keys.

When you type a command, the system will search for a command with that name in the list of directories known as the `PATH`. This is done because a complete search of the entire file system could take a very long time, and restricting the portions of the file system examined to only a small subset speeds things up significantly. Unfortunately, the current directory, where the shell "is", isn't necessarily in the `PATH`. Because of this, you might be in a directory named `/home/wizbot/spin/`, and there might be a command named `spinnin` in the directory, but typing `spinnin` produces only the error `command not found`. In this case, you can run the command by specifying either the full name of the path to the command (`/home/wizbot/spin/spinnin`), or by specifying the relative path to the command (`./spinnin`). You can also solve the problem by adding the path to the directory holding `spinnin` to the `PATH` list, or by adding the current directory to the `PATH`. You'll learn about this and more in Chapter 18. You'll also learn considerably more about paths in the immediately following section, covering the file system and basic navigation.

Occasionally, you might do something that leaves your shell in an apparently unusable state. Frequently, this is because you've started a process that is expecting input from you. There are several key combinations you can try that might help you regain control of your shell:

- **Ctrl+D**—This key combination sends an End Of Form (`EOF`) signal to the current process, usually terminating input. If the process is designed to continuously accept data until reaching the EOF, sending it this key combination will cause it to stop accepting input and go about whatever it was designed to do next.

Caution

Be careful with Ctrl+D. If you're not currently running a process in the shell, you'll send the `EOF` to the shell itself, and it will summarily stop accepting input.

- **Ctrl+Z**—This key combination suspends the current foreground process (more on foreground and background processes in the "Process Management" section of Chapter 14, "Advanced Shell Concepts and Commands"). The process won't continue to run; it will simply sit there in suspended animation until you either close the shell (perhaps by logging out), thereby killing it, or until you re-enable it using one of the techniques discussed in "Process Management."

- **Ctrl+C**—This key combination is the Unix break character. This key combination usually (you can configure the behavior) kills the current process and returns you to the shell prompt.

Don't be afraid to test the commands shown in this book. The system can do a pretty good job of protecting itself from anything a normal user can type, and we'll be sure to place conspicuous warnings with any commands that are capable of causing mischief in any case. With a little experimenting, we think you'll find that you can do a surprising number of things with only a few keystrokes.

The Online Manual Pages

The very first command that you should familiarize yourself with is the `man` (manual) command. All good Unix systems provide an online collection of manual pages that detail almost every command available in the system. OS X is no exception. Simply type `man` *`<commandname>`* at any shell prompt, and if there is a manual page documenting the command, it will be shown to you. For example, to see the man pages for the `time` command (which, coincidentally, tells you what time it is), you could type

```
[localhost:~] miwa% man time

    TIME(1)                   System Reference Manual                  TIME(1)

    NAME
         time - time command execution

    SYNOPSIS
         time [-lp] utility

    DESCRIPTION
     The time utility executes and times utility. After the utility finishes,
     time writes the total time elapsed, the time consumed by system overhead,
     and the time used to execute utility to the standard error stream. Times
     are reported in seconds.

         Available options:

         -l      The contents of the rusage structure are printed.
         -p      The output is formatted as specified by .

       The csh(1) has its own and syntactically different builtin version of .
       The utility described here is available as /usr/bin/time to csh users.

    DIAGNOSTICS
         The time utility shall exit with one of the following values:

         1-125   An error occurred in the time utility.
```

```
     126     The utility was found but could not be invoked.
     127     The utility could not be found.

     Otherwise, the exit status of time shall be that of utility.

SEE ALSO
     csh(1),  getrusage(2)

FILES
     /usr/include/sys/resource.h
/usr/share/man/cat1/time.0 (81%)
```

Tip

If your terminal shows you a line that says `more` at the bottom of the window, or a pathname and a percentage figure, it means that there is more output to be seen. Simply press the spacebar and the next page of output will scroll into view.

It is not unusual for Unix systems to be shipped with the man pages unformatted to conserve space, and OS X is no exception. Formatting the pages consumes a bit of disk space, but today's disk storage is cheap, and you get not only the benefit of faster display, but also a searchable man page system. To format your man pages, follow these instructions, and don't worry about the warning messages that you see. So long as the warning messages look like what is shown here, everything is working okay.

```
 [localhost:~] joray% su
Password:
[localhost:/Users/joray] root# catman /usr/share/man/man1

     catman: can't open /usr/share/man/man/: No such file or directory
     catman: can't open /usr/share/man/manu: No such file or directory
     catman: can't open /usr/share/man/mans: No such file or directory
     .
     <lots of errors deleted>
     .
     catman: can't open /usr/share/man/manm: No such file or directory
     catman: can't open /usr/share/man/mana: No such file or directory
     catman: can't open /usr/share/man/mann: No such file or directory
     mkdir /usr/share/man/cat1
     nroff -mandoc /usr/share/man/man1/a2p.1 > /usr/share/man/cat1/a2p.0
     nroff -mandoc /usr/share/man/man1/addftinfo.1 > cat1/addftinfo.0
     nroff -mandoc /usr/share/man/man1/afmtodit.1 > cat1/afmtodit.0
     .
     <lots of output nroff lines>
     .
```

```
    nroff -mandoc /usr/share/man/man1/zshmisc.1 > cat1/zshmisc.0
    nroff -mandoc /usr/share/man/man1/zshoptions.1 > cat1/zshoptions.0
    nroff -mandoc /usr/share/man/man1/zshparam.1 > cat1/zshparam.0
    nroff -mandoc /usr/share/man/man1/zshzle.1 > /usr/share/man/cat1/zshzle.0
    /usr/libexec/makewhatis /usr/share/man
[localhost:/Users/joray] root#
```

Next, run catman for each of the directories man4, man5, man6, man7, and man8 like so:

```
[localhost:/Users/joray] root# catman /usr/share/man/man4
     .
     .
     .
[localhost:/Users/joray] root# catman /usr/share/man/man5
     .
     .
     .
[localhost:/Users/joray] root# catman /usr/share/man/man6
     .
     .
     .
[localhost:/Users/joray] root# catman /usr/share/man/man7
     .
     .
     .
[localhost:/Users/joray] root# catman /usr/share/man/man8
     .
     .
     .
```

Note

For the inquisitive, the su command used at the beginning of the examples here is the switch user command. If you have enabled the root account, the su command allows you to switch to an even more powerful administrative user. We don't recommend that you spend much time in an su-ed shell because you can do a lot of damage in this mode, but it's required for doing some sorts of maintenance like this. The catman command uncompresses, indexes, and formats the contents of the compressed man page data files.

Now that you've formatted your man pages, you can use the `-k` option to `man`. (This is equivalent to the `apropos` command; wherever you see `man -k`, you can substitute `apropos`, if that's easier for you to remember.) This option searches the man pages for pages with keywords matching what you've entered. For example, if you'd like to know which man pages might have information on the subject of `time`, you could issue a `man` command like this:

```
man -k time

Benchmark(3)              - benchmark running times of Perl code
CPAN::FirstTime(3), s-1CPAN:s0 - Util for s-1CPAN:s0:Config file Initialization
Net::Time(3)              - time and daytime network client interface
TCL_MEM_DEBUG(3)         - Compile-time flag to enable Tcl memory debugging
.
.
.
sleep(1)                  - suspend execution for an interval of time
strftime(3)               - format date and time
time(1)                   - time command execution
time(3)                   - get time of day
time2posix(3), posix2time(3) - convert seconds since the Epoch
times(3)                  - process times
timezone(3)               - return the timezone abbreviation
touch(1)                  - change file access and modification times
tzfile(5)                 - time zone information
tzset(3)                  - initialize time conversion information
ualarm(3)                 - schedule signal after specified time
uptime(1)                 - show how long system has been running
utime(3)                  - set file times
utimes(2)                 - set file access and modification times
vtimes(3)                 - get information about resource utilization
zdump(8)                  - time zone dumper
zic(8)                    - time zone compiler
```

This command lists each of the man pages that the system knows about that match the keyword (in this case, `time`) that you've requested.

Finally, it's important to know that the man page system has several sections into which the content is divided. Because of this, there might be commands that have multiple man pages, each in a different section. The system is divided into sections roughly segregated into the following topics:

- `Man1`—Typical user commands. Documentation of commands that can be executed by the normal user at the command line.
- `Man2`—System calls. Documentation of routines internal to the system that programmers can use in programs.

- `Man3`—User-level library calls. Documentation of C and other library functions for programmers.
- `Man4`—Device drivers, protocols, and network interfaces. Documentation of the internals of hardware support and software APIs for these items.
- `Man5`—File formats. Documentation of file format details for both system control files and certain program data files.
- `Man6`—Games and demos. Documentation for amusement software.
- `Man7`—Miscellaneous. Various tables of useful information, such as ASCII tables.
- `Man8`—Maintenance commands. Documentation for maintenance and system administration commands.

Caution

The segregation of the man pages into the directories `Man1`–`Man8` is not absolute. Third-party software providers have a bad habit of breaking convention and placing their man pages in inappropriate sections.

If you look at the earlier listing for the `man -k time` command, you will notice that each topic listed includes a number or letter in parentheses after the name of the topic. This is the man page section in which the item occurs.

Note

Your system might not show exactly these same items. The available man pages will depend on whether you've installed the developer toolkit, and on any other software that is installed on the system. If the following examples using manual section 3 do not work for you, read through them now, and try them again after you've installed the developer tools in Chapter 16, "Command-Line Software Installation." We're including them here because we expect that many users will have "installed ahead," or are reading this book while trying to learn on a completely configured machine at work or school. If you're following along in a from-the-ground-up installation, bookmark this section on man pages, and try it out again after finishing the developer tools install in the next chapter.

To look at man pages that are in other sections of the manual, specify the numeric or character identifier for the section between the `man` command and the item you want to look up. For example, the system includes man pages for both the `time` command and the `time()` C library function. `man time` will default to showing you the man page for the command line–related item, if one exists, so both `man time` and `man 1 time` will show you the man page for the `time` command:

```
[localhost:~] joray% man 1 time

     TIME(1)                  System Reference Manual                  TIME(1)

     NAME
          time - time command execution

     SYNOPSIS
          time [-lp] utility

     DESCRIPTION
      The time utility executes and times utility. After the utility finishes,
      time writes the total time elapsed, the time consumed by system overhead,
      and the time used to execute utility to the standard error stream.  Times
      are reported in seconds.

          Available options:

          -l      The contents of the rusage structure are printed.

          -p      The output is formatted as specified by .

        The csh(1) has its own and syntactically different builtin version of .
        The utility described here is available as /usr/bin/time to csh users.

     DIAGNOSTICS
          The time utility shall exit with one of the following values:

          1-125   An error occurred in the time utility.

          126     The utility was found but could not be invoked.

          127     The utility could not be found.

     /usr/share/man/cat1/time.0 (70%)
```

If you want to know about the C library function named `time()`, however, you will need to look in the program-functions-related section of the man pages, using `man 3 time` as your command:

```
[localhost:~] joray% man 3 time
```

```
TIME(3)                System Programmer's Manual                TIME(3)

NAME
     time - get time of day

SYNOPSIS
     #include <time.h>

     time_t
     time(time_t *tloc)

DESCRIPTION
 The time() function returns the value of time in seconds since 0 hours, 0
 minutes, 0 seconds, January 1, 1970, Coordinated Universal Time.

 A copy of the time value may be saved to the area indicated by the point-
  er tloc. If tloc is a NULL pointer, no value is stored.

 Upon successful completion, time() returns the value of time.  Otherwise
 a value of ((time_t) -1) is returned and the global variable errno is set
 to indicate the error.

ERRORS
     The following error codes may be set in errno:

     [EFAULT]      An argument address referenced invalid memory.

SEE ALSO
     gettimeofday(2),  ctime(3)

HISTORY
     A time() function appeared in Version 6 AT&T UNIX.
/usr/share/man/cat3/time.0 (93%)
```

Note

If you add any software to the system, it may place man pages into the system `man` directories (located in `/usr/share/man` on OS X), or into the local `man` directories (located in either `/opt/man` or `/usr/local/man`, or both). If you do this, you will need to rebuild the `catman` database before the new manual pages will show up when you use the `man -k` option.

The `man` system is self-documenting, of course, so if you would like to read further about the `man` command, simply type `man man`.

The command documentation table for `man` is shown in Table 12.3.

TABLE 12.3 The command documentation table for `man`

`man`	Displays online manual pages.
`man [-achw] [-C <file>] [-M <path>] [-m <path>] [<section>] <name1> <name2> ...`	
`man [-M <path>] [-m <path>] -k <keyword1> <keyword2> ...`	
`-a`	Displays all the manual pages for a specified section and name combination. (The default is to display only the first page found.)
`-c`	Copies the manual page to the standard output instead of using `more(1)` for pagination.
`-h`	Displays the `SYNOPSIS` lines of the requested manual pages.
`-w`	Lists the pathnames of manual pages that would be displayed for the specified section and name combination.
`-C` *<file>*	Uses the specified file instead of the default configuration file. This allows users to configure their own manual environment. See `man.conf(5)` for more details.
`-M` *<path>*	Overrides the list of standard directories where `man` searches for manual pages. The path specified must be a colon-separated list of directories. The search path may also be specified by the `MANPATH` environment variable.
`-m` *<path>*	Adds to the list of standard search directories. The path specified must be a colon-separated list of directories. These directories are searched before the standard list or directories specified by `-M` or `MANPATH`.
`-k` *<keyword>*	Displays a list of manual pages that contain the *<keyword>*.

The optional *<section>* argument restricts `man`'s search to the specified section.

The Unix File System

To the novice Unix user—especially one coming from a GUI environment as nice as the Mac's—venturing into the Unix file system will probably feel like a journey back to the Stone Age. Files upon files, nothing to indicate what any of them do, and not a friendly icon in sight. Although the file system might initially appear cryptic and primitive, you will find that with experience, it actually affords you considerable sophistication and control. This sophistication comes from the ability to combine the functions of many small programs into larger programs with arbitrarily complex functions.

Before the use of most Unix commands will make sense, you'll need to understand a few things about the design of the Unix file system. The Mac OS X HFS+ file system doesn't strictly adhere to the model that most Unixes use, but from the point of view of the BSD subsystem, it functions in an analogous manner. You'll find a number of differences between the way Unix thinks of files, and what you're probably used to, but after you get used to them, you'll probably find these differences are to your liking.

Basic Unix File Principles

Unix file systems have a single root directory. Unlike Macintosh file systems with their multiple drive icons on the desktop, and Windows machines with their ABCs, Unix file systems have only a single top-level designator for the file system. This is the root directory named `/`. Unix considers all its files to belong to a tree-shaped structure, with the root directory at its base and files as the leaves. Directories are the branching points between the branches. Unix trees are upside down with respect to real trees, as the root directory is at the top of the tree. Any directory can contain files and other directories.

Note

The term *root* is used for multiple meanings in Unix. The `root` user is the most authoritative user of the system, with essentially absolute control over any process or configuration. The root of the file system is the top directory of the file system, beneath which all other files and directories occur.

Every file in the Unix file system has a unique and unambiguous name that points to it. This complete name is known as the "full path" to the file, and can be specified from any directory in the file system to indicate any file in the file system. The full path to a file always starts with the root directory, and ends in the filename, indicating directory names along the way, separated by the separator character `/`. A full path may be thought of as the shortest list of directories that must be traversed from the root to reach the file. A file with the full path `/home/wizbot/spin/spinnin` is named `spinnin`, and is located in the directory `spin`, which is located in the directory `wizbot`, which is located in the directory `home`, which is located in the root directory `/`.

Files have both full paths and relative paths. A *relative path* is a path from the current directory, instead of from the root directory. There are two special relative directory names. One of these is `.`, which indicates the current directory; the other is `..`, which indicates the directory that is the parent of this directory. For example, assume that there is a directory named `spun` in the same directory as the directory named `spin` in the earlier path (it would have a full path of `/home/wizbot/spun`). If we are in the directory `spun` and want to specify the relative path to `spinnin`, we can do so with the relative path `../spin/spinnin`.

Tip

Full paths always start with `/`; relative paths never do.

Not only don't you have multiple drives at the top level of the system, you, as the user, don't need to know what drives are where. Additional drives (or, more properly, *partitions*) appear as directories, and can be mounted at any point in the file system to appear as an extended branch in the system. Sound strange? After a while it won't. In one of the nice feats of Unix abstraction, the system removes from the user's sphere of concern what hardware devices actually exist, and where they are or how they're connected. After you get used to this system, you'll see that it makes good sense. So long as you can uniquely identify a file by name in the file system, why would you care which spinning chunk of metal it lives on? This system has additional nice features. If you find one day that you've run out of space to put files in some particular location, you can simply add a drive to the system and mount it where you need space. There's no need to reconfigure things or move files around, because the additional space will simply appear as new space in whatever directory you mount it as.

As a matter of fact, you don't even need to know what country your files physically reside in. Again, Unix abstraction comes into play, and a remote file server is mounted as a directory under the local file system just like additional physical storage is. From your point of view, a remote file server is just another directory; the only difference between accessing files on it and on local storage is the possible network delay associated with transporting the files.

Regardless of whether you know where your files actually are, the shell, as previously mentioned, is always somewhere in the file system structure.

Also as previously mentioned, Unix is a case-sensitive system, and Unix filenames are case sensitive from the command line. From OS X, this isn't necessarily the case (depending on which base disk format you chose for your installation), but when you're working from the command line, remember that what you type must have the correct capitalization.

A file has three attributes that control who can access the file. These attributes control access at the level of whether the file can be read, written to, and executed. Additionally, these attributes can be specified separately for the user who owns the file, a group of selected users, and everybody on the system. These attributes can be set to any combination of values, although some combinations do not make much sense. For example, you would expect an application to be executable, a configuration file for a program to be readable, and something like your daily schedule to be both readable and writeable. Unix, however, will do whatever you tell it to with the file permissions. If you make your daily schedule executable, Unix will do its best to execute it, which most likely will result in an error message and no damage done. If you tell Unix that an application is writeable, it will be happy to let you edit it in a word processor, which will probably make the application useless. We'll cover file permissions in more detail later in the "Introduction to File Permissions" section of Chapter 14.

Everything in the file system has an owner. Every file and directory in the Unix file system has auxiliary information attached to it that specifies the individual user who owns it, and also the group of users that owns it. Depending on the permissions, this user or group of users control access to the file and can set its permissions.

Each user has a home directory. This is one special directory in the file system that is owned by the user, and is used to contain configuration files and other content that is specific to the user. From the point of view of the file system, the user's home directory is no different than any other directory, but it is significant in that it is the directory where you start when you open a terminal and shell on the system. To make things simpler for you, Unix doesn't require that you remember the path to your directory; it can always be specified by the special full path `~<username>`.

Keep these basic principles in mind when reading about the commands to work within the file system. We'll cover some of them in more detail later in this chapter, but it will help you to have a basic understanding of them as we move to the explanations and examples of commands.

Note

When discussing your interaction with the shell, we'll frequently use *you* interchangeably with *the shell*. It's much shorter to write *in the directory where you type the command* than *in the current working directory of the shell that you're interacting with when you type the command.*

Basic File System Navigation

The most basic commands for dealing with the Unix file system are those for moving around the file system (changing that "somewhere" that the shell always is), and for listing the contents of directories (finding out what's in the same location as the shell or in some other directory). Before you start moving around, however, it's a good idea to be able to find out where you are.

Where Are You? pwd

The pwd command (print working directory) prints the full path to the current working directory—the location where you "are" at the moment in this particular shell.

```
[localhost:~] nermal% pwd
     /Users/nermal
```

The command documentation table for pwd is as shown in Table 12.4.

TABLE 12.4 The Command Documentation Table for pwd

pwd	Prints current working directory
pwd [-L|P]	
-L	Prints the logical path to the current working directory, as defined by the shell in the environment variable PWD.
-P	Default. Prints the physical path to the current working directory, with symbolic links resolved.

Listing Files: ls

The ls command lists files in the directory where you currently are. More properly, the ls command will list files anywhere in the file system, presuming you have permissions with which to do so. If you don't specify any other directory for it to list, ls defaults to listing the files in the current working directory.

For example, to list the files in the current working directory, simply type ls.

```
[localhost:~] nermal% cd /
[localhost:/] nermal% pwd
     /
[localhost:/] nermal% ls
     AppleShare PDS          Network                  etc
```

```
Applications                System                    mach
Applications (Mac OS 9)     System Folder             mach.sym
Cleanup At Startup          TheFindByContentFolder    mach_kernel
Desktop DB                  TheVolumeSettingsFolder   private
Desktop DF                  Trash                     sbin
Desktop Folder              Users                     tmp
Developer                   Volumes                   usr
Documents                   bin                       var
Late Breaking News          cores                     vol.tar
Library                     dev                       ???T+???Blank1
```

This example shows that the directory `/` contains 33 things. From this listing, you can't tell which of those things are directories and which of those things are files.

There's really no need to issue the `pwd` command as shown in the preceding example. It's been included here for the sake of clarity. If you already know where you are in the file system, there's no need to ask the computer to tell you.

Note

Many of the command listings shown here are based on a user account we've created for demo purposes, with the username `nermal`. You're welcome to use your own account instead of `nermal` for the examples.

If you would like to list the files in a directory other than the one that you are currently in, simply specify the path to the directory after the `ls` command. The path to specify can be either a relative or an absolute path. For example, to list the files in a directory named `/Users/nermal/` if you're in the directory `/Users/`, simply type `ls nermal/`.

```
[localhost:/] nermal% cd /Users/
[localhost:/Users] nermal% ls

     Shared joray  miwa   nermal

[localhost:/Users] nermal% ls nermal/

     Desktop                  Network Trash Folder      chown-output
     Documents                Pictures                  myfile
     Library                  Public                    output-sample6
     Movies                   Sites                     su-output
     Music                    TheVolumeSettingsFolder   typescripts
```

You could also produce this same output by using the absolute path. Instead of the relative path `nermal/` from the current directory `/Users/`, you could look explicitly in `/Users/nermal/`:

```
[localhost:/] nermal% cd /Users/
[localhost:/Users] nermal% ls
```

```
     Shared joray  miwa   nermal
[localhost:/Users] nermal% ls /Users/nermal/
     Desktop                   Network Trash Folder     chown-output
     Documents                 Pictures                 myfile
     Library                   Public                   output-sample6
     Movies                    Sites                    su-output
     Music                     TheVolumeSettingsFolder  typescripts
```

Or, if you're in the directory `/Users/nermal/Documents/` and would like to list the files in the directory that is the parent of this directory (`/Users/nermal/`), you can type `ls ../`.

```
[localhost:/Users] nermal% cd /Users/nermal/Documents
[localhost:~/Documents] nermal% ls ../
     Desktop                   Network Trash Folder     chown-output
     Documents                 Pictures                 myfile
     Library                   Public                   output-sample6
     Movies                    Sites                    su-output
     Music                     TheVolumeSettingsFolder  typescripts
```

Likewise, if you want to list the contents of `/Users/nermal/typescripts/`, and you're in `/Users/nermal/Documents/`, you could type

```
[localhost:/Users] nermal% cd /Users/nermal/Documents
[localhost:~/Documents] nermal% ls ../typescripts/
     typescript         typescript-copy-2   typescript2         typescript5
     typescript-copy    typescript-copy-3   typescript4
```

Like most Unix commands, the `ls` command has a plethora of options from which to choose. These options allow you to specify which files you want to list and what information you want to list about them. Table 12.5 shows the available options and outputs for `ls`.

TABLE 12.5 The Command Documentation Table for `ls`

`ls`	Lists files or directory contents.
`ls [-ACFLRSTWadfgilnoqrsktcux1] <file1> <file2> ...`	
`ls [-ACFLRSTWadfgilnoqrsktcux1]`	
`-A`	Lists all entries except for "`.`" and "`..`". Always set for super user.
`-C`	Forces multi-column output. This is the Default when output is to a terminal.
`-F`	Displays a symbol, if applicable, after each file to denote the following: slash (`/`) for a directory; asterisk (`*`) for an executable; an at sign (`@`) for a symbolic link; a percent sign (`%`) for a whiteout; an equal sign (`=`) for a socket; a vertical bar (`|`) for a FIFO.

TABLE 12.5 continued

`-L`	If the argument is a symbolic link, the file or directory the link references rather than the link itself is displayed.
`-R`	Recursively lists subdirectories.
`-S`	Sorts by size, largest file first.
`-T`	Displays complete time information, including month, day, hour, minute, second, and year.
`-W`	Displays whiteouts.
`-a`	Lists all files in the directory, including files whose names begin with a dot (`.`).
`-d`	If the argument is a directory, it is listed as a plain file, rather than listing its contents. If the argument is a symbolic link, its link information is not displayed.
`-f`	Does not sort output.
`-g`	Does nothing. Is kept for compatibility with older versions of `ls`.
`-i`	Lists the argument's serial number (inode number) .
`-l`	Lists in long format. Displays file mode, number of links, owner name, group name, size of the file in bytes, date and time file was last modified, and the file. If displayed to a terminal, the first line of output is the total number of 512-byte blocks used by the files in the directory.
`-n`	Displays user and group ID as numbers rather than names in a long (`-l`) output.
`-o`	Includes file flags in a long (`-l`) output.
`-q`	Forces printing of non-graphic characters in filenames as character `?`. This is the default when output is to a terminal.
`-r`	Reverses sort order to reverse alphabetic order; smallest first or oldest first, as appropriate.
`-s`	Displays file size in 512-byte blocks, where partial units are rounded up to the next integer value. If the output is to a terminal, first line displayed is the total number of 512-byte blocks used by files in the directory.
`-k`	Modifies the `-s` option to report sizes in kilobytes.
`-t`	Sorts by time modified (most recently modified first) before sorting in alphabetic order.
`-c`	Uses time when file status was last changed for sorting (`-t`) or printing (`-l`).

TABLE 12.5 continued

`-u`	Uses time of last access for sorting (`-t`) or printing (`-l`).
`-x`	Forces multi-column output sorted across the page rather than down the page.
`-v`	Forces unedited printing of non-graphic characters. This is the default when output is not to a terminal.
`-1`	Forces output to one entry per line. This is the default when output is not to a terminal.
`-1`, `-C`, `-l`, and `-x` options override each other. The last one specified determines the format used.	
`-c` and `-u` options override each other. The last one specified determines the file time used.	

You can use an `ls` command like this to produce a listing that shows the contents of the root directory and indicates the following for each file (or directory): who the owner of the file is, what the group that the file belongs to is, as well as the size of files.

```
[localhost:/] nermal% ls -l

    total 13232
    -rwxrwxrwx   1 root  wheel    106496 Apr 20 14:59 AppleShare PDS
    drwxrwxrwx  25 root  admin       806 Apr 18 11:05 Applications
    drwxrwxrwx  18 root  wheel       568 Apr 20 14:54 Applications (Mac OS 9)
    drwxrwxrwx   2 root  wheel       264 Apr  6 12:24 Cleanup At Startup
    -rwxrwxrwx   1 root  wheel    212992 Apr 20 14:59 Desktop DB
    -rwxrwxrwx   1 root  wheel   1432466 Apr 20 14:57 Desktop DF
    drwxrwxrwx   6 root  staff       264 Apr  4 11:51 Desktop Folder
    drwxrwxr-x  12 root  admin       364 Mar  1 20:29 Developer
    drwxrwxrwx   6 root  wheel       264 Apr  4 14:20 Documents
    -rwxrwxrwx   1 root  wheel         0 Apr  4 14:11 Late Breaking News
    drwxrwxr-x  21 root  admin       670 Apr 18 11:04 Library
    drwxr-xr-x   6 root  wheel       264 Apr  4 12:47 Network
    drwxr-xr-x   3 root  wheel        58 Apr 12 00:51 System
    drwxrwxrwx  40 root  wheel      1316 Apr 20 14:50 System Folder
    drwxrwxrwx   2 root  wheel       264 Mar 23 14:59 TheFindByContentFolder
    drwxrwxrwx   4 root  wheel       264 Mar 23 14:46 TheVolumeSettingsFolder
    drwxrwxrwx   2 root  wheel       264 Apr 20 14:58 Trash
    drwxr-xr-x   6 root  wheel       160 Apr 16 12:37 Users
    drwxrwxrwt   6 root  wheel       264 Apr 20 15:00 Volumes
    drwxr-xr-x  33 root  wheel      1078 Apr 16 09:40 bin
    lrwxrwxr-t   1 root  admin        13 Apr 20 15:00 cores -> private/cores
    dr-xr-xr-x   2 root  wheel       512 Apr 20 15:00 dev
    lrwxrwxr-t   1 root  admin        11 Apr 20 15:00 etc -> private/etc
    lrwxrwxr-t   1 root  admin         9 Apr 20 15:00 mach -> /mach.sym
    -r--r--r--   1 root  admin    652352 Apr 20 15:00 mach.sym
    -rw-r--r--   1 root  wheel   4039744 Mar 30 23:46 mach_kernel
    drwxr-xr-x   7 root  wheel       264 Apr 20 15:00 private
```

```
drwxr-xr-x  56 root  wheel      1860 Apr 16 09:41 sbin
lrwxrwxr-t   1 root  admin        11 Apr 20 15:00 tmp -> private/tmp
drwxr-xr-x  10 root  wheel       296 Apr 12 14:45 usr
lrwxrwxr-t   1 root  admin        11 Apr 20 15:00 var -> private/var
-rw-r--r--   1 root  admin     10240 Apr 16 09:35 vol.tar
-rwxrwxrwx   1 root  wheel    221696 Apr  4 13:57 ???T+???Blank1
```

The output might look a little confusing at first, but it breaks down into parts that are easy to understand.

The first line contains information telling you the total sum for all the file sizes contained in the directory. The total is in 512-byte blocks.

Next come lines detailing the contents of the directory, one file or directory listed per line.

At the beginning of each line are 10 characters. These indicate the values of 10 flags that belong to the file. The first flag indicates whether the file is a directory, a symbolic link (Unix for *alias*), or just a plain normal file. If the first flag is a `d`, the indicated item is a directory. If it is an `l`, the item is a link. If it is only a `-`, the item is a file. Next is a repeating a set of three values `r`, `w`, and `x` repeated three times. These specify the read flag, the write flag, and the execute flag for each user who owns the file, the group that owns the file, and all other users on the system. If a `-` is shown instead of an `r`, `w`, or `x`, the user, the group, or everybody on the system is not allowed to perform whatever action—read, write, or execute—that the flag is missing for.

Shortly following the 10 flag characters, each line contains an entry indicating the user who owns the file; in this case, `root` owns many of the files shown.

Following the information indicating the owner of the file is another entry indicating the group that owns the file. Group ownership of a file is not as stringent as the user ownership of a file. The individual owner of a file is the only user allowed to modify the permissions of a file. So, although a user who belongs to the group that owns the file may be able to write to the file, he or she cannot modify the flags indicating what the permissions are for the file.

Next is an entry indicating the size of the file in bytes. Entries for files indicate the full size of the file on disk. Entries for directories indicate another value that is loosely associated with the number of entries that the directory contains.

Following the size of the file comes an entry indicating the date of the most recent modification of the file. If the file was modified within the last year, the date and time are given; otherwise, the month, day, and year are given.

Finally, each entry lists the filename. Note that the filenames are identical to the name shown by the use of `ls` from our very first example, with the exception of `core`, `etc`, `tmp`, `mach`, and `var`. Each of these entries is followed by an odd arrow that points to a path. Note the file type for these is indicated by `ls` as a symbolic link. Just as a Mac OS alias points to a file or directory in another location, a symbolic link also points to a file or directory in another location. The information shown following the arrow is the path to which each particular entry points.

To prevent clutter, the `ls` command, by default, will not show certain files and directories that are expected to be configuration files or to contain maintenance or control information. Specifically, files or directories whose names begin with a dot (`.`) are not shown. Still, if you want to see them, there is an `ls` option that will allow this. If you want to see absolutely everything in the directory, add the `-a` option to the `ls` command; for example, `ls -la`.

```
[localhost:/] nermal% ls -al
    total 13264
    drwxrwxr-t  39 root  admin     1282 Apr 20 15:00 .
    drwxrwxr-t  39 root  admin     1282 Apr 20 15:00 ..
    -rwxrwxrwx   1 root  admin     8208 Apr 18 11:05 .DS_Store
    d-wx-wx-wx   2 root  admin      264 Apr  4 12:20 .Trashes
    -r--r--r--   1 root  wheel      142 Feb 25 03:05 .hidden
    dr--r--r--   2 root  wheel      224 Apr 20 15:00 .vol
    -rwxrwxrwx   1 root  wheel   106496 Apr 20 14:59 AppleShare PDS
    drwxrwxrwx  25 root  admin      806 Apr 18 11:05 Applications
    drwxrwxrwx  18 root  wheel      568 Apr 20 14:54 Applications (Mac OS 9)
    drwxrwxrwx   2 root  wheel      264 Apr  6 12:24 Cleanup At Startup
    -rwxrwxrwx   1 root  wheel   212992 Apr 20 14:59 Desktop DB
    -rwxrwxrwx   1 root  wheel  1432466 Apr 20 14:57 Desktop DF
    drwxrwxrwx   6 root  staff      264 Apr  4 11:51 Desktop Folder
    drwxrwxr-x  12 root  admin      364 Mar  1 20:29 Developer
    drwxrwxrwx   6 root  wheel      264 Apr  4 14:20 Documents
    -rwxrwxrwx   1 root  wheel        0 Apr  4 14:11 Late Breaking News
    drwxrwxr-x  21 root  admin      670 Apr 18 11:04 Library
    drwxr-xr-x   6 root  wheel      264 Apr  4 12:47 Network
    drwxr-xr-x   3 root  wheel       58 Apr 12 00:51 System
    drwxrwxrwx  40 root  wheel     1316 Apr 20 14:50 System Folder
    drwxrwxrwx   2 root  wheel      264 Mar 23 14:59 TheFindByContentFolder
    drwxrwxrwx   4 root  wheel      264 Mar 23 14:46 TheVolumeSettingsFolder
    drwxrwxrwx   2 root  wheel      264 Apr 20 14:58 Trash
    drwxr-xr-x   6 root  wheel      160 Apr 16 12:37 Users
    drwxrwxrwt   6 root  wheel      264 Apr 20 15:00 Volumes
    drwxr-xr-x  33 root  wheel     1078 Apr 16 09:40 bin
    lrwxrwxr-t   1 root  admin       13 Apr 20 15:00 cores -> private/cores
    dr-xr-xr-x   2 root  wheel      512 Apr 20 15:00 dev
    lrwxrwxr-t   1 root  admin       11 Apr 20 15:00 etc -> private/etc
    lrwxrwxr-t   1 root  admin        9 Apr 20 15:00 mach -> /mach.sym
```

```
-r--r--r--   1 root  admin   652352 Apr 20 15:00 mach.sym
-rw-r--r--   1 root  wheel  4039744 Mar 30 23:46 mach_kernel
drwxr-xr-x   7 root  wheel      264 Apr 20 15:00 private
drwxr-xr-x  56 root  wheel     1860 Apr 16 09:41 sbin
lrwxrwxr-t   1 root  admin       11 Apr 20 15:00 tmp -> private/tmp
drwxr-xr-x  10 root  wheel      296 Apr 12 14:45 usr
lrwxrwxr-t   1 root  admin       11 Apr 20 15:00 var -> private/var
-rw-r--r--   1 root  admin    10240 Apr 16 09:35 vol.tar
-rwxrwxrwx   1 root  wheel   221696 Apr  4 13:57 ???T+???Blank1
```

Moving Around the File System: cd, pushd, popd

Now that you know how to determine where you are in the file system and how to list the files in a particular location, it's time to learn how to change your location. Unix provides two primary mechanisms by which you can do this. The first of these is the `cd` (change directory) command. This command does exactly what you would expect from its name: It changes your location in the file system to whatever location you ask it. If you would like to change the current working directory from `/var` to `/var/log/`, you can type `cd /var/log/`. Because `cd`, like most Unix commands, accepts either relative or absolute paths, you can also make this change by typing `cd log/`, as shown here:

```
[localhost:/var] nermal% cd /var/log

[localhost:/var/log] nermal%

[localhost:/var] nermal% cd log

[localhost:/var/log] nermal%
```

Tip

Remember that you can always use ~ as a quick absolute path to your home directory. You can also use ~ to construct absolute paths to directories or files that are beneath your home directory. If you want to change into the directory named `fizbin` that is located in your home directory, you can use the `cd` command `cd ~/fizbin`.

The `cd` command can also be used without an argument, in which case it will assume that you want to go to your home directory, and will take you to that location:

```
[localhost:/var/log] nermal% cd

[localhost:~] nermal%
```

The command documentation table for `cd` is shown in Table 12.6.

TABLE 12.6 The Command Documentation Table for cd

cd	Changes working directory
cd <directory>	
cd	
<directory> is an absolute or relative pathname. The interpretation of the relative pathname depends on the CDPATH environment variable.	
The following environment variables affect the execution of cd:	
HOME	If cd is invoked without any arguments and the $HOME exists, $HOME becomes the new working directory.
CDPATH	If *<directory>* does not begin with /, ., or .., cd searches for the directory relative to each directory named in CDPATH variable, in the order listed. If the new working directory is derived from $CDPATH, it is printed to standard output.

The tcsh shell (similar to most others) also supports a considerably more powerful way of navigating through the file system. This method, accessed through the pushd and popd commands, makes use of a computer structure called a *stack*. Using a stack allows you to go to another location, and return to wherever you came from, without needing to remember the location and cd back.

> **Note**
>
> Computer scientists use the term *stack* as a friendly term for a data structure also known as a Last In, First Out (LIFO) structure. A classical LIFO structure has one place into which data can be put or retrieved from the structure. If you put one piece of data into the structure, and then put in a second, you can't get the first back out again until you remove the second. See? The last thing you put in must be the first thing you take out. It's also called a stack because it works just like a stack of plates at a cafeteria. The last plate put on the stack (the one at the top of the stack) is the one that you take off first.

The pushd and popd commands work in concert. pushd puts the current directory on the stack, and takes you to whatever directory you tell it to. popd takes you to whatever directory is on top of the stack, and removes that directory from the stack.

For example, if you're in /var/tmp/ and you'd like to temporarily change to the directory /etc/httpd/, you could do so by issuing the following set of commands:

```
[localhost:/var/tmp] nermal% cd /var/tmp
[localhost:/var/tmp] nermal% pwd

     /private/var/tmp

[localhost:/var/tmp] nermal% cd /etc/httpd
[localhost:/etc/httpd] nermal% pwd

     /private/etc/httpd

[localhost:/etc/httpd] nermal% cd /var/tmp
[localhost:/var/tmp] nermal% pwd

     /private/var/tmp
```


Note

Note that pwd doesn't respond with the same information that we cded to. This is because Apple has put some of the normal Unix directories in weird places, and pulled some trickery to get them to appear as though they're where they should be. This is a compromise forced on the system because it must be able to co-exist with Mac OS on the same drive. If you'd like to see pwd return the same information as where you cded to, use pwd -L.

But moving around like this is relatively inefficient, and if you do much in directory /etc/httpd/ before deciding to return, you might forget where it was that you'd come from. Instead, you might want to use the pushd and popd commands. To do the same thing using them, you could type

```
[localhost:/var/tmp] nermal% cd /var/tmp
[localhost:/var/tmp] nermal% pwd -L

     /var/tmp

[localhost:/var/tmp] nermal% pushd /etc/httpd

     /etc/httpd /var/tmp

[localhost:/etc/httpd] nermal% pwd -L

     /etc/httpd

[localhost:/etc/httpd] nermal% popd

     /var/tmp

[localhost:/var/tmp] nermal% pwd -L

     /var/tmp
```

Because the stack of directories is arbitrarily deep, you can push multiple items on before you start popping them off. For example:

```
[localhost:/var/tmp] nermal% cd /var/tmp
[localhost:/var/tmp] nermal% pushd /etc/httpd

      /etc/httpd /var/tmp

[localhost:/etc/httpd] nermal% pwd -L

      /etc/httpd

[localhost:/etc/httpd] nermal% pushd /Users

      /Users /etc/httpd /var/tmp

[localhost:/Users] nermal% pwd -L

      /Users

[localhost:/Users] nermal% popd

      /etc/httpd /var/tmp

[localhost:/etc/httpd] nermal% pwd -L

      /etc/httpd

[localhost:/etc/httpd] nermal% popd

      /var/tmp

[localhost:/var/tmp] nermal% pwd -L

      /var/tmp
```

To be able to switch back and forth between a pair of directories, don't give an argument to `pushd`. It will pop the directory on top of the stack, push the current directory on, and switch you to the directory that it popped off. If that's a little confusing, just remember that if you've just come from somewhere using `pushd`, you can get back again using `pushd` with no arguments. When you're back, you've again just come from somewhere using `pushd`, so to get back you just…. For example, you might do something like this:

```
[localhost:/var/tmp] nermal% cd /var/tmp
[localhost:/var/tmp] nermal% pushd /etc/httpd

      /etc/httpd /var/tmp

[localhost:/etc/httpd] nermal% pwd -L

      /etc/httpd

[localhost:/etc/httpd] nermal% pushd

      /var/tmp /etc/httpd
```

```
[localhost:/var/tmp] nermal% pwd -L
     /var/tmp
[localhost:/var/tmp] nermal% pushd
     /etc/httpd /var/tmp
[localhost:/etc/httpd] nermal% pwd -L
     /etc/httpd
( And this can go on forever)
```

Finally, note that the stack used by tcsh isn't technically a classical LIFO structure because it has a side door. You might have noticed that pushd prints out the stack of directories after it's used each time. If you need to switch to a directory that's not at the top, issue pushd *+n*, where *n* is the depth of the directory you want to go to. Doing so shuffles that directory out to the top of the stack, and switches you to it.

The command documentation table for pushd is shown in Table 12.7.

TABLE 12.7 The Command Documentation Table for pushd

pushd	Pushes a directory on to the directory stack.
pushd [-p] [-l] [-n | -v] [<*dir*> | +<*n*>]	
pushd	
Without arguments, pushd exchanges the top two elements of the directory stack. If pushdtohome is set, pushd without arguments does pushd ~, like cd.	
-p	Overrides the pushdsilent shell variable. (The pushdsilent shell variable can be set to prevent pushd from printing the final directory stack.)
-l	Lists the output in long form.
-v	Prints one entry per line, preceded by their stack positions.
-n	Wraps entries before they reach the edge of the screen.
<*dir*>	Pushes the current directory into the stack and changes to the specified <*dir*>.
+<*n*>	Rotates the <*n*>th directory to the top of the stack and changes to that directory.
If both -n and -v are specified, -v takes precedence.	

The command documentation table for popd is shown in Table 12.8.

TABLE 12.8 The Command Documentation Table for `popd`

`popd`	Pops the directory stack and changes to the new top directory.
`popd [-p] [-l] [-n | -v] [+<n>]`	
`popd`	
Without arguments, `popd` pops the directory stack and returns to the new top directory. Elements in the directory stack are numbered from `0` starting at the top.	
`-p`	Overrides the `pushdsilent` shell variable. (The `pushdsilent` shell variable can be set to prevent `popd` from printing the final directory stack.)
`-l`	Lists the output in long form.
`-v`	Prints one entry per line, preceded by their stack positions.
`-n`	Wraps entries before they reach the edge of the screen.
`+<n>`	Discards the <*n*>th directory in the stack.
If both `-n` and `-v` are specified, `-v` takes precedence.	

Summary

In this chapter, we began the introduction to what is, for most practical purposes, a second operating system living under the hood of your OS X computer. The BSD Unix variant underlying the graphical interface to OS X is a fully featured Unix, and provides you with a command-line interface to your operating system.

This chapter covered some of the background information that you need to know for interacting with the command line, as well as a few commands for getting around the file system. However, the most important thing to remember from this chapter is not the particular commands or syntax detailed here, but rather the general way that these commands work and feel. The most powerful tool in a Unix user's toolbox is an understanding of "The Unix Way." Learned best by experience and experimentation, you will soon find that you can use your understanding of the way things work in Unix to rearrange and recombine examples that we've shown to synthesize new solutions.

CHAPTER 13

Common Unix Shell Commands: File Operations

IN THIS CHAPTER

Having mastered navigating about the file system, it's now time to learn how to interact with some of the files. We'll start off with basic file manipulation commands that do things such as rename files and make copies of them, and then cover more complicated things such as finding files, extracting portions of their contents, and archiving them.

As mentioned previously, Unix commands tend to be small, single-function commands that can be combined to form more complex functionality. You will see this demonstrated by many of the commands in this chapter; their functionality might seem oddly limited, if you're not used to the Unix command philosophy. By the time you're done with this chapter, however, you should begin to see how the commands could be fit together, and you should be able to abstract what you learn here to most Unix commands.

Rearranging Files

If you're a long-time Macintosh user, you are probably familiar with the notion of moving files about by way of the Macintosh's drag-and-drop formalism. Unix and its command line might not seem like a particularly appealing way to deal with moving files—having to type the names and paths to directories can't possibly be much fun! There's no way to deny that there are certain tasks for which the drag-and-drop way works much better than the command line. But, although you might not have thought about it, there are also situations in which drag-and-drop makes your life much more difficult. Interestingly, these are frequently situations in which the command line works particularly well; for example, when a folder contains a great number of files of the same type and you're interested in using a number of them that are related by name rather than by icon position. In a situation like this, rearranging things in the Finder, or Shift-clicking your way through the list of files to pick the ones you want, is usually less efficient than choosing them from the command line by using a shell filename wildcard. Similarly, it's frequently faster to type a filename, if you know it, than to scroll around in a Finder window looking for the file. For these reasons, as well as conveniences that really become apparent only from experience rather than explanation, the command line makes for a useful complement to the Finder for certain operations.

Renaming Files: `mv`

Renaming files in Unix is accomplished with the `mv` (move) command. It might seem odd at first that renaming a file is accomplished by moving it, but it makes sense in the Unix sense of accomplishing things in simple, abstract ways. Why create two commands that do essentially the same thing, when one command can do both with the same syntax, the same way. To rename a file from one name to another, simply use `mv` *`<oldfilename>`*

<newfilename>. For example, if you're in a directory with a file named `mynewfile`, and you'd like to rename it as `myoldfile`, you might do something like this:

```
[localhost:~/Documents] nermal% ls

     lynx       lynx.cfg   mynewfile  test

[localhost:~/Documents] nermal% mv mynewfile myoldfile

[localhost:~/Documents] nermal% ls

     lynx       lynx.cfg   myoldfile  test
```

Remember that most commands can take absolute paths or relative paths to files? Well, being in the same directory and using just the filenames is using the relative paths. On the other hand, you can accomplish the same thing using the absolute paths to the files like this:

```
[localhost:~/Documents] nermal% ls

     lynx       lynx.cfg   mynewfile  test

[localhost:~/Documents] nermal% pwd

     /Users/nermal/Documents

[localhost:~/Documents] nermal% mv /Users/nermal/Documents/mynewfile
➥/Users/nermal/Documents/myoldfile
[localhost:~/Documents] nermal% ls

     lynx       lynx.cfg   myoldfile  test
```

Because you can do that, why should you need to be in the same directory as the files at all? As a matter of fact, because you can specify the full paths to the files, what is to stop you from changing something other than the filename when you use the `mv` command? What if you decide to change one of the directories in the full path while you're at it? For example, let's look at what happens if you move a file from the `Documents` directory at the same time that you change its name:

```
[localhost:~/Documents] nermal% cd ~
[localhost:~] nermal% ls

     Desktop                   Network Trash Folder     chown-output
     Documents                 Pictures                 myfile
     Library                   Public                   output-sample6
     Movies                    Sites                    su-output
     Music                     TheVolumeSettingsFolder  typescripts

[localhost:~] nermal% ls Documents

     lynx       lynx.cfg   mynewfile  test
```

```
[localhost:~] nermal% mv /Users/nermal/Documents/mynewfile
➥/Users/nermal/Public/myoldfile
[localhost:~] nermal% ls Documents/

     lynx      lynx.cfg test

[localhost:~] nermal% ls Public/

     Drop Box   myoldfile
```

The end result is that Unix's abstraction of file access and naming causes the full path to the file to be, essentially, the full proper name of the file. "Renaming" it using the `mv` command can result in a change to any part of that name, including the parts that indicate the directory in which the file exists. See? Nothing odd about using the same syntax to rename files as used to move them about at all.

Note

Moving or renaming directories is exactly the same as moving or renaming files, with the exception of trying to move a directory from physical media that belongs to one disk partition or network device to media belonging to another. If you try to do this, the system will warn you that you're trying to move a directory across partition boundaries, and will disallow the action. There's no simple way around this, so we'll cover a trick that you can use to get around this limitation of the file system in the section on `tar` later in the chapter. The obvious, and somewhat brute-force solution, is to do it the way it's always been done on the Mac: Copy the directory to the location on the other drive or partition, and then delete the original. But this changes the modification times of the files, and you might not want that.

Caution

You can't create a directory structure by the action of a move command. If you try to move `/usr/local/wizbot` to `/usr/remote/wizbot`, and the directory `/usr/remote/` does not exist, the `mv` command will exit and notify you of the error.

The command documentation table for `mv` is shown in Table 13.1.

TABLE 13.1 The Command Documentation Table for `mv`

`mv`	Moves files.
`mv [-fi] <source> <target>`	
`mv [-fi] <source1> <source2> <source3> ... <directory>`	
In the first form, `mv` renames `<source>` to the name provided by `<target>`. If `<source>` is a file, a file is renamed. Likewise, if `<source>` is a directory, a directory is renamed.	
In the second form, `mv` moves the list enumerated by `<source1> <source2> <source3> ...` to the directory named by `<directory>`.	
`-f`	Forces an existing file to be overwritten.
`-i`	Invokes an interactive mode that prompts for a confirmation before overwriting an existing file.
The last of any `-f` or `-i` options determines the behavior of `mv`.	

Creating Directories: mkdir

The `mkdir` command is used to create directories. The usual syntax is very simple, being most commonly used as

```
mkdir <new directory name>
```

This will create a new directory named `<new directory name>` in the current directory. Full and relative paths are allowed to the new directory being specified. If the path to the directory that you are attempting to create does not completely exist, `mkdir` will not create the entire directory structure. For example, if you want to create `/usr/local/tmp/testing/morefiles/`, and the directory `/usr/local/tmp/testing/` does not exist, you will have to create it before you can create `/usr/local/tmp/testing/morefiles/`. This holds for all levels in the directory hierarchy. The command reference is shown in Table 13.2.

TABLE 13.2 The Command Documentation Table for `mkdir`

`mkdir`	Makes directories.
`mkdir [-p] [-m <mode>] <dir1> <dir2> ...`	
`mkdir` creates the named directories in the order specified, using mode `rwxrwxrwx (0777)` as modified by the current `umask (2)`.	
The user must have write permission in the parent directory.	

Table 13.2 continued

`-p`	Creates all nonexistent parent directories first. If this option is not specified, the full path prefix of each operand must already exist. Intermediate directories are created with permission bits `rwxrwxrwx (0777)` as modified by the current `umask (2)`, plus write and execute permission for the owner.
`-m <mode>`	Sets the permission bits of the created directory to *`<mode>`*. *`<mode>`* can be in any formats specified to the `chmod (1)` utility. If a symbolic mode is specified, the operation characters + and - are interpreted relative to an initial mode of `a=rwx`.

Copying Files: cp

The `cp` (copy) command functions in a similar fashion to the `mv` command, but instead of renaming a file between two locations, the `cp` command creates a duplicate of the file. The syntax is also similar, copying a file from one location to another or copying a number of files into a directory.

If our user `nermal` would like to copy some images to the `/Users/shared` directory so that all users can conveniently find the images without having to remember which user has the images, she can copy them with the `cp` command to the desired location.

Because `nermal` is new to Unix, she first decides to double-check that the images are located where she thinks they ought to be with the following:

```
[localhost:~] nermal% ls -l Public/Drop\ Box/shar*tiff

    -rw-r--r--  1 nermal  staff  872714 Apr 16 16:17 Public/Drop Box/sharing-
    1.tiff
    -rw-r--r--  1 nermal  staff  873174 Apr 16 16:17 Public/Drop Box/sharing-
    2.tiff
```

Then she actually copies them and verifies that they copied:

```
[localhost:~] nermal% cp Public/Drop\ Box/shar*tiff /Users/shared/

[localhost:~] nermal% ls -l /Users/shared

    total 3424
    -rw-r--r--  1 nermal  wheel  872714 Apr 23 11:08 sharing-1.tiff
    -rw-r--r--  1 nermal  wheel  873174 Apr 23 11:08 sharing-2.tiff
```

She could have copied each file individually, but `cp` can fortunately take multiple files in its arguments, so she can use `shar*tiff` to refer to both files. Note that the copies in the `/Users/shared` directory show the date that they were copied, rather than the original date. If everyone knows that the images from April 16 are the ones they need to use, they might be confused by the April 23 date. `nermal` could remove this confusion by specifying the `-p` option, which preserves as much as possible of the original modification time, user information, and so on:

```
[localhost:~] nermal% cp -p Public/Drop\ Box/shar*tiff /Users/shared/

[localhost:~] nermal% ls -l /Users/shared

     total 3424
     -rw-r--r--  1 nermal  staff  872714 Apr 16 16:17 sharing-1.tiff
     -rw-r--r--  1 nermal  staff  873174 Apr 16 16:17 sharing-2.tiff
```

Note the use of the `\` character to escape the space in the folder named `Drop Box` so that the shell doesn't interpret `Public/Drop` as one argument and `Box/shar*.tiff` as another.

If user `joray` has promised `nermal` some test data in a subdirectory named `tests-for-nermal` in `joray`'s home directory, `nermal` can recursively copy the test directory to her own home directory as follows:

```
[localhost:~] nermal% cp -R ~joray/tests-for-nermal ./
```

A check shows that a directory was indeed copied:

```
[localhost:~] nermal% ls -ld tests-for-nermal

     drwxr-xr-x  9 nermal  staff  262 Apr 23 11:29 tests-for-nermal
```

Not only that, but there was a directory under that directory, and `cp` copied it:

```
[localhost:~] nermal% ls -l tests-for-nermal

     total 48
     -rw-r--r--  1 nermal  staff   15 Apr 23 11:29 broken
     -rw-r--r--  1 nermal  staff   20 Apr 23 11:29 broken-again
     -rw-r--r--  1 nermal  staff   23 Apr 23 11:29 fix
     -rw-r--r--  1 nermal  staff   17 Apr 23 11:29 fix2
     -rw-r--r--  1 nermal  staff  848 Apr 23 11:29 test
     drwxr-xr-x  4 nermal  staff   92 Apr 23 11:29 test-data
     -rw-r--r--  1 nermal  staff  848 Apr 23 11:29 test2
```

You have seen just some of what you can do with `cp`. The complete syntax and options for `cp` are in Table 13.3, the command documentation table.

TABLE 13.3 The Command Documentation Table for `cp`

`cp`	Copies files.
`cp [-R (-H | -L | -P)] [-f	-i] [-p] <source> <target>`	
`cp [-R (-H | -L | -P)] [-f	-i] [-p] <source1> <source2> ... <directory>`	

TABLE 13.3 continued

In its first form, `cp` copies the contents of *<source>* to *<target>*.	
In its second form, `cp` copies the contents of the list enumerated by *<source1>* *<source2>* `...` to the directory named by *<directory>*. The names of the files themselves are not changed. If `cp` detects an attempt to copy to itself, that attempt fails.	
`-R`	If *<source>* is a directory, cp recursively copies the directory. This option also causes symbolic links to be copied, rather than indirected through. Created directories have the same mode as the corresponding source directory.
`-H`	If `-R` is specified, symbolic links on the command line are followed, but symbolic links in the tree traversal are not.
`-L`	If `-R` is specified, all symbolic links are followed.
`-P`	If `-R` is specified, no symbolic links are followed.
`-f`	Forces an existing file to be overwritten. If permissions do not allow the copy to succeed, this forces the existing file to be removed and a new file to be created, without prompting for confirmation. The `-i` option is ignored if the `-f` option is specified.
`-i`	Invokes an interactive mode that prompts for a confirmation before overwriting an existing file.
`-p`	Causes `cp` to retain as much of the modification time, access time, file flags, file mode, user ID, and group ID information as permissions allow.

Creating Symbolic Links: `ln`

Sometimes it is useful to be able to link a name with a particular file or directory. This can be done with the `ln` command. It is especially useful for administrative purposes, but even a regular user might have the need to link a filename or directory name to some other particular name. The best way to do this is to use a symbolic link. The simplest syntax for making a symbolic link is

```
ln -s <source> <target>
```

Because the syntax is similar to the basic `cp` syntax, you won't have much trouble remembering it.

You might be wondering just what sort of use you might have for symbolic links. An instance in which you might use a symbolic link is for your Web site. Suppose that you are using a Web editing suite that uses `home.html` for the default name for the main page of your Web site. Suppose, however, that your Web server is set to read only files named `index.html` as the default page for a directory. If you use `home.html`, you might have to give out something like `http://ryoohki.biosci.ohio-state.edu/~nermal/home.html` as your URL. If, on the other hand, your `home.html` file were really called `index.html`, you could give out a slightly shorter URL instead: `http://ryoohki.biosci.ohio-state.edu/~nermal/`.

What could you do to get an `index.html` file in your directory if your Web editing suite won't create one? And how could you keep it conveniently updated to match `home.html`? Well, as you just saw, you could copy `home.html` to `index.html`. But the next time you edited `home.html`, you would then have to remember to copy `home.html` to `index.html` when you were done. Although you might be very good about remembering to do that, you undoubtedly will eventually forget, probably when it matters most. If you simply link `index.html` to `home.html`, every time you update `home.html`, you don't have to remember to do anything else! To create the symbolic link, do the following:

```
[localhost:~/public_html] nermal% ln -s home.html index.html
```

A quick check shows us that `index.html` is now a link to `home.html`.

```
[localhost:~/public_html] nermal% ls -l

     total 16
     -rw-r--r--  1 nermal  staff  52 Apr 23 11:56 home.html
     lrwxr-xr-x  1 nermal  staff   9 Apr 23 11:56 index.html -> home.html
```

A common administrative use for symbolic links is to move a directory from one partition to another, while leaving the path that a user would use to get to the directory the same. This makes the change that the administrator has made transparent to the user for most purposes. An example of this follows. On this machine, `/usr` partition was getting full, so the local directory of `/usr/local` was moved to the `/home` partition. After the directory was moved, the `/usr/local directory` was replaced with a symbolic link that points to `/home/local`.

```
Rosalyn joray 201 > ls -l /usr/local

     lrwxrwxrwx   1 root     other    11 Mar 20  1997 /usr/local -> /home/local
```

If a user changes to the `/usr/local directory` and then checks her location with `pwd`, she finds the following:

```
Rosalyn joray 202 > cd /usr/local

Rosalyn local 203 > pwd

     /home/local
```

So, as the user might have grown to expect, she can still `cd` to `/usr/local`, but without having to know any of the "administrivia" behind its actual location.

The complete syntax and options for `ln` are in Table 13.4, the command documentation table.

TABLE 13.4 The Command Documentation Table for `ln`

`ln`	Makes links.
`ln [-fhns] <source> <target>`	
`ln [-fhns] <source1> <source2> <source3> ... <directory>`	
In the first form, `ln` links `<source>` to `<target>`. If `<target>` is a directory, a link named `<source>` is placed in `<target>`.	
In the second form, `ln` makes links to the files enumerated by `<source1> <source2> <source3> ...` in `<directory>`. The links have the same names as the sources in the list.	
There are two types of links: hard links and symbolic links. The default is hard links. A hard link to a file is indistinguishable from the original directory entry. Hard links may not normally refer to directories and may not span file systems.	
A symbolic link refers by name to the file to which it is linked. Symbolic links may refer to directories and may span file systems.	
`-f`	Forces the link to occur by unlinking any already existing links.
`-h`	If `<target>` or `<directory>` is a symbolic link, it is not followed. This is most useful when used with `-f`, to replace a symbolic link that might point to a directory.
`-n`	Same as `-h`. Retained for compatibility with other implementations of `ln`.
`-s`	Creates a symbolic link--this is most like the idea of aliases with which you're already familiar.

Changing Modification Times, Creating Empty Files: `touch`

The `touch` command is used to update the last-modified time for a file. This command also has the side effect of creating a new, empty file, if the file that you attempt to `touch` does not exist.

Neither of these functionalities probably sounds particularly interesting at the outset, but, in fact, they both have good uses. For example, most archiving and backup software is frequently configured to back up only files that have changed since the last backup. Using `touch` on a file makes it appear to have been changed, which results in it being flagged for backup. Because the `touch` command can be quickly applied from the command line to a large number of files, it allows you to conveniently force some files to be backed up without having to open and resave each in its parent applications.

Creating empty files doesn't have much use at the command line, but turns out to be a very useful thing to be able to do when you start writing programs in the shell scripting language (Chapter 18 "Programming with the Shell: Shell Scripting"). In this case, multiple simultaneously running scripts can be made to talk to each other by the creation of empty files known as *flag files*—essentially the electronic ability for a script to raise a flag to tell another script that something has happened.

To create a new (empty) file with `touch`, or to update the modification date of the file to the current time, the syntax for the `touch` command is simply

```
touch <filename to modify>
```

The `touch` command can actually update files to have any modification time that you'd like, although the preceding is by far the most common usage. Table 13.5 shows the command documentation table for `touch`.

TABLE 13.5 The Command Documentation Table for `touch`

`touch`	Changes file access and modification times.
`touch [-acfhm] [-r <file>] [-t [[CC]YY]MMDDhhmm[.SS]] <file> ...`	
`touch` sets modification and access times of files to the current time of day. If the file does not exist, it is created with default permissions.	
`-a`	Changes the access time of the file. Does not change modification time unless `-m` is also specified.
`-c`	Does not create the file if it does not exist.
`-f`	Attempts to force the update, even if file permissions do not currently permit it.
`-h`	If `<file>` is a symbolic link, changes access and/or modification time of the link. This option also implies `-c`.
`-m`	Changes the modification time of the file. Does not change the access time unless `-a` is also specified.
`-r <file>`	Replaces access and modification time with that of `<file>`, rather than using the current time.
`-t`	Changes the access and modification time to the specified time.

TABLE 13.5 continued

The argument for `-t` should be in the form `[[CC]YY]MMDDhhmm[.SS]`, where each pair of letters represents the following:

`CC`	First two digits of the year (the century).
`YY`	Second two digits of the year. If `YY` is specified but `CC` is not, a value for `YY` between `69` and `99` results in a `CC` value of `19`. Otherwise, a value of `20` is used.
`MM`	The month of the year, from `1` to `12`.
`DD`	The day of the month, from `1` to `31`.
`hh`	The hour of the day, from `0` to `23`.
`mm`	The minute of the hour, from `0` to `59`.
`SS`	The second of the minute, from `0` to `61`.

If `CC` and `YY` letter pairs are not specified, the values default to the current year. If the `SS` letter pair is not specified, the value defaults to `0`.

Examining File Contents

Moving around the file system, and moving files around the file system, isn't all that interesting if you can't look at what's in the files. Unix provides a number of facilities for examining the contents of files, and frequently these are more convenient to use than their graphical counterparts. BBEdit, for example, is a wonderful text editor, and it's light enough in memory footprint to load quickly. However, if what you want to do is see whether the file you're thinking about deleting is really the file you mean to delete, and the information is readily apparent by looking at the beginning of the text, there are much more efficient ways to examine the contents from the command line than starting up a GUI program just to glance at the file.

Looking at the Contents of Files: `cat`, `more`, `less`

Now that you have learned a little bit about how to list your files and copy your files, it is time to learn how to examine the contents of your files.

`cat` reads files and displays their contents. In this example, you see that `myfile` is very short.

```
[localhost:~] nermal% cat myfile
     Hi.  this is nermal.

     I hope you enjoyed myfile.
```

If the file were longer, it would keep scrolling by on the screen either until you pressed Ctrl+C to break the process or the file came to an end.

It might seem odd that anyone would want a program that just dumped all the output to the terminal, with no convenient way to slow it down or page through it. However, this is part of the Unix philosophy. The `cat` command reads files and sends their contents to the terminal. (Actually, `cat` sends their contents to `STDOUT`, a way of connecting commands that you'll learn more about in Chapter 18. `STDOUT` just happens to be connected to the terminal, unless you tell the command line otherwise.) In the Unix way of doing things, it is the job of some other program to provide paged display of data.

The complete syntax and options for `cat` are shown in Table 13.6, the command documentation table.

TABLE 13.6 The Command Documentation Table for `cat`

`cat`	Concatenates and prints files.
`cat [-nbsvetu] <file1> <file2> ...`	
`cat [-nbsvetu] [-]`	
`cat` reads files in sequential, command-line order and writes them to standard output. A single dash represents standard input.	
`-n`	Numbers all output lines.
`-b`	Numbers all output lines, except `b` or blank lines.
`-s`	Squeezes multiple adjacent empty lines, causing single-spaced output.
`-v`	Displays nonprinting characters. Control characters print as `^X` for Control+X; delete (octal 0177) prints as `^?`; non-ASCII characters with the high bit set are printed as `M-` (for meta) followed by the character for the low 7 bits.
`-e`	Implies `-v` option. Displays a dollar sign (`$`) at the end of each line as well.
`-t`	Implies `-v` option. Displays tab characters as `^I` as well.
`-u`	Guarantees unbuffered output.

You could also use cat to read the contents of longer files. However, the contents of your file scroll quickly. If you hope to read the contents as they appear, it would be better to use more, which also reads and displays files, but it pauses the display after a screenful.

The contents of nermal's short file look the same when viewed with more:

```
[localhost:~] nermal% more myfile
```

```
Hi.  this is nermal.

I hope you enjoyed myfile.
```

With a longer file, though, more pauses after a screenful:

```
[localhost:/var/log] joray% more system.log
```

```
Apr 23 03:15:02 localhost syslogd: restart
Apr 23 03:15:02 localhost sendmail[7423]: NOQUEUE: SYSERR(root):
➥/etc/mail/sendmail.cf:
 line 81: fileclass: cannot open /etc/mail/local-host-names:
➥Group writable directory
Apr 23 03:15:02 localhost sendmail[7424]: NOQUEUE: SYSERR(root):
➥/etc/mail/sendmail.cf:
 line 81: fileclass: cannot open /etc/mail/local-host-names:
➥Group writable directory
Apr 23 03:15:02 localhost CRON[7390]: (root) MAIL (mailed 108 bytes of
➥output but got status 0x0047 )
Apr 23 09:01:03 localhost WindowServer[56]: CGXGetSharedWindow:
➥Invalid window -1
Apr 23 09:01:03 localhost /System/Library/Frameworks/ScreenSaver.framework
➥/Versions/A/Resources/ScreenSaverEngine.app/Contents/MacOS/
➥ScreenSaverEngine: kCGSErrorIllegalArgument :
➥CGSLockWindowRectBits: Invalid window
Apr 23 09:01:03 localhost /System/Library/Frameworks/ScreenSaver.framework
➥/Versions/A/Resources/ScreenSaverEngine.app/Contents/MacOS
➥/ScreenSaverEngine: kCGSErrorCannotComplete : Cannot create
➥context device
Apr 23 09:01:03 localhost /System/Library/Frameworks/ScreenSaver.framework
➥/Versions/A/Resources/ScreenSaverEngine.app/Contents/MacOS
➥/ScreenSaverEngine: kCGSErrorFailure : Cannot initialize
➥context RIPContext
Apr 23 10:15:46 localhost WindowServer[56]: CGXGetSharedWindow:
➥Invalid window -1
Apr 23 10:15:46 localhost /System/Library/Frameworks/ScreenSaver.framework
➥/Versions/A/R
esources/ScreenSaverEngine.app/Contents/MacOS/ScreenSaverEngine:
➥kCGSErrorIllegalArgument : CGSLockWindowRectBits: Invalid window
Apr 23 10:15:46 localhost /System/Library/Frameworks/ScreenSaver.framework
➥/Versions/A/Resources/ScreenSaverEngine.app/Contents/MacOS/
➥ScreenSaverEngine: kCGSErrorCannotComplete : Cannot create
➥context device
```

```
Apr 23 10:15:46 localhost /System/Library/Frameworks/ScreenSaver.framework
➥/Versions/A/Resources/ScreenSaverEngine.app/Contents/MacOS/
➥ScreenSaverEngine: kCGSErrorFailure : Cannot initialize
➥context RIPContext
Apr 23 10:17:26 localhost WindowServer[56]: CGXGetSharedWindow:
➥Invalid window -1
Apr 23 10:17:26 localhost /System/Library/Frameworks/ScreenSaver.framework
➥/Versions/A/Resources/ScreenSaverEngine.app/Contents/MacOS/
➥ScreenSaverEngine: kCGSErrorIllegalArgument :
➥CGSLockWindowRectBits: Invalid window
Apr 23 10:17:26 localhost /System/Library/Frameworks/ScreenSaver.framework
➥/Versions/A/Resources/ScreenSaverEngine.app/Contents/MacOS
➥/ScreenSaverEngine: kCGSErrorCannotComplet
system.log (11%)
```

In this display, we can see at the bottom of the screen that we are looking at a file called `system.log`, and that we have viewed about 11% of the file. After we are done looking at that screenful, we can press the space bar and look at the next screenful of text. Although `more` has many options to it, probably the most common syntax you will use is

```
more <filename>
```

The complete syntax and options for `more` are in Table 13.7, the command documentation table.

TABLE 13.7 The Command Documentation Table for `more`

`more`	Pages through data or text files.
`more [-cdflsu] [-n] [+<linenumber>] [+/<pattern>] <file1> <file2> ...`	
`more` pages through data a screenful at a time. When the user presses a carriage return at the `More` prompt at the bottom of the screen, one more line is displayed. When the user presses the space bar, another screenful of data is displayed. When `more` is invoked as `page`, each screenful is cleared before the next is displayed.	
`-c`	Draws each page by beginning at the top of the screen and erasing each line just before it draws on it. This option is ignored if the screen is unable to clear to the end of a line.
`-d`	Prompts user with `Press space to continue, 'q' to quit.` at the end of each screenful. Responds to illegal user input with `Press 'h' for instructions.` instead of ringing the bell.
`-f`	Counts logical rather than screen lines. Long lines are not folded. Useful when trying to display lines containing non-printing characters or escape sequences.

TABLE 13.7 continued

`-l`	Does not treat `^L` (form feed) as a page break. Where form feeds occur, `more` pauses after them, as if the screen were full. Particularly recommended if piping `nroff` output through `ul`.
`-s`	Squeezes multiple blank lines of output into one blank line of output. Useful for viewing `nroff` output.
`-u`	Suppresses underlining or stand-out mode, whichever the terminal is capable of displaying.
`-n`	Specifies the number of lines to use per screenful rather than the default.
`+`*`<linenumber>`*	Starts at *`<linenumber>`*.
`+/`*`<pattern>`*	Starts two lines before the line containing the regular expression pattern *`<pattern>`*.
Additional options for interacting with `more` when it pauses (*`i`* is an optional integer argument, defaulting to 1):	
`i<return>`	Displays *`i`* more lines. Advances one line, if *`i`* is not given.
`i<space>`	Displays *`i`* more lines. Advances another screenful if *`i`* is not given.
`^D`	Displays 11 more lines. If *`i`* is given, scroll size is set to *`i`*.
`d`	Same as `^D`.
`iz`	Same as typing *`<space>`*, except that if *`i`* is given, scroll size becomes *`i`*.
`is`	Skips *`i`* lines and prints a screenful of lines.
`if`	Skips *`i`* screenfuls and prints a screenful of lines.
`i^F`	Same as *`if`*.
`ib`	Skips back *`i`* screenfuls and prints a screenful of lines.
`i^B`	Same as *`ib`*.
`q`	Exits.
`Q`	Exits.
`=`	Displays the current line number.
`v`	Starts the editor at the current line number, if the environment variable `EDITOR` is set to `vi` or `ex`. If no `EDITOR` is specified, `vi` is the default.
`h`	Displays the help menu.

TABLE 13.7 continued

`i/<expression>`	Searches for the `i`th occurrence of the regular expression `<expression>`. If the input is a file rather than a pipe, and there are less than `i` occurrences, the file remains unchanged. Otherwise, the display advances to two lines before the line containing `<expression>`.
`in`	Searches for the `i`th occurrence of the last regular expres-
sion entered.	
`'`	(Single quote) Goes to the point where the last search was started. If no search has been done on the file, it goes back to the beginning of the file.
`!<command>`	Invokes a shell that executes `<command>`. The characters `%` and `!`, when used in the `<command>`, are replaced with the current filename and the previous shell command, respectively. If there is no current filename, `%` is not expanded. To escape expansion, use `\%` and `\%`, respectively.
`i:n`	Skips to the `i`th next file given in the command line, or to the last file if `i` is beyond range.
`i:p`	Skips to the `i`th previous file in the command line, or to the first file if `i` is beyond range. If `more` is in the middle of displaying a file, it goes to the beginning of the file. If `more` is displaying from a pipe, the bell rings.
`:f`	Displays current filename and line number.
`:q`	Exits.
`:Q`	Exits.
`.`	(Dot) Repeats the previous command.

`less` is another pager. Because it does not have to read the entire file first, it starts faster. In addition, it has more backward and forward movement. Its commands are based both on `more` and `vi`, a text editor which we will examine in Chapter 15, "Command-Line Applications." Although `less` is frequently thought of as a command, it has enough complex functionality for the user who desires it that `less` might be better called an *application*. The fact that it is most frequently used for its command-like capabilities leads to its inclusion here.

The appearance of `less` output is similar to that from `more`:

```
[localhost:/var/log] joray% less system.log

    Apr 23 03:15:02 localhost syslogd: restart
    Apr 23 03:15:02 localhost sendmail[7423]: NOQUEUE: SYSERR(root):
    ➥/etc/mail/sendmail.cf: line 81: fileclass: cannot open
    ➥/etc/mail/local-host-names: Group writable directory
```

```
Apr 23 03:15:02 localhost sendmail[7424]: NOQUEUE: SYSERR(root):
➥/etc/mail/sendmail.cf: line 81: fileclass: cannot open
➥/etc/mail/local-host-names: Group writable directory
Apr 23 03:15:02 localhost CRON[7390]: (root) MAIL (mailed 108 bytes of
➥output but got status 0x0047 )
Apr 23 09:01:03 localhost WindowServer[56]: CGXGetSharedWindow:
➥Invalid window -1
Apr 23 09:01:03 localhost /System/Library/Frameworks/ScreenSaver.framework
➥/Versions/A/Resources/ScreenSaverEngine.app/Contents/MacOS
➥/ScreenSaverEngine: kCGSErrorIllegalArgument : CGSLockWindowRectBits:
➥Invalid window
Apr 23 09:01:03 localhost /System/Library/Frameworks/ScreenSaver.framework
➥/Versions/A/Resources/ScreenSaverEngine.app/Contents/MacOS/
➥ScreenSaverEngine: kCGSErrorCannotComplete : Cannot create context device
Apr 23 09:01:03 localhost /System/Library/Frameworks/ScreenSaver.framework
➥/Versions/A/Resources/ScreenSaverEngine.app/Contents/MacOS/
➥ScreenSaverEngine: kCGSErrorFailure : Cannot initialize context
➥RIPContext
Apr 23 10:15:46 localhost WindowServer[56]: CGXGetSharedWindow:
➥Invalid window -1
Apr 23 10:15:46 localhost /System/Library/Frameworks/ScreenSaver.framework
➥/Versions/A/Resources/ScreenSaverEngine.app/Contents/MacOS/
➥ScreenSaverEngine: kCGSErrorIllegalArgument : CGSLockWindowRectBits:
➥Invalid window
Apr 23 10:15:46 localhost /System/Library/Frameworks/ScreenSaver.framework
➥/Versions/A/Resources/ScreenSaverEngine.app/Contents/MacOS/
➥ScreenSaverEngine: kCGSErrorCannotComplete : Cannot create context device
Apr 23 10:15:46 localhost /System/Library/Frameworks/ScreenSaver.framework/
➥Versions/A/Resources/ScreenSaverEngine.app/Contents/MacOS/
➥ScreenSaverEngine:
➥kCGSErrorFailure : Cannot initialize context RIPContext
Apr 23 10:17:26 localhost WindowServer[56]: CGXGetSharedWindow:
➥Invalid window -1
Apr 23 10:17:26 localhost /System/Library/Frameworks/ScreenSaver.framework
➥/Versions/A/Resources/ScreenSaverEngine.app/Contents/MacOS/
➥ScreenSaverEngine: kCGSErrorIllegalArgument : CGSLockWindowRectBits:
➥Invalid window
Apr 23 10:17:26 localhost /System/Library/Frameworks/ScreenSaver.framework
➥/Versions/A/Resources/ScreenSaverEngine.app/Contents/MacOS/
➥ScreenSaverEngine:
➥ kCGSErrorCannotComplet
system.log
```

Like `more`, `less` has paused after a screenful. At the bottom, we also see that the file is called `system.log`, but it is not displaying the percentage of the file that we have examined.

The most common syntax you will use for `less` is

```
less <filename>
```

less is very powerful. The most important thing to remember about less is how to invoke help, which can be done by issuing either less -? or less —help. Depending on how your shell interprets a question mark, you might have to try -\? or "-\?" for help. The man page is quite overwhelming, but the —help option is easy to read and organized nicely. The output from the —help option is included in Table 13.8.

Many options are available in less, and there is much that you can do after you are in less. The syntax and options for less are in Table 13.8, the command documentation table.

TABLE 13.8 The Command Documentation Table for less

less Opposite of more.

Pages through data or text files.

less -?

less --help

less -V

less --version

less [-[+]aBcCdeEfgGiImMnNqQrsSuUVwX][-b *<bufs>*][-h *<lines>*][-j *<line>*] [-k *<keyfile>*] [--{oO} *<logfile>*] [-p *<pattern>*][-t *<tag>*] [-T *<tags-file>*] [-x *<tab>*] [-y *<lines>*] [-[-z] *<lines>*][+[+]*<cmd>*] [--] [*<file1>*...]

Summary Of Less Commands

Commands marked with * may be preceded by a number, *N*.

Notes in parentheses indicate the behavior if *N* is given.

h H Display this help.

q :q Q :Q ZZ Exit.

MOVING

e ^E j ^N CR * Forward one line (or *N* lines).

y ^Y k ^K ^P * Backward one line (or *N* lines).

f ^F ^V SPACE * Forward one window (or *N* lines).

TABLE 13.8 continued

```
b ^B ESC-v     * Backward one window (or N lines).
z              * Forward one window (and set
                 window to N).
w              * Backward one window (and set
                 window to N).
ESC-SPACE      * Forward one window, but don't
                 stop at end-of- file.
d ^D           * Forward one half-window (and
                 set half-window to N).
u ^U           * Backward one half-window
                 (and set half-window to N).
ESC-( RightArrow * Left 8 character positions (or
                 N positions).
ESC-) LeftArrow  * Right 8 character positions (or
                 N positions).
F                Forward forever; like "tail -f".
r ^R ^L          Repaint screen.
R                Repaint screen, discarding
                 buffered input.
      ---------------------------------------------------
   Default "window" is the screen height.
   Default "half-window" is half of the screen height.
 ---------------------------------------------------------

                  SEARCHING

/pattern   * Search forward for (N-th) matching line.
?pattern   * Search backward for (N-th) matching line.
n          * Repeat previous search (for N-th
             occurrence).
N          * Repeat previous search in reverse direction.
ESC-n      * Repeat previous search, spanning files.
ESC-N      * Repeat previous search, reverse
```

TABLE 13.8 continued

```
            dir. & spanning files.
  ESC-u         Undo (toggle) search highlighting.
      ---------------------------------------------------
  Search patterns may be modified by one or more of:
  ^N or !  Search for NON-matching lines.
  ^E or *  Search multiple files (pass thru END OF FILE).
  ^F or @  Start search at FIRST file (for /) or last
          file (for ?).
  ^K      Highlight matches, but don't move (KEEP position).
  ^R      Don't use REGULAR EXPRESSIONS.
  ---------------------------------------------------------


                    JUMPING


  g  <  ESC-<       *  Go to first line in file (or line N).
  G  >  ESC->       *  Go to last line in file (or line N).
  p  %              *  Go to beginning of file (or N
                       percent into
                      file).
  {  (  [           *  Find close bracket } ) ].
  }  )  ]           *  Find open bracket { ( [.
  ESC-^F <c1> <c2>  *  Find close bracket <c2>.
  ESC-^B <c1> <c2>  *  Find open bracket <c1>
      ---------------------------------------------------
  Each "find close bracket" command goes forward to the close
  bracket matching the (N-th) open bracket in the top line.
  Each "find open bracket" command goes backward to the open
  bracket matching the (N-th) close bracket in the bottom
  line.

  m<letter>          Mark the current position
                 with <letter>.
  '<letter>          Go to a previously marked position.
```

TABLE 13.8 continued

```
''              Go to the previous position.
^X^X            Same as '.

    -----------------------------------------------
    A mark is any upper-case or lower-case letter.
    Certain marks are predefined:
        ^  means  beginning of the file
        $  means  end of the file
-------------------------------------------------------


                CHANGING FILES

:e [file]      Examine a new file.
^X^V           Same as :e.
:n           * Examine the (N-th) next file
               from the command line.
:p           * Examine the (N-th) previous file
               from the command line.
:x           * Examine the first (or N-th) file
               from the command line.
:d             Delete the current file
               from the command line list.
= ^G :f        Print current filename.
-------------------------------------------------------


            MISCELLANEOUS COMMANDS

-<flag>            Toggle a command line option
                   [see OPTIONS below].
--<name>           Toggle a command line option, by name.
_<flag>            Display the setting of a command
                   line option.
__<name>           Display the setting of an option,
                   by name.
```

TABLE 13.8 continued

```
+cmd            Execute the less cmd each time a
                new file is examined.

!command        Execute the shell command with $SHELL.
|Xcommand       Pipe file between current
                pos & mark X to shell command.
v               Edit the current file with $VISUAL
                or $EDITOR.
V               Print version number of "less".
---------------------------------------------------------

                OPTIONS

Most options may be changed either on the command line,
or from within less by using the - or -- command.
Options may be given in one of two forms: either a single
character preceded by a -, or a name preceded by --.

-? ........ --help
          Display help (from command line).
-a ........ --search-skip-screen
          Forward search skips current screen.
-b [N] .... --buffers=[N]
          Number of buffers.
-B ........ --auto-buffers
          Don't automatically allocate buffers for pipes.
-c -C .... --clear-screen --CLEAR-SCREEN
          Repaint by scrolling/clearing.
-d ........ --dumb
          Dumb terminal.
-D [xn.n] . --color=xn.n
          Set screen colors. (MS-DOS only)
```

TABLE 13.8 continued

```
-e -E .... --quit-at-eof --QUIT-AT-EOF
             Quit at end of file.
-f ........ --force
             Force open non-regular files.
-g ........ --hilite-search
             Highlight only last match for searches.
-G ........ --HILITE-SEARCH
             Don't highlight any matches for searches.
-h [N] .... --max-back-scroll=[N]
             Backward scroll limit.
-i ........ --ignore-case
             Ignore case in searches.
-I ........ --IGNORE-CASE
             Ignore case in searches and in
              search patterns.
-j [N] .... --jump-target=[N]
             Screen position of target lines.
-k [file] . --lesskey-file=[file]
             Use a lesskey file.
-m -M .... --long-prompt --LONG-PROMPT
             Set prompt style.
-n -N .... --line-numbers --LINE-NUMBERS
             Use line numbers.
-o [file] . --log-file=[file]
             Copy to log file (standard input only).
-O [file] . --LOG-FILE=[file]
             Copy to log file (unconditionally
              overwrite).
-p [pattern] --pattern=[pattern]
             Start at pattern (from command line).
-P [prompt] --prompt=[prompt]
             Define new prompt.
```

TABLE 13.8 continued

-q -Q .... --quiet --QUIET --silent --SILENT

Quiet the terminal bell.

-r .... --raw-control-chars

Output "raw" control characters.

-s .... --squeeze-blank-lines

Squeeze multiple blank lines.

-S .... --chop-long-lines

Chop long lines.

-t [tag] .. --tag=[tag]

Find a tag.

-T [tagsfile] --tag-file=[tagsfile]

Use an alternate tags file.

-u -U .... --underline-special --UNDERLINE-SPECIAL

Change handling of backspaces.

-V .... --version

Display the version number of "less".

-w .... --hilite-unread

Highlight first new line after forward-screen.

-W .... --HILITE-UNREAD

Highlight first new line after any forward movement.

-x [N] .... --tabs=[N]

Set tab stops.

-X .... --no-init

Don't use termcap init/deinit strings.

-y [N] .... --max-forw-scroll=[N]

Forward scroll limit.

-z [N] .... --window=[N]

Set size of window.

-" [c[c]] . --quotes=[c[c]]

Set shell quote characters.

-~ .... --tilde

TABLE 13.8 continued

```
                    Don't display tildes after end of file.

 ---------------------------------------------------------

                          LINE EDITING

        These keys can be used to edit text being entered
        on the "command line" at the bottom of the screen.

 RightArrow            ESC-l     Move cursor right one
                         character.
 LeftArrow             ESC-h     Move cursor left one
                         character.
 CNTL-RightArrow  ESC-RightArrow  ESC-w     Move cursor
                              right one word.
 CNTL-LeftArrow   ESC-LeftArrow   ESC-b     Move cursor
                              left one word.
 HOME                  ESC-0     Move cursor to
                         start of line.
 END                   ESC-$     Move cursor to
                         end of line.
 BACKSPACE                       Delete char to
                         left of cursor.
 DELETE                ESC-x     Delete char
                         under cursor.
 CNTL-BACKSPACE   ESC-BACKSPACE     Delete word to
                         left of cursor.
 CNTL-DELETE   ESC-DELETE  ESC-X     Delete word
                         under cursor.
 CNTL-U                    Delete entire line.
 UpArrow               ESC-k     Retrieve previous
                         command line.
 DownArrow             ESC-j     Retrieve next
                         command line.
```

TABLE 13.8 continued

TAB		Complete filename & cycle.
SHIFT-TAB	ESC-TAB	Complete filename & reverse cycle.
CNTL-L		Complete filename, list all.

Looking at Portions of the Contents of Files: head, tail

Sometimes, however, you need to see only a portion of a file, rather than the entire contents. To see only portions of a file, use either `head` or `tail`. As the names suggest, `head` displays the first few lines of a file, whereas `tail` displays the last few lines of a file.

Let's look at the first few lines of `system.log`:

```
[localhost:/var/log] joray% head system.log
     Apr 23 03:15:02 localhost syslogd: restart
     Apr 23 03:15:02 localhost sendmail[7423]: NOQUEUE: SYSERR(root):
     ➥/etc/mail/sendmail.cf: line 81: fileclass: cannot open
     ➥/etc/mail/local-host-names: Group writable directory
     Apr 23 03:15:02 localhost sendmail[7424]: NOQUEUE: SYSERR(root):
     ➥/etc/mail/sendmail.cf: line 81: fileclass: cannot open
     ➥/etc/mail/local-host-names: Group writable directory
     Apr 23 03:15:02 localhost CRON[7390]: (root) MAIL (mailed 108 bytes of
     ➥output but got status 0x0047 )
     Apr 23 09:01:03 localhost WindowServer[56]: CGXGetSharedWindow:
     ➥Invalid window -1
     Apr 23 09:01:03 localhost /System/Library/Frameworks/ScreenSaver.framework
     ➥/Versions/A/Resources/ScreenSaverEngine.app/Contents/MacOS/
     ➥ScreenSaverEngine:
     ➥kCGSErrorIllegalArgument : CGSLockWindowRectBits: Invalid window
     Apr 23 09:01:03 localhost /System/Library/Frameworks/ScreenSaver.framework
     ➥/Versions/A/Resources/ScreenSaverEngine.app/Contents/MacOS/ScreenSaverEng
     ine:
     ➥kCGSErrorCannotComplete : Cannot create context device
     Apr 23 09:01:03 localhost
     ➥/System/Library/Frameworks/ScreenSaver.framework/Versions/
     ➥A/Resources/ScreenSaverEngine.app/Contents/MacOS/ScreenSaverEngine:
```

```
➥kCGSErrorFailure : Cannot initialize context RIPContext
Apr 23 10:15:46 localhost WindowServer[56]: CGXGetSharedWindow:
➥Invalid window -1
Apr 23 10:15:46 localhost
➥/System/Library/Frameworks/ScreenSaver.framework/Versions/
➥A/Resources/ScreenSaverEngine.app/Contents/MacOS/ScreenSaverEngine:
➥ kCGSErrorIllegalArgument : CGSLockWindowRectBits: Invalid window
```

Nothing other than the first few lines of the file are displayed. Because `head` is not a pager, we do not see the name of the file displayed at the bottom of the screen. The complete syntax and options for `head` are in Table 13.9, the command documentation table.

TABLE 13.9 The Command Documentation Table for `head`

`head`	Displays the first lines of a file.
`head [-n` *<number>*`]` *<file1> <file2>* `...`	
`head [-n` *<number>*`]`	
-n <number>	Displays the first *<number>* of lines. If *n* is not specified, the default is `10`.

`tail` behaves in the same way as `head`, except that only the last few lines of a file are displayed, as you see in this sample:

```
[localhost:/var/log] joray% tail system.log
```

```
Apr 23 17:30:09 localhost sshd[807]: lastlog_perform_login: Couldn't stat
➥/var/log/lastlog: No such file or directory
Apr 23 17:30:09 localhost sshd[807]: lastlog_openseek: /var/log/lastlog
➥is not a file or directory!
Apr 23 17:30:10 localhost sshd[807]: lastlog_perform_login: Couldn't stat
➥/var/log/lastlog: No such file or directory
Apr 23 17:30:10 localhost sshd[807]: lastlog_openseek: /var/log/lastlog
➥is not a file or directory!
Apr 23 17:31:31 localhost su: joray to nermal on /dev/ttyp4
Apr 23 17:34:07 localhost su: joray to nermal on /dev/ttyp4
Apr 23 17:36:43 localhost sshd[298]: Generating new 768 bit RSA key.
Apr 23 17:36:45 localhost sshd[298]: RSA key generation complete.
Apr 23 17:42:45 localhost su: BAD SU nermal to joray on /dev/ttyp4
Apr 23 17:42:58 localhost su: nermal to joray on /dev/ttyp4
```

The complete syntax and options for `tail` are in Table 13.10, the command documentation table.

TABLE 13.10 The Command Documentation Table for `tail`

`tail`	Displays the last part of a file.
`tail [-f	-F	-r] [-b` *<number>* `| -c` *<number>* `|` *-n <number>*`]` *<file>*	
`tail [-f	-F	-r] [-b` *<number>* `| -c` *<number>* `|` *-n <number>*`]`	

TABLE 13.10 continued

`-f`	Waits for and displays additional data that `<file>` receives, rather than stopping at the end of the file.
`-F`	Similar to `-f`, except that every five seconds, `tail` checks whether `<file>` has been shortened or moved. If so, `tail` closes the current file, opens the filename given, displays its entire contents, and waits for more data. This option is especially useful for monitoring log files that undergo rotation.
`-r`	Displays the file in reverse order, by line. The default is to display the entire file in reverse. This option also modifies the `-b`, `-c`, and `-n` options to specify the number of units to be displayed, rather than the number of units to display from the beginning or end of the input.
`-b <number>`	Specifies location in number of 512-byte blocks.
`-c <number>`	Specifies location in number of bytes.
`-n <number>`	Specifies location in number of lines.
If `<number>` begins with `+`, it refers to the number of units from the beginning of the input. If `<number>` begins with `-`, it refers to the number of units from the end of the input.	

Deleting Files

Removing files and directories with Unix are fairly straightforward tasks, so you need to know only two commands to accomplish them.

Removing Files and Directories: rm, rmdir

Now that you have filled up your directory with lots of files, it is time to learn how to clean it up a bit. You can remove a file with `rm`.

Our user `nermal` has decided that her file called `myfile` is no longer needed. To remove it she does the following:

```
[localhost:~] nermal% ls -l myfile
     -rw-r--r--  1 nermal  staff  51 Apr 12 15:11 myfile
[localhost:~] nermal% rm myfile
     remove myfile? Y
```

As you notice in this example, `rm` prompts for confirmation before removing the file. Your system might not be configured to make `rm` prompt you for the removal of files. Information on how to make it ask you (`rm`'s interactive mode) is provided in Appendix B, and we very highly recommend that you follow the instructions to make your `rm` command interactive at the first possible opportunity. After you're a seasoned Unix user, you're welcome to run with `rm` in noninteractive mode by default, but until you've been certain that you're ready for a few years, it's probably safest to have it operate interactively by default.

Our user `nermal` has also decided that she is done with the data that she copied from user `joray`'s directory, and that she wants to remove the entire directory. The easiest way to do this is to force `rm` to recursively remove the directory, using options `-r` for recursive, and `-f` to override the interactive mode she has enabled by default, as shown here:

```
[localhost:~] nermal% ls -ld tests-for-nermal

     drwxr-xr-x  9 nermal  staff  262 Apr 23 11:29 tests-for-nermal

[localhost:~] nermal% rm -rf tests-for-nermal

[localhost:~] nermal% ls -ld tests-for-nermal

     ls: tests-for-nermal: No such file or directory
```

Removing a directory and all its contents using the recursive, and force options to `rm` is easy, but it is also silent and very, *very* fast. Remember to use those options only when you really mean it. Double-check everything before you run it. As you can see in the example, there is no recourse if you type the wrong thing.

The complete syntax and options for `rm` are in Table 13.11, the command documentation table.

TABLE 13.11 The Command Documentation Table for `rm`

`rm`	Removes directory entries.
`rm [-f | -i] [-dPRrW] <file1> <file2> ...`	
`-f`	Forces the removal of files without prompting the user for confirmation. If the file does not exist, no error diagnostic is displayed. The `-f` option overrides any previous `-i` options.
`-i`	Invokes an interactive mode that prompts for confirmation before removing a file. The `-i` option overrides any previous `-f` options.
`-d`	Attempts to remove directories as well as other types of files.

TABLE 13.11 continued

`-P`	Overwrites regular files before deleting them. Files are overwritten three times before being deleted; first with byte pattern `0xff`, and then `0x00`, and then `0xff`.
`-R`	Attempts to recursively remove files. Implies `-d` option.
`-r`	Same as `-R`.
`-W`	Attempts to undelete files. This option can be used to recover only files covered by whiteouts.
`rm` removes symbolic links, but not the files referenced by the links.	
Also, attempting to remove the files `.` and `..` is an error.	

There is also a command available for removing directories: `rmdir`. Unfortunately, it is only useful for removing empty directories. Its complete syntax and options are in the command documentation table, Table 13.12.

TABLE 13.12 The Command Documentation Table for `rmdir`

`rmdir`	Removes directories.
`rmdir [-p] <directory1> <directory2> ...`	
`rmdir` removes each *`<directory>`* argument specified, provided it is empty. Arguments are processed in the order listed on the command line. To remove a parent directory and subdirectories of the parent directory, the subdirectories must be listed first.	
`-p`	Attempts to remove the specified directory and its parent directories, if they are empty.

Searching for Files, Directories, and More

Unix traditionally has provided very useful tools for searching for files by name and by content, and Apple has expanded on these by making available an interface into the Sherlock databases from the command line. Unix's traditional tools don't work from a database as Sherlock does, so they run a little slower. But they aren't hampered by needing a database to run, or by being only as current in their results as the last database update.

Finding Files: `locate`, `find`

Sometimes you want to find some files, but you are not sure where they are. There are two tools available to search for files: `locate` and `find`. If you know some of the name of a file, you can use the `locate` utility to try to find it.

For example, our user `nermal` looked earlier at a file called `system.log`. Does our machine have other files that have `log` in their name? You bet! The syntax for `locate` is

`locate <pattern>`

We encourage you to try the `locate` command for files with `log` in them (`locate log`) to see the output, but it is much too long to include here. `locate` searches a database of pathnames on the machine.

> **Note**
>
> If you try `locate log` and produce no output, it's because your machine hasn't generated the database of paths yet. This database starts off empty, and is automatically rebuilt once a week. We've provided an example of how to force the database to be built in Chapter 1. Also, if you're particularly adventurous, you will find what you need to know to build it by hand in the `/etc/weekly` script, but this is a bit more complex than a novice will want to face.

Further information on `locate` is in the command documentation table, Table 13.13.

TABLE 13.13 The Command Documentation Table for `locate`

`locate`	Finds files.
`locate <pattern>`	
Searches a database for all pathnames that match `<pattern>`. The database is rebuilt periodically and contains the names of all publicly accessible files.	
Shell and globbing characters (`*`, `?`, `\`, `[`, and `]`) may be used in `<pattern>`, although they must be escaped. Preceding a character by `\` eliminates any special meaning for it. No characters must be explicitly matched, including `/`.	
As a special case, a pattern with no globbing characters (`foo`) is matched as (`*foo*`).	
Useful files:	
`/var/db/locate.database`	Database
`/usr/libexec/locate.updatedb`	Script to update database

A more powerful and more ubiquitous tool for finding files is `find`. It is much slower than the `locate` command because it actually searches the file system every time it's used, rather than consulting a database, but that also means it doesn't depend on a database for its information and the information is always completely up to date.

After running her search for files containing `log` in the name, our sample user `nermal` was overwhelmed by the results. However, she thinks that she might have heard that general system log files might be located in `/usr` or `/var`. To check whether what she recalls is correct, she decides to run `find`:

```
[localhost:~] nermal% find /var /usr -name \*log\*
      /usr/bin/logger
      /usr/bin/login
      /usr/bin/logname
      /usr/bin/rcs2log
      /usr/bin/rlog
      /usr/bin/rlogin
      /usr/bin/slogin
      /usr/include/hfs/hfscommon/headers/CatalogPrivate.h
      /usr/include/httpd/http_log.h
      /usr/include/mach/mig_log.h
      /usr/include/netinet6/natpt_log.h
      /usr/include/php/ext/standard/php_ext_syslog.h
      /usr/include/php/main/logos.h
      /usr/include/php/main/php_logos.h
      /usr/include/php/main/php_syslog.h
      /usr/include/sys/syslog.h
      /usr/include/syslog.h
      /usr/libexec/emacs/20.7/powerpc-apple-darwin1.0/rcs2log
      /usr/libexec/httpd/mod_log_config.so
      /usr/libexec/rlogind
      /usr/sbin/logresolve
      /usr/sbin/rotatelogs
      /usr/sbin/sliplogin
      /usr/sbin/syslogd
      /usr/share/emacs/20.7/lisp/add-log.el
      /usr/share/emacs/20.7/lisp/add-log.elc
      /usr/share/emacs/20.7/lisp/gnus/gnus-logic.el
      /usr/share/emacs/20.7/lisp/gnus/gnus-logic.elc
      /usr/share/emacs/20.7/lisp/progmodes/prolog.el
      /usr/share/emacs/20.7/lisp/progmodes/prolog.elc
      /usr/share/emacs/20.7/lisp/rlogin.el
      /usr/share/emacs/20.7/lisp/rlogin.elc
      /usr/share/groff/font/devps/prologue
      /usr/share/init/tcsh/login
      /usr/share/init/tcsh/logout
      /usr/share/man/cat1/logger.0
      /usr/share/man/cat1/login.0
```

```
/usr/share/man/cat1/logname.0
/usr/share/man/cat1/rlog.0
/usr/share/man/cat1/rlogin.0
/usr/share/man/cat2/getlogin.0
/usr/share/man/cat3/login.0
/usr/share/man/cat3/Sys::Syslog.0
/usr/share/man/cat3/syslog.0
/usr/share/man/cat5/.k5login.0
/usr/share/man/cat5/syslog.conf.0
/usr/share/man/cat8/logresolve.0
/usr/share/man/cat8/nologin.0
/usr/share/man/cat8/rlogind.0
/usr/share/man/cat8/rotatelogs.0
/usr/share/man/cat8/sliplogin.0
/usr/share/man/cat8/syslogd.0
/usr/share/man/man1/logger.1
/usr/share/man/man1/login.1
/usr/share/man/man1/logname.1
/usr/share/man/man1/rlog.1
/usr/share/man/man1/rlogin.1
/usr/share/man/man1/slogin.1
/usr/share/man/man2/getlogin.2
/usr/share/man/man3/login.3
/usr/share/man/man3/Sys::Syslog.3
/usr/share/man/man3/syslog.3
/usr/share/man/man5/.k5login.5
/usr/share/man/man5/syslog.conf.5
/usr/share/man/man8/logresolve.8
/usr/share/man/man8/nologin.8
/usr/share/man/man8/rlogind.8
/usr/share/man/man8/rotatelogs.8
/usr/share/man/man8/sliplogin.8
/usr/share/man/man8/syslogd.8
/usr/share/vi/catalog
```

In the preceding statement, `nermal` searches `/usr` and `/var`. The results, though, do not include the `system.log` file that `nermal` knows user `joray` was looking at earlier. According to these results, there are many files in `/usr` that contain `log`, but nothing in `/var`. But `nermal` is sure that `/var` is the other possibility she has heard. So, she decides that maybe the problem has something to do with `/var` actually being a symbolic link in OS X. She adds another option, `-H`, for `find` to return information on the referenced file, rather than the link:

```
[localhost:~] nermal% find -H /var -name \*log\*

    find: /var/cron: Permission denied
    find: /var/db/dhcpclient: Permission denied
    find: /var/db/netinfo/local.nidb: Permission denied
    /var/log
    /var/log/ftp.log
```

```
/var/log/ftp.log.0.gz
/var/log/ftp.log.1.gz
/var/log/lookupd.log
/var/log/lookupd.log.0.gz
/var/log/lookupd.log.1.gz
/var/log/lpr.log
/var/log/lpr.log.0.gz
/var/log/lpr.log.1.gz
/var/log/mail.log
/var/log/mail.log.0.gz
/var/log/mail.log.1.gz
/var/log/netinfo.log
/var/log/netinfo.log.0.gz
/var/log/netinfo.log.1.gz
/var/log/secure.log
/var/log/system.log
/var/log/system.log.0.gz
/var/log/system.log.1.gz
/var/log/system.log.2.gz
/var/log/system.log.3.gz
/var/log/system.log.4.gz
/var/log/system.log.5.gz
/var/log/system.log.6.gz
/var/log/system.log.7.gz
find: /var/root: Permission denied
/var/run/syslog
/var/run/syslog.pid
find: /var/spool/lpd: Permission denied
find: /var/spool/mqueue: Permission denied
find: /var/spool/output: Permission denied
find: /var/spool/printing/74FE197C-2928-11D5-AFCC.Q: Permission denied
find: /var/spool/printing/95E0CC6A-2F6F-11D5-B43C.Q: Permission denied
find: /var/spool/printing/B6E8E296-2EB1-11D5-98A5.Q: Permission denied
/var/tmp/console.log
```

There, in the middle of that output, is the `system.log` file, as well as some additional files with `system.log` in their name. As we see from the output, `nermal` does not have permission to search everywhere, but `find` responds with information for areas where permissions permit it. `nermal` was lucky that her machine's logs appear to include `log` in the name. That is not the case on all systems.

There are numerous options available in `find`. In addition to being able to search on a pattern, `find` can also run searches based on ownership, file modification times, file access times, and much more. The complete syntax and options for `find` are in the command documentation table, Table 13.14.

TABLE 13.14 The Command Documentation Table for `find`

`find`	Finds files.

`find [-H | -L | -P] [-Xdx] [-f <file>] <file> .... <expression>`

`find` recursively descends the directory tree of each file listing, evaluating an `<expression>` composed of primaries and operands.

Options

`-H`	Causes the file information and file type returned for each symbolic link on the command line to be those of the file referenced, rather than those of the link itself. If the file does not exist, the information is for the link itself. File information of symbolic links not on the command line is that of the link itself.
`-L`	Causes the file information and file type returned for each symbolic link to be those of the referenced file, rather than those of the link itself. If the referenced file does not exist, the information is for the link itself.
`-P`	Causes the file information and file type returned for each symbolic link to be those of the link itself.
`-X`	Permits `find` to be safely used with `xargs`. If a filename contains any delimiting characters used by `xargs`, an error message is displayed and the file is skipped. The delimiting characters include single quote, double quote, backslash, space, tab, and newline.
`-d`	Causes a depth-first traversal of the hierarchy. In other words, directory contents are visited before the directory itself. The default is for a directory to be visited before its contents.
`-x`	Excludes `find` from traversing directories that have a device number different from that of the file from which the descent began.
`-h`	Causes the file information and file type returned for each symbolic link to be those of the referenced file, rather than those of the link itself. If the referenced file does not exist, the information returned is for the link itself.
`-f`	Specifies a file hierarchy for `find` to traverse. File hierarchies may also be specified as operands immediately following the options listing.

TABLE 13.14 continued

Primaries (expressions)

All primaries that can take a numeric argument allow the number to be preceded by +, -, or nothing. *n* takes on the following meanings:

+*n* More than *n*

-*n* Less than *n*

n Exactly *n*

`-atime` *n*	True if the file was last accessed *n* days ago. Note that `find` itself will change the access time.
`-ctime` *n*	True if the file's status was changed *n* days ago.
`-mtime` *n*	True if the file was last modified *n* days ago.
`-newer` *<file>* than *<file>*.	True if the current file has a more recent modification time
`-exec` *<command>*`;`	True if *<command>* returns a zero-value exit status. Optional arguments may be passed to *<command>*. The expression must be terminated by a semicolon. If `{}` appear anywhere in the command name or arguments, they are replaced by the current pathname.
`-follow`	Follows symbolic links.
`-fstype`	True if the file is contained in a file system specified by `-fstype`. Issue the command `sysctl vfs` to determine the available types of file systems on the system. There are also two pseudo types: `local` and `rdonly`. `local` matches any file system physically mounted on the system where `find` is being executed; `rdonly` matches any mounted read-only file system.
`-group` *<gname>*	True if the file belongs to the specified group name. If *<gname>* is numeric and there is no such group name, *<gname>* is treated as the group ID.
`-user` *<uname>*	True if file belongs to the user *<uname>*. If *<uname>* is numeric and there is no such user *<uname>*, it is treated as the user ID.
`-nouser`	True if the file belongs to an unknown user.
`-nogroup`	True if the file belongs to an unknown group.
`-inum` *n*	True if the file has inode number *n*.
`-links` *n*	True if the file has *n* links.

TABLE 13.14 continued

-ls	Always true. Prints the following file statistics: inode number, size in 512-byte blocks, file permissions, number of hard links, owner, group, size in bytes, last modification time, and filename. If the file is a symbolic link, the display of the file it is linked to is preceded by ->. The display from this ls is identical to that displayed by ls -dgils.
-ok *<command>*	Same as -exec, except that confirmation from the user is requested before executing *<command>*.
-name *<pattern>*	True if the filename contains *<pattern>*. Special shell pattern matching characters ([,], *, ?) may be used as part of *<pattern>*. A backslash (\) is used to escape those characters to explicitly search for them as part of *<pattern>*.
-path *<pattern>*	True if the pathname contains *<pattern>*. Special shell pattern matching characters ([,], *, ?) may be used as part of *<pattern>*. A backslash (\) is used to escape those characters to explicitly search for them as part of *<pattern>*. Slashes (/) are treated as normal characters and do not need to be escaped.
-perm [-]*<mode>*	<mode> may be either symbolic or octal (see chmod). If *<mode>* is symbolic, a starting value of 0 is assumed, and *<mode>* sets or clears permissions without regard to the process's file mode creation mask. If *<mode>* is octal, only bits 0777 of the file's mode bits are used in the comparison. If *<mode>* is preceded by a dash (-), this evaluates to true if at least all the bits in *<mode>* are set in the file's mode bits. If *<mode>* is not preceded by a dash, this evaluates to true if the bits in *<mode>* match exactly the file's mode bits. If *<mode>* is symbolic, the first character may not be a dash.
-print0	Always true. Prints the current pathname followed by a null character.
-print	Always true. Prints the current pathname followed by a newline character. If none of -exec, -ls, -ok, or -print0 is specified, -print is assumed.
-prune	Always true. Does not descend into current file after the pattern has been matched. If -d is specified, -prune has no effect.

TABLE 13.14 continued

`-size n[c]`	True if the file size, rounded up, is *n* 512-byte blocks. If `c` follows *n*, it is true if the file size is *n* bytes.
`-type t`	True if the file is of the specified type. Possible file types are `W` Whiteout `b` Block special `c` Character special `d` Directory `f` Regular file `l` Symbolic link `p` FIFO `s` Socket
Operators	
Primaries may be combined using the following operators (in order of decreasing precedence).	
`(expression)`	True if the parenthesized expression evaluates to true.
`!expression`	True if the expression is false. (`!` is the unary, not the operator)
`expression [-and] expression`	
`expression expression`	True if both expressions are true. The second expression is not evaluated if the first is false. (`-and` is the logical AND operator.)
`expression -or expression`	True if either expression is true. The second expression is not evaluated if the first is true. (`-or` is the logical OR operator.)

Finding Files with Specific Contents: grep

Trying to remember what you've named a file that you need can sometimes be a real chore, especially if you haven't used the file for a long time, or its name is similar to many other files on your system. For situations like these, it is useful to be able to search for files based on patterns contained within the contents of the files themselves, rather than just the filenames. The basic syntax for `grep` is

```
grep <pattern> <files>
```

Here is a sample of using grep:

```
[localhost:~] joray% grep me file*

     grep: file1: Permission denied
     file2:It's me.  Doing some
     file3:Yep, me again..
     file4:me again
     file5:Another test by me...
```

In the preceding statement, we see that grep provides output as permissions permit. We also see that the default output lists only the fil,e the filename, and lines containing the searched pattern. A number of options are available in grep. For example, we could ask grep to list the line numbers on which our pattern, me, appears in the files:

```
[localhost:~] joray% grep -n me file*

     grep: file1: Permission denied
     file2:2:It's me.  Doing some
     file3:2:Yep, me again..
     file4:6:me again
     file5:1:Another test by me...
```

Another available option is the recursive option, for descending a directory tree searching all the contents.

The grep command is even more powerful than might be immediately apparent because it is also very useful for searching for patterns in the output of other commands. It could, for example, have been used to filter the rather verbose output from the preceding finds, to print out only the specific lines containing exact matches to the filename of interest. Although we haven't gotten to the syntax of the more complex matter of chaining Unix commands together to make sophisticated commands, keep grep in mind as a building block, and consider its possible uses when you reach the end of Chapter 14, "Advanced Shell Concepts and Commands."

The complete syntax and options for grep are shown in the command documentation table, Table 13.15.

TABLE 13.15 The Command Documentation Table for grep

grep	Prints lines matching a pattern
egrep	
fgrep.	
grep [*options*] <*pattern*> <*file1*> <*file2*> ...	
grep [*options*] [-e <*pattern*> | -f <*file*>] <*file1*> <*file2*>	

TABLE 13.15 continued

`grep` searches the list of files enumerated by *<file1> <file2>* ..., or standard input if no file is specified or if - is specified. By default, the matching lines are printed.	
Two additional variants of the program are available as `egrep` (same as `grep -E`) or `fgrep` (same as `grep -F`).	
`-A` *<num>*	Prints *<num>* lines of trailing context after matching lines.
`--after-context=`*<num>*	Same as `-A` *<num>*.
`-a`	Processes a binary file as if it were a text file. Equivalent to `-binary-files=text` option.
`--text`	Same as `-a`.
`-B` *<num>*	Prints *<num>* lines of leading context before matching lines.
`--before-context=`*<num>*	Same as `-B` *<num>*.
`-C` *<num>*	Prints *<num>* lines of output context. Default is 2.
`-`*<num>*	Same as `-C` *<num>*.
`--context[=`*<num>*`]`	Same as `-C` *<num>*.
`-b`	Prints the byte offset within the input file before each line of output.
`--byte-offset`	Same as `-b`.
`--binary-files=`*<type>*	Assumes a file is type *<type>* if the first few bytes of a file contain binary data.
Default *<type>* is `binary`, and `grep` normally outputs a one-line message indicating the file is binary, or nothing if there is no match.	
If *<type>* is `without-match`, it is assumed that a binary file does not match. Equivalent to `-I` option.	
If *<type>* is `text`, it processes the file as though it were a text file. Equivalent to `-a` option. Warning: Using this option could result in binary garbage being output to a terminal, some of which could be interpreted by the terminal as commands, resulting in unwanted side effects.	
`-I`	Assumes that a binary file does not match. Equivalent to `-binary-files=without-match` option.
`-c`	Prints a count of matching lines for each file. Combined with `-v`, counts nonmatching lines.
`--count`	Same as `-c`.
`-v`	Inverts matching to select nonmatching lines.
`--invert-match`	Same as `-v`.
`-d` *<action>*	If input file is a directory, uses *<action>* to process it.

TABLE 13.15 continued

If `<action>` is `read`, `grep` reads directories as if they were normal files. This is the default.	
If `<action>` is `skip`, `grep` silently skips directories.	
If `<action>` is `recurse`, `grep` recursively reads files under the directory. Equivalent to `-r`.	
--directories=*<action>*	Same as `-d <action>`.
-r	Recursively reads files under directories. Equivalent to `-d recurse` option.
--recursive	Same as `-r`.
-f *<file>*	Reads a list of patterns from `<file>`, which contains one pattern per line. An empty file has no patterns and matches nothing.
--file=*<file>*	Same as `-f <file>`.
-e *<pattern>*	Uses `<pattern>` as the pattern. Useful for protecting patterns beginning with `-`.
-regexp=*<pattern>*	Same as `-e <pattern>`.
-G	Interprets `<pattern>` as a basic regular expression. This is the default behavior.
--basic-regexp	Same as `-G`.
`-E`	Interprets `<pattern>` as an extended regular expression. Equivalent to `egrep`.
`-extended-regexp`	Same as `-E`.
`-F`	Interprets `<pattern>` as a list of fixed strings, separated by newlines, any of which is to be matched. Equivalent to `fgrep`.
`--fixed-strings`	Same as `-F`.
`-H`	Prints the filename for each match.
`--with-filename`	Same as `-H`.
`-h`	Suppresses filenames on output when multiple files are searched.
`--no-filename`	Same as `-h`.
`--help`	Displays a brief help message.
`-i`	Ignores case in `<pattern>` and input files.
`--ignore-case`	Same as `-i`.
`-L`	Prints a list of files that do not have matches. Stops scanning after the first match.

TABLE 13.15 continued

`-l`	Prints a list of files that contain matches.
`--mmap`	If possible, uses `mmap(2)` system call rather than the default `read(2)` system call. Sometimes `-mmap` results in better performance. However, it can cause unexpected behavior, such as core dumps, if the file shrinks while `grep` is reading it or if an I/O error occurs.
`-n`	Output includes the line number where the match occurs.
`--line-number`	Same as `-n`.
`-q`	Quiet. Suppresses normal output. Scanning stops on the first match. Also see the `-s` and `-no-messages` options.
`--quiet`	Same as `-q`.
`--silent`	Same as `-q`.
`-s`	Suppresses error messages about nonexistent or unreadable files.
`--no-messages`	Same as `-s`.
`-V`	Prints the version number of `grep` to standard error. Includes the version number in all bug reports.
`--version`	Same as `-V`.
`-w`	Selects only lines that have matches that form whole words.
`--word-regexp`	Same as `-w`.
`-x`	Selects only those matches that exactly match the whole line.
`--line-regexp`	Same as `-x`.
`-Z`	Outputs a zero byte (the ASCII NUL character) instead of the character that normally follows a filename. This option makes the output unambiguous, even for filenames containing unusual characters such as newlines.
`--null`	Same as `-Z`.
`-y`	Obsolete equivalent for `-i`.
`-U`	Has no effect on platforms other than MS-DOS and MS Windows. On those platforms, `-U` treats files as binary files to affect how CR characters are handled.
`--binary`	Same as `-U`.

TABLE 13.15 continued

`-u`	Has no effect on platforms other than MS-DOS and MS Windows. On those platforms, reports Unix-style byte offsets; that is, with CR characters stripped off.
`--unix-byte-offsets`	Same as `-u`.

File Compression and Archiving

As with the Macintosh world, a number of standards have arisen in the Unix world for compressing and archiving files. Unlike the Mac world, however, these programs don't tend to be do-all programs such as StuffIt that can archive, compress, password protect, and perform a wealth of other useful file archive functions. Following the Unix tradition, software that compresses files, mostly just compresses files. Software that collects lots of files together into a single-file archive, mostly just collects lots of files together into a single-file archive. These functions are used together to collect files into an archive (uncompressed), and then subsequently used to compress the files into a compressed archive. Likewise, the analogous procedure to "UnStuffiting" a file requires two steps in Unix because decompression of the archive and unpacking of its contents are two separate steps.

> **Tip**
>
> For those looking for a more seamless solution than the Unix way, take heart. The newer versions of GNU's `tar` program also include compression/decompression facilities. (GNU stands for GNU's Not Unix, and is the operating moniker for software developed or supported by the Free Software Foundation—the pioneers of the Open Source movement.) It's not too awfully Unix-like a way to do things, but if you insist on using the convenience, we won't hold it against you.

Compressing and Decompressing Files: `compress`, `gzip`, `uncompress`, `gunzip`

Unix has various tools available for compressing and decompressing files. Compressing files, of course, causes them to take up less space. As drive space becomes cheaper, this is perhaps not as great a concern. However, if you will be transferring files over the network, smaller files transfer faster. In addition, you might find it useful to compress files—especially archives of software packages you have installed—for writing to CD-ROM, where space is limited.

compress and gzip are the compressing tools available on your system; uncompress and gunzip are the decompression tools. compress and uncompress are more widely available by default on systems. The gzip tool, however, can compress further than compress.

Software packages that you download are frequently distributed as files compressed by compress or gzip. Files that you download ending in .Z are files compressed with compress. Files ending in .gz are compressed with gzip. Decompress files ending in .Z with uncompress; decompress files ending in .gz with gunzip. You will also occasionally see files ending in .tgz, which is the result of shoehorning .tar.gz (for tar archive, compressed with gzip) into a three-letter file extension).

Here is a sample of compressing a file using gzip:

```
Rosalyn source 19 >ls -l sendmail-src.tar

     -rw-r--r--   1 miwa  class  4454400 Jul  6  2000 sendmail-src.tar

Rosalyn source 20 >gzip -9 sendmail.8.10.2-src.tar

Rosalyn source 21 >ls -l sendmail.8.10.2-src.tar*

     -rw-r--r--   1 miwa  class  1250050 Jul  6  2000 sendmail-src.tar.gz
```

As we see from the ls listing, the size of the file has been reduced and .gz has been appended to the filename. The syntax and options for compress and uncompress are in the command documentation table, Table 13.16. The syntax and options for gzip and gunzip are in the command documentation table, Table 13.17.

TABLE 13.16 The Command Documentation Table for compress and uncompress

compress	Compresses data.
uncompress	Expands data.

compress [-cfv] [-b <*bits*>] <*file1*> <*file2*> ...

uncompress [-cfv] <*file1*> <*file2*> ...

compress reduces the size of a file and renames the file by adding the .Z extension. As much of the original file characteristics (modification time, access time, file flags, file mode, user ID, and group ID) are retained as permissions allow. If compression would not reduce a file's size, the file is ignored.

uncompress restores a file reduced by compress to its original form, and renames the file by removing the .Z extension.

-c	Writes compressed or uncompressed output to standard output without modifying any files.

TABLE 13.16 continued

`-f`	Forces compression of a file, even when compression would not reduce its size. Additionally, forces files to be overwritten without prompting for confirmation.
`-v`	Prints the percentage reduction of each file.
`-b <bits>`	Specifies the upper-bit code limit. Default is 16. Bits must be between 9 and 16. Lowering the limit results in larger, less compressed files.

TABLE 13.17 The Command Documentation Table for `gzip`, `gunzip`, and `zcat`

`gzip`	Compresses or expands files.
`gunzip`	
`zcat`	

`gzip [-acdfhlLnNrtvV19] [-S <suffix>] <file1> <file2> ...`

`gunzip [-acfhlLnNrtvV] [-S <suffix>] <file1> <file2> ...`

`zcat [-fhLV] <file1> <file2> ...`

`gzip` reduces the size of a file and renames the file by adding the `.gz` extension. It keeps the same ownership modes, and access and modification times. If no files are specified, or if the filename `-` is specified, standard input is compressed to standard output. `gzip` compresses regular files, but ignores symbolic links.

Compressed files can be restored to their original form by using gunzip, gzip -d, or zcat.

`gunzip` takes a list of files from the command line, whose names end in `.gz`, `-gz`, `.z`, `-z`, `_z`, or `.Z`, and which also begin with the correct magic number, and replaces them with expanded files without the original extension. `gunzip` also recognizes the extensions `.tgz` and `.taz` as short versions of `.tar.gz` and `.tar.Z`, respectively. If necessary, `gzip` uses the `.tgz` extension to compress a `.tar` file.

`zcat` is equivalent to `gunzip -c`. It uncompresses either a list of files on the command line or from standard input and writes uncompressed data to standard output. `zcat` uncompresses files that have the right magic number, whether or not they end in `.gz`.

Compression is always formed, even if the compressed file is slightly larger than the original file.

`-a`	ASCII text mode. Converts end-of-lines using local conventions. Supported only on some non-Unix systems.
`--ascii`	Same as `-a`.
`-c`	Writes output to standard output and keeps the original files unchanged.
`--stdout`	Same as `-c`.

TABLE 13.17 continued

`--to-stdout`	Same as `-c`.
`-d`	Decompresses.
`--decompress`	Same as `-d`.
`--uncompress`	Same as `-d`.
`-f`	Forces compression or decompression, even if the file has multiples links, or if the corresponding file already exists, or if the compressed data is read from or written to a terminal. If `-f` is not used, and `gzip` is not working in the background, the user is prompted before a file is overwritten.
`-h`	Displays a help screen and quits.
`--help`	Same as `-h`.
`-l`	Lists the following fields for each compressed file: `compressed` (compressed size) `uncompressed` (uncompressed size) `ratio` (compression ratio; `0.0%` if unknown) `uncompressed_name` (name of uncompressed file) Uncompressed size is `-1` for files not in `gzip` format. To get an uncompressed size for such files, use `zcat <file1.Z> | wc -c` Combined with `-verbose`, it also displays `method` (compression method) `crc` (32-bit CRC of the uncompressed data) `date and time` (time stamp of the uncompressed file) Compression methods supported are `deflate`, `compress`, `lzh`, and `pack`. `crc` is listed as `ffffffff` when the file is not in `gzip` format.
`--list`	Same as `-l`.
`-L`	Displays the `gzip` license and quits.
`--license`	Same as `-L`.
`-n`	When compressing, it does not save the original filename and time stamp by default. (Always saves the original name if it has to be truncated.) When decompressing, it does not restore the original name (removes only `.gz`) and time stamp (only copies it from compressed file), if present. This is the default.
`--no-name`	Same as `-n`.

TABLE 13.17 continued

`-N`	When compressing, it always saves the original filename and time stamp. This is the default. When decompressing, it restores the original time stamp and filename, if present.
`--name`	Same as `-N`.
`-q`	Suppresses all warnings.
`--quiet`	Same as `-q`.
`-r`	Traverses the directory structure recursively. If a filename specified on the command line is a directory, `gzip/gunzip` descends into the directory and compresses/decompresses the files in that directory.
`--recursive`	Same as `-r`.
`-S` *<suffix>*	Uses *<suffix>* instead of `.gz`. Any suffix can be used, but we recommend that suffixes other than `.z` and `.gz` be avoided to avoid confusion when transferring the file to another system. A null suffix (`-S ""`) forces `gunzip` to try decompression on all listed files, regardless of suffix.
`--suffix` *<suffix>*	Same as `-S` *<suffix>*.
`-t`	Test. Checks the integrity of the compressed file.
`--test`	Same as `-t`.
`-v`	Verbose. Displays the name and percentage reduction for each file compressed or decompressed.
`--verbose`	Same as `-v`.
`-V`	Version. Displays the version number and compilation options and quits.
`--version`	Same as `-V`.
`-`*<n>*	
`--fast`	
`--best`	Regulates the speed of compression as specified by `-`*<n>*, where `-1` (or `--fast`) is the fastest compression method (least compression) and `-9` (or `--best`) is the slowest compression method (most compression). Default compression option is `-6`.

Archiving Files: tar

tar is a useful tool for archiving files. Although originally intended for archiving to tape, tar is commonly used for archiving files or directories of files to a single file. After you have the archive file, it is common to compress it for further storage or distribution.

The most common options that you will probably use with tar are -c for creating a file, -t for getting a listing of the contents, -x for extracting the file, -f for specifying a file to create or act on, and -v for verbose output.

Here is an example of looking at the contents of a tar file. It is often useful to look at the contents of a tar file before extracting it. Because a tar file can be an archive of files rather than an archive of a directory of files, it is helpful to see the contents. That way, you know whether you should create a separate directory for extracting the file so that you have its contents in one place, or whether it will create a directory into which the files will be extracted.

Although not all the output is shown in this example, we can see nonetheless that the archive will create a directory into which the files will be extracted:

```
Rosalyn source 18 >tar -tvf sendmail.8.10.2-src.tar
     drwxr-xr-x 103/700       0 2000-06-07 13:01 sendmail-8.10.2/
     -rw-r--r-- 103/700     795 1999-09-27 17:39 sendmail-8.10.2/Makefile
     -rwxr-xr-x 103/700     327 1999-09-23 17:31 sendmail-8.10.2/Build
     -rw-r--r-- 103/700     321 1999-02-06 22:21 sendmail-8.10.2/FAQ
     -rw-r--r-- 103/700    1396 1999-04-04 03:01 sendmail-8.10.2/INSTALL
     -rw-r--r-- 103/700    8923 1999-11-17 13:56 sendmail-8.10.2/KNOWNBUGS
     -rw-r--r-- 103/700    4116 2000-03-03 14:24 sendmail-8.10.2/LICENSE
     -rw-r--r-- 103/700   23017 1999-11-23 14:08 sendmail-8.10.2/PGPKEYS
     -rw-r--r-- 103/700   13703 2000-03-16 18:46 sendmail-8.10.2/README
     -rw-r--r-- 103/700  348392 2000-06-07 03:39 sendmail-8.10.2/RELEASE_NOTES
     drwxr-xr-x 103/700       0 2000-06-07 13:00 sendmail-8.10.2/devtools/
     ...
```

The syntax and options for tar are in the command documentation table, Table 13.18.

TABLE 13.18 The Command Documentation Table for tar

tar	Creates, extracts, or appends to tape archives.
tar [-] <c | t | x | r | u> [fbemopvwzZhHLPX014578] [<*archive*>] [<*blocksize*>] [-C <*directory*>] [-s <*replstr*>] <*file1*> <*file2*> ...	
tar saves files to and restores files from a single file. Although that single file might have originally been intended to be magnetic tape, magnetic tape is not required.	
One of the following flags is required:	
-c	Creates a new archive or overwrites an existing one.
-t	Lists the contents of an archive. If any files are listed on the command line, only those files are listed.

TABLE 13.18 continued

`-x`	Extracts files from an archive. If any files are listed on the command line, only those files are extracted. If more than one copy of a file exists in an archive, earlier copies are overwritten by later copies.
`-r`	Appends the specified files to an archive. This works only on media on which an end-of-file mark can be overwritten.
`-u`	Alias to `-r`.
In addition to the required flags, any of these options may be used:	
`-f` *<archive>*	Filename where the archive is stored. Default is `/dev/rmt8`.
`-b` *<blocksize>*	Sets the blocksize to be used in the archive. Any multiple of 512 between 10240 and 32256 may be used.
`-e`	Stops after the first error.
`-m`	Does not preserve modification time.
`-o`	Does not create directories.
`-p`	Preserves user ID, group ID, file mode, and access and modification times.
`-v`	Verbose mode.
`-w`	Interactively renames files.
`-z`	Compresses the archive using `gzip`.
`-Z`	Compresses the archive using `compress`.
`-h`	Follows symbolic links as if they were normal files or directories.
`-H`	Follows symbolic links given on the command line only.
`-L`	Follows all symbolic links.
`-P`	Does not follow any symbolic links.
`-X`	Does not cross mount points in the file system.
`[-014578]`	Selects a backup device, `/dev/rmtN`.
`-C` *<directory>*	Sets the working directory for the files. When extracting, files are extracted into the specified directory. When creating, specified files are matched from the directory.
`-s` *<replstr>*	Modifies the filenames or archive member names specified by the pattern or file operands according to the substitution expression *<replstr>*, using the syntax of `ed(1)` in this format:

TABLE 13.18 continued

	/*old*/*new*/[gp]
	old is the old expression. *new* is the new expression.
	The optional trailing g applies the substitution globally. That is, it continues to apply the substitution. The first unsuccessful substitution stops the g option.
	The optional trailing p causes the final result of a successful substitution to be written to standard error in this format:
	<original pathname> >> *<new pathname>*
	Multiple -s *<replstr>* options can be specified. They are applied in the order listed.

Summary

This chapter introduced the most common Unix command-line file manipulation commands. Commands to copy files, move files, delete files, search and display files, as well as archive and compress files were covered. You will most likely type at least one command from this chapter, or the previous chapter, for every other command or application that you invoke from the Unix command line.

These commands also provide a good introduction to the Unix concept of small, single-function commands. What you've learned here about how a task can be accomplished the Unix way should serve you well in determining how to use other Unix commands that we don't have the time to cover in such depth.

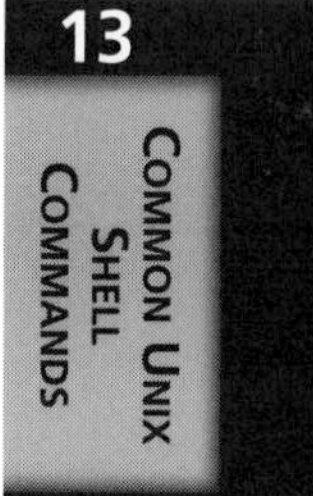

Advanced Command-Line Concepts

PART V

IN THIS PART

CHAPTER

Advanced Shell Concepts and Commands

In This Chapter

Now that we've covered the use of some of the most common Unix commands and their individual options and quirks, it's time to step back and examine some of the factors that affect the use of all shell commands.

In this chapter, we'll cover the Unix permission system, whereby you can control who is allowed to access your files, and what access rights they have.

We'll also cover process management from the command line, including how to identify and terminate processes that are causing problems for you.

Finally, we'll cover one of the most powerful shell formalisms, the notion of input and output redirection. This formalism is the root of much of the real power of the Unix command line. You should think about how commands that you've already learned might be enhanced by what you learn in that section when you reach it.

Introduction to File Permissions

This section expands on the topic of file permissions that was introduced in the section on the `ls` command. It's likely that you won't have an immediate use for modifying file permissions, and it's possible that you'll never need to deal with them at all. However, if you want to work with other users on the same system, or decide to start writing your own programs, understanding the permission system will be necessary.

Read, Write, and Execute

Permissions are specified as a collection of three flags. These flags (also called *bits*) control whether data in the file may be read, whether it may be written, and whether it may be executed. Unix takes these flags literally. So, if you have a program and you unset its execute flag, you won't be able to run the program—the system simply won't understand that the program is executable. Likewise, if you set the execute flag for a file containing a word processor document, Unix will assume that the file contents are a program and will try its best to run the file. This is unlikely to do anything but produce an error message.

In the case of directories, the same bits apply, but the meanings are slightly different. The read and write bits control whether the contents of the directory may be read, and whether the directory can be written to, respectively. The execute bit, however, controls whether the directory can be `cd`ed to, or otherwise moved into by a shell or program.

The permissions for whether a directory listing can be read or written to are separate from the permission that controls whether you, or programs, can move into it. Also, the permissions for files contained in the directory do not necessarily need to agree with the permissions of the directory. The significance of this might not be immediately apparent, but the meaning is quite literal. If you have files that have world read permission turned on, you can put them in a directory and set the bits on the directory so that the files in it can be read, but the files can't be listed. Likewise, you can set the permissions so that the directory allows anyone on the system to write files into it, but nobody can read the files or list the contents.

The execute permission for directories interacts with the read and write permission for files in it, in a slightly nonintuitive fashion. Read permission for the directory allows you to read the directory listing, but not the files. Read permission for a file in the directory allows you to read the file, but not list the directory. However, to be able to read the file, you, or rather the software you're using to read the file, need to be able to go into the directory. Because of this, if you turn on read permission for a directory and not execute permission, you can list the directory, but not read the files, no matter what the permissions on the files are. Likewise, you (or software under your control) can't write into a directory with only write permission turned on; execute permission must be enabled as well.

If you know that the file `fizbin` exists in the directory `thozbot`, but read and execute are turned off for `thozbot`, you can still read `fizbin` (assuming that you have read permission on `fizbin` itself) by using its full or relative path from outside the `thozbot`. If you don't know that `fizbin` exists in the directory, there's no way for you to find out, because you can't enter the directory or list the contents.

Note

Interesting applications for separated directory/file permissions immediately spring to mind. For example, perhaps you want to have a "drop box" directory where people could leave you files, but could not snoop around and see or read what anyone else had written. A directory with permissions set to write and execute permissions only would accomplish this.

Alternatively, a directory set to execute permission only, containing files with read permission enabled, would allow you to distribute files privately from a directory. With this setup, you could use one directory to distribute different files to a number of people privately, by giving each person only the filenames of the files he is allowed to read. Nobody can list the contents of the directory, but he can read files from it, if he knows the correct filenames.

Owner, Group, and World

Adding a layer of complexity to the permission system, the read, write, and execute permissions detailed earlier can be specified separately for three subsets of users. They can be set for each owner of the file, the group owner of the file, and the world.

The owner of a file is, as the name implies, the user who owns the file. Each file on a Unix system has information stored about it that indicates to which user account the file belongs. Files that you create will automatically belong to your user ID. Other files on the system will belong to other users, or to one of the system accounts that exists to help the operating system keep its processes sorted out and secure.

Files have an additional piece of ownership information: the group ownership of the file. The group ownership specifies, by group name, a collection of users who share the group permissions to the file. This additional information facilitates the sharing of information among more than one user. Creating groups and controlling their membership were covered in Chapter 11, "Additional System Components."

Finally, there is a set of permission bits that control the access level enjoyed by the world, or at least all the other users on the system. If you provide any sort of guest access to your machine, it's best to assume that the file's world permissions do in fact apply to just about everyone, independent of location.

Tip

Remember that the permissions allowed each type of user, owner, group, and world do not need to be the same. If you want to allow your friends to look at the data in your daily calendar file and the correlated data in your address/contacts file, you can set permissions on these files so that you (the user) can read and write them, but the group to which your friends belong can only read them. You might even want to let the world read the contents of your schedule, so you could turn on read access for the world for it. But you probably don't want the world picking though your personal address book, so you could shut off all access from the world by turning off all three flags for the world on that file.

Extended Bits

In addition to the read, write, and execute bits for each file and directory, a few additional bits exist as well. These bits are typically used by system administrators, but they occasionally come in handy for other users.

The complete set of bits, including the extended bits, that control the permissions and properties of a file or directory are called the *mode bits* for the file.

Special Flags

Further extending the classical set of mode bits are a set of special flags. These are definitely not for use by anyone but the administrator, but are mentioned here because one particular bit can sneak up and bite you.

The most important of these for you to watch out for is the immutable flag. This flag is set by the Finder's locked status for a file. It's not currently clear why Apple chose this particular flag to map to the Finder's locked status, but it causes a few problems on the Unix side.

Checking the Permissions: `ls -l`

Remember that the `ls -l` command shows you the permissions associated with files. To find out the permissions associated with a single file, give it a filename to list:

```
[localhost:~] nermal% ls -l /etc/passwd
     -rw-r--r--  1 root  wheel  564 Feb 25 03:05 /etc/passwd
```

Controlling Permissions: `chmod`

After you are comfortable examining the permissions of files, you'll probably want to be able to change them. This is accomplished with the `chmod` (change mode) command. This command operates in either a "fully specified mode bits" manner, or in a "change this specific mode bit" manner, depending on the arguments you give it on the command line.

The "change this specific mode bit" form is the more friendly of the two, and works by allowing you to specify a bit to change, how to change it, and which type of user to change it for. The complete syntax for this form of the command is

```
chmod <u|g|o|a><+|-><r|w|x> <filename> ...
```

To use it, simply do the following:

1. Pick whether you want to change the permissions for the user (yourself), the group, or the world. If you want to change the user, the first argument is `u`; `g` is for group; and `o` is for other (world).
2. Pick whether you want to add or delete a permission. If you want to add a permission, follow your first argument with a `+` sign; otherwise, follow it with a `-` sign.

3. Indicate the permission you want to add or delete using `r` for read, `w` for write, or `x` for execute. Follow these by the names of the files or directories for which you would like to change the permissions.

You might also use an `a` to indicate all, in place of the `u`, `g`, or `o` argument, if you want to make the change for the file to all three user types.

For example, consider a file named `fizbin` with the current permission set so that the user has full read, write, and execute permission, and the group and world have no permissions at all.

```
[localhost:~/Documents/test] nermal% ls -l
    total 0
    -rwx------   1 nermal  staff  0 Apr 22 23:32 fizbin
```

Perhaps this file is not actually a program, and to prevent yourself from accidentally trying to run it, you'd like to remove the execute permission from the user.

```
[localhost:~/Documents/test] nermal% chmod u-x fizbin
[localhost:~/Documents/test] nermal% ls -l
    total 0
    -rw-------   1 nermal  staff  0 Apr 22 23:32 fizbin
```

Now you would like to make it readable by both the group and the world.

```
[localhost:~/Documents/test] nermal% chmod g+r fizbin
[localhost:~/Documents/test] nermal% chmod o+r fizbin
[localhost:~/Documents/test] nermal% ls -l
    total 0
    -rw-r--r--   1 nermal  staff  0 Apr 22 23:32 fizbin
```

As you can see, this method of changing file permissions is fairly simple, but it does not lend itself to setting many permissions at once. More importantly, it changes the current permissions for the file one at a time. It can't set all the permission bits at once to force the file's mode bits into some particular pattern in a single command. To solve this, the `chmod` command also includes an "all at once" option, whereby you can specify the full complement of mode bits simultaneously.

This form of the command is slightly more complicated because it requires you to do a little math. In this form, the `chmod` command considers the mode bits for the file to be binary bits. To use the command, you need to specify which bits to set and which to unset.

Unfortunately, you can't do this in a manner as nice as just giving `chmod` a set of nine `rwxrwxrwx` characters, or ones and zeros. Instead, you must break up the nine bits of the mode bit set into three sets of three bits (`rwx rwx rwx`), and calculate the decimal equivalent of the bits that you want set.

Put another way, you could think of the elements in `rwx` as specifying where, in a binary string, a `1` occurs. This is done as shown here:

```
100 - read permission.    100 in binary = 4 in decimal.
010 - write permission.   010 in binary = 2 in decimal.
001 - execute permission. 001 in binary = 1 in decimal.
```

To find the decimal value equivalent of a particular combination of `r`, `w`, and `x` bits, you sum the decimal values that correspond to the bit patterns that represent them. So, if you wanted read and execute permission, with no write permission, you'd add `4 + 1 = 5`, and for user, group, or world, would put a `5` in the pattern where needed.

A full example should help to explain this. Let's again consider the `fizbin` file, which, due to the use of `chmod` previously, has mode bits of `rw-r--r--`. That is to say, the user can read and write, and both the group and world can read. If you wanted to change this to mode bits `r-xr-x--x`, the syntax shown for the friendlier mode of `chmod` would require several commands. Instead, you could make this change in a single command by using the "all at once" form. To do so, follow these steps:

1. Split the desired permissions into user, group, and world bits. This results in `r-x` belonging to the user, `r-x` belonging to the group, and `--x` belonging to the world.
2. Calculate the decimal values for each: `r-x` is read permission and execute permission, which is `4+1 = 5`. `r-x` for the group is the same. `--x` for the world is execute permission alone, which is simply `1`.
3. Put these together with the `chmod` command and the filename to change the mode bits for the file. In this case, `chmod 551 fizbin`.

Let's see whether it works:

```
[localhost:~/Documents/test] nermal% ls -l
     total 0
     -rw-r--r--  1 nermal  staff  0 Apr 22 23:32 fizbin
[localhost:~/Documents/test] nermal% chmod 551 fizbin
[localhost:~/Documents/test] nermal% ls -l
     total 0
     -r-xr-x--x  1 nermal  staff  0 Apr 22 23:32 fizbin
```

The command documentation table for `chmod` is shown in Table 14.1.

TABLE 14.1 The Command Documentation Table for `chmod`

`chmod`	Changes file modes
`chmod [-R [-H | -L | -P]] [-h]` *<absolute_mode> <file1> <file2>* ...	
`chmod [-R [-H | -L | -P]] [-h]` *<symbolic_mode> <file1> <file2>* ...	
`-R`	Recursively descends through directory arguments to change file modes.
`-H`	If `-R` is specified, symbolic links on the command line are followed. Symbolic links encountered in tree traversal are not followed.
`-L`	If `-R` is specified, all symbolic links are followed.
`-P`	If `-R` is specified, no symbolic links are followed.

Unless `-H` or `-L` is specified, `chmod` on a symbolic link always succeeds and has no effect. The `-H`, `-L`, and `-P` options are ignored unless `-R` is specified. Furthermore, `-H`, `-L`, and `-P` override each other. The last option specified determines the action that is taken.

Permissions are described by three sequences of letters in the order listed here. Each sequence describes the permissions for user, group, and other. If a certain permission has not been granted, a `-` (dash) appears in its place.

User	Group	Other
`rwx`	`rwx`	`rwx`

The permissions on a file can be viewed using `ls -l` and changed using `chmod`.

Absolute mode

Absolute mode is constructed by `OR`ing any of the following modes:

`4000`	Sets user ID on execution
`2000`	Sets group ID on execution
`1000`	Turns on sticky bit
`0400`	Allows read by owner
`0200`	Allows write by owner
`0100`	Allows execute (search in a directory) by owner
`0600`	Allows read, write by owner
`0500`	Allows read, execute by owner
`0300`	Allows write, execute by owner
`0700`	Allows read, write, execute by owner
`0040`	Allows read by group
`0020`	Allows write by group
`0010`	Allows execute (search in a directory) by group

TABLE 14.1 continued

0060	Allows read, write by group
0050	Allows read, execute by group
0030	Allows write, execute by group
0070	Allows read, write, execute by group
0004	Allows read by other
0002	Allows write by other
0001	Allows execute (search in a directory) by other
0006	Allows read, write by other
0005	Allows read, execute by other
0003	Allows write, execute by other
0007	Allows read, write, execute by other

Symbolic mode

Symbolic mode is a comma-separated list, with no intervening white space, of the form:

`[`*<who>*`]`*<operator>*`[`*<permissions>*`]`

<who> has the following form:

`< u | g | o | a>`

u	User's permissions
g	Group's permissions
o	Other's permissions
a	All permissions (user, group, other); equivalent to ugo

<operator> has the following form:

`< + | - | =>`

+	Adds <permissions>.

If <permissions> is not specified, no changes occur.

If <who> is not specified, <who> defaults to a, and <permissions> are added as specified, except that chmod does not override the file mode creation mask.

If <who> is specified, <permissions> are added as specified.

-	Removes <permissions>.

If <permissions> is not specified, no changes occur.

If <who> is not specified, <who> defaults to a, and <permissions> are removed as specified, except that chmod does not override the file mode creation mask.

If <who> is specified, <permissions> are removed as specified.

TABLE 14.1 continued

=	Assigns the absolute <permissions> specified.

If <who> is not specified, <who> defaults to a.

If <permissions> is not specified, <permissions> defaults to remove.

If `<who>` is specified and `<permissions>` is not, all permissions for `<who>` are removed.

If `<who>` is not specified and `<permissions>` is specified, `<permissions>` for all are set to `<permissions>`, except that `chmod` does not override the file creation mask.

If `<who>` is specified and `<permissions>` is specified, `<permissions>` for `<who>` are set as specified.

`<permissions>` has the following form:

`<r | w | x | X | s | t | u | g | o>`

`r`	Sets read bits.
`w`	Sets write bits.
`x`	Sets execute/search bits.
`X`	Sets execute/search bits if the file is a directory, or if any execution/search bits are already set in the file before `X` would act upon the file. `X` is used only with `+`, and is ignored in all other cases.
`s`	Sets the `set-user-ID-on-execution` and `set-group-ID-on-execution` bits. A process runs as the user or group specified by `s`.
`t`	Sets the sticky bit.
`u`	User permission bit in the mode of the original file.
`g`	Group permission bits in the mode of the original file.
`o`	Other permission bits in the mode of the original file.

Operations on `<who>` `o` in combination with `<permissions>` `s` or `t` are ignored.

Controlling a File's Group Ownership: `newgrp`, `chgrp`

As covered in Chapter 11, a user may belong to multiple different groups. Each of those groups may have different purposes on the system. For example, allowing groups of individual users to collaborate on projects, and allowing some users to belong to multiple different project groups.

A user who is a member of a group can access files that have that group as their group owner. As with real-life groups of people, however, each user can be in only one group at a time, no matter how many groups that user is a member of.

The group you are currently in is your *effective group ID*, and any files that you create while in this group will have the group ownership set to this group ID. If you are a member of multiple groups, you can pick the group ID that you are currently in by the use of the `newgrp` command. Issuing `newgrp <groupname>` switches your current group to `<groupname>`.

Note

For some reason, the `newgrp` command is missing from the current distribution (10.02) of OS X. This command is important, so we expect that its omission is another oversight on the part of Apple, and will be addressed in a future update.

In addition to being created as belonging to the user's current group ID, group ownership of a file can be further controlled by the file's owner. The owner of a file has the ability to change the group ownership of a file to any group to which the owner belongs. Issuing `chgrp <groupname> <filename>` will switch the group ownership of `<filename>` to `<groupname>`, assuming that you are a member of `<groupname>`. The command documentation table for `chgrp` is shown in Table 14.2.

TABLE 14.2 The Command Documentation Table for `chgrp`

`chgrp`	Changes group.
`chgrp [-R [-H | -L | -P]] [-fh] <group> <file1> <file2> ...`	
`-R`	Recursively descends through directory arguments to change the group ID.
`-H`	If `-R` is specified, symbolic links on the command line are followed. Symbolic links encountered in tree traversal are not followed.
`-L`	If `-R` is specified, all symbolic links are followed.
`-P`	If `-R` is specified, no symbolic links are followed.
`-f`	Forces an attempt to change group ID without reporting any errors.
`-h`	If the file is a symbolic link, the group ID of the link is changed.

TABLE 14.2 Continued

Unless -h, -H, or -L is specified, chgrp on symbolic links always succeeds and has no effect.

The -H, -L, and -P options are ignored unless -R is specified. Because they also override each other, the last one specified determines the action that is taken.

The group may be either a numeric group ID or a group name. If a group name exists for a group ID, the associated group name is used for the group.

The user invoking chgrp must belong to the specified group and be the owner of the file, or be the super user.

Unless invoked by the super user, chgrp clears the set-user-id and set-group-id bits.

Controlling the Special Flags

To modify the special flags, you use the `chflags` command. It's not at all clear what Apple is using the special flags for at the moment, although we do know that the Finder's locked status of a file sets the immutable bit on the Unix side. For example:

```
localhost testing 172> ls -l

      total 0
      -rw-r--r--  1 ray  staff  -    0 Jun 27 14:22 test
      -rw-r--r--  1 ray  staff  -    0 Jun 27 14:22 test2

localhost testing 173> su

      Password:

[localhost:/Users/ray/testing] root# chflags schg test
[localhost:/Users/ray/testing] root# ls -ol

      total 0
      -rw-r--r--  1 ray  staff  schg 0 Jun 27 14:22 test
      -rw-r--r--  1 ray  staff  -    0 Jun 27 14:22 test2

[localhost:/Users/ray/testing] root# chflags noschg test

      chflags: test: Operation not permitted

[localhost:/Users/ray/testing] root# rm test

      override rw-r--r--  ray/staff for test? y
      rm: test: Operation not permitted
```

The immutable flag is a relatively recent Unix invention, and indicates that the file *cannot* be changed. It's clear from the example that *immutable* really means just that: Even root can't delete the file, and what's more, root can't even *remove* the immutable flag after it has been set.

Even booting back into Mac OS 9.1 and trying to unlock the file from a Get Info dialog in the Finder turns out to be insufficient. The only successful route that we've found thus far is to remove the locked flag by the use of the venerable ResEdit program!

We don't really recommend experimenting with the `chflags` command much because it has the potential to make a real mess of things, and there's no documentation of what Apple is using the rest of the flags for. We've included the documentation table in Table 14.3, in case you should run across command examples using this in the future, as adventurous hackers pry the secrets out of OS X.

TABLE 14.3 The Command Documentation Table for `chflags`

`chflags`	Changes file flags
`chflags [-R [-H | -L | -P]] <flags> <file1> <file2> ...`	
`-R`	Recursively descends through directory arguments to change file flags.
`-H`	If `-R` is specified, symbolic links on the command line are followed. Symbolic links encountered in tree traversal are not followed.
`-L`	If `-R` is specified, all symbolic links are followed.
`-P`	If `-R` is specified, no symbolic links are followed.
Symbolic links do not have flags. Unless `-H` or `-L` is specified, `chflags` on a symbolic link always succeeds and has no effect. `-H`, `-L`, and `-P` options are ignored unless `-R` is specified. Furthermore, `-H`, `-L`, and `-P` override each other. The last option specified determines the action that is taken.	
`<flags>` is a comma-separated list of keywords. Currently available keywords are as follows:	
`arch`	Sets the `archived` flag (super user only)
`opaque`	Sets the `opaque` flag (owner or super user only)
`nodump`	Sets the `nodump` flag (owner or super user only)
`sappnd`	Sets the system `append-only` flag (super user only)
`schg`	Sets the system `immutable` flag (super user only)
`uappnd`	Sets the user `append-only` flag (owner or super user only)
`uchg`	Sets the user `immutable` flag (owner or super-user only)
Prepending the letters `no` to a flag turns the flag off.	

Process Management

In Chapter 6, "Native Utilities and Applications," you were introduced to the way that OS X is composed of many different cooperating processes. This is not particular to OS X, but instead is also the norm for Unix. Instead of a monolithic OS and user interface environment, Unix and (even more so) the Mach kernel on which OS X is based both operate as collections of a large number of cooperating programs. These programs create the illusion and functional experience of a seamless interface, but provide considerably more flexibility in the user's ability to modify things to suit his or her particular needs.

For example, with Mac OS, you're used to having a clock in the menu bar, and having the option to turn it on or off and perhaps set the font. This functionality is a built-in part of the OS and user interface. With Unix, if you want a clock, you run a separate program that displays a clock. Because the clock is a program and not an integral part of the OS, it can be any program. By selecting different programs, the clock can be made to appear as any type that you choose, anywhere on the screen that you choose.

It might take a while for you to come to appreciate the flexibility that this "everything is a process" idea of building operating systems provides for you. Monolithic OS and user interface environments have the advantage of being able to guide the user somewhat more strictly. They also are able to "guarantee" some types of responsiveness in ways that can't be done when all the user interface components are controlled by separate programs. Many of the things we will say are advantages of the new Unix environment—such as processes that run and provide some sort of functionality with no user interface (background processes), or programs that start at some pre-specified time—you might think are not so impressive because they were available in earlier versions of Mac OS. It is true that these advantages have been available. But as much as we love the Mac OS, we have to admit that they have been, at best, hacks; attempts to implement what you now have available to you, the Unix way of managing processes.

Listing Processes: ps

The ps command is used for listing the process status report. This is the command-line version of the Process View utility. There are many options to ps, but you might find issuing ps with the following options informative:

```
ps -aux
```

The following provides a sample of what to expect the output to look like:

```
[localhost:/] joray% ps -aux
USER    PID %CPU %MEM    VSZ   RSS  TT  STAT      TIME COMMAND
joray   345 85.1  2.6  89016 20428  ??  R   3619:50.28 /Applications/SETI@hom
root    277  6.1  0.1  51492   920  ??  S     63:19.47 /Library/S@hScreenSave
joray   290  3.0  0.1   5708   728 std  Ss     0:00.32 -tcsh (tcsh)
root    205  3.0  0.1   2420   560  ??  Rs     0:00.95 lookupd
joray    56  0.0  2.6  62568 20160  ??  Ss    20:50.78 /System/Library/CoreSe
root     58  0.0  0.0   1248    84  ??  Ss     1:39.07 update
root     61  0.0  0.0   1268    72  ??  Ss     0:00.00 dynamic_pager -H 40000
root    106  0.0  0.0   1996   316  ??  Ss     0:00.38 autodiskmount -v -a
root    130  0.0  0.1   3280  1048  ??  Ss     0:00.54 configd
root    138  0.0  0.0   1456   228  ??  Ss     0:00.01 ipconfigd
root    175  0.0  0.0   1260   140  ??  Ss     0:00.93 syslogd
root    194  0.0  0.0   1252   116  ??  Ss     0:00.01 portmap
root    197  0.0  0.0   1288   140  ??  Ss     0:00.00 nibindd
root    198  0.0  0.1   1632   484  ??  S      0:00.49 netinfod local (master
root    214  0.0  0.0   1524   276  ??  S<s    0:21.68 ntpd -f /var/run/ntp.d
root    221  0.0  0.2   9800  1560  ??  S      0:34.79 AppleFileServer
root    225  0.0  0.0   1692   256  ??  Ss     0:00.02 DesktopDB
root    230  0.0  0.0   1260   100  ??  Ss     0:00.02 inetd
root    239  0.0  0.0   1248    68  ??  S      0:00.00 nfsiod -n 4
root    240  0.0  0.0   1248    68  ??  S      0:00.00 nfsiod -n 4
root    241  0.0  0.0   1248    68  ??  S      0:00.00 nfsiod -n 4
root    242  0.0  0.0   1248    68  ??  S      0:00.01 nfsiod -n 4
root    251  0.0  0.2   4560  1648  ??  S      0:00.73 DirectoryService
root    256  0.0  0.0   2260   324  ??  Ss     0:00.01 automount -m /Network/
root    268  0.0  0.2   5048  1788  ??  Ss     0:02.36 /System/Library/CoreSe
root    272  0.0  0.0   1532   120  ??  Ss     0:00.73 cron
root    276  0.0  0.0   1248    60  ??  Ss     0:00.00 /Library/S@hScreenSave
joray   279  0.0  0.4  70752  2976  ??  Ss     0:20.96 /System/Library/CoreSe
root    281  0.0  0.1   3000   432  ??  Ss     0:08.09 slpd -f /etc/slpsa.con
joray   285  0.0  0.3  16000  1972  ??  S      0:01.52 /System/Library/CoreSe
joray   286  0.0  3.3 111080 25680  ??  S      0:28.51 /System/Library/CoreSe
joray   287  0.0  0.7  69216  5260  ??  S      0:01.67 /System/Library/CoreSe
joray   288  0.0  0.2  55260  1488  ??  S      0:00.45 /System/Library/CoreSe
joray   289  0.0  0.9  78860  7328  ??  R      0:21.15 /Applications/Utilitie
joray   302  0.0  2.2  89748 17224  ??  S     44:58.58 /Applications/Internet
joray   304  0.0  5.2 117528 41016  ??  R     62:49.21 /System/Library/CoreSe
root    321  0.0  0.0   1312   100  ??  Ss     0:00.00 /usr/libexec/lpd
joray   346  0.0  0.1   5708   700  p2  Ss     0:00.27 -tcsh (tcsh)
joray   376  0.0  0.0   1604   180  ??  Ss     0:00.07 /usr/bin/hdid -f /User
joray   383  0.0  0.8  76460  6096  ??  S      0:07.24 /Applications/TextEdit
joray   595  0.0  0.1   1676   464  p2  S+     0:00.02 vi output-ps
root    280  0.0  0.0      0     0  ??  Zs     0:00.00  (slpdLoad)
root    598  0.0  0.0   1316   284 std  R+     0:00.00 ps -aux
```

```
root      1  0.0  0.0   1260   240  ??  SLs    0:00.03 /sbin/init
root      2  0.0  0.0   1276   140  ??  SL     0:14.17 /sbin/mach_init
root     38  0.0  0.1   2676  1080  ??  Ss     0:00.76 kextd
joray    54  0.0  0.4  20816  2796  ??  Ss     0:02.58 /System/Library/Framew
```

The output from ps using these flags includes the owner of the process (USER), the process ID (PID), the percentage of the CPU (%CPU) and memory (%MEM) being consumed by the process, the virtual size of the memory space used by the program (VSZ) as well as the amount of that size that's resident in main memory (RSS), the controlling terminal (TT = ?? for no terminal), the run state of the process (STAT = R for running, S for short sleep, others), the accumulated CPU time (TIME), and the command that is running (COMMAND). More display options and orderings are available with the ps command, and command options, syntax, and keyword definitions for ps are included in the command documentation table in Table 14.4.

TABLE 14.4 The Command Documentation Table for ps

ps	Displays process status report
ps [-aCcefhjMmrSTuvwx] [-O *<fmt>*] [-o *<fmt>*] [-p *<pid>*] [-t *<tty>*] [-U *<username>*]	
ps [-L]	
-a	Includes information about processes owned by others in addition to yours.
-C	Changes the way CPU percentage is calculated by using a raw CPU calculation that ignores resident time. This normally has no effect.
-c	Changes the command column output to contain just the executable name rather than the full command line.
-e	Displays the environment.
-f	Shows command line and environment information about swapped-out processes. This is honored only if the user's user ID is 0.
-h	Repeats the header information so that there is one header per page of information.
-j	Prints information associated with the following keywords: user, pid, ppid, pgid, sess, jobc, state, tt, time, and command.
-l	Displays information associated with the following keywords: uid, pid, ppid, cpu, pri, nice, vsz, rss, wchan, state, tt, time, and command.

TABLE 14.4 continued

`-M`	Prints the threads corresponding with each task.
`-m`	Sorts by memory usage, rather than by process ID.
`-r`	Sorts by current CPU usage, rather than by process ID.
`-S`	Changes the way the process time is calculated by summing all exited children to their parent process.
`-T`	Displays information about processes attached to the device associated with standard output.
`-u`	Displays information associated with the following keywords: `user`, `pid`, `%cpu`, `%mem`, `vsz`, `rss`, `tt`, `state`, `start`, `time`, and `command`. The `-u` option implies the `-r` option.
`-v`	Displays information associated with the following keywords: `pid`, `state`, `time`, `sl`, `re`, `pagein`, `vsz`, `rss`, `lim`, `tsiz`, `%cpu`, `%mem`, and `command`. The `-v` option implies the `-m` option.
`-w`	Uses 132 columns to display information, instead of the default, which is your window size. If the `-w` option is specified more than once, `ps` uses as many columns as necessary, regardless of your window size.
`-x`	Displays information about processes without controlling terminals.
`-O` *<fmt>*	Adds the information associated with the space- or comma-separated list of keywords specified, after the process ID, in the default information displayed. Keywords may be further defined with an = and a string. Keywords further specified in this manner are displayed in the header as specified rather than using the standard header.
`-o` *<fmt>*	Displays information associated with the space- or comma-separated list of keywords specified. Keywords may be further defined with an = and a string. Keywords further specified in this manner are displayed in the header as specified rather than using the standard header.
`-p` *<pid>*	Displays information associated with the specified process ID *<pid>*.
`-t` *<tty>*	Displays information about processes attached to the specified terminal device *<tty>*.
`-U` *<username>*	Displays information about processes belonging to the specified *<username>*.

TABLE 14.4 continued

`-L`	Lists the set of available keywords.
The following is a list of the definitions of the keywords that some of the options already include. There are more keywords available than are defined here.	
`%cpu`	Percentage CPU usage (alias `pcpu`)
`%mem`	Percentage memory usage (alias `pmem`)
`command`	Command and arguments
`cpu`	Short-term CPU usage factor (for scheduling)
`jobc`	Job control count
`lim`	Memory use limit
`nice`	Nice value (alias to `ni`)
`pagein`	Pageins (total page faults)
`pgid`	Process group number
`pid`	Process ID
`ppid`	Parent process ID
`pri`	Scheduling priority
`re`	Core residency time (in seconds; `127` = infinity)
`rss`	Resident set size (real memory)
`rsz`	Resident set size + (text size/text use count) (alias `rs-size`)
`sess`	Session pointer
`sl`	Sleep time (in seconds; `127` = infinity)
`start`	Time started
`state`	Symbolic process state (alias `stat`)
`tsiz`	Text size (in kilobytes)
`tt`	Control terminal name (two-letter abbreviation)
`uid`	Effective user ID
`user`	Username (from `uid`)
`vsz`	Size of process in virtual memory in kilobytes (alias `vsize`)
`wchan`	Wait channel (as a symbolic name)

Listing Shell Child Processes: jobs

The term *jobs* and the term *processes* are frequently used interchangeably when discussing programs running on a Unix machine. But there is also a more specific meaning of *jobs* that has to do with processes that are run within, or by, a shell process.

Unix processes have the notion of parent and child processes. For example, consider `Terminal.app`. If you run a shell in a terminal window (which is what you most frequently will do to get access to a shell), the running process that is that shell will be a child of `Terminal.app`. If you run a process in the shell, such as `ls`, or any other commands we discuss in this book, the process that is that command will be a child of the shell. Likewise, the shell will be the parent of the `ls` command run in it, and `Terminal.app` will be the parent of the shell. `Terminal.app` itself in this case will most likely be the child of the OS X Finder, and the Finder will be the child of whatever process controls OS X logins. Every process in this way can trace its execution lineage back to the ancestor of all executing programs `/sbin/init`, which will have process ID `1`.

Therefore, a *user's jobs* refers to all processes running on a machine that belong to a particular user. *Shell jobs*, on the other hand, refer to processes that are children of (that is, were run by) a particular running instance of a shell.

The `jobs` command displays current processes that are children of the shell where the command is issued. This might not make much sense just yet because we haven't introduced any way for you to run a command and have it execute to completion before returning to the command prompt, but we will cover this material shortly. The `jobs` command gives you the ability to find out what jobs are present and what state they are in. For example, the shell shown in the following output has three jobs running in the background, and one job that is suspended:

```
localhost ray 160> jobs
      [1]      Running                       ./aaa.csh
      [2]  -   Running                       ./bbbb.csh
      [3]      Running                       ./test.csh
      [4]  +   Suspended                     ./test2.csh
```

Suspended jobs are jobs that are not executing for one reason or another. In this case, the suspended job was stopped with the Ctrl+Z shell key sequence discussed in Chapter 12, "Introducing the BSD Subsystem,"and is waiting for the user to resume it, send it to the background, or kill it off.

The `+` and `-` characters indicate the most current job, and the previously most current job, respectively.

The command documentation for `jobs` in Table 14.5 also includes information on how a job may be referenced, based on the output of `jobs`, for use in other job-control commands.

TABLE 14.5 The command Documentation Table for `jobs`

`jobs`	Displays the table of current jobs.
`jobs [-l]`	
`-l`	Lists jobs in long format. This includes the job number and its associated process ID.

After you know what jobs belong to the current shell, there are several ways to refer to a job. `%` introduces a job name. Job number `1` is `%1`. An unambiguous string of characters at the beginning of the name can be used to refer to a job; the form is `%<`*`first-few-characters-of-job`*`>`. An unambiguous string of characters in the job name can also be used to refer to a job; for example, the form `%?<`*`text-string`*`>` specifies a job whose name contains `<`*`text-string`*`>`.

Output pertaining to the current job is marked with `+`; output from a previous job, `-`. `%+`, `%`, and `%%` refer to the current job. `%-` refers to the previous job.

Backgrounding Processes: bg

The `bg` command backgrounds a suspended job. The process continues, only in the background. The most noticeable effect for the user is the return of the command prompt. Backgrounding processes is particularly useful for commands and programs that do not produce command-line output. Although the user's prompt returns, the process continues. It does not make sense to background something like `ls`, which is trying to show you output to the terminal. On the other hand, backgrounding the process responsible for a long `cp` or `compress` can be very convenient. The usual method for suspending a running process is to press Ctrl+Z, which stops, but does not kill, the process. For example:

```
localhost ray 185> jobs

     [1]  - Running                          ./aaa.csh
     [4]  + Running                          ./test.csh
localhost ray 186> ./test2.csh
^Z

     [1]      468 Running                          ./aaa.csh
     [4]  -   504 Running                          ./test.csh
     [5]  +   635 Suspended                        ./test2.csh
```

```
localhost ray 187> jobs
     [1]    Running                          ./aaa.csh
     [4]  - Running                          ./test.csh
     [5]  + Suspended                        ./test2.csh
localhost ray 188> bg
     [5]    ./test2.csh &
     /Users/ray
localhost ray 189>
localhost ray 189> jobs
     [1]  - Running                          ./aaa.csh
     [4]  + Running                          ./test.csh
     [5]    Running                          ./test2.csh
```

When stopped with Ctrl+Z, the shell automatically tells me the current list of jobs, and includes their process IDs for convenience.

Caution

Watch out for the potentially confusing output of the current directory (`/Users/ray` in the preceding example) after backgrounding a job. Output timing issues frequently result in the shell displaying its prompt before the `bg` command prints the current directory. This causes the working directory to be printed as though it were a command, sitting after the prompt at the command line. Pressing the Enter key if this happens will not harm anything.

If there were multiple suspended jobs, I could pick which one to send to the background, by the use of an optional job specifier, as shown in the documentation for the `bg` command in Table 14.6.

TABLE 14.6 The Command Documentation Table for `bg`

`bg`	Backgrounds a job
`bg [%job> ...]`	
`%<job>%`	
`bg`	
Backgrounds the specified jobs, or if no argument is given, the current job, and continues as though each has stopped. `<job>` may be any acceptable form described in `jobs`.	

Backgrounding Processes with &

Processes can also be put in the background by the use of the & symbol at the end of the command line. Simply add this symbol to the end of any command line, and the resulting process will be run in the background automatically.

```
localhost ray 190> jobs

     [1]  - Running                          ./aaa.csh
     [4]  + Running                          ./test.csh
     [5]    Running                          ./test2.csh

localhost ray 191> ./bbbb.csh  &

     [6] 691
      /Users/ray

localhost ray 192>
localhost ray 192> jobs

     [1]  - Running                          ./aaa.csh
     [4]  + Running                          ./test.csh
     [5]    Running                          ./test2.csh
     [6]    Running                          ./bbbb.csh
```

When a job is put into the background using the & suffix for a command line, it automatically prints out its job number and process ID.

Foregrounding Processes: fg

The command fg returns a job to the foreground, where it continues to run. The command may be either a background job or a suspended job.

```
localhost ray 207> jobs

     [1]  - Running                          ./aaa.csh
     [5]  + Running                          ./test2.csh

localhost ray 208> fg %1

     ./aaa.csh
```

Documentation for fg is in the command table, Table 14.7.

TABLE 14.7 The Command Documentation Table for fg

fg	Foregrounds a job
fg [%<*job*>...]	
%<*job*>	
fg	
Brings the specified jobs (or, if no argument is given, the current job) to the foreground, continuing each as though it had stopped. <*job*> may be any acceptable form as described in jobs.	

Stopping Processes, Sending Signals: kill

The `kill` command sends a signal to a process or terminates a process. It is most commonly used in conjunction with `ps`, which provides the process ID of the process to which you want to send a signal.

You will probably most often use this command either to terminate a process, or to send a hang up signal (HUP) to force a process to reread its configuration file.

The syntax that you will probably most often use is one of the following forms:

```
kill -9 <pid>

kill -HUP <pid>
```

In the first example, the `-9` sends a definite termination signal to the process specified. In the second example, the `-HUP` sends a hangup signal to a process, which then rereads its configuration file and starts over. You will see at least one example of this later in the book.

The command documentation table for `kill` is shown in Table 14.8.

TABLE 14.8 The Command Documentation Table for `kill`

`kill`	Sends a signal to a process or terminates a process
`kill [-<signal>] %<job> | <pid>`	
`kill -l`	
`-l`	Lists the signal names
`<signal>`	Specifies which signal to send to a process. If `<signal>` is not specified, the `TERM` (terminate) signal is sent. `<signal>` may be a number or name.
`%<job>`	Specifies the job that should receive a signal.
`<pid>`	Specifies the process ID that should receive a signal. The process ID can be determined by running `ps`.

Signal `KILL (9)` is a sure way to kill a process. Signal `HUP` is another common signal to send to a process. You might want to send a `HUP` signal to a process to get it to reread its configuration file.

Listing Resource-Consuming Processes: top

The `top` command displays system usage statistics, particularly of those processes making the most use of system resources. Processes are displayed at one-second intervals. It can be useful for diagnosing unusual behavior with a process. It is worthwhile to run `top` from time to time so that you learn what the typical behavior for your system is.

When `top` is displaying processes, it takes over your screen. You can quit the display by pressing the Q key. The following is a sample of what `top` output looks like:

```
Processes:  41 total, 3 running, 38 sleeping... 102 threads            10:52:23
Load Avg:  1.50, 2.01, 1.99     CPU usage:  89.0% user, 11.0% sys, 0.0% idle
SharedLibs: num =   71, resident = 14.9M code, 1.05M data, 3.62M LinkEdit
MemRegions: num = 1544, resident = 39.0M + 5.67M private, 26.6M shared
PhysMem:  46.5M wired, 30.6M active, 84.4M inactive,  161M used,  607M free
VM: 1.01G + 38.9M   7300(1) pageins, 0(0) pageouts

  PID COMMAND      %CPU   TIME   #TH #PRTS #MREGS RPRVT  RSHRD  RSIZE  VSIZE
  295 top          7.3%  0:00.80   1    19    14   172K   224K   392K  1.31M
  290 tcsh         0.0%  0:00.14   1    17    14   260K   460K   700K  5.57M
  289 Terminal     0.9%  0:01.23   4    76    58  1.40M  3.86M  4.49M+ 73.8M+
  287 ProcessVie   0.0%  0:01.07   2    67    51  1.11M  4.43M  4.57M  73.7M
  286 SETI@home_  88.1%  3:04.39   3    97   131  17.3M  4.32M  20.1M  87.3M
  285 DocklingSe   0.0%  0:00.39   1    56    32   428K  1.53M  1.34M  53.7M
  284 Dock         0.0%  0:00.67   2    93    87  4.18M  3.12M  5.62M  68.2M
  283 Finder       0.0%  0:06.18   3    86   230  10.7M  12.4M  18.2M  98.0M
  282 pbs          0.0%  0:01.52   3    84    51   564K  1.28M  1.87M  15.6M
  278 slpd         0.0%  0:00.03   4    21    19   124K   320K   420K  2.93M
  276 loginwindo   0.0%  0:01.23   2    89    65  1.22M  2.51M  2.90M  69.1M
  274 S@hScreenS   0.9%  0:03.47   1    48    26   364K  1.01M   924K  50.3M
  273 SETI@homeI   0.0%  0:00.00   1    10    12    44K   192K    64K  1.22M
  269 cron         0.0%  0:00.00   1    10    14    84K   220K   132K  1.50M
  265 SecuritySe   0.0%  0:00.04   2    24    27   256K  1020K  1.23M  4.43M
```

The command documentation table for `top` is shown in Table 14.9.

TABLE 14.9 The Command Documentation Table for `top`

`top`	Displays system usage statistics
`top [-u] [-w] [-k] [-s <interval>] [-e | -d | -a] [-l <samples>] [<number>]`	
`top`	
`-u`	Sorts by CPU usage and displays usage starting with the highest usage.
`-w`	Generates additional columns of output data. The additional columns include `VPRVT` and the delta information for `#PRTS`, `RSHRD`, `RSIZE`, and `VSIZE`.
`-k`	Causes `top` to traverse and report the memory object map for pid 0 (kernel task). This option is optional because it is expensive to traverse the object maps, as the kernel task may have a large number of entries.

TABLE 14.9 continued

`-s <interval>`	Samples processes at the specified `<interval>`. Default is one-second intervals.
`-e`	Switches to event counting mode where counts reported are absolute counters. Options `-w` and `-k` are ignored.
`-d`	Switches to an event counting mode where counts are reported as deltas relative to the previous sample. Options `-w` and `-k` are ignored.
`-a`	Switches to an event counting mode where counts are reported as cumulative counters relative to when `top` was launched. Options `-w` and `-k` are ignored.
`-l <samples>`	Switches from default screen mode to a logging mode suitable for saving the output to a file. If `<samples>` is specified, `top` samples the number of samples specified before exiting. The default is `1`.
`<number>`	Limits the number of processes displayed to `<number>`.
Pressing the Q key causes `top` to exit immediately.	
Columns displayed in default data mode:	
`PID`	Unix process ID
`COMMAND`	Unix command name
`%CPU`	Percentage of CPU used (kernel and user)
`TIME`	Absolute CPU consumption (min:secs.hundredths)
`#TH`	Number of threads
`#PRTS` (delta)	Number of MACH ports
`#MERG`	Number of memory regions
`VPRVT` (`-w` only)	Private address space currently allocated
`RPRVT` (delta)	Resident shared memory (as represented by the resident page count of each shared memory object)
`RSHRD` (delta)	Total resident memory (real pages that this process currently has associated with it; some may be shared by other processes)
`VSIZE` (delta)	Total address space currently allocated (including shared)
Columns displayed in event counting modes:	
`PID`	Unix process ID
`COMMAND`	Unix command name
`%CPU`	Percentage of CPU used (kernel and user)

TABLE 14.9 continued

`TIME`	Absolute CPU consumption (min:secs.hundredths)
`FAULTS`	Number of page faults
`PAGEINS`	Number of requests for pages from a pager
`COW_FAULTS`	Number of faults that caused a page to be copied
`MSGS_SENT`	Number of mach messages sent by the process
`MSGS_RCVD`	Number of mach messages received by the process
`BSDSYSCALL`	Number of BSD system calls made by the process
`MACHSYSCALL`	Number of MACH system calls made by the process
`CSWITCH`	Number of context switches to this process

Communication Between Processes: Redirection, Pipes

Building an operating system out of a multitude of small, cooperating processes would not provide such flexibility and power to the user were it not for a simple method of making all of these processes speak to each other. At the heart of the interprocess communications model of Unix, is a simple but amazingly effective abstraction of the idea of input and output.

To paraphrase the model on which Unix bases input and output, you can imagine that Unix thinks of user input to a program as a stream—a stream of information. Output from the program back to the user can be thought of in the same way. A stream of information is simply a collection of information that flows in or out of the program in a serial (ordered) fashion. A user can't send two pieces of information to a program at the same time—two key presses, no matter how closely they occur, are ordered, one first and one second. A cursor moving across a screen provides information serially as to where it is now, and where it was then. Even if two events manage to occur simultaneously, the electronics of the machine can't really deal with simultaneous events, and so they end up being registered as separate events occurring very close in time. Output must be similarly serially ordered. Whether drawing data to the screen or sending data over an Internet connection, no two data items leave a program at exactly the same time; therefore, they are also a serial stream of information.

Because both input and output from processes are streams of information, and every function of the system from user programs to reading files to parts of the OS is a running process, Unix models the implementation of communication between the processes as simply tying the output stream of one process to another's input stream. Tying the output stream (named STDOUT) from one process to the input stream (named STDIN) of another is called *creating a pipe* between them. When you understand the view of data moving into or out of a process as being a data stream, it is immediately obvious that there is no need for the system to concern itself over the endpoints of the stream. One endpoint (STDOUT) might be a process taking input from a user, and the other endpoint (STDIN) might be a process manipulating that input and writing it into a file. On the other hand, the same input could be placed in a file, and a process could read that file, creating the same output on STDOUT, and sending it via STDIN into the same manipulation program. There would be absolutely no difference between these two situations from the OS's point of view.

In short, this abstraction provides that so long as the input coming to a process "looks like" the input the process expects, it does not matter to the process or the OS where that input comes from. Likewise, provided that the destination of the output from the process "acts like expected," it does not matter where the output is actually going.

Redirection: STDIN, STDOUT, STDERR

Unix makes this input/output model available to the user through a concept known as redirection. This is implemented as a requirement that all processes adhere to certain conventions regarding input and output.

At the base is the notion that input and output from programs is generally from, and to, a user typing information at the command line. Even programs that are not intended to be used by a person at a command line are expected to adhere to the model that input comes from a user, and output goes to a user.

This might seem counterintuitive, but further conventions are required that allow this seeming restriction to be less restrictive, while generalizing the input/output model sufficiently that it can be applied to almost any need. Two of these are the idea of input arriving in a program through a virtual interface known as STDIN (standard input), and output leaving the program through a virtual interface known as STDOUT (standard output). It also requires the convention of a third virtual interface by which error messages can be conveyed, which is STDERR (standard error).

Redirection is accomplished by attaching these virtual interfaces to each other in various combinations—essentially redirecting the input or output from a process to a different location than to a user or from a user.

Standard In: STDIN

The virtual input interface to programs is called STDIN, for standard input. A program can expect the incoming data stream from the user (or any other source) to arrive at STDIN.

When you interact with a command-line program, the program is reading the data you are entering from STDIN. If you prefer not to enter the data by hand, you can put it in a file and redirect the contents of the file into the program's STDIN—the program will not know the difference.

A program that you can use for an example is the spell program. Apple hasn't distributed spell with OS X as of this writing, but we've provided instructions on how to install it in Chapter 15, "Command Line Applications and Application Suites." If you're using a system on which it's already been installed, follow along here. If not, spell still makes a good program for explanation because it has exactly the features we want to exhibit—just read along and imagine that it's really working until you get to Chapter 15.

The spell command finds misspellings. Given input from STDIN, spell parses through it, checks the input against a dictionary, and returns any misspellings it finds. Issued from the command line, you might type something like the following:

```
% spell
Now is the tyem for all good authors to come to thie ayde of some very
good Unix users
Ctrl+d
```

Pressing Ctrl+d finishes the input, sending an end-of-data signal into STDIN, effectively telling the program that there is no further information to come. The spell program goes to work, and returns the following:

```
tyem
thie
ayde
```

Each of the misspelled words (or at least words that aren't in the dictionary) is displayed, exactly as expected.

This might not seem to be a particularly useful program at first glance—how often do you want to type a sentence, just to find out what words are misspelled in it? The key to its usefulness, however, is that the spell program does not care whether you typed the input, or whether the input came from a file.

Note

Actually, it's more proper to think of spell as not caring whether the input comes from a file, or from you instead. The spell program is designed to work with input coming from a file or a program. It just happens that because of the input/output model abstracting all system input and output as from/to a file-like interface, spell doesn't mind if the input comes from a user instead. Many programs you'll find available for Unix fall into this category—they are designed to take input or provide output to or from other programs or files rather than from users. The input/output model, however, allows a user to interact with the software anyway. Because of this, you might occasionally find the syntax in which these programs converse to be slightly odd. Just remember, they weren't really designed to talk directly to you.

Now to try it with data from a file. Fire up your favorite text editor, and create a file containing the same text you typed to spell previously. Then try `spell` by redirecting this file into its `STDIN` interface. If you named your file `reallydumbfile`, you can run spell on it by typing the following:

```
% spell < reallydumbfile

     tyme
     thie
     ayde
```

The < character redirects `STDIN` for the program to its left to come from the file named to its right. Here, it redirects `STDIN` for the `spell` program so that it comes from the file `reallydumbfile`, rather than from your keyboard.

Standard Out: STDOUT

The virtual output interface that Unix provides to programs is called `STDOUT`, for standard output. Just as you can redirect `STDIN` from a file, if you want to store the output of a command in a file, you can redirect `STDOUT` from the program into the file. The > character directs the `STDOUT` of the program to its left into the file named to its right. For example, if you would like to collect the last few lines of `/var/log/system.log` into a file in your home directory, you could type

```
% tail -20 /var/log/system.log > ~/my-output
```

> **Note**
>
> You can't read /var/log/system.log, unless you're either root or an administrative user.

This command directs the shell to create the file my-output in your home directory, and to redirect STDOUT from the tail command into it. If my-output already exists in your home directory, it will be overwritten by the output from tail.

If you'd prefer to collect and archive the data, by appending it to my-output instead of overwriting it, the shell can be directed to append rather than replace the data. In this case, STDOUT is redirected with >> instead of the single >. The >> character pair appends the STDOUT of the program to the left into the file named on its right.

You can also combine STDOUT and STDIN, like so:

```
[localhost:~/Documents] nermal% spell < reallydumbfile > reallydumbspelling
[localhost:~/Documents] nermal% ls

     get_termcap          lynx.cfg            reallydumbspelling  termcap-1.3.tar
     lynx                 reallydumbfile      termcap-1.3         test

[localhost:~/Documents] nermal% cat reallydumbspelling

     tyem
     thie
     ayde
```

Standard Error: STDERR

To make your life easier, Unix actually has two different output interfaces that it defines for programs. The first, STDOUT, has just been covered. The second, STDERR, is used to allow the program to provide error and diagnostic information to the user. This is done for two reasons. First, it allows error information to be reported in such a way that it does not interfere with data on the STDOUT interface. Second, if you are redirecting STDOUT from a program to another program or to a file, you would not see error messages if they were carried on STDOUT. By providing a separate error channel, the user is given the choice of how and where error and diagnostic information should be displayed, independent of data that is actually correct output data.

If you want to redirect STDERR into the same stream as STDOUT, effectively combining these two different pieces of information, you can do so by using the character pair >& to indicate redirection in the command, instead of >.

Again, if you've chosen to use a shell other than `tcsh` or `csh`, the redirection syntax is likely to vary considerably. See your online man pages to learn how the shell of your preference behaves.

Pipes

Finally, there is nothing in the input/output model that restricts redirection to coming from or going into files. `STDIN` and `STDOUT` can just as easily be tied together instead of being tied into files or the command line.

Perhaps more correctly, the OS never really redirects to or from files. What the OS is really doing when you redirect into a file is invisibly creating a process that writes into a file, and redirecting your output to the `STDIN` of the process writing the file. Likewise, when you redirect a file into a program's `STDIN`, the OS is invisibly creating a process that opens and reads the file, and is tying the `STDOUT` from this process into your process's `STDIN`. For the user's convenience, these common actions are abbreviated into the < and > redirection characters.

Programs, on the other hand, are connected by directly redirecting their `STDOUT` and `STDIN` interfaces with a pipe. To create a pipe in Unix, you simply use a `|` character between the programs on the command line.

Again, an example is more illustrative than a considerable amount of explanation. Consider a situation in which you would like to examine the content of a file that is larger than will fit on one screen. You can accomplish this easily by piping the output from the `cat` command into a pager, such as the `more` command.

```
[localhost:~/Public/spell-1.0] nermal% cat /etc/magic | more

#! file
#       $OpenBSD: Header,v 1.2 1996/06/26 05:33:03 deraadt Exp $

# Magic data for file(1) command.
# Machine-genererated from src/cmd/file/magdir/*; edit there only!
# Format is described in magic(files), where:
# files is 4 on V7 and BSD, 4 on SV, and ?? in the SVID.
#------------------------------------------------------------------------------
# Localstuff:  file(1) magic for locally observed files
#
# $OpenBSD: Localstuff,v 1.3 1997/02/09 23:58:40 millert Exp $
# Add any locally observed files here.  Remember:
# text if readable, executable if runnable binary, data if unreadable.

#------------------------------------------------------------------------------
# OpenBSD:  file(1) magic for OpenBSD objects
#
```

```
# All new-style magic numbers are in network byte order.
#

0       lelong                  000000407      OpenBSD little-endian object file
>16     lelong                  >0             not stripped
0       belong                  000000407      OpenBSD big-endian object file
>16     belong                  >0             not stripped

0       belong&0377777777       041400413      OpenBSD/i386 demand paged
>0      byte                    &0x80
>>20    lelong                  <4096          shared library
>>20    lelong                  =4096          dynamically linked executable
>>20    lelong                  >4096          dynamically linked executable
>0      byte                    ^0x80          executable

more
```

Of course, you already know that you could have accomplished this by just using `more /etc/magic`. The point, though, is that although we told you how to use `more` to read a file before, `more` *actually* wants to take its input from `STDIN`, and uses a file specified as an argument only as a last resort.

Knowing this, you now know how to make any other output from any other program viewable with the `more` pager. This lets you do things such as look at the full contents of your file system, without needing an immensely large scroll buffer in your terminal:

```
[localhost:~/Public/spell-1.0] nermal% ls -lRaF / | more

     ls: .Trashes: Permission denied
     total 13264
     drwxrwxr-t  39 root  admin     1282 Apr 20 15:00 ./
     drwxrwxr-t  39 root  admin     1282 Apr 20 15:00 ../
     -rwxrwxrwx   1 root  admin     8208 Apr 18 11:05 .DS_Store*
     d-wx-wx-wx   2 root  admin      264 Apr  4 12:20 .Trashes/
     -r--r--r--   1 root  wheel      142 Feb 25 03:05 .hidden
     dr--r--r--   2 root  wheel      224 Apr 20 15:00 .vol/
     -rwxrwxrwx   1 root  wheel   106496 Apr 20 14:59 AppleShare PDS*
     drwxrwxrwx  25 root  admin      806 Apr 18 11:05 Applications/
     drwxrwxrwx  18 root  wheel      568 Apr 20 14:54 Applications (Mac OS 9)/
     drwxrwxrwx   2 root  wheel      264 Apr  6 12:24 Cleanup At Startup/
     -rwxrwxrwx   1 root  wheel   212992 Apr 20 14:59 Desktop DB*
     -rwxrwxrwx   1 root  wheel  1432466 Apr 20 14:57 Desktop DF*
     drwxrwxrwx   6 root  staff      264 Apr  4 11:51 Desktop Folder/
     drwxrwxr-x  12 root  admin      364 Mar  1 20:29 Developer/
     more
```

These are, of course, simplistic examples of connecting programs, but keep an eye out for how pipes are used throughout the rest of the book. The ability to create small programs with small functions, and to tie these together into arbitrarily large programs with arbitrarily complex behaviors is a very powerful one, and is one of the largest reasons that having access to the BSD half of your new OS is such a valuable feature.

Think back to programs such as `grep`, and you can probably begin to see how you could apply this to creating custom solutions to problems that you might have encountered. You should also begin to see why this functionality cannot be conveniently duplicated with a GUI-only interface.

Joints in Pipes: `tee`

On occasion, you might want to redirect `STDOUT` to both a file and another program at the same time. In such a case, you can use the `tee` command. This command accepts data on `STDIN`, writes it to a filename specified on the command line, and continues to send the data, unaltered on `STDOUT`.

Consider an example in which you would like to search through your files, looking for files that match a particular name pattern. You would like to both browse the found names as they appear, and collect the names into a log file so that you can use the information again later. In this example, we will look in a rather inefficient fashion for files with names that contain `java`. Because there are probably lots of them on the system, we want the output piped through a pager (`more`). We also want to collect the filenames into a file in our home directory named `my_output`.

```
find / -name \*java\* -print | tee ~/my_output | more

     /Applications (Mac OS 9)/Apple...Applet
     Runner/Applets/Animator/Animator.java
     /Applications (Mac OS 9)/Apple...Applet Runner/Applets/ArcTest/ArcTest.java
     /Applications (Mac OS 9)/Apple...Applet Runner/Applets/BarChart/Chart.java
     /Applications (Mac OS 9)/Apple...Applet
     Runner/Applets/DrawTest/DrawTest.java
     .
     .
     .
```

If you let this run to completion, you can then look at the file `my_output`, and it will have all the stuff you just scrolled through with `more`. This isn't a very valuable listing, so you might not actually want to wait for this to finish. But, if you press Ctrl+C out of it, you'll kill the `tee` process and it won't write its output.

There's a chance you can't run `find` from the root directory as anything other than the root user. This appears to be a bug on Apple's part. If you've got a single, single-partition drive, it seems to work okay; if you don't, `find` dies with a permission denied at the root level. We've worked out a fix for this, but we can't guarantee that our fix doesn't break something else. If you'd like to try it, do exactly the following:

```
su
umount /.vol
chmod 555 /.vol
sync;sync;sync;reboot
```

At this point, your machine should reboot. If you typed everything properly, after your machine comes back up, `find` will work from the root directory. Be patient if it seems that your machine is not responding immediately.

The `tee` command is invaluable if you need to split one `STDOUT` stream to be used by multiple different processes, or if you need to collect logging or partial output from intermediate steps in a large, multiprogram piped command.

Summary

This chapter detailed some of the general concepts and commands that can be used to interact with and control the behavior of other shell commands. File permissions, process management, and output redirection are all fundamental Unix concepts, although ones that many Unix users frequently choose to ignore.

Most anything that you can do with Unix, you can do without paying particularly close attention to this chapter, although the process might be many times as hard and take many times as long to accomplish. For this reason, we recommend that you familiarize yourself with these ideas and commands—they are fundamental to using Unix effectively, if not to simply using it.

CHAPTER 15

Command-Line Applications and Application Suites

IN THIS CHAPTER

In the last few chapters, we covered what you need to know to get around in the command line–based BSD environment. We also introduced you to the use of simple programs. In this chapter, we'll cover command-line programs with more complex interfaces. If you're from a Mac background, the previous chapter's small building block–type programs are probably a slightly foreign concept because most Mac applications have historically been self-contained. The Unix applications introduced in this chapter will be somewhat more familiar because they are more similar to the functionally complete programs you're used to.

Networking Applications

Many of the command-line network applications are simply textual equivalents of graphical network applications with which you're likely to already be familiar. There are command-line applications for browsing the Web, transferring files over the Internet, reading your e-mail, and most other network functions you're familiar with. Most of these have both advantages and disadvantages with respect to their graphical counterparts. The mouse has proven a very efficient tool for tasks involving complex selections, and the command-line applications fail in situations that would require fast and furious mousing. On the other hand, if you're using a terminal and at a command-line prompt, it's almost always faster to use a textual tool to do something quick, such as transfer a file via FTP, than it is to start a graphical client. An additional difference is that some command-line applications can function in both an interactive fashion and as a building-block program. This allows many of them to be used in shell scripts or other programs to provide their functionality to a more complex program that needs to use it.

Note

URLs are one the most ubiquitous formalized ways of specifying the place a program should look for a particular network resource. You're almost certainly familiar with URLs in a practical sense—many of them look like `http://www.apple.com/`. What you might not be aware of is that this string `http://www.apple.com/` has meaning beyond simply specifying the name of a machine, `www.apple.com`, to which software should connect. The `http://` part of the expression is also used, and specifies the connection protocol, which should be used for accessing this resource. Other connection protocols can be specified by the use of other prefixes before the machine name, such as `ftp://`.

As we've pointed out previously, Unix is a particular and precise environment. Specifying `www.apple.com` as a URL to a Web browser is sloppy and imprecise, and works only in certain cases in which the browser manufacturer has decided to write its software to try to compensate for poor habits on the part of the user.

A considerable amount of Unix software isn't written to support sloppy usage on the part of the user, and requires that you enter complete and correct URLs, including the `http://`, or other prefix, part of the URL to function correctly.

Some recent Unix software is starting to go the route of the large browsers and support the sloppy usage without a specified protocol, but much still does not, and we don't believe this is a positive trend. We've made every effort to provide complete and correct URLs in the text here, and we hope that you'll get used to using them properly—it will eventually save you a considerable headache when you meet an application that requires you to be as precise as it is.

Browsing the Web: `lynx`

`lynx` is a command-line Web client. Surprising as it might seem, many people prefer browsing the Web in a text-only application. There are, of course, many pages that simply can't be browsed without a graphics-capable application, but those pages are written by people who aren't concerned with making their information as widely available as possible, and don't seem to be of interest to people who prefer to browse in text only.

Tip

For more information on why you might want, or not want, to make your pages available as plain text, see Chapter 27, "Web Serving."

Note

There's a reasonable chance that `lynx` isn't installed on your system. We're going to use it for a few things later in the chapter, so if you don't have it, you'll be installing it in the section on compiling and installing software. The install we do for `lynx` will be of the easiest possible command-line install style, so you might even want to flip forward a few pages and do the install now.

The basic syntax of `lynx` is `lynx <URL>`. This will give you a textual representation of the page, and a few lines of prompting information as to what you can do from there. For example, looking at `http://www.apple.com/`, `lynx` produces the following output:

```
[localhost:~] nermal% lynx http://www.apple.com

      #home index

   Apple The Apple Store iTools iCards QuickTime Apple Support Mac OS X
   Hot News Hardware Software Made4Mac Education Creative Small Biz Developer
   Where to Buy

      Blue Dalmation Rip. Mix. Burn. The new iMac. With iTunes + CD-RW drive.
                        Headphones

                            Hot News Headlines Hot News Ticker

       Now Shipping. Mac OS X. QuickTime 5: Download the new digital media
   ➥standard.
            Final Cut Pro 2 PowerBook G4 - 1" think - 5.3 pounds - Titanium.

                                       [spacer.gif]
                                         Gray line

                             _________________________ Search
                             Site Map | Search Tips | Options


                             Find Job Opportunities at Apple.

                         Visit other Apple sites around the world:
                                    [Choose...___________]

                                Contact Us | Privacy Notice
               Copyright © 2001 Apple Computer, Inc. All rights reserved.
                                      1-800-MY-APPLE


                                 Powered by MacOSXServer


   (NORMAL LINK)   Use right-arrow or <return> to activate.
   Arrow keys: Up and Down to move.  Right to follow a link; Left to go back.
   H)elp O)ptions P)rint G)o M)ainscreen Q)uit /=search [delete]=history list
```

If you want to move down the page, you can follow the instruction that suggests the spacebar to move down a page.

Tip

I mentioned "follow the instruction that suggests...move down a page" because a significant amount of human-computer-interface research indicates that to many people, omnipresent onscreen help is almost invisible. Keep your eye on the onscreen hints—even if it's not the best user interface design, it is there to help, and it's a lot faster than searching the help pages.

The up-arrow and down-arrow keys will move you up and down the page, and will also select between the links on the page. The right-arrow and left-arrow keys will take you, somewhat predictably, to the target of the currently selected link, or back to the previous page.

Common one-key commands within `lynx` are as shown in Table 15.1.

TABLE 15.1 Common One-Key Commands Within the `lynx` Interactive Web Browser

Key	*Action*
`+/-`	Move down, or up the page.
`<space bar>`	Move down the page.
`<right arrow>`, `<return>`	Go to selected link.
`<left arrow>`	Go back.
`<up arrow>`	Select previous link, downloadable element, or form field.
`<down arrow>`	Select next link, downloadable element, or form field.
`d`	Download the target of the currently selected link or downloadable element.
`H`	Go to the `lynx` help pages. These pages are implemented as HTML pages, so you can go forward and back in them with the forward and back arrows.
`O`	Go to the `lynx` Options page. Here you can set an assortment of internal parameters such as where your `lynx` bookmarks are stored.
`P`	Print the current page.
`G`	Go to a new URL.
`M`	Go back to the Main page, by which `lynx` means the page that you first started on.
`Q`	Quit the program.
`/`	Search in the page.
`<delete>`	Show the history for the current browser window.

There is a veritable plethora of additional one-key options that are explained in the `lynx` help, under the `Key-stroke commands` heading.

The `lynx` browser also sports a wide range of command-line options that enable or modify advanced behaviors. These include items like sending the data to `STDOUT`, or collecting a list of the URLs contained in the document.

Finally, it should be mentioned that `lynx`, like much Unix software, works great as a command-line building-block utility. Ever wanted to process the contents of a Web page, perhaps to do something like collect all the links from someone's page of interesting links, without having to dig through the source by hand? Using the `-dump` option will cause `lynx` to send the target document of the URL to `STDOUT`, followed by a list of the URLs in the document. For example, if you wanted to collect a list of URLs to all the Darwin patches shown on `http://www.darwinfo.org/` (specifically, the stuff in the `patches` subdirectory), you could use `lynx` like this:

```
[localhost:~] nermal% lynx -dump http://www.darwinfo.org/patches/

         Hexley Darwinfo Logo
           _________________________________________________________________

             [1]Home [2]The FAQ [3]How To... [4]Patches [5]Ports [6]Links
           _________________________________________________________________

                                   Darwin Patches
           _________________________________________________________________

         This section if for patches to source code in order to alter it in
         some way, either to add functionallity, fix bugs, or just compile on
         Darwin.
           * [7]bootx patch - This is a patch to bootx to allow you to boot
             /mach_kernel.backup during startup by holding down 'cmd-b'. By
             Louis Gerbarg.
           * [8]gcc crosscompile - This is a patch to the current (Nov. 7th)
             gcc source to be able to build a cross compiler under Darwin. By
             Stan Shebs.
           * [9]/dev/random - This is a /dev/random for Darwin! Now, you can
             actually have decent random number generation for Darwin!
             [10](Read more...) By Louis Gerbarg
           * [11]noffs.patch: A patch that cleans up some of the configuration
             files to allow one to build xnu without UFS in the kernel. By
             Louis Gerbarg
           * [12]Tcl 8.3.1 for Darwin - patch to TCL 8.3.1 to compile as a
             framework for Darwin, so that almost all of the incuded tests
             pass. [13](Read more...) By Chris Douty
           * [14]Screen 3.9.5 - patch to get Screen to compile for darwin
             [15](Read More...) By Graham Orndorff
```

```
    * [16]mfs.tar.gz - A patch to add a struct buf *b_actf to the struct
      buf definition in xnu/bsd/sys/buf.h. The mfs.tar.gz file should
      replace xnu/bsd/ufs/mfs. [17](Read More...) By Rob Braun
    * [18]newfs.diff - I also added the option where you can do a
      mount_mfs swap /mntpt, and that'll create fake settings for the
      size of the mounted filesystem. The fake settings were ripped off
      from NetBSD's newfs. By Rob Braun
    * [19]bigmem.diff - A patch to allow xnu to boot on Intel systems
      with 256MB or more of memory. Thanks to John Kullmann.
    * [20]iocatalog.intel.diff - Fixes a syntax error in
      xnu/iokit/IOCatalog.cpp for Intel machines. Without this, the
      kernel won't boot on Intel. By Naoki Hamada.
    * [21]groff.diff - Fixes a bus error when using grops in the groff
      package. By Scott Thompson.
    * [22]diskdev_cmds-man.diff - Modifies the build environment to
      install the man pages. By Torrey Lyons.
    * [23]xnu 103.0.1 for 604 - A patch from Markus Hitter for booting
      xnu 103.0.1 on a 604. Originally posted in [24]this mail. By
      Markus Hitter .
    * [25]UniEnet - A patch to make the UniEnet driver only display
      supported media types. By Louis Gerbarg.
    * [26]Intel Cursor - A patch to fix the invisible cursor on Intel
      machines. By Rob Braun.

Deprecated Patches

   These patches are either out of date, or have already been integrated
   into the cvs tree.
    * [27]sysctl.diff - Makes sysctl deal with the hostid variable
      correctly. By Ryan Rempel.
    * [28]xnu-intel.diff - This is a collection of patches to bring the
      current cvs version of xnu up on Intel. This patch incorporates
      Naoki Hamada's patch to fix iokit/KernelConfigTables.cpp to allow
      the kernel to boot on Intel, Justin Walker's fix for bpf under
      Intel, and my patch to get the cursor working on the console.
    * [29]/dev/zero - Adds a /dev/zero to Darwin. Especially useful. By
      Louis Gerbarg
    * [30]cons.diff - Fixes the Darwin console to display at the proper
      width&height. From me.. By Rob Braun
    * [31]inetd-pid.diff - Make inetd write it's pid to
      /var/run/inetd.pid. By Rob Braun
    * [32]mach_init.diff - Makes sure mach_init properly hands off
      arguments to init. Prior to this patch, mach_init would not
      properly hand off multiple args to init (such as -v and -s
      sumultaneously). And [33]here is a gzipped binary of the patched
      mach_init. By Rob Braun
    * [34]pwd_mkdb.diff - In an attempt to run Darwin without netinfo
      and the host of daemons surrounding it, I needed the utilities
      pwd_mkdb and vipw. I found that the current versions in cvs have
      minor bugs preventing their correct execution. These are minor
      patches to each to make them work properly. ---Sat, 12 Aug 2000
```

```
     16:46:38 -0600 By Rob Braun
   * [35]vipw.diff - See the notes on pwd_mkdb above. By Rob Braun
   ________________________________________________________________

 copyright © 2000 [36]Tom Hackett and [37]Rob Braun
 Hexley image created and copyright Jon Hooper

References

  1. http://www.darwinfo.org/
  2. http://www.darwinfo.org/faq.shtml
  3. http://www.darwinfo.org/howto/
  4. http://www.darwinfo.org/patches/
  5. http://www.darwinfo.org/ports
  6. http://www.darwinfo.org/links.shtml
  7. http://www.rpi.edu/~gerbal/darwinpatches/bootx_backup.patch
  8. http://www.darwinfo.org/pub/darwin/fixes/xcompile.diff
  9. http://www.rpi.edu/~gerbal/darwin-patches/devrandom.patch
 10. http://www.darwinfo.org/patches/dev_random_patch.shtml
 11. http://www.rpi.edu/~gerbal/darwin-patches/noffs.patch
 12. http://www.darwinfo.org/patches/tcl831ForDarwin-2.patch
 13. http://www.darwinfo.org/patches/tcl831patch.shtml
 14. http://www.darwinfo.org/patches/screen_patch.diff
 15. http://www.darwinfo.org/patches/screen_port.shtml
 16. http://www.darwinfo.org/patches/mfs.tar.gz
 17. http://www.darwinfo.org/patches/mfs.shtml
 18. http://www.darwinfo.org/patches/newfs.diff
 19. http://www.darwinfo.org/patches/big_mem.diff
 20. http://www.darwinfo.org/patches/iocatalog.intel.diff
 21. http://www.darwinfo.org/patches/groff.diff
 22. http://www.darwinfo.org/patches/diskdev_cmds-man.diff
 23. http://www.darwinfo.org/patches/604-103.0.1.diff
 24. http://www.darwinfo.org/devlist.php3?number=2809
 25. http://www.darwinfo.org/patches/UniEnet.cpp.patch
 26. http://www.darwinfo.org/patches/intel-cursor.diff
 27. http://www.darwinfo.org/patches/sysctl.diff
 28. http://www.darwinfo.org/patches/xnu-intel.diff
 29. http://www.rpi.edu/~gerbal/devzero.patch.gz
 30. http://www.darwinfo.org/patches/cons.diff
 31. http://www.darwinfo.org/patches/inetd-pid.diff
 32. http://www.darwinfo.org/patches/mach_init.diff
 33. http://www.darwinfo.org/patches/mach_init.gz
 34. http://www.darwinfo.org/patches/pwd_mkdb.diff
 35. http://www.darwinfo.org/patches/vipw.diff
 36. mailto:tomhackett@darwinfo.org
 37. mailto:bbraun@darwinfo.org
```

If you wanted to parse just the URLs out of this output, you could simply run `lynx`, and pipe the output though `grep` looking for URL patterns. Something like `lynx -dump` `http://www.darwinfo.orf/patches/ | grep "http:"` will do the trick, and produces the following output:

```
[localhost:~] nermal% lynx -dump http://www.darwinfo.org/patches/ | grep "http:"

        1. http://www.darwinfo.org/
        2. http://www.darwinfo.org/faq.shtml
        3. http://www.darwinfo.org/howto/
        4. http://www.darwinfo.org/patches/
        5. http://www.darwinfo.org/ports
        6. http://www.darwinfo.org/links.shtml
        7. http://www.rpi.edu/~gerbal/darwin-patches/bootx_backup.patch
        8. http://www.darwinfo.org/pub/darwin/fixes/xcompile.diff
        9. http://www.rpi.edu/~gerbal/darwin-patches/devrandom.patch
       10. http://www.darwinfo.org/patches/dev_random_patch.shtml
       11. http://www.rpi.edu/~gerbal/darwin-patches/noffs.patch
       12. http://www.darwinfo.org/patches/tcl831ForDarwin-2.patch
       13. http://www.darwinfo.org/patches/tcl831patch.shtml
       14. http://www.darwinfo.org/patches/screen_patch.diff
       15. http://www.darwinfo.org/patches/screen_port.shtml
       16. http://www.darwinfo.org/patches/mfs.tar.gz
       17. http://www.darwinfo.org/patches/mfs.shtml
       18. http://www.darwinfo.org/patches/newfs.diff
       19. http://www.darwinfo.org/patches/big_mem.diff
       20. http://www.darwinfo.org/patches/iocatalog.intel.diff
       21. http://www.darwinfo.org/patches/groff.diff
       22. http://www.darwinfo.org/patches/diskdev_cmds-man.diff
       23. http://www.darwinfo.org/patches/604-103.0.1.diff
       24. http://www.darwinfo.org/devlist.php3?number=2809
       25. http://www.darwinfo.org/patches/UniEnet.cpp.patch
       26. http://www.darwinfo.org/patches/intel-cursor.diff
       27. http://www.darwinfo.org/patches/sysctl.diff
       28. http://www.darwinfo.org/patches/xnu-intel.diff
       29. http://www.rpi.edu/~gerbal/devzero.patch.gz
       30. http://www.darwinfo.org/patches/cons.diff
       31. http://www.darwinfo.org/patches/inetd-pid.diff
       32. http://www.darwinfo.org/patches/mach_init.diff
       33. http://www.darwinfo.org/patches/mach_init.gz
       34. http://www.darwinfo.org/patches/pwd_mkdb.diff
       35. http://www.darwinfo.org/patches/vipw.diff
```

The `-dump` option turns out to be useful for doing things that don't relate to processing the URLs as well, such as downloading files from FTP or HTTPD servers. You'll see examples of this use of `lynx` during the software installs in Chapter 16, "Command Line Software Installation."

The `lynx` command documentation table is shown in Table 15.2.

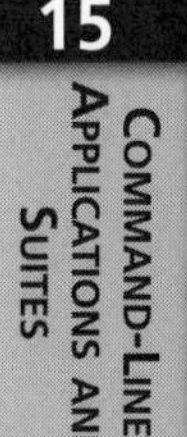

TABLE 15.2 The Command Documentation Table for `lynx`

`lynx`	Textual Web browser
`lynx [options] [file]`	
You can find out which options are available by running `lynx -help`. Here is the listing of command-line options for the current version of `lynx`:	
`-`	Receive options and arguments from `STDIN`.
`-accept_all_cookies`	Accept cookies without prompting if `Set-Cookie` handling is on (off).
`-anonymous`	Apply restrictions for anonymous account; see also `-restrictions`.
`-assume_charset=MIMEname`	Charset for documents that don't specify it.
`-assume_local_charset=MIMEname`	Charset assumed for local files.
`-assume_unrec_charset=MIMEname`	Use this instead of unrecognized charsets.
`-auth=id:pw`	Authentication information for protected documents.
`-base`	Prepend a request URL comment and BASE tag to `text/html` for `-source` dumps.
`-book`	Use the bookmark page as the start file (off).
`-buried_news`	Toggle scanning of news articles for buried references (on).
`-cache=`*`NUMBER`*	*`NUMBER`* of documents cached in memory.
`-case`	Enable case-sensitive user searching (off).
`-cfg=`*`FILENAME`*	Specify a `lynx.cfg` file other than the default.
`-child`	Exit on left arrow in start file, and disable save to disk.
`-connect_timeout=`*`N`*	Set the *N*-second connection timeout (`18000`) .
`-cookie_file=`*`FILENAME`*	Specify a file to use to read cookies.
`-cookie_save_file=`*`FILENAME`*	Specify a file to use to store cookies.
`-cookies`	Toggle handling of `Set-Cookie` headers (on).
`-core`	Toggle forced core dumps on fatal errors (off).
`-crawl`	With `-traversal`, output each page to a file with `-dump`, format output as with `-traversal`, but to `STDOUT`.
`-debug_partial`	Incremental display stages with `MessageSecs` delay (off).
`-display=`*`DISPLAY`*	Set the display variable for X `exec`'ed programs.
`-dont_wrap_pre`	Inhibit wrapping of text in `<pre>` when `-dumping` and `-crawling`, mark wrapped lines in interactive session (off).
`-dump`	Dump the first file to `STDOUT` and exit.

TABLE 15.2 continued

`-editor=EDITOR`	Enable edit mode with specified editor.
`-emacskeys`	Enable `emacs`-like key movement (off).
`-enable_scrollback`	Toggle compatibility with comm programs' scrollback keys (might be incompatible with some `curses` packages) (off) .
`-error_file=FILE`	Write the HTTP status code here.
`-force_empty_hrefless_a`	Force HREF-less `A` elements to be empty (close them as soon as they are seen) (off)
`-force_html`	Force the first document to be interpreted as HTML (off).
`-force_secure`	Toggle forcing of the secure flag for SSL cookies (off).
`-forms_options`	Toggle forms-based versus old-style options menu (on).
`-from`	Toggle transmission of From headers (on).
`-ftp`	Disable FTP access (off).
`-get_data`	User data for `get` forms, read from `STDIN`, terminated by `'---'` on a line.
`-head`	Send a `HEAD` request (off).
`-help`	Print this usage message.
`-hiddenlinks=[option]`	Hidden links options are `merge`, `listonly`, and `ignore`.
`-historical`	Toggle use of `'>'` or `'-->'` as a terminator for comments (off).
`-homepage=URL`	Set home page separate from start page.
`-image_links`	Toggles inclusion of links for all images (off) .
`-index=URL`	Set the default index file to *`URL`*.
`-ismap`	Toggle inclusion of ISMAP links when client-side MAPs are present (off).
`-link=NUMBER`	Starting count for `lnk#.dat` files produced by `-crawl` (0).
`-localhost`	Disable URLs that point to remote hosts (off).
`-mime_header`	Include MIME headers and force source dump.
`-minimal`	Toggle minimal versus valid comment parsing (off).
`-newschunksize=NUMBER`	Number of articles in chunked news listings.
`-newsmaxchunk=NUMBER`	Maximum news articles in listings before chunking.
`-nobold`	Disable bold video attribute.
`-nobrowse`	Disable directory browsing.
`-nocc`	Disable Cc: prompts for self copies of mailings (off).

TABLE 15.2 continued

`-nocolor`	Turn off color support.
`-nofilereferer`	Disable transmission of Referer headers for file URLs (on).
`-nolist`	Disable the link list feature in dumps (off).
`-nolog`	Disable mailing of error messages to document owners (on).
`-nonrestarting_sigwinch`	Make window size change handler non-restarting (off).
`-nopause`	Disable forced pauses for status-line messages.
`-noprint`	Disable some print functions, like `-restrictions=print` (off) .
`-noredir`	Don't follow Location: redirection (off).
`-noreferer`	Disable transmission of Referer headers (off).
`-noreverse`	Disable reverse video-attribute
`-nostatus`	Disable the miscellaneous information messages (off).
`-nounderline`	Disable underline video attribute.
`-number_fields`	Force numbering of links as well as form input fields (off).
`-number_links`	Force numbering of links (off)
`-partial`	Toggle display partial pages while downloading (on) .
`-partial_thres [=`*NUMBER*`]`	Number of lines to render before repainting display with partial-display logic (-1).
`-pauth=id:pw`	Authentication information for protected proxy server.
`-popup`	Toggle handling of single-choice `SELECT` options via pop-up windows or as lists of radio buttons (off).
`-post_data`	User data for `post` forms, read from `STDIN`, terminated by `'---'` on a line.
`-preparsed`	Show parsed text/HTML with `-source` and in source view to visualize how `lynx` behaves with invalid HTML (off).
`-print`	Enable print functions (DEFAULT); opposite of `-noprint` (on).
`-pseudo_inlines`	Toggle pseudo-`ALT`s for inlines with no `ALT` string (on).
`-raw`	Toggle default setting of 8-bit character translations or CJK mode for the startup character set (off).
`-realm`	Restrict access to URLs in the starting realm (off).
`-reload`	Flush the cache on a proxy server (only the first document affected) (off).
`-restrictions=[`*options*`]`	Use `-restrictions` to see list.

TABLE 15.2 continued

`-resubmit_posts`	Toggles forced resubmissions (no cache) of forms with method `POST` when the documents they returned are sought with the `PREV_DOC` command or from the History List (off).
`-rlogin`	Disable `rlogins` (off).
`-selective`	Require `.www_browsable` files to browse directories.
`-short_url`	Enable examination of beginning and end of long URL in status line (off).
`-show_cursor`	Toggle hiding of the cursor in the lower-right corner (on).
`-soft_dquotes`	Toggle emulation of the old Netscape and Mosaic bug that treated `'>'` as a co-terminator for double quotes and tags (off).
`-source`	Dump the source of the first file to `STDOUT` and exit.
`-stack_dump`	Disable `SIGINT` cleanup handler (off).
`-startfile_ok`	Allow non-HTTP start file and home page with `-validate` (off) .
`-tagsoup`	Use `TagSoup` rather than `SortaSGML` parser (off).
`-telnet`	Disable telnets (off).
`-term=TERM`	Set terminal type to `TERM`.
`-tlog`	Toggle use of a `lynx` Trace Log for the current session.
`-tna`	Turn on Textfields Need Activation mode (off).
`-trace`	Turn on `lynx` trace mode.
`-traversal`	Traverse all HTTP links derived from start file.
`-underscore`	Toggle use of `_underline_` format in dumps (off).
`-useragent=`*`Name`*	Set alternative Lynx User-Agent header.
`-validate`	Accept only HTTP URLs (meant for validation); implies more restrictions than `-anonymous`,but `goto` is allowed for HTTP and HTTPS.
`-verbose`	Toggle `[LINK]`, `[IMAGE]`, and `[INLINE]` comments with filenames of these images (on).
`-version`	Print `lynx` version information.
`-vikeys`	Enable `vi`-like key movement (off) .
-width=NUMBER	Screen width for formatting of dumps (default is 80).
`-with_backspaces`	Omit backspaces in output if `-dumping` or `-crawling` (like `man` does) (off).

Accessing FTP Servers: `ftp`

`ftp` is the command name for the program that implements the FTP protocol (creative, no?). Historically on the Macintosh, the `Anarchie` and `Fetch` programs have been the FTP clients of preference, and both of these provide features that are sadly lacking in the default command-line `ftp` interface. The command-line interface, however, is again a quick and convenient way to get or put a file or three, without needing to launch a graphical client. It also tends to be better for diagnosis purposes when an FTP transfer fails, or when a file can't be found. All the messages from the server can be seen immediately, and are directly in response to the commands you issue, so if something's wrong, it's much clearer at what point it goes that way.

To connect to a remote site using `ftp`, simply issue the command as `ftp <ftp site>`. This will, presuming all goes well, connect you to the remote site and request your user ID and password. If you're trying to connect to a public site, the default guest user ID is `anonymous`. After that, the site will ask you for a password, which if you're connecting as an anonymous user, should be given as your e-mail address. Responding properly to both of these queries (anonymous and your e-mail address, or your correct user ID and password) will take you to an internal prompt in the `ftp` program from where you can traverse the site's directories and upload or download files.

Following is a sample of what you might see after connecting to a site that doesn't really want you there. This sort of information is largely hidden in the graphical FTP clients, frequently leaving you clicking Retry indefinitely; in reality, the site is trying to give you some helpful information.

```
[localhost:~] nermal% ftp ftp.cis.ohio-state.edu

     220 www.cis.ohio-state.edu FTP server (Version wu-2.6.1(4) Fri Jul
                                             14 13:02:07 EDT 2000) ready.
     Name (ftp.cis.ohio-state.edu:nermal): anonymous
     331 Guest login ok, send your complete e-mail address as password.
     Password:
     530-Sorry, the limit of 20 users logged in has been exceeded (20).
     530-We've had to cut back to avoid swamping our outside link.
     530-
     530-Please try again later.
     530-
     530-To report problems, please contact ftp@cis.ohio-state.edu.
     530 Login incorrect.
```

And this is an example of what you might see if you have connected properly.

```
[localhost:~] nermal% ftp ftp.cis.ohio-state.edu

     Connected to www.cis.ohio-state.edu.
     220 www.cis.ohio-state.edu FTP server (Version wu-2.6.1(4)
```

```
Fri Jul 14 13:02:07 EDT 2000) ready.
Name (ftp.cis.ohio-state.edu:nermal): anonymous
331 Guest login ok, send your complete e-mail address as password.
Password:
230-Hello [unknown]@ryoohki.biosci.ohio-state.edu.
230-
230-This is the anonymous FTP archive of the Computer and Information
230-Science Department and The Ohio State University.
230-
230-You are user 1 out of 30 users currently allowed in.
230-
230-This FTP server is running on a Sun Enterprise 250, with approximately
230-100 GB of disk space.  The directory space was recently reorganized
230-and cleaned.
230-
230-Mirrors of other sites are in /mirror
230-Everything else is in /pub
230-
230-Please report any problems to ftp@cis.ohio-state.edu
230-
230 Guest login ok, access restrictions apply.
Remote system type is UNIX.
Using binary mode to transfer files.
ftp>
```

Note

If you attempt to access these servers and get different results, don't be alarmed. These are simply examples of various results that can occur, and your results might be different depending on when you connect, where you're connecting from, and whether the site has changed its configuration since these dialogs were captured.

From this `ftp>` prompt, you can issue one of the following commands, such as `help`, `rhelp`, `get`, `put`, `cd`, `ls`, `pwd`, and potentially others, depending on the server configuration. The output from the `help` command will give you a list of what commands are available to you in your client, and the output of `rhelp` will tell you about commands on the server:

```
ftp> help
    Commands may be abbreviated.  Commands are:

    !               debug           mget            put             size
    $               dir             mkdir           pwd             status
    account         disconnect      mls             quit            struct
```

```
    append      form        mode        quote       system
    ascii       get         modtime     recv        sunique
    bell        glob        mput        reget       tenex
    binary      hash        newer       rstatus     trace
    bye         help        nmap        rhelp       type
    case        idle        nlist       rename      user
    cd          image       ntrans      reset       umask
    cdup        lcd         open        restart     verbose
    chmod       ls          passive     rmdir       ?
    close       macdef      prompt      runique
    cr          mdelete     proxy       send
    delete      mdir        sendport    site
ftp> rhelp
    214-The following commands are recognized (* =>'s unimplemented).
       USER    PORT    STOR    MSAM*   RNTO    NLST    MKD     CDUP
       PASS    PASV    APPE    MRSQ*   ABOR    SITE    XMKD    XCUP
       ACCT*   TYPE    MLFL*   MRCP*   DELE    SYST    RMD     STOU
       SMNT*   STRU    MAIL*   ALLO    CWD     STAT    XRMD    SIZE
       REIN*   MODE    MSND*   REST    XCWD    HELP    PWD     MDTM
       QUIT    RETR    MSOM*   RNFR    LIST    NOOP    XPWD
    214 Direct comments to ftp@cis.ohio-state.edu.
```

Additionally, you can ask for help on specific commands—one of the more interesting ones to ask about in the listing shown is the `site` command:

```
ftp> rhelp site
    214-The following SITE commands are recognized (* =>'s unimplemented).
       UMASK           GROUP           INDEX           GROUPS
       IDLE            GPASS           EXEC            CHECKMETHOD
       CHMOD           NEWER           ALIAS           CHECKSUM
       HELP            MINFO           CDPATH
```

The `site` command implements FTP-site specific command options, and you'd need to contact the administrator to find out exactly what the command options are, and which you are allowed to use.

Files that you get from the FTP server will be placed (unless you specify otherwise by giving a download path along with the `get` command at the prompt) into the same directory from which you issued the `ftp` command.

Another thing that the command-line `ftp` client does much better than the graphical clients is let you know and access special features that the server has available for your use. Because the command-line client can't recursively download directories like the graphical clients can, and because it predates the graphical clients by many years, the most popular Unix FTP servers provide facilities to compensate. For example, many sites provide automatic `tar`ring and `compress`ing of directories, so that even though you can't recursively download a directory, you can still retrieve it all, conveniently `tarred` and `compressed` with a single command. To access these special facilities, though, you have to `get` files that don't exist—typically named `<directoryname>.tar` or `<directory-name>.tar.gz`. The server intercepts the request for the nonexistent name and dynamically creates the `tar`file or compressed `tar`file. This facility could be accessed, even with graphical clients, but because the clients by default hide the server messages, the user rarely knows they're available, and the nonexistent filenames are notoriously difficult to click on.

The following is an example of interaction with a server that provides this sort of special facilities to the user.

Note

Don't be worried if your connection doesn't look exactly like this. Specifically, if you end up at what appears to be a different server, with similar content, all is well. The CPAN sites are very popular, and use a dynamic load-balancing system to hand off connections between a large number of servers so that no one installation becomes overloaded.

```
[localhost:~/osx-test] joray% ftp ftp.cpan.org

    Connected to onion.valueclick.com.
    220 onion.valueclick.com FTP server (Version wu-2.6.1(1)
    ➥Thu Nov 23 12:15:07 PST 2000) ready.
    Name (ftp.cpan.org:joray): anonymous
    331 Guest login ok, send your complete e-mail address as password.
    Password:
    230-
    230-Welcome to onion.valueclick.com, also known as ftp.perl.org,
    230-ftp.cpan.org and others.
    230-
    230-
    230-        ValueClick - The Pay-for-Results Advertising Network
    230-           http://www.valueclick.com/ sponsors this site.
    230-
    230-Comments to ask@valueclick.com and jacob@netcetera.dk. If you ask
    nicely we
    230-might want to mirror or host your Open Source project too. It needs to
    be
    230-accessible for us via rsync though.
    230-
    230-most popular things around here:
```

```
     230-
     230-  /pub/CPAN/              - Comprehensive Perl Archive Network
     230-  /pub/FreeBSD/           - FreeBSD mirror
     230-  /pub/apache/dist/       - the Apache webserver
     230-  /pub/perl/              - Other Perl bits (APC, ...)
     230-  /pub/mysql/Downloads/   - the MySQL database
     230-  /pub/perl/backup.pause/ - mirror of the historical PAUSE archive
     230-
     230-Most things here are also available at
     230-
     230-  http://mirrors.valueclick.com/
     230-
     230-which probably will be faster if you are using a webbrowser.
     230-
     230-
     230-Please read the file README
     230-  it was last modified on Thu Apr 19 06:23:27 2001 - 3 days ago
     230 Guest login ok, access restrictions apply.
     Remote system type is UNIX.
     Using binary mode to transfer files.
ftp> cd /pub/CPAN/authors/id/W/WI
     250 CWD command successful.
ftp> ls -l
     200 PORT command successful.
     150 Opening ASCII mode data connection for /bin/ls.
     total 4
     -r--r--r--  1 mirror  mirror   307 Jan 28 01:33 CHECKSUMS
     drwxrwxr-x  2 mirror  mirror   512 Feb 22 16:04 WICKLINE
     drwxrwxr-x  2 mirror  mirror  1024 Apr  9 22:57 WIMV
     drwxr-xr-x  2 mirror  mirror   512 Dec 20  1998 WINKO
     226 Transfer complete.
ftp> cd WINKO
     250 CWD command successful.
ftp> ls -l
     200 PORT command successful.
     150 Opening ASCII mode data connection for /bin/ls.
     total 10
     -r--r--r--  1 mirror  mirror   548 Dec 13 18:31 CHECKSUMS
     -rw-r--r--  1 mirror  mirror  965 Dec 11  1996 String-BitCount-1.11.readme
     -rw-r--r--  1 mirror  mirror 2316 Dec 11  1996 String-BitCount-1.11.tar.gz
     -rw-r--r--  1 mirror  mirror   925 Dec 10  1996 String-Parity-1.31.readme
     -rw-r--r--  1 mirror  mirror  3586 Dec 11  1996 String-Parity-1.31.tar.gz
     226 Transfer complete.
ftp> cd ..
     250 CWD command successful.
```

```
ftp> binary

     200 Type set to I.

ftp> get WINKO.tar.gz

     local: WINKO.tar.gz remote: WINKO.tar.gz
     200 PORT command successful.
     150 Opening BINARY mode data connection for /bin/tar.
     226 Transfer complete.
     7375 bytes received in 0.166 seconds (44521 bytes/s)

ftp> quit

     221-You have transferred 7375 bytes in 1 files.
     221-Total traffic for this session was 10107 bytes in 3 transfers.
     221-Thank you for using the FTP service on onion.valueclick.com.
     221 Goodbye.

[localhost:~/osx-test] joray% ls

     WINKO.tar.gz

[localhost:~/osx-test] joray% gunzip WINKO.tar.gz
[localhost:~/osx-test] joray% tar -tvf WINKO.tar

     drwxr-xr-x  2 1001     1001           0 Dec 20  1998 WINKO
     -r--r--r--  1 1001     1001         548 Dec 13 13:31 WINKO/CHECKSUMS
     -rw-r--r--  1 1001     1001         965 Dec 10  1996
     ➥WINKO/String-BitCount-1.11.readme
     -rw-r--r--  1 1001     1001        2316 Dec 11  1996
     ➥WINKO/String-BitCount-1.11.tar.gz
     -rw-r--r--  1 1001     1001         925 Dec 10  1996
     ➥WINKO/String-Parity-1.31.readme
     -rw-r--r--  1 1001     1001        3586 Dec 11  1996
     ➥WINKO/String-Parity-1.31.tar.gz
```

In this example, we've retrieved a `tar`red and `gzip`ped copy of the `WINKO` directory, with a single command, even though that `.tar.gz` file doesn't exist on the system. As shown, it arrives on our local machine with the contents expected.

> **Note**
>
> Even more sophisticated things can be done with the servers, but their implementation tends to be site specific. Pay attention to the introductory and help messages presented by servers that you connect to. The site administrators will often use these messages to inform you of any special capabilities, as well as how you can use them.

The command documentation table for `ftp` is shown in Table 15.3.

TABLE 15.3 The Command Documentation Table for `ftp`

`ftp`	File transfer program.
`ftp [-dgintv] [`*<hostname>* `[`*<port>*`]]`	
The remote host with which `ftp` is to communicate can be specified on the command line. Done this way, `ftp` immediately tries to establish a connection with the remote host. Otherwise, `ftp` enters its command interpreter mode, awaits commands from the user, and displays the prompt `ftp>`.	
`-d`	Enables debugging.
`-g`	Disables filename globbing.
`-I`	Turns off interactive mode when transferring multiple files.
`-n`	Does not attempt auto-login upon initial connection. If auto-login is not disabled, `ftp` checks for a `.netrc` file in the user's directory for an entry describing an account on the remote machine. If no entry is available, `ftp` prompts for the login name on the remote machine (defaults to the login name on the local machine), and if necessary, prompts for a password.
`-t`	Enables packet tracing.
`-v`	Enables verbose mode. Default if input is from a terminal. Shows all responses from the remote server as well as transfer statistics.
When `ftp` is in its command interpreter mode awaiting instructions from the user, there are many commands that the user might issue. Some of them include:	
`ascii`	Sets the file transfer type to network ASCII. Although this is supposed to be the default, it is not uncommon for an FTP server to indicate that `binary` is its default.
`binary`	Sets the file transfer type to support binary image transfer.
`bye`	Terminates the `ftp` session and exits `ftp`. An end of file also terminates the session and exits.
`quit`	Same as `bye`.
`Cd` *<remote_directory>*	Changes the current working directory on the remote host to *<remote_directory>*.
`cdup`	Changes the current working directory on the remote host to the parent directory.
`close`	Terminates the `ftp` session with the remote host and returns to the command interpreter.

TABLE 15.3 continued

`disconnect`	Same as `close`.
`dir [<remote-directory> [<local_file>]]`	Prints a listing of the directory on the remote machine. Most Unix systems produce an `ls -l` output. If `<remote_directory>` is not specified, the current directory is assumed. If `<local_file>` is not specified, or is `-`, the output is sent to the terminal.
`ftp <hostname> [<port>]`	Same as `open`.
`open <hostname> [<port>]`	Attempts to establish an `ftp` connection on `<hostname>` at `<port>`, if `<port>` is specified.
`glob`	Toggles filename expansion for `mdelete`, `mget`, and `mput`. If globbing is turned off, filename arguments are taken literally and not expanded.
`delete <remote_file>`	Deletes the specified `<remote_file>` on the remote machine.
`mdelete <remote_files>`	Deletes the specified `<remote_files>` on the remote machine.
`get <remote_file> [<local-file>]`	Downloads `<remote_file>` from the remote machine to the local machine. If `<local_file>` is not specified, the file is also saved on the local machine with the name `<remote_file>`.
`recv <remote_file> [<local_file>]`	Same as `get`.
`mget <remote_files>`	Downloads the specified `<remote_files>`.
`put <local_file> [<remote_file>]`	Uploads the specified `<local_file>` to the remote host. If `<remote_file>` is not specified, the file is saved on the remote host with the name `<local_file>`.
`send <local_file> [<remote_file>]`	Same as `put`.
`mput <local_files>`	Uploads the specified `<local_files>`.
`msend`	Same as `mput`.
`help [<command>]`	Displays a message describing `<command>`. If `<command>` is not specified, a listing of known commands is displayed.
`?`	Same as `help`.
`lcd <directory>`	Changes the working directory on the local machine. If `<directory>` is not specified, the user's home directory is used.

TABLE 15.3 continued

`ls [<remote_directory> [<local_file>]]`	Prints a list of the files in a directory on the remote machine. If `<remote_directory>` is not specified, the current working directory is assumed. If `<local_file>` is not specified, or is `-`, the output is printed to a terminal. Note that if nothing is listed, the directory might only have directories in it. Try `ls -l` or `dir` for a complete listing.
`mkdir <directory>`	Makes the specified `<directory>` on the remote machine.
`rmdir <directory>`	Removes the specified `<directory>` from the remote machine.
`passive`	Toggles passive mode. If passive mode is turned on (off by default), the `ftp` client sends a `PASV` command for data connections rather than a `PORT` command. `PASV` command requests that the remote server open a port for the data connection and return the address of that port. The remote server listens on that port and the client then sends data to it. With the `PORT` command, the client listens on a port and sends that address to the remote host, who connects back to it. Passive mode is useful when FTPing through a firewall. Not all `ftp` servers are required to support passive mode.
`pwd`	Prints the current working directory on the remote host.
`verbose`	Toggles verbose mode. Default is on. In verbose mode, all responses from the `ftp` server are shown as well as transfer statistics.

Terminals in Terminals: `telnet`, `rlogin`, `ssh`

Because one of the primary methods for interacting with a Unix machine that you're sitting in front of is via a textual terminal, it should come as no surprise that there are a number of network tools available to allow you to access remote machines through that same interface. The three primary examples of these are the `telnet`, `rlogin` and `ssh`/`slogin` (secure shell) clients. Each of these provides a connection to a remote machine that is analogous to the one that `Terminal.app` provides to your local machine—you get access to a command prompt and can run software on the remote machine just like software in `Terminal.app` on the local machine.

The telnet Program

telnet is a venerable connection program that speaks a language compatible with the over-the-wire communication protocol used by many Internet services. The protocol is a fundamental building block of much of the Internet, and has been used to provide everything from Web services, to file transfer services, to terminal services. It is, unfortunately, as trivial as it is ubiquitous, and provides almost no built-in security. Because of this, terminal services implemented directly in the protocol are inherently insecure, and the telnet client and server fall into this category.

The syntax of the telnet command is telnet *<host>* *[port number]*.

If you're communicating with a system that's either not connected to the Internet, or run by a particularly security-unconscious system administrator, you might actually be able to use it as a terminal application. In that case, if you issue the telnet command you might see something like the following:

```
[ray@venice ~]$ telnet krpan.killernuts.org

    Trying 192.168.1.10...
    Connected to krpan.killernuts.org (192.168.1.10).
    Escape character is '^]'.

    Red Hat Linux release 7.0 (Guinness)
    Kernel 2.4.2 on a 2-processor i686
    login: adam
    Password:
    Last login: Thu Apr 19 19:36:23 on vc/1
    You have mail.

    Terminal: vt100.
    Printer set to newsioux

    krpan adam %
```

At that point, you're at a shell prompt on the remote machine, and can interact with it just as you interact with your local machine via its shell prompt in the terminal.

Note

Don't expect to actually be able to telnet to krpan.killernuts.org to test this. We don't know any system administrators who leave telnet available on their machine, and had to enable it specifically for the example.

If everyone you know is concerned about security and has their `telnet` daemons disabled, there are still a number of interesting uses for the `telnet` client. Because many servers for other Internet applications speak the same protocol, you can use the `telnet` protocol to talk to them as well. It might not seem like a useful idea to be able to talk to a Web-server with a terminal program that doesn't understand anything about the HTTP language and can't display the data properly, but it turns out to have a number of interesting applications.

For example, your Web browser tells you that a server isn't responding—can you tell whether it's the Web server software that's not responding, or the machine that hosts it that's not responding? `telnet` to the HTTP port (port 80) on the server, and see what the response is. If the Web server software and machine are both okay, your session should look something like this:

```
[localhost:~] nermal% telnet www.biosci.ohio-state.edu 80

     Trying 140.254.12.240...
     Connected to ryoko.biosci.ohio-state.edu.
     Escape character is '^]'.
```

If the machine is okay, but the Web server software isn't speaking, the session might instead look more like:

```
[localhost:~] nermal% telnet rosalyn.biosci.ohio-state.edu 80

     Trying 140.254.12.151...
     telnet: Unable to connect to remote host: Connection refused
```

If the machine is completely absent from the network, such as `catbert` in the following example, the response will get only to the `Trying` line, and hang there, well, trying—I press Ctrl+C in the example to convince it to give up.

```
[localhost:~] nermal% telnet catbert.biosci.ohio-state.edu 80

     Trying 140.254.12.236...
     ^C
```

Finally, if there really isn't a machine by that name at all, you'll see:

```
[localhost:~] nermal% telnet dingbat.biosci.ohio-state.edu 80

     dingbat.biosci.ohio-state.edu: Unknown host
```

Caution

Please don't use the `telnet` program as a terminal program unless you are connecting to a machine that has no connection to the Internet. The program transfers all data in plain text, and anyone with physical access to any of the communication hardware involved in the connection (like the phone lines, ethernet wiring, the air, if you're using AirPort) can read everything you type, including user IDs and passwords out of the data stream.

The `rlogin` Program

Whereas the `telnet` communication package was conceived with hardly any concern for security, the `rlogin` communications package was developed under the seemingly quaint notion that certain connections could be trusted, based only on their self-proclaimed credentials. Passing its data using the same unprotected protocol as `telnet`, `rlogin` is supposed to give the administrator some confidence in the identity of a connecting visitor by virtue of the fact that the connection came from a trusted port. Using it is similar to `telnet`, except that it doesn't accept an optional connection port, and it automatically fills in your user ID on the remote system based on your local system user ID. The syntax is simply `rlogin` *<remotehost>*.

Note

A long, long time ago, in a decade almost two removed, the Internet and the perceptions regarding users who could connect to it were a very different place. Along with the lack of `this.dot.that.dot.coms` all over the place, and the lack of spam in your e-mail, Unix was an expensive commercial operating system. Machines that ran it were expensive, and the people who ran them, even people on different ends of the earth who had never met each other, thought of each other as fellow members of a professional fraternity. Professional courtesies were extended, and if you were a system administrator, a concern about another's security was the same as a concern about your own security.

Due to this expectation that any person running a Unix machine was another security-conscious professional, early security measures were based on utilizing this trust as a form of security credential. Security-conscious professionals were as worried about allowing security risks on others machines as incurring security risks on their own, so they would never let a "bad" user use their system. The

continues

only people who could connect using the `rlogin` client were users on other Unix machines. Taken together, any user with valid credentials on a Unix machine, verified by their being allowed to run the `rlogin` program, must, by association, be a trustable user.

Taken in the context of today's rampant attacks against system security, this might sound like a naively bad security method, but until the advent of "personal Unixes" such as Linux, it worked surprisingly well. Given that much of today's data is passed around with equally insecure connections, without even a trust-based attempt to verify the authenticity of the content, we probably shouldn't poke too much fun at the naiveté of the early communication packages.

As you are coming into the world of having your very own personal Unix machine connected to the Internet, we'd like to encourage you to adopt some of the historic notions regarding administrator responsibility and fraternity, but not their naïve notions regarding security.

Like the `telnet` program, if you're connecting to machines that aren't connected to the Internet, the `rlogin` client is just as good as any. If you're connecting to machines that are connected to the Internet, please don't use the `rlogin` program, even if the remote machine makes it available. Doing so only risks your accounts and data on both local and remote machines, and the security of both machines as well.

The Secure-Shell Software Suite: `slogin`, `scp`, `sftp`, and Others

The Secure Shell collection of programs provides strongly encrypted communications between your machine and a remote server. The implementation that Apple has chosen to provide is based on the OpenSSH (`http://www.openssh.org/`) distribution of the protocols. The protocol requires both client software, which we will cover in this chapter, and server software that will be covered in Chapter 26. Here, we will assume that you already have a server to talk to, and will detail the use of the client software on the Unix side of your OS X machine to talk to your remote server.

`slogin`

The starting point for use of the Secure Shell client is the `slogin` program. This program replaces the functionality of the `telnet` and `rlogin` programs, and provides some additional capabilities as well. Unlike `telnet` and `rlogin`, `slogin` passes all information between the machines as encrypted data, using a public-key encryption method.

Note

Public-key encryption is a clever method of encrypting data. Basically, in public-key encryption schemes, every person interested in exchanging encrypted information creates two keys. One of the created keys is the person's private key, and the other is the person's public key. These keys are mathematically related, but one cannot be derived from the other. The cleverness resides in the mathematical relationship between the keys. When you encrypt data, you encrypt it using two keys: your private key and the public key of the message's intended recipient. The keys are related in such a fashion that data encrypted with your private key, and another's public key, can be decrypted only with a combination of your public key and the other person's private key. This encryption method is used in both systems such as the PGP (Pretty Good Privacy) e-mail encryption software, and in data transmission software such as `ssh`. In e-mail encryption, you use your private key, and the e-mail recipient's public key, to encrypt mail destined for them, and they use your public key and their private key to encrypt mail destined for you. In the encryption of data transmission in software such as `ssh`, the system again uses your private and public keys, and a pair of private and public keys belonging to the remote system to which you are connecting.

The basic use of `slogin` is much like that for `rlogin`—simply issue the command `slogin <machinename>`, where `<machinename>` is the name or IP address of the remote machine to which you'd like to connect. If the remote machine is running a Secure Shell server and it is configured to allow you to connect, the server will respond asking for your password. If you respond correctly, you will be left at a shell prompt on the remote machine, and can type into it and execute commands, just as though you were in a `Terminal.app` window typing to your local machine. A successful `slogin` attempt might look something like this:

```
[localhost:~] joray% slogin rosalyn.biosci.ohio-state.edu

     joray@rosalyn's password:
     Last login: Sat Apr 21 19:55:15 2001 from dhcp9574211.colu
     You have new mail.
     /home/joray

     ...Remote login...

     /net/rosalyn/home2/joray

     Rosalyn joray 201 >
```

Again, at this point we're at a shell prompt on the remote machine `rosalyn.biosci.ohio-state.edu`.

Some system administrators choose not to allow remote logins through simple password authentication. Passwords are generally too short to be difficult for a computer to guess by simple brute-force methods. Instead, the Secure Shell suite allows the use of arbitrarily long, multiword passphrases. A `slogin` connection requiring this type of login looks like this:

```
[localhost:~/test-stuff] miwa% slogin rosalyn

     Enter passphrase for RSA key 'miwa@ryoohki':
     Last login: Sat Apr 21 15:55:55 2001 from ryoohki.biosci.o
     You have mail.
     Rosalyn miwa 1 >
```

If the remote machine is running this more restrictive security (and we recommend that you do so, if you choose to enable remote connections to your machine when we get to Chapter 26), you will be asked, not for your password, but for your passphrase if you have created one. The connection will be refused if you have not created a passphrase.

Creating a passphrase involves a bit of work on your part. This is because if you really want security, you can't allow the encrypted keys that identify you to be seen on the network. Therefore, after the key is created, you need to transfer it to the remote machine via some old-fashioned, physical method, such as writing it on a floppy disk and taking this directly to the remote machine.

Tip

If you're in charge of setting up both machines, you could leave password access under Secure Shell on long enough for you to copy the keys back and forth on the encrypted channel, and then turn off password access to tighten security.

Creating a passphrase for yourself involves the following:

On your OS X machine, generate a key pair by running

```
ssh-keygen -d -C <username>@<osx-hostname>
```

The `-d` option specifies DSA authentication, which is the default encryption mode for SSH2. The `-C` specifies what kind of comment to make. In other versions of `ssh-keygen`, the comment is typically of the form *<username>@<hostname>*. Sometimes comments contain more information. On the OS X machine where the sample was run, `ssh-keygen` generates a comment of `<user>@<localhost>` if you don't specify a more specific comment.

When you run `ssh-keygen`, you are asked for a passphrase to protect the private key. It is recommended that the passphrase be at least 11 characters long and include as many character types as possible: uppercase letters, lowercase letters, numbers, and special characters. Spaces may be included as part of the passphrase.

Here is a sample run:

```
[localhost:~] miwa% ssh-keygen -d -C miwa@ryoohki

     Generating DSA parameter and key.
     Enter file in which to save the key (/Users/miwa/.ssh/id_dsa):
     ➥Enter passphrase (empty for no passphrase):
     Enter same passphrase again:
     Your identification has been saved in /Users/miwa/.ssh/id_dsa.
     Your public key has been saved in /Users/miwa/.ssh/id_dsa.pub.
     The key fingerprint is:
     54:ae:7a:73:2e:12:3b:2e:68:ce:8d:61:33:95:83:81 miwa@ryoohki
```

As `ssh-keygen` tells us, user `miwa` does indeed have the promised keys, as shown in the following output. The private key was saved as `id_dsa`, and the public key was saved as `id_dsa.pub`; both are stored in the directory `~/.ssh/`.

```
[localhost:~/.ssh] miwa% ls -al

     total 32
     drwx------    6 miwa  staff   160 Apr 16 16:55 .
     drwxr-xr-x   15 miwa  staff   466 Apr 16 15:46 ..
     -rw-------    1 miwa  staff   736 Apr 16 16:56 id_dsa
     -rw-r--r--    1 miwa  staff   602 Apr 16 16:56 id_dsa.pub
     -rw-r--r--    1 miwa  staff   353 Apr 16 15:31 known_hosts
     -rw-------    1 miwa  staff  1024 Apr 16 16:56 prng_seed
```

Next, we need to transfer the file `id_dsa.pub` to the remote host. Because you might be generating different keys for different hosts, it's most convenient if you rename the file first—this also helps prevent you from overwriting it the next time you create a key, or overwriting the key on the remote host when you transfer it. Because it's your public key, it doesn't matter if the world can see it—you can copy it to your remote host via FTP, move it there with a floppy, or paste it across a logged-in terminal session.

On the remote host, in the `.ssh` directory in your home directory (`~/.ssh/`), the public key you just created needs to be added to the file `authorized_keys2` (`~/.ssh/authorized_keys2`). If the file does not exist, it must be created. When adding the new key to the file, be sure that the key is added as a single long line of data.

Tip

Many terminals will be friendly and line-wrap the key, if you try to paste it though a logged-in terminal window. If your passphrase refuses to work, make sure that there are no extra blank lines in your `~/.ssh/authorized_keys2` file, and that the key hasn't accidentally accumulated any line breaks.

Having done all this, if you now try to `slogin` to the remote host where you just added your key (and assuming the remote host is running `sshd2`!), you should be greeted with a login process asking for your passphrase instead of your password. Enter the passphrase exactly as you did to create the keys, and you will enjoy a data connection that is almost impossible to decrypt, and an access code (your passphrase) that is much more secure than a simple password.

Note

Note that there are a number of variations on the movement of the public key and its installation on the remote host. These revolve around the version of server running on the remote machine. Considerably more detail and examples of these options are given in Chapter 26, "Remote Access and Administration," where we cover getting these outside machines to talk to your OS X box.

The `slogin` program also provides a neat method for protecting data transmissions other than terminals. This is implemented as an encrypted tunnel between the two machines connected by the `slogin` terminal connection. Essentially, `slogin` can be instructed to watch for connections that come to your local machine, package the data from these connections up, encrypt it, ship it off to the other end of the tunnel, and unpackage it again. You then use your `ftp`, or any other network connection program, to connect to your local machine (not the remote machine!), and `slogin` will tunnel that connection to the remote machine and make the connection at the other end. Because your user ID and password for the FTP server are carried over the encrypted tunnel, they're never in clear text on the network, and your login information and any data you transmit are protected.

To demonstrate this, the following `slogin` connection sets up a tunnel from the local machine to a remote machine named `waashu`, over which `ftp` connections can be carried.

```
[localhost:/Users/joray] root# slogin waashu.biosci.ohio-state.edu
➥-l joray -L21:waashu:21
```

```
The authenticity of host 'waashu.biosci.ohio-state.edu' can't be
➥established.
RSA key fingerprint is 54:d2:85:b2:fa:2f:f1:b8:c7:16:6f:ca:75:d8:0b:ea.
Are you sure you want to continue connecting (yes/no)? yes
Warning: Permanently added
➥'waashu.biosci.ohio-state.edu,140.254.12.239' (RSA)
                            to the list of known hosts.
joray@waashu.biosci.ohio-state.edu's password:
Last login: Tue Apr 17 15:50:07 2001 from rosalyn.biosci.ohio-state.edu
You have new mail.
...Remote login...
/home/joray

WAASHU joray 201 >
```

Again, this leaves the terminal connected to the remote machine, and sitting at a shell prompt on the remote machine.

Note

Note that only the `root` user can map to ports numbered lower than `1024`. For this reason, the `slogin` forwarding as here isn't quite what you want to do for day-to-day use. It's the easiest for basic illustration, though—a more practical example comes a little later.

After `slogin` is connected like this, it is connecting port `21`, the normal `ftp` port on our machine (`localhost`) to port `21` on the remote host we're logged in to. Fire up another terminal window. The second terminal window will be used to invoke `ftp` to connect over the tunnel like so:

```
[localhost:~] joray% ftp localhost

    Connected to localhost.biosci.ohio-state.edu.
    220 waashu.biosci.ohio-state.edu FTP server ready.
    Name (localhost:joray): joray
    331 Password required for joray.
    Password:
    230 User joray logged in.
    Remote system type is UNIX.
    Using binary mode to transfer files.

ftp> passive

    Passive mode on.

ftp> cd osx-misc

    250 CWD command successful.
```

```
ftp> binary
     200 Type set to I.
ftp> put developer-1.tiff
     local: developer-1.tiff remote: developer-1.tiff
     227 Entering Passive Mode (140,254,12,239,60,59)
     150 Opening BINARY mode data connection for 'developer-1.tiff'.
     226 Transfer complete.
     1255376 bytes sent in 16.2 seconds (77490 bytes/s)
ftp> quit
     221 Goodbye.
```

To check whether it arrived okay, we go to the waashu terminal:

```
WAASHU osx-misc 203 > ls -l dev*tiff
     -rw-r--r--    1 joray    user     1255376 Apr 21 20:35 developer-1.tiff
```

Note that when we ftp to localhost, ftp reports that we're connected to localhost, but waashu responds. The tunnel is working as expected.

As noted earlier, use of port 21 is restricted to the root user, but for your first introduction, it made sense to direct the ftp port to the ftp port. There is nothing that limits the forwarding to connecting identically numbered ports, though, and ftp can also connect to ports other than the usual port 21. For use on a day-to-day basis, a normal user can replace the -L21:<machinename>:21 section of the command with -L2000:<machinename>:21. The ftp command then is extended by adding the port number for the local connection, as ftp localhost 2000.

Additional options for the operation of slogin are as shown in Table 15.4.

TABLE 15.4 The Command Documentation Table for ssh and slogin

ssh	
slogin	Secure shell remote login client
ssh [-l *<login_name>*] [*<hostname>* | *<user>*@*<hostname>*] [*<command>*]	
ssh [-aAfgknqtTvxXCNP246] [-c *<cipher_spec>*] [-e *<escap_char>*] [-i *<identity_file>*] [-l *<login_name>*] [-o *<option>*] [-p *<port>*] [-L *<port>*:*<host>*:*<hostport>*] [-R *<port>*:*<host>*:*<hostport>*] [*<hostname>* | *<user>*@*<hostname>*] [*<command>*]	
-a	Disables forwarding of the authentication agent.
-A	Enables forwarding of the authentication agent. This can also be specified on a per-host basis in a configuration file.

TABLE 15.4 continued

`-f`	Requests ssh to go to background just before command execution. This implies -n. The recommended way to start X11 programs at a remote site is ssh -f host xterm.
`-g`	Allows remote hosts to control local forwarded ports.
`-k`	Disables forwarding of Kerberos tickets and AFS tokens. This may also be specified on a per-host basis in a configuration file.
`-n`	Redirects stdin from /dev/null.
`-q`	Quiet mode. Causes warning and diagnostic messages to be suppressed.
`-t`	Forces pseudo-tty allocation. Useful for executing arbitrary screen-based programs on a remote machine.
`-T`	Disables pseudo-tty allocation (SSH2 only).
`-v`	Verbose mode. Causes debugging messages to be printed.
`-x`	Disables X11 forwarding.
`-X`	Enables X11 forwarding. This can also be specified on a per-host basis in a configuration file.
`-C`	Requests compression of all data.
`-N`	Does not execute a remote command. Useful for just forwarding ports. SSH2 only.
`-P`	Uses a nonprivileged port for outgoing connections. Useful if your firewall does not permit connections from privileged ports. Turns off RhostsAuthentication and RhostsRSAAuthentication.
`-L` *<port>*`:`*<host>*`:` *<hostport>*	Specifies that the given port on the client (local) host is to be forwarded to the given host and port on the remote side.
`-R <port>:<host>: <hostport>`	Specifies that the given port on the remote (server) host is to be forwarded to the given host and port on the local side.
`-2`	Forces SSH2 protocol.
`-4`	Forces ssh to use IPv4 addresses only.
`-6`	Forces ssh to use Ipv6 addresses only.
`-c blowfish|3des`	Selects the cipher to use for the session. 3des is the default.
`-c 3des-cbc,blowfish-arc, arcfour,cast128-cbc`	For SSH2, a comma-separated list of ciphers can be specified in order of preference. SSH2 supports 3DES, Blowfish, CAST128 in CBC mode and Arcfour mode.

TABLE 15.4 continued

`-e ch|^ch|none`	Sets escape character for sessions with a pty (default: ~). The escape character is only recognized at the beginning of a line. Followed by a . closes the connection; followed by ^Z suspends the connection; followed by itself sends the escape character once. Setting it to none disables any escapes and makes the session fully transparent.
`-i <identity_file>`	Specifies the file from which the identity (private key) for RSA authentication is read. Default is $HOME/.ssh/identity
`-l <login_name>`	Specifies the user to log in as on the remote machine. This may also be specified on a per-host basis in a configuration file.
`-o <option>`	Can be used for giving options in the format used in the configuration file. Useful for specifying options that have no separate command-line flag. Option has the same format as a line in the configuration file.
`-p <port>`	Specifies the port to connect to on the remote host. This can be specified on a per-host basis in the configuration file.

scp, sftp, and Others

In addition to the `slogin` program, the Secure Shell suite of programs provides additional data encryption and protection functions to the user. There are components that function analogously to the `cp` command that you learned about in the previous chapter (`scp`), and to the `ftp` command that you learned about earlier in this one (`sftp`).

The `scp` command can copy a file either from, or to, a Secure Shell remote host. The syntax, like `cp`, is `scp <from> <to>`. Either `<from>` or `<to>` can be specified as a remote machine and file, in the syntax of `[<username>@]<remotemachine>:<pathtofile>`. For example, the following command copies `~ray/public_html/my_bookmarks.html` from the machine `soyokaze` (`soyokaze` is a host alias to `soyokaze.biosci.ohio-state.edu` on this machine) to a file by the same name in the local folder `~/Documents/`.

```
[localhost:~] nermal% scp ray@soyokaze:public_html/my_bookmarks.html
➥~/Documents/

    The authenticity of host 'soyokaze' can't be established.
    RSA key fingerprint is
    ➥95:2f:55:91:57:4b:42:ad:63:fb:62:ce:b1:33:ba:eb.
    Are you sure you want to continue connecting (yes/no)? yes
    Warning: Permanently added 'soyokaze.biosci.ohio-state.edu,140.254.12.137'
```

```
                         (RSA) to the list of known hosts.
    ray@soyokaze.biosci.ohio-state.edu's password:
    warning: Executing scp1 compatibility.
    my_bookmarks.html     100% |***************************|   271 KB    00:01
```

The complaints regarding the host key aren't something to be concerned about—they simply mean that this host hasn't been accessed yet, and isn't a known host yet.

Likewise, the following copies the file `myfile` from the current directory to the directory `/tmp`, and names it `yourfile` on the remote machine `soyokaze`, again logging in using the user ID `ray`.

```
[localhost:~] nermal% scp ./myfile ray@soyokaze:/tmp/yourfile

    ray@soyokaze's password:
    warning: Executing scp1 compatibility.
    myfile                 100% |*************************|     0        --:-- ETA
```

Note that `scp` doesn't make complaints about the host key the second time because it's already accepted and stored it.

The command documentation table for `scp` is shown in Table 15.5.

TABLE 15.5 The Command Documentation Table for scp

`scp`	Secure remote copy
`scp [-pqrvC46] [-S <program>] [-P <port>] [-c <cipher>] [-i <identity_file>] [-o <option>] [[<user>@]<host1>:]<file1> [...] [[<user>@]<host2>:]<file2>`	
`-p`	Preserves modification times, access times, and modes from the original file.
`-q`	Disables the progress meter.
`-r`	Recursively copies entire directories.
`-v`	Verbose mode. Causes `scp` and `ssh` to print debugging messages.
`-C`	Enables compression. Passes the flag to `ssh(1)` to enable compression.
`-4`	Forces `scp` to use IPv4 addresses only.
`-6`	Forces `scp` to use IPv6 addresses only.
`-S <program>`	Specifies `<program>` to use for the encrypted connection. Program must understand `ssh(1)` options.
`-P <port>`	Specifies the port to connect to on the remote host.
`-c <cipher>`	Selects the cipher to use for encrypting the data transfer. Option is passed directly to `ssh(1)`.

TABLE 15.5 continued

`-i <identity_file>`	Specifies the file from which the identity (private key) for RSA authentication is read.
`-o <option>`	Passes specified option to `ssh(1)`.

Apple currently isn't distributing an `sftp` client as part of the OS X secure shell package, even though it is distributing an `sftpd` daemon with which you can allow other machines to connect to your OS X box. We've detailed using `sftp` to talk to your OS X box from another Unix box in Chapter 26. If Apple should start to distribute an `sftp` client for OS X, those instructions should be applicable to using `sftp` from your OS X box to elsewhere as well.

Mail Clients

Depending on how your machine is configured, you might not have a use for the first e-mail reading command discussed in this chapter. It is detailed here partly for historical completeness, and partly because it is an excellent utility for your use, if you have the opportunity to use it.

The `mail` program is an e-mail reading and sending program that works on e-mail that is actually received and managed by your local machine. If all you've ever used is a POPmail or IMAP client, such as Eudora or Mailsmith, you're probably unfamiliar with the idea of your local machine being its own e-mail server. Unix machines have, since the dawn of e-mail, been part of the backbone by which e-mail makes its way around the Internet. Configured properly, they don't need POPmail servers, they *are* POPmail (and IMAP) servers. E-mail gets around between them by way of the SMTP (Simple Mail Transfer Protocol), and is delivered (with a few minor exceptions) directly from the sender's machine to the receiver's machine.

What does this mean to you? If your machine is set up to receive and deliver mail itself, mail doesn't arrive at 10-minute intervals (or however frequently you have your POPmail client configured to connect). It arrives as instantaneously as it can make its way across the Internet—usually within a few seconds of being sent. It doesn't require your ISP's mail service to be up and running for you to receive mail because you (for e-mail purposes) are your own ISP. Old-time Unix users are frequently amused by the instant messaging services that seem to be all the rage as the hot new Internet technology. Unfettered by the POPmail and IMAP protocols, plain old e-mail *is* an instant messaging technology.

Building Block Simplicity: mail

The `mail` program is a simple command-line program for sending and reading e-mail. Invoked with no arguments, its default behavior is to display the list of messages in your system mailbox, and provide you with a prompt from which further interaction can occur. Used in this fashion, `mail` will produce output similar to the following:

> **Note**
>
> If you're just setting up your system, you're unlikely to have any mail, and will probably get only a message that says `No mail for` *<username>*. If you never set up your machine as its own mail server, you'll have no reason to read your mail this way. You might still want to set up your machine to do its own mail delivery, which will allow you to use the `mail` command as a building block application for shell scripts. We'll talk more about this in Chapter 18, "Advanced Unix Shell Use: Configuration and Programming (Shell Scripting)."

```
rodan joray 205> mail
    Mail version SMI 4.0 Fri Oct 14 12:50:06 PDT 1994 Type ? for help.
    "/var/spool/mail/joray": 11 messages 11 new
    >N  1 joray          Tue Nov  7 08:30   14/296    testing
     N  2 joray          Thu Nov  9 10:30   15/359    testing new sendmail
     N  3 joray          Thu Nov  9 10:43   15/384    another test
     N  4 joray          Thu Nov  9 11:00   13/370    another test...
     N  5 joray          Thu Nov  9 11:21   15/402    Testing sendmail and geth
     N  6 MAILER-DAEMON  Thu Nov  9 11:32   64/2324   Returned mail: see transc
     N  7 joray          Thu Nov  9 11:40   15/480    testing gethostbyaddr fix
     N  8 MAILER-DAEMON  Thu Nov  9 11:42   65/2283   Returned mail: see transc
     N  9 joray          Thu Nov  9 11:55   14/374    testing...
     N 10 joray          Thu Nov  9 12:13   14/407    Hi there.
     N 11 joray          Tue Dec 19 13:00   14/374    hi there
    &
```

The `&` on the last line is the internal mail prompt from which you can enter commands.

> **Note**
>
> Wondering how we got a mail version that claims to be compiled in 1994? There is an annoying feature making Apple's Sendmail difficult to use as of this writing, and getting mail to work on OS X requires jumping through some additional hoops as compared to a normal Unix installation. The hoops aren't particularly difficult, and we'll show you how to fix the system when you enable the Sendmail daemon in Chapter 29. The example shown here is from a version of the same program running on an older Unix varient

At the & prompt internal to mail, you have a number of options. These include the expected functions of reading, sending, and deleting messages, as well as a few others. Table 15.6 details command options available for the mail program.

TABLE 15.6 The Command Documentation Table for mail

mail	Sends and receives mail
mail [-iInv] [-s <*subject*>] [-c <*cc-addr*>] [-b <*bcc-addr*>] <*to-addr*>...	
mail [-iInNv] -f [<*name*>]	
mail [-iInNv] [-u <*user*>]	
mail	
-I	Ignores tty interrupt signals. Especially useful for communication on noisy phone lines.
-I	Forces interactive mode, even when input isn't a terminal. Particularly useful for using the ~ character, which is only available in interactive mode.
-n	Ignores /etc/mail.rc upon startup.
-v	Verbose mode.
-s <*subject*>	Specifies the subject. Uses only the first argument after the flag. Be certain to use quotes for any subjects with spaces.
-c <*cc-addr*>	Sends a carbon copy to the users specified in <*cc-addr*>.
-b <*bcc-addr*>	Sends a blind copy to the users specified in <*bcc-addr*>. The list should be a comma-separated list.
-f [<*name*>]	Reads the contents of your mbox or the file specified by <*name*>. When you quit, mail writes undeleted messages back to this file.
-u <*user*>	Equivalent to -f /usr/mail/<user>.
Here are some of the useful options available within mail:	
-<*n*>	Displays the previous message, if <*n*> is not specified; otherwise, displays the <*n*>th previous message.
?	Displays a brief summary of commands.
help	Same as ?.
^D	Sends the composed message.
!<*shell_command*>	Executes the shell command that follows.
<return>	
n	
+	Goes to the next message in sequence.

TABLE 15.6 continued

`Reply`	
`R`	Replies to the sender of the message. Does not reply to any other recipients of the message.
`reply`	
`r`	Replies to the sender and all other recipients of the message.
`respond`	Same as `reply`.
`mail` *`<user>`*	
`m`	Sends mail to the *`<user>`* specified. Takes login names and distribution group names as arguments.
`delete`	
`d`	Takes as its argument a list of messages and marks them to be deleted. Messages marked for deletion are not available for most other commands.
`dp`	
`dt`	Deletes the current message and prints the next message.
`undelete`	
`u`	Takes a message list as its argument and unmarks the messages for deletion.
`edit`	
`e`	Takes as its argument a list of messages and points a text editor at each one in turn.
`inc`	Checks for any new incoming messages that have arrived since the session began and adds those to the message list.
`save`	
`s`	Takes as its argument a list of messages and a filename and saves the messages to the filename. Each message is appended to the file. If no message is given, saves the current message.
`write`	
`w`	Similar to `save`, except saves only the body of messages.
`unread`	
`U`	Takes as its argument as list of messages and marks them as not read.

TABLE 15.6 continued

`alias`	
`a`	With no arguments, prints out the list of currently defined aliases. With one argument, prints out the specified alias. With multiple arguments, creates a new alias or edits an old one.
`unalias`	Takes as its argument a list of names defined by alias commands and discards the remembered groups of users.
`exit`	
`ex`	
`x`	Exits `mail` without making any changes to the user's `mbox`, system mailbox, or the `-f` file that was being read.
`xit`	Same as `exit`.
`quit`	
`q`	Terminates the session, saving all undeleted messages in the user's `mbox`.

Caution

Be aware that Apple has provided a program named `Mail`, as well as a program named `mail`. (Remember, capitalization makes a difference in the Unix world; these programs have different capitalization and therefore are not the same thing.) In most Unixes, there is a difference in functionality between `Mail` and `mail`. Specifically, `mail` is usually a simple application mostly useful for quick shell-scripting applications—it usually produces a dump of all new messages as its default action. `Mail`, on the other hand, usually provides the interface discussed here. Intentionally or unintentionally, Apple's `mail` acts like the traditional `Mail`, and Apple's `Mail`, at the time of writing, appears to be broken.

Full-Featured Power: `pine`

`pine` is a command-line-based modern e-mail client. It provides access to system mailboxes, as well as remote (or local if you choose) POPmail and IMAP servers. The `pine` e-mail client provides an interface that will be much more familiar to users of applications such as Eudora. Although text-based, it provides a menu driven interface with multiple mailboxes, sophisticated filtering, and other friendly conveniences. As of this writing, Apple doesn't distribute `pine` as a default application with OS X, but it's a popular enough mail client that many sites will have it installed. If you're playing system administrator for your own machine, the installation of `pine` is covered later in this chapter.

`pine`, being a menu-driven, windowed system, doesn't lend itself to command documentation tables, so we give you a pair of screenshots from the running program. Figure 15.1 shows the first `pine` screen you'll see when you start it up. Unless you have `sendmail` working properly, *don't* press the Return key to send the requested statistic information!

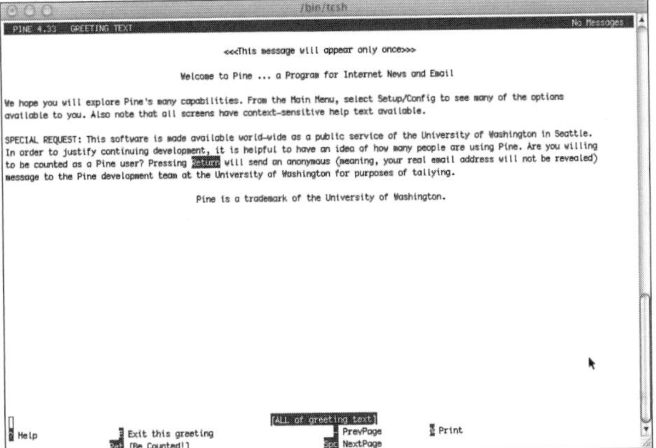

FIGURE 15.1
The initial `pine` *window. From this window, you can choose from any of the keys shown at the bottom to start using the program.*

Figure 15.2 shows the more typical `pine` screen from which you'll work. You can choose items from the textual menu shown on the screen, and also choose commands from those shown at the bottom of the screen. One thing that you should be aware of is that `pine` usually expects you to go back to get out of any situation. It's sort of like wandering around on the Web—there isn't necessarily a link back to the first page from any sub-pages several layers down in the system. Look for options that take you to the previous screen and so on to assist in navigating the system.

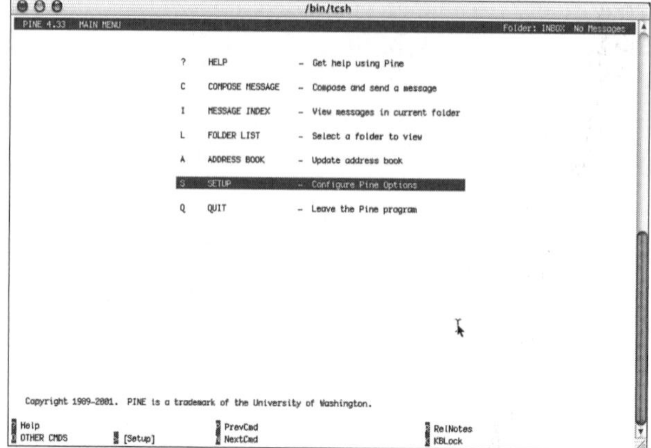

FIGURE 15.2
The normal top-level window for the `pine` *e-mail reading program.*

Text Editors

Even though you might think that you'll never have a reason to use anything other than a GUI text editor such as `Pepper` or `BBEdit`, there are a few arguments to be made for text-only mode editing in a terminal. Among them are that the text-only editors can even be used when the system can't display a GUI interface, and that an editor in a terminal can start much faster than most GUI editors. There's also the advantage that if you have occasion to work on Unix machines other than OS X boxes, the command-line editors are what you will have available.

Finally, at this point, the GUI clients available currently seem to have a bit of a problem figuring out whether they should convert a file that they load into Mac-style text (for newlines), or Unix-style text. The Unix command-line editors are a bit more predictable in preferring Unix-format text.

When it comes to editing text on the Unix side, you'll find that many Unix programs use text files as input, create text files as output, or are configured using commands and variables set up in text files. To change the contents of these files, you'll need to make use of a text editor.

As a matter of fact, most Unix software doesn't know the difference between a text file and any other file. Unlike in Mac OS, from the OS X operating system's point of view, files are files are files. If the user chooses to view some of them as containing text, and some as containing programs, that's the user's business. An interesting consequence of this lack of concern about a file's contents is that the operating system is just as happy to allow you to use a text editor to edit the contents of your spreadsheet program as it is to enable you to attempt to run your e-mail. Of course, if you actually have execute permission turned on for your e-mail and try to run it, it's almost certainly going to result in nothing more interesting than a Bus Error and an immediate exit of the command—but the OS will try.

Tip

If you are a programmer, you might find this lack of distinction (yet another example of Unix abstraction at work) to be useful. On occasion, you might find a program that needs a minor change, such as the correction of a misspelling or a change of wording. In these instances, it is sometimes more convenient to simply load the executable file into a text editor and make the correction directly into the binary. This isn't a trick for the faint of heart, but sometimes it's the quick fix you need, and occasionally it's the only fix available for software for which you don't have access to the source.

If you spend much time discussing Unix editors with longtime Unix users, you'll find that there is a disagreement of warlike proportions between the users of the two most common editors: `vi` and `emacs`. Although these editors are actually rather complementary in their functions and are both useful tools to have in your toolbox, chances are that you will run into many users who insist that one or the other editor is completely useless. If you listen to them, you'll be depriving yourself of the better solution to at least some tasks.

Many Unix editors have immense power. `emacs`, for example, not only contains its own built-in programming language, but can also function as a complete windowing system, a compiler/debugger interface, a news reader, and many other things. Even with a book of this size, however, there isn't space to do more than address the basics of using these editors. After you've mastered the basics, if you're interested in learning more, we encourage you to stop by your local bookstore or library and choose from among the several books available on each of the major Unix editors.

Quick, Dirty, and Omnipresent: `vi`

The `vi` editor is Unix's most universal editor. Some users pronounce it *vee-eye*, and some pronounce it *vye*, and a growing contingent who claim it's pronounced *six*, when used on OS-X. There seems to be no concrete consensus which pronunciation is correct (but the people who say *vye* are still wrong). `vi` isn't an easy editor, and it isn't friendly.

It is, however, a quick-starting editor with a small memory footprint, which you will find on every Unix machine you encounter, regardless of flavor. `vi`, although annoying to learn, is frequently the most convenient editor to use for doing things like making single-line changes to configuration files.

When you start `vi`, there are a number of things you need to know to make it useful. The Return key has been included in the explanations here because some commands take effect immediately, and some require you to press Return after you enter them.

`vi` operates in one of two modes: command mode or insert mode. In command mode, you have control over things such as cursor position, deleting characters, and saving files. In command mode, every keyboard character you type will be interpreted as part of a command of some sort. In insert mode, every keyboard key you type is inserted into the file you are editing. This distinction is bound to be confusing at first, but if you use `vi`, you'll find that its speed makes it a preferred editor for quick changes to files.

Some of the most used keys and tasks are shown in Table 15.7.

TABLE 15.7 Common Key Presses and the Resultant Actions in `vi`

Mode	Key(s)/Key Combination(s)	Action
Command	l	Move right
	h	Move left
	j	Move to next line
	k	Move to previous line
	Put cursor on character and press x key	Delete character under cursor
	Press d key twice	Delete an entire line, including an empty line
	A	Enter insert mode at end of current line
	i	Enter insert mode before the character under the cursor
	a	Enter insert mode after the character under the cursor
	:w Return	Save the file
	:w <*filename*> Return	Save the file to <*filename*>
	:q Return	Quit
	:q! Return	Quit without saving
	:wq!	Save file and exit

TABLE 15.7 continued

Mode	Key(s)/Key Combination(s)	Action
Insert Mode	Esc key	Switch to command mode
	Backspace or Delete key	Backspaces or deletes, but only for data entered in current insert mode session on the current line
	Any printable keyboard character	Insert the character at the cursor

Instead of trying to walk through a screenshot by screenshot example of using `vi`, try typing the following example. Remember to compare what you're typing to the commands in the previous table, and watch what happens. Although the finer details are not revealed by this example, you will pick up enough to get you started doing useful work, and to get you out of any sticky situations you might get yourself into while editing a file.

Try typing the following exactly as it appears here, and observe what happens. Where a new line appears in the text, press Return. Remember that `<esc>` is the Escape key.

```
% vi mynewfile

    iThis is my new file
    This is line one of my new file
    This is a test
    This is line four of my new file<esc>kddkA
    This is line three of my new file<esc>khhhhhhhhhhhhhhhhhxxxitwo<esc>:wq!
```

Your machine should respond

```
"mynewfile" [New file] 4 lines, 119 characters
```

Now look at what you've got:

```
% cat mynewfile

    This is my new file
    This is line two of my new file
    This is line three of my new file
    This is line four of my new file
```

Table 15.8 shows the command documentation table for the `vi` command.

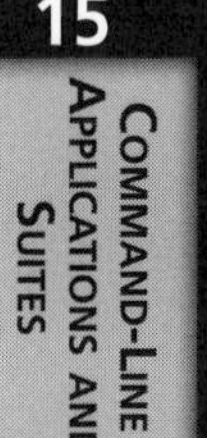

TABLE 15.8 The Command Documentation Table for `vi`

`vi`	
`ex`	
`view`	Screen-oriented text editor

TABLE 15.8 continued

Line-oriented screen editor

Read-only version of vi

`vi [-eFlRrSv] [-c <cmd>] [-t <tag>] [-w <size>] [<file1> <file2> ...]`

`ex [-eFlRrSsv] [-c <cmd>] [-t <tag>] [-w <size>] [<file1> <file2> ...]`

`view [-eFlRrSv] [-c <cmd>] [-t <tag>] [-w <size>] [<file1> <file2> ...]`

`vi` is a screen-oriented text editor; `ex` is a line-oriented editor. `vi` and `ex` are different interfaces to the same program. view is equivalent to `vi -R`, the read-only option to `vi`.

The following options are available:

`-e`	Starts to edit in ex mode.
`-F`	Doesn't copy the entire file when first starting to edit. Default is to make a copy in case someone else modifies the file during your edit session.
`-l`	Starts editing with the lisp and showmatch options set.
`-R`	Starts editing in read-only mode.
`-r`	Recovers the specified file. If no file is specified, it lists the files that could be recovered. If no recoverable files with the specified name exists, vi starts editing as if the option has not been issued.
`-S`	Runs with secure edit option set, which disallows all access to external programs.
`-s`	Enters batch mode. Applicable only to ex. It is useful for running ex scripts.
`-v`	Starts editing in vi mode.
`-c <cmd>`	Executes *<cmd>* immediately after starting the edit session. It is especially useful for initial positioning in the file, but is not limited to positioning commands.
`-t <tag>`	Starts editing at the specified *<tag>*.
`-w <size>`	Sets the initial window size to `<size>` lines.

vi has two modes: command mode and input mode. Command mode is the initial and normal mode. Completion of the input mode returns the user to command mode. Pressing the Esc key ends a partial command.

Input mode is required to input some types of edits. Input mode is terminated by pressing the Esc key. Upon termination of input mode, the user is returned to command mode.

Some commands for moving around in a file:

`h`	Moves the cursor one character to the left.
`l`	Moves the cursor one character to the right.

TABLE 15.8 continued

`j`	Moves the cursor one line down.
`k`	Moves the cursor one line up.
`<arrow keys>`	The arrow keys often also function properly.
`<num>G`	Moves the cursor to the line number specified by `<num>`. If `<num>` is not specified, the cursor moves to the last line of the file.
Some commands for inputting text (input mode):	
`i`	Inserts text before the cursor.
`a`	Appends new text after the cursor.
`A`	Appends new text at the end of the line where the cursor is.
`o`	Opens a new line below the line where the cursor is and allows the user to start entering text on the new line.
`O`	Opens a new line above the line where the cursor is, and allows the user to start entering text on that new line.
Some commands for copying text:	
`yy`	Copies the line the cursor is on.
`p`	Appends the copied line after the line the cursor is on.
Some commands for deleting text:	
`dd`	Deletes the line the cursor is on.
`<num>dd`	Deletes *<num>* lines, starting with the line the cursor is on.
`dw`	Deletes the word the cursor is on.
`x`	Deletes the character the cursor is on.
Some other useful text manipulation:	
`r<x>`	Replaces the character the cursor is on with *<x>*.
`J`	Joins the line the cursor is on with the line below.
Some commands for pattern searching:	
`/<pattern>`	Searches forward in the file for *<pattern>*, starting with the location of the cursor.
`?<pattern>`	Searches backward in the file for *<pattern>*, starting with the location of the cursor.
`n`	Repeats the last / or ? pattern search.
`N`	Repeats the last / or ? pattern search in reverse.

TABLE 15.8 continued

Some commands to write the file:	
`:w<return>`	Writes the file back to the filename originally specified when vi was started.
`:w <filename><return>`	Writes the file to the filename specified by *<filename>*.
Some commands to quit editing and exit vi:	
`:q<return>`	Exits vi. Refuses to quit if there are any unsaved modifications, or if the file is read-only.
`:q!`	Exits vi, even if there are any unsaved modifications.
`ZZ`	Exits vi, saving changes.

Everything and the Kitchen Sink: emacs

On the other end of the spectrum from `vi`'s odd syntax and tiny footprint is `emacs`. In certain circles, it is thought that `emacs` is an acronym for Emacs Makes a Computer Slow because `emacs` epitomizes the notion of an everything package, and has the memory footprint to prove it. Including a windowing system, an e-mail reading client, a news reading client, a programming language, and an online help database, to name only a few of its features, `emacs` can almost certainly do anything you want a plain text editor to do.

Note

Don't believe me? `emacs` also includes an implementation of the aged Eliza psychoanalyst, and a Zippy the Pinhead quote generator. Do you really think there's anything that's *not* in there? If you're creative, you can convince Zippy to have a conversation with Eliza inside `emacs`.

With today's fast machines and nearly unlimited memory, the major complaints against `emacs` aren't a significant impediment to its use.

From the point of view of the average user, `emacs` has a much more intuitive interface than `vi`. You're always in insert mode, just like you're used to in GUI-based word processors. Commands are handled by the use of Control+*<key>* combinations, instead of the use of a separate mode.

To use `emacs`, there are some basics that you need to know—you can get more information from the online tutorial mentioned at the end of this section. In the following list, whenever you see Ctrl+ preceding a character, it means that you need to hold down the

Control key and type that character. Whenever you see Esc- preceding a character, it means to press the Esc key, and then the character.

- The `emacs` editor doesn't have a separate mode for entering commands. You are always either typing a command or typing text—no switching between modes for them. This is just like most word processors that you are probably familiar with. To enter text, just type what you want to appear. To enter a command (usually Ctrl+<key> or Esc-x <*somecommand*>), just type the command as shown.
- You can position the cursor keys in `emacs` by using the arrow keys. If you're working across a network connection, the arrow keys might not work, but you can also position the cursor with Ctrl+<*key*> combinations. Ctrl+f moves the cursor forward. Ctrl+b moves it back. Ctrl+n moves to the next line. Ctrl+p moves up one line.
- You can delete everything from the cursor to the end of the line with Ctrl+k. A second Ctrl+k will delete the now blank line.
- Ctrl+g is the `emacs` "quit what you're doing" command. If you've started typing a command and change your mind, press Ctrl+g to abort.
- If you use Ctrl+k to delete a line or lines, you can use Ctrl+y to yank it (them) back. You don't have to yank them to the same location from which you deleted them.
- To save the file you're working on, press Ctrl+x Ctrl+s.
- To save the file to a new name, press Ctrl+x Ctrl+w <*filename*>Return.
- To exit `emacs`, press Ctrl+x Ctrl+c. If `emacs` proceeds to ask you about unsaved buffers, it's because you have unsaved work. You can either answer no, and save your work, or answer yes to the "quit anyway?" questions and exit without saving.

Beyond the Ctrl+ commands available in `emacs`, there's also an amazingly extensible set of commands that come into play if you use the Escape key. These commands are usually known as `emacs` meta commands, even though the machine with the meta key from which the commands draw their name has long since faded into history. These commands, even though they're initiated by pressing the Escape key, are usually abbreviated in the documentation with a leading *M*, for meta. The complete set of these commands is the subject of more than one book, and we recommend that you investigate your library or bookstore options, if you really want to understand the inner workings. If you're a puzzle solver, many of the interesting items are documented in Table 15.9. A good place to start on meta commands will be with testing out the `emacs` online help system. Start `emacs` by simply typing `emacs` at the prompt. After it starts, press Esc-x, and then type `help-` and press the spacebar. You will be presented with a list of `emacs` commands starting with `help-`, including useful things such as `help-for-help`, a very good place to start.

Instead of a quick example like we used for `vi` above, we suggest you take the `emacs` tutorial. To enter the `emacs` tutorial, all you need to do is start `emacs`, and type `Ctrl+h i` (hold the Ctrl key, press the h key, release them both, and press the i key). If you type a ? after the Ctrl+h instead of the i, you'll see that there is actually a whole world of alternatives to the i. These alternatives give you access to a range of different types of helpful information. For now, take the tutorial. If you're curious, you can probably spend a near eternity exploring the rest of the options available.

Table 15.9 shows the a portion of the command documentation table for `emacs`, as well as a listing of some of the help topics detailing a number of the available meta commands. The synopses of the help topic areas should give you an idea of some of the things that you can do, and some of the information that you can look for in the online documentation. This table is derived from the `emacs` internal documentation, and it can be accessed in `emacs` itself by typing `M-x info`, and selecting the `emacs` documentation line. It should be clear from this listing that the complete documentation for `emacs` is rather voluminous.

TABLE 15.9 The Command Documentation Table for `emacs`

`emacs`	Editor
`emacs [`*`<command-line switches>`*`] [`*`<file1> <file2>`*`...]`	
`emacs` is a powerful editor that can actually do more than edit files. It has an extensive information system, which can be accessed in `emacs` with the key sequence <Ctrl+h i> (holding the Control key and h and then i). The information system can be navigated using the arrow keys to move around and pressing the Enter key to make a selection.	
`emacs` has an interactive help facility, <Ctrl+h>. The information facility is one of the types of help available. A help tutorial is available with <Ctrl+h t>. Help Apropos <Ctrl+h a> helps the user find a command given its functionality. Help Character <Ctrl+h c> describes a given character's effect.	
The following are `emacs` options of general interest:	
`<file>`	Edits the specified *`<file>`*.
`+`*`<number>`*	Moves the cursor to the line number specified by *<number>*. (Do not include a space between + and *<number>*.)
`-q`	Does not load an init file.
`-u` *`<user>`*	Loads the init file of the specified *`<user>`*.

TABLE 15.9 continued

`-t <file>`	Uses the specified `<file>` as the terminal instead of using stdin/stdout. This must be the first argument specified in the command line.
`-nw`	Tells `emacs` not to use its special X interface. If this option is given when invoking `emacs` in an `xterm(1)` window, the `emacs` display is done in that window. This must be the first option specified in the command line.

The following are basic `emacs` key sequences. Remember that two keys pressed simultaneously have a plus sign between them, and a space indicates pressing them sequentially. Most Unix documentation, including the online man pages and info pages will document Esc-x as M-x, for the Meta key:

Up Arrow	Move cursor up one line.
Left Arrow	Move cursor to the left one character, to end of previous line if at left side of current line.
Right Arrow	Move cursor to the right one character, move to the beginning of the next line if at the right side of the current line.
Down Arrow	Move cursor down one line. Adds a new line to the file, if currently on the last line of the file.
Ctrl+p	Move cursor up one line.
Ctrl+b	Move cursor to the left one character, to end of previous line if at left side of current line.
Ctrl+f	Move cursor to the right one character, move to the beginning of the next line if at the right side of the current line.
Ctrl+n	Move cursor down one line. Adds a new line to the file, if currently on the last line of the file.
Ctrl+v	Move down one page in file.
Esc-v	Move up one page in file
Ctrl+l	Move current line to the center of the page
Ctrl+a	Move cursor to the beginning of the current line.
Ctrl+e	Move cursor to the end of the current line.
Esc-a	Move cursor to the beginning of the current sentence.
Esc-e	Move cursor to the end of the current sentence.
Ctrl+x Ctrl+h	Bring up list of Ctrl+x prefixed commands. (If you do this, you will see that this table is a *very* abbreviated list!)
Ctrl+x Ctrl+s	Saves the file.
Ctrl+x Ctrl+w	Prompt for new name to save file.

TABLE 15.9 continued

Ctrl+x Ctrl+c	Exits `emacs`.
Ctrl+x Ctrl+f	Prompt to open file.
Ctrl+x Ctrl+b	List current file buffers.
Ctrl+x b	Prompt to switch to another buffer.
Esc-x `find-file-literally`	Prompt to open file in literal mode—no Mac/Unix linefeed interpretation and so on.
Ctrl+x Ctrl+d	List directory in `emacs` buffer (allows opening files by browsing directory rather than by typing name).
Ctrl+x Ctrl+o	Delete blank lines in file.
Ctrl+x Ctrl+t	Transpose lines.
Ctrl+spacebar	Set mark at the current cursor position.
Ctrl+x Ctrl+l	Downcase region. The region is the area between the cursor, and where the current mark is set.
Ctrl+x Ctrl+u	Upcase region. The region is the area between the cursor, and where the current Mark is set.
Ctrl+w	Delete from mark to cursor. Deleted text goes to kill-ring buffer.
Esc-w	Copy from mark to cursor into kill-ring buffer.
Ctrl+k	Delete from cursor to end of line. Place deleted text in kill-ring buffer.
Ctrl+y	Yank top data from kill-ring buffer into the text at the current cursor position.
Ctrl+x 2	Split current window vertically into two editing windows (two full-width windows, half the previous height).
Ctrl+x 3	Split current window horizontally into two editing windows (two full-height windows, half the previous width).
Ctrl+x o	Switch to next editing window in split-window mode.
Ctrl+x 1	Switch to single-window mode, keeping the current window open.
Ctrl+x 0	Remove current editing window, keeping others.
Ctrl+x (	Start recording keyboard macro.
Ctrl+x)	Stop recording keyboard macro.
Ctrl+x e	Execute recorded keyboard macro.
Ctrl+u <####>	Creates a numeric argument for the next command.
Ctrl+u <####> *<keyseq>*	Execute *<keyseq>* ##### times.

TABLE 15.9 continued

Ctrl+x f	Set fill column for word wrap. Requires a numeric argument set with Ctrl+u <####>.
Esc-x `fill-region`	Word wrap region between cursor and mark.
Ctrl+h Ctrl+h	Bring up menu of help subjects.
Ctrl+h t	Bring up `emacs` tutorial.
Ctrl+h i	Bring up `emacs` info-mode manual browser. Browsing through the `emacs` info through this interface is recommended.
Esc-x `info`	Bring up `emacs` info-mode manual browser.
Esc-x `apropos`	Prompt for command or key sequence to document.
Ctrl+h h	Bring up list of ways to say hello in 34 different languages—we told you `emacs` had *everything* in it!

The following is a listing of some of the interesting parts of the information system's main menu for `emacs`:

File: emacs, Node: Top, Next: Distrib, Prev: (dir), Up: (dir)

The Emacs Editor

****

Emacs is the extensible, customizable, self-documenting real-time display editor. This Info file describes how to edit with Emacs and some of how to customize it; it corresponds to GNU Emacs version 20.3. For information on extending Emacs, see *Note Emacs Lisp: (elisp)Emacs Lisp.

* Menu:

* Distrib:: How to get the latest Emacs distribution.

* Copying:: The GNU General Public License gives you permission to redistribute GNU Emacs on certain terms; it also explains that there is no warranty.

* Intro:: An introduction to Emacs concepts.

* Glossary:: The glossary.

* Antinews:: Information about Emacs version 19.

TABLE 15.9 continued

```
* MS-DOS::            Using Emacs on MS-DOS (otherwise known as "MS-DOG").
* Manifesto::         What's GNU?  Gnu's Not Unix!
* Acknowledgments::   Major contributors to GNU Emacs.

Indexes (nodes containing large menus)
* Key Index::         An item for each standard Emacs key sequence.
* Command Index::     An item for each command name.
* Variable Index::    An item for each documented variable.
* Concept Index::     An item for each concept.

Important General Concepts
* Screen::            How to interpret what you see on the screen.
* User Input::        Kinds of input events (characters, buttons, function keys).
* Keys::              Key sequences: what you type to request one editing action.
* Commands::          Named functions run by key sequences to do editing.
* Text Characters::   Character set for text (the contents of buffers and strings).
* Entering Emacs::    Starting Emacs from the shell.
* Exiting::           Stopping or killing Emacs.
* Command Arguments:: Hairy startup options.

Fundamental Editing Commands
* Basic::             The most basic editing commands.
* Minibuffer::        Entering arguments that are prompted for.
* M-x::               Invoking commands by their names.
* Help::              Commands for asking Emacs about its commands.

Important Text-Changing Commands
* Mark::              The mark: how to delimit a "region" of text.
* Killing::           Killing text.
* Yanking::           Recovering killed text.  Moving text.
* Accumulating Text:: Other ways of copying text.
* Rectangles::        Operating on the text inside a rectangle on the screen.
.
```

TABLE 15.9 continued

```
* Registers::       Saving a text string or a location in the buffer.
* Display::         Controlling what text is displayed.
* Search::          Finding or replacing occurrences of a string.
* Fixit::           Commands especially useful for fixing typos.

Major Structures of Emacs
* Files::           All about handling files.
* Buffers::         Multiple buffers; editing several files at once.
* Windows::         Viewing two pieces of text at once.

* Postscript Variables::
                    Customizing the PostScript printing commands.
* Sorting::         Sorting lines, paragraphs, or pages within Emacs.
* Narrowing::       Restricting display and editing to a portion of the buffer.
* Two-Column::      Splitting apart columns to edit them in side-by-side windows.
* Editing Binary Files::
                    Using Hexl mode to edit binary files.
* Saving Emacs Sessions::
                    Saving Emacs state from one session to the next.
* Recursive Edit::  A command can allow you to do editing
                    "within the command".  This is called a
                    `recursive editing level'.
* Emulation::       Emulating some other editors with Emacs.
* Dissociated Press:: Dissociating text for fun.
* Amusements::      Various games and hacks.
* Customization::   Modifying the behavior of Emacs.

Recovery from Problems
* Quitting::        Quitting and aborting.
* Lossage::         What to do if Emacs is hung or malfunctioning.

* Bugs::            How and when to report a bug.
* Contributing::    How to contribute improvements to Emacs.
* Service::         How to get help for your own Emacs needs.
```

TABLE 15.9 continued

Here are some other nodes which are really inferiors of the ones already listed, mentioned here so you can get to them in one step:

— The Detailed Node Listing —

The Organization of the Screen

* Point:: The place in the text where editing commands operate.
* Echo Area:: Short messages appear at the bottom of the screen.
* Mode Line:: Interpreting the mode line.
* Menu Bar:: How to use the menu bar.

Basic Editing Commands

* Inserting Text:: Inserting text by simply typing it.
* Moving Point:: How to move the cursor to the place where you want to change something.
* Erasing:: Deleting and killing text.

* Undo:: Undoing recent changes in the text.
* Files: Basic Files. Visiting, creating, and saving files.
* Help: Basic Help. Asking what a character does.
* Blank Lines:: Commands to make or delete blank lines.
* Continuation Lines:: Lines too wide for the screen.
* Position Info:: What page, line, row, or column is point on?
* Arguments:: Numeric arguments for repeating a command.

The Minibuffer

* Minibuffer File:: Entering file names with the minibuffer.
* Minibuffer Edit:: How to edit in the minibuffer.
* Completion:: An abbreviation facility for minibuffer input.

TABLE 15.9 continued

* Minibuffer History::	Reusing recent minibuffer arguments.
* Repetition::	Re-executing commands that used the minibuffer.
Help	
* Help Summary::	Brief list of all Help commands.
* Key Help::	Asking what a key does in Emacs.
* Name Help::	Asking about a command, variable or function name.
* Apropos::	Asking what pertains to a given topic.
* Library Keywords::	Finding Lisp libraries by keywords (topics).
* Language Help::	Help relating to international language support.
* Misc Help::	Other help commands.
The Mark and the Region	
* Setting Mark::	Commands to set the mark.
* Transient Mark::	How to make Emacs highlight the region when there is one.
* Using Region::	Summary of ways to operate on contents of the region.
* Marking Objects::	Commands to put region around textual units.
* Mark Ring::	Previous mark positions saved so you can go back there.
* Global Mark Ring::	Previous mark positions in various buffers.
Deletion and Killing	
* Deletion::	Commands for deleting small amounts of text and blank areas.
* Killing by Lines::	How to kill entire lines of text at one time.
* Other Kill Commands::	Commands to kill large regions of text and syntactic units such as words and sentences.

TABLE 15.9 continued

Yanking

* Kill Ring::   Where killed text is stored. Basic yanking.
* Appending Kills::   Several kills in a row all yank together.
* Earlier Kills::   Yanking something killed some time ago.

Registers

* RegPos::   Saving positions in registers.
* RegText::   Saving text in registers.
* RegRect::   Saving rectangles in registers.
* RegConfig::   Saving window configurations in registers.
* RegFiles::   File names in registers.
* Bookmarks::   Bookmarks are like registers, but persistent.

Controlling the Display

* Scrolling::   Moving text up and down in a window.
* Horizontal Scrolling:: Moving text left and right in a window.
* Follow Mode::   Follow mode lets two windows scroll as one.
* Selective Display::   Hiding lines with lots of indentation.

* Optional Mode Line::   Optional mode line display features.
* Text Display::   How text is normally displayed.
* Display Vars::   Information on variables for customizing display.

Searching and Replacement

* Incremental Search::   Search happens as you type the string.
* Nonincremental Search:: Specify entire string and then search.
* Word Search::   Search for sequence of words.
* Regexp Search::   Search for match for a regexp.
* Regexps::   Syntax of regular expressions.

TABLE 15.9 continued

```
* Search Case::          To ignore case while searching, or not.
* Replace::              Search, and replace some or all matches.
* Other Repeating Search:: Operating on all matches for some regexp.

Replacement Commands

* Unconditional Replace::  Replacing all matches for a string.
* Regexp Replace::         Replacing all matches for a regexp.
* Replacement and Case::   How replacements preserve case of letters.
* Query Replace::          How to use querying.


Commands for Fixing Typos

* Kill Errors::         Commands to kill a batch of recently entered text.
* Transpose::           Exchanging two characters, words, lines, lists...
* Fixing Case::         Correcting case of last word entered.
* Spelling::            Apply spelling checker to a word or a whole buffer.

File Handling

* File Names::          How to type and edit file-name arguments.
* Visiting::            Visiting a file prepares Emacs to edit the file.
* Saving::              Saving makes your changes permanent.
* Reverting::           Reverting cancels all the changes not saved.
* Auto Save::           Auto Save periodically protects against loss of data.
* File Aliases::        Handling multiple names for one file.
* Version Control::     Version control systems (RCS, CVS and SCCS).
* Directories::         Creating, deleting, and listing file directories.
* Comparing Files::     Finding where two files differ.
* Misc File Ops::       Other things you can do on files.
* Compressed Files::    Accessing compressed files.
```

TABLE 15.9 continued

* Remote Files:: Accessing files on other sites.

* Quoted File Names:: Quoting special characters in file names.

Saving Files

* Backup:: How Emacs saves the old version of your file.

* Interlocking:: How Emacs protects against simultaneous editing of one file by two users.

Version Control

* Introduction to VC:: How version control works in general.

* VC Mode Line:: How the mode line shows version control status.

* Basic VC Editing:: How to edit a file under version control.

* Old Versions:: Examining and comparing old versions.

* Secondary VC Commands:: The commands used a little less frequently.

* Branches:: Multiple lines of development.

* Snapshots:: Sets of file versions treated as a unit.

* Miscellaneous VC:: Various other commands and features of VC.

* Customizing VC:: Variables that change VC's behavior.

Using Multiple Buffers

* Select Buffer:: Creating a new buffer or reselecting an old one.

* List Buffers:: Getting a list of buffers that exist.

* Misc Buffer:: Renaming; changing read-onlyness; copying text.

* Kill Buffer:: Killing buffers you no longer need.

* Several Buffers:: How to go through the list of all buffers and operate variously on several of them.

* Indirect Buffers:: An indirect buffer shares the text of another buffer.

TABLE 15.9 continued

Multiple Windows

* Basic Window:: Introduction to Emacs windows.
* Split Window:: New windows are made by splitting existing windows.
* Other Window:: Moving to another window or doing something to it.
* Pop Up Window:: Finding a file or buffer in another window.
* Force Same Window:: Forcing certain buffers to appear in the selected window rather than in another window.
* Change Window:: Deleting windows and changing their sizes.

Frames and X Windows

* Mouse Commands:: Moving, cutting, and pasting, with the mouse.
* Secondary Selection:: Cutting without altering point and mark.
* Mouse References:: Using the mouse to select an item from a list.

* Menu Mouse Clicks:: Mouse clicks that bring up menus.
* Mode Line Mouse:: Mouse clicks on the mode line.
* Creating Frames:: Creating additional Emacs frames with various contents.
* Multiple Displays:: How one Emacs job can talk to several displays.
*Special Buffer Frames:: You can make certain buffers have their own frames.
* Frame Parameters:: Changing the colors and other modes of frames.
* Scroll Bars:: How to enable and disable scroll bars; how to use them.
* Menu Bars:: Enabling and disabling the menu bar.
* Faces:: How to change the display style using faces.
* Font Lock:: Minor mode for syntactic highlighting using faces.
* Support Modes:: Font Lock support modes make Font Lock faster.
* Misc X:: Iconifying and deleting frames. Region highlighting.
Non-Window Terminals:: Multiple frames on terminals that show only one.

Font Lock Support Modes

TABLE 15.9 continued

* Fast Lock Mode:: Saving font information in files.

* Lazy Lock Mode:: Fontifying only text that is actually displayed.

* Fast or Lazy:: Which support mode is best for you?

International Character Set Support

* International Intro:: Basic concepts of multibyte characters.

* Enabling Multibyte:: Controlling whether to use multibyte characters.

* Language Environments:: Setting things up for the language you use.

* Input Methods:: Entering text characters not on your keyboard.

* Select Input Method:: Specifying your choice of input methods.

* Coding Systems:: Character set conversion when you read and write files, and so on.

* Recognize Coding:: How Emacs figures out which conversion to use.

* Specify Coding:: Various ways to choose which conversion to use.

* Fontsets:: Fontsets are collections of fonts that cover the whole spectrum of characters.

* Defining Fontsets:: Defining a new fontset.

* Single-Byte European Support:: You can pick one European character set to use without multibyte characters.

Major Modes

* Choosing Modes:: How major modes are specified or chosen.

Indentation

* Indentation Commands:: Various commands and techniques for indentation.

* Tab Stops:: You can set arbitrary "tab stops" and then indent to the next tab stop when you want to.

* Just Spaces:: You can request indentation using just spaces.

TABLE 15.9 continued

Commands for Human Languages

* Words:: Moving over and killing words.
* Sentences:: Moving over and killing sentences.
* Paragraphs:: Moving over paragraphs.
* Pages:: Moving over pages.
* Filling:: Filling or justifying text.
* Case:: Changing the case of text.
* Text Mode:: The major modes for editing text files.
* Outline Mode:: Editing outlines.
* TeX Mode:: Editing input to the formatter TeX.
* Nroff Mode:: Editing input to the formatter nroff.
* Formatted Text:: Editing formatted text directly in WYSIWYG fashion.

Filling Text

* Auto Fill:: Auto Fill mode breaks long lines automatically.
* Fill Commands:: Commands to refill paragraphs and center lines.
* Fill Prefix:: Filling paragraphs that are indented or in a comment, etc.
* Adaptive Fill:: How Emacs can determine the fill prefix automatically.

Editing Programs

* Program Modes:: Major modes for editing programs.
* Lists:: Expressions with balanced parentheses.
* List Commands:: The commands for working with list and sexps.
* Defuns:: Each program is made up of separate functions. There are editing commands to operate on them.
* Program Indent:: Adjusting indentation to show the nesting.
* Matching:: Insertion of a close-delimiter flashes matching open.
* Comments:: Inserting, killing, and aligning comments.
* Balanced Editing:: Inserting two matching parentheses at once, etc.

TABLE 15.9 continued

```
* Symbol Completion::   Completion on symbol names of your program or language.
* Documentation::       Getting documentation of functions you plan to call.
* Change Log::          Maintaining a change history for your program.

* Tags::                Go directly to any function in your program in one command.  Tags remem-
bers which file it is in.
* Emerge::              A convenient way of merging two versions of a program.
* C/Java Modes::        Special commands of C, C++, Objective-C and Java modes.
* Fortran::             FORTRAN mode and its special features.
* Asm Mode::            Asm mode and its special features.

Indentation for Programs

* Basic Indent::        Indenting a single line.
* Multi-line Indent::   Commands to reindent many lines at once.
* Lisp Indent::         Specifying how each Lisp function should be indented.
* C Indent::            Choosing an indentation style for C code.

Tags Tables

* Tag Syntax::          Tag syntax for various types of code and text files.
* Create Tags Table::   Creating a tags table with `etags'.
* Select Tags Table::   How to visit a tags table.
* Find Tag::            Commands to find the definition of a specific tag.
* Tags Search::         Using a tags table for searching and replacing.

* List Tags::           Listing and finding tags defined in a file.

Merging Files with Emerge

* Overview of Emerge::  How to start Emerge.  Basic concepts.
* Submodes of Emerge::  Fast mode vs. Edit mode.
```

TABLE 15.9 continued

Skip Prefers mode and Auto Advance mode.

* State of Difference:: You do the merge by specifying state A or B for each difference.

* Merge Commands:: Commands for selecting a difference, changing states of differences, etc.

* Exiting Emerge:: What to do when you've finished the merge.

* Combining in Emerge:: How to keep both alternatives for a difference.

* Fine Points of Emerge:: Misc.

Compiling and Testing Programs

* Compilation:: Compiling programs in languages other than Lisp (C, Pascal, etc.).

* Compilation Mode:: The mode for visiting compiler errors.

* Compilation Shell:: Customizing your shell properly for use in the compilation buffer.

* Debuggers:: Running symbolic debuggers for non-Lisp programs.

* Executing Lisp:: Various modes for editing Lisp programs, with different facilities for running the Lisp programs.

* Lisp Libraries:: Creating Lisp programs to run in Emacs.

* Lisp Interaction:: Executing Lisp in an Emacs buffer.

* Lisp Eval:: Executing a single Lisp expression in Emacs.

* External Lisp:: Communicating through Emacs with a separate Lisp.

Running Debuggers Under Emacs

* Starting GUD:: How to start a debugger subprocess.

* Debugger Operation:: Connection between the debugger and source buffers.

* Commands of GUD:: Key bindings for common commands.

* GUD Customization:: Defining your own commands for GUD.

Abbrevs

* Abbrev Concepts:: Fundamentals of defined abbrevs.

* Defining Abbrevs:: Defining an abbrev, so it will expand when typed.

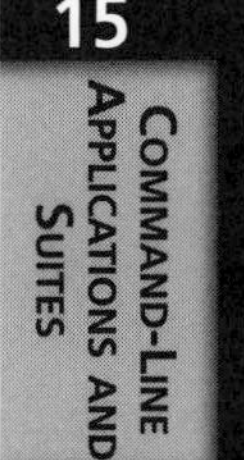

TABLE 15.9 continued

* Expanding Abbrevs::	Controlling expansion: prefixes, canceling expansion.
* Editing Abbrevs::	Viewing or editing the entire list of defined abbrevs.
* Saving Abbrevs::	Saving the entire list of abbrevs for another session.
* Dynamic Abbrevs::	Abbreviations for words already in the buffer.
Editing Pictures	
* Basic Picture::	Basic concepts and simple commands of Picture Mode.
* Insert in Picture::	Controlling direction of cursor motion after "self-inserting" characters.
* Tabs in Picture::	Various features for tab stops and indentation.
* Rectangles in Picture::	Clearing and superimposing rectangles.
Sending Mail	
* Mail Format::	Format of the mail being composed.
* Mail Headers::	Details of permitted mail header fields.
* Mail Aliases::	Abbreviating and grouping mail addresses.
* Mail Mode::	Special commands for editing mail being composed.
* Distracting NSA::	How to distract the NSA's attention.
* Mail Methods::	Using alternative mail-composition methods.
Reading Mail with Rmail	
* Rmail Basics::	Basic concepts of Rmail, and simple use.
* Rmail Scrolling::	Scrolling through a message.
* Rmail Motion::	Moving to another message.
* Rmail Deletion::	Deleting and expunging messages.
* Rmail Inbox::	How mail gets into the Rmail file.
* Rmail Files::	Using multiple Rmail files.
* Rmail Output::	Copying message out to files.
* Rmail Labels::	Classifying messages by labeling them.

TABLE 15.9 continued

* Rmail Attributes::	Certain standard labels, called attributes.
* Rmail Reply::	Sending replies to messages you are viewing.
* Rmail Summary::	Summaries show brief info on many messages.
* Rmail Sorting::	Sorting messages in Rmail.
* Rmail Display::	How Rmail displays a message; customization.
* Rmail Editing::	Editing message text and headers in Rmail.
* Rmail Digest::	Extracting the messages from a digest message.
* Out of Rmail::	Converting an Rmail file to mailbox format.
* Rmail Rot13::	Reading messages encoded in the rot13 code.
* Movemail::	More details of fetching new mail.
Dired, the Directory Editor	
* Dired Enter::	How to invoke Dired.
* Dired Commands::	Commands in the Dired buffer.
* Dired Deletion::	Deleting files with Dired.
* Flagging Many Files::	Flagging files based on their names.
* Dired Visiting::	Other file operations through Dired.
* Marks vs Flags::	Flagging for deletion vs marking.
* Operating on Files::	How to copy, rename, print, compress, etc. either one file or several files.
* Shell Commands in Dired::	Running a shell command on the marked files.
* Transforming File Names::	Using patterns to rename multiple files.
* Comparison in Dired::	Running `diff' by way of Dired.
* Subdirectories in Dired::	Adding subdirectories to the Dired buffer.
* Subdirectory Motion::	Moving across subdirectories, and up and down.
* Hiding Subdirectories::	Making subdirectories visible or invisible.
* Dired Updating::	Discarding lines for files of no interest.
* Dired and Find::	Using `find' to choose the files for Dired.

TABLE 15.9 continued

```
The Calendar and the Diary

* Calendar Motion::     Moving through the calendar; selecting a date.
* Scroll Calendar::     Bringing earlier or later months onto the screen.
* Counting Days::       How many days are there between two dates?
* General Calendar::    Exiting or recomputing the calendar.

* LaTeX Calendar::      Print a calendar using LaTeX.
* Holidays::            Displaying dates of holidays.
* Sunrise/Sunset::      Displaying local times of sunrise and sunset.
* Lunar Phases::        Displaying phases of the moon.
* Other Calendars::     Converting dates to other calendar systems.
* Diary::               Displaying events from your diary.
* Appointments::        Reminders when it's time to do something.
* Daylight Savings::    How to specify when daylight savings time is active.

Movement in the Calendar

* Calendar Unit Motion::      Moving by days, weeks, months, and years.
*  Move to Beginning or End:: Moving to start/end of weeks, months, and years.
* Specified Dates::           Moving to the current date or another specific date.

Conversion To and From Other Calendars

* Calendar Systems::     The calendars Emacs understands (aside from Gregorian).
* To Other Calendar::    Converting the selected date to various calendars.
* From Other Calendar::  Moving to a date specified in another calendar.

* Mayan Calendar::       Moving to a date specified in a Mayan calendar.
```

TABLE 15.9 continued

The Diary

* Diary Commands:: Viewing diary entries and associated calendar dates.
* Format of Diary File:: Entering events in your diary.
* Date Formats:: Various ways you can specify dates.
* Adding to Diary:: Commands to create diary entries.
* Special Diary Entries:: Anniversaries, blocks of dates, cyclic entries, etc.

GNUS

* Buffers of Gnus:: The group, summary, and article buffers.
* Gnus Startup:: What you should know about starting Gnus.
* Summary of Gnus:: A short description of the basic Gnus commands.

Running Shell Commands from Emacs

* Single Shell:: How to run one shell command and return.
* Interactive Shell:: Permanent shell taking input via Emacs.

* Shell Mode:: Special Emacs commands used with permanent shell.
* Shell History:: Repeating previous commands in a shell buffer.
* Shell Options:: Options for customizing Shell mode.
* Remote Host:: Connecting to another computer.

Customization

* Minor Modes:: Each minor mode is one feature you can turn on independently of any others.
* Variables:: Many Emacs commands examine Emacs variables to decide what to do; by setting variables, you can control their functioning.
* Keyboard Macros:: A keyboard macro records a sequence of keystrokes to be replayed with a single command.

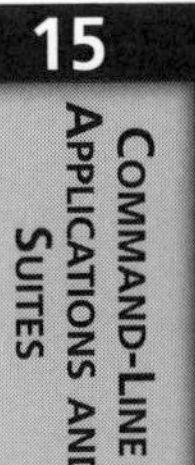

TABLE 15.9 continued

* Key Bindings:: The keymaps say what command each key runs. By changing them, you can "redefine keys".

* Keyboard Translations::

If your keyboard passes an undesired code for a key, you can tell Emacs to substitute another code.

* Syntax:: The syntax table controls how words and expressions are parsed.

* Init File:: How to write common customizations in the `.emacs' file.

Variables

* Examining:: Examining or setting one variable's value.

* Easy Customization:: Convenient and easy customization of variables.

* Hooks:: Hook variables let you specify programs for parts of Emacs to run on particular occasions.

* Locals:: Per-buffer values of variables.

* File Variables:: How files can specify variable values.

Keyboard Macros

* Basic Kbd Macro:: Defining and running keyboard macros.

* Save Kbd Macro:: Giving keyboard macros names; saving them in files.

* Kbd Macro Query:: Making keyboard macros do different things each time.

Customizing Key Bindings

* Keymaps:: Generalities. The global keymap.

* Prefix Keymaps:: Keymaps for prefix keys.

* Local Keymaps:: Major and minor modes have their own keymaps.

* Minibuffer Maps:: The minibuffer uses its own local keymaps.

* Rebinding:: How to redefine one key's meaning conveniently.

* Init Rebinding:: Rebinding keys with your init file, `.emacs'.

* Function Keys:: Rebinding terminal function keys.

TABLE 15.9 continued

* Named ASCII Chars:: Distinguishing <TAB> from `C-i', and so on.

* Mouse Buttons:: Rebinding mouse buttons in Emacs.

* Disabling:: Disabling a command means confirmation is required before it can be executed. This is done to protect beginners from surprises.

The Init File, `~/.emacs'

* Init Syntax:: Syntax of constants in Emacs Lisp.

* Init Examples:: How to do some things with an init file.

* Terminal Init:: Each terminal type can have an init file.

* Find Init:: How Emacs finds the init file.

Dealing with Emacs Trouble

* DEL Gets Help:: What to do if <DEL> doesn't delete.

* Stuck Recursive:: `[...]' in mode line around the parentheses.

* Screen Garbled:: Garbage on the screen.

* Text Garbled:: Garbage in the text.

* Unasked-for Search:: Spontaneous entry to incremental search.

* Memory Full:: How to cope when you run out of memory.

* Emergency Escape:: Emergency escape— what to do if Emacs stops responding.

* Total Frustration:: When you are at your wits end.

Reporting Bugs

* Criteria: Bug Criteria. Have you really found a bug?

* Understanding Bug Reporting:: How to report a bug effectively.

* Checklist:: Steps to follow for a good bug report.

* Sending Patches:: How to send a patch for GNU Emacs.

TABLE 15.9 continued

Command Line Options and Arguments

* Action Arguments:: Arguments to visit files, load libraries, and call functions.
* Initial Options:: Arguments that take effect while starting Emacs.
* Command Example:: Examples of using command line arguments.

* Resume Arguments:: Specifying arguments when you resume a running Emacs.
* Environment:: Environment variables that Emacs uses.

* Display X:: Changing the default display and using remote login.
* Font X:: Choosing a font for text, under X.
* Colors X:: Choosing colors, under X.
* Window Size X:: Start-up window size, under X.
* Borders X:: Internal and external borders, under X.
* Title X:: Specifying the initial frame's title.
* Icons X:: Choosing what sort of icon to use, under X.
* Resources X:: Advanced use of classes and resources, under X.
* Lucid Resources:: X resources for Lucid menus.
* Motif Resources:: X resources for Motif menus.

Environment Variables

* General Variables:: Environment variables that all versions of Emacs use.
* Misc Variables:: Certain system specific variables.

Printing Tools

You already have some printing capability from the `Terminal`'s printing menu options, and built in to the rest of your OS X system. The command line, however, has its own printing facility, allowing you to direct the output of commands to a printer, without having to select that output in the terminal and use the menu options to print. These command line tools are actually fairly sophisticated, although they provide only a minimalist interface to the printing architecture. Print queuing, job-status notification, and print-job logging are all part of the standard Unix `lpr` printing system.

Sending Jobs to the Printer: lpr

The command to send a job to the printer is `lpr`. Although there are a number of options to `lpr`, the most common forms that you will probably use are

```
lpr <filename>

lpr -P<printer> <filename>
```

The first example sends *<filename>* to the system's default printer. The second example sends *<filename>* to an alternative printer named *<printer>*. If your system has more than one printer available to it at the command line, the second form might be of use. Note that there is no space between the `-P` and *<printer>*. You can send multiple jobs to the printer at once, and they will be queued and printed in sequence.

The command provides no feedback other than a return to your prompt:

```
[localhost:~] joray% lpr file2

[localhost:~] joray%
```

The command documentation table for `lpr` is shown in Table 15.10.

TABLE 15.10 The Command Documentation Table for `lpr`

`lpr`	Sends a job to the printer
`lpr [-P<printer>] [-#<num>] [-C <class>] [-J <job>] [-T <title>] [-U <user>] [-i [<numcols>]] [-1234<font>] [-w<num>] [-cdfglnptv] <file1> <file2> ...`	
`lpr` creates a printer job in a spooling area to be printed when facilities become available. A print job consists of a control file and one or more data files, which are copies of the specified files. `lpr` uses a spooling daemon, `lpd`, to print the files or to send the files to a remote host if the printer is on a remote host.	
`-c`	Assumes that files contain data produced by `cifplot(1)`.
`-d`	Assumes that files contain data from `tex` (DVI format from Stanford) .
`-f`	Uses a filter that interprets the first character of each line as a standard FORTRAN carriage control character.

TABLE 15.10 continued

`-g`	Assumes that files contain standard plot data as produced by plot routines.
`-l`	Uses a filter that allows control characters to be printed and suppresses page breaks.
`-n`	Assumes that files are assumed to contain data from `ditroff` (device independent `troff`).
`-p`	Uses `pr(1)` to format the files (equivalent to `print`).
`-t`	Assumes that files contain data from `troff(1)` (`cat` phototypesetter commands).
`-v`	Assumes that files contain a raster image for devices such as Benson Varian.
The following options apply to the handling of the print job:	
`-P`*<printer>*	Forces output to a specific printer. Normally the default printer for the site is used, or the value of the environment variable `PRINTER` is used.
`-h`	Suppresses the printing of a banner page.
`-m`	Sends mail on completion.
`-r`	Removes the file on completion of the spooling or on completion of printing (with the `-s` option).
`-s`	Uses symbolic links. Usually files are copied to the `spool` directory. The `-s` option uses a symbolic link to the data files rather than copying them to the spool directory. Files sent to the printer in this manner should not be modified or removed until they are printed.
The following options apply to copies, the page display, and headers:	
`-#`*<num>*	Prints the number of copies specified by *<num>*.
`-[1234]`*<font>*	Specifies a *<font>* to be mounted on font position `i`. The daemon constructs a `.railmag` file referencing the font pathname.
`-C` *<class>*	Specifies the job classification to be used on the banner page. Replaces the name returned by `hostname(1)` with *<class>*.
`-J` *<job>*	Specifies the job name to be used on the banner page. Normally, the first filename is used.
`-T` *<title>*	Uses *<title>* for `pr(1)` instead of the filename.

TABLE 15.10 continued

-U *<user>*	Specifies *<user>* as the name to print on the banner page. It is only honored if the real user ID is daemon, and is intended for instances where print filters requeue jobs.
-i [*<numcols>*]	Indents the output. If *<numcols>* is specified, it prints *<numcols>* of blank spaces before each line. Otherwise, eight characters are printed.
-w*<num>*	Uses *<num>* as the page width for pr(1).

Checking the Print Queue: lpq

Because lpr provides no feedback other than a return to your prompt, you might sometimes find it useful to check the print queue to check on the status of your print job. The lpq command displays the print queue:

```
[localhost:~] joray% lpq

     lw360 is ready and printing
     Rank    Owner   Job     File(s)                         Total Size
     active  joray   4       file2                           34 bytes
```

Surprisingly, it provides quite a bit of information. We see from the lw360 that the machine that hosts the printer knows it as lw360. The remote machine actually could provide arbitrarily complete data for the printer name, so, depending on your setup, the remote administrator could even include location and printer model information here if he chose.

The output displays each print job on one line. In this example, there is only one print job. The line describing the print job includes a print job number and the filename, size, and owner. If there were multiple jobs queued on the printer, however, each would be listed here, along with the job owner, making it very convenient to track down who's hogging all the printer time!

The command documentation table for lpq is shown in Table 15.11.

TABLE 15.11 The Command Documentation Table for lpq

lpq	Displays the queue of print jobs.
lpq [-la] [-P*<printer>*] [*<job#>*...] [*<user>*...]	
-P*<printer>*	Specifies *<printer>* as the printer. Otherwise, the site's default printer is used or the value of the PRINTER environment variable.

TABLE 15.11 continued

`-l`	Displays the queue information in long format. Includes the name of the host from which the job originated.
`-a`	Displays the local queues for all printers.
`<job#>`	Displays information on the specified job numbers.
`<user>`	Displays information on all jobs for the specified users.

Removing Printer Jobs: `lprm`

If you decide that you would like to remove a print job from the queue, use the `lprm` command. You might find it useful to use in conjunction with `lpq`.

Here are two examples of using `lprm`:

```
[localhost:~] joray% lpq

     lw360 is ready and printing
     Rank    Owner   Job     File(s)                          Total Size
     active  joray   17      file3                            30 bytes
     1st     joray   18      file4                            46 bytes

[localhost:~] joray% lprm 17

     lw360-17: cancelled

[localhost:~] joray% lprm  joray

     lw360-18: cancelled
```

In the first example, we used `lpq` to get a print job number, and then used `lprm` to cancel the specific job number. In the second example, we used the username and cancelled all jobs owned by the specified user. You can cancel jobs only if you are the user they belong to or if you are the super user.

The command documentation table for `lprm` is shown in Table 15.12.

TABLE 15.12 The Command Documentation Table for `lprm`

`lprm`	Removes print jobs from the queue.
`lprm [-P<printer>] [-] [<job#>...] [<user>...]`	
`-P<printer>`	Specifies `<printer>` as the printer. Otherwise, the site's default printer is used or the value of the `PRINTER` environment variable.
`-`	Removes all print jobs in the queue owned by the user invoking the command. If invoked by a super user, removes all print jobs from the queue.

TABLE 15.12 continued

`<job#>`	Removes from the queue the print job specified by `<job#>`. The `<job#>` can be determined by using `lpq(1)`.
`<user>`	Removes jobs in the print queue owned by the specified `<user>`.

Summary

In this chapter, you were introduced to command line tools for accessing network resources of a number of types. The chapter also covered the two premier Unix text editors, and the Unix printing environment that functions as a small suite of cooperating commands.

As of now, you have been introduced to a range of command line programs that is representative of the types of interactions you will experience with almost any Unix software at the command line. Many of these commands and applications probably still seem cumbersome, and it is likely that you find a need to refer back to the book frequently to remember an option. Don't be discouraged at this. There is probably not a single person alive who actually remembers all the possible commands in the `emacs` environment. Use the commands when the opportunity occurs, and reference the book or the man pages to help recall what you've forgotten. Even the best Unix users refer back to the man pages or a book with considerably more frequency than Mac OS users look at their user manuals. Eventually the parts of the programs that you use with regularity will sink in to "muscle memory," and you'll be able to whiz around the command line doing what you do on an everyday basis, without needing to consult your references at all.

CHAPTER

Command-Line Software Installation

In This Chapter

This chapter introduces software installation at the command line. We'll focus specifically on command-line installs that are for command-line software because these are the variety that will be the least familiar.You should be aware, however, that some GUI software might require you to install it by using a command-line program such as `tar`.

Because of its long-standing position at the forefront of the Open Source software movement, the majority of traditional Unix programs are distributed as source code, rather than an executable application. If you're like most Macintosh users, you've probably never even looked at the code it takes to create a program, let alone tried to convince a machine to turn it into a fully-functional application. As OS X becomes more popular and more prevalent in the market, we'll probably see much more software distributed in precompiled form to appease those of you who really don't want to know this stuff. Until then, however, building your own really isn't that difficult.

The components needed to compile and install many pieces of Unix software right out of the box (or more accurately, right out of the `ftp` directory), are already located on your system. You need some support files that tell software how to interact with the hardware, the source for whatever application you'd like to build, and a compiler to build it with. In the good tradition of Unixes everywhere, Apple has provided the first and last of these for you; all that remains is for you to pick the software you'd like, and issue a few fairly standard commands.

Note

Just so you don't take this the wrong way—not all Unix software will compile as easily as what we demonstrate here. Apple has arranged some things in a sufficiently nonstandard fashion, so some software seems almost impossible to compile as of Mac OS X version 10.04. We expect that things will continue to improve over time, and that more and more software will compile cleanly. For the adventurous, Chapter 17, "Troubleshooting Software Installs, and Compiling and Debugging Manually," will detail some of the steps that can be taken if things shown in this chapter don't work properly for the software you want. Even if you're comfortable rolling up your sleeves and jumping into the code, we can't guarantee that everything you try can be compiled.

Installing the Developer Tools

The OS X Developer Tools include compilers, libraries, and assorted programs. The parts that we're most interested in are the compilation and debugging tools. If you're interested in details regarding the libraries and so forth, remember those man commands, and spend some time digging around in the system man pages to learn what other neat things exist after the installation.

Installing

Installation of the Developer Tools is much like installing other software from the GUI. Insert the CD, and click the installer package.

Figure 16.1 shows the installer package selected.

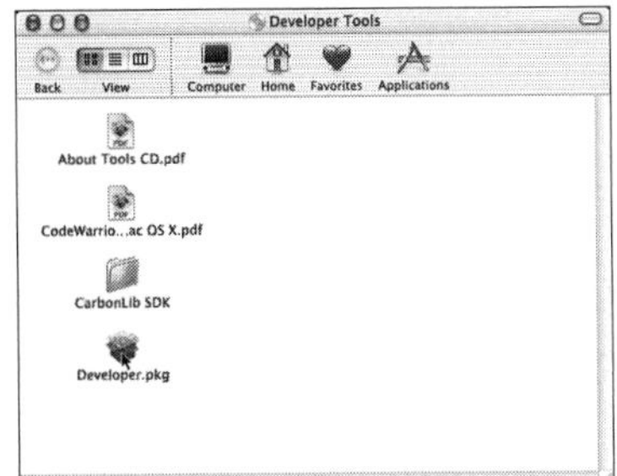

FIGURE 16.1
Double-click the installer package to start the Developer Tools install.

To run the install, you need an administrator (group `wheel`) account. If you're already familiar with installation under OS X, you'll breeze right through this install. If you've skipped ahead to do this installation early, just work through the following steps.

1. Click the lock shown in Figure 16.2.

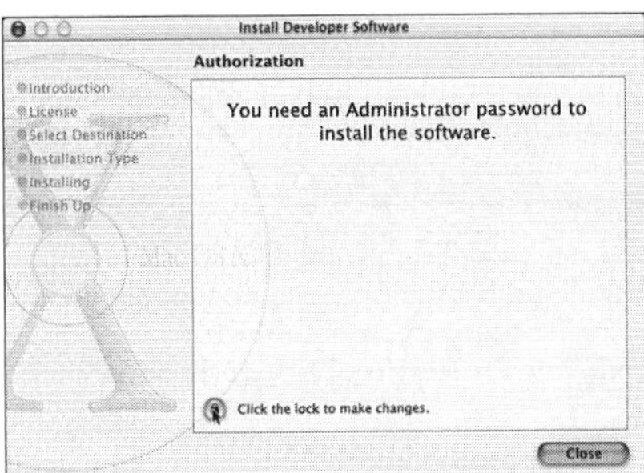

FIGURE 16.2
Click the lock to tell it you're an administrator.

2. Enter your administrator account and password in the dialog that appears, as shown in Figure 16.3.

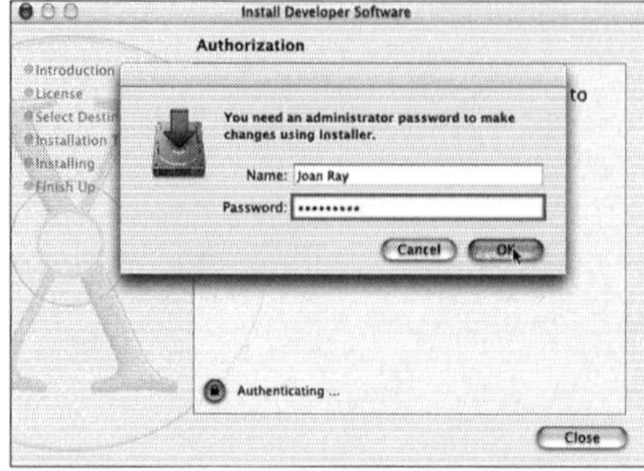

FIGURE 16.3 *Enter your administrator user ID and password.*

3. Click Continue at the welcome screen, as shown in Figure 16.4.

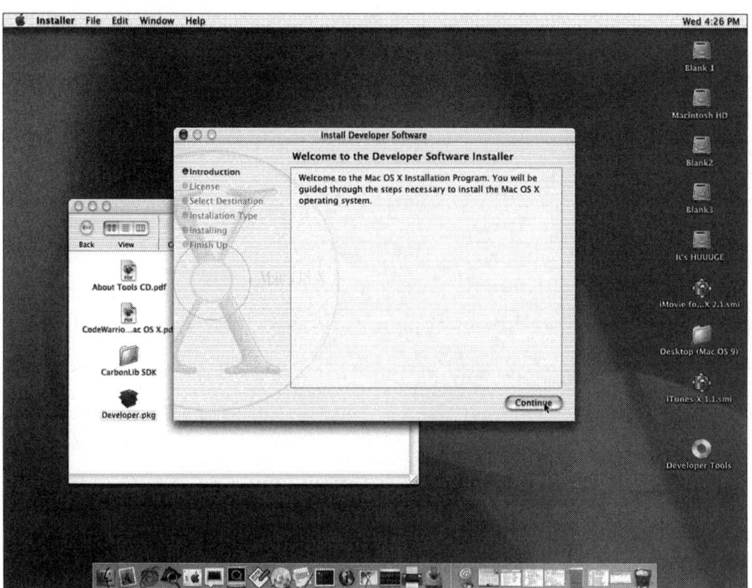

FIGURE 16.4 *Click Continue here to start the install.*

4. Read the license agreement shown in Figure 16.5 and then click Continue.

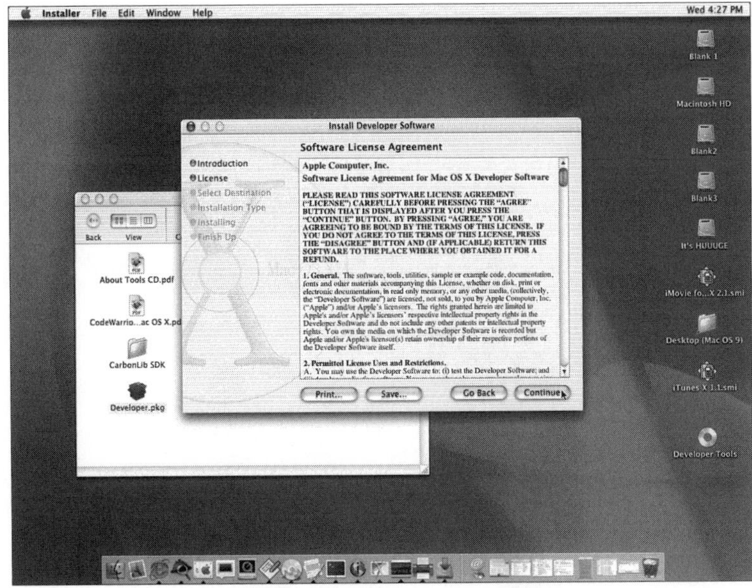

FIGURE 16.5
Read the Developer Tools license information. There's actually some interesting information in there (well, if you're a programmer anyway).

5. Click the Agree button, as shown in Figure 16.6, to indicate that you really did read the agreement.

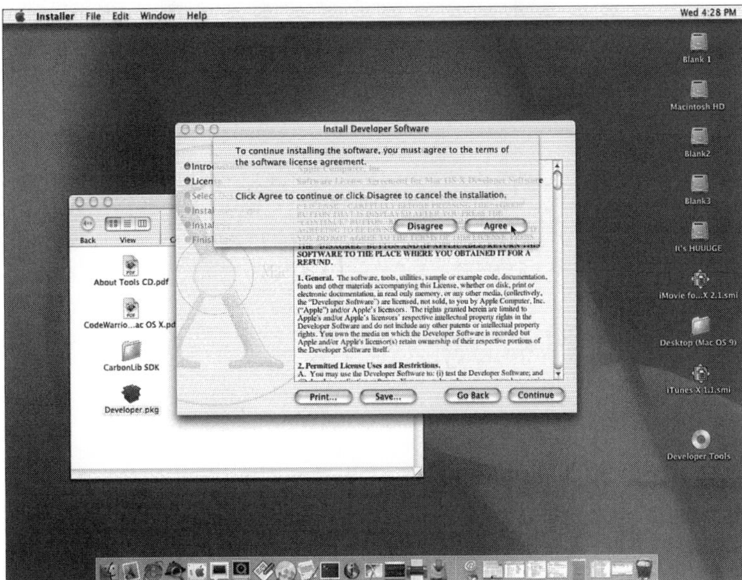

FIGURE 16.6
They really want you to have read that license agreement. Click Agree here to go on.

6. Select the disk on which to install, as shown in Figure 16.7. Be aware that the install wants more than 600MB free space. Your life will probably be easier if you can pick the same drive on which you've installed OS X. Click Continue when you're happy with where the installation will go.

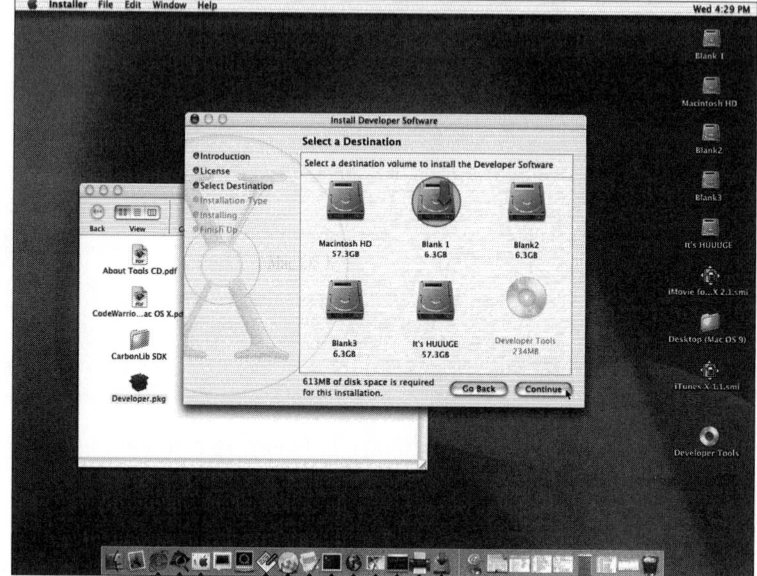

FIGURE 16.7
Picking the disk to install on. It's probably best to pick the same one on which you installed OS X, if there's enough space.

Your only choice is an Easy Install, as shown in Figure 16.8.

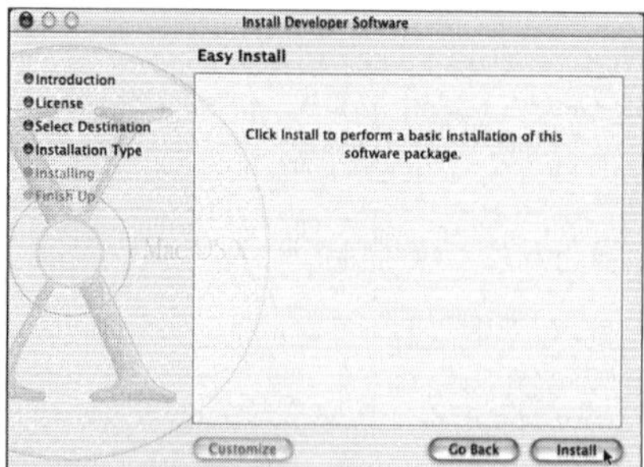

FIGURE 16.8
There is no custom option, at least in the initial release of the Developer Tools, so just click Install to continue with the Easy Install option.

The install proceeds through preparation, as shown in Figure 16.9.

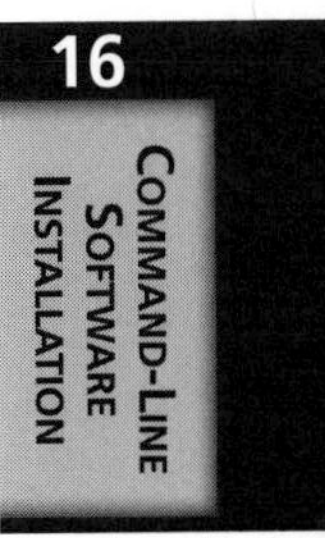

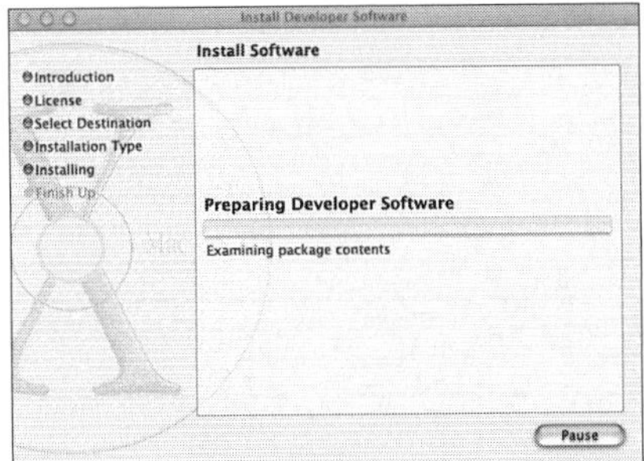

FIGURE 16.9
The Developer Tools preparing to install.

The install then proceeds to writing files, as shown in Figure 16.10.

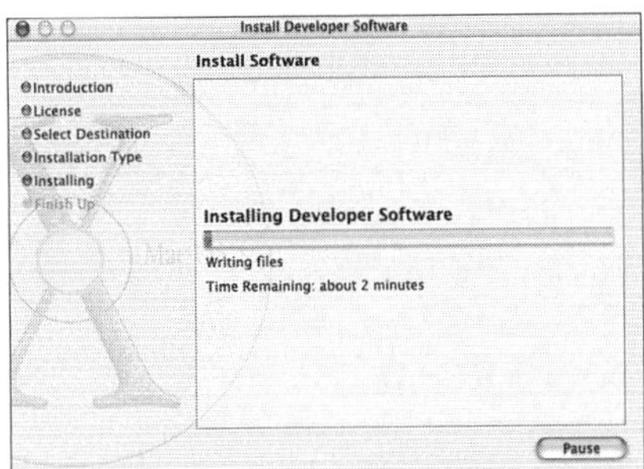

FIGURE 16.10
The Developer Tools writing files.

Running the installer script, shown in Figure 16.11, and optimizing system performance, shown in Figure 16.12, can take some time. The optimizing step makes a number of changes in the system; some are reported to increase system responsiveness, but others appear to actually slow things down.

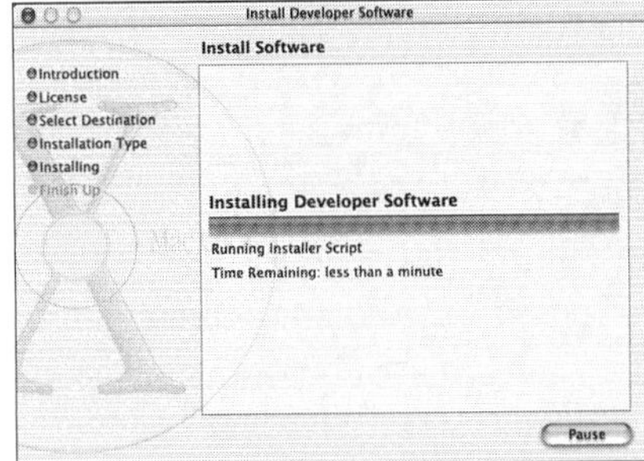

FIGURE 16.11
The Developer Tools running the installer script.

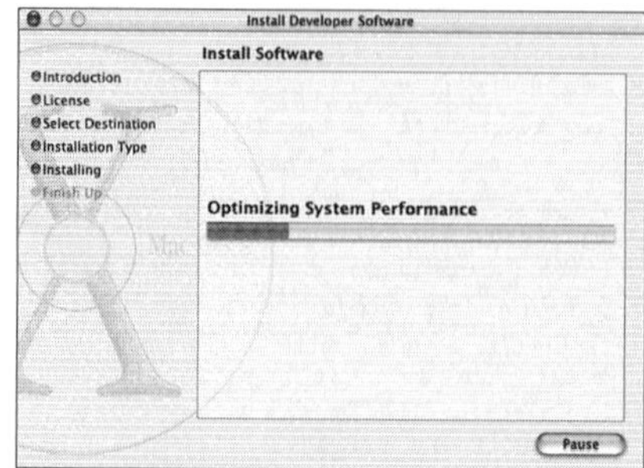

FIGURE 16.12
The Developer Tools optimizing system performance. If there's going to be a problem with the install, it will most likely be here.

The install is finished when you reach, surprisingly enough, the screen indicating a successful install, shown in Figure 16.13.

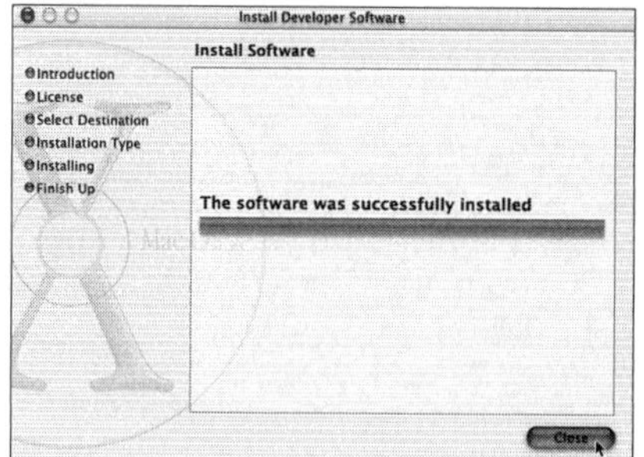

FIGURE 16.13
Everything has been installed, and you're ready to start using the tools.

About the only possible complication is that some people have reported problems and system hangs at the Optimizing System step. There doesn't seem to be any observable commonality in the symptoms reported. We suspect it has something to do with the users having perhaps installed unauthorized system updates, or experimented with Internet-reported, but unapproved, modifications of the system.

Installing Software at the Command Line

The majority of the Unix software you'll find that hasn't been specifically made for OS X is created by other users just like you. Because of the wide range of individuals involved, the possibilities for how it might be delivered and what you will need to do to install it are truly limitless. We'll do our best to give an overview of the techniques used, but you should pay attention to the author's instructions to see whether or where they differ from our suggestions. Also, don't be afraid to use your own common sense if you find something that doesn't have instructions and our samples don't appear to apply.

Regardless of the actual steps involved in the installation, there are some things to keep in mind if you want to keep your system in some semblance of order.

- You'll usually have as much flexibility about where you install software in Unix as in Mac OS. Unfortunately, although Mac OS invisibly and automatically updates the database of software that's installed for you, Unix doesn't. If you install software in random places throughout the system, you will need to continuously update your `PATH` variable to reflect the changes. For this reason, despite having the option to install just about anywhere, there are a few common and highly recommended locations where you'll probably be happiest if you confine your installs. Specifically, those locations are the `/usr/local` and `/opt` directory trees. They are the most common and best places to install software if you want convenience in your system.
- If you have multiple users on the system, even if you update your own `PATH`, other users' paths won't be updated, and, consequently, they might not be able to run the software. This can be an advantage, or disadvantage, depending on whether you want to hide the software from others or make it publicly available.
- If you decide to reconfigure your system or reinstall something, it will be much easier if you keep a complete copy of the distribution and any special options you picked to make it work. Use the `tar` command and `compress` or `gzip` commands (explained in Chapter 13, "Common Unix Shell Commands: File Operations"), after you've successfully managed to install it. You'll probably want to `make clean` the distribution first, if possible—that incantation will be explained shortly.
- If you want to maintain your sanity, it will help if you always download software packages into the same location, and do all your configuration and software building in the same directory.
- Never compile or install software as the `root` user. Some would suggest that we append *unless absolutely necessary* to that dictum, but we won't. Some software might require that you install it as `root`, but the `root` user is the single user with the capacity to destroy your system with a single command. It might be preachy to suggest that you're probably better off without any software that requires you to be `root` to install it, but until you *know* when it's safe to ignore this suggestion, you'll be much safer following it.
- Another useful trick for keeping your system in order is to create a special user ID that is used solely for software installations and management. The ownership of the `/usr/local` and `/opt` directories can be set to this user ID, as well as the ownership of wherever you download software and where you store it. This user ID does not need to have, and should not have, administrator privileges on the system. This

minimizes both the risk of simply doing something wrong, and accidentally damaging the running system. It also minimizes the impact that a malicious user, distributing damaging scripts in the guise of useful software, can do to your system.

Downloading

You'll find Unix software being distributed in Usenet newsgroups, on Web pages, FTP servers, through e-mail, and other mechanisms. No matter how it's distributed, you are going to need to transfer a copy of the software, from wherever it is stored, onto your local machine.

You've got all the tools necessary to accomplish any of these in both the command-line programs discussed here and in the previous chapter, as well as the GUI clients covered earlier.

Keep in mind while acquiring the software that things will go smoothest if

- It is downloaded by the user who will be responsible for the installation.
- It is downloaded into a directory where it can be unpackaged and compiled, if necessary. This includes the requirement for sufficient disk space, as well as the appropriate permissions for the user ID that will be doing the installation.
- If you're using `ftp`, use binary mode.

Unarchiving

Some software will come as source code (the language that compilers read) and that explains to the compiler how to create a finished program. Some will come as final executable programs. Either way, most will come as a tarfile compressed with either the compress program (usually denoted by a `.Z` file suffix), or the `gzip` program (usually denoted by a `.gz` suffix).

The first thing you'll need to do after downloading, therefore, is usually to uncompress or `gunzip` the tarfile.

Next you'll usually need to untar the tarfile (with `tar -xvf <tarfile>`). Before you do that, however, it's usually a good idea to make sure what's in the tarfile. You're interested in the contents, as well as where the tarfile wants to put the stuff that's in it. The second item is of particular importance—some software authors have the sloppy habit of letting their tarfiles place files in the current directory rather than a subdirectory (as mentioned in the section on `tar` in Chapter 13). Additionally, some packages are distributed as tarfiles that are designed to untar in place in the system. That is, they place files directly into their final locations (such as `/usr/local/bin`), rather than into a temporary subdirectory for subsequent installation.

Finally, keep in mind that if you download with a Web browser, it isn't unusual for the browser to remove the file suffix without actually doing anything to the file. This results in downloaded `gzip` files that are missing their `.gz` suffix. If you have downloaded a piece of software with a Web browser that arrives as a `.tar` file but `tar` refuses to unpack it, try adding a `.Z` or `.gz` suffix and see whether `uncompress` or `gunzip` will process the renamed file.

If you've downloaded a precompiled application that only needs you to unpack it in place, or for you to put it in a final location after unpacking the distribution, you're all set. If you've downloaded a package that is distributed as source code, then skip to the next section on compiling software.

Installing `lynx`

The `lynx` command-line Web browser is such a useful tool that we'll do a download and unarchive install right now. A precompiled version of `lynx` is available from `http://www.osxfaq.com/downloads/`.

Before you install `lynx`, we recommend that you make a change in your system's configuration that will help keep your system safe from malicious software and accidents during software installs. If you didn't create the unprivileged `software` user with group `tire` that we recommended in Chapter 11, "Additional System Components," go back and create that user now. Next, `su` to the `root` user. Finally, change the ownership of the directory `/usr/local/` on your machine to belong to the software user and group. From the command line, this looks like

```
[localhost:~nermal] ray% su
Password:
[localhost:/Users/nermal] root# cd /usr
[localhost:/usr] root# chown software.tire /usr/local
[localhost:/usr] root# ls -ld local
drwxr-xr-x  4 software  tire  92 Apr 21 22:00 local
```

1. Now, log out and log back in as the unprivileged software user that you created earlier.
2. Start a terminal and create the directories `/usr/local/lib` and `/usr/local/bin` (`mkdir /usr/local/lib`; `mkdir /usr/local/bin`).
3. Next, point your browser at `http://www.macosxunleashed.com/downloads/` and download the files `lynx.gz` and `lynx.cfg`.

Chances are if you're using Internet Explorer, its going to insist on decompressing `lynx.gz` automatically. If not, you will need to find the file (double-click `lynx.gz` in the download manager, and hit reveal in finder), and then drag it to your software user's `Documents` folder.

4. In the terminal, `cd ~/Documents`. Uncompress the `lynx.gz` archive with the command `gunzip lynx.gz`. If your browser already did this for you, a file named `lynx` might be in your `Desktop` folder.
5. Wherever the file `lynx` ends up, copy it to `/usr/local/bin/`. Use `cp <path to lynx> /usr/local/bin/`. `<path to lynx>` might just be `lynx`, or it might be `~/Desktop/lynx`.
6. Read the beginning of `lynx.cfg`. You can do this with `less lynx.cfg`. You can set a lot of configuration defaults in this file, but for now, leave the defaults as they are and copy the file to its intended destination. It should tell you that it belongs in `/usr/local/lib/lynx.cfg`, so `cp <path to lynx.cfg> /usr/local/lib/lynx.cfg`.
7. Just to make sure that the `lynx` file is executable, `chmod 755 /usr/local/bin/lynx`.
8. Log out and back in as your normal user. You might need to set your path to include `/usr/local/bin`, if it doesn't already. The easiest way to do this, as explained in Chapter 12, "Introducing the BSD Subsystem," is to extend your path with `set path=($path /usr/local/bin)` placed in your `.cshrc` file.

The `lynx` application should now be executable and behave just as detailed in Chapter 15, "Command-Line Applications and Application Suites."

Compiling

Compilation is the process that a program-language compiler uses to take source code and convert it into an actual executable application. It is also used to describe running the compiler to perform the compilation. The idea of having to cook your own software from the raw ingredients probably evokes images of impossibly cryptic commands and more headaches than you would ever want to deal with to those coming from a Macintosh or Windows background. Thankfully, compiling prepackaged source code isn't quite cooking from the raw ingredients—it's usually more like warming up a TV dinner. (If you're interested in learning to cook software from scratch, we recommend Kernigan and Ritchie's excellent *The C Programming Language*, and Donald Knuth's *The Art of Computer Programming* books on software architecture.

It's still complicated enough—and there are plenty of places it can go wrong—that most users will at least initially find it less than fun. It'll be the last *scary* topic we introduce in this book though—everything after this is applications of what you've learned in the last few chapters and this one, and the introduction of new programs for you to use. In actuality, this stuff isn't that scary either—if you make it through this chapter and we haven't scared you away from the BSD subsystem, you're home free—we promise!

Basic Steps: `configure, make`

Let's start with an example of a software install—things can get more complicated than this, but for many applications that have been written by conscientious programmers these steps will suffice. We'll assume that the software package `pine4.33` has been successfully downloaded, uncompressed, and untarred. Installs shown here are also done assuming you're logged in as your `software` user, and that you've downloaded software into the `Documents` directory.

Almost universally, the first command you'll issue to compile software is either `./configure` (if it's present) or `make` (if `./configure` is not present). For `pine`, the only things you have to type are

```
make
build osx
cp bin/pine /usr/local/bin/
mkdir /usr/local/man/
mkdir /usr/local/man1/
cp docs/pine.1 /usr/local/man/man1/
```

That doesn't look too hard, does it? The basic operations are simply `make`, `build`, and copying some files into standard locations in the file system.

If you'd like to try this example, the `pine` package shown here can be downloaded from `ftp://ftp.cac.washington.edu/pine/pine4.33.tar.gz`. The simplest way to do this is with `lynx`, by issuing the following:

> **Note**
>
> The developers of `lynx` are changing and rearranging the way that some of the download functions work in the program. If your version of `lynx` produces files that can't be gunzipped as shown in the examples, you've been unlucky and gotten one of the versions that automatically uncompresses and gunzips files on download, even when storing them to disk. In this case, remove the gunzip step from the process, and start off with the file as a `.tar` file instead.

```
cd ~/Documents
lynx -dump ftp://ftp.cac.washington.edu/pine/pine4.33.tar.gz > pine4.33.tar.gz
gunzip pine4.33.tar.gz
tar-xf pine4.33.tar
[localhost:~/Documents] software% cd pine4.33/

[localhost:~/Documents/pine4.33] software% ls

     CPYRIGHT  README build  build.cmd contrib
     doc   imap   makefile  pico  pine
```

There's no file named `configure`, so try `make`.

```
[localhost:~/Documents/pine4.33] software% make

     Use the "build" command (shell script) to make Pine.
     You can say "build help" for details on how it works.
```

So, this software install isn't quite standard—it doesn't use `make`, other than to tell us that it doesn't use `make`. If you read the `README`, and look at the output of build help, you'll observe that there's an `osx` option already available, so give that a try:

```
[localhost:~/Documents/pine4.33] software% ./build osx

     make args are CC=cc

     Making c-client library, mtest and imapd
     make CC=cc osx
     Applying an process to sources...
     tools/an "ln -s" src/c-client c-client
     .
     ...much output deleted...
     .
     Building c-client for osx...
     echo GSSDIR=/usr/local  > c-client/SPECIALS
     cd c-client;make osx EXTRACFLAGS=''\
      EXTRALDFLAGS=''\
     .
     .
     .
     Once-only environment setup...
     echo cc > CCTYPE
     echo -g -O '' > CFLAGS
     echo -DCREATEPROTO=unixproto -DEMPTYPROTO=unixproto \
     .
     .
     .
     ln -s os_osx.h osdep.h
     ln -s os_osx.c osdepbas.c
     ln -s log_std.c osdeplog.c
     .
     .
```

```
.
`cat CCTYPE` -c `cat CFLAGS` mail.c
`cat CCTYPE` -c `cat CFLAGS` misc.c
`cat CCTYPE` -c `cat CFLAGS` newsrc.c
.
.
.
`cat CCTYPE` -c `cat CFLAGS` phile.c
`cat CCTYPE` -c `cat CFLAGS` mh.c
`cat CCTYPE` -c `cat CFLAGS` mx.c
sh -c 'rm -rf c-client.a || true'
.
.
.
Building bundled tools...
cd mtest;make
cc -I../c-client `cat ../c-client/CFLAGS`   -c -o mtest.o mtest.c
cc -I../c-client `cat ../c-client/CFLAGS` -o mtest mtest.o ../c-client/
➥c-client.a `cat ../c-client/LDFLAGS`
.
.
.
Making Pico and Pilot
make CC=cc -f makefile.osx
rm -f os.h
ln -s osdep/os-osx.h os.h
cc   -g -DDEBUG  -Dbsd -DJOB_CONTROL   -c -o main.o main.c
cc   -g -DDEBUG  -Dbsd -DJOB_CONTROL   -c -o attach.o attach.c
.
.
.
Making Pine.
make CC=cc -f makefile.osx
rm -f os.h
ln -s osdep/os-osx.h os.h
./cmplhlp2.sh  < pine.hlp > helptext.h
cc   -g -DDEBUG   -DBSDDEF -DSYSTYPE=\"OSX\"   -c -o addrbook.o addrbook.c
cc   -g -DDEBUG   -DBSDDEF -DSYSTYPE=\"OSX\"   -c -o adrbkcmd.o adrbkcmd.c
.
.
.
Links to executables are in bin directory:
__TEXT  __DATA  __OBJC  others  dec     hex
3465216 253952  0       2539520 6258688 5f8000  bin/pine
622592  12288   0       643072  1277952 138000  bin/mtest
667648  20480   0       688128  1376256 150000  bin/imapd
262144  12288   0       319488  593920  91000   bin/pico
258048  12288   0       315392  585728  8f000   bin/pilot
Done
```

Wow, that's a lot of output! Still at the end, it tells you that there are executables in the bin directory, so let's look in there.

```
[localhost:~/Documents/pine4.33] software% ls -l bin
```

```
total 19560
-rwxr-xr-x  2 software  staff  1363248 Apr 22 01:53 imapd
-rwxr-xr-x  2 software  staff  1270632 Apr 22 01:53 mtest
-rwxr-xr-x  2 software  staff   582664 Apr 22 01:53 pico
-rwxr-xr-x  2 software  staff   577008 Apr 22 01:53 pilot
-rwxr-xr-x  2 software  staff  6212364 Apr 22 01:55 pine
```

We were building `pine`, and in fact there is an executable `pine` in the `bin` directory, as well as a number of other applications. Installing `pine` now is simply copying it to `/usr/local/bin` with `cp bin/pine /usr/local/bin`. After that, `pine` should function as shown earlier.

There are a number of other executable applications in that `bin` directory, too. You might want to spend the time to find out whether they do anything that you'd find useful, but we'll leave that exercise up to you.

Also, as you might have noticed at the first listing of the directory, there is a `doc` directory. Things such as man pages are probably found there, so let's have a look:

```
[localhost:~/Documents/pine4.33] software% ls doc
```

```
brochure.txt   mime.types    pilot.1       pine.1        tech-notes.txt
mailcap.unx    pico.1        pine-ports    tech-notes
```

Great! Things that end in `.#` are usually man pages that belong in the `man#` section of the manual. Let's put the `pine.1` page for `pine` into the appropriate `man1` directory in `/usr/local/man`:

```
[localhost:~/Documents/pine4.33] software% cp doc/pine.1 /usr/local/man/man1
```

```
cp: /usr/local/man/man1: No such file or directory
```

There isn't a `/usr/local/man/man1` (remember, we had to create `/usr/local/bin` and `/usr/local/lib` to install `lynx`).

```
[localhost:~/Documents/pine4.33] software% mkdir /usr/local/man/man1
```

```
mkdir: /usr/local/man/man1: No such file or directory
```

Of course! We haven't made the `/usr/local/man` directory either. Thankfully, this install will be the only time you have to create these directories—if another application needs another directory, you'll need to create it, but you've got almost everything standard covered by now.

```
[localhost:~/Documents/pine4.33] software% mkdir /usr/local/man
[localhost:~/Documents/pine4.33] software% mkdir /usr/local/man/man1
[localhost:~/Documents/pine4.33] software% cp doc/pine.1 /usr/local/man/man1
```

And now we can try looking at the man page:

```
[localhost:~/Documents/pine4.33] software% man pine

     man: no entry for pine in the manual.
```

Remember the MANPATH variable mentioned in Chapter 12? I've forgotten to set it in this example. Again, fixing these things is best done in your .cshrc file. Setting it by hand now can be accomplished as follows:

```
[localhost:~/Documents/pine4.33] software% echo $MANPATH

     /Users/ray/man:/usr/local/share/man:/usr/share/man:/usr/X11R6/man
[localhost:~/Documents/pine4.33] software%
[ic:ccc]setenv MANPATH {$MANPATH}:/usr/local/man
[localhost:~/Documents/pine4.33] software%  man pine

     man: Formatting manual page...

     pine(1)                                                   pine(1)

     NAME
            pine - a Program for Internet News and Email

     SYNTAX
            pine [ options ] [ address , address ]

            pinef [ options ] [ address , address ]

     DESCRIPTION
            Pine  is  a screen-oriented message-handling tool.  In its
            default configuration, Pine offers an  intentionally  lim-
            ited  set  of functions geared toward the novice user, but
            it also has a growing list of  optional  "power-user"  and
            personal-preference  features.  pinef is a variant of Pine
            that uses function keys rather than mnemonic single-letter
            commands.  Pine's basic feature set includes:
     .
     .
     .
```

Finally, clean up after yourself, and put the pine stuff into your installed software directory in case you need it again:

```
[localhost:~/Documents/pine4.33] software% cd ../
[localhost:~/Documents] software% gzip pine4.33.tar
[localhost:~/Documents] software% mv pine4.33.tar.gz installed
[localhost:~/Documents] software% \rm -rf pine4.33
```

That's it! If you've been following along, you've just compiled and installed a piece of software. Is your heart racing or are your palms sweaty? Do you feel like a different person? No? Didn't think so. Most software installations, by and large, are exactly this anticlimactic.

Next, let's do a couple of quick installs that use a more standard installation protocol. They're a setup for a considerably more difficult install we'll do in the troubleshooting section of the next chapter. The first of these is `libjpeg`, the second is `libpng`. These are library packages that will be needed later to support the `netpbm` package—an amazingly powerful command-line graphics processing program. The complete standard invocation for configuration and compiling is usually

```
configure
make
make test
make install
```

If you read the `README` file for this software, you'll see it gets an additional `make install-lib` step—always read the `README` and `INSTALL` files if they are present!

1. Download both `libjpeg` and `libpng` with `lynx`:

   ```
   cd ~/Documents/
   lynx -dump ftp://ftp.uu.net/graphics/jpeg/jpegsrc.v6b.tar.gz
   [ic:ccc] > jpegsrc.v6b.tar.gz
   lynx -dump ftp://swrinde.nde.swri.edu/pub/png/src/libpng-1.0.10.tar.gz
   [ic:ccc] > libpng-1.0.10.tar.gz
   ```

2. Uncompress and unarchive the `libjpeg` archive:

   ```
   [localhost:~/Documents] software% gunzip jpegsrc.v6b.tar.gz
   [localhost:~/Documents] software% tar -xf jpegsrc.v6b.tar
   ```

3. `cd` into the directory, check to see whether there's a `configure` file, or only a `makefile`, and either `./configure`, or `make`, as appropriate:

   ```
   [localhost:~/Documents] software% cd jpeg-6b/
   [localhost:~/Documents/jpeg-6b] software% ls
   README          jcmarker.c      jdhuff.h        jpegint.h       maktjpeg.st
   ansi2knr.1      jcmaster.c      jdinput.c       jpeglib.h       makvms.opt
   ansi2knr.c      jcomapi.c       jdmainct.c      jpegtran.1      rdbmp.c
   cderror.h       jconfig.bcc     jdmarker.c      jpegtran.c      rdcolmap.c
   cdjpeg.c        jconfig.cfg     jdmaster.c      jquant1.c       rdgif.c
   cdjpeg.h        jconfig.dj      jdmerge.c       jquant2.c       rdjpgcom.1
   change.log      jconfig.doc     jdphuff.c       jutils.c        rdjpgcom.c
   cjpeg.1         jconfig.mac     jdpostct.c      jversion.h      rdppm.c
   cjpeg.c         jconfig.manx    jdsample.c      libjpeg.doc     rdrle.c
   ckconfig.c      jconfig.mc6     jdtrans.c       ltconfig        rdswitch.c
   coderules.doc   jconfig.sas     jerror.c        ltmain.sh       rdtarga.c
   config.guess    jconfig.st      jerror.h        makcjpeg.st     structure.doc
   config.sub      jconfig.vc      jfdctflt.c      makdjpeg.st     testimg.bmp
   ```

```
configure      jconfig.vms    jfdctfst.c     makeapps.ds     testimg.jpg
djpeg.1        jconfig.wat    jfdctint.c     makefile.ansi   testimg.ppm
djpeg.c        jcparam.c      jidctflt.c     makefile.bcc    testimgp.jpg
example.c      jcphuff.c      jidctfst.c     makefile.cfg    testorig.jpg
filelist.doc   jcprepct.c     jidctint.c     makefile.dj     testprog.jpg
install-sh     jcsample.c     jidctred.c     makefile.manx   transupp.c
install.doc    jctrans.c      jinclude.h     makefile.mc6    transupp.h
jcapimin.c     jdapimin.c     jmemansi.c     makefile.mms    usage.doc
jcapistd.c     jdapistd.c     jmemdos.c      makefile.sas    wizard.doc
jccoefct.c     jdatadst.c     jmemdosa.asm   makefile.unix   wrbmp.c
jccolor.c      jdatasrc.c     jmemmac.c      makefile.vc     wrgif.c
jcdctmgr.c     jdcoefct.c     jmemmgr.c      makefile.vms    wrjpgcom.1
jchuff.c       jdcolor.c      jmemname.c     makefile.wat    wrjpgcom.c
jchuff.h       jdct.h         jmemnobs.c     makelib.ds      wrppm.c
jcinit.c       jddctmgr.c     jmemsys.h      makeproj.mac    wrrle.c
jcmainct.c     jdhuff.c       jmorecfg.h     makljpeg.st     wrtarga.c
```

There's a configure file, so call `./configure`:

> **Note**
>
> Why `./configure`, instead of just `configure`? Because there might be many different executables named `configure` on your machine and you want to be sure to run only this one in this directory.

```
[localhost:~/Documents/jpeg-6b] software% ./configure

    checking for gcc... no
    checking for cc... cc
    checking whether the C compiler (cc  ) works... yes
    checking whether the C compiler (cc  ) is a cross-compiler... no
    checking whether we are using GNU C... yes
    checking how to run the C preprocessor... cc -E -traditional-cpp
    checking for function prototypes... yes
    checking for stddef.h... yes
    checking for stdlib.h... yes
    checking for string.h... yes
    checking for size_t... yes
    checking for type unsigned char... yes
    checking for type unsigned short... yes
    checking for type void... yes
    checking for working const... yes
    checking for inline... __inline__
    checking for broken incomplete types... ok
    checking for short external names... ok
    checking to see if char is signed... yes
    checking to see if right shift is signed... yes
```

```
checking to see if fopen accepts b spec... yes
checking for a BSD compatible install... /usr/bin/install -c
checking for ranlib... ranlib
checking libjpeg version number... 62
creating ./config.status
creating Makefile
creating jconfig.h
```

`configure` runs and drops you back to the command line with no complaints, so now it's time to run `make`:

```
[localhost:~/Documents/jpeg-6b] software% make
```

```
cc -02  -I.   -c -o jcapimin.o jcapimin.c
cc -02  -I.   -c -o jcapistd.o jcapistd.c
cc -02  -I.   -c -o jctrans.o jctrans.c
cc -02  -I.   -c -o jcparam.o jcparam.c
cc -02  -I.   -c -o jdatadst.o jdatadst.c
.
.
.
rm -f libjpeg.a
ar rc libjpeg.a  jcapimin.o jcapistd.o jctrans.o jcparam.o jdatadst.o \
jcinit.o jcmaster.o jcmarker.o jcmainct.o
[ic:ccc]jcprepct.o jccoefct.ojccolor.o \
jcsample.o jchuff.o jcphuff.o jcdctmgr.o
[ic:ccc]jfdctfst.o jfdctflt.o jfdctint.o \
jdapimin.o jdapistd.o jdtrans.o jdatasrc.o
[ic:ccc]jdmaster.o jdinput.o jdmarker.o \
jdhuff.o jdphuff.o jdmainct.o jdcoefct.o
[ic:ccc]jdpostct.o jddctmgr.o jidctfst.o \
jidctflt.o jidctint.o jidctred.o jdsample.o
[ic:ccc]jdcolor.o jquant1.o jquant2.o \
jdmerge.o jcomapi.o jutils.o jerror.o jmemmgr.o jmemnobs.o
ranlib libjpeg.a
cc -02  -I.   -c -o cjpeg.o cjpeg.c
cc -02  -I.   -c -o rdppm.o rdppm.c
.
.
.
cc -02  -I.   -c -o wrjpgcom.o wrjpgcom.c
cc  -o wrjpgcom wrjpgcom.o
```

Again, you arrive back at the command line, so it's time to try `make test`:

```
[localhost:~/Documents/jpeg-6b] software% make test
```

```
rm -f testout*
./djpeg -dct int -ppm -outfile testout.ppm  ./testorig.jpg
./djpeg -dct int -bmp -colors 256 -outfile testout.bmp  ./testorig.jpg
./cjpeg -dct int -outfile testout.jpg  ./testimg.ppm
./djpeg -dct int -ppm -outfile testoutp.ppm ./testprog.jpg
```

```
./cjpeg -dct int -progressive -opt -outfile testoutp.jpg ./testimg.ppm
./jpegtran -outfile testoutt.jpg ./testprog.jpg
cmp ./testimg.ppm testout.ppm
cmp ./testimg.bmp testout.bmp
cmp ./testimg.jpg testout.jpg
cmp ./testimg.ppm testoutp.ppm
cmp ./testimgp.jpg testoutp.jpg
cmp ./testorig.jpg testoutt.jpg
```

If there was a problem, `make test` would have spit out some error diagnostics and told you that it had encountered trouble. Because it didn't, you're on to `make install`:

```
[localhost:~/Documents/jpeg-6b] software% make install

    /usr/bin/install -c cjpeg /usr/local/bin/cjpeg
    /usr/bin/install -c djpeg /usr/local/bin/djpeg
    /usr/bin/install -c jpegtran /usr/local/bin/jpegtran
    /usr/bin/install -c rdjpgcom /usr/local/bin/rdjpgcom
    /usr/bin/install -c wrjpgcom /usr/local/bin/wrjpgcom
    /usr/bin/install -c -m 644 ./cjpeg.1 /usr/local/man/man1/cjpeg.1
    /usr/bin/install -c -m 644 ./djpeg.1 /usr/local/man/man1/djpeg.1
    /usr/bin/install -c -m 644 ./jpegtran.1 /usr/local/man/man1/jpegtran.1
    /usr/bin/install -c -m 644 ./rdjpgcom.1 /usr/local/man/man1/rdjpgcom.1
    /usr/bin/install -c -m 644 ./wrjpgcom.1 /usr/local/man/man1/wrjpgcom.1
```

Notice that it's making use of the `/usr/local/man/man1` directory that you created earlier. If you hadn't, it would be complaining here.

Note

Most Unix flavors have `install` programs that automatically create directories that are needed for installation, but the `install` application Apple has provided apparently doesn't do this. We hope that things eventually get fixed so that directories are created automatically, but for now, you're going to have to do some by hand.

Finally, if you read the `README`, you'd see that we need a `make install-lib` step here, too:

```
[localhost:~/Documents/jpeg-6b] software% make install-lib

    /usr/bin/install -c -m 644 jconfig.h /usr/local/include/jconfig.h
    /usr/bin/install: /usr/local/include/jconfig.h: No such file or directory
    make: *** [install-headers] Error 1
```

What did I say about that installer not creating directories? Now it needs a `/usr/local/include` directory as well.

```
[localhost:~/Documents/jpeg-6b] software% mkdir /usr/local/include
[localhost:~/Documents/jpeg-6b] software% make install-lib
      /usr/bin/install -c -m 644 jconfig.h /usr/local/include/jconfig.h
      /usr/bin/install -c -m 644 ./jpeglib.h /usr/local/include/jpeglib.h
      /usr/bin/install -c -m 644 ./jmorecfg.h /usr/local/include/jmorecfg.h
      /usr/bin/install -c -m 644 ./jerror.h /usr/local/include/jerror.h
      /usr/bin/install -c -m 644 libjpeg.a /usr/local/lib/libjpeg.a
```

Then you're done. If you're being neat, delete the directory you've been working in, `gzip` the `tar` file, and store it in your `installed` directory.

Now let's take a look at what you just did. Other than creating a directory to fix the not-quite-functional installer, the entire process was: `./configure`, which guessed a few settings about your machine, and then a series of `make`, `make test`, `make install`, and `make install-lib`. Other than the `./configure`, the actual program called in each case was `make`, and it was directed to make different things with each call. The identities of these things are defined by the software author in a control file called a makefile, and named, unsurprisingly, either `Makefile` or `makefile`. With any well-written software package, the makefile will direct `make` with no arguments to compile the software with default settings. Frequently, but not always, there will be a test suite provided that can be invoked with `make test`. Finally, an installer routine will be invoked, by convention, with `make install`. In the case of `libjpeg`, the package provides both a few small executables, and some library functions for other software, should you want them. The basic `make install` process puts the small executables in `/usr/local/bin`, but doesn't install the libraries because not everyone wants them. Therefore, there's an optional `make install-lib` step to install the libraries and support files. If you've followed along this far, your `/usr/local` structure should be fairly mature, and most software won't need you to create any more directories for it.

Note

Some software that you try to install will want you to use the `bsdmake` version of the `make` program instead of just `make`. Apple has also provided a separate `gnumake` executable, should you find software that wants `gnumake` or `gmake`. If you find this requirement in a `README` file, just substitute `bsdmake` or `gnumake` for `make` in the discussion. If you find a program that outputs what seems to be incomprehensible gibberish when you type `make`, give the other versions a try and see whether they do any better.

The `configure` step is typical as well, although the mechanics will vary depending on the application you're compiling. Most of the time, it can either examine your system and determine, or make an educated guess about, configuration options. Occasionally, it will require you to provide it with some information, but in most cases it's all right to accept the default answers suggested by `configure` if you don't have a better answer or don't know the answer.

Finally, let's run through the install of `libpng` because without it, the broken `netpbm` we're going to fix in the next section is truly hopeless:

```
[localhost:~/Documents/libpng-1.0.10] software% gunzip libpng-1.0.10.tar.gz
[localhost:~/Documents/libpng-1.0.10] software% tar -xv libpng-1.0.10.tar
[localhost:~/Documents/libpng-1.0.10] software% cd libpng-1.0.10
[localhost:~/Documents/libpng-1.0.10] software% ls

     ANNOUNCE    Y2KINFO      png.5        pngerror.c   pngrio.c     pngvcrd.c
     CHANGES     configure    png.c        pngggccrd.c  pngrtran.c   pngwio.c
     INSTALL     contrib      png.h        pngget.c     pngrutil.c   pngwrite.c
     KNOWNBUG    example.c    pngasmrd.h   pngmem.c     pngset.c     pngwtran.c
     LICENSE     libpng.3     pngbar.jpg   pngnow.png   pngtest.c    pngwutil.c
     README      libpng.txt   pngbar.png   pngpread.c   pngtest.png  projects
     TODO        libpngpf.3   pngconf.h    pngread.c    pngtrans.c   scripts
```

It has a `configure`, so use it:

```
[localhost:~/Documents/libpng-1.0.10] software% ./configure

        There is no "configure" script for Libpng-1.0.10.  Instead, please
        copy the appropriate makefile for your system from the "scripts"
        directory.  Read the INSTALL file for more details.
```

Another nonstandard installation, so follow the instructions:

```
[localhost:~/Documents/libpng-1.0.10] software% ls scripts

     SCOPTIONS.ppc    makefile.bor       makefile.knr       makefile.std
     descrip.mms      makefile.cygwin    makefile.linux     makefile.sunos
     libpng.icc       makefile.dec       makefile.macosx    makefile.tc3
     makefile.acorn   makefile.dj2       makefile.mips      makefile.vcawin32
     makefile.aix     makefile.gcc       makefile.msc       makefile.vcwin32
     makefile.amiga   makefile.gcmmx     makefile.os2       makefile.watcom
     makefile.atari   makefile.hpgcc     makefile.sco       makevms.com
     makefile.bc32    makefile.hpux      makefile.sggcc     pngdef.pas
     makefile.bd32    makefile.ibmc      makefile.sgi       pngos2.def
     makefile.beos    makefile.intel     makefile.solaris   smakefile.ppc
```

Fantastic! A `macosx` file! Copy it to the `libpng` directory as `makefile` and run `make`, `make test` (the output of which we're omitting here), and `make install`:

```
[localhost:~/Documents/libpng-1.0.10]
[ic:ccc]software% cp scripts/makefile.macosx ./makefile
[localhost:~/Documents/libpng-1.0.10] software% make
```

```
cc -I../zlib -O    -c -o png.o png.c
cc -I../zlib -O    -c -o pngset.o pngset.c
cc -I../zlib -O    -c -o pngget.o pngget.c
.
.
.
cc -I../zlib -O    -c -o pngerror.o pngerror.c
cc -I../zlib -O    -c -o pngpread.o pngpread.c
ar rc libpng.a  png.o pngset.o pngget.o pngrutil.o pngtrans.o \
pngwutil.o pngread.o pngrio.o pngwio.o pngwrite.o pngrtran.o \
pngwtran.o pngmem.o pngerror.o pngpread.o
ranlib libpng.a
cc -I../zlib -O    -c -o pngtest.o pngtest.c
cc -o pngtest -I../zlib -O  pngtest.o -L. -L../zlib -lpng -lz
/usr/bin/ld: warning -L: directory name (../zlib) does not exist
```

It had a warning, but no errors! You can run `make test` here to verify that it works—we'll just show the output of make install:

```
[localhost:~/Documents/libpng-1.0.10] software% make install
```

```
mkdir: /usr/local/include: File exists
make: [install] Error 1 (ignored)
mkdir: /usr/local/lib: File exists
make: [install] Error 1 (ignored)
cp png.h /usr/local/include
cp pngconf.h /usr/local/include
chmod 644 /usr/local/include/png.h
chmod 644 /usr/local/include/pngconf.h
cp libpng.a /usr/local/lib
chmod 644 /usr/local/lib/libpng.a
```

```
[localhost:~/Documents] software%
```

It survived the whole thing without you needing to do anything other than follow some simple instructions. The vast majority of Unix software installs are this easy. Unfortunately, OS X isn't as well supported in the `configure` scripts as most Unix flavors just yet, but after it is, expect that 90% of all software will install with `./configure`, `make`, `make test`, `make install`, and no further interaction from you.

You can make more installs work using the `configure` command by copying some files that Apple has provided into the software directory where you will be running `configure`. None of the installs shown here benefits from this, but copying `/usr/libexec/config.guess` and `/usr/libexec/config.sub` to the directory where you run `configure` might help with some compilations.

Summary

In this chapter, you did something the vast majority of Macintosh users have never done—compile and install your own software. We hope that you found this experience completely anticlimactic. OS X is still rough enough around the edges that if you try to install every program out there, you will run across some that raise your blood pressure. But on Unix flavors that have existed for a longer time, almost every piece of source can be compiled with the same standard installation procedure: `./configure`, `make`, `make test`, `make install`. We expect that OS X will mature rapidly to the point that all installs are as simple as what we've gone through here.

Troubleshooting Software Installs, and Compiling and Debugging Manually

In This Chapter

Sometimes, when you try to compile and install a program, it won't work as easily as the examples we've shown in the previous chapter. Sometimes it's a matter of the program not being tweaked to run properly on OS X. Sometimes the program is just poorly written. Most often, however, it's because the vast majority of software written for Unix is in a constant state of revision, and minor bugs are introduced, and squashed again, on a regular basis. If you're in no hurry to use the software, don't worry that it doesn't compile. As long as you've paid attention to this suggestion: Never compile or install software as a user with a privileged account. The attempt to compile and run it has done nothing more than occupy some disk space and cause a little frustration. Write to the program's author, let him or her know that something's not right, and it will probably be fixed in a reasonable amount of time.

If you're in a hurry, or are either inquisitive or stubborn, there are some things that you can try to get the software working. A few of these involve updating certain parameters in your environment, one involves rolling up your sleeves and digging around in the program's guts. If the latter is something you've never imagined doing, don't worry—it's your choice! Just remember that as long as you're working in a nonprivileged account, you can't really do much damage—the software is already broken, you can't hurt the system. The worst that will happen is you don't improve anything.

This chapter will lay out a few common things to check when an install doesn't seem to work, and take you through an example of what is necessary to fix one particularly troublesome install. Because every problem install will be different, we can't give you an exhaustive list of things to look for. Instead, we hope the tour of a problematic install and the example of using the GNU debugger will give you an idea of what to look for and how to solve the problem.

If you find this material too complicated, don't let it bother you. What we aim to provide in this chapter is an example of the routes of attack that you can take, if you choose to pursue the issue. If you aren't inclined to fight with a recalcitrant install, feel free to skip this chapter. There is nothing in the rest of the book that requires that you be comfortable with the troubleshooting material.

At the end of the chapter, we've provided a short section outlining a number of useful applications that you might like to install at the command line. Where possible, we've included copies of the source and compiled binaries at `www.macosunleashed.com`. In general, the precompiled software will work for you, but if you want the most current and complete version of a piece of software, it's always best to go to the source and build it yourself.

Common Sense and Configuration Options

A reasonable number of problems can be solved by a suitable application of common sense. The biggest problem with this is users appear to have a difficult time figuring out what sense is common, and what is not. Repeatedly, I have seen users who were convinced their problems were the fault of a program or machine, and were hopping mad at the system for treating them poorly. Most frequently, however, it turns out that they've mistyped some command or entered an incorrect parameter, and fixing this also fixes the problem. Conversely, I've seen users who have spent hours fighting with a problem, firmly convinced that they were making some trivial error and were simply incapable of seeing it. Almost to the user, these cases turn out to be actual machine or software errors, rather than user errors. If you're new to the Unix environment, watch for this tendency—if you think something is the system's fault, stop to consider whether you really have done everything properly. If you think you're doing something wrong, but can't figure out what it is after suitable inspection, don't forget that the people who wrote the software are users too, and could have made an error just as easily.

That being said, we'll provide a general list of things that might help you figure out what's going wrong with a piece of compiled software. There is no such thing as a complete list, but these are relatively good places to start.

- The absolute first thing to try, if software doesn't install, is reading the instructions. I know, you've already read the instructions. Read them again.

> **Tip**
>
> Try taking out a marker and highlighting the specific places it says, type this and enter that. I've been coding on Unix machines for 15 years, and I still religiously highlight all relevant sections of installation and configuration instructions. Get into the habit—it's good for you.

- Make certain while reading the instructions that you've read any sections dealing specifically with OS X. If there's nothing that deals specifically with OS X, the instructions for BSD, NextStep, or OpenStep installation might be of interest.
- Examine the evidence of a problem. Error messages are generally trying to tell you something beyond the fact that there was an error. They sometimes do an abysmally bad job of it, but the average error message contains at least some clues as to what the error is and how to fix it.

- If the error involves something going wrong well after the compile—for example, when the program is running—check whether the program outputs log files. Many programs write progress reports and debugging information into log files. The location of these files is frequently defined in the program's configuration options, but programs can also log via the SYSLOG facility and write log information into files in the /var/log/ directory.
- If the program doesn't have a log file, check to see whether it has a debug or verbose mode (usually invoked with -d or —debug and -v or —verbose, respectively). Adding these to the programs invocation will either enable log output to a file, or cause the program to produce useful output to the terminal.
- If the problem is that at the compilation step, the program makes a complaint that it can't find a library (typically a file ending in .o or .so), it might be because the compiler doesn't know where to find it, not because it doesn't exist. If you can find the file it's complaining about, you can attempt to fix the problem in one of two ways. The first involves editing the makefile. If you can find where the library is used in the makefile (look for the <*filename*>.o string in the makefile), you can try adding -L<*pathtodirectory*> to the makefile. <*pathtodirectory*> should be the full path to the directory that the library was found in. The second involves informing the compiler of the location in a more general fashion. At the command line, enter setenv LD_LIBRARY_PATH <*pathtodirectory*>. The LD_LIBRARY_PATH environment variable tells the compiler that there is an additional place for it to check for all libraries. The problem with this approach is it's not convenient to enter every possible library path this way, and you might need to add more than one, depending on how your system is arranged.
- A syntax error from the compiler that indicates a line number is a statement that invalid code has been found in the file. This is an indication that there's something wrong with the program, or perhaps that you've downloaded it incorrectly, or that it has become corrupted on your local machine. Something fixable in the syntax is, for example, an edit done in a Mac OS side editor that's been saved with Macintosh end-of-line characters instead of Unix end-of-line characters (or has accumulated an assortment of each through the use of different editors).

File Locations, and Fighting with Installers

For this example, you will need the netpbm package, available from http://download.sourceforge.net/netpbm/netpbm-9.12.tgz. The easy solution is

```
lynx -dump http://download.sourceforge.net/netpbm/netpbm-9.12.tgz
➥> netpbm-9.12.tgz
```

The file should be 2057293 bytes in length. Uncompress it, `untar` it, and check whether it wants `configure` or `make`:

```
[localhost:~/Documents] software% gunzip netpbm-9.12.tgz
[localhost:~/Documents] software% tar -xf netpbm-9.12.tar
[localhost:~/Documents/netpbm-9.12] software% ls
    COPYRIGHT.PATENT         README.VMS          pbmplus.h
    GNUmakefile              amiga               pgm
    GPL_LICENSE.txt          compile.h           pnm
    HISTORY                  configure           ppm
    Makefile                 empty_depend        scoptions
    Makefile.common          installosf          shhopt
    Makefile.config.djgpp    libopt.c            stamp-date
    Makefile.config.in       libtiff             stamp-date.amiga
    Makefile.depend          magic               testgrid.pbm
    Netpbm.programming       make_merge.sh       testimg.ppm
    README                   mantocat            urt
    README.CONFOCAL          mkinstalldirs       version.h
    README.DJGPP             netpbm.lsm          vms
    README.JPEG              pbm                 zgv_bigmaxval.patch
```

There's a `configure` file, so run it. This one is going to make some guesses, and ask you some questions. Pick the options shown in the following example, because they're necessary to get the rest of the example to work:

```
[localhost:~/Documents/netpbm-9.12] software% ./configure
    ./configure: Command not found.
```

Hold on, problem number one—that wasn't the expected behavior. The file configure is right here in the directory with you, yet you're getting a command not found error. It could be `./configure` isn't executable, but in this case, it's a less obvious, more common problem:

```
[localhost:~/Documents/netpbm-9.12] software% head ./configure
    #!/bin/perl -w

    use strict;

    # This program generates Makefile.config, which is included by all of the
    # Netpbm makefiles.  You run this program as the first step in building
    # Netpbm.  (The second step is 'make').

    # This program is only a convenience.  It is supported to create
    # Makefile.config any way you want.  In fact, an easy way is to copy
    .
    .
    .
```

The problem is OS X doesn't have Perl as `/bin/perl`, it's `/usr/bin/perl`. Fire up `vi` (or your favorite text editor) and change that first line to `#!/usr/bin/perl -w`.

```
[localhost:~/Documents/netpbm-9.12] software% head ./configure
     #!/usr/bin/perl -w

     use strict;
     .
     .
     .
```

Now try again:

```
[localhost:~/Documents/netpbm-9.12] software% ./configure
     Which of the following best describes your platform?
     1) GNU/Linux
     2) Solaris or SunOS
     3) AIX
     4) Tru64
     5) Irix
     6) Windows (Cygwin or DJGPP)
     7) BeOS
     8) NetBSD
     9) none of these are even close

     Your choice ==> 1

     Enter the installation directory (the prefix on all installation
     paths for 'make install'). This is not built into any programs;
     It is used only by 'make install'.

     install prefix (/usr/local/netpbm)=>

     Do you want static-linked Netpbm libraries or shared?

     static or shared (shared)=> static

     Can't exec "ginstall": No such file or directory at ./configure line 195.

     We have created the file 'Makefile.config'. You can now
     proceed to enter the 'make' command.

     Note, however, that we have only made a rough guess at your
     configuration, and you may want to look at Makefile.config and
     edit it to your requirements and taste before doing the make.
```

Note

By the way, we picked GNU/Linux even though OS X is a BSD flavor, because many of the tools are GNU tools. Still, this will cause problems later because Linux typically has things in nonstandard places with respect to BSD, and Apple has maintained a lot of the typical BSD file system structure.

The results of the configure are better, but there's an ominous complaint in there about `can't exec ginstall`. To get things working will take editing that `Makefile.config` and making a few changes—mostly to patch things back to standard locations, where Linux tends to store them. Fire up `vi` and look through `Makefile.config` for lines that look similar to the following; then change them until they're exactly as shown in the following listings:

It seems to have ignored the `static` option given to `configure`, so set it here, too.

```
# STATICLIB = N
STATICLIB = Y
```

`ginstall` is GNU's installation program. Apple has probably named it `install` instead, so comment out the `ginstall` line and uncomment the `install` line.

```
#INSTALL = ginstall
#Solaris:
#INSTALL = /usr/ucb/install
#Tru64:
#INSTALL = installbsd
#OSF1:
#INSTALL = installosf
#Red Hat Linux:
```

Linux installations tend to have taken a wrong turn in file system design, and include the binaries, libraries, and headers for optional packages in the `/usr/bin/`, `/usr/lib/` and `/usr/include` directories. This makes system maintenance a real problem because your unprivileged software management user would need `root` privileges to work in those directories. Fix the defaults so the `jpeglib` stuff comes from `/usr/local`, where we put it not too long ago:

```
#JPEGLIB_DIR = /usr/lib/jpeg
#JPEGHDR_DIR = /usr/include/jpeg
# Netbsd:
#JPEGLIB_DIR = ${LOCALBASE}/lib
#JPEGHDR_DIR = ${LOCALBASE}/include
# OSF, Tru64:
#JPEGLIB_DIR = /usr/local1/DEC/lib
#JPEGHDR_DIR = /usr/local1/DEC/include
# Typical:
JPEGLIB_DIR = /usr/local/lib
```

```
JPEGHDR_DIR = /usr/local/include
# Don't build JPEG stuff:
#JPEGLIB_DIR = NONE
#JPEGHDR_DIR = NONE
```

Do the same for the `libpng` stuff:

```
#PNGLIB_DIR = /lib
#PNGHDR_DIR = /usr/include/png
# NetBSD:
#PNGLIB_DIR = $(LOCALBASE)/lib
#PNGHDR_DIR = $(LOCALBASE)/include
# OSF/Tru64:
#PNGLIB_DIR = /usr/local1/DEC/lib
#PNGHDR_DIR = /usr/local1/DEC/include
# Typical:
PNGLIB_DIR = /usr/local/lib
PNGHDR_DIR = /usr/local/include
# No PNG:
#PNGLIB_DIR = NONE
#PNGHDR_DIR = NONE
```

Now you're ready to try the make:

```
[localhost:~/Documents/netpbm-9.12] software% make

    make -C pbm -f /Users/software/Documents/netpbm-9.12/pbm/Makefile all
    ln -s ../pbmplus.h pbmplus.h
    ln -s ../version.h version.h
    ../stamp-date
    gcc -c -I../shhopt -pedantic -O3 -Wall -Wno-uninitialized
    ➥  -o atktopbm.o ../pbm/atktopbm.c
    make[1]: gcc: Command not found
    make[1]: *** [atktopbm.o] Error 127
    make: *** [pbm] Error 2
```

Again, not the output we wanted! This time, it's complaining that it can't find the compiler. `cc` is the standard name for a C compiler, but `gcc` is the GNU C Compiler, and many software packages are written to take advantage of special features that the GNU compiler provides. Apple has been nice enough to provide the GNU compiler with the development tools, but has named it `cc`, instead of `gcc`. The error for this program could be fixed by modifying the `Makefile.config` file again to call `cc` instead of `gcc`, but this problem will crop up frequently, and many installers won't know that they can use the special `gcc` features unless the compiler is called `gcc`. Let's fix it by creating an alias (symbolic link) named `gcc` instead, and pointing it at the `cc` compiler:

```
[localhost:~/Documents/netpbm-9.12] software% pushd /usr/local/bin

    /usr/local/bin ~/Documents/netpbm-9.12
```

```
[localhost:/usr/local/bin] software% which cc

     /usr/bin/cc

[localhost:/usr/local/bin] software% ln -s /usr/bin/cc ./gcc
[localhost:/usr/local/bin] software% popd

     ~/Documents/netpbm-9.12
```

Try the make again:

```
[localhost:~/Documents/netpbm-9.12] software% make

make -C pbm -f /Users/software/Documents/netpbm-9.12/pbm/Makefile all
gcc -c -I../shhopt -pedantic -O3 -Wall -Wno-uninitialized  -o atktopbm.o
➥ ../pbm/atktopbm.c
In file included from /usr/include/machine/types.h:30,
                 from /usr/include/sys/types.h:70,
                 from /usr/include/stdio.h:64,
                 from ../pbm/atktopbm.c:13:
/usr/include/ppc/types.h:75: warning: ANSI C does not support `long long'
/usr/include/ppc/types.h:76: warning: ANSI C does not support `long long'
In file included from ../pbm/pbmplus.h:115,
                 from ../pbm/pbm.h:7,
                 from ../pbm/atktopbm.c:15:
/usr/include/stdlib.h:181: warning: ANSI C does not support `long long'
/usr/include/stdlib.h:183: warning: ANSI C does not support `long long'
gcc -c -I../shhopt -pedantic -O3 -Wall -Wno-uninitialized   -o libpbm1.o
➥ ../pbm/libpbm1.c
.
.
.
gcc -o pgmkernel pgmkernel.o -lm `../libopt libpgm.a ../pbm/libpbm.a`
make -C ppm -f /Users/software/Documents/netpbm-9.12/ppm/Makefile all
ln -s ../pbmplus.h pbmplus.h
ln -s ../pbm/pbm.h pbm.h
ln -s ../pbm/libpbm.h libpbm.h
ln -s ../pbm/pbmfont.h pbmfont.h
ln -s ../pgm/pgm.h pgm.h
ln -s ../pgm/libpgm.h libpgm.h
gcc -c -I../shhopt -I/usr/local/include -pedantic -O3 -Wall -Wno-uninitialized \
    -o 411toppm.o /Users/software/Documents/netpbm-9.12/ppm/411toppm.c
/Users/software/Documents/netpbm-9.12/ppm/411toppm.c:60: header file 'malloc.h'
➥ not found
cpp-precomp: warning: errors during smart preprocessing, retrying in basic mode
make[1]: *** [411toppm.o] Error 1
make: *** [ppm] Error 2
```

Did I mention I picked this install because it wasn't easy? Those error messages are just gcc being pedantic about the code. The C programming language has gone through a few revisions, and some programs still don't adhere to the most recent standards. The warnings won't hurt anything, but the error at the bottom of the output will. A few lines above the error is the complaint `header file malloc.h not found`. This is the actual source of the error. If you were to read the code looking for occurrences of `malloc.h` (`grep` might help with this), you'd find there are comments detailing the ambiguities of different Unix flavors and their oddball `malloc.h` implementations. In Apple's case, its that `malloc.h` isn't where the source expects it to be. You've got a choice of fixing all the code to point to `/usr/include/sys/malloc.h`, instead of `/usr/include/malloc.h`, or cheating a little and making it available somewhere that the makefile already has the compiler looking. We're going to take the cheating route, and make a link to `/usr/include/sys/malloc.h` in `/usr/local/include/malloc.h`, where the compiler should be able to find it. There's actually another option, adding a path to the places that the compiler will search for header files, but it turns out that fix will break something else later on, so stick with our cheat:

```
[localhost:~/Documents/netpbm-9.12] software% pushd /usr/include

      /usr/include ~/Documents/netpbm-9.12

[localhost:/usr/include] software% find ./ -name malloc.h -print

      .//objc/malloc.h
      .//sys/malloc.h
[localhost:/usr/include] software% popd

      ~/Documents/netpbm-9.12

[localhost:~/Documents/netpbm-9.12] software% pushd /usr/local/include

      /usr/local/include ~/Documents/netpbm-9.12

[localhost:/usr/local/include] software% ln -s /usr/include/sys/malloc.h ./
[localhost:/usr/local/include] software% popd

      ~/Documents/netpbm-9.12
```

And, back to `make` again:

```
[localhost:~/Documents/netpbm-9.12] software% make

make -C pbm -f /Users/software/Documents/netpbm-9.12/pbm/Makefile all
make -C pbmtoppa all
cd ../../pbm ; make libpbm.a
make[3]: `libpbm.a' is up to date.
make -C pgm -f /Users/software/Documents/netpbm-9.12/pgm/Makefile all
cd ../pbm ; make libpbm.a
make[2]: `libpbm.a' is up to date.
make -C ppm -f /Users/software/Documents/netpbm-9.12/ppm/Makefile all
```

```
gcc -c -I../shhopt -I/usr/local/include -pedantic -O3 -Wall -Wno-uninitialized \
    -o 411toppm.o /Users/software/Documents/netpbm-9.12/ppm/411toppm.c
In file included from /usr/include/machine/types.h:30,
                 from /usr/include/sys/types.h:70,
                 from /usr/include/stdio.h:64,
                 from /Users/software/Documents/netpbm-9.12/ppm/411toppm.c:58:
/usr/include/ppc/types.h:75: warning: ANSI C does not support `long long'
/usr/include/ppc/types.h:76: warning: ANSI C does not support `long long'
.
.
.
gcc   -o ppmtojpeg ppmtojpeg.o `../libopt libppm.a ../pbm/libpbm.a
➥../pgm/libpgm.a` \
  -L/usr/local/lib -ljpeg
/usr/bin/ld: table of contents for archive: /usr/local/lib/libjpeg.a
➥ is out of date; rerun ranlib(1) (can't load from it)
make[1]: *** [ppmtojpeg] Error 1
make: *** [ppm] Error 2
```

Well, at least this time it not only tells us what the error is, but how to fix it…

```
[localhost:~/Documents/netpbm-9.12] software% ranlib /usr/local/lib/libjpeg.a
[localhost:~/Documents/netpbm-9.12] software% make

.
.
.
gcc -c parallel.c -o parallel.o -pedantic -O3 -Wall -Wno-uninitialized
➥  -I. -Iheaders -I../../shhopt -I/usr/local/include
/usr/include/sys/socket.h:175: undefined type, found `u_char'
/usr/include/sys/socket.h:176: undefined type, found `u_char'
/usr/include/sys/socket.h:186: undefined type, found `u_short'
.
.
.
parallel.c:1790: sizeof applied to an incomplete type
parallel.c:1764: warning: unused variable `nameEntry'
make[2]: *** [parallel.o] Error 1
make[1]: *** [all] Error 2
make: *** [ppm] Error 2
```

This one is tough—tough enough that this would be where most people would throw up their hands and decide they don't need the software that badly. It hasn't complained that there's a file missing, but it's complaining about undefined types. It's bad to have undefined things in programs, and there doesn't seem to be anything missing to have caused things to be undefined. Still, it's not like doing some poking around is going to do anything worse than waste a bit of time, and you never know when you might get lucky, so let's press ahead. First, find the file that it's complaining about:

```
[localhost:~/Documents/netpbm-9.12] software% find ./ -name parallel.c -print
.//ppm/ppmtompeg/parallel.c
```

Looking at this file, we see

```
#include <sys/types.h>
#include <sys/socket.h>
#include <sys/times.h>
#include <time.h>
#include <netinet/in.h>
#include <unistd.h>
#include <netdb.h>
```

The `make` process complained that there were undefined things in `socket.h`, and the only thing included before `socket.h` that could have defined them is `types.h`. `types.h` almost certainly lives in `/usr/include/sys`, based on the angle brackets surrounding the `include` filename in `parallel.c`. Searching in `/usr/include/sys/types.h` for the undefined `u_char` type, we find

```
#ifndef _POSIX_SOURCE
typedef unsigned char   u_char;
typedef unsigned short  u_short;
typedef unsigned int    u_int;
typedef unsigned long   u_long;
typedef unsigned short  ushort;         /* Sys V compatibility */
typedef unsigned int    uint;           /* Sys V compatibility */
#endif
```

Interestingly, the type is defined, but there's a cryptic `#ifndef POSIX_SOURCE...#endif` surrounding the definition. If you were a programmer, the problem would be almost immediately obvious at this point. Because you're probably not a programmer, the most information you can get is that if something named `POSIX_SOURCE` is not defined, the needed `u_char` type is defined. Presumably, if `POSIX_SOURCE` is defined, `u_char` doesn't get defined here. Armed with this knowledge, if you search in `parallel.c` again, you'll find the following lines:

```
#define _POSIX_SOURCE
#define _POSIX_C_SOURCE 2
```

What do you know! Right there in `parallel.c`, it's shooting itself in the foot. Let's see what happens if we just comment that out, and have at it again. It already doesn't work, the most that can go wrong is that it still doesn't work, right? Fire up your editor again, and change those lines so they look like this:

```
/* #define _POSIX_SOURCE */
/* #define _POSIX_C_SOURCE 2 */
```

Note

No, I'm not quite sure what the `#define _POSIX_C_SOURCE 2` line is doing. I commented it out on a hunch, and things seem to have worked. You're welcome to try it without commenting it out, and see what happens. I can't guarantee that the rest of the install will follow the course shown if you do, but it's just as possible that it will work better.

And, `make` again:

```
[localhost:~/Documents/netpbm-9.12] software% make

     .
     .
     .
     gcc  -o pnmtopng pnmtopng.o `../libopt libpnm.a ../ppm/libppm.a
     ➥../pgm/libpgm.a ../pbm/libpbm.a ` \
       -L/lib, -lz -L/usr/local/lib -lpng -lm
     /usr/bin/ld: warning -L: directory name (/lib,) does not exist
     /usr/bin/ld: table of contents for archive:
     ➥/usr/local/lib/libpng.a is out of date; \
                  rerun ranlib(1) (can't load from it)
     make[1]: *** [pnmtopng] Error 1
     make: *** [pnm] Error 2
```

You've already seen that one before:

```
[localhost:~/Documents/netpbm-9.12] software% ranlib /usr/local/lib/libpng.a
[localhost:~/Documents/netpbm-9.12] software% make

.
.
.
make -C ../../pnm libpnm.a
make[3]: `libpnm.a' is up to date.
make -C ../../ppm libppm.a
make[3]: `libppm.a' is up to date.
make -C ../../pgm libpgm.a
make[3]: `libpgm.a' is up to date.
make -C ../../pbm libpbm.a
make[3]: `libpbm.a' is up to date.
gcc  -o pnmtofiasco binerror.o cwfa.o getopt.o getopt1.o params.o \
`../../libopt codec/libfiasco_codec.a input/libfiasco_input.a
➥output/libfiasco_output.a lib/libfiasco_lib.a ` \
 `../../libopt ../../pnm/libpnm.a ../../ppm/libppm.a ../../pgm/libpgm.a
➥../../pbm/libpbm.a ` -lm
/usr/bin/ld: archive: codec/libfiasco_codec.a has no table of contents,
➥add one with ranlib(1) (can't load from it)
/usr/bin/ld: archive: input/libfiasco_input.a has no table of contents,
```

```
➥add one with ranlib(1) (can't load from it)
/usr/bin/ld: archive: output/libfiasco_output.a has no table of contents,
➥add one with ranlib(1) (can't load from it)
/usr/bin/ld: archive: lib/libfiasco_lib.a has no table of contents,
➥add one with ranlib(1) (can't load from it)
make[2]: *** [pnmtofiasco] Error 1
make[1]: *** [all] Error 2
make: *** [pnm] Error 2
```

That's getting a little boring! Don't you wish it would just run `ranlib` for you, instead of telling you it needs to be run? Actually, the installers are supposed to take care of that stuff for you. Like the install not creating the needed directories, it also seems to have trouble `ranlib`ing things, so for some things you have to do it by hand:

```
[localhost:~/Documents/netpbm-9.12] software% ranlib codec/libfiasco_codec.a

     ranlib: can't open file: codec/libfiasco_codec.a (No such file or
     directory)
```

Oops! That wasn't expected. Something else you don't (usually) need to know about `make` is it might be recursively making things in subdirectories. The path shown in an error might not be the relative path from your location, but the relative path from wherever `make` is currently operating. In this case, we can just find the directories by name, and `ranlib` them that way:

```
software% find ./ -name libfiasco_codec.a -print

     .//pnm/fiasco/codec/libfiasco_codec.a

software% find ./ -name libfiasco_input.a -print

     .//pnm/fiasco/input/libfiasco_input.a

software% find ./ -name libfiasco_output.a -print

     .//pnm/fiasco/output/libfiasco_output.a

software% find ./ -name libfiasco_lib.a -print

     .//pnm/fiasco/lib/libfiasco_lib.a
software% ranlib .//pnm/fiasco/codec/libfiasco_codec.a
software% ranlib .//pnm/fiasco/input/libfiasco_input.a
software% ranlib .//pnm/fiasco/output/libfiasco_output.a
software% ranlib .//pnm/fiasco/lib/libfiasco_lib.a
```

And, `make` again:

```
[localhost:~/Documents/netpbm-9.12] software% make
.
.
.
```

```
                from ../../pnm/pnmtopalm/pnm.h:7,
                from ../../pnm/pnmtopalm/pnmtopalm.c:12:
/usr/include/stdlib.h:181: warning: ANSI C does not support `long long'
/usr/include/stdlib.h:183: warning: ANSI C does not support `long long'
gcc  -o pnmtopalm pnmtopalm.o palmcolormap.o `../../libopt ../../pnm/libpnm.a
➥../../ppm/libppm.a ../../pgm/libpgm.a ../../pbm/libpbm.a ` \

[localhost:~/Documents/netpbm-9.12] software%
```

Hard to believe, but it just finished the compile. Now you can do a `make install`, and you'll be all set. `netpbm` installs its applications into `/usr/local/netpbm/bin/`; its man pages and so on go into directories in `/usr/local/netpbm`. Because of this you'll again need to extend your path: `set path=($path /usr/local/netpbm/bin/)`, and your `MANPATH`: `setenv MANPATH {$MANPATH}:/usr/local/netpbm/man/`.

Finally, if you'd like to see whether it works, find something like a JPEG file, and try out the following:

```
jpegtopnm < ~/Pictures/<oldfile>.jpg | pnminvert |
➥ppmtojpeg > ~/Pictures/<newfile>.jpg
```

Take a look at the new file in your `Pictures` directory. The `netpbm` package is a large collection of programs that perform very specific graphics manipulations. They can be chained together in arbitrary combinations to create arbitrarily complex graphics manipulations. We'll cover a few of the things it can do in Chapter 18, "Advanced Unix Shell Use: Configuration and Programming (Shell Scripting)." The number of uses is almost unlimited, so you really should read through the man pages for more ideas.

Using the gdb Debugger

If thinking about the problem, trying to do things as correctly as possible, and examining all the debugging information yields only an application that doesn't run correctly, you still have the option of digging around in the code. Thankfully, Apple has provided the GNU debugger, `gdb`, as part of the development tools. The GNU debugger is to the Unix debugging world what the GNU compiler is to the Unix programming world—a flexible, community-supported, de facto standard for programmer productivity.

The easiest way to explain how to use `gdb` is to demonstrate its use. The program has copious online help, as well as man pages, and an INFO section available through the `emacs M-x info` command. Before the demonstration however, Table 17.1 contains a summary of command-line options and common internal commands.

TABLE 17.1 The Command Documentation Table for the `gdb` Debugger

gdb	GNU debugger

`gdb [-help] [-nx] [-q] [-batch] [-cd=`*<dir>*`] [-f] [-b `*<bps>*`] [-tty=`*<dev>*`] [-s `*<symfile>*`] [-e `*<prog>*`] [-se `*<prog>*`] [-c `*<core>*`] [-x `*<cmds>*`] [-d `*<dir>*`] [`*<prog>* `[`*<core>* `|` *<procID>*`]`

`gdb` can be used to debug programs written in C, C++, and Modula-2.

Arguments other than options specify an executable file and a core file or process ID. The fist argument encountered with no associated option flag is equivalent to the `-se` option; the second, if any, is equivalent to the `-c` option, if it is a file. Options and command-line arguments are processed in sequential order. The order makes a difference when the `-x` option is specified.

`-help`	
`-h`	Lists all options with brief explanations.
`-symbols=`*<file>*	
`-s `*<file>*	Reads symbol table from file *<file>*.
`-write`	Enables writing into executable and core files.
`-exec=`*<file>*	
`-e `*<file>*	ses *<file>* as the executable file to execute when appropriate, and for examining pure data in conjunction with a core dump.
`-se=`*<file>*	Reads symbol table from *<file>* and uses it as the executable file.
`-core=`*<file>*	
`-c `*<file>*	Uses *<file>* as a core dump to examine.
`-command=`*<file>*	
`-x `*<file>*	Executes `gdb` commands from *<file>*.
`-directory=`*<directory>*	
`-d `*<directory>* source files.	Adds *<directory>* to the path to search for
`-nx`	
`-n`	Does not execute commands from any `.gdbinit` files. Normally, commands in these files are executed after all the command options and arguments have been processed.
`-quiet`	
`-q`	Quiet mode. Does not print the introductory and copyright messages. Also suppresses them in batch mode.

TABLE 17.1 Continued

-batch	Batch mode. Exits with status 0 after processing all the command files associated with the -x option (and .gdbinit, if not inhibited). Exits with nonzero status if an error occurs in executing the gdb commands in the command files.
-cd=<*directory*>	Runs gdb using <*directory*> as the working directory rather than using the current directory as the working directory.
-fullname	
-f	Outputs information used by emacs-gdb interface.
-b <*bps*>	Sets the line speed (baud rate or bits per second) of any serial interface used by gdb for remote debugging.
-tty=<*device*>	Runs using <*device*> for your program's standard input and output.
These are some of the more frequently needed gdb commands:	
break [<*file*>]<*function*>	Sets a breakpoint at <*function*> (in <*file*>).
run [<*arglist*>]	Starts your program (with <*arglist*>, if specified).
bt	Backtrace. Displays the program stack.
print <*expr*>	Displays the value of an expression.
c	Continues running your program (after stopping, such as at a breakpoint).
next	Executes the next program line (after stopping); steps over any function calls in the line.
step	Executes the next program line (after stopping); steps into any function calls in the line.
help [<*name*>]	Sows information about gdb command <*name*>, or general information about using gdb.
quit	Exits gdb.

To use gdb, you first need something on which to use it. Type in the little program shown in Listing 17.1, just as it appears here. Name the file addme.c.

LISTING 17.1 The Source for the addme.c Demo C Program/* addme.c

```
A really silly C demo program */
/* 990325 WCR                              */
/* Usage is <progname> <filename>          */

#include <stdio.h>

int addem(a,b)
int a, b;
{
  return a+b;
}

void main(argc,argv)
int argc;
char *argv[];
{
  int i;
  char infilename[8];
  int j;
  FILE *infile;
  char number[100];
  char *infilename2=infilename;
  strcpy(infilename2,argv[1]);
  i=0; j=0;
  infile = fopen(infilename2,"r");

  if(infile==NULL)
  {
     printf("couldn't open file %s please try again\n",infilename2);
     exit(1);
  }

  i=0;
  while (fgets(number,90,infile) != '\0')
  {
     sscanf(number,"%d",&j);
     i=addem(i,j);
  }
  printf("Your total is %d\n",i);
  exit(0);
}
```

This simple little C program will take a list of integers from a file, one per line, and add them together. So that you'll have a file to work from, create a file named `numbers` with the following contents:

```
1
2
13
15
```

Make sure that there are no blank lines above or below the data.

Also create a file with a very long name, such as `supercalifradgilisticzowie`, and put the same data in it.

Note there's a bit of trickery involved in the way this code is written that's specifically there to generate an error. Even though there are a few errors in this code, some systems are sloppy enough with memory management that the program might run intermittently. Also, if you rearrange the definition of the variables `i` and `j`, you decrease the likelihood of a crash. Weird, huh?

So, let's see what we have. Time to compile the program. We don't have a makefile, so we'll have to do it by hand. Issue the command:

```
cc -g -o addemup addme.c
```

After a few seconds, your machine should return you to a command line. The compiler should respond with a warning similar to the following:

```
addme.c: In function `main':
addme.c:14: warning: return type of `main' is not `int'
```

It should return you to the command line. If it does anything else, for instance outputs

```
addme.c: In function `main':
addme.c:15: parse error before `char'
addme.c:23: subscripted value is neither array nor pointer
```

that means you've typed the program in incorrectly. Specifically, if you got this error, in all likelihood you forgot the semicolon after the line that says `int argc;`. The warning is just that: a warning, not an error. The most recent revision of the C programming language has a preference for a particular return type for the main program, and the compiler is just being pedantic.

After you get the program to compile cleanly with no errors you're ready for the next step—trying it out. Issue the command `./addemup` and see what happens. Note that the command is `addemup`, not something related to `addme`. I could actually have named it anything I wanted, simply by changing the `-o addemup` part of the `cc` command. If you don't specify any output filename, `cc` will name the output file `a.out` by default. Also, just so you know, the `-g` flag tells the compiler to turn on the debugging output. This slows the program, but it gives the debugger important information.

```
/addemup
Bus Error
```

Well, that doesn't sound good. What could be wrong? You can probably figure it out just by looking at the code at this point, but on a more complicated program that would be impossible. Instead, let's start the gdb debugger and take a look.

```
racer-x testaddme 274% gdb ./addemup
GNU gdb 5.0-20001113 (Apple version gdb-186.1)
➥(Sun Feb 18 01:18:32 GMT 2001) (UI_OUT)
Copyright 2000 Free Software Foundation, Inc.
GDB is free software, covered by the GNU General Public License, and you are
welcome to change it and/or distribute copies of it under certain conditions.
Type "show copying" to see the conditions.
There is absolutely no warranty for GDB.  Type "show warranty" for details.
This GDB was configured as "powerpc-apple-macos10".
Reading symbols for shared libraries .. done
(gdb)
```

Okay, we're at a prompt. What do we do? The gdb debugger actually has a rather complete selection of online help available. To access the help system, simply enter the command help.

```
(gdb) help
List of classes of commands:

running — Running the program
stack — Examining the stack
data — Examining data
breakpoints — Making program stop at certain points
files — Specifying and examining files
status — Status inquiries
support — Support facilities
user-defined — User-defined commands
aliases — Aliases of other commands
obscure — Obscure features
internals — Maintenance commands

Type "help" followed by a class name for a list of commands in that class.
Type "help" followed by command name for full documentation.
Command name abbreviations are allowed if unambiguous.
(gdb)
```

I'll leave some of the interesting items here for you to explore, rather than walk you through them. Right now, let's get back to debugging our program. To start the program, simply issue the command r.

```
(gdb) r
Starting program: /priv/home/ray/testaddme/./addemup
[Switching to thread 1 (process 390 thread 0x1903)]

Program received signal EXC_BAD_ACCESS, Could not access memory.
0x700047d4 in strcpy ()
(gdb)
```

So, gdb knows something. Not a very intelligible something at this point, but something none the less. Let's see whether it can be a bit more informative.

```
(gdb) where
#0  0x700047d4 in strcpy ()
#1  0x00001d18 in main (argc=1, argv=0xbffffb00) at addme.c:23
#2  0x00001bf4 in _start ()
#3  0x00001a34 in start ()
#4  0x00000000 in ?? ()
(gdb)
```


gdb says the program broke in a procedure named `strcpy`, which was called from a procedure named `main`, in line 23 of our file `addme.c`. The `start()`, and `??()` calls are OS X and gdb initializing and starting the program. Let's take a look at this region of the code.

```
(gdb) l 23
18        char infilename[8];
19        int j;
20        FILE *infile;
21        char number[100];
22        char *infilename2=&infilename;
23        strcpy(infilename2,argv[1]);
24        i=0; j=0;
25        infile = fopen(infilename2,"r");
26
27        if(infile==NULL)
(gdb)
```

Line 23 has a function `strcpy` on it. The debugger seems to be on to something here. Let's set a breakpoint (a place we want the program to stop running and wait for us) at line 23 and see what happens.

```
(gdb) b 23
Breakpoint 1 at 0x2320: file addme.c, line 23.
(gdb)
```

So far, so good. Now let's run the program again and see where this takes us.

```
(gdb) r
The program being debugged has been started already.
Start it from the beginning? (y or n) y
Starting program: /priv/home/ray/testaddme/./addemup
[Switching to thread 1 (process 395 thread 0x1a07)]


Breakpoint 1, main (argc=1, argv=0xf7fff744) at addme.c:23
23        strcpy(infilename2,argv[1]);
(gdb)
```

Note that gdb asked me whether I wanted to restart from the beginning and I told it to go ahead. Now it has run up to our breakpoint and is waiting for me to do something. Even if I don't know quite what strcpy does, there's still something obviously wrong with this line. I know I've got a variable named infilename2 and a funny variable named argv[1]. Let's see what gdb has to say about them.

```
(gdb) p infilename2
$1 = 0xbffff99c "L\000\000@"
(gdb)
```

The $1 indicates that it's telling us about the first variable we asked about. The 0xbfff99c is the memory location where it's stored—don't be surprised if yours is different. The L\000\000@ is the current contents of that memory, which currently isn't too informative. (Don't be surprised if yours has something else in whatever memory location shows up on your machine.) What can we tell about this argv[1]?

```
(gdb) p argv[1]
$2 = 0xbffffba9 0x0
(gdb)
```

Hmmm… 0x0 is a hexadecimal 0, or NULL in the C world. Examining the code again certainly suggests that something useful should be happening here. It looks like infilename2 gets used to open a file in just a few lines, and neither L\000\000@ nor NULL looks promising as a filename. Nulls get used in C, but frequently they're signs of a problem, so let's think about this.

The program is trying to do something with a variable named argv[1]. The only other place this variable (argv) appears is in the main statement, the statement that starts off the actual program execution. It certainly looks like there should be something other than a NULL here. Wait a minute, what did it say in the comments at the top? It said I needed to give it a filename! I didn't give it a filename, and it's trying to copy something that doesn't exist to get one. Aren't programmers supposed to check for that?

Let's see if I'm right. I'll rerun the program with a filename this time.

```
(gdb) r numbers
The program being debugged has been started already.
Start it from the beginning? (y or n) y
Starting program: /priv/home/ray/testaddme/./addemup numbers
[Switching to thread 1 (process 405 thread 0x250b)]

Breakpoint 1, main (argc=2, argv=0xf7fff73c) at addme.c:23
23          strcpy(infilename2,argv[1]);
(gdb)
```

I started it over, but I forgot to turn off my breakpoint. Still, this is a good opportunity for me to check to see whether I was right.

```
(gdb) p infilename2
$3 = 0xf7fff200 "\000\000\200\000\000\000 "
(gdb)
```

That's just as useless as before.

```
(gdb) p argv[1]
$4 = 0xf7fff80f "numbers"
(gdb)
```

Now we're getting somewhere! If we remember to give it a filename, it actually gets one! To continue past the breakpoint, I can enter `c`.


```
(gdb) c
Continuing.
Your total is 31

Program exited normally.
(gdb)
```

The program now does exactly what it should. If I'd like to test it again without stopping at the breakpoint, I can delete the breakpoint and run it again.

```
(gdb) d 1
(gdb) r
Starting program: /priv/home/ray/testaddme/./addemup numbers
[Switching to thread 1 (process 445 thread 0x2721)]

Your total is 31

Program exited normally.
(gdb)
```

The command `d 1` deletes breakpoint 1 (you can have multiples if you need them). Note that I didn't have to give it the command-line argument `numbers` this time when I hit `r` because it conveniently remembered command-line arguments between runs. As you can see, it runs properly to completion.

Quitting `gdb` with the `quit` command and trying it on the command line produces the same results.

```
racer-x testaddme 286% ./addemup numbers
Your total is 31
racer-x testaddme 287%
```

Now let's see whether we can demonstrate another type of error. Do you still remember what your very long filename is? Try using that filename instead of `numbers` and see what happens.

```
racer-x testaddme 287% ./addemup supercalifragilisticzowie
couldn't open file supercalifra please try again
racer-x testaddme 288%
```

Huh? I didn't call it `supercalifra`. Something happened to my filename. Time to break out gdb again and have another look.

```
gdb ./addemup
GNU gdb 5.0-20001113 (Apple version gdb-186.1)
➥ (Sun Feb 18 01:18:32 GMT 2001) (UI_OUT)
Copyright 2000 Free Software Foundation, Inc.
GDB is free software, covered by the GNU General Public License, and you are
welcome to change it and/or distribute copies of it under certain conditions.
Type "show copying" to see the conditions.
There is absolutely no warranty for GDB.  Type "show warranty" for details.
This GDB was configured as "powerpc-apple-macos10".
Reading symbols for shared libraries .. done
(gdb)  r supercalifragilisticzowie
Starting program: /priv/home/ray/testaddme/./addemup supercalifragilisticzowie
[Switching to thread 1 (process 551 thread 0x351b)]

couldn't open file supercalifra please try again

Program exited with code 01.
(gdb)
```

Basically, it says the same thing. There must be something more we can find out, though. Let's look at the code and see if we can figure out where that weird truncation came from.

```
(gdb) l
14        int argc;
15        char *argv[];
16        {
17          int i;
18          char infilename[8];
19          int j;
20          FILE *infile;
21          char number[100];
22          char *infilename2=infilename;
23          strcpy(infilename2,argv[1]);
(gdb)
24          i=0; j=0;
25          infile = fopen(infilename2,"r");
26
27          if(infile==NULL)
28          {
29             printf("couldn't open file %s please try again\n",infilename2);
30             exit(1);
31          }
32
33          i=0;
(gdb)
```

Line 29 seems to be where the error message is coming from. Let's set a breakpoint there and see what happens.

```
(gdb) b 29
Breakpoint 1 at 0x2374: file addme.c, line 29.
(gdb) r
Starting program: /priv/home/ray/testaddme/./addemup supercalifragilisticzowie
[Switching to thread 1 (process 583 thread 0x291b)]


Breakpoint 1, main (argc=2, argv=0xf7fff72c) at addme.c:29
29            printf("couldn't open file %s please try again\n",infilename2);
(gdb)
```


We're at our breakpoint. `infilename2` is supposed to be `supercalifragilisticzowie`, and it is

```
(gdb) p infilename2
$1 = 0xbffff99c "supercalifra"
(gdb)
```

Something's very wrong here! Time to back up to our trusty breakpoint at line 23 and watch what happens from the top down.

```
(gdb) r
Starting program: /priv/home/ray/testaddme/./addemup supercalifragilisticzowie

Breakpoint 1, main (argc=2, argv=0xf7fff72c) at addme.c:23
23         strcpy(infilename2,argv[1]);
(gdb) p argv[1]
$1 = 0xf7fff7ff "supercalifragilisticzowie"
(gdb)
```

So, the previous culprit isn't a problem here.

```
(gdb) p infilename2
$2 = 0xbffff99c "\000\000\200\000\000\000 "
(gdb)
```

There's nothing interesting there. Let's see what happens on the next line—use the `gdb` command `n` to step to the next line. When you step to the next line, this line executes, so you should expect to see the results of that `strcpy` after stepping forward.

```
(gdb) n
24         i=0; j=0;
(gdb) p infilename2
$1 = 0xf7fff6b0 "supercalifragilisticzowie"
(gdb)
```

As expected, `infilename2` contains our atrociously long filename. Nothing wrong here, but by the time it hit line 29, it was broken, so let's step forward again and see what happens.

```
(gdb) n
25          infile = fopen(infilename2,"r");
(gdb) p
$3 = 0xf7fff6b0 "supercalifra"
(gdb)
```

Wait a minute! Now it's wrong! What happened? All that the program did was assign both the variables `i` and `j` to be zero, and somehow it affected `infilename2`. You wouldn't think this could happen, variables just changing their values willy-nilly.

In fact, if the program were written properly, this wouldn't happen. As a non-programmer, this is where you usually give up. That isn't to say that the exercise has been useless. With this information, you can more easily explain to the author or online support community what problems you've observed, so they can fix it more easily and quickly. Program authors hate it when they get bug reports that say, "it didn't work." This doesn't mean anything to them because if they could duplicate the problem on their end, they'd probably have found and fixed it already.

By taking these extra steps, the information you can provide about the program's problems can mean the difference between a fix that takes a few minutes to appear and a fix that never appears.

> **Note**
>
> If you're curious, and keep a C handbook around, fixing this particular error isn't that difficult. The error here is the variable `infilename` has been defined to hold only eight characters. `infilename2` is essentially an alias to `infilename1` and is needed to fool the debugger into not telling you about the problem immediately. The assignment of the very long filename to `infilename2` actually works most of the time. It works because there's enough slop in the assignment of memory space that it's not going to write over anything important, although the `supercalifragilisticzowi` value hangs out the end of it and into unknown memory space.
>
> The thing that actually makes the error show up almost all the time is the placement of the definitions of `i` and `j` around the definition of `infilename`. Most compilers will order variables in memory in the same order they were defined in the program. Because the compiler doesn't know you're going to stuff a huge string into `infilename`, it chooses memory close to `infilename` for the storage

of i and j. With optimization turned off, most compilers will place i and j flanking infilename in memory, and a sufficiently long value in infilename will overlap the memory used by i and j. By assigning both i and j to 0 after assigning infilename, it's almost guaranteed that part of infilename will be damaged and that the program will fail. To fix the program so that this can't occur with any reasonable filename, simply change the definition of infilename to something like char infilename[256]; instead of char infilename[8];.

Recommended Command-Line Software Installations

As we've mentioned several times previously, there are thousands of freely available Unix programs that can be downloaded as source and compiled for your machine. We've included a small sample of these in this section—some that we've used in this book, and some that are simply useful utilities to have available. If you browse the FTP sites and Web directories where you can find these sources, you'll discover many more programs that might be of interest.

libtermcap

For some reason, Apple has not included a copy of libtermcap.a with OS X. This resource is required by programs so that they can look up, and make use of, the differing screen format controls that different types of terminals provide.

You can download a copy of the libtermcap source from any GNU mirror, such as ftp.gnu.org, although we strongly recommend that you follow the instructions provided immediately after connection, and use a local mirror of the FTP site rather than the parent GNU site. The source should be in /pub/gnu/termcap/.

Installation is straightforward: gunzip, tar -xf termcap-1.3.tar, cd termcap-1.3, cp /usr/libexec/config.* ./, ./configure, make, make install.

A problem with the install will be that it wants to put termcap.h into /usr/include/termcap.h. Because only the super user can write to that directory, you will have to make install as root, or you will have to change the permissions on /usr/include so that your software maintenance user can write to the directory.

It also might help some software installations if you ln -s /usr/share/misc/termcap /etc/termcap, and ln -s /usr/share/misc/termcap.db /etc/termcap.db.

spell and ispell

spell is the spelling checker program that we used as an example for the discussion of STDIN/STDOUT and pipes. The ispell program is actually the base driver for the spell program, and can do a number of things that we didn't demonstrate in the pipes section. You're encouraged to check out the man pages for more information.

This software has a somewhat convoluted install, but not because it's inherently difficult to install. The problem exists because the dictionaries that it uses are copyrighted, and can't be legally distributed by the author of the spell program. This necessitates a separate download for the dictionaries, and some fiddling with the source to point it at the downloaded dictionaries.

The ispell homepage is located at http://www.cs.ucla.edu/ficus-members/geoff/ispell.html.

```
ln -s /var/tmp /usr/tmp
```

(Lots of software will expect /usr/tmp to exist.)

```
lynx -dump ftp://ftp.tue.nl/pub/tex/GB95/ispell-english.zip > english.zip
lynx -dump ftp://ftp.cs.ucla.edu/pub/ispell-3.1/ispell-3.1.20.tar.gz
➥ > ispell-3.1.20.tar.gz
lynx -dump http://www.ibiblio.org/pub/gnu/spell/spell-1.0.tar.gz
➥ > spell-1.0.tar.gz
```

```
unzip english.zip
gunzip ispell-3.1.20.tar.gz
gunzip spell-1.0.tar.gz
tar -xf ispell-3.1.20.tar
tar -f spell-1.0.tar
cd ispell-english
mv american.med+ american.med
mv british.med+ british.med
mv * ../ispell-3.1/languages/english/
cd ./ispell-3.1
make all
```

This will compile for a little while, and then die with errors. After it does, edit the file local.h, and add the following line on the first empty line:

```
#define LANGUAGES "{american,MASTERDICTS=american.med,
➥HASHFILES=americanmed.hash}"
```

```
make all
make install
```

The make install step will need a number of directories, and permissions to write into them, in the /usr/local tree. If they don't all exist on your system, create them and rerun the make install step.

```
cd ../spell-1.0/
cp /usr/libexec/config.* ./
./configure
make
make install
```

Now you can run both the `ispell` program and the `spell` program as shown in Chapter 14, "Advanced Shell Concepts and Commands."

You're supposed to be able to compile this with the capability to add words to the dictionary. Unfortunately, the script that builds the dictionaries requires that `sort` accept a different syntax than OS X's `sort`. The adventurous are encouraged to attempt the repair—it's not too difficult, but it does require a number of changes to accomplish.

gdbm

This is the GNU `dbm` (database management) library. Software authors have chosen at least three different `dbm` flavors to support their applications. `gdbm` is the GNU-supported variant. These libraries don't conflict with each other, so it doesn't hurt to have extras installed, and `gdbm` is required for some installs.

The source can be downloaded from any GNU mirror (see `libtermcap` for suggestions).

Read the `READMEs`

```
./configure
make
make progs
make install
```

The `make progs` step makes test and conversion programs. Among other things, this step makes comparisons between the behavior of the `gdbm` and other `dbm` libraries installed on your machine. It is expected to fail on systems that do not have `dbm` or `ndbm` libraries (currently, Apple doesn't provide these, but this could change in the future).

Python

Python is a programming language designed for building "smart" applications. Some software authors use the Python libraries to build expert-system applications, and it has been growing in popularity in recent years. If you'd like to either experiment with writing applications in Python, or need to install it to support other applications you'd like to run, this should get you started.

Available from `http://www.python.org/`

Read the `READMEs`

```
./configure —with-suffix=.exe —with-dyld
```

Edit the `Modules/Setup` file if there are any modules that you know you want to use. For example, if you are thinking about installing `HostSentry`, you should uncomment the lines for `gdbm` and `syslog`. If you discover later that there are some modules you want to use, you can edit the `Modules/Setup` file as appropriate, recompile and reinstall `python`.

```
make
```

If you edited `Modules/Setup` you will see a comment in the early `make` output that you might have to rerun `make`. If you see the comment, rerun `make`. Otherwise, you can run `make test` next.

```
make test
```

You might find that the `make test` step fails, even though the `make` step does not. Try installing your compiled `python` anyway. So far, people are reporting success in using `python` on OS X anyway.

```
make install
```

PortSentry

PortSentry, available at `http://www.psionic.com/`, is a connection-monitoring program that attempts to determine if your machine is being attacked via the network, and blocks access from machines that appear to be attempting malicious connections. We will be covering the setup and monitoring of this program in Chapter 31, "Server Security and Advanced Network Configuration."

Read the `README`s.

Edit, if needed, the `portsentry_config.h` file for the following location definitions: `CONFIG_FILE`, `WRAPPER_HOSTS_DENY`, `SYSLOG_FACILITY`, `SYSLOG_LEVEL`. The software author recommends leaving the settings alone.

Edit `portsentry.conf`. This is the file you edit to set the scan and response level.

Edit `portsentry.ignore`. This is the file that contains a listing of hosts that `portsentry` should ignore.

```
make generic
```

As root, run `make install`.

Start `portsentry` for TCP and UDP:

```
/usr/local/psionic/portsentry/portsentry -tcp
/usr/local/psionic/portsentry/portsentry -udp
```

Adjust configuration settings until you are happy with them.

Add PortSentry to the system's startup scripts if you want PortSentry to start at boot.

nmap

nmap, available from http://www.insecure.com/, is a tool that can be used to scan ports on your machine or other machines. You may or may not be interested in nmap if you are already using some combination of ipfw and/or PortSentry. The latest version of nmap has an OS X port available. The config.guess and config.sub files that come with it are even more up to date than the OS X default config.guess and config.sub files.

Read the READMEs.

```
./configure
make
make install
```

Tripwire 1.3.1 (Academic Source Release)

Tripwire, available from http:// www.tripwire.com/, monitors the integrity of whatever important directories or files you configure it to monitor. Regular use of Tripwire can alert you to any unauthorized changes that have been made to files on your system.

Go to the GNU Darwin porting page at http://gnu-darwin.sourceforge.net/ports/ and follow the directions for setting up the porting engine. Don't start the bootstrap process. The current source is located at http://elisa.utopianet.net/~rlucia/devel/darwin_ports/. This package is intended to do much the same thing as the GNU Darwin porting engine, but both have minor problems, and seem to overlay and work better in tandem than either alone.

If you have not already done so, make a user called man. Follow the same method that you used for making a bin user. The porting engine used in FreeBSD expects certain user IDs to exist, and won't run properly without them.

These packages will enable you to compile and install far more software than just the Tripwire monitor.

Notes on compiling Tripwire via the ports system:

Tripwire wants to be compiled in /usr/ports/security/tripwire-131/.

Run bsdmake in that directory after you have installed the ports system, and it will tell you where to get the actual Tripwire source. You might need to run bsdmake again if it doesn't unpack the source after downloading.

This is all supposed to work straight from the bsdmake command, but it doesn't work cleanly as of this writing. Fixing it isn't too strenuous, but is somewhat annoying.

cd to work/tw_ASR_1.3.1_src/. Edit the Makefile. Add a # in front of the line that says

```
# LDFLAGS= -static        # Most systems, Linux / RedHat 5.2 and previous
```

and remove the # from in front of the line that says

```
# LDFLAGS= -ldl           # Solaris 2.x, Redhat 6.0
```

You need to make sure that the LDFLAGS has no spaces in front of it.

Run bsdmake in work/tw_ASR_1.3.1_src/.

The compiler provided by Apple doesn't like the compiler directive #if (TW_TYPE32 == int). You can look for these and replace them with #if (0). You'll need to do this for each of several subdirectories of the sigs subdirectory.

Depending on the state of the Darwin ports system, whichever you choose to use, you might need to build bits and pieces of the downloaded parts, such as the dlcompat library, and install them. There's an effort underway to get this all into a single clean install, but it's not quite there yet.

Eventually, you should get to a point that the make builds two executables: tripwire and siggen. make install, and if all goes well, it's time to read the instructions and learn how to use it (or, wait until Chapter 31, when we'll get you started on Tripwire configuration, along with a number of other network security topics). If the make install doesn't work, it'll be because of missing directories, or a need to create the man user for the installation to proceed.

Note that this make install moves files when it installs them, rather than copying them. If you need to reinstall, either to place it somewhere else or because the install didn't finish properly, you'll need to bsdmake it all again.

Edit tw.config. This is the file where you specify what files or directories you want Tripwire to monitor.

Initialize the Tripwire database:

```
tripwire -initialize
```

Run tripwire:

```
tripwire
```

Add tripwire to a daily cron job so that Tripwire regularly checks the integrity of your important files and sends you the results.

restore

The `restore` command is part of the `dump/restore` pair of traditional Unix commands used for creating and managing backups. Apple, for reasons yet unknown, has provided the `dump` command with the system, but not the `restore` command. Chapter 32, "Maintenance and Troubleshooting," details the use of the `dump` and `restore` commands.

The adventurous and intrepid can try their hand at building `restore` straight from the FreeBSD sources:

```
localhost work 230% setenv CVSROOT
➥:pserver:anoncvs@anoncvs.FreeBSD.org:/home/ncvs
localhost work 231% cvs login

     (Logging in to anoncvs@anoncvs.FreeBSD.org)

CVS password: anoncvs

localhost work 232% cvs co restore

     cvs server: Updating restore
     U restore/Makefile
     U restore/dirs.c
     U restore/extern.h
     U restore/interactive.c
     U restore/main.c
     U restore/restore.8
     U restore/restore.c
     U restore/restore.h
     U restore/symtab.c
     U restore/tape.c
     U restore/utilities.c

localhost work 233% ls

     restore

localhost work 234% cvs co dump

     cvs server: Updating dump
     U dump/Makefile
     U dump/dump.8
     U dump/dump.h
     U dump/dumprmt.c
     U dump/itime.c
     U dump/main.c
     U dump/optr.c
     U dump/pathnames.h
     U dump/tape.c
     U dump/traverse.c
     U dump/unctime.c
```

```
localhost rawrestore 235% cvs logout
     (Logging out of anoncvs@anoncvs.FreeBSD.org)
localhost work 237% ls
     dump      restore
```

Tip

You can learn considerably more about this system of obtaining source code from the FreeBSD Web page at `http://www.freebsd.org/doc/en_US.ISO8859-1/books/handbook/anoncvs.html` and the online manual at `http://www.FreeBSD.org/cgi/man.cgi?query=cvs&sektion=1`.

This shows downloads for both `dump` and `restore` because the compilation of `restore` requires one of the `dump` source files as well. You can start hacking away in the `restore` directory using `bsdmake`. Expect to have to modify at least one `.h` file and a couple of the `.c` files. The fix isn't terribly difficult, but it's a bit uglier than we feel it would be educational to discuss here.

Those less adventurous can download our patched source from `http://www.osxunleashed.com/fixes/`, and we're hoping that Apple will start distributing this as part of the standard software package soon.

Summary

This chapter took you through a tour of several types of installation, compilation, troubleshooting and debugging, as well as provided you with some suggestions for installing a number of useful command-line applications. After they have developed the necessary mindset regarding software installation, we have found that a large percentage of Unix users can productively fight though troublesome installs such as this by successively attacking small parts of the problem as shown here. The keys to remember are that the messages output from the compilers and debuggers do have meaning, and the worst that can happen by attempting to logically determine the cause of an error is that it doesn't help. Surprisingly frequently, a problem in a programming language can be fixed by working with error messages and making logical guesses, even if you don't know the language in the slightest.

Advanced Unix Shell Use: Configuration and Programming (Shell Scripting)

IN THIS CHAPTER

In the preceding several chapters, we have introduced you to the wide range of possibilities inherent in being able to access the Unix subsystem at the command line. Although we've said that being able to type to the command line can give you the power to do things that you've never been able to do before, we've also repeatedly hinted that there were ways that you could automate much of the typing and build your own mini programs. In this chapter, we'll cover the final things you need to know to make this a reality.

As in previous chapters, we'll focus on the use of `csh/tcsh` syntax and programming. Most available shells can do things similar to what we will cover here, although the syntax might be somewhat different. A few (such as `ksh`) can do considerably more, although a complete description of their use is sufficient to fill a book or two.

You might not realize it yet, but you already know shell syntax. To make the best use of the command-line environment, you'll also need to know about shell variables, conditional statements, and looping structures.

Customizing Your Shell Environment and Storing Data

Variables are a way of addressing bits of the computer memory so that we can store random pieces of information in it. It would be difficult to do much productive work with a computer if all we could store in any location was one particular, predetermined piece of information. Variables give us the ability to name a region X, and store whatever value we want in X, and change the value whenever we want. Variables in the shell are used both to hold data to be used in commands and programs written in the shell, and to control the behavior of certain aspects of the shell. You've already been introduced peripherally to this second use by way of the `path` variable, which affects where the shell looks to find executable programs. We'll go into somewhat more detail on this use in the next section, and cover the former later in this chapter.

Environment and Shell Variables

Many shells make a distinction between environment variables and shell variables in one way or another. Both are variables that you can set and use in a shell. The difference is that environment variables are inherited by any programs (such as subshells) that are children of (Unixism for "run by") that shell, whereas shell variables are not inherited. This might not seem a useful distinction, but there are significant uses for each type. Noninherited shell variables don't cost memory and startup time for subshells, and can be expected to be empty in any shell until they are used to store something. Inherited environment variables, on the other hand, must be copied into the memory space of child programs, taking room and time, and they can be used to pass information between a parent shell and programs that it executes.

Setting shell and environment variables is similar in `tcsh`, although there are a few syntactic differences between the way that they're used in some situations. To set a shell variable, the syntax is as follows:

```
set <shellvariablename> = <value>
```

To `set` a shell variable named `x` to contain the value `7`, the shell expression is simply

```
set x=7
```

To set an environment variable to a particular value, the syntax is

```
setenv <environmentvariablename> <value>
```

To set an environment variable named `Y` to contain the value `8`, the shell expression is

```
setenv Y 7
```

Note

It is traditional to use uppercase variable names for environment variables, and lowercase variable names for shell variables, although there is no requirement that this tradition must be followed in your own scripts. In fact, it's quite possible for you to create a shell variable and an environment variable with the same name, each containing a distinct value. In this case, most shell commands will see the variable as having the value of the shell variable, rather than the value of the environment variable.

Both shell and environment variables are addressed for use by the prepending of a `$` sign before the variable names. A simple demonstration can be accomplished with the `echo` command, which prints to the `STDOUT` of the shell, the value of the expression following it.

```
localhost ray 200> echo "Hi There"

     Hi there

localhost ray 201> echo $x

     x: Undefined variable.

localhost ray 202> set x=7
localhost ray 203> echo $x
```

```
     7
localhost ray 205> setenv Y 8
localhost ray 206> echo $y

     y: Undefined variable.

localhost ray 207> echo $Y

     8

localhost ray 208> @ z = ( $x + $Y )
localhost ray 209> echo $z

     15
```

Here, a shell variable x and an environment variable Y have been set to values 7 and 8, respectively, and their values have been printed to the terminal. The @ command is a tcsh shell built-in command, similar to the set command. However, the set command treats all its arguments as strings, whereas the @ command treats them as numbers, allowing math operations such as +, -, /, and *. The @ command, like the set command, sets a shell variable (or creates it if it does not exist). The set and @ commands can also be used as [set or @] *<variablename>*[*n*] = *<expression>*. In this form, the command attempts to treat the variable *<variablename>* as an array, and set item *n* (the *n*th word, if echoed) to the value of *<expression>*. Table 18.1 lists the most frequently used methods for setting variable values. (Frankly, the need for a separate command to operate on variables as numeric values, rather than string values, is one of the most annoying weaknesses of the csh/tcsh shell model.)

TABLE 18.1 tcsh Syntax Options for Setting Shell and Environment Variables to Values

Expression syntax	*Effect*
<word>	Used as a part of a command-line expression, *<word>* is a string of non-whitespace characters, or a quoted string that possibly contains spaces.
$*<variable>*	Expands to the contents of *<variable>*. This will typically be a *<word>* or *<wordlist>*. $*<variablename>* preferentially expands to the value of the shell variable by the name *<variablename>*, if both shell and environment variables with this name exist.
set *<variable>* = *<word>*	Sets the value of *<variable>* to *<word>*.
set *<variable>*[*n*] = *<word>*	Treats *<variable>* as an array of words, and sets the *n*th value to *<word>*. This has the effect of setting the *n*th word of a wordlist to *<word>*.

TABLE 18.1 continued

Expression syntax	*Effect*
`setenv <variable> <word>`	Sets the environment variable `<variable>` to contain the value `<word>`. Most variable manipulations must be done in shell variables, and the values transferred into environment variables if needed.
`@ <variable> = <expression>`	Treats `<expression>` as a mathematical expression, attempts to evaluate it, and assigns the result to `<variable>`. Most forms of errors in attempts at this result in the response `@: Expression Syntax`.
`@ <variable> = ( <expression> )`	Same as the previous item. Parentheses can be used to order the execution of parts of the expression, and it's frequently helpful to use them around any expression on general principles.
`@ <variable>[n] = <expression>`	Treats `<variable>` as an array, and sets the *n*th value of it to the value of `<expression>`.

Caution

The spacing between the parts of a command, like the `@ z = ( $x + $y )` command in the table, is one of the largest sources of difficulty to the beginning shell programmer. The spaces between "words" that are being operated on—here the $x, the $y, and the + symbol—are critical to the command being understood properly. You can have more spaces, but if you remove a space, the words become indistinct, and the shell becomes confused. For example, if you remove the space between the $x and the + sign, the shell will no longer see a variable named $x, a + sign, and a variable named $y. Instead, it will see a variable named $x+ and a variable named $y, with no mathematic operation between them. This turns out to be two errors because the + symbol isn't a valid part of a variable name, and some math operation is required in the expression.

To demonstrate the difference between shell and environment variables, you can create a subshell and test the variables you used in the previous example in it:

```
localhost ray 210> tcsh

    /Users/ray
```

```
localhost ray 151> echo $x
     x: Undefined variable.
localhost ray 152> echo $Y
     8
```

As you can see, after the subshell is started (notice that the command number in the prompt drops to `151`—the size of my retained command history list), the environment variable `Y` maintains its value and the shell value `x` becomes undefined.

Note

Here we're using a slightly modified shell environment than what comes as a default—this one shows the command number on the command line as part of the prompt. If you'd like to make this modification to your environment, the changes to make to your `.cshrc` file are shown in Appendix B.

As mentioned earlier, certain shell and environment variables affect the behavior of some parts of the shell, or of programs that run as children of the shell. Table 18.2 lists the `tcsh` shell variables that affect the behavior of `tcsh` and a few intimately related programs. Please remember that any program you run in a shell may be additionally affected by environment variables. For example, the `man` command determines where to look for man pages by examining the `MANPATH` environment variable. If you set this environment variable to some path in your shell, the `man` command will inherit it and search in that path for man pages. Because every program may independently choose to examine any environment variables it chooses, it's best to look at the man pages for any programs to determine whether there are environment variables with which you can affect the program's behavior.

TABLE 18.2 The `tcsh` Reserved Shell Variables

Shell Variable	*Effects*
`addsuffix`	Controls addition of `/` to the end of directories paths, and spaces after normal filenames when expanded by shell filename autocompletion.
`afsuser`	If set, the username to autologout under kerberos authentication.
`ampm`	If set, shows time in 12-hour AM/PM format.
`argv`	The list of arguments passed to the shell on startup.

TABLE 18.2 continued

Shell Variable	*Effects*
`autocorrect`	If set, attempts to fix command misspellings.
`autoexpand`	If set, passes command completion attempts through the expand-history processor. (See the `tcsh` man page for more details.)
`autolist`	If set, lists possible expansions for autocompletion, if the expansion is ambiguous. If the value is set to `ambiguous`, lists possibilities only when an autocompletion attempt does not add any new characters.
`autologout`	The number of minutes of inactivity before autologout. Optionally, the number of minutes before automatic locking of the terminal.
`backslash_quote`	If set, backslashes (\ characters) are automatically inserted before any backslash or quote character in a command completion.
`cdpath`	A list of directories in which `cd` should look for subdirectories if they aren't in the current working directory.
`color`	If set, enables color display for the `ls` command and shell built-in command `ls-F`.
`command`	If set, contains the command which was passed to the shell with a `-c` flag.
`complete`	If set to `enhance`, completion ignores filename case, considers periods, hyphens, and underscores to be word separators, and hyphens and underscores to be equivalent.
`correct`	If set to `cmd`, attempts automatic spelling correction for commands. If set to `complete`, commands are automatically completed. If set to `all`, the entire command line is corrected.
`cwd`	The full path of the current working directory.
`dextract`	If set, `pushd +n` extracts the *n*th subdirectory from the stack, rather than rotating it to the top.
`dirsfile`	The default location in which `dirs -S` and `dirs -L` look for their history.
`dirstack`	An array of all directories in the directory stack.
`dspmbyte`	If set to `euc`, enables display and editing of EUC-Kanji (Japanese) code. If set to `sjis`, enables display and editing of Shift-JIS (Japanese) code. Other options are available—see the `tcsh` man page for more details.

TABLE 18.2 continued

Shell Variable	*Effects*
`dunique`	If set, `pushd` removes any instances of the pushed directory from the stack, before pushing it onto the top of the stack.
`echo`	If set, each command and its arguments are echoed to the terminal before being executed.
`echo_style`	The style of the echo built-in. May be set to `bsd`, `sysv`, `both`, or `none` to control the behavior of the `echo` command. See the `tcsh` man page for more details on behavior affected.
`edit`	If set, allow command-line editing.
`ellipsis`	If set, use an ellipsis to represent portions of the path that won't fit in the prompt.
`fignore`	List of filename suffixes to be ignored in completion attempts.
`filec`	An unused `tcsh` shell variable, included to maintain backward compatibility with `csh`, which used this variable to control whether completion should be used.
`gid`	The user owning the shell's real group ID.
`group`	The user owning the shell's group name.
`histchars`	A string determining the characters used in history substitution. The first character replaces the default `!` character, and the second replaces the default `^` character.
`histdup`	Controls handling of duplicate entries in the history list. If set to `all`, only unique history events are entered into the history. If set to `prev`, a run of identical commands is reduced to a single entry in the history list. If set to `erase`, a repeat of a command already in the history list removes the previous occurrence from the history.
`histfile`	The default location in which `history -S` and `history -L` look for a history file. If unset, `~/.history` is used.
`histlit`	If set, the shell built-in, editor commands, and history-saving mechanism use the literal (unexpanded) form of lines in the history list.
`history`	The first word indicates the number of history events to save. The optional second word indicates a format for printing the history. See the `tcsh` man page for more details on format control strings.

TABLE 18.2 continued

Shell Variable	*Effects*
`home`	Initialized to the home directory of the user. Command-line expansion of ~ refers to this variable for its action.
`ignoreeof`	If set to the empty string or `0` and the input is a terminal, an end-of-file command sent to the terminal causes the shell to print an error, rather than exit.
`implicitcd`	If set, the shell treats a directory name entered on the command line as though it were entered as the argument of a `cd` command.
`inputmode`	Can be set to insert or overwrite to control the behavior of command-line editing.
`listflags`	Contains command-line flags to include with any used when issuing the `ls-F` shell built-in.
`listjobs`	If set, all current jobs are listed when a running job is suspended.
`listlinks`	If set, the `ls-F` shell built-in command shows the time of file to which symbolic links point.
`listmax`	The maximum number of items that the list-choices command-line editor and autocompletion will list, without prompting.
`loginsh`	Set by the shell if it is a login shell.
`logout`	Set by the shell to `normal` before a normal logout, `automatic` before an automatic logout, and `hangup` if the shell was killed by a hangup signal (typically generated by `kill -HUP`, or by a terminal connection being interrupted, rather than cleanly exited).
`mail`	The name of the files or directories to check for incoming mail. See both the `tcsh` and `mail` man pages for more information on the behaviors controlled by this variable.
`matchbeep`	Controls whether and when command-line completion rings the bell. Setting it to `never` prevents all beeps. `nomatch` beeps when there is no current match. `ambiguous` beeps when there are multiple matches. `notunique` beeps when there is an exact match, as well as other longer matches. If unset, the behavior is the same as `ambiguous`.
`nobeep`	If set, beeping is completely disabled.

TABLE 18.2 continued

Shell Variable	*Effects*
`noclobber`	If set, the shell attempts to prevent output redirection from overwriting existing files. See the `tcsh` man page for more details.
`noglob`	If set, filename substitution and directory substitution are inhibited. Normally used only as a performance enhancement for shell scripts where filenames are already known.
`nokanji`	If set, disables kanji support, so that the meta key is used.
`nonomatch`	If set, a filename or directory substitution that doesn't match any files does not cause an error.
`nostat`	A list of directories, or patterns that match directories, that should not be examined for matches during completion attempts.
`notify`	If set, announces job completions immediately, rather than waiting until just before the next command prompt appears.
`owd`	The previous working directory.
`path`	A list of directories in which to look for executable commands. The `path` shell variable is set at startup from the `PATH` environment variable.
`printexitvalue`	If set and a program exits with a non-zero status, prints the status.
`prompt`	The string that is printed as the prompt for command-line input. This can contain both literal strings for display as well as a number of special patterns indicating the substitution of everything from the current directory, to the user name. See the `tcsh` man page for the (rather extensive) list of options available.
`prompt2`	The string to use for the inner prompt in `while` and `foreach` loops. The same format sequences as used in the `prompt` variable may be used in `prompt2`.
`prompt3`	The string to use for prompting regarding automatic spelling corrections. The same format sequences as used in the `prompt` variable may be used in `prompt2`.
`promptchars`	If set, specifies a pair of characters to substitute between for a shell prompt when a normal user, and when `su`-ed to the super user.
`pushdtohome`	If set, `pushd` without any arguments is equivalent to `pushd ~`.

TABLE 18.2 continued

Shell Variable	*Effects*
`pushdsilent`	If set, `pushd` and `popd` don't print the directory stack.
`recexact`	If set, completion is finished with an exact match, even if a longer one is available.
`recognize_only_executables`	If set, command listings display only files in the path that are executable.
`rmstar`	If set, the user is prompted before `rm *` is allowed to execute.
`rprompt`	The string to print on the right-hand side of the screen when the prompt is displayed on the left. This prompt accepts the same formatting controls as the prompt variable. In your author's opinion, this is a bizarre shell capability.
`savedires`	If set, the shell does a `dirs -S` before exiting.
`savehist`	If set, the shell does a `history -S` before exiting.
`sched`	The format in which the `sched` built-in prints scheduled events. The string format is the same as that for `prompt`.
`shell`	The file in which the executable shell resides.
`shlvl`	The nested depth of the current shell beneath the login shell for this session.
`status`	The status returned by the last command to exit.
`symlinks`	Can be set to several different values to control the resolution of symbolic links. See the `tcsh` man page for more details.
`tcsh`	The version number of the `tcsh` shell.
`term`	The terminal type currently being used to work in the shell.
`time`	If set to a number, execute the `time` built-in after any command that takes longer than that number of seconds. Can also control the format of the output of the time commands so executed. See the `tcsh` man page for further information.
`tperiod`	The period, in minutes, between executions of the `tcsh` special alias, `periodic`.
`tty`	The name of the tty for the current terminal, or `empty` if the current shell is not attached to a terminal.
`uid`	The user's real numeric user ID.

TABLE 18.2 continued

Shell Variable	*Effects*
`user`	The user's login name.
`verbose`	If set, causes the words of each command to be printed after any history substitution. Can be set on startup by executing the shell with the `-v` command.
`version`	The shell's version ID stamp, as well as a considerable amount of information regarding compile-time options that were specified when the shell was compiled. See the `tcsh` man page for more information on interpreting the output.
`visiblebell`	If set, flash the screen, instead of using an audible terminal bell.
`watch`	A list of user/terminal pairs to watch for logins and logouts.
`who`	The format string for `watch` messages. See the `tcsh` man page for specific format information.
`wordchars`	A list of nonalphanumeric characters to be considered part of a word by the command-line editor.

Shell and environment variables can also be addressed in a number of ways other than with the simple $<*variablename*> method used to return the contents of the variable. Table 18.3 lists available alternatives for accessing other information in the shell or other information regarding the variable, such as the number of words in the variable or whether the variable actually has a value.

TABLE 18.3 Alternative Variable Addressing Methods

Addressing a Variable As	*Returns*
`$name`	
`${name}`	The value of the variable.
	If the variable contains multiple words, each is separated by a blank. The braces insulate name from characters following it.
`$name[selector]`	
`${name[selector]}`	Treats name as an array of words, and returns only the selected element from the list of words.
`$0`	Substitutes the name of the file from which command input is being read (used in shell scripts).

TABLE 18.3 continued

Addressing a Variable As	*Returns*
`$number`	
`${number}`	Equivalent to `$argv[number]`. Remember that argv is the array of command-line arguments passed to the shell.
`$*`	Equivalent to `$argv`.
`$?name`	
`${?name}`	Substitutes `1`, if variable `name` is set, 0, if it is not.
`$?0`	Substitutes `1` if the name of the program running the shell is known. This is specifically applicable to shell scripts, and is always `0` for interactive shells.
`$#name`	
`${#name}`	Substitutes the number of words in `name`.
`$#`	Equivalent to `$#argv`.
`$%name`	
`${%name}`	Substitutes the number of characters in `name`.
`$?`	Equivalent to `$status`.
`$$`	Substitutes the process number of the parent shell.
`$!`	Substitutes the process number of the most recent background process started by the shell.
`$<`	Substitutes a line from `STDIN`. This can be used to read input from the keyboard into a shell script.

Variable Substitution Modifiers

Along with the capability to set variables to specific values, and to manipulate variable values by the use of external programs, the shell also contains some capability to modify variables internally as well. This capability is mainly targeted to modification of command, filename, and path-like contents in variables. For example, this allows you to parse the extension part of a filename off a file with a name like `myfile.jpg`—keeping either the extension, `jpg`, or the main name, `myfile`. These manipulations are effected by appending to the variable one or more sets of a colon followed by a modifier string. Table 18.4 shows the allowable substitution modifier strings.

TABLE 18.4 Shell and Environment Variable Substitution :<*modifier*> Options

Modifier String	*Effect*
h	Removes a trailing pathname component, leaving the head.
t	Removes all leading path components, leaving only the trailing file component.
r	Removes a filename extension `.xxx`, leaving the head portion of the filename before this.
e	Removes everything from a filename except for the extension.
u	Changes the case of the first lowercase letter to uppercase.
l	Changes the case of the first uppercase letter to lowercase.
s/l/r/	Substitutes `l` for `r`. `l` can be any simple string, as can `r`.
g	Applies the next modifier to each word, rather than just to the first.
a	Applies the next modifier as many times as possible to a single word. Beware of creating modification loops with this option.

As a simple example, if the variable `x` contains `/home/ray/testfile.jpg`, we can extract and act upon several different parts of this variable by using the modifiers shown in Table 18.4.

```
localhost ray 152> set x=/home/ray/testfile.jpg
localhost ray 153> echo $x

     /home/ray/testfile.jpg

localhost ray 154> echo $x:h

     /home/ray

localhost ray 155> echo $x:t

     testfile.jpg

localhost ray 156> echo $x:r

     /home/ray/testfile

localhost ray 157> echo $x:e

     jpg

localhost ray 158> echo $x:u

     /Home/ray/testfile.jpg
```

```
localhost ray 159> echo $x:s/test/special/

     /home/ray/specialfile.jpg
localhost ray 171> set y=( /home/ray/testfile.jpg /home/ray/filetest.jpg )
localhost ray 172> echo $y

     /home/ray/testfile.jpg /home/ray/filetest.jpg

localhost ray 173> echo $y:u

     /Home/ray/testfile.jpg /home/ray/filetest.jpg

localhost ray 174> echo $y:gu

     /Home/ray/testfile.jpg /Home/ray/filetest.jpg

localhost ray 175> echo $y:au

     /HOME/RAY/TESTFILE.JPG /home/ray/filetest.jpg
```

Note

The four most important things to remember for working with variables in the shell are the `set` command, the `@` command, the `setenv` command, and the `$` prefix for accessing variables. Nearly everything you will want to do with variables will involve permutations of these.

Command History Substitution

As briefly mentioned earlier, the `tcsh` shell, as well as some others, maintains a history of commands that you have executed at the command line. Although we've mentioned only selecting previous commands out of the history by use of the arrow keys up to this point, the shell actually provides a number of options for the use of previous commands from the history in more sophisticated ways. Primary among these is the ability to select among the previous commands, and substitute new information for previous information in the commands. The modification strings for variables detailed earlier can be applied to commands in the history, and some additional history-specific modifiers can be used as well. The basic form of history substitution is simply the exclamation point, which indicates that a history substitution is to take place at that point in the command line. The characters following the exclamation point specify which item from the history is to be used and, optionally, what modifications need to be made to it. Table 18.5 lists the history item specifiers that can follow the exclamation point history substitution indicator.

TABLE 18.5 History Substitution Options

Item Following ! *Character*	*Meaning to the History Mechanism*
n (*n* is a number)	Execute the item with that number out of the history list.
-*n* (*n* is a number preceded by a minus sign)	Execute the command *n* items before the current one.
# (the pound sign)	The current command. This allows recursion, so be careful! To indicate a modification of the current event, the # sign indicating the current command can be omitted if there is a substitution modifier used also.
!	The previous command (equivalent to -1).
s (*s* is a character)	Execute the most recent command whose first word begins with *s*.
?*s*? (*s* is a string)	The most recent event that contains the string *s*.

For example, a user's command history (listable by use of the `history` command) is shown in part here:

```
localhost ray 191> history | tail -5

        186  21:34   ls -l
        187  21:37   cp file1.ps file1.ps.bak
        188  21:37   cp /usr/test/storage/file1.ps ./
        189  21:37   lpr file1.ps
        190 21:38  history | tail -5
```

We could execute another `lpr file1.ps` simply by typing `!l` on a command line. Alternatively, `!?ora?` would execute the copy from `/usr/test/storage` by matching the string `ora` from `storage`. `!!` would re-execute the `history` command, and `!-4` would execute the copy to `file1.ps.bak` again, as would `!187` These are shown here:

```
localhost ray 192> !l

     lpr file1.ps

localhost ray 193> !?ora?

     cp /usr/test/storage/file1.ps ./

localhost ray 194> !!

     history | tail

localhost ray 195> !-4

     cp file1.ps file1.ps.bak

localhost ray 196> !187

     cp file1.ps file1.ps.bak
```

These commands can be combined with substitution modifiers for variables as detailed earlier to further reduce the amount of typing effort needed:

```
localhost ray 201> !?ora?:s/1/2/

    cp /usr/test/storage/file2.ps ./

localhost ray 202> !187:gs/1/2

    cp file2.ps file2.ps.bak

localhost ray 203> !187:r.newbak

    cp file1.ps file1.ps.bak.newbak
```

Table 18.6 shows some `history`-specific `:<modifier>` strings that can be applied to history substitutions.

TABLE 18.6 History-Specific `:<modifier>` Options

Modifier String	*Action*
`&`	Repeat the previous substitution in this position.
`p`	Print out a history substitution with expanded substitutions, rather than execute the command.
`q`	Quote the value after this modification, preventing further modifications.
`0`	The leftmost argument of the command (typically, the command itself).
n	The *n*th argument of the command.
`^`	The first argument, equivalent to `1`. The colon can be omitted from before this modifier.
`$`	The last argument. The colon can be omitted from before this modifier.
`%`	The word matched by an `?s?` search. The colon can be omitted from before this modifier.
x`-`*y*	A range of arguments from the *x*th to the *y*th.
`-`*y*	Equivalent to `0-`*y*. The colon can be omitted from before this modifier.
`*`	Equivalent to `^-$`, but returns nothing if the command is the only argument. The colon can be omitted from before this modifier.
`x*`	Equivalent to `x-$`.
`x-`	Equivalent to `x*`, but omits the last word `$`.

Note

These tables and examples cover only the most commonly used history and variable modification options. The `tcsh` man page alone would occupy almost 100 pages of this book, and it is tersely written, to say the least. Entire books have been written on using shells effectively, and if you're interested in making the absolute best use of the shell, we really recommend that you pick up one or three. Don't let the volume of options available overwhelm you, though. Most people who use Unix don't make use of even 10% of the options shown in the abbreviated discussion here, and are perfectly happy with their productivity at that level. Be aware that these options exist; they can make your life much easier if you find that you need them, but don't feel obliged to try to actually learn them until you do find a need.

Aliases

The `alias` command is a simple tool that can help you customize your environment. It is the textual equivalent of the graphical Mac OS icon aliases (or Windows shortcuts) that you're probably already familiar with. It lets you specify a new name by which you can refer to an existing command. If you don't like typing `history` to list your command history, you can use the `alias` command to make typing `h` equivalent to typing `history`. We could have introduced this command much earlier in the discussion, but the information you have just learned about `history` and variable substitution makes the `alias` command much more powerful. The `alias` command has an almost trivial syntax: `alias <new-name> <definition>`. It accepts no command-line options, and has no arguments or flags to control it. To alias `h`, so that it calls `history` as described earlier, is simply `alias h history`.

The real power of the `alias` command, however, comes from the ability to use history substitutions in the `<definition>` part of the `alias`. For example, there are a number of machines in another domain that I access on a regular basis. It's inconvenient to have to type `slogin oak.cis.ohio-state.edu`, and `slogin shoe.cis.ohio-state.edu`, and so on whenever I need to access one of these machines. Using the trivial application of `alias`, I could change `slogin` so that I could type something shorter, such as `scis`. This would still leave me typing `scis oak.cis.ohio-state.edu`, and so on. Using the history substitution capability, however, this can be made much more useful. In this case, I can use the `*` modifier to the history, executed against the current command in the history (`#`), to pass the arguments given to my alias to another command of my choice. Specifically, what I've done is `alias scis 'slogin \!#:*.cis.ohio-state.edu'`. The backslash before the history expansion prevents it from being expanded immediately at the prompt when I entered the `alias` command. Now, all I have to do is type `scis oak`, and the `alias` command expands the command to `slogin !#:*.cis.ohio-state.edu`. The history substitution then replaces the `!#:*` with the argument given to the command, which in this case is `oak`. The final command executed is `slogin oak.cis.ohio-state.edu`.

Note

Note that there are several comments in the tables on history substitution and modifiers that relate to the `!#:*` expression. Most notably, if a modifier is acting on the current history event, the # can be omitted and the : can be omitted before *. This history substitution specifier therefore abbreviates to `!*`, and the alias could therefore be written `alias scis 'slogin \!*.cis.ohio-state.edu'`.

Also note that the `!*` substitution specifier substitutes the entire remainder of the command line from the current command. This is fine as long as I type `scis oak`, but if I type `scis oak apple pear`, the expansion is probably not going to be what I want. I could limit it to the first argument to the command with the ^ modifier, or the last argument with the $ modifier, instead of the * all arguments modifier I have used. It's a little bit sloppy, but I normally find it sufficient to just use the all modifier, and to remember to issue commands within the restrictions that doing so imposes. For me, this is easier than remembering to use the proper modifier, but you're welcome to use whatever you find easiest.

This might seem complicated, but a simple demonstration should suffice to make it clearer.

```
localhost ray 156> h

     h: Command not found.
localhost ray 157> alias h history
localhost ray 158> h | tail -3

        156  23:56   h
        157  23:56   alias h history
        158  23:56  h | tail -5
localhost ray 159> scis

     OK? sccs oak? no
     scis: Command not found.
localhost ray 160> alias scis 'slogin \!#:*.cis.ohio-state.edu'
localhost ray 161> scis oak

     ray@oak.cis.ohio-state.edu's password:
```

To remove an alias, simply use the `unalias` command on the *<newname>* that you've created for your command.

Tip

Several aliases that we suggest you configure in your environment are listed in Appendix B, which is available from this book's Web site. Some of these will reduce the amount of typing you have to do, some are simply conveniences we've grown to like over the years, and a few are recommended as safety precautions to help you avoid breaking things with typos.

Automating Tasks with Shell Scripts

With as many times as we've mentioned how powerful shell scripting can be and how much time and effort it can save you, you might be expecting that writing shell scripts is going to require dealing with some additional level of complexity on top of what you've already learned. Shell scripts are simple programs that you write in the language of the shell, and if you've made it this far in the book, you've been learning and working in the language of the shell for a few chapters now. If you consider this fact, and the notion that Unix, by design, attempts to abstract the notion of input and output so that everything looks the same to the OS, you might have a good guess at what we'll say next: That's right—you *already know* how to write shell scripts. There are a few more shell techniques that you can learn to enhance your ability to program the shell, but Unix itself doesn't care whether it's you typing at a command prompt or commands being read out of a file on disk. Everything you've typed so far in working with the shell could have been put in a file, and the computer could have typed it to itself—voila, a shell script.

At its most trivial, a shell script can be exactly what you type at a prompt to accomplish some set of tasks. If you find that you have a need to repeatedly execute the same commands over and over, you can type them once into a file, make that file executable, and forever after execute them all just by typing the name of the file.

It really is as simple as it sounds, but just in case it's not quite clear yet, an example should help. Consider the following situation: Let's say that every day when you log in to your computer, you like to check the time (with `date`), check to see who's online (using the `who` command), check to see how much space is left on the drive with your home directory (with `df`), and finally check who's most recently sent you mail (with `from`).

You could type in each of these things to a command prompt when you log in to your machine, or you could put them in a file, make it executable, and let the file "type" them for you.

```
soyokaze ray 226> date

     Mon Jun 18 23:35:55 EDT 2001

soyokaze ray 227> who

     joray    ttyp0   Jun 14 18:22   (140.254.12.151)
     ray      ttyp1   Jun 18 21:49   (24.95.74.211)
     ray      ttyp2   Jun 15 10:00   (rodan.chi.ohio-s)
     radman   ttyp3   Jun 18 23:33   (ac9d3e22.ipt.aol)

soyokaze ray 228> df .

     Filesystem            kbytes    used    avail capacity  Mounted on
     /dev/sd2g             953619  846078    12180    99%    /priv

soyokaze ray 229> from | tail -10

     From vanbrink@home.ffni.com  Mon Jun 18 16:20:23 2001
     From billp@abraxis.com  Mon Jun 18 17:28:33 2001
     From douglas_mille70@hotmail.com  Mon Jun 18 18:34:28 2001
     From owner-c-r-ffl@serge.shelfspace.com  Mon Jun 18 19:23:42 2001
     From owner-c-r-ffl@serge.shelfspace.com  Mon Jun 18 20:42:53 2001
     From owner-c-r-ffl@serge.shelfspace.com  Mon Jun 18 21:24:00 2001
     From buckshot@wcoil.com  Mon Jun 18 22:02:15 2001
     From jray@poisontooth.com  Mon Jun 18 22:28:56 2001
     From jray@poisontooth.com  Mon Jun 18 23:15:28 2001
     From owner-c-r-ffl@serge.shelfspace.com Mon Jun 18 23:34:43 2001

soyokaze ray 230> cat > imhere
#!/bin/csh

date
who
df .
from | tail -10
soyokaze ray 231> chmod 755 imhere
soyokaze ray 232> imhere

     Mon Jun 18 23:36:51 EDT 2001
     joray    ttyp0   Jun 14 18:22   (140.254.12.151)
     ray      ttyp1   Jun 18 21:49   (24.95.74.211)
     ray      ttyp2   Jun 15 10:00   (rodan.chi.ohio-s)
     Filesystem            kbytes    used    avail capacity  Mounted on
     /dev/sd2g             953619  846078    12180    99%    /priv
     From billp@abraxis.com  Mon Jun 18 17:28:33 2001
     From douglas_mille70@hotmail.com  Mon Jun 18 18:34:28 2001
     From owner-c-r-ffl@serge.shelfspace.com  Mon Jun 18 19:23:42 2001
     From owner-c-r-ffl@serge.shelfspace.com  Mon Jun 18 20:42:53 2001
     From owner-c-r-ffl@serge.shelfspace.com  Mon Jun 18 21:24:00 2001
```

```
From buckshot@wcoil.com  Mon Jun 18 22:02:15 2001
From jray@poisontooth.com  Mon Jun 18 22:28:56 2001
From jray@poisontooth.com  Mon Jun 18 23:15:28 2001
From owner-c-r-ffl@serge.shelfspace.com  Mon Jun 18 23:34:43 2001
From owner-c-r-ffl@serge.shelfspace.com Mon Jun 18 23:36:48 2001
```

As you can see, executing the file `imhere`, containing my commands, produces essentially the same output, with much less typing. (The output has a few changes because one user has left the system, and new mail has arrived between the by-hand runs and the execution of the shell script.)

The only part of the `imhere` script that might be confusing is the first line, `#!/bin/csh`. The shell interprets the first line of a shell script in a special manner. If a pattern such as this is found `#!`*`<path to an executable file>`*, the executable file named in that line is used as the shell for executing the contents of the script.

Note

The C shell, `csh`, and the Bourne shell, `sh`, are probably the best shells for you to write shell scripts in. Some shells offer somewhat more power in their scripting ability, but `csh` and `sh` are the only shells that can be considered ubiquitous. This might not be a concern, if you never intend your scripts to run anywhere but on your own personal machine. But if you think you might ever use another machine, or are interested in distributing your scripts to other people, you can't rely on any specialty shells being available.

Tip

In many scripting languages—`tcsh`/`csh` shell scripting being no exception—anywhere that a # appears indicates that the rest of the line is a comment. A `#!` on the first line is a special comment to the system, indicating which program is the intended interpreter for the script contained in the file.

Single-Line Automation: Combining Commands on the Command Line

Before we go too far with the notion of storing collections of commands in files, however, let's look at what can be done at just the command-line level. You already know about using pipes and variables. These concepts can be combined to produce very powerful expressions directly at the command line, without any need to store the collection of commands in a file.

Consider for a moment the `netpbm` collection of graphics manipulation programs that was installed in Chapter 17, "Troubleshooting Software Installations, and Compiling and Debugging Manually." Included in the capabilities of the suite are a number of conversions among various file formats, as well as a range of manipulations of the image content itself. With Mac OS, if you want to convert a GIF file into a PICT file, and convert it to four-color grayscale along the way, you have a number of options. You could fire up PhotoShop or GraphicConverter, and perform the changes there, and save the file. Alternatively, you could program a conversion filter in DeBabelizer to perform this manipulation for you. With `netpbm`, you can perform the manipulation from the command line:

```
soyokaze ray 277> ppmtogif < john.ppm > john.gif
     ppmtogif: computing colormap...
     ppmtogif: 192 colors found
soyokaze ray 278> giftopnm < john.gif > john.pnm
soyokaze ray 279> ppmtopgm < john.pnm > john.pgm
soyokaze ray 280> ppmquant 4 < john.pgm > john.pgm2
     ppmquant: making histogram...
     ppmquant: 120 colors found
     ppmquant: choosing 4 colors...
     ppmquant: mapping image to new colors...
soyokaze ray 281> ppmtopict < john.pgm2 > john.pict
     ppmtopict: computing colormap...
     ppmtopict: 4 colors found
```

Figure 18.1 shows a comparison of the original image `john.gif`, and the four-color grayscale image, `john.pict`.

FIGURE 18.1
A comparison of an original file and the result of processing it through one of a number of different `netpbm` *filters.*

Note

The netpbm suite provides most of its manipulation facilities on an internal format, variably named .ppm, .pgm, or .pnm. It provides a number of filters that can read data into this format, a number of filters that can act upon and modify the contents of files in this format, and a number of filters that can output into other file formats. Together, these facilities allow a wide range of image formats to be read, manipulated, and written. Additionally, the file format is well documented and simple for a programmer to write code to parse. This makes it easy for a programmer to write her own filters to perform any manipulations that the provided software cannot. See the netpbm man pages, if you've installed this suite, for considerably more information on the use of netpbm.

From the brief discussion at the beginning of this section, you should already have an idea of how you could combine all that into a single file, if for some reason you wanted to perform that conversion to the john.gif file over and over and over.

This seems to be not very useful a thing to automate, and quite a bit of typing to boot (although, frankly, not nearly as much work as starting up Photoshop to do something this simple!). Let's see what we can do with pipes and shell variables to cut down on the amount of typing.

First, observe that all the programs are taking the input files on STDIN, and are producing output on STDOUT. Unix command-line programs are frequently like this, and it's a very good thing. Using the power of pipes to connect one program's STDOUT to another program's STDIN, we can shorten that collection of commands to a single command line:

```
soyokaze ray 287> giftopnm < john.gif | ppmtopgm | ppmquant 4 |
➥ ppmtopict > john.pict

    ppmquant: making histogram...
    ppmquant: 120 colors found
    ppmquant: choosing 4 colors...
    ppmquant: mapping image to new colors...
    ppmtopict: computing colormap...
    ppmtopict: 4 colors found
```

I'll let you verify that the output is graphically identical on a file of your own.

You might think that it's probably not very likely that you'll want to perform this single manipulation repeatedly to the same image. However, there are many times when you'd like to be able to perform a collection of manipulations like that on a number of different images. With what you know about shell variables, you might be able to come up with a way to abstract that command line so that it could be reused for any GIF file. You might try something like this:

```
soyokaze ray 288> set infile=john.gif
soyokaze ray 289> giftopnm < $infile | ppmtopgm | ppmquant 4 |
➥ ppmtopict > $infile:r.pict

    ppmquant: making histogram...
    ppmquant: 120 colors found
    ppmquant: choosing 4 colors...
    ppmquant: mapping image to new colors...
    ppmtopict: computing colormap...
    ppmtopict: 4 colors found
```

Note

Note how I use the `:r` modifier to the shell variable `$infile` to remove the `.gif` suffix, and replace it with my new `.pict` suffix.

Now, you could simply use new values for `$infile`, and you'd have a reusable command that could perform the same manipulation on any GIF image.

It's still too much work though, right? Well, remember aliases? We can further automate things by using an `alias` command to compact that large command-line expression into something more manageable.

```
soyokaze ray 290> alias greyconvert 'set infile=\!#:* ; giftopnm < $infile |
➥ ppmtopgm | ppmquant 4 | ppmtopict > $infile:r.pict '
soyokaze ray 291> greyconvert john.gif

    ppmquant: making histogram...
    ppmquant: 120 colors found
    ppmquant: choosing 4 colors...
    ppmquant: mapping image to new colors...
    ppmtopict: computing colormap...
    ppmtopict: 4 colors found
```

Note

Notice how I've used the history substitution `\!#:*` to get the arguments passed into the alias, and then put those arguments (although I only expect one, a filename) into `$infile`?

That command is getting pretty long, isn't it? The good news is that for almost any task in Unix, you can figure out how to build up to an expression like this, just as shown here. Start by figuring out how to do it one step at a time on the command line, and work your way up to an elegant solution that solves the problem for you with as little repetitive work as necessary.

After you've invented useful aliases such as this one for yourself, remember to store them in your `.cshrc` or `.tcshrc` file in your home directory, or in your `aliases.mine` file in `~/Library/init/tcsh/`, so that you can use them again, whenever you log in to your computer.

Multi-Line Automation: Programming at the Prompt

Creating customized commands that perform special functions like the `greyconvert` command built in the previous sections is useful, but it still doesn't address the need to automate tasks. For that, we need some sort of looping command, and the `tcsh` shell offers two: the `foreach` command and the `while` command. Both commands repeat a block of shell commands. The first executes it "for each" of its arguments, and the second executes it "while" some condition is true.

The `foreach` command and `while` command of the shell are unlike other shell commands that you've become familiar with in that they require additional information beyond the first command line. For example, the syntax for the `foreach` command is

```
foreach <variablename> ( <item list> )
  <first command to execute>
  <second command to execute>
  .
  .
  .
  <nth command to execute>
end
```

The `while` command, on the other hand, has the syntax

```
while ( <comparison> )
  <first command to execute>
  <second command to execute>
  .
  .
  .
  <nth command to execute>
end
```

In the `foreach` command, the *`<item list>`* can be a space-separated list of items, or a command that produces a space-separated (or return-separated) list of items, or a command-line wildcard that matches a list of files. As a demonstration, consider a situation in which we want to execute our previous `greyconvert` command on every GIF file in a directory containing many files. This can be accomplished in several ways by the use of the `foreach` command. The following example demonstrates the wildcard match to all the files of interest:

```
localhost amg 246% ls
     AMG_cal-cover.gif          AhMyGoddess-v05.gif        AhMyGoddess-v10-f1.gif
     AhMyGoddess-v01-f1.gif     AhMyGoddess-v06-f1.gif     AhMyGoddess-v10-i1.gif
     AhMyGoddess-v01.gif        AhMyGoddess-v06.gif        AhMyGoddess-v10-i2.gif
     AhMyGoddess-v02-f1.gif     AhMyGoddess-v07-f1.gif     AhMyGoddess-v10-i3.gif
     AhMyGoddess-v02.gif        AhMyGoddess-v07.gif        AhMyGoddess-v10.gif
     AhMyGoddess-v03-f1.gif     AhMyGoddess-v08-f1.gif     amg-nt0694_cover.gif
     AhMyGoddess-v03.gif        AhMyGoddess-v08.gif        amg-nt0694_i1.gif
     AhMyGoddess-v04-f1.gif     AhMyGoddess-v09-f1.gif     amg-nt0694_i2.gif
     AhMyGoddess-v04.gif        AhMyGoddess-v09.gif
     AhMyGoddess-v05-f1.gif  AhMyGoddess-v10-b.gif
localhost amg 247% foreach testfile ( *.gif )
foreach -> greyconvert $testfile
foreach -> end
     ppmquant: making histogram...
     ppmquant: 165 colors found
     ppmquant: choosing 4 colors...
     ppmquant: mapping image to new colors...
     ppmtopict: computing colormap...
     ppmtopict: 4 colors found
     ppmquant: making histogram...
     ppmquant: 159 colors found
     ppmquant: choosing 4 colors...
     ppmquant: mapping image to new colors...
     ppmtopict: computing colormap...
     ppmtopict: 4 colors found
     .
     .
     .
     ppmquant: making histogram...
     ppmquant: 163 colors found
     ppmquant: choosing 4 colors...
     ppmquant: mapping image to new colors...
     ppmtopict: computing colormap...
     ppmtopict: 4 colors found
localhost amg 248% ls
     AMG_cal-cover.gif          AhMyGoddess-v05-f1.pict    AhMyGoddess-v10-b.gif
     AMG_cal-cover.pict         AhMyGoddess-v05.gif        AhMyGoddess-v10-b.pict
     AhMyGoddess-v01-f1.gif     AhMyGoddess-v05.pict       AhMyGoddess-v10-f1.gif
     AhMyGoddess-v01-f1.pict    AhMyGoddess-v06-f1.gif     AhMyGoddess-v10-f1.pict
     AhMyGoddess-v01.gif        AhMyGoddess-v06-f1.pict    AhMyGoddess-v10-i1.gif
     AhMyGoddess-v01.pict       AhMyGoddess-v06.gif        AhMyGoddess-v10-i1.pict
     AhMyGoddess-v02-f1.gif     AhMyGoddess-v06.pict       AhMyGoddess-v10-i2.gif
```

```
AhMyGoddess-v02-f1.pict    AhMyGoddess-v07-f1.gif     AhMyGoddess-v10-i2.pict
AhMyGoddess-v02.gif        AhMyGoddess-v07-f1.pict    AhMyGoddess-v10-i3.gif
AhMyGoddess-v02.pict       AhMyGoddess-v07.gif        AhMyGoddess-v10-i3.pict
AhMyGoddess-v03-f1.gif     AhMyGoddess-v07.pict       AhMyGoddess-v10.gif
AhMyGoddess-v03-f1.pict    AhMyGoddess-v08-f1.gif     AhMyGoddess-v10.pict
AhMyGoddess-v03.gif        AhMyGoddess-v08-f1.pict    amg-nt0694_cover.gif
AhMyGoddess-v03.pict       AhMyGoddess-v08.gif        amg-nt0694_cover.pict
AhMyGoddess-v04-f1.gif     AhMyGoddess-v08.pict       amg-nt0694_i1.gif
AhMyGoddess-v04-f1.pict    AhMyGoddess-v09-f1.gif     amg-nt0694_i1.pict
AhMyGoddess-v04.gif        AhMyGoddess-v09-f1.pict    amg-nt0694_i2.gif
AhMyGoddess-v04.pict       AhMyGoddess-v09.gif        amg-nt0694_i2.pict
AhMyGoddess-v05-f1.gif     AhMyGoddess-v09.pict
```

In this example, the `foreach testfile ( *.gif )` line could have been replaced, with the following variants, with identical results:

```
foreach testfile ( `ls *.gif` )
```

```
foreach testfile ( AMG_cal-cover.gif AhMyGoddess-v01-f1.gif ... amg-
nt0694_i2.gif )
```

Note

The second variant should be understood to contain a list of *all* GIF files in the directory, not just the three shown. The presence and direction of the single backquotes in the first line are also critical. Single backquotes around a command on the command line, if you remember, cause that command to be executed and its results substituted into the current command line in the place of the quoted command.

The `while` command works similarly, executing its code block while some *`<condition>`* holds:

```
localhost ray 225> set x = 10
localhost ray 226> while ( $x > 0 )
while -> echo $x
while -> @ x = ( $x - 1 )
while -> end
    10
    9
    8
    7
    6
```

```
    5
    4
    3
    2
    1
localhost ray 227> echo $x

    0
```

This example obviously doesn't have much day-to-day applicability. Most `while` expressions that are actually useful do things like watch for particular events to occur, such as the existence of temporary files, or disk space usage of more than or less than some value. None of these is particularly easy to demonstrate in a text-only format such as a book, but we expect that you'll get the idea fairly quickly. Table 18.7 shows the conditional operators that can be used to construct the *`<condition>`* part of `while` loops and `if` conditional statements.

TABLE 18.7 Logical, Arithmetical, and Comparison Operators Comparison Operators

Operator or Symbol	*Function*
`||`	Boolean `OR` arguments.
`&&`	Boolean `AND` arguments.
`|`	Bitwise Boolean `OR`.
`^`	Bitwise Exclusive `OR`.
`&`	Bitwise Boolean `AND`.
`==`	Equality comparison of arguments (`$x == $y` is true if the value in `$x` equals the value in `$y`).
	Compares arguments as strings.
`!=`	Negated equality comparison of arguments (`$x != $y` is true if the value in `$x` is not equal to the value in `$y`).
	Compares arguments as strings.
`=~`	Pattern-matching equality comparison (matches shell wildcards).
	Compares arguments as strings.
`!~`	Pattern-matching negated equality comparison.
	Compares arguments as strings.
`<=`	Less than or equal to.
`>=`	Greater than or equal to.
`<`	Less than.

TABLE 18.7 continued

Operator or Symbol	*Function*
`>`	Greater than.

`<<`	Bitwise shift left. To avoid the shell interpreting this as redirection, it must be in a parenthesized subexpression.
	For example,
	`set y = 32;`
	`@ x = ( $y << 2 )`

`>>`	Bitwise shift right. See preceding comment.
`+`	Add arguments.
`-`	Subtract arguments.
`*`	Multiply arguments.
`/`	Divide arguments.
`%`	Modulus operator (divide and report remainder).
`!`	Negate argument.
`~`	Ones complement of argument.
`(`	Open parenthesized subexpression for higher-order evaluation.
`)`	Close parenthesized subexpression for higher-order evaluation.

Another common use for the `while` command is to create infinite loops in the shell. This is a way to do things such as cause a shell command to execute over and over, potentially creating something like a "drop directory" that automatically processes files that are copied to it. For example, if we want to create a directory into which we could copy GIF files, and any files copied into it would have the `greyconvert` process run on it automatically, and then the GIF files would be deleted, we might try something like the following:

```
localhost Pictures 243> while (1)
while -> foreach testfile (*.gif)
while -> greyconvert $testfile
while -> rm $testfile
while -> end
while -> sleep 60
while -> end
```

Note

The first four lines, with the `while->` prompt, are actually part of the `foreach` command, but it doesn't display its prompt while the `while->` prompt is active.

This `while` command attempts to loop perpetually (the value of `1` is `true` for the purposes of a comparison expression), and to internally execute our previous `foreach` loop to convert any files that match the `*.gif` pattern in the current directory. An `rm` command has been added to the `foreach` loop to remove the GIF file after it has been converted. The `sleep 60` command after the `foreach` command's `end` causes the `while` loop to pause for `60` seconds before going on to its `end` statement and re-looping to the top of the `while`.

Unfortunately, this does not quite work properly, as when there are no files that match `*.gif`, the `foreach` line fails without creating its loop, and the `end` on line 4 is mistaken as intended to `end` the `while` loop.

Thankfully, you can work around this problem by applying the final topic in our discussion of shell scripts.

Storing Your Automation in Files: Proper Scripts

With all the power available to you directly at the command line, the move to putting shell scripts in files should seem almost anticlimactic in its lack of complexity. As mentioned at the beginning of this chapter, anything that you can type on the command line, you can put in a file, and the system will quite happily execute it for you, if you make the file executable. It really is that simple. There'd be little more to say, except that putting your script in a file allows you to conveniently separate parts of the execution into separate shells, preventing conflicts such as those just demonstrated earlier with the `while` and `foreach` loops.

Any script that is put in a file and directly executed (rather than source, in your current shell) creates its own shell in which to execute. To use this to make the previous example function properly, we can put the `foreach` section of the command into its own file:

```
localhost Pictures 244>cat > greyconv.csh

    #!/bin/csh
    foreach testfile (*.gif)
    greyconvert $testfile
    rm $testfile
    end
```

```
localhost Pictures 245> chmod 755 greyconv.csh
localhost Pictures 246> ls -l greyconv.csh

     -rwxr-xr-x  1 ray  staff  75 Jun 23 01:58 greyconv.csh

localhost Pictures 247> cat greyconv.csh

     #!/bin/csh
     foreach testfile (*.gif)
     greyconvert $testfile
     rm $testfile
     end
```

Then our perpetual `while` command can be run as

```
localhost Pictures 248> while (1)

     while -> ./greyconv.csh
     while -> sleep 60
     while -> end
```

Note

Remember to `chmod` the script file so that it's executable. The shell won't let you run the script if it's not set to be executable.

This command will loop perpetually in the current directory, executing the `greyconv.csh` shell script every 60 seconds. Any file with a `.gif` extension that is placed in the directory will be passed through the `greyconvert` alias that we created earlier, and then the original file will be deleted. This will run perpetually in the directory, allowing any file dropped in to be converted (within 60 seconds) automatically. Because the end of the `foreach` is in a completely separate shell, it can't accidentally end the `while`, and everything will work as expected. Of course, if there were a reason to do this on a regular basis, you could put that `while` loop into its own shell script file. It could be stored and executed as a single command from the command line just like any other command.

Note

Particularly astute readers will observe that the script does not attempt to make sure that the whole GIF file has been copied into the directory before it executes upon it. You might also expect that the behavior of the script could be rather unpredictable if the `greyconv.csh` script takes longer than a minute to execute. Shell scripts are generally an exercise in successive refinement to eliminate potential problems such as these, and these examples should be considered nothing more than the first step to a final application. You can get quite a bit of functionality out of simple scripts such as this. But if you're inclined to tackle the more complicated "correct" solutions, we can't recommend reading the man pages and checking out some books specifically on shell scripting strongly enough.

Two final things to note because we've now introduced independent shells invoked as the result of placing scripts in files: the `$argv[1]...$argv[n]` and corresponding `$1...$n` command-line argument variables. (Refer to the table of shell variables and the table of alternative variable addressing methods for a refresher on these.) This also allows us to introduce the `if ( <comparison> )` shell command, allowing conditional execution of code blocks.

If we'd like to make the `greyconv.csh` script somewhat more general, we can make use of the ability to pass arguments into the script. For example, it would be nice to be able to use `greyconv.csh` on the GIF files in a directory, without actually having to be in the directory when we run the `while` loop. This is easily accomplished by using the shell argument variables. The modified version of `greyconv.csh` is as follows:

```
#!/bin/csh

if ( $?1 == 1 ) then
cd $1
endif

foreach testfile (*.gif)
greyconvert $testfile
rm $testfile
end
```

This version of `greyconv.csh` demonstrates both an `if` conditional expression, and the use of a command-line argument. The `if` statement checks whether the variable `$1` is set (using the `$?<variablename>` alternative variable addressing to check for existence). If it is set, the script assumes that the value in `$1` is the name of a directory, and it `cd`s into that directory before executing the `foreach` loop to convert and delete the GIF files. `greyconv.csh` can now be called with a directory, to operate in that directory, or without a directory specified, to operate in the current directory.

We hope that gives you a few ideas for how powerful shell scripts can be, and how you can use them to make your use of OS X much more productive. We've only just scratched the surface in this chapter, and have trivialized some explanations to their simplest case to avoid a chapter that takes half the book. What's here can get you quite a way into shell scripting, and many Unix users with years of experience don't use more than a fraction of what's covered here. Still, if you're looking for more power and more capabilities, don't hesitate to go to the man pages and shell programming–specific reference books.

Making Shell Scripts Start at Login or System Startup

Now that you know how to write shell scripts and run them as commands, making them start when you log in to your account, or making them start when the system starts, is straightforward.

You're already familiar with the Login preferences settings, and your ability to customize what programs start when you log in from it. An executable shell script is just another program as far as Unix is concerned, so you can configure scripts to start on login from there. If you're going to be working from the command line with any frequency, you might want to consider adding a single shell script to your login preferences, and using that script to execute other scripts as necessary.

To add a shell script as an item that starts at system startup is also quite simple. Create a subdirectory for the script you want to run in the `/System/Library/StartupItems/` folder, and place the script or a link to the script in the directory, giving it the same name as the directory. When the system starts, the script will execute. Remember that it's not going to have a terminal attached, so if it does things such as echo data, the data will have nowhere to appear. In Chapter 20, "Command-Line Configuration and Administration," we'll cover the contents of the `plist` (properties list) file that you can add to the directory with your script to customize some of its behavior.

Summary

This chapter rounded out the remainder of the general topics you need to know to productively use the Unix command-line shell. We described environment variables and shell variables, both those that affect the behavior of the shell directly and those that can be used in scripts. The chapter also expanded on the use of `STDIN` and `STDOUT`, as well as pipes on the command line. Finally, the use of loops, conditional expressions, and the storage of your command-line expressions in executable files gives you the ability to create powerful and completely customized solutions to problems that you encounter.

Server/Network Administration

PART VI

IN THIS PART

CHAPTER 19

X Window System Applications

In this chapter, we introduce the X Window System, Unix's favored graphical user interface (GUI). If we haven't convinced you that this Unix stuff is too confusing, you shouldn't be too bothered by the fact that the X Window System is rather different from the Mac OS GUI and the OS X Aqua GUI, and that frequently it exists best as a completely separate graphical interface.

> **Note**
>
> We have a few too many Xs to go around. The X Window System, though, has had its X for two decades longer than Mac OS X, so we're going to have to get used to the nomenclature. The X Window System is usually referred to as X#, where # is the major revision number. Alternatively, you may see X#Rn, where # is the major revision, and n is the minor revision. As of this writing, X11R6 is the current version, but it is generally referred to as X11, or more simply, just X.

Both a bit of a boon and bane to the new Mac OS X user, the X Window System will be an important, if somewhat confusing, feature of OS X for some time to come. As the de facto standard for Unix GUI applications, you will find a considerable amount of software that has been written to use the X Window System. Much of this software probably will be slow in being ported to the OS X interface, and some might not be ported at all. Because of this, it is important that you install the software to allow you to use the X Window System, and get to know a little about the way that the interface works. For this you have a choice, at the time of this writing, between two different products: the XFree86 open source X11R6 distribution known as XonX, and the commercial X11R6 distribution available from Tenon systems, XTools. This chapter will cover the differences and benefits of each, as well as provide a basic introduction of how the X Window System interacts with the OS X interface.

Introduction to the X Window System

In attempting to explain the X Window System, in many ways it will be easier to explain how it is different from the interface that you're accustomed to than it will be to explain how it is similar. Certainly, whether you're from a Mac or a PC background, you're used to a graphical user interface, and both the X Window System and the interface to which you are accustomed display windows with program content and information in them. But beyond this, the X Window System is fundamentally a very different interface than the GUI present on either of the popular desktop operating systems.

At the most obvious, the X Window System is not a built-in part of the operating system. Whereas the Mac OS and Windows graphical user interfaces are intimately tied to the underlying OS, the X Window System is a completely separate system, with no real attachment to the operating system underneath it. This separation makes for inefficiencies in the way the window system interacts with the OS, and is the cause of certain performance issues that will be of some annoyance. As will be shown, however, it also provides a level of flexibility that cannot be readily accomplished with integrated systems.

Also different is the fact that the X Window System functions as a client/server system. Unlike OSes with integrated GUI functionality, programs that make use of the X Window System interface functionality do not actually display GUI elements. Instead they contact a completely separate program, the X server, and request that the server perform whatever display functions they require. This might seem like a bizarre and inefficient fashion of handling GUI element display, but it leads to the abstraction that is another major difference, and one of the sources of the extreme flexibility of the system.

The client/server model utilized for X Window System communication is a network-capable system. Messages requesting display functionality can be passed from client to server over a network connection. In fact, even connections from a client running on the same machine as the server are processed as though the client were speaking to the server over the network. A benefit of this model that is not immediately obvious is that to a user sitting in front of a machine running the X Window System, it is completely transparent whether the programs being displayed on the machine are actually running on that machine or on some other machine. Other than possible delays due to delays in the network, the X Window System server responds identically to programs running on other machines as it does to programs running on its own. Still not sure what this means to you? It means that you can display programs running on any machine anywhere (well, any machine running a Unix-like OS), on any other machine running an X Window System server. This doesn't require some high-priced and proprietary commercial application or an experimental program and protocol; it uses well-established and open source software that has been being developed by the online community for decades.

An additional difference between personal computer windowing systems and the X Window System is that the interface's look and feel is controlled by yet another separate program, rather than by the X Window System server or the OS itself. In the X Window System model, the X server is responsible for handling client display requests for displaying windows. Unless a client specifically draws things like title bars for itself, X won't give them to it. The convention with the X Window System is that a separate program is run to create title bars and to manage user interactions such as moving windows around, iconizing and minimizing windows, and providing application-dock or other similar functionality.

In this chapter, we will cover both the open source XFree86 distribution of X11 and the Tenon Systems XTools distribution. The XFree86 software currently provides a completely separate interface to the Unix side of OS X, and promises to eventually integrate X11 and the OS X–native Aqua interface. Tenon's commercial XTools already provides a surprisingly good integration between X11 windows and the Aqua interface.

Client/Server System

As mentioned briefly earlier, the heart of the X Window System is a server that provides display functionality to client applications. In a slight twist on the terminology that you are used to, the X Window System server is the application that runs on your local machine, and clients are the programs that run anywhere, including on remote machines. When you consider the functionality, this makes sense because a server provides a service: displaying data locally to you. The clients request the service, which is the displaying of data regardless of where the clients are. Figure 19.1 shows a typical X11 session with several programs displaying themselves on the X server. Among them are a number of `xterms`—applications that are similar to Terminal.app in functionality—as well as a text editor, an application dock, a game, and a mail application. The icons that appear as small computer terminals in the upper left are iconized applications; where the Mac OS uses windowshade title bars, the X Window System collapses applications into representative icons.

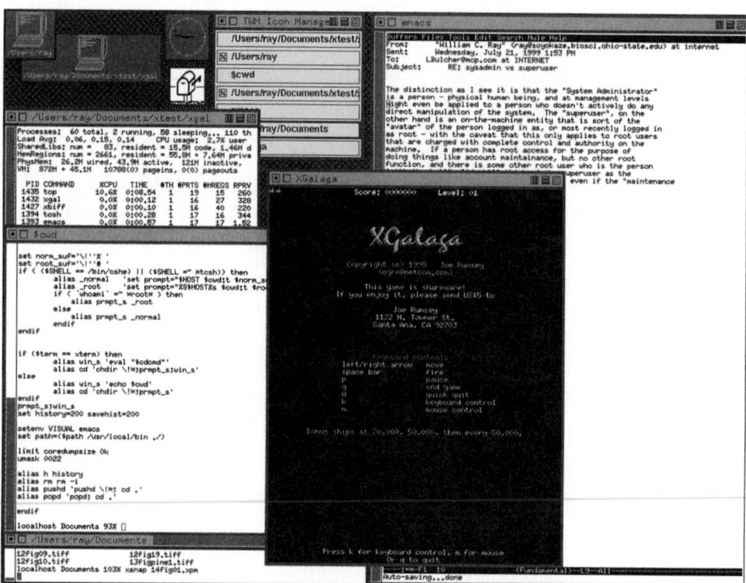

FIGURE 19.1
A typical X11 session with several programs running. The X Window System on a 1024×768 screen is a bit cramped, but still useable.

Remote Application Display

Conveniently, this client/server model, like much of the software designed for Unix, is extremely abstract. Just as the input/output model abstracts the notion of where data comes from and goes to (to the point that it doesn't matter whether the data source is a program, user, or file), the X Window System client/server model doesn't care how the client and server are connected. This allows clients to connect to the server from any location, allowing you to run software on remote machines and interact with its interface on your local machine.

In Figure 19.2, you again see the X Window System running on a machine. Other than the difference in a few running applications, there is little to distinguish it from Figure 19.1. This is exactly the point. In this screenshot, the Web browser, two of the terminal windows (find the ones with host `soyokaze` in the command prompt), and the game are being displayed from a machine running on the other side of the city from the actual screen. It would not matter—outside possible slowdowns associated with network delays—whether the applications were running across the city or across the planet.

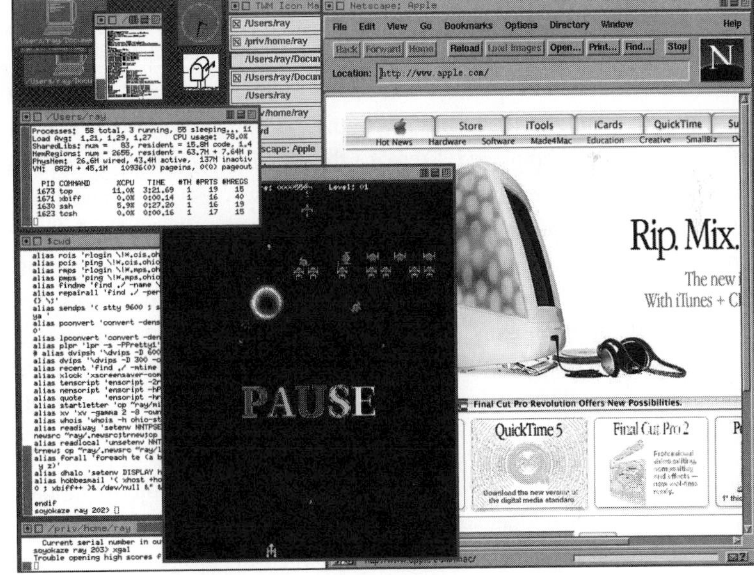

FIGURE 19.2
Another typical X11 session with several programs running. In this image, several of the windows actually belong to applications running on a remote machine.

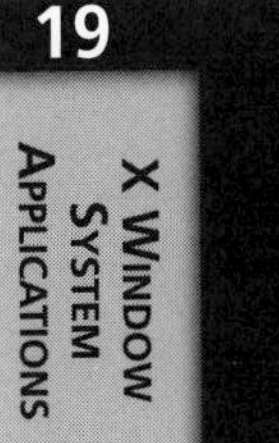

The impact of this might not be obvious to you yet, but consider that with this capability, the following become possible:

- Have a document at home that you were supposed to edit and e-mail to someone, but you forgot? Just connect to your home machine and fire up your editor with it displayed back to your local machine. Edit your document and send it on its way.
- Need to change something in a file and you don't have the software on the machine you're sitting at? No problem, just connect to your normal machine over the network, and use the software on it.
- Stuck behind a firewall and can't get to eBay to submit a last-minute bid? Don't tell your boss about this, but using what you know about tunneling connections with `slogin`, and a Web browser running on your home machine, you've got a recipe to browse from home, no matter where you're currently sitting.

Rooted Versus Nonrooted Displays

A quirk forced upon the X Window System by attempts to get it to coexist with GUIs such as Aqua is the idea of rooted versus nonrooted displays. The X Window System has existed for years under the same impression that Mac OS has—that it is "the" windowing system running on any particular machine. As such, it includes the idea of a root window, much like the Mac OS desktop. The root window is assumed to be a full-screen window that exists behind all other windows in the system, and into which certain restricted types of information can be placed. To make the X Window System coexist with another windowing system that also wants to have a single whole-screen background window, only a few possible compromises can be made. To coexist, either one of the systems has to give up its assumption of supremacy; one or the other could run entirely inside a window in the one that reigns supreme; or both could operate as usual, but display only one at a time, with the user toggling between them. If you've used `Timbuktu` or `VNC` before, you've used a system in which one display runs entirely inside a window on the other. There have been X11 implementations for Mac OS that have provided this option for X as well.

Displaying an entire windowing system rooted inside a window in another windowing system is a less than ideal solution. Outside the problem of not really integrating the functionality, and leaving the user with a poor workflow between applications in each of the environments, handling things like mouse events destined for the "in window" system (as opposed to the window containing the system) is difficult. The current XFree86 implementation provides the X Window System functionality as an entirely separate windowing system into which you can toggle. The screenshot in Figure 19.1 shows an X Window System session, and Figure 19.3 shows an Aqua session—these two are actually running on the same machine, at the same time. The X Window System environment can be toggled to by clicking the X icon in the Aqua dock, and the Aqua environment can be toggled to by pressing Command+Option+A. Even when one of the environments isn't being displayed, the applications in it keep on running. Although it's not very convenient to inter-operate between applications running in each, it's not a bad way to work, especially if you're mostly using Unix-side applications and not Aqua-native applications. XFree86's XonX project promises to eventually integrate X11 applications into the Aqua environment. As of this writing, this is not a viable option for any but the most courageous because it requires considerable crossbreeding of Mac OS X, the Darwin project, and additional minimally tested code.

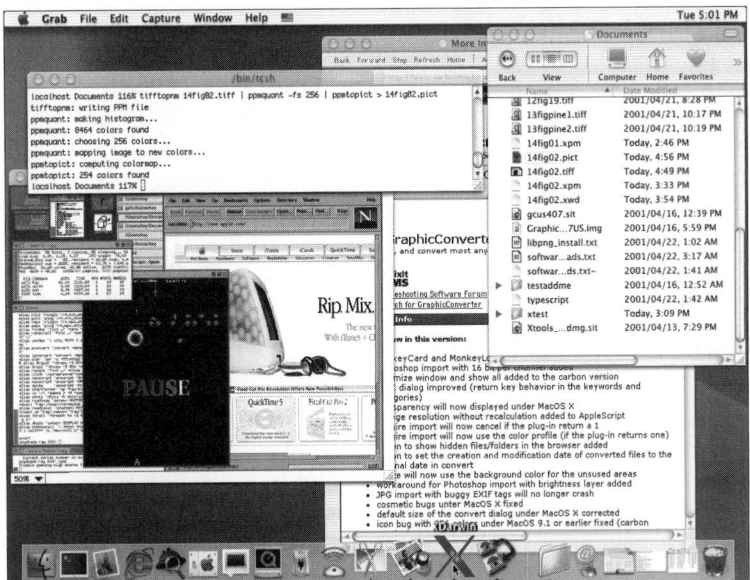

FIGURE 19.3

This Aqua session is running concurrently with the X11 session shown in Figure 19.1. The window containing what looks like an X11 session is Picture Preview showing the image for Figure 19.2.

Tenon's commercial XTools, on the other hand, is a surprisingly successful implementation of a nonrooted, or rootless X11 environment. To produce such an environment, the X Window System model must be gutted of its notion of having a root window, and it is not entirely clear how doing so might affect all possible X11 applications. However, it is clear that it works surprisingly well for at least most applications at this point. In addition, it manages to wrap the X Window System applications with an Aqua interface manager, rather than a native X11 interface manager. Figure 19.4 shows an Aqua session with X11 applications running side by side with native Aqua applications. In fact, the Web browser in Figure 19.2 is running on a remote machine, and is displaying happily integrated with Aqua applications on the local machine.

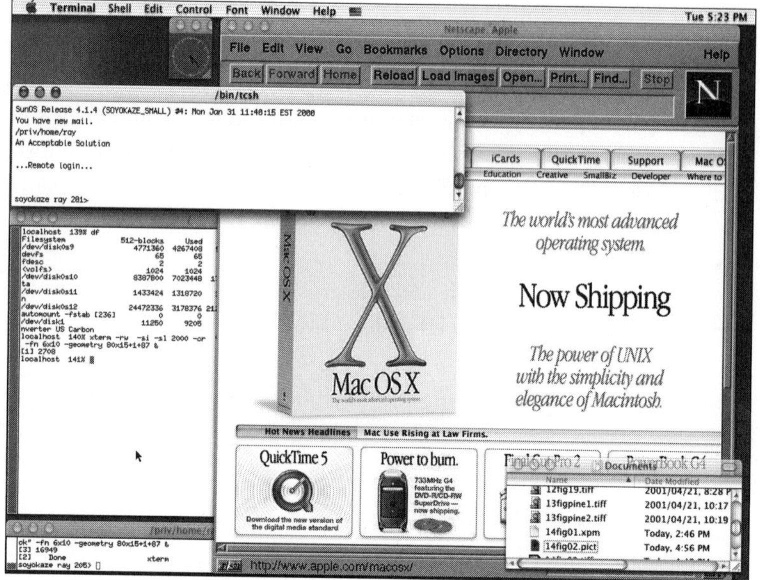

FIGURE 19.4
Tenon's XTools, shown displaying X11 applications side by side with Aqua applications.

Installing the XFree86 OS X Distribution

The XFree86 distribution changes on a regular basis, and the installation process for it is modified with almost the same regularity. Apple has begun providing an easy-installing distribution of X11 from its OS X software Web site, so if you relish simplicity, you might want to work with Apple's distribution. If you're itching for the most recent features available, you'll wnat to work with the distribution straight from XFree86. For the most current installation method, we suggest that you visit the SourceForge XonX site (go to `http://www.sourceforge.com/` and search for `xonx`), read the documentation, and follow what SourceForge has to say. Alternatively, as of the most recent XonX project release, the XFree86 distribution itself has had OS X/Darwin support rolled into it (but the XonX project might have more recent or experimental code available).

As of this writing, the XFree86 installation process involves downloading a number of files and running an installation script. Because we can't be sure that this process will be identical by the time you're reading this, we'll cover both the idealized and current installation protocols here.

Idealized XFree86 Installation

The idealized XFree86 X Window System installation involves a number of steps, all fairly simple to accomplish.

1. First, go to `http://www.xfree86.org/`.
2. Next, read the current release notes. Look for a paragraph describing online documentation and then follow the online documentation link and look for information on OS X/Darwin.
3. Go to the Getting Started/Installation section of the documentation, and follow the directions for either installing by downloading and compiling the code, or download the precompiled binaries.
4. Downloading the precompiled binaries involves following a link to an FTP server, and downloading files as instructed by the documentation.
5. Execute the installation script as root.

After these are accomplished, XFree86 will be ready to run, and you will be able to run X11 applications on an X Window System server running in parallel with Aqua. The current distribution claims that a rootless version of the server will be available soon. This will allow X11 applications to run intermingled with Aqua applications, as allowed by XTools, but this code is available only for the more adventurous who want to compile X11 for themselves.

Practical XFree86 Installation as of July, 2001

In practice, following the preceding instructions *almost* works for installing XFree86. There is currently an error in the xfree86.org Web site that prevents you from accessing the files by following the site's links. Also, there are currently errors in the installation instructions that indicate the necessity of a nonexistent Xvar.tgz file and omit the necessity of a Xquartz.tgz file.

The installation process that worked for us was as follows:

```
lynx -source ftp://ftp.xfree86.org/pub/XFree86/4.1.0/binaries/
Darwin-ppc/Xinstall.sh > Xinstall.sh

lynx -source ftp://ftp.xfree86.org/pub/XFree86/4.1.0/binaries/
Darwin-ppc/extract > extract

lynx -source ftp://ftp.xfree86.org/pub/XFree86/4.1.0/binaries/
Darwin-ppc/Xbin.tgz > Xbin.tgz

lynx -source ftp://ftp.xfree86.org/pub/XFree86/4.1.0/binaries/
Darwin-ppc/Xlib.tgz > Xlib.tgz

lynx -source ftp://ftp.xfree86.org/pub/XFree86/4.1.0/binaries/
Darwin-ppc/Xman.tgz > Xman.tgz

lynx -source ftp://ftp.xfree86.org/pub/XFree86/4.1.0/binaries/
Darwin-ppc/Xdoc.tgz > Xdoc.tgz

lynx -source ftp://ftp.xfree86.org/pub/XFree86/4.1.0/binaries/
Darwin-ppc/Xfnts.tgz > Xfnts.tgz
```

```
lynx -source ftp://ftp.xfree86.org/pub/XFree86/4.1.0/binaries/
Darwin-ppc/Xfenc.tgz > Xfenc.tgz

lynx -source ftp://ftp.xfree86.org/pub/XFree86/4.1.0/binaries/
Darwin-ppc/Xetc.tgz > Xetc.tgz

lynx -source ftp://ftp.xfree86.org/pub/XFree86/4.1.0/binaries/
Darwin-ppc/Xquartz.tgz > Xquartz.tgz

lynx -source ftp://ftp.xfree86.org/pub/XFree86/4.1.0/binaries/
Darwin-ppc/Xxserv.tgz > Xxserv.tgz

lynx -source ftp://ftp.xfree86.org/pub/XFree86/4.1.0/binaries/
Darwin-ppc/Xfsrv.tgz > Xfsrv.tgz

lynx -source ftp://ftp.xfree86.org/pub/XFree86/4.1.0/binaries/
Darwin-ppc/Xnest.tgz > Xnest.tgz

lynx -source ftp://ftp.xfree86.org/pub/XFree86/4.1.0/binaries/
Darwin-ppc/Xprog.tgz > Xprog.tgz

lynx -source ftp://ftp.xfree86.org/pub/XFree86/4.1.0/binaries/
Darwin-ppc/Xprt.tgz > Xprt.tgz

lynx -source ftp://ftp.xfree86.org/pub/XFree86/4.1.0/binaries/
Darwin-ppc/Xvfb.tgz > Xvfb.tgz

lynx -source ftp://ftp.xfree86.org/pub/XFree86/4.1.0/binaries/
Darwin-ppc/Xf100.tgz > Xf100.tgz

ls -l

total 80544

-rw-r—r—  1 ray  staff   3099299 Jul 16 13:32 Xbin.tgz
-rw-r—r—  1 ray  staff   1575927 Jul 16 13:35 Xdoc.tgz
-rw-r—r—  1 ray  staff    297200 Jul 16 13:43 Xetc.tgz
-rw-r—r—  1 ray  staff  12176196 Jul 16 13:59 Xf100.tgz
-rw-r—r—  1 ray  staff    309738 Jul 16 13:42 Xfenc.tgz
-rw-r—r—  1 ray  staff  16160286 Jul 16 13:39 Xfnts.tgz
-rw-r—r—  1 ray  staff     38160 Jul 16 13:50 Xfsrv.tgz
-rw-r—r—  1 ray  staff     33287 Jul 16 13:29 Xinstall.sh
-rw-r—r—  1 ray  staff    101185 Jul 16 13:32 Xlib.tgz
-rw-r—r—  1 ray  staff    607499 Jul 16 13:34 Xman.tgz
-rw-r—r—  1 ray  staff    588687 Jul 16 13:52 Xnest.tgz
-rw-r—r—  1 ray  staff   2962554 Jul 16 13:53 Xprog.tgz
-rw-r—r—  1 ray  staff    791789 Jul 16 13:53 Xprt.tgz
-rw-r—r—  1 ray  staff    695767 Jul 16 13:48 Xquartz.tgz
-rw-r—r—  1 ray  staff    694941 Jul 16 13:56 Xvfb.tgz
-rw-r—r—  1 ray  staff    656073 Jul 16 13:49 Xxserv.tgz
-rw-r—r—  1 ray  staff    389980 Jul 16 13:30 extract
-rw-r—r—  1 ray  staff      5130 Jul 16 14:01 typescript

sh Xinstall.sh

setenv PATH "${PATH}:/usr/X11R6/bin"

setenv MANPATH "${MANPATH}:/usr/X11R6/man"
```

At this point, you should be ready to run X11 applications. Remember that some versions of lynx insist on being helpful and unpacking gzipped files for you. If you encounter problems with the extraction of these `.tgz` files, you might need to find another way to download these files (such as by saving them, from within a Lynx or Explorer browser). You will probably want to add the `setenvs` for the `PATH` and `MANPATH` to your `.cshrc` file or to the system-wide configuration file.

If you've read the installation instructions from xfree86.org, you'll notice that we've installed a number of optional packages in addition to the base required install. These include:

- **`Xvfb`, the virtual framebuffer X server**—This is an X server that can run without actually displaying anything. It was originally designed to allow testing, but it turns out to be useful for things such as running applications that need a running X server, but that don't actually display anything on it.
- **The 100dpi font set**—This gives you more flexibility in choosing font sizes for display on your screen.
- **The X11 font server**—This package allows you to provide a central font store to a number of running X servers, without needing to install the fonts on each of them.
- **The nested X11 server**—This allows you to run an X11 server as a client, inside another X11 server. Also allows you to run additional X servers with different display properties for specialty applications, if the need arises.
- **The X11 headers and compilation support files**—These allow you to compile X11 applications for your machine.

You can read more about these, as well as the capabilities of the rest of the X Window System, from the man pages on X11. To get an idea of what you might want to ask man about, look in the subdirectories of `/usr/X11R6/man`.

Using XFree86

After you have XFree86 installed, starting it up is simply a matter of running the command from the shell. The XonX port of the XFree86 distribution suggests that you might be able to start it with `startx — -aqua`, but as of the version available on April 17th, 2001, this feature does not work. Instead, the software currently appears to require the invocation `startx — -quartz`. When started, you will shortly be presented with a dialog box like that shown in Figure 19.5. Pay attention to what the dialog box has to say. Remember, the current XFree86 implementation runs X11R6 as a completely separate windowing system; you will need to know how to switch between them, and that information is shown in this dialog box.

FIGURE 19.5
The Startup dialog for the XFree86 X Window System server gives you the information you need to know to switch back to the Aqua interface.

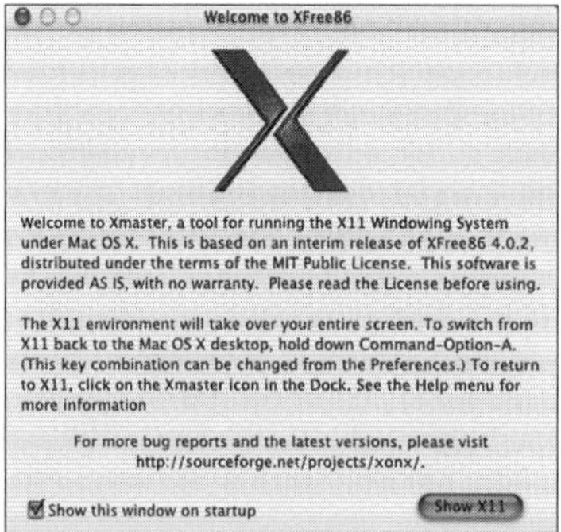

Tip

If you didn't pay attention to the dialog, the default is Command+Option+A to switch out of the X Window System back to the Aqua interface, and click on that big red X in the Dock to switch back to X11.

Caution

If it appears that you can't type into any of the windows (you move your cursor over the window and the in-window text cursor highlights, but nothing you type appears), congratulations, you've found an OS X bug. Currently the OS X kernel appears to have a bug in which it randomly unloads a table that contains a list of which keys exist on the keyboard. X11 needs this table to map what you type into data to be provided to a program. The best current recommendation is to kill X11, sleep the machine, wake it back up, and start X11 again. Apparently the keymap table is re-injected into the kernel on wakeup, and starting X11 immediately afterward seems to be the only consistent fix.

The look and feel of the X Window System is mostly the responsibility of the particular window manager you've chosen to run (you'll learn more about window managers in the immediately following section). But in the general operation of the environment, you'll find that there are a number of constants to the way the X Window System works, regardless of what the interface looks like. Some of these will be familiar to anyone who has previously used a computer with a mouse. A few, however, are likely to be new even to users who have been happily using a mouse since the earliest days of the Mac. The significant things to remember are described in the next section.

Common X11 Interface Features

The X Window System is designed for a three-button mouse. Most X software makes use of the left button for pointing, clicking, and selection. X uses the center button for general functions such as moving or resizing windows, and the right button for application-specific functions such as opening in-application pop-up windows. Of course, any application is capable of modifying these uses, so examination of a program's documentation is always in order.

X also uses its three-button mouse for selection, copying, and pasting in a way that won't be familiar, but that you will probably come to appreciate quickly. Unlike the Mac and Windows, there is no separate command to perform copy functions. Instead, X functions as though whatever has been most recently selected has been placed on the clipboard and can be pasted. The left mouse button allows click-and-drag type selection, and picking the start of a selection region. The right mouse button functions like Shift-clicking on the Mac; that is, it extends the selection. And clicking the center mouse button pastes whatever is selected—or has been most recently selected—into whichever window the cursor is in when clicked. This different paradigm for selection, copying, and pasting turns out to be a wonderfully efficient way of allowing you to work with text with the mouse, as it requires no coordinated use of a second hand.

The Mac of course, has no middle or right mouse buttons by default. XFree86 deals with this by allowing you to use keyboard modifiers to emulate the middle and right mouse buttons. To enable this mode, add the argument `-fakebuttons` to the `startx` invocation. This allows clicking while holding the left Command key to emulate the middle mouse button, and the left Option key to emulate the right mouse button. So, that benefit of not needing the second hand goes away again, at least on the Mac currently. It might be time to put away that cool pro mouse and buy one with multiple buttons, or petition Apple to get with the X program! For more information on compensatory changes of this nature that the XonX group have had to make to get X running on X, see the XonX FAQ (Frequently Asked Questions list) at `http://mrcla.com/XonX/FAQ.html`.

X has the concept of focused input. On the Macintosh and Windows platforms, if you type on the keyboard, you generally expect the typing to appear in whatever window or dialog box is in front. On the Mac and Windows, the window in front is the *active window*. In X, the window manager has the option of directing your input where it chooses. The location into which your input is directed is called the *input focus*. Most window managers can be configured to focus input on the frontmost window; focus input on a selected window (which, on X, does not have to be the front window); or focus input on whichever window the cursor is over. These are usually called, respectively, Focus to Front, Click to Focus, and Focus Follows Cursor modes. The last of these, although most unlike the interface you are probably familiar with, is usually considered to be the most powerful. With the window manager configured in Focus Follows Cursor mode, you can direct typing into a mostly hidden window (for example, to start a noninteractive program) by simply moving the cursor over any visible part of the mostly hidden window and typing. There is no need to waste time bringing a rear window to the front, typing the command, and then shuffling the window back underneath the window that you really wanted to be working in. Figures 19.6 though 19.8 show several examples of working in the different X11 focus modes. Configuration methods for the different window managers vary; we'll cover the options for several in the next section.

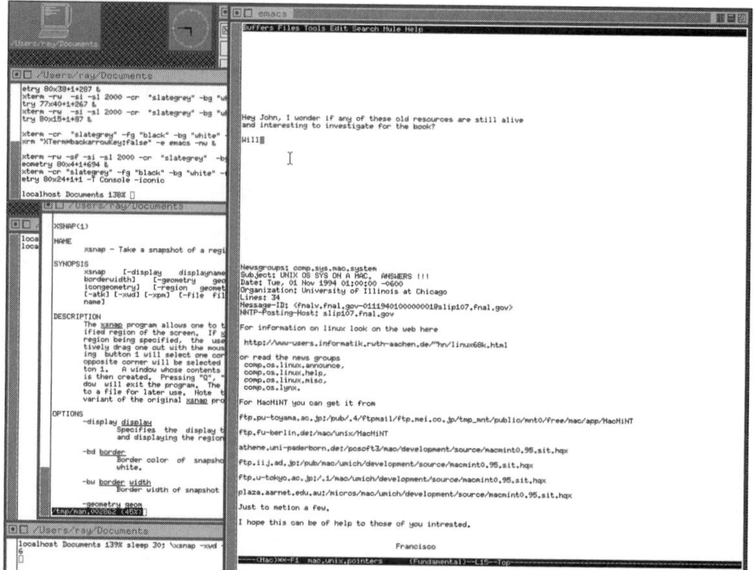

FIGURE 19.6
Focus-Follows-Cursor mode, with work being done in the frontmost window—this looks like the type of interaction with which you're probably familiar. Note that both the mouse pointer (the I-bar text cursor) and the text-insertion point (the dark filled rectangle in the emacs window) are inside the same window.

Tip

If you're typing and you notice that what you're typing isn't appearing where you think it is supposed to, chances are you've got your input focused in some other window. Make certain that your cursor is where it belongs, or if your system is configured to Click-to-Focus mode, be sure that you've clicked where you intend to type. It's very easy to get confused when moving between platforms using different input focus methods.

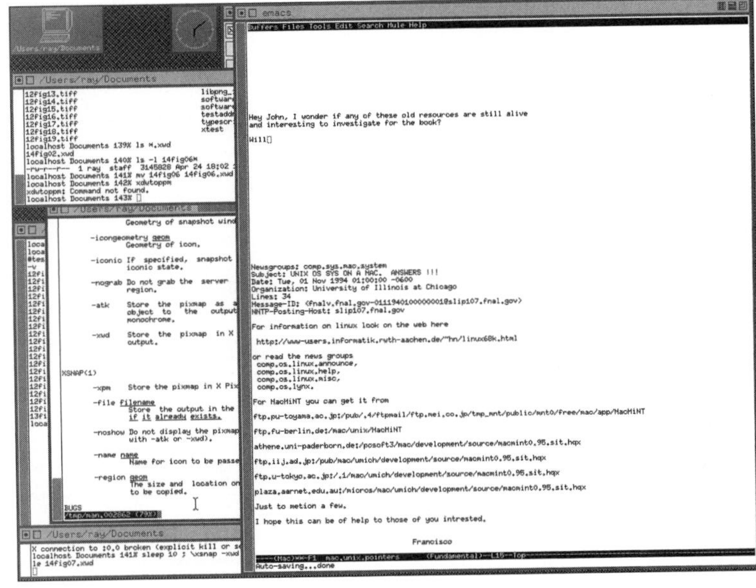

FIGURE 19.7
Focus-Follows-Cursor mode, with work being done in a window that is behind the front window. Notice that the in-window cursor of the emacs window (frontmost) has gone hollow, to indicate that it is no longer active. The dark active cursor has followed the mouse pointer to indicate that a different window is active. The window border also changes colors, but that probably doesn't show up well in a black-and-white printed image.

In the X Window System, the window manager or any other program can attach arbitrary commands to arbitrary user actions. For example, a program can attach the action of displaying a menu when a user right-clicks on the title bar. The window manager could pop up a variety of menus when the user left-, right-, or center-clicks in the empty background (root window or desktop) of the windowing system. Or it could happen when the user Shift-left-clicks, Shift-right-clicks, or Shift-center-clicks—the possibilities are endless. One popular terminal program, `xterm`, pops up its configuration menus when the user holds down the Control key and left-, right-, or center-clicks in the window. Some window managers attach a standard menu with common commands such as close and resize to icons in each window's title bar. Others attach these functions to pop-up menus in the title bar. You'll find variations in program behavior even among different installations of X11 on the same version of Unix because local configuration options can exert a significant influence over the interface. Don't be too surprised if your installation of X11 doesn't look or behave quite like what is shown here. With the short generation times for open source software, there is plenty of time for the software to be updated a dozen times between typing this and you reading it. Also, don't be afraid to read the documentation and the FAQ to find out how things work today, regardless of when *today* happens to be.

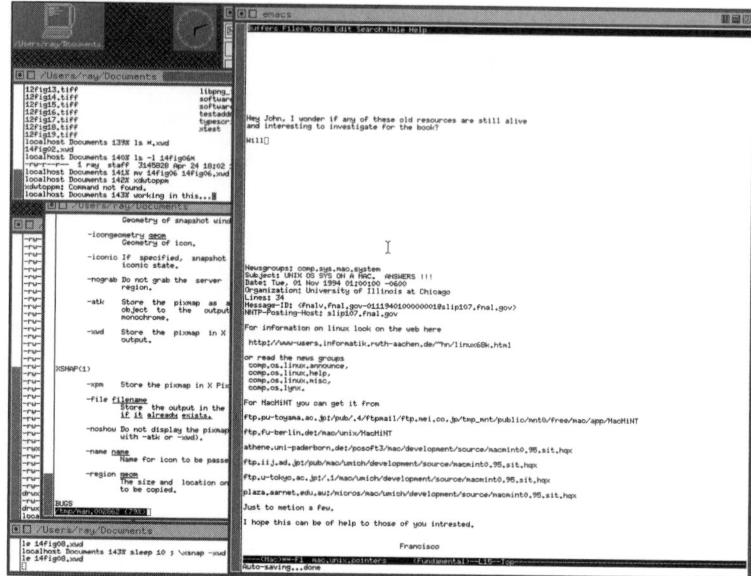

FIGURE 19.8
Click-to-Focus mode, with a window selected other than the one that the cursor is in—this does not have to be the front window. Note how the mouse pointer and active text cursor are not in the same window. After input has been focused into a window in this mode, it will not leave until the mouse is clicked elsewhere.

Most window managers can iconize windows. Because the actual display of a client's windows isn't handled by the client, but by the server at the request of the client, the X server and window manager are free to make some useful contributions to the user experience. One of these contributions is that when a client requests a window with particular characteristics, the server isn't obliged to represent the window that way to the user. The server is only obliged to treat it as though it had those characteristics. This enables the server, for example, to scale the window arbitrarily, or to shrink it down and display it as an icon. You're familiar with the concept of files and folders being represented with icons. X11 doesn't know a thing about files or folders. It knows about drawing pictures on the screen (there are file browser applications for X11, much like the OS X Finder, and we'll talk about them later in this chapter), and it knows that you don't always want all those pictures fighting for display space. So, X11 includes the notion that a window can be turned into an icon displayed in the root window, if you don't care to have it taking up space. This is sort of like OS X's capability to minimize a running application into the Dock, but you aren't limited to just placing things in one location on the screen. Likewise, some applications can be dynamically resized to provide different functionality than you are familiar with from Mac OS. The `xterm` terminal window, for example, interacts dynamically with the size of the font it's using. Increase the size of the font, and the window will increase to show the same data. You can also decrease the font size to a single point—in which case, the terminal will shrink to icon size, while remaining a usable terminal and continuing to display output.

Configuring the X Window System

Most configuration of the X Window System is handled by a server resource database. When a client makes a request of the server, the server checks the server resource database to determine user preferences for that client. The server resource database is loaded on a per-user basis via the command `xrdb`, which needs to be executed automatically after starting X11. `xrdb` loads configuration information from a dotfile, usually named `.X11defaults`. `.X11defaults` usually contains lines similar to the following:

```
1    xbiff*onceOnly:                on
2    xbiff*wm_option.autoRaise:     off
3    xbiff*mailBox                  /usr/spool/mail/mymail
```

If you were to include these lines in your `.X11defaults` file, you would be telling your X server that if `xbiff` (an X11 program that notifies you when you have new mail) starts, it needs to set certain options.

Line 1 sets an `xbiff`-specific option regarding how frequently to ring the alarm to tell you that you have mail. Here, it's set to ring a single time when mail arrives. Other options are available to set how many times the alarm should ring, and at what intervals, if you prefer something other than a single ring.

Line 2 sets an option that belongs to the window manager and tells it how you want `xbiff` treated. Specifically, this tells the window manager not to bring `xbiff` to the front if it's behind other windows when it needs to notify you. Remember, X11 provides the display, and a separate window manager provides such things as window controls.

Line 3 tells `xbiff` where to find the mailbox that it's supposed to look at.

Because each client supports different options and allows the window manager different levels of control, and you'll need to consult each client's documentation to learn what you can configure, and what you need to do to configure it. As an idea of what you can do, and perhaps a sample you might like to play with, Listing 19.1 includes a commented listing of my `.X11defaults` file.

LISTING 19.1 A Typical `.X11defaults` File

```
!  ~/.X11defaults
!   This file is used by xrdb to initialize the server resource
!   database, which is used by clients when they start up.
!
! Default defaults
!
```

LISTING 19.1 continued

```
*Font:          *-courier-medium-r-*-*-*-120-*-*-*-*-*-*
*MenuFont:      *-courier-medium-r-*-*-*-140-*-*-*-*-*-*
*BoldFont:      *-courier-bold-r-*-*-*-120-*-*-*-*-*-*
!
! GNU Emacs
!
emacs*BorderWidth:      1
! emacs*Font:           9x15
!
! Clock
!
xclock*borderWidth:             0
xclock*wm_option.title:         off
xclock*wm_option.gadgets:       off
xclock*wm_option.borderContext: off
xclock*wm_option.autoRaise:     off
!
! Load meter
!
xload*font:                 *-courier-medium-r-*-*-*-100-*-*-*-*-*-*
xload*wm_option.title:          off
xload*wm_option.gadgets:        off
xload*wm_option.borderContext:  off
xload*wm_option.autoRaise:      off
!
! Mail notifier
!
xbiff*wm_option.title:          off
xbiff*wm_option.gadgets:        off
xbiff*wm_option.borderContext:  off
xbiff*wm_option.autoRaise:      off
xbiff*wm_option.volume:         20
!
! Terminal Emulator
!
!XTerm*Font:            9x15
XTerm*c132:             true
XTerm*curses:           true
XTerm*jumpScroll:       true
XTerm*SaveLines:        2048
XTerm*scrollBar:        true
XTerm*scrollInput:      true
XTerm*scrollKey:        true
!
XTerm*fontMenu.Label:                VT Fonts
XTerm*fontMenu*fontdefault*Label:    Default
XTerm*fontMenu*font1*Label:          Tiny
XTerm*VT100*font1:                   nil2
XTerm*fontMenu*font2*Label:          10 Point
```

LISTING 19.1 continued

```
XTerm*VT100*font2:            -*-lucidatypewriter-medium-r-*-*-*-080-*-*-*-*-*-*
XTerm*fontMenu*font3*Label:          14 Point
XTerm*VT100*font3:            -*-lucidatypewriter-medium-r-*-*-*-140-*-*-*-*-*-*
XTerm*fontMenu*font4*Label:          18 Point
XTerm*VT100*font4:            -*-lucidatypewriter-medium-r-*-*-*-180-*-*-*-*-*-*
XTerm*fontMenu*font5*Label:          24 Point
XTerm*VT100*font5:                   12x24
XTerm*fontMenu*fontescape*Label:     Escape Sequence
XTerm*fontMenu*fontsel*Label:        Selection
XTerm*VT100.Translations:         #override \n\
     <Key>L1:     set-vt-font(1) set-scrollbar(off) \n\
     <Key>L2:     set-vt-font set-scrollbar(on) \n\
     <Key>R4:     string("0x1b") string("[211z") \n\
     <Key>R5:     string("0x1b") string("[212z") \n\
     <Key>R6:     string("0x1b") string("[213z") \n\
     <Key>R7:     string("0x1b") string("[214z") \n\
     <Key>R9:     string("0x1b") string("[216z") \n\
     <Key>R11:    string("0x1b") string("[218z") \n\
     <Key>R13:    string("0x1b") string("[220z") \n\
     <Key>R15:    string("0x1b") string("[222z")
!
! Netscape
!
netscape*defaultHeight:      850
netscape*anchorColor:        maroon
netscape*visitedAnchorColor:    blue3
!
! screensaver config
!
xscreensaver*programs: \
     xfishtank -c black -r .1 -f 20 -b 20 \n \
     /usr/local/X11R5/bin/flame -root \n \
     /usr/local/X11R5/bin/maze -root
xscreensaver*colorPrograms:
xscreensaver*monoPrograms:
```

In addition to the server resources database, clients frequently have command-line options that can control the client's interaction with X11. For example:

```
> xterm -fg "black" -bg "white" -fn 6x10 -geometry 85x30+525+1
```

This starts an `xterm` terminal session with the following configuration: black foreground color, white as the background color (black text on a white window), and a 6×10 point font. It also sets the geometry information so that the window is 85 characters wide, 30 characters high, and is placed 525 pixels from the left edge of the screen and 1 pixel down from the top.

Again, different programs have different options available and your location documentation is your best source for up-to-date information on your exact configuration.

Finally, the applications that start when you start X11 (or most standardized installations of X11, including the default XFree86 installation) are configured by the execution of a file named `.xinitrc` in your home directory. This is a shell script file, containing a collection of commands that you want executed when X11 starts. Therefore, you can put in it lines that start `xterm` terminals, clocks, editors, and any other X11-based applications that you'd like to have start in your environment. The lines are exactly the commands you'd type at the command line to start these applications, so the earlier comments about the wide variability of the configuration options apply here as well. Listing 19.2 shows the contents of my `.xinitrc` file, which produces the X11 environment shown in Figure 19.1.

LISTING 19.2 A Typical `.xinitrc` File

```
#!/bin/sh

xrdb -load $HOME/.X11defaults
xset m 2 5 s off
xset fp+ /usr/X11R6/lib/X11/fonts

# xmodmap -e 'keysym BackSpace = Delete'
echo  "XTerm*ttyModes:erase ^H" | xrdb -merge

/usr/X11R6/bin/twm &

/usr/X11R6/bin/xclock -bg "slategrey" -fg "lightgrey"  -analog
    ➥-geometry 60x60+220+1 -padding 4 &

xterm -rw  -si -sl 2000 -cr  "slategrey" -bg "white" -fg "black"
    ➥-fn 6x10 -geometry 80x38+1+287 &
xterm -rw  -si -sl 2000 -cr  "slategrey" -bg "white" -fg "black"
    ➥-fn 6x10 -geometry 77x40+1+267 &
xterm -rw  -si -sl 2000 -cr  "slategrey" -bg "white" -fg "black"
    ➥-fn 6x10 -geometry 80x15+1+87 &

xterm -cr  "slategrey" -fg "black" -bg "white" -fn 6x10 -geometry 82x73+507+1
    ➥-xrm "XTerm*backarrowKey:false" -e emacs -nw &

xterm -rw -sf -si -sl 2000 -cr  "slategrey"  -bg "white" -fg "black"
    ➥-fn 6x10 -geometry 80x4+1+694 &
xterm -cr "slategrey" -fg "black" -bg "white" -fn 6x10 -title "CONSOLE"
    Â-C -geometry 80x24+1+1 -T Console -iconic
```

Finally, window managers have their own configuration files that control display options and, possibly, other parameters regarding the user experience.

Window Managers: `twm`, `mwm`

After you've started the X Window System environment, and confirmed that you want to switch into it with the dialog, you will be presented with a screen much like the one shown in Figure 19.9. This is the current default for a user who has no `.xinitrc` file to control what applications to start and where to put them, and no `.twmrc` file to control what the applications look and feel like. Remember that the X Window System provides only interface, component, and display functionality; additional programs are required to provide a useful user interface. In Figure 19.1, you are actually looking at the result of 10 programs running simultaneously (not counting the X Window System server and associated programs necessary for it to function) just to create the interface. Six are displaying windows, one is providing an application dock, one a clock, one an editor, and finally, the window manager, `twm`, is providing the title bars and border controls shown associated with the windows. Start up of the programs occurs in `.xinitrc`, and the configuration of their appearance is controlled by `twm`.

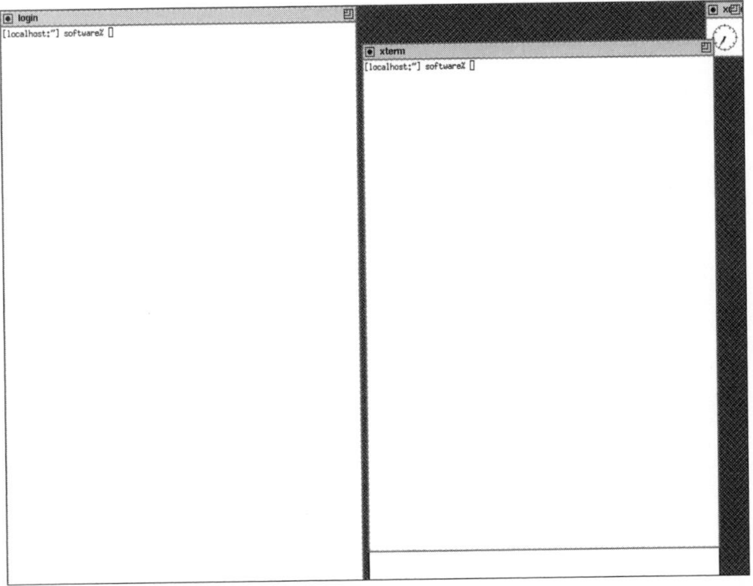

FIGURE 19.9
The current default startup environment for XFree86. More interesting collections of windows and utilities are created by the use of `.xinitrc` *startup scripts.*

`twm`

One of the most common window managers is `twm` (tabbed window manager). Shown managing the display in Figure 19.1, `twm` provides very basic window management functions, and is the default window manager used by XFree86. Even though it is one of the less feature-filled window managers, twm is convenient and allows an extreme amount of user customization of the environment. If you choose to do so, you can create your own standard buttons that appear in your twm title bars, and cause them to execute arbitrary commands. You can also build your own pop-up menus, automatically execute commands when the cursor enters windows, customize window manager colors and actions by an application name and type, and a host of other customizations. Listing 19.3 is a portion of my .twmrc file, giving you an idea of the range of configuration options. It's only a portion because the entire file contains 284 individual configuration parameters. I'm particular about how my interface functions, and twm gives me the flexibility to configure every last one of the 284 tweaks it takes to get it how I like it.

LISTING 19.3 A Representative Sample of a .twmrc Configuration File for the twm X Window System Window Manager

```
Color
{
    BorderColor "maroon4"

    BorderTileForeground "bisque4"
    BorderTileBackground "darkorchid4"

    TitleForeground "darkslategray"
    TitleBackground "bisque3"

    DefaultBackground "bisque"
    DefaultForeground "slategrey"

    MenuForeground "slategrey"
    MenuBackground "moccasin"

    MenuTitleForeground "slategrey"
    MenuTitleBackground "bisque3"
    MenuShadowColor "bisque4"
    IconForeground "lightgrey"
    IconBackground "slategray"
    IconBorderColor "darkslategray"
    IconManagerForeground "darkslategrey"
    IconManagerBackground "bisque"
    IconManagerHighlight  "maroon4"
}

BorderWidth      4
FramePadding     2
TitleFont       "8x13"
MenuFont        "8x13"
IconFont        "6x10"
```

LISTING 19.3 continued

```
ResizeFont      "fixed"
NoTitleFocus

IconManagerGeometry    "=200x10+290+1"

ShowIconManager

IconManagerFont                 "variable"
IconManagerDontShow
{
    "xclock"
    "xbiff"
    "perfmeter"
}

ForceIcons
Icons
{
    "xterm"     "terminal"
}

NoTitle
{
  "TWM"
  "xload"
  "xclock"
  "xckmail"
  "xbiff"
  "xeyes"
  "oclock"
}

NoHighlight
{
  "xclock"
  "dclock"
  "xload"
  "xbiff"
}

AutoRaise
{
  "nothing"
}

DefaultFunction f.menu "default-menu"
#WindowFunction f.function "blob"
```

LISTING 19.3 continued

```
#Button = KEYS : CONTEXT : FUNCTION
#——————————————————
Button1 =       : root   : f.menu "button1"
Button2 =       : root   : f.menu "button2"
Button3 =       : root   : f.menu "button3"

Button1 =       : title  : f.function "blob"
Button2 =       : title  : f.lower

Button1 =       : frame  : f.raiselower
Button2 =       : frame  : f.move
Button3 =       : frame  : f.lower

Button1 =       : icon   : f.function "blob"
Button2 =       : icon   : f.iconify
Button3 =       : icon   : f.menu "default-menu"
Button1 = m     : icon   : f.iconify
Button2 = m     : icon   : f.iconify
Button3 = m     : icon   : f.iconify
Button3 = c     : root   : f.function "beep-beep"

Function "beep-beep"
{
    f.beep
    f.beep
    f.beep
    f.beep
    f.beep
}

menu "button1"
{
"Window Ops"        f.title
"(De)Iconify"       f.iconify
"Move"              f.move
"Resize"            f.resize
"Lower"             f.lower
"Raise"             f.raise
"Redraw Window"     f.winrefresh
"Focus Input"       f.focus
"Unfocus Input"     f.unfocus
"Window Info"       f.identify
}

menu "button2"
{
"Window Mgr"        f.title
"Circle Up"         f.circleup
"Circle Down"       f.circledown
```

LISTING 19.3 continued

```
"Refresh All"       f.refresh
"Source .twmrc"     f.twmrc
"Beep"              f.beep
"Show Icon Mgr"     f.showiconmgr
"Hide Icon Mgr"     f.hideiconmgr
"Feel"              f.menu "Feel"
}

menu "button3"
{
"Clients"              f.title
"Xterm"                ! "xterm &"
"Emacs"                ! "emacs -i &"
"Lock Screen"          ! "xnlock &"
"Xman"                 ! "xman &"
"X Text Exitor"        ! "xedit &"
"Calculator"           ! "xcalc &"
}

menu "default-menu"
{
"Default Menu"         f.title
"Refresh"              f.refresh
"Refresh Window"       f.winrefresh
"twm Version"          f.version
"Focus on Root"        f.unfocus
"Source .twmrc"        f.twmrc
"Cut File"             f.cutfile
"Move Window"          f.move
"ForceMove Window"     f.forcemove
"Resize Window"        f.resize
"Raise Window"         f.raise
"Lower Window"         f.lower
"Focus on Window"      f.focus
"Raise-n-Focus"        f.function "raise-n-focus"
"Zoom Window"          f.zoom
"FullZoom Window"      f.fullzoom
"Kill twm"             f.quit
"Destroy Window"       f.destroy
}

RightTitleButton "down" = f.zoom
RightTitleButton "right" = f.horizoom
LeftTitleButton "icon" = f.destroy
```

mwm

The Motif window manager (`mwm`) is a popular window manager evolved from a commercial product, and is also a popular window manager for others to attempt to emulate. It provides a somewhat different user experience than `twm`. The difference is partly because it automatically attaches things such as resize corners to all windows, and partly because of the pretty 3D look it gives to the controls. Figure 19.10 shows `mwm` managing the same collection of windows managed by `twm` in Figure 19.1.

FIGURE 19.10
The `mwm` *window manager, managing the same collection of windows shown in Figure 19.1.*

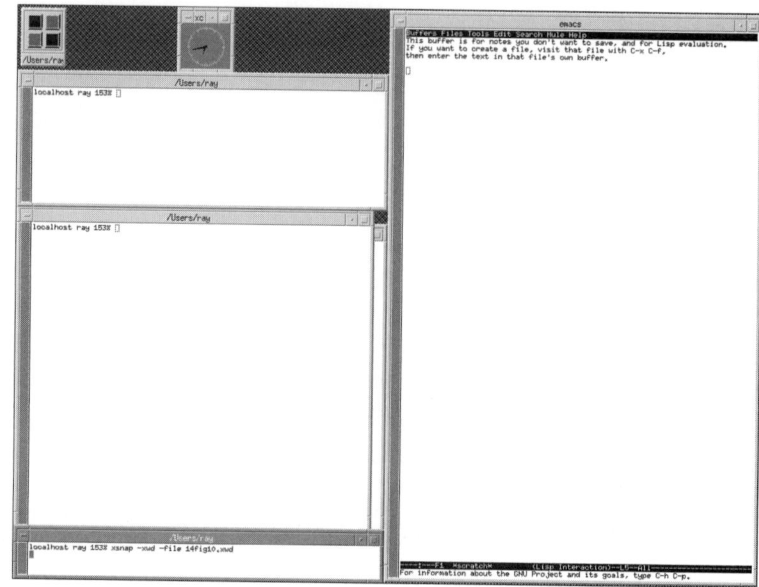

The XFree86 distribution doesn't include any documentation for the `mwm` window manager, so we don't recommend that you choose it as your window manager unless you're already familiar with it.

Other Window Managers

There aren't many other X Window System window managers available for the XonX project just yet, but people will be creating ports regularly. Several will probably appear by the time this book is published, so we'll give a quick list of some of the interesting ones here:

- `tvtwm`—An extension of `twm` that allows you to create an arbitrarily large number of virtual windows and switch between them conveniently.
- `fvwm`—A 3D-"ish" version of `twm`, with even more flexible configuration options.
- Enlightenment—A heavyweight window manager that belongs to the GNOME desktop environment. GNOME and Enlightenment are popular on the Linux platform because of the user-friendly environment created under X11, and will probably be a natural for OS X as well.
- Window Maker—Another heavyweight window manager, Window Maker is designed to give special support for the GNUstep applications, and attempts to provide the elegant look and feel of the OpenStep environment.

Keep in mind, when running the X Window System, that the window controls such as title bars and scroll bars are provided by a separate window manager application. The point of repeating this yet again is that it is possible for the window manager to exit, leaving you with a collection of unmanaged windows. This is a slightly disconcerting state in which to find the X Window System because the window manager also controls the input focus. Figure 19.11 shows an X Window System session that has lost its window manager.

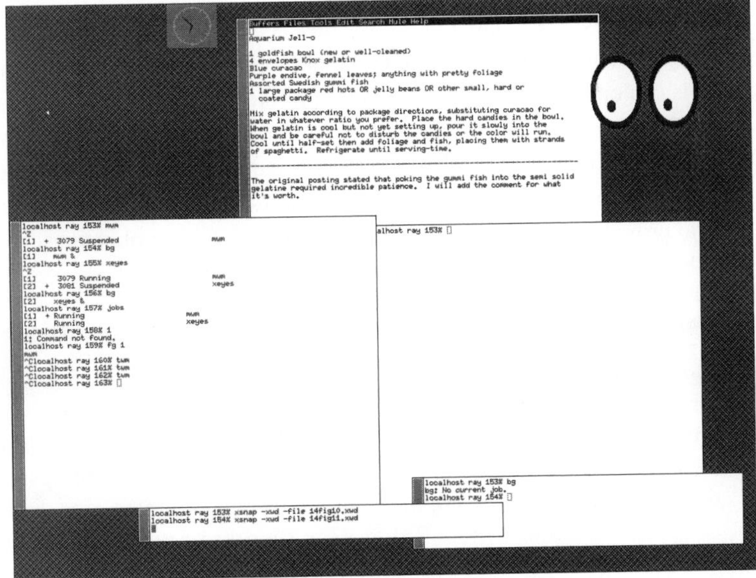

FIGURE 19.11
An X Window System session that has lost its window manager.

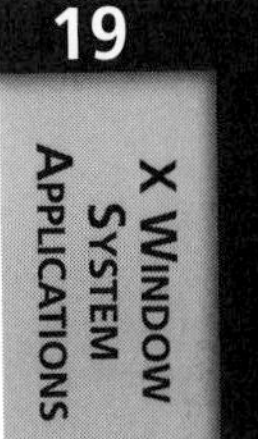

Note

If your window manager dies while your input is focused somewhere other than a terminal window, you won't be able to refocus. Therefore, you won't be able to type into a window (meaning you can't type something like `twm` at a prompt, and so can't restart your window manager). In this case, all is not necessarily lost because the mouse cursor selection and paste method usually still works, even without a window manager. If you can find the letters t, w, and m anywhere on your screen, you can select and paste them at a command prompt, and then select and paste a return/newline, which will usually rescue things.

This is a problem with no elegant solution, but if you desperately need to save something you've been working on, it's nice to know there's a fix, even if it's a nuisance. Thankfully, window managers don't frequently die of their own accord. Usually, it takes a user clicking on something like `kill twm` in the menu—in which case, you'll probably be more annoyed at yourself than at having to copy and paste a couple of letters to fix things.

Using Tenon XTools

Tenon's XTools is a commercial X Window System server version for OS X, with one very significant feature difference that makes it well worth the cost for some users. XTools can operate both in a rooted fashion like the current implementation of XonX/XFree86, as well as in a rootless environment. In the rootless environment, it does away with the traditional X11 root window, and allows the X server to display windows directly into the Aqua GUI environment. Additionally, it allows the Aqua window manager to provide window manager functions for the X11 applications, creating an almost seamless integration between the two environments.

Note

It's not entirely clear what Tenon's done with the root window, or what the implications of the choice will be for all X Window System applications. The root window is an integral part of the X Window System philosophy, and it is a testimonial to both the creativity of the Tenon programmers, and the power of Unix-like abstraction models that XTools works so well without it. There's a good chance that Tenon has done something like implemented its X Window System server so that it displays the root window somewhere else. *Somewhere else* is likely into an invisible and unused buffer in memory, and Tenon has fooled the applications into thinking that they are working in a normal X11 environment. We know, it's geeky—but we think that the ability to do things like that with Unix applications is pretty cool.

XTools is a lot easier to start and work with than the XFree86 implementation currently is—just click the application icon, and away it goes. Because XTools doesn't display a root window, though, it's a lot harder to tell that it's running. And if there are no X11 applications running in it, XTools just looks like another application in your Dock.

Advantages

The big advantage of XTools comes when you start running X Window System applications. Figure 19.12 shows a screenshot with some X11 applications running beside some Aqua applications—can you tell which are which?

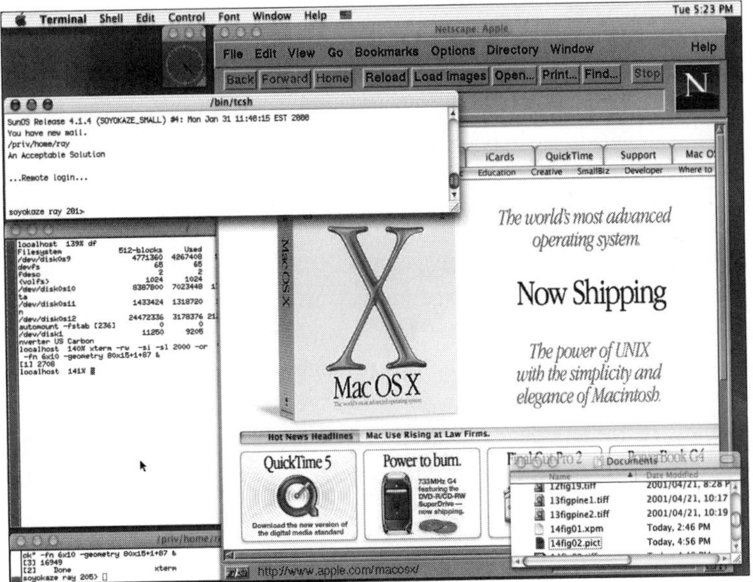

FIGURE 19.12
The Tenon XTools X Window System server displaying X11 applications in the Aqua interface.

Another significant advantage is the fact that it's a commercial application. Open source software is great, and the rapidity with which bugs are addressed in open source code is simply amazing. However, if a bug isn't being addressed, it's much nicer if it is in a commercial application so that it's somebody's fault that the problem isn't fixed. If you rely on X11 software for some business purpose, you might want to consider the benefits of paying for software, and being able to hold another company liable for bugs in its software.

Installation

XTools installs like most other OS X applications: Download the installer from Tenon's Web site (`http://www.tenon.com/products/xtools/`) or buy it on CD, run the installer, and follow the directions. Pay special attention to the note that says that XTools uses the same X11 libraries as XFree86. If you decide to delete XTools from your system using the uninstaller, it will delete the libraries that XFree86 needs as well. Tenon provides instructions on how to uninstall the software without deleting the libraries, and we suggest that you follow those instructions if you need to remove XTools. The instructions with the install we examined said to remove it by dragging the XTools application to the trash if you have XFree86 installed, but we expect that this might change because the software is still under development.

Using XTools

Using XTools is trivially easy—start it up, and you're using it. After XTools is started, any X11 applications that you execute will display into the XTools server, and will appear alongside the applications in your Aqua environment. If you don't like having to start a terminal and execute X11 applications from the command line, you can always use what you know about shell scripts to write scripts that will start them all up for you.

XTools will allow you to manage your X11 applications with a window manager other than the Aqua manager if you choose. Current options are `twm` and `mwm`. If you choose to use one of these, be aware that Tenon cautions that OpenGL might not function properly in windows managed by non-Aqua managers. Still, the alternatives give a few benefits of their own, so you might be inclined to experiment and see what works best for you. Figures 19.13 through 19.15 show XTools with X11 applications integrated among Aqua applications, running each of the windows managers currently supported.

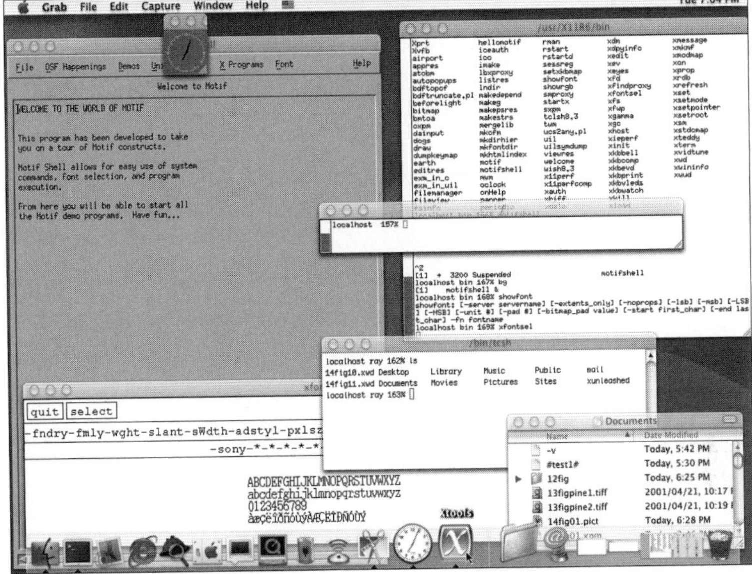

FIGURE 19.13
Tenon XTools using Aqua to manage its windows. Note that there are X Window System applications running here, as well as Aqua-only applications.

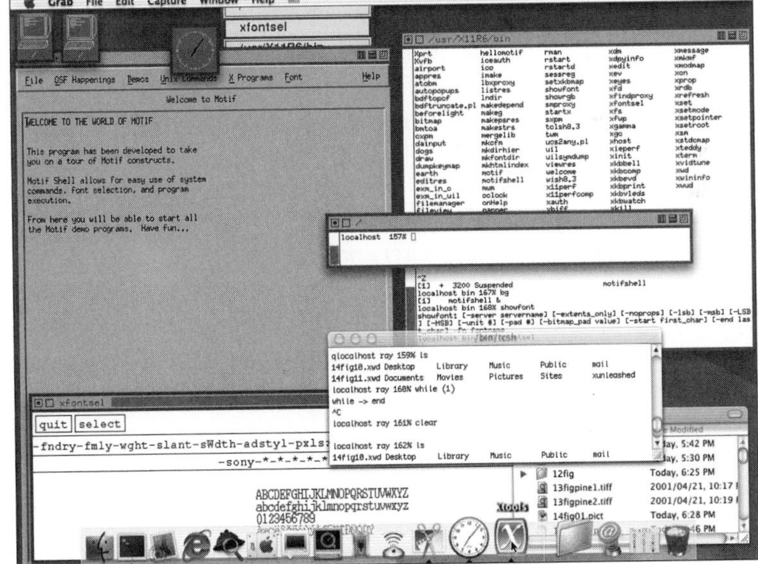

FIGURE 19.14
Tenon XTools using `twm` *to manage its windows. Now the difference between Aqua applications and X Window System applications is clearer.*

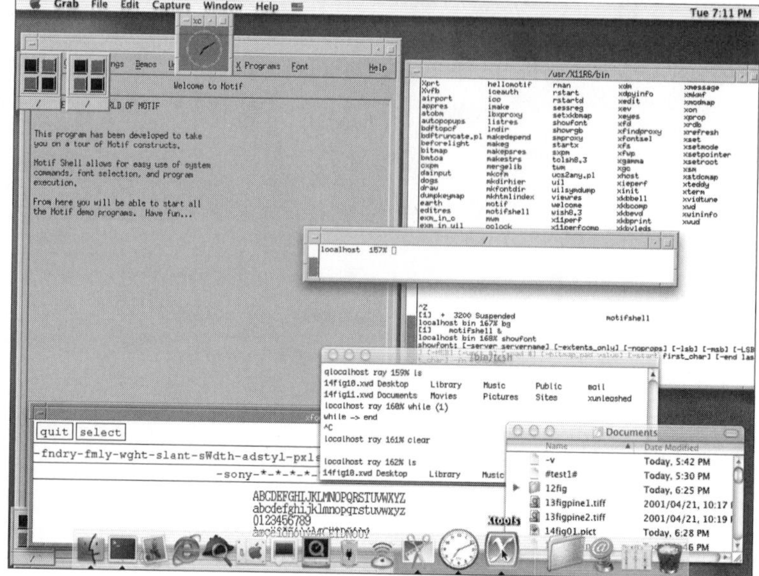

FIGURE 19.15
Tenon XTools using `mwm` *to manage its windows.*

Summary

With the installation of the X Window System on your machine, a whole world of graphical Unix applications has been opened up to you. The particulars of the installation process for the X11 servers might change by the time you read this, but the availability of software that will compile and run under X11—however you install it—will only continue to increase. For a taste of the range of X11 applications available, peruse the archives of X.org, located at `http://www.x.org/`.

CHAPTER 20

Command-Line Configuration and Administration

You've already been introduced to configuring and controlling the system through GUI utilities such as the control panels. When using older versions of Mac OS, the only access you have to the configuration for the system is through the GUI interface. Now, you have the option of using a GUI or modifying things through the command line. Although you might wonder whether you'd ever want to use the command line for configuration when Apple has provided such nice GUI tools for configuration, we think there are a few arguments to be made for the command line.

- Generally, we agree that Apple's GUI tools are nice. Still, they're GUI tools, and that means you need access to the GUI to use them. If you're trying to manage your machine from a remote location (more on this in Chapter 26, "Remote Administration"), access to the GUI might not be possible.
- Even if you're at the console, GUI tools generally take more time to load up and display their interface than it takes to tweak configuration files. Sometimes this doesn't make any difference, but sometimes it's simply annoying to wait for a GUI interface to load, when only a few keystrokes are necessary to make the same change.
- Configuration files don't need you to change them. A piece of software can make changes to configurations for you. More interestingly, software can change your configurations on a schedule or based on changes that it detects in the operation of the system. This can let you automate things such as location or network settings, as well as a range of other possibilities.
- Finally, just to be pedantic, we'll point out that the GUI interface is software running on top of a non-GUI interface. It's possible for the software that creates the GUI interface to be damaged, and for the rest of the system still to be intact enough to run. If you're limited to knowledge of the GUI tools only, you're very limited in your ability to fix the situation. Generally, when dealing with Unix-based things, it's safest to have a handle on the command-line configuration and administration tools. For a pure Unix book, we'd say that it is imperative that you avoid the GUI tools and learn to do everything with the command line. For this book, we'll say that it's a good idea to know the command-line tools—Apple has done a *very* good job.

In this chapter, we'll introduce you to the tools that you need to modify your machine's configuration from the command line, and give you a few examples of things that you can do. You'll learn further specifics about the use of these tools in chapters such as Chapter 24, "User Management," where we detail specific system configuration topics.

Locating and Editing the OS X Configuration Files

Locating OS X configuration files and figuring out what can be put in them can sometimes be a bit of an adventure. It's difficult to determine the correct information to provide for some items in this chapter. Many configuration options and files that exist in OS X are not actually intended for you to use in the OS X client version. These parts of the configuration system are actually managed by tools provided only (for the moment, at least) by OS X Server. It's possible to diddle around with them, and to do some interesting things, but OS X doesn't provide the tools or the information to do a complete job of documentation or configuration. We'll do our best to provide you with up-to-the-minute information on what's been discovered to be tweakable in the system as of when the book hits the shelves. Please do check online information sources such as `http://www.osxunleashed.com/` and `http://www.macosxhints.com/`, and understand that it seems clear that Apple doesn't intend for the user to ever understand or modify some of these things.

Preference Locations

Unlike previous versions of Mac OS, which kept almost all its preferences in the Preferences folder of the System folder, OS X keeps its preferences in several different locations. Primarily these are the `/etc/` folder, the NetInfo database, and the `~/Library/Preferences/` folders. Many preferences that affect the running of the system, such as what network services are started, the machine name, and such global information that does not change from login to login, are kept in the `/etc/` folder or its subfolders. Other preferences of this nature are kept in the NetInfo database. Preferences that affect individual user configuration are primarily kept in files stored in `~/Library/Preferences/`.

Preference Format

Preferences stored in files in the `/etc/` directory generally follow longstanding Unix tradition, and are formatted according to their own individual file formats. For example, the file `/etc/inetd.conf` configures a number of the network services that your machine will provide to the outside world. The default `inetd.conf` file as it comes from Apple is shown in Listing 20.1. The `#` symbol in front of each item indicates that the line is commented out and will not be run. Apple very wisely leaves all these network services off by default. Many of them can be security holes, and it's best if you enable them only as you need and understand them.

LISTING 20.1 A Typical `/etc/inetd.conf` File

```
#
# Internet server configuration database
#
#        @(#)inetd.conf    5.4 (Berkeley) 6/30/90
#
# Items with double hashes in front (##) are not yet implemented in the OS.
#
#finger    stream   tcp    nowait   nobody  /usr/libexec/tcpd  fingerd -s
#ftp       stream   tcp    nowait   root    /usr/libexec/tcpd  ftpd -l
#login     stream   tcp    nowait   root    /usr/libexec/tcpd  rlogind
#nntp      stream   tcp    nowait   usenet  /usr/libexec/tcpd  nntpd
#ntalk     dgram    udp    wait     root    /usr/libexec/tcpd  ntalkd
#shell     stream   tcp    nowait   root    /usr/libexec/tcpd  rshd
#telnet    stream   tcp    nowait   root    /usr/libexec/tcpd  telnetd
#uucpd     stream   tcp    nowait   root    /usr/libexec/tcpd  uucpd
#comsat    dgram    udp    wait     root    /usr/libexec/tcpd  comsat
#tftp      dgram    udp    wait     nobody  /usr/libexec/tcpd
➥tftpd /private/tftpboot
#bootp     dgram    udp    wait     root    /usr/libexec/tcpd  bootpd
##pop3     stream   tcp    nowait   root    /usr/libexec/tcpd
➥/usr/local/libexec/popper
##imap4    stream   tcp    nowait   root    /usr/libexec/tcpd
➥/usr/local/libexec/imapd
#
# "Small servers" — used to be standard on, but we're more conservative
# about things due to Internet security concerns.  Only turn on what you
# need.
#
#chargen  stream   tcp    nowait  root    internal
#chargen  dgram    udp    wait    root    internal
#daytime  stream   tcp    nowait  root    internal
#daytime  dgram    udp    wait    root    internal
#discard  stream   tcp    nowait  root    internal
#discard  dgram    udp    wait    root    internal
#echo     stream   tcp    nowait  root    internal
#echo     dgram    udp    wait    root    internal
#time     stream   tcp    nowait  root    internal
#time     dgram    udp    wait    root    internal
#
# Kerberos (version 5) authenticated services
#
##eklogin  stream tcp   nowait root    /usr/libexec/tcpd   klogind -k -c -e
##klogin   stream tcp   nowait root    /usr/libexec/tcpd   klogind -k -c
##kshd     stream tcp   nowait root    /usr/libexec/tcpd   kshd -k -c -A
#krb5_prop stream tcp   nowait root    /usr/libexec/tcpd   kpropd
#
# RPC based services (you MUST have portmapper running to use these)
#
##rstatd/1-3    dgram rpc/udp wait root    /usr/libexec/tcpd    rpc.rstatd
```

LISTING 20.1 continued

```
47 ##rusersd/1-2    dgram rpc/udp wait root    /usr/libexec/tcpd    rpc.rusersd
48 ##walld/1    dgram rpc/udp wait root    /usr/libexec/tcpd    rpc.rwalld
49 ##pcnfsd/1-2    dgram rpc/udp wait root    /usr/libexec/tcpd    rpc.pcnfsd
50 ##rquotad/1    dgram rpc/udp wait root    /usr/libexec/tcpd    rpc.rquotad
51 ##sprayd/1    dgram rpc/udp wait root    /usr/libexec/tcpd    rpc.sprayd
52 #
53 # The following are not known to be useful, and should not be enabled unless
54 # you have a specific need for it and are aware of the possible implications
55 #
56 #exec    stream    tcp    nowait  root  /usr/libexec/tcpd    rexecd
57 #ident   stream    tcp    wait    root  /usr/libexec/tcpd    identd -w -t120
```

This is probably the most important `/etc/` preference file to be familiar with. Its lines tell the system what programs to start in response to certain network events. Briefly, the intent of the services on each line is as follows:

- Line 8—The `fingerd` daemon allows external users to finger a user ID and find out whether the ID exists; if it does, how recently, and on what terminals the ID has been logged in.
- Line 9—The `ftpd` daemon provides an FTP (file transfer protocol) server.
- Line 10—The `login` service provides service for the `rlogin` remote login terminal program. Don't turn this on.
- Line 11—The `nntp` service is a Usenet newsgroups server. If your machine is configured to receive news from other servers, you can point your newsreader to your local machine to read news.
- Line 12—The `ntalk` (new protocol talk) daemon provides for real-time chat services. If you're familiar with ICQ or IRC, this service is somewhat similar.
- Line 13—Provides remote shell service—another way to remotely access machines. This service is required to use certain remote services, such as remote tape archive storage. Because Apple hasn't provided all the software necessary to make full use of these services, we suggest that this be left off as well; it's almost as large a security risk as `rlogin` and `telnet`.
- Line 14—Provides the `telnet` daemon to allow remote `telnet` terminal connections. Don't turn this on.
- Line 15—The `uucpd` service implements the Unix-to-Unix Copy Protocol. This is an antiquated method for networking Unix machines that can't always be connected to the network. Essentially, it allows network traffic between two sites to be queued until both sites are available on the network, and then exchanges the data. This service is of very limited utility today, and presents a significant security risk because it hasn't really been maintained since the days of 1200 baud modems.

- Line 16—The `comsat` daemon provides notification of incoming mail to mail-reader clients.
- Line 17—`tftp` is trivial file transfer protocol, and is one of the methods of providing file service to completely diskless network clients. You won't need to enable this service unless you're providing network boot services for diskless Unix clients.
- Line 18—`bootp` is a way of transmitting network configuration information to clients. Chances are you'll use DHCP for this, if you have a need to do so, although it's possible that OS X server could use `bootp` for netboot clients.
- Line 19—`pop3` is a POPmail (Post Office Protocol Mail) server. In the file, Apple indicates that this service is not yet available.
- Line 20—`imap4` is an IMAP mail server. Again, this service is not available as of the 10.0.2 release.
- Lines 26–33—Provide a number of network and network-software diagnostic servers. Unless you are performing network diagnosis and specifically need these, leave them off. They do not cause any known security problems, but if you're not using them, they occupy resources needlessly.
- Lines 34 and 35—Provide the time service (some servers require both stream and datagram connectivity, and these must be defined on separate lines). If you want your machine to be a time server, these can be turned on.
- Lines 39–42—Start a number of kerberos (security authentication) related servers, but most are unavailable from Apple as of the 10.0.2 release. The `krb5_prop` service (starting `krpropd`) is the server that propagates a master kerberos server's database to slave servers.
- Line 46—The `rstatd` daemon allows systems to connect through the network and get machine status information.
- Line 47—The `rusersd` daemon allows systems to connect through the network and to find information about this system's users. This is generally considered to be a bad idea.
- Line 48—The `walld` daemon allows users to write to the screens of all users on the system. This facility is nice, if you're root and need to tell your users that the machine is going to go down for maintenance. It's annoying if one of your users starts using it to incessantly ask anyone connected to the machine for help with trivial Unix problems.
- Line 49—The `pcnfsd` daemon provides service for a PC network file system product named `pcnfs`. Almost everybody uses `samba` instead nowadays.

- Line 50—The `rquotad` daemon provides disk quota information to remote machines, so that they can enforce quotas that your machine specifies on disks that it is serving to them.
- Line 51—`sprayd` is another network diagnostic server. Simply put, it responds, as rapidly as it can, to packets placed on the network by some other machine's spray process, which places packets on the network as fast as it can. This one would be nice if Apple provided it in a later release because it can be very useful for finding problem hardware in your network.
- Line 56—The `rexecd` daemon allows for the remote execution of parts of programs. Apple claims that it isn't known to be useful, but a programmer can make very good use of this service to perform distributed processing tasks by sending parts of programs to many different machines. Of course, it is also a security risk.
- Line 57—Another service that Apple considers to be of no practical use. The `identd` daemon provides a method for a remote machine to verify the identity of a user causing a connection, in as much as any identity can be verified over the network. The service was created because it is very easy for a user accessing, for example, a remote FTP site, to pretend to be a different user on your system, and potentially cause trouble for the person he is pretending to be.

The service this file controls, `inetd`, (the Internet services daemon) is a bit of a special case because it is a service that is configured by the `inetd.conf` file. Its function is to start other services. The configuration of `inetd`, and how it configures other services, will be covered in greater detail later in this chapter.

The `/etc/` preference file with the next most significance to you will be the `/etc/hostconfig` file. This file contains a number of variable assignments that provide information to assorted programs that run on your behalf. The values in the `/etc/hostconfig` come partly from settings in the System Preferences panels and partly from manual modification (even though the file says that it should be touched only by the controls). The `/etc/hostconfig` on your machine should look similar to Listing 20.2.

LISTING 20.2 A Typical `/etc/hostconfig` File

```
##
# /etc/hostconfig
##
# This file is maintained by the system control panels
##

# Network configuration
HOSTNAME=Racer-X
ROUTER=-AUTOMATIC-
```

LISTING 20.2 continued

```
10
11 # Services
12 AFPSERVER=-NO-
13 APPLETALK=en1
14 AUTHSERVER=-NO-
15 AUTOCONFIG=-YES-
16 AUTODISKMOUNT=-REMOVABLE-
17 AUTOMOUNT=-YES-
18 CONFIGSERVER=-NO-
19 IPFORWARDING=-NO-
20 MAILSERVER=-NO-
21 MANAGEMENTSERVER=-NO-
22 NETBOOTSERVER=-NO-
23 NISDOMAIN=-NO-
24 TIMESYNC=-YES-
25 QTSSERVER=-NO-
26 SSHSERVER=-NO-
27 WEBSERVER=-NO-
28 APPLETALK_HOSTNAME=Racer-X
```

Briefly, the lines of this listing specify the following information:

- Line 8 sets the `HOSTNAME` variable to `Racer-X`. This is used in the system startup scripts to tell the machine what name it has been given in the DNS (Domain Name Service). If you will be using your machine on a network, you can't just pick this value arbitrarily; it must be assigned by your network manager. The default value is `AUTOMATIC`, which currently seems to automatically do nothing particularly useful. If you're not going to be using your machine on a network, feel free to place any name here that you'd like to see replace `localhost` in your prompt.
- Line 9 configures a variable that specifies that network routing is handled automatically. That means it is going to use the gateway or DHCP information that you've provided via the GUI `Locations` manager.
- Line 12 indicates that the machine isn't providing AppleShare Filing Protocol services, which are necessary for serving files via AppleShare.
- Line 13 indicates that the ethernet interface is `en1`; in this case, the AirPort card. The twisted-pair interface would usually be `en0`.
- Line 14 specifies that the machine isn't providing authentication services.
- Line 15 affects whether the undocumented server `configd` starts, and whether AppleTalk services should obey values coming from it.
- Line 16 controls what types of media should automatically mount. Automatically mounting drives (floppies, Zip disks, CDs, and so on) is actually a big security

problem for Unix-based operating systems. Allowing this makes the user's life easier, but also allows a malicious user to compromise the root account much more easily.

- Line 17 controls whether the NFS Automounter will run. If you're not using NFS, it seems to make no difference. We aren't fans of NFS automounting for normal Unix installations, and aren't quite certain what to think of it on OS X. You'll learn more about NFS in Chapter 23, "File and Resource Sharing."
- Line 18 controls whether this machine serves as a configuration server for other machines. This appears to be an OS X Server–specific function.
- Line 19 controls IP forwarding. This is a technique by which one machine with a real network connection can make that connection available to other machines connected to it, as though they were also connected to the Internet. Configuration of this, and other network security–related options, will be covered in Chapter 31, "Server Security and Advanced Network Configuration."
- Line 20 configures whether the machine functions as its own mail server. Configuration using this option will be covered in Chapter 29, "Creating a Mail Server."
- Line 21 determines whether the machine functions as a management server for other machines. This is another OS X Server–specific function.
- Line 22 configures whether the machine functions as a netboot server for other machines. Again, this is best left to OS X Server, which contains GUI tools for configuring this option.
- Line 23 specifies which, if any, NIS domain the machine belongs to. NIS is the normal Unix way of distributing user ID and password information to multiple machines in a cluster. If you have an existing Unix installation, you can subscribe your OS X machine to the Unix machine's account information. This will be covered in Chapter 23.
- Line 24 determines whether the machine should use a remote time server to synchronize its clock.
- Line 25 specifies whether the machine functions as a QuickTime streaming server. This technology will be detailed in Chapter 27, "Web Serving."
- Line 26 controls whether the machine provides `sshd` (Secure Shell daemon) services. This is a high-security network connection suite that will be covered in Chapter 26, "Remote Administration."
- Line 27 controls whether the machine functions as a Web (HTTPD) server. How to enable and configure your machine as a high-power Web server will be covered in Chapter 27.

- Line 28 sets the name with which the machine registers itself on the AppleTalk network. In this case, I've registered this Mac with the same name that it has on the Internet.

Note

Please note that we've abbreviated the language in the preceding list a bit. The first few entries are worded correctly—the file literally sets the values of variables, and these variables are used elsewhere to configure the properties of the system described. Later items that state that the line *controls* something should be read to mean that it sets a variable that is used by a program elsewhere to control the item.

Other `/etc/` directory preference and configuration files that you will want to be familiar with are

- `/etc/services`—Configures the service name to port number mapping required for `inetd`, and some other network-based services.
- `/etc/printcap`—Configures printing for the `lpr`/`lpd` BSD-based printing subsystem. (Setting up this printing subsystem will be given as a NetInfo example in Chapter 23, "File and Resource Sharing.")
- `/etc/hosts`—Configures the set of other machines that this machine knows about, without having to go to the DNS server to get a hostname or IP address.
- `/etc/passwd`—Configures user IDs, and associated home directories, passwords, and shells.
- `/etc/group`—Configures groups and group memberships.

These files all use specific internal preferences formats that are rooted in Unix tradition and are documented in the man pages (`man printcap`, for example, to read about the `printcap` file format). In OS X, these files are directly used only in single-user mode because Apple has replaced their use with databases from NetInfo. Learning about them isn't completely irrelevant, though. It's often much easier to load the NetInfo database from these files with well-defined formats than it is to enter the data directly into NetInfo. In Chapter 23, we show how to use the traditional `/etc/` configuration file formats to load data into NetInfo.

You might also want to be familiar with the formats for `/etc/fstab` and `/etc/exports`. These files traditionally control the mounting of disks and the serving of disks, respectively. Apple, however, doesn't seem to use them even in single-user mode. But the

NetInfo server can load data from these file formats, so it might be useful to learn them if you will be interacting with other types of Unix machines.

Defaults Database

Preferences stored in the `~/Library/Preferences/` files are stored in XML (Extensible Markup Language), an emerging data storage standard. Readers familiar with HTML (Hypertext Markup Language) will find many similarities in the structure of HTML documents and of documents written in XML. The primary differences are that HTML is intended to be (but has wandered away from being) a structurally tagged language in a specified tag set, whereas XML is a language in which structural tagging may be arbitrarily defined.

For those unfamiliar with either language, both are essentially languages in which the content of a document is indicated by surrounding content items with tags. The beginning tag is usually of the form `<TAGNAME>`, where the < and > are required parts of the tag. The ending tag is of the form `</TAGNAME>` where the `TAGNAME` part of the begin/end pair must match. Tags in both languages may be nested, but neither supports tag pairs that overlap. (That is, `<TAG1> some data <TAG2> more data</TAG1> and more data</TAG2>` is not acceptable.) HTML has a defined set of tags that are part of the language, but XML is actually a language in which arbitrary tags can be defined. HTML tags also imply to a browser that the data enclosed by the tags has certain intended display characteristics. XML tags, however, imply only document structure and require an additional style definition to provide display properties. Finally, through design and through degeneration by lack of standards, HTML has come to include a number of tags with purposes and syntaxes outside the logic described earlier. For example, HTML allows "half tags" for certain types of tags, as it uses some tags exclusively for display control, rather than for structural tagging. HTML's `<P>` (paragraph) tag, for instance, can be used alone with no closing `</P>` tag because it specifies only that the browser should move down and start a new line with the next text. It does not delimit the boundaries of a paragraph.

For comparison, Listing 20.3 shows a syntactically correct HTML file, and Listing 20.4 shows similar data encoded in XML.

LISTING 20.3 A File with Typical HTML Tagging

```
<HTML>
<HEAD>
    <META HTTP-EQUIV="Content-type" CONTENT="text/html; charset=iso-8859-1">
    <TITLE>Animate! Ohio State - Not Quite All About Animate!</TITLE>
<LINK REL="stylesheet" HREF="../animate.css" type="text/css">
</HEAD>
```

LISTING 20.3 continued

```
<BODY MARGINWIDTH="0" MARGINHEIGHT="0" LEFTMARGIN="0" TOPMARGIN="0"
      BGCOLOR="#FFFFFF" TEXT="#000000" LINK="#C00F00" VLINK="#C00F00"
      ALINK="#808080">
<TABLE BACKGROUND="../scarlet.gif" BORDER=0 CELLSPACING=0 CELLPADDING=0
       WIDTH="100%">
  <TR>
    <TD ALIGN=LEFT VALIGN="TOP"> 
      <IMG SRC="../images/TopMenu/all-animate.gif" WIDTH=146 HEIGHT=30
           BORDER=0 ALT="[ All About Animate! ]" ALIGN="MIDDLE">
    </TD>
    <TD ALIGN=CENTER><IMG SRC="space_scarlet.gif" WIDTH=1 HEIGHT=1></TD>
    <TD ALIGN=RIGHT><A HREF="../animate.html">
      <IMG SRC="../images/TopMenu/association.gif" WIDTH=284 HEIGHT=40
           BORDER=0 ALT="[ The Ohio State University Japanese
           Animation Association ]"></A>
    </TD>
  </TR>
</TABLE>

<TABLE WIDTH="100%" BORDER="0" CELLSPACING="0" CELLPADDING="0"
       BACKGROUND="../grey.gif">
  <TR>
    <TD HEIGHT="25" ALIGN="LEFT" VALIGN="TOP" CLASS="date">
    <IMG SRC="../space_grey.gif" WIDTH=1 HEIGHT=1 BORDER=0>
    <A HREF="find.html" CLASS="date">Find Animate!</A>
    |
    <A HREF="joining.html" CLASS="date">Join Animate!</A>
    |
    <A HREF="officers.html" CLASS="date">The Officers</A>
    |
    <A HREF="helpers.html" CLASS="date">Helpers</A>
    |
    <a href="bylaws.html" CLASS="date">The Bylaws</A>
    |
    <a href="constitution.html" CLASS="date">The Constitution</A>
    </TD>
    <TD ALIGN=CENTER><IMG SRC="space_scarlet.gif" WIDTH=1 HEIGHT=1></TD>
    <TD VALIGN="top" ALIGN="right"><IMG SRC="../space_grey.gif" WIDTH=1
        HEIGHT=1 BORDER=0>
    </TD>
  </TR>
</TABLE>

<TABLE WIDTH="660" BORDER="0" CELLSPACING="0" ALIGN="CENTER">
  <TR>
    <TD ALIGN="left" VALIGN="top" COLSPAN="2"><img src="../space.gif"
        height="20" width="1"></TD>
  </TR>
  <TR>
```

LISTING 20.3 continued

```
    <TD WIDTH="360">
    <P CLASS="header">All About Animate!
    <P CLASS="text">As this is a new year, we're busy readying the
    newest club information, so this section is still a little thin.
    Make sure to visit the <A HREF="officers.html">Club Officers</A>
    index and meet the people who keep you in the anime pink, as it
    were,and <A HREF="find.html">how to get to them</A>.
    <P CLASS="text">In the meantime, you can go over the
    <A HREF="constitution.html">constitution</A>
    and <A HREF="bylaws.html">club bylaws</A> to learn just how things
    are run at Animate! Ohio State. Also check out the <A HREF="helpers.html">
    helpers</A> page and see just who else lends a hand at Animate!
    <P CLASS="text">This section will be updated as we receive and revise
    the neccessary information. Stay tuned!
    </TD>
    <TD WIDTH="340" ALIGN="RIGHT" VALIGN="TOP">
    <P CLASS="caption">
      <IMG SRC="../images/anime/seraphim.jpg" BORDER=1 WIDTH=325 HEIGHT=249
         ALT="[ The 266,613,336 wings of Seraphim. ]">
      The 266,613,336 wings of Seraphim.
    </TD>
  </TR>
    </TD>
  </TR>
  <TR>
    <TD COLSPAN=3>
      <IMG SRC="../space.gif" WIDTH=1 HEIGHT=1 VSPACE=400 BORDER=0>
    </TD>
  </TR>
</TABLE>

</BODY>
</HTML>
```

LISTING 20.4 A File with Typical XML Tagging

```
<PAGE>
<SUMMARY>
    <ITEM>charset</ITEM>
      <VALUE>iso-8859-1</VALUE>
    <ITEM>Title</ITEM>
      <VALUE>Animate! Ohio State - Not Quite All About Animate!</VALUE>
</SUMMARY>

<CONTENTS>
<TABLE_FORMAT_1>
  <TABLE_ROW>
    <DATA_1>
```

LISTING 20.4 continued

```
      <!ENTITY all-animate SYSTEM "../images/TopMenu/all-animate.gif"
               NDATA GIF87A>
    </DATA_1>
    <DATA_2>
      <!ENTITY spacer SYSTEM "space_scarlet.gif" NDATA GIF87A>
    </DATA_2>
    <DATA_3>
      <LINK XML-LINK="SIMPLE" HREF="animate.html">
        <!ENTITY "The Ohio State University Japanese Animation Association"
                 SYSTEM "../images/TopMenu/association.gif" NDATA GIF87A>
      </LINK>
    </DATA_3>
  </TABLE_ROW>
</TABLE_FORMAT_1>

<TABLE_FORMAT_2>
  <TABLE_ROW>
    <DATA_4>
      <!ENTITY spacer2 SYSTEM "../space_grey.gif" NDATA GIF87A>
      <LINK XML-LINK="SIMPLE" HREF="find.html">Find Animate!</LINK>
      |
      <LINK XML-LINK="SIMPLE" HREF="joining.html">Join Animate!</LINK>
      |
      <LINK XML-LINK="SIMPLE" HREF="officers.html">The Officers</LINK>
      |
      <LINK XML-LINK="SIMPLE" HREF="helpers.html">Helpers</LINK>
      |
      <LINK XML-LINK="SIMPLE" HREF="bylaws.html">The Bylaws</LINK>
      |
      <LINK XML-LINK="SIMPLE" HREF="constitution.html">The Constitution</LINK>
    </DATA_4>
    <DATA_5><!ENTITY spacer SYSTEM "space_scarlet.gif" NDATA GIF87A></DATA_5>
    <DATA_6><!ENTITY spacer2 SYSTEM "../space_grey.gif" NDATA GIF87A></DATA_6>
  </TR>
</TABLE_FORMAT_2>

<TABLE_FORMAT_3>
  <TABLE_ROW>
    <DATA_7>
    <!ENTITY spacer3 SYSTEM "../space.gif" NDATA GIF87A>
    </DATA_7>
  </TABLE_ROW>

  <TABLE_ROW>
    <DATA_8>
    <HEADER_PARAGRAPH>All About Animate!</HEADER_PARAGRAPH>
    <NORMAL_PARAGRAPH>As this is a new year, we're busy readying the newest
    club information, so this section is still a little thin. Make sure
    to visit the <LINK XML-LINK="SIMPLE" HREF="officers.html">Club Officers
```

LISTING 20.4 continued

```
    </LINK>index and meet the people who keep you in the anime pink, as it
    were, and <LINK XML-LINK="SIMPLE" HREF="find.html">how to get to them
    </LINK>.</NORMAL_PARAGRAPH>
    <NORMAL_PARAGRAPH>In the meantime, you can go over the
    <LINK XML-LINK="SIMPLE" HREF="constitution.html">constitution</LINK>
    and <LINK XML-LINK="SIMPLE" HREF="bylaws.html">club bylaws</LINK>
    to learn just how things are run at Animate! Ohio State. Also check
    out the <LINK XML-LINK="SIMPLE" HREF="helpers.html">helpers</LINK>
    page and see just who else lends a hand at Animate!</NORMAL_PARAGRAPH>
    <NORMAL_PARAGRAPH>This section will be updated as we receive and revise
    the neccessary information. Stay tuned!</NORMAL_PARAGRAPH>
    </DATA_8>
    <DATA_9>
    <CAPTION_PARAGRAPH>
      <!ENTITY "The 266,613,336 wings of Seraphim" SYSTEM
               "../images/anime/seraphim.jpg" NDATA GIF87A>
      The 266,613,336 wings of Seraphim.
    </CAPTION_PARAGRAPH>
    </DATA_9>
  </TABLE_ROW>

  <TABLE_ROW>
    <WIDE_DATA>
      <!ENTITY spacer3 "../space.gif" NDATA GIF87A>
    </WIDE_DATA>
  </TABLE_ROW>
</TABLE_FORMAT_3>

</CONTENTS>
</PAGE>
```

The HTML file will render in a Web browser similar to what is shown in Figure 20.1. The XML file actually has no visual representation because XML is a structural definition, and requires an auxiliary style definition to indicate the appropriate visual representation. The auxiliary style definition provides all the style mappings so that tags that have explicit styles in the HTML file (such as `<TD>` elements) with assigned widths, and so on, can be given display style directions. This is why the XML representation has many different `<DATA_*>` tags, instead of a single `<TD>` type tag with parameters. The appropriate display options characteristics for each `<DATA_*>` type are defined in the external style file. We won't provide the style file here because learning its syntax won't help you with Apple's preferences. Still, for this example, you can probably imagine reasonable visual intentions from the tag names and a comparison with the HTML file.

FIGURE 20.1
A Web browser renders the HTML shown in Listing 20.3 like this. The XML shown in Listing 20.4 could render like this as well, but it also could render in any number of other manners as well.

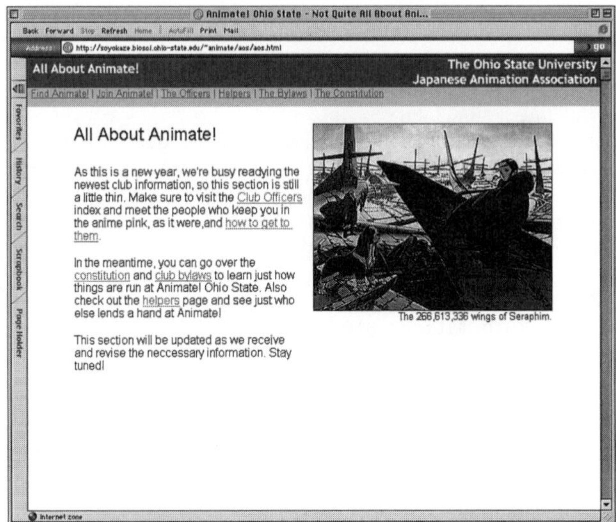

The observant reader will note that the similarities are significant, but that where HTML allows implicitly closed tags for items such as `<P>` (paragraph), XML requires explicitly closed tags. For completely nonenclosing tags, such as HTML's `<HR>` tag (horizontal line), XML substitutes a tag type that is understood to open and close itself in the statement. The XML equivalent would look like `<HR/>`, which is read by the parser as `<HR></HR>`. Apple uses this type of tagging frequently in its XML preferences files. Listing 20.5 shows the `Terminal.app` preference file (located in `~/Library/Preferences/com.apple.terminal.plist`) from an installed, but little-used user account.

LISTING 20.5 An Almost Bare Preference File for `Terminal.app`

```
<?xml version="1.0" encoding="UTF-8"?>
<!DOCTYPE plist SYSTEM "file://localhost/System/Library/DTDs/PropertyList.dtd">
<plist version="0.9">
<dict>
        <key>WinLocULY</key>
        <integer>-53</integer>
        <key>WinLocX</key>
        <integer>23</integer>
        <key>WinLocY</key>
        <integer>827</integer>
</dict>
</plist>
```

The terminal preferences currently contain little of interest other than some variables that control the location of the window. If the file were to be opened in a text editor and the values changed, the location on the screen where the Terminal opens would be changed.

Listing 20.6 shows the `Terminal.app` preferences from a considerably more used account. As you can see, the `plist` files are not required to contain all the preferences for an application, and can grow as the user specifies more preferences that aren't just the defaults. One annoyance that this causes is that sometimes hidden preferences aren't accessible through any of the application's preferences panes. These preferences can find their way into the XML `plist` files only if somebody discovers their existence and adds the preference line to the `plist` file manually. The terminal opacity setting that will be discussed shortly is exactly this sort of discovered preference.

Tip

If you'd like to search for this type of hidden preference for yourself, you might want to check out the `strings` command. If you run the `strings` command on `/Applications/Utilities/Terminal.app/Contents/MacOS/Terminal` (`strings Applications/Utilities/Terminal.app/Contents/MacOS | more` might be a reasonable attempt), you'll see a list of all textual strings in the program. It's reasonable to expect that for the program to read strings out of a `.plist` file, it must contain the string, so the strings found in the program make for potentially interesting things to try as preferences.

LISTING 20.6 A Preferences File for `Terminal.app` That Has Accumulated Some Settings over Time

```
<?xml version="1.0" encoding="UTF-8"?>
<!DOCTYPE plist SYSTEM "file://localhost/System/Library/DTDs/PropertyList.dtd">
<plist version="0.9">
<dict>
    <key>AlwaysPromptOnQuit</key>
    <integer>1</integer>
    <key>AppleSavePanelExpanded</key>
    <string>YES</string>
    <key>AutoFocus</key>
    <true/>
    <key>Autowrap</key>
    <true/>
    <key>BlinkCursor</key>
    <true/>
    <key>CleanCommands</key>
    <string>rlogin;telnet;ssh;slogin</string>
    <key>Columns</key>
```

LISTING 20.6 continued

```
<integer>132</integer>
<key>CursorShape</key>
<integer>0</integer>
<key>CustomTitle</key>
<string>Wowzers! </string>
<key>DisableAnsiColors</key>
<false/>
<key>DockLaunchHide</key>
<false/>
<key>DoubleBold</key>
<true/>
<key>Keypad</key>
<true/>
<key>LastCommand</key>
<string>emacs</string>
<key>Meta</key>
<integer>-1</integer>
<key>MonitorProcs</key>
<true/>
<key>NSColorPanelMode</key>
<string>6</string>
<key>NSDefaultOpenDirectory</key>
<string>~/Documents</string>
<key>NSFixedPitchFont</key>
<string>Monaco</string>
<key>NSFixedPitchFontSize</key>
<integer>10</integer>
<key>NSPreferencesContentSize</key>
<string>{460, 470}</string>
<key>NSPreferencesSelectedIndex</key>
<integer>3</integer>
<key>NSWindow Frame NSColorPanel</key>
<string>3 379 205 367 0 55 1024 691 </string>
<key>NSWindow Frame TermInspector</key>
<string>454 200 268 387 0 4 1024 742 </string>
<key>Rows</key>
<integer>35</integer>
<key>RunningBackgroundClean</key>
<false/>
<key>SaveLines</key>
<integer>10000</integer>
<key>Scrollback</key>
<true/>
<key>Shell</key>
<string>/bin/tcsh</string>
<key>ShellExitAction</key>
<integer>2</integer>
<key>SourceDotLogin</key>
<true/>
```

LISTING 20.6 continued

```
    <key>StartupAction</key>
    <integer>1</integer>
    <key>StartupFile</key>
    <string></string>
    <key>StrictEmulation</key>
    <true/>
    <key>TextColors</key>
    <string>0.000 0.000 0.000 1.000 1.000 1.000 0.000 0.000 0.000 0.333 0.333
             0.333 1.000 1.000 1.000 0.333 0.333 0.333 1.000 0.988 0.033 0.333
             0.333 0.333 </string>
    <key>TitleBits</key>
    <integer>1</integer>
    <key>Translate</key>
    <true/>
    <key>WinLocULY</key>
    <integer>19</integer>
    <key>WinLocX</key>
    <integer>42</integer>
    <key>WinLocY</key>
    <integer>723</integer>
</dict>
</plist>
```

Instead of requiring you to edit XML files directly, Apple has provided a convenient command-line program for editing the preferences stored in these files. The `defaults` command allows you to specify a preference to be modified and a value with which to modify it. As an example of the `defaults` command in use, the following command modifies the transparency of the `Terminal.app` windows to produce those wonderful semi-opaque terminals you undoubtedly have seen in OS X screenshots on the Web:

```
defaults write com.apple.terminal TerminalOpaqueness 0.5
```

Specifically, this command modifies the value of the preference `TerminalOpaqueness` in the file `~/Library/Preferences/com.apple.terminal.plist`, and sets the value to `0.5` (or 50% opacity). If you were to run this command on the account with the `Terminal.app` preferences shown in Listing 20.5, the `~/Library/Preferences/com.apple.terminal.plist` would change to that shown in Listing 20.7.

LISTING 20.7 A `Terminal.app` Preferences File After Forcing a New Value into It (`TerminalOpaqueness`) with the `defaults` Command

```
<?xml version="1.0" encoding="UTF-8"?>
<!DOCTYPE plist SYSTEM "file://localhost/System/Library/DTDs/PropertyList.dtd">
<plist version="0.9">
<dict>
```

LISTING 20.7 continued

```
        <key>TerminalOpaqueness</key>
        <string>0.5</string>
        <key>WinLocULY</key>
        <integer>-53</integer>
        <key>WinLocX</key>
        <integer>23</integer>
        <key>WinLocY</key>
        <integer>827</integer>
</dict>
</plist>
```

As you can see in Listings 20.6 and 20.8, the items stored in the `~/Library/Preferences/` files are many and varied. You also can see that some preferences are not intuitively parseable.

LISTING 20.8 The `plist` File for `GraphicConverter`

```
<?xml version="1.0" encoding="UTF-8"?>
<!DOCTYPE plist SYSTEM "file://localhost/System/Library/DTDs/PropertyList.dtd">
<plist version="0.9">
<dict>
    <key>AppleNavServices:GetFile:0:Path</key>
    <string>file://localhost/Users/ray/Documents/</string>
    <key>AppleNavServices:GetFile:0:Position</key>
    <data>
    ALwA+A==
    </data>
    <key>AppleNavServices:GetFile:0:Size</key>
    <data>
    AAAAAAG0AhA=
    </data>
    <key>AppleNavServices:PutFile:0:Disclosure</key>
    <data>
    AQ==
    </data>
    <key>AppleNavServices:PutFile:0:Path</key>
    <string>file://localhost/Users/ray/Documents/</string>
    <key>AppleNavServices:PutFile:0:Position</key>
    <data>
    AQcA+A==
    </data>
    <key>AppleNavServices:PutFile:0:Size</key>
    <data>
    AAAAAAEdAhA=
    </data>
</dict>
</plist>
```

Unfortunately, Apple hasn't provided a definitive list of preference options for each application. Even a listing of the options that each file contains would not be complete because some applications accept preferences that are not yet stored in the XML files. There are preference options that some programs take as defaults, but that can be overridden by the insertion of specific preferences into the XML files. Because no current preference is stored, we can only make intelligent guesses as to what preference names and values might be accepted. The command for controlling the Terminal.app opacity is the result of such a serendipitous preference discovery. As a matter of fact, making intelligent guesses is exactly what the online community is doing regarding these preferences, and a number of interesting options have been discovered. Table 20.1 lists a number of preferences options that have been reported to be interesting, when configured using the `defaults` command. Not all these have known or well-documented functions.

TABLE 20.1 A Number of the Interesting `defaults` Preferences Options That Have Been Reported as Having Interesting Effects on the Interface

Issuing `defaults write` *this domain*	*and this key*	*and one of these values*	*affects this feature of the interface*
`com.apple.finder`	`Desktop.HasLocalVolumes`	`1` `0`	Display drives on the desktop
	`Desktop.HasTrash`	`1` `0`	Put the trash back on the desktop (where some say it belongs)
	`ZoomRects -bool`	`yes` `no`	Zoom or don't zoom Finder windows

	`DesktopViewOptions -dict ArrangeBy`	`dnam`
		`size`
		`kind`
			Arrange icons by name, size, or kind

	`Desktop.HasDarkDesktop`	`0`	1
	`Desktop.HasRemovableMedia`	`1` `0`	Removable media does or does not appear on the desktop
	`OpenWindowForNewRemovableDisk`	`1` `0`	Mounting removable media does or does not open a new window
	`CreateDesktop`	`0`	Don't show a desktop picture

TABLE 20.1 continued

Issuing `defaults write` *this domain*	*and this key*	*and one of these values*	*affects this feature of the interface*
	`AppleShowAllFiles`	`True`	Show even files that are normally hidden
`com.apple.terminal`	`TerminalOpaqueness`	`0.0 to 1.0`	Change the opacity of the Terminal window

`NSGlobalDomain`	`NSInterfaceStyle`	`nextstepdefaults`
		`macintoshdefaults`
		`windowsdefaults`	

	`Desktop.HasDark` `Background`	`1` `0`	
	`NSFixedPitchFontSize`	<*fontsize*>	
	`NSFontSize`	<*fontsize*>	
	`NSSystemFontSize`	<*fontsize*>	
`com.apple.dock`	`showhidden -boolean`	`yes` `no`	
	`showforeground -boolean`	`no`	`yes`
	`showforeground`	`1`	Colors the triangle indicating a running application in the Dock blue
	`showhidden`	`1`	Dims the Dock icons for hidden applications

	`mineffect`	`genie`
		`suck`
		`scale`
			Known values for different minimize into Dock effects

	`showshadow`	`1` `0`	Dock shadows back ground
<any application domain>	`NSUserKeyEquivalents`	'{"<menuitem>" ="<keystring>";}'	<menuitem> is any named menu item in a Cocoa application <keystring> is built from

TABLE 20.1 continued

Issuing defaults write *this domain*	*and this key*	*and one of these values*	*affects this feature of the interface*
			@ = Command $ = Shift ~ = Option ^ = Control and any character Modifies the key equivalent for a menu item

Note

This table is excerpted from information collected from the Internet from a variety of places, including

`http://www.macosxhints.com/search.php?query=defaults+write&mode=search&datestart=0&dateend=0&topic=0&type=stories&autho=0`

`http://osx.macnn.com/`

`http://www.pixits.com/defaults.htm`

Table 20.2 shows the command documentation table for the `defaults` command.

TABLE 20.2 Command Documentation Table for the `defaults` Command

`defaults`	*Accesses the Mac OS X user defaults system*

```
defaults read [ <domain name> [ <key> ] ]
defaults write <domain name> [ {'<domain rep>' | <domain name> <key>
'<value rep>'}
defaults delete [ <domain name> [ <key> ] ]
defaults { domains | find <word> | help }
```

`defaults` allows users to read, write, and delete Mac OS X user defaults from the command line. Applications use the defaults system to record user preferences and other information that must be maintained when applications aren't running, such as the default font for new documents. Because applications do access the defaults system while they are running, you should not modify the defaults of a running application.

TABLE 20.2 Command Documentation Table for the `defaults` Command

`defaults`	*Accesses the Mac OS X user defaults system*

User defaults belong to domains, which typically correspond to individual applications. Each domain has a dictionary of keys and values to represent its defaults. Keys are always strings, but values can be complex data structures comprised of arrays, dictionaries, strings, and binary data.

Although all applications, system services, and other programs have their own domains, they also share a domain called `NSGlobalDomain`. If a default is not specified in the application's domain, it uses the default listed in the `NSGlobalDomain` instead.

`read`	Prints all of the user's defaults for every domain to standard output.
`read` *`<domain name>`*	Prints all of the user's defaults for the specified *`<domain name>`* to standard output.
`read` *`<domain name>`* *`<key>`*	Prints the value for the default of the *`<domain name>`* identified by *`<key>`*.
`write` *`<domain name>`* *`<key>`* `'`*`<value rep>`*`'`	Writes *`<value rep>`* as the value for *`<key>`* in *`<domain name>`*. *`<value rep>`* must be a property list, and must be enclosed in single quotes. For example: `defaults write MyApplication "Default Color" '(255, 0, 0)'` sets the default color in `MyApplication` to the array containing 255, 0, 0 (red, green, blue components). Note that the key is in quotes because of the space in its name.
`write` *`<domain name>`* `'`*`<domain rep>`*`'`	Overwrites the defaults information in *`<domain name>`* with that specified in *`<domain rep>`*. *`<domain rep>`* must be a property list representation of a dictionary, and must be enclosed in single quotes. For example, `defaults write MyApplication '[ "Default Color" = (255, 0, 0); "Default Font" = Helvetica; } '` overwrites any previous defaults for `MyApplication` and replaces them with the ones specified.
`delete` *`<domain name>`*	Deletes all default information for *`<domain name>`*.
`delete` *`<domain name>`* *`<key>`*	Deletes the default named *`<key>`* in *`<domain name>`*.
`domains`	Prints the names of all domains in the user's defaults system.
`find` *`<word>`*	Searches for *`<word>`* in the domain names, keys, and values of the user's defaults, and prints out a list of matches.
`help`	Prints a list of possible command formats.

System Services

Many programs run on your system to provide an assortment of services to you as a local user and to remote users contacting your system. These services range from obvious things (such as terminal services that allow you to connect to your machine from remote locations and file-sharing services) to less obvious but still useful services (such as the ones that provide wall-clock time information and remote machine status information).

Programs that provide service for all users on a machine are generally started by one of two different mechanisms. Either they are started at machine startup, by a series of shell-scripts that execute programs during boot. Or they are executed by a daemon that waits for requests for service, and starts the appropriate program to handle the request.

Modifying Startup Services

Services that need to be continuously present, such as the software that configures and maintains network connections, are started from startup scripts. These startup scripts are kept in subdirectories of the `/System/Library/StartupItems` directory, and are simply shell scripts (such as you learned about in Chapter 18), that perform simple logic to make certain that everything is right with the system, and start the appropriate software.

Note

Remember that in Unix, if you can type it at the command line, you can write it into a shell script. Anything that you find that you want to run whenever the system is running, can simply be placed in a shell script and that script executed at system startup.

As shipped, your OS X machine should have a complement of items in the `StartupItems` folder similar to that shown in Table 20.3. Don't worry if your `/System/Library/StartupItems/` doesn't contain exactly these items. Depending on what installation options you've chosen, and whether any additional software has been installed by the time you're reading this, your system might display some differences.

TABLE 20.3 Typical Items in the `/System/Library/StartupItems/` Directory

Accounting	Handles process accounting, if you care to log every action that every user or process takes
Apache	The Web server
AppServices	Assorted support services for the overall GUI interface

TABLE 20.3 continued

AppleShare	AppleShare file sharing
AppleTalk	AppleTalk network services
AuthServer	User authentication services
Cleanup	A collection of routines that remove temporary files and log files that are probably just cluttering up space
ConfigServer	Allows the machine to tell itself and, potentially, other machines you want to function similarly, about its configuration
CrashReporter	Reports system crashes to Apple, if desired
Cron	A service that runs various programs at specified times or specified intervals
DirectoryServices	Manages directory information for exchanging data between the Unix subsystem and the GUI portions of the interface
Disks	Controls disk operations
Ipservices	Controls some services related to TCP/IP networking
NFS	Controls use of and access to the NFS (Network File System) Unix file sharing protocol
Network	Configures and controls the network interface
NetworkTime	Interacts with the network time server
Portmap	Provides connectivity between remote machines, and services on your machine that don't have defined TCP/IP ports that they run on
SSH	Secure Shell suite startup configuration
SecurityServer	Part of user authentication software
Sendmail	Configures and controls the mail server
SystemLog	Configures the system logging daemon
SystemTuning	Apple-specific script that turns on and off assorted services to optimize the system performance

Each of these directories contains a number of items—typically a file named after the name of the directory, a directory named Resources, and a file named `StartupParameters.plist` (which oddly, isn't an XML file). The file named after the directory (and service), is the actual shell script that is run at system boot time. The Resources directory typically contains directories of "resource-like" information, such as files that contain language-replacement strings for language localization. The `StartupParameters.plist` contains a collection of variables and associated values that affect the operation of the service started.

Listing 20.9 shows a simple `StartupItems` shell script—this one starts the Apache HTTPD (Web) server.

LISTING 20.9 The Apache `HTTPD` `StartupItems` Shell Script

```
1  #!/bin/sh
2
3  ##
4  # Start Web Server
5  ##
6
7 .  /etc/rc.common
8
9  if [ "${WEBSERVER:=-NO-}" = "-YES-" ]; then
10     ConsoleMessage "Starting web server"
11
12     apachectl start
13 fi
```

In this listing, items starting with the `#` sign are comments. The meaning of the lines in the script can be summarized in a simple manner:

- Line 7 sources the script `/etc/rc.common`, where many system-wide definitions are made.
- Line 9 checks the value of the variable `WEBSERVER`, and determines whether the value is `YES` or `NO`. This value actually is extracted from the `/etc/hostconfig` file shown in Listing 20.2.
- If Line 9 finds a `YES`, line 10 sends a message to the console that says `Starting web server`.
- Line 12 executes the program `apachectl` with the argument `start`. `apachectl` is actually another shell script, specific to the Apache installation, which handles all the real work of starting the service.
- Line 13 `fi` is *if* backwards, and it terminates the conditional expression started by the `if` on line 9.

The English language locale configuration for the Apache `StartupItems` (`Apache/Resources/English.lproj/Localizable.strings`) is shown in Listing 20.10.

LISTING 20.10 The English Language Locale Configuration for the Apache `StartupItems`

```
<?xml version="1.0" encoding="UTF-8"?>
<!DOCTYPE plist SYSTEM "file://localhost/System/Library/DTDs/PropertyList.dtd">
<plist version="0.9">
<dict>
        <key>Starting Apache web server</key>
        <string>Starting Apache web server</string>
</dict>
</plist>
```

This XML file specifies a key, the expression `Starting Apache web server`, and a local (English) replacement string for that expression `Starting Apache web server`. If everything works as intended, whenever the program attempts to print the key value, the system will instead output the replacement string value. Because this isn't quite obvious from the English example, Listing 20.11 shows the `Spanish.lproj` version of the `Localizable.strings` file.

LISTING 20.11 `Spanish.lproj` Version of the `Localizable.strings` File for the Apache Web Server

```
<?xml version="1.0" encoding="UTF-8"?>
<!DOCTYPE plist SYSTEM "file://localhost/System/Library/DTDs/PropertyList.dtd">
<plist version="0.9">
<dict>
        <key>Starting Apache web server</key>
        <string>Iniciando servidor Apache</string>
</dict>
</plist>
```

Here, it is more obvious that the localization file is requesting a search to find `Starting Apache web server`, and replacing it with the Spanish equivalent. Amusingly, the startup script itself doesn't output `Starting Apache web server`; it outputs `Starting web server`. So, although this is one of the most concise examples of the relation between the Resource items and the `StartupItems` script, it doesn't appear to be the most correct.

`inetd` Services

As mentioned earlier, the `inetd` service, configured by the `/etc/inetd.conf` file, actually is a service that starts and controls other services. It's not practical to start an unlimited number of some types of network services and leave them running, right from startup. Depending on the use of your machine, some services might be needed in great numbers; for example, the `ftpd` FTP server processes, if you serve particularly interesting data and have many people connecting simultaneously. Others might be used hardly at all, such as the sprayd network diagnostic daemon. Or, on your system, the use pattern might be the opposite—but regardless of the use, patterns are likely to vary over time. For many of these types of services, the system relieves you of the task of trying to provide the right number of these servers in some manual configuration process, by using the inetd daemon to configure and run them on an as-needed basis.

Note

If you'd like to learn much more about network services in general, you're invited to check out Que Publishing's *Special Edition Using TCP/IP* (ISBN 0-7897-1897-9), another book by John Ray.

The inetd.conf file then is the file that tells inetd which services it should start and how. A typical inetd.conf file is shown in Listing 20.12, and has the form of a set of lines, with each line containing a specification for a service. The service specification lines consist of a set of fields separated by tabs or spaces. The fields that must occur on each line are shown in the following list, with a brief description of the data that belongs in them.

- Service name (used to look up service port in NetInfo services map)
- Socket type (stream, dgram, raw, rdm, or seqpacket)
- Protocol (tcp or udp, rcp/tcp, or rcp/udp)
- Wait/nowait (for dgrams only—all others get nowait; should the socket wait for additional connections)
- User (user to run the service as)
- Server program (actual path to binary on disk)
- Server program arguments (how the command line would look, if typed, including server name)

Listing 20.12 shows an inetd.conf file from a running machine, with a few useful network services enabled.

LISTING 20.12 An inetd.conf File from a Running Machine, with a Few Useful Network Services Enabled

```
#
# Internet server configuration database
#
#    @(#)inetd.conf    5.4 (Berkeley) 6/30/90
```

LISTING 20.12 continued

```
#
# Items with double hashes in front (##) are not yet implemented in the OS.
#
#finger  stream   tcp   nowait    nobody  /usr/libexec/tcpd        fingerd -s
ftp      stream   tcp   nowait    root    /usr/libexec/tcpd        ftpd -l
#login   stream   tcp   nowait    root    /usr/libexec/tcpd        rlogind
#nntp    stream   tcp   nowait    usenet  /usr/libexec/tcpd        nntpd
ntalk    dgram    udp   wait      root    /usr/libexec/tcpd        ntalkd
#shell   stream   tcp   nowait    root    /usr/libexec/tcpd        rshd
#telnet  stream   tcp   nowait    root    /usr/libexec/tcpd        telnetd
#uucpd   stream   tcp   nowait    root    /usr/libexec/tcpd        uucpd
comsat   dgram    udp   wait      root    /usr/libexec/tcpd        comsat
#tftp    dgram    udp   wait      nobody  /usr/libexec/tcpd
    ➥        tftpd /private/tftpboot
#bootp   dgram    udp   wait      root    /usr/libexec/tcpd        bootpd
##pop3   stream   tcp   nowait    root    /usr/libexec/tcpd
    ➥        /usr/local/libexec/popper
##imap4  stream   tcp   nowait    root    /usr/libexec/tcpd
    Â        /usr/local/libexec/imapd
```

In Listing 20.12, service control lines that have a # symbol in front of them are turned off. Because this machine doesn't provide many network services to the outside world, the majority of the services are turned off. Only the `ftpd` (ftp server), `ntalkd` (talk daemon, provides chat-like services), and `comsat` (provides new mail notification service) are turned on. To turn on additional services, simply uncomment (remove the # sign) the line, and restart `inetd` by sending it an HUP signal.

```
kill -HUP <inetd pid>
```

We strongly recommend that you leave your `telnet` daemon and `rlogin` daemon disabled because these are both significant security risks. You're already familiar with the ssh (Secure Shell) programs for connecting to remote machines. Chapter 26 will cover installing and configuring the `sshd` daemon on your own machine, and this service will provide a secure replacement for the functionality of the `telnet` and `shell` daemons.

You will notice that according to the file format definition given earlier, the program started by many of the lines is exactly the same: `/usr/libexec/tcpd`. This is part of a security mechanism, whereby `inetd` doesn't start the actual service, but instead starts yet another service, which starts the desired final service. The intermediate service, the program `/usr/libexec/tcpd`, is the TCP Wrappers program. This program can be configured to intercept requests for network services, and allow them to continue only if the request comes from an authorized remote host. TCP Wrappers lives as an intermediate service between the `inetd` service and the end services that it delivers because the `inetd`-to-end-service method of providing network services was well established before the magnitude of potential Internet security problems were discovered. It turned out to be easier to sneak a wrapper around the end service, and not worry about modifying the model or about having to add security-conscious code to each and every possible service. Chapter 31, "Server Security and Advanced Network Configuration," covers how to configure TCP Wrappers to increase your system security.

Summary

This chapter provided an overview of the preference and configuration controls that are available from and through the command line. Because so much of the system is currently undocumented by Apple, we can't guess whether these items will remain in these places or continue to contain the same options. However, we have a pretty good guess that the general form and style of how the configuration is controlled will remain the same. With the tools provided here, you should be able to cope with any changes that might come your way.

CHAPTER 21

AppleScript

IN THIS CHAPTER

With the BSD subsystem, Mac OS X has become scriptable using very low-level components of the operating system. You might be surprised to learn, however, that the Macintosh has been scriptable for almost ten years, through a feature called AppleScript. AppleScript is often referred to as Apple's best-kept secret—it is a command line buried beneath many of the Mac's popular applications, including the Finder. Not surprisingly, Mac OS X integrates AppleScript into the operating system and provides access to the technology from both Carbon and Cocoa applications.

This chapter uncovers the mystery of using AppleScript and introduces the syntax and tools a user can employ to take control of his or her system at an entirely new level.

Introduction to AppleScript

When creating BSD shell scripts, you are limited to the input and output of the applications being scripted. Complex applications are often impossible to control because of their inability to process standard input. AppleScript works at an entirely different level—within the applications themselves.

To be controlled by AppleScript, an application must implement a scripting dictionary. A *scripting dictionary* is a collection of commands and functions that can be invoked through AppleScript. Each application determines the features that it makes available for scripting. The result of this approach is that applications can make their most useful functions available through a script, making it possible to create far more complex scripts.

It's also important to note the audience of Mac OS X's AppleScripting capabilities. Shell and Perl scripting are the tools of programmers and system administrators. AppleScript was intended to provide a means for normal, everyday Macintosh users to automate tasks on their computers. The syntax is surprisingly simple and can be understood even if you've never seen a programming language before. For example, take the following code:

```
tell application "Finder"
       activate
       close window "Applications"
end tell
```

It doesn't *look* like a programming language, but it is. This small example instructs Mac OS X to activate the Finder application, and then close an open window with the title Applications.

Using a language that can almost be read aloud and understood, normal users can write scripts that combine the capabilities of multiple applications.

Script Editor

The easiest way to get started with AppleScript is with the AppleScript editor. Besides being a context-sensitive programming editor, it also acts as a script recorder. A user can open the Script Editor, click record, and generate an AppleScript by using the editor to monitor his actions while interacting with an AppleScriptable application.

Note

It's critical to note that AppleScript (and the AppleScript editor) should not be considered a macro system. Macro applications, such as QuicKeys, work by simulating user input to applications. This is very similar to shell scripting. From the application's perspective, a user is controlling it.

When AppleScript controls an application, the application understands what is happening. It can return error codes and extended status to the script, enabling it to react and adapt to changing conditions. AppleScript is a very powerful tool and offers flexibility beyond simple macros. The drawback? An application is AppleScriptable only if it is designed to be.

(This isn't to downplay tools such as QuicKeys, which integrate virtual user capabilities with AppleScript for complete scripting solutions. In fact, I recommend users take a look at QuicKeys for an example of an excellent integrated Mac OS X scripting solution. The Web site is `http://www.cesoft.com/products/qkx.html`.)

Apple has made remarkable strides in making Mac OS X 10.1 scriptable. Applications such as the Finder and Terminal are now fully scriptable. The Script Editor will serve as your primary entry and testing point for any AppleScript development—either recorded or entered by hand.

Basic Usage

Launch the Script Editor (`Applications/AppleScript/Script Editor`) to begin scripting. The basic editor window is shown in Figure 21.1.

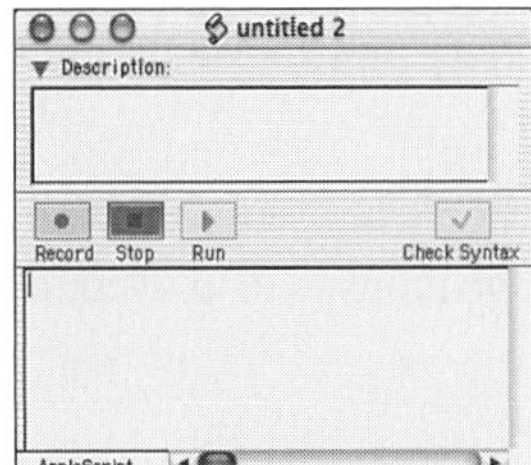

FIGURE 21.1
The Script Editor is used when editing or recording AppleScripts.

The Script Editor is composed of script recording and editing controls, which include:

- **Description**—This area is used to advertise the purpose and use instructions of your AppleScript.
- **Recording/Playback**—Similar to a tape deck, these buttons are used to control recording and playback of an AppleScript. Click the Record button (Command+D) to start monitoring your system for Apple events within scriptable applications. These events are then stored in a script. The Stop button (Command+.) is used to stop recording, whereas the Run button (Command+R) executes the actions.
- **Check Syntax**—Reviews the syntax of the current script for errors and automatically reformats the script if needed.
- **Content**—The content area is used to compose and edit script content. It functions like any Mac OS X text editor, but has the benefit of auto-formatting code when syntax is checked or the script is run.

Start using the editor by clicking the Record button and moving a few Finder windows around. As you move and open windows, the script will build in the editor window. Click Stop to finish off the code block and prepare it for execution. Figure 21.2 displays a script that has just finished generating.

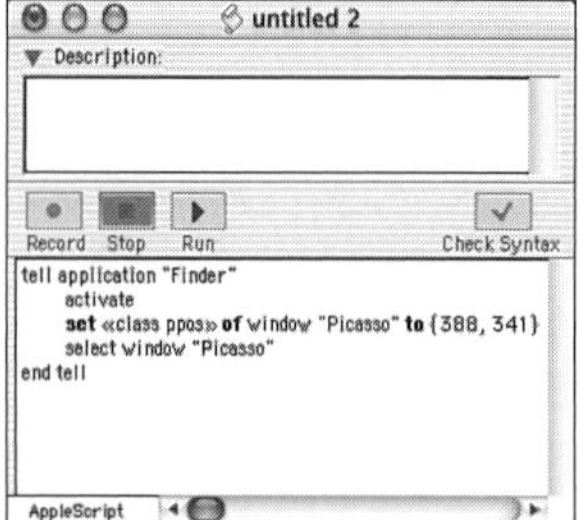

FIGURE 21.2
Click Record to monitor your actions and build an AppleScript, and then click Stop to finish the script.

Scripting Dictionary

Obviously, the biggest draw to AppleScript is the capability to create scripts from scratch. Recording is a good way to get a quick start, but can't be used to generate anything truly useful. The basic AppleScript syntax will be covered later in this chapter. Even this, however, is useless without knowledge of what commands an application can accept. Luckily, you can view a scripting dictionary that shows the functions and properties offered by a given piece of software.

To access a scripting dictionary for any application, choose Open Dictionary from the File menu. A list of the available scriptable applications is displayed, as demonstrated by Figure 21.3.

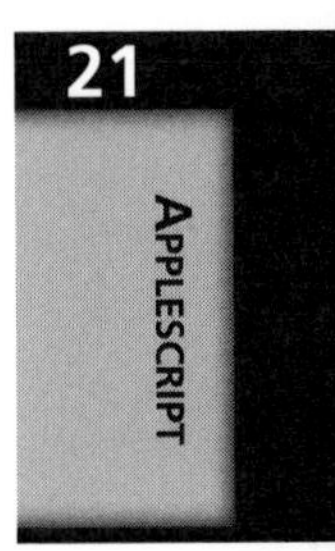

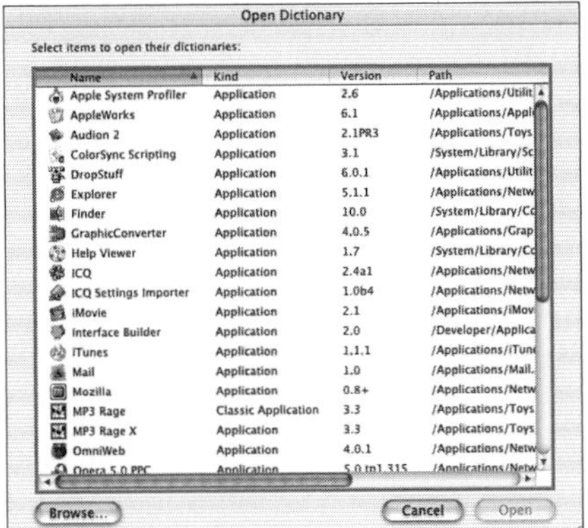

FIGURE 21.3
Choose from the available scriptable applications.

Be aware that some applications might not be shown—the Browse button at the bottom of the window opens a standard File Open dialog box for choosing an arbitrary file. After picking an application, from the default or browse view, a dictionary window should appear, as seen in Figure 21.4.

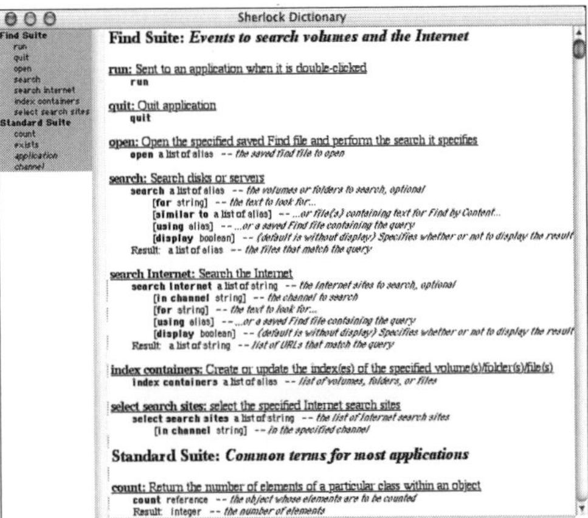

FIGURE 21.4
The dictionary documents the available AppleScript functions.

Along the left side of the dictionary window is a list of the AppleScript functions that are provided. These functions are divided into categories, depending on their purpose. These categories are called *suites*. To display the syntax for a given item, click its name in the list. Highlighting a suite name displays a description of the functions within that grouping, and a complete view of the syntax for each.

Tip

Hold down Shift and click each of the suite headings to create a master list of the available scripting functions. Use Print (Command+P) from the File menu to print a hard-copy reference guide for AppleScripting your favorite applications.

AppleScript abstracts the parts of an application into objects within classes. These objects have properties that can be set or modified to effect changes to the object. The properties can also be retrieved with `get` to return results for evaluation. For example, the Finder has a file object with a file type property. The following script gets and displays the type for an arbitrary file:

```
1: tell application "Finder"
2:     set thisFile to (choose file with prompt "Pick the file to examine:")
3:     set theType to get the file type of thisFile
4:     display dialog theType
5: end tell
```

Line 1 sends instructions to the Finder. Line 2 sets a variable called `thisFile` to point to a file. The `choose` command opens a file selection dialog box for visually selecting a file. Line 3 sets a variable called `theType` to the results of a command that gets the file type of the file reference by `thisFile`. Line 4 displays a dialog box containing the contents of `theType`. Finally, line 5 stops talking to the Finder.

This example introduces the structure you will see in most AppleScript programs. The `tell`, `set`, and `get` statements form the basis of scripts. The objects and the parameters that can be modified, however, will have to be looked up in the application's dictionary.

Note

The `display dialog` command used in this script isn't even a function of basic AppleScript. It is provided by the Standard Additions scripting extension, automatically installed on Mac OS X. You can view additional functions offered by the Standard Additions by displaying its dictionary.

Results

When an AppleScript function returns a result, it is stored in a special temporary variable called `result`. This can be used to access a value without the need for additional variables. For example, lines 3 and 4 of the preceding script could be changed to

```
get the file type of thisFile
display dialog the result
```

To display the contents of the `result` container within the Script Editor, choose Show Result (Command+L) from the Controls menu. Mac OS X will open a small window that contains the current value of result.

Syntax Highlighting

The Script Editor automatically highlights and formats AppleScript as you type. To change the default font styles and sizes, choose AppleScript Formatting from the Edit menu. The format dialog box can be seen in Figure 21.5.

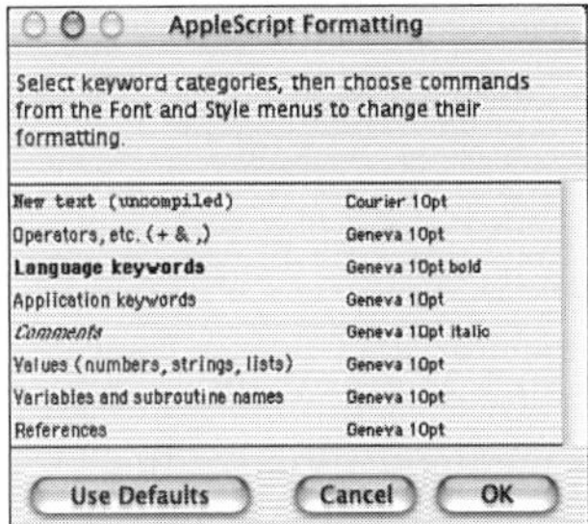

FIGURE 21.5
AppleScript Formatting controls enable the user to adjust the appearance of the Script Editor.

Choose one of the lines in the formatting dialog box, and use the Font and Style menus to pick a new appearance for the item. To reset to the built-in defaults, click Use Defaults.

Script Tracing

To trace the execution of a script as it runs, use the Event Log (Command+E). This log keeps track of the events (commands) sent to an application and, if the Show Event Results button is checked, displays the results that are returned, immediately. Figure 21.6 shows the Event Log after replaying a simple script to `get` the location of a Finder window.

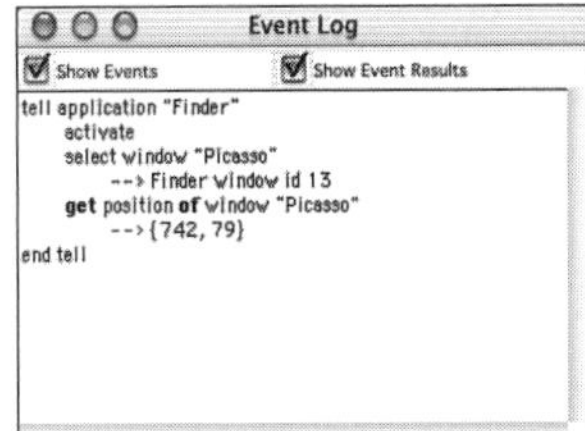

FIGURE 21.6
The Event Log can be used to monitor script execution.

Saving

After creating a script that functions the way you want, you can save it for double-click execution whenever you'd like. Choose Save As or Save As Run-Only from the File menu. The Run-Only option should be used to protect the script from future edits. Figure 21.7 displays the Save As dialog box.

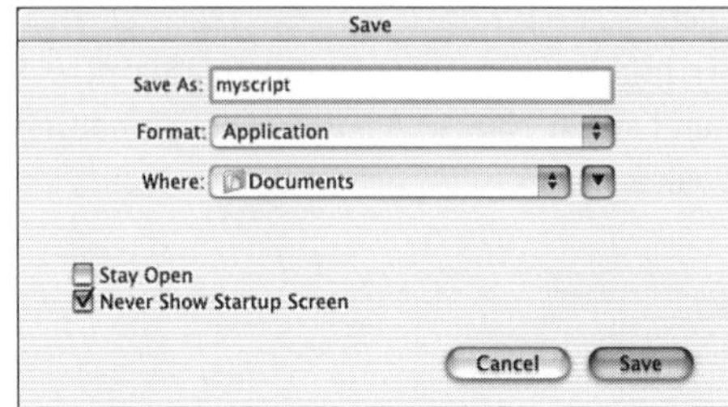

FIGURE 21.7
Save a script for later execution.

There are three possible file formats for scripts:

- **Text**—Save the contents of the script in a plain-text file.
- **Compiled Script**—Save the script as a compiled binary file.
- **Application**—Save the script for double-click execution under Mac OS X.

When saving the script as an Application, there are two additional options in the lower-left corner of the dialog box. Choose Stay Open to have a script remain open after running, or Never Show Startup Screen to remove the AppleScript startup screen when the program runs.

Scripting Syntax

Describing the AppleScript syntax to a programmer familiar with C or Perl isn't as straightforward as you might think. AppleScript uses an entirely different programming model based on an English-like structure that, after a few minutes of use, will leave the programmer feeling as though he is having a deep, intellectual conversation with his computer.

tell

The basic building block of an AppleScript is the `tell` statement. `tell` is used to address an object and give it instructions to perform. A `tell` line is written in one of two common forms: a block or a single statement. The block format enables the programmer to send multiple commands to an application without stating its name each time.

Single:

```
tell <object> <object name> to <action>
```

Block:

```
tell <object> <object name>
        <action>
        <action>
        <action>
        ...
end tell
```

For example, the following two statements are identical, but are structured using the simple and block forms of `tell`:

```
tell application "Finder" to empty trash
```

and

```
tell application "Finder"
        empty trash
end tell
```

Both of these short scripts will cause the Finder to empty the Trash can. Although the second form might seem more verbose, it is likely to be the most commonly encountered form. Most scripts interact with objects to perform complex compound operations rather than simple commands. In addition, the second version of the AppleScript is easier to read and view the functional components. Maintaining readable code is a good idea no matter what programming platform you're using.

Tip

In addition to breaking up code with `tell` blocks, long lines are typically split using a code-continuation character. To break a single long code line across multiple lines, press Option+Return to insert a code-continuation character.

Variables: set/get

In AppleScript, variables are automatically created when they are `set`. A variable name can be any combination of alphanumerics as long as the first character is a letter. There are no special prefixes required to denote a variable within the code.

Although type conversions happen automatically in many cases, a variable type can be explicitly given directly in the `set` statement:

```
set <variable/property> to <value> [as <object type>]
```

For example, both of the following lines set variables (`thevalue` and `thevalue2`) to `5`, but the second line forces the variable to be a string:

```
set thevalue to 5
set thevalue2 to 5 as string
```

Variables can take on simple values, such as numbers or strings, or more complex values in the form of lists. Lists are equivalent to arrays in more traditional programming languages. A list is represented by a comma-separated group of values, enclosed in curly brackets `{}`. For example, the following line sets a variable, `theposition`, to a list containing two values:

```
set theposition to {50, 75}
```

This is often used to set coordinate pairs for manipulating onscreen objects, but can be comprised of any object. In fact, lists can even contain lists of lists. For example:

```
set thelistofpositions to {{50, 75}, {65, 45}, {25, 90}}
```

Here, a variable called `thelistofpositions` is set to a list of lists. Item 1 of the list is `{50,75}`, item 2 `{65,45}`, and so on.

In addition to setting variables, the `set` command can act on the properties of an object to effect changes on the system. Earlier you saw how an AppleScript could `get` the file type of a given file. Similarly, `set` can alter the file type. For example:

```
1: tell application "Finder"
2:     set thisFile to (choose file with prompt "Pick the file to examine:")
3:     set the file type of thisFile to "JOHN"
4: end tell
```

In line 3 of this code fragment, `set` is used to alter the file type of the chosen file to equal `JOHN`.

Note

This is just an example, but chances are you don't want to set your file's type code to JOHN. It will require an application that can handle files of type JOHN to be able to open it, and I am unaware of what that application would be.

To retrieve values from variables, or properties from objects, you would use the get command. get, by itself, retrieves the value of an object or variable and stores it in the result variable:

```
get the <property/variable> [of <object>]
```

Traditional programmers might feel uncomfortable with retrieving results into a temporary variable (result); in that case, they can combine the get and set commands to immediately store the results of a get in another variable or object property:

```
set <variable/property> [of <object>] to
    ➥get the <property/variable> [of <object>]
```

When dealing with list values, you can reference individual items within a list by referring to them as just that: items. For example, assume that you've run the following command:

```
set theposition to {50, 75}
```

To retrieve the value of the first item in the list, you can use

```
get item 1 of theposition
```

When dealing with lists within lists, just embed item statements within one another. Assume that this list has been entered

```
set thelistofpositions to {{50, 75}, {65, 45}, {25, 90}}
```

To retrieve the value of the second item of the second list within a list, you could write

```
get item 2 of item 2 of thelistofpositions
```

Again, the power of these commands is based in the dictionaries of AppleScript applications. With products such as FileMaker Pro, your AppleScript can edit, insert, and delete records.

If

A common programming construct is the `If-then-else` statement. This is used to check the value of an item, and then react appropriately. The syntax for a basic `If` statement is

```
If <condition> then
        <action>
end if
```

For example, the following code asks the user to input a value, check to see whether it equals 5, and outputs an appropriate message if it does.

```
1: display dialog "Enter a number:" default answer ""
2: set thevalue to (text returned of the result) as integer
3: if thevalue = 5 then
4:     display dialog "Five is my magic number."
5: end if
```

Line 1 displays a dialog prompt for a user to enter a value. Line 2 sets a variable `thevalue` to the text returned from the dialog, and forces it to be evaluated as an integer. Line 3 checks `thevalue`; if it is equal to the number 5, line 4 is executed. Line 4 displays an onscreen message, and line 5 ends the `If` statement.

The `If` statement can be expanded to include an `else` clause that is executed if the original condition is not met.

```
1: display dialog "Enter a number:" default answer ""
2: set thevalue to (text returned of the result) as integer
3: if thevalue = 5 then
4:     display dialog "Five is my magic number."
5: else
6:     display dialog "That is NOT my magic number."
7: end if
```

In this modified version of the code, line 6 contains an alternative message that will be displayed if the condition in line 3 is not met.

Finally, the `else` itself can be expanded to check alternative conditions using `else if`. This enables multiple possibilities to be evaluated within a single statement:

```
display dialog "Enter a number:" default answer ""
set thevalue to (text returned of the result) as integer
if thevalue = 5 then
    display dialog "Five is my magic number."
else if thevalue = 3 then
    display dialog "Three is a decent number too."
else
    display dialog "I don't like that number."
end if
```

The latest version of the code includes an `else if` in line 5. If the initial comparison in line 3 fails, line 5 is evaluated. Finally, if line 5 fails, the `else` in line 8 is executed.

repeat

Another common programming construct is the loop. AppleScript uses a single-loop type to handle a variety of looping needs. The `repeat` statement has several different forms that cover `while`, `until`, and other types of traditional loops.

There are six different forms of the `repeat` statement:

- **Repeat Indefinitely**—Repeat a group of statements indefinitely, or until the `exit` command is called.

  ```
  repeat
     <statements>
  end repeat
  ```

- **Repeat #**—Using the second loop format, the user can choose the number of times a loop repeats.

  ```
  repeat <integer> times
      <statements>
  end repeat
  ```

- **Repeat While**—Loop indefinitely while the given condition evaluates to true.

  ```
  repeat while <condition>
      <statements>
  end repeat
  ```

- **Repeat Until**—Loop indefinitely until the given condition evaluates to true. This is the inverse of the `repeat while` loop.

  ```
  repeat until <condition>
      <statements>
  end repeat
  ```

- **Repeat With**—Called a `for/next` loop in more traditional languages, this form of the repeat loop counts up or down from a starting number to an ending number. Each iteration updates a variable with the latest loop value.

  ```
  repeat with <variable> from <starting integer> to
  ➥<ending integer> [by <increment>]
      <statements>
  end repeat
  ```

- **Repeat with List**—Like the standard `repeat with` style loop, the `repeat with list` loop runs over a range of values, storing each value in a named variable during the iterations of the loop. The difference is the value range is specified with a list, rather than an upper and lower integer value. This enables the loop to operate over anything from numbers to strings, to lists of lists.

```
repeat with <variable> in <list>
    <statements>
end repeat
```

Subroutines

The final building block that we will cover in AppleScript is the subroutine. Subroutines help modularize code by breaking it into smaller, more manageable segments that can return specific results to a controlling piece of code. There are two types of subroutines in AppleScript: those with labeled parameters and those that use positional parameters. A *parameter* is a piece of information that is passed to a subroutine when it is called.

Positional parameters will be the most familiar to anyone who has used another programming language. This type of subroutine, which is the easiest to define and use, depends on being called with a certain number of parameters in a certain order.

Labeled parameters, on the other hand, rely on a set of named parameters and their values, which can be sent to the subroutine in any order. This can be used to create an English-like syntax, but adds a level of complexity when reading the code.

Because positional parameters can be used for almost any type of development and fit in with the structure of other languages discussed in this book, they will be the focus here.

The syntax of a positional parameter subroutine is shown here:

```
on <subroutine name> ([<variable 1>,<variable 2>,<variable n>,...])
    <statements>
    [return <result value>]
end <subroutine name>
```

Each positional parameter–based subroutine requires a name, a list of variables that will be supplied when called, and an optional value that will be returned to the main application. For example, the following `BeAnnoying` routine will take a string and a number as parameters, and then display a dialog box with the message. The display will be repeated until it matches the number given.

```
1: on BeAnnoying(theMessage, howAnnoying)
2:     repeat howAnnoying times
3:         display dialog theMessage
4:     end repeat
5: end BeAnnoying
```

Line 1 declares the subroutine `BeAnnoying` and its two parameters: `theMessage` and `howAnnoying`. Line 2 starts a loop that repeats for the number of times set in the `howAnnoying` variable. Line 3 displays a dialog box with the contents `theMessage`. Line 4 ends the loop, and line 5 ends the subroutine.

As expected, running this piece of code does absolutely nothing—it is a subroutine, and, as such, requires that another piece of code call it. To call this particular routine, you could use a line such as

```
BeAnnoying("Am I annoying yet?",3)
```

This will cause the subroutine to activate and display the message `Am I annoying yet?` three times.

A more useful subroutine is one that performs a calculation and returns a result. For example, the following example accepts, as input, an integer containing a person's age in years. It returns a result containing the given age in days.

```
on yearsToDays(theYears)
    return theYears * 365
end yearsToDays
```

Because this subroutine returns a value, it can be called from within a `set` statement to store the result directly into a variable:

```
set dayAge to yearsToDays(90)
```

When working in subroutines, one must explicitly define variables that are *only* used in the subroutine, as opposed to those that can be accessed from anywhere in the AppleScript application. A variable that is visible to all portions of a script is called a global variable and is defined using the `global` declaration. Similarly, the `local` keyword can be used to limit the scope of a variable to only the code contained within a subroutine. For example, try executing the following AppleScript:

```
1: set theValue to 10
2: reset()
3: display dialog theValue
4:
5: on reset()
6:     local theValue
7:     set theValue to 0
8: end reset
```

In line 1, a variable called `theValue` is set to `10`. In line 2, the `reset` subroutine is called, that appears to set the contents of `theValue` to zero. Yet, when the result is displayed in line 3, the original value remains. The reason for this strange behavior is the inclusion of line 6. Line 6 defines `theValue` as a local variable to the `reset` subroutine. This means that any changes to that variable will not extend outside of the subroutine.

To gain the behavior we expect (the contents of `theValue` are set to zero *everywhere*), swap the `local` keyword with `global`:

```
1: set theValue to 10
2: reset()
3: display dialog theValue
4:
5: on reset()
6:     global theValue
7:     set theValue to 0
8: end reset
```

This tiny modification tells the `reset` subroutine that it should use the global representation of the variable `theValue`. When `theValue` is set to zero in line 7, it replaces the initial value set in line 1.

Other Sources of Information

AppleScript is a very capable language that offers many advanced features impossible to cover in the amount of space this title allows. What is provided here should be an ample start to creating scripts of your own and editing scripts included with Mac OS X. If you're interested in more information on advanced AppleScript syntax, I strongly suggest that you check the following resources:

AppleScript Language Guide—`http://developer.apple.com/techpubs/macos8/InterproCom/AppleScriptScripters/AppleScriptLangGuide/`

AppleScript Guide Book—`www.apple.com/applescript/begin/pgs/begin_00.html`

AppleScript in Mac OS X—`www.apple.com/applescript/MacOSX_Overview/index.htm`

AppleScript in a NutShell, Bruce W. Perry, ISBN: 1565928415, O'Reilly, 2001

Caution

If, by chance, you are still running Mac OS X 10.0.x, it's a good idea to upgrade before trying to use AppleScript. Many of the application dictionaries in the original release contain warning messages such as "This is for debugging only." building serious AppleScript applications on such a shaky foundation is not recommended.

Scripting Additions

Enterprising developers who open the power of their software to the AppleScript model constantly expand AppleScript. The most common type of scripting addition is a new application. Applications that you install under Mac OS X may or may not be scriptable—be sure to check the documentation or try opening the software's dictionary using the Script Editor.

In addition, some developers may deliver extensions to AppleScript in the form of a scripting extension. These extensions are not applications themselves, but libraries of additional functions that can be used in any AppleScript. There are currently very few AppleScript extensions compiled for Mac OS X, but, if you're interested, check out `www.pasoftware.com/products/#AppleScript` for a few examples of extensions.

Downloaded AppleScript extensions should be stored in `~/Library/ScriptingAdditions` or the system-level directory `/Library/ScriptingAdditions` for access by all users.

Mac OS X Power Additions

An extremely useful addition for Mac OS X users who have decided to start shell scripting their applications are the OS X Power Additions found at `www.vampiresoft.com/Products/MacOS/osxpoweraddos.html`. These additions let AppleScript send commands directly to the Mac OS X Shell. For example, to return the results of the Unix command `uptime`, you could use the script:

```
return «event OSxaShel» "uptime"
```

Any command or Unix script can be run with the syntax:

```
return »event OsxaShel» "<unix command name>"
```

Users who are interested in working with only the GUI portion of Mac OS X might not be interested in this addition, but it is an invaluable extension for system administrators and Unix developers.

> **Tip**
>
> Users who just want to activate a shell script can do so by scripting the terminal. Unfortunatlely, at the time of this writing, this method does not provide a means of returning shell results back to the AppleScript.
>
> An example of a Terminal script that uses the 1s command to display a list of files is shown here:

```
tell application "Terminal"
    do script with command "1s"
end tell
```

Script Runner

In Mac OS X 10.0 and 10.1, there is a significant change in how user interaction takes place during a script. Dialogs and other scripting additions are not recognized when running a compiled script. This results in errors when using functions such as `display dialog`.

Until Apple addresses this issue, there are two potential workarounds: run all scripts from within the Script Editor, or use the Script Runner to execute your AppleScripts. The Script Runner will correctly load additions and enables AppleScripts to function identically to their Mac OS 9 counterparts.

The Script Runner (path: `Applications/AppleScript/Script Runner`) is a *very* low-key application. It creates a single floating window, pictured in Figure 21.8.

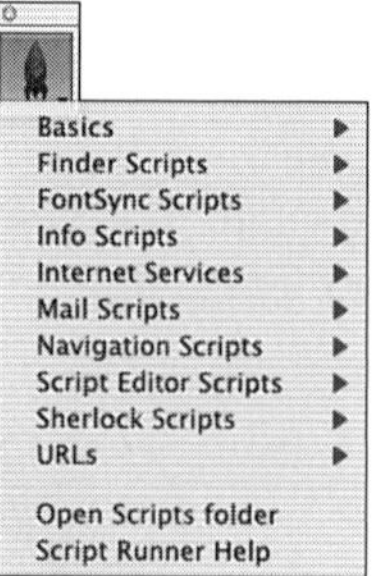

FIGURE 21.8
The Script Runner creates a small floating window to serve as a script launch point.

Click and hold the Script Runner icon in the floating palette. A pop-up appears listing available scripts along with "Open Scripts folder" and "Script Runner help."

The Open Scripts folder opens both the `~/Library/Scripts` and `/Library/Scripts` folders. Any compiled scripts placed in these locations will become accessible from the pop-up menu. To create submenus for categorizing scripts, just create multiple folders within the Scripts folder.

Script Runner Help displays help information for the Runner application.

Unlike normal applications, the Script Runner doesn't have a menu, a Dock icon, or any other interactive elements beyond the floating window and pop-up menu. To quit the application, click the close box in the upper-left corner of the window. This violates standard Macintosh user interface guidelines, but it's the best we have for now.

To maintain compatibility with changes to the AppleScript system that are likely to occur in the near future, it is recommended that you use the Script Runner to activate your AppleScripts.

Command-Line Tools

AppleScript compilation and execution has been extended to the BSD shell through the use of the `osacompile` and `osascript` commands.

The `osacompile` utility accepts a text file containing AppleScript as input, and outputs a compiled script file using the syntax:

```
osacompile -o <output file> <script file>
```

Although this is likely the form you'll use most, there are several additional command-line options that can fine-tune the compile process. Table 21.1 documents the additional options.

TABLE 21.1—Compile Options for `osacompile`

Option	*Purpose*
`-o`	Name the output file. The default output name is `a.scpt`.
`-e`	Save the compiled file as execute-only.
`-d`	Save the script in the data fork of the output file.
`-r <type:id>`	Save the output script as the named resource type and ID.
`-c <creator>`	Set a creator code for the output script.
`-t <file type>`	Set a file type code for the output script.

The `osascript` utility can be invoked to run as script by typing

```
osascript <script filename>
```

If a filename is not set specified on the command line, `osascript` will attempt to run AppleScript from standard input. This is a great way to test scripts, or run a quick AppleScript command without needing to start the Script Editor.

Summary

AppleScript carries on the tradition of being one of the best secret Apple technologies. Programmers who are accustomed to C-like syntax are likely to find AppleScript verbose and less than intuitive. The Script Editor is the centerpiece of script development and offers the novice users the ability to record their interactions directly to an AppleScript. Although there are very few applications that currently use AppleScript, this situation is bound to change as more mainstream applications are released. Learn it today, use it tomorrow.

CHAPTER 22

Perl Scripting and SQL Connectivity

In This Chapter

The Macintosh community has had access to scripting languages such as Perl for many years. Unfortunately, however, the Macintosh port of Perl, like many other applications, lags behind its Unix and Windows counterparts and lacks many of the features available on other platforms. Mac OS X's underlying Unix base finally brings parity to the platform by giving users access to the latest version of Perl along with the myriad of accompanying add-ons.

Additionally, Macintosh users now enjoy first-class open source database packages such as MySQL. Instead of forking over several hundred (or thousand) dollars for a server-class database system, users can take 20 minutes, compile MySQL, and have a full-featured relational database system. We've never had it so good.

This chapter covers both Perl and MySQL and how they can be combined to create a powerful database development environment. At first glance, this might seem an unlikely pairing, but they both serve as excellent examples of the power Unix gives to the new Mac OS X, and how these technologies can be integrated.

Perl

Perl (Practical Extraction and Reporting Language) has grown from a cult following in the early 1990s to a massive hit today. Originally designed to make working with text data simple, Perl has been expanded by developers to handle tasks such as image manipulation and client/server activities. Because of its ease of use and capability to work with ambiguous user input, Perl is an extremely popular Web development language. For example, assume that you want to extract a phone number from an input string. A user might enter 555-5654, 5552231, 421-5552313, and so on. It is up to the application to find the area code, local exchange, and identifier numbers. In Perl, this is simple:

```
#!/usr/bin/perl
print "Please enter a phone number:";
$phone=<STDIN>;
$phone=~s/[^\d]//g;
$phone=~s/^1//;
if (length($phone)==7) {
    $phone=~/(\d{3,3})(\d{4,4})/;
    $area="???"; $prefix=$1; $number=$2;
} elsif (length($phone)==10) {
    $phone=~/(\d{3,3})(\d{3,3})(\d{4,4})/;
    $area=$1; $prefix=$2; $number=$3;
} else { print "Invalid number!"; exit; }
print "($area) $prefix-$number\n";
```

This program accepts a phone number as input, strips any unusual characters from it, removes a leading 1, if included, and then formats the result in an attractive manner.

Applying this capability to mine data from user input to Web development creates opportunities for programmers to make extremely user-friendly software.

Perl programs are similar to shell scripts in that they are interpreted by an additional piece of software. Each script starts with a line that includes the path to the Perl interpreter. In Mac OS X, this is typically `#!/usr/bin/perl`. Upon entering a script, it must be made executable by typing `chmod +x <script name>`. Finally, it can be run by entering its complete path at the command line, or by typing `./<script name>` from the same directory as the script. For more information on this process, please refer to Chapter 18, "Advanced Unix Shell Use: Configuration and Programming (Shell Scripting)."

Although this chapter provides enough information to write a program like the one shown here, it is not a complete reference to Perl. Perl is an object-oriented language with thousands of functions. *Sams Teach Yourself Perl in 21 Days* is an excellent read and a great way to beef up on the topic.

Tip

In addition to this introduction, Chapter 28, "Web Programming," discusses using Perl as a Web development language.

Variables and Data Types

Perl has a number of different variable types, but the most common are shown in Table 22.1. Perl variable names are comprised of alphanumeric characters and are case sensitive, unlike much of Mac OS X. This means that a variable named `$mymacosx` is entirely different from `$myMacOSX`. Unlike some languages, such as C, Perl performs automatic type conversion when possible. A programmer can use a variable as a number in one statement, and a string in the next.

TABLE 22.1 Common Perl Variable Types

Type	*Description*
`$variable`	A simple variable that can hold anything is prefixed with a `$`. You can use these variables as strings or numbers. These are the most common variables.
`FILEHANDLE`	Filehandles hold a reference to a file that you are writing or reading. Typically, these are expressed in uppercase and do not have the `$` prefix.

TABLE 22.1 continued

Type	*Description*
`@array`	The `@` references an array of variables. The array does not need to be predimensioned and can grow to whatever size memory allows. You reference individual elements of an array as `$array[0]`, `$array[1]`, `$array[2]`, and so on. The array as a whole is referenced as `@array`.
`%array`	This is another type of an array—an associative array. Associative arrays are another one of Perl's power features. Rather than using numbers to reference the values stored in this array, you use any string you'd like. For example, if you have 3 apples, 2 oranges, and 17 grapefruit, you could store these values in the associative array as `$array{apple}=3`, `$array{orange}=2`, `$array{grapefruit}=17`. The only difference between the use of a normal array and an associate array (besides the method of referencing a value) is the type of brackets used. Associative arrays use curly brackets `{}` to access individual elements, whereas standard arrays use square brackets `[]`.

Input Output Functions

Because Perl is so useful for manipulating data, one of the first things you'll want to do is get data into a script. There are a number of ways to do this, including reading from a file or the Terminal window. To Perl, however, command-line input and file input are very much the same thing. To use either, you must read from an input stream.

Input Streams

To input data into a variable from a file, use `$variable=<FILEHANDLE>`. This will input data up to a newline character into the named variable. To read from the command line, the filehandle is replaced with a special handle that points to the standard input stream—`<STDIN>`.

When data is read from an input stream, it contains the end of line character (newline) as part of the data. This is usually an unwanted piece of information that can be stripped off using the `chomp` command. Failure to use `chomp` often results in debugging headaches as you attempt to figure out why your string comparison routines are failing. For example, the following reads a line from standard (command line) input and removes the trailing newline character:

```
$myname=<STDIN>;
chomp($myname);
```

To read data in from an actual stored file, it must first be opened with `open` *`<FILEHANDLE>, <filename>`*. For example, to read the first line of a file named `MacOSX.txt`:

```
open FILEHANDLE, "MacOSX.txt";
$line1=<FILENAME>;
close FILEHANDLE;
```

When finished reading a file, use `close` followed by the filehandle to close.

Outputting Data

Outputting data is the job of the `print` command. `print` can display text strings or the contents of variables. In addition, you can embed special characters in a `print` statement that are otherwise unprintable. For example:

```
print "I love Mac OS X!\n---------------\n";
```

In this sample line, the `\n` is a newline character—this moves the cursor down a line so that subsequent output occurs on a new line, rather than the same line as the current `print` statement. Table 22.2 contains other common special characters.

TABLE 22.2 Common Special Characters

Escape Sequence	*Description*
`\n`	Newline, the Unix equivalent of return/enter
`\r`	A standard return character
`\t`	Tab
`\"`	Double quotes
`\\`	The \ character

Many characters (such as `"`) have a special meaning in Perl; if you want to refer to them literally, you must prefix them with `\`—this is called *escaping the character*. In most cases, nonalphanumeric characters should be escaped just to be on the safe side.

File Output

To output data to a file rather than standard output, you must first `open` a file to receive the information. This is nearly identical to the `open` used to read data, except for one difference. When writing to a file, you must prefix the name of the file with one of two different character strings:

>—Output to a file, overwriting the contents.

>>—Append to an existing file. Creates a new file if none exists.

With a file open, the `print` command is again used for output. This time, however, it includes the filehandle of the output file. For example, this code saves `Mac OS X` to a file named `MyOS.txt`:

```
open MYFILE, "> MyOS.txt";
print MYFILE "Mac OS X\n";
close MYFILE;
```

Again, the `close` command is used to close the file when all output is complete.

External Results (` `)

One of the more novel (and powerful) ways to get information into Perl is through an external program. For example, to quickly and easily grab a listing of running processes, you could use the output of the Unix `ps axg` command:

```
$processlist=`ps axg`;
```

The backtick (` `) characters should be placed around the command of the output you want to capture. Perl will pause and wait for the external command to finish executing before it continues processing.

This is both a dangerous and powerful tool. You can easily read an entire file into a variable by using the `cat` command with backticks. Unfortunately, if the external program fails to execute correctly, the Perl script might hang indefinitely.

Expressions

Although Perl variables can hold numbers or strings, you still need to perform the appropriate type of comparison based on the values being compared. For example, numbers can be compared for equality using ==, but strings must be compared with `eq`. If you attempt to use == to compare two strings, the expression will evaluate to `true` because the numeric value of both strings is zero, regardless of the text they contain. Table 22.3 displays common Perl expressions.

TABLE 22.3 Use the Appropriate Comparison Operators for the Type of Data Being Compared

Expression Syntax	*Description*
`$var1==$var2`	Compares two numbers for equality.
`$var1!=$var2`	Compares two numbers for inequality.
`$var1<$var2`	Checks `$var1` to see whether it is less than `$var2`.

TABLE 22.3 continued

Expression Syntax	*Description*
`$var1>$var2`	Tests `$var1` to see whether it is a larger number than `$var2`.
`$var1>=$var2`	Tests `$var1` to see whether it is greater than or equal to `$var2`.
`$var1<=$var2`	Compares `$var1` to see whether it is less than or equal to `$var2`.
`$var1 eq $var2`	Checks two strings for equality.
`$var1 ne $var2`	Checks two strings for inequality.
`$var1 lt $var2`	Checks to see whether the string in `$var1` is less than (by ASCII value) `$var2`.
`$var1 gt $var2`	Tests the string in `$var1` to see whether it is greater than `$var2`.
`()`	Parentheses can be used to group the elements of an expression together to force an evaluation order or provide clarity to the code.
`&&/and`	Used to connect two expressions so that both must evaluate to `true` in order for the complete expression to be `true`.
`||/or`	Used to connect two expressions so that if either evaluates to `true`, the entire expression will evaluate to `true`.
`!`	Used to negate an expression. If the expression previously evaluated to `true`, you can place a `!` in front of the expression to force it to evaluate `false`—or vice versa.

Regular Expressions

Regular expressions (REs) are a bit more interesting than the expressions in the preceding section. Like one of the previous expresses, REs evaluate to a `true` or `false` state. In addition, they are used to `local` and `extract` data from strings.

For example, assume that the variable `$mycomputer` contains the information

```
My computer is a Mac.
```

To create a regular expression that would test the string for the presence of the word `mac`, you could write

```
$mycomputer=~/mac/i
```

Although this line might look like an assignment statement, it is in fact looking inside of the variable `$mycomputer` for the pattern `mac`. The pattern that a regular expression matches is contained within two `/` characters, unless changed by the programmer. The `i` after the expression tells Perl that it should perform a case-insensitive search, allowing it to match strings such as `MAC` and `mAC`.

To understand the power of regular expressions, you must first understand the pattern matching language that comprises them.

Patterns

Regular expressions are made up of groups of pattern matching symbols. These special characters symbolically represent the contents of a string and can be used to build complex pattern matching rules with relative ease. Table 22.4 contains the most common components of regular expressions and their purpose.

TABLE 22.4 Use These Pattern Matching Components to Build a Regular Expression

Pattern	*Purpose*
`$`	Matches the end of a string.
`^`	Matches the beginning of a string.
`.`	Matches any character in the string.
`[]`	Matches any of the characters within the square brackets.
`\s`	Matches any type of white space (space, tab, and so on).
`\n`	Matches the newline character.
`\t`	Matches the tab character.
`\w`	Matches a word character.
`\d`	Matches a digit.

The bracket characters enable you to clearly define the characters that you want to match if a predefined sequence doesn't already exist. For example, if you'd like to match only the uppercase letters A through Z and the numbers 1, 2, and 3, you could write

```
[A-Z123]
```

As seen in this example, you can represent a contiguous sequence of letters or numbers as a range—specifying the start and end characters of the range, separated by a –.

Pattern Repetition

With the capability to write patterns, you can match arbitrary strings within a character sequence. What's missing is the capability to match strings of varying lengths. These repetition characters modify the pattern they follow and enable it to be matched once, twice, or as many times as you'd like:

`*`—Match any number (including *zero*) copies of a character.

`+`—Match at least one copy of a character.

`{x,y}`—Match at least `x` characters and as many as `y`.

When a repetition sequence is followed by a `?`, the pattern will match as few characters as possible to be considered `true`. For example, the following expression will match between 5 and 10 occurrences of the numbers `1`, `2`, or `3`:

```
$testnumbers=~/[1-3]{5,10}/;
```

The capability to match an arbitrary number of characters enables the programmers to deal with information they might not be expecting.

Extracting Information from a Regular Expression

Although it's useful to be able to find strings that contain a certain pattern, it's even better if the matching data can be extracted and used. To extract pieces of information from a match, enclose the pattern with parentheses `()`. To see this in action, let's go back to the original telephone number program that introduced Perl in this chapter. One of the regular expressions extracted the parts of a 10-digit phone number from a string of 10 digits:

```
$phone=~/(\d{3,3})(\d{3,3})(\d{4,4})/;
```

There are three parts to the regular expression, each enclosed within parentheses. The first two `(\d{3,3})` capture strings of three consecutive digits, and the third `(\d{4,4})` captures the remaining four.

For each set of parentheses used in a pattern, a `$#` variable is created that corresponds to the order that the parentheses are found. Because the area code is the first set of parentheses in the example, it is `$1`, the local prefix is `$2`, and the final four digits are held in `$3`.

Search and Replace

Because you can easily find a pattern in a string, wouldn't it be nice if you could replace it with something else? Perl enables you to do just that by writing your regular expression line a little bit differently:

```
$a=~s/<search pattern>/<replace pattern>/
```

This simple change enables you to modify data in a variable so it is exactly what you're expecting—removing extraneous data. For example, to match a phone number in the variable `$phone`, and then change it to a standard format could be accomplished in a single step:

```
$phone=~s/(\d{3,3})(\d{3,3})(\d{4,4})/($1) $2-$3/;
```

A new string in the format `(xxx) xxx-xxxx` replaces the phone number found in the original string. This enables a programmer to modify data on the fly, transforming user input into a more useable form.

Regular expressions are not easy for many people to learn and a single misplaced character can trip them up. Don't feel bad if you're confused at first, just keep at it. An understanding of regular expressions is important in many languages and, if properly used, can be a very powerful development tool.

Flow Control

Flow control statements give Perl the capability to alter its execution and adapt to different conditions on-the-fly. Perl uses very standard C-like syntax for its looping and conditional constructs. If you've used C or Java before, these should all look very familiar.

`if-then-else`

Perl's `if-then-else` logic is very simple to understand. If a condition is met, a block of code is executed. If not, a different piece of programming is run. The syntax for this type of conditional statement is

```
if <expression> {
       <statements...>
} else {
       <statements...>
}
```

For example, to test whether the variable `$mycomputer` contains the string `Mac OS X` and print `Good Choice!` if it does, you could write:

```
if ($mycomputer=~/mac os x/i) {
        print "Good Choice!\n";
} else {
        print "Buy a Mac!\n";
}
```

The curly brackets `{}` are used to set off code blocks within Perl. These denote the portion of code that a conditional, looping, or subroutine construct applies to.

unless-then-else

The `unless` statement is syntactically identical to the `if-then` statement, except that it operates on the inverse of the expression (and uses the word `unless` rather than `if`). To change the previous example so that it uses `unless`, write

```
unless ($mycomputer=~/mac os x/i) {
        print "Buy a Mac!\n";
} else {
        print "Good Choice!\n";
}
```

The `unless` condition is rarely used in Perl applications and is provided mainly as a way to write code in a more readable manner.

while

The `while` loop enables you to execute *while* a condition remains true. At the start of each loop, an expression is evaluated; if it returns `true`, the loop executes. If not, it exits. The syntax for a Perl `while` loop is

```
while <expression> {
        <statements>
}
```

For example, to monitor a process listing every 30 seconds to see if the application `Terminal` is running, the following code fragment could be employed:

```
$processlist=`ps axg`;
while (!($processlist=~/terminal/i)) {
        print "Terminal has not been detected.\n";
        sleep 30;
        $processlist=`ps axg`;
}
print "The Terminal process is running.";
```

Here the output of the `ps axg` command is stored in `$processlist`. This is then searched using a regular expression in the `while` loop. If the pattern `terminal` is located, the loop will exit and the message `The Terminal process is running.` is displayed. If not, the script sleeps for 30 seconds, and then tries again.

for-next

The `for-next` loop is the bread and butter of all looping constructs. This loop iterates through a series of values until a condition (usually a numeric limit) is met. The syntax for a `for-next` loop is

```
for (<initialization>;<execution condition>;<increment>) {
        <code block>
}
```

The *initialization* sets up the loop and initializes the counter variable to its default state. The *execution condition* is checked with each iteration of the loop; if it evaluates to `false`, the loop ends. Finally, the *increment* is a piece of code that defines an operation performed on the counter variable each time the loop is run. For example, the following loop counts from 0 to 9:

```
for ($count=0;$count<10;$count++) {
        print "Count = $count";
}
```

The counter, `$count`, is set to `0` when the loop starts. With each repetition, it is incremented by 1 (`$count++`). The loop exits when the counter reaches 10 (`$count<10`).

Subroutines

Subroutines help modularize code by dividing it into smaller functional units. Rather than creating a gigantic block of Perl that does everything under the sun, you can create subroutines that are easier to read and debug.

A subroutine is started with the `sub` keyword and the name the subroutine should be called. The body of the subroutine is enclosed in curly brackets `{}`. For example, here is a simple subroutine that prints `Mac OS X`.

```
sub printos {
        print "Mac OS X\n";
}
```

You can include subroutines anywhere in your source code and call them at any time by prefixing their name with `&` (`&printos`). Subroutines can also be set up to receive values from the main program and return results. For example, this routine accepts two strings and concatenates them together (useful, huh?):

```
sub concatenatestring {
        my ($x,$y)=@_;
        return ("$x$y");
}
```

To retrieve the concatenation of the strings `Mac` and `OS X`, the subroutine would be addressed as

```
$result=&concatenatestring("Mac","OS X");
```

Data is received by the subroutine through the use of the special variable `@_`. The two values it contains are then stored in local variables (denoted by the `my` keyword) named `$x` and `$y`. Finally, the `return` statement returns a concatenated version of the two strings.

Additional Information

The information in this chapter should be enough to get you started authoring and editing Perl scripts. Later in the chapter, you'll learn how to extend Perl to another free software package—MySQL. In Chapter 28, "Web Programming," you'll see how Perl can be used to author online applications.

As with many topics in the book, the space just isn't available for a completely comprehensive text. If you like what you see, you can learn more about Perl through these resources:

The Perl Homepage—`www.perl.org/`—All that is Perl. This page can provide you with links to the latest and most useful Perl information online.

CPAN—`www.cpan.org/`—The Comprehensive Perl Archive Network contains information on all the available Perl modules (extensions). Later in this chapter, you'll learn how to add modules to your Mac OS X Perl distribution.

Programming Perl—O'Reilly Publishing, Larry Wall, ISBN: 0596000278. Written by the inventor of Perl, you can't get much closer to the source than this.

Sams Teach Yourself Perl in 21 Days—Laura Lemay, ISBN: 0672313057. An excellent step-by-step guide to learning Perl and putting it to use on your system.

MySQL

The MySQL database system is a free implementation of an SQL-based (Structured Query Language) database system. MySQL has been successfully deployed for a number of high-end applications on Web sites such as NASA, Yahoo!, and Slashdot. In addition to the database package itself, MySQL has JDBC and ODBC drivers available, making it accessible from any platform supporting these standards, including Microsoft Windows.

> **Note**
>
> This note is for those of you who are familiar with Microsoft's SQL Server offering. The letters *SQL* are pronounced S-Q-L, not *Sequel* as Microsoft wants you to believe. MySQL, as documented on `www.mysql.com`, is pronounced *My S-QL*.

Installing MySQL

To install MySQL, download the latest source code distribution. The server software is updated on an almost daily basis, but there is a stable release listed along with the latest developmental releases. We highly recommend that you stick with the stable release for any serious development projects.

The MySQL source `tarball` can be downloaded from `www.mysql.com/downloads/`:

```
[primal:~] jray% curl-o http://www.mysql.com/Downloads/MySQL-3.23/
➥mysql-3.23.39.tar.gz
```

Next, unarchive the distribution, `cd` into the resulting MySQL directory and run `./configure` to prepare for compilation:

```
[primal:~] jray% cd mysql-3.23.39/
[primal:~/mysql-3.23.39] jray% ./configure
creating cache ./config.cache
checking host system type... powerpc-apple-darwin1.3.3
checking target system type... powerpc-apple-darwin1.3.3
checking build system type... powerpc-apple-darwin1.3.3
checking for a BSD compatible install... /usr/bin/install -c
checking whether build environment is sane... yes
checking whether make sets ${MAKE}... yes
checking for working aclocal... missing
checking for working autoconf... found
checking for working automake... missing
checking for working autoheader... found
...
```

After a few minutes of analyzing your system, the configuration process will complete. Use `make` to compile the software. This will take 5 to 10 minutes, depending on your system:

```
[primal:~/mysql-3.23.39] jray% make
cd include; make link_sources
/bin/cp ../config.h my_config.h
echo timestamp > linked_include_sources
cd libmysql; make link_sources
set -x; \
...
```

Finally, install the software with `sudo make install`:

```
[primal:~/mysql-3.23.39] jray% sudo make install
Making install in include
make[2]: Nothing to be done for `install-exec-am'.
/bin/sh ../mkinstalldirs /usr/local/include/mysql
mkdir /usr/local/include
mkdir /usr/local/include/mysql
 /usr/bin/install -c -m 644 dbug.h /usr/local/include/mysql/dbug.h
 /usr/bin/install -c -m 644 m_string.h /usr/local/include/mysql/m_string.h
 /usr/bin/install -c -m 644 my_sys.h /usr/local/include/mysql/my_sys.h
 /usr/bin/install -c -m 644 mysql.h /usr/local/include/mysql/mysql.h
```

The software is installed (`/usr/local/bin`), but isn't ready to run. Before you're finished, you'll need to initialize the default databases and create a startup script to initialize the server when Mac OS X boots.

Creating the Initial MySQL Database

MySQL uses an internal database to manage access permissions to databases and tables. Before the software can start for the first time, you must initialize these tables using the `mysql_install_db` command, located in `/usr/local/bin`:

```
[primal:/usr/local/bin] jray% sudo ./mysql_install_db
Preparing db table
Preparing host table
Preparing user table
Preparing func table
Preparing tables_priv table
Preparing columns_priv table
Installing all prepared tables
010614 14:50:09  /usr/local/libexec/mysqld: Shutdown Complete

To start mysqld at boot time you have to copy support-files/mysql.server
to the right place for your system

PLEASE REMEMBER TO SET A PASSWORD FOR THE MySQL root USER !
This is done with:
/usr/local/bin/mysqladmin -u root -p password 'new-password'
/usr/local/bin/mysqladmin -u root -h primal -p password 'new-password'
See the manual for more instructions.

You can start the MySQL daemon with:
cd /usr/local ; /usr/local/bin/safe_mysqld &

You can test the MySQL daemon with the benchmarks in the 'sql-bench' directory:
cd sql-bench ; run-all-tests

Please report any problems with the /usr/local/bin/mysqlbug script!

The latest information about MySQL is available on the web at
http://www.mysql.com
Support MySQL by buying support/licenses at https://order.mysql.com
```

As the documentation says, you should reset the `root` password immediately using the command `/usr/local/bin/mysqladmin -u root -p` *<password> <new-password>*.

> **Note**
>
> When creating the new `root` password, just press Enter when prompted for the current password. Also, be aware that this password has no effect on the actual Mac OS X `root` account.

Creating a Startup Script

Mac OS X uses a special directory structure located in `/Library/StartupItems` or `/System/Library/StartupItems` to automatically start processes when the machine boots. Although some applications install these startup files in the `/System` path, the design of the operating system indicates that add-on software should use the `/Library` directory, rather than altering the main system folder.

There are three components to a Mac OS X startup script:

- A folder named after the service you are installing (such as `MySQL`).
- A shell script that bears the same name as the folder. This script should contain the commands needed to start the server process.
- An XML file named `StartupParameters.plist` that contains a description of the process. This currently isn't used by any Mac OS X admin tool, but presumably will provide an Extension Manager–type control of services in the future.

Let's take a look at what is exactly needed for Mac OS X and MySQL.

Create the folder `MySQL` in `/Library/StartupItems`. Within this folder, add a text file named `MySQL` containing the following shell script:

```
#!/bin/sh

##
# Start MySQL
##

. /etc/rc.common

if [ "${MYSQL:=-NO-}" = "-YES-" ]; then
    ConsoleMessage "Starting MySQL"
    cd /usr/local ; /usr/local/bin/safe_mysqld &
fi
```

This script will check the `/etc/hostconfig` file for a line that reads `MYSQL=-YES-` and, if it exists, add start the server. Use a text editor to add this to the `hostconfig` file, or just type

```
echo "MYSQL=-YES-" >> /etc/hostconfig
```

Next, add the `StartupParameters.plist` file to the directory. The contents of this file are arbitrary—until Apple releases official specifications.

```
{
  Description     = "MySQL database server";
  Provides        = ("MySQL");
```

```
    Requires        = ("Resolver");
    OrderPreference = "None";
    Messages =
    {
      start = "Starting MySQL server";
      stop  = "Stopping MySQL server";
    };
  }
```

After you add these files, your Mac OS X machine will automatically start MySQL upon booting. It's time to start using your new SQL server.

Creating a Database

The key to using MySQL is an understanding of the SQL syntax itself. If you've used Oracle or another SQL-based system, you'll be right at home interacting with MySQL. For beginners, this introduction should be enough to get started, but we recommend a more complete text such as *Sams Teach Yourself MySQL in 21 Days* (ISBN: 0672319144).

To start MySQL, invoke the client (mysql) using mysql -u<*username*> -p<*password*>. To start, there should only be the root account available. If you didn't set the password for root, there will be no password required.

The first step when working with MySQL is to create the database itself. If you've worked with FileMaker Pro or AppleWorks, this is a *very* different concept. In MySQL, a database is a container that holds a collection of tables. These tables, in turn, hold actual information. The FileMaker database model has a single table in a single database. To create relationships between different collections of data requires multiple databases. In MySQL, a single database can contain multiple tables each with unique data.

To create a database, make sure that you've started MySQL and are at a command prompt:

```
[primal:~] jray% mysql -uroot
Welcome to the MySQL monitor.  Commands end with ; or \g.
Your MySQL connection id is 183 to server version: 3.23.27-beta-log

Type 'help;' or '\h' for help. Type '\c' to clear the buffer

mysql>
```

Next, use create database <*database name*> to set up an empty database. This database will be completely empty, but not for long. After creating the database, type use <*database name*> to work with the new database.

Note

The MySQL client requires that all commands end with a semicolon (;). Input can span multiple lines, as long as a semicolon appears at the end.

For example, let's start with an employee database:

```
mysql> create database employee;
Query OK, 1 row affected (0.07 sec)

mysql> use employee;
Database changed
mysql>
```

If you want to delete the database that you've defined, you can use the `drop` command, just like `create`:

```
drop database <database name>
```

Caution

Remember, a MySQL database can contain multiple tables, each with its own data. Deleting a database removes *all* information that has been stored in any of the tables.

After a database has been created, you need to set up the internal tables that will actually hold the data you want to store.

Tables and Data Types

When making a table, use another `create` command to tell the system what type of data you want to store—if any.

```
create table <tablename> (<columns...>)
```

For example, let's create some tables for a fictitious employee database:

```
create table tblemployee (
    employeeID  int not null,
    firstname   varchar(50),
    lastname    varchar(50),
    titleID     int,
    salary      float,
    primary key (employeeID)
);
```

```
create table tbljobclassification (
    titleID      int not null,
    title        text,
    minsalary    float,
    maxsalary    float,
    primary key (titleID)
);
```

The first table, `tblemployee`, holds information about each person in the database, such as his name and salary. The second table, `tbljobclassification`, contains job classification data—a general position description, and the minimum and maximum salary ranges for that position.

When defining a database table, there are numerous data types used to build the collection of information that can be stored. Table 22.5 contains a description of the available data types. This is a summarized version of the documentation supplied at `www.mysql.com/`.

TABLE 22.5 Database Tables Are Built with MySQL Data Types

Data Type	*Description*
`TINYINT [UNSIGNED]`	A very small integer. The signed range is –128 to 127. The unsigned range is 0 to 255.
`SMALLINT [UNSIGNED]`	A small integer. The signed range is –32768 to 32767. The unsigned range is 0 to 65535.
`MEDIUMINT [UNSIGNED]`	A medium-size integer. The signed range is –8388608 to 8388607. The unsigned range is 0 to 16777215.
`INT [UNSIGNED]`	A normal-size integer. The signed range is –2147483648 to 2147483647. The unsigned range is 0 to 4294967295.
`INTEGER [UNSIGNED]`	The same as `INT`.
`BIGINT [UNSIGNED]`	A large integer. The signed range is –9223372036854775808 to 9223372036854775807. The unsigned range is 0 to 18446744073709551615.
`FLOAT`	A small (single precision) floating-point number. Cannot be unsigned. Allowable values are –3.402823466E+38 to –1.175494351E–38, 0 and 1.175494351E–38 to 3.402823466E+38
`DOUBLE`	A normal-size (double-precision) floating-point number. Cannot be unsigned. Allowable values are –1.7976931348623157E+308 to –2.2250738585072014E–308, 0 and 2.2250738585072014E–308 to 1.7976931348623157E+308.

TABLE 22.5 continued

Data Type	*Description*
`DECIMAL`	An unpacked floating-point number. Cannot be unsigned. Behaves like a `CHAR` column: *unpacked* means the number is stored as a string, using one character for each digit of the value.
`DATETIME`	A date and time combination. The supported range is 1000-01-01 00:00:00 to 9999-12-31 23:59:59. MySQL displays `DATETIME` values in YYYY-MM-DD HH:MM:SS format, but enables you to assign values to `DATETIME` columns using either strings or numbers.
`TIMESTAMP`	A timestamp. The range is 1970-01-01 00:00:00 to sometime in the year 2037.
`YEAR`	A year in two- or four-digit format (the default is four-digit). The allowable values are 1901 to 2155, and 0000 in the four-digit format and 1970–2069 if you use the two-digit format (70–69).
`CHAR(<M>) [BINARY]`	A fixed-length string that is always right-padded with spaces to the specified length when stored. The range of *M* is 1 to 255 characters. Trailing spaces are removed when the value is retrieved. `CHAR` values are sorted and compared in case-insensitive fashion according to the default character set unless the `BINARY` keyword is given.
`VARCHAR(<M>) [BINARY]`	A variable-length string. Note: Trailing spaces are removed when the value is stored. The range of *M* is 1 to 255 characters. `VARCHAR` values are sorted and compared in case-insensitive fashion unless the `BINARY` keyword is given.
`TINYBLOB / TINYTEXT`	A `BLOB` or `TEXT` column with a maximum length of 255 (2^8–1) characters.
`BLOB / TEXT`	A column with a maximum length of 65535 (2^16–1) characters.
`MEDIUMBLOB / MEDIUMTEXT`	A `BLOB` or `TEXT` column with a maximum length of 16777215 (2^24–1) characters.
`LONGBLOB / LONGTEXT`	A `BLOB` or `TEXT` column with a maximum length of 4294967295 (2^32–1) characters.

Fields are defined within a table creation statement by using the syntax `<fieldname> <datatype> <options>`. There are two common options that are employed to force certain conditions on a database:

not null—Forces the field to contain a value. If a user attempts to insert data into the database and a not null field is left blank, an error will occur.

auto_increment—When used with an integer field, the value for the field will be determined automatically by MySQL and be incremented with each subsequent record.

The final line of a table creation command should define a primary key (or keys) for the table primary key (<*fieldname 1,fieldname 2,...*>). Defining keys are a necessary part of creating a normalized database structure. For more information on normalization, see www.devshed.com/Server_Side/MySQL/Normal/. We highly recommend reading through this tutorial, at the very least, before designing large-scale database models.

To remove a table that has been defined, type drop table <*table name*>.

Inserting Data

There are two ways to insert data into a table; both use the insert command with this structure:

```
insert into <table name> [(<field1,field2,...>)] values
(<'value1','value2',...>)
```

The difference between the methods comes from the optional field listing. If you want to insert into only a few fields of a table, and want to manually specify the order, you would include the field names, like this example using the tblemployee table created earlier:

```
insert into tblemployee (lastname,firstname,employeeID)
       values ('Ray','John','1');
```

In this example, only the lastname, firstname, and employeeID fields are given in the record, and they don't occur in the same order they were defined in the original table.

The second way you can use insert is to provide all the field values at once, in the table definition order. This method doesn't require the field names to be listed:

```
insert into tblemployee values ('1','John','Ray','1','35000.00');
```

It is important to note that you must obey the not null clause for a table definition at all times. In these examples, we had to include a value for the employeeID field; otherwise, the insert would have caused an error message to be generated.

To demonstrate the rest of the MySQL syntax, you'll need some data to work with. Go ahead and insert some information into the tables:

```
insert into tbljobclassification
       ➥values ('1','Programmer/Analyst','20000','80000');
```

```
insert into tbljobclassification
       ➥values ('2','Web Developer','20000','50000');
insert into tbljobclassification
       ➥values ('3','CEO/President','40000','5000000000');

insert into tblemployee values ('1','John','Ray','1','25300.65');
insert into tblemployee values ('2','Will','Ray','1','32100.25');
insert into tblemployee values ('3','Joan','Ray','1','55300.75');
insert into tblemployee values ('4','Robyn','Ness','2','35000.20');
insert into tblemployee values ('5','Anne','Groves','2','35000.65');
insert into tblemployee values ('6','Julie','Vujevich','2','30300.01');
insert into tblemployee values ('7','Jack','Derifaj','1','12000.00');
insert into tblemployee values ('8','Russ','Schelby','1','24372.12');
insert into tblemployee values ('9','Bill','Gates','3','50000.01');
insert into tblemployee values ('10','Steve','Jobs','3','380000000.00');
```

These statements add three different job classifications (Programmer/Analyst, Web Developer, and CEO/President) to the system, as well as ten employees that fall under these classifications.

After your database has been populated, you can update or delete individual records using the commands `update`, `delete`, and `replace into`.

Modifying Data

Obviously, data in a database must be able to change; otherwise, it would only be useful for a short period of time or very limited applications.

Update

To change existing data, use the `update` command:

```
update <table name> SET <field name 1>=<expression 1>,
        ➥<field name 2>=<expression 2>,<field name n>=<expression n>
        ➥ [WHERE <search expression>]
```

To use `update`, you must supply a table name, as well as the names of the fields that need to be updated, and the new values that they should take on. This leaves one important part of the equation missing: the search expression. Without telling `update` which fields to modify, it will modify *all* the tables. For example, issuing the command

```
update tblemployee set salary='3000';
```

will modify every listed employee so that their `salary` field contains `'3000'`. If this is the desired action, great! If not, you're likely to be smacking your forehead when you discover what you've done.

To be a bit more selective about the update, you must define the `WHERE` search expression. This will select only the records that you want to update. For example, assume that we'd like to set the salary for `employeeID 1` to equal `30000.99`. The `update` statement would look like this:

```
update tblemployee set salary='30000.99' where employeeID='1';
```

This `update` statement will search the database for a field where `employeeID` is equal to `1`, and then update the value in that record's `salary` field.

In addition to `=`, there are a number of common ways to select a record based on comparing a field to a value; that is, you can select records by creating an expression that evaluates to `true` or `false`. Table 22.6 shows some of the most common expression operators and syntax.

TABLE 22.6 Some of the Common Expression Operators and Syntax

Expression Syntax	*Description*
`<fieldname> = <value>`	Select records based on a direct comparison to a value.
`<fieldname> > <value>`	Select records where the value of a field is greater than a given value.
`<fieldname> < <value>`	Select records where the value of a field is less than a given value.
`<fieldname> >= <value>`	Select records where the value of a field is greater than or equal to a given value.
`<fieldname> <= <value>`	Select records where the value of a field is less than or equal to a given value.
`<fieldname> LIKE <value>`	Select records based on a simple SQL pattern matching scheme. The character `%` matches any number characters, while _ matches a single character.

These basic expressions can be combined to form more complex searches:

`NOT` *<expression>*—Evaluates to `true` if the expression evaluates to `false`.

<expression> **`OR`** *<expression>*—Evaluates to `true` if either of the expressions is `true`.

<expression> **`AND`** *<expression>*—Evaluates to `true` if both of the expressions are `true`.

(<*expression*>**)**—Use parentheses to combine expressions to force an order of evaluation.

Check the MySQL documentation for further information on available mathematical expressions, string comparisons, and other operators that can be used in expression syntax.

Delete

To delete data from a MySQL system, you use a command similar to `update`, but without supplying new field values:

```
delete from <table name> [WHERE <search expression>]
```

As with the `update` command, you *can* leave out the `WHERE` portion of the statement entirely. Unfortunately, the result would be the elimination of all data from the named table. Again, if this is your intention, by all means, use it! For example, to delete employees who make more than $50,000 from the database, you would enter

```
delete from tblemployee where salary>'50000';
```

Replace

There is one final way to conveniently replace existing records with new data. Using the `INSERT` command to try to save a record more than one that already exists will result in an error. This happens because only one record with a given primary key can exist at a time. For example, assuming that we've filled the database with the following employee record:

```
insert into tblemployee values ('1','John','Ray','1','25300.65');
```

Attempting to insert another record using the same employee ID (`1`) will cause an error:

```
mysql> insert into tblemployee values ('1','Maddy','Green','1','41000.00');
ERROR 1062: Duplicate entry '1' for key 1
```

To circumvent this, you could `update` the existing record; or `delete` the record and then re-run the `insert`; or use the `replace into` command.

`replace` replaces an existing record with new data or, if no record exists, simply inserts a record. Think of `replace` as a more powerful version of the basic `insert` command. It can be used to add new records to a table, or replace existing records with new data. The syntax is identical to `insert`. For example, let's retry the `insert` into the `tblemployee` table—this time using `replace`:

```
mysql> replace into tblemployee values ('1','Maddy','Green','1','41000.00');
Query OK, 2 rows affected (0.00 sec)
```

Success!

Caution

replace is a useful command that is unique to the MySQL instruction set. Although replace is convenient, it is best to stick to the basic insert statement for most database operations to avoid inadvertently deleting data.

Querying MySQL

After you add data to the tables in a database, you would obviously want to display it. Querying a MySQL database is performed with the select statement. The power of relational databases comes from the capability to relate data in one table to that of another, and select can do just that:

```
select <field name1>,<field name2>,… from <table name 1>,<table name 2>,...
    ➥[where <search expression>] [ORDER BY <expression> ASC|DESC]
```

If this isn't confusing for you, fantastic. If you're like the rest of us, however, some explanation is necessary.

The simplest query that select can perform is to pull all the data out of a single table (select * from <*table name*>). For example:

```
mysql> select * from tbljobclassification;
+---------+-------------------+----------+----------+
| titleID | title             | minsalary | maxsalary |
+---------+-------------------+----------+----------+
|       1 | Programmer/Analyst |    20000 |    80000 |
|       2 | Web Developer     |    20000 |    50000 |
|       3 | CEO/President     |    40000 |    5e+09 |
+---------+-------------------+----------+----------+
3 rows in set (0.00 sec)
```

Ordering Information

To sort the information based on one of the fields, use order by with an expression (often one or more comma separated field names), and asc for ascending order or desc for descending order:

```
mysql> select * from tbljobclassification order by maxsalary desc;
+---------+-------------------+----------+----------+
| titleID | title             | minsalary | maxsalary |
+---------+-------------------+----------+----------+
|       3 | CEO/President     |    40000 |    5e+09 |
|       1 | Programmer/Analyst |    20000 |    80000 |
|       2 | Web Developer     |    20000 |    50000 |
+---------+-------------------+----------+----------+
```

In this example, the `tbljobclassification` table is displayed and the records are sorted by the maximum salary in descending order (most to least). Obviously, this is great for getting data out of a single table and manipulating its order, but it still doesn't draw on the relational power of MySQL.

Joining Tables

To fully exploit MySQL's capabilities, relationships must be created and used. A relationship links two or more tables based on a common attribute. For example, the `tblemployee` and `tbljobclassification` tables share a `titleID` field. Each employee record has a `titleID` field that can be used to *relate* to the `tbljobclassification` table. The process of relating tables together is called a `join`.

To see a `join` in action, let's take a look at how you would display a list of each employee's name, along with his or her job title. The `select` statement looks like this:

```
select firstname,lastname,title from tblemployee,tbljobclassification
      ➥WHERE tblemployee.titleID=tbljobclassification.titleID;
```

Translating this query into English is simple: Select the `firstname`, `lastname`, and title fields (`select firstname,lastname,title`) from the `tblemployee` and `tbljobclassification` database tables (`from tblemployee,tbljobclassification`). Relate the two tables by matching the `titleID` field in `tblemployee` to the `titleID` field in `tbljobclassification` (`WHERE tblemployee.titleID=tbljobclassification.titleID`).

The result is a neat display of the employees and their corresponding job titles:

```
mysql> select firstname,lastname,title from tblemployee,tbljobclassification
      ➥WHERE tblemployee.titleID=tbljobclassification.titleID;
+-----------+----------+-------------------+
| firstname | lastname | title             |
+-----------+----------+-------------------+
| Maddy     | Green    | Programmer/Analyst |
| Will      | Ray      | Programmer/Analyst |
| Joan      | Ray      | Programmer/Analyst |
| Jack      | Derifaj  | Programmer/Analyst |
| Russ      | Schelby  | Programmer/Analyst |
| Robyn     | Ness     | Web Developer     |
| Anne      | Groves   | Web Developer     |
| Julie     | Vujevich | Web Developer     |
| Bill      | Gates    | CEO/President     |
| Steve     | Jobs     | CEO/President     |
+-----------+----------+-------------------+
10 rows in set (0.03 sec)
```

Tip

In this example, the two `titleID` fields are referenced by an extended version of their name—*`<table name>.<field name>`*.

By using this syntax, you remove ambiguity in the SQL statements that would result from multiple tables containing the same names. You can use this format when referring to *any* field. In large database projects, with dozens of tables, it helps document the relationships that are being used and is suggested as the standard query format.

A `select` statement can be combined with the `WHERE` search expressions that you've already seen in this chapter. For example, the last query can be modified to show only the employees who are making more than $50,000:

```
select firstname,lastname,title,salary from tblemployee,tbljobclassification
      ➥WHERE tblemployee.titleID=tbljobclassification.titleID
      ➥AND tblemployee.salary>'50000';
```

For example:

```
mysql> select firstname,lastname,title,salary from
      ➥tblemployee,tbljobclassification WHERE
      ➥tblemployee.titleID=tbljobclassification.titleID
      ➥AND tblemployee.salary>'50000';
+-----------+----------+--------------------+---------+
| firstname | lastname | title              | salary  |
+-----------+----------+--------------------+---------+
| Joan      | Ray      | Programmer/Analyst | 55300.8 |
| Bill      | Gates    | CEO/President      |   50000 |
| Steve     | Jobs     | CEO/President      | 3.8e+08 |
+-----------+----------+--------------------+---------+
3 rows in set (0.00 sec)
```

Of course, expressions can be combined with other expressions to create truly complex queries.

Calculations

Using built-in MySQL functions, you can create virtual fields that contain data that is calculated as the query is performed. The syntax for an inline calculation is

```
<expression> as '<variable name>'
```

For example, the expression required to calculate the percentage of the maximum salary that each person makes could be represented by

```
tblemployee.salary/tbljobclassification.maxsalary*100 as 'percent'
```

Adding this code into a query of all the employees names and salaries results in

```
mysql> select firstname,lastname,salary,tblemployee.
       ➥salary/tbljobclassification.maxsalary*100 as 'percent'
       ➥from tblemployee,tbljobclassification where
       ➥tblemployee.titleID=tbljobclassification.titleID;
+-----------+----------+---------+------------------+
| firstname | lastname | salary  | percent          |
+-----------+----------+---------+------------------+
| Maddy     | Green    |   41000 |            51.25 |
| Will      | Ray      | 32100.2 |       40.1253125 |
| Joan      | Ray      | 55300.8 |       69.1259375 |
| Jack      | Derifaj  |   12000 |               15 |
| Russ      | Schelby  | 24372.1 |  30.465148925781 |
| Robyn     | Ness     | 35000.2 |    70.0003984375 |
| Anne      | Groves   | 35000.6 |     70.001296875 |
| Julie     | Vujevich |   30300 |   60.60001953125 |
| Bill      | Gates    |   50000 | 0.00100000023437 5 |
| Steve     | Jobs     | 3.8e+08 |              7.6 |
+-----------+----------+---------+------------------+
10 rows in set (0.01 sec)
```

Suddenly, the database has provided information that didn't even exist previously! Using these methods, you can use the MySQL database engine to perform much of the mathematical work of database applications, leaving the logic to other programming languages.

Summarization and Grouping

Summarizing data is another very useful part of any query. Using the summarization functions, you can easily find totals for numeric columns, or count the number of records of a particular type. Here are a few summarization functions that can be used in a query:

max()—The maximum of a given field. Used to match the highest value. For example, if you use `max` on the salary field of the employee table, it should return the highest salary in the group.

min()—The minimum of a given field. Has the exact opposite of the `max` function.

sum()—The sum of the values in a given field. For example, to find the total amount paid in salaries.

count()—Provides a count of the number of occurrences of a given field.

For example, you could find the minimum salary of all the employees by typing

```
mysql> select min(salary) from tblemployee;
+-------------+
| min(salary) |
+-------------+
|       12000 |
```

```
+-------------+
1 row in set (0.01 sec)
```

Or a count of the occurrences of the `titleID` field:

```
mysql> select count(titleID) from tblemployee;
+----------------+
| count(titleID) |
+----------------+
|             10 |
+----------------+
1 row in set (0.00 sec)
```


This second example obviously isn't very useful—all it did was return the number of times the `titleID` field was used—that is, ten times, once in each record. Displaying the count of each of the types of `titleIDs` would make more sense. This can be accomplished with one last construct—the `group by` clause.

`group by` organizes the data based on a field name, and then makes it available to the summarization function. For example, the previous query could be modified like this:

```
select titleID,count(titleID) from tblemployee group by (titleID);
```

Instead of simply counting the field occurrences and reporting a result, the query groups the `records` by the `titleID` field, and then counts the occurrences within each group. The output looks like this:

```
mysql> select titleID,count(titleID) from tblemployee group by (titleID);
+---------+----------------+
| titleID | count(titleID) |
+---------+----------------+
|       1 |              5 |
|       2 |              3 |
|       3 |              2 |
+---------+----------------+
3 rows in set (0.00 sec)
```

As with all queries, this could be turned into a `join` to provide information from more than one table. To show the actual job titles rather than just ID numbers, you could modify the query like this:

```
mysql> select title,count(tblemployee.titleID) from
       ➥tblemployee,tbljobclassification where
       ➥tblemployee.titleID=tbljobclassification.titleID
       ➥group by (tblemployee.titleID);

+-------------------+----------------------------+
| title             | count(tblemployee.titleID) |
+-------------------+----------------------------+
| Programmer/Analyst |                         5 |
```

```
| Web Developer      |                          3 |
| CEO/President      |                          2 |
+--------------------+----------------------------+
```

This output should be a bit more presentable. Note that in the modified query, the extended name (table name *and* field name) was used to refer to the `titleID` field. Failure to do this would result in an ambiguity error.

Tip

We highly recommend looking through the official MySQL documentation to get an idea of the full capabilities of the product. This chapter should not be seen as a complete reference to the capabilities of this wonderful application.

Helpers and Alternatives

There are several helper applications that are available for graphically controlling MySQL and its databases. Personally, I prefer the command-line interface, but your mileage may vary. In addition, Mac OS X boasts several industrial-strength commercial SQL database solutions. If you're interested in pointing and clicking, take a look these products:

EstellaSQL—Provides a Cocoa interface to MySQL databases, as well as a Service menu item to perform searches from within any other Cocoa application. `http://homepage.mac.com/mxcantor/FileSharing.html`.

SQL4x Manager—Manage MySQL users and databases from this Cocoa application. This is, by far, the most elegant front end available for MySQL on any platform. `www.macosguru.de/download.html`.

FrontBase—A Mac OS X–native SQL database system that features a fully graphical administration and RealBASIC integration. `www.frontbase.com/cgi-bin/WebObjects/FrontBase`.

OpenBase—Another commercial SQL system for Mac OS X. OpenBase features GUI tools for designing database schema, as well as application development using either RealBASIC or RADStudio. `www.frontbase.com/cgi-bin/WebObjects/FrontBase`.

Perl/MySQL Integration

Perl and MySQL can be combined to create database applications that can be used for anything from storing your personal movie collection to enterprise-wide solutions. This portion of the chapter will introduce you to the MySQL and Perl connection. You can later apply this knowledge to create Web applications in Chapter 28.

This section is intended to provide an example of Perl module installation, as well as the integration of Perl and MySQL functionality. Even if you don't intend to use these two applications together, the installation instructions apply to just about any Perl module.

CPAN

Perl can be extended to offer additional functionality ranging from Internet access to graphics generation. Just about anything you could ever want to do can be done using Perl—you just need the right module. The best place to find the right Perl module is CPAN—the Comprehensive Perl Archive Network. CPAN contains an ever-increasing list of Perl modules with their descriptions and documentation. To browse CPAN, point your Web browser to `www.cpan.org`.

There are two ways to install modules that are located in the CPAN archive. The first is using a built-in Perl module that interacts directly with CPAN from your desktop computer. The second is the traditional method of downloading, unarchiving, and installing—just like with any other software. Perl modules are a bit easier to install than most software because the installed software ends up in the Perl directory, rather than needing to be placed in a variety of directories across the entire system hierarchy.

There are two Perl modules (`DBI::DBD` and `DBD::mysql`) that are needed to interact with MySQL. Conveniently, this corresponds to the two available installation methods. So, let's take a look at how these modules can be installed using the interactive connection to CPAN and by downloading, and working with, the module archive directly.

CPAN Installation (`DBI::DBD`)

Using the interactive method of installing Perl modules is as simple as `install` *`<module name>`*. To start the interactive module installation shell, type `sudo perl -MCPAN -e shell` at a command line. The CPAN installer shell will start:

```
cpan shell — CPAN exploration and modules installation (v1.52)
ReadLine support available (try ``install Bundle::CPAN'')

cpan>
```

> **Note**
>
> `sudo` is used to start the CPAN shell because Perl modules must be installed in privileged directories. If you attempt to use the command without running it as `root`, it will work through most of the installation, and then fail at the final step.

The `DBI::DBD` module provides a database interface to Perl's arsenal of capabilities. At the cpan> prompt, type `install DBI::DBD` to begin the installation process:

```
cpan> install DBI::DBD

Issuing "/usr/bin/ftp -n"
Local directory now /private/var/root/.cpan/sources/modules
GOT /var/root/.cpan/sources/modules/03modlist.data.gz
Going to read /var/root/.cpan/sources/modules/03modlist.data.gz
Running make for T/TI/TIMB/DBI-1.18.tar.gz
Issuing "/usr/bin/ftp -n"
Local directory now /private/var/root/.cpan/sources/authors/id/T/TI/TIMB
GOT /var/root/.cpan/sources/authors/id/T/TI/TIMB/DBI-1.18.tar.gz

  CPAN: MD5 security checks disabled because MD5 not installed.
  Please consider installing the MD5 module.

DBI-1.18
DBI-1.18/DBI.xs
DBI-1.18/lib
DBI-1.18/lib/DBD
DBI-1.18/lib/DBD/NullP.pm
DBI-1.18/lib/DBD/Sponge.pm
DBI-1.18/lib/DBD/ADO.pm
DBI-1.18/lib/DBD/ExampleP.pm
DBI-1.18/lib/DBD/Multiplex.pm
DBI-1.18/lib/DBD/Proxy.pm
DBI-1.18/lib/DBI
DBI-1.18/lib/DBI/FAQ.pm
...
Installing /usr/bin/dbiproxy
Installing /usr/bin/dbish
Writing /Library/Perl/darwin/auto/DBI/.packlist
Appending installation info to /System/Library/Perl/darwin/perllocal.pod
  /usr/bin/make install  — OK
```

Depending on your Perl installation and version, you might notice several additional messages during the installation. Each time the CPAN shell is used, it checks for new versions of itself. If a new version is found, it will provide instructions on how to install the update. Don't concern yourself too much about these messages unless the installation fails.

Tip

Many Perl modules ask some basic questions during the install process. Even the highly automated CPAN shell installation method will pause to collect information it needs—so pay attention to your screen during an install.

That's it. The `DBD::DBI` module, which provides the basis for database access from within Perl, is now installed.

For more control within the CPAN shell, you can use these additional commands:

> **`get`** ***`<module name>`***—Download the named module.
>
> **`make`** ***`<module name>`***—Download and compile the module, but do not install.
>
> **`test`** ***`<module name>`***—Download, compile, and run the named module's tests.
>
> **`install`** ***`<module name>`***—Download, compile, test, and install the module.

Modules that have been downloaded are stored in the `.cpan` directory within your home directory. Keep track of the size of this directory because it will continue to grow as long as you install new modules.

Archive-Based Installation (`DBD::mysql`)

To complete the integration of Perl with MySQL, we need the `DBD::mysql` module. This package provides the MySQL driver that works with the `DBI::DBD` software. Instead of using the CPAN shell, let's take a look at installation of the module distribution archive directly. This is almost identical to installing other types of software, so there shouldn't be many surprises here.

First, download the package to install from CPAN:

```
[primal:~] jray% curl -o ftp://ftp.cpan.org/pub/CPAN/modules/
        ➥by-module/DBD/DBD-mysql-2.0901.tar.gz
```

Next, unarchive the module:

```
[primal:~] jray% tar zxf DBD-mysql-2.0901.tar.gz
```

Enter the distribution directory and enter this command: `perl Makefile.PL —cflags="-I'/usr/local/mysql/include'"`. In this particular example, you need to add the `—cflags` option to tell Perl where the MySQL header directory is located. Typically, module installations need nothing more than `perl Makefile.PL` at this stage.

```
[primal:~/DBD-mysql-2.0901] jray% perl Makefile.
        ➥PL —cflags="-I'/usr/local/mysql/include'"
This is an experimental version of DBD::mysql. For production
environments you should prefer the Msql-Mysql-modules.

I will use the following settings for compiling and testing:

  testpassword  (default     ) =
  testhost      (default     ) =
  testuser      (default     ) =
  nocatchstderr (default     ) = 0
  libs          (mysql_config) = -L/usr/local/lib/mysql -lmysqlclient -lz -lm
```

```
  testdb        (default     ) = test
  cflags        (Users choice) = -I'/usr/local/mysql/include'

To change these settings, see 'perl Makefile.PL —help' and
'perldoc INSTALL'.

Using DBI 1.18 installed in /Library/Perl/darwin/auto/DBI
Writing Makefile for DBD::mysql
```

Now, the installation becomes identical to any other software. The same `make` commands apply. The best step to take next is to type `make` to compile and then `make test` to test the compiled software:

```
[primal:~/DBD-mysql-2.0901] jray% make
cc -c -I/Library/Perl/darwin/auto/DBI -I'/usr/local/mysql/include'
        ➥ -g -pipe -pipe -fno-common -DHAS_TELLDIR_PROTOTYPE
        ➥ -fno-strict-aliasing -O3     -DVERSION=\"2.0901\" -DXS_VERSION=
        ➥\"2.0901\"  -I/System/Library/Perl/darwin/CORE  dbdimp.c
...
t/00base............ok
t/10dsnlist.........ok
t/20createdrop......ok
t/30insertfetch.....ok
t/40bindparam.......ok
t/40blobs...........ok
t/40listfields......ok
t/40nulls...........ok
t/40numrows.........ok
t/50chopblanks......ok
t/50commit..........ok, 14/30 skipped: No transactions
t/60leaks...........skipped test on this platform
t/ak-dbd............ok
t/akmisc............ok
t/dbdadmin..........ok
t/insertid..........ok
t/mysql2............ok
t/mysql.............ok
All tests successful, 1 test and 14 subtests skipped.
Files=18, Tests=758, 25 wallclock secs ( 3.59 cusr +  0.35 csys =  3.94 CPU)
```

Finally, `sudo make install` to install the Perl module:

```
[primal:~/crud/DBD-mysql-2.0901] jray% sudo make install
Skipping /Library/Perl/darwin/auto/DBD/mysql/mysql.bs (unchanged)
Installing /Library/Perl/darwin/auto/DBD/mysql/mysql.bundle
Files found in blib/arch: installing files in blib/lib into
         ➥architecture dependent tree
...
Installing /usr/share/man/man3/Bundle::DBD::mysql.3
Installing /usr/share/man/man3/DBD::mysql.3
Installing /usr/share/man/man3/DBD::mysql::INSTALL.3
```

```
Installing /usr/share/man/man3/Mysql.3
Writing /Library/Perl/darwin/auto/DBD/mysql/.packlist
Appending installation info to /System/Library/Perl/darwin/perllocal.pod
```

The module is installed and ready to use. To view documentation for any of the installed modules, type perldoc *<module name>*.

Using Perl and MySQL (DBD::mysql)

The DBD::mysql module uses an object-oriented model to carry out database translations. Because object-oriented programming is a bit beyond the scope of this book, we'll take a look at two examples: Adding information to a database and displaying information contained in a table. You should be able to modify these examples to your own applications, or, if you need more functionality, I recommend adding a Perl book to your library.

Displaying a Table

The easiest way to retrieve information from a MySQL database is to compose a query and retrieve the results, one record at a time. To be able to do this, you must connect to the database, issue the query, determine the number of results, and loop through a display of each one. Listing 22.1 shows the surprisingly short code necessary to do just that.

LISTING 22.1 Display the Result of a MySQL Query

```
#!/usr/bin/perl

use DBI;

$user="";
$pass="";
$database="employee";
$dsn="DBI:mysql:database=$database;host=localhost";
$sql="select firstname,lastname,title from tblemployee,tbljobclassification
    ➥where tblemployee.titleID=tbljobclassification.titleID";

$dbh=DBI->connect($dsn,$user,$pass);
$sth=$dbh->prepare($sql);
$sth->execute;

$numrows=$sth->rows;
$numfields=$sth->{'NUM_OF_FIELDS'};
$nameref=$sth->{'NAME'};

for ($x=0;$x<$numrows;$x++) {
    $valueref = $sth->fetchrow_arrayref;
    print "---------------------------\n";
    for ($i=0;$i<$numfields;$i++) {
```

LISTING 22.1 continued

```
23:             print "$$nameref[$i] = $$valueref[$i]\n";
24:     }
25: }
```

The following lines describe how the Perl code interacts with the MySQL database through the DBI module:

> **Line 3**—Use the DBI module. This must be included in any Perl application that accesses MySQL.
>
> **Lines 5–9**—Set up the username, password, database name, and sql that will be used to access the database. The `$dsn` variable contains a string that will be used to set up the connection to MySQL. The format of this string cannot change, although the database and hostname can.
>
> **Line 11**—Connect to the database using the previously defined connection string and username and password. The variable `$dbh` is a handle that references the database connection.
>
> **Line 12**—Prepare the SQL for execution.
>
> **Line 13**—Execute the SQL statement, and return a reference to the results in the variable `$sth`.
>
> **Line 15**—Store the number of returned rows in the `$numrows`.
>
> **Line 16**—Store the number of fields (columns) in the result within `$numfields`.
>
> **Line 17**—Store a reference to an array containing the field names in the variable `$nameref`.
>
> **Lines 19–25**—Loop through each of the rows in the result.
>
> **Line 20**—Fetch a row of the result and return the field values in an array referenced by `$valueref`.
>
> **Line 21**—Print a divider between each output record.
>
> **Line 22–24**—Loop based on the number of fields in the result. Display each fieldname followed by the value stored in that field.

Executing the code (assuming that the employee database from earlier in the chapter is in place) produces output like this:

```
[primal:~/perlex] jray% ./display.pl
----------------------------
firstname = Maddy
lastname = Green
title = Programmer/Analyst
----------------------------
firstname = Will
lastname = Ray
```

```
title = Programmer/Analyst
----------------------------
firstname = Joan
lastname = Ray
title = Programmer/Analyst
----------------------------
firstname = Jack
lastname = Derifaj
title = Programmer/Analyst
----------------------------
firstname = Russ
lastname = Schelby
title = Programmer/Analyst
----------------------------
firstname = Robyn
lastname = Ness
title = Web Developer
----------------------------
firstname = Anne
lastname = Groves
title = Web Developer
----------------------------
firstname = Julie
lastname = Vujevich
title = Web Developer
----------------------------
firstname = Bill
lastname = Gates
title = CEO/President
----------------------------
firstname = Steve
lastname = Jobs
title = CEO/President
```


Obviously, the syntax of this code is a bit different from the Perl that you've seen so far, but it should be easy enough to understand that you can modify the code to fit your application.

Storing Data

You probably noticed that the code for displaying the results of a query was very modular. In fact, you can use the same code to insert a record into the database. Listing 22.2 demonstrates the code needed to store data in the `tblemployee` table.

LISTING 22.2 Display the Result of a MySQL Query

```
#!/usr/bin/perl

use DBI;
```

LISTING 22.2 continued

```
4:
5: $user="";
6: $pass="";
7: $database="employee";
8: $id="11"; $firstname="Troy"; $lastname="Burkholder";
9: $titleID="2"; $salary="45000";
10: $dsn="DBI:mysql:database=$database;host=localhost";
11: $sql="insert into tblemployee values ('$id','$firstname','
      ➥$lastname','$titleID','$salary')";
12:
13: $dbh=DBI->connect($dsn,$user,$pass);
14: $sth=$dbh->prepare($sql);
15: $sth->execute;
```

The only difference between this code and the previous script is the definition of the values for an insert (lines 8 and 9) and the definition of the `insert` statement itself (line 11). The SQL statement can be whatever arbitrary SQL code you'd like. If the statement returns results, they can be read and displayed with the techniques in the previous code.

Summary

This chapter introduced two of the most popular and useful open source applications available and showed how they are integrated to create a truly powerful database development platform. Perl offers features from languages such as C, but is friendly and flexible enough to appeal to both beginners and experienced programmers. MySQL, on the other hand, provides a powerful database system that can be used to develop commercial solutions for a fraction of the price. By installing a few Perl modules, the power of both products can be combined. Moving Mac OS to a Unix base has opened an entirely new world of software to the Mac user.

File and Resource Sharing with NetInfo

IN THIS CHAPTER

Although OS X is a Unix-based operating system, there is a remaining vestige from its NEXTSTEP heritage that most Unix users won't recognize: the NetInfo database. The NetInfo database is a hierarchical database that stores information on your machine's configuration and resources.

The NetInfo hierarchy is composed of directories. Each directory has properties. Each property has a name and value. The main directory on a given machine is the root directory, represented by `/`. Each machine has a local database with information about the machine's local resources.

The NetInfo hierarchy can extend beyond your local machine. As you might have guessed, your machine could be part of a NetInfo network. A NetInfo network is a hierarchical collection of domains, where each has a corresponding NetInfo database. A NetInfo network could have an unlimited number of domains, but up to three domains is most common. Your machine has its own local domain, but it could belong to a domain composed of it and other machines. That domain could describe resources available to your local cluster of machines. That domain could also belong to another domain that might include information on yet another level of resources available, and so on.

Your machine could be part of a larger NetInfo network. However, because NetInfo is not a widespread network type, we expect that it is more likely your machine will be using its NetInfo database either as a standalone machine or, possibly, as part of a Unix cluster.

In this chapter, we will examine the NetInfo database using the graphical interface, NetInfo Manager, as well as command-line tools. You will learn how to work with the NetInfo database by adding, in a variety of ways, a PostScript printer served by a remote Unix host to our system as a useable printer. Learning how to add a printer to the NetInfo database will provide the background needed for the rest of the chapter. You will learn how to customize a local user so that you can also use it on another system. You will finish by learning how to mount file systems served by a remote Unix host on your local OS X machine, as well as how to serve a file system on your OS X machine to a remote Unix host.

Getting to Know the NetInfo Database

In this section, we will get to know the NetInfo database. We will use the NetInfo Manager to examine parts of the NetInfo database. Then we will actually make a change to the NetInfo database by adding a printer to the system. We will demonstrate how to add a printer using the NetInfo Manager entirely. Then we will add a printer by using the Print Center in conjunction with the NetInfo Manager. In the final portion of this section, we will integrate command-line usage while examining some of the NetInfo database and adding a printer.

Using the NetInfo Manager to Examine the NetInfo Database

The NetInfo Manager (path: `/Applications/Utilities/NetInfo Manager`) is the graphical interface to the NetInfo database. Using the NetInfo Manager to examine some of the contents of your NetInfo database is the easiest way to see the hierarchical arrangement of the database.

When you first start the NetInfo Manager, under the Domain menu, you open the NetInfo database on your machine by choosing Open. This opens a window from which you can select a domain. The only choice is to select the `/` domain, as shown in Figure 23.1.

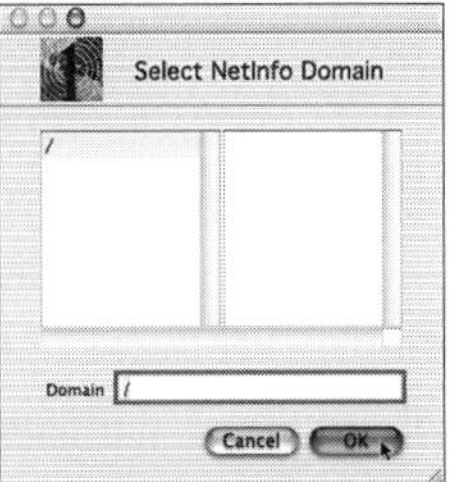

FIGURE 23.1
Opening your machine's NetInfo database from the top level.

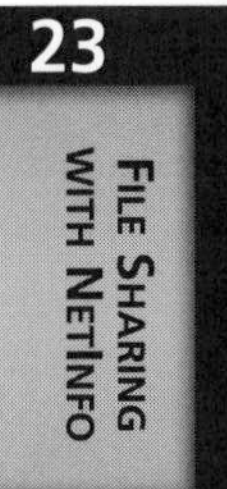

Your machine's local NetInfo database also has the name, or tag, local. When you looked at the Domain menu, you might have noticed the option to Open by Tag. If you try to Open by Tag rather than Open, the dialog box shown in Figure 23.2 asks for the host name or IP address and the NetInfo database tag. Possible entries you can use for your own host include its IP address, `localhost`, or `127.0.0.1`. For the tag, enter `local`.

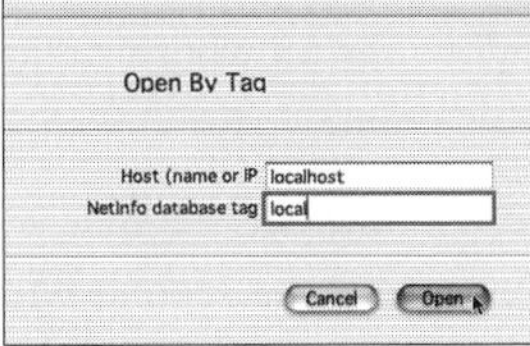

FIGURE 23.2
Opening your machine's NetInfo database by tag.

No matter which way you choose to open your NetInfo database, the result is the same, except that how the name of the local database is displayed might vary. Figure 23.3 shows what you get if you choose to open your NetInfo database using Open and selecting the default domain. Here the name is displayed as `local@localhost.biosci.ohio-state.edu - /`. In our case, the Open By Tag window displays the database as `local@localhost`.

FIGURE 23.3
The top level of your NetInfo database, as seen in the NetInfo Manager.

As you can see in Figure 23.3, the hierarchical nature of the NetInfo database is immediately apparent. In the left window, it's in the top level, `/`. In the second window, there is a list of directories. If you scroll through the list, you will see some of the types of information that the NetInfo database stores. In the lower window are the properties for a given directory. In Figure 23.3, we see the properties for the `/` directory. We see that our machine is the master of its local database, and we see that we could add a list of trusted networks.

Let's examine the NetInfo database a bit using the NetInfo Manager. If we click the `aliases` directory in the second window, more data appears in the third window. In the bottom window, we see the property values for the `aliases` directory. It only has a property called `name` with a value of `aliases`. Yes, the `name` property is indeed the name of the directory. The third window displays the actual contents of the `aliases` directory. The folder to the right, just above the right window, shows where we are currently in the hierarchy. Figure 23.4 shows where we are at this point.

If we click a directory, `postmaster`, in the third window, we see that we have reached the end of the hierarchy. What was the third window is now the second window. The third window has no data. The folder above the right window shows where we are in the hierarchy, `/aliases/postmaster`. The bottom window shows the properties of the `postmaster` directory. In addition to the `name` property, we see that the `postmaster` directory also has a `members` property with a value of `root`. What we learn from Figure 23.5 is that `postmaster` is aliased to `root`. The portion of the NetInfo database that we just looked at is what, in Unix machines, is usually stored in the file `/etc/aliases` or `/etc/mail/aliases`, depending on the system.

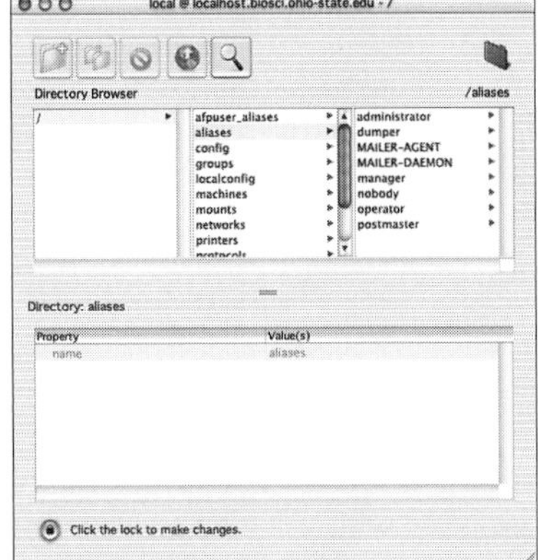

FIGURE 23.4
The third window shows the contents of the `aliases` *directory. The bottom window shows any properties associated with the* `aliases` *directory.*

FIGURE 23.5
The bottom window shows the contents of the `postmaster` *directory. The lack of data in the third window shows that we have reached the end of the hierarchy.*

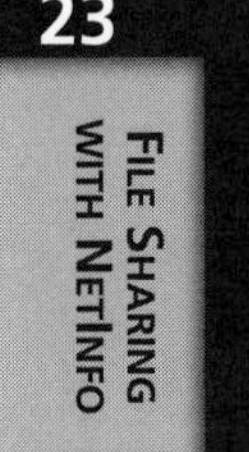

Let's look at something else in the NetInfo database. If we scroll back one window and click `services`, we see the same behavior we saw with the `aliases` directory. It only has a name property. Similar to the `aliases` directory, it has additional directories under it as displayed in the third window. The third window has enough directories to have to scroll through the listing. If you scroll to the `ssh` service and click it, you see what is shown in Figure 23.6.

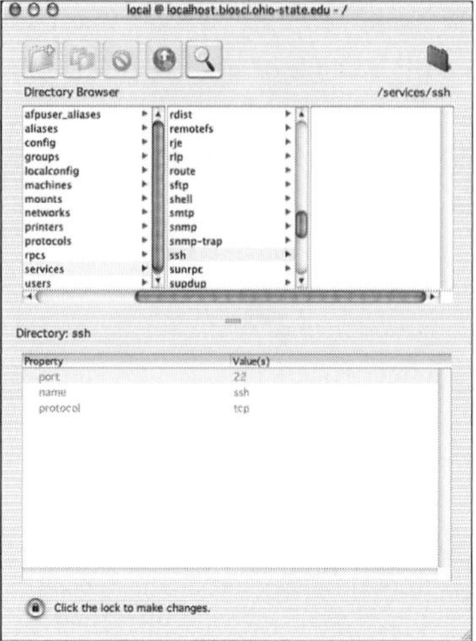

FIGURE 23.6
The contents of the `/services/ssh` *directory of the NetInfo database.*

In Figure 23.6, we see that the `/services/ssh` directory of the NetInfo database contains a `name` property with value `ssh`, a `port` property with value `22` and a `protocol` property with value `tcp`. As you might have guessed, this is NetInfo's way of displaying information that would normally be stored in a file, `/etc/services`, on a typical Unix machine. The `ssh` service itself, will be discussed in greater detail in Chapter 26, "Remote Administration."

As we have seen in our brief tour of the NetInfo database, the hierarchical nature of the database indeed becomes apparent when viewed in the NetInfo Manager.

Single-User Mode

Now that you have had the opportunity to briefly tour the NetInfo database, you might be starting to see that the NetInfo database is an important part of OS X. Consequently, it is good practice to regularly back up the NetInfo database before you make any changes to it. We will learn how to do that shortly.

You might be making your backups of the database in single-user mode. Even if you don't end up making the backups in single-user mode, there is bound to be a time when you make a change to the NetInfo database that does not work at all. Or, you might accidentally delete all of it, if you selected the wrong directory. In any case, at some point in time, you might have to restore your NetInfo database from single-user mode.

Whether it is for backing up or restoring, it is best to familiarize yourself with single-user mode ahead of time. The appearance of single-user mode on a Macintosh can be quite disturbing. It is best to have some idea of what to expect before you really need to be in single-user mode.

So, what is single-user mode? It is a quiet state of the machine. In single-user mode, `root` is the only user who can access the machine. Only a minimum number of processes are running. Only a minimum number of partitions are mounted.

To get into single-user mode, press Command + S, while the machine is booting or rebooting. When the Macintosh boots into single-user mode, it looks much like a PC. You will see a black background and text in various colors scroll by. The final portion of what appears on the screen is this:

```
Singleuser boot - fsck not done
Root device is mounted read-only
If you want to make modifications to files,
run '/sbin/fsck -y' first and then '/sbin/mount -uw /'
localhost#
```

Not all OS X machines appear to boot into single-user mode with the root device mounted read-only. Be sure to look carefully at the lines of output before the `localhost` prompt. If you need to modify any files, such as making a backup or restoring the NetInfo database, be sure to follow the indicated instructions. Otherwise, you will not be able to make any changes. It is helpful to know what behavior to expect from your system ahead of time, so that you don't panic. Because `root` is the only user in single-user mode, it is important to be calm and pay close attention to what you're doing.

While you are in single-user mode, you might be interested in running `ps`, just to see what processes run in single-user mode. When you return to multi-user mode, try running `ps` again to see the difference.

To return to multi-user mode, issue the command

```
sync;sync;sync;reboot
```

The first three commands, `sync`, force the system to complete any disk writes before rebooting. It is tradition to issue the command three times. Then `reboot` is executed.

After seeing your machine once in single-user mode, you are better prepared for any emergencies you might encounter by the end of the chapter.

Using the NetInfo Manager to Add a Printer

After a brief tour of the NetInfo database, you should feel a bit more comfortable navigating through the database in the NetInfo Manager. This is a useful skill for what we are about to do—add a printer to the NetInfo database. Because it is common in a Unix environment for one host to serve a printer that can be used by other hosts, the printer we will add to our system is a PostScript printer that is served by another Unix machine. After we are done adding the printer, we will be able to print directly from the command line, rather than having to resort to selecting Print in the `Terminal` application.

Creating a Backup of the Local NetInfo Database

Given the importance of the NetInfo database to your machine's functioning, it is best to back up the NetInfo database before making any major changes to it. You can back up the NetInfo database at either the command line or in the NetInfo Manager. In the command line, you could use `cp` or `tar` to create your backup. The NetInfo database is the directory `/var/db/netinfo/local.nidb`. When backing up the NetInfo database from the command line, Apple recommends making the back up in single-user mode.

```
localhost# cp -R local.nidb local.nidb-backup
lccalhost# tar -cf local.nidb-backup.tar local.nidb
```

If you prefer, you can back up the database in the NetInfo Manager. Click the lock in the bottom left side of the window to make changes, enter the administrator username and password, and click OK. Under the Domain menu, select Save Backup. Then pick a name and location. As shown in Figure 23.7, the default name is `local.nibak` and the default location is in `/var/db/netinfo/`. Please note that backing up the NetInfo database through the NetInfo Manager can take a long time. We recommend that you back up the NetInfo database using the command line, especially as you customize the database more and more.

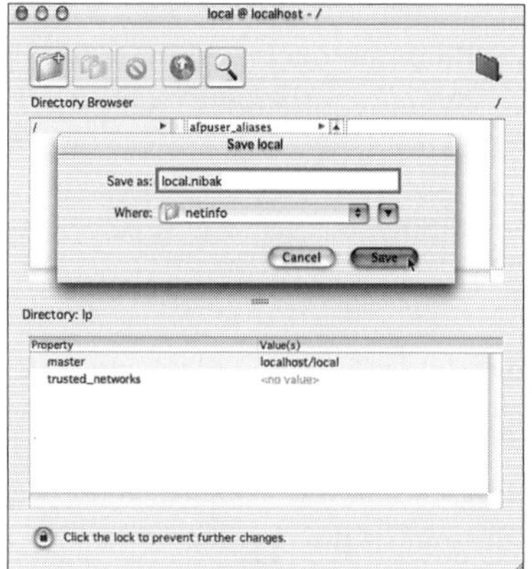

FIGURE 23.7
In addition to using the command line, the NetInfo database can be backed up directly in the NetInfo Manager.

No matter which method you use to make your backup, remember to double-check `/var/db/netinfo` to verify that it has been made:

```
localhost# ls -l local.nidb-backup

     total 136
     -rw-------  1 root  wheel     4 May  3 10:09 Clean
     -rw-r--r--  1 root  wheel     4 May  3 10:09 Config
     -rw-------  1 root  wheel  2656 May  3 10:09 Index
     -rw-r--r--  1 root  wheel  9216 May  3 10:09 Store.128
```

```
    -rw-------  1 root  wheel   1472 May  3 10:09 Store.1472
    -rw-r--r--  1 root  wheel  10720 May  3 10:09 Store.160
    -rw-r--r--  1 root  wheel   1344 May  3 10:09 Store.192
    -rw-------  1 root  wheel    224 May  3 10:09 Store.224
    -rw-r--r--  1 root  wheel   2464 May  3 10:09 Store.352
    -rw-------  1 root  wheel    416 May  3 10:09 Store.416
    -rw-------  1 root  wheel   2560 May  3 10:09 Store.640
    -rw-------  1 root  wheel    672 May  3 10:09 Store.672
    -rw-r--r--  1 root  wheel   1344 May  3 10:09 Store.96
localhost# ls -l local.nidb-backup.tar

    -rw-r--r--  1 root  wheel  51200 May  3 10:10 local.nidb-backup.tar
[localhost:/var/db/netinfo] root# ls -l local.nibak

    total 136
    -rw-------  1 root  wheel      4 May  3 09:58 Clean
    -rw-r--r--  1 root  wheel      4 Apr  4 12:20 Config
    -rw-------  1 root  wheel   2656 May  3 09:58 Index
    -rw-r--r--  1 root  wheel   9216 Apr 27 17:15 Store.128
    -rw-------  1 root  wheel   1472 Apr  4 12:47 Store.1472
    -rw-r--r--  1 root  wheel  10720 Apr 27 17:15 Store.160
    -rw-r--r--  1 root  wheel   1344 Apr 27 17:15 Store.192
    -rw-------  1 root  wheel    224 May  1 10:29 Store.224
    -rw-r--r--  1 root  wheel   2464 Apr  4 14:55 Store.352
    -rw-------  1 root  wheel    416 Apr 27 13:08 Store.416
    -rw-------  1 root  wheel   2560 Apr 27 17:15 Store.640
    -rw-------  1 root  wheel    672 Apr 16 12:37 Store.672
    -rw-r--r--  1 root  wheel   1344 May  1 10:29 Store.96
```

Modifying the NetInfo Database

After you are satisfied that your backup does indeed exist, you are ready to change your NetInfo database. To add a printer through the NetInfo Manager, we have widened the view a bit and increased the amount of space available for the `values` section. If you have a remote LaserWriter printer, we recommend that you do the same.

As we observed in the previous section, the NetInfo database is the information warehouse used by your OS X machine, instead of where files would ordinarily be used on other Unix systems. For printers, the equivalent file on some Unix systems is `/etc/printcap`. You might want to take a look at the man page for `printcap` to familiarize yourself with some of the values we will enter. Other Unix systems do not use `/etc/printcap` at all. Although printing on those systems seems a bit more magical, when the magic is working, it works well and seamlessly from the user's perspective.

To add a PostScript printer served by another Unix machine, do the following:

1. If you are not already in NetInfo Manager, start it up; then open your local database.

2. As you probably noticed in the previous section, the values shown in the bottom window of the NetInfo Manager were grayed out, and therefore could not be edited. To make changes to the NetInfo database, click the lock in the bottom-left side of the window. Enter the administrator username and password, and click OK. If you backed up your NetInfo database using the NetInfo Manager, this step is unnecessary.
3. Click the `printers` directory. In the bottom window, you will see that the `printers` directory only has a `name` property with a value of `printers`. In the right window, you will see nothing. At this time, we are at the end of the hierarchy.
4. Under the Directory menu, select New Directory. Notice that a directory, called `new_directory`, appears in the window to the right of where `printers` is located. Notice also that, in the bottom window, the `new_directory` only has a `name` property with value `new_directory`, as shown in Figure 23.8.

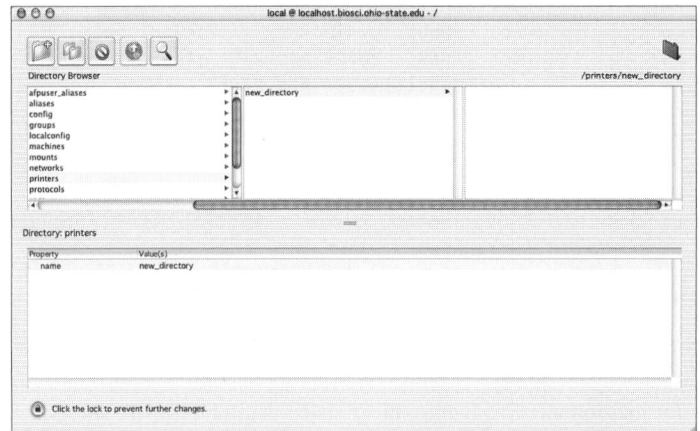

FIGURE 23.8
To add a printer definition to the `printers` *directory, select New Subdirectory under the Directory menu. A new directory called* `new_directory` *is created.*

5. Change the name of `new_directory` to the name that we want to call our printer—`lp`. Double-click `new_directory` in the bottom window, and change the name to `lp`. You might have to wait a couple seconds before you can edit the value.
6. Now `new_directory` has one property called `name` with a value of `lp`. We need more values than that to define our printer, though. Under the Directory menu, select Insert Property, New Property, or Append Property. Insert Property and New Property add a new property above the `name` line. Append Property adds a new line following the `name` line. For this example, it shouldn't matter which you pick. Now

a new line with a `new_property` with a grayed-out `value` of `<no_value>` is added, as shown in Figure 23.9. It doesn't matter where in the list the `new_property` lands. The NetInfo database will sort everything.

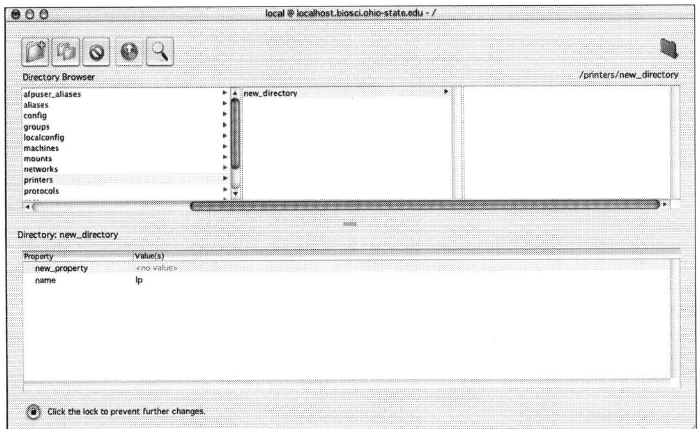

FIGURE 23.9
Under the Directory menu, select either Insert Property or Append Property to add a new property. A new property called `new_property` *with a grayed-out value of* `<no_value>` *is added.*

7. As you did before for the `lp` value, double-click `new_property`. Change it to `lo`. To change the value, select New Value or Insert Value under the Directory menu. Now `<no_value>` becomes an editable new value. Change it to lock. You should have two lines that look like the ones shown in Figure 23.10.

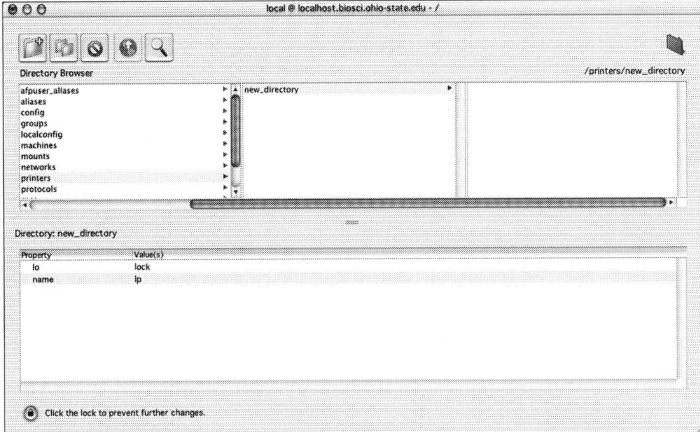

FIGURE 23.10
After adding a new property and editing its values, we now have two lines in our printer definition.

8. Using the techniques described in the previous steps, add the following lines to further define `lp`:

Property	*Value(s)*
rp	*<name of the remote printer as it is known to the remote host>*
rm	*<IP address or name of the remote machine>*
lp	/dev/null
sd	/var/spool/lpd/lp
LPR_PRINTER	1

9. In a terminal window, look at this directory: `/System/Library/Printers/PPDs/Contents/Resources`. You should see a listing of directories of the form `<language>.lproj`. Here is what the `English.lproj` directory looks like:

```
[localhost:PPDs/Contents/Resources] joray% ls English.lproj
LaserWriter
LaserWriter 12_640 PS
LaserWriter 16_600 PS
LaserWriter 16_600 PS Fax
LaserWriter 16_600 PS-J
LaserWriter 4_600 PS
LaserWriter 8500 PPD v1.2
LaserWriter Color 12_600 PS
LaserWriter Color 12_600 PS-J
LaserWriter Color 12_660 PS
LaserWriter II NT
LaserWriter II NTX
LaserWriter II NTX v50.5
LaserWriter II NTX v51.8
LaserWriter II NTX-J v50.5
LaserWriter IIf v2010.113
LaserWriter IIf v2010.130
LaserWriter IIg v2010.113
LaserWriter IIg v2010.130
LaserWriter Personal 320
LaserWriter Personal NT
LaserWriter Personal NTR
LaserWriter Pro 400 v2011.110
LaserWriter Pro 405 v2011.110
LaserWriter Pro 600 v2010.130
LaserWriter Pro 630 v2010.130
LaserWriter Pro 810
LaserWriter Pro 810f
LaserWriter Select 360
LaserWriter Select 360f
LaserWriter Select 610
```

That directory contains the default English PPDs that come with OS X. If you see a PPD for your remote printer, add a line to the `lp` definition that follows the form shown here for a LaserWriter Select 360:

```
        Ppdurl        file://localhost/System/Library/Printers/PPDs
➥/Contents/Resources/English.lproj/LaserWriter%20Select%20360
```

If your printer could be described as a generic PostScript printer, this line should be fine:

```
    ppdurl        <no_value>
```

If you have another PPD file for your printer on the system, specify its location.

10. Now you have entered all the values to define a PostScript printer attached to a remote host. Figure 23.11 shows what values for a remote LaserWriter 360 attached to another Unix system would look like.

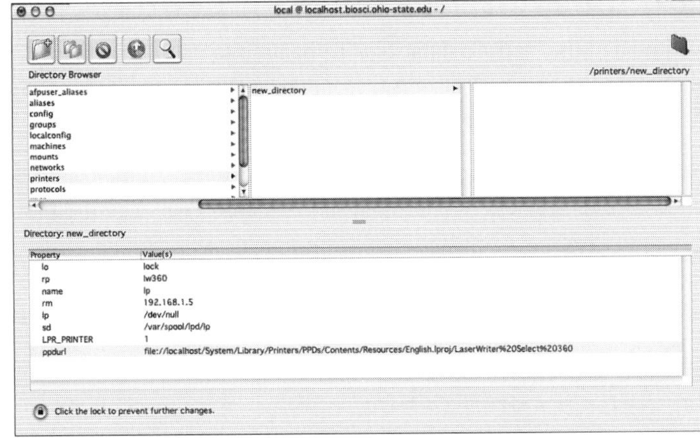

FIGURE 23.11
Completed values for a remote PostScript printer. In this case, we know that the remote PostScript printer is a LaserWriter Select 360.

11. To save our changes to the NetInfo database, select Save, under the Domain menu.
12. A request to Confirm Modification appears. Click Update this copy. Now the `new_directory` has been changed to `lp`, as shown in Figure 23.12.

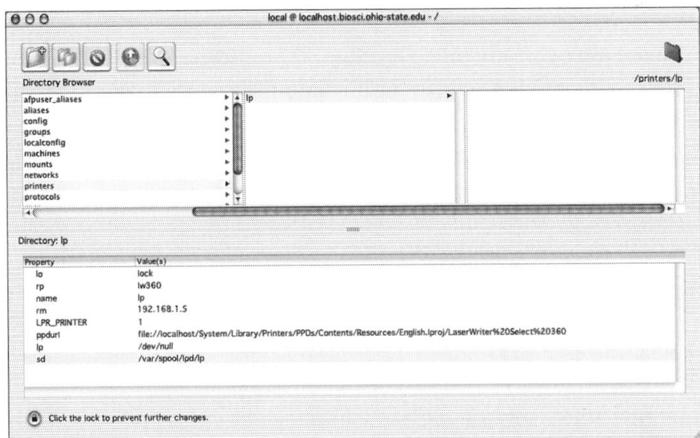

FIGURE 23.12
After saving our changes to the NetInfo database, we see that the directory called `new_directory` *has become* `lp`. *We have successfully added a new hierarchy level to the NetInfo database.*

13. Under the Options menu, select Restart All NetInfo Domains on Local Host. An alert asking if you really want to restart the machine's NetInfo servers appears. Click Yes.

14. Click the lock at the bottom-left side of the window to end your ability to make changes at this time; then close the NetInfo Manager. You may find it sufficient to just click on the lock to save your changes.

Adding the Printer to the Print Center

We have updated the NetInfo database. To be able to use this printer in regular applications, including the capability to print from the menu in the Terminal application, we need to add the printer to the Printer List in the Print Center.

1. Start the Print Center (path: `/Applications/Utilities/Print Center`). Either under Printers, select Add Printer, or click Add Printer in the Printer List.
2. Select the Directory Services connection type. You should `lp` listed as NetInfo host, as shown in Figure 23.13. Click `Add`.

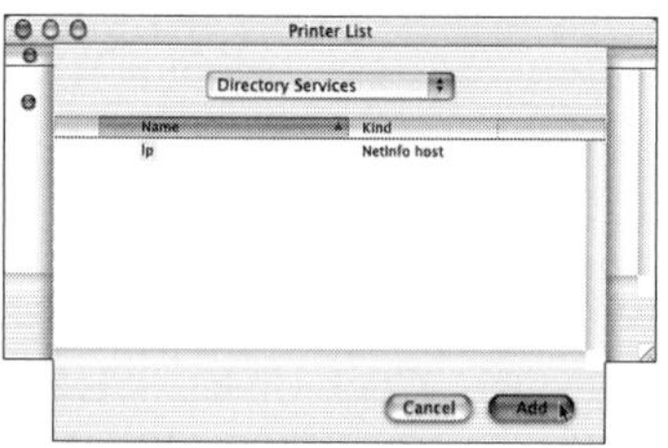

FIGURE 23.13
When we add our printer `lp` to the list of printers in the Print Center, `lp` appears as a choice under Directory Services and is described as a NetInfo host.

3. You are almost ready to try printing. If you try to print via the command line using `lpr`, you should get an error at this point. The spool directory (the `sd` property) does not yet exist. In a terminal window, make the spool directory, `/var/spool/lpd/lp`. The directory `/var/spool/lpd` should already exist.

```
[localhost:/var/spool/lpd] root# mkdir lp
[localhost:/var/spool/lpd] root# chmod 770 lp
[localhost:/var/spool/lpd] root# chown daemon.daemon lp
```

4. Test your printer from the command line by running `lpr`.

```
[localhost:~] joray% lpr file2
```

To see your print job in the queue, check the queue.

```
[localhost:~] joray% lpq
lw360 is ready and printing
Rank     Owner    Job     File(s)                              Total Size
active   joray    0       file2                                34 bytes
```

5. Test `lp` from an OS X application, such as Internet Explorer.

Add `lpd` to Your Startup Scripts

After you are satisfied that the printer works, it is probably a good idea to make a backup copy of the NetInfo database. It is also necessary to set up `lpd`, the daemon that handles sending print jobs to the printer, to start up at boot time. Until `lpd` is set to start at boot time, your ability to print will last only through your current session. To add `lpd` to your startup scripts, do the following:

1. Make a backup copy of `/etc/hostconfig`:

   ```
   [localhost:~joray] root# cp /etc/hostconfig /etc/hostconfig.backup
   ```

2. Create a directory called `/System/Library/StartupItems/LPD`:

   ```
   [localhost:/Users/joray] root# cd /System/Library/StartupItems
   [localhost:/System/Library/StartupItems] root# mkdir LPD
   ```

3. In `/System/Library/StartupItems/LPD`, using your favorite text editor, make a file called `LPD` with the following contents:

   ```
   #!/bin/sh

   ##
   # start lpd
   ##

   . /etc/rc.common

   if [ "${LPD:=-NO-}" = "-YES-" ]; then
       ConsoleMessage "Starting lpd"

       /usr/libexec/lpd

   fi
   ```

   You can start to create the file by copying `/System/Library/StartupItems/Apache/Apache` to the `LPD` directory as `LPD` and editing the appropriate lines. If you choose to start by copying a file from another `StartupItems` directory, recall that `cp -p` retains the permissions of the original file.

4. In `/System/Library/StartupItems/LPD`, using your favorite text editor, make a file called `StartupParameters.plist`. Again, you can start it by copying a simple `StartupParameters.plist` in another directory, such as the one in the `Apache` directory, to the `LPD` directory and editing it so that it looks like this:

   ```
   {
     Description    = "let's you print";
     Provides       = ("lpd");
     Requires       = ("Resolver");
     Uses           = ("Network Time");
     Preference     = "None";
   ```

```
  Messages =
  {
    start = "Starting lpd";
    stop  = "Stopping lpd";
  };
}
```

5. The `Provides`, `Requires`, and `Uses` entries are suggestions to the startup system regarding when and whether it is appropriate to run the script. It is not clear at this point that the startup system actually uses these specifications, but many parts of OS X are still evolving. Although it doesn't seem necessary to provide correct information in these fields at this time, we suggest trying to make your entries as intelligent as possible. What we've chosen here are certainly not the only possible choices—feel free to tweak it as you see fit. So far, this `StartupParameters.plist` appears to work for us.

   Make sure that your files have the permissions as listed here.

   ```
   [localhost:Library/StartupItems/LPD] root# ls -l
   total 16
   -r-xr-xr-x  1 root  wheel  147 Apr 24 12:18 LPD
   -r—r—r—  1 root  wheel  241 Apr 25 19:48 StartupParameters.plist
   ```

   If your files do not have the permissions listed previously, use the commands below to change them.

   ```
   [localhost:Library/StartupItems/LPD] root# chmod 555 LPD
   [localhost:Library/StartupItems/LPD] root# chmod 444 StartupParameters.plist
   ```

After you are satisfied that you have completed the previous steps, reboot the machine. When you log back in you should be able to print from the command line using the `lpr` command, as shown in Chapter 15, "Command-Line Applications and Application Suites."

Using the Print Center and NetInfo Manager to Add a Printer

Although you can often work completely in the NetInfo Manager to update the NetInfo database, there are some instances when another tool in the system can enter part of the NetInfo properties for you. Determining what properties you need to add to the NetInfo database for a given item can sometimes seem like guesswork. Carefully reading the man pages will give you some clues. Sometimes, using another system tool can do some of the work for you. In this example, we will add a printer to the system by using the Print Center and NetInfo Manager in combination with each other. What we will do is add a printer in the Print Center, use the NetInfo Manager to modify the settings the Print Center adds to the NetInfo database, and modify the printer in the Print Center using the updated information from the NetInfo database.

To add a PostScript printer served by another Unix host to the NetInfo database using the Print Center and the NetInfo Manager, do the following:

1. Make a backup of the NetInfo database.
2. Start the Print Center. Under Printers, select Add Printer; or click Add Printer in the Printer List.
3. In the window that comes up, select `LPR Printers using IP`. Enter the IP address or name of the remote Unix host. Select a printer description, if one is available. The choices are various types of LaserWriter printers (the same ones we saw listed in the `/System/Library/Printers/PPDs/Contents/Resources/<language>.lproj` directory), `generic`, and `other`. Selecting `other` enables you to specify a PPD that you might have elsewhere on your machine. Figure 23.14 shows our printer defined in the Print Center.

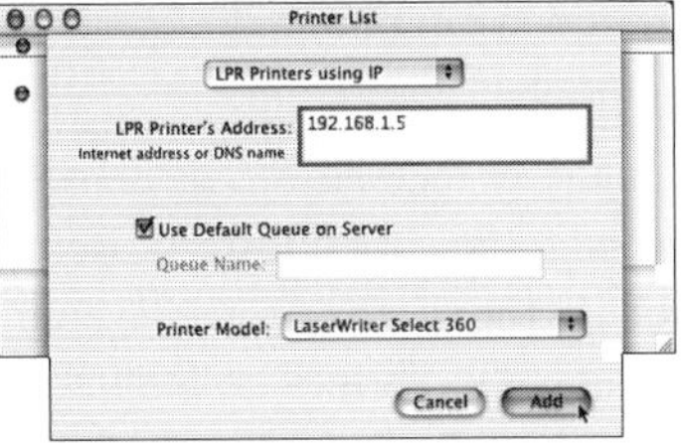

FIGURE 23.14
Defining our printer in the Print Center. We have listed the remote host's IP address and selected a PPD file.

4. When you are returned to the Printer List, note that the new printer is described as an `lpr` host, as shown in Figure 23.15.

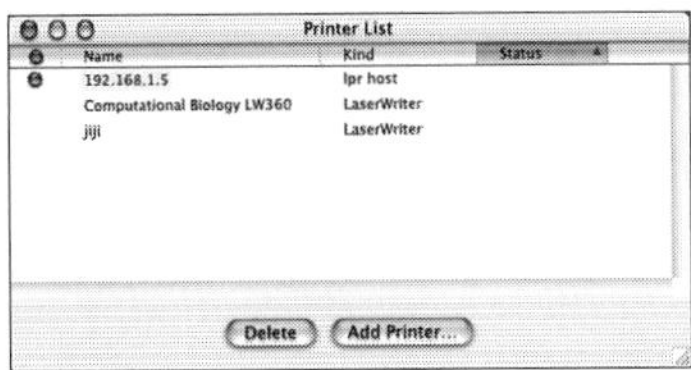

FIGURE 23.15
Our printer has been added to the Printer List as an `lpr` *host.*

5. Now you are ready to interact with the NetInfo database using the NetInfo Manager. Open the NetInfo Manager and select your local domain, if it is not already open. Click `printers`, and then click the IP address/name in the window to the right. Click in the lock to make changes, and then enter your administrator username and password. Figure 23.16 shows the default NetInfo entry that the Print Center added to the database.

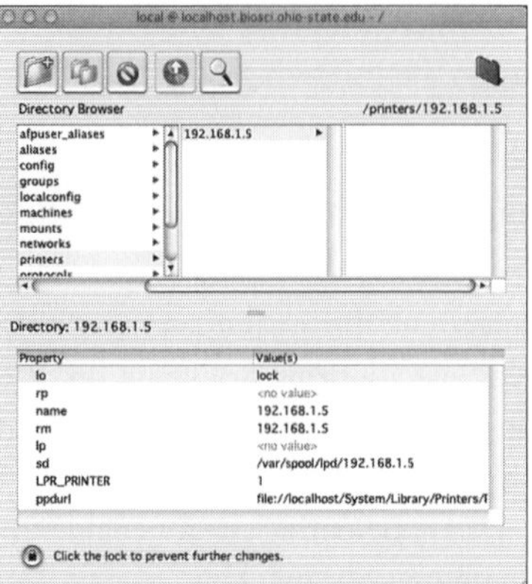

FIGURE 23.16
Print Center has already added our printer to the NetInfo database in a directory labeled with the IP address/name of the remote Unix host and created a number of properties for us.

It should be getting clearer how some tools integrate and interoperate with the NetInfo database. The Print Center added not only a directory for our printer, but also a number of properties for the printer.

6. Rather than adding properties manually in the NetInfo database, following this path, a few precreated properties need to be edited instead. Before editing the properties, take a look at your `/var/spool/lpd` directory. You'll note that the `Print Center` not only added information about the printer to NetInfo, but also created the spool directory. At this time, the spool directory has the same name as the directory entry that was created in the NetInfo database, which came from the IP address or name of the remote host.

   Edit the properties accordingly:

Property	*Value(s)*
`rp`	*`<name of the remote printer as it is known to the remote host>`*
`rm`	*`<IP adddress or name of the remote machine>`*
`lp`	`/dev/null`
`sd`	`/var/spool/lpd/lp`
`LPR_PRINTER`	`1`
`ppdurl`	*`<as appropriate>`*

7. Double-check your edits and then save them. Select Save under the Domain menu. A request to Confirm Modification appears. Click Update this copy. Note that the directory named with the IP address/remote hostname is now called `lp`.

8. Under the Options menu, select Restart All NetInfo Domains on Local Host. An alert asking if you really want to restart the machine's NetInfo servers appears. Click Yes. Click the lock at the bottom left of the window to end your ability to make changes at this time. Then close the NetInfo Manager.
9. Start the Print Center. Either under Printers, select Add Printer, or click Add Printer in the Printer List.
10. Select the Directory Services connection type. You should see `lp` listed as a NetInfo host. Click `Add`.
11. Now there is a listing for `lp` as a NetInfo host and a listing for the printer as an `lpr` host, as shown in Figure 23.17. Select the printer as an `lpr` host definition and delete it.

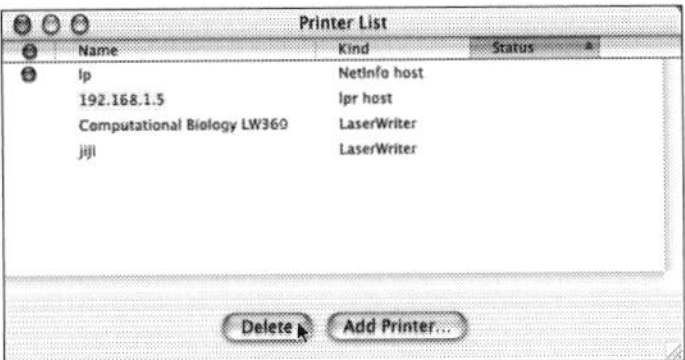

FIGURE 23.17
Now the printer has been added as `lp`*, a NetInfo host. The original description of the printer as an* `lpr` *host is still in the Printer List, but can be deleted now.*

You can now test the printer by running `lpr` in the command line and printing from an OS X application. After you are satisfied that it prints, add `lpd` to your startup scripts as described in the previous section. You might also want to make a backup copy of your NetInfo database.

Using the Command Line to Examine the NetInfo Database

As you have seen throughout this book, command-line tools are frequently available to do what can be done in the graphical tools in OS X. This is also the case with the NetInfo database. You can manage the database graphically in the NetInfo Manager, and you can manage the database through command-line tools. As you become more familiar with the NetInfo database, you will learn that sometimes the graphical tools are more suitable for accomplishing your task, whereas at other times the command-line tools are more suitable.

In this section we will take some of the same tour of the NetInfo database that we did using the NetInfo Manager, only this time we will use the command line. Having already used the NetInfo Manager will make the introduction to the command line easier.

Before we even begin our tour, we can verify that our machine is indeed a NetInfo server, serving its own local domain by running `ps`:

```
[localhost:~] joray% ps -aux | grep netinfo

     root   196  0.0 0.1  1632  496  ?? S  0:00.49 netinfod local (master)
     joray  558  0.0 0.0  5708  0 std   RV 0:00.00 grep netinfo
```

As we can see from the `ps` listing, our machine is indeed running a NetInfo server for its `local` domain, and it is the master of its `local` domain.

Now let's look directly at the NetInfo database. We will be examining the NetInfo database using the `niutil` command, the NetInfo utility. You can do more than just examine the database with `niutil`, but we will get to that later.

The primary form of `niutil` is

```
niutil <action> [opts] <domain> <path>
```

One of the most confusing parts about using the command-line tools is remembering what term to use to refer to the local domain. As you might guess from the NetInfo Manager, `/` would probably refer to the `local` domain. However, you will also see in man pages and online documentation the use of `.` to refer to the `local` domain. Which is it?

```
[localhost:~] joray% niutil -domainname .

     /
[localhost:~] joray% niutil -domainname /

     /
```

As we see from the `niutil` command, we can use either `.` or `/` to refer to the local domain, as long as the local domain is the only domain we have. As you research things on the Internet, you might see both terms being used to refer to the local domain. As we continue with this chapter, we will use the notation described in the man pages.

Let's look at the `root` directory of our local domain:

```
[localhost:~] joray% niutil -list . /

     1          users
     7          groups
     27         machines
     31         networks
     33         protocols
     48         rpcs
```

```
77        services
141       aliases
150       mounts
151       printers
152       localconfig
156       config
164       afpuser_aliases
```

This looks familiar! The result we get on the command line looks much like what we saw in NetInfo Manager in the right window, except that the NetInfo Manager listed the directories in alphabetical order rather than by numeric ID.

We can look at the properties of the `root` directory of the local domain:

```
[localhost:~] joray% niutil -read . /

    master: localhost/local
    trusted_networks:
```

This looks like the same view we had in the bottom window of the NetInfo Manager.

Let's do the command-line equivalent of clicking on the `aliases` directory in the NetInfo Manager:

```
[localhost:~] joray% niutil -list . /aliases

    142       administrator
    143       postmaster
    144       MAILER-DAEMON
    145       MAILER-AGENT
    146       nobody
    147       dumper
    148       manager
    149       operator
```

If we were in the NetInfo Manager, the window to the right would show more data now. If we click the `postmaster` directory, we also see in the command line that we have reached the end of the hierarchy:

```
[localhost:~] joray% niutil -list . /aliases/postmaster
```

Again, we can look at the properties of `postmaster`:

```
[localhost:~] joray% niutil -read . /aliases/postmaster

    name: postmaster
    members: root
```

As we saw in the NetInfo Manager, `postmaster` appears to be aliased to `root`.

We can also view a specific property using the command line. Here we ask for the value of the `port` property of the `ssh` directory of the `services` directory in our `local` domain:

```
[localhost:~] joray% niutil -readprop . /services/ssh port
     22
```

Now we have taken a brief tour of our local NetInfo database using `niutil`. So far, we have seen that using `-list` or some form of `-read` is much like clicking on values in the NetInfo Manager. Specifically, `-list` lists directories in the specified name and path, and `-read` lists associated values of a directory. In NetInfo Manager terms, the `-list` action is like navigating the upper windows, but using `-read` is like viewing the contents of a directory being displayed in the upper window in the bottom window. The command documentation table for `niutil` is shown in Table 23.1.

TABLE 23.1 The NetInfo Utility `niutil` Is Used to Edit the NetInfo Database.

Niutil	*NetInfo utility*

```
niutil -create [opts] <domain> <path>
niutil -destroy [opts] <domain> <path>
niutil -createprop [opts] <domain> <path> <key> [<val>...]
niutil -appendprop [opts] <domain> <path> <key> <val>...
niutil -mergeprop [opts] <domain> <path> <key> <val>...
niutil -insertval [opts] <domain> <path> <key> <val> <index>
niutil -destroyprop [opts] <domain> <path> <key>
niutil -destroyval [opts] <domain> <path> <key> <val>
niutil -renameprop [opts] <domain> <path> <oldkey> <newkey>
niutil -read [opts] <domain> <path>
niutil -list [opts] <domain> <path>
niutil -rparent [opts] <domain>
niutil -resync [opts] <domain>
niutil -statistics [opts] <domain>
```

`niutil` enables you to perform arbitrary reads and writes on the specified NetInfo *<domain>*. To perform writes, `niutil` must be run as `root` on the NetInfo master for the database, unless `-p`, `-P`, or `-u` is specified. The directory specified by *<path>* is separated by `/` characters. A numeric ID may be used for a path in place of a string. Property names might be given in a path with an =. The default property name is `name`. The following examples refer to a user with user ID 3:

```
/name=users/uid=3
/users/uid=3
```

TABLE 23.1 continued

Options	
`-t <host>/<tag>`	Interprets the domain as a tagged domain. For example, `parrish/network` is the domain tagged network on machine `parrish`.
`-p`	Prompts for the `root` password or the password of `<user>` if combined with `-u`.
`-u <user>`	Authenticates as `<user>`. Implies `-p`.
`-P <password>`	Provides the `root` password or the password of `<user>` if combined with `-u`. Overrides `-p`.
`-T <seconds>`	Sets the read and write timeout to `<seconds>`. Default is 30 seconds.
Operations	
`-create <domain> <path>`	Creates a new directory with the specified path.
`-destroy <domain> <path>`	Destroys the directory with the specified path.
`-createprop <domain> <path> <key> [<val>...]`	Creates a new property in the directory `<path>`. `<key>` is the name of the property. Zero or more property values may be specified. If the named property already exists, it is overwritten.
`-appendprop <domain> <path> <key> <val>...`	Appends new values to an existing property in directory `<path>`. `<key>` is the name of the property. Zero or more property values may be specified. If the named property does not exist, it is created.
`-mergeprop <domain> <path> <key> <val>...`	Merges new values into an existing property in the directory `<path>`. `<key>` is the name of the property. Zero or more property values might be specified. The values are appended to the property only if they do not already exist. If the named property does not exist, it is created.
`-insertval <domain> <path> <key> <val> <propindex>`	Inserts a new value into an existing property in the directory `<path>` at position `<propindex>`. `<key>` is the name of the property. If the named property does not exist, it is created.
`-destroyprop <domain> <path> <key>`	Destroys the property with name `<key>` in the specified `<path>`.

TABLE 23.1 continued

-destroyval <domain> <path> <key> <val>	Destroys the specified value in the property named <key> in the specified <path>.
-renameprop <domain> <path> <oldkey> <newkey>	Renames the property with name <oldkey> in the specified <path>.
-read <domain> <path>	Reads the properties associated with the directory <path> in the specified <domain>.
-list <domain> <path>	Lists the directories in the specified <domain> and <path>. Directory IDs are listed along with directory names.
-readprop <domain> <path> <key>	Reads the value of the property named <key> in the directory <path> of the specified <domain>.
-readval <domain> <path> <key> <index>	Reads the value at the given index of the named property in the specified directory.
-rparent <domain>	Prints the current NetInfo parent of a server. The server should be explicitly given using the -t <host>/<tag> option.
-resync <domain>	Resynchronizes NetInfo. If a domain name is given, the master resynchronizes all clones. If the -t <clone>/<tag> option is used instead, only that clone is resynchronized. Using -t <master>/<tag> resynchronizes the whole domain.
-statistics <domain>	Prints server statistics on the specified <domain>.
-domainname <domain>	Prints the domain name of the given domain.
<domain>	A value of . for <domain> refers to the local NetInfo database.

Using the Command Line to Add a Printer

With all the values we saw in the previous sections, you might feel that adding a printer through the command-line tools would be especially painful. However, this method can be as easy as the method described in the section on using the Print Center with the NetInfo Manager.

As you might recall, OS X uses the NetInfo database to store information on printers, whereas some versions of Unix store this information in a file called /etc/printcap.

OS X has a nice command-line tool available that understands certain typical Unix flat files and can convert them to NetInfo data. One of the flat-file formats that the tool, niload, understands is the printcap.

To add a PostScript printer served by a remote Unix host using primarily command-line tools, do the following:

1. Make a backup of the NetInfo database.
2. Look at the man page and sample /etc/printcap that comes with the system to familiarize yourself with the basic format of the /etc/printcap file.
3. Using your favorite text editor, create a printcap file in some location. Do not overwrite or even edit the sample that comes with the system, so that you have your original sample intact.
4. Add a line of this form to your printcap file:

   ```
   lp:\
   :lp=/dev/null:rm=192.168.1.5:rp=lw360:\
   :sd=/var/spool/lpd/lp:
   ```

   These values should already look familiar. The lp on the first line is the name of our printer. The lp on the second line will become the lp property with value /dev/null. The rm on the second line will become the rm property with the value of the IP address or name of the remote machine. The rp on the second line will become the rp property with the value of the name of the printer as it is known on the remote host. The sd on the third line will become the sd property with a value of the spool directory, /var/spool/lpd/lp.

   Please note that this file is virtually only one line long, even though it is entered on three lines. The \ indicates that the current line continues to the next line in the file.
5. As root, use the niload command to load the flat file you made into the NetInfo Database.

   The basic form of the command we will use is niload *<format>* *<domain>* < *<filename>*.

   ```
   [localhost:~] root# niload printcap . < printcap-test
   ```

   The command documentation table for niload is shown in Table 23.2.

   Look at the results of what you just did using the command niutil and/or the NetInfo Manager. In our command-line result, lp2 appears, rather than lp, because we created a second definition of the same printer for demonstration purposes.

   ```
   [localhost:~] joray% niutil -read . /printers/lp2
   lp: /dev/null
   ```

```
rp: lw360
sd: /var/spool/lpd/lp
name: lp2
rm: 192.168.1.5
```

Figure 23.18 shows a sample of what the `niload` version of the `printcap` data looks like in the NetInfo Manager.

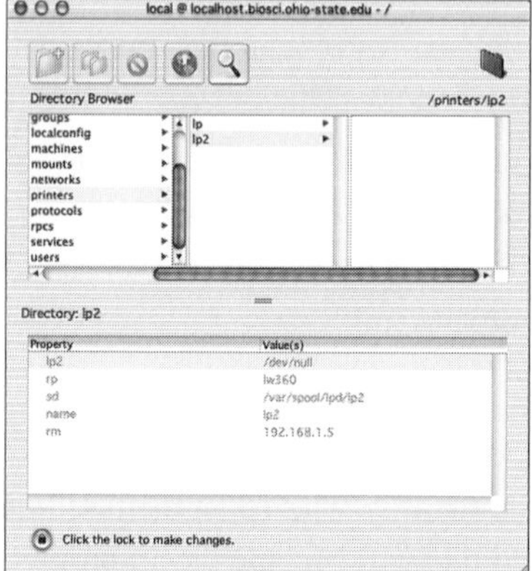

FIGURE 23.18
`niload` *has been successfully used to load* `printcap` *information into the NetInfo database.*

Notice that the `printcap` does not necessarily use all the values that the Print Center generates. The minimum values that can be defined in a typical `printcap` file are acceptable to the NetInfo database.

6. Create the spool directory. In a terminal window, make the spool directory, `/var/spool/lpd/lp`. The directory `/var/spool/lpd` should already exist.

```
[localhost:/var/spool/lpd] root# mkdir lp
[localhost:/var/spool/lpd] root# chmod 770 lp
[localhost:/var/spool/lpd] root# chown daemon.daemon lp
```

7. Start the Print Center. Either under Printers, select Add Printer, or click Add Printer in the Printer List. Select the Directory Services connection type. You should see `lp` listed as a NetInfo Host. Click `Add`.
8. Test printing via `lpr` in the command line, as well as through the normal print menu of an OS X application.

After you are satisfied that it prints, add `lpd` to your startup scripts as described in the section on adding a printer directly through the NetInfo Manager. You might also want to make a backup copy of your NetInfo database.

TABLE 23.2 Use `niload` to Load Data into NetInfo Domains

`niload [-v] [-d | m] [-p] [-t] {-r <directory> | <format>} <domain>`

`niload` loads information from standard output into the specified NetInfo `<domain>`. If `<format>` is specified, the input is interpreted according to the flat-file format `<format>`. Acceptable values for `<format>` are `aliases`, `bootparams`, `bootptab`, `fstab`, `group`, `hosts`, `networks`, `passwd`, `printcap`, `protocols`, `rpc`, and `services`.

If `-r <directory>` is specified instead of `<format>`, the input is interpreted as raw NetInfo data, as generated by `nidump -r`, and is loaded into `<directory>`.

`niload` overwrites entries in the existing directory with those contained in the input. Entries that are in the directory, but not in the input, are not deleted unless `-d` is specified. `niload` must be run as the `superuser` on the master NetInfo server for `<domain>`, unless `-p` is specified.

`-v`	Verbose mode. Prints + for each entry loaded, and - for each entry deleted (flat-file formats only).
`-d`	Deletes entries that are in the directory, but not in the input.
`-m`	Merges new values into the directory when the input contains a duplicate name.

Note: Only one of `-d` or `-m` might be specified. If neither option is specified, existing entries in the NetInfo database will remain unchanged when the input contains a duplicate name.

`-p`	Prompts for the `root` password of the given domain so that the command might be run from locations other than the master.
`-u <user>`	Authenticates as `<user>`. Implies `-p`.
`-P <password>`	Provides `<password>` on the command line. Overrides `-p`.
`-t <host>/<tag>`	Interprets the domain as a tagged domain. For example, `trotter/network` refers to the domain network on the machine trotter. Machine name can be specified as an actual name or an IP address.
`-T <seconds>`	Sets the read and write timeout to `<seconds>`. Default is 30 seconds.
`-r <directory>`	Loads entries in raw format, as generated by `nidump -r`. The first argument should be the path of a NetInfo directory into which the information is loaded. The specified directory might be renamed as a result of contents of the input, particularly if the input includes a top-level `name` property. If the specified directory does not exist, it is created.
`<domain>`	NetInfo `<domain>` that is receiving input. If `.` is the value for `<domain>`, it is referring to the local NetInfo database.

NetInfo Manager Interface

Now that you have had a chance to use the NetInfo Manager, let's take a brief look at the NetInfo Manager interface itself. The NetInfo Manager and NetInfo database can seem so overwhelming at first, that now is a good time to take a step back and look at the interface itself.

As you have seen throughout this chapter, there are many options available under the menu items of the NetInfo Manager. Because there are so many options, it can be easy to overlook the buttons that are included in the upper left of the NetInfo Manager window.

The buttons, provide some useful shortcuts for some actions. Descriptions are provided for the buttons, from left to right:

- **Create New Directory**, the button with a folder and a plus sign, is used to add a new subdirectory to the NetInfo database.
- **Duplicate Selected Directory**, the one with two folders, causes the selected folder to be duplicated. You might find this button particularly useful as you create more groups and some types of users.
- **Delete Selected Directory**, the circle with a slash in the middle, deletes the selected directory when clicked.
- **Open Parent Domain**, the button with an earth and an up arrow, causes NetInfo to move to the parent domain of the current domain. If your machine is not part of a complicated network, you might not find much use for this button. For the typical user whose machine is only a part of its own local NetInfo domain, this button does nothing.
- **Show Find Panel**, represented by a magnifying glass, is used to open the Find dialog box. You might find this button useful for searching the NetInfo database. Figure 23.19 shows the results of using Find on `lp` in our NetInfo database.

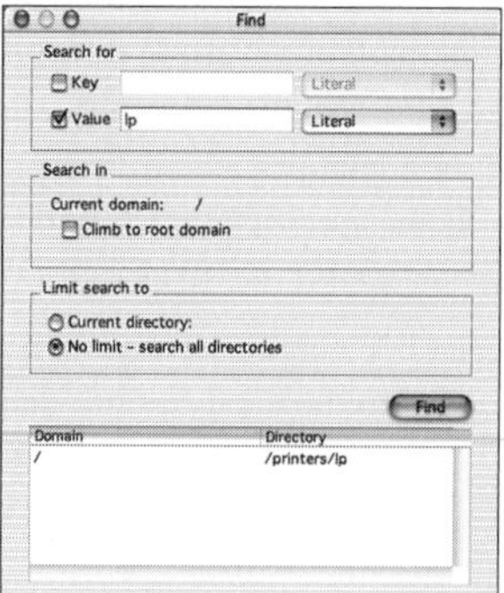

FIGURE 23.19
The Find button can be used to search the NetInfo database.

In addition to the buttons, you might also have noticed the folder at the right. Your present location in the NetInfo database is displayed underneath this folder. The upper window is where you navigate through the NetInfo database. The lower window is where you view the contents of a specific directory in the NetInfo database.

Using the NetInfo Database to Customize a User

Now that you have had the opportunity to examine the NetInfo database, back it up, and try using it. In the previous section, you saw that changes can be made in the NetInfo database in conjunction with other tools. We will make use of that idea in this section, where we will learn how to customize the creation of a user account. We will use the Users control panel to create a user, but we will customize our user by editing information in the NetInfo database.

In our example, we will make a user that we want to use as our general software user. This is a specialized user whose account we want to use when compiling software for the system, but we do not want to be one of the administrators for the machine. We would like our user to belong to a group called `tire`, with group ID `100`. We would also like to have a specific user ID, `502`, for our user, whose account we intend to call `software`. To create this user, do the following:

1. Open the Users control pane in the System Preferences. Click the lock icon if it is set to not allow changes. Next enter the administrator username and password; then click New User, as shown in Figure 23.20.

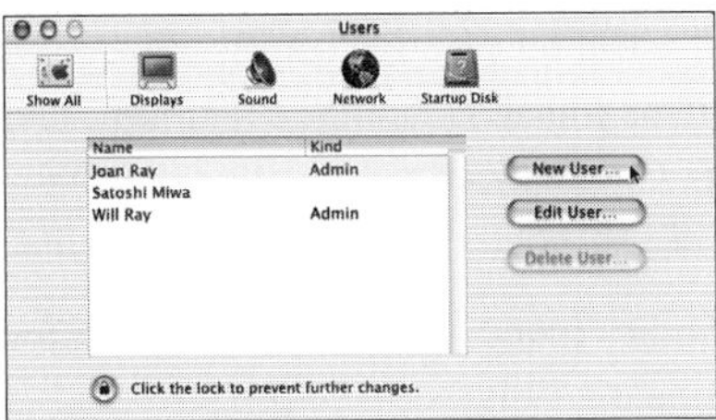

FIGURE 23.20
The Users control pane is where you create users.

2. A New User window appears, as seen in Figure 23.21. Enter the following information for the user:
   - **Name**—Enter a name for your user.
   - **Short Name**—The short name is the username, that is, the name of the account. This is the name that the user uses to log in to the machine. In our case, the username is `software`.

- **Password**—The password should be at least four characters. Many systems recommend at least six characters, with a variety of character types included in the password.
- **Verify**—Re-enter the password for verification purposes.
- **Password Hint**—This is an optional field. If you include a hint, make sure that the hint is not so obvious that other users can guess the password.

3. Do not check the box enabling administrative privileges. Click Save.

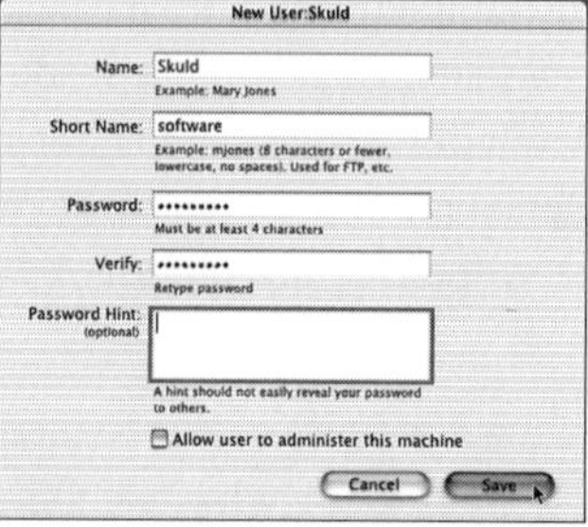

FIGURE 23.21
A New Users window appears where a name, username, and password are entered for the new user. A box can be checked to allow a user administrative privileges.

4. You are returned to the Users control pane, which now lists your new user by name. If you were not interested in customizing your user, you would be done. However, to customize the user, the NetInfo database must be edited. Make a back up of the NetInfo database, if you do not already have a recent backup. Open the NetInfo Manager, and select the `local` domain if it is not already selected. Click the lock to make changes, and enter the administrator username and password.
5. Click the `groups` directory and scroll through the list. Because `tire` is not a default group that comes with the system, you should not see a group called `tire`. So, you will have to make a new group. Click any group to see what values are typically included in a group. Figure 23.22 shows the types of properties that belong to a group.
6. Click `groups`. Under the Directory menu, select New Subdirectory. A new directory called `new_directory` appears. Edit the `name` property and add properties as follows:

Property	*Value*
`name`	`tire`
`passwd`	`*`
`gid`	`100`
`users`	`software`

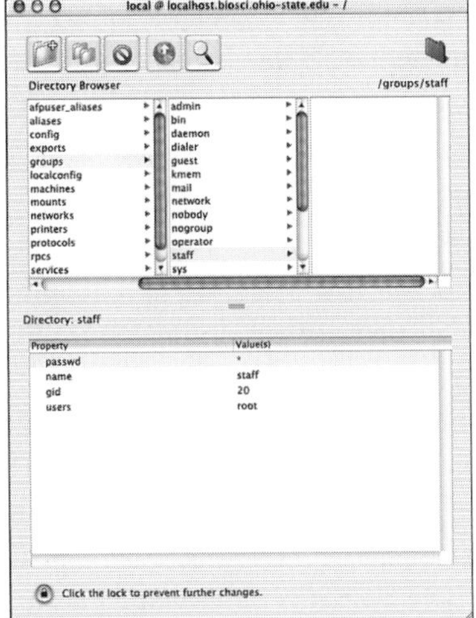

FIGURE 23.22
Looking at the `staff` *directory, we see that the typical properties for a group are* `passwd`, `name`, `gid`, *and* `users`.

The `*` in the password field means that a group password is not being assigned. So far, we have only one user in our group, user `software`. As the term group implies, we can have more than one user in a group.

7. Select Save under the Domain menu. The question to Confirm Modification appears. Click Update this copy. Now `new_directory` has become `tire`, as shown in Figure 23.23.

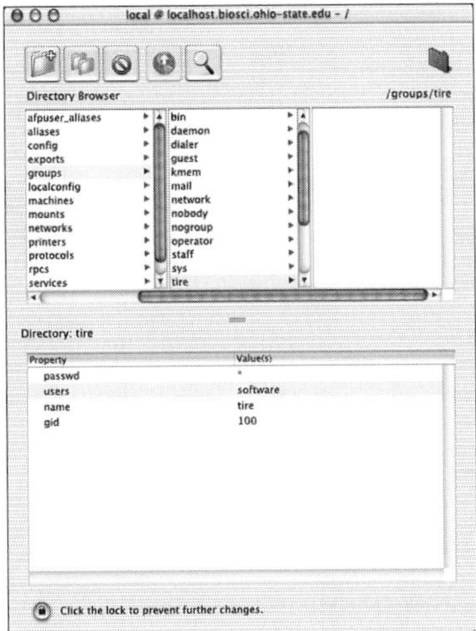

FIGURE 23.23
We now have a new group called `tire`, *with GID* `100`. *At this time, only one user,* `software`, *belongs to the group.*

8. Click `users`, and then click `software`. Now the default information on user `software` appears in the bottom window. If this is one of your first users, `502` might already be the user ID. A group ID of `20` is probably what was made. If you look at the information on software, you can see that the Users pane added quite a bit of information about `software` to the NetInfo database. The password you see is an encrypted version of the password.

   Because `software` was not one of our first users, we have to either change the user ID of our original user or delete it. Because our original user with UID `502` was simply a demonstration user to run various commands, we chose to delete it. If we had wanted to keep our user, we could have changed the user ID of the original user to one that was not already taken, and then changed the UID of `software` to `502`. For your purposes, the user ID for `software` might not be important. Because we would like to share some of our resources with another machine that also has a user called `software`, whose UID is `502`, it is important for us to make `software`'s UID `502` for compatibility purposes. In either case, we want user `software` to belong to group `tire`. Change the `GID` to `100`. Change the UID as is appropriate for your situation. Select Save under the Domain menu, and click Update this copy in the Confirm Modification box. Figure 23.24 shows the updated information for our user `software`.

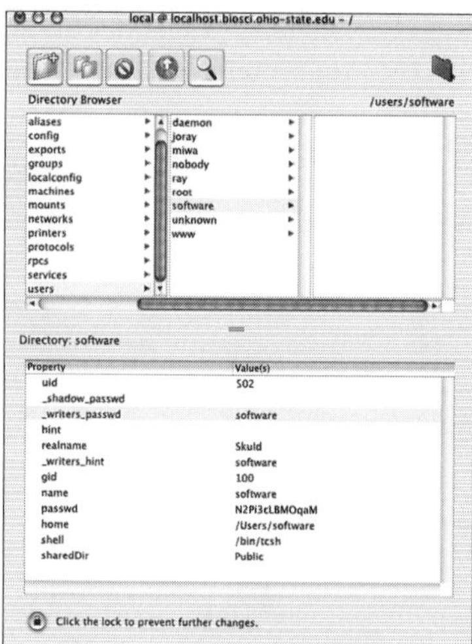

FIGURE 23.24
Now our user software has UID `502` *and GID* `100`*. We can see from this information that user* `software` *has been assigned a password, a home directory in* `/Users/software`*, and a default shell of* `/bin/tcsh`*.*

9. Under the Options menu, select Restart All NetInfo Domains on Local Host. An alert asking if you really want to restart the machine's NetInfo servers appears. Click Yes. Click the lock to prevent further changes.

10. Open a terminal window, go to software's home directory, and look at the directory's contents. Take note that the directory was created by the Users pane with the default values. The update to the information in the NetInfo database, however, was not entirely reflected in the system. So, you will have to manually implement those changes. First, here is the default information for the software user that was created on our system:

```
[localhost:~software] joray% ls -al
total 8
drwxr-xr-x  11 505  staff  330 Jan 30 18:17 .
drwxr-xr-x   8 root wheel  228 May  4 13:45 ..
-rw-r--r--   1 505  staff    3 Nov 14 13:39 .CFUserTextEncoding
drwx------   3 505  staff  264 Feb 20 12:29 Desktop
drwx------   2 505  staff  264 Nov 14 16:45 Documents
drwx------  15 505  staff  466 Feb  2 19:40 Library
drwx------   2 505  staff  264 Nov 15 17:14 Movies
drwx------   2 505  staff  264 Nov 15 17:14 Music
drwx------   2 505  staff  264 Nov 15 17:14 Pictures
drwxr-xr-x   3 505  staff  264 Nov 15 17:09 Public
drwxr-xr-x   4 505  staff  264 Feb 13 19:31 Sites
```

In our example, software's original UID was 505. If you did not change your software user's UID, you should see software in that column, not 505. The default GID that the Users pane used for creating software was GID 20, which is the staff group on OS X. So, the information that we see for software's home directory is the information that was originally assigned to software. We have to update the information to software's directory to reflect the new information.

As root, in the /Users directory, change the ownership of software's directory to the software user in group tire:

```
[localhost:/Users] root# chown -R software.tire software
```

Check the results:

```
[localhost:/Users] root# ls -ld software
    drwxr-xr-x  11 software  tire  330 Jan 30 18:17 software
[localhost:/Users] root# ls -l software
    total 8
    -rw-r--r--   1 software  tire    3 Nov 14 13:39 .CFUserTextEncoding
    drwx------   3 software  tire   58 Feb 20 12:29 Desktop
    drwx------   2 software  tire   24 Nov 14 16:45 Documents
    drwx------  15 software  tire  466 Feb  2 19:40 Library
    drwx------   2 software  tire   24 Nov 15 17:14 Movies
    drwx------   2 software  tire   24 Nov 15 17:14 Music
    drwx------   2 software  tire   24 Nov 15 17:14 Pictures
```

```
drwxr-xr-x   3 software  tire    58 Nov 15 17:09 Public
drwxr-xr-x   4 software  tire    92 Feb 13 19:31 Sites
```

If you had changed the UID of a user who was originally assigned UID `502`, look at that user's home directory and make appropriate ownership changes.

Using the NetInfo Database to Share Resources

In this section we will demonstrate ways that your OS X machine can share resources with other Unix machines using NFS, Network File System. We will demonstrate two ways to set up your OS X machine as an NFS client and one way to use it as an NFS server.

A Common Way to Set Up an NFS Client in OS X

In this section, we will demonstrate a common method for setting up an NFS client on an OS X machine. We show you this method because you will see references to this type of code, for this and other NetInfo-related activities, regularly on the Internet. Sometimes this type of method is the only method you can choose, so you need to be familiar with it. Sometimes, though, an alternative method might work better. For your OS X machine to be a client machine, there has to be another Unix machine that is an NFS server. In other words, there has to be a Unix machine (Mac OS X or another flavor of Unix) on your network that is willing to export one of its file systems to your OS X machine. So, you cannot just set up your machine as a client and assume that everything will work fine. Discuss your interest in being able to use your OS X machine to access a file system on another Unix machine with that machine's system administrator. There is a security risk involved, particularly for the other machine, when it shares its resources with your machine. Therefore, in that machine's interest, the system administrator might not be willing to export its file systems to your machine.

There might be some additional details to work out with your NFS server system administrator that we will not discuss in depth here, assuming that he feels you will responsibly control your machine and your use of the NFS server's resources. To avoid confusion on the remote host machine, it would be a good idea for users that are accessing the other machine's file system from your machine to have the same user and group IDs that they might already have on the remote host machine. Depending on how the remote host is set up, there might not be much confusion. For example, if the remote host does not have user IDs in the same range as the users on your machine, the unusual user IDs might not be a problem. However, if users on your machine have user IDs in the same range as users on the remote host, files you create on the remote host with your user ID might be viewed by the remote host as being owned by a different user with the same user ID on its system. At any rate, if the system administrator of the remote machine agrees to export to your machine whichever file system you are interested in using, be aware that you still might have to work out some additional details with the system administrator. As your understanding of how to update the NetInfo database continues to improve in this chapter, any changes the system administrator of the remote host might request for your OS X machine should not be difficult to change.

With that said, let's continue to the details of setting up an NFS client on your OS X machine. To be an NFS client, your machine needs to be running the right services. If you did not turn off any of the major default services, you do not need to worry about this. If you turned off NFS in the `/System/Library/StartupItems/` directory, you will have to turn it back on to be able to run your NFS client.

It would also be a good idea to read the man pages for `mount`, `mount_nfs`, and `fstab`. The information that you will be adding to the NetInfo database is information where your machine should mount a particular file system that resides on a remote host. When you are done updating the NetInfo database, the remote host's file system will appear to be local to your own machine.

To add a file system from a remote host to your OS X machine, do the following:

1. Back up your NetInfo database.
2. Plan where you want your OS X machine to mount the remote host's file system. The purpose of the remote file system might guide you in how to mount it on your machine. For example, it is common practice, when a file system with a users' home directories are involved, that a machine mounting such a file system frequently does so in a directory hierarchy of `/net/`*`<remote_host>`*`/home`. If the remote file system is simply a file system used for storage, any way you want to mount it is probably suitable. Of course, you can change the name of the mount point if you find that you do not like what you picked. Extra thought is particularly important when the remote file system is used for users' home directories.

   In our example, we are going to mount a file system used for storage. On our machine we want it to be mounted in a directory called `/morespace`. If we were to decide later to mount a number of storage file systems from remote hosts, we might consider a hierarchy similar to the `user` hierarchy, and choose something like `/net/<remote_host>/morespace` or `/morespace/<remote_host>/`, where the mount point clearly includes the host of origin.

   After you have decided what to call the mount point, make it:

   ```
   [localhost:/] root# mkdir morespace
   ```

3. Using your favorite text editor, create a file with the contents of the following form:

```
{
"opts" = ( "w" );
"dir" = ( "/<mountpoint>/" );
"name" = ( "<remote_host>:<remote_filesystem>");
"type" = ( "nfs" );
}
```

Although many options are available for mounting, the one you will probably find most important is the read/write option. On most systems, that option is `rw`. In OS X, that option is `w`, although using the traditional `rw` also appears to work.

Here is a copy of the file we used:

```
{
"opts" = ( "w" );
"dir" = ( "/morespace/" );
"name" = ( "rosalyn:/mnt2");
"type" = ( "nfs" );
}
```

4. Run `niutil` to create a new directory in the `mounts` directory of the NetInfo database:

```
[localhost:~joray/nfs] root# niutil -create . /mounts/new1
```

5. Run `niload` to load the file into the NetInfo database:

```
[localhost:~joray/nfs] root# niload -r /mounts/new1 . < mount-test.txt
```

If you type as well as we do, you might have to run that statement a few times before it works. You might get messages indicating that there is an error at some line number. Just look at your file carefully and fix whatever needs to be fixed.

6. Look at the updates in the `mounts` section of the NetInfo database either using the command line or the NetInfo Manager. If you are using the command line, you might find it easier to see the values by directory number rather than directory name.

Here are the command-line results in our example as seen using `niutil`:

```
[localhost:~] joray% niutil -list . /mounts
167      rosalyn:/mnt2

[localhost:~] joray% niutil -read . 167

opts: w
dir: /morespace/
name: rosalyn:/mnt2
type: nfs
```

7. After you have verified that the updates to your NetInfo database are correct, reboot the machine and test the results.

It might seem like it takes your machine a little longer to reboot. This is to be expected.

First, check whether the file system mounted. You could run `mount` to see what is mounted where:

```
[localhost:~] joray% mount
     /dev/disk1s6 on / (local)
     devfs on /dev (local)
     fdesc on /dev (union)
     <volfs> on /.vol (read-only)
     /dev/disk0s5 on /Volumes/Macintosh HD (local)
     /dev/disk1s7 on /Volumes/Blank2 (local)
     /dev/disk1s8 on /Volumes/Blank3 (local)
     /dev/disk1s9 on /Volumes/huge (local)
     rosalyn:/mnt2 on /morespace
     automount -fstab [259] on /Network/Servers
```

You could even skip running `mount` and directly run `ls`:

```
[localhost:~] joray% ls /morespace
     0012129-unison.tar installed           patches-0104        restoresymtable
     deleted_web_pages  lost+found          public              unison
```

Now you can access a remote file system as if it were local to your machine.

As we mentioned earlier, you might have to work out some details with the system administrator of the remote machine. One of the details you might have to work out is making sure that there is a directory on that file system that you are allowed to write to. In our example, there is a public directory on the remote file system that we are allowed to use.

An Easier Way to Set Up an NFS Client in OS X

As you might recall from the section on adding a printer through the command line, the `niload` command can recognize some regular Unix flat-file formats. The format we saw earlier, `printcap`, is one of them. It turns out the file that controls mount points, `fstab`, is another of those formats.

We recommend that, where possible, you use `niload` in combination with formats it might already recognize rather than having it load in raw NetInfo format. Because the Unix flat-file formats are easier to type, you will make fewer typos. In addition, if you take the time to familiarize yourself with the regular Unix flat files, you will be even better prepared to understand information that relates to other Unix platforms. Always be sure to check the NetInfo database results, not only to confirm that everything was done properly, but also to learn the OS X formats.

In this section, we will show you an easier way to enter the mounts information into the NetInfo database. Although this is easier, be aware that you still have to coordinate with the system administrator of the remote host.

To set up an NFS client on an OS X machine, you can also do the following:

1. Back up the NetInfo database.
2. Create the local mount point for the remote file system.
3. Create a one-line file containing the mount information. The one-line file has these fields, which can be separated by spaces or tabs:

Field	*Value*
1	Remote file system to be mounted
2	Local `mount` point
3	File system type
4	`mount` options
5	Interval between dumps
6	Order in which `fsck` is run at boot time

Fields `5` and `6` do not apply to remote file systems. Those values can either not be present or can be `0`.

Here is the `fstab` used in these examples:

```
rosalyn:/space /extraspace  nfs rw 0 0
```

4. Run `niload` to load the `fstab` format file into the NetInfo database. In our example, we used "fstab-test" as the `fstab` formatted file:

```
[localhost:/Users/joray/nfs] root# niload fstab . < fstab-test
```

Verify that the data was loaded properly into the NetInfo database using either the command line or the NetInfo Manager. Figure 23.25 shows the results of this load.

5. Reboot the machine, and then test the results.

Run the same sorts of command-line tools you ran in the previous section, such as `mount` and `ls`. But you might also want to check `system disk` in your OS X desktop, as you will hopefully find a pleasant surprise there too. Figure 23.26 shows the remote file systems as they appear on our OS X system disk. Unfortunately, choosing a mount point of `/Volumes/`*`<mount_point>`*`/` does not result in the remote file system appearing in the lineup on the desktop.

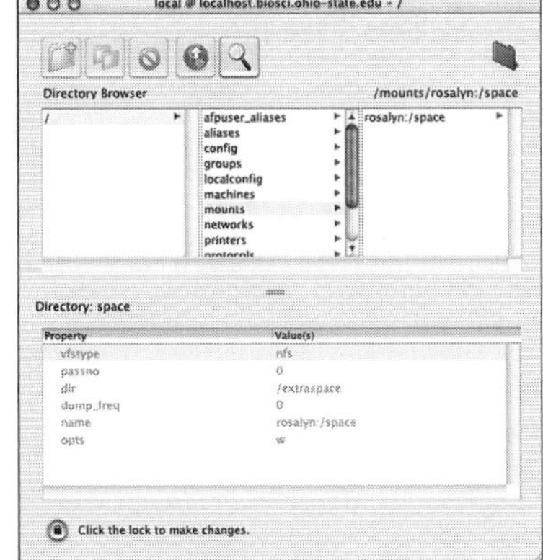

FIGURE 23.25
The `fstab` *format file was successfully loaded into the NetInfo database.*

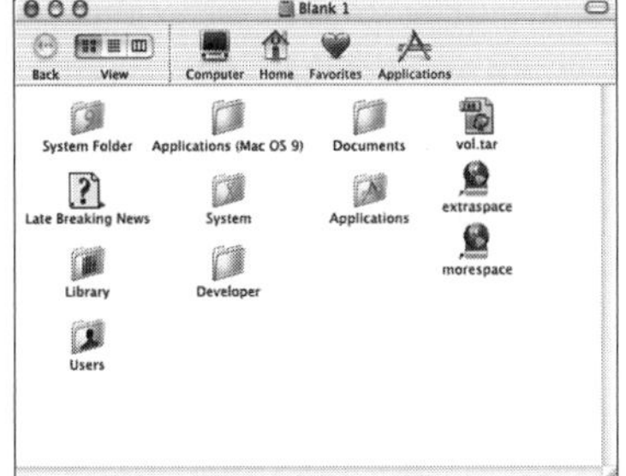

FIGURE 23.26
The remote file systems appear on our OS X disk, exactly as we specified in the NetInfo database.

You can open the remote file systems in the graphical interface as well, as shown in Figure 23.27.

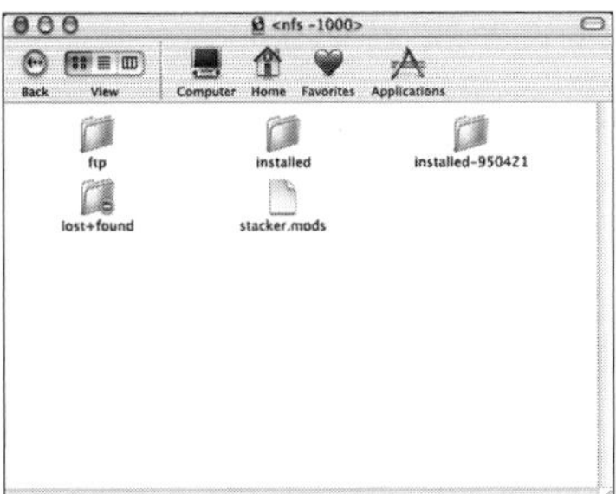

FIGURE 23.27
Here are the contents of the remote file system mounted as `/extraspace` *on our OS X machine. This is not obvious from the title bar.*

Any changes you make to the NFS mounts by just restarting the NetInfo domain servers will be available immediately via the command line. If you want to make the NFS mounts available via the graphical interface immediately as well, be sure to reboot after making your changes to the mounts in the NetInfo database.

Setting Up Your OS X Machine to Be an NFS Server

As the prices of IDE storage continue to drop, you might be interested in serving one of your file systems to another Unix machine. You might, for example, want to export one of your file systems to another Unix machine you use regularly, so as to have some of your storage conveniently available.

Just as setting up your machine to be an NFS client requires coordination with the system administrator of the remote Unix machine, so does serving a file system to a remote Unix machine. Remember, this reduces security on both systems, especially yours. Do not consider doing this unless you can trust the remote host.

Depending on the system setups, coordination between user IDs might be necessary, especially if you want to make the drive available to users other than yourself. The other system administrator should be able to guide you through any additional details that might need to be coordinated.

The other Unix system administrator will set up the remote host to be able to mount your file system. You will have to set up your machine to export a file system to a remote host. At this time, you should read the `exports` man page.

If you plan to create your exports through the command line, you might want to take this opportunity to look at the `nidump` command. As the name suggests, `nidump` dumps information from the NetInfo database to standard output. It can dump information to a flat file, if you should have a need for the information in the format of a traditional flat file. It can also dump information in a format that can be understood by the NetInfo database. You might find running `nidump` on one of the NetInfo directories to be a useful way of seeing the syntax that is used to create a new directory and directories under it.

Here is what the `nidump` output from the `mount` examples in the previous section looks like:

```
[localhost:~] software% nidump -r /mounts .

     {
       "name" = ( "mounts" );
       CHILDREN = (
         {
           "vfstype" = ( "nfs" );
           "passno" = ( "0" );
           "dir" = ( "/extraspace" );
           "dump_freq" = ( "0" );
           "name" = ( "rosalyn:/space" );
           "opts" = ( "w" );
         },
         {
```

```
            "opts" = ( "w" );
            "dir" = ( "/morespace" );
            "name" = ( "rosalyn:/mnt2" );
            "type" = ( "nfs" );
        }
    )
}
```

Not only does `nidump` provide an example of the syntax used to create a directory and subdirectories, but the output from an `nidump` command can also provide the basis for a file that you could edit for setting up your exports. This would already provide much of the complicated part of the syntax, and enable you to just edit values suitable for exports instead.

The complete documentation for `nidump` is in Table 23.3.

TABLE 23.3 The `nidump` Utility Can Export NetInfo Data to Plain Text Formats

`nidump`	Extracts text or flat-file-format data from NetInfo
`nidump [-t] { -r <directory> | <format> } <domain>`	
`nidump` reads the specified NetInfo domain and dumps a portion of its contents to standard output. When a flat-file administration format is specified, `nidump` provides output in the syntax of the corresponding flat file. Allowed values for *<format>* are `aliases`, `bootparams`, `bootptab`, `exports`, `fstab`, `group`, `hosts`, `networks`, `passwd`, `printcap`, `protocols`, `rpc`, and `services`.	
If `-r` is used, the first argument is interpreted as a NetInfo directory path, and its contents are dumped in a generic NetInfo format.	
`-t`	Interprets the domain as a tagged name.
`-r`	Dumps the specified directory in raw format. Directories are delimited in curly brackets. Properties within a directory are listed in the form `property = value;`. Parentheses introduce a comma-separated list of items. The special property name `CHILDREN` is used to hold a directory's children, if any. Spacing and line breaks are significant only within double quotes, which might be used to protect any names with meta characters.

To set up your OS X machine to export a file system to a remote Unix host, do the following:

1. Back up the NetInfo database.
2. If you plan to export a file system that currently contains a space in the name, change its name to something that does not have a space. The remote host will understand a file system name that does not contain a space in its name.

3. Enter `exports` information into the NetInfo database. Unfortunately, despite what the man page says, the `niload` command currently does not understand the typical `exports` format. So, in this case, you cannot make an `exports` format file and load that into NetInfo. You must either make a file that follows the same kind of format we saw in the first `mount` example, the format with braces, parentheses, and quotes, or you must enter the information into the NetInfo database using the NetInfo Manager.

   Because I am so poor at typing all the appropriate characters needed to make one of the raw NetInfo files, I prefer to do this through the NetInfo Manager. Our instructions are specifically for the NetInfo Manager. However, you should choose whichever method you are most comfortable with.

   Open the NetInfo Manager, and select the `local` domain. Click in the lock to make changes, and enter the administrator username and password. With the root directory selected, select New Subdirectory under the Directory menu. Change the name of `new_directory` to be `exports`, and save the change.

4. Click the `exports` directory. Select New Subdirectory from the Directory menu. Give this subdirectory the name of the file system you want to export. Add a `clients` property whose value is a list of clients that the file system should be exported to. Add an `opts` property with any options you want to specify, based on the `exports` man page.

Figure 23.28 shows the settings that we used for exporting our file system.

FIGURE 23.28
Here are the settings we used for exporting our `/Volumes/huge` *filesystem. Note that you should not use the maproot mapping we have used,* `maproot=root`*, unless you can trust the remote system.*

5. Save your changes to the `exports` directory, and then restart the NetInfo servers for your local domain. Click the lock to prevent further changes.

6. Reboot the machine and then test the results. You might find that the exports are exported right away after restarting the NetInfo servers; however, we have found that rebooting the machine consistently works.

   A quick test you can do on your OS X machine is to run `mount`:

   ```
   [localhost:~] joray% mount
   /dev/disk1s6 on / (local)
   devfs on /dev (local)
   fdesc on /dev (union)
   <volfs> on /.vol (read-only)
   /dev/disk0s5 on /Volumes/Macintosh HD (local)
   /dev/disk1s7 on /Volumes/Blank2 (local)
   /dev/disk1s8 on /Volumes/Blank3 (local)
   /dev/disk1s9 on /Volumes/huge (NFS exported, local)
   rosalyn:/space on /extraspace
   rosalyn:/mnt2 on /morespace
   automount -fstab [259] on /Network/Servers
   ```

   Note that the OS X machine indicates that `/Volumes/huge` is being served as an NFS export as well as mounted locally.

   Test that the remote host agrees with the OS X machine:

   ```
   Rosalyn joray 87 > ls /net/ryoohki/huge
   AppleShare PDS          TheFindByContentFolder   osx-misc.tar
   Desktop DB              TheVolumeSettingsFolder  test
   Desktop DF              Trash                    â¢T+â¢It's HUUUGE
   Desktop Folder          lpd-spool-working.tar
   ```

   If we check the file system locally, we find the same `ls` listing:

   ```
   [localhost:~] joray% ls /Volumes/huge
   AppleShare PDS               TheFindByContentFolder       osx-misc.tar
   Desktop DB                   TheVolumeSettingsFolder      test
   Desktop DF                   Trash                        ???T+???It's
   HUUUGE
   Desktop Folder               lpd-spool-working.tar
   ```

   After you are satisfied that the export is working properly, you should remember that your machine is now serving data to another machine. Consequently, it might seem like it takes a little longer for it to shut down at shutdown or reboot time. Do not panic. This is expected. If you plan for your exported file system to be of regular use, try to keep the number of reboots to a minimum. After your machine starts serving data to another machine, it is not just your machine or a machine for your local users, it is a machine that users on a remote host could come to rely on.

If the basic ways available to you in OS X for sharing resources seem a bit overwhelming, you might be interested in a shareware product called NFS Manager, available at `http://www.bresink.de/osx/`. It provides GUI interface controls for both NFS mounts and exports. A sample of the interface is shown in Figure 23.29.

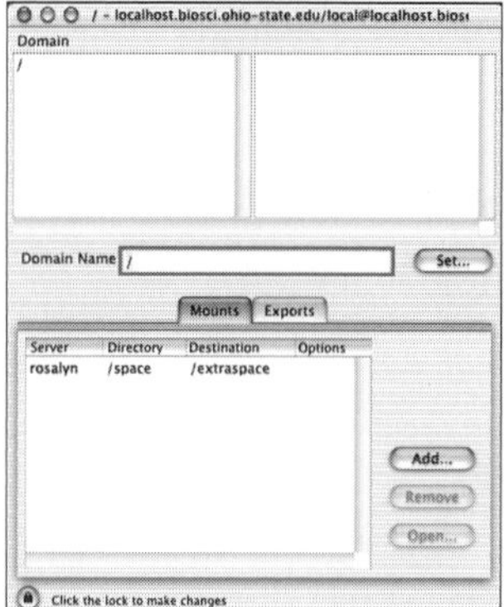

FIGURE 23.29
Here is a sample of what the interface for the shareware product called NFS Manager looks like.

Restoring the Local NetInfo Database

Knowing how to restore your local NetInfo database is just as important as knowing how to back it up.

Exactly how you restore it depends on what method you chose for backing it up or whether you backed up the database as a directory or as a `tar` file. Depending on the situation, you might be running your restore in multi-user mode or in single-user mode. If you are in single-user mode, remember to follow the instructions that appear at the very end of the startup so that you are allowed to make modifications.

Be sure not to rush and pay close attention to what you are doing.

1. If your modification to the NetInfo database was made in conjunction with a change to the `/etc/hostconfig` file, replace the modified `/etc/hostconfig` file with the backup copy.
2. Go to the `/var/db/netinfo`:

   ```
   [localhost:/Users/joray] root# cd /var/db/netinfo
   ```

   List the contents of the directory. You might have multiple backup copies. Make sure that you know which one you want to use for restoring the NetInfo database. The directory called `local.nidb` is the local NetInfo database.
3. Either remove the broken `local.nidb` or rename it to something that lets you know that it is broken. If you rename it, you can remove it later when you have your NetInfo database restored.

   To remove the broken NetInfo database:

   ```
   [localhost:/var/db/netinfo] root# \rm -rf local.nidb
   ```

To rename the broken NetInfo database:

```
[localhost:/var/db/netinfo] root# mv local.nidb local.nidb-broken
```

4. If you made your backup as a `tar` file, extract the back-up copy:

```
[localhost:/var/db/netinfo] root# tar -xf local.nidb-20010512.tar
```

If you made your backup as a copy of the directory, rename the backup copy to `local.nidb`:

```
[localhost:/var/db/netinfo] root# mv local.nidb-backup local.nidb
```

5. Send a `kill -HUP` to the `nibindd` process, if you are in multiuser mode:

```
[localhost:/Users/joray] root# ps -aux | grep nibind
root    6993  0.0  0.0   1288   136  ??  Ss     0:00.04 /usr/sbin/nibindd
root    7777  0.0  0.0   5708     0 std  RV     0:00.00 grep nibind
[localhost:/Users/joray] root# kill -HUP 6993
```

If the NetInfo database does not appear to be restored after sending a `kill -HUP` to the `nibindd` process, reboot the machine.

If you are in single-user mode, reboot the machine:

```
localhost# sync;sync;sync;reboot
```

After the restored NetInfo database is up and determined to be fine, if you saved the broken NetInfo database, it is all right to remove it now.

Please note that you could also restore the local NetInfo database using the NetInfo Manager's Restore From Backup option under the Domain menu. Given how long a backup can take using the NetInfo Manager, we have not actually tried restoring the local database using the NetInfo Manager. If something goes wrong when you try to restore this way, be prepared to restore the database via the command line.

Summary

The NetInfo database system is used by Mac OS X to store many of its system-critical settings. This database can be used to store and share administrative information across a network. Users can access NetInfo via the NetInfo Manager, or a handful of command-line utilities such as `niutil`, `nidump`, and `niload`.

In this chapter you learned the basics of the NetInfo system and how it is used to store user and printer information. It is extremely important to remember to back up your NetInfo database before making any changes. Without a properly functioning NetInfo system, Mac OS X will be rendered inoperable. Apple, to this point, has released very little information about the data that *is* and can be stored in NetInfo. It is a tool for hardcore administration and should not be considered a beginner's utility.

CHAPTER 24

User Management and Machine Clustering

In This Chapter

As has been mentioned several times already, Mac OS X, being based on Unix, is designed from the ground up as a multi-user operating system. Where previous versions of Mac OS have supported some types of multiple user functionality, internally only a single user could be using the machine at once, and the separation of data and resources between user accounts was not particularly strict. With OS X, a nearly unlimited number of users can be simultaneously logged in to a single machine, and from the point of view of each user, the machine is essentially devoted to his own use. One of the consequences of this type of multiple user operating system, and of the Unix notion of abstraction, is that it is natural to do away with the personal computer notion of one machine keeping each user's data, when there are several users, and several machines in proximity to each other. Instead, in the Unix world, it is traditional to set the machines up so that all the users can use all the machines, and to distribute the user account information and contents via the network. A collection of machines cooperating in this fashion is called a *cluster*. In a cluster, any user with an account on the cluster can log in to any machine in the cluster and be presented with his account just as if it were his own personal machine.

In the previous chapter, you learned almost all the techniques necessary to implement a cluster with OS X. This chapter covers some of the management details that you will need to keep in mind to manage a cluster successfully, and provides the details needed to actually put a cluster together.

Skeleton User Accounts

If you're going to have any significant number of users on your machine (or machines), you'll soon find that being able to provide a more customized environment than what comes out of the system Users control pane by default, is a benefit.

Apple has provided a convenient method for you to perform some customization of accounts as created by the Users control pane.This is the inclusion of a `UserTemplate` directory, from which the accounts made by the pane are created by duplication. The family of `UserTemplate` directories, individualized by locale, are kept in `/System/Library/UserTemplate`. This system works for simple configuration settings that you might like to configure for each newly created user, but it has some limitations if you'd like to work with more complex setups. The largest of these is that if you're trying to set up complicated startup scripts, and sophisticated environment settings, it's nice to be able to log in for testing and tweaking.

The easiest way to do this is to create a skeleton user account as a real user account, and to keep it up to date with any environmental customizations that you want to provide for new users when you create accounts. If you create the skeleton user as simply another user account, you can log in to it and then conveniently tweak its settings. Using this method, you can create as many skeleton accounts as you need for different collections of settings.

Even if you prefer to use the Users control pane, the creation of skeleton users as real users on the system can be useful for you. You can configure skeleton users that you can log in as for testing, and then populate the `/System/Library/UserTemplate` directories as required for customizing the configuration of users under the Users pane.

As covered in Chapter 12, "Introducing the BSD Subsystem," every user's shell environment is configured by the `.login` and `.cshrc` (presuming you're using the `tcsh` or `csh` shell) scripts in the user's home directory. You might also want to provide a more customized starter Web page or assorted bits of default data.

After you configure an account in the fashion you'd like your new users to have, the hard part is done. It would be nice to have a way to use this account directly from the Users pane as the seed for new accounts as they are created but, unfortunately, we aren't yet so lucky. Instead, you have two options for how to use the starter account information. First, you can create a new user through the Users control pane. After the account is created, you can replace the user's home directory (that the Users control pane created) with a copy of the skeleton account home directory.

Your other option is to create a new user by duplicating an existing user node from the NetInfo hierarchy, making a copy of the skeleton account home directory for the new user's home directory, and then editing the copy of the NetInfo entry for the new user to reflect the correct information for that user.

The first option is probably easier, but the second has the benefit of being able to be done from the command line with `nidump` and `niload`.

For the rest of the discussion, it will be assumed that you've created a skeleton account in which you have made any customizations that you want to install for all new users. The account `UID` will be assumed to be `5002`, with a home directory of `/Users/skel` and a `GID` of `20`.

To implement the first method of providing local customization for a new user, follow these steps:

1. Create the new user with the Users control pane. Make any necessary changes to the user's configuration, such as the default `GID`, as shown in the previous chapter.
2. Become root (`su`, provide password).
3. Change directories to the skeleton user's directory (`cd ~skel`).
4. Tar the contents of the current directory, using the option to place the output on `STDOUT` (`tar -cf - .`) and then pipe the output of `tar` into a subshell. In the subshell, `cd` to the new user's directory, and untar from `STDIN` (`| ( cd ~`*<newusername>* `; tar -xf - ) )`.
5. Change directories to one level above the new user's directory (`cd ~`*<newusername>* `; cd ../`).

6. Change the ownership of everything in the new user's directory to belong to the new user and, potentially, to the user's default group if it's not the same as the `skel` account default group (`chown -R` *<newusername>*:*<newusergroup>* *<newuserdirectoryname>*). We'll cover the complete documentation for `chown` at the end of this chapter.

For example, if you've just created a new user named `jim`, assigned to the group `users` with the Users control pane, and want to put the `skel` account configuration into `jim`'s home directory, you would enter the following:

```
su (provide password)

cd ~skel

tar -cf - . | ( cd ~jim ; tar -xf - )

cd ~jim

cd ../

chown -R jim:users jim
```

If you'd rather create new users from the command line, either because you can't access the physical console conveniently or because you want to use what you know about shell scripting to automate the process, you can use the second method suggested earlier. You might find this method more convenient for creating users in a NetInfo domain other than `localhost/local`. The Users control pane in the non-server version of OS X seems incapable of creating users in other NetInfo domains, and this makes using it for managing cluster users difficult.

Caution

This process creates a new user by manipulating the NetInfo database directly, so the cautions to back up your database frequently are important to remember here.

To implement the second method, follow these steps:

1. Become root (`su`, give password).
2. Change directories to the directory in which you'd like to place the new user's home directory (`cd /Users`, for example).

3. Make a directory with the short name of the user you're about to create (mkdir *<newusername>* to create a directory for a new user named *<newusername>*).
4. Change directories to the home directory of the skel account (cd ~skel).
5. Tar the contents of the current directory, and use the option to place the output on STDOUT (tar -cf - .)
6. Pipe the output of the tar command into a subshell. In the subshell, cd to the new user's directory, and untar from STDIN (| (cd *<pathtonewuserdirectory>* ; tar -xf -). Note that you can't use ~*<newusername>* because *<newusername>* doesn't actually exist on the system yet.)
7. Dump your skel account (UID 5002 here, remember) NetInfo entry, or some other user's entry, into a file that you can edit (nidump -r /name=users/uid=5002 -t localhost/local > ~/*<sometempfile>*).
8. Edit ~/*<sometempfile>*, changing the entries so that they are appropriate for the new user you want to create. You'll want to change at least _writers_passwd, uid, _writers_hint, gid, realname, name, passwd, and home. It's probably easiest to leave passwd blank for now.
9. Use niutil to create a new directory for the uid that you've picked for the new user (niutil -p -create -t localhost/local /name=users/uid=*<newuserUID>*, give the root password when asked).
10. Use niload to load the data you modified in ~/*<sometempfile>* back into the NetInfo database (cat ~/*<sometempfile>* | niload -p -r /name=users/uid=<newuserUID> -t localhost/local).
11. Set the password for the new user (passwd *<newusername>*;). Provide a beginning password—another BSD utility documented at the end of this chapter.
12. Change back to the directory above the new user's home directory (cd ~*<newuser-name>*; cd ../).
13. Change the ownership of the new user's directory to the new user's *<username>* and *<defaultgroup>* (chown -R *<username>*:*<usergroup>* *<newuserdirec-tory>*).

If you've made a mistake somewhere along the way, just restore your NetInfo database from the backup that you made before you started this. You also might need to find the nibindd process, and send it a HUP signal (\ps -auxww | grep "nibindd"; kill -HUP *<whatever PID belongs to nibindd>*).

To produce results similar to those from the first method earlier, the following example will create a new user with the username of james, UID 600, GID 70, with home directory /Users/james. This again assumes the skel account with UID 5002 and characteristics as described earlier.

su (provide the password)

`cd /Users`

`mkdir james`

`cd ~skel`

`tar -cf - . | ( cd /Users/james ; tar -xf - )`

`nidump -r /name=users/uid=5002 -t localhost/local > ~/skeltemp`

`vi ~/skeltemp` and change the contents from

```
{
  "_shadow_passwd" = ( "" );
  "_writers_passwd" = ( "skel" );
  "hint" = ( "" );
  "uid" = ( "5002" );
  "_writers_hint" = ( "skel" );
  "gid" = ( "20" );
  "realname" = ( "Skeleton Account" );
  "name" = ( "skel" );
  "passwd" = ( "*" );
  "home" = ( "/Users/skel" );
  "shell" = ( "/bin/tcsh" );
  "sharedDir" = ( "Public" );
}
```

to

```
{
  "_shadow_passwd" = ( "" );
  "_writers_passwd" = ( "james" );
  "hint" = ( "" );
  "uid" = ( "600" );
  "_writers_hint" = ( "james" );
  "gid" = ( "70" );
  "realname" = ( "James the friendly Giant" );
  "name" = ( "james" );
  "passwd" = ( "" );
  "home" = ( "/Users/james" );
  "shell" = ( "/bin/tcsh" );
  "sharedDir" = ( "Public" );
}
```

`niutil -p -create -t localhost/local /name=users/uid=600` (give the root password when asked)

`cat ~/skeltemp | niload -p -r /name=users/uid=600 -t localhost/local` (give the root password when asked)

`passwd james` (fill in a good starting value)

`cd ~james`

`cd ../`

`chown -R james:www james` (`GID 70` is group www on this machine)

Note

Depending on whether your NetInfo daemon is feeling well, you might have to HUP the nibindd process to get it to recognize that you've made the change. Remember that you can always restore your NetInfo database backup to get out of a mess, if you've created one.

Tip

If you need to delete a user account from the command line, you can destroy the NetInfo information for the user by using the command `niutil -p -destroy -t localhost/local /name=users/uid=<userUIDtobedeleted>`. Then `\rm -rf` the user's home directory to delete it and all of its contents from the system.

Just to make sure that your user has been created as you think it should have been, you can use niutil to list the /users NetInfo directory:

```
[localhost:/Users/ray] root# niutil -list -t localhost/local /users
     2        nobody
     3        root
     4        daemon
     5        unknown
     6        www
     154      joray
     166      miwa
     161      ray
     163      software
     171      nomad
     173      ftp
     174      marvin
     175      skel
     177      bin
     179      betty
     181      ralph
     184      james
```

As shown, james does now exist in the NetInfo /users directory, although this listing shows only the NetInfo node numbers, rather than the users and property values. To see whether james has the properties intended, you can use niutil to read the info from the node named james:

```
[localhost:/Users/ray] root# niutil -read -t localhost/local /users/james

    _shadow_passwd:
    _writers_passwd: james
    hint:
    uid: 600
    _writers_hint: james
    gid: 70
    realname: James the friendly Giant
    name: james
    passwd:
    home: /Users/james
    shell: /bin/tcsh
    sharedDir: Public
```

Multiple Users and Multiple Machines: Creating Clusters

Since almost the dawn of computing, the Unix operating system has supported the notion of a cooperating group of machines that share user information between them. The concept of clustering includes the idea that the machines should share not only information, but also sufficient resources so that any user with an account on the cluster can use any machine in the cluster, and the experience will be indistinguishable from using any other machine.

The user information traditionally is shared among the machines in the cluster by using a technology known as NIS (the Network Information System, originally known as the Yellow Pages) that was developed by Sun Microsystems. File systems (containing user accounts and software) are shared to members of the cluster using NFS (the Network File System). NFS is still the preferred way of sharing file systems under OS X, but Apple has provided a slightly more complex, and considerably more powerful, method of sharing user information: the NetInfo system. Not only is the information in NetInfo databases used for configuration of your own machine, but if you choose, this information can be shared to other machines.

As you might guess from what you know of Unix abstraction by now, a machine shouldn't really care whether its NetInfo configuration information comes from its local NetInfo server, or from another NetInfo server that it's talking to over the network. As a matter of fact, a hierarchy of NetInfo servers can be linked together to provide a significant level of sophistication in the distribution of user information.

Creating and managing many-level NetInfo hierarchies is a topic best left for Mac OS X Server, but the creation of a two-level hierarchy is something that can be reasonably done with OS X.

The normal two-level hierarchy includes a local NetInfo domain, and a parent NetInfo domain that is delivered via the network. Each machine that participates in the cluster subscribes to the parent NetInfo domain. (This includes the machine that runs the parent server as well; it subscribes via the network to a domain that it serves via the network. Don't worry, these things will make sense eventually.) Any users defined in the parent domain can use any of the machines that subscribe to the domain. Users that are defined in the local domain on any machine can use the machine on which they are defined, but do not have access to any other machines in the cluster.

Subscribing to a NetInfo Parent Domain

If you would like your machine to participate in a cluster, there are two options for participation: Your machine can either subscribe to a parent NetInfo domain or it can be the provider of the domain. Because subscribing to a domain is necessary in both cases, we'll cover subscription to a domain supplied by another machine first.

For a technique that provides such a powerful method of integrating machines and user accounts, joining a cluster implemented through the NetInfo service is surprisingly easy. There are essentially only two things that you need to do. First, you need to mount the file systems from the remote machine so that users' home directories appear on your machine in the same places that they are defined to be in the NetInfo domain to which you will be subscribing.

Second, subscribe to a parent NetInfo domain using the Directory Setup utility.

The first of these tasks you've already learned how to do in the previous chapter. For this example, we will assume that users who are intended to be cluster users, with the ability to log in on any of the machines in the cluster, have home directories defined to exist in the directory `/netusers`. Therefore, if we want to be able to log in on our machine as one of the users defined in the parent NetInfo database, we need to mount the remote directory on the server (`192.168.1.16` in this case) named `/netusers` as a local directory `/netusers`. This will allow logins to user accounts listed in the `localhost/local` NetInfo database, as well as to accounts listed in the remote `192.168.1.16/network` database. The following listing shows the `mounts` entry for the machine that is subscribing to the NetInfo cluster:

```
[kimagure:~/] ray% nidump -r /mounts -t localhost/local

     {
       "name" = ( "mounts" );
       CHILDREN = (
         {
           "vfstype" = ( "nfs" );
           "dir" = ( "/mnt" );
```

```
            "name" = ( "venice.iwaynet.net:/home" );
            "opts" = ( "-i", "net", "-P", "-b", "ro" );
          },
          {
            "vfstype" = ( "nfs" );
            "dir" = ( "/netusers" );
            "name" = ( "192.168.1.16:/netusers" );
            "opts" = ( "-b", "-s", "-P" );
          }
        )
      }
```

Note that it is mounting the `/netusers` directory to participate in the cluster, as well as another directory from an entirely different machine. NFS can be used to create arbitrarily complex networks of interconnected file systems.

Satisfying the second requirement involves only opening the Directory Setup utility, and entering the machine name or IP address and the NetInfo directory to which to subscribe. For a machine subscribing to the `network` database, served by `192.168.1.16`, this is shown in Figures 24.1 and 24.2.

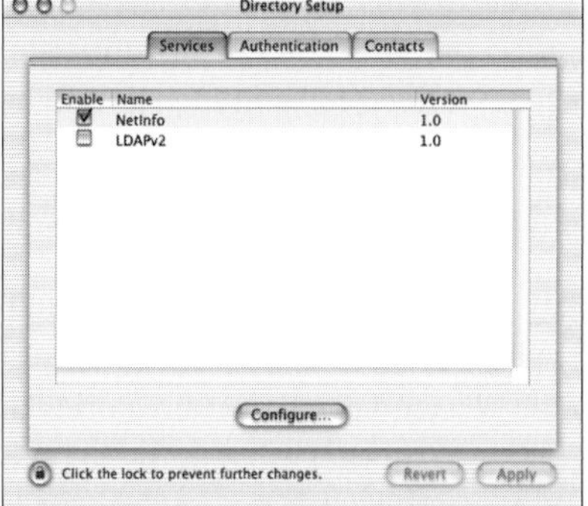

FIGURE 24.1
To subscribe to a parent NetInfo domain, open the Directory Setup utility, enable changes, and check the NetInfo box. Then click the Configure button.

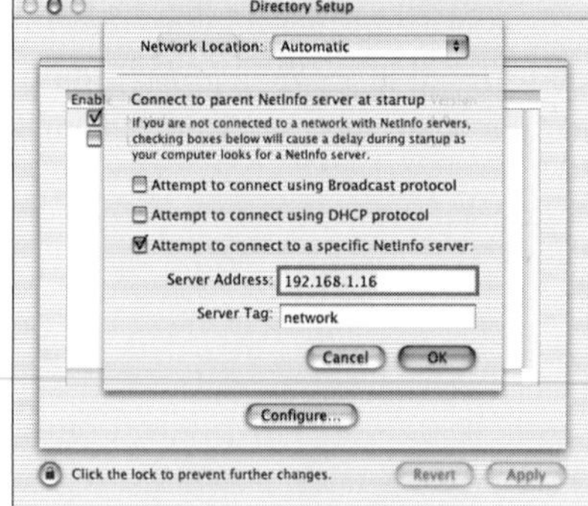

FIGURE 24.2
Subscribing to the parent `network` *NetInfo database, served from a machine at IP address* `192.168.1.16`. *This dialog is reached by clicking Configure as shown in the previous figure.*

The network NetInfo database, to which our machine's NetInfo database is now parented in this example contains the following users;

```
[kimagure:~] ray% niutil -list -t 192.168.1.16/network /users
     3          root
     4          skel
     5          bellchan
```

Tip

Depending on how your name service is configured, you might be able to use an IP address to refer to the remote server's NetInfo domain, or you might have to refer to it by hostname. It's also possible to create a machine entry in your localhost/local database that relates the IP address and a machine name, if you prefer to use a nickname for the remote server.

Figures 24.3 and 24.4 show the same user, bellchan, logged in to 192.168.1.16 and 192.168.1.105. 192.168.1.16 is the server of the NetInfo network domain, and 192.168.1.105 is subscribed to this as a child of the network domain. If you look closely at the figures, you won't see much of a difference—and that is exactly the point. The bellchan user has its home directory in the /netusers directory on 192.168.1.16, and this directory is mounted in the same location on 192.168.1.105. All of bellchan's user information is served via NetInfo and subscribed to by 192.168.1.105. So, due to Unix abstraction and the power of clustering, there is no difference to the user (other than possible network performance issues) between sitting down in front of either of these machines.

Parenting a NetInfo Domain to Other Machines

If you would like to set up your machine to be the server of a NetInfo parent domain to which other machines can subscribe, the process is also straightforward. There are three requirements. First, as you should realize from the previous example, for users who exist in the parent domain to be useable on machines that are clients to the domain, their home directories (or, more usefully, the directory containing all their home directories) must be made available to the client machines.

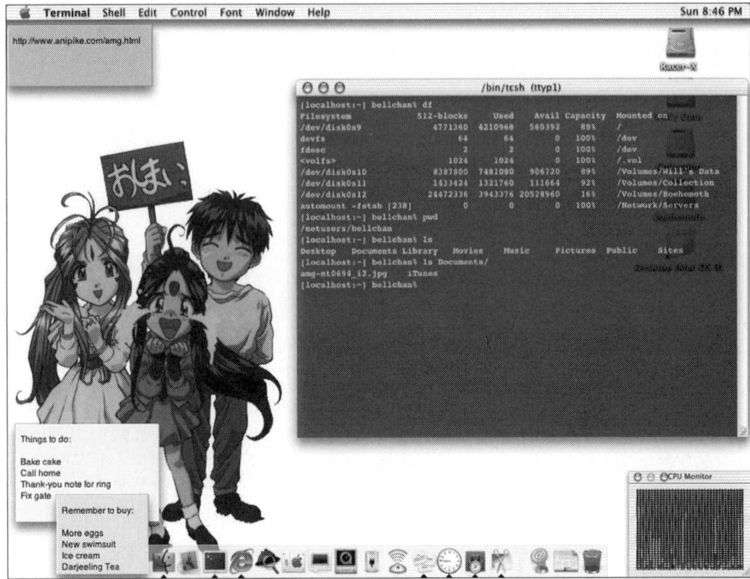

FIGURE 24.3
The user `bellchan` *logged into* `192.168.1.16` *(locally named* `racer-x`*) at the console.* `bellchan`*'s account physically resides on this machine, as does the* `network` *NetInfo database.*

FIGURE 24.4
The user `bellchan` *logged into* `192.168.1.105` *(locally named* `kimagure`*) at the console.* `bellchan`*'s account physically resides on another machine, and is coming to this machine via the power of NetInfo,* NFS*, and the notion of Unix clustering.*

Next, your machine must be set up to serve a NetInfo directory to the network, and users must exist in it.

Finally, your machine must be subscribed to the `network` NetInfo server that it serves, so that your `local` NetInfo database is a child of the `network` NetInfo database.

After these requirements are met, others can subscribe as children of your network-served `network` NetInfo database by following the directions given in the section "Subscribing to a NetInfo Parent Domain" earlier in this chapter.

Caution

It isn't particularly useful to parent a domain with a machine that switches "locations" frequently. It is difficult to configure the machine to properly parent and not parent the domain when desired. Also, if you're providing domain parenting information to other machines, it's rude to yank their parent domain away when you take the machine down to move it. For this reason, we recommend parenting NetInfo domains only from machines with fixed IP addresses and that are generally intended to be always on.

To configure the server similarly to the one on `192.168.1.16` that was used in the previous example, the following steps need to be taken:

1. The directory `/netusers` needs to be created, owner set to `root`, and group set to `wheel`, just as the `/Users` directory is set.
2. The directory `/netusers` needs to be exported via NFS. The following listing shows the NetInfo `exports` entry used:

```
[localhost:~/Documents] ray% nidump -r /exports -t localhost/local
{
  "name" = ( "exports" );
  CHILDREN = (
    {
      "clients" = ( );
      "name" = ( "/netusers" );
      "opts" = ( "maproot=root", "network=192.168.1.0",
    ➥"mask=255.255.255.0" );
    }
  )
}
```

Tip

Remember that the `export` needs to be done in the `local` domain. If you try to use the shareware NFS Manager GUI tool to create this `export`, it will create the `export` in the parent NetInfo domain. If you've already created a parent master NetInfo server, the `export` information will go into it, and not into the `localhost/local` domain where it is needed.

3. A new master NetInfo server needs to be created on your server machine (ours was `192.168.1.16`). To do this, simply go to the NetInfo Manager, enable modifications to the `localhost/local` domain, select Manage Domains from the Domain menu, and Hierarchy under that. In the dialog box that appears, choose `Create a new master server on this host`. A new master server serving a domain named `network` will be created by default.
4. Choose the newly created NetInfo `network` domain as a parent domain. To do this, follow the instructions in the prior example for selecting a parent domain. You will use the Directory Setup utility to enable parenting to a NetInfo domain, and provide your IP address and `network` as the domain to use as a parent.
5. Rebooting the machine at this point is probably a wise choice. If the `network` domain was not correctly created, or your NetInfo service doesn't want to connect to it as a parent domain, you'll need to delete the domain and try again.

   Unfortunately, this step seems a little hit or miss at the moment. What appears to be a bug or three in the NetInfo server occasionally results in it dying, instead of accepting the changes. The symptom is that the colorful spinning wait cursor appears for the NetInfo Manager, and never returns to a pointer cursor. In this case, Force-Quit the NetInfo Manager, restore your NetInfo database from a backup (as discussed in Chapter 23), and reboot your machine).
6. If everything goes well, your machine will reboot cleanly, and you will be able to log in. Verify that your local NetInfo domain is now a child of the `network` domain by opening the `local` domain on `localhost` from the `NetInfo Manager`, and then clicking the `Open Parent Domain` button (world with up-pointing arrow). The `network` domain you created earlier should open.
7. Create some users in the `network` domain by duplicating the root user and changing the user's information as appropriate. For the example given earlier, we created the `skel` skeleton account so that we could use it to create other customized users, and then used it as shown in previous examples in this chapter to create the

bellchan account. If you're going to create the account using the nidump, niutil, and niload command-line tools, remember that you're not inserting users into localhost/local, but instead into *<yourip>*/network.

8. Log out, and try to log in at your console as one of your users from the network domain. If you're successful, you've completed the basic configuration of your machine as a NetInfo and NFS server to provide cluster information to other machines. Other machines can now mount your exported directories, and subscribe to your NetInfo network domain, as shown in the previous example.

If you aren't successful, check the user information that you've created in the network domain carefully to make certain that you haven't overlapped any UIDs or usernames with users that exist in your local domain. Also, check that things you've specified, such as the home directories, really exist. If your NetInfo Manager shows that your local domain is a child of the network domain (by being able to open the network domain as its parent), you're 99% of the way there, and the problem must be in the user account information itself.

Note

When you're modifying the network domain, the user ID and password required to modify it will belong to one of the users in that domain. Unless you've created a non-root administrative user in the network domain, you'll need to use root, and the root password to enable modifications in the network domain.

Command-Line Administration Tools

There are a number of command-line tools that are of assistance in the configuration and maintenance of user accounts. Some of these have functionality duplicated in graphical tools and some do not. For truly sophisticated user management, we again suggest looking to Mac OS X Server because it provides tools that are considerably more powerful.

NetInfo Utilities

The nidump, niutil, and niload commands are particularly useful for user account creation and deletion. It's also a good idea to be familiar with the tar command for backing up NetInfo databases. The command documentation table for each of the NetInfo-specific commands is provided in the previous chapter. tar is documented in Chapter 12. We wouldn't be surprised if someone creates a graphical tool that scripts the sort of account maintenance that has been shown in this chapter, and makes it available on the Net. If we managed to pique your interest in shell programming in the earlier chapters, this would be an ideal problem to attack as a learning experience. Because NetInfo is so vital to the operation of the machine, we recommend that you verify, by using print statements, that the scripts you create output exactly what you want—before you turn them loose on the NetInfo database.

Common BSD Tools

In addition to the NetInfo commands for creating and modifying user accounts themselves, you have access to a number of standard BSD utilities. Primarily, these allow you to operate on the files in user accounts; but one, the `passwd` command, inserts `crypted` passwords into the NetInfo user record. (This is a little odd because Apple has circumvented most BSD tools of this nature, and incorporated their functionality into the NetInfo commands. It wouldn't be too surprising if Apple replaces or supercedes this command with another in the future.)

Changing File Ownership: `chown`

The `chown` command is used to change the ownership of files. Only the root user can execute the `chown` command. The simplest form, and the one in which you'll end up using it the most frequently, is `chown` *<username> <filename>*, which changes the ownership property of *<filename>* to belong to the user *<username>*. The command can optionally be given as `chown` *<username>*:*<groupname> <filename>* to change the user and group at the same time. Additionally, `-R` can be specified after the command to cause a recursive change in an entire directory, instead of to a single file. The command documentation table is shown in Table 24.1.

TABLE 24.1 The Command Documentation Table for `chown`

`chown`	*Changes file owner and group.*
`chown [-R [-H	-L	-P]] [-fh]` *<owner> <file1> <file2> ...*	
`chown [-R [-H	-L	-P]] [-fh]` *:<group> <file1> <file2> ...*	
`chown [-R [-H	-L	-P]] [-fh]` *<owner>:<group> <file1> <file2> ...*	
`-R`	Recursively descends through directory arguments to change the user ID and/or group ID.
`-H`	If `-R` is specified, symbolic links on the command line are followed. Symbolic links encountered in tree traversal are not followed.
`-L`	If `-R` is specified, all symbolic links are followed.

TABLE 24.1 continued

chown	*Changes file owner and group.*
`-P`	If `-R` is specified, no symbolic links are followed.
`-f`	Forces an attempt to change user ID and/or group ID without reporting any errors.
`-h`	If the file is a symbolic link, the user ID and/or group ID of the link is changed.

The `-H`, `-L`, and `-P` options are ignored unless `-R` is specified. Because they also override each other, the last option specified determines the action that is taken.

The `-L` option cannot be used with the `-h` option.

It is not necessary to provide both *<owner>* and *<group>*; however, one must be specified. If group is specified, it must be preceded with a colon (:).

The owner may be either a numeric user ID or a username. If a username exists for a numeric user ID, the associated username is used as for the owner. Similarly, the group may be either a numeric group ID or a group name. If a group name exists for a group ID, the associated group name is used for the group.

Unless invoked by the super user, `chown` clears `set-user-id` and `set-group-id` bits.

Changing File Group Ownership: `chgrp`

The `chgrp` command functions like the `chown` command, except that it changes only the group ownership of a file. This can be particularly useful when you want to give a user, or group of users, access to files owned by a number of different users. Instead of changing the ownership of each, or issuing a separate `chown <userid>:<groupid>` for each file, you can instead change the file's groups *en masse* to one that the intended user or group can read, while not affecting the actual ownership of the files.

The command documentation table for `chgrp` is shown in Table 24.2.

TABLE 24.2 The Command Documentation Table for `chgrp`

chgrp	*Changes group.*
`chgrp [-R [-H | -L | -P]] [-fh] <group> <file1> <file2> ...`	
`-R`	Recursively descends through directory arguments to change the group ID.
`-H`	If `-R` is specified, symbolic links on the command line are followed. Symbolic links encountered in tree traversal are not followed.

TABLE 24.2 continued

chgrp	*Changes group.*
-L	If -R is specified, all symbolic links are followed.
-P	If -R is specified, no symbolic links are followed.
-f	Forces an attempt to change group ID without reporting any errors.
-h	If the file is a symbolic link, the group ID of the link is changed.

Unless -h, -H, or -L is specified, chgrp on symbolic links always succeeds and has no effect.

The -H, -L, and -P options are ignored unless -R is specified. Because they also override each other, the last option specified determines the action that is taken.

The group may be either a numeric group ID or a group name. If a group name exists for a group ID, the associated group name is used for the group.

The user invoking chgrp must belong to the specified group and be the owner of the file, or be the super user.

Unless invoked by the super user, `chgrp` clears `set-user-id` and `set-group-id` bits.

Setting a User's Password: `passwd`

The `passwd` command, somewhat unexpectedly, changes a user's password. If you look at the man page for `passwd`, you will see that there are a number of related password and account management commands that come from BSD Unix. With the exception of the `passwd` command, all the others appear to operate on the local files only, and do not seem to affect the NetInfo database information. Because the local authentication files (such as `/etc/passwd` and `/etc/group`) are used only in single-user mode, none of the other commands currently have any significant use in OS X. (We'd like to think that Apple is working on making more of them operate with the NetInfo database, but we've really got no idea whether the BSD utilities are coming or going.)

Simply issued as `passwd`, with no other options, the `passwd` command enables a user to change her password. The root user has the ability to issue `passwd` *`<username>`* to force the password for the user *`<username>`* to change. The command documentation table for `passwd` is shown in Table 24.3.

TABLE 24.3 The Command Documentation Table for `passwd`

`passwd`	*Modifies a user's password*

`passwd [-l] [-k] [-y] [<user>]`

`passwd` changes the user's local, Kerberos, or YP password. The user is first prompted for her old password. The user is next prompted for a new password, and then prompted again to retype the new password for verification.

The new password should be at least six characters in length. It should use a variety of lowercase letters, uppercase letters, numbers, and metacharacters.

`-l`	Updates the user's local password.
`-k`	Updates the Kerberos database, even if the user has a local password. After the password has been verified, passwd transmits the information to the Kerberos authenticating host.
`-y`	Updates the YP passwd, even if the user has a local password. The rpc.yppasswdd (8) daemon should be running on the YP master server.

If no flags are specified, the following occurs:

If Kerberos is active, the user's Kerberos password is changed, even if the user has a local password.

If the password is not in the local database, an attempt to update the YP password occurs.

To change another user's Kerberos password, run `kinit (1)` followed by `passwd`. The super user is not required to supply the user's password if only the local password is being modified.

Summary

This chapter covered the techniques used to make your machine into a member of a cooperating cluster of computers, or to make it into a server for such a cluster. It also covered techniques that can be used to automate the creation and customization of user accounts on your machine or in your cluster.

The most important thing to remember is the Unix abstract notion that it doesn't matter where things like user account information are coming from or where drives are coming from. The OS is designed so that it can acquire such information and resources from any compatible system, and so can be combined with any compatible systems to provide a seamless user experience across any number of machines.

Although Mac OS X uses slightly different protocols by default than most Unix systems, the principles are identical to those used by other Unix flavors. If you find that you'd like to construct a system that is more complex than what we've covered here, don't hesitate to consult references for other Unixes—you'll have to use the information here to do a bit of translation, but you should be able to interpret such references readily.

If you're planning on using your machine only as a personal machine, you'll have only minor need for the material covered here. Do keep in mind that you can use these techniques to network multiple computers in your home or office, so that you have less maintenance and less software configuration to do. If you've no interest in doing even this, don't let the seemingly complex processes outlined here intimidate you. You've got no real need to understand them unless you plan on clustering your machine.

CHAPTER 25

FTP Serving

Sometimes it is helpful to be able transfer files between machines. If you are collaborating on a project, you or your collaborators might need to exchange files. As mail spools frequently have file size limits, an FTP server can provide an alternative means to exchange files. If you have built a Web site on one machine, but would like to transfer it to your OS X machine because you have a Web server running on it, an FTP server can provide a way to do so. With little effort, your OS X machine can run an FTP server to facilitate this activity. In this chapter, we will look at the FTP server that is included in the OS X distribution. Then we will look at an alternative, highly configurable FTP server that you could install in place of the default FTP server. Lastly, we will take a brief look at alternatives that can be used in place of, or in conjunction with, an FTP server.

Turning On the FTP Server

The OS X distribution includes the FreeBSD FTP server. Because Apple is concerned about the security of your machine, this service is not turned on by default. At this point in time, you can ftp only from your OS X machine to other FTP servers. After you have turned on the FTP service, you will be able to ftp directly to your OS X machine. Unfortunately, this service also makes your machine more vulnerable to outside attacks. Throughout the chapter, we will provide suggestions for some simple precautions that you can take to protect your machine. Of course, the best protection is to not turn on the FTP server.

If you choose to turn on the FTP server, first make a backup copy of your `/etc/inetd.conf` file. Then in the `Sharing` pane, check the `Allow FTP` access box, as shown in Figure 25.1.

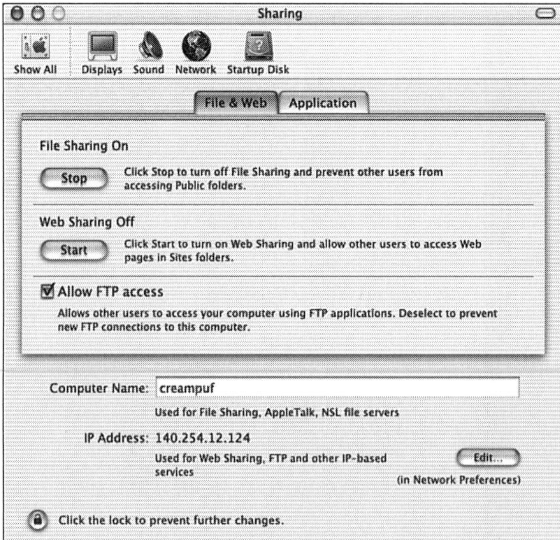

FIGURE 25.1
The FTP server is turned on in the Sharing pane.

If you look at your /etc/inetd.conf file now, you will notice that the line for the FTP server is no longer commented out. The Sharing pane has, among other things, edited this file.

Available Options in the FTP Server

You have just turned on your FTP server. If you looked at the ftp entry in your /etc/inetd.conf file, you noticed that the server runs by default with the -l option, which is the option that forces the logging of successful and unsuccessful FTP sessions.

Many other options are available in the FTP server, and they are detailed in the command documentation table, Table 25.1. To implement any of the options, edit the ftp entry in the /etc/inetd.conf file. Remember to back up /etc/inetd.conf before making any changes.

To cause the changes you have made to the /etc/inetd.conf file to take effect, you must make the inetd process reread its configuration file. To do so, find the process ID and issue a kill -HUP to that process ID, as shown here:

```
[localhost:/Users/joray] root# ps -aux | grep inetd
     root    233   0.0  0.0     1260     112  ??  Ss      0:00.01 inetd
     root    768   0.0  0.0     5708       0 std  T       0:00.00 grep inetd
[localhost:/Users/joray] root# kill -HUP 233
```

Nothing obvious will occur after you have issued the preceding commands. You might not even see anything in the log file to indicate that the hangup signal was issued. Test the FTP server to make sure that the options you specified are being observed. If you find they are not, you can always reboot the machine to ensure that the inetd process rereads its configuration file. But in a multi-user environment, it is polite to keep the number of times you have to reboot to a minimum.

TABLE 25.1 Command Documentation Table for ftpd

ftpd	Internet File Transfer Protocol server.
ftpd [-AdDhlMSU] [-T *<maxtimeout>*] [-t *<timeout>*] [-u *<mask>*]	
ftpd is the Internet File Transfer Protocol process. It uses the TCP protocol and runs on the port specified as ftp in services directory of the NetInfo database.	
-A	Permits only anonymous FTP connections. All others are refused.

TABLE 25.1 continued

`-d`	Turns on debugging. Debugging information is written to the syslog using `LOG_FTP`.
`-D`	Detaches and becomes a daemon. Accepts connections on the FTP port and forks child processes to handle them. This has a lower overhead than starting the service from `inetd(8)` and is useful on busy servers to reduce the load.
`-h`	Uses data ports in the high port range (usually 40000–44999) for passive connections.
`-l`	Each successful and failed `ftp (1)` session is logged to the syslog using `LOG_FTP`. If specified twice (`-l -l`), the logging of retrieve (get), store (put), append, delete, make directory, remove directory, and rename operations and their arguments also occurs.
`-M`	Enables multihomed mode. Instead of using `~ftp` for anonymous transfers, a directory matching the fully qualified domain name of the IP address of the connected client, located in `~ftp`, is used instead.
`-S`	Logs all anonymous transfers to `/var/log/ftpd`, if the file exists.
`-U`	Logs each concurrent `ftp (1)` session to the file `/var/log/ftpd`, making them visible to commands such as `who (1)`.
`-T` *`<maxtimeout>`*	A client may also request a different timeout period. The maximum period may be set to *`<timeout>`* in seconds. Default is two hours.
`-t` *`<timeout>`*	Sets the inactivity timeout period to *`<timeout>`* seconds. Default is 15 minutes.
`-u` *`<mask>`*	Changes default `umask` from `027` to *`<mask>`*.
ftpd supports the following FTP requests, case ignored.	
`ABOR`	Aborts previous command.
`ACCT`	Specifies account (ignored).
`ALLO`	Allocates storage (vacuously).
`APPE`	Appends to a file.
`CDUP`	Changes to the parent directory of the current working directory.

Table 25.1 continued

CWD	Changes current working directory.
DELE	Deletes a file.
HELP	Gives help information.
LIST	Gives list files in a directory (`ls -lgA`).
MKD	Makes a directory.
MDTM	Shows last modification time of file.
MODE	Specifies data transfer mode.
NLST	Gives name list of files in directory.
NOOP	Does nothing.
PASS	Specifies password.
PASV	Prepares for server-to-server transfer.
PORT	Specifies data connection port.
PWD	Prints current working directory.
QUIT	Terminates session.
REST	Restarts incomplete transfer session.
RETR	Retrieves a file.
RMD	Removes a directory.
RNFR	Specifies rename-from filename.
RNTO	Specifies rename-to filename.
SITE	Nonstandard commands (see next section).
SIZE	Returns size of file.
STAT	Returns status of server.
STOR	Stores a file.
STOU	Stores a file with a unique name.
STRU	Specifies data transfer structure.
SYST	Shows operating system type of server system.
TYPE	Specifies data transfer type.
USER	Specifies username.
XCUP	Changes to parent of current working directory (deprecated).
XCWD	Changes working directory (deprecated).
XMKD	Makes a directory (deprecated).

TABLE 25.1 continued

XPWD	Prints the current working directory (deprecated)
XRMD	Removes a directory (deprecated).
The following nonstandard commands are supported by the SITE request:	
UMASK	Changes the umask; for example, `SITE UMASK 002`.
IDLE	Sets the idle timer; for example, `SITE IDLE 60`.
CHMOD	Changes the mode of a file; for example, `SITE CHMOD0 0CHMOD1 1CHMOD2`.
HELP	Gives help information.
The remaining FTP requests specified in Internet RFC 959 are recognized, but not implemented.	
`ftpd` interprets filenames according to the globbing conventions by `csh (1)`. This allows users to use the metacharacters: `*`, `?`, `[]`, `{}`, and `~`.	
`ftpd` authenticates users according to these rules:	
1. Login name must be in the password database and not have a null password.	
2. Login name must not appear in `/etc/ftpusers`.	
3. User must have a standard shell returned by `getusershell (3)`.	
4. If the username appears in `/etc/ftpchroot`, the sessions root is changed to the user's home directory by `chroot (2)`, as for an anonymous or FTP account. The user must still supply a password. This feature is a compromise between an anonymous account and a fully privileged account. This account should also be set up as for an anonymous account.	
5. If the username is `anonymous` or `ftp`, an anonymous FTP account must be present in the password file for user `ftp`. The connecting user may specify any password, customarily an e-mail address.	
Associated files:	
`/etc/ftpusers`	List of unwelcome/restricted users.
`/etc/ftpchroot`	List of normal users who should be chrooted.
`/etc/ftpwelcome`	Welcome notice.

Restricting Access to the FTP Server Using Its Tools

The FTP server provides some ways for you to limit access to the service. An `/etc/ftpusers` file comes by default. This file contains the list of users who are not allowed FTP access to the machine:

```
[localhost:~] joray% more /etc/ftpusers
     # list of users disallowed any ftp access.
     # read by ftpd(8).
     Administrator
     administrator
     root
     uucp
```

If you have any additional users who should not be granted FTP access, include them in this file.

The FTP server also allows for `chroot`ed FTP access, which is a compromise between full access and anonymous-only access. With this compromise access, a user is granted FTP access only to his home directory. List any users who should have this type of access in the `/etc/ftpchroot` file. Note, however, that if you decide to make anonymous FTP available, OS X currently ignores the `/etc/ftpchroot` file. In other words, if you decide to make anonymous FTP available, only anonymous FTP receives the behavior of `chroot` being used to limit the root directory of the FTP session to that of the user's home directory. Real users have full access.

Logging

The FTP server logs connections to `/var/log/ftp.log`. Typical entries in the log look like this:

```
Jul 19 14:56:00 localhost ftpd[20313]: connection from
➥calvin.biosci.ohio-state.edu
Jul 19 14:56:01 localhost ftpd[20313]: FTP LOGIN FROM
➥calvin.biosci.ohio-state.edu as marvin
Jul 19 15:01:44 localhost ftpd[20327]: connection from
➥calvin.biosci.ohio-state.edu
Jul 19 15:01:45 localhost ftpd[20327]: FTP LOGIN FROM
➥calvin.biosci.ohio-state.edu as marvin
Jul 19 15:19:39 localhost ftpd[20358]: connection from
➥calvin.biosci.ohio-state.edu
Jul 19 15:19:39 localhost ftpd[20358]: ANONYMOUS FTP LOGIN FROM
➥calvin.biosci.ohio-state.edu, marvin@
```

The `ftp.log` file shows who logged in and where the user logged in from. In the case of an anonymous connection, the password used identifies the user. The file logs only the initial connections, not anything about the transfers.

Setting Up Anonymous FTP

As you have seen, setting up the FTP server to allow real users to have FTP access is not difficult. Setting up the FTP server to allow anonymous FTP takes some work. Be warned that setting up anonymous FTP makes your machine vulnerable to yet more attacks. For whatever reason, you might have a need to conveniently distribute or receive files. An anonymous FTP server can provide an easy cross-platform way to accomplish those goals.

To set up an anonymous FTP site, do the following:

1. Create an `ftp` user in the NetInfo database. Follow the pattern of one of the generic users, such as user `unknown`. You might start by duplicating the `unknown` user and editing the duplicate user. Create your `ftp` user with the basic parameters shown in Table 25.2.

TABLE 25.2 Basic Parameters for an `ftp` User

Property	*Value*
`name`	`ftp`
`realname`	*<some generic reference to ftp>*
`uid`	*<some unused uid number>*
`passwd`	`*`
`home`	*<some suitable location>*
`shell`	`/dev/null`
`gid`	*<some unused gid number>*
`change`	`0`
`expire`	`0`

Figure 25.2 shows the values we used for our `ftp` user.

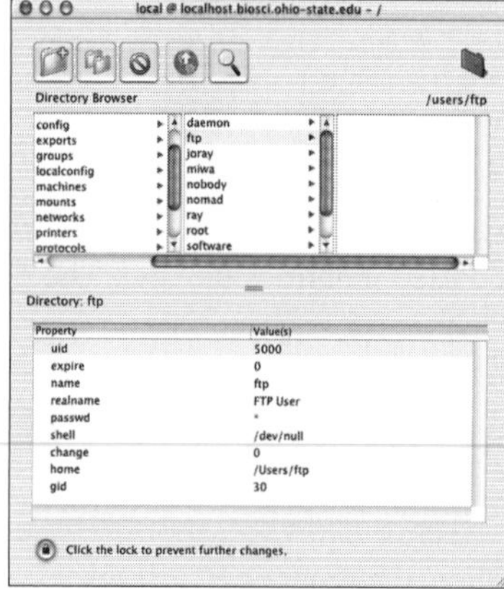

FIGURE 25.2
Here is how we chose to create our `ftp` user, as seen in the NetInfo Manager.

2. Create an `ftp` group in the NetInfo database. Make sure that you assign the `ftp` group the same `gid` that you indicated for the `ftp` user.
3. Create a home directory for user `ftp`. Make sure that you create the directory that you specified in the NetInfo database. The directory should be owned by `root` and have permissions `555`.
4. Create a `~ftp/bin` directory, owned by `root` with permissions `555`.
5. Copy the system's `/bin/ls` to `~ftp/bin/`.
6. Create `~ftp/usr/lib`. Each of those directories should be owned by `root` with permissions `555`.
7. Copy the system's `/usr/lib/dyld` to `~ftp/usr/lib`. This is one of the files that helps `ls` function properly in this `chroot`ed environment.
8. Copy the system's `/usr/lib/libSystem.B.dylib` to `~ftp/usr/lib`. This is another file that helps `ls` function properly in the `chroot`ed environment.
9. Create `~ftp/System/Library/Frameworks/System.framework/Versions/B`. Each of those directories should be owned by `root` with permissions `555`.
10. Copy the system's `/System/Library/Frameworks/System.framework/Versions/B/System` to `~ftp/System/Library/Frameworks/System.framework/Versions/B`. This is another file that helps `ls` function properly in the `chroot`ed environment.
11. Create a `~ftp/pub` directory where files could be stored for download. Recommended ownership of this directory includes some user and group `ftp` or user `root`. Typical permissions for this directory are `755`.
12. If you also want to make a drop location where files could be uploaded, create `~ftp/incoming`, owned by `root`. Recommended permissions include `753`, `733`, `1733`, `3773` or `777`. You could also create `~ftp/incoming` with permissions `751` and subdirectories that are used as the drop locations with any of the recommended drop-off permissions.

If you decide to allow anonymous FTP, make sure that you regularly check the anonymous FTP area and your logs for any unusual activity. In addition, regularly check Apple's Web site for any updates for OS X that include `ftp` updates. Security holes are regularly found in `ftpd` and regularly fixed.

For your convenience, we include a listing of our `ftp` user's home directory:

```
[localhost:/Users] root# ls -lRaF ftp

     total 0
     dr-xr-xr-x   7 root  wheel  194 May  8 14:59 ./
     drwxr-xr-x  12 root  wheel  364 May 10 14:24 ../
```

```
dr-xr-xr-x   3 root  wheel   58 May  8 13:28 System/
dr-xr-xr-x   3 root  wheel   58 May  8 13:22 bin/
drwxr-x-wx   2 root  wheel   24 May 10 14:32 incoming/
drwxr-xr-x   2 root  wheel   24 May  8 15:01 pub/
dr-xr-xr-x   3 root  wheel   58 May  8 13:22 usr/

ftp/System:
total 0
dr-xr-xr-x  3 root  wheel   58 May  8 13:28 ./
dr-xr-xr-x  7 root  wheel  194 May  8 14:59 ../
dr-xr-xr-x  3 root  wheel   58 May  8 13:28 Library/

ftp/System/Library:
total 0
dr-xr-xr-x  3 root  wheel  58 May  8 13:28 ./
dr-xr-xr-x  3 root  wheel  58 May  8 13:28 ../
dr-xr-xr-x  3 root  wheel  58 May  8 13:29 Frameworks/

ftp/System/Library/Frameworks:
total 0
dr-xr-xr-x  3 root  wheel  58 May  8 13:29 ./
dr-xr-xr-x  3 root  wheel  58 May  8 13:28 ../
dr-xr-xr-x  3 root  wheel  58 May  8 13:30 System.framework/

ftp/System/Library/Frameworks/System.framework:
total 0
dr-xr-xr-x  3 root  wheel  58 May  8 13:30 ./
dr-xr-xr-x  3 root  wheel  58 May  8 13:29 ../
dr-xr-xr-x  3 root  wheel  58 May  8 13:31 Versions/

ftp/System/Library/Frameworks/System.framework/Versions:
total 0
dr-xr-xr-x  3 root  wheel  58 May  8 13:31 ./
dr-xr-xr-x  3 root  wheel  58 May  8 13:30 ../
dr-xr-xr-x  3 root  wheel  58 May  8 13:35 B/

ftp/System/Library/Frameworks/System.framework/Versions/B:
total 2464
dr-xr-xr-x  3 root  wheel       58 May  8 13:35 ./
dr-xr-xr-x  3 root  wheel       58 May  8 13:31 ../
-r-xr-xr-x  1 root  wheel  1260748 May  8 13:35 System*

ftp/bin:
total 56
dr-xr-xr-x  3 root  wheel     58 May  8 13:22 ./
dr-xr-xr-x  7 root  wheel    194 May  8 14:59 ../
-r-xr-xr-x  1 root  wheel  26984 May  8 13:22 ls*

ftp/incoming:
total 0
```

```
drwxr-x-wx  2 root  wheel   24 May 10 14:32 ./
dr-xr-xr-x  7 root  wheel  194 May  8 14:59 ../

ftp/pub:
total 0
drwxr-xr-x  2 root  wheel   24 May  8 15:01 ./
dr-xr-xr-x  7 root  wheel  194 May  8 14:59 ../

ftp/usr:
total 0
dr-xr-xr-x  3 root  wheel   58 May  8 13:22 ./
dr-xr-xr-x  7 root  wheel  194 May  8 14:59 ../
dr-xr-xr-x  3 root  wheel   58 May  8 13:26 lib/

ftp/usr/lib:
total 640
dr-xr-xr-x  3 root  wheel      58 May  8 13:26 ./
dr-xr-xr-x  3 root  wheel      58 May  8 13:22 ../
-r-xr-xr-x  1 root  wheel  327528 May  8 13:26 dyld*
-r-xr-xr-x  1 root  wheel 1260748 May 11 13:25 libSystem.B.dylib*
```

For additional thoughts on anonymous FTP configuration, you might want to check these Web sites:

CERT Coordination Center Tech Tips	`http://www.cert.org/tech_tips/`
WU-FTPD Resource Center's Related Documents link	`http://www.landfield.com/wu-ftpd/`
AppleCare Tech Info Library	`http://til.info.apple.com`

Using wu-ftpd as a Replacement for the Default ftpd

If you decide to activate anonymous FTP, especially anonymous FTP with an upload directory, you should consider replacing the default `ftpd` with a modifiable `ftpd`. A popular, highly configurable replacement `ftpd` is `wu-ftpd`, available at `http://www.wu-ftpd.org`. In addition to being highly configurable, it easily compiles under OS X.

Although popular and highly configurable, `wu-ftpd` is not exempt from security problems. It is still important to regularly monitor the anonymous FTP area, if you have one, as well as make sure that you have the latest version of `wu-ftpd`, which is version 2.6.1, as of this writing.

How to Replace ftpd with wu-ftpd

To replace the default ftpd with wu-ftpd, first download, compile, and install wu-ftpd. Fortunately, wu-ftpd is one of the packages that follows this basic format for compilation and installation:

```
./configure
make
make install
```

When you download the wu-ftpd source files, also download any patches available for the source. Currently there are three patch files. Copy the patch files to the root directory of the source, and then run patch on the files as follows:

```
[localhost:~/wu-ftpd-2.6.1] software% patch -p0 < missing_format_strings.patch
[localhost:~/wu-ftpd-2.6.1] software% patch -p0 < nlst-shows-dirs.patch
[localhost:~/wu-ftpd-2.6.1] software% patch -p0 < pasv-port-allowcorection.patch
```

Please note that for display purposes, one of the actual patch filenames has been altered. The patches for the CHANGES file won't all work quite right, but don't worry about it because the CHANGES file is not as important as the other files that are patched.

The default config.guess and config.sub files that come with the wu-ftpd source do not work with OS X. Use the files that come with OS X:

```
[localhost:~ /wu-ftpd-2.6.1] software% cp /usr/libexec/config.guess ./
[localhost:~ -/wu-ftpd-2.6.1] software% cp /usr/libexec/config.sub ./
```

If you have not already done so, create a bin user. The bin user is needed for wu-ftpd to install properly. The bin user should have a relatively low uid. OS X already comes with a bin group with gid 7. In many other Unix variants, the bin user has the same uid and gid. As with the ftp user, follow the basic paramaters of a generic user, such as the unknown user. You might consider duplicating the unknown user and editing values. Suggested values for the bin user are shown in Table 25.3.

TABLE 25.3 Suggested Parameters for a bin User

Property	*Value*
name	bin
realname	System Tools Owner
uid	7
passwd	*
home	/bin
shell	/bin/sync

Table 25.3 continued

Property	*Value*
gid	7
change	0
expire	0

Next, you are ready to run `./configure`. Being the highly configurable package that it is, you can pass many parameters to `configure`, as detailed in Table 25.4.

Table 25.4 Available Options to `configure` for `wu-ftpd`

`--with-etc-dir=PATH`	Path for configuration files; usually `/etc`.
`--with-pid-dir=PATH`	Path for `run/pid` files; usually `/var`.
`--with-log-dir=PATH`	Path for log files (`xferlog`); usually `/var/log`.
`--disable-upload`	Disables support for the `upload` keyword in the `ftpaccess` file.
`--disable-overwrite`	Disables support for the `overwrite` keyword in the `ftpaccess` file.
`--disable-hostxs`	Disables support for the `allow` and `deny` keywords in the `ftpaccess` file.
`--disable-logfailed`	Disables logging of failed attempts (wrong password, wrong username, and so on).
`--disable-logtoomany`	Disables logging of failed attempts that failed because too many users were already logged in.
`--disable-private`	Disables support for private files (site group/site `gpass` FTP commands).
`--disable-dnsretry`	Disables retrying failed DNS lookups at connection time.
`--enable-anononly`	Allows only anonymous FTP connections.
`--enable-paranoid`	Disables some features that might possibly affect security.
`--disable-quota`	Disables support of disk quotas, even if your operating system supports them.
`--disable-pam`	Does not use PAM authentication, even if your operating system supports it.
`--enable-skey`	Supports S/Key authentication (needs S/Key libraries).
`--enable-OPIE`	Supports OPIE (One Password In Everything) authentication (needs OPIE libraries).

TABLE 25.4 continued

`--disable-new-cd`	Causes `cd ~` to not return to the `chroot`-relative home directory.
`--enable-chmod`	Allows FTP users to set `SETUID`, `SETGID`, and `STICKY` bits on file permissions.
`--disable-rfc931`	Does not do RFC931 (`IDENT`) lookups (worse logging, but faster).
`--disable-daemon`	Does not support running as a normal daemon (as opposed to running from `inetd`).
`--disable-map-chdir`	Does not keep track of user's path changes. This leads to worse symlink handling.
`--disable-throughput`	Does not keep track of user's throughput.
`--disable-count`	Does not keep track of transferred bytes (for statistics).
`--disable-newlines`	Suppresses some extra blank lines.
`--enable-crackers`	Does not wait for password entry if someone tries to log in with a wrong username. Although convenient, it is a security risk in that crackers can find out names of valid users.
`--disable-verbose`	Disables verbose error logging.
`--enable-NOOP`	`NOOP` command resets idle time.
`--disable-log-rp`	Logs the relative path rather than the real path.
`--disable-virtual`	Disables support of virtual servers. See `doc/HOWTO/VIRTUAL.FTP.SUPPORT` for details on virtual servers.
`--disable-closedvirt`	Allows guests to log in to virtual servers.
`--disable-dns`	Skips all DNS lookups.
`--disable-port`	Disallows port mode connections.
`--disable-pasv`	Disallows passive mode connections.
`--disable-plsm`	Disables PID lock sleep messages. Recommended for busy sites.
`--disable-pasvip`	Does not require the same IP for control and data connection in passive mode. This is more secure, but can cause trouble with some firewalls.
`--disable-anonymous`	Allows only real users to connect.
`--enable-ls`	Uses the internal `ls` command instead of `/bin/ls` in the `chroot` directory. This is experimental and has known problems.

TABLE 25.4 continued

`--enable-numericuid`	Makes the internal `ls` display `UID` and `GID` instead of user/group names. This is faster, but the `ls` output looks worse.
`--disable-hidesetuid`	Causes the internal `ls` command not to hide `setuid/setgid` bits from the user. Default is for the internal `ls` to hide them as a security precaution.
`--disable-mail`	Disables support of the mail on upload feature. The feature allows you to automatically send an e-mail message to the FTP administrator whenever an anonymous user uploads a file.
`--enable-badclients`	Supports broken clients. See the `CHANGES` file for details.
`--with-bufsize=x`	Sets the buffer size to `x`. (You won't usually have to adjust this value.)
`--with-backlog=x`	Sets the number of incoming processes to backlog in daemon mode to `x`. Default is `100`.

To distinctly separate the `wu-ftpd` installation from the default `ftpd`, you should consider specifying paths in the various path parameters. In addition, you might consider running `./configure` with `-prefix=<some-directory-for-wu-ftpd>`, so that the `wu-ftpd` binaries and man pages are all in one place. Although not documented, the `-prefix` parameter appears to work. You might also find it interesting that you can create either an anonymous-only or a real users-only FTP server. Next, run `make` and `make install`.

After you have a `wu-ftpd` binary, you should update the `/etc/inetd.conf` file to reflect the location of the new `ftpd` as well as any options that should be used. Options available in `wu-ftpd` are detailed in Table 25.5.

TABLE 25.5 Options Available in `wu-ftpd`

`ftpd`	Internet File Transfer Protocol server
`ftpd [-d] [-v] [-l] [-t <timeout>] [-T <maxtimeout>] [-a] [-A] [-L] [-i] [-I] [-o] [-p <ctrlport>] [-P <dataport>] [-q] [-Q] [-r <rootdir>] [-s] [-S] [-u <mask>] [-V] [-w] [-X]`	
`ftpd` is the Internet File Transfer Protocol process. It uses the TCP protocol and runs on the port specified as `ftp` in the `services` directory of the NetInfo database.	
`-d`	Logs debugging information to the syslog.
`-v`	Logs debugging information to the syslog.
`-l`	Logs each FTP session to the syslog.

TABLE 25.5 continued

`-t <timeout>`	Sets the inactivity timeout period to *<timeout>* seconds. Default is 15 minutes.
`-T <maxtimeout>`	A client may also request a different timeout period. The maximum period may be set to *<maxtimeout>* seconds. Default is two hours.
`-a`	Enables the use of the `ftpaccess (5)` configuration file.
`-A`	Disables the use of the `ftpaccess (5)` configuration file. This is the default.
`-L`	Logs commands sent to the `ftpd` server to the syslog. Overriden by the use of the `ftpaccess` file. With the `-L` command, logging occurs as soon as the FTP server is invoked. All `USER` commands are logged. If a user accidentally enters a password for a username, the password is logged.
`-i`	Logs files received by the `ftpd` server to the `xferlog (5)`. Overridden by the use of the `ftpaccess (5)` file.
`-I`	Disables use of RFC931 (`AUTH/ident`) to attempt to determine the username on the client.
`-o`	Logs files transmitted by the `ftpd` server to the `xferlog (5)`. Overridden by the use of the `ftpaccess (5)` file.
`-p <ctrlport>` `-P <dataport>`	Overrides port numbers used by the daemon. Normally, the port number is determined by the `ftp` and `ftp-services` values in `services`. If there is no entry for `ftp-data` and `-P` is not specified, the daemon uses the port just prior to the control connection port. The `-p` option is available only for the standalone daemon.
`-q` `-Q`	Determines whether the daemon uses the PID files, which are required by the limit directive to determine the number of current users in each access class. Disabling the use of PID files disables user limits. Default, `-q`, is to use PID files. Specify `-Q` as a normal user testing the server when access permissions prevent the use of PID files. Large, busy sites that do not want to impose a limit on the number of concurrent users might consider disabling PID files.

Table 25.5 continued

`-r` *<rootdir>*	Instructs the daemon to `chroot (2)` to *<rootdir>* immediately upon loading. This can improve system security by limiting the files that can be damaged in a break-in. Setup is much like anonymous FTP, with additional files required.
`-s` `-S`	Sets the daemon to standalone mode. The `-S` option runs - the daemon in the background and is useful in startup scripts during system initialization (that is, `rc.local`). The `-s` option leaves the daemon in the foreground and is useful when running from `init` (that is, `/etc/inittab`).
`-u` *<umask>*	Sets the default umask to *<umask>*.
`-V`	Displays the copyright and version information, and then terminates.
`-w`	Records every login and logout. This is the default.
`-W`	Does not record user logins in the `wtmp` file.
`-X`	Does not save output created by `-i` or `-o` to the `xferlog` file, but saves it via syslog so that output from several hosts can be collected on one central loghost.

This `ftpd` supports the same FTP requests as the OS X default `ftpd`. The following nonstandard commands are supported by the `SITE` request:

`UMASK`	Changes the umask; for example, `SITE UMASK 002`
`IDLE`	Sets the idle timer; for example, `SITE IDLE 60`
`CHMOD`	Changes the mode of a file; for example, `SITE CHMOD 755` *`filename`*
`HELP`	Gives help information; for example, `SITE HELP`
`NEWER`	Lists files newer than a particular date
`MINFO`	Like `SITE NEWER`, but gives extra information
`GROUP`	Requests special group access; for example, `SITE GROUP foo`
`GPASS`	Gives special group access password; for example, `SITE GPASS bar`
`EXEC`	Executes a program; for example, `SITE EXEC` *`program params`*

Have `inetd` reread its configuration file:

```
[localhost:/Users/joray] root# ps -aux | grep inetd
    root        228  0.0  0.0     1260    108  ??  Ss      0:00.03 inetd
    root       6529  0.0  0.0     5708      0 std  T       0:00.00 grep inetd
[localhost:/Users/joray] root# kill -HUP 228
```

Editing the `ftpaccess` File

Although `wu-ftpd` provides a lot of configurability with its compile-time and run-time options, more controls can be set in the `ftpaccess` file. To enable the use of the `ftpaccess` file, be sure to run `wu-ftpd` with the `-a` option.

Selected useful controls in `ftpaccess` are documented in Table 25.6. Be sure to read the `ftpaccess` man page thoroughly for information on these and other available controls.

TABLE 25.6 Selected Controls Available for `ftpaccess`

Control	*Function*
`loginfails <number>`	Logs a "repeated login failures" message after `<number>` login failures. Default is `5`.
`class <class> <typelist> <address> [<address>...]`	Sets up classes of users and valid access addresses. `<typelist>` is a comma-separated list of any of these keywords: `real`, `anonymous`, or `guest`. If `real` is included, the class can include users FTPing to real accounts. If `anonymous` is included, the class can include anonymous FTP users. If `guest` is included, the class can include members of guest access accounts.
`guestgroup <groupname> [<groupname>...]`	Defines what groups are considered guests.
`limit <class> <number> <times> <message_file>`	Limits the number of users belonging to `<class>` to access the server during the `<times>` indicated and posts `<message_file>` as the reason for access denial.
`file-limit [<raw>] <in | out | total> <count> [<class>]`	Limits the number of files a user in `<class>` may transfer. Limit may be placed on files in, out, or total. If no class is specified, the limit is the default for classes that do not have a limit specified. `<raw>` applies the limit to the total traffic rather than only data files.

TABLE 25.6 continued

Control	*Function*
data-limit [*<raw>*] *<in | out | total>* *<count>* [*<class>*]	Limits the number of data bytes a user in *<class>* may transfer. Limit may be placed on bytes in, out, or total. If no class is specified, the limit is the default for classes that do not have a limit specified. *<raw>* applies the limit to the total traffic rather than just data files.
limit-time {* | anonymous | guest} *<minutes>*	Limits the total time a session can take. By default, there is no limit. Real users are never limited.
log commands *<typelist>*	Logs individual commands issued by users in *<typelist>*, where *<typelist>* is a comma-separated list of any of the keywords real, anonymous, or guest.
log transfers *<typelist>* *<directions>*	Logs the transfers of users belonging to *<typelist>* in the specified *<directions>*. *<typelist>* is a comma-separated list of any of the keywords real, anonymous, or guest. *<directions>* is a comma-separated list of the keyword inbound or outbound, where inbound refers to transfers to the server and outbound refers to transfers from the server.
log syslog	Redirects logging messages for incoming and outgoing transfers to the system log. Default is xferlog.
log syslog+xferlog	Logs transfer messages to both the system log and xferlog.
defaultserver deny *<username>* [*<username>*...]	
defaultserver allow *<username>* [<username>...]	By default, all users are allowed access to the default, non-virutal FTP server. defaultserver *<deny>* denies access to specific users. You could use defaultserver *<deny>* * to deny access to all users, then default-server *<allow>* to allow specific users.
passwd-check *<level>* *<enforcement>*	Defines the level and enforcement of password checking done by the server for anonymous ftp. *<level>* can be none, trivial (must contain an @), or rfc822 (must be an RFC822-compliant address). *<enforcement>* can be warn (warns the user but allows him to log in) or enforce (warns the user and logs him out).
chmod <yes | no> *<typelist>*	
delete <yes | no> *<typelist>*	

TABLE 25.6 continued

Control	*Function*
`overwrite <yes | no> <typelist>` `rename <yes | no> <typelist>` `umask <yes | no> <typelist>`	Sets permissions for `chmod`, `delete`, `overwrite`, `rename`, `umask` as `yes` or `no` for users in `<typelist>`, where `<typelist>` is a comma-separated list of any of the keywords `real`, `anonymous`, or `guest`.
`upload [absolute | relative] [class=<classname>]... [-] <root-dir> <dirglob> <yes | no> <owner> <group> <mode> [dirs | nodirs] [<d_mode>]`	Specifies upload directory information. `<root-dir>` specifies the FTP root directory. `<dirglob>` specifies a directory under the `<root-dir>`. `<yes | no>` indicates whether files can be uploaded to the specified directory. If `yes`, files will be uploaded as belonging to `<owner>` and `<group>` in `<mode>`. `[dirs | nodirs]` specifies whether new subdirectories can be created in the upload directory. If `dirs`, they are created with mode `<d_mode>`, if it is specified. Otherwise, they are created as defined by `<mode>`. If `<mode>` is not specified, they are created with mode 777. Upload restrictions can be specified by class with `class=<classname>`.
`path-filter <typelist> <mesg> <allowed_charset> [<disallowed regexp>...]`	Defines regular expressions that control what a filename can or cannot be for users in `<typelist>`, where `<type list>` is a comma-separated list of any of the keywords `real`, `anonymous`, or `guest`.
`throughput <root-dir> <subdir-glob> <file-glob-list> <bytes-per-second> <bytes-per-second-multiply> <remote-glob-list>`	Restricts throughput to `<bytes-per-second>` on down load of files in the comma-separated `<file-glob-list>` in the subdirectory matched by `<subdir-glob>` under `<root-dir>` when the remote host or IP address matches the comma-separated `<remote-glob-list>`.
`anonymous-root <root-dir> [<class>]`	Specifies `<root-dir>` as the `chroot` path for anonymous users. If no anonymous-root is matched, the old method of parsing the home directory for the FTP user is used.
`guest-root <root-dir> [<uid-range>]`	Specifies `<root-dir>` as the chroot path for guest users. If no guest-root is matched, the old method of parsing the user's home directory is used.

TABLE 25.6 continued

Control	*Function*
`deny-uid <uid-range> [...]` `deny-gid <gid-range> [...]` `allow-uid <uid-range> [...]` `allow-gid <gid-range> [...]`	The `deny` clauses specify UID and GID ranges that are denied access to the FTP server. The `allow` clauses are then used to allow access to those who would otherwise be denied access. `deny` is checked before `allow`. Default is to allow access. Use of these controls can remove the need for the `/etc/ftpusers` file. Throughout the `ftpaccess` file where `uid` or `gid` can be specified, either names or numbers may be used. Put `%` before numeric `uid` or `gid`.
`restricted-uid <uid-range> [...]` `restricted-gid <gid-range> [...]` `unrestricted-uid <uid-range> [...]` `restricted-gid <gid-range> [...]`	Controls whether real or guest users are allowed access to areas on the FTP server outside their home diretories. Not intended to replace the use of `guestgroup` and `guestuser`. The unrestricted clauses may be used to allow `unrestricted-gid <gid`-users outside their directories when they would have been otherwise restricted.
`passive ports <cidr> <min> <max>`	Allows control of the TCP port numbers that may be used for a passive data connection. If the control connection matches `<cidr>`, a port in the `<min>` to `<max>` range is randomly selected for the daemon to listen on. This control allows firewalls to limit the ports that remote clients use for connecting to the protected network. `<cidr>` is shorthand for an IP address in dotted-quad notation, followed by a slash and the number of leftmost bits that represent the network address. For example, for the reserved class-A network 10, instead of using a net mask of 255.0.0.0, use a CIDR of 8, and 10.0.0.0/8 represents the network. Likewise, for a private class-C home network, you could use 192.168.1.0/24 to represent your network.
`dns refuse_mismatch <filename> [override]`	Refuses FTP sessions when the forward and reverse lookups for the remote site do not match. Displays `<filename>` to warn the user. If `override` is specified, allows the connection after complaining.
`dns refuse_no_reverse <filename> [override]`	Refuses FTP sessions when there is no reverse DNS entry for the remote site. Displays `<message>` to warn the user. If `override` is specified, allows the connection after complaining.

Understanding Basic ftpaccess Controls

As you saw in Table 25.6, even a selective list of ftpaccess controls is large. Because many controls are available, let's take a look at some of the basic configuration controls in the ftpaccess file.

class

Look at this statement:

```
class    staff    real     *.biosci.ohio-state.edu
```

In this example, a class called staff is defined as being a real user coming from anywhere in the biosci.ohio-state.edu domain.

In the following statement, a class called local is defined as being a guest user coming from anywhere in the ohio-state.edu domain:

```
class    local    guest    *.ohio-state.edu
```

In the following statement, a class called remote is defined as being an anonymous user whose connection comes from anywhere:

```
class    remote   anonymous        *
```

You can create as many classes as suit your needs.

limit

In the following statement, there is a limit of five users belonging to class remote who can access the FTP server on Saturdays and Sundays and on any day between 6:00 p.m. and 6:00 a.m.:

```
limit    remote   5        SaSu|Any1800-0600        /usr/local/etc/msgs/msg.toomany
```

When the limit has been reached, any additional user will see a posting of the message file, msg.toomany, in /usr/local/etc/msgs.

In the following statement, no users belonging to the class staff can access the FTP server at any time:

```
limit    staff  0        Any                /usr/local/etc/msgs/msg.notallowed
```

Whenever any user in class staff attempts to log in, she sees a message indicating that she is not allowed to access the FTP server.

upload

In the following statements, the guest user, bioftp, can upload files to the ~ftp/public directory. The files will be uploaded with permissions 600 (that is, read and write permissions) for guest user bioftp:

```
upload  /home/ftp   /public       yes     bioftp   ftponly      0600
upload  /home/ftp   /public/*     yes     bioftp   ftponly      0600
```

However, in the following statement, no user can upload to the ~ftp/bin directory:

```
upload  /home/ftp   /bin          no
```

Please note that the upload control also has a nodirs option that does not allow directories to be uploaded. If you decide to run an anonymous FTP server, make sure that you include the nodirs option to the upload control.

restricted-uid and restricted-gid

Although restricted-uid and restricted-gid are straightforward controls, it is useful to note that these controls function like the /etc/ftpchroot file for the default ftpd.

A restricted control entry such as this:

```
restricted-uid marvin
```

restricts user marvin to his home directory for FTP access. The numeric uid for marvin, preceded by %, could be used instead, as well as a range of uids.

Understanding the xferlog

By default, wu-ftpd logs transfers to a file called xferlog. Each entry in the log consists of an entry in this format:

```
<current-time> <transfer-time> <remote-host> <file-size> <filename>
<transfer-type> <special-action-flag> <direction> <access-mode> <username>
<service-name> <authentication-method> <authenticated-user-id>
<completion-status>
```

At a casual glance, that format might seem a bit overwhelming. Let's look at some sample entries to better understand that format.

Here is an entry resulting from someone contacting the anonymous FTP server:

```
Fri May 11 13:32:19 2001 1 calvin.biosci.ohio-state.edu 46
/Users/ftp/incoming/file4 b _ i a joray@ ftp 0 * c
```

Immediately apparent are the date and time when the transfer occurred. The next entry, the 1, indicates that the transfer time was only one second. The remote host was calvin.biosci.ohio-state.edu. The file size was 46 bytes. The file transferred was file4 in the incoming area of the anonymous FTP server. The transfer was a binary transfer. No special action, such as compressing or tarring, was done. From the i, we see that this was an incoming transfer; that is, an upload. From the a, we see that this was an anonymous user. The string identifying the username in this case is joray@. That is the password that the user entered. The ftp indicates that the FTP service was used. The 0 indicates that no authentication method was used. The * indicates that an authenticated user ID is not available. The c indicates that the transfer completed.

Here is an entry resulting from a guest user contacting the FTP server:

```
Fri May 11 16:32:24 2001 5 calvin.biosci.ohio-state.edu 5470431
/Users/guests/betty/dotpaper.pdf b _ i g betty ftp 0 * c
```

It looks much like the anonymous entry. In this entry, we see that the transfer time was five seconds. The file transfer was larger than in the previous example, 5470431 bytes. The i indicates that this transfer was also an incoming transfer, an upload. The g indicates that the user involved was a guest user. The guest user was user betty.

Here is an entry resulting from a real user contacting the FTP server:

```
Fri May 11 15:34:14 2001 1 ryoohki.biosci.ohio-state.edu 277838
/Users/marvin/introduction.ps b _ o r marvin ftp 0 * c
```

Again, this entry is much like the other two entries we have seen. In this example, we learn from the o that the transfer was an outgoing transfer; that is, a download. The r indicates that a real user made the transfer. In this case, the real user was marvin.

You will probably find that wu-ftpd logs to /var/log/ftpd.log as well. However, the log entries are more detailed than what you saw for the default FTP server. Take a look at it, too. It contains a lot of the same information as the xferlog, but it also includes information on passive mode, ports that were used, and so on.

Guest User Accounts

As you have seen, wu-ftpd understands three types of users: real, anonymous, and guest. Real users are users who have full login access to your machine. As you have also seen, you can restrict your real users' FTP access to their home directories, if you so choose. Whether you choose to do so is up to you. If you trust your users enough to give them full login access to your machine in the first place, you might also trust them with full FTP access. Anonymous users are users who have access to only the anonymous area of your machine, if you chose to create an anonymous FTP area. Guest users are users who have accounts on your machine, but are not granted full access to your machine. Guest user accounts might be suitable for users who have Web sites on your machine and only need FTP access to occasionally update their Web sites.

A guest user account is a cross between a real user account and an anonymous FTP account. A guest user has a username and password, but does not have shell access to his account. Guest user accounts are also set up similarly to the anonymous FTP account. The users are restricted to only their home directories, as is the anonymous FTP account, and their accounts contain the commands that they might need to run while accessing their accounts via FTP.

If you decide that you need guest user accounts, do the following to implement the guest user:

1. Decide where the guest user's home directory should be. You could put your guest users in the same location as your regular users. You also could create a directory somewhere for guest users and place guest user directories in that location.
2. After you have decided where the guest account should reside, make a guest account. You could create your user in the User control panel. Your guest user, however, might not really have a need for all the directories that are made in a user account created by the User control panel. You can decide what directories might be necessary. If you anticipate having many guest users, you could create a guest skeleton user as your basis for guest accounts.
3. The guest user should belong to some sort of guest group. Create a guest group with an unused GID number. Edit the guest user's account to belong to the guest group. The guest user's shell should be modified to some nonexistent shell.
4. There are two possible ways to list the guest user's home directory. The traditional way is to include a `.` where the FTP server should `chroot` to as the root FTP directory. For example, we could create a guest user called `betty`, with a home directory located in `/Users/guests/betty`. To indicate that the root directory that we want `betty` to see when she accesses the FTP server to be `/Users/guests/betty`, we would edit the home directory to be `/Users/guests/betty/./`. If we wanted `betty` to be able to see a listing of other guest users' directories before changing to her directory, we could list her home directory as `/Users/guests/./betty`. By listing her home directory this way, her guest root directory does not need to be specifically listed in the `ftpaccess` file. Figure 25.3 shows how the guest user's home directory appears in the NetInfo Manager when indicated by this method.

   The other way to list a guest user's home directory is to list the home directory as usual in the NetInfo Manager. Then in the `ftpaccess` file, list the guest user's root directory with the `guest-root` control. With this method, the user's directory in the NetInfo database looks like the notation for any real user's home directory, as we see for guest user `ralph` in Figure 25.4.

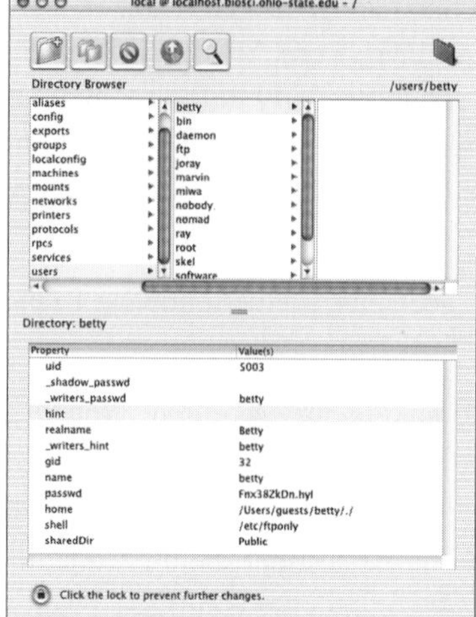

FIGURE 25.3
Here are the parameters we used for our guest user `betty`*. Her home directory is listed in the traditional notation for a guest user, which includes a* **.** *to indicate the root directory the user will see when she FTPs.*

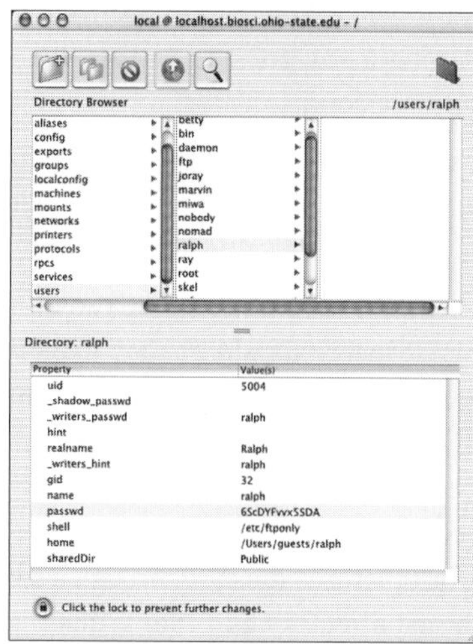

FIGURE 25.4
The home directory for this guest user is indicated in the regular fashion. The root directory for FTP for this guest user is indicated instead using the guest-root control in the `ftpaccess` *file.*

The entry for the guest user's root directory in `ftpaccess` looks like this:

```
guest-root /Users/guests/ralph
```

5. Include the shell that you use for the guest in `/etc/shells`. You might want the contents of your fake guest user shell to be something like this:

```
#! /bin/sh
exit 1
```

6. Update the ownership information of the guest user's account to include the guest group GID that is indicated in the NetInfo database.
7. Copy the same system files that are used for the anonymous FTP user to the guest user's account. Specifically, make sure the system's

```
/bin/ls
/usr/lib/dylib
/usr/lib/libSystem.B.dylib
/System/Library/Frameworks/System.framework/Versions/B/System
```

are included in the guest user's home directory in `~/bin`, `~/usr/lib` and `~/System/Library/Frameworks/System.framework/Versions/B` with the same permissions and ownerships that are used for an anonymous FTP account.

If you create a skeleton guest user account, these are files that would be useful to include in the skeleton guest user account.

Alternatives to FTP

As we have mentioned, turning on the FTP server makes your machine more vulnerable to attacks from the outside. There are other, more secure options you could consider using as alternatives to FTP.

scp and sftp

If you turn on the SSH server, two alternatives become available. You could transfer files either with secure copy (`scp`) or secure FTP (`sftp`). Transfers made using `scp` or `sftp` are encrypted, thereby providing an extra level of security. With FTP, passwords are transmitted in clear text, adding yet another vulnerability to FTP itself.

With the SSH server turned on, you will be able to transfer files to other machines running SSH servers. Likewise, those machines will be able to transfer files to your machine using `scp` or `sftp`. In addition, there is a freely available Mac OS client that has built-in `scp` capabilities. For PCs, there is a client which has a built-in `sftp` client. Running SSH removes almost any need for an FTP server. We will discuss SSH in detail in Chapter 26, "Remote Administration."

FTP and SSH

As you might recall, the wu-ftpd can be built as an anonymous-only FTP server. If your real users are transferring files via scp or sftp, but you still have a need to distribute files to anonymous users, you might then consider compiling an anonymous-only FTP server and running that alongside your SSH server.

Regularly checking the anonymous FTP area for any irregularities and keeping your wu-ftpd current are still important activities to do.

Tunneling FTP over SSH

If, for whatever reason, running the SSH server is not sufficient to meet your users' needs, you could further exploit wu-ftpd's configurability by creating a real users–only FTP server, using the --disable-anonymous compile-time option. In addition, you will probably need the --disable-pasvip option to get the tunneling to function properly. Then you could have your users tunnel their FTP connections to the FTP server via SSH. In the next chapter, we will discuss in detail how to set up a client to tunnel an FTP connection.

To make tunneling work on the server side, you have to wrap the FTP server to accept connections only from itself. The easiest way to set up the restriction is to make use of the TCP Wrappers program that comes with the OS X distribution.

In a FreeBSD-style /etc/hosts file, you would do this with this syntax:

```
in.ftpd: <machine-IP> 127.0.0.1 localhost: allow
in.ftpd: deny
```

If you also need to have an anonymous FTP server running, you could build one anonymous-only FTP server running on the standard FTP ports (21 for ftp, 20 for ftp-data). As you have seen, you don't need to edit anything anywhere to run an FTP server on the standard ports. Then you could build a real users-only FTP server and run it on an alternative set of ports. For ease of administration, it is a good idea to have each FTP server installed in a distinctly separate location. For example, you could install your anonymous FTP server in /usr/local/ftp and your real users FTP server in /usr/local/wuftp. Pick a close set of unused port numbers. Edit the services directory of the NetInfo database to include the alternative services. You could call them something like wuftp and wuftp-data. Whichever port number you assign to the wuftp service is the one that the client would tunnel. Name the alternative FTP server itself something similar to the service name, such as wuftpd. It will automatically be installed as in.ftpd in whatever location you specify, but you can rename that file. Then wrap the alternative FTP server to only itself, but allow the anonymous FTP server access to all machines.

If you also decide to run OS X's built-in firewall, `ipfw`, you will have to add statements to allow `ipfw` to grant access to the alternative FTP server. In addition, set the `passive ports` control to the `ftpaccess` file to a range of ports, such as 15001–19999. Then add a statement to the rules for `ipfw` to allow access to whatever range of ports you specfied with `passive ports`. You might find that you have to keep tweaking your `ipfw`, and anonymous and real FTP configurations, until everything works in harmony. Be sure to check your logs as you are doing this. They are more informative than you might realize now.

Don't worry if the wrapping concept or `ipfw` seems confusing right now. Use of TCP Wrappers and `ipfw` is discussed in Chapter 31. These details are mentioned here so that you can quickly find a summary of the important information about running two FTP servers in one place. Shortly, `scp` and `sftp` should suit most of your needs. We recommend that, where possible, you use `scp` and `sftp` instead of running an FTP server.

If you decide to run the types of FTP servers suggested in this section, you might find that guest accounts do not work.

Summary

In this chapter, you learned how to do a variety of tasks involving FTP. First, you learned how to turn on the default FTP server and restrict access to it. Then you learned how to set up an anonymous FTP area that would work with the default FTP server or a third-party FTP server. In addition, you learned how to replace the default `ftpd` with a highly configurable FTP server, `wu-ftpd`. You learned that `wu-ftpd` comes with many compile-time and run-time options, as well as additional controls when using the `ftpaccess` file. You saw how typical entries in the `xferlog` file appear for real, guest, and anonymous users. You learned how to create a guest user to access `wu-ftpd`. You also learned about some alternatives to running an FTP server. You learned that, if you have a need to transfer files between machines running SSH, that `scp` and `sftp` are more secure alternatives. You also learned that you could potentially tunnel your FTP connection over SSH, making accessing your FTP server more secure. With `wu-ftpd`, you learned that you could consider running both an anonymous-only FTP server and a real-users-only FTP server.

You might have found some parts of the chapter confusing. However, as your needs evolve, so will your understanding. You can always return to this chapter to get a start on customizing your FTP needs.

CHAPTER 26

Remote Access and Administration

In This Chapter

Apple advertises that with OS X, you now have the power of Unix. With the power of Unix also come some unfamiliar security issues. Many Unix machines run various types of services, such as telnet, which increase your machine's vulnerability to attacks from crackers. In general, crackers are interested in either wiping your machine or installing a packet sniffer that saves passwords transmitted on your network for future devious uses. To keep your machine most secure, you should not hook it up to the Internet. Given that that solution is rather impractical in an age in which Internet communication is one of the many reasons why people buy computers, it becomes your responsibility to pay attention to security issues, if not for yourself, for the other machines on your network.

Fortunately, Apple realizes that Macintosh users are not used to worrying about security issues. In fact, Macintosh users have always had the luxury of knowing that their Macintosh is practically impenetrable. So, unlike some Unix operating systems, OS X ships with all the services turned off. You have to decide, as you start using your machine more, which services, if any, you should try to turn on. Remember that the more services you turn on, the more vulnerable your machine becomes.

Security-Minded Thinking

Although Chapter 31, "Server Security and Advanced Network Configuration," goes into security details in considerably more depth, it's a good idea to start thinking about security issues now. In this chapter, you're going to configure your machine so that you can connect to it from other machines. If you can connect to it, so can anyone else, and it's time to start thinking about security. Here are some common sense guidelines that you can use when thinking about your machine's security:

- Regularly apply updates to the operating system. It is common for the Unix vendors to fix security problems and make the fixes available as downloadable updates, usually called *patches*.
- Do not turn on any unnecessary services. If you don't know what the service is, you probably don't need it.
- Do not turn on the `telnet` service. `telnet` transmits passwords in clear text. That is exactly what some of the crackers are looking for.
- Restrict as many of the TCP-based services as possible with `tcpwrappers`. OS X already comes with `tcpwrappers` installed, and is configured to assume that you will use `tcpwrappers`. Using `tcpwrappers` allows you to control access to some services. You can, for example, restrict access to the `ftp` service by using `tcpwrappers`.
- Use secure shell (SSH) for remote logins to your machine.

It is the last item, secure shell, that we will discuss in depth in this chapter. You were first introduced to the secure shell software, via `slogin`, in Chapter 13, "Common Unix Shell Commands: File Operators." In that chapter, you learned how to use `slogin` on your Mac OS X box to connect to outside machines. Now that you're more familiar with the Unix side of your operating system, we'll discuss it in a bit more depth, and also explain how to start it as a service so that you can connect from remote back to your OS X machine. Then we will discuss how to use clients in Mac OS 9.1 and earlier to remotely access your OS X machine.

What Is Secure Shell?

Secure shell is a common term used to describe a secure remote login protocol. Anyone using the term *secure shell* is also referring to the SSH protocol. In particular, the SSH protocol encrypts traffic and permits tunneling; that is, port forwarding over a secure channel.

There are two SSH protocols: SSH1 and SSH2. As you might have guessed, SSH1 is the original protocol, and SSH2 is a later development. Currently, SSH2 is the protocol under development. Where possible, use the SSH2 protocol rather than the SSH1 protocol. However, there are still Unix machines out there running only SSH1 servers. Consequently, we will discuss using both protocols. In most areas, the usage is similar.

The SSH protocol was originally developed by Tatu Ylonen, the chairman of SSH Communications Security, Ltd. The product was further developed by SSH Communications Security and F-Secure Corporation (formerly Data Fellows). Both companies still work on the protocol. F-Secure has marketing rights and rights to further modify the code. The SSH2 servers from these companies are similar.

There is also an SSH open source project called OpenSSH. It is also based on Tatu Ylonen's SSH. OpenSSH provides support for both SSH1 and SSH2 protocols. There is little noticeable difference in using one of the SSH servers from one of the companies and the OpenSSH package.

Because you now have the power of Unix, our examination of SSH will include not only what you need to know to connect to your OS X machine, but also what you need to know to connect to other Unix boxes that might be running the other SSH packages. As security concerns grow throughout the Internet community, using secure shell as a `telnet` replacement is becoming more common. Consequently, it is worthwhile to learn general basic SSH usage.

Starting SSH in OS X

If you are running the first non-public beta release of OS X, SSH is not included. Run Software Update, which is located in System Preferences, to get the update (patch) that includes SSH. The first official release that contains SSH is OS X 10.0.1. Software Update places your SSH server, `sshd`, in `/usr/sbin` and your SSH tools in `/usr/bin`.

After you have SSH installed, you are ready to turn on your SSH service. Just go to the Sharing pane in System Preferences and check the Allow Remote Login option, as shown in Figure 26.1. The first time you do this, you might experience a delay.

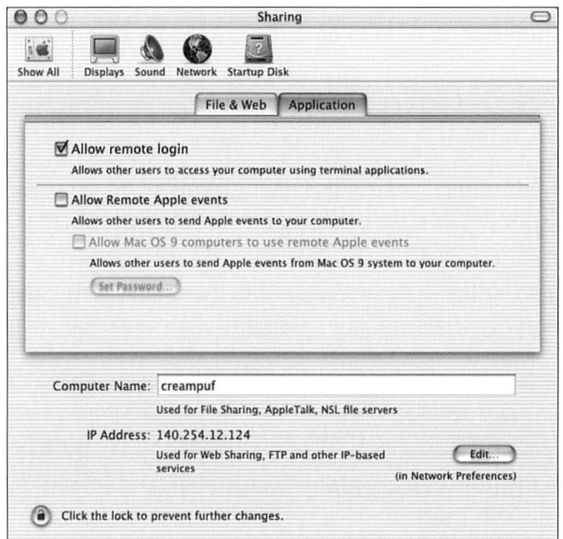

FIGURE 26.1
Check the Allow Remote Login box in the Sharing pane to start the SSH service.

One of the main activities that checking this box performs is updating your `/etc/hostconfig` file, shown following this paragraph, to indicate that the SSH service should be turned on. Note that `SSHSERVER` is set to `YES`. If you were to turn off the service, this would revert to `NO`. Because this file has the comment that it is maintained by the system control panels, it might not be wise to edit this file directly yourself. However, it is interesting to be able to occasionally see some of what the operating system is doing for you behind the scenes.

```
##
# /etc/hostconfig
##
# This file is maintained by the system control panels
##
```

```
# Network configuration
HOSTNAME=-AUTOMATIC-
ROUTER=-AUTOMATIC-

# Services
AFPSERVER=-YES-
APPLETALK=en0
AUTHSERVER=-NO-
AUTOCONFIG=-YES-
AUTODISKMOUNT=-REMOVABLE-
AUTOMOUNT=-YES-
CONFIGSERVER=-NO-
IPFORWARDING=-NO-
MAILSERVER=-NO-
MANAGEMENTSERVER=-NO-
NETBOOTSERVER=-NO-
NISDOMAIN=-NO-
TIMESYNC=-YES-
QTSSERVER=-NO-
SSHSERVER=-YES-
WEBSERVER=-NO-
APPLETALK_HOSTNAME=creampuf
```

If you check your process listing for ssh, you will now see an sshd process:

```
[localhost:~] joray% ps aux | grep ssh
      root    614   0.0  0.0     1476    340  ??  Ss       0:00.50 /usr/sbin/sshd
      joray   676   0.0  0.0     1384    300 std  S+       0:00.01 grep ssh
```

For the 10.1 update, what you have just turned on is the open source package SSH package, OpenSSH –2.9p2. It is SSH1- and SSH2-capable. Because it supports both protocols, a connection from either type of SSH client works.

Using SSH: From Unix Box to Unix Box

SSH provides for secure encrypted traffic transmission across a network. Most SSH software, including that provided by Apple, includes both the encrypted transmission facility and rudimentary tools for making use of that functionality. These tools include the ability to use the encryption to provide secure terminal services and file transfer support. Other functionality can be added as needed by the user, by making use of just the secure transport portion of the software to encrypt the traffic between otherwise insecure external software packages.

Terminal-to-Terminal Connections

With SSH installed on your machine, you are now ready to connect to remote machines running secure shell.

To connect to another machine, use either `ssh` or `slogin`. The command you will most often use is

```
ssh [-2] <hostname>
```

Sometimes you might have to log in to a remote machine as a user other than as the user you are known as on the local machine. The `-2` option forces the use of the SSH2 protocol. For example, a user might have an account named `jray` on one machine, and an account named `rayj` on another. The syntax to use to log in as another user on a remote machine is

```
ssh [-2] [-l <login_name>] [<hostname> | <user>@<hostname>]
```

If you are accustomed to using `telnet`, these are the commands that you will now use instead of `telnet`. If you are used to using `rlogin`, you might find `slogin` to be the more natural alternative. To quickly test that `sshd` works on your machine, it is easiest to login to your own machine, as shown here:

```
[localhost:~] joray% ssh ryoohki

     The authenticity of host 'ryoohki' can't be established.
     RSA key fingerprint is 29:1f:f6:25:1c:17:41:50:2e:43:d9:d5:1b:ca:3d:6b.
     Are you sure you want to continue connecting (yes/no)? yes
     Warning: Permanently added 'ryoohki,140.254.12.124' (RSA) to the list of
     known hosts.
     joray@ryoohki's password:
     Welcome to Darwin!

[localhost:~] joray% exit

     logout
     Connection to ryoohki closed.
```

Note that the first time you try an `ssh` action to a remote host, you are told that the remote machine's identity can't be verified and you are asked whether it should be trusted. The precise message varies with the version of SSH.

Transferring Files

To transfer files between machines, there are a couple of options: secure copy (`scp`) and secure FTP (`sftp`). The version of OpenSSH that comes with the 10.0.1 update does not include an `sftp` client. In earlier versions of OSX, `scp` is your only option. In later versions, both `scp` and `sftp` are available. The basic form of the scp command is

```
scp [<user@>]<host1>] <file1> [[<user@>]<host2>:]<file2>
```

Here's an example of using the `scp` command to copy a file on an OS X machine to a remote machine:

```
[localhost:~] joray% scp developer-1.tiff rosalyn.biosci.ohio-state.edu:
    The authenticity of host 'rosalyn.biosci.ohio-state.edu'
    ➥can't be established.
    RSA key fingerprint is 49:97:6b:54:18:40:0b:d3:17:25:fd:03:37:b2:09:68.
    Are you sure you want to continue connecting (yes/no)? yes
    Warning: Permanently added 'rosalyn.biosci.ohio-state.edu'
    ➥(RSA) to the list of known hosts.
    joray@rosalyn.biosci.ohio-state.edu's password:
    warning: Executing scp1 compatibility.
    developer-1.tiff
    ➥100% |**********************************************| 1225 KB    00:04
```

Note that the remote host, `rosalyn`, gives a warning about invoking `scp1` for compatibility. Although this version of the OpenSSH `sshd` is SSH1- and SSH2-compatible, the version of `scp` included appears to be an SSH1 version. This might mean that you might not be able to successfully run `scp` to a remote host running an SSH2-only server, rather than the hybrid-style that OpenSSH appears to be. This is not a problem with remote host `rosalyn` because `rosalyn` is running both SSH2 and SSH1 servers.

To verify that the file has indeed been copied to the remote machine, let's log in and check:

```
[localhost:~] joray% slogin rosalyn.biosci.ohio-state.edu
    joray@rosalyn.biosci.ohio-state.edu's password:
    Last login: Mon Apr 16 21:49:23 2001 from dhcp9574211.colu
    You have new mail.
    You have mail.
    /home/joray

    ...Remote login...

    /home/joray
Rosalyn joray 201 > ls -l developer*
    -rw-r--r--   1 joray    user     1255376 Apr 18 16:24 developer-1.tiff
```

In addition, some of the remote hosts might also have an SSH2 version of `scp`. For these remote machines to use their `sftp` or SSH2 version of `scp` to transfer files to your machine, you have to turn on the `sftp` subsystem of your `sshd`.

To turn on your `sftp` subsystem, use your favorite text editor to edit the `/etc/sshd_config` file. Even if you are not interested in providing this extra compatibility at this time, you might want to glance at the `/etc/sshd_config` file to see what configuration options are currently in place. If you are using an editor such as `vi`, which does not make a backup copy of your file, you should make a copy of the file before you do any editing. By default, the line that turns on the `sftp` subsystem is commented out. To activate the subsystem, uncomment it. After you have uncommented the `sftp` subsystem line, the `sftp` related lines in `/etc/sshd_config` should look like this:

```
# Uncomment if you want to enable sftp
Subsystem       sftp    /usr/libexec/sftp-server
```

Next, tell `sshd` to reread its configuration file. This is done by sending a hangup signal to the process:

```
[localhost:/Users/joray] root# ps aux | grep sshd

     root     298   0.0  0.0     1476    324  ??  Ss      0:03.26 /usr/sbin/sshd
     root    1743   0.0  0.0     1084    188 std  R+      0:00.00 grep sshd

[localhost:/Users/joray] root# kill -HUP 298
```

In `/var/log/system.log`, you can see the system's response to your signal:

```
Apr 19 09:36:37 localhost sshd[298]: Received SIGHUP; restarting.
```

If you check the process listing again, you will also notice that the process ID has changed; in this case, from `298` as it was earlier to `1764`:

```
[localhost:~] joray% ps aux | grep sshd

     root    1764   0.0  0.0     1476    308  ??  Ss      0:00.58 /usr/sbin/sshd
     joray   1924   0.0  0.0     5708      0 std  R       0:00.00 grep sshd
```

If you feel uncomfortable with sending the hangup signal, or if the system does not seem to have paid attention to the hangup signal, you can always reboot.

The message that `sshd` logs to `/var/log/system.log` stating that it is restarting is the only obvious sign you will see that anything has changed. You will not see any obvious `sftp` processes until there is a connection request for the `sftp` subsystem. When there is an `sftp` connection in progress, here is what the process listing will look like:

```
[localhost:~] joray% ps -aux | grep ftp

     joray   1389   0.0  0.0     1324    344  ??  S       0:00.03
     /usr/libexec/sftp-ser
     joray   1391   0.0  0.0     5708      0 std  T       0:00.00 grep ftp
```

The version of the OpenSSH package that is provided in the 10.0.1 update is not the latest version of OpenSSH. Perhaps a later update will also include an `sftp` client.

Using an SSH2 Client in Mac OS

The SSH2 client we will use is F-Secure SSH 2.1. Although there is at least one freely available SSH2 client for the Macintosh, we choose to demonstrate the basic concepts with a product developed by one of the companies originally involved in creating the SSH protocol.

Install F-Secure SSH 2.1 as you would any other Macintosh software. It installs in a folder called `F-Secure SSH` in whatever location you specify.

The client can be used to make terminal connections and to forward arbitrary TCP connections. Because FTP and e-mail are the most popular kinds of TCP connections to tunnel, we will demonstrate setting up those tunnels. F-Secure SSH also has a Connection Manager feature to manage your connections. We will finish by taking a brief look at the Connection Manager.

Setting Up a Terminal

To set up a terminal, do the following:

1. Start F-Secure SSH 2.1. The Connection Manager will probably appear.
2. Click on the terminal window icon in the Connection Manager (the second icon) or choose New Terminal from the File menu. A Properties dialog box appears with Connect highlighted. Note that in the top left of the window the term *Terminal* appears.
3. Enter the remote machine as the SSH server.

   The default server port is `22`. There is no need to change this unless you have been informed that the SSSH2 server is running on a different port.
4. Enter your username and password, as shown in Figure 26.2; then click Connect.
5. The first time you connect to an unknown host, you are asked whether you should accept the host key for the unknown host. If you plan to connect regularly to the remote host, click Accept & Store in the message box shown in Figure 26.3.

Assuming that you have entered your username and password correctly, you should be logged in to the remote host.

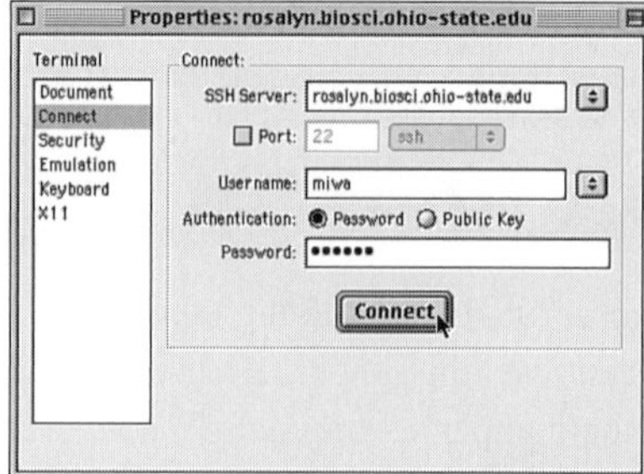

FIGURE 26.2
Fill in the connection parameters in the Connect section of the Properties dialog box.

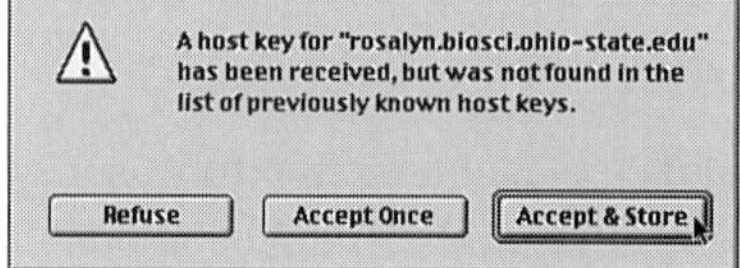

FIGURE 26.3
Click Accept & Store to store the remote host's host key.

Note that the status connection of the terminal appears in the bottom left of the terminal window. In Figure 26.4, the status is SSH Shell Connected. When you have logged out, the status changes to Disconnected.

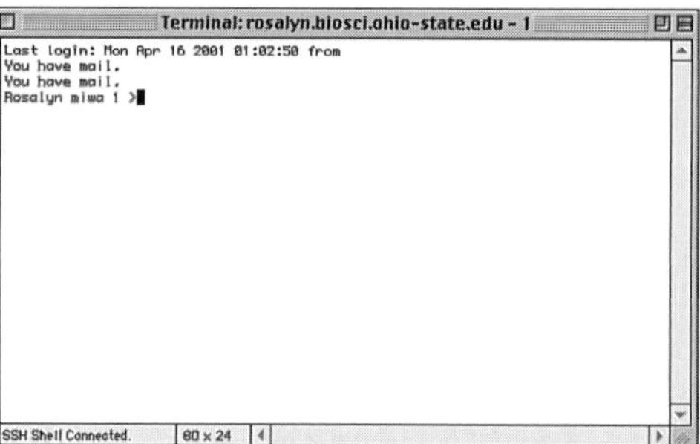

FIGURE 26.4
Connected terminal window.

If you plan to connect to the remote host regularly, you might want to choose Save under the File menu and then save the connection as an alias to your desktop.

There are various ways to end your terminal connection. You can type `exit` at the command line. You can also select the terminal connection in the Connection Manager, and then click on the Disconnect button. You will likely find that the connection to the remote host times out after some period of time. Of course, you can quit the F-Secure program. If you have a connection in progress, it will, of course, ask whether you really want to close the connection.

Setting Up an FTP Tunnel

As shown in the section detailing the use of SSH from the command line in Chapter 15, the SSH tools can also be used to secure other network protocols, such as FTP, by tunneling their connections through an SSH-encrypted network connection.

To set up an FTP tunnel, perform the following steps:

1. Click on the FTP icon in the Connection Manager, or select FTP Tunnel in the Tunnel list under the File menu.

   A Properties box appears, with Connect highlighted. Note that in the top left of the window, the description *FTP Tunnel* appears.

2. Name your tunnel by first clicking Document in the FTP Tunnel menu, and then add a tunnel name in the Name box. Next, check the Auto-Connect on Open box. Note that there is an Auto-launch on Connect feature, as shown in Figure 26.5. With this feature enabled, you can set F-Secure to automatically open another application upon connection.

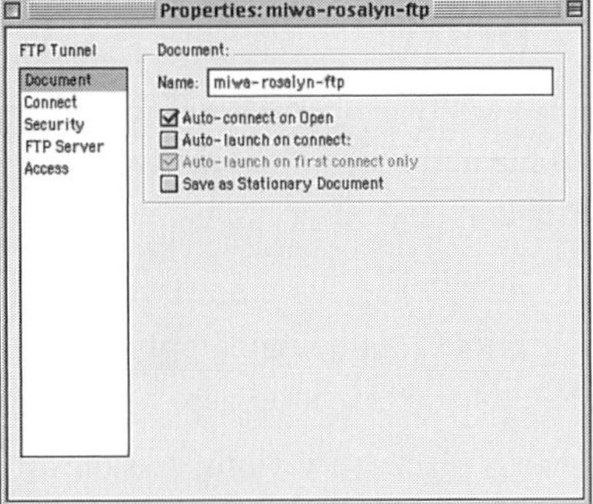

FIGURE 26.5
You can set a name for your FTP tunnel in the Document section of the Properties box. You can also do this for a terminal connection.

3. Next, select FTP Server in the FTP Tunnel menu, as shown in Figure 26.6. It is all right to click in the FTP Server Port boxes, even if you are using the default `21` port. SSH Server comes selected as the default item. If you do not do anything with this section, the client will assume port `21` for the local and remote ports and that the SSH server is the remote server.

   If you will be accessing a machine that might be running an FTP server on an alternate port, be sure to change the port number appropriately. If you should ever have to do that, you will lose the `ftp` descriptor, but the tunnel will still work.

4. Select Connect in the left menu, and enter the remote machine as the SSH server.

FIGURE 26.6
FTP server settings are set in the FTP Server section of the Properties box.

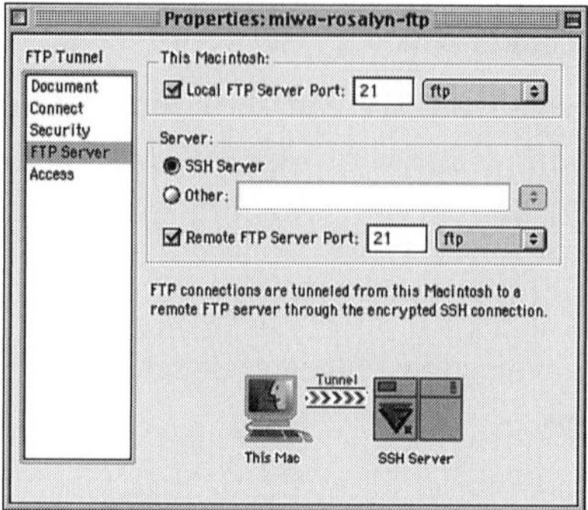

5. Next, enter your username and password; then click Connect. Note that the Properties window now says Connected at the bottom left, and that the Connection Manager shows an FTP connection.
6. Under the File menu, choose Save. For your convenience, also save this alias directly to your desktop.

Setting Up the FTP Client

After your FTP tunnel is set up, you are ready to set up the FTP client. Although we have only done our testing with Anarchie and Fetch, the basic concepts shown here should prepare you to use other FTP clients, too.

1. If you are using Anarchie as your FTP client, you need to set it to use Passive Transfer (PASV) mode for connections. Although simply stated, this can sometimes be the most complicated step in setting it up.

   This setting can be found in various places in various versions of Anarchie, most notably in the Internet or Internet Config control panel. Some menu paths to follow to get Anarchie to launch Internet/Internet Config include:

   - Settings - Preferences—Automatically launches Internet/Internet Config
   - Settings - Preferences—Edits Internet Config
   - Edit - Firewalls—Automatically launches Internet/Internet Config
   - Edit - Preferences—Launches Internet Config

2. The Internet control panel will bring up a set of tabs. If Advanced is not one of them, select User Mode under the Edit menu, and set it to Advanced. An Advanced tab should appear directly. Click on File Transfer, if it is not already selected, and then check the Use FTP Passive (PASV) box. Figure 26.7 shows the advanced settings.

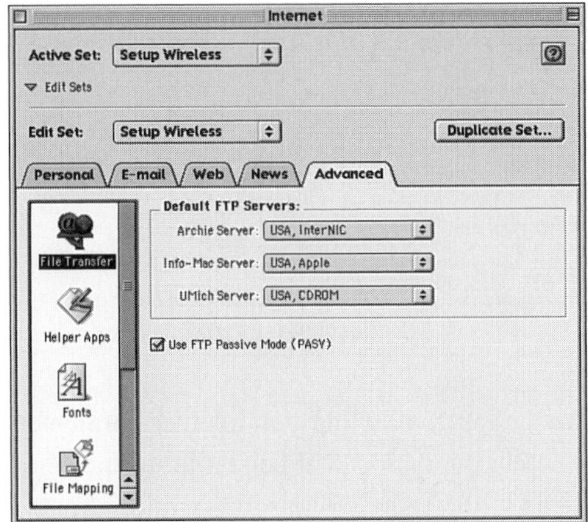

FIGURE 26.7
Set PASV mode in the Internet control panel by checking the Use FTP Passive Mode (PASV) box on the Advanced tab.

3. Alternatively, your system might be using the Internet Config control panel, instead of the Internet control panel. To configure PASV mode with this control panel, select the Firewalls option in the Internet Config control panel, as shown in Figure 26.8, and then check the Use FTP Passive (PASV) box.

   In older versions, PASV is an option in Firewalls, under the Edit menu.

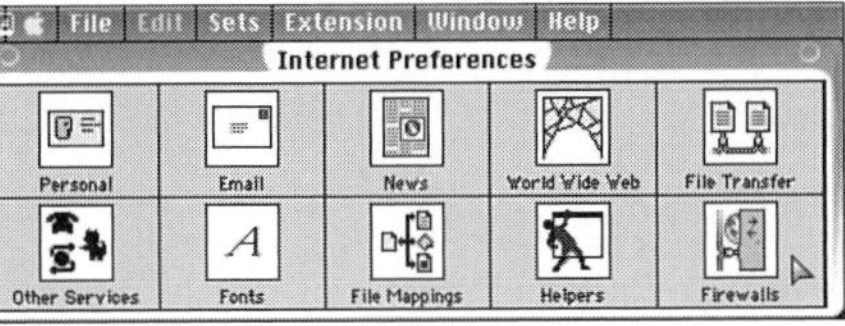

FIGURE 26.8
The Internet Config control panel has a Firewalls option, where PASV mode can be set.

4. If you are using Fetch as your FTP client, you can set Fetch to FTP using PASV mode, by selecting Preferences in the Customize menu.
5. Click the Firewall tab in the Preferences dialog box, as shown in Figure 26.9. Check the Use Passive Mode Transfers (PASV) box and then click OK.
6. After you have your FTP client configured, which should need to be done only once for each client, you are ready to initiate a connection. In Anarchie, either select FTP under the FTP menu or select Get via FTP under the File menu. In older versions of Anarchie, select Get under the FTP menu. In Fetch, select New Connection under the File menu.

FIGURE 26.9

Set PASV mode in Fetch at the Firewall tab in Preferences under the Customize menu.

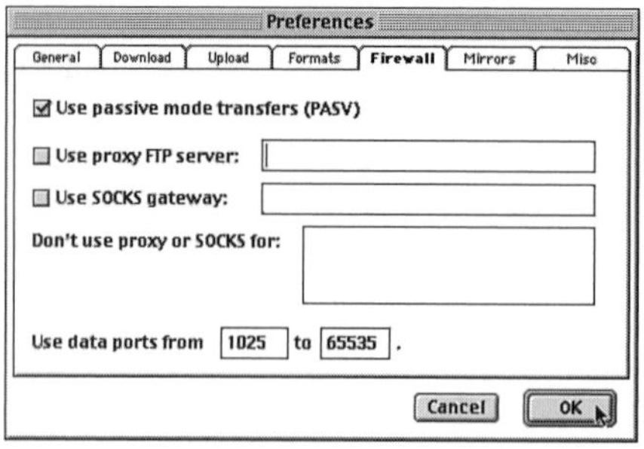

7. A connection dialog will appear, allowing you to enter parameters for the connection. If you are using Fetch, the dialog will be similar to that shown in Figure 26.10—other FTP clients will require similar information. Enter `localhost` or `127.0.0.1` as Server/Host; then enter a path/directory, if you know what directory you are looking for. Entering `127.0.0.1` should always work, but whether `localhost` is acceptable will vary with the setup of your machine and network.
8. Enter your username and password; then click OK or List, as appropriate.

FIGURE 26.10

Initiating a connection in Fetch to a remote host via an FTP tunnel in the SSH client.

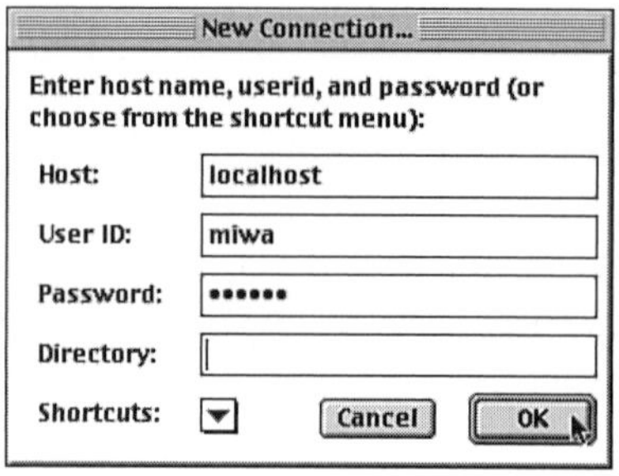

You should see a listing of your home directory. If you encounter a host error, try entering the alternative host suggestion from the previous step. If you were watching the FTP tunnel in the Connection Manager before the connection was made you saw that the data in/out transfer indicator was 0/0, indicating that the tunnel was not being accessed. Now that you have a connection, the data in/out indicator has changed. In Figure 26.11, that number changed from 0/0 to 52/1905.

9. Choose File, Save Bookmark. If Anarchie asks about your password, select Ask Later. Save the alias to the desktop for your convenience.

To briefly summarize the FTP process, whenever you want to FTP, first open an FTP tunnel connection to the FTP server in the F-Secure SSH client. Then make a connection to `localhost` in the FTP client. The connection will be tunneled from one server, the Mac OS machine, to the other server, the remote FTP server, as you have specified in the F-Secure client.

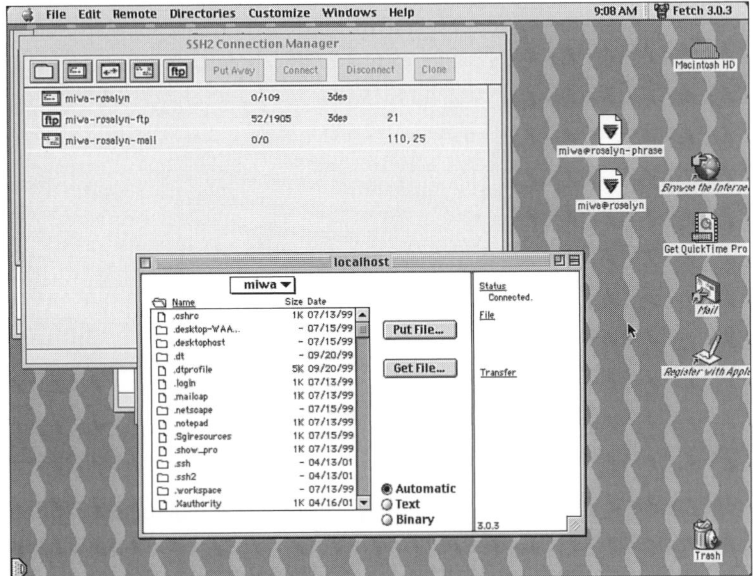

FIGURE 26.11
A connection to a remote host using Fetch via an FTP tunnel in the SSH client.

Note

If you try your Fetch bookmark later (after connecting to the remote host in the F-Secure client, of course), and you get strange behavior, such as Fetch unsuccessfully attempting to download whatever the first file in your account is, throw away this Fetch bookmark and create another one.

Setting Up an E-Mail Tunnel

Another type of tunnel that you might want to make is a tunnel for your POP/IMAP account. Making a mail tunnel is much like making an FTP tunnel. Follow these steps:

1. In the F-Secure Connection Manager, click the e-mail icon (fourth icon) or select E-Mail Tunnel from the Tunnel list under the File menu.

   A Properties box appears with Connect highlighted. Note that in the top left of the window the description *E-Mail Tunnel* appears.

2. To name your tunnel, click Document in the menu at the left of the dialog box, and then provide a tunnel name in the Name text box. Check the Auto-connect on Open box. As with the FTP tunnel, the e-mail tunnel also has an Auto-launch on Connect feature, if you are interested in using it.
3. Click Services in the left-side menu to display the services dialog shown in Figure 26.12. If you will be accessing a POP account, deselect the IMAP tunnel service. If you will be accessing an IMAP account, deselect the POP tunnel service.

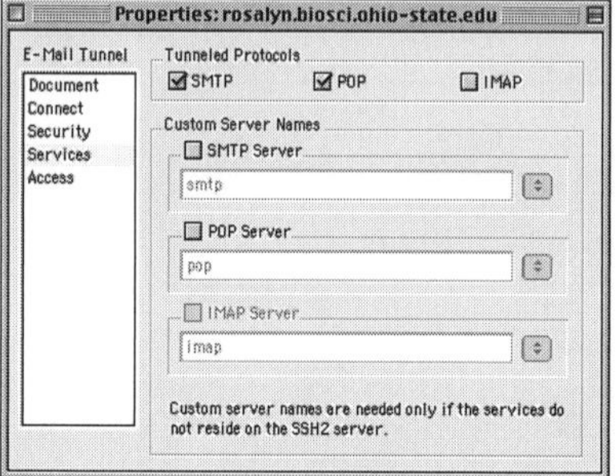

FIGURE 26.12
The Services section of the Properties box is where you specify what e-mail services are to be tunneled.

The Services section of the Properties box also includes a section to enter server names. These need to be filled out only if the e-mail services are on a host other than the server to which you are connecting. When in doubt, provide the complete information, even if the e-mail services are on the host to which you are connecting.

4. Select Connect in the left menu and then enter the remote machine as the SSH server.
5. Enter your username and password; then click Connect.

   Note that the Properties window now says Connected at the bottom left, and that the Connection Manager shows an e-mail connection.
6. Choose File, Save to save the connection properties for your e-mail tunnel. For your convenience, you might also want to make an alias from the saved file directly to your desktop.

Setting Up an E-mail Client

You will have to experiment with e-mail clients and some settings to see what ultimately works for you. Setting up Claris Emailer works for reading POPmail via an e-mail tunnel in SSH. However, Claris Emailer is no longer supported, so we cannot recommend it. The most important setting where you might see some variation is for your e-mail account. What account you list for your email client to check can vary, depending on the sendmail settings of the mail server. Expect either *<username>*@localhost or *<username>*@*<your-local-mac's-fully-qualified-domain-name>*. You might have to talk with the mail server's administrator to tweak that setting. However, to give you visual examples of the most likely ways to enter your account information to successfully read your e-mail through an e-mail tunnel, check out the following figures. In Figure 26.13, the e-mail account to be checked in the e-mail reader is in the form *<username>*@localhost. Sendmail on the mail server is likely configured to accept mail from machines without a fully qualified domain name (FQDN).

FIGURE 26.13
The e-mail connection dialog for Claris Emailer, with representative tunnel settings for a mail server configured to accept mail from machines not using an FQDN.

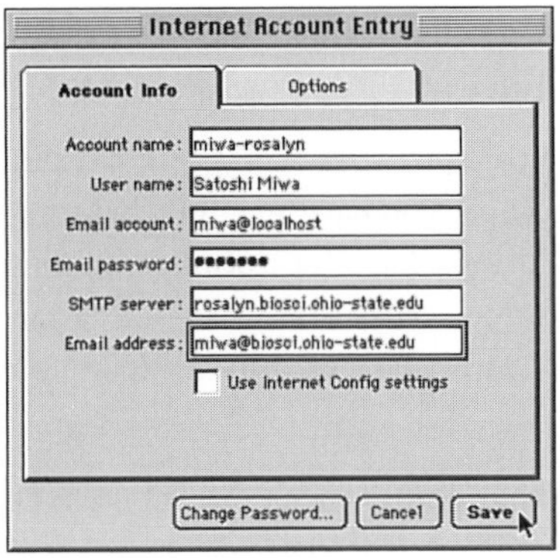

Internet Account Entry
Account Info | Options
Account name: miwa-rosalyn
User name: Satoshi Miwa
Email account: miwa@localhost
Email password: •••••••
SMTP server: rosalyn.biosci.ohio-state.edu
Email address: miwa@biosci.ohio-state.edu
Use Internet Config settings
Change Password... | Cancel | Save

In Figure 26.14, the e-mail account to be checked in the e-mail reader is of the form *<username>*@*<mac's FQDN>*. Sendmail on the mail server is likely configured to accept mail only from machines with an FQDN.

FIGURE 26.14
The e-mail connection dialog for Claris Emailer, with representative tunnel settings for a mail server configured to require an FQDN.

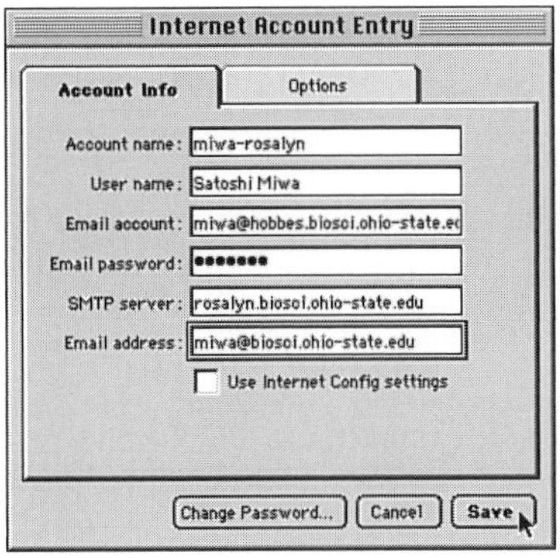

Internet Account Entry
Account Info | Options
Account name: miwa-rosalyn
User name: Satoshi Miwa
Email account: miwa@hobbes.biosci.ohio-state.e
Email password: •••••••
SMTP server: rosalyn.biosci.ohio-state.edu
Email address: miwa@biosci.ohio-state.edu
Use Internet Config settings
Change Password... | Cancel | Save

Setting Up Other Tunnels

F-Secure SSH 2.1 also allows you forward arbitrary TCP services, for which prelabeled services might not already be listed in the TCP Tunnel Properties box. If you need to tunnel other TCP services, tunnel them using the TCP Tunnel type, which is the third icon in the Connection Manager, or the TCP Tunnel in the Tunnels section under the File menu.

For example, if you typically accessed a program on a remote host by a special `telnet` client (one that did something more special than show you a command-line prompt; otherwise, the SSH terminal is a perfectly sufficient alternative), you could forward the `telnet` connection through an arbitrary TCP Tunnel in the SSH client. As with FTP clients, the remote host you would list in the `telnet` client would be `localhost`.

In addition to arbitrary TCP tunnels, you can also tunnel X11 connections. Even though OS X does not come with an X11 package, you have seen in Chapter 19 how to install one. After you have been using your X11 package for a while, you might find some applications that run on it that you want to access from your older Mac. The ability to tunnel X11 connections can also be of particular use with applications on other Unix machines.

If you discover a need for X11 tunneling, simply check the Tunnel X11 Connections box in the X11 section of the Properties box for a terminal connection, as shown in Figure 26.15. The option to specify eXodus (a commercial X Window System server for Mac OS and Windows) as the local X server is even available.

FIGURE 26.15
Enable X11 tunneling in the X11 section of the Properties box for terminal connection in the SSH client.

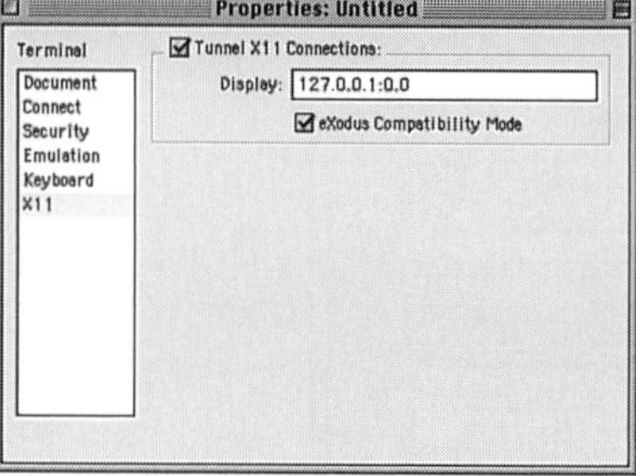

If you are tunneling an X11 connection to your remote OS X machine, edit the X11 forward line in `/etc/sshd_config` to

```
X11Forwarding yes
```

Because this would be making a change to the default configuration of `sshd`, you need to have `sshd` reread its configuration file, as was demonstrated in the earlier section on enabling the `sftp` server.

Managing Your Connections

So far in this section, we have been creating independent tunnels in F-Secure 2.1. Because our tunnels are independent, we can choose, for example, to use only the FTP tunnel without having to log in to the remote host. We have been saving our independent tunnels as separate aliases on the desktop. If you made at least a terminal alias and an FTP alias, you now have two aliases on your desktop. This might be precisely what you need, especially if you regularly plan to access the remote host with only one type of connection. However, if you expect to regularly use both types of connections to the host, you might be interested in grouping your independent tunnels together.

When you group a set of independent tunnels that you have already made, the group alias you save on the desktop replaces the aliases for the independent tunnels. When you use the group alias, you automatically make all the desired connections at once. If you decide to terminate all the connections at once, you can select the appropriate folder in the Connection Manager, and then select Disconnect. You still have the freedom to terminate any given connection without terminating the other connections in your group by selecting the appropriate connection in the Connection Manager, and then selecting Disconnect.

Although we tend to group our connections by host, you can also group connections to different hosts, if that is more suitable to your needs. For example, you might regularly use a terminal connection to one host, but the FTP server might be on another host. You can set up your individual connection types, group them together, and save that group as an alias on the desktop. When you connect using that alias, you are asked for both passwords right away.

If you are interested in organizing your connections into groups, do the following:

1. Click on the group icon (the first icon) in the Connection Manager, or select New Group under the file menu.
2. Double-click the folder that appears in the Connection Manager to display the Properties dialog box.
3. Fill in the Document section.
4. Click the Override Connection Parameters box in the Connect section, shown in Figure 26.16, to cause any connect and security parameters specified for the group to override specifications in the individual connections that belong to the group.

This might be particularly useful if all the connections in the group are to the same host. If you select the override option, fill in the appropriate host, username, and password information.

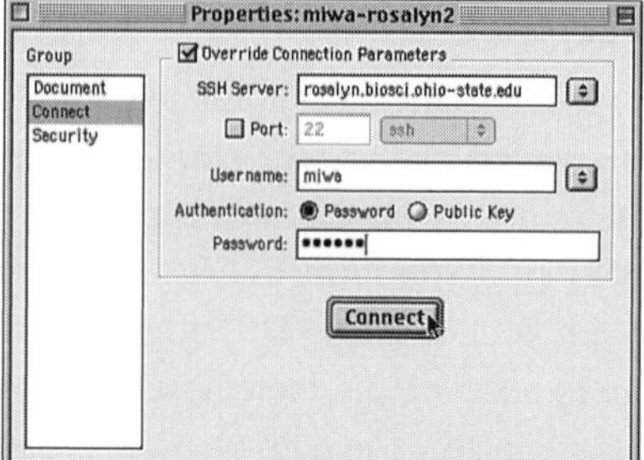

FIGURE 26.16
The Connect section of the Properties box for a new group.

5. In the Connection Manager, shown, in Figure 26.17, drag whichever connections you want to include in the group.

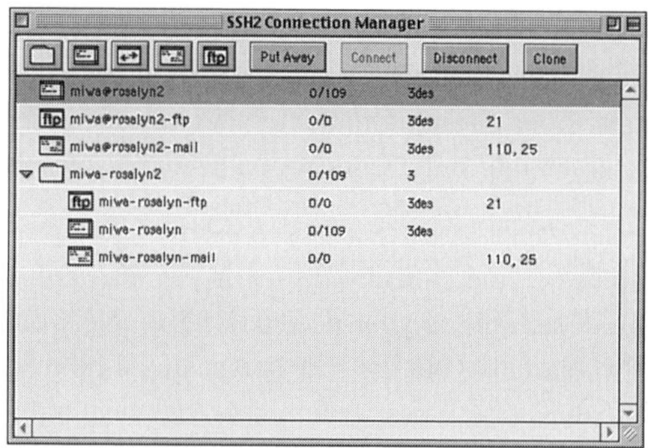

FIGURE 26.17
The Connection Manager with a set of independent connections as well as a set of grouped connections.

6. Save the group alias to your desktop. After you have quit the program, the desktop no longer has the independent aliases, but it does have the group alias.

Whether you make the tunnels first or the group first does not matter. In either case, you drag the appropriate connections to the appropriate group.

Using an SSH1 Client in Mac OS

The SSH1 client we will primarily use is F-Secure SSH 1.0.2. We again choose to demonstrate the basic concepts with a product developed by one of the companies originally involved in creating the SSH protocol.

Install F-Secure SSH 1.0.2 as you would any other Macintosh software. Like F-Secure SSH 2.1, it installs in a folder called F-Secure SSH in whatever location you specify. There is no reason not to store both in the same F-Secure SSH folder.

Like the SSH2 client, this client can also be used to make terminal connections and to tunnel arbitrary TCP connections. We will only demonstrate making an FTP tunnel in this section. From the user's perspective, the tunnel concepts are the same for both clients; only the interfaces differ.

From a technical perspective, the SSH1 client speaks to only machines that are running SSH1 servers. Because the OS X 10.0.1 update includes an OpenSSH package, which is SSH1- and SSH2-compatible, you do not specifically need an SSH1 package. However, if you have to connect to machines that are running only an SSH1 server, you might find an SSH1 client useful. Be sure to use F-Secure 1.0.2 rather than 1.0.1 because 1.0.2 includes some fixes that make it more compatible with more SSH1 servers.

On another note, even though OpenSSH is SSH1- and SSH2-compatible, we have seen some unusual characteristics to the package, specifically its SSH1-only implementation of `scp`. We do bring to your attention a freely available SSH1 client that you might find useful: Nifty Telnet SSH. Although Nifty Telnet SSH does not have any tunneling capabilities, it does have an `scp` feature, which the F-Secure 1.0.2 client does not include.

In this section, we will demonstrate the use of the terminal and tunnel features in the commercial package, F-Secure 1.0.2. However, we will also demonstrate the `scp` feature in the freely available package, Nifty Telnet.

Setting Up a Terminal

To set up a terminal, do the following:

1. Start F-Secure SSH 1.0.2, as shown in Figure 26.18. The first time you start the program, you will be asked to initialize the random number generator. Just move your cursor around in the window.

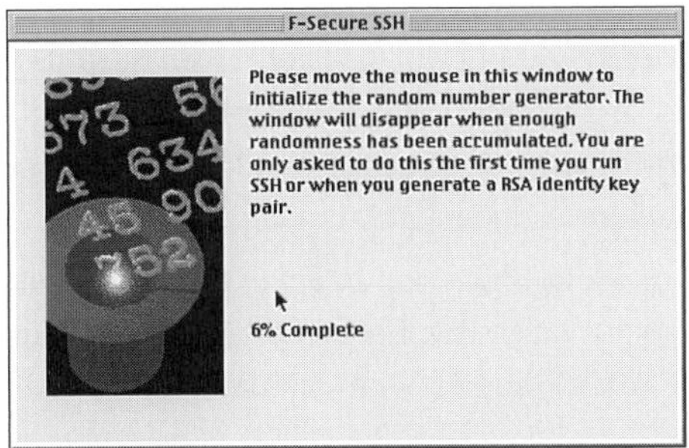

F-Secure SSH
Please move the mouse in this window to initialize the random number generator. The window will disappear when enough randomness has been accumulated. You are only asked to do this the first time you run SSH or when you generate a RSA identity key pair.
6% Complete

FIGURE 26.18
Move your cursor around in the window to generate randomness.

2. When you are finished generating enough randomness, a terminal window appears, as shown in Figure 26.19.

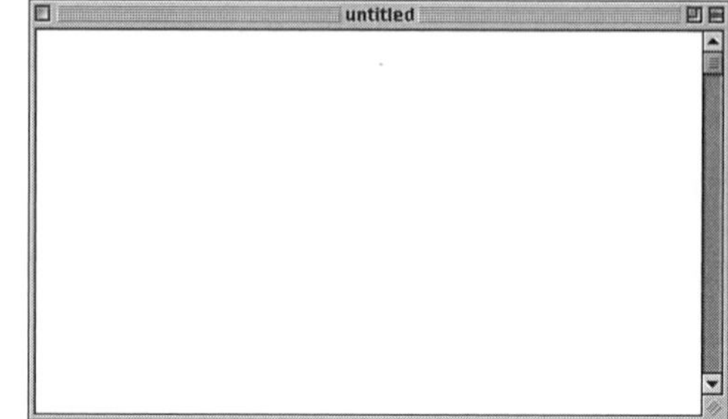

FIGURE 26.19
The terminal window is the primary user interface in F-Secure 1.0.2. There is no Connection Manager in this version.

3. Press Enter in the terminal window to display the Connect Using Password Authentication dialog box, shown in Figure 26.20. Enter the remote machine as the host name. Enter your username and password; then click OK.

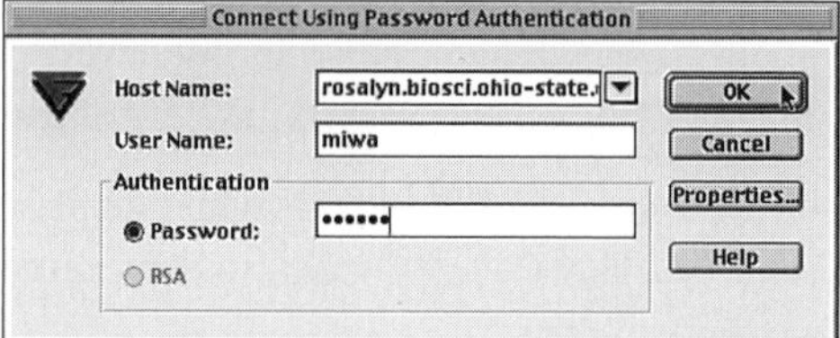

FIGURE 26.20
Enter the appropriate information in the Connect Using Password Authentication dialog to connect to the remote host.

Note

Be careful when you enter the host name. If you accidentally enter your password in that slot, your password forever remains one of the optional hosts in the list of hosts that it keeps for you.

4. As with SSH2, the default server port is `22`. There is no need to change this unless you have been informed that the SSSH1 server is running on a different port. If you have been so informed, click on Properties before you enter the rest of the information for the Password Authentication dialog.

   The Properties dialog shown in Figure 26.21 appears, where you can enter an alternate port, should this be necessary. Enter the correct port number and then click OK. Complete the rest of the Password Authentication dialog.

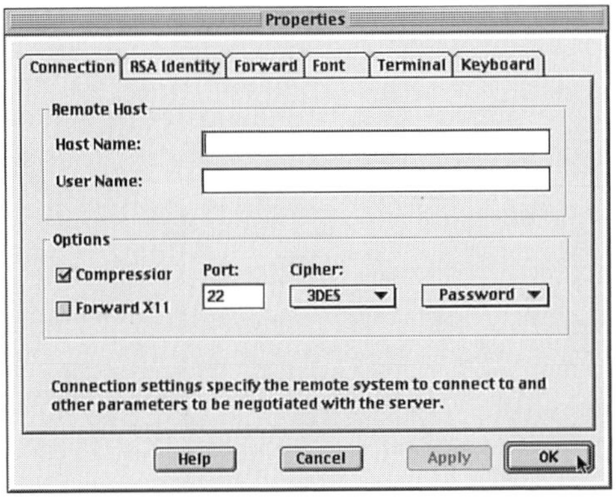

FIGURE 26.21
If necessary, change the port setting in the Connection tab in the Properties box.

5. Whenever you connect to an unknown host the first time, a dialog like that in Figure 26.22 is shown, where you are asked whether you want to accept the new host key. If you will be connecting to the remote host regularly, choose Accept & Save.

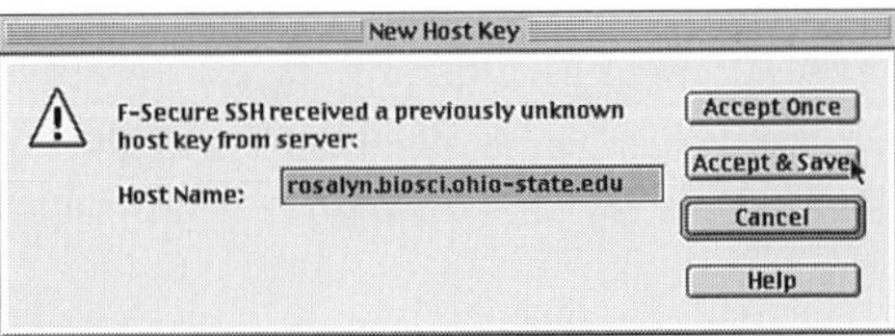

FIGURE 26.22
If you will be regularly connecting to the unknown remote host, click Accept & Save.

6. Choose Save Settings under the File menu, and save the alias to the desktop for your convenience.
7. Log out of your terminal session and quit the program.

Setting Up an FTP Tunnel

Like the 2.1 client, the 1.0.2 client has tunneling capabilities. The interface for setting up tunnels is not as friendly as in the 2.1 client. We recommend that you make any tunnels that you need for a particular host and save them all to the same alias. Because the only way to use the tunnels in 1.0.2 is through a terminal session, it is not to your advantage to save an alias to the host with an FTP tunnel, another alias to the same host with an e-mail tunnel, and so on. To set up an FTP tunnel in the 1.0.2 client, follow these steps:

1. Start F-Secure using the alias you saved to the desktop.
2. Click Properties and then click Forward. Make sure that Local is selected.

3. Click New. The Edit Local Forwarding dialog box appears, as shown in Figure 26.23.

FIGURE 26.23
Manually enter the information for your tunnel in the Edit Local Forwarding dialog box.

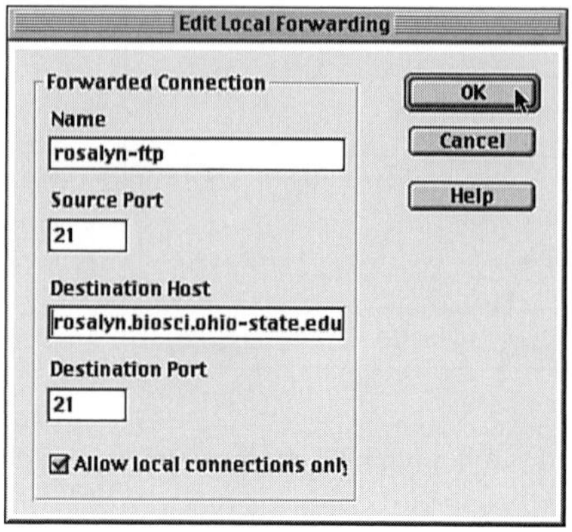

4. In the Edit Local Forwarding dialog box, enter a name for your tunnel and then enter a source port. This is the port to be used (listened to) on your local machine. Port 21 is the default FTP port.
5. Enter a destination host. Again, port 21 is the default FTP port. Use port 21, unless you have been told otherwise. Make sure that Allow local connections only is checked, and click OK.
6. Once you have entered your tunnel information, you are returned to the Forward tab of the Properties dialog box. Click OK. Figure 26.24 shows what the Forward tab looks like after you have made a tunnel.

FIGURE 26.24
An FTP tunnel has been created for the remote host.

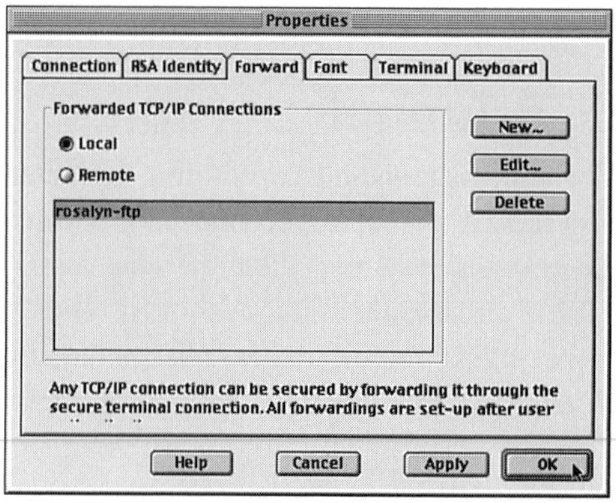

7. Continue to log in. After you have successfully logged in to the remote machine, choose Save under the File menu to save your changes. Now your desktop alias includes the additional tunnel information.

Setting Up an FTP or E-mail Client

Use the same procedures described in the section on the F-Secure 2.1 client to set up an FTP or e-mail client for F-Secure 1.0.2. Note that because philosophies are the same, any special setup work that you might already have made for 2.1 tunnels might work for 1.0.2 tunnels.

If you are making 1.0.2 aliases for a host that you already made 2.1 tunnels for, the same FTP or e-mail client settings that you made earlier should work. If you are making 1.0.2 tunnels for a different host, you will want to make sure that you don't have connections to both hosts open at the same time. Otherwise, your FTP and e-mail clients will be confused about which tunnel to use.

If you are making 1.0.2 tunnels for a different host, you might want to try to make new settings in your FTP and e-mail clients. You can do this by trying to use different ports on your local machine. If you can do this in your FTP and e-mail clients, be sure to edit the local port information of your 1.0.2 tunnels to reflect the ports in the FTP and e-mail clients. For example, you might want to set up your FTP client to FTP through a tunnel to host A, which has an FTP server on port `21`. You might also want to set up a tunnel to host B, which also has an FTP server on port `21`. Because the FTP client obeys the F-Secure tunnel information, it does not care which port the server runs on. It only cares which port it should use locally. If you wanted to be able to have both FTP tunnels open at the same time, you could set the local port for the host whose FTP you would use most often to the default, `21`. Then you could set an alternative port, such as `31`, as the local port for the host that you would not FTP to as often. For the host for which you would use the default port setting of `21`, there is nothing special you need to do in the FTP client. For the host for which you would use the alternate port setting of `31`, you do need to specify that port in the FTP client. Anarchie does not have a separate port setting. In Anarchie, to specify the alternative port, use this syntax for the host:

```
localhost:31
```

The latest version of Fetch, Fetch 4.0, has a nonstandard port number box in the New Connection dialog box, where you can specify an alternate port setting. In that box, enter `31`. Of course, for this setting to work, the local source port should be set to `31` in the F-Secure SSH package.

Setting Up Other Tunnels

As you have seen in the section on setting up an FTP tunnel, setting up any arbitrary TCP tunnel in F-Secure 1.0.2 is no different than setting up an FTP tunnel. Make as many tunnels as you need in the Forward section of the Properties box. You can make tunnels only before you have logged in. After you have logged in, you can only view your tunnels.

Because 1.0.2 does not give you any hints, it might be useful to know that the default POP port is `110`; IMAP, `143`; SMTP, `25`. If you want to tunnel any other common services, check the default TCP tunnel services that the 2.1 client lists.

The only other type of connection that you might be interested in forwarding is an X11 connection. As with the 2.1 client, activating X11 forwarding in the 1.0.2 is also a matter of checking the X11 forwarding box, which is located in the Connection section of Properties, as shown in Figure 26.25.

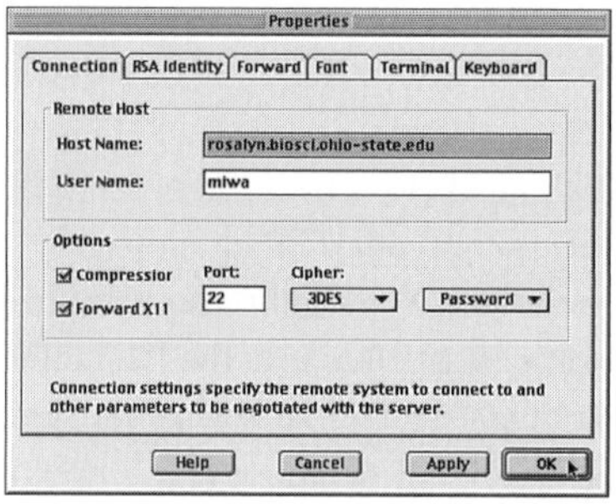

FIGURE 26.25
Check the Forward X11 box in the Connection section of Properties to enable X11 forwarding.

Using `scp` in Nifty Telnet SSH

The freely available package, Nifty Telnet 1.1 SSH r3, available from `http://www.lysator.liu.se/^jonasw/freeware/niftyssh`, was for a while illegal to use in the United States. However, some patent restrictions have been lifted, and it is now legal to use here. Nifty Telnet does not provide any tunneling capabilities—only `terminal` and `scp`. Because the package was illegal to use in the United States, we have not done much testing. However, its `scp` feature might be of interest to you. Because Nifty Telnet is an SSH1 client, and OpenSSH's `scp` is at this time only SSH1-capable, the products work nicely together. Where possible, however, we still recommend that you use the SSH2 protocol, which is under current development, rather than the SSH1 protocol.

We will now provide an example of using Nifty Telnet's `scp` to copy a file from a remote OS X host to our local Mac OS machine.

1. When you first start Nifty Telnet, the New Connection dialog appears, as shown in Figure 26.26. Fill in your host information and then click on scp.

FIGURE 26.26
Enter the remote host name and select scp *in the New Connection dialog.*

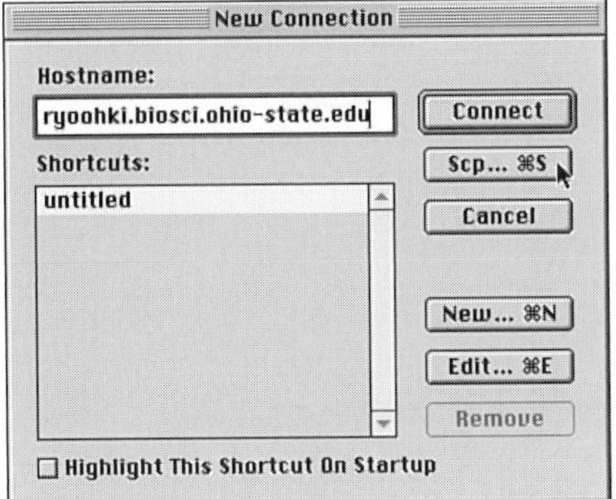

2. After you have selected scp, a new dialog box appears, as shown in Figure 26.27. In this dialog, you should first specify whether you want to receive files from the remote host or send files to the remote host.

FIGURE 26.27
Specify which files are to be copied, where, and how in the dialog box that comes up next.

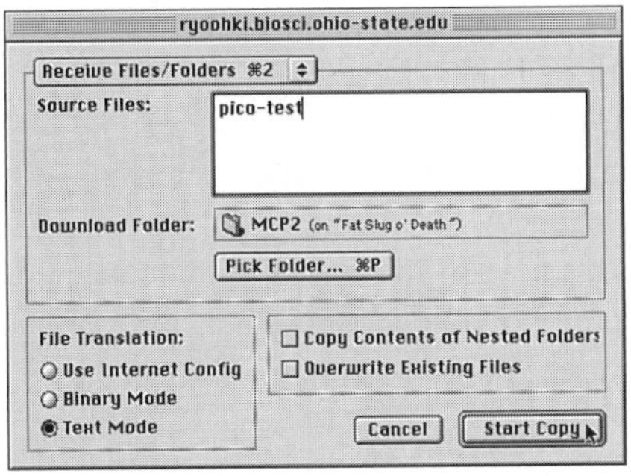

3. Next, specify which files are to be transferred and provide a destination path. Select a file transfer mode and then click OK.
4. If this is the first time that you are connecting to a host, the Host Identification Alert dialog appears, as shown in Figure 26.28. If you expect to regularly connect to the host, click Accept & Save. In this example, we have chosen to Accept Once for the time being.
5. Before the transfer is actually initiated, the SSH Login dialog appears, as seen in Figure 26.29. Enter your username and password so that the scp process can begin.

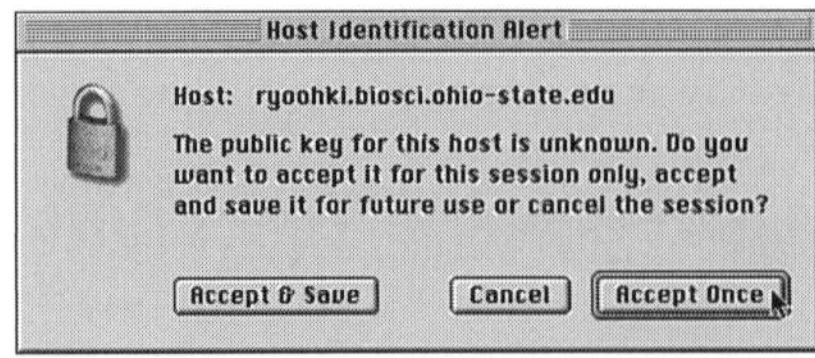

FIGURE 26.28
Tell Nifty Telnet in the Host Identification Alert dialog box whether it should accept and save the host key from an unknown host, or whether it should accept once.

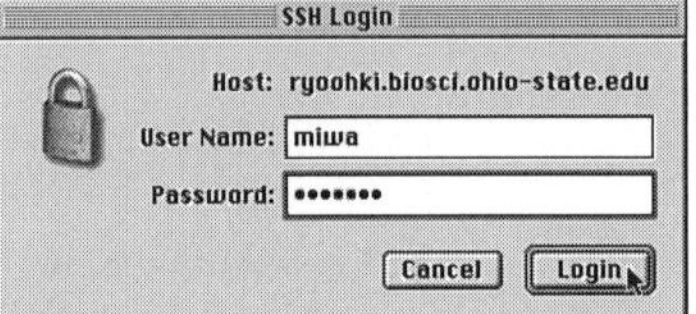

FIGURE 26.29
The SSH Login dialog for Nifty Telnet.

Public Key Authentication

In addition to the standard method of user authentication—a username and password—SSH provides another method: public key authentication. With the traditional authentication method, the remote host stores a username and password pair for a user. With public key authentication, the user creates a key-pair on a given host. The key-pair consists of a private key and a public key. Then the user transfers the public key to the remote host to which she would like to connect. So, the remote host stores a set of public keys for machines on which you have generated a key-pair and transferred a copy of your public key. Furthermore, you can protect your key with a passphrase, rather than a password.

The procedure for enabling public-key authentication is similar in SSH1 and SSH2. We will concentrate our efforts on transferring keys between Mac OS machines and Unix machines. We will also demonstrate generating key-pairs on the Unix side. Finally, we will demonstrate key authentication between Unix machines.

Public Key Authentication in SSH2

In this section, we will demonstrate how to enable public key authentication for two types of SSH2 servers. The difference between types of SSH2 servers is most apparent in how public key authentication is done. We will first look at public-key authentication between a Mac OS machine and an OS X machine. Then we will demonstrate how to enable public key authentication between a Mac OS machine and a Unix machine running an SSH2 server based on a non-OpenSSH package.

Authentication Between a Mac OS Machine and an OS X Machine

It is easiest to start the process of enabling public key authentication on the OS X machine. In particular, starting with the OS X machine provides an opportunity to more quickly see what the F-Secure client will do on your Mac OS machine. It also starts to prepare the user on the OS X machine to be able to connect from the OS X machine to other machines via public key authentication. To set up public key authentication, perform these steps, substituting your user ID and machine information as appropriate:

1. On your OS X machine, generate a key-pair by running

   `ssh-keygen -d -C <username>@<osx-hostname>`

   The *-d* option specifies DSA authentication, which is the default encryption mode for SSH2. The `-C` specifies what kind of comment to make. In other versions of `ssh-keygen`, the comment is typically of the form `<username>@<hostname>`. Sometimes comments contain more information. On the OS X machine where the sample was run, `ssh-keygen` generates a comment of `<user>@<localhost>`, without specifying a more specific comment.

   When you run `ssh-keygen`, you are asked for a passphrase to protect the private key. It is recommended that the passphrase be at least 11 characters long and include as many character types as possible: uppercase letters, lowercase letters, numbers, and special characters. Spaces may be included as part of the passphrase.

   Here is a sample run:

```
[localhost:~] miwa% ssh-keygen -d -C miwa@ryoohki

    Generating DSA parameter and key.
    Enter file in which to save the key (/Users/miwa/.ssh/id_dsa):
    ➥Enter passphrase (empty for no passphrase):
    Enter same passphrase again:
    Your identification has been saved in /Users/miwa/.ssh/id_dsa.
    Your public key has been saved in /Users/miwa/.ssh/id_dsa.pub.
    The key fingerprint is:
    54:ae:7a:73:2e:12:3b:2e:68:ce:8d:61:33:95:83:81 miwa@ryoohki
```

   As `ssh-keygen` tells us, user `miwa` does indeed have the promised keys, as shown below. The private key was saved as `id_dsa`, and the public key was saved as `id_dsa.pub`, both are stored in the directory `~/.ssh/`.

```
[localhost:~/.ssh] miwa% ls -al

     total 32
     drwx------   6 miwa  staff   160 Apr 16 16:55 .
     drwxr-xr-x  15 miwa  staff   466 Apr 16 15:46 ..
     -rw-------   1 miwa  staff   736 Apr 16 16:56 id_dsa
     -rw-r--r--   1 miwa  staff   602 Apr 16 16:56 id_dsa.pub
     -rw-r--r--   1 miwa  staff   353 Apr 16 15:31 known_hosts
     -rw-------   1 miwa  staff  1024 Apr 16 16:56 prng_seed
```

2. In the `.ssh` directory on your OS X machine, copy `id_dsa.pub` to `authorized_keys2`:

```
[localhost:~/.ssh] miwa% cp id_dsa.pub authorized_keys2
```

   The file `authorized_keys2` is where your OS X machine stores the SSH2 public keys of authorized hosts. Anyone who has the matching private key for a given public key in this file is authorized to connect to this host as this user.

3. Test that your passphrase works if you connect to your OS X machine from your OS X machine. The `-2` option forces `ssh` to use the SSH2 protocol.

```
[localhost:~] miwa% ssh -2 ryoohki

     The authenticity of host 'ryoohki' can't be established.
     DSA key fingerprint is e8:3f:30:28:ca:ac:f0:92:05:ab:95:2d:59:80:67:bd.
     Are you sure you want to continue connecting (yes/no)? yes
     Warning: Permanently added 'ryoohki,140.254.12.124' (DSA) to the list of
     known hosts.
     Enter passphrase for DSA key '/Users/miwa/.ssh/id_dsa':
     Welcome to Darwin!

[localhost:~] miwa% exit

     logout
     Connection to ryoohki closed.
```

4. On the Mac OS machine, connect to the OS X machine using your saved desktop alias.

5. Select Create Public Key under the File menu. The Public Key Authentication Key Generator dialog box appears, as shown in Figure 26.30.

6. In the Public Key Authentication Key Generator dialog box, enter a comment in the comment field. A comment of the form *<user>*@*<macos-host>* would follow the default comment form when a key is generated on a Unix machine.

7. Make sure that DSA is selected. DSA is the default encryption for SSH2. RSA encryption is an option, and therefore not present in all versions of SSH2. DSA is already selected here by default.

8. Enter a length of no less than 1024 bits and no longer than 2048 bits. 1024 is the default.

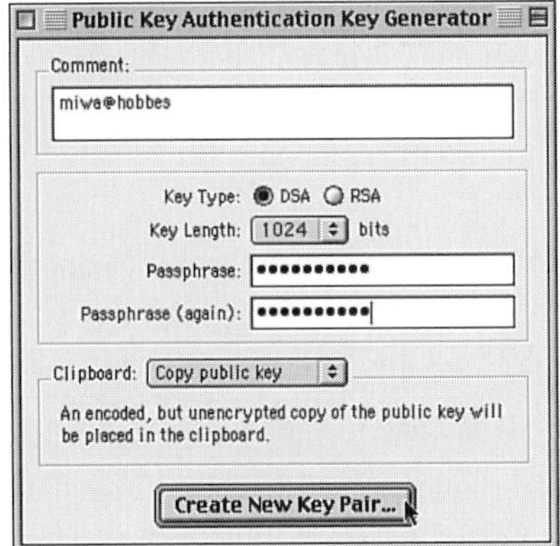

FIGURE 26.30
Indicate parameters for public key generation in the Public Key Authentication Key Generator dialog.

9. Enter a passphrase to encrypt the private key. Again, it is recommended that the passphrase be at least 11 characters long and include as many character types as possible: uppercase letters, lowercase letters, numbers, and special characters. Spaces may be included as part of the passphrase.
10. Select a clipboard option. The Copy Install Script option copies a script to the clipboard for transferring the public key to the server. Although it is probably all right to use this option, we avoid this as a precaution. The Copy Public Key option copies only the contents of the public key to the clipboard. We recommend this option. The Leave alone option does nothing.
11. Click on Create New Key Pair.
12. Save the public key and private key. Do not add an extension to the private key, and do not change the `.pub` extension of the public key. The filenames default to `key` and `key.pub`. If multiple users use the Mac OS machine, it is recommended that, for easy sorting, each user store his keys in his own folder in the F-Secure SSH folder.
13. In the OS X terminal window connection, create a file in your `.ssh` directory with a name that lets you know which host this public key belongs to and that you created it in the SSH2 client. You might consider something of the form `<macos-host>-ssh2.pub`.

    The public key that was created in F-Secure SSH has this form:

```
---- BEGIN SSH2 PUBLIC KEY ----
Comment: "miwa@hobbes"
AAAAB3NzaC1kc3MAAACBALPMiCqdPDGxcyB1IwPrPXk3oEqvpxR62EsspxGKGGbOM6mf60
i1hwTvjZzDhUSR7ViGeCopKtjJIqn2ljgeLbhFsQUX2UyJ6A1cFVuef0x6GVAsybqbtJc8
JBh41U+iSXJKppEY5BI+REMydpBXJf2qT/8yZeq3NPjiOiMb6TyjAAAAFQDYvvV4WQK1Zu
23q/7iLKg5j/zi5wAAAIBR7vgrQpjKW2cprIUJsnenTm4hnBrEO7NMUomjgezrY23iZdIS
```

```
QlU1ESMgx9W9nnZstd2vjeqHDSmmcD2p/aGqhl3N1WlYk8zgFYYJilPwRxVm77Np/vXz/M
QpygJE7ToXGvfHqVmdBpUyakyfx6DveWhFPis1Ab8N1RCPWm6PMwAAAIAytHjAAMYscqX2
tl4icw3oOku3HIvoHBCx9D6Q9LjCqt7DqqgMN2e5vuvNz0hzqBaBDJsjNA/A4bI88ZrgLh
fJM/Nhs2xkcb7AYeHEtuGKVbsbB0EjsECtLRHydfmk3wDQjUVT92HsodFvsIl4Je7seWUu
iAEe0V1xfF7XrXuwNQ==
---- END SSH2 PUBLIC KEY ----
```

This form is not quite compatible with the form that the OpenSSH package uses. The form that is acceptable for OpenSSH's SSH2 public key is

```
ssh-dss lots-of-characters== comment
```

The form for SSH2 in OpenSSH is contained on one line.

On the OS X machine, you can run an option to `ssh-keygen` that converts the format created in F-Secure to an OpenSSH-compatible format. Use

```
ssh-keygen -X -f <macos-host>-ssh2.pub > <macos-host>-ssh2-open.pub
```

The preceding statement converts the SSH2-format public key to an OpenSSH format public key and outputs it to a file called *<macos-host>*`-ssh2-open.pub`.

Here is a sample of what the command does:

```
[localhost:~/.ssh] miwa% ssh-keygen -X -f hobbes-ssh2.pub > hobbes-ssh2-open.pub

ignore: ---- BEGIN SSH2 PUBLIC KEY ----
ignore: Comment: "miwa@hobbes"
ignore: ---- END SSH2 PUBLIC KEY ----
```

We see some output on ignoring some lines, but it creates `hobbes-ssh2-open.pub` in OpenSSH format.

You can also use a text editor to edit the public key file that you created so that it has the appropriate form. Before you edit the file, even if you are using an editor that makes a backup file, make a backup copy. The OpenSSH format is also not difficult to create in an editor.

14. Add the public key from your Mac OS machine to the `authorized_keys2` file in your `.ssh` directory on the OS X host. Before you edit the `authorized_keys2` file, make a backup copy. As you might recall, the first key in the `authorized_keys2` file is the public key that you generated on your OS X machine. Add a blank line after that key, and then add a copy of the public key from your Mac OS machine that you modified to fit the form of the `authorized_keys2` file. For our user `miwa`, the `authorization_keys2` file looks like this:

```
[localhost:~/.ssh] miwa% more authorized_keys2

ssh-dss AAAAB3NzaC1kc3MAAACBALzT9RbceziStHPmMiHmg78hXUgcMP14sJZ/7MH/p2NX/fB0cmbU
LPNgEN8jrs8w9N73J7yUFHSPR/LVfBj+UwkIzwjyXUW/z/VmCs25IDF/UBn1OQK5PCi16rF0F+Cx0hMN
```

```
4R3AaFAetXBdLqoom5x4Yo9gdspPqhhB44QnT43JAAAAFQDWTkKDJ2m4SApHZ/qRnRpMN5whTQAAAIAV
ADOsHpnUdUOFKjIgxZ0Hwh7IaMQ2ofG/6PmbmNG/8zXRdxmu/JrBzieWHq6sSRSkWDSDIjuEuTkZyJ4w
x3KsLmhIrtlBw3NCcsJT2GfGQ9gEBm8fkUpeQyKAQcirbx4Hw93iMFC3g9A8cwqmA4DalKSX3un7cweN
U32Irhq+gAAAIAz+lDSjqjFzuTV4vJ/P83nH2uwb62/iCSIB9cL32hrOm234imaAceu8pN9qqEAPr9Ai
lCWa+lqGvgcdyDK0vZTvKQnk6KOU3TJfDyMR7i/gzW4P4TA/k/+YbognMCZ7SWYQXhZXWBhiPObVLYPf
fDJsLdpkyBXjZbx+Zmrmi4Bxg== miwa@ryoohki

ssh-dss AAAAB3NzaC1kc3MAAACBALPMiCqdPDGxcyB1IwPrPXk3oEqvpxR62EsspxGKGGbOM6mf60i1h
wTvjZzDhUSR7ViGeCopKtjJIqn2ljgeLbhFsQUX2UyJ6A1cFVuef0x6GVAsybqbtJc8JBh41U+iSXJKpp
EY5BI+REMydpBXJf2qT/8yZeq3NPjiOiMb6TyjAAAAFQDYvvV4WQK1Zu23q/7iLKg5j/zi5wAAAIBR7vg
rQpjKW2cprIUJsnenTm4hnBrEO7NMUomjgezrY23iZdISQlU1ESMgx9W9nnZstd2vjeqHDSmmcD2p/aGq
hl3N1WlYk8zgFYYJilPwRxVm77Np/vXz/MQpygJE7ToXGvfHqVmdBpUyakyfx6DveWhFPis1Ab8N1RCPW
m6PMwAAAIAytHjAAMYscqX2tl4icw3oOku3HIvoHBCx9D6Q9LjCqt7DqqgMN2e5vuvNz0hzqBaBDJsjNA
/A4bI88ZrgLhfJM/Nhs2xkcb7AYeHEtuGKVbsbB0EjsECtLRHydfmk3wDQjUVT92HsodFvsIl4Je7seWU
uiAEe0V1xfF7XrXuwNQ== miwa@hobbes
```


Although this looks like several lines, it is really a three-line file. Line 1 contains the public key for the OS X machine. Line 2 is blank. Line 3 contains the public key for the Mac OS machine.

15. Log out of the OS X machine.
16. Start another connection to your OS X machine in F-Secure SSH 2.1. So that you have the option to connect via public key authentication, do not use your desktop alias to make this connection.
17. In the Connect section of the Properties dialog box, shown in Figure 26.31, enter your OS X machine as the SSH server. Select Public Key and then select your private key file by clicking the Select button and navigate the file system to your key file, as shown in Figure 26.32. Click Connect.
18. After a connection with the remote machine has been established, you will be prompted for your passphrase as shown in Figure 26.33. Enter the passphrase for the public key that you created on your Mac OS machine and click OK.

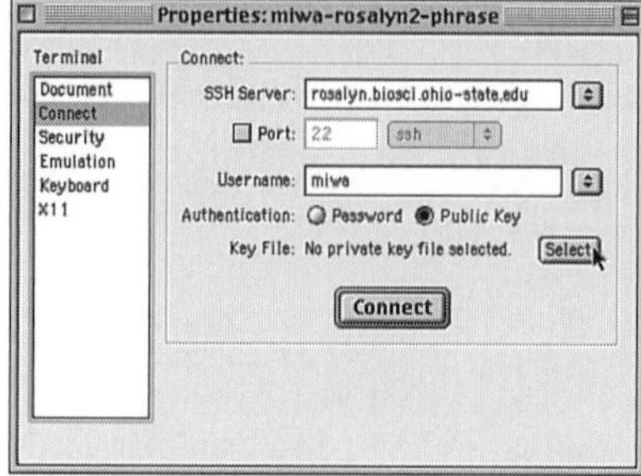

FIGURE 26.31
You can choose to connect via public key authentication or password authentication in the Connect section of the Properties dialog.

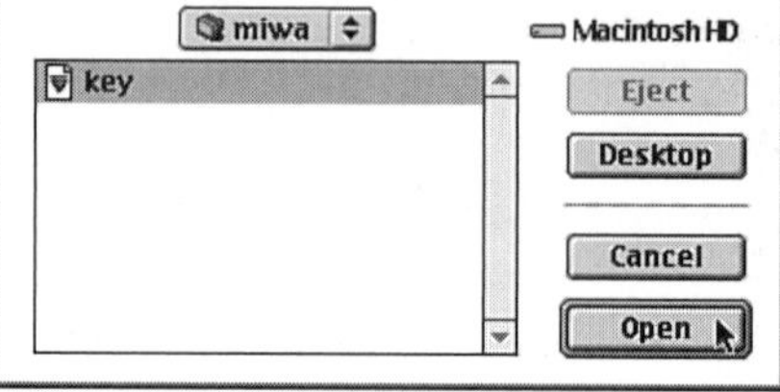

FIGURE 26.32
Find the private key file you created by browsing your system in the file dialog.

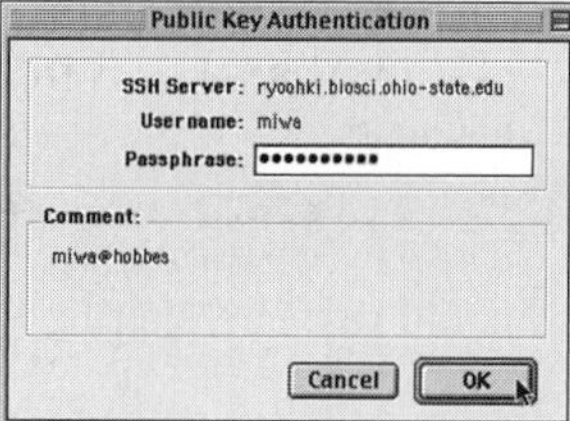

FIGURE 26.33
Enter the passphrase for the public key created on the Mac OS machine to complete the login procedure.

If all went well, you are now connected to your OS X machine. If you end up having to connect via password instead, the public key for the Mac OS machine in your `authorized_keys2` might not yet be in the right form. Make sure that you have removed any spaces and returns that have been in the original public key file, without altering any of the characters in the long string. If all else fails, start over from scratch.

If you would like to connect to your OS X machine from your Mac OS machine by regularly using a passphrase, be sure to save these new settings, or an alias to them, to your desktop. You can also modify your tunnel connections so that you connect via public key authentication. Unfortunately, you still have to use a password in the FTP or e-mail client.

Authentication Between a Mac OS Machine and a Unix Machine Running a Separate SSH2 Server

Believe it or not, you have already completed the complicated part. The remote host we will use in this section is running an SSH2 server that comes from the SSH Communications Security/F-Secure product line. Some of the commands you will run are slightly different than in the previous section, and the keys are stored differently than in the previous section. However, because you might have to connect to SSH2 servers running this product line, it is useful to see a different demonstration of enabling public key authentication.

Again, it is easiest to start the process of enabling public key authentication on the Unix machine. In particular, this provides an opportunity to see, more quickly, what the F-Secure client will do on your Mac OS machine. It also starts to prepare the user on the Unix machine to be able to connect from the Unix machine to other machines via public key authentication. To do this, follow these steps:

1. On the remote host, generate a key-pair by running

   ```
   ssh-keygen
   ```

   On systems like this one, the `ssh` commands default to the SSH2 protocol. However, if you want to be certain that you are invoking an SSH2 protocol, append `2` to the end of the command. In this example, you could specify `ssh-keygen2` to be absolutely certain that you are specifying the desired protocol.

   As was the case on the OS X machine, when you run `ssh-keygen` you are asked for a passphrase to protect the key. Follow the same guidelines as you used on the OS X machine. Make sure that the passphrase is at least 11 characters long and includes a variety of characters.

   Here is a sample run:

```
Rosalyn miwa 69 >ssh-keygen

      Generating 1024-bit dsa key pair
         2 oOo.oOo.oOo.
      Key generated.
      1024-bit dsa, miwa@Rosalyn, Mon Apr 16 2001 17:23:31
      Passphrase :
      Again      :
      Private key saved to /home/miwa/.ssh2/id_dsa_1024_a
      Public key saved to /home/miwa/.ssh2/id_dsa_1024_a.pub
```

   Just as you saw on our OS X machine, `ssh-keygen` has generated a private key and a public key. On this system, the private key is called `id_dsa_1024_a`, and the public key is called `id_dsa_1024_a.pub`. On our OS X machine, the keys are stored in a directory called `.ssh`. On this system, they are stored in a directory called `.ssh2`.

If we check the results of our run, we do indeed see that the keys have been generated and stored as `ssh-keygen` specified they would:

```
Rosalyn .ssh2 71 >ls -al

    total 12
    drwxr-xr-x   3 miwa     class        512 Apr 16  2001 .
    drwxr-xr-x  14 miwa     class       1024 Apr 16 11:55 ..
    drwx------   2 miwa     class        512 Apr 13 16:12 hostkeys
    -rw-------   1 miwa     class        868 Apr 16  2001 id_dsa_1024_a
    -rw-r--r--   1 miwa     class        729 Apr 16  2001 id_dsa_1024_a.pub
    -rw-------   1 miwa     class        512 Apr 16  2001 random_seed
```

2. In the `.ssh2` directory on the remote host, create a file called identification, whose contents are this line:

   ```
   IdKey id_dsa_1024_a
   ```

   This file identifies which key is your private key.

3. In the `.ssh2` directory on the remote host, create a file called authorization, whose contents are this line:

   ```
   Key id_dsa_1024_a.pub
   ```

   The `K` must be capitalized.

   The file authorization is where the remote host stores the listing of SSH2 public keys for authorized hosts. Anyone who has the matching private key for a given public key in this file is authorized to connect to this host as user `miwa`. As you might recall, on the OS X machine, the file that stores this information is `authorized_keys2`.

4. Test that your passphrase works if you connect to the remote host from the remote host. Again, on this system, the `ssh` commands default to the SSH2 protocol. To be more specific, you could also use `ssh2` instead of `ssh`.

```
Rosalyn miwa 4 >ssh rosalyn

    Passphrase for key "/home/miwa/.ssh2/id_dsa_1024_a"
    ➥with comment "1024-bit dsa, miwa@Rosalyn, Mon Apr 16 2001 17:23:31":
    Last login: Mon Apr 16 2001 17:20:56 from
    You have mail.
    You have mail.

Rosalyn miwa 1 >exit
```

5. End your terminal session with the remote host.

   Assuming that you are connecting to this remote host from the same Mac OS machine that you used for connecting to the OS X host in the previous section, you have already created your key-pair for this machine. If you are using a different Mac OS machine, follow the steps in the previous section for creating your key-pair.

6. Now transfer a copy of your public key (if you saved by the default name, this is `key.pub`) to the remote host. Use your ingenuity to make this happen. As you might recall, we recommended that you paste this key into a file called something like `<macos-host>-ssh2.pub` in your `.ssh` directory on your OS X machine. One reason we suggested this was to make it easier to edit the public key into an acceptable form for OpenSSH. The other reason we suggested it was to make it easier for you to transfer the key to other remote Unix hosts. With the key already on your OS X machine, you can now `scp` or `sftp` the key to the other remote Unix host with the knowledge that nothing odd happened. Copying these keys in Mac OS can sometimes be frustrating. Of course, if the remote host is running an FTP server, you could certainly `ftp` the key from your Mac OS machine through an SSH tunnel to the remote host. At any rate, choose a method you are comfortable with to transfer the public key to this remote host. Whatever method you choose, make sure that nothing about the formatting changes. We know this to be the case using the `scp`/`sftp` method.

   After transferring his Mac OS machine's public key, user `miwa`'s `.ssh2` directory looks like this:

```
Rosalyn .ssh2 81 >ls -al

total 18
drwxr-xr-x   3 miwa     class          512 Apr 16  2001 .
drwxr-xr-x  14 miwa     class          512 Apr 16 13:39 ..
-rw-------   1 miwa     class           15 Apr 16  2001 authorization
-rw-------   1 miwa     class          675 Apr 16 13:56 hobbes.pub
drwx------   2 miwa     class          512 Apr 13 16:12 hostkeys
-rw-------   1 miwa     class          868 Apr 16 13:32 id_dsa_1024_a
-rw-r--r--   1 miwa     class          729 Apr 16 13:32 id_dsa_1024_a.pub
-rw-r--r--   1 miwa     class           20 Apr 16 13:38 identification
-rw-------   1 miwa     class          512 Apr 16 13:32 random_seed
```

7. On the remote host, make a backup copy of the authorization file. Remember, this is the file the host uses to identify authorized public keys.

8. Edit the file authorization. Add a line that points to the file that contains the public key for your Mac OS machine. In our example, user `miwa`'s authorization file looks like this:

```
Key id_dsa_1024_a.pub
Key hobbes.pub
```

9. End the terminal session.

10. Start a new terminal session. Do not start the terminal session from your already existing desktop alias.
11. In the Connect section of the Properties dialog box, enter your OS X machine as the SSH server. Select Public Key and then select your private key file. Click Connect.
12. Enter the passphrase for the public key that you created on your Mac OS machine and click OK.

If all went well, you are now connected to the remote host. If you have to connect via password instead, check whether the authorization file points to the right file. Check to see that the file it points to is of the accepted format. Remember, that an acceptable format looks like this:

```
---- BEGIN SSH2 PUBLIC KEY ----
Comment: "<user>@<macos-host>"
String-of-characters-70-characters-wide-with-returns-at-each-line==
---- END SSH2 PUBLIC KEY ----
```

If all else fails, start over from scratch.

If you would like to connect to this remote host from your Mac OS machine by regularly using a passphrase, be sure to save these new settings to your desktop. You can also modify your tunnel connections so that you connect via public key authentication. Unfortunately, you still have to use a password in the FTP or e-mail client.

Public Key Authentication Between an OS X Machine and Another Unix Host

In this section, we will demonstrate enabling public key authentication between an OS X machine and a Unix machine running a non-OpenSSH style SSH2 server. Based on the previous two sections, you are probably formulating ideas on how you might do this.

If we skip the little details on dealing with the Mac OS client, what we did in the other sections can be summarized as follows:

- Create keys on host A, which you would like to use for remotely accessing host B.
- Transfer a copy of the public key that was just created on host A to the remote host B.
- Make the remote host B aware that it has a copy of a public key from host A.
- Log in to host B from host A using a passphrase. Your private key from host A and your public key from host A together authenticate the login. In practice, this means that your host A private key (stored on host A) combined with the copy of your host A public key (stored on host B) authenticates your login to host B from host A.

How does this translate to public key authentication between an OS X machine and another Unix host? In the examples carried out in this chapter thus far, we already generated private and public keys on our OS X machine using `ssh-keygen -d`. We also already created public and private keys on our remote Unix host by running `ssh-keygen` (or `ssh-keygen2`). So, we are already part of the way there! Next, we need to format our public keys appropriately for the different types of SSH2 servers and then transfer our public keys between the hosts. We could, of course, skip the formatting step if we were attempting public key authentication between machines running the same type of SSH2 server. But before we continue further, we will outline the procedure from start to finish.

1. On the OS X machine:

- Generate public and private keys by running:

  ```
  ssh-keygen -d -C <username>@<osx-hostname>
  ```

- Create the file that holds the set of authorized public keys:

  ```
  cp .ssh/id_dsa.pub .ssh/authorized_keys2
  ```

- Test that the passphrase works by connecting from the OS X machine to the OSX machine. Make a backup copy of your public key. Name it something that is easily identifiable to you when you are on a remote host. If given a good name, the backup copy is probably the most informative copy to transfer to other hosts.

  ```
  cp .ssh/id_dsa.pub .ssh/<this-osx-host>-ssh2.pub
  ```

- Make a copy of the file that is in a form acceptable to other SSH2 servers. Remember that this is the basic form:

  ```
  ---- BEGIN SSH2 PUBLIC KEY ----
  Comment: "<user>@<osx-host>"
  String-of-characters-70-characters-wide-with-returns-at-each-line==
  ---- END SSH2 PUBLIC KEY ----
  ```

You can make your public key in an acceptable format for other machines by manually editing the file to the form above, or by running an `ssh-keygen` command that does it for you:

```
ssh-keygen -x -f id_dsa.pub > <this-osx-host>-ssh2-ssh2.pub
```

With the `-x`, this `ssh-keygen` command converts an OpenSSH format private key to an SSH2-format public key, and then outputs it to a file named `<this-osx-host>-ssh2-ssh2.pub`. You can use any filenames you want.

Here is an example:

```
[localhost:~/.ssh] miwa% ssh-keygen -x -f id_dsa > ryoohki-ssh2-ssh2.pub

     Enter passphrase:
```

If we look at the first couple of lines of the file, we see that the comment includes *<user>@<localhost>*. You might want to change that comment to something more informative to you, such as *<user>@<hostname>*.

```
[localhost:~/.ssh] miwa% more ryoohki-ssh2-ssh2.pub

     ---- BEGIN SSH2 PUBLIC KEY ----
     Comment: "1024-bit DSA, converted from OpenSSH by miwa@localhost"
```

You can also edit the public key file in an editor. If you do, be sure to remember that the length of the lines is 70 characters.

- Transfer the newly formatted public key to the remote host. You can keep whatever name you used on the OS X machine or change it to something else. Do whatever helps you remember things best. Here is what our user `miwa` did:

```
[localhost:~/.ssh] miwa% scp ryoohki-ssh2.pub rosalyn:.ssh2/ryoohki.pub

     miwa@rosalyn's password:
     warning: Executing scp1 compatibility.
     ryoohki-ssh2.pub     100% |*****************************|   677       00:00
```

2. On the remote Unix host:

- Generate public and private keys by running:

  `ssh-keygen2`

- Create `.ssh2/identification`, whose content is this line:

  `IdKey id_dsa_1024_a.pub`

- Create `.ssh2/authorization`, whose content is this line:

  `Key id_dsa_1024_a.pub`

- Test that the passphrase works by connecting from the Unix host to the Unix host
- Make a backup copy of the public key

  `cp .ssh2/id_dsa_1024_a.pub <remote-host>.pub`

  If you feel comfortable with your editor, create a copy of the public key so that it is in OpenSSH format. This format is easy to create in an editor. Remember that this is the basic form, all on one line:

  `ssh-dsa Lots of characters== <user>@<remote-host>`

If you don't feel comfortable doing that in your editor, wait until you have transferred the file to the OS X machine so that you can convert formats.

Transfer a copy of the public key to the OS X machine. Again, use whatever name is useful to you. Here is what our user `miwa` did to transfer his public key:

```
Rosalyn .ssh2 9 >scp rosalyn-ssh2.pub ryoohki:.ssh/rosalyn.pub

     miwa@ryoohki's password:
     Transfering rosalyn-ssh2.pub -> ryoohki:.ssh/rosalyn.pub  (1k)
     |.....................................................................
     ...|
     602 bytes transferred in 0.06 seconds [9.68 kB/sec].
```

- If you did not edit the format of the key on the remote host to OpenSSH format, do it now on the OS X machine using:

```
ssh-keygen -X -f <remote-host>-ssh2.pub > <remote-host>-ssh2-open.pub
```

As you might recall, the above command converts the remote host's SSH2-format public key to an OpenSSH format public key and outputs that to the file `<remote-host>-ssh2-open.pub`. Remember, you can use whatever filenames you want.

- Edit the `.ssh2/authorization` file to have a new line pointing to the pubic key file of the OS X machine. Here is what our user's authorization file looks like after adding the OS X machine:

```
Rosalyn .ssh2 4 >more authorization

     Key id_dsa_1024_a.pub
     Key hobbes.pub
     Key ryoohki.pub
```

The first line points to the public key for the host itself. The second line points to our Mac OS machine's public key. The third points to the OS X machine's public key.

3. Now that the remote Unix host's `.ssh2/authorization` file includes a pointer to the OS X machine's public key, test the connection from the OS X machine to the remote host:

```
[localhost:~/.ssh] miwa% ssh -2 rosalyn

     The authenticity of host 'rosalyn' can't be established.
     DSA key fingerprint is ee:b3:21:1b:3f:6a:57:90:59:8a:54:8d:e9:3b:24:75.
     Are you sure you want to continue connecting (yes/no)? yes
     Warning: Permanently added 'rosalyn,140.254.12.151' (DSA) to the list of
     known hosts.
     Enter passphrase for DSA key '/Users/miwa/.ssh/id_dsa':
     Last login: Fri Apr 20 2001 20:48:15 from ryoohki.biosci.o
     You have mail.
     You have mail.

Rosalyn miwa 1 >
```

4. On the OS X machine, add the contents of the public key file that you transferred from the remote host to your `.ssh/authorized_keys2` file. After doing this, our user's `authorized_keys2` file looks like this:

```
[localhost:~/.ssh] miwa% more authorized_keys2

ssh-dss AAAAB3NzaC1kc3MAAACBALzT9RbceziStHPmMiHmg78hXUgcMP14sJZ/7MH/p2NX/fB0cmbU
LPNgEN8jrs8w9N73J7yUFHSPR/LVfBj+UwkIzwjyXUW/z/VmCs25IDF/UBn1OQK5PCi16rF0F+Cx0hMN
4R3AaFAetXBdLqoom5x4Yo9gdspPqhhB44QnT43JAAAAFQDWTkKDJ2m4SApHZ/qRnRpMN5whTQAAAIAV
ADOsHpnUdUOFKjIgxZ0Hwh7IaMQ2ofGt/6PmbmNG/8zXRdxmu/JrBzieWHq6sSRSkWDSDIjuEuTkZyJ4
wx3KsLmhIrtlBw3NCcsJT2GfGQ9gEBm8fkUpeQyKAQcirbx4Hw93iMFC3g9A8cwqmA4DalKSX3un7cwe
NU32Irhq+gAAAIAz+lDSjqjFzuTV4vJ/P83nH2uwb62/iCSIB9cL32hrOm234imaAceu8pN9qqEAPr9A
ilCWa+lqGvgcdyDK0vZTvKQnk6KOU3TJfDyMR7i/gzW4P4TA/k/+YbognMCZ7SWYQXhZXWBhiPObVLYP
ffDJsLdpkyBXjZbx+Zmrmi4Bxg== miwa@ryoohki

ssh-dss AAAAB3NzaC1kc3MAAACBALPMiCqdPDGxcyB1IwPrPXk3oEqvpxR62EsspxGKGGbOM6mf60i1
hwTvjZzDhUSR7ViGeCopKtjJIqn2ljgeLbhFsQUX2UyJ6A1cFVuef0x6GVAsybqbtJc8JBh41U+iSXJK
ppEY5BI+REMydpBXJf2qT/8yZeq3NPjiOiMb6TyjAAAAFQDYvvV4WQK1Zu23q/7iLKg5j/zi5wAAAIBR
7vgrQpjKW2cprIUJsnenTm4hnBrEO7NMUomjgezrY23iZdISQlU1ESMgx9W9nnZstd2vjeqHDSmmcD2p
/aGqhl3N1WlYk8zgFYYJilPwRxVm77Np/vXz/MQpygJE7ToXGvfHqVmdBpUyakyfx6DveWhFPis1Ab8N
1RCPWm6PMwAAAIAytHjAAMYscqX2tl4icw3oOku3HIvoHBCx9D6Q9LjCqt7DqqgMN2e5vuvNz0hzqBaB
DJsjNA/A4bI88ZrgLhfJM/Nhs2xkcb7AYeHEtuGKVbsbB0EjsECtLRHydfmk3wDQjUVT92HsodFvsIl4
Je7seWUuiAEe0V1xfF7XrXuwNQ== miwa@hobbes

ssh-dss AAAAB3NzaC1kc3MAAACBAIFBAfGPtfG2xUqjT21La84K8huT12bXE1UZ8pKqBZpTFYmIbAbI
oPVvWVP0ihgWCmLKa8nGypCGx71z+9RoiDSivkCUqmIeu1vzAwFYab+F0pXc/F1Kiy1NYdvJsniPz7fP
H6btMZFkisdVFiLUfwn0mun+gdwmjbVx+V71hXZLAAAAFQCq7worKGceMLms0kPRyvcucPPqcQAAAIAu
EnKtaWkeTDqm31MC/4hr241o8E5NOqLJKcWTkOPg52a846288mihc05XUk+wa02KUvsqE+b84Q315qCM
0vDMoqofKAhvlL63XfUHO0vL94YTKJHtfvO0DhmsY7Hzk+kocSS1HtyIicA51E/EHAAvKPdi9kIliQ4d
jDVielDFbwAAAIBiUM/Wl3aPdmNgXQMTZ0b8ql6fxwbHKarBiAE3/DGpPIoDK7tWxbnS66ey0EdVQ9xh
jT/sHP9+NGykRkQg1OUv6ND8BdzJUEbhri1OosWKeVO3S/d4FitIfjNnE9CQEUj9A3AL1N1sGN5whFSI
v12T9e49ubniYjWoLVwG8KH+Jw== miwa@Rosalyn
```

The first line is the public key for the OS X machine itself. The second is a blank line. The third is the public key for the Mac OS machine. The fourth line is a blank line. The fifth line is the public key for the remote Unix host.

5. Now that the `.ssh/authorized_keys2` file includes a copy of the public key for the remote Unix host, test a connection from the remote host to the OS X machine:

```
Rosalyn miwa 1 >ssh2 ryoohki

    Passphrase for key "/home/miwa/.ssh2/id_dsa_1024_a"
    ➥with comment "1024-bit dsa, miwa@Rosalyn, Mon Apr 16 2001 17:23:31":
    Welcome to Darwin!

[localhost:~] miwa%
```

Pubic Key Authentication in SSH1

In this section, we will demonstrate how to enable public key authentication for SSH1 servers. Unlike public key authentication with the two most popular types of SSH2 servers, the two most popular types of SSH1 servers implement public key authentication in the same way. We will demonstrate enabling public key authentication between a Mac

OS machine and a Unix machine. Then we will enable public key authentication between an OS X machine and another Unix machine.

Authentication Between a Mac OS Machine and Unix Machine

As with SSH2, it is easiest to start the process of enabling public-key authentication on the Unix machine. Starting with the Unix machine provides an opportunity to more quickly see what the F-Secure client will do on your Mac OS machine. Additionally, it starts to prepare the user to be able to connect from the Unix machine to other machines via public key authentication.

1. On the Unix machine, generate public and private keys by running `ssh-keygen` or `ssh-keygen1`. Which one you will use depends on the host. On some systems, `ssh-keygen` defaults to the SSH2 protocol. To do anything SSH1-specific on those systems, append `1` to the end of the command. In OpenSSH, `ssh-keygen` defaults to SSH1 unless the option for generating an SSH2 protocol key is used.

This Unix host is running SSH2 and SSH1 servers, so `ssh-keygen1` has to be used:

```
Rosalyn miwa 1 >ssh-keygen1
    Initializing random number generator...
    Generating p:  ...............++ (distance 224)
    Generating q:  .....++ (distance 92)
    Computing the keys...
    Testing the keys...
    Key generation complete.
    Enter file in which to save the key
    (/home/miwa/.ssh/identity):
    Enter passphrase:
    Enter the same passphrase again:
    Your identification has been saved in
    /home/miwa/.ssh/identity.
    Your public key is:
    1024 35  1233312813655580342629444440019705730527794755700146
    ➥2510447921204589975264176684977834967422442955486232
    ➥2759148790022277518022104954840563331735710347611258
    ➥4401245696271560346079612184349553815058693112556130
    ➥9028548711559684218705529622437924369765037766990458
    ➥8920718940456117968631232063576786600240415013401
    miwa@Rosalyn
    Your public key has been saved in
    /home/miwa/.ssh/identity.pub
```

On this remote host, the private and public keys are saved to the directory called `.ssh`. This is where the files for both SSH1 and SSH2 keys are stored in OS X.

As you also saw with SSH2, the user is prompted for a passphrase to protect the private key. The same recommendations for creating a passphrase still apply. It should be at least 11 characters long and include as many character types as possible: uppercase letters, lowercase letters, numbers, and special characters. Spaces may be also included as part of the passphrase.

2. In the `.ssh` directory, copy `identity.pub` to `authorized_keys.pub`. The file `authorized_keys` is where the host stores the SSH1 public keys of authorized hosts. As with SSH2, anyone who has the matching private key for a given public key in this file is authorized to connect to this host as this user.
3. Test that your passphrase works if you connect from this remote host to this remote host. As shown here, this works for our user:

```
Rosalyn miwa 9 >ssh1 rosalyn

    Enter passphrase for RSA key 'miwa@Rosalyn':
    Last login: Fri Apr 13 16:05:09 2001 from rosalyn.biosci.o
    You have mail.

Rosalyn miwa 1 >
```

4. In the `.ssh` directory, save another copy of `identity.pub` to some other name that lets you know that it is the public key for this remote host, such as `<hostname>-ssh1.pub`.
5. On the Mac OS machine, connect to the remote host via the usual password authentication method in F-Secure SSH 1.0.2.
6. Under the Edit menu, select Connection Properties. Click on the RSA Identity tab, which brings up the panel shown in Figure 26.34, if it is not already the tab showing.

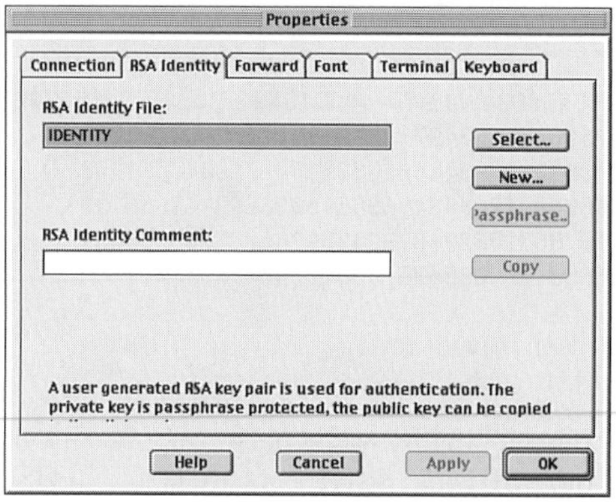

FIGURE 26.34
Generating a key pair in F-Secure SSH 1.0.2 starts with the RSA Identity section of the Properties dialog.

7. Click on New. An RSA identity generation dialog box like that shown in Figure 26.35 appears. Do the following:
   - Enter a comment in the suggested form of `<user>@<macintosh>`.
   - Enter a passphrase using the same guidelines you saw earlier.
   - Enter the passphrase again for verification.
   - The default and recommended key length is 1024 bits. It is not necessary to adjust the default.
   - Click on Generate key.

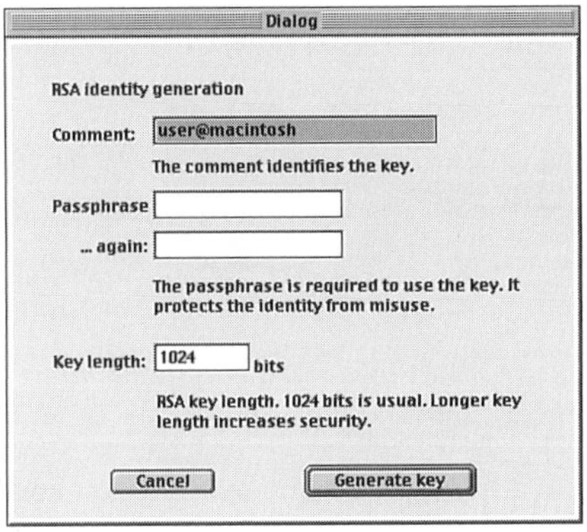

FIGURE 26.35
Specify the parameters of your keys in the RSA identity generation dialog.

8. Just as when you first started F-Secure SSH 1.0.2, move your cursor around in the window to initialize the random number generator.
9. Save the key pair as instructed. The name of the file defaults to `IDENTITY`. If multiple users use the Mac OS machine, it is recommended that for easy sorting, each user store her keys in her own folder in the F-Secure SSH folder.
10. Click OK in the dialog box that tells you that your identity has been filed as you specified it should be.
11. The RSA Identity section of the Properties box reappears, with some additional information filled in as shown in Figure 26.36. Verify that the identity file has been properly selected.
12. If Copy is available as a selection, click on it. If it is not, click on OK. Then bring up the RSA Identity window again and click on Copy, assuming that your identity file is still selected. Copy copies your public key to the clipboard. An information dialog like that shown in Figure 26.37 should appear.

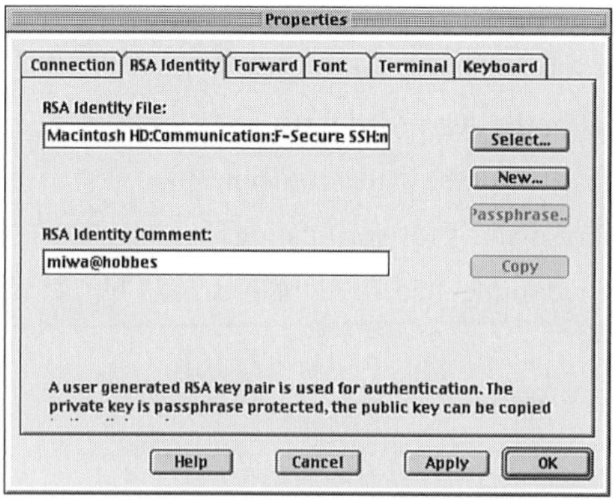

FIGURE 26.36
The selection of the identity file now appears in the RSA Identity section of the Properties dialog.

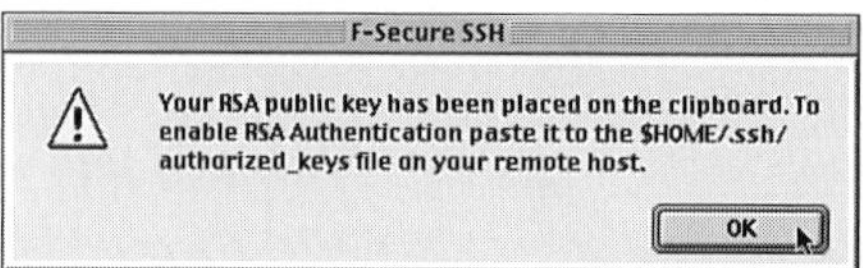

FIGURE 26.37
The informative dialog box that appears when you copy tells you where on the Unix side to paste your public key.

13. On the Unix machine, create a file with a name that lets you know it is the SSH1 public key for your Mac OS machine. You could call it something like `<macos-host>-ssh1.pub`.

14. Make a backup copy of `.ssh/authorized_keys`. Edit `.ssh/authorized_key` in your favorite text editor. Add to it a blank line and a line that contains the contents of `<macos-host>-ssh1.pub`. Here is what the `.ssh/authorized_keys` file of our user `miwa` looks like at this stage:

```
1024 35 123331281365558034262944444001970573052779475570014625104479212045899752
64176684977834967422442955486232275914879002227751802210495484056333173571034761
12584401245696271560346079612184349553815058693112556130902854871155968421870552
96224379243697650377669904588920718940456117968631232063576786600240415013401 mi
wa@Rosalyn

1024 35 909400270068835789365340764432579481890601265942027673338014578714246240
08941333767613393457884572605367686913264231165534818281623120501426552405476133
86011470780123940481672833879017816652256472285975437039764248048300592030161507
1190666939214904116358241550344838704220243882868572485328230167776925913357 miw
a@hobbes
```

Notice that the form of a public key for SSH1 is one line containing:

```
1024 two-digit-number lots-of-characters <user>@<host>
```

The `1024` is the key length, though we've never seen it generate anything other than 1024 bit keys.

This looks familiar, doesn't it? It looks like the OpenSSH SSH2 public key follows a form similar to SSH1 public keys!

If what you copy to the Unix side looks nothing like the form shown here, go back to the copy step and try again. Sometimes the copy step goes very smoothly. Other times, it is very frustrating, and random data can be pasted over instead of your key. We've observed no pattern to the problematic instances, so if you have problems, read the instructions and try it over again—chances are it will work properly the second time around.

15. Log out of the remote host.
16. Start another connection to the Unix host in F-Secure SSH 1.0.2. So that you have the option to connect via public key authentication, do not use your desktop alias to make this connection.
17. This time, rather than entering your password, select the RSA. Then click OK. Save your settings to an alias to your desktop, if you expect to log in regularly with your passphrase.
18. A dialog asking you to enter your passphrase appears. At this point, you're back on familiar territory. Enter your passphrase and click OK.

You should now be logged in to the remote host. If you end up having to connect via password instead, check some of the basics. Make sure that F-Secure SSH 1.0.2 selected your identity file. Make sure your `.ssh/authorized_keys` really does have the additional key included. If the additional key is included, make sure that it is on one long line, rather than separate lines with returns. If all else fails, start over from scratch.

If you were successful, you might want to update the passphrase alias you saved to the desktop by including your tunnels, too. You can also modify your tunnel connections so that you connect via public key authentication. Unfortunately, you still have to use a password in the FTP or e-mail client.

Public Key Authentication Between Unix Machines

Because the SSH1 format does not vary among the popular SSH1 servers, public key authentication between Unix machines is also easier than what you saw in SSH2. In this example, we will look at public key authentication between an OS X machine, which runs OpenSSH, and a Unix machine running the other popular SSH1 server.

At this point, you should be able to figure out what to do. If one of the Unix hosts involved is also the one that your Mac OS machine connected to, you have even already done some of the work. Because we know that the procedure for enabling public key authentication is easy to forget if you don't have to do it often, we include the procedure from start to finish.

1. On Unix host A:
    - Generate public and private keys by running the SSH1 version of `ssh-keygen`.
    - Create the file that holds the set of authorized public keys:

      ```
      cp .ssh/identity.pub .ssh/authorized_keys
      ```

    - Test that your passphrase works by connecting from Unix host A to Unix host A.

   Make a backup copy of your public key. Name it something that is easily identifiable to you when you are on a remote host. If given a good name, the backup copy is probably the most informative copy to transfer to other hosts.

   ```
   cp .ssh/identity.pub .ssh/<host-A>-ssh1.pub
   ```

    - Transfer a copy of your public key on host A to host B.
2. On Unix host B:
    - Generate public and private keys by running the SSH1 version of `ssh-keygen`.
    - Create the file that holds the set of authorized public keys:

      ```
      cp .ssh/identity.pub .ssh/authorized_keys
      ```

    - Test that your passphrase works by connecting from Unix host B to Unix host A.
    - Make a backup copy of your public key. Name it something that is easily identifiable to you when you are on a remote host. If given a good name, the backup copy is probably the most informative copy to transfer to other hosts.

      ```
      cp .ssh/identity.pub .ssh/<host-B>-ssh1.pub
      ```

    - Transfer a copy of your public key on host B to host A.

Edit `.ssh/authorized_keys` to include the public key from host A. Remember that the public key for a host is on one line only. Each public key contained in `.ssh/authorized_keys` should be only one line long without any returns or spaces. This is the same behavior we saw with `.ssh/authorized_keys2` on an OS X machine. Here is a sample `.ssh/authorized_keys` file on host B for our user, `miwa`:

```
[localhost:~/.ssh] miwa% more authorized_keys

1024 35 143360183656224498601121073193820768197357701013476215869370944931688223
70498617132214779624465699914141070434905449681454367814018069875143895388524470
```

```
1935281558951482716003278779890735070473366177974045270721691760053943622355l843
189297104449029777380930950785153164849125052551675778129451064997244608804 49 mi
wa@ryoohki

1024 35 9094002700688357893653407644325794818906012659420276733380145787l4246240
0894133376761339345788457260536768691326423116553481828162312050142655240547 6133
8601147078012394048167283387901781665225647228597543703976424804830059203016 1507
1190666939214904116358241550344838704220243882868572485328230167776925913357 miw
a@hobbes

1024 35 12333128136555803426294444400197057305277947557001462510447921204589 9752
6417668497783496742244295548623227591487900222775180221049548405633317357103 4761
1258440124569627156034607961218434955381505869311255613090285487115596842187 0552
96224379243697650377669904588920718940456117968631232063576786600240415013401 mi
wa@Rosalyn
```

In this example, line 1 contains the public key for the host itself, host B, which is our OS X machine. Line 2 is a blank line. Line 3 is the public key for the Mac OS machine. Line 4 is a blank line. Line 5 is the public key for host A, another Unix machine.

3. Now that the `.ssh/authorized_keys` file on host B includes host A's public key, test a connection from host A to host B. For our user `miwa`, the test is successful:

```
Rosalyn .ssh 4 >ssh1 ryoohki

    Host key not found from the list of known hosts.
    Are you sure you want to continue connecting (yes/no)? yes
    Host 'ryoohki' added to the list of known hosts.
    Enter passphrase for RSA key 'miwa@Rosalyn':
    Warning: Remote host denied X11 forwarding, perhaps xauth program
    ➥could not be run on the server side.
    Welcome to Darwin!

[localhost:~] miwa%
```

4. Edit `.ssh/authorized_keys` on host A to include the public key from host B.
5. Now that the `.ssh/authorized_keys` file on host A includes host B's public key, test a connection from host B to host A. For our user `miwa`, this test is also successful:

```
[localhost:~] miwa% ssh rosalyn

    Enter passphrase for RSA key 'miwa@ryoohki':
    Last login: Sat Apr 21 01:46:08 2001
    You have mail.
    You have mail.

Rosalyn miwa 1 >
```

Are There Any Graphical SSH Clients for OS X?

As of this writing, there is no native OS X graphical SSH client. To use SSH in OS X, you will have to learn the command-line SSH tools. Hopefully, as OS X becomes more widely used, more native OS X applications will be developed. Whether they are SSH products or other types of applications, be certain you let the software companies know that you are interested in having native OS X applications on the market.

In the meantime, you might be wondering how the graphical SSH clients work as Classic applications in OS X. Unless you enjoy the thrill and excitement of seeing a machine with floppy icon with a question mark, we recommend that you do not even try it. We had a particularly bad experience with the F-Secure SSH 2.1 client running as a Classic application. We have not experimented with the freely available SSH clients running as Classic applications.

Are There SSH Clients Available for the PC?

Although the Macintosh is your preferred platform, you might have to use a PC from time to time. Don't worry—SSH clients are also available for the PC. F-Secure 4.3 is the latest SSH product for Windows 95/98/Me/NT/2000 by F-Secure Corporation. It is supposed to support SSH1 and SSH2. In the past, F-Secure Macintosh products and PC products have functioned similarly. SSH Communications Security also makes an SSH client, SSH Secure Shell 2.4.0. It is an SSH1 and SSH2 client that also includes a built-in `sftp` client. SSH Secure Shell is free to certain types of noncommercial users. There are freely available SSH packages for the PC.

Although the interfaces between the various products vary, you will find the basic concepts behind them to be the same. If you understand how to use the Mac clients, you will be able to use PC clients and Mac clients that have not been discussed here.

Summary

In this chapter, we looked at how to use SSH to connect between Mac OS machines and OS X machines, Mac OS machines and other Unix machines, and OS X machines and Unix machines. We saw how to use SSH1 and SSH2 clients. Additionally, we learned how to enable public key authentication in the Mac OS clients as well as Unix clients.

CHAPTER 27

Web Serving

IN THIS CHAPTER

The Macintosh has never been a major contender in the Web-serving space. As a platform, it has been unstable, and suffered from a slow network stack. Users had only a few choices—either expensive proprietary software, or Apple's built-in Web Sharing application. As an enterprise-level Web server, the Macintosh had almost nothing to offer. Being personally involved in Web development, I became accustomed to sitting in front of my Mac and remotely accessing Linux servers for development and production.

The introduction of the Mac OS X Server signaled the end of the agony. The Mac OS X Server includes the world-class Apache Web server. Apache, an open source project similar to Mac OS X itself, is a high-speed extensible server that is supported by thousands of developers nationwide. Mac OS X also ships with Apache as a replacement to the Mac OS 8/9 Web Sharing server. Never before has a personal Web server been so powerful. This chapter introduces Apache, its capabilities, extensions, and basic administration.

Apache

Apache is an open source project developed by a worldwide group of volunteers known as the Apache group (`www.apache.org`). It is available on dozens of operating systems including Microsoft Windows. Apache's appeal comes from its flexibility and extensibility. The base server package excels at serving HTML, but to truly exploit the power of Apache, you can install a number of extension modules, including MP3 streaming servers, SSL security, Java Server Pages, and much more. With a total expenditure of $0, you can set up a secure e-commerce server that processes credit cards in real-time and delivers SQL database access.

Apache Versus Personal Web Sharing

If you're looking for the features of the Mac OS 8/9 personal Web server, look elsewhere. The Apache server under Mac OS X does not offer the Finder mode, nor does it offer the SimpleText to HTML conversion of the previous operating system. To place information online, you'll need to create HTML documents. This isn't difficult, but there is no direct upgrade path if you have a collection of SimpleText documents you've been serving off the Internet.

Although Mac OS 8/9 allowed you to use the primary address of your computer as the address for your Web site, the Mac OS X Web sharing system forces a URL based on your username. For example, if your computer's address is `http://192.168.0.1` and your username is `joeuser`, your Web site address would be `http://192.168.0.1/~joeuser`. This change is due to the multiuser capabilities of Mac OS X. Regardless of how many users are on the system, each can have his or her personal Web site online, simultaneously. To use this feature, users must place their Web pages with the `Site` folder of their home directory. If you want a single server without usernames, a master Web site can be created by placing documents in the `/Library/Webserver/Documents` folder.

Regardless of whether Apache is being used for an entire Web site or a few personal pages, users can take advantage of the server's advanced features. A personal page can execute CGI applications, use embedded programming languages, and so on.

Capabilities

This chapter addresses the base features of Apache, but it also includes some interesting add-ons that will make your system into a Web serving powerhouse. There are literally hundreds of Apache modules available for download (`http://modules.apache.org/`), so we'll try and focus on a select few:

`mod_ssl`—The standard for Web server security is SSL, the Secure Socket Layer. Through the use of OpenSSL and the `mod_ssl` module, Apache can be configured for completely secure transactions.

`mod_dav`—Mac OS X supports built-in WebDAV (Distributed Authoring and Versioning) file system access. This open standard defines a file-sharing protocol based on standard HTTP. The cross-platform nature of WebDAV means both Macintosh and Windows users can access the same files, from the same server.

`mod_mp3`—Have an MP3 library? Want to stream it to the world? This module creates an MP3 stream accessible by any MP3 player supporting the Shoutcast protocol.

If you're not interested in these features, take a look at the other Apache modules available. It's best to install only the modules you really use. Additional modules can add overhead and potentially weaken the overall security of the server.

> **Note**
>
> I don't mean to imply that the modules included in this chapter are inherently dangerous. The common rule that less is better is a good rule of thumb, whether talking about Apache modules or full-blown server applications.

Activating Web Sharing

To activate Web sharing (and the Apache Web server), open the System Preferences application (Path: `/Applications/System Preferences`) and click the Sharing icon. You've seen this screen, shown in Figure 27.1, before.

Assuming the screen reads Web Sharing Off, click the Start button to start Apache. After a few seconds, the server status should change to Web Sharing On. Your Web pages are now online.

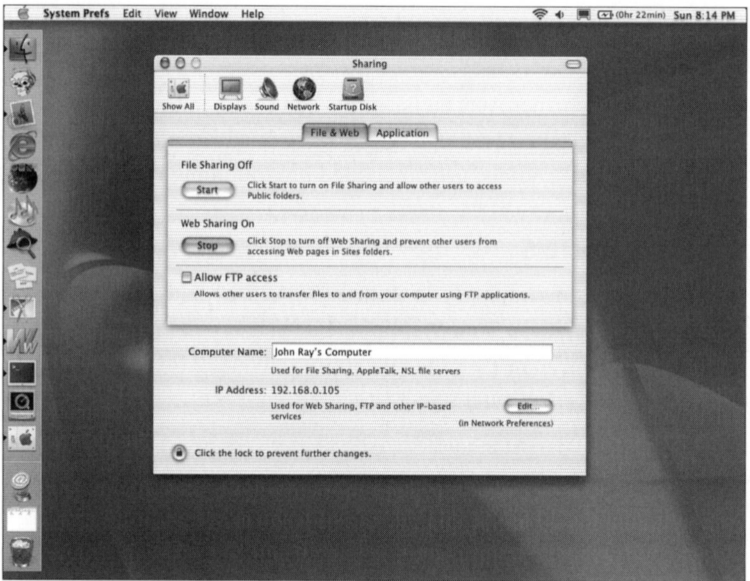

FIGURE 27.1
Use the Sharing Preference panel to activate Apache.

The Sharing button does two things. First, it configures the Mac OS X Server to start Apache when it boots. The `/etc/hostconfig` file is modified to read `WEBSERVER=-YES-`:

```
##
# /etc/hostconfig
##
# This file is maintained by the system control panels
##

# Network configuration
HOSTNAME=-AUTOMATIC-
ROUTER=-AUTOMATIC-

# Services
AFPSERVER=-YES-
APPLETALK=en1
AUTHSERVER=-NO-
AUTOCONFIG=-YES-
AUTODISKMOUNT=-REMOVABLE-
AUTOMOUNT=-YES-
CONFIGSERVER=-NO-
IPFORWARDING=-NO-
MAILSERVER=-NO-
MANAGEMENTSERVER=-NO-
NETBOOTSERVER=-NO-
NISDOMAIN=-NO-
TIMESYNC=-YES-
QTSSERVER=-NO-
```

```
SSHSERVER=-YES-
WEBSERVER=-YES-
APPLETALK_HOSTNAME="John Ray's Computer"
```

Second, it activates the Apache server with no need to reboot. You can start, stop, and restart Apache at any time using the `/usr/sbin/apachectl` utility. For example, to restart the server, type

```
$ /usr/sbin/apachectl restart
```

Tip

The Start/Stop buttons within the Sharing System Preference panel can also be used to start and stop the Apache process.

Table 27.1 documents all of the available `apachectl` options.

TABLE 27.1 The `apachectl` Administration Application Accepts These Commands

Options	*Functions*
`start`	Start the Apache server.
`stop`	Stop the Apache server.
`restart`	Restart Apache. This is equivalent to stopping then starting the server. Current connections are closed.
`fullstatus`	Display a full status of the server. This requires `lynx` to be installed.
`status`	Display a summary of the server status. The `lynx` text browser is required.
`graceful`	Restart the server gracefully. Current connections are not dropped.
`configtest`	Check the configuration files for errors. Can be used regardless of the current server state.

There is an interface problem that occurs with Apple's use of the Personal Web Sharing metaphor when it is applied to Apache. Each user has his or her own directory. When Web sharing is turned on for one user, it is activated for everyone.

If the computer is a multiuser system, you cannot be certain that Web sharing is on or off. The only ways to guarantee that your files aren't being displayed on the Web is to manually disable viewing files using Apache configuration directives, or to remove the files from your `Site` directory.

Note

This isn't Apple's fault, but just part of the growing pains associated with moving to a multiuser environment. The `/etc/hostconfig` file is the definitive checkpoint for figuring out what your server will be doing when it starts up.

Apache Configuration

Apache is a *very* large piece of software that has hundreds of configuration options and possible setups. There are a number of books that have been written about Apache. This section will look at the most common attributes that can be configured and how they affect your system. It is not meant to be a complete reference to Apache. Version 2.0 is expected to be released within the next year, and with it will come numerous changes and additions. The current shipping version, 1.3.x, is discussed here.

File Locations

Apple has done an excellent job of making the Apache Web server configuration manageable for machines with large numbers of personal Web sites. Instead of a single monolithic configuration, like the standard Linux or Windows installation, the server can be configured on two different levels:

System-wide configuration—(path: `/etc/httpd/httpd.conf`) This is the master configuration file. It contains information about the system as a whole—what directories are accessible, what plug-ins are in use, and so on. Changes to the Web server as a whole are included here.

User-directory configuration—(path: `/etc/httpd/users/`*`username.conf`*) When the Mac OS X Users System Preference panel creates a new account, it automatically adds a basic configuration file for that user within the `/etc/httpd/users` directory. This mini configuration file determines the security for the Web pages within a user's `Sites` folder.

By splitting up the configuration, the administrator can quickly adjust Web permissions on a given account. To edit the user or system configuration, you must either log in (or `su`) as `root`, or use `sudo`.

> **Note**
>
> Although the user configuration files are stored based on the user's name, they have no real connection to the actual user other than containing the path to a personal `Sites` folder. These files can contain any Apache configuration option, including those that affect other users. The division by username is for ease of editing only.

Apache approaches configuration in a very object-oriented manner. The configuration files are XML-like, but not compliant, so don't attempt to edit them using the `plist` editor. Apache calls each configuration option a directive. There are two types of configuration directives:

Global—Global directives affect the entire server. Everything from setting a name for the Web server to loading and activating modules.

Container-based—An Apache container is one of a number of objects that can hold Web pages. For example, a directory is a container, a virtual host is a container, and an aliased location is also a container. If you don't know what these are, don't worry, we'll get there. For now, just realize that each container can be configured to limit who has access to what it contains, and what pages within it can do.

Global Options

The global options can fall anywhere within the server configuration file. If you're running a heavy-traffic Web site you'll definitely want to change the defaults. By default, Apache starts only one server and keeps a maximum of five running at any given time. These numbers do not allow the server to quickly adapt to increased server load.

Table 27.2 documents the most important configuration directives contained in the `/etc/httpd/httpd.conf` file. They are listed in the order that you're likely to encounter them in the `httpd.conf` file.

> **Note**
>
> Several of the Apache directives refer to the number of server processes that should be started. These processes are subprocesses of the master Apache process. When you use `apachectl` to control the server, you are controlling *all* the Apache processes.

TABLE 27.2 Global Apache Directives

Directive	*Description*
`ServerType <standalone|inetd>`	The Server type determines how Apache starts. Standalone servers are the default. Inetd-based servers use the `inetd` process to activate a server only when it is accessed. This is inefficient and not recommended for all but the lowest-traffic systems.
`ServerRoot <path>`	The base path of the Apache binary files.
`PidFile <path/filename>`	The path (and filename) of the file that should store Apache's process ID.
`Timeout <seconds>`	The number of seconds that Apache will wait for a response from a remote client. After the time period expires, the connection will be closed.
`KeepAlive <On|Off>`	Allow more than one request per connection. This is the default behavior of HTTP/1.1 browsers. Shutting this off might result in a higher server load and longer page load times for clients.
`MaxKeepAliveRequests <#>`	The maximum number of requests that can be made on a single connection.
`KeepAliveTimeout <seconds>`	The amount of seconds to wait between requests on a single connection.
`MinSpareServers <#>`	Apache automatically regulates the number of running servers to keep up with incoming requests. This is the minimum number of servers kept running at any given time.
`MaxSpareServers <#>`	The maximum number of servers that will be kept running when there is no load. This is not a limit on the total number of server processes to start—it limits the number of unused processes that will be kept running to adapt to changes in load.
`StartServers <#>`	The number of servers to start when Apache is first launched.
`MaxClients <#>`	The `MaxClients` directive sets an upper limit on the number of servers that can be started at a given time.
`MaxRequestsPerChild <#>`	Some systems have memory leaks. A memory leak is a portion of the system software in which memory usage slowly grows in size. Apache recognizes that memory leaks might exist and will automatically kill a server after it has processed a given number of requests, freeing up any memory it was using. The server process is then restarted—fresh and ready to go.

TABLE 27.2 continued

Directive	*Description*
LoadModule *<modulename>* *<modulepath>*	Loads an Apache module. Many modules will be installed automatically, so you'll rarely need to adjust anything.
AddModule *<modulename.c>*	Activates a loaded module.
Port *<#>*	The port number that the Apache server will use. The standard HTTP port is 80.
User *<username>*	The user ID that Apache will run under. Apache has the full access permissions of this user, so never, ever, EVER, set this to the root account.
Group *<groupname>*	The group ID that Apache will run under. Like the User directive, this should never be set to a privileged account. If it is, any broken Web applications could compromise your entire computer.
ServerAdmin *<Email Address>*	The e-mail address of the Web server operator.
ServerName *<Server Name>*	If your server has several different hostnames assigned, use the ServerName directive to set the one that will be returned to the client browser. This cannot be an arbitrary name, it *must* exist!
DocumentRoot *<path to html files>*	This defines the path to the main server HTML files. The Mac OS X default is /Library/WebServer/Documents.
UserDir *<name of user's website directory>*	The personal Web site directory within each user's home directory. As you already know, OS X uses Sites—the default used in most Apache installs is public_html.
DirectoryIndex *<Default HTML file>* with this name.	When a URL is specified using only a directory name, the Web server will attempt to display a default HTML file
AccessFileName *<Access Filename>*	The name of a file that, if encountered in a directory, will be read for additional configuration directives for that directory. Typically used to password-protect a directory. The default name is .htaccess.
DefaultType	The default MIME type for outgoing documents. HTML files should be served using the text/html type.
HostnameLookups *<On|Off>*	If activated, Apache will store the full hostname of each computer accessing the server rather than its IP address. This is *not* recommended for servers with more than a trivial load. Hostname lookups can greatly slow down response time and overall server performance.

TABLE 27.2 continued

Directive	*Description*
`TypesConfig <mime-type configuration file>`	The path to a file that contains a list of MIME types and file extensions that should be served using that MIME type. For example, the type `text/html` is applied to files with the `.html` extension. The default MIME types are located at `/private/etc/httpd/mime.types`.
`LogLevel <level>`	One of eight different error log levels: `debug`, `info`, `notice`, `warn`, `error`, `crit`, `alert`, or `emerg`.
`LogFormat <Log Format> <short name>`	Defines a custom log format and assigns it to a name. Discussed shortly.
`CustomLog <Log filename> <short name>`	Sets a log filename and assigns it to one of the `LogFormat` types.
`Alias <URL path> <server pathname>`	Creates a URL that aliases to a different directory on the server.
`ScriptAlias <URL path> <server pathname>`	Creates a URL that aliases to a directory containing CGI applications on the server.
`Redirect <old URL> <new URL>`	Redirects (transfers) a client from one URL to another. Can be used to transfer between URLs on the same server, or to transfer a client accessing a local Web page to a remote site.
`AddType <MIME-type> <extension(s)>`	Adds a MIME-type without editing the `mime.types` file.
`AddHandler server-parsed <file extension>`	Activates server-side includes for files with the specified extension. The default SSI extension is `.shtml`.
`AddHandler send-as-is <file extension>`	When activated, files with the defined extension will be sent directly to the remote client as is.
`AddHandler imap-file <file extension>`	Sets the extension for server-side imagemap features. All modern Web browsers use client-side image maps, but, if you need compatibility with Netscape 1.0 browsers, you'll need to use server-side clients.
`ErrorHandler <error number> <Error Handler>`	Sets an error handler from any one of the standard HTML error messages. This will be discussed in greater detail shortly.
`Include <directory>`	Reads multiple configuration files from a directory. This is set to `/etc/httpd/users`.

This is only a partial list of commonly used directives—for a complete list, visit Apache's Web site. To get a handle on configuration, let's take a look at a few different directives in use. Each of these commands, because of its global nature, can be used anywhere within the `/etc/httpd/httpd.conf` configuration file.

Aliases

As you build a complex Web server, you'll probably want to spread files out and organize them using different directories. This can lead to extremely long URLs, such as `/mydocuments/work/project1/summary/data/`. This URL is a bit bulky to be considered convenient if it were commonly accessed or publicly advertised.

Thankfully, you can shorten long URLs by creating an alias. Aliases work in a similar manner as the Mac OS X Finder aliases. A short name is given that, when accessed, will automatically retrieve files from another location. To alias the long data URL to something shorter, such as `/data/`, you would use the following command:

```
Alias /data/ /mydocuments/work/project1/summary/data
```

Aliases can be used to access files anywhere on the server, not just within the server document root. Obviously, the files in the alias directory need to be readable by the Apache process owner.

Redirection

Web sites change. URLs change. For established Web sites, changing the location of a single page can be a nightmare for users—bookmarks break and advertised URLs fail. Although this might seem trivial to experienced Web surfers, some users might not be persistent enough to figure out where the page has gone.

Many Web sites put a redirection page up in place of the missing page. This type of redirection relies on a browser tag to take the user to another URL after a set timeout period. This is effective for most modern browsers, but it takes several seconds between loading the original page and the redirection. In addition, a page needs to be created for each location that might be accessed by the client. This could be hundreds of pages!

A simpler, faster, neater way is to use the `Redirect` directive. `Redirect` forces the client browser to transfer to a different URL before the original page even opens. Entire URL structures can be redirected using a single command. The destination URL can even be on a remote server!

For example, if you've decided to move all of the files under a URL called `/ourcatalog/toys` to a new server with the URL `www.mynewstoreonline.com/toys`, you could use

```
Redirect /ourcatalog/toys http://www.mynewstoreonline.com/toys.
```

If a user attempted to access the URL `/ourcatalog/toys/cooltoy1.html`, he would immediately be transferred to `www.mynewstoreonline.com/toys/cooltoy1.html`.

Using redirects is more reliable and transparent for the end user. Avoid using HTML-based redirects and rely on the Apache `Redirect` directive to hide changes in the structure of your Web site.

Logs

Apache on Mac OS X stores its log files in the directory `/var/log/httpd`. By default, there are two logs—`access_log` and `error_log`.

The `access_log` file contains a record of what remote computers have accessed Apache, what they asked for, and when they did it. For example:

```
140.254.85.2 - - [02/May/2001:16:49:47 -0400] "GET /extimage/images/
                    ➥26_thumb.jpg HTTP/1.1" 200 27012
140.254.85.2 - - [02/May/2001:16:49:47 -0400] "GET /extimage/images/
                    ➥27_thumb.jpg HTTP/1.1" 200 35793
140.254.85.2 - - [02/May/2001:16:49:47 -0400] "GET /extimage/images/
                    ➥28_thumb.jpg HTTP/1.1" 200 26141
140.254.85.2 - - [02/May/2001:16:49:47 -0400] "GET /extimage/images/
                    ➥30_thumb.jpg HTTP/1.1" 200 29316
140.254.85.2 - - [02/May/2001:16:49:47 -0400] "GET /extimage/images/
                    ➥29_thumb.jpg HTTP/1.1" 200 33626
```

This log excerpt shows five requests for `.jpg` images from the Apache server. There are five fields stored with each log entry:

Remote Client—The machine accessing the Apache Web server. In these examples, that client is `140.254.85.2`.

Date and Time—A time and date stamp for when the request was made. These five requests were made on May 2, 2001 at 4:49 p.m.

Request String—The actual request that the remote machine made. Most requests begin with `GET` and are followed by the resource to retrieve, then the version of the HTTP protocol to retrieve it with. The five requests in the example are for files within the `/extimage/images/` directory of the server's documents folder.

Response Code—Identifies how the remote server responded to the request. The code 200 shows that the request was successfully served. A 404, on the other hand, indicates that the request couldn't be satisfied because the resource wasn't found. The response codes for HTTP 1.1 are available from `http://www.w3.org/Protocols/rfc2616/rfc2616-sec6.html`.

Response Size—The number of bytes sent to the remote client to satisfy the request.

Note

There are actually seven fields in this log format. The second and third fields contain a `-` that indicates a value could not be determined. It is unlikely you'll see values here.

Apache knows this style of access log as the common log format. Log formats are completely customizable using the `LogFormat` directive. The common format is defined as

```
LogFormat "%h %l %u %t \"%r\" %>s %b" common
```

Each of the `%h` elements denotes an element to be stored in the log file. The `\"` is an escaped quote, meaning that a quote will also be stored in that location. You can build a log format using:

`%h`—Hostname of the requesting computer.

`%a`—IP address of the remote computer.

`%r`—Request string.

`%t`—Time of request.

`%T`—Amount of time taken to serve the request.

`%b`—Bytes sent.

`%U`—URL Path requested.

`%P`—Process ID of the child that served the request.

`%>s`—The last status reported by the server.

`%{Referer}i`—The referring URL (the URL that contained the link to current page).

`%{User-Agent}i`—The string identifies the remote browser.

Tip

This is only a partial listing. You can find a complete list of the Apache Log elements at `http://httpd.apache.org/docs/mod/mod_log_config.html#logformat`.

You define a log format by using the `LogFormat` line, a string containing the format elements, and a name for the file. For example, to define a log called `mylog` that stores only the hostname of the remote client for each request, you would use:

```
LogFormat "%h" mylog
```

Except for custom solutions, you'll be best served by one of Apache's default log formats. Although the `common` log *is* common, it probably isn't the best thing for doing extensive reporting. A better choice is Apache's `combined` log format. The `combined` log format includes `referer` and `user-agent` strings with each request. Most Web analysis packages use the combined log style.

To activate a log format, use the `CustomLog` directive, followed by the pathname for the log and the log name. To activate the `combined` log format, use within the `/etc/httpd/httpd.conf` file:

```
CustomLog "/private/var/log/httpd/access_log" combined
```

Log files are an important part of any Web server. They can provide important data on the popular pages of the server, errors that have occurred, and how much traffic your system is getting.

Note

The `error_log` is not shown here because it should only contain startup and shutdown messages. If a security violation or configuration error occurs, it is recorded to this file. In addition, programmers can find detailed information about program errors written to this location. We'll see it again later, so don't worry!

Log Analysis Software

There is an abundance of log analysis software available for Unix operating systems (and thus Mac OS X). Log analysis is more of an art than a science. As you've seen by looking at the logfile formats, you can determine the remote host, requested resource, and time of request from the logfile. Unfortunately, many analysis packages try to go even further by providing information on how long visitors were at your page, or where (geographically) they are located. Neither of these pieces of information is tracked in the Apache logs.

To determine how long someone has been at your site, the analysis software must look at all accesses and determine which are related, and the amount of time between them. This is entirely guesswork on the part of the server. Assume a user opens her browser, views a page, walks away for 15 minutes, and then accidentally clicks on another page before closing her browser. If the software is set with a session timeout period greater than 15 minutes, it sees two separate hits on the page. The software assumes the user spent at least 15 minutes reading both pages, and registers that the browser spent 30 minutes on the site. In reality, only a minute or two was spent looking at the site content.

When determining geographic information, analysis software performs an even more amazing task—locating what city a user is coming from. To do this, the analysis utility looks up the domain of the client accessing the system. It retrieves the city and state that the domain was registered in. Unfortunately, this is almost completely worthless data. I recently ran a WebTrends report on a local (Columbus, Ohio) e-commerce site to see how it would perform.

The results showed that more than 95% of the remote requests are coming from Herndon, VA. In fact, an analysis of other (non-related) sites shows a similar amount of traffic from Virginia. The reason is simple—the RoadRunner cable model network. The `rr.com` domain is registered in Herndon, VA. There are thousands of users with RoadRunner-based access—no matter where they are *actually* coming from, the report displays Herndon, VA. That isn't very useful, is it?

The final Web statistic fallacy is the number of hits a page receives. Many people are delighted when they find that they're getting a few thousand hits a day, but they don't realize what constitutes a hit. The Apache Web server counts *any* information requested as a hit. If a Web page has ten tiny icons on it, it takes at least 11 hits to load the page (1 for the page, 10 for the icons). As pages become more graphically rich, it takes even more requests to load them. A 10,000-hit-per-day site might only be serving a few hundred pages per day!

As long as you realize that log analysis data can be deceiving, it can still provide useful information. Here are a few popular Web statistics packages available for Mac OS X:

Analog—The world's most popular statistics software, Analog provides all the basics in a very simple layout. Analog doesn't create DTP-quality graphs or have the snazziest interface you've ever seen, but it's fast, does a good job, and it's free. `http://www.summary.net/soft/analog.html`.

Sawmill—The Sawmill software provides complete statistics including search engine identification and a unique Calendar view for located information by month and date. Sawmill is a commercial package costing $99 and up. `http://www.flowerfire.com/sawmill/samples.html`.

Summary—Summary is a great entry-level piece of software with advanced reporting features. Data can be exported directly to spreadsheet format for external graphing. Single-user licenses for Summary start at $59. `http://summary.net/download.html`.

Urchin—Urchin has, without a doubt, the most user-friendly and attractive interface, as shown in Figure 27.2. Behind the interface is one of the most comprehensive Web statistics applications available—exceeding such industry stand-bys as WebTrends. Urchin is the ultimate stats solution for serious Web sites. Urchin starts at $199 for an individual server license, but can operate in Lite mode for free. `http://www.urchin.com/download/`.

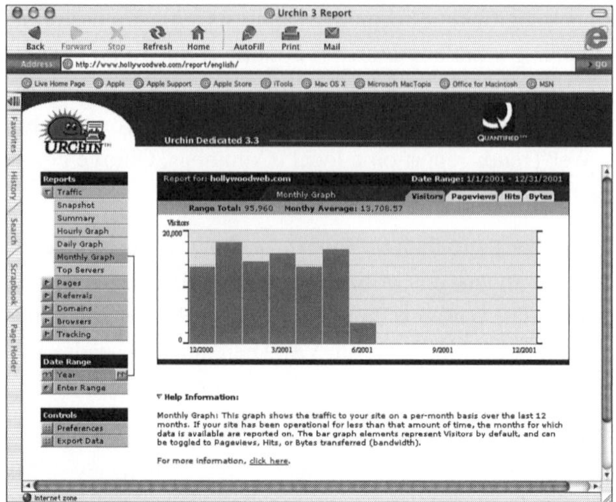

FIGURE 27.2
Web statistics can provide valuable information about your site's operation. The Urchin log analysis software is shown here.

> **Note**
>
> I do not endorse any stats package over another. The primary difference in Web statistics packages is the interface and data presentation. Remember, there is a *very* finite amount of data stored in the log file. The best log analysis software is one that creates the reports with the information you need, in the format you need it.

Container Options

The second type of Apache directives are container based. These directives control how Apache serves a certain group of files. Files are chosen based on pattern or location and are denoted by a start and end tag in the Apache configuration file. For example, the `/etc/httpd/users/` configuration files define a container consisting of each user's `Sites` directory. This is the configuration file created for my `jray` user account (in my case, that file would be `/etc/httpd/httpd.conf`):

```
<Directory "/Users/jray/Sites/">
    Options Indexes MultiViews
    AllowOverride None
    Order allow,deny
    Allow from all
</Directory>
```

In this example, the directory `/Users/jray/Sites` is the container. Web pages within this container can use the `Indexes` and `Multiviews` options. The `AllowOverride`, `Order`, and `Allow` directives control who has access to the files within this container. This will be explained in more detail shortly.

Besides a directory container, there are other constructs that can also be added to the configuration file(s):

Directory—Creates a directory-based container. All files within the named directory are part of the container.

DirectoryMatch—Like Directory, but uses a regular expression to match directory names. Check Chapter 22, "Perl Scripting and SQL Connectivity," for more information on regular expressions.

Files—Groups files based on their name. All files matching the specified name are included in the container. The filename should be given exactly, or using the `?` and `*` wildcards to match a single unknown character or any number of unknown characters.

FilesMatch—Similar to Files, but matches filenames based on a regular expression rather than an exact name.

Location—The Location container is similar to Directory but matches Web content based on a URL, rather than a full-server directory.

LocationMatch—If you've been following along, you'll probably guess correctly that LocationMatch is the same as Location, but matches the URL based on a regular expression.

VirtualHost—The VirtualHost container defines a virtual server within the main server. For external clients, the virtual host appears identical to any other Web server. To you, the system administrator, it is a directory on your server that gets its very own domain name. You'll see how this can be set up shortly.

Within the container objects, the administrator can add a number of directives to control access to the contents, or what special features are available in that location. Table 27.3 includes the container directives you'll encounter most often. We're going to explicitly set up password protection and virtual hosting shortly because this can be a bit tricky just going on the directive definitions alone.

TABLE 27.3 Apache Container Directives

Directive	*Description*
`Options <Option List>`	Sets the special abilities of the server container. There are eight possible options; each can be preceded by an optional + or - to add or remove it. `ExecCGI`—Enables CGI execution; `FollowSymLinks`—Follow symbolic links in the directory; `Includes`—Enable server-side includes, `IncludeNOEXEC`—Enable server-side includes without allowing application execution; `Indexes`—Displays a directory listing if an index document doesn't exist; `MultiViews`—Activates multiple views using content negotiation; `SymLinksIfOwnerMatch`—Follow symbolic links only if the owner of the link matches the owner of the linked directory; and `All`—Enable all options.
`AllowOverride <All>|<None>|<Directive Type>`	Chooses the server-defined directives that a local `.htaccess` file can override. The `.htaccess` file is used to apply directives outside of the main Apache server configuration and can be edited by any user with access to the directory. For that reason, it is important to allow only trusted users to override options. `None`—disables all overrides; `All`—allows all server directives to be overridden, or specifies a combination of `AuthConfig`, `FileInfo`, `Indexes`, `Limit`, or `Options` to allow these directive types to be overridden.
`Order <Deny|Allow>, <Deny|Allow>`	Controls the order in which security controls are evaluated. Whether or not the list of allowed hosts (`Allow`) or denied hosts (`Deny`) is checked first.
`Allow from <allowed networks|all>`	A list of IP addresses, networks and subnets, or domain names that can be *allowed* access to the resource.
`Deny from <allowed networks|all>`	A list of IP addresses, networks and subnets, or domain names that should be *denied* access to the resource.
`AuthType <Basic|Digest>`	Attaches HTTP authorization password protection to a directory.
`AuthName <text string>`	Identifies the password-protected resource to the end user.
`AuthUserFile <userfile path>`	Sets a path to the userfile being used for authentication.
`Require user|group|valid-user <user/group list>`	Allows only listed users, groups, or any valid user to access a directory. The users and groups are *not* Mac OS X users. They are created with the `htpasswd` command.

TABLE 27.3 continued

Directive	*Description*
`ErrorDocument` *<Error ID>* *<Document Path>*	Used to substitute a custom-error page in place of the default Apache pages. Use the standard HTTPD error codes (such as 404) and a path to the HTML page to display when the error occurs within the given resource.
`ServerAdmin`	The e-mail address of the administrator of a virtual host.
`DocumentRoot`	The root-level directory for a virtual host.
`ServerName`	The fully qualified domain name for a virtual host, such as `www.poisontooth.com`.

Now let's see how these directives can be used to refine and secure your Apache Web server.

Password Protection: `htpasswd`

Password protecting a directory is extremely simple. For example, suppose a user wants to password protect his entire public Web site for development purposes. The first step is to set up a username and password file that will contain the login information for those who are allowed to access the resource. This is accomplished using `htpasswd`. There are two steps to the process—first, create a new password file with a single user; second, add additional usernames/passwords to it.

To create a new file, use the syntax `htpasswd -c` *<pathname> <initial username>*. For example:

```
[primal:~/Sites] jray% htpasswd -c /Users/jray/webpasswords jray
New password:
Re-type new password:
Adding password for user jray
```

A new password file (`/Users/jray/webpasswords`) is created, and the initial user `jray` is added.

Subsequent users can be added by calling `htpasswd -b` *<pathname><username> <password>*:

```
[primal:~/Sites] jray% htpasswd -b /Users/jray/webpasswords testuser testpass
Adding password for user testuser
```

The password file now has two entries: the initial `jray` user, and now `testuser`.

Next, create a directory container that encompasses the files that need to be protected. Because this example is protecting a personal Web site, the container already exists as a `username.conf` file in `/etc/httpd/users`:

```
<Directory "/Users/jray/Sites/">
    Options Indexes MultiViews ExecCGI
    AllowOverride None
    Order allow,deny
    Allow from all
</Directory>
```

Note

This example file has been modified slightly since the initial Mac OS X installation. The Options directive includes `ExecCGI` to allow CGI development to take place.

To this directory container, add `AuthType`, `AuthName`, `AuthUserFile`, and `Require` directives. You must be `root` or using `sudo` to edit the file:

```
<Directory "/Users/jray/Sites/">
    AuthType Basic
    AuthName "John's Development Site"
    AuthUserFile /Users/jray/webpasswords
    Require valid-user
    Options Indexes MultiViews ExecCGI
    AllowOverride None
    Order allow,deny
    Allow from all
</Directory>
```

The `AuthUserFile` is set to the name of the password file created with `htpasswd`, whereas the `Require valid-user` directive allows *any* user in the password file to gain access to the protected resource. To activate the authentication, use `sudo /usr/sbin/apachectl restart`:

```
[primal:~/Sites] jray% sudo /usr/sbin/apachectl restart
/usr/sbin/apachectl restart: httpd restarted
```

Attempting to access the `/Users/jray/Sites` directory (`~jray`) now opens an HTTP authentication dialog, as seen in Figure 27.3.

Access to a directory can be restricted even further using the `Allow`, `Deny`, and `Order` directives.

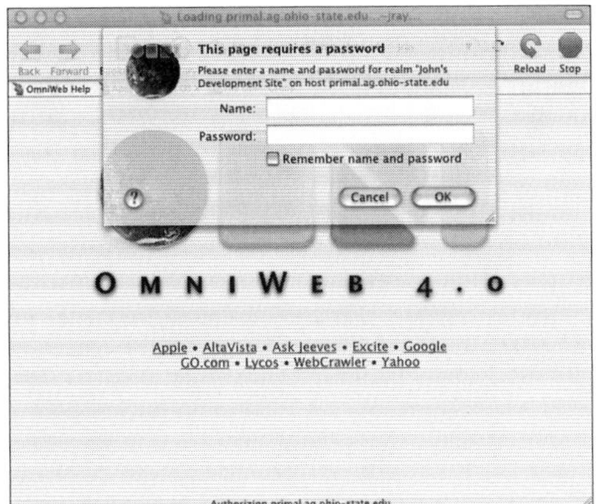

FIGURE 27.3
The directory is now password protected.

Restricting Access by Network

To create more stringent control over the users who can access a given resource, use `Allow` and `Deny` to set up networks that should or shouldn't have access to portions of your Web site. This is extremely useful for setting up intranet sites that should only be accessible by a given subnet. For example, assume that you want to restrict access to a resource from everyone except the subnet `192.168.0.x`. The following rules define the access permissions:

```
Allow from 192.168.0.0/255.255.255.0
Deny from all
```

Because there isn't an ordering specified, what really happens with these rules is ambiguous. Is the connection allowed because of the `allow` statement? Or denied because all the connections are denied?

To solve the problem, insert the `Order` directive:

```
Order Deny,Allow
Allow from 192.168.0.0/255.255.255.0
Deny from all
```

With this ordering, an incoming connection is first compared to the deny list. Because `all` access is denied by default, *any* address matches this rule. However, the `Allow` directive is used for the final evaluation of the connection and will allow any connection from the network `192.168.0.0` with the subnet `255.255.255.0`.

Using different orderings and different `Allow/Deny` lists, you can lock down a Web site to only those people who should have access, or disable troublesome hosts that misuse the site.

Tip

As with any change to the Apache configuration file, you must use `/usr/sbin/apachectl` to restart the server.

An alternative to restarting is to add an `.htaccess` file to the directory you want to protect. This file can contain any of the standard directory container directives and will be automatically read when Apache attempts to read any file from the directory.

Virtual Hosts

A virtual host is a unique container object, in that it can define an entirely separate Web space unrelated to the main Apache Web site or user sites. For example, the three domains `poisontooth.com`, `vujevich.com`, and `shadesofinsanity.com` are all being served from a single computer. To the end user, these appear to be different and unique hosts. To Apache, however, they're just different directories on the same hard drive.

There are two types of virtual hosts, name-based and IP-based:

Name-based—Name-based virtual hosts rely on the HTTP/1.1 protocol to work. A single IP address is used on the server, but there are multiple DNS name entries for that single address. When connecting to the server, the client browser sends a request for a Web page, along with the name of the server it should come from. Apache uses that information to serve the correct page. This works for all but the oldest 2.0 revision browsers.

IP-based—IP-based virtual hosts rely on Apache's capability to listen to multiple IP addresses simultaneously. Each domain name is assigned to a different IP address. Apache can differentiate between the different incoming addresses and serve the appropriate documents for each. This works on *any* browser, but is costly in terms of the IP addresses that it consumes.

To set up a virtual host, you must first have an IP address and a domain name assigned for the host. If you're using name-based hosts, you will have a single IP address but multiple hostnames. Your ISP or network administrator should be able to help set up this information.

Tip

Mac OS X users who are attempting to configure IP-based virtual hosts will find that no GUI currently exists for adding multiple addresses to a single machine. Luckily, they can be added from the command line using `ifconfig <interface>`

alias <*additional IP address*> 255.255.255.255. For most single network card systems, the interface will be en0. AirPort cards are usually identified with en1. For example:

```
ifconfig en0 alias 192.168.0.200 255.255.255.255
```

This adds the IP address 192.168.0.200 as an additional address to the Mac OS X system.

There are only two differences in the Apache configuration of name-based and IP-based virtual hosts. Name-based hosts must include the NameVirtualHost directive, whereas IP-based hosts will need to use Listen to inform Apache of all the available addresses.

Let's take a look at two different ways to configure the virtual hosts www.mycompany.com and www.yourcompany.com. First, using named-based hosting:

Assume that both mycompany and yourcompany domain names point to the IP address 192.168.0.100. To configure name-based virtual hosts, you could add the following directives to the end of the /etc/httpd/httpd.conf file:

```
NameVirtualHost 192.168.0.100

<VirtualHost 192.168.0.100>
        ServerName www.mycompany.com
        DocumentRoot /Users/jray/mycompany
        ServerAdmin president@mycompany.com
</VirtualHost>

<VirtualHost 192.168.0.100>
        ServerName www.yourcompany.com
        DocumentRoot /Users/jray/yourcompany
        ServerAdmin president@yourcompany.com
</VirtualHost>
```

The NameVirtualHost sets up the IP address that Apache will expect multiple domain name requests to come in on. The two VirtualHost directives define the basic properties of the two sites: what their real domain names are, where the HTML documents are loaded, and the e-mail address for the person who runs the site.

Creating this same setup using IP-based hosts doesn't require much additional effort. For this sample configuration, assume that www.mycompany.com has the address 192.168.0.100 and www.yourcompany.com uses 192.168.0.101. The configuration becomes:

```
Listen 192.168.0.100
Listen 192.168.0.101

<VirtualHost 192.168.0.100>
        ServerName www.mycompany.com
        DocumentRoot /Users/jray/mycompany
        ServerAdmin president@mycompany.com
</VirtualHost>

<VirtualHost 192.168.0.101>
        ServerName www.yourcompany.com
        DocumentRoot /Users/jray/yourcompany
        ServerAdmin president@yourcompany.com
</VirtualHost>
```

This time, the `Listen` directive is used to tell Apache to watch for incoming Web connections on both of the available IP addresses. The `VirtualHost` containers remain the same, except they now use different IP addresses for the two different sites.

Virtual hosting provides an important capability to the Mac OS X Web server. Although available with a GUI configuration tool in the Mac OS X Server, the Apache distribution included in Mac OS X is every bit as powerful. It just takes a bit of manual editing to get things done!

Rebuilding and Securing Apache

Many of today's hot Web sites include e-commerce or other private areas that require secure communications. Unfortunately, although Mac OS X *does* ship with SSL support built into Apache, it is neither enabled nor easily configured. In addition, the version of Apache shipped with Mac OS X lags behind the current release by several version numbers. Don't worry, this isn't cause for great alarm, but it does make things tricky for system administrators who want to stay current with the supplied BSD software.

There are two goals to rebuilding and securing Apache. The first is to, obviously, rebuild Apache with the latest source code from `Apache.org`. The second, and intimately related, goal is to configure Apache for SSL communications during the rebuild process. If you have no need for secure Web services, just skip this section.

What Is SSL?

SSL stands for Secure Sockets Layer. It is a protocol developed by Netscape for transmitting sensitive data over the HTTP protocol. All data that passes over SSL is encrypted using a variable-length key. The key size determines the level of encryption. SSL-enabled Web sites are typically used in banking and e-commerce applications to provide security during credit card and other money transactions. In addition, SSL provides support for digitally signed certificates that are used to verify that a server or client is who it claims to be. We highly recommend that anyone who hasn't set up an SSL server before read this introduction before continuing: www.modssl.org/docs/2.8/ssl_intro.html.

Building Apache

To build Apache with SSL support, we need a few components before we can get started. Unlike most Apache modules, the mod_ssl software must be compiled at the same time as the Apache source code. In addition, you will need to download the OpenSSL software that mod_ssl uses for security. Some of this software is included on Mac OS X, but is missing the necessary header files to complete the installation. Rather than muddling with partially broken software, it's easiest to just install from scratch.

First, download the latest Apache source from http://www.apache.org/, the most current version of mod_ssl from http://www.modssl.org, and the Darwin-patched OpenSSL distribution from http://www.stepwise.org. Place them in a common build directory:

```
[localhost:~] jray% mkdir apachebuild
[localhost:~] jray% cd apachebuild/
[localhost:~/apachebuild] jray% wget http://www.modssl.org/source/mod
                   ➥_ssl-2.8.4-1.3.20.tar.gz
[localhost:~/apachebuild] jray% wget http://httpd.apache.org/dist/httpd/apache
                   ➥_1.3.20.tar.gz
[localhost:~/apachebuild] jray% wget http://www3.stepwise.com/Articles/Workbench
                   ➥/OpenSSL-0.9.5a-3.1.tar.gz
```

Now, decompress and untar (`tar zxf <filename>`) each of the archives:

```
[localhost:~/apachebuild] jray% tar zxf apache_1.3.20.tar.gz
[localhost:~/apachebuild] jray% tar zxf mod_ssl-2.8.4-1.3.20.tar.gz
[localhost:~/apachebuild] jray% tar zxf OpenSSL-0.9.5a-3.1.tar.gz
```

All done! Let's move on.

Preparing mod_ssl

The next step is to prepare mod_ssl—this can be skipped if you are simply upgrading Apache and have no desire to add SSL support. Use the command `./configure --with-apache=<path to apache source distribution>` from within the mod_ssl distribution directory, substituting in the appropriate name of your Apache distribution:

```
[localhost:~/apachebuild/mod_ssl-2.8.4-1.3.20] jray% ./configure --with-apache=.
./apache_1.3.20
Configuring mod_ssl/2.8.4 for Apache/1.3.20
 + Apache location: ../apache_1.3.20 (Version 1.3.20)
 + Auxiliary patch tool: ./etc/patch/patch (local)
 + Applying packages to Apache source tree:
   o Extended API (EAPI)
   o Distribution Documents
   o SSL Module Source
   o SSL Support
   o SSL Configuration Additions
   o SSL Module Documentation
   o Addons
Done: source extension and patches successfully applied.
```

The `mod_ssl` configuration will include several additional instructions on how to finish the Apache installation—*do not* follow them or your compiled Apache server will be missing some important functions.

Preparing OpenSSL

Now it's time to set up the OpenSSL system—again, skip this step if you have no intention of running an SSL-enabled server. Compiling might take quite awhile, depending on your system speed. You might want to start this process, then walk away for a few minutes. To configure OpenSSL for compilation, `cd` into the distribution directory (`OpenSSL-3-1/openssl`) and type `./config`:

```
[localhost:~/apachebuild/OpenSSL-3-1/openssl] jray% ./config
Operating system: powerpc-apple-darwin1.3.3
Configuring for Darwin
IsWindows=0
...
```

After the software has been configured, use `make` to compile OpenSSL:

```
[localhost:~/apachebuild/OpenSSL-3-1/openssl] jray% make
making all in crypto...
( echo "#ifndef MK1MF_BUILD"; \
echo "  /* auto-generated by crypto/Makefile.ssl for crypto/cversion.c */"; \
echo "  #define CFLAGS \"cc -O3 -fomit-frame-pointer -Wall\""; \
echo "  #define PLATFORM \"Darwin\""; \
echo "  #define DATE \"`date`\""; \
echo "#endif" ) >buildinf.h
...
and on...
and on...
...
```

Finally, it's time to compile and install Apache.

Building Apache

Building Apache is straightforward—Apple has worked with the Apache group to incorporate information about the Mac OS X (Darwin) operating system into the source code distribution. What this means to *you* is that Apache, when compiled and installed, will correctly integrate itself with the Mac OS X operating system.

To configure Apache for installation, first `cd` into the source distribution directory. If you are compiling with SSL support, you must set the `SSL_BASE` environment variable to point to the directory containing the OpenSSL source distribution:

```
[localhost:~/apachebuild/apache_1.3.20] jray% setenv SSL_BASE=../
            ➥OpenSSL-3-1/openssl
```

Next, use `./configure --enable-module=all --enable-shared=max` to setup the distribution for the Mac OS X environment:

```
[localhost:~/apachebuild/apache_1.3.20] jray% sudo ./configure --enable-module=a
ll --enable-shared=max
Password:
Configuring for Apache, Version 1.3.20
 + using installation path layout: Darwin (config.layout)
Creating Makefile
Creating Configuration.apaci in src
Creating Makefile in src
 + configured for Darwin platform
 + setting C compiler to cc
 + setting C pre-processor to cc -E -traditional-cpp
 + checking for system header files
 + adding selected modules
    o rewrite_module uses ConfigStart/End
      enabling DBM support for mod_rewrite
    o dbm_auth_module uses ConfigStart/End
    o db_auth_module uses ConfigStart/End
      using Berkeley-DB/1.x for mod_auth_db (-lc)
    o ssl_module uses ConfigStart/End
      + SSL interface: mod_ssl/2.8.4
...
```

If an error occurs, make sure that you have correctly set the `SSL_BASE` and typed the command-line options exactly as they appear here.

Now, one tiny correction needs to be made to the SSL module `Makefile`. From within the main Apache source distribution, `cd` into `src/modules/ssl/`. Open the file `Makefile` in your favorite text editor, and look for the line that reads:

```
SSL_LIBS= ldbm -lssl -lcrypto
```

Change it to

```
SSL_LIBS= -lssl -lcrypto
```

If you fail to follow these steps, the compilation process will complain of a missing library.

Finally, compile your new version of Apache by typing `make` from within the root level of the Apache source directory:

```
[localhost:~/apachebuild/apache_1.3.20] jray% make
===> src
===> src/regex
<=== src/regex
===> src/os/unix
cc -c  -I../../os/unix -I../../include   -DDARWIN -DMOD_SSL=208104 -DUSE
  ➥_HSREGEX -DEAPI -DUSE_EXPAT -I../../lib/expat-lite `../../apaci` os.c
...
```

The compile should finish in roughly five minutes on a base 500MHz G4. When the compile finishes, Apache will display a success message with the following instructions:

```
+--------------------------------------------------------------------+
| Before you install the package you now should prepare the SSL      |
| certificate system by running the 'make certificate' command.      |
| For different situations the following variants are provided:      |
|                                                                    |
| % make certificate TYPE=dummy    (dummy self-signed Snake Oil cert) |
| % make certificate TYPE=test     (test cert signed by Snake Oil CA) |
| % make certificate TYPE=custom   (custom cert signed by own CA)    |
| % make certificate TYPE=existing (existing cert)                   |
|        CRT=/path/to/your.crt [KEY=/path/to/your.key]               |
|                                                                    |
| Use TYPE=dummy    when you're a  vendor package maintainer,        |
| the TYPE=test     when you're an admin but want to do tests only,  |
| the TYPE=custom   when you're an admin willing to run a real server |
| and TYPE=existing when you're an admin who upgrades a server.      |
| (The default is TYPE=test)                                         |
|                                                                    |
| Additionally add ALGO=RSA (default) or ALGO=DSA to select          |
| the signature algorithm used for the generated certificate.        |
|                                                                    |
| Use 'make certificate VIEW=1' to display the generated data.       |
|                                                                    |
| Thanks for using Apache & mod_ssl.       Ralf S. Engelschall       |
|                                          rse@engelschall.com       |
|                                          www.engelschall.com       |
+--------------------------------------------------------------------+
```

You now have the most recent version of Apache, and it is ready to start handling secure Web traffic! All that remains is a few more minutes of setting up a basic certificate. If you are not using SSL, you can type `sudo make install` start using the new version of Apache immediately.

Creating a Certificate and Installing

Secure Web servers rely on a CA (Certifying Authority) signed certificate to prove their identity and open a secure connection with a client. Unfortunately, obtaining a certificate isn't as simple as going to a Web site and buying one. An official certificate can be issued only by a CA, and only after generating and sending a CSR (Certificate Signing Request) to it. Luckily, for the purposes of testing SSL-enabled Apache, you can sign your own certificate. This will create a secure server, but most Web browsers will display a dialog box when accessing a server that isn't signed by a known CA. For the purposes of this chapter, we'll assume that you want to get up and running quickly, and that you'll want to use a VeriSign or other CA signed certificate later on.

Assuming that you're still in the Apache distribution directory, type `make certificate TYPE=test`. This will take you through the steps of setting up a certificate, automatically signing it using a fictional CA so that it can be used immediately, and then creating a CSR file so that you can send in a request for a real certificate in the future. Sound good? Let's give it a shot. During the certification creation, you'll be asked a series of questions related to your business or organization. Of all the questions, it is most important to correctly answer the Common Name prompt. This is the hostname of your Web server (for example, `www.poisontooth.com`). Any questions you are unsure of can be left with their default values:

```
[localhost:~/apachebuild/apache_1.3.20] jray% make certificate TYPE=test
SSL Certificate Generation Utility (mkcert.sh)
Copyright (c) 1998-2000 Ralf S. Engelschall, All Rights Reserved.

Generating test certificate signed by Snake Oil CA [TEST]
WARNING: Do not use this for real-life/production systems
______________________________________________________________________

STEP 0: Decide the signature algorithm used for certificate
The generated X.509 CA certificate can contain either
RSA or DSA based ingredients. Select the one you want to use.
Signature Algorithm ((R)SA or (D)SA) [R]:
______________________________________________________________________

STEP 1: Generating RSA private key (1024 bit) [server.key]
2529186 semi-random bytes loaded
Generating RSA private key, 1024 bit long modulus
...........................++++++
......++++++
e is 65537 (0x10001)
______________________________________________________________________

STEP 2: Generating X.509 certificate signing request [server.csr]
Using configuration from .mkcert.cfg
```

```
You are about to be asked to enter information that will be incorporated
into your certificate request.
What you are about to enter is what is called a Distinguished Name or a DN.
There are quite a few fields but you can leave some blank
For some fields there will be a default value,
If you enter '.', the field will be left blank.
-----
1. Country Name             (2 letter code) [XY]:US
2. State or Province Name   (full name)     [Snake Desert]:Ohio
3. Locality Name            (eg, city)      [Snake Town]:Dublin
4. Organization Name        (eg, company)   [Snake Oil, Ltd]:PoisonTooth, Ent.
5. Organizational Unit Name (eg, section)   [Webserver Team]:
6. Common Name             (eg, FQDN)      [www.snakeoil.dom]:www.poisontooth.com
7. Email Address           (eg, name@FQDN) [www@snakeoil.dom]:jray@poisontooth.com
8. Certificate Validity     (days)          [365]:
______________________________________________________________________

STEP 3: Generating X.509 certificate signed by Snake Oil CA [server.crt]
Certificate Version (1 or 3) [3]:
Signature ok
subject=/C=US/ST=Ohio/L=Dublin/O=PoisonTooth, Ent./OU=Webserver
Team/CN=www.poisontooth.com/Email=jray@poisontooth.com
Getting CA Private Key
Verify: matching certificate & key modulus
read RSA key
Verify: matching certificate signature
../conf/ssl.crt/server.crt: OK
______________________________________________________________________

STEP 4: Enrypting RSA private key with a pass phrase for security [server.key]
The contents of the server.key file (the generated private key) has to be
kept secret. So we strongly recommend you to encrypt the server.key file
with a Triple-DES cipher and a Pass Phrase.
Encrypt the private key now? [Y/n]: n
Warning, you're using an unencrypted RSA private key.
Please notice this fact and do this on your own risk.
______________________________________________________________________

RESULT: Server Certification Files

o  conf/ssl.key/server.key
   The PEM-encoded RSA private key file which you configure
   with the 'SSLCertificateKeyFile' directive (automatically done
   when you install via APACI). KEEP THIS FILE PRIVATE!

o  conf/ssl.crt/server.crt
   The PEM-encoded X.509 certificate file which you configure
   with the 'SSLCertificateFile' directive (automatically done
   when you install via APACI).

o  conf/ssl.csr/server.csr
```

```
    The PEM-encoded X.509 certificate signing request file which
    you can send to an official Certificate Authority (CA) in order
    to request a real server certificate (signed by this CA instead
    of our demonstration-only Snake Oil CA) which later can replace
    the conf/ssl.crt/server.crt file.

WARNING: Do not use this for real-life/production systems
```

In this example, there is only one nonintuitive response—the use of encryption for the server key (`Encrypt the private key now? [Y/n]: n`). If the server key *is* encrypted, you will have to manually enter a password to unlock the key each time the server is started, or write a script to supply the password to the server. When the key is left unencrypted, the assumption is made that your server protection is sufficient to keep the file safe from prying eyes. The Apache server and certificate are ready to install. Type `sudo make install` to prepare the software:

```
[localhost:~/apachebuild/apache_1.3.20] jray% sudo make install
===> [mktree: Creating Apache installation tree]
./src/helpers/mkdir.sh /usr/bin
./src/helpers/mkdir.sh /usr/sbin
...
+--------------------------------------------------------+
| You now have successfully built and installed the      |
| Apache 1.3 HTTP server. To verify that Apache actually |
| works correctly you now should first check the         |
| (initially created or preserved) configuration files   |
|                                                        |
|   /etc/httpd/httpd.conf
|                                                        |
| and then you should be able to immediately fire up     |
| Apache the first time by running:                      |
|                                                        |
|   /usr/sbin/apachectl start
|                                                        |
| Or when you want to run it with SSL enabled use:       |
|                                                        |
|   /usr/sbin/apachectl startssl
|                                                        |
| Thanks for using Apache.       The Apache Group        |
|                                http://www.apache.org/  |
+--------------------------------------------------------+
```

Unfortunately, the installation of the newly compiled Apache needs a modified version of the configuration file, so there are still two final changes to be made before we're done. Open the file `/etc/httpd/httpd.conf.default` and add the following line to the bottom of the file:

```
Include /private/etc/httpd/users
```

Next, search for the directive

```
UserDir public_html
```

and change it to

```
UserDir Sites
```

Save the configuration file, and copy it to take the place of `/etc/httpd/httpd.conf`. *Now* we're ready to go. Stop the existing Apache server (`apachectl stop`) and start the new SSL-enabled server with `apachectl startssl`.

```
Include /private/etc/httpd/users
[localhost:/etc/httpd] root# /usr/sbin/apachectl stop
/usr/sbin/apachectl stop: httpd stopped
[localhost:/etc/httpd] root# /usr/sbin/apachectl startssl
Processing config directory: /private/etc/httpd/users
 Processing config file: /private/etc/httpd/users/jray.conf
 Processing config file: /private/etc/httpd/users/robyn.conf
 Processing config file: /private/etc/httpd/users/test.conf
 Processing config file: /private/etc/httpd/users/test2.conf
/usr/sbin/apachectl startssl: httpd started
```

To configure Mac OS X to automatically start Apache in SSL mode each time it boots, edit the file `/System/Library/StartupItems/Apache/Apache` and change the line

```
apachectl start
```

to read

```
apachectl startssl
```

That wasn't so bad, was it? Your Mac OS X machine is now a full- fledged secure Web server. To test it, open a Web browser and point to a URL on the machine, prefacing the URL with `https://` rather than the usual `http://`. Your browser might display a message about the certificate and signing authority not being recognized. You can expect to see these messages until you send in a certificate-signing request to a recognized CA.

Certifying Authorities

When you created your server certificate, you also created a CSR that can be sent to a CA to generate a real certificate. The certificate signing request file is stored in `/etc/httpd/ssl.csr/server.csr`. This file can be sent to a CA, such as

VeriSign—`http://digitalid.verisign.com/server/apacheNotice.htm`

Thawte—`www.thawte.com/certs/server/request.html`

After processing your request, the CA will return a new digitally signed certificate file. Replace the existing `/etc/httpd/ssl.crt/server.crt` certificate with the CA signed certificate, and your server will be official.

Note

There are a large number of SSL configuration directives that you can include to fine-tune Apache's secure services. The default configuration file is sufficient for most, but if you'd like to alter the setup, please read the `http://www.modssl.org/` documentation. SSL is *not* a simple topic and will require resources beyond the scope of this book.

WebDAV—mod_dav

Something that Apple hasn't advertised with Mac OS X is the integration of WebDAV as a native file-sharing format. WebDAV (Distributed Authoring and Versioning) is a relatively new protocol that operates on top of HTTP. What makes this attractive is the fact it doesn't require additional `inetd` or system daemons to be present.

WebDAV is entirely cross-platform, is integrated into the Windows operating system, and supported natively in software such as Macromedia Dreamweaver as well. Using WebDAV, you can distribute authoring and editing Web sites across a number of different computers and operating systems. Best of all, WebDAV is easy to use and, because it operates through Apache, the same configuration directives you've already seen can apply directly to its setup.

Installing and Configuring WebDAV

You can download the WebDAV Apache module (`mod_dav`) from `www.webdav.org/mod_dav/`. Installing WebDAV is an excellent example of a typical Apache module compilation.

First, unarchive and uncompress the software:

```
[primal:~] jray% tar zxf mod_dav-1.0.2-1.3.6.tar.gz
```

Next, configure the application. You should use the `--with-apxs` directive to enable automatic configuration and installation of the Apache module:

```
[primal:~/mod_dav-1.0.2-1.3.6] jray% ./configure --with-apxs
creating cache ./config.cache
checking for gcc... no
checking for cc... cc
checking whether the C compiler (cc  ) works... yes
checking whether the C compiler (cc  ) is a cross-compiler... no
checking whether we are using GNU C... yes
checking whether cc accepts -g... yes
checking for ranlib... ranlib
```

Finally, make and install the module:

```
[primal:~/mod_dav-1.0.2-1.3.6] jray% sudo make install
cc -c   -I/usr/include/httpd -I/usr/include/httpd/xml -g -O2 -DDARWIN -DUSE
        ➥_HSREGEX -DUSE_EXPAT -I../lib/expat-lite -g -O3 -pipe
        ➥ -DHARD_SERVER_LIMIT=1024 -DEAPI -DSHARED_MODULE
        ➥   dav_props.c -o dav_props.o
...
cp libdav.so /usr/libexec/httpd/libdav.so
chmod 755 /usr/libexec/httpd/libdav.so
[activating module `dav' in /private/etc/httpd/httpd.conf]
```

Note

Modules that are installed using the `apxs` utility are automatically placed in the appropriate location and have the appropriate `LoadModule` and `AddModule` directives added to the `http.conf` file.

To finish the configuration and activation of WebDAV service on your Apache server, you need to create a directory that will hold WebDAV lock files and then turn on the service for a particular directory or location.

Use the `DAVLockDB` directive to set the directory and base filename for WebDAV's lockfiles. This should fall anywhere after the `LoadModule/AddModule` lines in the `/etc/httpd/httpd.conf` file:

```
DAVLockDB /var/tmp/davlock
```

This example specifies that the directory `/var/tmp` will be used to hold lock files, and that `davlock` will be the base filename for the lock files. Be sure to include the base filename, not just a directory name. If the lockfile is not properly set, `mod_dav` will start, but won't operate correctly.

Now, choose one of the directory or container objects that will support WebDAV service and add the `DAV On` directive:

```
<Directory "/Library/WebServer/Documents">
     DAV On
     Options Indexes FollowSymLinks MultiViews
     AllowOverride None
     Order allow,deny
     Allow from all
</Directory>
```

You should limit access to the DAV services using the same `require` directive in the standard Apache configuration. WebDAV relies on the HTTP protocol to authenticate users for editing. This means you will need to create a password file just like we did earlier. Unlike the previous example, however, a valid user will be required only when performing a modification to the file system. To create this sort of selective authentication, we'll use the `Limit` directive. For example, the following configuration file fragment defines an authentication scheme and limits it to the operations that WebDAV uses to add and update files.

```
AuthType Basic
AuthName "The Poisontooth Webserver"
AuthUserFile /Users/jray/webpasswords
<Limit PUT DELETE PROPPATCH MKCOL COPY MOVE LOCK UNLOCK>
          Require valid-user
</Limit>
```


To finish things up, just combine the authentication block with the resource that WebDAV support has been enabled (`DAV On`):

```
1: <Directory "/Library/WebServer/Documents">
2:       DAV On
3:       Options Indexes FollowSymLinks MultiViews
4:       AllowOverride None
5:       Order allow,deny
6:       Allow from all
7:       AuthType Basic
8:       AuthName "The Poisontooth Webserver"
9:       AuthUserFile /Users/jray/webpasswords
10:      <Limit PUT DELETE PROPPATCH MKCOL COPY MOVE LOCK UNLOCK>
11:          Require valid-user
12:      </Limit>
13: </Directory>
```

Line 1 sets up the directory to WebDAV enable. This can be a directory that is already defined in the main Apache `http.conf` or one of the user configuration files.

Line 2 turns on DAV support, and lines 3 through 6 are standard directory security directives—not WebDAV related.

Lines 7 through 9 set up basic HTTP authentication. This will be used to authenticate potential WebDAV clients. Lines 10–12 limit the HTTP authentication to only those actions that would be triggered by a WedDAV client.

There's still one small thing that needs to be adjusted before WebDAV can be used—the permissions on the directory that has DAV support enabled. Because WebDAV is nothing more than an extension to Apache, it has no more user rights than the Apache server process. This means that if Apache can't write to a resource (that is, it isn't owned by www or isn't set to world-writable), WebDAV won't be able to modify the resource either. To make a directory editable using DAV, you must use `chown` to modify the file and directory ownership. Type `chown -R www:admin <directory to DAV-enable>` and you're done!

Restart Apache (`/usr/sbin/apachectl restart`) to begin using WebDAV.

Mounting WebDAV Shares

First, from within a Finder window, use the Go menu to choose Connect to Server (Command+K). The dialog box shown in Figure 27.4 will appear.

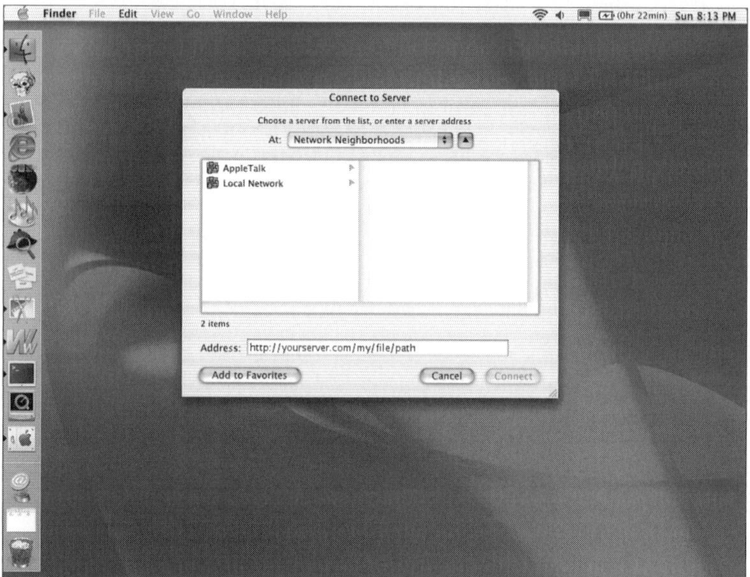

FIGURE 27.4
Use the Connect to Server menu item to connect to WebDAV-enabled servers.

Fill in the URL of the directory with DAV access in the Address field. This should be the *Web* path to the resource, not the actual file path on the server. In the screenshot shown, the main root directory of the Web server has been enabled, so the URL given is just set to the main Web site URL. When satisfied that your settings are correct, click Connect. You will be prompted for a username and password for the resource. Use the username/password pair defined with `htpasswd`.

After a few seconds, the remote site should be mounted as if it were a local drive on your computer.

Tip

Although not entirely practical (it's *really* slow), WebDAV volumes work just like AppleShare or NFS volumes under Mac OS X. Unlike the implementation on certain other platforms, Mac OS X users can store and execute applications directly on WebDAV shares. In Mac OS X 10.1, your iDisk is accessed entirely via the WebDAV protocol. This enables it to appear to be connected all the time. The end result is more convenient access for you, and less of a load on Apple's servers.

Using WebDAV on Windows

Like Mac OS X, WebDAV is integrated into recent releases of the Windows operating system. To access a WebDAV share from your Linux Web server, you must create a new Network Place.

Double-click My Network Places to open the Network Places window. Next, double-click Add Network Place to start the Network Place wizard, as seen in Figure 27.5.

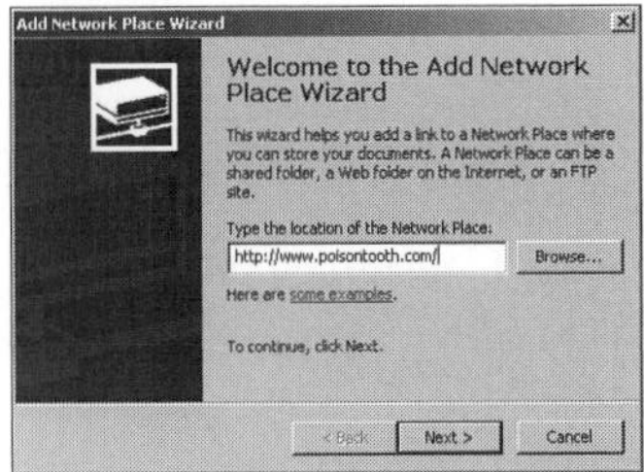

FIGURE 27.5
The Network Place connection wizard will help set up a WebDAV resource in Windows.

Fill in the URL of the WebDAV resource, and then click Next. As with Mac OS X, you will be prompted for the username and password that were set using `htpasswd`. Click Next to finish and mount the resource.

WebDAV support is an integral part of Mac OS X and Windows, and can be used to unite a multiplatform environment for collaboration on Web sites and other projects. In a pinch, WebDAV can even serve as a file server for things other than Web-related files.

That's enough work for now. On to something a bit more entertaining—streaming audio from Apache!

Streaming MP3s—mod_mp3

If you've been using iTunes, you've probably got quite a collection of MP3 files that have been building up on your drive. Rather than taking the MP3s with you wherever you go, you can create your own Internet radio station and broadcast music to your computer at work, home, or wherever your MP3s aren't. Using the Apache mod_mp3 module, you can create a Shoutcast-compatible streaming MP3 server in a matter of minutes. Of course, it goes without saying that anyone who listens to your streams has a legitimate copy of the music. Absolutely no sarcasm intended. None.

Installing mod_mp3 only takes a few minutes of time. Download the latest release from http://www.modmp3.com/, and then decompress the archive:

```
[primal:~/mod_mp3] jray% tar zxf mod_mp3-0.19.tar.gz
```

Next, cd into the distribution directory, and use make install to compile the module:

```
[primal:~/mod_mp3] jray% cd mod_mp3-0.19/
[primal:~/mod_mp3/mod_mp3-0.19] jray% make install
apxs -o mod_mp3.so -c    directives.c ice.c load.c mod_mp3.c shout.c utility.c o
gg.c common.c
cc -DDARWIN -DUSE_HSREGEX -DUSE_EXPAT -I../lib/expat-lite -g -O3 -pipe -
                   ➥DHARD_SERVER_LIMIT=1024 -DEAPI -DSHARED_MODULE
                   ➥ -I/usr/include/httpd  -c directives.c
cc -DDARWIN -DUSE_HSREGEX -DUSE_EXPAT -I../lib/expat-lite -g -O3 -pipe -
                   ➥DHARD_SERVER_LIMIT=1024 -DEAPI -DSHARED_MODULE
                   ➥ -I/usr/include/httpd  -c ice.c
cc -DDARWIN -DUSE_HSREGEX -DUSE_EXPAT -I../lib/expat-lite -g -O3 -pipe -
                   ➥DHARD_SERVER_LIMIT=1024 -DEAPI -DSHARED_MODULE
                   ➥-I/usr/include/httpd  -c load.c
```

Although the included installation instructions say to use make install to install the module, this does not work correctly under Mac OS X. Use sudo apxs -i -a -n 'mp3' mod_mp3.so to complete the process:

```
[primal:~/mod_mp3/mod_mp3-0.19] jray% sudo apxs -i -a -n 'mp3' mod_mp3.so
cp mod_mp3.so /usr/libexec/httpd/mod_mp3.so
chmod 755 /usr/libexec/httpd/mod_mp3.so
[activating module `mp3' in /private/etc/httpd/httpd.conf]
```

The MP3-streaming module is now installed and ready for use.

Configuring mod_mp3

The mod_mp3 module is activated by setting up an Apache virtual host that will serve as the contact point for iTunes or any other streaming MP3 client. There are two ways to approach this—either by using a name-based or IP-based host, as we've already seen, or using a virtual host running on a port address rather than the standard Web server port 80. We shall use the latter.

There are a handful of directives used to control the mod_mp3 streaming features. These are documented in Table 27.4.

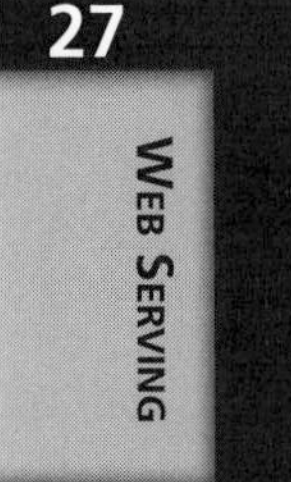

TABLE 27.4 These Directives Control mod_mp3's Capability to Stream Music.

<table>
<tr><th>Directive</th><th>Purpose</th></tr>
<tr><td>MP3 <file or pathname></td><td>Adds an MP3 file or directory containing MP3 files to the list of files to be served.</td></tr>
<tr><td>MP3Engine <on|off></td><td>Turns on the streaming engine.</td></tr>
<tr><td>MP3CastName <stream name></td><td>Sets a name for the streaming music collection.</td></tr>
<tr><td>MP3Genre <stream genre></td><td>Sets a music genre for the stream.</td></tr>
<tr><td>MP3Random <on|off></td><td>Randomizes the order that MP3 files will be served.</td></tr>
<tr><td>MP3Loop <on|off></td><td>Loops through the music files indefinitely.</td></tr>
<tr><td>MP3LimitPlayConnections <connection limit></td><td>The number of simultaneous streaming connections that will be supported.</td></tr>
<tr><td>MP3ReloadRequest <on|off></td><td>If turned on, mod_mp3 will reload all files with each request. This is useful if you're adding to the available files during the broadcast.</td></tr>
<tr><td>MP3Playlist <playlist file></td><td>Accepts the name of a file that contains a list of MP3 filenames.</td></tr>
<tr><td>MP3Cache <on|off></td><td>When on, the module will attempt to cache all MP3 files in memory. This can speed up the server, but will likely take up waaaay too much memory if you have more than a handful of files.</td></tr>
</table>

Use these directives, coupled with a virtual host, to set up and start streaming. The following is a typical sample virtual host entry for the /etc/httpd/httpd.conf file:

```
Listen 8000
<VirtualHost music.poisontooth.com:8000>
   ServerName music.poisontooth.com
   MP3Engine On
   MP3CastName "Johns Tunes"
   MP3Genre "Hard Rock and 80s"
   MP3 /Users/jray/Music
   MP3Random On
   Timeout 1200
</VirtualHost>
```

Line 1 sets the port number for listening to incoming streaming requests. The default Web port is 80, so if you're using the hostname for a Web site as well as streaming music, be sure to pick a different port.

Line 2 sets up the virtual host and port number for connections. Line 4 turns on MP3 support, and Lines 5 and 6 set some identifying information for the streaming server.

Line 7 adds a directory containing MP3 files to the stream (you can add as many `MP3` directives as you'd like). Line 8 randomizes the playback order; and line 9 sets a high timeout so that connections are properly serviced.

Restart Apache to turn on your new `mod_mp3`-streaming server: `/usr/sbin/apachectl restart`.

> **Note**
>
> Starting the Apache Web server with `mod_mp3` and a reasonably sized MP3 collection can take several seconds. Don't worry if the system appears to stall occasionally.

To access your new MP3 server using iTunes, select Open Stream (Command+U) and enter the URL of your MP3 virtual host. The sample `mod_mp3` configuration used in this chapter would be referenced with the URL `http://music.poisontooth.com:8000`, as seen in Figure 27.6.

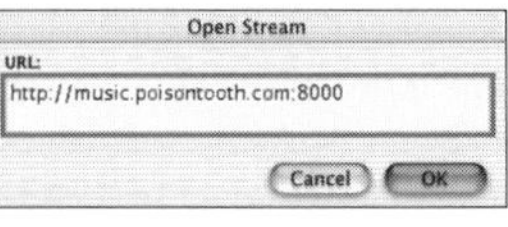

FIGURE 27.6
Open the Apache-served MP3 stream from within iTunes.

Summary

Apache is an extremely configurable and a very powerful Web server platform. The basic Apache software can be configured with network and user-level security and used to set up multiple virtual hosts on a single computer. If the basic software isn't enough, Apache can be expanded to include SSL support, MP3 streaming, and integrated file-sharing capabilities. The Apache module library continues to grow and add new features daily. As you might have guessed, Apache is a very large and capable server application. If you'd like to learn more, I suggest looking at an Apache-dedicated title, such as *Sams Apache Server Unleashed*, ISBN 0672318083. Apple's Personal Web server is capable of publishing a few pages, or your entire corporate Web site.

Server Health

Part VII

In This Part

CHAPTER 28

Web Programming

In This Chapter

A Web server is only as good as its content. Creating a Web site that changes over time is an important step in keeping users interested. The Mac OS X BSD base provides access to dozens of different programming and scripting languages, each of which can be used for creating dynamic Web applications that run from within Apache.

This chapter should serve as a beginner's guide to CGI (common gateway interface) programming, and will introduce topics ranging from CGI security to Perl and PHP programming. Like many of the Unix chapters in *Mac OS X Unleashed*, it is important to remember that the information provided is appropriate for learning about the technology available in the operating system. If you're starting from scratch, you might want to look into additional references on Web development.

Introduction to Web Programming

Writing an application for the Web is not quite as simple as writing an application or script that executes on a local machine. Web applications must obey the HTTP protocol, which, by design, is stateless and connectionless. This poses quite a problem for anything beyond simple programs that submit a form.

To understand the problem, consider the steps in running a normal piece of software from the Mac OS X desktop (this is a generic fictitious application):

1. Double-click the application to display the Welcome screen.
2. Provide basic input into the application screen by typing or clicking.
3. The application provides feedback based on your input.
4. Repeat steps 2 and 3 as necessary.
5. Choose Quit from the application menu.
6. The application saves your changes and preferences, and then exits.

To translate these operations into a Web application, however, requires working around the limitations of the HTTP protocol.

HTTP

When the HTTP (Hypertext Transfer Protocol) was developed, the Web was never expected to become the consumer-driven mish-mash that it is today. HTTP was created to be simple and fast. When retrieving a Web page, the client performs four actions. It first opens a connection to the remote server. The client then requests a resource from the server and sends form data, if necessary. Next, the client receives the results, and finally, it closes the connection.

This happens repeatedly for different page elements (or, depending on the browser and server, multiple requests can be made in one connection). When the browser has finished downloading data, that data is displayed on the user's screen. At this point in time, there is no connection between the client computer and the server. They have effectively forgotten each other's existence.

If the user clicks a link to visit another page on the server, the same process is repeated. The server has no advance knowledge of who the client is, even though they've just been talking. If you've seen the movie *Memento*, you'll understand this concept. The HTTP protocol suffers from a severe lack of short-term memory (statelessness).

Applying this new knowledge to the steps of using an application, the problems become obvious:

1. **Double-click the application**—This is the equivalent of clicking a link on a Web page or entering a URL into a browser. Launching a Web application is nothing more than browsing its URL. No problems so far.
2. **It starts, displaying a welcome screen**—An HTML welcome page is easily built with a link into the main application. Still no problems.
3. **You provide basic input into the application screen by typing or clicking**—The trouble begins. Data that is entered on an HTML form is sent all at once. Providing live feedback to data isn't possible, except for rudimentary JavaScript functionality. Clicking links will transport the browser to other pages, effectively losing any information you've already entered.
4. **The application provides feedback based on your input**—The Web application has access only to information that was provided as input in the form immediately preceding it. For example, assume that there are two forms in which a user inputs data, one right after the other. The first form submits to the second form. The second form, in turn, submits its data to a page that calculates results based on the entries in both form pages. Only the data in the second form will be taken into account. The first form's information no longer exists after submitting the second.
5. **Repeat steps 3 and 4 as necessary**—During each repetition, the server is entirely unaware of what has come before. The application cannot build upon previous input.
6. **Choose Quit from the application menu**—This is a tough one. Remember that the connection to the Web server lasts only long enough to retrieve a single page and send form data. This means that the Web application effectively quits after any step of execution. Web software must be developed with the knowledge that the user can quit his browser at any given point in time. Doing so must not pose either a functional or security risk to the original software.

7. **The application saves your changes and preferences, and then exits**—If a user quits in the middle of running an online application, there is no way for the software to know that it has occurred. It is up to the programmer to ensure that Web software saves as much information, each time it is accessed.

So, how do you work around a protocol that was never designed to keep information between accesses? By employing session management techniques.

Session Management

A *session*, in Web-speak, is the equivalent to the process of running an application from start to finish. The goal of session management is to help the Web server remember information about a user and what that user has done in previous requests for the server. Using session management techniques, you can quickly create Web applications that function like conventional desktop apps. Unfortunately, there is no perfect session management technique. There are several ways to approach the problem, but none offers a completely satisfying solution.

URL Variable Passing

URL variable passing is the simplest form of session management. To make a value available on any number of Web pages, you can use the URL to pass information from page to page. For example, suppose that I had a variable, `name`, with the value of `johnray` that I wanted to be available even after clicking a link to another portion of the program. I could create links that looked like this:

```
www.acmewebsitecomp.com/webapp.cgi?name=johnray
www.acmewebsitecomp.com/reportapp.cgi?name=johnray
www.acmewebsitecomp.com/accountapp.cgi?name=johnray
```

Each of the three Web applications would receive the variable `name` with the value `johnray` upon clicking the links. These applications could then pass the values along even further by appending the same information (`?name=johnray`) to links within themselves. Obviously, this would require the Web applications to generate links dynamically, but it's a small price to pay for being able to reliably pass information from page to page.

This technique relies on the `GET` method. When a browser sends a `GET` request for a Web resource, it can append additional data onto the request by adding it in the format:

```
?<variable>=<value>[&<variable>=<value>...]
```

The trouble with this approach is that to send large amounts of data between pages, you must construct extremely large URLs. Visually, this creates an ugly URL reference in the browser's URL field, and could lead users to bookmark a URL that contains information about the current execution of the Web application that might not be valid in subsequent executions.

In addition, users can easily modify the URL line of the browser to send back any information to the server that they want. If you've just created a shopping cart application that passes a user's total to a final billing page where it is charged against that user's credit card, it is unlikely that you want him to be able to adjust the price of the merchandise he's purchasing.

Form Variable Passing

Similar to passing variables within a URL is using hidden form fields to hold values before they are needed. Assume that you have two forms: the first collects a first and last name, and the second collects an e-mail address and phone number. Submitting the first form opens the second form, which, when submitted, saves the data to a file.

Each form could save its data to a file independently, but this is problematic when considering applications in which all data must be present before it can be saved. Session management can be used to ensure that all data is present when the final form is submitted.

For example, assume that the first form looks something like this:

```
<form action="form2.cgi" method="post">
First Name: <input type="text" name="first"><br>
Last Name: <input type="text" name="last"><br>
<input type="submit">
</form>
```

This form submits two fields (`first` and `last`) to the `form2.cgi`. If the second form must collect an e-mail address and phone number and submit them *simultaneously* with the `first` and `last` values, the `form2.cgi` could dynamically create a form that stored the original two fields in two hidden input fields:

```
<form action="savedata.cgi" method="post">
Email Address: <input type="text" name="email"><br>
Phone Number: <input type="text" name="phone"><br>
<input type="hidden" name="first" value="first-value">
<input type="hidden" name="last" value="last-value">
<input type="submit">
</form>
```

Submitting this form would make *all* the field data available to the subsequent page (`savedata.cgi`).

> **Note**
>
> These examples show how you might use different techniques to pass data between Web pages. For them to be effective, you must be able to dynamically generate the URLs and forms that contain your data. We're getting to that—don't panic!

Unfortunately, the trouble with this approach is that only pages with forms can transfer data between one another. Form variable passing is usually used in conjunction with URL passing to cover all bases.

Data integrity is also an issue with this method because a savvy user could easily save an HTML form locally, edit the hidden field values, and then submit the data from the edited form.

> **Note**
>
> The URL and form variable passing methods are much more closely related than they appear. The technique of specifying variables and values within a URL is actually also a way of submitting a form called the `GET` method. When using the `GET` method, the values sent from a form are appended to the URL that is requested from the server. By doing this manually, we are simulating a form submission using `GET`.
>
> The `POST` method, shown in these examples, sends the variable/value data to the server after requesting a resource. It does not allow information to be appended to the URL and can only be used to send data via an actual form submission.

Cookies

Another way to pass information is to use a cookie. *Cookies* are variable/value pairs that are stored on a user's computer and can be retrieved by the remote Web server. Many people are cautious of cookies because of the fear of information being stolen from the cookie without their knowledge. Cookies, however, can be a very valuable tool for Web developers and users alike.

From the developer's perspective, assigning a cookie is very much like setting a variable. You can name the cookie, and give it a value and an expiration day/time. That value then becomes globally available regardless of whether the user jumps to another page, retypes the URL, or starts over. Only if the cookie is reassigned or reaches its expiration does the value cease to exist. This is as close to persistent variables as a Web developer can hope to get.

From the user's perspective, cookies offer both security and ease-of-use advantages. If a Web application stores a user's identifier in a cookie, that user can immediately be recognized when visiting a Web site. This is commonly used on sites such as Amazon.com and Excite.com to provide a personalized appearance. Because cookies can span multiple pages and applications, a single login can apply to many different portions of a Web site. Using URL or form variable passing, each link and form on a site must be constructed on the fly. No changes need to be made to the links when cookies are used. In the case of the former, the chance of programming error is much greater.

Cookies are saved to the local computer's drive and can be viewed in many popular browsers. Internet Explorer, for example, enables the user to examine stored cookies within the Cookies Preference panel, shown in Figure 28.1.

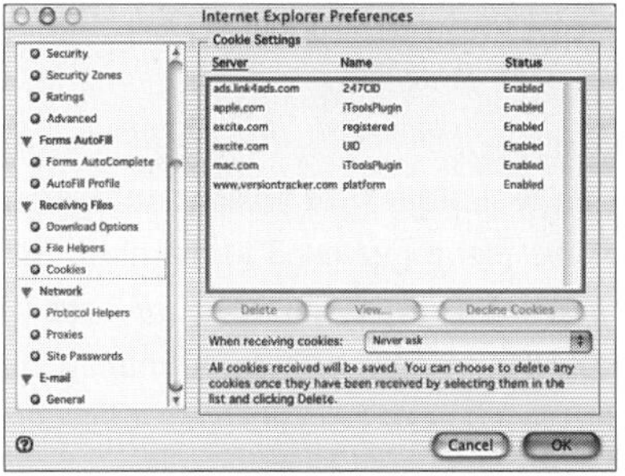

FIGURE 28.1
Popular browsers, such as Internet Explorer, enable the user to browse stored cookies.

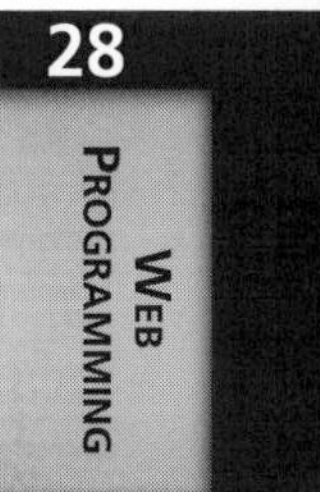

A special type of expiration also exists that limits a cookie's lifetime to the current browser session. In this case, the values are never stored on the client computer and are forgotten when the user exits the program. Using this special type of expiration, a programmer can create a Web application that, after the user exits, leaves no remnants of the login information.

Cookies—Are They Evil?

Many people *still* view cookies as evil. I've heard everything from concerns about a cookie stealing credit card numbers to cookies being used to upload viruses to client computers.

continues

Contrary to popular belief, cookies are not retrieved by a remote server; they are made available by the client browser. When a cookie is first set, it is given a path (URL) for which it is valid. If your browser comes across a request for a resource (HTML page, image, and so forth) that includes the path, the cookie is automatically sent to that server along with the request. Your browser will send cookies only to the paths where they belong, not to *all* Web sites you view.

The contents of a cookie are, indeed, determined by the remote server and can be set to any arbitrary string. They do not provide the capacity to upload binary files or executable applications. It's certainly possible that a cookie *could* hold a credit card number, but you would have had to enter that number into a Web page before it could be stored in a cookie. I have never seen an e-commerce or banking site that worked in this manner, but it is possible that one might exist.

If you're concerned about using cookies on your system, the best advice is to inform your users about how cookies are being employed and make sure that they are comfortable with the information being stored. The dangers of cookies have been greatly exaggerated. Use of common sense and caution while programming with cookies will lead to applications that users will trust and enjoy.

Although it is possible to use the other techniques for passing information, cookies are the fastest and easiest. Regardless of the technique used to maintain information, there are still two final elements that are missing from the big picture—the session database and session ID. Together they form the Holy Grail of session management, session variables.

Session Variables

A *session variable* is a variable that can be set to any value, will be accessible by any portion of a Web application, and will last only while the Web application is being used. In principle, any of the techniques we've looked at so far can do this. Unfortunately, they all fall short when applied to a large system.

For example, imagine that you're passing variables using the URL method:

```
www.mywebsite.com/mywebapp.cgi?variable1=value&variable2=value
```

This works great for one or two variables, but extend it to a few thousand! Suddenly a two- or three-line URL seems short. There is a limit to the amount of data that can be contained within a URL, making this impossible for large amounts of information.

When using cookies or forms to pass data, you aren't necessarily limited by the size of the request string, but by the overhead and complexity of the coding. For each variable that must be stored, a hidden field must be added to a form, or a cookie sent back to the server. This process must be repeated on every page. This adds up, in terms of transmission time and processing.

Luckily, there is a solution that can be used with any of the approaches to variable passing—the use of a session database and a session ID.

The concept is simple—when a user comes to a Web site, his session starts. He is assigned a unique ID, called the session ID, by the remote Web application. As the user interacts with the Web site, the Web application passes the session ID from page to page. This process can be done using the URL, forms, or cookies. When the Web application software wants to store a value, it stores it on the server, in a local database that is keyed to that particular session ID.

For programmers, this is a dream come true. They can store any information they'd like (including sensitive data), and it is never transmitted over the network. The only piece of data that is visible on the network wire is the session ID.

Because a single piece of information can keep track of an unlimited number of variables, the session management system can be written to pass the session ID using URL/form methods, or a cookie. Either way is entirely feasible. To make things even easier, developers have included these capabilities in programming languages such as JSP and PHP. For example, in PHP, you can activate session management and store a variable for use on another Web page using syntax like this:

```
<?php
session_start();
$x=$x+1;
session_register('x');
print $x;
?>
```

This example uses `session_start()` to create a new session ID, which is automatically stored in a cookie. Next, the variable `x` is incremented, and then registered (stored) with the session. Finally, the value of `x` is displayed. The result is a Web page that displays an increasing count, each time a user loads it.

Note

It is important to make the distinction that this is *not* the same as a Web counter. A session ID is specific to a single user, as are all the variables registered with that session. If 50 users were accessing this script simultaneously, each would see a result that is independent of all the others.

More traditional languages (such as Perl or C) weren't created with Web programming in mind. To implement session variables within Perl, you must create, manipulate, and manage session IDs and session databases. This has already been done so many times that there are a number of pre-built solutions to work with, but none is as elegant as a language that was designed for the purposes of creating Web applications.

That said, let's look at using Perl for creating simple CGI applications. What? Didn't I just say that Perl is not nearly as elegant as languages such as PHP? Although this is true, Perl is an excellent starting point for anyone learning Web application development. Perl is robust, easy to use, and forces the user to understand the basics of Web programming.

What Is a CGI?

CGI stands for Common Gateway Interface. A CGI application is one that is written to conform to a Web server/application communication standard (the CGI). CGI applications pass and read their information to and from an underlying Web server. The generic definition of CGI is just a standalone Web application.

This chapter will look at two types of CGI applications. Those programmed within a traditional language, such as Perl, and others that are based on embedded programming languages, such as PHP. The latter is not truly considered a CGI language because it uses a different mechanism for exchanging information with the Web server, but the end result of each is a Web application.

Programming CGIs in Perl

This chapter assumes that you either know a reasonable amount of Perl basics, or have diligently read the introduction to Perl scripts in Chapter 22, "Perl Scripting and SQL Connectivity." In addition, you must have set `ExecCGI` permissions for the directory you are programming in and the CGI `AddHandler` directive uncommented, as described in Chapter 27, "Web Serving."

Let's start with the most basic example possible—Hello World. Your initial reaction is probably (hopefully!) to create a Perl script (`helloworld.cgi`) along the lines of

```
#!/usr/bin/perl
print "Hello World! I have a Mac, do you?";
exit;
```

After enabling execution (`chmod +x helloworld.cgi`), try running the application from the command line (`./helloworld.cgi`), and then by accessing its URL through a Web browser. Although the command-line version runs fine, the browser will report an execution error message, as shown in Figure 28.2.

FIGURE 28.2
A simple Hello World isn't quite so simple.

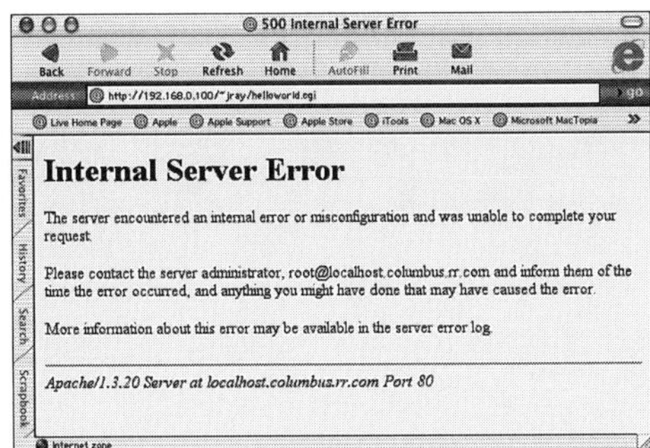

So, what went wrong? Why is this program, which runs perfectly from a command prompt, broken when it tries to send its results over the Web?

The answer lies in the way the Web servers communicate their results back to a client browser.

HTTP Headers

For the simple Hello World application to work, it must produce the sort of output that a Web browser expects. To the browser, it should send the same response as when a standard `.html` static Web page is loaded. The easiest way to see that response is to generate one manually by using `telnet` to connect to a Web server and request a page. For example, to retrieve the primary page from the local Mac OS X box, you would telnet to `localhost` (or `127.0.0.1`) on port 80, and then use `GET / HTTP/1.0` to retrieve the root level of the Web site:

```
[localhost:~] jray% telnet localhost 80
Trying 127.0.0.1...
Connected to localhost.columbus.rr.com.
Escape character is '^]'.
GET / HTTP/1.0

HTTP/1.1 200 OK
Date: Thu, 24 May 2001 00:55:56 GMT
Server: Apache/1.3.14 (Darwin)
Content-Location: index.html.en
Vary: negotiate,accept-language,accept-charset
TCN: choice
```

```
Last-Modified: Fri, 31 Mar 2000 01:45:46 GMT
ETag: "3c390-54e-38e4034a;3aac49b0"
Accept-Ranges: bytes
Content-Length: 1358
Connection: close
Content-Type: text/html
Content-Language: en
Expires: Thu, 24 May 2001 00:55:56 GMT
```

Note

This example does not include the text of the Web page, just the headers that are sent from the server. If you attempt this on your own machine, you'll get similar results, along with the contents of the `index.html` file within your `/Library/WebServer/Documents` folder.

There are quite a few interesting lines in the group of headers that are returned, such as the language content and an expiration date (used to keep a page from being cached beyond a certain day and time). Only one of these headers, however, is required.

The Content-type header tells the remote Web browser what `MIME` type of file it is about to receive. When a user requests a JPEG image file, the server sends a header that reads

```
Content-type: image/jpeg
```

Each type of file has a different `MIME` type (determined by the file `/private/etc/mime.types`) The server can decide what type of file it is about to serve based on the filename. Unfortunately, when working with CGIs, the Web server cannot be certain what type of information is going to be sent back. In fact, a single CGI could very easily send an image with one request, and an HTML page with another.

To create a fully working CGI, the first thing that the Web application must send is an appropriate `MIME` type. The initial version of `helloworld.cgi` did nothing but print out the Hello World message. The browser, however, was expecting a Content-type header; when the header didn't appear, an error was generated. To correct the problem, the Content-type must be printed before any other output occurs:

```
#!/usr/bin/perl
print "Content-type: text/html\n\n";
print "Hello World! I have a Mac, do you?";
exit;
```

After making the small change to the script, this smallest of Web applications will happily run, as demonstrated in Figure 28.3.

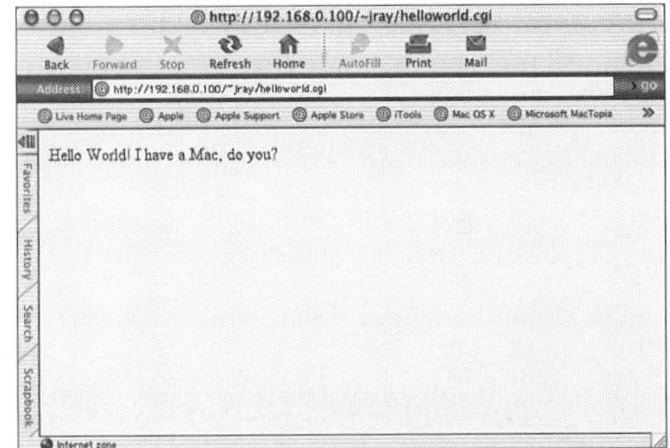

FIGURE 28.3
When the appropriate header is added to the CGI script, everything works as planned.

Note

You can add any valid headers to the output that you'd like. The Content-type header is the only one that is required. Each header needs to be printed with a single newline character at the end of each line. The final header must have two newline characters at the end.

These headers must come before any other output, but not necessarily at the start of the program. As long as no parts of the page body are produced before a Content-type header is sent, the headers can occur anywhere within the script.

HTML Output

Creating the output of a CGI is the second step of developing a Web application. Unlike normal Perl scripts that produce plain text output, Web applications produce HTML. This can take awhile to get used to, but keep in mind that the goal is to produce a dynamic Web page, not a plain text file.

When creating output from a CGI script, you can use any tags that you normally would in an HTML document. The trouble with doing this in Perl is that you have to escape all quotes when printing the HTML.

For example:

```
<TABLE BORDER="0" CELLPADDING="0" CELLSPACING="0">
```

When printed in Perl, this becomes

```
print  "<TABLE BORDER=\"0\" CELLPADDING=\"0\" CELLSPACING=\"0\">";
```

When creating complicated output, this can get a bit tedious. It can also lead to programmers taking shortcuts and leaving out quotes around HTML tag attributes. The easiest way to display large amounts of complex HTML is to use Perl's alternative print method:

```
print <<ENDOFHTML;
   <TABLE BORDER="0" CELLPADDING="0" BGCOLOR="#FFDDDD" CELLSPACING="0">
   <TR><TD align="right">This is more HTML</TD></TR>
   </TABLE>
ENDOFHTML
```

So, let's go ahead and take a look at an example of CGI output in action. This is CGI *output*, so don't think that you won't be able to get information into your Web application. We're going to get there, just be patient!

Let's start with something simple, such as creating a script that will display all the images and the associated filenames in a given folder.

To start the CGI, build a simple Perl script that lists all the JPEG (`.jpg`) files in a folder. Listing 28.1 shows such as script.

LISTING 28.1 When Building a CGI, It's Often Easiest to Start with Something That Runs from the Command Line

```
1: #!/usr/bin/perl
2:
3: $imagedir="imagefolder";
4: @imagelist=glob("$imagedir/*jpg");
5:
6: for ($x=0;$x<@imagelist;$x++) {
7:         $imagename=$imagelist[$x];
8:         print "Image $x = $imagename\n";
9: }
```

Line 3 sets the variable `$imagedir` to the directory that contains the images. In this case, I'm using `imagefolder` inside my `Sites` directory, which is also where this script is located. I have not specified the entire path because I'm only interested in the location of the images relative to the script.

Line 4 loads all the filenames within `$imagedir` that end in .jpg into the array `@imagelist`. The Perl `glob` function takes a path and filename pattern as input, and then returns any results that match.

Lines 6–9 loop through each element in the `@imagelist` array, temporarily storing them in the `$imagename` variable. Print a line that displays the image and its name.

When run, the CGI-in-the-making, which I've named `showimages.cgi`, produces the list we were hoping for:

```
[localhost:~/Sites] jray% ./showimages.cgi
Image 0 = imagefolder/4jr2.jpg
Image 1 = imagefolder/BLvividLotuses1600x1024.jpg
Image 2 = imagefolder/BLyellows1600x1024.jpg
Image 3 = imagefolder/berries.jpg
Image 4 = imagefolder/bluesilk.jpg
Image 5 = imagefolder/door.jpg
Image 6 = imagefolder/flower.jpg
Image 7 = imagefolder/flowers.jpg
Image 8 = imagefolder/forjohn.jpg
Image 9 = imagefolder/funnyflow.jpg
Image 10 = imagefolder/snow.jpg
Image 11 = imagefolder/snowstorm.jpg
```

So, how can this be translated into a CGI that displays the actual images in a Web browser? The first step, as mentioned earlier, is to produce a Content-type header. Without this information, the browser has no idea what type of data it is receiving. At the same time, it's a good idea to translate any `\n` (newline) characters in the program into their HTML equivalent: `<br>`. Listing 28.2 shows the new CGI, which is capable of running in a browser.

LISTING 28.2 Adding a Content-Type and Fixing Line Breaks Is All You Need to Turn a Simple Command-Line Script into a CGI

```
#!/usr/bin/perl
print "Content-type: text/html\n\n";
$imagedir="imagefolder";
@imagelist=glob("$imagedir/*jpg");

for ($x=0;$x<@imagelist;$x++) {
        $imagename=$imagelist[$x];
        print "Image $x = $imagename<br>";
}
```

Note

The `\n` (newline) characters that come after the `Content-type` header should not be translated to HTML breaks. The browser interprets data *after* the header lines, and always expects the final (and in this case, only) header to be followed by two newlines.

Figure 28.4 shows the result of running the new CGI in a Web browser.

FIGURE 28.4
The command-line application now runs within a Web browser.

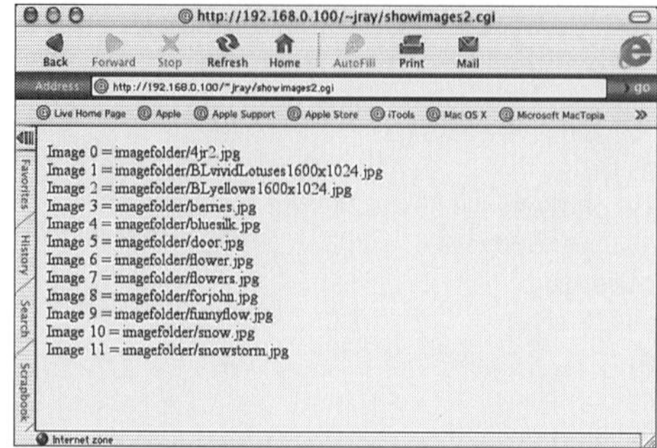

Unfortunately, things still aren't quite where we want them. What good is a CGI that lists pictures but doesn't display them? To be able to show the pictures, the CGI must be modified so that the name is used within an `<IMG>` (image) tag, rather than just displayed on the screen. Try adding a new line that uses an image, rather than the image name, as seen in Listing 28.3.

LISTING 28.3 The Revised Code Will Display an Image as Well as Its Name

```
1: #!/usr/bin/perl
2: print "Content-type: text/html\n\n";
3: $imagedir="imagefolder";
4: @imagelist=glob("$imagedir/*jpg");
5:
6: for ($x=0;$x<@imagelist;$x++) {
7:         $imagename=$imagelist[$x];
8:         print "<IMG SRC=\"$imagename\" width=\"120\" height=\"90\"><br>";
9:         print "Image $x = $imagename<br>";
10: }
```

Line 8 performs the magic in the application. Using the same `$imagename` variable used to print an image's name (now in line 9), the variable is instead used to set an image source within an `<IMG>` tag. I've also added a width and height to the image tag to maintain some consistency in the display.

When viewed in a Web browser, the result resembles Figure 28.5.

Note

When setting an image size within the image tag, be aware that it doesn't change the physical size of the images being sent to the browser. The amount of data transmitted is identical to what would be sent if the width and height tags were not included. To resize the image in real-time requires the use of additional software, such as the `GD` Perl module, downloadable from `CPAN.org`.

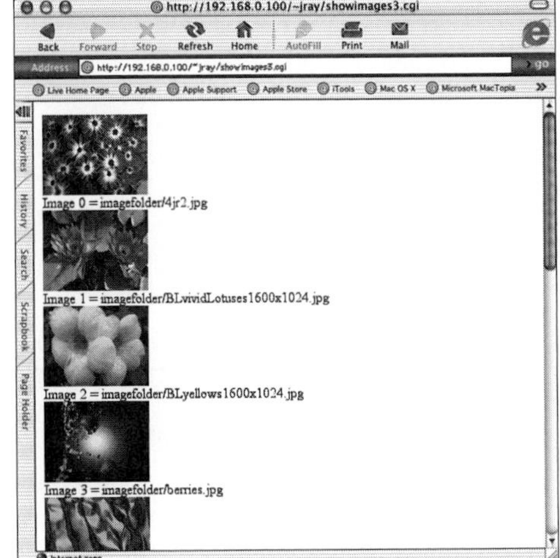

FIGURE 28.5
With the addition of the IMG *tag, the images themselves can now be seen in the listing.*

Hopefully, by now, you're starting to see the method to the madness. CGIs are just applications that write HTML as their output. The example we've been looking at is barely modified from the original command-line version, yet it includes full images for each file it finds. To fully realize the potential of a CGI, you must use HTML to its fullest. So far, the Perl script we've been developing is nothing but a simple port of the initial command-line utility. With only a small amount of work, we can turn it into something far more useful. Listing 28.4 shows a more developed version of the application. Unlike the previous version of the CGI, this revision uses an HTML table to structure the layout of the images.

LISTING 28.4 With a Little Work, the CGI Can Take Advantage of All of HTML's Layout Capabilities

```
#!/usr/bin/perl
print "Content-type: text/html\n\n";

$imagedir="imagefolder";
$columns=3;

@imagelist=glob("$imagedir/*jpg");

print "<TABLE BGCOLOR=\"#FFFFFF\" BORDER=\"1\" BORDERCOLOR=\"#000000\">";
while ($x<@imagelist) {
    print "<TR>";
    for ($y=0;$y<$columns;$y++) {
        $imagename=$imagelist[$x];
        if ($x<@imagelist) {
            $x++;
```

LISTING 28.4 continued

```
16:               print "<TD align=\"center\">";
17:              print "<IMG SRC=\"$imagename\" width=\"120\" height=\"90\"><br>";
18:               $imagename=~s/$imagedir\///;
19:               print "<FONT TYPE=\"Arial\">$imagename</FONT>";
20:               print "</TD>";
21:           }
22:       }
23:       print "</TR>";
24: }
25: print "</TABLE>";
```

Line 5 sets a limit for the number of columns in the table (how many images will be displayed in a single line), whereas line 9 sets up the table structure using a table with a white (`#FFFFFF`) background and a black (`#000000`) border. In line 10, instead of using a `for` loop to go through each image, the counter `$x` is incremented when an image tag is output. The `while` loop will continue as long as the counter is less than the total number of images.

Line 11 starts a new table row (`<TR>`). Lines 12–22 loop through the number of columns set for the table. For each column, increment the variable `$x`. If `$x` has not exceeded the total number of images available, output a table data cell (`<TD>`) that contains the image and its name. Line 18 removes the path from the image filename. This is done using a simple Perl regular expression search and replace. After displaying all the data cells for a row, line 23 ends the table row (`</TR>`). Line 24 repeats lines 11–23 until all images have been displayed, and line 25 ends the table (`</TABLE>`).

Figure 28.6 shows the output from the finalized CGI.

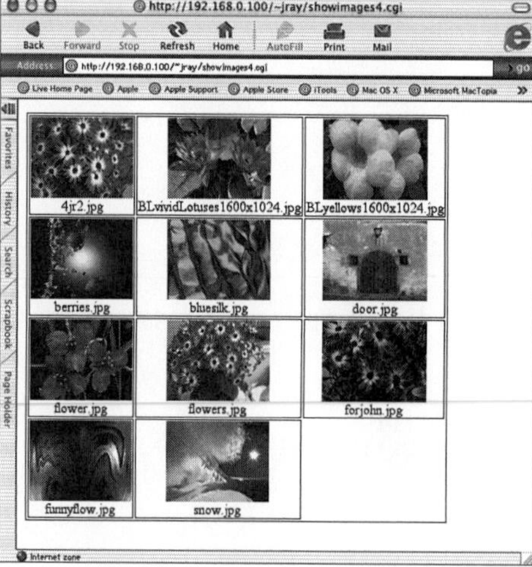

FIGURE 28.6
The final version of the CGI outputs the image directory in a nicely formatted table.

Note

The most common type of CGI/Web-application output is `text/html`. This doesn't mean that a Web application can't output other types of data. If your script opens, reads, and outputs a JPEG file, it would use `Content-type: image/jpeg`. Any type of media that can be sent by a Web server can also be sent from a CGI.

CGI Input

This quick-and-dirty image viewer provides a reasonable start to CGI programming, but it is lacking in the one area that can be used to create truly dynamic and user-driven sites—user input. Getting input into a CGI can be a bit of a challenge if you're starting from scratch.

Thankfully, others have been here before, so there are some well-developed routines that will help you get data into your CGIs in only a few minutes. Listing 28.5 contains the additional code that you'll need for parsing input from URLs and HTML forms.

LISTING 28.5 These Functions Enable Data Input from Remote Browsers

```
sub MethGet {
  return ($ENV{'REQUEST_METHOD'} eq "GET");
}

sub MethPost {
  return ($ENV{'REQUEST_METHOD'} eq "POST");
}

 sub ReadParse {
  local (*variable) = @_ if @_;
  local ($i, $key, $val);

  if (&MethGet) {
    $variable = $ENV{'QUERY_STRING'};
  } elsif (&MethPost) {
    read(STDIN,$variable,$ENV{'CONTENT_LENGTH'});
  }

  @variable = split(/[&;]/,$variable);

  foreach $i (0 .. $#variable) {
    $variable[$i] =~ s/\+/ /g;
    ($key, $val) = split(/=/,$variable[$i],2); # split on the equal sign
    $key =~ s/%(..)/pack("c",hex($1))/ge;
```

LISTING 28.5 continued

```
25:     $val =~ s/%(..)/pack("c",hex($1))/ge;
26:     $variable{$key} .= "\0" if (defined($variable{$key}));
27:     $variable{$key} .= $val;
28:   }
29:   return scalar(@in);
30: }
```

> **Note**
>
> The original author of this code is not known. It has been used in hundreds of Perl CGIs and is available in countless variations. This version is included in the text because of its readability.

You can place this code anywhere you want within your CGI. To save some space, place it in its own file, such as cgiinput.pl. You can then require this file at the start of any CGI that needs to access the routines. You will also need to add a line 1; at the bottom of the file. This is a requirement for any included Perl libraries—it produces a value of true when the file is read. If the line is missing, the CGI will exit with an error.

There are three functions in the code:

MethGet—Returns true if the data submitted to the CGI was submitted using the GET (URL-based/form) method.

MethPost—Returns true if the data submitted to the CGI was submitted using the POST (form) method.

ReadParse—ReadParse performs the brunt of the workload. This routine decodes the incoming CGI data and creates an associative array (%variable) that stores each variable and its value. For example, if a form had an input field defined as <INPUT TYPE="text" NAME="mydata">, the ReadParse function would assign the value to the %variable array so that it could be accessed using $variable{"mydata"}. It's that simple.

The MethGet and MethPost functions (lines 1–7 of Listing 28.5) should be mostly self-explanatory. Each checks the environment variable REQUEST_METHOD to determine how data was transferred to the CGI. This variable is automatically set by Apache. If the GET method was used, MethGet returns true. If POST is used, MethPost is true.

Because the real work occurs in ReadParse, let's take a look at how it works its magic:

Lines 13–17 of Listing 28.5 check MethGet to see whether GET was used to send the data. If it was, the variable $variable is set equal the contents of the environment variable QUERY_STRING. If the MethPost function returns true, $variable is instead filled by reading in a number of bytes from standard input. The amount of input is determined by the environment variable CONTENT_LENGTH.

Line 19 creates an array @variable that contains each of the variable=value pairs.

Lines 21–28 loop through each of the variable pairs, extracting the key and value, and storing them in the %variable associative array.

Line 22 coverts any encoded spaces (+) in the variable to real spaces. Line 23 sets $key and $val equal to the incoming variable and value, respectively, and line 24 decodes any hex characters in $key. For example, a space is encoded as %20 (hex 20 = 2x16 = 32 ASCII).

Line 25 decodes any hex characters in the variable $val. If the key in the %variable array is already defined, line 26 adds a NULL (for separating multivalue fields, such as <SELECT> fields) and line 27 stores the key and value in the %variable associative array. If you found that enlightening, great! If not, don't worry, there's no real need to know too much about these functions beyond typing them in and saving them. To read input into a CGI application, use ReadParse on a line by itself—that's all there is to it.

Note

If you're an experienced Perl or CGI programmer, you probably also know that there is a CGI Perl module that includes an entire library of functions for creating CGI applications.

Unfortunately, the CGI module does not provide beginner-level programmers easy access to its capabilities. If you're a Perl programmer who understands Perl's OO model, take a look. Personally, I find CGI.pm to be overkill in many cases, and cumbersome when handling forms and other HTML elements.

Let's take a look at practical CGI input by altering the Hello World application we used previously so that it personalizes the message. If your name happens to be World, you might skip this exercise. Listing 28.6 shows the helloworld.cgi modified to display a person's name. I'll refer to this new version as helloworld2.cgi.

LISTING 28.6 Using the ReadParse Function, Any Script Can Receive Input

```
#!/usr/bin/perl
require "cgiinput.pl";

&ReadParse;
$myname=$variable{"name"};

print "Content-type: text/html\n\n";
print "Hello $myname! I have a Mac, do you?";
```

> **Note**
>
> This code makes the assumption that the MethGet, MethPost, and ReadParse functions are stored in a file named cgiinput.pl in the same directory as helloworld2.cgi. If you'd rather not spread your source across multiple files, just add the input functions to the end of the main CGI.

Although mostly apparent, the breakdown of the code is as follows:

Line 2 loads the input functions defined earlier in this section. The `cgiinput.pl` file must exist in the same directory as the CGI in order for the `require` statement to work.

Line 4 uses the `ReadParse` function to load the `%variable` associative array with any incoming variables and values. Line 5 sets the variable `$myname` to the submitted variable `name`. Line 7 sends the required content-type, and line 8 prints a greeting containing the name submitted to the CGI in the `name` variable.

As you can see, the number of changes to the original application is very small. This CGI should now correctly allow a name to be sent to it for use in a customized greeting. The problem remains, however, how do you go about actually *sending* the variable and value to the application?

Because the `ReadParse` routing handles either `POST` or `GET` method transmission, there are two ways that this new CGI can be called. Using the URL to pass a variable is the easiest, so let's start there. Start a Web browser and enter the URL for the new CGI, adding `?name=John` (or whatever is appropriate for you) to the end:

```
http://<your host>/<your cgi path>/helloworld2.cgi?name=<your name>
```

My test system, for example, looks like this:

```
http://primal.ag.ohio-state.edu/~jray/bookstuff/helloworld2.cgi?name=John
```

Figure 28.7 shows the new personalized message.

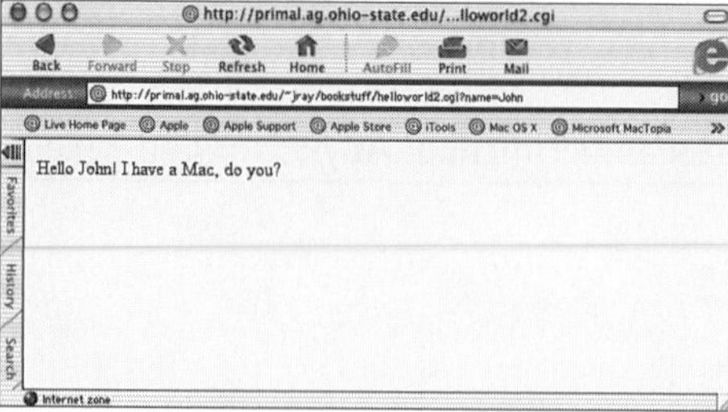

FIGURE 28.7
Providing an input method for CGIs enables you to customize their output.

To use the POST method to send information to the CGI, create an HTML form that will submit its data to the Web application. For helloworld2.cgi, the form needs nothing more than a name field and a submit button:

```
<form action="helloworld2.cgi" method="post">
Enter your name: <input type="text" name="name">
<input type="submit" name="submit">
</form>
```

Save the form code in a new HTML file (hello.html) in the same directory as the helloworld2.cgi. Open the new Web page in your browser, type a name, and click Submit. You should see results almost identical to the earlier URL-based input seen in Figure 28.7.

> **Note**
>
> If you don't include the method="post" attribute for the form, or use method="get", submitting the form will actually pass the name data through the URL.

As it stands, if using a separate HTML page to submit information to the CGI, two files comprise the entire project: helloworld2.cgi and hello.html. This isn't excessive, but it can be consolidated. Rather than hello.html containing the form, it can be added directly to helloworld2.cgi. Listing 28.7 consolidates the form and application into a single CGI file.

LISTING 28.7 A CGI Can Encapsulate HTML and Application Logic

```
#!/usr/bin/perl
require "cgiinput.pl";

&ReadParse;
$myname=$variable{"name"};
print "Content-type: text/html\n\n";

if ($myname eq "") {
    print <<ENDOFHTML;
        <form action="helloworld2.cgi" method="post">
        Enter your name: <input type="text" name="name">
        <input type="submit" name="submit">
        </form>
ENDOFHTML
```

LISTING 28.7 continued

```
15:     exit;
16: }
17:
18: print "Hello $myname! I have a Mac, do you?";
```

Consolidating the code into the single CGI brings into play some of the session management techniques discussed earlier in the chapter. This revision of `helloworld2.cgi` has two states—prior to entering the name and after entering the name. To determine what the program should be doing, it checks the value of `$myname`—if a name hasn't been set, the HTML form should be displayed. If a name *is* defined, the `Hello` message is shown. A more detailed analysis of the changes follows:

Line 8 checks to see whether the `$myname` variable is empty. If it is, this is the first time the CGI has been executed—the user hasn't entered his name yet.

Lines 9–14 display the HTML form, and line 15 exits the CGI. This line is more important than it might appear. If it is not included, the CGI will continue to execute after displaying the HTML form; this will generate an empty hello message immediately following the form. Finally, line 18 displays the hello message with the user's name.

This demonstrates the fundamental workings of CGI applications. Although the example is only a two-step process, it could easily be extended to multiple steps by passing data from screen to screen. For an encore, let's add another form to the hello page that collects the user's age. After submitting this second form, a third page is shown with the user's name, age, and a few comments. Listing 28.8 shows the final version of this overly long Hello World application.

LISTING 28.8 The Extended Version of Hello World Now Includes Three Steps and Demonstrates CGI Input and Variable Passing

```
#!/usr/bin/perl
require "cgiinput.pl";

&ReadParse;
$myname=$variable{"name"};
$myage=$variable{"age"};

print "Content-type: text/html\n\n";

if ($myname eq "") {
    print <<ENDOFHTML;
        <form action="helloworld2.cgi" method="post">
        Enter your name: <input type="text" name="name">
        <input type="submit" name="submit">
```

LISTING 28.8 continued

```
15:          </form>
16: ENDOFHTML
17:     exit;
18: }
19:
20: if ($myage eq "") {
21:     print "Hello $myname!";
22:     print "<BR>";
23:     print <<ENDOFHTML2;
24:         <form action="helloworld2.cgi" method="post">
25:         Enter your age: <input type="text" name="age"><br>
26:         <input type="hidden" name="name" value="$myname">
27:         <input type="submit" name="submit">
28:         </form>
29: ENDOFHTML2
30:     exit;
31: }
32:
33: $dayage=$myage*365;
34: $hourage=$dayage*24;
35: $minage=$hourage*60;
36: print "Hello again $myname!<BR>";
37: print "You have lived for $dayage days...<br>";
38: print "... or $hourage hours...<br>";
39: print "... or $minage minutes!<br>";
```

This final revision adds an additional form and output screen. Lines 20–31 display the standard `hello` message, but also show a form where the user is prompted for his age. What makes this form unique is that it includes a hidden `name` field that is set to the original `$myname` value. This shows how information can be carried from page to page.

The final page, generated in lines 33–39, calculates a user's name in days, hours, and minutes. This demonstrates that the name has indeed been carried through each of the CGI screens.

As an exercise, you might want to try adding a `search` screen to the image catalog creator that was built earlier in the chapter. Suppose, for instance, that there are multiple image folders to view, a need for the number of columns to be adjusted, or even searching based on the image filename—these features can all be added very easily to the application. Listing 28.9 is a two-step version of the image catalog application.

LISTING 28.9 This New Version of the Image Catalog CGI Now Offers Searching and Display Settings

```
#!/usr/bin/perl

```

LISTING 28.9 continued

```
3: require "cgiinput.pl";
4: &ReadParse;
5: $imagedir=$variable{"imagedir"};
6: $imagename=$variable{"imagename"};
7: $columns=$variable{"columns"};
8: $match=$variable{"match"};
9: if ($imagedir=~/\//) { $imagedir="imagefolder"; }
10: if ($imagename=~/\//) { $imagename=""; }
11:
12: print "Content-type: text/html\n\n";
13: if ($imagedir eq "") {
14:      print <<ENDOFHTML;
15:         <form action="showimages5.cgi" method="post">
16:Choose image dir: <input type="text" name="imagedir" value="imagefolder"><br>
17:         Select the number of columns in the display: <select name="columns">
18:             <option>1</option>
19:             <option>2</option>
20:             <option>3</option>
21:             <option>4</option>
22:         </select><br>
23:         Show images that match: <input type="text" name="match">
24:         <input type="submit" name="submit">
25:         </form>
26: ENDOFHTML
27: }
28:
29: @imagelist=glob("$imagedir/*$match*jpg");
30:
31: print "<TABLE BGCOLOR=\"#FFFFFF\" BORDER=\"1\" BORDERCOLOR=\"#000000\">";
32: while ($x<@imagelist) {
33:     print "<TR>";
34:     for ($y=0;$y<$columns;$y++) {
35:         $imagename=$imagelist[$x];
36:         if ($x<@imagelist) {
37:             $x++;
38:             print "<TD align=\"center\">";
39:            print "<IMG SRC=\"$imagename\" width=\"120\" height=\"90\"><br>";
40:             $imagename=~s/$imagedir\///;
41:             print "<FONT TYPE=\"Arial\">$imagename</FONT>";
42:             print "</TD>";
43:         }
44:     }
45:     print "</TR>";
46: }
47: print "</TABLE>";
```

The only modifications to the original image catalog are the addition of lines 3–27. The rest remains the same.

Lines 3–4 load the `cgiinput` library, and then use the `ReadParse` function to read any submitted form information.

Lines 5–8 store values for the columns to display, image directory to use, and a string to search for in the image names.

Lines 9–10 are *very* important. When processing user input an application can never trust the incoming data. If the image catalog blindly accepted an arbitrary path, it could pose a serious security risk and give the user access to other parts of the file system. For that reason, any input that includes a `/` is disregarded. This eliminates the potential for the user to input *any* path information.

If an image directory has not been set (such as the application has not received the search criteria yet), lines 13–27 display a search form. This is a simple HTML form that includes elements for setting the image directory, number of columns, and a search string for the image name.

A modification to the original `glob`, this line 29 variation adds the `$match` string to the pattern, displaying only images that match the specified string.

By now, you should have a grasp of the basics of CGI programming, and how Perl can be used to create quick-and-dirty Web applications.

Note

If you're set on using Perl for your Apache development environment, you might want to look into the `mod_perl` module. This add-on attaches a Perl interpreter to the Apache process, greatly speeding up CGI execution. If your site makes extensive use of very large Perl applications, give it a try. `mod_perl` can be downloaded from `http://perl.apache.org/`.

Although Perl is certainly capable of generating large-scale applications, it isn't necessarily the best choice in terms of speed and ease of use. It's time to look at something a bit more suited to Web development: PHP.

PHP

PHP, the PHP Hypertext Preprocessor (it's recursive), is a relatively new language that integrates with the Apache Web server. Whereas Perl is a general-purpose programming language, PHP provides Web-specific functions that can speed up development time significantly.

Note

As you read this, the push is on to transition PHP into a programming language that can generate desktop software as well as dynamic Web applications. Given PHP's birth as a Web language, it's safe to say that it will retain its lead over Perl for developing online applications.

One of the primary differences between Perl and PHP is how it is programmed. With Perl, the focus is on the application logic; integrating an interface is secondary. When using PHP, the logic is embedded into the HTML. A PHP developer can use traditional Web development tools, such as Macromedia Dreamweaver or Adobe GoLive, to create an interface, and then attach logic. For example, in Perl, we used code like this to print a variable within some HTML:

```
print <<HTML;
        print "<TR>";
        print "<TD align=\"center\">$myname</TD>";
        print "</TR>";
HTML
```

The equivalent code in PHP looks like this:

```
<TR>
<TD align="center"><?php print $myname; ?></TD>
</TR>
```

As you can see, the application code is entirely isolated from the HTML. PHP code is contained with its own tags: `<?php` to start and `?>` to end. As Apache reads a PHP file, it executes the code in the PHP tags, and then sends the final result to the waiting browser. The remote user cannot see these special tags in the HTML source—your application logic is safe from prying eyes. In addition to a clean programming model, PHP offers features such as built-in database access, advanced security, and real-time graphic generation.

Installing PHP

If you've poked around through the files on your system, you might have noticed that there is a PHP folder installed with Mac OS X (path: `/System/Library/PHP`). Unfortunately, with the initial release of Mac OS X, this PHP distribution is inherently broken. I don't recommend that you try to get it running; the result will be a partially functioning, bug-ridden version of PHP. So, the first step in using PHP is getting it installed. Before starting, make sure that you `su` to `root`, or execute the commands shown here using `sudo`.

First, download the latest PHP distribution from www.php.net/downloads.php and unarchive it:

```
[primal:~] jray% tar zxf php-4.0.5.tar.gz
```

Next, download the support files from Stepwise.com that will enable compilation on Mac OS X. The 4.0.5 distribution of PHP has a few errors that require an additional script to work around. This is likely to change in the future. The 4.0.4pl1 release of PHP did not suffer from this problem. You can download the 4.0.5 patch from http://graphics.stepwise.com/Articles/Workbench/php-4.0.5-genif.sh.

The download, php-4.0.5-genif.sh, should be moved to build/genif.sh within the php 4.0.5 directory. This will replace an existing genif.sh file:

```
[primal:~/php-4.0.5] jray% mv php-4.0.5-genif.sh build/genif.sh
```

cd into the distribution directory and use ./configure --with-apxs --with-xml to prepare the software for compilation.

```
[primal:~] jray% cd php-4.0.5
^C[primal:~/php-4.0.5] jray% sudo ./configure --with-apxs --with-xml
loading cache ./config.cache
checking for a BSD compatible install... (cached) /usr/bin/install -c
checking whether build environment is sane... yes
checking whether make sets ${MAKE}... (cached) yes
checking for working aclocal... missing
checking for working autoconf... found
checking for working automake... missing
checking for working autoheader... found
...
```

You might want to run ./configure --help to see other compilation options. By default, PHP includes MySQL support along with all base functions discussed in this chapter. For extended features, such as Flash generation, PostgreSQL support, and so on, you'll need to enable these options during the install step.

Next, use make to compile the software:

```
[primal:~/php-4.0.5] jray% sudo make
Making all in Zend
/bin/sh ../libtool --silent --mode=compile cc -DHAVE_CONFIG_H -I. -I. -I../main
   ➥-traditional-cpp -DSUPPORT_UTF8 -DXML_BYTE_ORDER=21
   ➥-  -g -O2 -c zend_language_scanner.c
/bin/sh ../libtool --silent --mode=compile cc -DHAVE_CONFIG_H -I. -I. -I../main
   ➥-    -traditional-cpp -DSUPPORT_UTF8 -DXML_BYTE_ORDER=21
   ➥-  -g -O2 -c zend_ini_scanner.c
/bin/sh ../libtool --silent --mode=link cc  -g -O2  -o libZend_c.la
   ➥-zend_language_scanner.lo zend_ini_scanner.lo
...
```

After a few minutes, the compilation will finish. The software is now ready to be installed, so use `make install` to complete the process:

```
[primal:~/php-4.0.5] jray% sudo make install
Making install in Zend
make[2]: Nothing to be done for `install-exec-am'.
make[2]: Nothing to be done for `install-data-am'.
Making install in main
make[2]: Nothing to be done for `install-p'.
...
```

Next, copy the default PHP configuration file into its final location:

```
[primal:~/php-4.0.5] jray% cp php.ini-dist /usr/local/lib/php.ini
```

If you'd like to fine-tune the PHP configuration, open `/usr/local/lib/php.ini`.

First, make sure that any system-specific settings are set. Usually, the default settings work perfectly fine. You might want to look at the resource settings, however, because they can be used to make sure that renegade scripts don't eat up the memory and CPU time on your system. Look in the `php.ini` for these lines:

```
;;;;;;;;;;;;;;;;;;;
; Resource Limits ;
;;;;;;;;;;;;;;;;;;;

max_execution_time = 30     ; Maximum execution time of each script, in seconds
memory_limit = 8M           ; Maximum amount of memory a script may consume (8MB)
```

By default, scripts might use up to 8MB of memory and take 30 seconds to execute. For many CGIs, these are rather liberal values. You can reduce them as you'd like; I've cut them in half on my system and haven't had any problems thus far.

Additionally, you should enable safe mode (`safe_mode = On`) on a public-use production server. This virtually eliminates the need to worry about environment variables being modified and misused:

```
; Safe Mode
safe_mode                  =       On
safe_mode_allowed_env_vars = PHP_ ; Setting certain environment variables
                                  ; may be a potential security breach.
                                  ; This directive contains a comma-delimited
                                  ; list of prefixes.  In Safe Mode, the
                                  ; user may only alter environment
                                  ; variables whose names begin with the
                                  ; prefixes supplied here.
                                  ; By default, users will only be able
                                  ; to set environment variables that begin
                                  ; with PHP_ (e.g. PHP_FOO=BAR).
                                  ; Note:  If this directive is empty, PHP
```

```
                                      ; will let the user modify ANY environment
                                      ; variable!
safe_mode_protected_env_vars = LD_LIBRARY_PATH; This directive is a comma-
                                      ; delimited list of environment variables,
                                      ; that the end user won't be able to
                                      ; change using putenv().
                                      ; These variables will be protected
                                      ; even if safe_mode_allowed_env_vars is
                                      ; set to allow to change them.
disable_functions        =            ; This directive allows you to disable certain
                                      ; functions for security reasons.  It receives
                                      ; a comma separated list of function names.
                                      ; This directive is *NOT* affected by whether
                                      ; Safe Mode is turned on or off.
```

This combination of settings enables you, the administrator, to prohibit environment variables from being modified unless they begin with one of the listed prefixes (`safe_mode_protected_env_vars`). You can also specify environment variables that, under no circumstances, should ever be allowed to change, regardless of the prefix settings. Finally, if there are certain functions you'd rather not be available to users, you can list these here as well (`disable_functions`).

The final step is enabling the PHP module in Apache, which consists of nothing more than uncommenting a few lines in your `/private/etc/httpd/httpd.conf`:

```
LoadModule php4_module        libexec/httpd/libphp4.so
AddModule mod_php4.c
```

and

```
AddType application/x-httpd-php .php
AddType application/x-httpd-php-source .phps
```

Search the existing `httpd.conf` file and remove the # (comment) character from in front of each of these lines. To activate the changes, restart the Apache Web server using the Sharing Preference panel, or by typing `sudo /usr/sbin/apachectl restart` from the command line.

To verify that PHP is working, create a file (`test.php`) within one of your Web directories:

```
<?php
   phpinfo();
?>
```

Load this test page using a Web browser. If the installation was successful, you should see a screen similar to Figure 28.8.

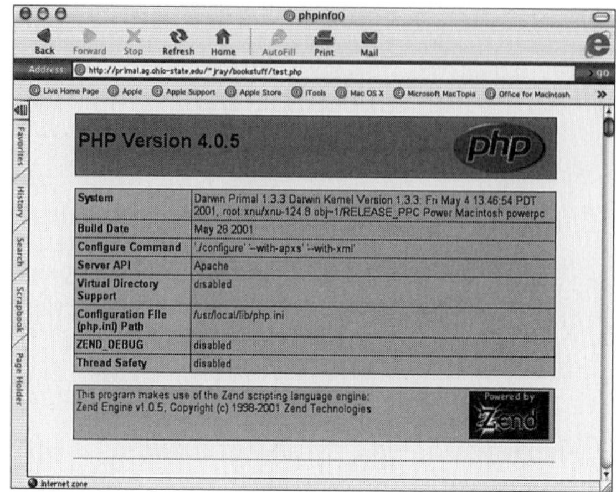

FIGURE 28.8
The `phpinfo()` function generates a screen of PHP installation information.

PHP Syntax

The best introduction to programming PHP is a background in C or Perl. Check out Chapter 22 as a starter guide for that language. PHP borrows heavily from Perl's free-form open scripting model and auto data conversion. What truly makes PHP shine is the built-in Web functions. Let's take a brief look at what you need to get you started, then examine some of the unique features.

Syntax

PHP programs are created as standard text files within any of your Web-enabled directories. To execute, the script you must have the extension `.php`. This does not have a bearing on the HTML contents of the file. In fact, you can have an HTML file that contains no PHP code, but ends in `.php`—it will still be served correctly, albeit with a slight performance penalty as the server checks the file for executable code.

PHP code itself is typically embedded within the `<?php` and `?>` brackets. Failing to place these tags around code will result in the programming being interpreted as text within an HTML document. Even if you are working with a file that contains no HTML at all, it must still place all the PHP script within the brackets. There can be multiple PHP start and end tags in a single document.

If you've written JavaScript, this is similar to the behavior of the `<script>` and `</script>` tags that embed JavaScript code into a document. Regardless of how many PHP code segments are in your program, the code can be considered all part of one big global block. The variables that are defined in one section are available in another. For example:

```
<?php $myname="John"; ?>
This is some standard HTML in the middle...<BR><BR>
<?php print $myname; ?>
```

This code fragment assigns the value John to `$myname`, and then includes a bit of HTML, and finally prints the value of `$myname` (John). Even though `$myname` occurs within two separate PHP blocks, the value is still maintained.

Note

Perhaps not surprisingly, PHP can be embedded with the `<script>` and `</script>` tags. To use this format, just include PHP as the scripting language within the first tag: `<script language="php">`.

Each line of PHP code must end in a semicolon (`;`) to be correctly executed. Because of this requirement, extremely long lines of code can be broken across multiple lines to improve legibility.

Data Types

Like Perl, PHP's data types are typecast from one to another internally. Although there is one primary data type, PHP is an object-oriented language and is used to create arbitrary object types with their own properties. Object-oriented programming is beyond the scope of this text, so only the basics will be covered here—don't worry, there's more than enough to start building complex Web applications.

`$<variable name>`—PHP defines a variable as an alphanumeric string prefaced by a `$`. Variable names *cannot* begin with a number. The variable can contain text, binary data, numbers, and so on. Type conversion happens automatically during program execution.

`$<variable name>[<index>]`—Arrays offer more flexibility than Perl. An array can be defined during the course of program execution by adding an `[index]` to the end of a variable name. Unlike Perl, which differentiates between a standard array and associative arrays, an array index in PHP can be either a number or a string.

PHP variables are unique creatures and can be used in very interesting ways. For example, the contents of a variable can be interpreted as variables themselves. Assume that you have a variable named `$peach`. Obviously, you can reference this variable by name (`$peach`). Now assume that a second variable, `$fruit`, contains the string peach `"peach"`. Using this second variable, you can reference the contents of the first variable through

$$fruit. This works because $$fruit is functionally identical to typing $"peach", which in turn is equivalent to $peach. This same technique can be applied to function calls to create a logic flow that changes itself based on variables in the program.

Note

Although not commonly used in simple applications, PHP does support passing variables by reference. As in C, you can pass a reference to a variable by placing an ampersand (&) in front: &<*$variable name*>.

Basic Operators

The comparison and assignment operations work much like a simplified version of their Perl counterparts. The primary difference is that string comparisons are identical to numeric comparisons in syntax within PHP. Table 28.1 contains the common PHP operators.

TABLE 28.1 Common PHP Operators

Operator	*Action*	*Description*
==	Equals	Tests for equality
!=	Not equal	Tests for inequality
=	Assignment	Assigns the value on the right to the variable on the left
*	Multiplication	Multiplies two values together
/	Division	Divides two values
+	Addition	Adds two numbers together
-	Subtraction	Subtracts one number from another
.	Concatenation	Concatenates two strings together
&&	AND	Performs a logical AND on two values
||	OR	Performs a logical OR on two values

As previously mentioned, PHP automatically handles type conversions for you, making it possible to write code that looks like this:

```
<?php
$a="1";
$b="3";
$c=$a.$b;
```

```
$c=$c*2;
?>
```

Here, two strings, 1 and 3, are concatenated together and stored in $c. This new value is then multiplied by 2. Printing the result would display 26—even though the only true number used in the calculation was 2 (during the multiplication).

There are a few shortcuts to the assignment as well. For example, incrementing or decrementing a number is very common. Written in long form, adding 1 to the existing value of a variable $a looks like this:

```
$a=$a+1;
```

This can be shortened to

```
$a++;
```

The same applies to subtraction, using the minus (-) symbol.

Another shortcut applies to concatenating, adding, or subtracting to an existing value. For example, this line of code concatenates $b onto the end of $a:

```
$a=$a.$b;
```

The same thing can be written as

```
$a.=$b;
```

For addition and subtraction, just substitute in the appropriate operator in place of .. The basic syntax remains the same.

Control Structures

Two types of control structures will be discussed here: linear flow operators and looping constructs. Linear flow operators can change the course of a program based on variables and other conditions. Looping constructs, on the other hand, can repeat sections of code based on similar criteria. Together they enable software to adapt to a particular task, rather than being hard-coded to work with one set of input.

if-then-else

The most common linear flow control structure is the if-then-else statement. This can evaluate one or more conditions and act on them accordingly. The basic PHP if-then statement is structured like this:

```
if <condition> {
        <do something>;
}
```

This statement can be expanded to include an alternative course of action if the original condition is not met. This is considered an `if-then-else` statement:

```
if <condition> {
        <do something>;
} else {
        <do something else>;
}
```

One final variation of the statement exists that can evaluate multiple conditions within the single statement. This last variation is the `if-then-elsif` statement.

```
if <condition> {
        <do something>;
} elsif <another condition> {
        <do something else>;
} else {
        <do yet another thing>;
}
```

This example includes a single `elsif` line, but, depending on the needs of the programmer, this can be repeated as many times as he or she feels necessary. A less verbose way to accomplish the same goal is to use the `switch` statement.

switch

The `switch` statement takes a value as input, and defines a set of possible outcomes that can occur, depending on that value. The best way to understand how this works is to take a look at an example:

```
switch ($x) {
        case 0:
                print "x=0";
                break;
        case 1:
                print "x=1";
                break;
        case 2:
                print "x=2";
                break;
        default:
                print "none of the above";
                break;
}
```

This piece of code examines the value of `$x`. If it is `0`, PHP prints `x=0`. If `$x` equals `1`, the code prints `x=1`… and so on. If `$x` doesn't match any of the listed values (`0`, `1`, `2`), it uses the `default` value and prints `none of the above`.

The `switch` statement can be extended to include as many cases as needed. In addition, the cases do not have to be numeric. You can just as easily include strings:

```
switch ($name) {
        case 'John':
                print "John has a dog named Maddy";
                break;
        case 'Robyn':
                print "Robyn has a dog named Coco";
                break;
        case 'Jack':
                print "Jack has a bag of M&Ms";
                break;
        case default:
                print "I don't know you!";
                break;
}
```

The two portions of the `switch` statement that might require a bit more explanation are the `break` statement and the `default` case.

The `break` causes the `switch` statement to exit. If `break` is not executed, all code after the matching case is executed. If `John` is matched, all the print statements are executed until a `break` is encountered.

The `default` case is optional. It is executed only if none of the other cases is matched. It's usually a good idea to have a default case to keep untrapped errors from occurring.

`for`

The `for` loop is the most commonly encountered loop in programming, regardless of the language. This loop executes a block of code until a condition is met. Each iteration of a `for-next` loop increments (or decrements) a counter variable. The loop is constructed using this syntax:

```
for (<initialization>;<execution condition>;<increment>) {
        <code block>
}
```

The *initialization* sets up the loop and initializes the counter variable to its default state. The *execution condition* is checked in each iteration of the loop; if it evaluates to false, the loop ends. Finally, the increment is a piece of code that defines an operation performed on the counter variable each time the loop is run. For example, the following loop counts from 0 to 9:

```
for ($count=0;$count<10;$count++) {
        print "Count = $count";
}
```

The counter, `$count`, is set to `0` when the loop starts. With each repetition, it is incremented by 1 (`$count++`). The loop exits when the counter reaches 10 (`$count<10`).

The format for the PHP `for` loop is identical to the Perl syntax.

while

The `while` loop executes while a condition evaluates to true. Unlike a `for` loop, which usually ends based on a change in the counter, the `while` loop requires that something change within the code block that will cause the condition to evaluate as false.

```
while (<execution condition>) {
        <code block>
}
```

The previous `for` example counted from 0 to 9. This same loop translated into a `while` loop looks like this:

```
$count=0;
while ($count<10) {
        print "Count = $count";
        $count++;
}
```

When using `while`/`do-while` loops, be sure that the execution condition will eventually evaluate to false. It's easy to write infinite loops using this structure.

do-while

Similar to the basic `while` loop, a `do-while` loop runs until a preset condition evaluates to false. The difference between the two loop styles is *where* the execution condition is checked. In a `while` loop, the condition is evaluated at the start of the loop. `Do-while` loops, on the other hand, evaluate the condition at the end:

```
do {
        <code block>
} while (<execution condition>);
```

Again, let's translate the count from 0 to 9 into a `do-while` loop. As you can see, the difference is slight.

```
$count=0;
do {
        print "Count = $count";
        $count++;
} while ($count<10);
```

Note

Many languages have a similar loop structure known as a `do-until` loop. The only difference is that the `do-until` loop exits after a condition is met, not after it has become false.

Functions

Like any good programming language, PHP supports the notion of functions—independent pieces of code that can act on input and return a result. As you develop Web applications, you'll find that a reasonable amount of code is reused each time. If applications are programmed as modularly as possible, you can create a library of commonly used functions to share among multiple applications and developers.

A function is set up using the `function` keyword; values are returned to the main program using `return`. For example:

```
function addnumbers($arg1,$arg2) {
        $result=$arg1+$arg2;
        return($result);
}
```

This function accepts two arguments (`$arg1` and `$arg2`), adds them together, and then returns the result to the main program. The `addnumbers` function could be called like this:

```
$theresult=&addnumbers(1,5);
```

In this example, the function is called with a preceding ampersand (`&`). This is optional, but is required in code where the function's definition occurs *after* the function call is used in the code.

By default, all variables used in a function are automatically considered local to that function and cannot be accessed outside of the function code. To make a variable's scope global, use the `global` keyword within a function:

```
global <variable name>;
```

A variable that is declared global can be accessed from the main program block as well as the declaring function.

Common Functions

It's pointless to try and document all PHP's capabilities in this chapter. There are more than 1,500 functions available in the PHP 4.0.6 release. Table 28.2 provides a quick reference to some of the more interesting and useful functions. For those of you interested, when compiling this list I surveyed more than a dozen PHP scripts and noted the most frequently used operations as well as those needed for the examples in the chapter.

TABLE 28.2 With More Than 1,500 Available Functions, PHP Is Anything but Limited

Function	*Purpose*
addslashes(<*string*>)	Escapes special characters within strings (such as ' " ') and returns the resulting string.
chop(<*string*>)	Removes trailing white spaces from a string and returns the result.
file(<*url*>)	Reads a file from a URL (local, FTP, Web) and returns an array of each line in the file.
header(<*string*>)	Outputs a header before processing any HTML output.
join(<*glue string*>, <*array*>)	Returns a single string containing all the elements of a given array joined together with the "glue" string. Same as implode.
preg_replace(<*regex*>, <*replace string*>,<*string*>)	Searches a string for a Perl-style regular expression, replaces it with another, and returns the new string.
print "<*output*>"	Displays an output string. This is identical to the echo keyword.
opendir(<*directory name*>)	Opens a directory for reading and returns a file handle.
readdir(<*file handle*>)	Returns the next filename within a directory opened with opendir. Returns false if no more files are available.
require(<*filename*>)	Includes the contents of another file within the PHP code.
session_start()	Initializes a new session.
session_register (<*variable*>)	Registers a variable with a session—making it available in subsequent Web page accesses. Do *not* include the $ with the name of the variable.
session_unregister (<*variable*>)	Unregisters a session variable.
session_destroy()	Removes the active session.
sort(<*array*>)	Sorts an array.

TABLE 28.2 continued

Function	*Purpose*
soundex(<*string*>)	Returns a soundex value for a given string. This value is based on the sound of a string and can be used to compare two strings that sound similar but are spelled differently.
split(<*pattern*>,<*string*>)	Splits a string based on the characters in <*pattern*> and returns each of the results as the element in an array.
stripslashes(<*string*>)	Removes slashes from a string—the opposite of addslashes—and returns the result.
strlen(<*string*>)	Returns the length of a given string.

Visit www.php.net/quickref.php for a full list of the PHP functions.

PHP in Practice

In the Perl portion of this chapter, we created a simple image catalog. Let's see how that catalog can be rewritten in PHP. Listing 28.10 shows a PHP version of the Perl-image catalog.

LISTING 28.10 The Image Catalog, Rewritten in PHP

```
<?php if (!$imagedir) { ?>
        <form action="showimages1.php" method="post">
Choose image dir: <input type="text" name="imagedir" value="imagefolder"><br>
        Select the number of columns in the display: <select name="columns">
            <option>1</option>
            <option>2</option>
            <option>3</option>
            <option>4</option>
        </select><br>
        Show images that match: <input type="text" name="match">
        <input type="submit" name="submit">
        </form>
<?php exit; } ?>

<TABLE BGCOLOR="#FFFFFF" BORDER="1" BORDERCOLOR="#000000">
<?php
$handle=opendir("$imagedir");
while ($imagename = readdir($handle)) {
    if ($count==0 && $loop==0) { print "<TR>"; $loop=1; }
    if (preg_match("/.*$match.*\.jpg$/i",$imagename)) { ?>
        <TD align=center>
<IMG SRC="<?php print"$imagedir/$imagename"; ?>" width="120" height="90"><br>
        <FONT TYPE="Arial"><?php print $imagename; ?></FONT>
```

LISTING 28.10 continued

```
24:         </TD><?php
25:         $count++;
26:         if ($count==$columns) { print "</TR>"; $count=0; $loop=0; }
27:     }
28: }
29: if ($count!=0) { print "</TR>"; }
30: ?>
31: </TABLE>
```

The first two things you should notice looking at this code are that it is shorter and that the PHP is embedded *in* the HTML, rather than the HTML being embedded in the programming.

As the PHP application begins sending output, it automatically adds a `text/html` content-type header. In addition, no external library, such as `cgiinput.pl`, is required. When a form posts information to a PHP program, the form variables are automatically translated into PHP variables. For example, an input field with the name `address` becomes the variable `$address` when submitted to a PHP script. These shortcuts enable you to focus on the code, rather than the specifics of HTTP.

A breakdown of the changes in the code follows:

Lines 1–13 check whether the variable `$imagedir` is defined. If it isn't, the user hasn't submitted a search request yet and the search form should be displayed. Unlike Perl, which used `print` to show the form, PHP `if-then` tags can encompass HTML blocks. In this case, if the variable isn't defined, the HTML in the `if-then` is sent to the browser—otherwise, it is skipped.

Line 15 starts the HTML output table. Line 17 opens the image directory for reading. PHP, sadly, doesn't support a `glob` function, like Perl. While there are files in the opened directory, lines 18–28 read them into `$filename`.

If at the start of a row, send a `<TR>` tag. Line 19 must also set a flag (`$loop`) to indicate that the loop has started—this prevents multiple `<TR>` from being sent if the first few files read in the directory are *not* image files. Line 20 uses a Perl regular expression to match the filename to a file that ends in `.jpg` and includes the search string (`$match`).

Lines 21–24 display the table data cell for the image. Note that the image name is added to the HTML by embedded PHP `print` statements. Lines 25–26 increment the number of images displayed. If it is equal to the selected number of image columns, output a `</TR>`.

If the last file displayed occurred in the middle of a row, the program must add a final `</TR>` to close the row. This is done with line 29. Line 31 closes the output table.

For the most part, the programming syntax should closely resemble what you've seen in Perl. The lack of a `glob` function adds a few extra lines, but doesn't prevent the PHP version from coming in 20% shorter.

You might have noticed that this version of the script does not attempt to check the input variables for `/`. This is because PHP automatically escapes troublesome characters in user input. For example, `/example` becomes `\/example`. This gives developers some peace of mind during programming.

PHP and Sessions

I've made such a big deal about sessions and how they make life easier; it's probably time to see one in use. Unfortunately, it's very difficult to fabricate the use for a session in a reasonable amount of space. So, let's take a look at a simple case of sessions at work.

Imagine having a Web page that remembers how many times you've visited it during your current browser session (since you last quit out of your Web browser). This can't be done using a form because an action would be needed to submit the form each time you load the page. URL parameters can't be used because, likewise, the page would have to alter all the links it contains to include the number of visits using URL variable passing. With sessions, this is beyond simple. In fact, the following example keeps track of the cumulative number of visits to two distinct pages.

Create two Web pages (`one.php` and `two.php`) that link to one another. In `one.php`, type the following:

```
<?php
session_start();
$x++;
session_register(x);
print "You've been to page one and two $x times";
?>
<BR>
<A HREF="two.php">Go to page two</A>
```

And in `two.php`, type this:

```
<?php
session_start();
$x++;
session_register(x);
print "You've been to page one and two $x times";
?>
<BR>
<A HREF="one.php">Go to page one</A>
```

Loading one of the pages (either one) creates a page similar to that shown in Figure 28.9.

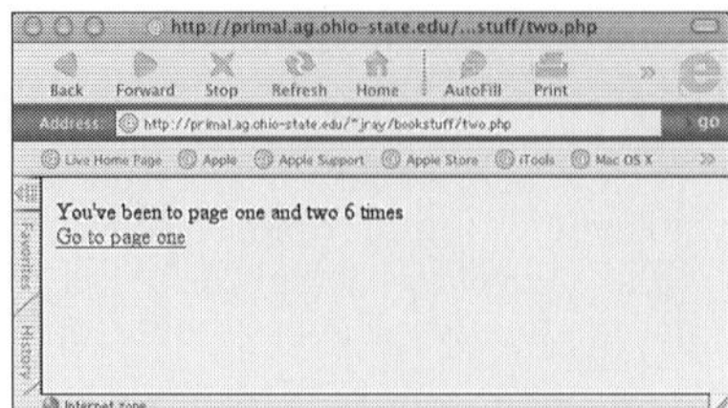

FIGURE 28.9
The two Web pages (`one.php` *and* `two.php`*) share a single variable* `$x`.

Clicking the link to toggle between the two pages increments the counter and the displayed number starts counting up. Although this is not a groundbreaking Web site, it demonstrates the capabilities of built-in session management. The two pages share a single counter variable `$x`. The `session_start()` command starts a new PHP session, if one doesn't already exist. The `session_register(x)` registers the variable `$x` with the current session—effectively saving its value until another page is accessed. It is important to provide variables to `session_register` *without* the preceding dollar sign (`$`).

The incrementing of `$x` doesn't depend in any way on the links between `one.php` and `two.php`. You can reload one of the pages 30 times and the counter will increment 30 times. You can even visit another Web site, then come back to either of the Web pages and the count is still present. The only way to lose the value of `$x` is to drop the session—that is close your Web browser.

The virtues of PHP could be touted for pages and pages, but, unfortunately, the room is not available. If you'd like more information on PHP development, I urge you to look at any of these fine sites:

PHP Homepage—`www.php.net/`

PHP Builder—`www.phpbuilder.net/`

PHPHead—`www.phphead.net/`

The PHP Resource—`www.php-resource.de/`

PHPInfo—`www.phpinfo.net`

Alternative Development Environments

There are a large number of alternative Web development environments that can run under Mac OS X, including Apple's own WebObjects. I, personally, have a thing for open source products, but depending on your needs, PHP or Perl might not be appropriate.

WebObjects, for example, is a Java-based development environment that includes RAD tools, distributed application logic and load handling, and a steep learning curve. WebObjects is used to deploy large-scale applications, and requires a decent knowledge of the Mac OS X object model to begin programming. WebObjects comes with a reasonable price tag ($1,500), which prices it outside the range of smaller groups. On the plus side, it is widely recognized as a superior Web application server and has won numerous awards in the enterprise marketplace (`www.apple.com/webobjects/`).

Active Server Pages (ASP) is usually associated with the Windows platform. Halcyon Software's iASP product brings Active Server Pages to the Mac OS X platform. This offers a great opportunity to ISPs and those entrenched in an NT environment to migrate to a better solution. iASP pricing ranges from $500 to $1,500 depending on your deployment requirements. PHP offers a great solution to the cross-platform scripting problem, but doesn't necessarily fit the corporate model just yet (that is, it's free). iASP is a great way to incorporate a Mac into a Windows-centric development environment (`http://www.halcyonsoft.com/`).

Java Server Pages (JSP) is a fast-growing application development solution that leverages the cross-platform nature of Java. Like WebObjects, JSP requires knowledge of the Java programming language, and has a similarly steep learning curve. A big advantage to JSP is that it is a supported server platform in software packages such as Macromedia's Dreamweaver UltraDev—enabling graphical development of Web applications. In addition, there are several free JSP server solutions that run on Mac OS X and even Mac OS 9.x. The two easiest to set up servers are Jetty (`http://jetty.mortbay.com/`) and Jakarta Tomcat (`http://jakarta.apache.org/tomcat/`). Jetty is simple to configure, whereas Tomcat can integrate seamlessly with Apache. A Tomcat setup helper application is available from VersionTracker: `www.versiontracker.com/`.

Summary

Professional Web application development *finally* comes to the Macintosh platform. There are a number of issues to overcome when transitioning from a standard programming model to the Web—most notably, session management. Perl offers a great starting language for programmers. A more Web-centric development environment is PHP, which works by embedding development code into HTML, rather than HTML into the code.

Even if the Perl/PHP development solutions don't meet your needs, there are a number of other options available that can create enterprise-level Web sites and online applications.

Creating a Mail Server

IN THIS CHAPTER

The Unix operating system houses the server application that started the e-mail phenomenon—Sendmail. Sendmail is an extremely complex and capable SMTP server. It can provide e-mail services for a small workgroup or an entire corporation. It's little surprise that this software is bundled with Mac OS X.

This chapter will explore the steps needed to activate the dormant Mac OS X Sendmail installation and implement basic security features. In addition, you'll learn how to install POP3 and IMAP servers to deliver e-mail to client computers across a network.

Running a Mail Server

The first step in running a successful e-mail server is determining that you actually *need* an e-mail server. Unlike more basic services, such as Apache, e-mail is a more intrusive process that enables complete strangers to store information on your computer. In addition, administration of an e-mail server is an ongoing process. Monitoring and detecting problems is a must. Sendmail has been around for more than 20 years, but it's still growing and evolving. Because it is one of the most highly utilized pieces of software on the Internet, it is also one of the most prone to attacks.

Mail server security is unlike basic server security because it occurs on two levels. First, you must protect the physical server software from being exploited. Remote users have found numerous holes in earlier versions of Sendmail that granted root access to the e-mail server, or enabled them to gain other forms of unauthorized access. Monitoring server logs for unexplained connections and abnormal mail transmissions is standard practice. This aspect of mail server security should seem familiar, because it should be a common practice for other basic system services, such as FTP or HTTP.

The second security problem is mail server abuse. This doesn't necessarily equate to compromising the e-mail server, but the results can be even more far reaching. E-mail spam, for example, is the result of poorly implemented e-mail security. In the case of spam, there are two possible problems. The first is an authorized user is inappropriately using your e-mail resources; the second is an unauthorized user is taking advantage of an open relay on your mail server to do the work of distributing his or her spam.

In either case, the result is the same. The second scenario is the most serious when considering the security of your network. It is very much akin to hacking, but without necessarily needing to exploit any program flaws on your system.

What Is an Open Relay?

An *open relay* is an SMTP server that accepts and delivers mail for *any* user from *any* user. Mail servers should be configured to allow only certain clients to send e-mail; otherwise, they can be used by anyone in the world to send spam or other harmful data.

For these reasons, you should seriously consider alternatives to running your own mail server. Users in need of controlling their own e-mail accounts, the privacy of storing their own messages, or requiring complex mail relaying or automated processing, are the best candidates for running their own server.

A properly configured server requires little maintenance and will perform extremely well on Mac OS X. An improperly configured server, however, could be a disaster.

Activating Sendmail

Assuming that you've decided to go ahead and create a mail server, the first step is to turn on the server application itself. Mac OS X includes the Sendmail software, but it is not activated when the system first boots.

Tip

The assumption is made that the Mac OS X machine you're going to use as a mail server already has a registered hostname. If this is not the case, be sure to register with a domain name system (DNS) before continuing. In addition to the standard A record (address record), a mail server typically also registers an MX record for the base-level domain. For example, although the server `postoffice.ag.ohio-state.edu` receives mail for accounts addressed directly to itself, there also is an MX record setup for `ag.osu.edu` that points to `postoffice.ag.ohio-state.edu`. This enables mail sent to an account at `ag.osu.edu` to be sent to the `postoffice.ag.ohio-state.edu` hostname transparently.

To automate Sendmail startup, open the file `/etc/hostconfig` in your favorite text editor. Edit the line that reads `MAILSERVER=-NO-` to `MAILSERVER=-YES-`:

```
##
# /etc/hostconfig
##
# This file is maintained by the system control panels
##

# Network configuration
HOSTNAME=Primal
ROUTER=-AUTOMATIC-

# Services
AFPSERVER=-YES-
APPLETALK=en0
AUTHSERVER=-NO-
AUTOCONFIG=-YES-
AUTODISKMOUNT=-REMOVABLE-
AUTOMOUNT=-YES-
CONFIGSERVER=-NO-
IPFORWARDING=-NO-
MAILSERVER=-YES-
MANAGEMENTSERVER=-NO-
NETBOOTSERVER=-NO-
NISDOMAIN=-NO-
...
```

Next, you must adjust the Sendmail configuration so that it doesn't detect a security error. By default, Sendmail detects any group-writable directories that contain its configuration files and fails to start if it finds even one. Because of the user and group structure in Mac OS X, if you were to change the permissions on the Sendmail configuration directories, you'd lose other administrative features. If you fail to complete this step, Sendmail will start at boot time, but will immediately quit, saving errors such as this to the `/var/spool/mail.log` file:

```
Jun 23 04:30:36 Primal sendmail[501]:
   ➥NOQUEUE: SYSERR(root): /etc/mail/sendmail.cf:
   ➥line 81: fileclass:
   ➥cannot open /etc/mail/local-host-names: Group writable directory
Jun 23 04:30:37 Primal sendmail[502]:
   ➥NOQUEUE: SYSERR(root): /etc/mail/sendmail.cf:
   ➥line 81: fileclass:
   ➥cannot open /etc/mail/local-host-names: Group writable directory
```

To fix the problem, open the `/etc/mail/sendmail.cf` and look for the line

```
#O DontBlameSendmail=safe
```

Change the line to read

```
O DontBlameSendmail=GroupWritableDirPathSafe
```

This adds the option DontBlameSendmail with flag GroupWritableDirPathSafe. This instructs Sendmail to define group-writable directories as being safe.

You can now restart your Mac OS X computer. The Sendmail e-mail server will start. You can verify that the server is running and responding by using telnet to connect to port 25 (SMTP):

```
[primal:/etc/mail] root# telnet localhost 25
Trying 127.0.0.1...
Connected to localhost.ag.ohio-state.edu.
Escape character is '^]'.
220 primal.ag.ohio-state.edu ESMTP Sendmail 8.10.2/8.10.2;
    ➥Mon, 25 Jun 2001 21:08:27 -0400 (EDT)
```

If your connection fails, verify that you *do* have a DNS-registered hostname for your computer and check for error messages in the /var/log/mail.log file. The Sendmail messages are quite verbose and a great deal of help with debugging a faulty installation.

Try sending yourself a test message from a remote computer. Be sure to specify the destination as the hostname and username used on your Mac OS X machine. Incoming messages are stored in /var/spool/<*username*>. Use the command-line mail utility to read the contents of your mailbox:

```
[primal:/etc/mail] root# mail
Mail version 8.1 6/6/93.  Type ? for help.
"/var/mail/jray": 1 message 1 new
>N  1 jray@poisontooth.com  Mon Jun 25 21:11  20/838   "Testing"
```

Congratulations. Your Mac OS X computer is now running an enterprise-class SMTP server.

Sendmail Configuration

Setting up Sendmail is an interesting experience. Although it might appear that the main configuration file /etc/mail/sendmail.cf is the central setup point, it is and it isn't. The Sendmail configuration file is generated by a series of macros run by the m4 macro processor. By adding very simple directives to the macro files, users can create extremely complex configurations. The final output is the /etc/mail/sendmail.cf file, but some of the most useful configuration options are specified in the macro files before sendmail.cf is even generated.

Generating sendmail.cf

You've already seen a very basic change that must be made to the /etc/mail/sendmail.cf file to accommodate the Mac OS X file system. Let's backtrack a bit and see how sendmail.cf is created and can be fine-tuned using m4 macros.

To re-create the default sendmail.cf file at any time, use these commands:

```
cd /usr/share/sendmail/conf/m4
m4 cf.m4 ../cf/generic-darwin.mc > /etc/mail/sendmail.cf
```

Note

The assumption is made that you are acting with root permissions. If this is not the case, you might need to preface commands with sudo.

This will overwrite the existing /etc/mail/sendmail.cf file and return the system to its initial state. To add macro-level features to the configuration, first copy the generic-darwin.mc file to a copy that you can edit:

```
cd /usr/share/sendmail/conf/cf
cp generic-darwin.mc myosxconfig.mc
```

You'll be making changes to the new /usr/share/sendmail/conf/cf/myosxconfig.mc file from this point forward. These changes can then be compiled into the master sendmail.cf file with

```
cd /usr/share/sendmail/conf/m4
m4 cf.m4 ../cf/myosxconfig.mc > /etc/mail/sendmail.cf
```

Tip

If you rebuilt the /etc/mail/sendmail.cf file, you must make the DontBlameSendmail change discussed at the start of the chapter. Although I've already said this, it's important to remember; otherwise, you might end up beating your head against a wall wondering why your server stopped working.

The following configuration directives (called *features*) can be added to your myosxconfig.mc file to increase functionality and security. You should not remove any of the default lines, or your mail server might not start.

RealTime Blacklisting

One of the first features to enable on any Internet-connected Sendmail server should be realtime blacklisting (RBL). RBL services maintain a list of known open relay mail servers and spammers. By enabling RBL service on the Mac OS X mail server, it automatically checks each incoming message to determine whether it is from a known open relay or spammer. If it is, the message is returned as undeliverable. Include this feature to your `myosxconfig.mc` file by adding the line

```
FEATURE(`dnsbl')
```

Blacklisting does run a slight risk of denying messages from legitimate sources that happen to be using a mail server configured as an open relay. This, however, is becoming increasingly rare and shouldn't dissuade you from implementing RBL on your system.

Relaying

The version of Sendmail that ships with Mac OS X (8.10.2) is not configured as an open relay. This means that you can start the server without worrying about whether or not it will be used to send spam. As the administrator, you will, however, need to make choices on what relaying capabilities the server should have.

If a server must be accessible by clients across the country or around the globe, it becomes very difficult to nail down what client computers should be allowed to use Sendmail as a relay. The best possible situation is to be running a mail server that allows relaying for a local domain and perhaps a few ISPs. In a situation such as this, you should create and edit the file `/etc/mail/relay-domains`. Add to this file a list of domains or IP addresses that should be allowed to send e-mail via the server. For example

```
[primal:/etc/mail] jray% more relay-domains
192.168.0.50
poisontooth.com
ag.ohio-state.edu
osu.edu
```

Here, there are three named domains (`poisontooth.com`, `ag.ohio-state.edu`, `osu.edu`) and one specific client (`192.168.0.50`), that are allowed to access the SMTP server.

After editing the relay file, open and edit the `/etc/mail/local-host-names` file. Enter into this file all the names for which your mail server should accept e-mail. Even if relays are properly configured, mail might be rejected if addressed to an alternative hostname for the server. For example, I want to be able to accept e-mail for `poisontooth.com`, `mail.poisontooth.com`, and `mail.shadesofinsanity.com`. Each of these hostnames' DNS entry points directly to the server. To make sure that Sendmail accepts e-mail for all the names, my `local-host-names` file would look like this:

```
[primal:/etc/mail] jray% more local-host-names
poisontooth.com
mail.poisontooth.com
mail.shadesofinsanity.com
```

For most small organizations, or even some large ones, this should be sufficient. Unfortunately, as was mentioned earlier, some organizations might need more control over the relay system. The following features provide more exacting control over the relay process:

`FEATURE(`relay_entire_domain')`—This is the most dangerous feature available. When used, the Mac OS X Sendmail server becomes an open relay, accessible by any user. This should not be used unless the server traffic is limited by another means, such as a firewall.

`FEATURE(`relay_local_from')`—Although not as bad as the first feature, this option is still quite dangerous. When used, the server enables any remote host to relay, as long as the messages being sent include a from header that consists of an address in your local domain. E-mail headers (including the mail from header) are easily forged, so this provides protection from only the most simplistic spam attacks.

`FEATURE(`accept_unresolvable_domains')`—This feature enables messages to be accepted with an invalid hostname in the mail from header.

`FEATURE(`relay_hosts_only')`—Activates relaying for hosts on your local network. If a client hostname has the same base domain name as the server, it is allowed to access the SMTP server. This is a very good feature to include if your network is the only place that should be able to send e-mail via the Mac OS X Sendmail daemon.

Advanced Access Control

In addition to blacklisting/relay-control features, you can create an access table that controls user access at an even lower level—down to the individual e-mail addresses that are being used. To enable this table, add these lines to your `myosxconfig.mc` file:

```
FEATURE(`access_db')
FEATURE(`blacklist_recipients')
```

The first line enables the access database, whereas the second enables the administrator to add individual e-mail accounts to which the server will refuse to send e-mail.

The access table is built as a plain text file, such as `/etc/mail/access`. To be used by Sendmail, it must be hashed using the following command:

```
makemap hash /etc/mail/access < /etc/mail/access
```

The access control table is built using simple single-line commands. Each line consists of a host, domain, or e-mail address and an action to take if it is matched. Table 29.1 lists the possible reactions to a match.

TABLE 29.1 Access Control Actions

Action	*Description*
`OK`	Accept mail regardless of other rules. This overrides any other relay configuration.
`RELAY`	Accept e-mail to or from the named domain.
`REJECT`	Reject e-mail from or to the recipient with a generic message.
`DISCARD`	Discard e-mail from or to the recipient.
`ERROR:<### *Text*>`	Identical to `REJECT`, but enables the administrator to set a customized error message.

For example, consider the following file:

```
wespamalot.com          ERROR:"550 We don't accept mail from your domain"
goodguy.wespamalot.com  OK
poisontooth.com         RELAY
192.168.0               RELAY
spammer@yahoo.com       REJECT
```

In this example, the mail from domain `wespamalot.com` is rejected with a custom error message. The host `goodguy.wespamalot.com` is allowed because the `OK` action overrides the initial `ERROR`. The domain `poisontooth.com` and subnet `192.168.0` are both allowed to use the server as a relay. Finally, e-mail from or to `spammer@yahoo.com` is rejected.

As you can see, this file can be built upon to grow with the needs of the server. Adding the `access_db` feature is recommended for any Sendmail installation.

Tip

These are only a few of the available Sendmail `m4` features. For more information on other features, view the Sendmail documentation at `www.sendmail.org/m4/features.html`.

`Sendmail.cf` Options

Assuming that you've made your changes to the macro setup files and then used `m4` to rebuild the main configuration, there are still several things you might want to change in the `sendmail.cf` file before calling your server done. There are literally hundreds of configuration options—most books on Sendmail are 800–1000 pages long—this will be the abbreviated version of what's important. Open the `/etc/mail/sendmail.cf` file and adjust what is appropriate for your machine. Table 29.2 has a few of the more interesting and useful options. Note: These options are already included in `sendmail.cf`, but must be uncommented (remove the #) and edited to suit the system requirements.

TABLE 29.2 Interesting and Useful `Sendmail.cf` Options

Option	*Purpose*
`O AliasFile=/etc/mail/aliases`	Actives e-mail aliases on the system. Enables e-mail to be sent to one address and then directed to multiple people or an entirely different e-mail address.
`O MaxMessageSize=1000000`	Sets a maximum message size on the server. When using a system with relaxed relaying, setting a maximum size is a good idea.
`O MeToo`	When using aliases, the server will cc the sender if he or she is included as part of the alias list.
`Dj$w.Foo.COM`	Manually sets a hostname for the Sendmail server. Used when Sendmail can't determine the name of the Mac OS X computer.
`O Timeout.queuereturn=5d`	Sets the length of time an e-mail will attempt to be delivered before it is returned undeliverable. Formatted using a number followed by `d` (days) or `h` (hours).
`O Timeout.queuewarn=4h`	Sets a warning period after which the server will notify a sender that the message has not yet reached its destination.

Aliases

Most systems employ the `AliasFile` option to provide simple mailing list functionality, enable users to receive e-mail under multiple names, or forward messages to another e-mail account. Aliases are added to the file `/etc/mail/aliases`. When inserted, the Sendmail alias database must be rebuilt by running `newaliases` at the command line. This utility must be run each time a change is made to the alias file.

The alias file contains lines with the username that will receive e-mail, followed by a colon, and then the e-mail address (local or remote) that should get the message

```
<email username> : <recipient email address>
```

For example

```
webmaster: jray
jraywork: ray.30@osu.edu
root: jray, hlaufman
```

In this simple alias file, e-mail addressed to `Webmaster` would be sent to the local user `jray`, whereas e-mail addressed to `jraywork` would be forwarded to the account `ray.30@osu.edu`. Finally, any messages sent to `root` are automatically sent to both `jray` and `hlaufman`—two local-user accounts.

To simplify and modularize aliases that direct e-mail to multiple users, you can `include` files that list several e-mail addresses. Take a line such as

```
job-info: :include:/etc/mail/job.list
```

When this entry is added in the `aliases` file, it includes the list of e-mail addresses in the file `/etc/mail/job.list`. This is a convenient way to create a mailing list with very little work.

Mac OS X's Sendmail implementation offers an alternative way to add mail aliases: via the NetInfo database system. This will result in a setup that isn't directly transferable to other Unix systems, but it will allow you to use the NetInfo Manager or `nicl` command-line utility to quickly add aliases.

To add aliases directly to the `/aliases` directory within the NetInfo database, you must first create a NetInfo directory with the name of the alias, and then add a members key with the appropriate alias information. Think of this as splitting the lines in the alias file on the first `:` character. The information to the left of the `:` is the NetInfo alias name, and the information to the right is the member name. For example, consider this line, as it appears in `/etc/mail/aliases`:

```
jraywork: ray.30@osu.edu
```

This information could be added directly to NetInfo using

```
[primal:~] jray% sudo nicl / -create /aliases/jraywork
[primal:~] jray% sudo nicl / -append /aliases/jraywork members ray.30@osu.edu
```

The NetInfo GUI tools can be used to perform this action as well. Chapter 23, "File and Resource Sharing with NetInfo," discusses the use of the NetInfo Manager utility.

Note

Although the `/etc/mail/aliases` file or NetInfo `/aliases` database can set up system-wide forward information for e-mail addresses, individual users can do the same for their accounts by creating a `.forward` file in their home directory (path: `~/.forward`).

continues

Within the `.forward` file, add a single line containing the e-mail address where e-mail should be forwarded. To prevent mail looping, add the forwarding address prefixed with a / character. This will prevent potential recursive loops caused by circular mail forwards.

Mail

When your server is properly configured, incoming messages will be stored within the `/var/mail` directory in a text file named after the intended recipient. You can use command-line tools to read these messages, or configure the Mail client to read e-mail directly from the local mail file. Setting up Mail is covered in Chapter 7, "Internet Communications."

Most system administrators, however, will want to serve their e-mail to remote clients rather than just local users. The next section of this chapter will deal with compiling and installing `POP` and `IMAP` servers to create a complete e-mail server package.

Additional Resources

Sendmail has had almost three decades of service, and has continued to grow larger and more powerful with each revision. Advanced configuration will require additional resources. A few excellent sources of information are provided here.

Sendmail.org—`www.sendmail.org/`—The home of the free Sendmail software, this site contains information on all the Sendmail features and options. Although the information is extensive, it is not a tutorial.

UIUC Sendmail Tutorial—`www-wsg.cso.uiuc.edu/sendmail/tutorial/`—An excellent tutorial on Sendmail and e-mail servers in general. Good for building a solid background in server terminology.

Sendmail: Theory and Practice, Butterworth-Heinemann Publishing, Frederick M. Avolio, Paul Vixie, ISBN: 155558229X.

Sendmail, O'Reilly Publishing, Bryan Costales, Eric Allman, ISBN: 1565922220.

University of Washington `imapd`

Sendmail makes up only part of the mail-server picture. Although Sendmail handles sending and receiving e-mail on the server side, it does not have any provisions for the client software, such as Eudora or Outlook Express. To provide e-mail for remote clients, Mac OS X will need an IMAP server, a POP3 server, or both. Thankfully, the University of Washington has created an easy-to-install software package that will kill two birds with one stone.

The UW `imapd` server is capable of handling both IMAP *and* POP3 traffic and it is already Mac OS X–aware, so it takes very little work to install. Even better, there is absolutely no configuration file for the software, so after it's installed, it's ready to use.

Note

If you're scratching your head wondering what POP3 and IMAP are, refer to Chapter 7. These two mail delivery protocols are explained during the introduction to the Mail application.

A straightforward comparison between POP3 and IMAP can be found at the IMAP Connection: `www.imap.org/imap.vs.pop.brief.html`.

Installing UW imapd

Installing `imapd` is straightforward, but will require a few additional modifications to be able to perform smoothly on your OS X computer. To start, fetch the current sources from `ftp://ftp.cac.washington.edu/imap/`. Unarchive the source and `cd` into the distribution directory:

```
[primal:~] jray% curl -o ftp://ftp.cac.washington.edu/imap/imap.tar.Z
[primal:~] jray% tar zxf imap.tar.Z
[primal:~] jray% cd imap-2001.BETA.SNAP-0106252013/
```

Before compiling, there is a *very* important change that should be made to the file `src/osdep/unix/env_unix.c`. By default, the IMAP server will attempt to create all mailboxes directly in the user's home directory. In fact, it assumes that *any* directory in the home directory is an IMAP folder. This results in potentially hundreds (or thousands) of folders being downloaded and displayed. To get around this, the `env_unix.c` file must be adjusted so that a directory other than the main home directory is used. This can be any directory, as long as it exists in every user's account. A good choice is `~/Library/Mail/Mailboxes` because it contains the mailboxes created by the Mail application. This enables remote access to mail downloaded onto the Mac OS X computer. Just remember to create the directory name you choose in each account that will access the IMAP server.

Edit the `src/osdep/unix/env_unix.c` file to add the mailbox directory name you've chosen. Look for a line reading

```
static char *mailsubdir = NIL;   /* mail subdirectory name */
```

Change the text to include the directory you've chosen. For example

```
static char *mailsubdir = "Library/Mail/Mailboxes";      /* mail subdirectory
name */
```

The source code is now ready to compile using `make osx`:

```
[primal:~/imap-2001.BETA.SNAP-0106252013] jray% make osx
Applying an process to sources...
tools/an "ln -s" src/c-client c-client
tools/an "ln -s" src/ansilib c-client
tools/an "ln -s" src/charset c-client
tools/an "ln -s" src/osdep/unix c-client
tools/an "ln -s" src/mtest mtest
...
```

The compile process takes only a minute or two because the server application is really quite small. Unfortunately, installation of the compiled software is not automated, so you will need to copy the binary files to an appropriate location.

The Mac OS X `/etc/inetd.conf` file already has entries for the IMAP and POP servers, so we'll just use the standard settings (`/usr/local/libexec/`). You'll have to create the `libexec` directory within `/usr/local`, then copy the files `imapd` and `ipop3d` to the new directory:

```
[primal:~/imap-2001] jray% mkdir /usr/local/libexec
[primal:~/imap-2001] jray% sudo cp imapd/imapd /usr/local/libexec/
[primal:~/imap-2001] jray% sudo cp ipopd/ipop3d /usr/local/libexec/
```

> **Note**
>
> Depending on what additional BSD software you've installed (such as MySQL), you might already have the `/usr/local/libexec` directory on your system..

Next, edit the `/etc/inetd.conf` file to uncomment the `imap` and `pop` server entries. You need uncomment (remove the # character) only the line for the server you want to run. If you want both, uncomment both lines. In addition, you'll need to change the name of the POP3 server to match the installed binary (`ipopd`). The original two lines read:

```
##pop3  stream  tcp  nowait  root  /usr/libexec/tcpd  /usr/local/libexec/popper
##imap4 stream  tcp  nowait  root  /usr/libexec/tcpd  /usr/local/libexec/imapd
```

The modified versions should look like this

```
pop3  stream  tcp  nowait  root  /usr/libexec/tcpd    /usr/local/libexec/ipop3d
imap4 stream  tcp  nowait  root  /usr/libexec/tcpd    /usr/local/libexec/imapd
```

Adding Services to NetInfo

On most Unix systems, you would finish the install by adding entries for the protocols `pop3` and `imap4` to the `/etc/services` file. Under Mac OS X, however, this file is replaced by the NetInfo database. Chapter 23 provides an introduction to NetInfo.

There are two different methods for adding service definitions to the NetInfo database—through the command line and via the graphical NetInfo manager. This chapter will examine the command-line version, and Chapter 30, "Accessing and Serving a Windows Network," will demonstrate the GUI procedure. Either way, the result is the same.

Two protocol definitions must be added to the NetInfo database:

> **Name**: `pop3`
>
> **Protocol**: `tcp`
>
> **Port**: `110`

and

> **Name**: `imap4`
>
> **Protocol**: `tcp`
>
> **Port**: `143`

To add these entries to your local NetInfo database, use the `nicl` utility as follows. First, the `IMAP4` protocol:

```
[primal:~] jray% sudo nicl / -create /services/imap4 name imap
[primal:~] jray% sudo nicl / -append /services/imap4 port 143
[primal:~] jray% sudo nicl / -append /services/imap4 protocol tcp
```

Next, `POP3`:

```
[primal:~] jray% sudo nicl / -create /services/pop3 name pop3
[primal:~] jray% sudo nicl / -append /services/pop3 port 110
[primal:~] jray% sudo nicl / -append /services/pop3 protocol tcp
```

Finally, reboot the Mac OS X computer, or force the `inetd` process to reload its configuration using `kill -1` and the `inetd` process ID.

Test to make sure that the services you want to run are running by telneting into port 110 (POP3) and port 143 (IMAP):

```
[primal:/Users/jray] root# telnet localhost 110
Trying 127.0.0.1...
Connected to localhost.ag.ohio-state.edu.
+OK POP3 primal.ag.ohio-state.edu v2001.76 server ready
Escape character is '^]'.
Connection closed by foreign host.
```

and

```
[primal:/Users/jray] root# telnet localhost 143
Trying 127.0.0.1...
Connected to localhost.ag.ohio-state.edu.
Escape character is '^]'.
* OK [CAPABILITY IMAP4REV1 LOGIN-REFERRALS AUTH=LOGIN]
      ➥localhost.ag.ohio-state.edu IMAP4rev1
      ➥2001.309 at Wed, 27 Jun 2001 19:01:15 -0400 (EDT)
```

Both services are running, as we intended. As a rule, remember that less is more when it comes to servers. If you aren't going to use the IMAP or POP3 servers, don't activate them in the `/etc/inetd.conf` file.

The UW `imapd` server is now ready for use. You can connect to the Mac OS X machine to pick up e-mail that has been received by the Sendmail SMTP daemon.

Tip

The IMAP and POP3 servers are both installed and configured to use TCP Wrappers. TCP Wrappers, as you'll learn in Chapter 31, "Server Security and Advanced Network Configuration," can be used to limit access to any `inetd`-controlled services. It is recommended that you use TCP Wrappers to block mail services except for those domains that must have access—these servers offer hackers an excellent entry point for their activities.

Web-Based E-mail

There are a number of packages that you can install to create Web-based e-mail, such as FocalMail from `http://home.focalmail.com/`. In addition, the PHP Web development language has the capability to talk directly to the IMAP servers. The Horde Project has created a Web-based e-mail package called IMP that is available as a free download from `www.horde.org/imp/2.3/`.

If you're interested in an extremely easy to set up solution, you might want to check out the Majora software, which can be downloaded from `www.poisontooth.com/`.

Written in Perl, Majora is easy to understand and simple to set up. Assuming that you've enabled CGI support in Apache, you can add a Web front end to your mail server in a minute or two.

First, download and unarchive the Majora distribution, placing it in a Web-accessible directory. In this example, the files are placed in my local `Sites` directory:

```
[primal:~/Sites] jray% curl -o http://www.poisontooth.com/software/majora.tar.gz
[primal:~/Sites] jray% tar zxf majora.tar.gz
```

Next, cd into the Majora directory and open the file majora.cgi. There are a few lines at the start of the file that can be configured to better suit your site.

The following lines affect the coloring of the message output table. Alter the colors to adjust the HTML display in the client browser:

```
#### Color information for the display
$NormalColor="BGCOLOR=\"#FFFFE9\"";
$SelectedColor="BGCOLOR=\"#A0A0DD\"";
$HeadingColor="BGCOLOR=\"#D3D3FA\"";
$NumberColor="BGCOLOR=\"#CDCDDD\"";
$SubjectColor="BGCOLOR=\"#FFEDED\"";
$DateColor="BGCOLOR=\"#EDFFED\"";
```

When viewing messages in a Web browser, you don't want to worry about downloading several megabytes of attachments to the remote Web browser. To get around this potential problem, set the $bigmessage variable to the largest message size (in bytes) to transfer.

```
#### Largest message (in bytes) to allow the user to view online
$bigmessage=10000;
```

The variable $popmailcgi should only be changed if, for some reason, you've modified the name of the Majora CGI.

```
#### URL to this CGI
$popmailcgi="majora.cgi";
```

Finally, the $smtpserver and $thishost variables should be set to the SMTP server that will be used for sending e-mail, and the hostname of the local computer, respectively.

```
#### SMTP server used to send mail...
$smtpserver="poisontooth.com
#### This server's hostname (in case `hostname` doesn't work)
$thishost="poisontooth.com";
```

Save these changes to the Majora CGI file, and the system will be ready to go. To test it, start your Web browser and open the URL where Majora has been installed. Figure 29.1 shows the Majora login screen.

After logging in to the system, the available options Compose, Get Mail, and Logout are displayed along the right side of the browser window. Those should be reasonably self-explanatory.

Clicking Get Mail might take quite awhile, depending on the size of your inbox. After collecting information about each message, a listing will be displayed for each one, as shown in Figure 29.2. Click the number at the start of each line to read the corresponding message.

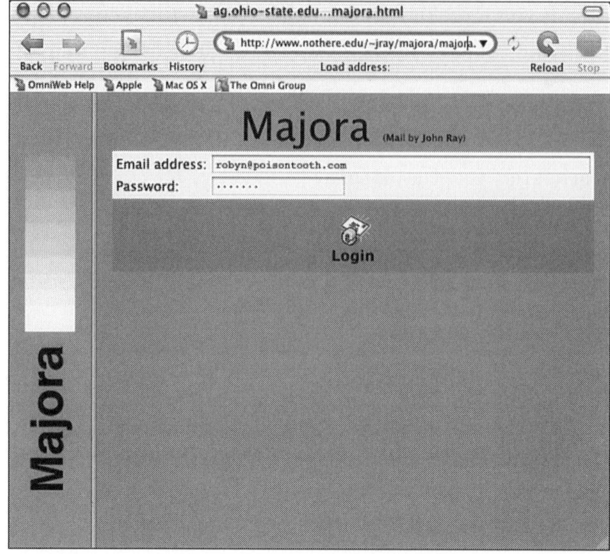

FIGURE 29.1
Log in to your e-mail account.

FIGURE 29.2
The messages in the inbox are listed.

The Majora code is open and can be modified as you see fit. Feel free to edit the Perl code to your heart's content.

Tip

Majora doesn't *have* to download messages from a local Mac OS X server. The software will attempt to access whatever e-mail server is specified in the e-mail login line.

Summary

Mail servers require disk space and a commitment from the administrator to monitor traffic and usage. An improperly configured mail server can be used to spread spam and viruses to remote clients around the world. Before setting up a server, you should first evaluate whether a local server is truly needed, and what alternative solutions are available.

When setting up an SMTP server such as Sendmail, you should be familiar with both the `m4` macro configuration files as well as the main `sendmail.cf` file. Additional resources might be necessary if you're running a large-scale server with special routing requirements. After configuring Sendmail, most installations will want to install a server such as UW `imapd` to deliver messages to client applications such as Eudora, Outlook Express, and Mail. In addition, Web clients can be added to create a mail solution that enables users to access e-mail from anywhere there is Web access.

Accessing and Serving a Windows Network

IN THIS CHAPTER

There's no denying it. There's no ignoring it. We live in a world dominated by Windows-based computers. Granted, this dominance will last only a few more years until the current generation of Unix-heads (Mac OS X users included!) take over. In the meantime, despite the example set by the opposition, it's still a good idea to play nice with Windows computers.

This chapter will introduce three pieces of software—Samba, Sharity, and the Mac OS X Finder—for Mac OS X that will help your computer exchange files over a Windows network, and even take the place of a Windows NT server for file and print sharing. Best of all, you can do everything from within the familiar Mac OS X interface.

SMB and CIFS

The SMB, Simple Message Block, protocol provides the basis for Windows file and print sharing. SMB provides support for file browsing, and two levels of security:

User—A user must authenticate with the SMB server during the initial connection. The supplied username and password determine what resources the user can access.

Share—Share-level security operates on an individual shared resource. The resource has a single password. Anyone with access to the password can access the resource.

SMB is implemented on top of a transport protocol. Think of this as similar to the way that AppleTalk exists on top of LocalTalk (serial networking) and EtherTalk (ethernet-based networks).

The SMB protocol has gone through several phases in its existence. Early in life, it used NetBEUI as its transport protocol. NetBEUI is independent of TCP/IP and, as such, was only suited for local-area networks. Today, most SMB services run on top of NetBIOS (NetBT/NBT). NetBIOS is the equivalent of NetBEUI, but running on top of TCP/IP. This creates a routable file/print serving system that can be used across the Internet as well as LAN situations.

Unfortunately, things aren't that clean and simple. The NetBEUI protocol used a simple broadcast protocol to enable browsing of local resources. When SMB moved to NetBIOS (and thus TCP/IP), finding remote resources became a bigger problem. Machines needed a new way to locate each other, besides sending broadcast packets—this was the only way to successfully handle spanning across multiple subnets.

The WINS protocol was created to provide a central registration point for Windows computers. When coming online, a computer can register itself with a WINS server, as well as look up other machines for creating a connection.

Note

Yes, WINS is a proprietary name resolution system that bares a resemblance to DNS (domain name service). Versions of Windows later than 98 and NT 4.0 support DNS resolution of remote computer names. Microsoft's latest attempt at a proprietary directory service is the Active Directory Service. ADS offers greater support for open standards, but continues to be based on a proprietary system.

The latest version of SMB is known as CIFS (Common Internet File System) and is backed by Microsoft as well as several third-party companies. CIFS is an open version of SMB with Internet-specific modifications. For the sake of remaining reasonably sane, you can assume that CIFS and SMB are synonymous.

Tip

The history of SMB, NetBEUI, NetBIOS, and how everything fits together is documented on the "What is SMB?" page: `http://samba.anu.edu.au/cifs/docs/what-is-smb.html`.

This makes AppleShare and NFS look like child's play.

SMB Server

The Macintosh operating system has never been a strong team player when it comes to interacting with Windows systems. Windows-centric networks usually rely on an NT or 2000-based server with Macintosh services installed to interoperate. Things have changed for the better. The Unix basis of Mac OS X has opened up the possibilities tremendously.

Over the past few years, Windows-only shops have been slowly adding Linux systems to their server arsenal. The reason for this seemingly unnatural acceptance of an alternative operating system is a piece of software called Samba (see "Samba" later in this chapter for more detailed information). Samba is named for the SMB protocol and provides a drop-in replacement for Windows NT services. Although many companies are converting to 2000-based and ADS-based servers, Samba offers comparable performance, features, and a price that can't be beat (free, of course). To quote *eWEEK*:

> Samba is capable, flexible, mature, and fairly well-documented; runs on several Unix operating systems; offers Web-based configuration and administration; and is free.
>
> Samba is now a viable option as a file and print server for many more Windows shops than before and earns an *eWEEK* Labs Analyst's Choice award for this remarkable technical accomplishment.
>
> To add this functionality, Samba Team developers (including those who are part of the Samba: The Next Generation project) had to reverse-engineer the proprietary protocols Microsoft Corp. uses to authenticate users and systems over the network, using, in many cases, nothing but a packet sniffer.

The entire article is available at: `www.zdnet.com/eweek/stories/general/0,11011,2712294,00.html`.

Samba offers Web-based configuration and administration. Even if you've never used a Windows computer and don't know the first thing about Windows file sharing, you'll be able to get a basic server up and running in only a few minutes.

Samba supports several advanced features, including file/printer sharing, user/share security, WINS, and emulation of a Windows NT domain. Best of all, it now runs natively on Mac OS X. Now Windows users can come to the Mac, rather than vice versa.

What Is an NT Domain?

A *domain* is a collection of computers, much like a basic Windows workgroup or a zone in the traditional Mac AppleShare model. Besides organizing multiple computers into a unit, a domain provides centralized authentication and administration. When starting a computer, a user logs in to a domain. Doing so grants him or her access to resources within the domain.

In addition, a domain controller can manage roaming profiles for users; wherever they log in to the network, they see their personal desktop.

Interestingly enough, these features are available natively on Mac OS X using the NetInfo network directory system. NetInfo has existed since the late 1980s, and predates the NT domain model by several years. Learn more about NetInfo in Chapter 23, "File and Resource Sharing with NetInfo."

SMB Client

Samba provides SMB server support, but we still need a Mac client for Windows networks. There have been several attempts to produce a stable Mac client that works well with Windows. Although your experience might be different, I have yet to find a Mac OS 8/9 solution that doesn't cause incredible system instability.

Again, Mac OS X's Unix basis gives it an advantage. Within a few days of the original Mac OS X release, Objective Development had released the first version of Sharity for Mac OS X. Sharity is a CIFS client that works on a large number of Unix platforms and is backed by years of stress testing. Sharity integrates the Windows network neighborhood into Mac OS X and is remarkably simple to use.

Objective Development offers licensing options that are very reasonable, including free hobbyist, student, and educational licenses. You can download Sharity and get started immediately, and then upgrade later if needed.

Samba

Samba is a very large piece of software—approaching Apache in terms of complexity and number of configuration options. In this chapter, the focus will be on setting up solid, general-purpose servers. High-end needs are best served by other sources, such as *Sams Teach Yourself Samba in 24 Hours* (ISBN: 0672316099). The Samba Web site is also a great source for information (`www.samba.org`).

Let's get down to business.

Installing Samba

There are two ways to install the Samba server software. The easiest method is to download a precompiled binary, double-click it, and go! Unfortunately, Samba is rapidly developed, and the only precompiled distribution is not an official distribution, and relies on a single person to keep it up to date. If you're interested, download a Mac OS X installer binary version of Samba from `http://xamba.sourceforge.net/sambax/index.shtml`.

If you have about thirty minutes and aren't afraid of the command line, you can easily compile and install Samba on your own. To get started, download the latest Samba source from `www.samba.org/`, and then unarchive the server:

```
[primal:~/samba] jray% tar zxf samba-latest.tar.gz
[primal:~/samba] jray% cd samba-2.2.0/
```

Next, cd into the Samba source directory and execute the configure command. You'll need to add the option --host=powerpc to configure; otherwise, the process will fail:

```
./configure --host=powerpc

loading cache ./config.cache
checking for gcc... (cached) cc
checking whether the C compiler (cc -O  ) works... yes
checking whether the C compiler (cc -O  ) is a cross-compiler... no
checking whether we are using GNU C... (cached) yes
checking whether cc accepts -g... (cached) yes
checking for a BSD compatible install... (cached) /usr/bin/install -c
checking for gawk... (cached) awk
checking host system type... powerpc-unknown-none
...
```

The configure process will take several minutes. When completed, use make to compile Samba:

```
[primal:~/samba/samba-2.2.0/source] jray% make

Using FLAGS =  -O  -Iinclude -I./include -I./ubiqx -I./smbwrapper
➥-DLOGFILEBASE="/usr/local/samba/var"
➥-DCONFIGFILE="/usr/local/samba/lib/smb.conf"
➥-DLMHOSTSFILE="/usr/local/samba/lib/lmhosts"
➥-DSWATDIR="/usr/local/samba/swat"
➥-DSBINDIR="/usr/local/samba/bin"
➥-DLOCKDIR="/usr/local/samba/var/locks"
➥-DCODEPAGEDIR="/usr/local/samba/lib/codepages"
➥-DDRIVERFILE="/usr/local/samba/lib/printers.def"
➥-DBINDIR="/usr/local/samba/bin"
➥-DHAVE_INCLUDES_H
➥-DPASSWD_PROGRAM="/bin/passwd"
,,,
```

The compilation easily took 10 minutes on a 500MHz G4, so this might be a good time to take a nap. Finally, when the compilation finishes, install the software with make install.

Tip

You must be root to install Samba. Be sure that you are either logged in or su'd to root, or use the sudo command when executing this step.

```
[primal:~/samba/samba-2.2.0/source] jray% sudo make install

/bin/sh ./install-sh -d -m 0755 \
/usr/local/samba /usr/local/samba/bin /usr/local/samba/bin /usr/local/samba/lib\
```

```
/usr/local/samba/var /usr/local/samba/lib/codepages
Installing bin/smbd as /usr/local/samba/bin/smbd
Installing bin/nmbd as /usr/local/samba/bin/nmbd
Installing bin/swat as /usr/local/samba/bin/swat
======================================================================
The binaries are installed. You may restore the old binaries (if there
were any) using the command "make revert". You may uninstall the binaries
using the command "make uninstallbin" or "make uninstall" to uninstall
binaries, man pages and shell scripts.
======================================================================
...
```

Samba is now mostly installed. The binaries are in place, but the server is not configured to start when the computer boots. Creating a new startup item easily solves this. Follow these steps closely; otherwise, Samba might not start at boot time.

1. Check to see whether the folder `/Library/StartupItems` exists; if it doesn't, create it.
2. Create a new folder named `Samba` within `StartupItems`.
3. Create a file called `StartupParameters.plist` in the `StartupItems` folder. The file should contain these lines:

   ```
   {
     Description     = "Samba Server";
     Provides        = ("smb");
     Requires        = ("Resolver");
     OrderPreference = "None";
     Messages =
     {
       start = "Starting Samba server";
       stop  = "Stopping Samba server";
     };
   }
   ```

4. Create a second file named `Samba` (the same as the enclosing folder). This file contains a short script that will activate the SMB and WINS server:

   ```
   #!/bin/sh
   /usr/local/samba/bin/smbd -D
   /usr/local/samba/bin/nmbd -D
   ```

Samba is now ready to run. It is still, however, lacking one very important thing—a configuration file. In its early days, Samba was configured entirely by hand—it worked, but wasn't really useful to anyone but the most die-hard Unix users. Today, however, configuration is handled entirely through a Web-based GUI called SWAT.

Although Samba can still be configured by hand (which you're welcome to do!), it is recommended that SWAT be used at all times.

> **Caution**
>
> Some small changes are easy enough to accomplish by hand with a text editor, but the Samba configuration file is extremely sensitive to invalid settings.

When Samba was installed with `make install`, it also included the SWAT application. SWAT, however, requires additional set up that will enable it to activate when a Web browser accesses port 901 on the Samba server. This involves editing `/etc/inetd.conf` and making some changes to the NetInfo database.

Open `/etc/inetd.conf` in your favorite browser and add the following line to the end:

```
swat    stream  tcp     nowait.400  root    /usr/local/samba/bin/swat swat
```

This tells the `inetd` (Internet Daemon) to start `/usr/local/samba/bin/swat` when it gets a request for the SWAT service. Unfortunately, Mac OS X does not know what SWAT is, so you'll have to define in it NetInfo.

First, open the NetInfo Manager from `/Applications/Utilities/NetInfo Manager`. NetInfo was discussed in depth in Chapter 23, so, if you haven't looked at the application yet, now would be a good time to do so.

Next, click the Lock icon so that changes will be permitted. A new service type must be added to the NetInfo database that defines the SWAT service.

> **Caution**
>
> Linux and Unix users are probably used to seeing services defined in `/etc/services`. Mac OS X stores these settings in NetInfo, but includes a `/etc/services` file that is not queried unless the computer is booted in single-user mode. You cannot add SWAT to this file and expect it to work.

With NetInfo running and changes enabled, navigate to the services properties using the NetInfo path of `/services`. Create a new service in this location by selecting an existing service such as `finger` and choosing Duplicate (`Command+D`) from the Edit menu, and then highlighting the duplicate in the listing.

To finish setting up the service type, set the service properties as seen in Table 30.1.

TABLE 30.1 Edit the Service Properties to Have These New Values

Property	*Value*
Name	`swat`
Port	`901`
Protocol	`tcp`

Choose Save (Command+S) from the Domain menu. The new service, as defined in NetInfo, is seen in Figure 30.1.

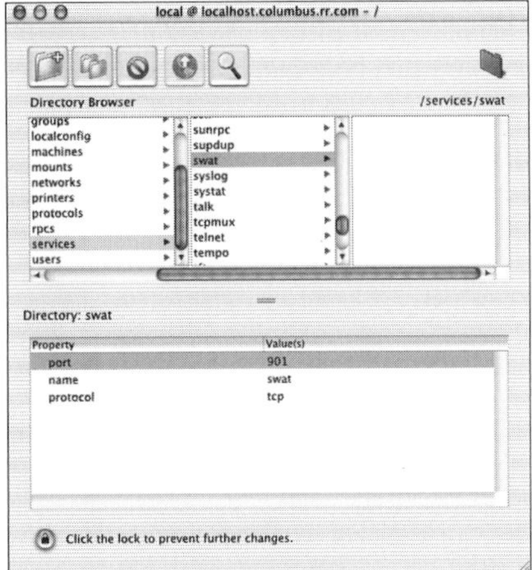

FIGURE 30.1
Add a new SWAT service to the NetInfo database.

Finally, you need to install a basic configuration file. The Samba distribution comes with `smb.conf.default` in the `examples` directory. Copy this file to `/usr/local/samba/lib/smb.conf`. You'll also need to update the permissions in the file. These permissions determine who will be able to administer the server. If you only want `root` enabled, `chmod 700` should be fine. If any Mac OS X admin user should be able to control the server, use `chown root:admin /usr/local/samba/lib/smb.conf`, followed by `chmod 775 /usr/local/samba/lib/smb.conf`.

SWAT is ready to run. Rebooting Mac OS X is the easiest way to make sure that everything starts as it should. Impatient users can manually execute the `/Library/StartupItems/Samba/Samba` file, then `kill -1` the `inetd` process to start Samba and prepare SWAT for execution.

Note

Interestingly enough, SWAT is not related, in any way, to the Apache process. Even if Apache is not activated, you'll still be able to use a Web browser to configure the Samba server. The `inetd` process listens on port 901 for incoming TCP connections, and then launches `/usr/local/samba/bin/swat` to service the request.

Configuring Samba

To configure Samba, start a Web browser and point it at port 901 of the Samba server (`http://localhost:901`). If everything has gone according to plan, SWAT will prompt for an administrative username and password. All screenshots shown in this section will assume that the controlling user is `root`. The SWAT home screen is shown in Figure 30.2.

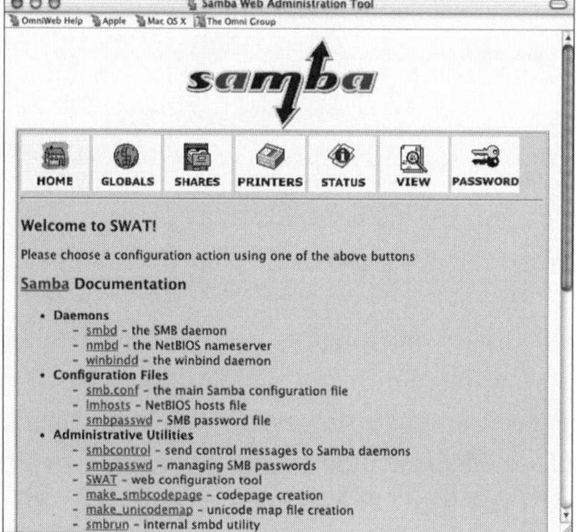

FIGURE 30.2
SWAT opens with a page providing easy access to Samba documentation.

The top of the SWAT display includes seven buttons to control the operation of the server:

Home—Provides links to Samba documentation and supplemental material.

Globals—Settings that affect the entire server, such as its name and security model.

Shares—Shared file resources. If you used the sample configuration file that came with the Apache distribution, there should be a single home directory share already configured.

Printers—Shared printers. In order to share a printer, it must first be set up so that it can be accessed from the `lpr` command in Unix.

Status—Monitor and view the status of the server. If logged in as `root`, you can restart or stop the server process.

View—View a copy of the text configuration file.

Password—Set and edit Samba user passwords.

Let's step through these configuration screens to see the options used in a typical sharing environment.

Globals

The Global Variables page, seen in Figure 30.3, is the starting point for setting up your Samba server. Many people jump the gun and immediately start setting up file shares. Failure to properly configure the global options might make it impossible to mount or browse shared resources.

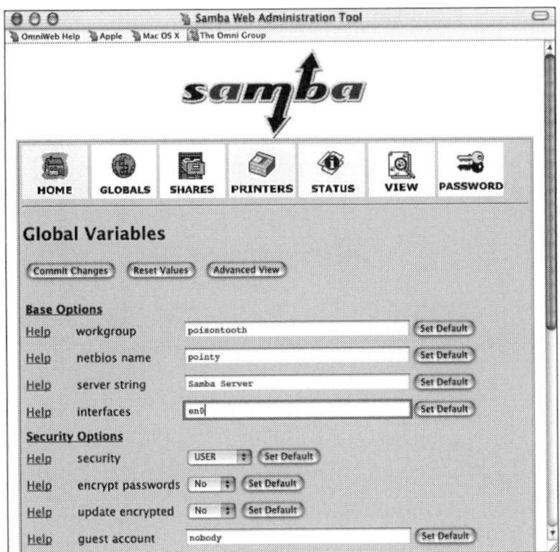

FIGURE 30.3
Global options set the operating parameters for the Samba server.

Three buttons can save (Commit Changes) server settings, reset changes (Reset Values), or access advanced options (Advanced View). Choosing Advanced View shows a number of additional options that are listed in Table 30.2. If you don't see the setting you're looking for, move to the Advanced mode.

TABLE 30.2 Global Options and Their Purpose

Option	*Purpose*
`workgroup`	Sets the workgroup or domain that the server belongs to. Set this to the same value as the workgroup/domain of local Windows clients; otherwise, they will not be able to browse the server.
`netbios name`	The Windows (NetBIOS) name of the server.
`netbios aliases`	A list of additional NetBIOS names to which the Samba server will respond. (Advanced)
`password level`	The number of case-changes that will be checked between the client login and the server password. Because client operating systems might transmit passwords in uppercase, they'll have to be altered to authenticate with the server. (Advanced)
`username level`	The same as the password level, but alters the username in a similar manner. For example, if I have a Mac OS X username of `jray` and a Windows login of `JRAY`, I'll have to set this value to `4` for it to be successfully permuted into the lowercase version. (Advanced)
`server string`	The text used to identify the server.
`interfaces`	The network interfaces that Samba will broadcast over. For example, Mac OS X's primary interface is `en0`. By default, all active interfaces will be used. To limit the interfaces, enter the interface names to use, or the network address followed by a subnet mask (that is, `192.168.0.0/255.255.255.0`).
`security`	The type of security model to use. User-level security bases access upon a user login. Share-level password protects individual shared resources. Domain and server security passes authentication duties to other NT or Samba servers, respectively. You'll probably want user or share-level security.
`encrypt passwords`	Sets encrypted password negotiation with the client. If you are using Windows 98 or later, set this to `Yes`. Encrypted passwords also require the use of the `smbpasswd` file, which is configured using the SWAT Password page.
`update encrypted`	Used when migrating from an unencrypted password on an existing server to a local encrypted `smbpassword` file. This shouldn't be needed unless in an advanced configuration.

TABLE 30.2 continued

Option	*Purpose*
`guest account`	The local user that should be used for guest access and resource browsing. Mac OS X should use `nobody`.
`hosts allow`	A list of hostnames, IP addresses, IP addresses and subnet masks (`192.168.0.0/255.255.255.0`), or partial addresses (`192.168.0.`) that can access the server. The `except` keyword can create an exception to a rule. For example, `192.168.0.0/255.255.255.0 except 192.168.0.5` would allow any host in the `192.168.0.0` subnet, except `192.168.0.5`, to access the server. If left blank, all remote hosts can access the server.
`hosts deny`	Like `hosts allow` but used to list servers that should not have access to the server. Configuring using the same method as `allow`.
`log file`	The logfile to store server accesses in. The `%m` in the default path appends the name of the remote machine to the logfile name.
`max log size`	The maximum size in kilobytes that a logfile should be allowed to reach before rolling over.
`os level`	A number used to determine the ranking of Samba when a master browser is being elected on a Windows network. If Samba is the only server on the network, use the default `20`. If NT 4.0 or 2000 machines are on the network, and you'd like Samba to be the master browser, set this to a value greater than `32`.
`domain logon`	Accept domain logins. This is part of the experimental domain controller code and should be activated only after becoming a Samba god. (Advanced)
`preferred master`	If set to `yes`, the Samba server will attempt to force an election for master browser. Do not use on networks with multiple servers that want to be masters.
`local master`	Enables Samba to try to become the master browser for the local area network. If set to `no`, it will not attempt to assume this role.
`domain master`	Enables Samba's `nmbd` component to become a domain master browser that collects browse lists from remote subnets.

TABLE 30.2 continued

Option	*Purpose*
`dns proxy`	Attempts to resolve WINS queries through DNS if they cannot be resolved from locally registered machines.
`wins server`	A remote WINS server that Samba should query to service NetBIOS name requests.
`wins support`	Enables Samba's WINS service. Only a single machine should act as a WINS server on a given subnet.

The default settings should be sufficient for most small networks, with the exception of the base and security options. The best rule for Samba is that if you aren't sure what something does, or whether you even need it, you shouldn't touch it!

Shares

The Share Parameters page sets up file shares that can be mounted on networked Windows-based computers. To create a new share, type a share name in the Create Share field, and then click the Create Share button. To edit an existing share, choose its name from the pop-up list, and then click Choose Share—or click Delete Share to remove it completely. With the default Samba configuration file, there should already be a single `homes` share available. `homes` is unique because it is equivalent to each user sharing his home directory with himself. This share is shown loaded in Figure 30.4.

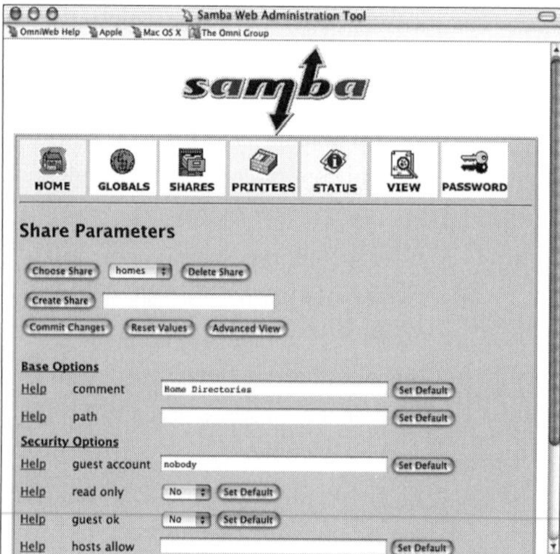

FIGURE 30.4
Use the Share Parameters page to set up your Windows SMB file shares.

The basic share parameters are listed in Table 30.3. Again, a few advanced options are also included. Like the Globals Variables page, there is an Advanced button to show all possible configuration features for file sharing.

TABLE 30.3 File-Sharing Options and Values

Option	*Purpose*
`comment`	A comment to help identify the shared resource.
`path`	The pathname of the directory to share. Be aware that in user-level security, you must make sure that the corresponding Mac OS X user accounts have access to this directory. When using share-level security, a single-user account is used—usually the `guest account`. In that case, the next setting becomes very important.
`guest account`	The account used to access the share if the remote client is logged in as a guest. The default is `nobody`, but, if set to another username, the guest user will have the read/write permissions of that local user account. If you want to use share-level access control, you can set this value to the account whose permissions should be used when accessing the share.
`force user`	If entered, the `force user` username will be used for all accesses (read/write) to the file share, regardless of the username used to log in. (Advanced)
`force group`	Similar to force user but forces a group rather than a user. (Advanced)
`read only`	When set to `Yes`, users cannot write to the share, regardless of the Mac OS X file permissions.
`create mask`	A set of permissions that newly created files will have. By default, the mask is set to 0744. (Advanced)
`guest ok`	If set to `Yes`, guests can log into the server without a password.
`hosts allow`	A list of hostnames, IP addresses, IP addresses and subnet masks (`192.168.0.0/255.255.255.0`), or partial addresses (`192.168.0.`) that can access the share. The `except` keyword can create an exception to a rule. For example, `192.168.0.0/255.255.255.0 except 192.168.0.5` would allow any host in the `192.168.0.0` subnet, except `192.168.0.5`, to access the server. If left blank, all remote hosts can access the server.

TABLE 30.3 Continued

Option	*Purpose*
`hosts deny`	Like `hosts allow` but used to list servers that should not have access to the server. Configure using the same method as `allow`.
`max connections`	Restricts the number of simultaneous users who can access the share. (Advanced)
`browseable`	When set to `Yes`, the share will show up in the Windows network browser. If `no`, the share still exists, but remote users cannot see its name.
`available`	If set to `Yes`, the share will be made available over the network. Setting to `No` will disable access to the share.

The trickiest part of setting up a share is figuring out user access rights. Regardless of whether Samba is using user-level or share-level access, a Unix user *must* be mapped to the incoming connection.

The easiest security model is user-level, which requires Windows users to log in to their computers using the same username set up on the Mac OS X machine and a password determined by the `smbpasswd` file (set using the Password SWAT screen). When using user-level access, Windows users are mapped directly to Samba users. The Mac OS X file permissions apply directly to the permissions of the connected user. Assume, for example, the Mac OS X user `jray` has read/write permissions to the folder `/Stuff`, which is also set to be a Samba share. If `jray` logs in to a Windows computer using the same username as on Mac OS X, he will be able to access the Stuff share and have read/write access. The SWAT Password page must be used to map Unix users to the passwords that they will use on the remote Windows client.

Things are a bit different with share-level access. In these cases, a single password is needed to access the share, but a valid user account must be used by Samba when interacting with the Mac OS X file system. To simplify share-level security, create a Mac OS X user and set a password for a user with the SWAT Password page. Then set the guest account for the share equal to the Mac OS X username.

Printers

Samba can act as a full print server for a Windows network. The one small catch is that your printers must first be accessible via `lpr` at the command line, which involves some NetInfo configuration. You might want to check out the NetInfo and printer chapters before setting up any printer shares. You'll also want to use the advanced features during set up; otherwise, some information will be missing.

To create a new shared printer, enter its name in the Create Printer field, and then click the Create Printer button. An existing printer can be selected from the pop-up menu, and edited by clicking Choose Printer or Delete Printer to remove it from the Samba configuration. A printer configuration screen is displayed in Figure 30.5.

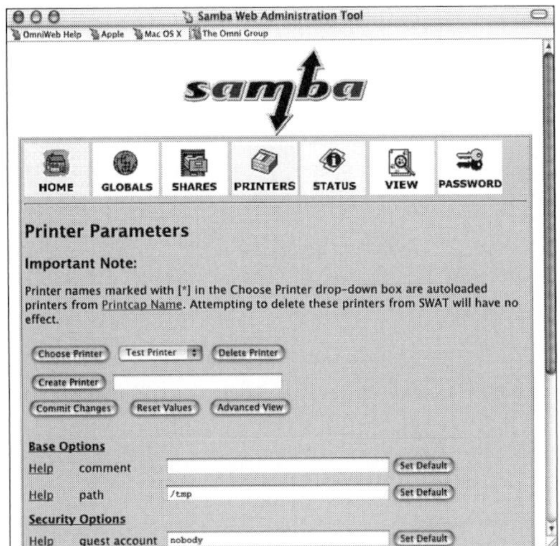

FIGURE 30.5
To use Samba's printer sharing, you must first configure the printer using NetInfo.

By default, Mac OS X users will see two printers already defined: `printers` and `lp[*]`. The `printers` selection operates much like `homes`—it automatically attempts to share out all the printers found on your system. These printers are then listed with their own separate share names appended with `[*]`. Unfortunately, Samba searches `/etc/printcap` to locate printers, whereas Mac OS X stores printer configuration in the NetInfo database. Because of this, the two initial shared resources (`printers/lp`) are harmless, but cannot be used for printing.

To create a new printer share, first configure it for use from the command line, and then create a new printer and set the options shown in Table 30.4.

TABLE 30.4 Printer Sharing Options

Option	*Purpose*
`comment`	A comment used to identify the printer share.
`path`	A directory where print spool files will be saved before printing. The directory must be configured to be world-writable and have the sticky bit set.
`guest account`	The `guest` account used to access the printer resource, if guest access is enabled.
`guest ok`	If set to `Yes`, guests may access the printer. This is not a wise idea on a publicly networked device.
`hosts allow`	A list of hostnames, IP addresses, IP addresses and subnet masks (`192.168.0.0/255.255.255.0`), or partial addresses (`192.168.0.`) that can access the share. The `except` keyword can create an exception to a rule. For example, `192.168.0.0/255.255.255.0 except 192.168.0.5` would allow any host in the `192.168.0.0` subnet, except `192.168.0.5`, to access the server. If left blank, all remote hosts can access the server.
`hosts deny`	Like `hosts allow` but used to list servers that should not have access to the server. Configure using the same method as `allow`.
`printable`	Allows authenticated clients to write to the print spool directory.
`printer name`	The NetInfo name for the printer. You must switch to Advanced View to see this option.
`browseable`	When set to `Yes`, the printer will show up in the Windows network browser. If `no`, the printer share still exists, but remote users cannot see its name.
`available`	If set to `Yes`, the printer will be made available over the network. Setting to `No` will disable access to the printer.

Status

The SWAT Status page is shown in Figure 30.6. This page gives a quick overview of the server's current conditions, including active connections, shares, and files. The administrator can use this screen to restart the server or disable any active connections.

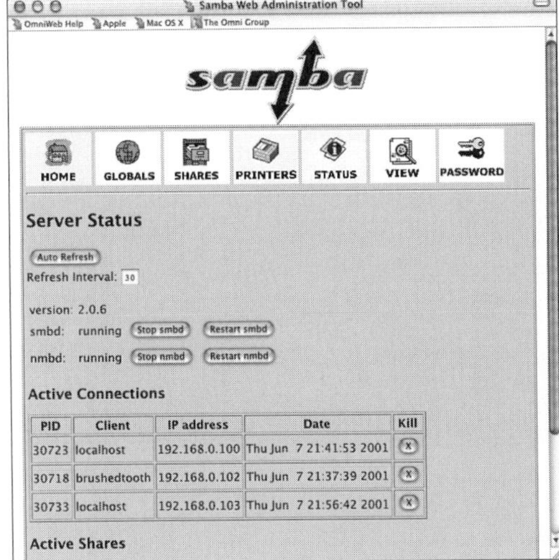

FIGURE 30.6
Use the Status page to monitor active connections.

Each of the visible buttons affects a change on the server:

Auto Refresh—Sets the SWAT status page to auto-refresh based on the Refresh Interval field. This is useful for monitoring server activity.

Stop/Start/Restart smbd—Stops, starts, or restarts `smbd`—the Samba SMB file/print server. All active connections are terminated.

Stop/Start/Restart nmbd—Stops, starts, or restarts `nmbd`—the Samba NetBIOS name server. Does not affect active connections.

Kill—The Kill button appears to the right of every listed connection. Clicking the button immediately terminates the link.

> **Note**
>
> Terminating an active connection might result in data loss for the remote user. Although certainly a tempting prank, it isn't a very nice thing to do.

View

View offers a glimpse at the configuration file behind SWAT's GUI. Sometimes it's easier to scan through a text file to locate a problem than to work with the Web interface. There are two modes in the View page. The Normal view shows the minimum configuration file needed to implement your settings. An example of this view is demonstrated in Figure 30.7.

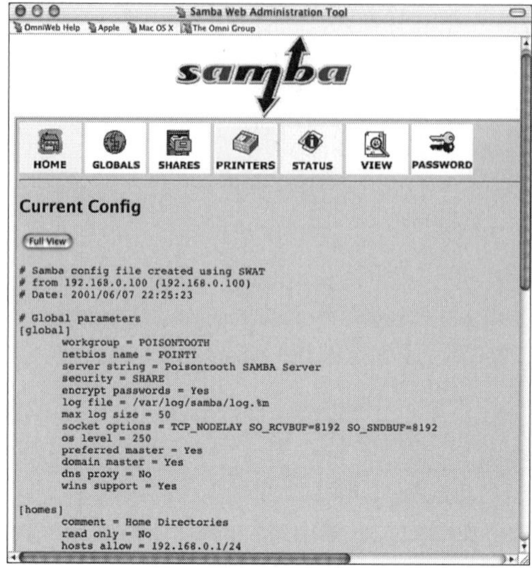

FIGURE 30.7
The Normal view contains the bare configuration.

Switching to the Full View displays all the settings, including default options, for the Samba configuration. Each option is explicitly listed, regardless of its necessity.

Password

The Password page is used to set up Samba passwords for existing Mac OS X users, or change remote user passwords if using domain-level security and a remote host for user authentication (Windows NT/2000 Server). The password page can be seen in Figure 30.8.

FIGURE 30.8
Set local and remote user passwords.

The Server Password portion of the screen configures local users and passwords. Be aware that these options *do not* affect the actual Mac OS X usernames and passwords, but must be based on a valid local username.

User Name—The Mac OS X username to add to the `smbpassword` file.

New Password—The Samba password to set for that user.

Re-type New Password—The same as the New Password option; used to verify typing.

Change Password—Changes the password for the specified user.

Add New User—Adds the new username/password mapping to the `smbpasswd` file.

Delete User—Deletes the named user from `smbpasswd`. This does not affect the Mac OS X user.

Disable User—Disables a user's ability to access Samba. Again, Mac OS X does not alter its user account whatsoever.

Enable User—Enables a disabled user account.

If Samba is using domain-level security, another server (such as a Windows primary domain controller) is the source for all authentication information. To change a user's password on the remote server, use the Client/Server Password Management features of the Password screen:

User Name—The remote user to change.

Old Password—The user's existing password.

New Password—The new password to set on the remote server.

Re-type New Password—The same as the New Password option; used to verify typing.

Remote Machine—The remote server that contains the username/password mappings.

Click the Change Password button to send the password changes to the server.

Accessing a Share from Windows

Now let's go through the process of accessing a shared volume from a Windows computer. This example will use Windows 2000. By the time you read this, there will probably be five or six new versions of Windows available, so I apologize if the instructions don't match up entirely.

Creating a Sample Share

First, set up the server defaults. For my machine, POINTY, I've created a very bare global configuration. Rather than including a screenshot for the share, I'm including the configuration from the `/usr/local/samba/lib/smb.conf` file. Each resource has its own block in the `config` file. Within that block, the options we've covered are listed, along with their associated value. This is the global configuration block for my simple Samba server:

```
[global]
          workgroup = POISONTOOTH
          netbios name = POINTY
          server string = Poisontooth SAMBA Server
          encrypt passwords = Yes
          log file = /var/log/samba/log.%m
          max log size = 50
          preferred master = Yes
          dns proxy = No
          wins support = Yes
```

The workgroup, NetBIOS name, and server string are personalized for my server and local area network. I've also chosen to have the server act as a WINS server and register as the preferred master browser on the network. It's important to note that encrypted passwords are enabled; otherwise, new Windows clients (such as Windows 2000) wouldn't be able to connect.

Next, the file share. I've created a folder `/filestorage/mp3s` on my Mac OS X computer to hold my library of iTunes (Napster? never heard of it) MP3 files. My user account (`jray`) owns the folder and has read/write permission to it. This very simple share, named My MP3s, is defined as

```
[My MP3s]
          path = /filestorage/mp3
          read only = No
```

As a final step, using the Password page within SWAT, I register the user `jray` with the password I use to log in to my Windows computer.

With only a few clicks of the mouse, I'll be happily listening to my iTunes music on a Windows computer.

Mapping the Share in Windows

There are a number of different ways to mount a network drive under Windows. If your Windows computer is set up with the same workgroup name as the Samba server, you can simply double-click My Network Places, and then Computers Near Me. The Samba server should appear using the NetBIOS name you specified in the Global configuration.

Right-clicking My Network Places (or My Computer) and choosing Map Network Drive from the pop-up menu is the fastest mounting method. The screen shown in Figure 30.9 will be displayed.

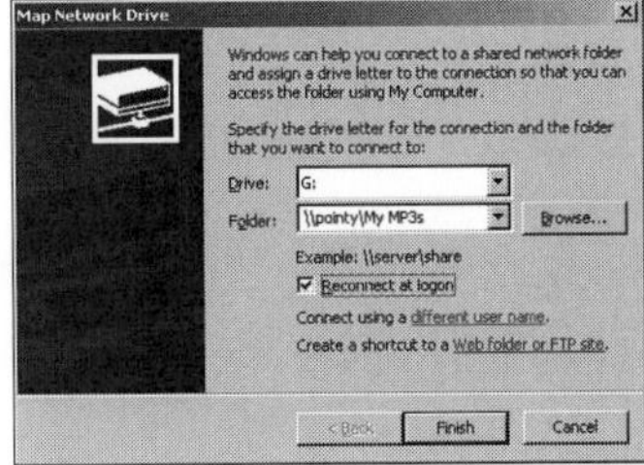

FIGURE 30.9
Map the shared folder in one simple step.

Choose a drive letter to use for the mounted volume, and then enter the share path in the Folder field. The share path is entered as `\\<NetBIOS name>\<share name>`. For the sample share I've set up, the path is `\\pointy\My MP3s\`. Click Reconnect at logon to automatically mount the shared resource when you log in to the Windows computer.

The Mac OS X Folder, shared through Samba, is now accessible like any other network drive on Windows. Figure 30.10 shows the mounted drive.

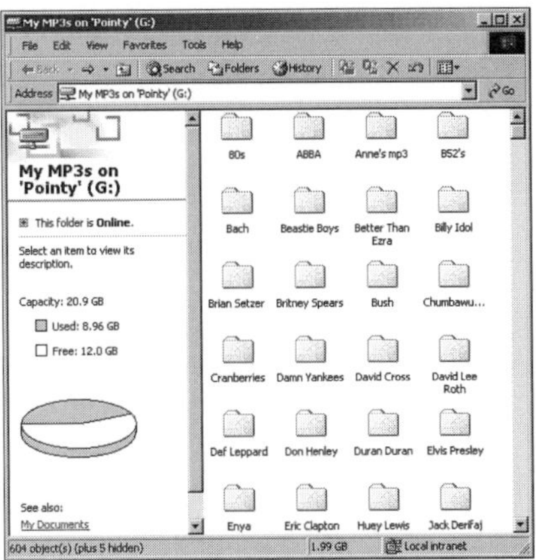

FIGURE 30.10
Access your Mac OS X files from a Windows computer.

It's too bad that Windows doesn't play as nicely, isn't it?

Samba Command-Line Utilities

Samba comes with a few command-line utilities that you might find useful when interacting with your server. Personally, I've always found SWAT to be more than sufficient, but if you've become a guru of the terminal prompt, you might appreciate this information.

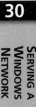

smbstatus

The smbstatus utility provides information about the active connections and users. This is equivalent to the Status page within the SWAT management tool. For example:

```
[primal:~] jray% /usr/local/samba/bin/smbstatus

Samba version 2.2.0
Service    uid    gid    pid     machine
--------------------------------------------
Programs  jray jray  12746   brushedtooth (192.168.0.107) Sat Jun 2 23:56:47
2001
My MP3s   jray jray  12746   brushedtooth (192.168.0.107) Sat Jun 2 23:47:05
2001

No locked files

Share mode memory usage (bytes):
   1048464(99%) free + 56(0%) used + 56(0%) overhead = 1048576(100%) total
```

The available smbstatus options are shown in Table 30.5.

TABLE 30.5 smbstatus Options

Option	*Purpose*
-b	Summary of connected users.
-d	Detailed connection listing. This is the default mode.
-L	Lists locked files only.
-p	Lists the smbd process IDs and exit.
-S	Lists connected shares only.
-s *<config file>*	Chooses the smb.conf file to use.
-s *<username>*	Displays only information relevant to a given username.

smbpasswd

The smbpasswd command is used to alter user information in the /usr/local/samba/lib/smbpasswd file. This can be used to set up Samba user account passwords from the command line or shell scripts.

By default, the smbpasswd command will change the Samba password for the currently logged in Mac OS X user:

```
[primal:~] jray% /usr/local/samba/bin/smbpasswd
Old SMB password:
New SMB password:
```

```
Retype new SMB password:
Password changed for user jray
```

As an administrative user, you can perform several additional functions with the command. The complete syntax for the smbpasswd is smbpasswd *<options>* *<username>* *<password>*. Table 30.6 shows the available options.

TABLE 30.6 smbpasswd Options

Option	*Purpose*
-a	Adds a new username to the local smbpasswd file.
-d	Disables the named user.
-e	Enables the named user.
-D <0-10>	Sets a debug level between 0 and 10 to control the verbosity of error reporting.
-n	Sets a user's password to null.
-r *<remote host>*	Sets the remote host to send password changes.
-j *<domain name>*	Joins a domain.
-U *<username>*	The username to send to the remote host when using -r.
-h	Displays a command summary.
-s	Silent output. Accept all input from standard input. This is useful for scripting smbpasswd.

Note

The smbclient utility allows FTP-like access to remote SMB (Samba/Windows/etc) shares. Because of the similarity to the next program in this chapter, and some known problems under Mac OS X, you will be left to explore smbclient on your own. Given the extensive documentation located on the SWAT home page, this shouldn't be an issue.

Mac OS X 10.1 SMB/CIFS Client

With Mac OS X 10.1, Apple has finally acknowledged that Mac users do need to access Windows networks. Although it does not providing nearly as friendly service as AppleShare, the Mac OS X CIFS client is still relatively straightforward.

Before trying to connect to a Windows or Samba share, you must first know the resource string required to access the share. Those accustomed to Microsoft Windows may have seen these strings denoted in the fashion:

```
\\<server name>\<resource name>
```

Mac OS X changes this into a more conventional URL, prefixed by either `cifs` or `smb` to denote the protocol. For example, the Windows connection string of `\\pointy\mp3` becomes `smb://pointy/mp3` in Mac OS X. Besides using the names of local servers, you can also enter the domain name or IP address for the server you want to access.

Unfortunately, it does not appear that Apple will be including the capability of browsing Windows networks (unless they are using SLP—the service locator protocol) at this time, so you will need to know the name of the resource you're accessing before you connect. If you'd like a more user-friendly method of connection, read about the Sharity application in the next section of this chapter.

After you determine the CIFS/SMB URL for the connection youwant to make, choose Connect to Server (Command+K) from the Finder's Go menu, enter the URL into the Address field (as shown in Figure 30.11), and then click Connect.

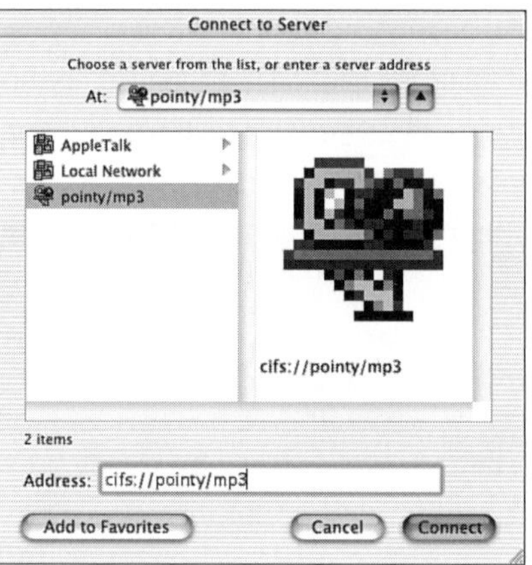

FIGURE 30.11
Enter the CIFS/SMB URL to connect to.

After a few seconds, the system should prompt you for Domain/Workgroup information as well as the username and password for the connection, demonstrated in Figure 30.12.

FIGURE 30.12
Provide the login information for your CIFS/SMB server, then click OK.

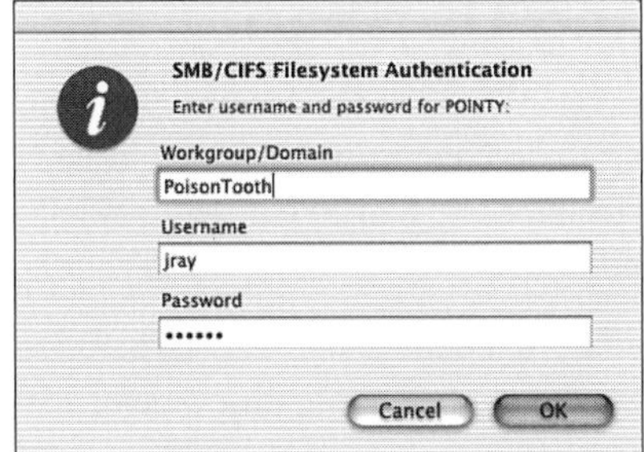

Fill in the requested information appropriately. For peer-to-peer connections, you can typically leave the Workgroup/Domain field blank. The username and password are determined by the administrator of the Windows or Samba resource and are not related to your Mac OS X login. When finished, click OK.

After a few seconds, the network share will be mounted on your system and will be virtually indistinguishable from a standard AppleShare connection. This capability is extremely important for the acceptance of the Mac inside existing networks. Some users, however, might need a more advanced solution, such as Sharity.

Sharity

The Sharity SMB/CIFS client offers transparent access to Windows and Samba servers from the Mac OS X Finder. Unlike the built-in SMB/CIFS client, Sharity offers a wide range of customization and integration with Mac OS X. If you need more control over your connection, Sharity is the way to go. It can be used to mount volumes on a local area network, or anywhere on the Internet.

Sharity acts as a go-between for the SMB/CIFS protocol and NFS. To Mac OS X, the mounted volumes are nothing but NFS mounts. The power of this becomes apparent when you realize that not only does this give access to stored Windows files, but also to storage areas for Mac OS X software. In fact, using Sharity and Samba on a cluster of Mac OS X machines is actually a more powerful file sharing solution than the Mac OS X built-in Shared Folders.

Installing and Setting Up Sharity

The Sharity installation process is very Mac-like, but requires some knowledge of the Windows network that you're going to be connecting to. It would be helpful if you collected the name of a WINS server (remember, Samba can serve WINS!), and the shares you want to connect to, before continuing.

Download Sharity from `www.obdev.at/products/sharity/`. There are currently several packaging formats for the application, including a `dmg` disk image. This is the preferred distribution format. After downloading, decompress the archive using StuffIt Expander (or your compression tool of choice) and double-click the disk image to mount it. The Sharity distribution appears in Figure 30.13.

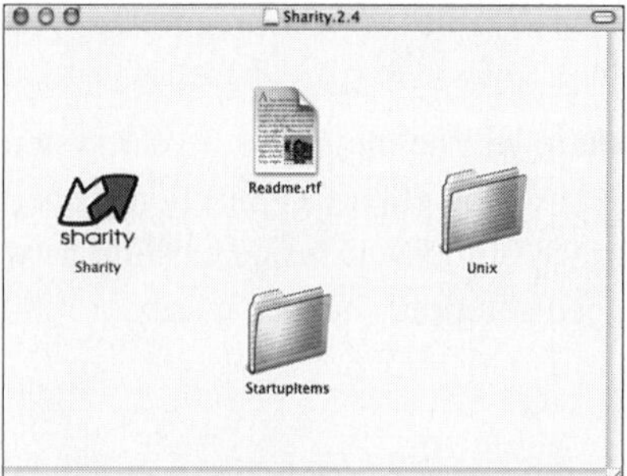

FIGURE 30.13
The Sharity distribution consists of a startup item and an application.

To install Sharity, drag the Sharity icon into the Mac OS X `/Applications` folder. Next, check the System `/Library` directory to see if a `StartupItems` folder exists. If it *does not*, drag the `StartupItems` folder from the Sharity distribution directly into `/Library`.

If there *is* an existing `/Library/StartupItems` directory, open `StartupItems` in the Sharity distribution and drag the `Sharity` folder into `/Library/StartupItems`.

Reboot the machine to start the Sharity process.

Sharity First-Run

The first time you run Sharity, it will guide you through an easy set up process. The initial welcome screen, displayed in Figure 30.14, collects the workgroup and WINS information for your Windows network. If you set up a Samba server in the beginning of the chapter, use the same values you used when configuring Samba.

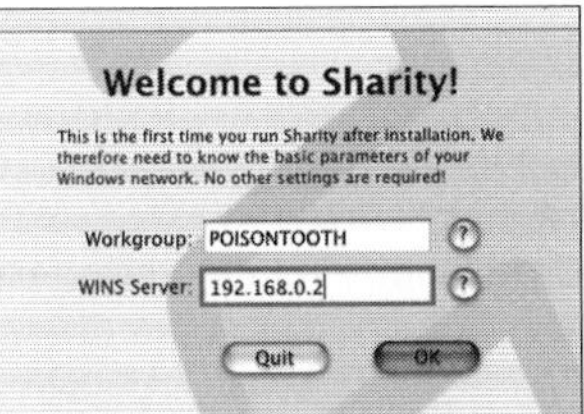

FIGURE 30.14
Enter your workgroup and WINS server names.

Click OK to confirm your choices and join the Windows network. Within a few seconds, Sharity will automatically open the Network level within the Finder. You will notice that there is a new icon available—CIFS, seen in Figure 30.15. This is actually a mounted Sharity drive called a *browser*—navigating through the browser lets you find network volumes just like using Network Places in Windows.

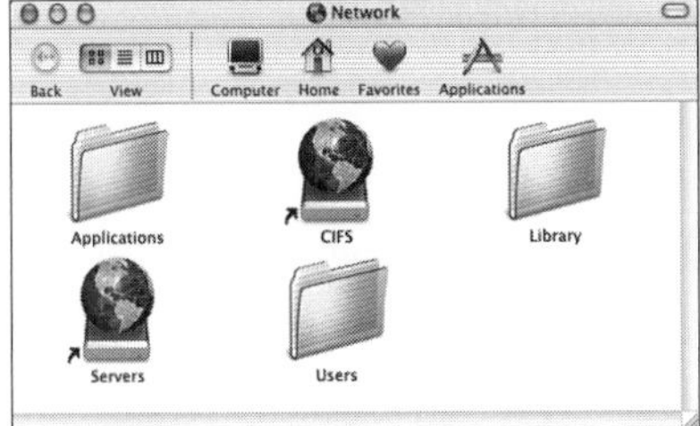

FIGURE 30.15
The CIFS mount is equivalent to the Windows Network Places icon.

Browsing

Double-click the CIFS icon to start browsing the Windows network. The first level of CIFS contains a list of computers (represented by folder icons) that are part of the workgroup you joined when opening Sharity. In addition, there is an `Entire_Network` folder that enables you to view all workgroups and hosts that are registered on the network. My local area network has two hosts—Inky and Pointy, as seen in Figure 30.16.

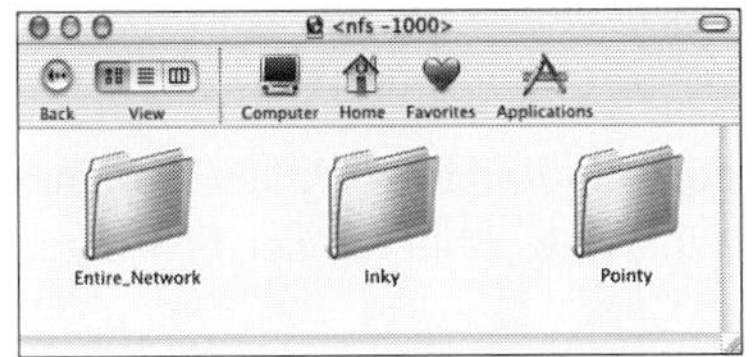

FIGURE 30.16
The first level of the CIFS hierarchy displays local servers within the same workgroup as well as an Entire_Network icon for browsing all available workgroups.

Mounting a Volume

As you learned in the Samba discussion, there are two types of security that can be implemented for a share: user level and share level. The difference between the two, in terms of Sharity use, is what happens when you double-click a computer folder. If the computer has user-level access, you must supply a username and password before you can see the contents. Figure 30.17 shows a login prompt for a user-level shared resource.

FIGURE 30.17
User-level access requires that a username and password be supplied before viewing shared volumes.

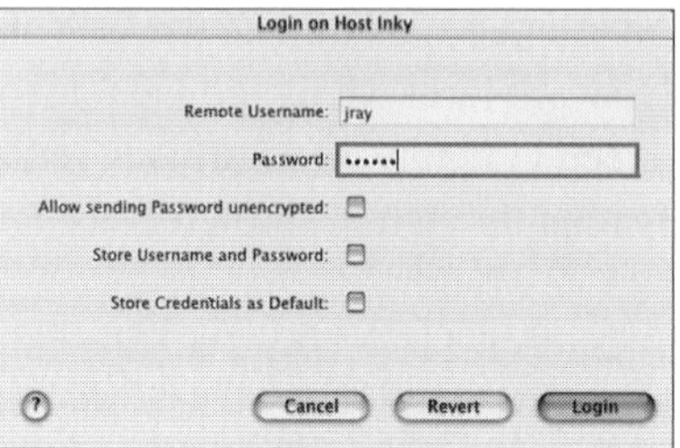

Fill in the login dialog box using the information that was set up on the Windows server:

Remote Username—The username used on the remote Windows computer.

Password—The corresponding Windows password.

Allow Sending Password Unencrypted—If connecting to an older Windows system, you might need to check this box. For most modern systems (NT 4/2000), leave this unchecked.

Store Username and Password—Save the username and password for the share so that it doesn't have to be entered in the future.

Store Credentials as Default—Saves the supplied username and password as the default name and password for resources on the network. This saved set is used to attempt to access other resources. If you use a different login/password on all the computers on the network, this won't be of much use.

Click Login to send authentication information to the server and view its available resources, or click Revert to return the form settings to their original values.

If the remote server uses share-level control, double-clicking the computer folder in the CIFS browser will show the available shares without the need for a password. A share list is displayed in Figure 30.18.

To mount a shared resource, double-click the name of the volume you want to mount. If the resource has a share-level password, you'll be prompted for the connection information, as demonstrated in Figure 30.19.

FIGURE 30.18
After logging in to a user-level server, or when accessing a server with share-level access, you'll see the available volumes.

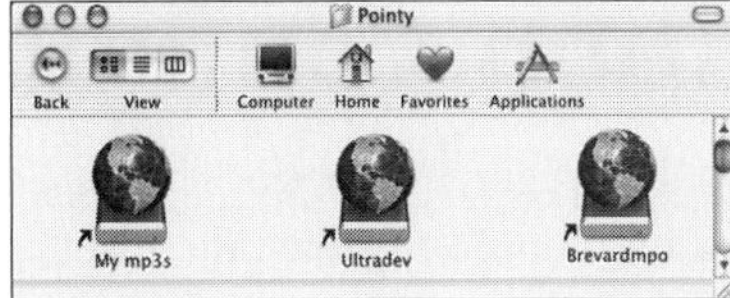

FIGURE 30.19
Share-level security control displays a connection dialog box when accessing the resource.

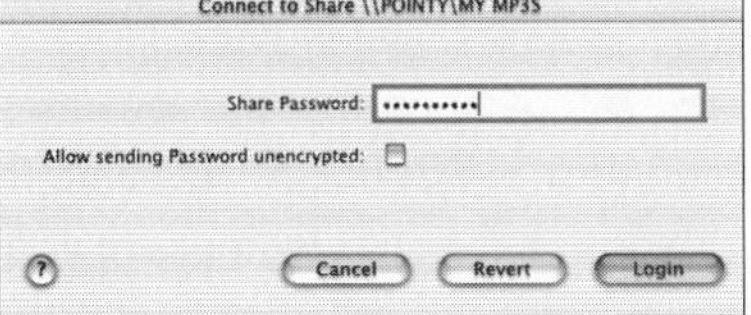

Enter the password for the share, and click the Allow sending Password unencrypted check box if you are attempting to connect to an older Windows server. Click Login to mount the share. Within a few seconds, the share will open in the Finder.

Tip

For easier access to a volume in the future, create a shortcut to its icon in the CIFS browser. Double-clicking the shortcut will attempt to log in to the resource.

That's all there is to it. To make sure that you can log in to shared resources immediately upon booting, you must drag the Sharity application into the Login Items pane of the Login System Preferences (path: `/Applications/System Preferences`) panel, as seen in Figure 30.20.

FIGURE 30.20
Add Sharity to your Login items.

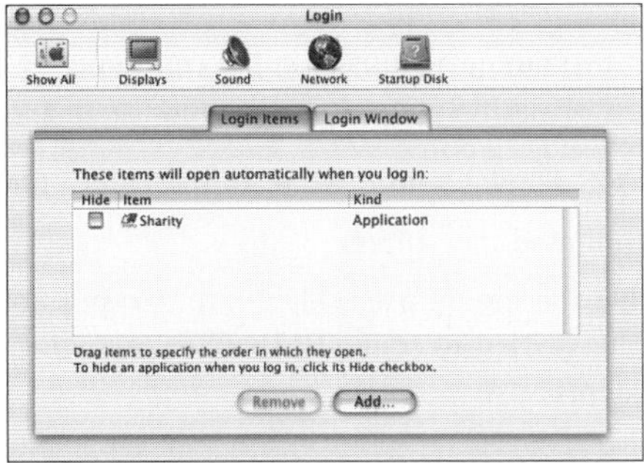

Sharity Application Configuration

The Sharity application offers additional configuration options beyond what you can do simply by browsing your network. You might need to adjust these settings if you're part of a large Windows network, or want greater control over when and how shares are mounted.

To access the advanced configuration, open the Sharity application, and then choose Configuration from the Configuration menu. There are seven different panes for setting up Sharity and two different access modes: Expert and Novice. Novice mode disables some of the available settings. Let's take a look at each of the screens and its purpose. Click between the available configuration panes by clicking its name from the list on the far left of the Sharity Configuration window. Let's start by looking at the Sharity Mounts pane.

Sharity Mounts

Using the Sharity Mounts pane, as shown in Figure 30.21, the Sharity user can manually mount additional browsers or shares on the Mac OS X computer.

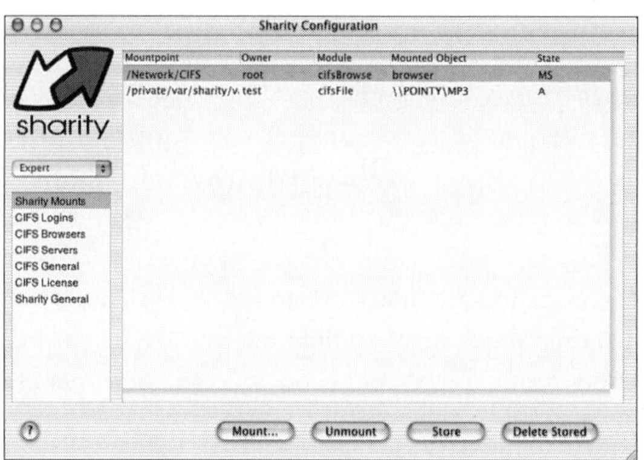

FIGURE 30.21
Sharity Mounts configures and stores mounted drives manually.

Sharity mounts displays a list of mounted volumes on the right side of the screen. The list has five columns showing information about the resource:

Mountpoint—The Mac OS X path where the resource is mounted.

Owner—The user that mounted the volume.

Module—The module that the mount uses. There are two possibilities: `cifsBrowse`, which enables browsing of the SMB/CIFS network, and `cifsFile` for mounting remote file systems.

Mounted Object—The Windows share path for the mounted resource. In the case of a `cifsBrowse` module, this is the name of the browser, as defined in CIFS Browsers.

State—The status of the mount, represented as a combination of (M)ounted, (A)utomounted through the CIFS browser, (R)ead-Only, or (S)tored.

Shares can be selected from the list and acted on by clicking the buttons at the bottom of the screen. Unmount disconnects from the selected share. Store saves a share so that it automatically mounts when Sharity starts at login time. Delete Stored, conversely, removes Stored status from the chosen Share.

To manually add a new volume mount, click the Mount button. A mount sheet will slide down from the top of the window, as shown in Figure 30.22.

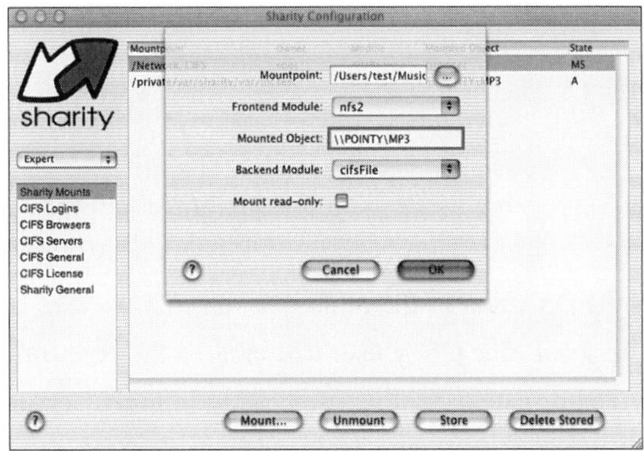

FIGURE 30.22
Click Mount to manually mount a shared resource.

Fill in the information necessary to create the mount. The Mountpoint and Mounted Object fields are usually all that should be changed:

Mountpoint—The path where the shared resource will be mounted. If this is confusing, please read Chapter 23 for more information.

Frontend module—The `nfs2` module is used for all mounts. This is not changeable.

Mounted Object—The Windows share path. This can include an IP address in addition to a NetBIOS name. If mounting another browser, use the browser name, as defined in the CIFS Browsers pane.

Backend Module—Choose `cifsFile` to mount windows shares, or `cifsBrowse` to create another CIFS browser.

Mount read-only—Mount the resource read-only.

Click OK to mount the resource and add it to the Sharity Mounts list.

Sharity Logins

The Sharity Logins screen is similar to the Mounts screen. It provides a quick view of the servers that you are currently logged in to, and enables you to log in to additional servers. Figure 30.23 shows the CIFS Logins pane.

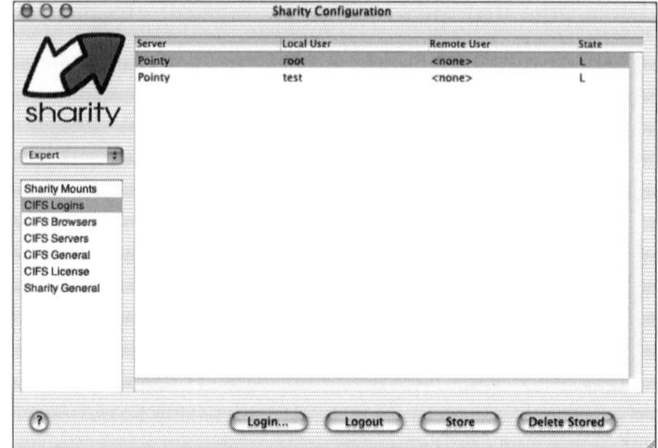

FIGURE 30.23
Use the CIFS Logins screen to log in and out of servers.

The currently mounted servers are listed, with information about the connection and the user account used:

Server—The NetBIOS name of the remote server that the user is connected to.

Local User—The local Mac OS X user that created the connection.

Remote User—The remote username used to log in to the server.

State—The state of the connection: (L)ogged in or (S)tored.

Use the buttons at the bottom of the window to Logout of a selected server, Store the connection information, or Delete Stored information. Clicking the Login button will open a sheet containing a list of the servers available for login. Selecting a server from the list will attempt to log in to the server in exactly the same manner as double-clicking it from the browser.

CIFS Browsers

By default, Sharity sets up a single CIFS Browser called browser. It is then mounted at `/Network/CIFS` and can be used for graphically browsing network resources. Using the CIFS Browsers pane, seen in Figure 30.24, you can create additional browsers that are specific to a workgroup.

A list of available browsers is located at the left side of the panel, although the configuration options for the selected browser are on the right. Use the Add and Delete buttons at the bottom of the screen to add or remove browsers from the list of available browser configurations.

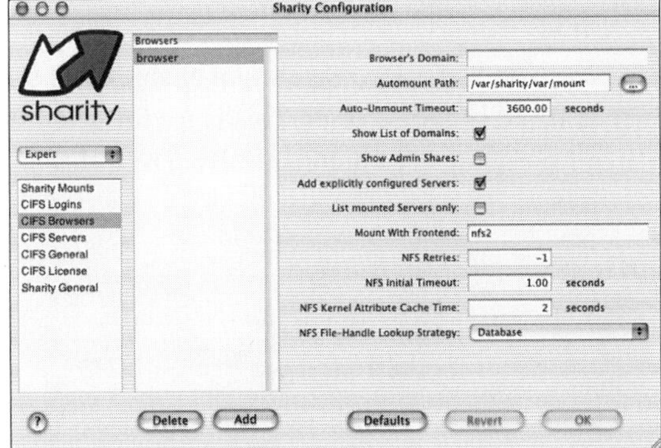

FIGURE 30.24
Configure additional network browsers using CIFS Browsers.

Edit the selected browser by setting the options on the right:

Browser's Domain—The workgroup name that the browser should operate in.

Automount Path—The path where automatically mounted volumes are placed. This should not be changed.

Auto-Unmount Timeout—The amount of time (in seconds) after which a mount will be automatically unmounted.

Show List of Domains—Adds the Entire_Network object to a mounted browser for viewing additional workgroups.

Show Admin Shares—Lists Windows administrative shares along with regular shares.

Add Explicitly Configured Servers—Adds servers manually configured in the CIFS Servers pane to the browser.

List Mounted Servers Only—Disables browsing, but retains automount capability. This is not normally needed.

Mount With Frontend—`nfs2` is the only available option.

NFS Retries—Number of retries a mount attempt will make. The default `-1` value means retry forever.

NFS Initial Timeout—The initial timeout period before a retry is started.

NFS Kernel Attribute Cache Time—The length of time the operating system kernel will cache file system information.

NFS File-Handle Lookup Strategy—Determines the method the NFS front end will use to store file identifiers.

Click OK to save the settings, or Revert to reset the options to their defaults.

CIFS Servers

Like the CIFS Browsers pane, the Servers configuration enables you to explicitly configure servers that will then be listed in the browser. This is useful when adding servers to the CIFS browser that aren't normally seen automatically. The CIFS Servers pane is seen in Figure 30.25.

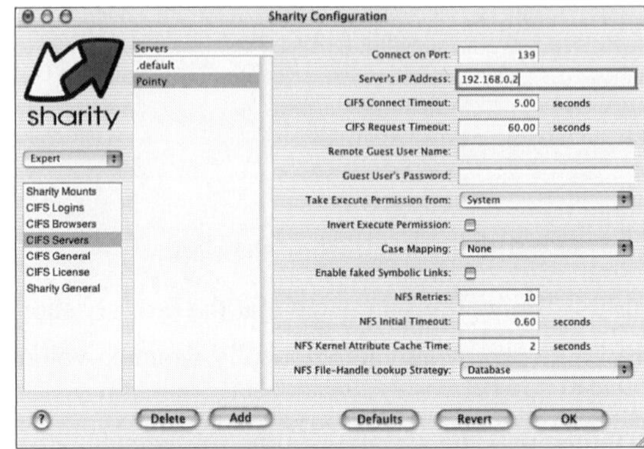

FIGURE 30.25
Manually set up servers that can't be browsed directly.

Like the previous panel, the CIFS servers are listed along the left side of the window, although the configuration options for the selected item are shown on the right. Use the Add and Delete buttons to create and remove new servers in the list.

Each server is defined with the following information:

Connect on Port—The SMB/CIFS TCP/IP port to use. The default is `139`.

Server's IP Address—The IP address of the remote server.

CIFS Connect Timeout—The timeout (in seconds) for the connection process.

CIFS Request Timeout—The timeout (in seconds) for a server request to be completed after the initial connection.

Remote Guest User Name—A guest user name that should be used for logging in to the server, regardless of the Mac OS X user logged in.

Guest User's Password—The password for the Remote Guest user.

Take Execute Permission From—CIFS permissions are mapped directly from DOS file attributes. Unfortunately, DOS attributes do not include an execute bit. This setting determines which DOS attribute is equivalent to execute on the Mac OS X side. If necessary, you can choose to turn execute permissions Always On or Always Off.

Invert Execution Permission—Inverts the DOS attribute that the execution permission is mapped from.

Case Mapping—Enables mapping remote filenames to all uppercase, lowercase, or as-is.

Enable faked Symbolic Links—Enables faked symbolic links on a mounted server.

NFS Options—The NFS options are identical to those defined in the CIFS Browsers pane.

Click OK to save the settings, Revert to return to the original configuration, or Defaults to set up the current Server using the Sharity defaults.

CIFS General

Things begin to thin out a bit with the CIFS General panel. These settings can override the initial Domain and WINS server that were configured during the first Sharity run. The CIFS General pane is displayed in Figure 30.26.

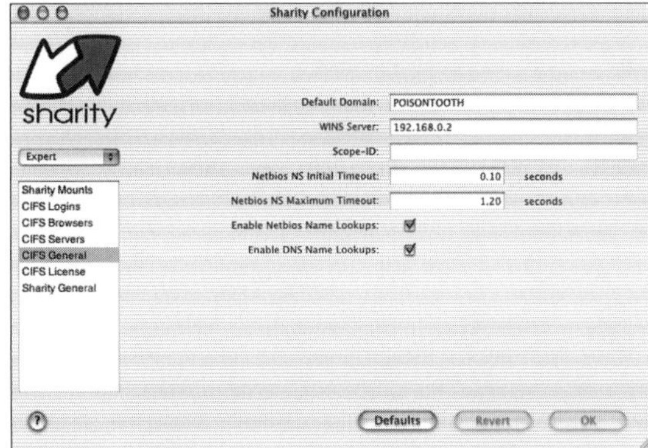

FIGURE 30.26
Set the default workgroup and WINS server for Sharity.

Fill in the following information to set WINS and NetBIOS defaults:

Default Domain—The default workgroup that Sharity should join.

WINS Server—The name or IP address of a WINS server.

Scope-ID—Scopes limit the viewable resources on a network. If your network is configured to use scopes, enter the Scope-ID in this field. This is not likely to be necessary.

NetBIOS NS Initial Timeout—The initial timeout (in seconds) that Sharity will wait for a response from a WINS server before resending the request.

NetBIOS NS Maximum Timeout—The maximum amount of time to wait for a WINS reply. If the server does not respond in this amount of time, DNS is used to resolve the name.

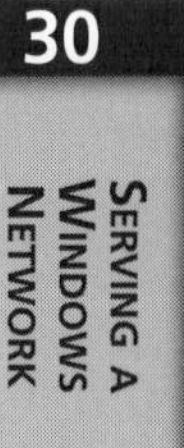

Enable NetBIOS Name Lookups—Enables WINS resolution.

Enable DNS Name Lookups—Enables DNS resolution of NetBIOS names.

Click OK to save the settings, Revert to return to the original configuration, or Defaults to set up the current server using the Sharity defaults.

Sharity License

If you purchase a license for Sharity, enter it in this pane. There are no other configuration options available on this screen.

Sharity General

Use the Sharity General pane to set up character mapping between Mac OS X and the remote Windows server. If you are logged in as `root`, you can also choose whether Mac OS X users can alter the Sharity set up. Figure 30.27 displays the Sharity General configuration pane.

FIGURE 30.27
A few more settings and we're done.

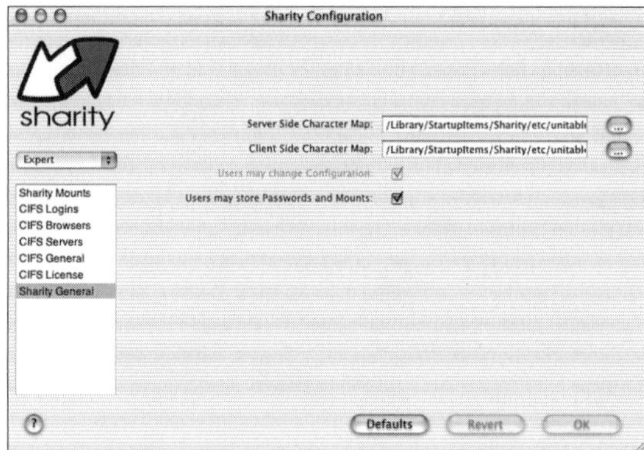

The Sharity general settings control the mapping of characters between Mac OS X and Windows as well as the ability to store passwords for mounted volumes:

Server Side Character Map—Defines the character mapping used by the remote server. By default, Sharity attempts to use Unicode names, so this is rarely needed in modern (NT/2000) environments.

Client-Side Character Map—The client-side character mapping. NFS does not use Unicode, so this must be defined properly. Mac OS X users should use the default, `UTF-8`.

Users May Change Configuration—The option can be set only by `root`. It enables any Mac OS X user to alter the Sharity configuration.

Users May Store Passwords and Mounts—If unchecked, users will not be able to store passwords or mounts. This might be necessary to ensure network security in strict environments.

Click OK to save the settings, Revert to return to the original configuration, or Defaults to set up the current server using the Sharity defaults.

Sharity provides excellent Mac OS X integration and compatibility with existing Windows networks. Although there are bound to be additional players in the PC interoperability arena, Sharity, being a native Cocoa application, is likely to lead the pack.

Note

Sharity, in addition to including a wonderful Mac OS X GUI, is also usable from the command line. The Sharity distribution includes a `readme` file in the folder Unix that describes the operation of these utilities. To start using Sharity from the Terminal, `cd` to `/Library/StartupItems/Sharity/bin`. There are several links to `Sharity` that can be used as shortcuts to all the functions of the GUI:

`cifslicense`—Views and sets Sharity license information.

`cifslist`—Lists the active hosts, users, and shares.

`cifslogin`—Logs in to a Windows server.

`cifslogout`—Logs out of a Windows server.

`cifsmount`—Mounts a Windows-shared resource.

`cifsstore`—Stores server credentials in a local database for passwordless access.

`cifsstoremnt`—Stores a mounted volume for automatic remounting.

`cifsumount`—Unmounts a shared resource.

Summary

This chapter introduced the reader to the Windows SMB/CIFS file-sharing protocols and how they can be used on the Mac OS X platform. Samba is a full-featured server product that is easy to install and set up, and can replace a Windows NT/2000 server for file and print sharing. Samba has such a large number of configuration options that additional resources, such as *Sams Teach Yourself Samba in 24 Hours*, are recommended for complex configuration. To access Samba or Windows shares from a Mac OS X desktop, you can use the built-in SMB/CIFS client, or, for more power, use Sharity. The Sharity application creates the equivalent of the Windows Network Places network browser that can be used to graphically locate and mount SMB/CIFS shares.

Server Security and Advanced Network Configuration

In This Chapter

In earlier chapters, we touched on the idea of making your machine as secure as possible. In this chapter, we will cover the topic in greater depth. We will discuss why security is important, types of attacks you might encounter, some suggestions for securing your machine, and some security tools that can help you.

Why Bother with Network Security

Before we can reasonably discuss ways to make your OS X machine more secure, it is important to understand why you should care and what you are facing.

You might be wondering, "Why bother with security?" You've never cared about securing your Mac before. In fact, prior to OS X, security has rarely been an issue for a Mac owner. However, as a Unix-based operating system, OS X brings with it not only the advantages, but also the disadvantages, of a Unix operating system. Unfortunately, one of those disadvantages is security, which has always been a problem for Unix operating systems. This will be unsettling at the beginning, but the simple fact is that nothing can be done to make any network-connected Unix machine (OS X or otherwise) completely secure. To paraphrase one system administrator's feeling about securing a Unix machine, "I'd pull the plug and the network, put the machine in a safe, fill the safe with concrete, lock it, and drop it in the middle of Hudson Bay—and even then I wouldn't be sure."

This take might be a little extreme, but you get the point. If your machine is on a network, and/or the hardware is physically accessible, it's vulnerable to something, somehow. Your best efforts at security are only capable of increasing the effort, time, and creativity required for a cracker to access your hardware—you simply can't make it impossible.

Crackers target anything they can find on your computer or network. Your Mac OS X computer has a variety of server processes running on it that enable it to communicate with the outside world. A single programming flaw in one of these daemons could open administrative access to anyone. If a cracker can't find a way in directly, he can direct attacks on your network hardware, or your ISP's hardware. Switches, routers, and other devices are also susceptible to attack. If your computer has blocked access to outside networks, the intruder might resort to IP spoofing to fake his real location.

The threat of computer break-ins is very real, and a very real concern—even if you're doing everything right. For example, earlier versions of Sendmail (the mail server included on your Mac OS X installation) suffered from a bug that allowed remote crackers to send a specially formatted e-mail to the server and force it to execute pieces of code with full administrator privileges. Imagine it: A person, anywhere in the world, could potentially take over control of your computer by sending it an e-mail message. Even experienced administrators were at risk from this bug. Although Sendmail has since been patched (and doesn't run by default on Mac OS X), this is an excellent example of the type of attack that is possible. For more information about this particular exploit, check out `http://ciac.llnl.gov/ciac/bulletins/h-23.shtml`.

Note

Crackers, not hackers: There seems to be a popular misconception that the term *hacker* means someone who breaks into computers. This has not always been the case, and annoys the hackers out there who do not break into computers. To many hackers, the term *hacker* means a person who *hacks* on code to make it do new and different things—frequently with little regard to corporate-standard good programming but also frequently with a Rube Goldberg-like, elegant-but-twisted logic.

Hackers, to those who don't break into computers, are some of the true programming wizards—the guys who can make a computer do almost anything. These are people you want on your side, and dirtying their good name by associating them with the average scum that will try to break into your machine isn't a good way to accomplish this.

So, to keep the real hackers happy we're going to refer to the people who compromise your machine's security as crackers in this book. We hope you'll follow our lead in your interactions with the programmers around you.

You might still be wondering, "Why bother?" If the machine can't be made completely secure, why try? When your machine is brand new, and not very customized, perhaps you can afford to have that attitude. Reinstalling the operating system is not all that traumatic at that stage. However, because you have made it to this chapter, you've seen OS X from many angles, and perhaps even implemented some customizations to your system. Hence, you might not feel like doing it all over again.

So, if you can't be completely secure, what can you do? You can be reasonably secure. Exactly how secure is reasonable differs from case-to-case, and depends on a wide range of factors. Later in this chapter, we'll discuss some of these factors, and how to assess your needs. For now, understand that when designing security measures, there is a threshold beyond which expending extra effort does not produce a sufficient increase in security to make that effort worthwhile. You can liken this to the somewhat facetious advice given for how to protect yourself when hiking in bear country—"always hike with someone who runs slower than you do." Your goal in securing your system is to make your machine and your network less attractive than the next guy's system to the cracker. In this chapter, we will look at some ways to accomplish that goal.

Security Assessment

There are a number of factors that you need to keep in mind when assessing what reasonable security means to you. How you weigh each of these factors and the decisions you make regarding implementation details are up to you. There are, however, some good rules of thumb that you can live by. Some of these you might not fully understand, but we recommend that you follow them anyway. Some of them might sound like overt paranoia, until you've been in the trenches for a while. After you've been there, and done that a few times, you'll probably come to realize that when it comes to security, paranoia is usually your friend.

The four questions that you should ask yourself before deciding on a strategy are "Why do I want security?" "Who is going to try to compromise my security?" "How worried about it am I?" and "How much effort do I want to invest in stopping them?"

Because is a perfectly reasonable answer to the first question, but if you have a better answer, such as because my system contains sensitive financial transaction data, your mission in securing your machine will be much more focused.

The answer to the second question will be instrumental in deciding what security precautions are appropriate for your site. If you're trying to secure a system that contains important industrial secrets, you have much more at stake. Therefore, you will also meet a very different kind of cracker than on something like a student-organization Web server at a college.

The answer to the third question should be *very*. First off, if you aren't very worried, you're putting forth a lot of effort to protect something for which you're not very worried. Secondly, paranoia is an admirable quality in a system administrator. You might not feel like a system administrator, but with your OS X machine, not only have you become a Unix user, but you're also a system administrator. A good system administrator always prepares for the worst possible scenario that she can imagine. The worst, or something closely approximating it, happens to everyone eventually, and it's the paranoid system administrator, who planned for it three years ago, who keeps the system up and running like nothing ever happened. When the job is done right, nobody ever notices that she's done it, and nobody ever says thank you. You might not have many users on your OS X machine, so you might not be in quite the same shoes as your system administrator. Nevertheless, you should take the time to brighten your system administrator's day and say thank you. If you want to make her even happier, let her know that you are taking steps to make your machine reasonably secure.

On the final question, if your answer isn't *a lot*, you should realize up front that your system won't be very secure for very long. All flavors of Unix are such complex systems that it's impossible to completely debug them and new holes and exploits are being found on a weekly basis. Although there are more interesting things to do on your OS X machine, as a responsible Unix machine owner, you should try to keep up with the latest patches to software and watch the latest developments in the cracker world.

Private Data Versus Secret Data

Understanding the reasons that the data or contents of your system need to be protected is important. If you're proposing to create a secure system for something like a K–12 student-teaching lab network, your main reason for wanting to protect your system is probably simply the principle of the matter. On the other hand, if you're protecting a system that contains important industrial secrets, preventing intrusion is probably more of a necessity. Essentially, this assessment comes down to a question of whether your data is simply private or actually secret. Allowing the disclosure of private data is never a good thing, but you won't find many people with the motivation to try to compromise your system if the data in it is simply private. On the other hand, if your data contains secrets, such as industrial trade secrets, financial records, or some types of highly sensitive personal information, you will find attackers that are much more motivated to crack your system.

The point of this examination goes back to that issue of making your system less attractive than the next guy's. If your system contains only private data, you won't have much trouble making it more secure than the vast majority of other systems out there. If your only concern is the random curious cracker, rather than the dedicated and motivated one, you can make your system unattractive to him with little work.

If, on the other hand, you're in the unfortunate position of needing to defend truly secret data, you might find crackers motivated enough that they won't leave you alone, no matter what you do. Against these individuals, you've little choice but to simply do your best to stay one step ahead of them.

Types of Attackers

We divide the types of attackers you're likely to meet into three subsets. Although it might not seem obvious at first consideration, the variety that you're the most likely to meet, regardless of the type of data you're protecting, are frequently both the most and least dangerous.

The Motivated Cracker

The type of cracker you're probably least likely to meet is the dedicated and motivated professional or amateur cracker with a mission. This person might be an industrial spy trying to discover your company's trade secrets, a student trying to change his grade, or a hobbyist who simply finds your security measures a challenge.

> **Caution**
>
> Obscurity isn't to be relied on, but it sure doesn't hurt!
>
> Many system administrators, and even OS vendors, have historically had a bad habit of attempting to implement security measures based only on the fact that people didn't know about the holes in them. This is a concept known as *security through obscurity*, and is generally considered a bad thing to rely on. On the other hand, obscurity in addition to other security measures certainly doesn't hurt. Keeping your system and security measures low profile is always a good idea. If you have a system with extra-tight security measures, telling people just how tight they are is the surest way to attract the person who delights in cracking systems "just because."
>
> Rely neither on security through obscurity, nor on the invincibility of your security measures. The best way to motivate a person to try to crack your system just because it's there is to let on that you think it can't be done.

The motivated cracker isn't likely to leave a large amount of evidence of his comings and goings. These types vary between unlikely to do any significant damage (other than observing your data), to making insidious and difficult-to-detect modifications to the contents of your system.

To defeat this type of cracker, you need to understand his motivation, and either remove it or resign yourself to a constant battle to stay ahead. The only way to actually stop these people permanently is to track them down and pursue legal remedies against them.

The Casual Experimenter

The next type of attacker you're likely to meet is the casual experimenter. These individuals don't usually intend any significant harm, and aren't usually very motivated to invade your system. They're frequently just a bit over-curious, and are trying out something that they stumbled across somewhere on the Internet. This doesn't mean that they're not dangerous—their lack of intent can't prevent simple typing mistakes that can be disastrous to a person with root access. Thankfully, these individuals aren't usually too difficult to defend against because they're usually not particularly sophisticated. They also don't tend to be worth investing much effort in tracking down legally.

The Script Kiddie

The most common type of cracker doesn't even deserve to be called a cracker. Historically, crackers have been frequently thought of as Robin Hood characters, with a sort of romantic fascination with their exploits. Not to minimize the impropriety of the legendary crackers' actions, but you can appreciate the creativity and tenacity of these individuals without approving of their actions. By the standards set by the crackers of old, the vast majority of today's crackers barely qualify as cracker-wannabe-wannabes.

Today's prototypical cracker is a young adult with too much free-time who found a cracking script on a Web site somewhere and is trying to use it to show his friends he's an "lEEt HaCkEr dOOd." In fact, these new crackers are called *script kiddies*.

These individuals are both a trivial and significant concern. If you keep your system up to date, and pay attention to the latest cracking scripts and to the patches against them, you are almost invulnerable to actual intrusion at the hands of these people. They don't generally try anything more complicated than running a script they've borrowed from someone else, so if you keep your system secure against these scripts, you're usually secure against cracker wannabes. This doesn't mean that they're completely innocuous though, as they can still consume your network resources while trying to break into your system.

They can also be very dangerous, however, if you don't keep your system completely up to date because there are so darned many of them, and because they're basically glory-hounds interested in nothing more than self-aggrandizement. To give you a perspective on the magnitude of their numbers, here at The Ohio State University, we see unsophisticated cracking attempts of this sort multiple times every week, directed at the thousands of machines on campus. A Linux machine, installed out of the box and not immediately secured against intrusion, stands a better than 50% chance of being cracked within 24 hours if it's attached to the network here. Fortunately, an OS X machine installed out of the box is a bit more secure, but that does not mean that it is invincible.

Also, because their basic goal is self-aggrandizement, and because they don't get that much glory for using someone else's script, these people are rarely content to break into a system, tread lightly, and leave without a trace. Instead, they're more likely to erase the contents of your hard drive, or replace your corporate Web page with pornography, so they have some evidence to show their "lEEt HaCkEr dOOd" friends.

Securing your system against these attacks is simply a matter of watching every security discussion list and cracker site for signs of trouble and postings of new cracking scripts, and then applying every security patch as quickly as it becomes available. Simple, no? As satisfying as tracking them down and squashing them like the insects they are might be, it's usually impractical. Ninety percent of these attacks come from users with transient accounts, and the best you'll usually do is chase them to a different account. If you do happen to catch one though, please do let the Internet system administration community know—the newsgroup `alt.sysadmin.recovery` would be a good venue—public lynchings are always well attended.

Types of Attacks

Next, let's look at what methods attackers might use to access your machine. This is especially important if your machine is connected to an unprotected network, or if it serves as a firewall.

Software and OS Flaws

The most common type of attack you will encounter is one that attempts to exploit flaws in application or operating system software. There is probably not much you can do about most software flaws other than hoping that the providers find and fix the problems promptly. Although this is a problem from a security standpoint, the positive side is that if you're spending the time to watch the cracking Web pages and the security mailing lists, you'll know about the problems as soon as the crackers do. With the information you get from these sources, and your understanding of the special risks your site incurs, you can assess whether leaving that software on your machine is an acceptable risk until the vendor fixes it.

You need to be aware that some of these flaws require prior access to your system to exploit, whereas others can be exploited from a remote site over the network. Don't make the mistake of assuming that because no one has actually logged in to your machine, you can't or haven't been attacked.

Brute Force Attacks

Although not a particularly elegant form of attack, the brute force attack is one that you can only partially prevent. In its simplest form, this attack is a cracker attempting to log in to a system by sitting at a machine and iteratively typing attempts at passwords into the prompt. There's not much you can do to keep people from trying this sort of thing.

Keep an eye on the system logs, and you'll see the trivial attempts as they occur. Typically, however, there is much more danger from this sort of attack when a cracker manages to get your password file and can attempt to crack the passwords on his own machine, at his leisure. To prevent this, some systems use a shadow password facility to keep the password file from being readable by a normal user. However, OS X does not have a shadow password facility. Instead, you might want to consider restricting the executable permission on your NetInfo utilities, such as `nidump` and `niutil`, to `root` only.

Denial of Service

Denial of service (DoS) attacks are generally destructive attempts rather than attempts to access your system. When the attacks come from a network of multiple machines, they are known as *distributed denial of service attacks*. Both types of attacks are targeted at preventing you and your users from using your machines instead of allowing an intruder access. Because this can be effectively accomplished without the aid of your system, there's little that you can do about many of these. Because the denial of service attack rarely results in an actual security violation or illegitimate access of your system, your best defense is detection and elimination.

Although the specific methods employed in different varieties of denial of service attacks vary, they share a common feature—the exhausting of some service or resource that your machines require or provide. Why do people do this? Good question. You might expect this sort of behavior from a disgruntled ex-employee attacking a former employer, or from a student who thinks it's a funny practical joke. Less expected are denial of service attacks that seem to happen as random vandalism, just because the attacker can do it.

Certain denial of service attacks can be mitigated or prevented with software or hardware updates. In general, these updates tend to be installation of OS patches to disallow certain types of connections, or installation of filtering hardware to block certain types of network traffic. Denial of service attacks range from flooding users' e-mail, to absorbing all your HTTP server connections, to running your printer out of paper, to flooding your network with ICMP ping packets. Unfortunately, there's little you can count on to be reliably effective other than constant vigilance and swift retribution.

Caution

Not all denial of service attacks are devoid of security risks. Some attacks are targeted at services that are known to break inelegantly, and that sometimes allow privileged access when broken. Just because a denial of service attack looks relatively harmless, don't allow yourself to be complacent. It could be less harmless than it looks, or it could be a prelude to more unpleasant attacks.

Generally most attacks can be thwarted by taking the following precautions:

- Against denial of service attacks, vigilance is your best defense. Watching your machine's load and network performance are the best ways to discover an attack in progress.
- Consider building a monitoring Web page that collects this information from all your machines and provides you with a continuously updated representation of the state of the world.
- A gateway between your cluster and the outside world can be used to deny traffic from a problematic outside host. Unfortunately, this can't prevent an outside host from effectively denying your network services just by banging away at your gateway until your network bandwidth is consumed.
- Enlist the help of system administrators upstream from your site in tracking and blocking denial of service attacks as they occur. Because you can't effectively prevent a user on the other side of the world from running `flood-ping` against your machines, you'll need to find someone between you and them who can help.

Physical Attacks

Many administrators in charge of system security overlook this area of obvious weakness in their security strategy. Computers don't need to be logged in for a person to access their data. A person unscrupulous enough to crack your machines will be just as happy to simply yank a hard drive out of your machine to steal the data on it. These sorts of attacks are usually easy to detect, but can cause significant downtime while critical hardware is replaced.

Although distributed computing and distributed storage are popular in certain environments, if security is a goal, especially data security, you should severely restrict access to all hardware with mission-critical data.

By far the easiest physical attack on your hardware is the power switch or reset button combined with the capability to boot the machine into single-user mode without a password, or to boot off of a device specified at startup, also without a password. When in single-user mode, an attacker can get a dump of your passwords, change your root password, and so on.

Disabling Access

An important part of securing your machine is limiting access to it. In this section, we will look at choosing services that run on your machine, using TCP Wrappers to restrict access, and some common-sense preventive measures you can take.

Selecting Services in the Graphical User Interface

As you might recall, Apple ships OS X with many services disabled. In many of the Unix operating systems, you have to be careful to disable some common services that are turned on by default, but that you might not actually need. With OS X, however, many of these common services are disabled. Instead, if you want to run a common service, such as a remote login service, you specifically have to turn it on in OS X.

In the Sharing pane of the System Preferences panel, controls to enable or disable the SSH, FTP, Web, and AppleShare servers are available. Choose only those services that you really need. Remember, the more services you turn on, the more vulnerable to attack your machine becomes.

Selecting Services Manually

As you saw earlier in the book, the actual controls that can be accessed via a graphical user interface are stored in a variety of places on the system.

`/etc/inetd.conf`

Some of the common services on your system, such as FTP and telnet, are controlled in the `/etc/inetd.conf` file. If you remembered to look at the `/etc/inetd.conf` file before turning on FTP in the Sharing pane, you noticed that all the lines were commented out. In other words, all the services controlled in `/etc/inetd.conf` are turned off by default in OS X.

If you decide to turn on a service, as a precaution, make a backup copy of the `/etc/inetd.conf` file. Next, uncomment the line containing the service you want to enable and save the file. Finally, restart the `inetd` process. If you decide to disable a service that starts out of `inetd`, simply comment the line that contains the service, save the file, and restart the `inetd` process—either by rebooting your machine or using `kill -HUP` *`<inetd pid>`*.

One of the services that comes disabled in `/etc/inetd.conf` is the `identd` service. Although this is not a problem, you might experience some `sendmail` delays as a result, if you choose to run `sendmail`.

You might have also noticed that some of the services listed in `/etc/inetd.conf` have `##` at the beginning of the line, rather than `#`. These services are not yet implemented in the operating system.

StartupItems

As you also saw earlier in the book, some of the services that run in OS X are started in `/System/Library/StartupItems`. Some of the services started in `/System/Library/StartupItems` also have controls in `/etc/hostconfig` that the startup scripts in `/System/Library/StartupItems` check. The Web server, SSH server, and AppleShare server are controlled in such a fashion.

If you enabled those services, but later decided to disable them, set the appropriate `/etc/hostconfig` variable to `NO` and kill their current processes. The next time you reboot, the services won't start. To manually start one of those services, set the appropriate variable in `/etc/hostconfig` to `YES`, and manually execute the startup script. For example, for the SSH server, you would make the `SSHSERVER` line in `/etc/hostconfig` read `SSHSERVER=-YES-`. Then you would execute `/System/Library/StartupItems/SSH/SSH`. To disable a service that does not have a control in `/etc/hostconfig`, simply rename the startup script and kill its process.

Tip

Some third-party applications install their startup scripts in the `/Library/StartupItems` folder. Be sure to check this location as well as the main System-level folder.

Using TCP Wrappers

A common way to restrict access to some TCP services is to use the TCP Wrappers program. TCP Wrappers is a package that monitors and filters requests for TCP (Transmission Control Protocol) services. We will not look at the protocol in any detail—that is a book subject in itself. Suffice it to say the protocol has enough control information in it that we can use a package like TCP Wrappers to filter some of that traffic. TCP Wrappers can be used to restrict certain network services to individual computers or networks.

To make use of this program on some flavors of Unix, TCP Wrappers has to be installed by the system administrator. This is not a necessary step in OS X because the TCP Wrappers program comes pre-installed on the system. The `/etc/inetd.conf` file in OS X already assumes that you will use TCP Wrappers, as evidenced by a line such as

```
#ftp    stream  tcp     nowait  root    /usr/libexec/tcpd               ftpd -l
```

The `/usr/libexec/tcpd` portion of the previous line indicates that TCP Wrappers will be used to call `ftpd`.

Configuring TCP Wrappers

The particularly difficult part about using TCP Wrappers is configuring it. We will look at two ways you can configure TCP Wrappers in OS X: the traditional method of using two control files and a newer method that uses only one control file.

Traditionally, TCP Wrappers has two control files: `/etc/hosts.allow` and `/etc/hosts.deny`. We will look at the traditional method in more detail because it is the default setup for a machine when extended processing options are not enabled. An understanding of the traditional method should carry over to the new method. Be sure to read the `hosts_access` and `hosts_options` man pages for detailed information.

Here is the format of the access control files:

```
daemon_list : client_list : option : option ...
```

Through `/etc/hosts.allow`, you can allow specific services for specific hosts.

Through `/etc/hosts.deny`, you can deny services to hosts and provide global exceptions.

The easiest way to think of and use these configuration files is to think of TCP Wrappers putting a big fence up around all the services on your machine.

The specifications in `/etc/hosts.deny` tell the fence what services are on the outside of the fence, and therefore *not* denied. The fence can appear to be around different sets of services for different clients. For example, an `/etc/hosts.deny` file might look like this:

```
ALL EXCEPT ftpd : 192.168.1. : banners /usr/libexec/banners
ALL : 140.254.12.100 140.254.12.135 : banners /usr/libexec/banners
ALL EXCEPT ftpd sshd : ALL : banners /usr/libexec/banners
```

This file says:

- For the subdomain `192.168.1.`, deny all connections except connections to the FTP daemon, `ftpd`.
- For the specific machines `140.254.12.100` and `140.254.12.135` (maybe they're troublemakers), deny absolutely all connections.
- For all other IP addresses, deny everything except connections to `ftpd` and to the secure-shell daemon `sshd`.

The `banners /usr/libexec/banners` entry is an option that tells `tcpd` that if it denies a connection to a service based on this entry, try to find an explanation file in this location. Use this option if you have a need to provide an explanation as to why the service is not available.

The specifications in /etc/hosts.allow make little gates through the fences erected by /etc/hosts.deny for specific host and service combinations. For example, an /etc/hosts.allow file might look like this:

```
ALL: 140.254.12.137 192.168.2. 192.168.3.
popd: 140.254.12.124 140.254.12.151 192.168.1.36
```

This file says:

- Allow connections to any TCP service from the host 140.254.12.137 and all hosts in the 192.168.2. and 192.168.3. subdomains. (Perhaps the 192.168.2. and 192.168.3. subdomains are known highly secure networks, and we really trust 140.254.12.137 because it's so well run.)
- Allow connections to the popd service for three specific machines 140.254.12.124, 140.254.12.151, and 192.168.1.36.

If used in combination with the previous /etc/hosts.deny file, these allowances still stand. They override the denials in /etc/hosts.deny, even though the 192.168.1. subdomain is denied all access except to ftpd by /etc/hosts.deny, the specific machine 192.168.1.36 has its own private gate that allows it access to the popd service as well.

Note

Services with a smile or without? There can be a bit of confusion as to the name of the service to put in an /etc/hosts.allow or /etc/hosts.deny file. If it's a service out of inetd.conf, generally the name to use is the service name from the leftmost column of the file. If this doesn't work, try adding a d to the end of the service name (ftp -> ftpd).

Other services use names that don't seem to be recorded officially anywhere. Other services that you encounter and decide to wrap with TCP Wrappers might require a bit of experimenting on your part. Thus far, my experience has been that their names are relatively easy to guess.

Now that we have seen how the traditional method of controlling TCP Wrappers works, let's take a brief look at a newer method that uses only the /etc/hosts.allow file. The newer method can be used on systems where extended option processing has been enabled. This is indeed the case with OS X. Nevertheless, either method works in OS X.

In the single file, /etc/hosts.allow, you specify allow and deny rules all in the same file. With the /etc/hosts.allow only method, tcpd reads the file on a first-match-wins basis. Consequently, it is important that your allow rules appear before your deny rules.

For example, to restrict access to `ftpd` only to our host, `140.254.12.124`, we would use these rules:

```
ftpd: 140.254.12.124 127.0.0.1 localhost: ALLOW
ftpd: ALL: DENY
```

In the first line, we allow our host, `140.254.12.124`, access to `ftpd` using various addresses that it knows for itself. On the second line, we deny access to all other hosts. If we reversed these lines, even the host that we want to allow `ftpd` access to would be denied access.

After you have sufficiently tested that you have properly set up your allow and deny rules, there is nothing else you need to do to keep TCP Wrappers running. As you are testing your rules, check your logs carefully to see where, if at all, the behaviors are logged. You will rarely see entries for `tcpd` itself in your logs, but you might see additional logging for a wrapped service under that service.

Wrapping Services to Allow Tunneling over SSH

As you saw earlier in the book, it is possible to tunnel connections over SSH. If you do decide to run the FTP service on your machine, you might be interested in restricting access to the service so that anyone who uses the service has to tunnel it through SSH. You saw in detail how to configure a Mac client running traditional Mac OS to do this. We have not yet officially seen how to configure the OS X machine to permit this.

The key to setting this up is restricting access to the desired service to your host by its IP address and as `localhost` addresses. Sometimes it can be helpful to include your machine by its name, too, but we have not encountered this problem on an OS X machine.

To restrict access to `ftpd` so that a user would have to tunnel her FTP connection, you could have an `/etc/hosts.deny` file like this:

```
ALL EXCEPT sshd: ALL
```

In this example, all services are denied except `sshd`.

In the `/etc/hosts.allow` file, add a line for your host that includes your host's IP address, `127.0.0.1` and `localhost`.

```
ftpd: 140.254.12.124 127.0.0.1 localhost
```

In this example, our host, `124.254.12.124`, is the only host allowed access to `ftpd`.

In the `/etc/hosts.allow` only method:

```
sshd: ALL: ALLOW
ftpd: 140.254.12.124 127.0.0.1 localhost: ALLOW
ftpd: ALL: DENY
```

Common Sense Preventive Measures

Before we continue any further in this chapter, we have reached a good time to point out some common sense preventive measures to provide basic security for your machine. They do not guarantee the safety of your machine, of course, but they provide good basic guidelines for you. These common sense activities apply not only to OS X, but also to any other operating system.

Common sense preventive security measures that you should always keep in mind are

- Keep your operating system current. You can easily do this by setting Software Update to a regular update schedule. If you prefer not to have Software Update check for updates automatically, make sure that you check Apple's Web site regularly for any updates and subsequently run Software Update. This is perhaps the most important common sense activity you can do.
- For OS X, do not turn on any network services that you don't need. For other operating systems, this often means turning off services you don't need, because many operating services tend to come with many network services turned on by default.
- Restrict access to the services you have to run. Using TCP Wrappers is one method for restricting access to some services.
- Replace insecure services with secure services. For many systems, this advice especially targets using `sshd` instead of `telnetd` because `sshd` typically has to be installed separately. For OS X, enabling remote login in the `Sharing` pane automatically starts `sshd`, which is included in the OS X distribution, rather than `telnetd`.
- Run services with the least privilege necessary for the job. Check the documentation for the service to see advice on this.

Using BrickHouse as an Interface to the Built-in Firewall Package

As we have already seen, OS X has basic tools available to help you secure your machine. In addition to the basic tools, OS X comes with a firewall package called `ipfw`. A nice graphical interface to configuring and using `ipfw` is a shareware product called BrickHouse, available at `http://personalpages.tds.net/~brian_hill/`.

There is another shareware graphical interface to configure the firewall package, called Firewalk X, which we will not discuss. It is available from `http://www.users.qwest.net/~mvannorsdel/firewalkx/`. We have not investigated this package. However, from the picture of the interface on the Web site, BrickHouse appears to be a friendlier package for the first-time `ipfw` user.

Preparation

Because you will probably want to see some of the before and after effects of BrickHouse, we suggest a couple commands that you might want to take a quick look at now before you get started with the application.

Run this command:

```
[localhost:/Users/joray] root# ipfw show

     65535 82606 46703351 allow ip from any to any
```

What you just did was ask `ipfw` to show you the current firewall settings. As you probably guessed, `ipfw` on OS X ships in an open state.

In order to correctly configure a firewall, you'll need to know the network interfaces being used on your system. The "ifcconfig" command displays and sets interface information on your system. Try this command, especially if you are hoping to use BrickHouse to help you set up your OS X machine as a gateway for your home network. This process will require you to correctly identify the interface of your internal (private) network and main Internet connection. `ifconfig` will be discussed at more length later in the chapter.

```
[localhost:~/security-misc] joray% ifconfig -a
lo0: flags=8049<UP,LOOPBACK,RUNNING,MULTICAST> mtu 16384
        inet 127.0.0.1 netmask 0xff000000
en0: flags=8863<UP,BROADCAST,b6,RUNNING,SIMPLEX,MULTICAST> mtu 1500
        inet 140.254.12.124 netmask 0xffffff00 broadcast 140.254.12.255
        ether 00:30:65:ca:f9:a2
        media: autoselect (100baseTX <half-duplex>) status: active
        supported media: none autoselect 10baseT/UTP <half-duplex>
            10baseT/UTP <full-duplex> 100baseTX <half-duplex> 100baseTX
➥<full-duplex>
```

The utility `ifconfig` enables you to configure interface parameters. As shown previously, `ifconfig -a` produces a full listing of available interfaces.

Because the firewall package can be tricky to work with, what you try to do in BrickHouse might make your machine completely unusable. This is no fault of BrickHouse, but you should be prepared to remove components that you might have BrickHouse install. Depending on your situation, this might be possible only in single-user mode. If you have not yet put your machine in single-user mode, we suggest you do so before doing anything in BrickHouse. If you tried single-user mode a while ago, but have forgotten what you did, take this moment to try again. Use Command+S while rebooting to get into single-user mode. The last few lines that appear are

```
Singleuser boot - fsck not done
Root device is mounted read-only
If you want to make modifications to files,
run '/sbin/fsck -y' first and then '/sbin/mount -uw /'
localhost#
```

Using BrickHouse

After you have downloaded and uncompressed the BrickHouse disk image, you are ready to start using it.

1. The Setup Assistant appears. Please note that you can also use the Setup Assistant at any time later by clicking on the Assistant button in the main BrickHouse window. The first part of the Setup Assistant is the External Network sheet, shown in Figure 31.1. Select your connection type and IP address assignment method (dynamic or static). Connection-type choices are DSL or Cable Ethernet (Regular Ethernet), Dialup Modem (PPP), DSL or Cable PPPoE, AirPort (+ External AirPort Base Station).

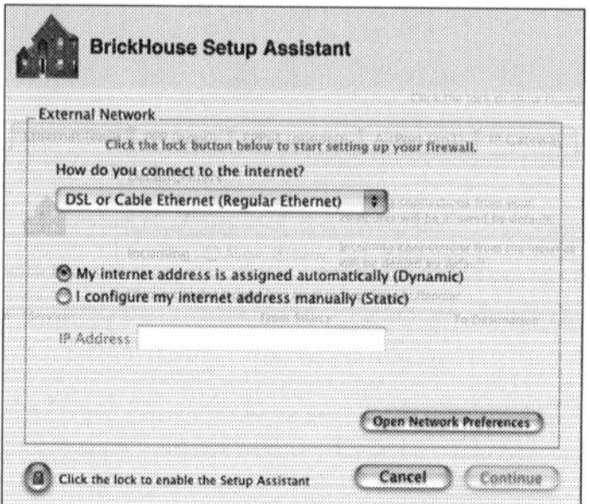

FIGURE 31.1
The BrickHouse Setup Assistant begins with your External Network settings.

2. The Public Services sheet, shown in Figure 31.2, is next. Check the boxes by the services that you want your machine to run. If you are not sure what a service is, select it and a description appears at the bottom of the window. Don't forget to check the appropriate AppleTalk services, if you typically share your machine over an AppleTalk network.
3. The Blocked Services sheet, shown in Figure 31.3, is where you select specific ports to be blocked. The list primarily includes ports aimed at various known attacks. The sheet notes that incoming traffic is blocked by default.

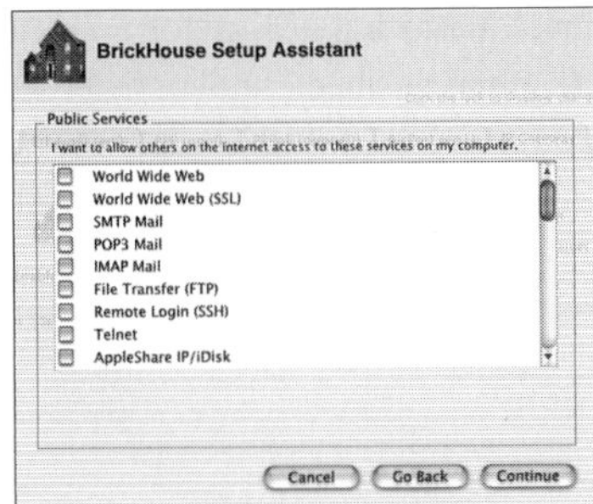

FIGURE 31.2
In the Public Services sheet, select the services you want your machine to run.

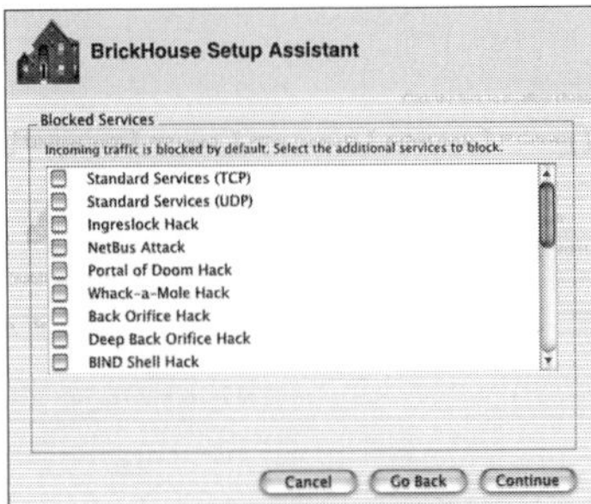

FIGURE 31.3
In the Blocked Services sheet, select additional ports to have blocked.

4. The next sheet to appear is the Firewall Setup Complete sheet, shown in Figure 31.4. To enable the configuration, click Apply Configuration. To install a startup script, click Install Startup Script. If you are interested in using your OS X machine as a gateway for an internal network, click the Setup IP Sharing button. If you decide you want to make changes to your configuration, you can make changes in the main window and apply a new configuration. Additionally, you can install or remove a startup script under the application's `Options` menu.

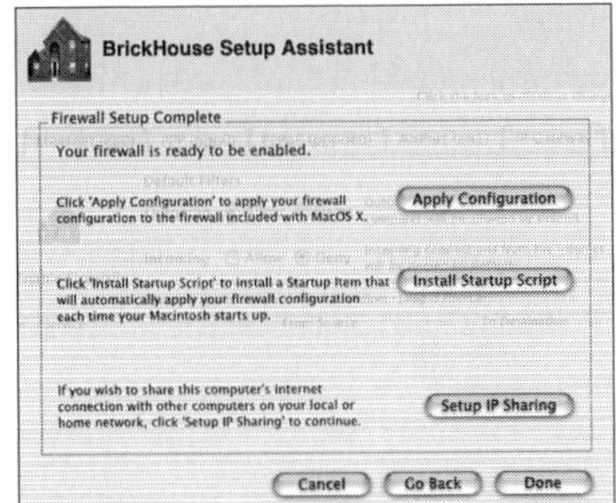

FIGURE 31.4
In the Firewall Setup Complete sheet, you can preliminarily finalize your setup, or you can continue your setup by clicking on the Setup IP Sharing button to configure your machine to serve as a gateway for an internal network.

5. If you plan to set up your OS X machine as a gateway for your internal network, the next sheet that appears is the IP Sharing sheet, shown in Figure 31.5. Here you select how your machine connects to the internal network and what internal IP address should be used for the machine. Connection choices are Ethernet Card (en0), AirPort or Second Ethernet Card (en1).

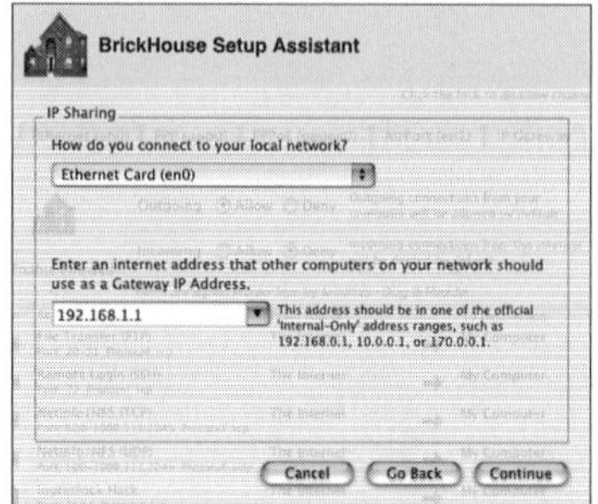

FIGURE 31.5
Make specifications about your local network in the IP Sharing sheet.

After you are done with this sheet, this version of BrickHouse then displays another sheet giving you instructions on starting IP Sharing in BrickHouse. At this time, BrickHouse does not configure IP Sharing to start at boot time.

You have just completed the initial BrickHouse setup. Now let's take the time to examine the rest of the BrickHouse interface. The default interface is the Quick Configuration, shown in Figure 31.6. The filters you selected during the setup process are shown under the tab for your interface. The IP Gateway tab shows information that pertains to any IP sharing that you might have set up.

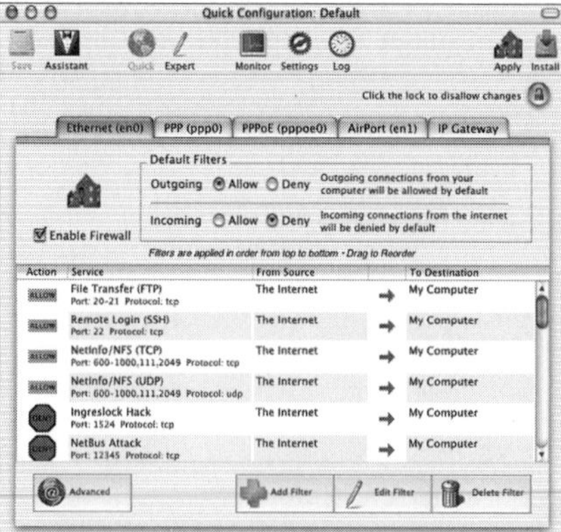

FIGURE 31.6
The default BrickHouse interface is the Quick Configuration interface.

The Advanced button, shown in Figure 31.7, allows you to edit some additional settings involving rules for some select protocols, DHCP, and your domain name service. The bottom-right buttons allow you to add, edit, and delete filters. When you add a filter, you can choose among the same options you saw in the Setup Assistant, as well as Custom Service, which allows you to specify a port or port range. The interface for adding a filter is shown in Figure 31.8. You can rearrange the order of filter rules by dragging them around in the main window.

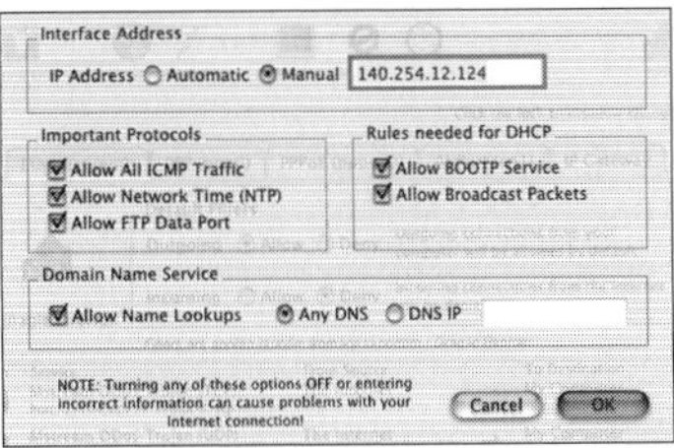

FIGURE 31.7
The Advanced button allows you to edit rules involving some select protocols, DHCP, and your domain name service.

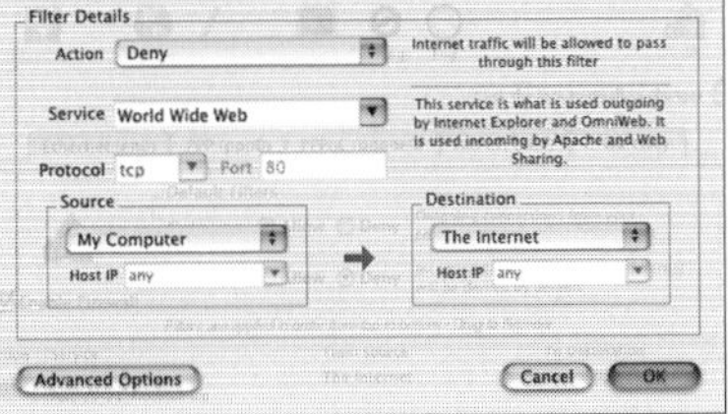

FIGURE 31.8
The Add Filter button opens this sheet, where you can add another filter. Specify the action, service, protocol, port, source host, and destination host.

From the toolbar, you can access the Setup Assistant anytime by clicking on the Assistant button. The Setup Assistant always starts from scratch. The Monitor button allows you to monitor the firewall. A sample of what it looks like is shown in Figure 31.9.

Settings allows you to manipulate settings files. You can duplicate, rename, delete, import, or export. By clicking the Log button, you can access the Daily Firewall Log window, shown in Figure 31.10, from which you can enable logging. If you want to have logging enabled at startup, be sure to reinstall the startup script, which you can do by either clicking the Install button or under the Options menu. Even if you don't think you want to have logging all the time, you might find having logging on at this stage to be a way to help you troubleshoot problems with the firewall configuration.

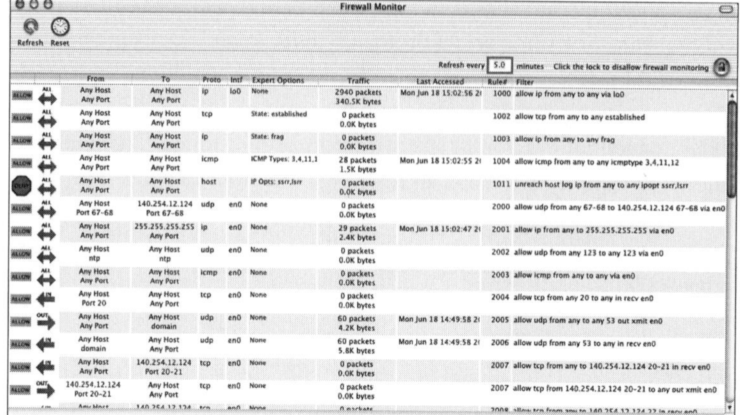

FIGURE 31.9
The Firewall Monitor window is where you can monitor the firewall's activity.

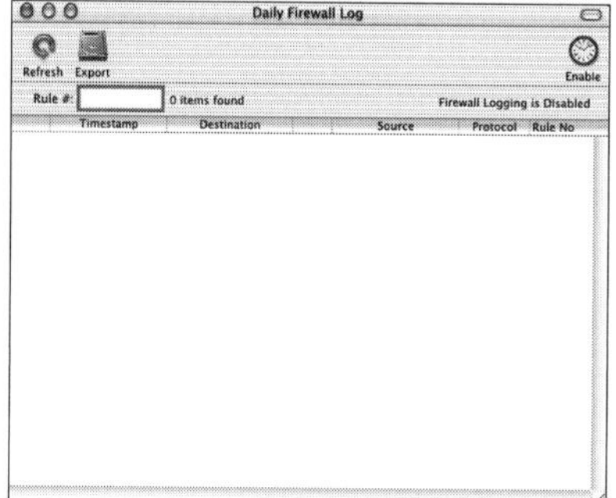

FIGURE 31.10
Click the Enable button at the right in the Daily Firewall Log window to enable firewall logging. If you want to enable logging at startup, reinstall the startup script.

In addition to the default Quick Configuration mode is an Expert Configuration mode, accessible from the Expert button. The Expert Configuration window, shown in Figure 31.11, is a split window that displays the rules that are being passed to `ipfw` as well as a configuration file for `natd`, which redirects packets to another machine if you configured your machine as a gateway.

It is worthwhile to experiment with some filters that you might be most concerned about while you are still in the BrickHouse interface. With each set you want to try, just click the Apply button to apply those settings. The Quick Configuration mode is useful for adding basic filters, whereas the Expert Configuration mode allows you to tweak the configuration. After you have a set that you are happy with, don't forget to save the settings. If you were working in the Expert Configuration mode, you might also want to save the settings in a text file in a terminal window, just to be sure that you can easily find the file without the graphical interface. After you are relatively satisfied with the results, install the startup script if you want the firewall to start at startup.

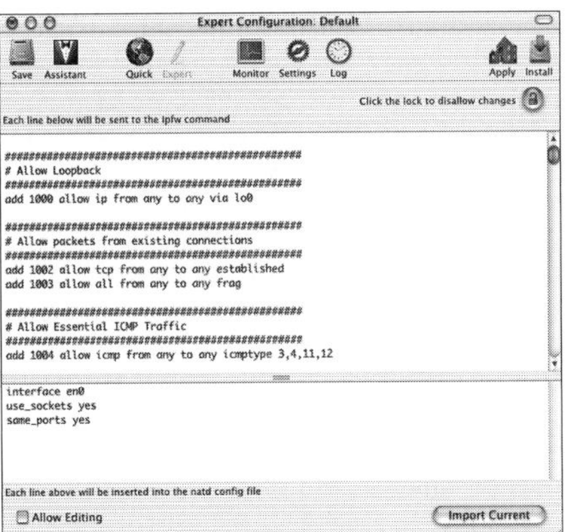

FIGURE 31.11
In the Expert Configuration window, you can edit the firewall rules more precisely.

If your OS X machine is an NFS client, do not test to see whether the mounts still work in the graphical interface. If your mounts are not working properly, you will hang your console when you check. If you check in the terminal, you will be able to continue testing until you are finally satisfied. For an OS X machine that is an NFS client, you might ultimately find it necessary to add a line in the Expert mode that allows all traffic from your NFS server.

Finally, you should be aware of the options available under the Options menu: Allow Changes, Quick Configuration, Expert Configuration, Apply Settings, Install Startup Script, Clear All Rules, Remove Startup Script. Only some of those options are available in the toolbar.

When you are satisfied with your firewall configuration, reboot your machine—especially if you had BrickHouse install a startup script for you. This tells you exactly what behavior to expect from the firewall starting from scratch. If something undesirable occurs, the potential cause for the behavior is fresh in your mind and more easily fixed.

Behind the Scenes

So, what are some of the things that BrickHouse did for you?

First, if you decided to have BrickHouse install a startup script for you, you should have noticed a comment about the firewall starting.

Run the first command that you ran before you started:

```
[localhost:/Users/joray] root# ipfw show

01000 10656 1346992 allow ip from any to any via lo0
01002   607   40266 allow tcp from any to any established
01003     0       0 allow ip from any to any frag
```

```
01004   408   22848 allow icmp from any to any icmptype 3,4,11,12
01011     0       0 unreach host log ip from any to any ipopt ssrr,lsrr
01999     0       0 allow udp from any 67-68 to 140.254.12.124 67-68 via en0
02000   244   29380 allow ip from any to 255.255.255.255 via en0
02001     0       0 allow udp from any 123 to any 123 via en0
02002     0       0 allow icmp from any to any via en0
02003     0       0 allow tcp from any 20 to any in recv en0
02005    89    6372 allow udp from any to any 53 out xmit en0
02006    89   10357 allow udp from any 53 to any in recv en0
02007     0       0 allow tcp from any to 140.254.12.124 20-21 in recv en0
02007     0       0 allow tcp from 140.254.12.124 20-21 to any out xmit en0
02008     3     144 allow tcp from any to 140.254.12.124 22 in recv en0
02008     0       0 allow tcp from 140.254.12.124 22 to any out xmit en0
02010     0       0 allow tcp from any to 140.254.12.124 548 in recv en0
02010     0       0 allow tcp from 140.254.12.124 548 to any out xmit en0
02011     0       0 allow udp from any to 140.254.12.124 427 in recv en0
02011     0       0 allow udp from 140.254.12.124 427 to any out xmit en0
02012     0       0 allow tcp from any to 140.254.12.124 600-1000,111,2049 in
                  ➥recv en0
02012     0       0 allow tcp from 140.254.12.124 600-1000,111,2049 to any out
                  ➥xmit en0
02013     0       0 allow udp from any to 140.254.12.124 600-1000,111,2049 in
                  ➥recv en0
02013     0       0 allow udp from 140.254.12.124 600-1000,111,2049 to any out
                  ➥xmit en0
02014     0       0 deny log tcp from any to 140.254.12.124 1524 in recv en0
02015     0       0 deny log tcp from any to 140.254.12.124 12345 in recv en0
02016     0       0 deny log udp from any to 140.254.12.124 10067 in recv en0
02017     0       0 deny log tcp from any to 140.254.12.124 12361 in recv en0
02018     0       0 deny log udp from any to 140.254.12.124 31337 in recv en0
02019     0       0 deny log udp from any to 140.254.12.124 31338 in recv en0
02020     0       0 deny log tcp from any to 140.254.12.124 31337 in recv en0
02021     0       0 deny log udp from any to 140.254.12.124 2140 in recv en0
02022     0       0 deny log udp from any to 140.254.12.124 31785 in recv en0
02023     0       0 deny log tcp from any to 140.254.12.124 31789,31791 in recv
                  ➥ en0
02024     0       0 deny log tcp from any to 140.254.12.124 21554 in recv en0
02025     0       0 deny log tcp from any to 140.254.12.124 6969 in recv en0
02026     0       0 deny log tcp from any to 140.254.12.124 23456 in recv en0
02027     0       0 deny log tcp from any to 140.254.12.124 1243,6776 in recv
                  ➥en0
02028     0       0 deny log tcp from any to 140.254.12.124 15104,12754 in recv
                  ➥en0
02029     0       0 deny log udp from any to 140.254.12.124 10498,6838 in recv
                  ➥en0
02030     0       0 deny log udp from any to 140.254.12.124 31335 in recv en0
02031     0       0 deny log tcp from any to 140.254.12.124 27665,27444 in recv
                  ➥en0
02032     0       0 deny log tcp from any to 140.254.12.124 20432 in recv en0
02033     0       0 deny log udp from any to 140.254.12.124 18753,20433 in recv
                  ➥en0
```

```
52034   304   20021 allow ip from 140.254.12.124 to any out xmit en0
52035     0       0 deny log ip from any to 140.254.12.124 in recv en0
65535 13048 1498445 allow ip from any to any
```

You should now have a bit more output than you did previously. The open rule, which was the only rule before you started, is now the last rule. The Firewall Monitor in BrickHouse appears to be a graphical view of `ipfw show`.

Next run `ifconfig -a` again:

```
[localhost:~/brickhouse-misc] joray% ifconfig -a

lo0: flags=8049<UP,LOOPBACK,RUNNING,MULTICAST> mtu 16384
        inet 127.0.0.1 netmask 0xff000000
en0: flags=8863<UP,BROADCAST,b6,RUNNING,SIMPLEX,MULTICAST> mtu 1500
        inet 140.254.12.124 netmask 0xffffff00 broadcast 140.254.12.255
        inet 192.168.1.1 netmask 0xffffff00 broadcast 192.168.1.255
        ether 00:30:65:ca:f9:a2
        media: autoselect (100baseTX <half-duplex>) status: active
        supported media: none autoselect 10baseT/UTP <half-duplex> 10baseT/UTP
        <full-duplex> 100baseTX <half-duplex> 100baseTX <full-duplex>
```

If you configured your machine to be a gateway, you should now see information about your machine's interface to the internal and external networks. If you did not configure your machine to be a gateway, you should see no changes. Command documentation for `ifconfig` is included in Table 31.1.

TABLE 31.1 Command Documentation Table for `ifconfig`

`ifconfig`	Configures network interface parameters.
`ifconfig` *<interface> <address_family>* [*<address>* [*<dest address>*]] [*<parameters>*]	
`ifconfig` *<interface>* [*<protocol family>*]	
`ifconfig -a [-d] [-u]` [*<address family>*]	
`ifconfig -l [-d] [-u]` [*<address family>*]	
`ifconfig` assigns an address to a network interface and/or configures network interface parameters. It must be used at boot time to define the network address of each network interface. It may also be used at a later time to redefine an interface's network address or other operating parameters.	
Only the super user can modify the configuration of a network interface.	
`-a`	Produces a full listing of all available interfaces.
`-l`	Produces a name-only listing of all available interfaces.
`-d`	Limits a listing to those interfaces that are down.

TABLE 31.1 continued

-u	Limits a listing to those interfaces that are up.
Available operands for `ifconfig` are	
<address>	For the DARPA-Internet family, the address is either a hostname in the hostname database or a DARPA-Internet address expressed in the Internet standard dot notation.
<address family>	Specifies the *<address family>*, which affects interpretation of the remaining parameters. The address or protocol families currently supported are `inet`, `iso`, and `ns`.
<interface>	*<interface>* parameter is a string of the form *<name physical unit>*, such as `en0`.
The following parameters may be set with `ifconfig`:	
alias	Establishes an additional network address for this interface. This is sometimes useful when changing network numbers, while still accepting packets for the old interface. A *<netmask>* should be used with this parameter. If the new *<alias>* address is on the same subnet as an existing address assigned to this interface, the netmask must be `255.255.255.255`. If a netmask is not supplied, the command will use the one implied by the address itself. If the *all ones* netmask is used, the system will handle route installation. If another is used, a route to that address may have to be added by hand; for example, `route add -host xx.xx.xx.xx -interface 127.0.0.1`, where `xx.xx.xx.xx` is the alias. In either case, the route might have to be deleted by hand when the alias is removed (`-alias` or `delete`).
arp	Enables the use of the Address Resolution Protocol in mapping between network-level addresses and link-level addresses (default). This is currently implemented for mapping between DARPA-Internet addresses and 10 Mb/s Ethernet addresses.
-arp	Disables the use of the Address Resolution Protocol.
broadcast	(`inet` only) Specifies the address to use to represent broadcasts to the network. The default broadcast address is the address with a host part of all 1s.
debug	Enables driver-dependent bugging code. This usually turns on extra console logging.
-debug	Disables driver-dependent debugging code.

TABLE 31.1 continued

`delete`	Removes the network address specified. This would be used if you incorrectly specified an alias or it was no longer needed.
`dest_addr`	Specifies the address of the correspondent on the other end of a point-to-point link.
`down`	Marks an interface down. When an interface is marked down, the system does not attempt to transmit messages through that interface. If possible, the interface is reset to disable reception as well. This does not automatically disable routes using the interface.
`ipdst`	Specifies an Internet host to receive IP packets encapsulating NS packets bound for a remote network.
`metric` *<n>*	Sets the routing metric of the interface to *<n>*, default `0`. The routing metric is used by the routing protocol. Higher metrics make a less favorable route. Metrics are counted as addition hops to the destination network or host.
`netmask` *<mask>*	(`inet` and `ISO`) Specifies how much of the address to reserve for subdividing networks into subnetworks. The mask includes the network part of the local address and the subnet part, which is taken from the host field of the address. The mask can be specified as a single hexadecimal number beginning with 0x, as a dot-notation Internet address, or as a pseudo-network name listed in the network table networks. The mask contains 1s for the bit positions in the 32-bit address that are to be used for the network and subnet parts, and 0s for the host part.
`nsellength` *<n>*	(ISO only) Specifies a trailing number of bytes for a received NSAP used for local identification, the remaining leading part of which, is taken to be the NET (Network Entity Title). The default is `1`, which is conformant to US GOSIP. When an ISO address is set in an `ifconfig`, it is really the NSAP that is being specified.
`trailers`	Requests the use of a trailer-link-level encapsulation when sending (default). If a network interface supports trailers, the system encapsulates outgoing messages so that the number of memory-to-memory-copy operations performed by the receiver is minimized. On networks that support Address Resolution Protocol, this flag indicates that the system should request that other systems use trailers when sending to this host. Currently used by Internet protocols only.

TABLE 31.1 continued

`-trailers`	Disables the use of a trailer link level encapsulation.
`link[0-2]`	Enables special processing of the link level of the interface.
`-link[0-2]`	Disables special processing at the link level with the specified interface.
`up`	Marks an interface up. Can be used to enable an interface after `ifconfig down` has been run. It happens automatically when setting the first address on an interface. If the interface was reset when previously marked down, the hardware is reinitialized.

If you had BrickHouse install a startup script, you now have a `/Library/StartupItems/Firewall` directory:

```
[localhost:~] joray% ls -l /Library/StartupItems/Firewall
     total 24
     -rwxrwxr-x  1 root  admin   535 Jun 19 11:30 Firewall
     -rw-rw-r—   1 root  admin   552 Jun 19 11:30 StartupParameters.plist
     -rwxrwxr-x  1 root  admin  2393 Jun 19 11:30 openniports.pl
```

Just as you saw earlier in the book with fonts and sounds, you can also place local startup items in the `/Library` directory, following the basic structure seen in `/System`; in this case, `/Library/StartupItems`. Here is a sample startup script installed by BrickHouse to start the firewall and its logging facilities:

```
[localhost:~] joray% more /Library/StartupItems/Firewall/Firewall
     #!/bin/sh
     # Firewall Boot Script
     # Generated by BrickHouse


     #============================================================
     # Enable IP Firewall Logging
     #============================================================
     /usr/sbin/sysctl -w net.inet.ip.fw.verbose=1

     # Put a limit on each rule's logging
     /usr/sbin/sysctl -w net.inet.ip.fw.verbose_limit=500

     #============================================================
     # Process Firewall Rules File
     #============================================================
     /sbin/ipfw -q /etc/firewall.conf
```

As you can see from the startup script, BrickHouse installed a configuration file that it called `firewall.conf` in `/etc`. Look at the configuration file, especially if you did not switch to the `Expert Configuration` mode in BrickHouse. The file is nicely commented. If you need to make additional changes to the ruleset, you can do so either in the BrickHouse interface, or you can edit the `/etc/firewall.conf` file directly. Be sure to check the `ifpw` man page for specific details. This configuration file works in a similar manner to the newer TCP Wrappers configuration method. The `ipfw` program reads the configuration file on a first-match-wins basis.

The general format of the lines the BrickHouse created in the `/etc/firewall.conf` file is

```
add <rule_number> <action> <protocol> from <source> to
    ➥<destination> [<options>] [via <interface>]
```

If you selected AppleShare as one of your services, you have entries that look approximately like this:

```
####################################################
## AppleShare IP/iDisk
####################################################
add 2010 allow tcp from any to 140.254.12.124 548 in via en0
add 2010 allow tcp from 140.254.12.124 548 to any out via en0
```

The first line is a rule that enables incoming `tcp` packets from any host to the host machine on port 548 via the interface `en0`. The second AppleShare rule enables outgoing `tcp` packets from the host machine on port 548 to any host via the `en0` interface.

As mentioned in the previous section, if your OS X machine is an NFS client, you might have to allow all incoming packets to the NFS server. You could do that with a rule like this:

```
add <rule_number> allow ip from <NFS_Server-IP> to <host_IP> via en0
```

The `ip` packet description means all packets. You can also use `all`. Command documentation for `ipfw` is included in Table 31.2.

TABLE 31.2 Command Documentation Table for `ipfw`

`ipfw`	Controlling utility for IP firewall
`ipfw [-q] [-p <preproc> [-D <macro>[=<value>]] [-U <macro>] <file>`	
`ipfw [-f | -q] flush`	
`ipfw [-q] zero [<number> ...]`	
`ipfw delete <number> ...`	
`ipfw [-aftN] list [<number>...]`	

TABLE 31.2 continued

```
ipfw [-ftN] show [<number>...]
```

```
ipfw [-q] add [<number>] <action> [log] <proto> from <src> to <dst>
[via <name> | <ipno>] [<options>]
```

If used as shown in the first line, a `<file>` is read line by line and applied as arguments to `ipfw`.

A preprocessor can be specified using `-p <preproc>` where `<file>` is to be piped through. Typical preprocessors include `m4` and `cpp`. Optional `-D` and `-U` macro specifications can be given to pass on to the preprocessor.

Each incoming and outgoing packet is sent through the `ipfw` rules. In the case of a host acting as a gateway, packets that are forwarded by the host are processed twice—once when entering and once when leaving. Each packet can be filtered based on the following associated information:

Receive Interface (`recv`)	Interface over which the packet was received.
Transmit Interface (`xmit`)	Interface over which packet would be transmitted.
Incoming (`in`)	Packet was just received.
Outgoing (`out`)	Packet would be transmitted.
Source IP Address	Sender's IP address.
Destination IP Address	Target's IP address.
Protocol	IP protocol, including but not limited to IP (`ip`), UDP (`udp`), TCP (`tcp`), ICMP (`icmp`).
Source Port	Sender's `UDP` or `TCP` port.
Destination Port	Target's `UDP` or `TCP` port.
Connection Setup Flag (`setup`)	Packet is a request to set up a TCP connection.
Connection Established Flag (`established`)	Packet is part of an established TCP connection.
All TCP Flags (`tcpflags`)	One or more of the TCP flags: close connection (`fin`), open connection (`syn`), reset connection (`rst`), push (`psh`), acknowledgement (`ack`), urgent (`urg`) .
Fragment Flag (`frag`)	Packet is a fragment of an IP packet.
IP Options (`ipoptions`)	One or more IP options: strict source route (`ssrr`), loose source route (`lsrr`), record route (`rr`), timestamp (`ts`).
ICMP Types (`icmptypes`)	One or more of the ICMP types: echo reply (`0`), destination unreachable (`3`), source quench (`4`), redirect (`5`), echo request (`8`), router advertisement (`9`), router solicitation (`10`), time-to-live exceeded (`11`), IP header bad (`12`), timestamp request (`13`), timestamp reply (`14`), information request (`15`), information reply (`16`), address mask request (`17`), address mask reply (`18`).

TABLE 31.2 continued

Note that it may be dangerous to filter on source IP address or source TCP/UDP port because either or both could be spoofed.

The `ipfw` utility works by going through the rule list for each packet until a match is found. All rules have two associated counters: a packet count and a byte count. These are updated when a packet matches the rule.

Rules are ordered by line number, from `1` to `65534`. Rules are tried in increasing order, with the first matching rule being the one that applies. Multiple rules might have the same number and are applied in the order they were added.

If a rule is added without a number, it is numbered `100` higher than the highest defined rule number unless the highest rule number is `65435` or greater, in which case the new rules are given that same number.

One rule is always present: `65535 deny all from any to any.`

This rule, not to allow anything, is the default policy.

If the kernel option `IPFIREWALL_DEFAULT_TO_ACCEPT` has been enabled, the default rule is `65535 allow all from any to any.`

The previous rule is the default rule in OS X.

`Add`	Adds a rule.
`delete`	Deletes the first rule with number *<number>*, if any.
`List`	Prints out the current rule set.
`show`	Equivalent to `ipfw -a list`.
`zero`	Zeroes the counters associated with rule number *<number>*.
`flush`	Removes all rules.

The following options are available:

`-q`	Uses quiet mode when adding, flushing, or zeroing (implies `-f`). Useful for adjusting rules by executing multiple `ipfw` commands in a script.
`-f`	Does not ask for confirmation for commands that can cause problems if misused (for example, `flush`).
`-a`	Shows counter values while listing. See also `show`.
`-t`	Shows last match timestamp while listing.
`-N`	Tries to resolve addresses and service names in output.

Available options for *<action>*:

`allow`	Allows packets that match rule. The search terminates. Aliases are `pass`, `permit`, `accept`.

TABLE 31.2 continued

`deny`	Discards packets that match rule. The search terminates. Alias is `drop`.
`reject`	(Deprecated) Discards packets that match `rule`, and tries to send an ICMP host unreachable notice. The search terminates.
`unreach <code>`	Discards packets that match rule, and tries to send an ICMP unreachable notice with code `<code>`, where `<code>` is a number from `0` to `255`, or one of these aliases: `net`, `host`, `protocol`, `port`, `needfrag`, `srcfail`, `net-unknown`, `host-unknown`, `isolated`, `net-prohib`, `host-prohib`, `tosnet`, `toshost`, `filter-prohib`, `host-precedence`, `precedence-cutoff`. The search terminates.
`reset`	TCP packets only. Discards packets that match rule, and tries to send a TCP reset (`RST`) notice. The search terminates.
`count`	Updates counters for all packets that match rule. The search continues with the next rule.
`divert <port>`	Diverts packets that match rule to divert (4) socket bound to port `<port>`. The search terminates.
`tee <port>`	Sends a copy of packets matching rule to the divert (4) socket bound to port `<port>`. The search terminates.
`fwd <ipaddr> [,<port>]`	Changes to the next hop on matching packets to `<ipaddr>`, which can be a dotted quad address or hostname. If `<ipaddr>` is not directly reachable, the route as found in the local routing table for that IP address is used instead. If `<ipaddr>` is a local address, when a packet enters the system from a remote host, it is diverted to `<port>` on the local machine, keeping the local address of the socket set to the original IP address for which the packet was destined. This is intended for use with transparent proxy servers. If `<ipaddr>` is not a local address, then `<port>`, if specified, is ignored, and the rule applies only to packets leaving the system. If `<port>` is not given, the port in the packet is used instead. The kernel must have been compiled with option `IPFIREWALL_FORWARD`.
`skipto <number>`	Skips subsequent rules numbered less than `<number>`. The search continues with the first rule numbered `<number>` or higher.

TABLE 31.2 continued

If a packet matches more than one divert and/or tee rule, all but the last are ignored.

If the kernel was compiled with IPFIREWALL_VERBOSE, when a packet matches a rule with the log keyword, a message is printed on the console. If the kernel was compiled with IPFIREWALL_VERBOSE_LIMIT, logging ceases after the number of packets specified by the option is received for that particular entry. Logging can then be re-enabled by clearing the packet counter for that entry.

Console logging and the log limit are adjustable dynamically through the sysctl (8) interface.

Available options for *<proto>*:

Ip	Matches all packets. The same as the alias all.
Tcp	Matches only TCP packets.
Udp	Matches only UDP packets.
Icmp	Matches only ICMP packets.
<number|name>	Matches only packets for the specified protocol. See

/etc/protocols for a complete list.

<src> and *<dst>* have the form

<address/mask> [*<ports>*]

<address/mask> may be specified as

Ipno	Has the form 1.2.3.4. Only this exact number matches the rule.
Ipno/bits	Has the form 1.2.3.4/24. In this case, all IP numbers from 1.2.3.0 to 1.2.3.255 match.
Ipno:mask	Has the form 1.2.3.4:255.255.240.0. In this case, all IP numbers from 1.2.0.0 to 1.2.15.255 match.

The sense of match can be inverted by preceding an address with the not modifier, causing all other addresses to match instead. This does not affect the selection of port numbers.

Rules can apply to packets when they are incoming or outgoing or both. The keyword in indicates that the rule should only match incoming packets. The keyword out indicates that the rule should only match outgoing packets.

To match packets going through a certain interface, specify the interface with via.

via *<ifX>*	Matches packets going through the interface *<ifX>*.
via *<if*>*	Matches packets going through the interface *<if*>*, where * is any unit.
via any	Matches packets going through some interface.
via ipno	Matches packets going through the interface having the IP address *<ipno>*.

TABLE 31.2 continued

The keyword `via` causes the interface to always be checked. If `recv` or `xmit` is used instead, only the `receive` or `transmit` interface (respectively) is checked. By specifying both, it is possible to match packets based on both `receive` and `transmit` interfaces; for example:

```
ipfw add 100 deny ip from any to any out recv en0 xmit en1
```

The `recv` interface can be tested on either incoming or outgoing packets, while the `xmit` interface can only be tested on outgoing packets. So `out` is required (an `in` is invalid) whenever `xmit` is used. Specifying `via` together with `xmit` or `recv` is invalid.

Options available for <*options*>:

`frag`	Matches if the packet is a fragment and it is not the first fragment of the datagram. `frag` cannot be used in conjunction with either `tcpflags` or TCP/UDP port specifications.
`in`	Matches if the packet was on the way in.
`out`	Matches if the packet was on the way out.
`ipoptions` <*spec*>	Matches if the IP header contains the comma-separated list of options specified in <*spec*>. The supported IP options are `ssrr` (strict source route), `lsrr` (loose source route), `rr` (record packet route), and `ts` (timestamp). The absence of a particular option may be denoted with a `!`.
`established`	TCP packets only. Matches packets that have the RST or ACK bits set.
`setup`	TCP packets only. Matches packets that have the SYN bit set but no ACK bit.
`tcpflags` <*spec*>	Matches if the TCP header contains the comma-separated list of flags specified in <*spec*>. The supported TCP flags are `fin`, `syn`, `rst`, `psh`, `ack`, and `urg`. The absence of a particular flag may be denoted by an `!`. A rule that contains a `tcpflags` specification can never match a fragmented packet that has a non-zero offset.
`icmptypes` <*types*>	Matches if the ICMP type is in the list <*types*>. The list may be specified as any combination of ranges or individual types separated by commas.

Important points to consider when designing your rules:

Remember that you filter both packets going in and out. Most connections need packets going in both directions.

Remember to test very carefully. It is a good idea to be at the console at the time.

Don't forget the `loopback` interface.

BrickHouse might also have installed a configuration file, `/etc/natd.conf`, for `natd`. Here is a sample `/etc/natd.conf` created by BrickHouse:

```
interface en0
use_sockets yes
same_ports yes
```

This configuration file specifies the interface to be used. In addition, the `use_sockets` option is included as well as the `same_ports` option. The `use_sockets` option allocates a socket for the connection, and is useful for guaranteeing connections when ports conflict. The `same_ports` option specifies that `natd` should try to keep the same port number when altering outgoing packets. This also aids in guaranteeing the success of the connection. Command documentation for `natd` is included in Table 31.3.

TABLE 31.3 Command Documentation Table for `natd`

`natd`	Network Address Translation Daemon
`natd [-ldsmvu] [-dynamic] [-i` *<inport>*`] [-o` *<outport>*`] [-p` *<port>*`]`	
`[-a` *<address>*`] [-n` *<interface>*`] [-f` *<configfile>*`]`	
`natd [-log] [-deny_incoming] [-log_denied] [-use_sockets] [-same_ports] [-verbose] [-log_facility` *<facility_name>*`] [-unregistered_only]`	
`[-dynamic] [-inport <inport>] [-outport` *<outport>*`] [-port` *<port>*`]`	
`[-alias_address` *<address>*`] [-interface` *<interface>*`] [-config` *<configfile>*`] [-redirect_port` *<linkspec>*`] [-redirect_address` *<localIP>* *<publicIP>*`] [-reverse] [-proxy_only] [-proxy_rule` *<proxyspec>*`] [-pptalias` *<localIP>*`]`	
`natd` provides a Network Address Translation facility for use with divert (4) sockets. It is intended for use only with NICs—if you want to do NAT on a PPP link, use the `-alias` switch to ppp (8).	
`natd` normally runs in the background as a daemon. It is passed raw IP packets as they travel into and out of the machine, and will possibly change these before reinjecting them back into the IP packet stream.	
`natd` changes all packets destined for another host so that their source IP number is that of the current machine. For each packet changed in this way, an internal table entry is created to record this fact. The source port number is also changed to indicate the table entry applying to the packet. Packets that are received with a target IP of the current host are checked against this internal table. If an entry is found, it is used to determine the correct target IP number and port to place in the packet.	
`-l`	
`-log`	Logs various aliasing statistics and information to the file `/var/log/alias.log`. This file is truncated each time `natd` is started.

TABLE 31.3 continued

`-d`	
`-deny_incoming`	Rejects packets destined for the current IP number that have no entry in the internal translation table.
`-s`	
`-use_sockets`	Allocates a socket (2) to establish an FTP data or `IRC DCC send` connection. This option uses more system resources, but guarantees successful connections when port numbers conflict.
`-m`	
`-same_ports`	Tries to keep the same port number when allocating outgoing packets. With this option, protocols such as `RPC` will have a better chance of working. If it is not possible to maintain the port number, it will be silently changed as per normal.
`-v`	
`-verbose`	Doesn't call `fork` (2) or `daemon` (3) on startup. Instead, it stays attached to the controlling terminal and displays all packet alterations to the standard output. This option should be used only for debugging.
`-u`	
`-unregistered_only`	Only alters outgoing packets with an unregistered source address. According to `RFC 1918`, unregistered source addresses are `10.0.0.0/8`, `176.16.0.0/12`, `192.168.0.0/16`.
`-log_denied`	Logs denied incoming packets via `syslog` (see also `log_facility`)
`-log_facility` <*facility_name*>	Uses specified log facility when logging information via `syslog`. Facility names as in `syslog.conf` (5).
`-dynamic`	If the `-n` or `-interface` option is used, `natd` monitors the routing socket for alterations to the <*interface*> passed. If the interface IP number is changed, `natd` will dynamically alter its concept of the alias address.
`-i` <*inport*>	
`-inport` <*inport*>	Reads from and writes to <*inport*>, treating all packets as packets coming into the machine.

TABLE 31.3 continued

`-o <output>`	
`-outport` *`<outport>`*	Reads from and writes to *`<outport>`*, treating all packets as packets going out of the machine.
`-p` *`<port>`*	
`-port` *`<port>`*	Reads from and writes to *`<port>`*, distinguishing packets as incoming or outgoing using the rules specified in divert. If *`<port>`* is not numeric, it is searched for in the `/etc/services` database. If this flag is not specified, the divert port named `natd` is used as a default.
`-a` *`<address>`*	
`-alias_address` *`<address>`*	Uses *`<address>`* as the alias address. If this option is not specified, the `-n` or `-interface` option must be used. The specified address should be the address assigned to the public-network interface. All data passing out through this address's interface is rewritten with a source address equal to *`<address>`*. All data arriving at the interface from outside is checked to see if it matches any already-aliased outgoing connection. If it does, the packet is altered accordingly. If not, all `-redirect_port` and `-redirect_address` assignments are checked and acted on. If no other action can be made, and if `-deny_incoming` is not specified, the packet is delivered to the local machine and port as specified in the packet.
`-n <interface>`	
`-interface` *`<interface>`*	Uses *`<interface>`* to determine the alias address. If there is a possibility that the IP number associated with *`<interface>`* might change, the `-dynamic` flag should also be used. If this option is not specified, the `-a` or `-alias_address` flag must be used. The specified *`<interface>`* must be the public network interface.
`-f <configfile>`	
`-config` *`<configfile>`*	Reads the configuration from *`<configfile>`*. *`<configfile>`* contains a list of options, one per line, in the same form as the long form of the command-line flags. For example, the line `alias_address 158.152.17.1` specifies an alias address of `158.152.17.1`. Options that don't take an argument are specified with an option of yes or no in the configuration file. For example, the line

TABLE 31.3 continued

	`-log yes` is synonymous with `-log`. Empty lines and lines beginning with # are ignored.
`-redirect_port` *<proto>* *<targetIP>*:*<targetPORT>* [*<aliasIP>*:]*<aliasPORT>* [*<remoteIP>*[:*<remotePORT>*]]	Redirects incoming connections arriving to given port to another host and port. *<proto>* is either `tcp` or `udp`; *<targetIP>* is the desired target IP number; *<targetPORT>* is the desired target PORT number; *<aliasPORT>* is the requested PORT Number and *<aliasIP>* if the aliasing address. *<remoteIP>* and *<remotePORT>* can be used to specify the connection more accurately, if necessary. For example, the argument `tcp inside1:telnet 6666` means that TCP packets destined for port `6666` on this machine will be sent to the `telnet` port on the `inside1` machine.
	`-redirect_address` *<localIP>* *<publicIP>* Redirects traffic for public IP address to a machine on the local network. This function, known as `static NAT`, is normally useful if your ISP has allocated a small block of IP addresses to you, but it can be used in the case of a single address: `redirect_address 10.0.0.8 0.0.0.0` The previous command would redirect incoming traffic to machine `10.0.0.8`. If several address aliases specify the same public address as follows `redirect_address 192.168.0.2` *<public_addr>* `redirect_address 192.168.0.3` *<public_addr>* `redirect_address 192.168.0.4` *<public_addr>* The incoming traffic will be directed to the last translated local address (`192.168.0.4`), but outgoing traffic to the first two addresses will be aliased to the specified public address.
`-reverse`	Reverses operation of `natd`. This can be useful in some transparent proxying situations when outgoing traffic is redirected to the local machine and `natd` is running on the incoming interface (it usually runs on the outgoing interface).
`-proxy_only`	Forces `natd` to perform transparent proxying only. Normal address translation is not performed.

TABLE 31.3 continued

-proxy_rule [<*type*> encode_ip_hdr | encode_tcp_stream] port <*xxxx*> server <*a.b.c.d:yyyy*>	Enables transparent proxying. Packets with the given port going through this host to any other host are redirected to the given server and port. Optionally, the original target address can be encoded into the packet. Use encode_ip_header to put this information into the IP option field or encode_tcp_stream to inject the data into the beginning of the TCP stream.
-pptpalias <*localIP*>	Enables PPTP packets to go to the defined local IP address. PPTP is VPN or secure IP-tunneling technology being developed primarily by Microsoft. For its encrypted traffic, it uses an old IP-encapsulation protocol called GRE. This natd option will translate any traffic of this protocol to a single server to be serviced with natd. If you are setting up a server, don't forget to allow the TCP traffic for PPTP setup. For a client or server, you must allow GRE (protocol 47) if you have firewall lists active.

Recovery

After you are done with BrickHouse, you might leave your machine in an unusable state. If you need to uninstall BrickHouse while you work out a solution, the documentation suggests that you select Remove Startup Script under the Options menu and reboot, or throw out the /Library/StartupItems/Firewall folder and reboot. The documentation also points out that Clear All Rules under the Options menu will temporarily uninstall the firewall.

If your machine is so unusable that you can't do any of the previous suggestions, reboot into single-user mode and remove the /Library/StartupItems/Firewall directory. You can also remove the /etc/firewall.conf and /etc/natd.conf files. Upon rebooting, your machine is restored to the condition it was in before you used BrickHouse. The next time you are ready to use BrickHouse, just start with the Setup Assistant and work from there.

Intrusion Detection

In the previous section, you saw some basic methods you can use for securing your machine, including the use of TCP Wrappers. Additionally, we saw that OS X comes with a firewall package, ipfw, which can be used for further securing your machine. In this section, we will look at a couple intrusion detection tools that you can install to further secure your machine, and discuss detecting and reacting to a break-in.

Tripwire

Tripwire is a utility that monitors the integrity of important files or directories. It stores information in a database about files and directories that you have specified. You can then use Tripwire to check whether there have been any changes to your files. It checks the current state of the files against the information in its database. The academic source release of Tripwire 1.3.1 is available from `http://www.tripwire.com/`. Tripwire Security Systems also has a commercial version of Tripwire, but it might not be available for OS X.

Remember that Tripwire can't detect any unauthorized changes that might have already been made on your system. If you have any doubts about the system's current integrity, you can reinstall the operating system and then install Tripwire.

Although we will not discuss details on compiling Tripwire, here are some tips that might be useful when compiling Tripwire via the ports system described in Chapter 17, "Troubleshooting Software Installs and Compiling and Debugging Manually."

- Try `/usr/bin/bsdmake` if `/usr/bin/gnumake` does not work.
- Compile the `dl` library.
- Whenever you encounter an error that is similar to `illegal expression found int`, manually run `make` in the offending directory. You will see many of these in subdirectories of the `sigs` directory.
- If you have not already done so, make a user called `man`. Follow the same method that you used for making a `bin` user.
- Note that `make install` moves files when it installs them, as opposed to copying them. If you have to recompile Tripwire for any reason, you also have to manually run `make` wherever you had to manually run it originally.

If you installed Tripwire via the ports system described in the chapter on additional software packages, `/var/adm/tcheck/tw.config` was installed on your system. If a typical manual installation does not specifically install a `tw.config` file for you, the source code does come with samples from which you can work.

To start using Tripwire, edit your `tw.config` file. The sample configuration file provides details on the syntax of the file. You can specify directories or files for Tripwire to check and what kind of checking it should do in the `tw.config` file. The basic form of a line in the file is `<file> <flags>`. The sample `tw.config` file provides a rather detailed description about the available flags and modifiers to `<file>`, and the man page provides even more details.

After you feel you have a good, basic `tw.config` file, you need to initialize the Tripwire database by running `tripwire -initialize`. In your `databases` directory, this creates a database called tw.db_<*hostname*>. Unless you customized your OS X machine's host-name, this database will likely be called `tw.db_localhost`.

The documentation suggests that you store your database in a read-only location and that you make a hardcopy of the database contents right away, as added protection. A hard-copy of the database contents will allow you to make a manual comparison, if you become suspicious of the database's integrity. Lastly, the documentation suggests that you might want to generate a set of signatures for the database, the configuration file, and the Tripwire executable by using the `siggen` utility that is included with the Tripwire package. Make a hardcopy of these as well.

Tripwire has four basic modes: database generation, integrity checking, database update, and interactive. You have already experienced the database generation mode. The integrity checking mode is the mode you are probably most interested in at this point. To run Tripwire in integrity checking mode, simply execute `tripwire`. In integrity checking mode, Tripwire checks the integrity of whatever you specified in `tw.config` and provides a report of what has changed.

Here is a sample of what the output looks like when Tripwire finds no changes:

```
[localhost:~joray] root# tripwire

     Tripwire(tm) ASR (Academic Source Release) 1.3.1
     File Integrity Assessment Software
      1992, Purdue Research Foundation,  1997, 1999 Tripwire
     Security Systems, Inc. All Rights Reserved. Use Restricted to
     Authorized Licensees.
     ### Phase 1:   Reading configuration file
     ### Phase 2:   Generating file list
     ### Phase 3:   Creating file information database
     ### Phase 4:   Searching for inconsistencies
     ###
     ###                      All files match Tripwire database.  Looks okay!
     ###
```

Here is a sample of what the outputs looks like when Tripwire finds changes:

```
[localhost:~joray] root# tripwire

     Tripwire(tm) ASR (Academic Source Release) 1.3.1
     File Integrity Assessment Software
      1992, Purdue Research Foundation,  1997, 1999 Tripwire
     Security Systems, Inc. All Rights Reserved. Use Restricted to
     Authorized Licensees.
     ### Phase 1:   Reading configuration file
     ### Phase 2:   Generating file list
     ### Phase 3:   Creating file information database
     ### Phase 4:   Searching for inconsistencies
     ###
```

```
###                     Total files scanned:           5528
###                           Files added:             0
###                           Files deleted:           0
###                           Files changed:           1
###
###                     Total file violations:         1
###
changed: -r-xr-xr-x root            0 8! /bin/ls
### Phase 5:   Generating observed/expected pairs for changed files
###
### Attr        Observed (what it is)         Expected (what it should be)
### =========== ============================= =============================
/bin/ls
      st_mtime: Thu Jun 21 18:28:06 2001      Thu Jun 21 18:22:26 2001
      st_ctime: Thu Jun 21 18:28:06 2001      Thu Jun 21 18:22:26 2001
```

If you were not expecting any changes, you should be suspicious. If you were expecting changes, there are two ways you can update your database to eliminate the false alarm. You can run `tripwire -interactive`. This puts Tripwire in interactive mode. Whenever it comes across a discrepancy, it prompts the user whether the database should be updated. You can also update your database by running `tripwire -update <filename>`, where *<filename>* can be a file or directory. This tells Tripwire to update the specified entry.

To make Tripwire useful, you should run it regularly. The easiest way to do that is to run Tripwire in a daily `cron` job and have the results mailed to you.

Be sure to read the man pages for `tripwire`, `tw.config` and `siggen` for more detailed information.

PortSentry

PortSentry is a utility available from `http://www.psionic.com/`. It is part of the Abacus Project, a project by Psionic Software to provide free host-based security and intrusion tools. Psionic Software also makes available LogChecker, which helps you monitor your system logs and HostSentry, which detects anomalous login behavior.

PortSentry monitors connections to ports specified in the `portsentry.conf` file. If PortSentry detects a connection on one of those ports, you can choose to have PortSentry simply log the connection. You can also configure PortSentry to immediately block the connection. PortSentry adds a deny line for the host to your `/etc/hosts.deny` or `/etc/hosts.allow`, depending on which way you are using TCP Wrappers. It then blocks the connection via `route` or `ipfw`. You can also provide PortSentry with a list of hosts whose connections it should ignore. You will have to do some testing until you are completely satisfied with your PortSentry configuration.

PortSentry cleanly compiles on OS X, so be sure to read the documentation carefully before you begin. The author clearly outlines the installation procedure step-by-step. Compiling with `make generic` works fine. By default, the package installs in `/usr/local/psionic/portsentry`.

The most important file you will work with is `portsentry.conf`. The first part of the configuration file is the Port Configurations section. Here you specify which TCP and UDP ports are monitored. The author has provided three basic selections: `anal`, `aware`, and `bare-bones`. Of course, you can add any additional ports to whichever set you select.

Next is the Advanced Stealth Scan Detection Options section. Because these options apply only to Linux, you can ignore this section.

The section that follows is the Configuration Files section, where you specify the location of `portsentry.ignore`, `portsentry.history`, and `portsentry.blocked`. The `portsentry.ignore` file is where you specify which hosts' connections the program should ignore. The `portsentry.history` file is where PortSentry logs a history of the actions it has taken. The `portsentry.blocked` file is where PortSentry logs a history of its actions for the current session.

The next section is the Response Options section. In this section, you specify what the automatic response should be for TCP and UDP connections. In the Ignore Options subsection, you specify what level of `ignore` PortSentry should follow for TCP and UDP connections. You can have PortSentry block scans, not block them, or execute some external command. The Dropping Options subsection is where you select what the blocking response should be. The program can be configured to block via `route` or via `ipfw`. The author recommends using `ipfw`, if you have it running. If you select `ipfw`, PortSentry, by default, adds a deny rule numbered `1` to `ipfw`. Of course, you can modify that rule. In the TCP Wrappers subsection, select the correct TCP Wrappers syntax for the way you are using it. In the External Commands subsection, an external command can be specified. In the Scan Trigger Value subsection, you configure the number of port connects that are allowed before an alarm is given. In the Port Banner section, you can specify what text, if any, should be displayed when PortSentry has been tripped.

After you have a basic `portsentry.conf` file, and you have installed the package, run the following to start PortSentry:

```
[localhost:~joray] root# /usr/local/psionic/portsentry/portsentry -tcp
[localhost:~joray] root# /usr/local/psionic/portsentry/portsentry -udp
```

Check `/var/log/system.log` for the PortSentry startup response. For each PortSentry, you will see some initial startup lines, a line for each port it is monitoring, and a final line indicating that PortSentry is active and listening.

If PortSentry is set to immediately block a connection, here is the type of response you will see in the log:

```
Jun 21 10:13:56 localhost portsentry[1065]: attackalert: Connect from host:
  ➥ryoko.biosci.ohio-state.edu/140.254.12.240 to TCP port: 21
Jun 21 10:13:56 localhost portsentry[1065]: attackalert: Host 140.254.12.240
  ➥has been blocked via wrappers with string: "ALL: 140.254.12.240"
Jun 21 10:13:56 localhost portsentry[1065]: attackalert: Host 140.254.12.240
  ➥has been blocked via dropped route using command:
  ➥"/sbin/ipfw add 1 deny all from 140.254.12.240:255.255.255.255 to any"
```

Check your `/etc/hosts.deny` and run `ipfw show`. You will see that it does add the offending host to the `/etc/hosts.deny` file and add an `ipfw` rule.

If PortSentry is not set to block connections, here is a sample response in the log file:

```
Jun 21 10:39:56 localhost portsentry[1301]: attackalert: Connect from host:
            ➥ryoko.biosci.ohio-state.edu/140.254.12.240 to TCP port: 20
Jun 21 10:39:56 localhost portsentry[1301]: attackalert:
            ➥Ignoring TCP response per configuration file setting.
```

Detecting the Break-in

In spite of all the tools we have looked at so far, it is not necessarily easy to detect a break-in, even with Tripwire. If your machine has been compromised, the intruder might update your Tripwire database for you. The tools certainly help, but they provide no guarantee of protection.

A Linux cluster that we put up a few years ago for a class experienced a break-in within days of being up. That Linux cluster was an out-of-the-box Linux installation and we did not follow the common sense, preventive security measures outlined earlier in this chapter. Unlike OS X, many Linux distributions come with services turned on by default. How did we detect the break-in? Actually, we didn't. The university's security group, which monitors the university's network traffic—among their various duties—told our administration staff that we had a break-in. Not only did they tell us we had a break-in, but they were able to tell us where on our machines to find the culprit software and evidence. Obviously, the security group keeps up-to-date on the latest vulnerabilities and popular cracking software. The break-in was well hidden from us. Common commands such as `ls` had been replaced and the software was put in a directory called `...` that not only usually requires using `ls -a` rather than `ls` to see, but their replacement version of `ls` wouldn't show at all. They also replaced the `ps` command with one that wouldn't show their sniffing processes, even as the processes were still running, and they tried to delete all other traces of their presence from the machines. A couple of people from the security group came with a floppy that had noncompromised versions of useful commands, and we were indeed able to see this `...` directory and the unusual processes that were running.

There are some things you and your facility, if your machine is part of a facility, can do to detect a break-in. Who knows? You might detect one in progress. Your network administrator, who is probably monitoring network traffic, might be able to tell you whether the network is being or was recently probed. This might give you the opportunity to check your logs for any unusual activity. If your machines seem sluggish, someone else could be tying up your resources. Check your logs; check to see who is logged on and check what processes are running. It's possible that you will discover that a normally inactive account has had a recent flourish of activity. Depending on how far along the cracker is your useful commands for detecting unusual activity might have been replaced. Try using `ls-F` in `tcsh`, instead of your normal `ls`, to see whether you can detect the presence of any unusual software or directories. Even if your network administrator hasn't alerted you to any unusual network activity, or even if your machine isn't sluggish, check your logs regularly. You never know what you might find. You might want to consider downloading the LogChecker utility to assist you with monitoring your logs.

Note

The `tcsh` shell has a built-in `ls` command named `ls-F`. Because most cracker wannabes don't know what they're doing, they won't add a fake `ls-F`, or replace `tcsh` with a broken version, as well as replace the normal `ls` command in `/usr/bin`. Of course, you shouldn't rely on this as a 100% certain way of detecting problem directories or compromised commands. As soon as you trust something, a cracker wannabe with above-average smarts will add it to one of the automated scripts. It's another tool in your arsenal, however, and you need all the tools you can get.

Regularly checking your machine's logs, processes, and so on really is useful. Recently, a machine on our building's network was compromised. How long it had been compromised is unknown. The system administrator noticed an odd `ftp` process that `root` was running, but had no reason to be running. When he killed the process, the machine became unusable. When the machine was finally restored, which involved reinstalling the operating system, it was compromised again within two weeks. This time the system administrator noticed that he had four new users that he did not create.

In addition, be especially paranoid around holidays. Crackers know that users won't be around on holidays, and that many system administrators won't be around either. This makes holidays, weekends, and early mornings prime time for crackers because they know they'll have at least a few hours to play before any human is likely to notice them.

Responding to the Break-in

How you respond to a break-in depends on the circumstances surrounding it.

If your security group personnel discovers the break-in, follow their instructions to the letter. What they tell you depends somewhat on the circumstances of the break-in. In the case of a sniffer, they will advise you to secure your machines and have everyone change their passwords. By changing passwords, they mean passwords for any accounts the users on your network might have accessed during the time in question. Yes, that's all passwords on any accounts they might have accessed from your network—including ones on other networks that they've accessed from your machines. However, even in the case of a sniffer, sometimes your security group will advise you to reinstall the operating system. If you have a sniffer, all the traffic that's been across your network has been compromised, including outgoing traffic to other sites, so this might impact machines far beyond yours.

What Is a Sniffer?

A *sniffer* is an application that watches network traffic as it moves past the sniffer machine. Most modern sniffers can extract usernames, passwords, and other sensitive information from the traffic flow. For an example of a network sniffer for Mac OS X, check out the Ettercap project at `http://ettercap.sourceforge.net/`. Note: You should *never* use a sniffer on a network that you do not administer, nor should you activate it without the knowledge of the other users on the network.

If your security group learns that your machine was used for attacking another site, the response they will suggest might surprise you. This time they might not ask you to secure your machine right away. The site that was attacked might request the cooperation of your site in capturing the culprit.

If, however, you detect a break-in before your security group does, you need to decide what the response will be. Do you close down the machine? Do you keep it open to try to catch the culprit? Do you ask your security group what to do? Certainly, there is nothing wrong with asking your security group, but depending on the time of day and number of security problems, you might not be able to find them. Think about how you might respond to a break-in before it actually occurs. If the break-in caused no obvious damage to anyone else's site, swiftly closing down services on your machine and fixing what was done might be the right solution. If damage is done to someone else's site, you might want to keep your machine open for a while in a cooperative effort to catch the culprit. On the other hand, if your site is being used to break into someone else's site and they don't know about it yet, you have the responsibility to stop the attack before the crackers can do any more damage. Cooperation is the name of the game here, and you should behave as reasonably and as professionally as possible. If a remote site requests your help, do everything you can to help—you'd want the same courtesy. If a remote site is being attacked through your site, bend over backwards to limit its damage—you wouldn't want someone to tell you, "Oh, we could have stopped that, but we were in the middle of a game of Quake and didn't want to shut down." Some of this might seem like advice to a system administrator, but remember, you are a system administrator for your OS X machine as well as one of its users.

No matter what you do decide to do, if you have a security group in your company, tell them about the incident and what you did. They need to know everything to best assess your company's security needs.

If your machine might have been compromised, but you can't find any obvious evidence in your logs or some helpful logs aren't available, you might have no recourse but to wipe out your machine and start over. Your users might not like this, but it is better for you to have a machine that you know you can trust, even if that means starting over from scratch. Your users probably prefer the downtime to the potential loss of their data. Again, tell your security group folks what you've done. In all likelihood, they will support your decision to wipe out your machine and start over from scratch. They would rather have you do that if you have any doubt about your machine, than have you let even one suspect machine stay on the network. Roughly one-third of our campus network and a related government site were taken down for several days a while ago when someone persisted in allowing one compromised machine to stay on the university's network. Fortunately, our machines weren't involved in that one.

Given that one day you may have to wipe your machine in response to an attack, there are some common sense measures you can take to make restoring your data easier:

- Keep a copy of your OS X CD in a location where you can find it.
- Keep your software CDs and registration numbers in a location where you can find them.
- Archive to CD-R any additional third-party software you downloaded and installed, especially if it was difficult to compile or is important to you.
- Archive to CD-R any data you don't want to lose.

Yes, that's it. Don't lose your OS X CD and software CDs. Back up any additional software you compiled and your data. That seems too obvious, doesn't it? It should be, but even the best of us need that reminder. Remember the machine on our network that was compromised twice in one month? The system administrator killed just one process, but the machine was hosed as a result. They probably spent at least $5,000 for their machine. They also lost a software package that was the key to a faculty member's research, but did not have a backup copy of it anywhere. After investing in the latest hardware, you can't afford to not spend a few dollars more and a little bit of time to preserve your data. With the current cost of CD-Rs, you should even be able to afford good CD-Rs for your data. In other words, if your machine has been compromised, it is best to be prepared to have the smoothest recovery possible. Backups and your original software CDs should help with this.

Where to Go from Here

The Ohio State University's security group says they have not experienced any security incidents involving OS X on campus, yet. They do point out, however, that as OS X becomes more widespread, crackers will start to target OS X machines. Of course, they recommend that you take a proactive security stance with your machine.

In this chapter, we have attempted to help you do just that. You have seen some basic security measures that you can follow in securing your machine. In addition, you have learned about `ipfw`, the built-in firewall package that comes with OS X. You have learned about some intrusion detection tools. After reading this chapter, you should at least follow those basic security measures. Hopefully, you will also decide to use some combination of the firewall package and intrusion detection tools.

Is there anything else you can do to protect your machine? If your company has a security group, contact the group to find out if they hold any security meetings or have a mailing list that they issue any security advisories that could be important for you. If you live near a university, find out whether the university has a security group. The university's security group probably holds meetings that are also open to the public. Attending meetings where you can meet some of the experts in security gives you the opportunity to ask any security question you might have face-to-face.

Earlier in this chapter, we mentioned that you should update OS X regularly. You can extend that to third-party-services software that you have installed, such as `wu-ftpd` and `sendmail`. In addition, we mentioned replacing basic services with secure services where possible. You might consider replacing `inetd` with `xinetd`, which is a secure replacement for `inetd` available from `http://www.xinetd.org/`.

You might also be interested in installing additional tools to enhance your security. Many of the sites listed here contain links to the various types of available tools.

Finally, it is important to keep informed on security issues. The following sections describe some resources that can be of assistance.

CERT Coordination Center—http://www.cert.org/

The CERT Coordination Center grew out of the Computer Emergency Response Team, which was formed in 1988 by the Defense Advanced Research Project Agency (DARPA), in response to the Internet worm of the day. The CERT Coordination Center issues security advisories that you can receive as they come out if you're on the mailing list. The site provides advice on many security matters, including those for the home user.

SecurityFocus.com—http://www.securityfocus.com/

This site provides a wealth of information on tools, vulnerabilities, and so on. In addition, this site hosts the BugTraq mailing list, a mailing list that discusses vulnerabilities, how to exploit them, and how to fix them. You can sign up to be on the mailing list or view the archives.

Apple Computer Product Security Incident Response— http://www.apple.com/support/security/security.html

This page is Apple's general security page, where Apple provides some formal information on Apple security as well as a link to a page where you can sign up to be on Apple's security announcement mailing list.

MacSecurity.org—http://www.macsecurity.org/

This is a nice site dedicated to Macintosh security issues.

SecureMac—http://www.securemac.com/

This site is dedicated to Macintosh security issues. At this time, it does not appear to be as current on security issues for OS X as MacSecurity.org.

OSX Security—http://www.osxsecurity.com/

This site is dedicated to OS X security. At this time, however, it does not appear to be as thorough as MacSecurity.org.

National Infrastructure Protection Center—http://www.nipc.gov/

The center provides some interesting security reports that break down into three sections: Bugs, Holes & Patches; Recent Exploit Scripts; and Viruses.

SANS Institute—http://www.sans.org/

The SANS (System Administration, Networking, and Security) Institute is a cooperative research and education organization. It sponsors a variety of conferences and training sessions. The site provides a wealth of security information, including an interesting article on the OS X Public Beta release.

CERIAS—http://www.cerias.purdue.edu/

Purdue University's Center for Education and Research in Information Assurance and Security is an education and research area for security issues. Probably the item of most interest here is the link to the FTP archive from which you can download a number of security tools. The archive includes many security tools, even ones that CERIAS didn't necessarily develop. Although you might prefer to download a specific tool from the home developing site, browsing this FTP archive is a convenient way to read the basic READMEs for many tools.

Summary

Network security has never been as important on the Macintosh as it is with Mac OS X. The new Mac operating system, based on a BSD core, provides a wider variety of network services than any previous release. Luckily, Mac OS X includes a variety of tools that can fend off attacks before they occur—without the need for additional software.

Many users will find that their needs are met by simply applying TCP wrappers to their critical services, and shutting down those protocols that aren't being used. Advanced users can employ `ipfw` or BrickHouse to provide low-level control over the flow of network traffic to and from the Mac OS X computer. In addition, administrators might want to take proactive measures by employing an intrusion detection tool such as Tripwire or PortSentry. These applications can detect an attack and react to it—potentially saving your system, data, and peace of mind.

System Maintenance

In This Chapter

With every book, there are topics that don't quite fit into any of the other chapters. In *Mac OS X Unleashed*, these topics, related to system maintenance and troubleshooting, have been included in this, the last chapter. Unfortunately, Mac OS X is still *extremely* immature, so there are large holes in the standard system services. Operations such as backing up critical data are left to the user's ingenuity, or a handful of third-party applications.

This chapter provides information on how to maintain your system and what products are available to aid your efforts.

Software Updates

An important part of maintaining a functioning and secure Mac OS X system is staying on top of the operating system updates. With a BSD core, Mac OS X requires more frequent attention than its predecessor, Mac OS 9.1. Critical security utilities such as SSH are revised on a regular basis and, unless updated, might open your system to outside attack. Within the first four months of Mac OS X's life, it has already seen four important updates.

Mac OS X automates the process of upgrading software through the use of the Software Update System Preference panel (path: `/Applications/System Preferences`), seen in Figure 32.1.

FIGURE 32.1
The Software Update panel controls automatic system updates.

Use the radio buttons to choose whether to run the software update application automatically, or invoke it manually. If you've chosen an automatic install, use the pop-up menu to select a schedule (Daily, Weekly, Monthly) for the update library to be queried.

> **Note**
>
> Unlike Mac OS 9.1, when the update runs automatically, it does not install the software it finds. It first prompts the user to select the module's installation.

To force the system to look for updates immediately, click the Update Now button. Your Mac OS X computer will contact Apple and detect available software packages.

Click the check box in front of each package that you want to download, and then click Install to start the process. You will be prompted for an administrator password before continuing.

During the download, the system will display a status bar within the same window that you used to choose the package to update. Some downloads could take a very long time, depending on your connection and how much bandwidth the latest Windows IIS virus is consuming, so you might want to take a break why your system is updated.

Depending on the software package, you might see a license agreement at some point in time during the installation. In addition, the install process is likely to pause for a *very* long period of time while it optimizes your installed packages. This is completely normal, albeit slightly annoying. I've seen the optimization process take longer than thirty minutes for a small update.

When finished, the software might prompt you to restart. All updates to the base operating system will require a reboot before becoming active.

> **Note**
>
> For users on modem connections, Apple offers normal file downloads for all the available system updates. If the automatic process fails, you might want to try downloading the entire update from Apple and installing it directly.

Installed Files

Many users, for good reason, want to keep track of what software has been installed on their system. Opening the Software Update preference panel and clicking the Show Log button will display a log of installed updates. This listing is shown in Figure 32.2.

FIGURE 32.2
The Software Update panel displays a list of installed update packages.

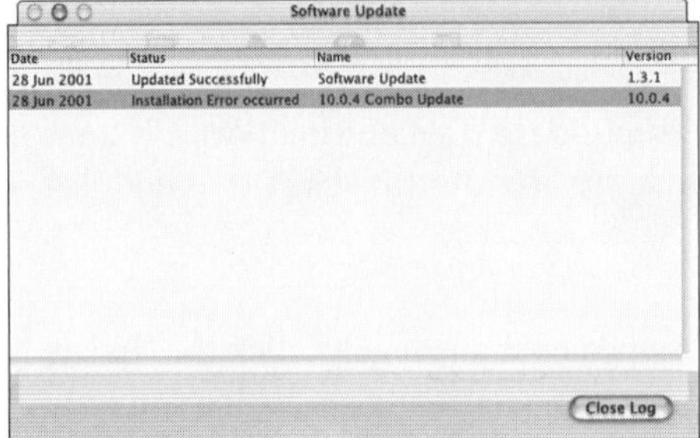

As you can see in Figure 32.2, one of the updates failed before it was correctly installed. In the event of a failure, Apple suggests manually forcing an update, and then reselecting and reinstalling the failed upgrade.

In some cases, the package might not show up as an available upgrade. This means that Mac OS X *thinks* the software was installed even if it wasn't. To make OS X forget about an update so that it can be reinstalled, open the directory `/Library/Receipts`. This folder contains receipt files for all software that is installed using Apple's built-in Installer program. The receipts are named based on the updated package; for example, Software Update 1.3.1 has the receipt file `SoftwareUpdate131.pkg`.

Throwing out a receipt file will effectively convince Mac OS X that the update was never installed.

Tip

If you have installed a developer update (or an illegally leaked and distributed update) and need to install an official release over the development release, this same technique should work for you. Remove the receipt file for the unofficial update, and the *real* update should install successfully.

The receipt files, in addition to keeping track of which packages have been installed, also contain a bill of materials (BOM) for every single file that was updated or installed. To view the file listing, you must "pretend" to install the receipt file. To Mac OS X, the receipts appear as packages that can be installed; they do not, however, contain any actual files.

Open the Installer application (path: `/Applications/Utilities/Installer`) and use Open from the File menu to choose one of the receipt files to examine. Alternatively, you can simply double-click the receipt file from the Finder. Authenticate with the Installer, if needed. Figure 32.3 displays a loaded receipt file for the Software Update 1.3.1 package.

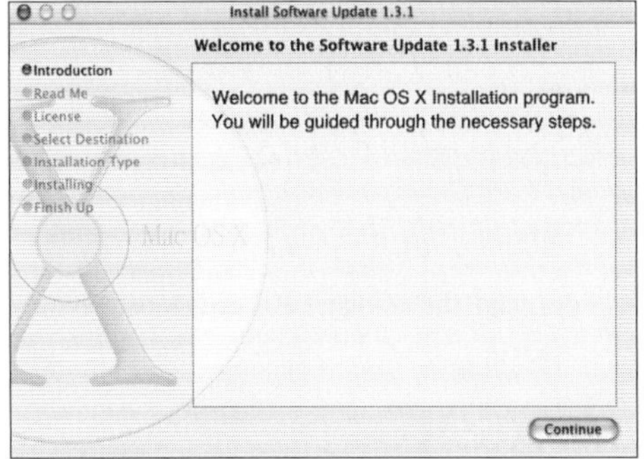

FIGURE 32.3
The Installer appears as if it were about to install a new package.

Proceed through the installation process exactly as if you were going to install the software. Stop when the Select a Destination screen is reached, as demonstrated in Figure 32.4.

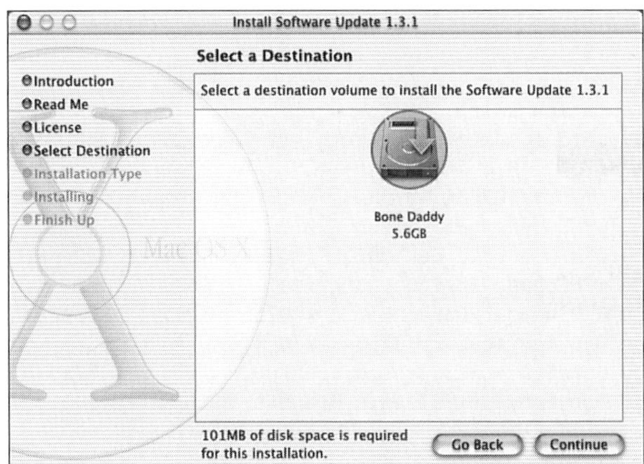

FIGURE 32.4
Proceed through the install process until you reach the Select a Destination screen.

Finally, choose Show Files from the Edit menu. A window displaying all the installed files will appear, as shown in Figure 32.5.

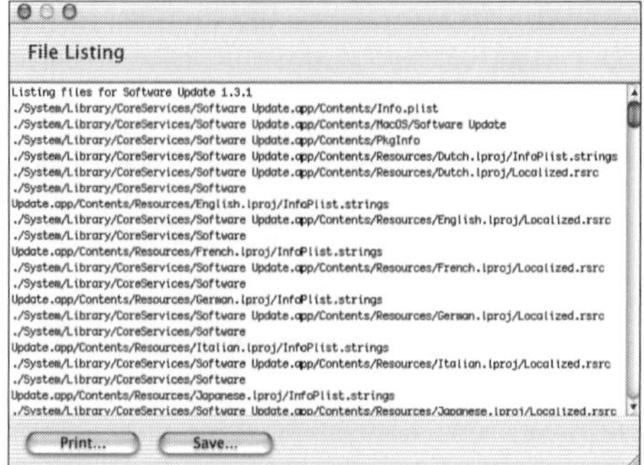

FIGURE 32.5
Choose Show Files to display a list of all files installed by the update package.

Use the Print button to output a copy of the listing to the default printer, or Save to save a text copy of the BOM.

Command-Line BOM Access

Command-line users can access the BOM directly using the `lsbom` command. You'll need to dig a bit deeper into the receipt files, usually accessing a directory with this pattern: `<receipt package>.pkg/Contents/Resources/<receipt package>.bom`. For example, to view the BOM for the 10.0.4 system update:

```
sudo lsbom /Library/Receipt/10.0.4Update.pkg/Contents/Resources/10.0.4Update.bom

.        40777   0/0
./Library        40755   0/0
./Library/Documentation 40755   0/0
./Library/Documentation/Acknowledgements.rtf    100664  0/80    62585    1730423858
./System         40755   0/0
./System/Library         40755   0/0
./System/Library/CFMSupport      40755   0/0
./System/Library/CFMSupport/._CarbonLib 100755  0/0      612      1897511375
./System/Library/CFMSupport/BridgeLibraries     40755   0/0
./System/Library/CFMSupport/CarbonLib   100755  0/0      363088  2965443096
./System/Library/CoreServices   40755   0/0
./System/Library/CoreServices/Classic Startup.app       40755   0/0
./System/Library/CoreServices/Classic Startup.app/Contents      40755   0/0
...
```

BOM files can be very useful in determining what has changed on your system. If you've modified the location of system software or configuration files, a system update might modify or move these files. Viewing the BOM can tell you exactly that happened during a system update.

Backups

Keeping an archive of your important applications and data is a crucial part of maintaining a Mac OS X computer, as it is with *any* operating system. The biggest problem with backups and Mac OS X is that there are currently no dedicated backup solutions shipping for the operating system.

The Unix users out there are probably scratching their heads out there asking, "What about `tar`, `dump`, and `restore`?" Although those are all perfectly good solutions for Mac OS X installations based on the UFS file system, or Unix and Cocoa apps based on HFS+, they are *not* suitable for Classic or Carbon applications. The dependency of these types of software on the HFS+ resource fork greatly limits what software can be used to back them up.

Traditional Unix utilities "see" the data fork only when looking at a dual-forked file. Attempting to back up a file with a resource fork will likely lead to an entirely unusable archive. This section of the chapter will look at what *is* currently available for backing up any Mac OS X file or application, and at the Unix tools that can be used to back up UFS and non-resource-forked files. Due to the overwhelming lack of GUI tools, the focus will be on what can be done from the Unix command line.

Mac OS X Native GUI Backup Utilities

When the table of contents for this book was in development, I had hoped that by the time this text was written, more backup tools for Mac OS X would be available. Unfortunately, the playing field is still open and waiting for a truly comprehensive native solution to be published.

The one piece of good news is that the Mac OS 8/9 tools, such as Retrospect, will continue to function and can back up a Mac OS X drive when booted into the older operating system. Another promising note is that the structure of Mac OS X makes it easy to back up individual user accounts and application preferences.

For most users, backing up the contents of their `/Users/`*`<username>`* home directories will suffice for protecting personal information. This, of course, doesn't help much with applications and Unix system services that have been installed. Let's go ahead and take a look at what is available, and then at a few Unix tools that can be employed to back up critical non-Carbon/Classic applications.

Retrospect

Retrospect is, by far, the most powerful backup solution for the Mac OS and Mac OS X, featuring the ability to back up and restore to Windows and Macintosh systems, store backups on FTP servers, and more. Figure 32.6 displays Retrospect Backup 5.0 for Mac OS X.

FIGURE 32.6
Retrospect 5.0 is a complete back up solution for Mac OS X.

The Retrospect client application is available for Mac OS X and, despite not being true backup software, is probably the best backup solution available at this point. The Retrospect client installs on the Mac OS X computer and Retrospect backup clients can be installed on any Mac OS X computer and accessed via either Retrospect Backup 4.5 for Mac OS 8 or 9 or Retrospect 5.0.

From a master Retrospect server the system administrator can locate the Mac OS X client, select the files to back up, and store them on a variety of media including CDRW, DAT, and Internet storage sites. Backups can be scripted for automatic execution, or run at any time with the click of a mouse. Restoring files from a backup is a simple point-and-click operation that automatically copies files from the source media back to the client.

Mixed platform networks will be happy to find that Retrospect clients are available for older Mac systems as well as Windows. Although not a native solution, it is an excellent system that makes possible backing up a Mac OS X computer in a Mac-like way.

Find out more about Retrospect Backup and download the Retrospect Mac OS X client from `http://www.dantz.com/`.

Synk X

The Synk X shareware application provides synchronization services between folders and volumes. Written as a Carbon application, this utility can work in either synchronize or backup mode. Additionally, the software can back up to an AppleShare volume and save common settings in a double-clickable "run" document. AppleScript programmers can automate the backup process by utilizing the built-in dictionary. Figure 32.7 shows the Synk X application in use.

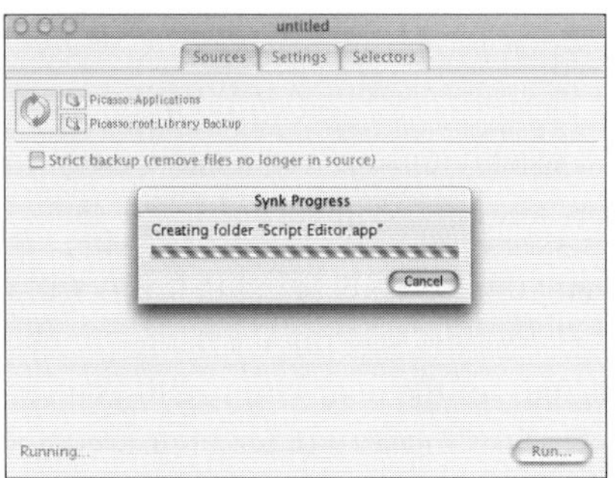

FIGURE 32.7
Synk X can synchronize or back up from a source folder to a local or remote destination.

Although Synk X does not provide support for external media, it is a quick-and-dirty backup method for those with removable disk storage devices or access to a network file server.

Download Synk X from `http://mypage.uniserve.ca/~rvoth/synkx.html`.

Tip

The command-line users out there might want to take a look at the utility `hfspax` from `http://homepage.mac.com/howardoakley`. This is a drop-in replacement for the `pax` utility that Apple uses in its own Installer application.

The `hfspax` software distribution works with both data and resource forks, and can be used to copy and archive *any* files on the computer. Unfortunately, the current distribution of `hfspax` does not come with the source code and is a "use at your own risk" piece of software.

Command-Line Backups

If you have created a Unix file system (UFS) partition for your OS X machine, you can use the `dump` utility to back up the data on that partition. The `dump` utility that currently comes with the OS X distribution cannot be used to back up HFS+ partitions. Because OS X does not provide an `mt` utility that can be used to communicate directly with a local tape drive, you might need to have access to a remote tape drive. If you do have access to a tape drive, we recommend that you store your important data on the UFS partition, because you will be able to back it up regularly.

Understanding Incremental Dumps

The version of `dump` that OS X provides supports incremental backups. As the phrase *incremental backups* might suggest, you will not back up everything on your UFS partition every time. Instead, you will decide on a backup schedule that consists of doing whatever is necessary to maintain reliability for your site. At the very least, you will run full backups every few months. At the very best, you will run full backups every few months, a monthly once a month, a weekly once a week, and a daily once a day. In practice, though, your schedule may fall somewhere in between.

The key to understanding incremental dumps is realizing that you will not be backing up everything on your UFS partitions every time you run the `dump` command. You will be able to issue different levels, or degrees, of the `dump` command. You can issue the `dump` command from levels 0 through 9. Except for level 0, which is the level used for a complete backup that backs up everything on the partition, you have the freedom to assign what a number means. Each dump level with a level number higher than 0 will back up only files that have changed since the most recent dump *that has a lower-level number.* Note that I didn't say since the most recent dump, but rather since the most recent with a lower-level number. This facility allows you to conserve tapes and save on equipment wear by doing most of your backups of only files that change, and infrequently backing up files that stay the same for long periods of time.

In the example we will look at, the level numbers I have chosen have the following meaning:

0	Full
2	Monthly
4	Weekly
6	Daily

I don't have to choose even numbers. Odd numbers are just fine, too. I've chosen to space mine out so that I can add an unexpected backup for whatever reason. It doesn't matter what arbitrary values you assign as long as the numeric values increase with the frequency of the scheduled dump, but, to make your life easier, be consistent from use to use.

It's fairly easy to be confused by the idea of incremental backups, but an example should help to clear things up.

Let's say that last month I ran a full dump (level 0) on a file system. Every day initially following the full dump, I ran dailies (level 6). A week after the full dump was made, I decided to run a weekly dump (level 4). In the days following the weekly dump, I ran dailies (level 6). The second week after the full dump, I ran another weekly (level 4). And I continued the pattern until today, a month after the full dump. Today I decide to run a monthly (level 2). Table 32.1 shows a sort of calendar of the sample backup schedule we will follow. For purposes of the example, today is the last identified day in the schedule, Monday of week 5.

TABLE 32.1 Sample Backup Schedule

Week	*Mon*	*Tues*	*Wed*	*Thurs*	*Fri*	*Sat*	*Sun*
1	0	6	6	6	6	6	6
2	4	6	6	6	6	6	6
3	4	6	6	6	6	6	6
4	4	6	6	6	6	6	6
5	2						

To reiterate, remember that dumps are incremental. Keeping that in mind, what do the numbers mean in Table 32.1? Here is what lands on each of the tapes:

On Monday of week 1, a full dump, level 0, was done. Everything on the file system was backed up to the dump level 0 tape.

On Tuesday of week 1, a daily, level 6 dump was done. That is, everything that had changed since the most recent dump with a lower level was backed up. In this case, Monday's dump level 0 has a lower level, and is the most recent dump with a lower level. So, anything that changed between Monday's level 0 dump and Tuesday's level 6 was backed up to the dump level 6 tape.

What about Wednesday of the first week? Again, with the Wednesday dump, level 6, only files that have changed since the most recent dump with a lower level have been backed up. What's the most recent dump with a lower-level number? Yes, it's the level 0 dump from Monday. Again, only files that changed between Monday, level 0, and Wednesday, level 6, were backed up. Wednesday's dump is not a reflection of the changes in files between Tuesday and Wednesday because both of those dumps were level 6.

Thursday, Friday, Saturday, and Sunday's dumps for the first week mimic the behavior of Tuesday's and Wednesday's. For each of these dumps, the most recent dump with a lower number will be Monday's level 0 dump, and each of these will contain a backup of all files that changed between Monday and the day of the dump.

On Monday of the second week, a dump level 4 was done. What does this mean? Again, the files that changed between the most recent dump with a lower dump level number and the current date were backed up. Again, the dump level 0 dump from the previous Monday was the most recent dump with a lower number. The dump from Monday of the second week reflects changes that were made between the previous Monday and that Monday. The significance of using level 4 for this dump will appear with the dump for the next day.

What about Tuesday of the second week? On this Tuesday we ran a dump level 6, but this time the most recent dump with a lower dump level than 6 is not the first Monday's level 0 dump, but the second Monday's level 4 dump instead. Tuesday's dump, then, consists of the files that changed between Monday of week 2 and Tuesday of week 2.

Likewise, the dump from Wednesday of week 2 reflects the changes between Monday of week 2 and Wednesday of week 2.

What files did the dump level 2 on Monday of week 5 capture? If we look at the chart, we see that the most recent dump with a dump level lower than our dump level of 2 is the dump level 0 of Monday on week 1. So, the dump level 2 on Monday of week 5 is a dump of the files that changed between Monday of week 1 and Monday of week 5.

Tomorrow Tomorrow, and All Tomorrow's Tomorrows

Notice that if we do a dump level 6 tomorrow, today's dump level 2 will be the most recent lower number. The *most recent lower number* isn't looking for any sort of order in the numbers, it just goes back looking for the most recent lower number dump performed in the past, and backs up everything since then.

When you are restoring files, the same incremental approach applies. Dumps are incremental, so the restores must be incremental as well. If a user deletes a directory, to rebuild that directory to its most recent state will take one restore at each of the dump levels that you use.

For example, if I accidentally deleted a directory mid-day on Tuesday of week 5, sometime after the daily dump (level 6) was done, I would have to restore my directory from the dump level 0 of Monday of week 1, the dump level 2 of Monday of week 5, and Tuesday morning's daily dump, level 6.

Why do I have to restore my directory from multiple different archives? Because other than the level 0 dump that provides a complete snapshot of my directory, the others only provide differences over time. I need to restore the dump level 0 to get back files that have been around in my directory for ages, the dump level 2 for changes in the last week, and the dump level 6 for changes since yesterday. What comes from each tape is as follows:

> The dump level 0 tape would provide the base level restore of my directory as it existed on Monday of week 1 because it's a full dump and captures everything as of when it is made.
>
> To this, the dump level 2 tape adds any changes that occurred between the dump level 0 dump of week 1 and the date of the level 2 dump, the day before I made the mistake. Any new files that I added during that time, or older files that I changed, would be backed up on this tape, but files that I had not changed would not be included.
>
> Tuesday's dump level 6 fills in any changes that occurred between the dump level 2 of the day before and Tuesday.

As you can see, the directory has to be restored incrementally. If Tuesday's daily dump ran at 4:00 a.m., and I made some spectacular changes at noon, just before I accidentally deleted everything after lunch, I can't get the spectacular changes back. I can only restore to the state of the directory as it was at 4:00 a.m.

Using `dump`

The `dump` utility has a variety of options. Options to make sure you include are the dump level, the blocking factor, any special tape size information you have to provide, and the name of the tape device. The blocking factor is information used by `dump` to determine how to group the data and control information on the tape. The man page mentions a maximum blocking size, which should probably be fine. The man page also mentions an option that could be used for automatic size detection. Unfortunately, this option is not currently available in the OS X distribution of `dump`. So, you probably will have to work out some density and feet numbers. For a remote tape device, definitely ask the system administrator of the machine with the tape drive for advice. If you are lucky, that system administrator has had to use a similar `dump`.

Always record on the tape packaging the date, dump level, blocking factor, and the file systems that were dumped in the order in which they were dumped. Record the blocking factor, even if you are just using the default. It might save someone else time restoring from your tape if she knows the blocking factor right away, instead of having to guess.

The clever system administrator will work out a schedule whereby tapes that are used for weekly or daily dumps will be rotated into duty as full-dump tapes and (semi-) permanently archived after some period of time. Magnetic media has a finite lifetime when running over record and playback heads, so moving a frequently used tape to a "use once and forget" status near the end (or middle, more practically) of its useful life is a way to economize on tape costs.

Here's the basic form of a dump command:

```
dump options <filesystem_to_dump>
```

Here is a sample of dump output:

```
root# dump 0bdsfu 64 83333 6000 rosalyn:/dev/rmt/0n /dev/rdisk2s9

        DUMP: Date of this level 0 dump: Fri Jun 29 12:31:03 2001
        DUMP: Date of last level 0 dump: the epoch
        DUMP: Dumping /dev/rdisk2s9 to /dev/rmt/0n on host rosalyn
        DUMP: mapping (Pass I) [regular files]
        DUMP: mapping (Pass II) [directories]
        DUMP: estimated 613411 tape blocks on 0.29 tape(s).
        DUMP: dumping (Pass III) [directories]
        DUMP: dumping (Pass IV) [regular files]
        DUMP: 23.54% done, finished in 0:16
        DUMP: 50.81% done, finished in 0:09
        DUMP: 75.19% done, finished in 0:04
        DUMP: 96.47% done, finished in 0:00
        DUMP: DUMP: 613410 tape blocks on 1 volumes(s)
        DUMP: level 0 dump on Fri Jun 29 12:31:03 2001
        DUMP: Closing /dev/rmt/0n
        DUMP: DUMP IS DONE
```

In this particular instance of `dump`, the level is 0. After the 0, you see the string `bdsfu`. This string specifies that it is followed by a collection of data values:

- `b` is the blocking factor
- `d` is the density in bytes per inch (bpi)
- `s` is the size of the tape in feet
- `f` is the tape device or file
- `u` is an indication to update `/etc/dumpdates` upon successful completion of dump

Following the `bdsfu` string are the numeric values corresponding to each item specified, in the order specified. The file system to be dumped is specified as the last thing on the line; here it's the raw device, `/dev/rdisk2s9`. With some versions of `dump`, you can specify the mount point of the file system, but that does not work with the `dump` that comes with OS X. As you can see by the naming convention, `rosalyn:/dev/rmt/0n`, the tape drive is not local to the machine. The magical numbers used for density and size have been determined from various man pages and trial and error as something that works on a 120m DAT tape for this particular tape drive on a different operating system.

The dump output includes this line:

```
DUMP: estimated 613411 tape blocks on 0.29 tape(s).
```

Some versions of dump also include output information in total MB, KB, or bytes dumped. Although the OS X dump does not provide that precise translation, from df -k we see a convenient correlation—the tape blocks must be approximately 1KB blocks:

```
[localhost:~] joray% df -k /dev/disk2s9

    Filesystem    1K-blocks      Used     Avail Capacity  Mounted on
    /dev/disk2s9     692795    612336     45820     93%    /new1
```

Command documentation for dump is included in Table 32.2. The dump syntax used in the earlier sample follows traditional dump syntax. However, from the man page, we would expect the following statement to work also:

```
dump -0u -b 64 -d 83333 -s 6000 -f rosalyn:/dev/rmt/0n /dev/rdisk2s9
```

If we look at the resulting /etc/dumpdates file, we see

```
[localhost:~] joray% more /etc/dumpdates

    /dev/rdisk2s9     0 Fri Jun 29 12:31:03 2001
```

From the file, we see that so far there has only been one dump of /dev/rdisk2s9 and that it was a level 0. When another dump level is performed on /dev/rdisk2s9, a new line will be added with the date and time for that dump level.

Note

Most classical versions of dump have arguments more appropriate for 9-track streaming tape drives of the type you see in 1960s and 1970s sci-fi films. The parameters were not really designed to accommodate today's high-capacity cartridge drives, so you must fudge the length and density values until you achieve a working selection that makes reasonable use of the tape's capacity. Usually it is sufficient to provide size and density values that are bigger than the actual tape capacity because most modern tape drives will detect when EOM (end of media) is reached. However, if the values are significantly larger, dump's estimate of the number of tapes required will be useless, so you probably will want to attempt to make a reasonably accurate guess. Usually the man pages make helpful suggestions on making these guesses, but given the rapid advances in tape capacity in recent years, even the man pages seem to be out-of-date as far as accurate predictions go.

TABLE 32.2 Command Documentation Table for `dump`

`dump`	File system backup
`dump [-0123456789cnua] [-B <records>] [-b <blocksize>] [-d <density>] [-f <file>] [-h <level>] [-s <feet>] [-T <date>] s`	
`dump [-W || -w]`	
(The 4.3BSD option syntax is implemented for backward compatibility, but is not documented.)	
`dump` examines files on a file system and determines which files need to be backed up. These files are copied to the given disk, tape, or other storage medium for safekeeping. A dump that is larger than the output medium is broken into multiple volumes. On most media, the size is determined by writing until an end-of-media indication is returned.	
On media that cannot reliably return an end-of-media, each volume is of a fixed size. The actual size is determined by the tape size and density and/or block count options. By default, the same output filename is used for each volume after prompting the operator to change media.	
`-0-9`	Dump levels. A level 0, full backup, guarantees the entire file system is copied. A level number above 0, an incremental backup, tells `dump` to copy all files new or modified since the last dump of the same or lower level. The default level is `9`.
`-c`	Changes the defaults for use with a cartridge tape drive, with a density of 8000 bpi and a length of 1700 feet.
`-n`	Notifies all operators in the group `operator` whenever `dump` requires operator attention.
`-u`	Updates the file `/etc/dumpdates` after a successful dump. The format of `/etc/dumpdates` is readable by people, consisting of one free format record per line: file system name, increment level, and `ctime (3)`. There may be only one entry per file system at each level.
`-B <records>`	The number of kilobytes per volume, rounded down to a multiple of the *`blocksize`*. This option overrides the calculation of the tape size.
`-b <blocksize>`	The number of kilobytes per dump record. Because the IO system slices all requests into chunks of `MAXBSIZE` (typically 64KB), it is not possible to use a larger block size without having problems later with `restore`. Therefore, `dump` constrains writes to `MAXBSIZE`.
`-d <density>`	Sets the tape density to *`<density>`*. The default is 1600 bpi.

TABLE 32.2 continued

`-f <file>`	Writes the backup to `<file>`. `<file>` may be a special device file, such as a tape drive or disk drive, an ordinary file, or `-` (standard output). Multiple filenames may be given as a single argument separated by commas. Each file will be used for one dump volume in the order listed. If the dump requires more volumes than the number of names listed, the last filename will be used for all remaining volumes after prompting for media changes. If the name of the file is of the form `<host>:<file>` or `<user>@<host>:file`, `dump` writes to the named file on the remote host using `rmt`.
`-h <level>`	Honors the user `nodump` flag only for dumps at or above the given `<level>`. The default honor level is `1`, so that incremental backups omit such files but full backups retain them.
`-s <feet>`	Attempts to calculate the amount of tape needed at a particular density. If this amount is exceeded, `dump` prompts for a new tape. It is recommended to be a bit conservative on this option. The default tape length is 2300 feet.
`-T <date>`	Uses the specified date as the starting time for the dump instead of the time determined from looking in `/etc/dumpdates`. The format of the date is the same as that of `ctime (3)`. This option is useful for automated dump scripts that want to dump over a specified period of time. The `-T` flag is mutually exclusive with the `-u` flag.
`-W`	Tells the operator what file systems need to be dumped. The information is gleaned from `/etc/dumpdates` and `/etc/fstab`. The `-W` flag causes `dump` to print out, for each file system in `/etc/dumpdates`, the most recent dump date and level and highlights of those file systems that should be dumped. If the `-W` flag is set, all other options are ignored, and `dump` exits immediately.
`-w`	Is like `W`, but prints only those file systems that need to be dumped.

`dump` requires operator intervention on these conditions: end of tape, end of dump, tape write error, tape open error, or disk read error (if there are more than a threshold of 32). In addition to alerting all operators implied by the `-n` flag, `dump` interacts with an operator on `dump`'s control terminal at times when `dump` can no longer proceed, or if something is grossly wrong. All questions `dump` poses must be answered by typing `yes` or `no`.

TABLE 32.2 continued

Because making a dump involves a lot of time and effort for full dumps, `dump` checkpoints itself at the start of each tape volume. If writing that volume fails for some reason, `dump` will, with operator permission, restart itself from the checkpoint after the old tape has been rewound and removed, and a new tape has been mounted.
`dump` tells the operator what is going on at periodic intervals, including (usually low) estimates of the number of blocks to write, the number of tapes it will take, the time to completion, and the time to the tape change.

Troubleshooting `dump`

If `dump` works fine on the machine with the tape drive, but not on your remote OS X client, you might need to double-check your coordination with the system administrator of the machine with the tape device.

Make sure that you are using the right device name for the remote tape drive. Ask the system administrator whether she has placed an entry for your OS X machine in `root`'s `.rhosts` file. An entry in the `.rhosts` file has a form like this:

```
mother.politically.correct.com  root
```

Also, if the system administrator has closed services on the machine with the tape drive, ask whether `rsh` has been enabled and if she has placed an entry in her `/etc/hosts.allow` for `rsh` for your OS X machine. Only machines that are allowed to have access to the tape drive should be given access to the `rsh` service. Make sure that any other possible firewall issues have been addressed.

Restoring Your Data from Tape: Using `restore`

It's one thing to get `dump` to work and another to successfully restore from tape. Make sure that you test restoring data from tape before you actually have to do it. Take notes as you do it. Do your testing in noncritical locations on your system. Get an approximate idea of what you have to do. You might not end up restoring to the exact location you hope for, but you can always move the data around.

Preparing to Restore

The information that you will most likely need for `restore` is the blocking factor and the name of the tape drive. If you choose an interactive `restore` session, you don't need to worry about too many other options.

Which tapes you will need for your `restore` will vary with what you have to restore. If you only have to restore a file that you last updated yesterday before today's dump, today's tape is sufficient. Recall, however, that you might need to restore from the appropriate combination of the most recent full, monthly, weekly, and daily tapes.

When you restore from tape, you have to navigate the tape to the location that has the file system with the data you need to restore. This shouldn't be too problematic, assuming that you have written, somewhere on the tape package, the dump date, dump level, blocking factor, and what was dumped in the order it was dumped. If you do not write this information down, your tapes are all but useless. With sufficient experimentation, you might be able to determine the contents of a tape that you haven't recorded this information for, but realistically you should consider the contents of a tape with no written information to be lost.

Doing a Restore

What I am going to restore first is actually data that was created by another operating system's dump of a UFS file system.

The data I am most interested in is a collection of patches for SunOS 4.1.4 and scripts to install the patches. Because my UFS partition is large enough to hold all the available data, I will restore all of it, and sort through it to see what I don't really need.

To complete this task, I will need the tapes from the most recent appropriate levels. In my case, I need the most recent level 0, level 2, and level 4 tapes.

I will first restore the base contents from the level 0 tape. My label indicates that a blocking factor of 126 was used, and that the directory I'm looking for is on the seventeenth file system on the tape.

On the remote host, I have to position the tape, using the `mt` command. First, I rewind the tape to make sure that I am at the beginning of the tape. Then I fast-forward the tape to the end of the sixteenth file system. As you saw in the `dump` example, the tape device on this host machine is `/dev/rmt/0n`.

```
rosalyn osx-misc 164 > mt -f /dev/rmt/0n rewind

rosalyn osx-misc 165 > mt -f /dev/rmt/0n fsf 16
```

The `fsf 16` instructs `mt` to fast-forward to the end of the sixteenth file. Some versions of `restore`, including the one for OS X, have a `-s` option that allows you to skip to the *n*th file on the tape. This `restore` option could alleviate some need for an `mt` utility.

With the tape properly positioned, I can now restore from it:

```
[localhost:/new1] root# restore ibf 126 rosalyn:/dev/rmt/0n

Connection to rosalyn.biosci.ohio-state.edu established.
```

```
restore > ls
.:
ftp/              installed-950421/ stacker.mods
installed/        lost+found/
```

The options I have indicated are `i` for interactive, `b` for blocking factor, and `f` for tape device. These are typical options available in traditional versions of `restore`. The man page with the OS X `restore` does not elaborate on available options.

Because I have chosen an interactive restore mode, I am given a prompt from which I can run `ls`, which as you might expect, lists the contents of the tape. A `/` at the end of a name indicates that the entry is a directory. Items that you want to restore can be selected with the `add` command. Because I want everything on this file system, I can just enter `add *`. If I wanted only certain files, I could navigate and select certain files and directories with the `add` command. Here is my `add` command:

```
restore > add *
```

After everything has been selected, I can tell `restore` to extract the data with the `extract` command:

```
restore > extract
```

The `restore` command responds with a request for which volume to read. I've always backed up one tape at a time, so I enter `1`. If you do multi-tape dumps for one file system, you will want to answer this question with the highest tape number for a given file system. The `restore` process will instruct you as to how to proceed from there. It's much more convenient to work with single-volume dumps and restores, however, and with today's high-capacity tape drives and a bit of planning, you should be able to avoid the necessity for multi-tape dumps entirely.

```
You have not read any tapes yet.
Unless you know which volume your file(s) are on you should start
with the last volume and work towards the first.
Specify next volume #: 1
```

Then I wait a while, or so it seems. Finally, `restore` asks whether I want to set modes:

```
set owner/mode for '.'? [yn] y
restore > quit
```

You might want to experiment with the set owner/modes question. The results of choosing yes and no are similar, but not exactly identical. When you choose `y`, the hierarchy of the file system on the tape is restored to the restore directory, with permissions and ownership of the restore directory itself (`'.'`) set to those of the file system on the tape. If `root` owns the file system that you're restoring from on the tape, and you used your home directory as the temporary restore location, your home directory is now owned by `root`.

If you choose n, the permissions and ownerships of the file system on the tape are not given to the directory that you're restoring in ('.'). But the hierarchy as it appears on the tape is still restored into the restore directory with the permissions and ownerships that belong to the hierarchy.

In this example, because I am restoring an entire file system, choosing yes is the best answer.

Because I am now done with the level 0 tape, I can continue with the level 2 tape. To eject the level 0 tape, or start the ejection process, depending on the tape drive, I can issue this command:

```
rosalyn osx-misc 166 > mt -f /dev/rmt/0n offline
```

Here is how the restore goes on the level 2 tape:

```
[localhost:/new1] root# restore ibf 126 rosalyn:/dev/rmt/0n

Connection to rosalyn.biosci.ohio-state.edu established.
restore > ls
.:
ftp/

restore > add ftp
warning: ./ftp: File exists
warning: ./ftp/incoming: File exists
warning: ./ftp/incoming/ISSR: File exists
warning: ./ftp/incoming/rtr: File exists
warning: ./ftp/incoming/galloway: File exists
warning: ./ftp/incoming/reeve: File exists
warning: ./ftp/incoming/reeve/990726: File exists
warning: ./ftp/incoming/reeve/05-1098: File exists
warning: ./ftp/incoming/reeve/05-1098-2: File exists
warning: ./ftp/incoming/njohnson: File exists
restore > extract
You have not read any tapes yet.
Unless you know which volume your file(s) are on you should start
with the last volume and work towards the first.
Specify next volume #: 1
set owner/mode for '.'? [yn] y
restore > quit
```

From the warnings that `restore` issues, I learn that there are probably new files in directories that now already exist on my machine.

Because the restore from the level 4 tape looks almost the same as the one from the level 2 tape, except for warnings about different directories, its output is not shown.

Always Something There to Rewind Me

If you can't seem to get off file number 1 on the tape drive, it's because you're using the rewind version of your tape device. Read the man pages on the tape host machine to find out how to use the nonrewinding interface to your tape. Currently, your tape is being helpful by automatically rewinding itself after every command. So, if you're using the rewind device and ask the drive to skip forward 16 files, it will dutifully do so. Then it will be most helpful, and automatically rewind itself again before you can issue another command.

So far, we have seen that the OS X `restore` can restore UFS data that was dumped from another operating system. It can also restore UFS data that was dumped from the OS X `dump`. Here is a demonstration of restoring a file from the OS X dump that you saw earlier:

```
[localhost:~joray/temp-restore2] root# restore ibf 64 rosalyn:/dev/rmt/0n

Connection to rosalyn.biosci.ohio-state.edu established.
restore > ls
.:
ftp/              installed-950421/ stacker.mods
installed/        lost+found/

restore > cd ftp
restore > ls
./ftp:
 /                              home.html
BuiltByNOF.gif                  incoming/
Home_HProfessional_down.gif     index.html
Home_NProfessionalBanner.gif    l3seqmotifs.pdf
INSTALL-BINARY                  l4datsearch.pdf
If-250.jpg                      l5apat.pdf
L1a-Intro.pdf                   l5bprotfam.pdf
L1b-Molbio.pdf                  public/
L2-database.pdf                 talks.htm
L2b-genomeDBs.pdf               usr/
L3a-homology.pdf                whatsnew.txt
L3b-globalaln.pdf               ws_ftp.exe
L6-phylogenetics.pdf            ws_ftp.ext
bin/                            ws_ftp.hlp
clearpixel.gif                  ws_ftp.ini
dev/                            ws_ftp.log
error.wav                       ws_ftp.txt
etc/                            ws_read.me
guest/
```

```
restore > cd public
restore > ls
./ftp/public:
.ADeskTop               dilbert.tar              patches-sunos-0010/
.IDeskTop               grasp.tar                patches-y2k/
.afpvols                jk1                      pfu_clean_leaders.tfa
.finderinfo/            lib-libMagick.tar        pfu_clean_leaders.tfa~
.resource/              mix                      ph_clean_leaders.tfa
BACK                    pab_clean_leaders        ph_clean_leaders.tfa~
ISSR.programs/          pab_clean_leaders.tfa    sendmail.8.11.1.tar.gz
Network Trash Folder/   pab_clean_leaders.tfa~   ssh-2.0.13-src.tar
assets/                 patches-aug98/           tbtupmc1.zip
bigfile.af-mt           patches-more/            yst.tar
delphin.tar             patches-security/

restore > cd patches-sunos-0010
restore > ls
./ftp/public/patches-sunos-0010:
100523-26/                 100626-10.tar          Solaris1.1.2.PatchReport
100523-26.tar              106859-01/             install-patches-0010
100626-10/                 106859-01.tar

restore > add Solaris1.1.2.PatchReport
restore > extract
You have not read any tapes yet.
Unless you know which volume your file(s) are on you should start
with the last volume and work towards the first.
Specify next volume #: 1
set owner/mode for '.'? [yn] n
restore > quit
```

If we do a quick check for the data, we see that the temporary restore directory, `~joray/temp-restore2`, has the desired file and that it was restored in the hierarchy seen while running `restore`.

```
[localhost:~] joray% ls -RaF temp-restore2

./   ../  ftp/

temp-restore2/ftp:
./      ../     public/

temp-restore2/ftp/public:
./                      ../                        patches-sunos-0010/

temp-restore2/ftp/public/patches-sunos-0010:
./                            ../                        Solaris1.1.2.PatchReport
```

Partial command documentation for `restore` is shown in Table 32.3. Just as you saw with the `dump` syntax, the `restore` syntax shown earlier is the traditional `restore` syntax. However, from the man page, we would also expect this `restore` statement to work:

```
restore -i -b 64 -f rosalyn:/dev/rmt/0n
```

After dumping to a tape, it is a good idea to randomly check the tape to make sure that your data is readable, especially on a level 0 dump tape. It should be sufficient to use `restore` and run `ls`, rather than actually restoring something. If the tape is not readable, the tape drive will inform you right away. Sometimes there is a bad tape in the package, and you find that out only when you try to restore from it.

TABLE 32.3 Command Documentation Table for `restore`

`restore`	Incremental file system restore
`restore -i -b` *<blocksize>* `-f` *<file>* `-s` *<filenumber>*	
(The 4.3BSD option syntax is implemented for backward compatibility, but is not documented.)	
`restore` restores files from backup media created with the `dump` command.	
A full backup of a file system may be restored and subsequent incremental backups layered on top of it. Single files and directory subtrees may be restored from full or partial backups.	
`-i`	Interactive. After reading in the directory information from the media, `restore` invokes an interactive interface that allows you to browse through the dump files directory hierarchy and select individual files to be extracted. See the listing of interactive commands later in this table.
`-b` *<blocksize>*	Specifies the block size, the number of kilobytes per dump record. If the option is not specified, it tries to determine the media block size dynamically.
`-f` *<file>*	Reads the backup from *<file>*. *<file>* may be a special device, such as a tape drive or disk drive, an ordinary file, or `-` (standard input). If *<file>* is of the form *<host>*:*<file>* or *<user>*@*<host>*:*<file>*, `restore` reads from the named file on the remote host using `rmt (8)`.
`-s` *<filenumber>*	Skips to *<filenumber>* when there are multiple files on the same tape. File numbering starts at `1`.
Interactive Commands	
`add` *<file>*	Adds the specified file or directory to the list of files to be extracted. If the argument is a directory, it and all its descendants are added to the list. Files that are on the extraction list are prepended with a `"*"` when they are listed by `ls`.

TABLE 32.3 continued

`delete <file>`	Deletes the current file or directory and its descendants from the list of files to be extracted.
`extract`	Extracts all files on the extraction list from the dump.
`cd <directory>`	Changes to the specified directory.
`ls <directory>`	Lists the current or specified directory.
`pwd`	Prints the full pathname of the current working directory.
`help`	Lists the available commands.
`quit`	Ends the session, even if there are files listed for extraction.

The utilities `dump` and `restore` are excellent examples of how the availability of Unix-based solutions often exceeds that of what is available natively on Mac OS X. Users who have abandoned non-native Classic and Carbon applications can easily use these utilities to back up their entire system. For everyone else, all we can do is wait.

Diagnostics

With a complex operating system like Mac OS X, things can sometimes go wrong, and the user is left with little recourse for solving the problem. Operations such as repairing damaged Mac OS X installations, resetting the `root` password, and fixing damaged disks can all be performed even if your machine is not booting into the operating system properly.

Verbose Boot

Mac OS 8 and 9, although hiding much of the system operation from the user, gave a clearer picture of what was going on during a system boot. When Mac OS X starts, dozens of support processes and drivers are loaded at the same time. If something fails, it is left to the imagination of the user to guess exactly what has gone wrong. In many cases, users might not even be aware that there are problems with their system configuration because the boot process hides behind a very simple GUI startup screen.

To view *exactly* what is happening as the Mac OS X system boots, you can hold down Command+V at power-on to force a verbose startup. The verbose boot displays all status and error messages while the computer starts. This can be a bit startling to many Mac users because instead of the usual blue or gray background present during startup, the screen is black and filled with text. Windows and Linux users will feel right at home.

The verbose startup messages are similar to those contained in /var/log/system.log. For example:

```
Jun 29 17:30:30 localhost mach_kernel: .Display_RADEON: i2cPower 1
Jun 29 17:30:30 localhost mach_kernel: .Display_RADEON:
➥user ranges num:1 start:9c008000 size:640080
Jun 29 17:30:30 localhost mach_kernel: .Display_RADEON:
➥using (1600x1024@0Hz,32 bpp)
Jun 29 17:30:30 localhost mach_kernel: AirPortDriver:
➥Ethernet address 00:30:65:11:37:15
Jun 29 17:30:30 localhost mach_kernel: ether_ifattach called for en
Jun 29 17:30:30 localhost mach_kernel: kmod_create:
➥com.apple.nke.ppp (id 58), 6 pages loaded at 0xc27a000, header size 0x1000
Jun 29 17:30:30 localhost mach_kernel: kmod_create:
➥ com.apple.nke.SharedIP (id 59), 5 pages loaded at 0xc28d000, header size
0x1000
Jun 29 17:30:30 localhost mach_kernel: kmod_create:
➥IPFirewall (id 60), 5 pages loaded at 0xc292000, header size 0x1000
Jun 29 17:30:30 localhost mach_kernel: ipfw_load
Jun 29 17:30:30 localhost mach_kernel:
➥IP packet filtering initialized, divert enabled, rule-based forwarding
➥enabled, default to accept, logging disabled
Jun 29 17:30:31 localhost sharity[161]: [0] Sharity daemon version 2.4 started
Jun 29 17:30:39 localhost ntpdate[204]:
➥ntpdate 4.0.95 Sat Feb 17 02:38:39 PST 2001 (1)
Jun 29 17:30:43 localhost ntpdate[204]:
➥no server suitable for synchronization found
Jun 29 17:30:43 localhost ntpd[206]:
➥ntpd 4.0.95 Thu Apr 26 13:40:11 PDT 2001 (1)
Jun 29 17:30:43 localhost ntpd[206]: precision = 7 usec
Jun 29 17:30:43 localhost ntpd[206]:
➥frequency initialized 0.000 from /var/run/ntp.drift
Jun 29 17:30:43 localhost ntpd[206]: server 128.146.1.7 minpoll 12 maxpoll 17
```

This small sample of the verbose output shows the Apple Radeon driver loading, followed by the AirPort software, Classic SharedIP driver, firewall, Sharity, and ntp (network time protocol) software.

Interestingly enough, in capturing this example, I ascertained what I had suspected for several weeks: The ntpdate utility, which is responsible for automatically contacting a remote time server for synchronization, has been failing:

```
Jun 29 17:30:39 localhost ntpdate[204]:
➥ntpdate 4.0.95 Sat Feb 17 02:38:39 PST 2001 (1)
Jun 29 17:30:43 localhost ntpdate[204]:
➥no server suitable for synchronization found
```

Similar feedback is provided for almost all the services on the computer, from low-level device drivers to Apache and Sendmail. If your computer hangs during boot, you can use the verbose startup mode to determine exactly where the sequence has gone amiss.

Single-User Mode

Another interesting modification to the startup process is booting into single-user mode. Holding down Command+S will start Mac OS X in single-user mode, allowing an administrator to directly access the system through a command-line interface. This is a last-resort method of booting your computer that should be used only if absolutely necessary.

Single-user mode boots in a text-only fashion, just like the verbose startup mode. The process finishes by dropping the user to a shell:

```
Singleuser boot — fsck not done
Root device is mounted read-only
If you want to make modifications to files,
run '/sbin/fsck -y' first and them '/sbin/mount -uw /'
localhost#
```

Caution

Be aware that the single-user mode command prompt carries with it full `root` access. This is not a place for playing games or learning Unix.

fsck

Using the `fsck` command, you can repair local file systems from the command line. To fix a damaged file system, type `fsck -y` at the single-user prompt. This is equivalent to running the First Aid Disk Utility:

```
localhost# fsck -y
** /dev/rdisk0s9
** Root file system
** Checking HFS Plus volume
** Checking Extents Overflow file.
** Checking Catalog file.
** Checking multi-linked files.
** Checking Catalog heirarchy.
** Checking volume bitmap.
** Checking volume information.
** The volume Rmac OS XS appears to be OK.
```

If an error occurs during this process, you might have to tell the system that it is okay to perform repairs. Table 32.4 lists additional command-line arguments for `fsck`.

TABLE 32.4 `fsck` Command-Line Options

Option	*Purpose*
`-d`	Debugging mode. Displays the commands that `fsck` will execute without actually carrying them out.
`-f`	Forces a check of the file systems, even if they are considered clean.
`-l <max parallel processes>`	Sets the number of scans that `fsck` will run in parallel. Usually defaults to one scan per disk.
`-n`	Assumes that the answer to all interactive questions is no.
`-p`	Preen (clean) the file systems marked as dirty.
`-y`	Answers yes to all interactive questions.

Tip

The Mac way of performing emergency disk repairs is to boot the system from the Mac OS X installation disk, and then choose Open Disk Utility from the Installer menu. The Disk Utility, covered in Chapter 6, "Native Utilities and Applications," includes a Disk First Aid component with a GUI for controlling disk checks and repairs.

Editing Files

When booted into single-user mode, the Mac OS X file system is mounted read-only as a precaution. If you've installed a new daemon or script that is stalling the system at startup, it would be useful to be able to edit files from within single-user mode. To mount the file system with write permissions, use `/sbin/mount -uw /`.

Again, be aware that changes made while in single-user mode are made as the `root` user. When dealing with stalled startups, take the same approach as with extensions and control panels under Mac OS 8 and 9: Remove the last item to load before the system failure, and then reboot.

As you already know, both the `/Library/Startupitems` and `/System/Library/Startupitems` directories contain the services that are started at boot time. Make these your starting locations for pinpointing hang-ups when Mac OS X is booting. In addition, the /etc/hostconfig and /private/var/db/SystemConfiguration/preferences.xml files hold information on your machine's network configuration and boot parameters. Although editing these files isn't a guaranteed cure for any problem, they're a good place to start.

Commercial Repair Tools

At the time of this writing, only a single disk repair utility is available under OS X: Drive 10 from MicroMat. This is expected to change in late 2001/early 2002, but that is of little consolation for those of us using the operating system currently.

Thankfully, because Mac OS X uses the same default file system as Mac OS 9, the big-name commercial disk repair utilities have been updated to work under the new operating system:

Drive 10 by Micromat Inc. (www.micromat.com/drive10) Drive 10 offers extensive disk diagnostic utilities ranging from power supply tests to buffer validation. Unfortunately, it is lacking several of the more useful features—such as more generalized system diagnostics and drive optimization—of its big brother, TechTool Pro.

TechTool Pro by Micromat Inc. (www.micromat.com/techTool_Pro3) TechTool Pro is the undisputed king of diagnostics. It can locate problems with almost any hardware component, from memory to CPU failures. It also includes extensive drive repair and optimization facilities.

Norton Utilities by Symantec, Inc. (www.symantec.com/product/home-mac.html) Norton Utilities is the oldest and best-known Macintosh repair software available. NU focuses entirely on drive repair, optimization, and data loss prevention.

It has been my experience that TechTool Pro and Norton Utilities can be used in conjunction with one another to successfully diagnose and solve problems that neither can handle alone. Drive 10, although effective as a complete disk drive diagnostic tool, does not offer as complete a package as the non-native TechTool Pro.

Reinstall

Most Windows users are familiar with the word *reinstall*. I've listened in on many support calls, only to hear the technician give up and tell the end user to reinstall. Unfortunately, Mac OS X users might find themselves doing the same thing. The difference, however, is that reinstalling Mac OS X *does not* replace your system accounts, information, or configuration.

I have found on numerous occasions that rerunning the Mac OS X installer is the fastest and easiest way to return to a viable system. There are, however, a few drawbacks—most notably, the system updates are replaced by the original version of the operating system. After running the Mac OS X Installer to recover a damaged system, be sure to open the `/Library/Receipts` folder and throw away any receipt files stored by system updates, and then manually force a software update to reinstall the latest versions of the Mac OS X support software.

Another anomaly is that if you've moved or removed any of the system-installed applications, they will be restored during the install process.

Restoring the Administrator Password

If the Mac OS X administrator password is forgotten or misplaced, Apple has provided a facility for restoring a password. Boot your computer from the Mac OS X install CD (hold down the C key while turning your computer on with the CD in the CD-ROM drive). When the Installer application starts, choose Reset Password from the Installer application menu. Figure 32.8 shows the interface to the Password Reset facility.

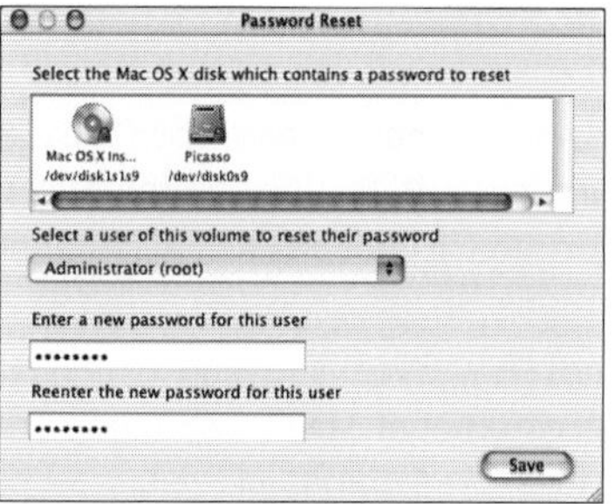

FIGURE 32.8
Use the boot CD and Password Reset application to ease your forgetful head.

Detected Mac OS X volumes are listed along the top of the Window. Click the main boot drive to load the password database for that volume.

Next, use the pop-up menu to choose the user account that you want to reset. Fill in the new password in both of the password fields provided.

Finally, click Save to store the new password.

This really isn't useful for much beyond resetting the administrator password. As long as there is access to the administrator account from the command line, you can easily use `passwd <username>` to reset the named user's password:

```
[primal:~] jray% sudo passwd robyn
Changing password for robyn.
New password:
Retype new password:
```

Tip

It is not possible to recover a password that has been forgotten—it is only possible to reset it. Mac OS X passwords are encrypted and can only be decrypted using the user's own password. If you're setting up a large-scale network with dozens of accounts, it's a good idea to develop a default password policy. Several organizations that I've worked for base the user's passwords on a combination of their initials and last four digits of the user's Social Security number. This enables the administrators to reset passwords to a safe default value that the user will be able to remember.

Housekeeping

The Mac OS X Unix subsystem can schedule tasks for automatic execution whenever you'd like. Like the automatic software installation, you can write your own maintenance scripts that execute at given intervals. In fact, there are already several scripts that help keep your system running clean.

cron

The `cron` process is used to schedule repeating tasks for execution by adding entries to either a user or system `crontab` file. The system-level file is located in `/etc/crontab`. The default `crontab` file looks like this:

```
#       $NetBSD: crontab,v 1.13 1997/10/26 13:36:31 lukem Exp $
#
# /etc/crontab - root's crontab
#
SHELL=/bin/sh
PATH=/bin:/sbin:/usr/bin:/usr/sbin
HOME=/var/log

#min    hour    mday    month   wday    user    command

# Disabled by default, since it causes disk access every 10 minutes,
# which is useless unless you use at(1).  Enable as needed.
#*/10   *       *       *       *       root    /usr/libexec/atrun

# do daily/weekly/monthly maintenance
15      3       *       *       *       root    sh /etc/daily
➥2>&1 | tee /var/log/daily.out   | mail -s "`hostname` daily output"   root
30      4       *       *       6       root    sh /etc/weekly
➥2>&1 | tee /var/log/weekly.out  | mail -s "`hostname` weekly output"  root
30      5       1       *       *       root    sh /etc/monthly
➥2>&1 | tee /var/log/monthly.out | mail -s "`hostname` monthly output" root
```

At the start of the file, a handful of environment variables are set (`SHELL`, `PATH`, `HOME`), which are made available to the commands executing from the file. Additional environment variables can be added using the same syntax: `<variable name>=<value>`.

One special `crontab` variable is the `MAILTO` variable, which can be set to a user account name. Output from the `crontab` commands (errors, and so on) will be sent via e-mail to that user's account.

The body of the `crontab` file is laid out in six columns, separated by spaces or tabs. These six fields control different aspects of when a command is run:

- **Minute**—The minutes after an hour that a command should be executed (`0–59`).
- **Hour**—The hour a command should run (`0–23`).
- **Day of the month**—The day of the month to run the command (`0–31`).
- **Month**—The month, specified numerically (`1–12`), or by name that the command should execute.
- **Weekday**—The day of the week the command should execute, set numerically (`0–7`, 0 or 7 specifies Sunday) or by name.
- **User**—The user ID to use while executing the command.
- **Command**—The command string to execute. This field can point to a shell script or other file to run a sequence of commands.

Fields that contain an asterisk (`*`) indicate that the command will run whenever the other columns values are matched. For example, assume that there is an asterisk in every column (except for the User and Command fields, obviously):

```
* * * * * <my user> <my command>
```

The command will be started every minute, of every hour, of every day, of every day of the week, and so on. In addition, you can add set a command to run at multiple different intervals within a time period without having to use additional lines. Just use integers separated by commas to set off multiple times within one of the columns.

For example, to run a command every ten minutes, you could use

```
0,10,20,30,40,50 * * * * <my user> <my command>
```

Even this, however, can be shortened to be a bit more manageable. Regular intervals can be shortened using the syntax `*/<interval length>`. The previous example, could be rewritten like this:

```
*/10 * * * * <my user> <my command>
```

Additions that are made to the /etc/crontab file are read every minute without additional user interaction.

Three scripts are run by default from the Mac OS X /etc/crontab file: /etc/daily, /etc/weekly, and /etc/monthly. As their names suggest, these files are run at repeating intervals each day, week, and month, respectively. They handle cleaning up temporary system files, log rotation, and other menial maintenance tasks. You can take advantage of these files or add additional script files to perform other common tasks.

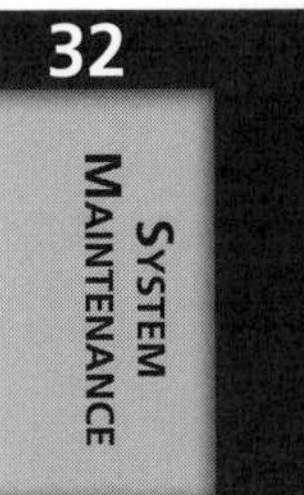

Caution

It might be tempting to set up scripts that run in very tight intervals (for monitoring system activity and so forth). If you set up commands to execute at extremely frequent intervals, be absolutely certain that they can finish executing within that interval. If a command tends to run long, you might find that your system slowly grinds to a halt as more and more copies are started and system resources are exhausted.

cron for Normal Users

The system-wide /etc/crontab file should be used only for system tasks. Users, however, might want to add their own commands and scripts that are executed within their accounts. To do this, a user can create a crontab-style file within his directory. This file should contain all the fields as the previously documented /etc/crontab file, with one notable exception: there is no User field. Any commands executed from a personal crontab file are executed with the permissions of that user.

For example:

```
*/15 * * * * /Users/jray/myscript.pl
```

Putting this line in a file gives me a personal crontab that executes a Perl script in my home directory every fifteen minutes.

Unlike the system-level crontab file, personal crontab files are loaded into a privileged system area, rather than being run directly from the file you've created. To load a personal crontab file into the system, use the crontab utility followed by the name of your personal file: crontab *<my crontab file>*.

Assuming that I've stored my crontab entries in mycrontab, I can load them into the system with

```
[primal:~] jray% crontab mycrontab
```

After the file is loaded into the system, you can safely delete the local copy of your crontab file—it is no longer needed. A user can display the loaded crontab information (and thereby regenerate the original file) by typing crontab -l:

```
[primal:~] jray% crontab -l
# DO NOT EDIT THIS FILE - edit the master and reinstall.
# (mycrontab installed on Sun Jul  1 10:01:20 2001)
# (Cron version — $FreeBSD: src/usr.sbin/cron/crontab/crontab.c,v 1.12
#  1999/08/28 01:15:52 peter Exp $)
*/15 * * * * /Users/jray/myscript.pl
```

A user can also use the -e option to edit her currently stored crontab information, or use -r to remove it entirely.

Note

The root user (or a user executing sudo) can work with the contents of any user's personal crontab file by adding -u<*username*> to the crontab -l command-line utility.

The crontab information is stored in /etc/cron/tabs/<*username*> if you'd like direct access to the data.

Tip

Users wanting to access cron services from a GUI interface might want to check out CronniX. CronniX can create and edit crontab files for any system user from within a point-and-click environment. Download it from www.koch-schmidt.de/cronnix/.

Limiting Access to cron Services

On a system with a large number of users, it isn't necessarily a good idea to give all of them access to cron services. You might find that your poor system performance is due to a few hundred copies of SETI@home that start automatically every night. To limit access to the crontab command for adding personal crontab entries, use either /var/cron/allow or /var/cron/deny.

As you might infer, the allow file controls who is allowed to access crontab. Adding entries to this file will *deny* access for anyone who isn't listed.

Likewise, the `deny` file, if it exists, will provide access to `crontab` for anyone who *isn't* listed.

This isn't intentionally tricky, but it is important to note that the act of creating one of these files implicitly denies or allows access to all the accounts on the system. Obviously, you should not be running a system where both files exist simultaneously because it leads to an ambiguity of what happens to "everyone else" who isn't listed in one of the files.

Over time, you'll discover that there are small tasks you carry out on a day-to-day basis. Using the power of the `cron` daemon along with shell scripts, Perl, or AppleScript can automate many of these processes.

Summary

Mac OS X is *not* the Mac OS of the 1990s. It is an entirely new creation that brings together the best parts of the traditional Mac OS with a Unix underpinning. This chapter demonstrated the use of single-user and verbose boot modes, introduced tools for backing up your system, and automating system processes.

Over the course of the next few years, Mac OS X will likely mature into a system that can be documented entirely without ever seeing a command line (unless you want to!). For now, we hope that this book has provided a balanced view of what you can do through the GUI and via the command line. Best of luck!

Sincerely,

John Ray (`jray@macosxunleashed.com`)

Will Ray (`wray@macosxunleashed.com`)

Command-Line Reference

Throughout *Mac OS X Unleashed*, you learned a number of different commands that can be used to interact with your system. There are literally hundreds of shell commands and utilities that can be used with the Mac OS X distribution, and, unfortunately, there simply isn't enough space to provide information on them all. This appendix provides an alphabetical reference to some of the more useful and/or interesting BSD commands.

As Apple updates Mac OS X, it is likely to add additional functionality behind the scenes. In the first few revisions, Apple added a number of security features accessible only from the command line. Keep track of the files added during each update to find out whether there are any new utilities available for your use. For more information on viewing the contents of system updates, see Chapter 32, "System Maintenance."

If you cannot find what you're looking for here, remember that you have instant access to command documentation through the use of the `apropos` and `man` utilities.

apropos

`apropos`	Displays a list of manual pages by keyword lookup.
`apropos [-M` *<path>*`] [-m` *<path>*`]` *<keyword1> <keyword2>* `...`	
`-M` *<path>*	Overrides the list of standard directories where `apropos` searches for the database, whatis.db. The path specified must be a colon-separated list of directories. The search path may also be specified by the `MANPATH` environment variable.
`-m` *<path>*	Adds to the list of standard search directories. The path specified must be a colon-separated list of directories. These directories are searched before the standard list or directories specified by `-M` or `MANPATH`.

at, atq, atrm, batch

`at`	Executes commands at a specified time.
`atq`	Lists the user's pending jobs, unless the user is super user. If the user is super user, lists all users' jobs.
`atrm`	Deletes jobs.
`batch`	Executes commands as soon as system load levels permit. This is either when the average load drops to below 1.5 or the value specified at the invocation of atrun.

```
at [-q <queue>] [-f <file>] [-m] <time>
atq [-q <queue>] [-v]
atrm [-q <queue>] <job> [<job2>...]
batch [-f <file>] [-m]
```

Both `at` and `batch` take input from either standard input or the file specified by `-f` option. The working directory, environment (except for variables TERM, TERMCAP, DISPLAY, and _) and `umask` are retained from the time of invocation. Any `at` or `batch` command invoked from an `su` shell retains the current user ID.

Permission to use these commands depends on the files /var/at/at.allow and /var/at/at.deny. The super user may use these commands. If /var/at/at.allow exits, only the users (one per line) listed in the file may use these commands. If /var/at/at.allow does not exist, /var/at/at.deny is checked. Only users listed in /var/at/at.deny may not use these commands. If an empty /var/at/at.deny exists, all users may use these commands. If neither file exists, only the super user may use these commands. This is the default configuration.

`-q <queue>`	Uses the specified queue. A queue consists of a single letter. Valid queue ranges are a to z and A to Z. If a job is submitted to a queue designated with an uppercase letter, it is treated as though it has been submitted to batch at that time. If atq is given a specific queue, it shows only the pending jobs in the specified queue.
`-f <file>`	Executes commands in the specified `<file>` rather than from standard input.
`-m`	Sends mail to the user when the job is complete, whether or not there was any output.
`-v`	For `atq`, shows completed, but not yet deleted, jobs in the queue. Otherwise, shows the time the job will be executed.
`<time>`	`<time>` may be given in a variety of formats. Times may be of the form `<HHMM>` or `<HH:MM>` for a specific time of day. If the time has already passed, the next day is assumed. You may also specify midnight, noon, or teatime (teatime for 4:00pm). You may also append AM, am, PM, or pm to a specific time. A time may also include a date in any of the following forms: `<month-name> <day>` [`<year>`] or MMDDYY or MM/DD/YY or DD.MM.YY. The date must follow the time specification. Time may also be given in increments, such as `<now>` + `<count><time_units>`, where `<time_units>` can be minutes, hours, days, or weeks. Terms today and tomorrow may also be used.

atrun

`atrun`	Runs jobs queued by `at`.

`atrun [-l <load_avg>] [d]`

`atrun` runs commands queued by at. `root`'s crontab (`/etc/crontab`) must contain this line:

```
*/10 * * * * root /usr/libexec/atrun
```

so that `atrun` is called every 10 minutes. By default, the `atrun` line is disabled to prevent disk access every 10 minutes. Enable the `atrun` line in order to use at.

At every invocation, every job whose start time has passed is started. A maximum of one batch job is started.

For `atrun` to work, a `cron` daemon must also be running.

`-l <load_avg>`	Specifies a limiting load average, over which batch runs should not be run, instead of the default value of 1.5.
`-d`	Debug mode. Prints error messages to standard error instead of using syslog.

automount

`automount`	Automatic NFS mount/unmount daemon.

`automount` is a daemon that automatically mounts NFS file systems when they are first accessed and later unmounts them when they are idle.

`automount` creates a virtual file system mounted at one or more places on the client's file and directory hierarchy. Actual NFS mount points within this virtual file system appear as symbolic links. Reading a symbolic link triggers `automount` to mount the associated remote file system.

To make the trigger symbolic links used by `automount` distinguishable from normal symbolic links, the sticky bit is set in the mode flags for the link. Programs that would normally traverse symbolic links can test for this bit and avoid triggering the mount. Workspace Manager and ls have been modified in this way.

Each virtual file system created by `automount` is governed by a corresponding map. One or more maps may be specified on the command line.

A map may be a file or a special map. A file map is a regular file containing a list of entries of the form:

```
location mount_options server:path
```

mount_options is a comma-separated list of options from the options known to mount and mount_nfs programs.

In addition to reading files specifying mount maps, `automount` supports the `-fstab` map. This causes `automount` to read the fstab database. All mounts with the net option are mounted within the `-fstab` map's filesytem using a path of the form:

`server/path`

If the `fstab` database contains an entry for `polaris:/Library/Fonts`, and if `automount` is started as

`automount -m /Useful -fstab`

the mount appears as `/Useful/polaris/Library/Fonts`.

`-m` *`<directory>`* *`<map>`*	Associates the specified *`<map>`* with the given *`<directory>`*. This directory is created if it does not exist. *`<map>`* may be the name of a file, or it may be the name of a special map.
`-d`	Runs `automount` in debug mode. The program remains attached to the command line and sends debugging information to standard output.
`-tm` *`<secs>`*	Sets the timeout for NFS mounts to *`<secs>`* seconds. Default is 20 seconds.
`-tl` *`<secs>`*	Sets the time-to-live for NFS mounts to *`<secs>`* seconds. Default is 3600 seconds.

biff

`biff`	Notification of incoming mail and who it is from during the current terminal session.
`biff [ny]`	
`n`	Disables notification.
`y`	Enables notification.

bg

`bg`	Backgrounds a job.
`bg [<%`*`<job>`* `...]`	
`%`*`<job>`*`&`	
`bg`	

Backgrounds the specified jobs; or if no argument is given, the current job continues as though each had stopped. *`<job>`* may be any acceptable form described in jobs.

bsdmake

`bsdmake`	Maintains program dependencies.

`bsdmake [-BPSeiknqrstv] [-D <variable>] [-d <flags>] [-E <variable>] [-f <makefile>] [-I <directory>] [-j <max_jobs>] [-m <directory>] [-V <variable>] [<variable>=<value>] [<target> ...]`

The `bsdmake` program simplifies the maintenance of other programs. Its input is a list of specifications describing the dependency relationships between the generation of files and programs. The first `makefile` or `Makefile` that can be found in either the current directory or a special object directory is read for the list of specifications. If the file `.depend` can be found, it is also read.

`-B`	Tries backward compatibility by executing a single shell per command and by executing the commands to make the sources of a dependency line in sequence. This is turned on by default unless `-j` is used.
`-P`	Collates the output of a given job and displays it only when the job finishes, instead of mixing the output of parallel jobs together. This option has no effect unless `-j` is also used.
`-S`	Stops processing when an error is encountered. Default behavior. This is needed to negate the `-k` option during recursive builds.
`-e`	Specifies that environment values override macro assignments within makefiles for all variables.
`-i`	Ignores nonzero exit of shell commands in the makefile. Equivalent to `specifying` `-` before each command line in the `makefile`.
`-k`	Continues processing after errors are encountered, but only on those targets that do not depend on the target whose creation caused the error.
`-n`	Displays the commands that would have been executed, but does not actually execute them.
`-q`	Does not execute any commands, but exits 0 if the specified targets are up-to-date, and 1 otherwise.
`-r`	Does not use built-in rules specified in the system makefile.
`-s`	Does not echo any commands as they are executed. Equivalent to specifying `@` before each command line in the makefile.

`-t`	Rather than rebuilding a target as specified in the `makefile`, creates it or updates its modification time to make it appear up-to-date.
`-v`	Is extra verbose. For multi-job makes, this causes file banners to be generated.
`-D <variable>`	Defines `<variable>` to be 1, the global context.
`-E <variable>`	Specifies a variable whose environment value (if any) will override macro assignments within makefiles.
`-f <makefile>`	Uses `<makefile>` as the `makefile`. If `<makefile>` is -, standard input is read. Multiple makefiles may be specified, and are read in the order specified.
`-I <directory>`	Specifies a directory in which to search for makefiles and included makefiles. The system makefile directory (or directories; see the `-m` option) is automatically included as part of this list.
`-j <max_jobs>`	Specifies the maximum number of jobs that bsdmake may have running at any one time. Turns compatibility mode off, unless the `-B` flag is also specified.
`-m <directory>`	Specifies a directory in which to search for sys.mk and `makefiles` included via the `<...>` style. Multiple directories can be added to form a search path. This path will override the default system include path: /usr/share/mk. Furthermore, the system `include` path will be appended to the search path used for `...-style` inclusions (see `-I` option).
`-V <variable>`	Prints gnumake's idea of the value of `<variable>`, in the global context. Does not build any targets. Multiple instances of this option may be specified; the variables will be printed one per line, with a blank line for each null or undefined variable.
`<variable>=<value>`	Sets the value of the variable `<variable>` to `<value>`.
`-d <flags>`	Turns on debugging, and specifies which portions of make are to print debugging information.

Argument `<flags>` is one or more of the following:

`A`	Prints all possible debugging information; equivalent to specifying all the debugging flags.
`a`	Prints debugging information about archive searching and caching.
`c`	Prints debugging information about conditional evaluation.

d	Prints debugging information about directory searching and caching.
f	Prints debugging information about the execution of loops. Currently at no-op.
g1	Prints the input graph before making anything.
g2	Prints the input graph after making everything, or before exiting on error.
j	Prints debugging information about running multiple shells.
l	Prints commands in makefiles regardless of whether they are prefixed by @ or other quiet flags. Also known as *loud behavior*.
m	Prints debugging information about making targets, including modification dates.
s	Prints debugging information about suffix-transformation rules.
t	Prints debugging information about target list maintenance.
v	Prints debugging information about variable assignment.

cat

`cat` Concatenates and prints files.

`cat [-nbsvetu] <file1> <file2> ...`

`cat [-nbsvetu] [-]`

`cat` reads files in sequential command-line order and writes them to standard output. A single dash represents standard input.

-n	Numbers all output lines.
-b	Numbers all output lines, except b or blank lines.
-s	Squeezes multiple adjacent empty lines, causing single-spaced output.
-v	Displays nonprinting characters. Control characters print as ^X for control-X; delete (octal 0177) prints as '^?'; non-ASCII characters with the high bit set are printed as `M-` (for meta) followed by the character for the low 7 bits.
-e	Implies `-v` option. Displays a dollar sign ($) at the end of each line as well.
-t	Implies `-v` option. Displays tab characters as `^I` as well.
-u	Guarantees unbuffered output.

catman

`catman`	Creates formatted files for the online manual reference.
`catman [-knpsw] [-M <directory>] [<sections>]`	
`-k`	Ignores errors from `nroff` when building man pages.
`-n`	Does not create the `whatis` database.
`-p`	Prints what would have been done, but does not actually do it.
`-s`	Works silently. Does not echo commands as they are executed. Ignored if `-p` is specified.
`-w`	Creates only the `whatis` database.
`-M <directory>`	Updates the manual pages in the `<directory>` specified.

The optional `<sections>` argument is a string containing the numbers of the sections to be regenerated. For example, if `<sections>` is 138, sections 1, 3, and 8 are regenerated.

When manual pages are regenerated, `catman` also rebuilds the `whatis` database.

cd

`cd`	Changes working directory.
`cd <directory>`	
`cd`	

`<directory>` is an absolute or relative pathname. The interpretation of the relative pathname depends on the `CDPATH` environment variable.

The following environment variables affect the execution of `cd`:

`HOME`	If `cd` is invoked without any arguments and the `$HOME` exists, `$HOME` becomes the new working directory.
`CDPATH`	If `<directory>` does not begin with `/`, `.`, or `..`, `cd` searches for the directory relative to each directory named in `CDPATH` variable, in the order listed. If the new working directory is derived from `$CDPATH`, it is printed to standard output.

chflags

`chflags`	Changes file flags.

`chflags [-R [-H | -L | -P]] <flags> <file1> <file2> ...`

`-R`	Recursively descends through directory arguments to change file flags.
`-H`	If `-R` is specified, symbolic links on the command line are followed. Symbolic links encountered in tree traversal are not followed.
`-L`	If `-R` is specified, all symbolic links are followed.
`-P`	If `-R` is specified, no symbolic links are followed.

Symbolic links do not have flags. Unless `-H` or `-L` is specified, `chflags` on a symbolic link always succeeds and has no effect. `-H`, `-L`, and `-P` options are ignored unless `-R` is specified. Furthermore, `-H`, `-L`, and `-P` override each other. The last one specified determines the action that is taken.

`<flags>` is a comma-separated list of keywords. Currently available keywords are

`arch`	Sets the archived flag (super user only).
`opaque`	Sets the opaque flag (owner or super user only).
`nodump`	Sets the nodump flag (owner or super user only).
`sappnd`	Sets the system append-only flag (super user only).
`schg`	Sets the system immutable flag (super user only).
`uappnd`	Sets the user append-only flag (owner or super user only).
`uchg`	Sets the user immutable flag (owner or super user only).

Prepending the letters "no" to a flag turns the flag off.

chgrp

`chgrp`	Changes group.

`chgrp [-R [-H | -L | -P]] [-fh] <group> <file1> <file2> ...`

`-R`	Recursively descends through directory arguments to change the group ID.
`-H`	If `-R` is specified, symbolic links on the command line are followed. Symbolic links encountered in tree traversal are not followed.
`-L`	If `-R` is specified, all symbolic links are followed.
`-P`	If `-R` is specified, no symbolic links are followed.

`-f`	Forces an attempt to change group ID without reporting any errors.
`-h`	If the file is a symbolic link, the group ID of the link is changed.

Unless `-h`, `-H`, or `-L` is specified, `chgrp` on symbolic links always succeeds and has no effect.

The `-H`, `-L`, and `-P` options are ignored unless `-R` is specified. Because they also override each other, the last option specified determines the action that is taken.

The group can be either a numeric group ID or a group name. If a group name exists for a group ID, the associated group name is used for the group.

The user invoking `chgrp` must belong to the specified group and be the owner of the file, or be the super user.

Unless invoked by the super-user, `chgrp` clears set-user-id and set-group-id bits.

chmod

`chmod`	Changes file modes.

`chmod [-R [-H | -L | -P]] [-h] <absolute_mode> <file1> <file2> ...`

`chmod [-R [-H | -L | -P]] [-h] <symbolic_mode> <file1> <file2> ...`

`-R`	Recursively descends through directory arguments to change file modes.
`-H`	If `-R` is specified, symbolic links on the command line are followed. Symbolic links encountered in tree traversal are not followed.
`-L`	If `-R` is specified, all symbolic links are followed.
`-P`	If `-R` is specified, no symbolic links are followed.

Unless `-H` or `-L` is specified, `chmod` on a symbolic link always succeeds and has no effect. `-H`, `-L`, and `-P` options are ignored unless `-R` is specified. Furthermore, `-H`, `-L`, and `-P` override each other. The last option specified determines the action that is taken.

Permissions are described by three sequences of letters in the order listed here. Each sequence describes the permissions for user, group, and other. If a certain permission has not been granted, a `-` (dash) appears in its place.

```
user    group    other
rwx     rwx      rwx
```

The permissions on a file can be viewed using `ls -l` and changed using `chmod`.

Absolute mode

Absolute mode is constructed by ORing any of the following modes:

`4000`	Sets user ID on execution.
`2000`	Sets group ID on execution.

`1000`	Turns on sticky bit.
`0400`	Allows read by owner.
`0200`	Allows write by owner.
`0100`	Allows execute (search in a directory) by owner.
`0600`	Allows read, write by owner.
`0500`	Allows read, execute by owner.
`0300`	Allows write, execute by owner.
`0700`	Allows read, write, execute by owner.
`0040`	Allows read by group.
`0020`	Allows write by group.
`0010`	Allows execute (search in a directory) by group.
`0060`	Allows read, write by group.
`0050`	Allows read, execute by group.
`0030`	Allows write, execute by group.
`0070`	Allows read, write, execute by group.
`0004`	Allows read by others.
`0002`	Allows write by others.
`0001`	Allows execute (search in a directory) by others.
`0006`	Allows read, write by others.
`0005`	Allows read, execute by others.
`0003`	Allows write, execute by other.
`0007`	Allows read, write, execute by others.

Symbolic mode

Symbolic mode is a comma-separated list with no intervening whitespace of the form:

`[<who>]<operator>[<permissions>]`

<who> has the following form:

`< u | g | o | a>`

u	User's permissions.
g	Group's permissions.
o	Others' permissions.
a	All permissions (user, group, other). Equivalent to ugo.

<operator> has the following form:

`< + | - | =>`

+	Adds *<permissions>*.
	If *<permissions>* is not specified, no changes occur.

	If `<who>` is not specified, `<who>` defaults to `a`, and `<permissions>` are added as specified, except that `chmod` does not override the file mode creation mask.
	If `<who>` is specified, `<permissions>` are added as specified.
-	Removes <permissions>.
	If <permissions> is not specified, no changes occur.
	If <who> is not specified, <who> defaults to a, and <permissions> are removed as specified, except that chmod does not override the file mode creation mask.
	If <who> is specified, <permissions> are removed as specified.
=	Assigns the absolute <permissions> specified.
	If <who> is not specified, <who> defaults to a.
	If <permissions> is not specified, <permissions> defaults to remove.
	If <who> is specified and <permissions> is not, all permissions for <who> are removed.
	If <who> is not specified and <permissions> is specified, <permissions> for all are set to <permissions>, except that chmod does not override the file creation mask.
	If <who> is specified and <permissions> is specified, <permissions> for <who> are set as specified.

`<permissions>` has the following form:

`<r | w | x | X | s | t | u | g | o>`

`r`	Sets read bits.
`w`	Sets write bits.
`x`	Sets execute/search bits.
`X`	Sets execute/search bits if the file is a directory, or if any execution/search bits are already set in the file before X would act upon the file. X is used only with +, and is ignored in all other cases.
`s`	Sets the set-user-ID-on-execution and set-group-ID-on-execution bits. A process runs as the user or group specified by s.
`t`	Sets the sticky bit.
`u`	User permission bit in the mode of the original file.
`g`	Group permission bits in the mode of the original file.
`o`	Other permission bits in the mode of the original file.

Operations on `<who>` or in combination with `<permissions>` `s` or `t` are ignored.

chown

`chown` Changes file owner and group.

`chown [-R [-H | -L | -P]] [-fh] <owner> <file1> <file2> ...`

`chown [-R [-H | -L | -P]] [-fh] :<group> <file1> <file2> ...`

`chown [-R [-H | -L | -P]] [-fh] <owner>:<group> <file1> <file2> ...`

`-R` Recursively descends through directory arguments to change the user ID and/or group ID.

`-H` If `-R` is specified, symbolic links on the command line are followed. Symbolic links encountered in tree traversal are not followed.

`-L` If `-R` is specified, all symbolic links are followed.

`-P` If `-R` is specified, no symbolic links are followed.

`-f` Forces an attempt to change user ID and/or group ID without reporting any errors.

`-h` If the file is a symbolic link, the user ID and/or group ID of the link is changed.

The `-H`, `-L`, and `-P` options are ignored unless `-R` is specified. Because they also override each other, the last option specified determines the action that is taken.

The `-L` option cannot be used with the `-h` option.

It is not necessary to provide both *<owner>* and *<group>*; however, one must be specified. If group is specified, it must be preceded with a colon (`:`).

The owner may be either a numeric user ID or a username. If a username exists for a numeric user ID, the associated username is used as for the owner. Similarly, the group may be either a numeric group ID or a group name. If a group name exists for a group ID, the associated group name is used for the group.

Unless invoked by the super user, `chown` clears set-user-id and set-group-id bits.

cmp

`cmp` Compares two files.

`cmp [-l | -s] <file1> <file2> [<skip1> <skip2>]`

`cmp` compares two files of any type and writes the results to the standard output. By default, `cmp` is silent if the files are the same; if they differ, the byte and line number where the first difference occurs is reported.

Bytes and line are numbered beginning with 1.

`-l`	Lists the byte number (decimal) and differing byte values (octal) for each difference.
`-s`	Prints nothing for differing files; returns exit status only.

The optional arguments <*skip1*> and <*skip2*> are the byte offsets, from the beginning of <*file1*> and <*file2*>, respectively, where the comparison will begin. The offset is decimal by default, but may be expressed as a hexadecimal or octal value by preceding it with a leading 0x or 0.

`cmp` exits with one of the following values:

`0`	Files are identical.
`1`	Files are different; this includes the case where one file is identical to the first part of the other. In the latter case, if -s has not been specified, cmp writes to standard output that EOF was reached in the shorter file before any differences were found.
`>1`	An error occurred.

compress

compress	Compresses data.
uncompress	Expands data.

compress [-cfv] [-b <*bits*>] <*file1*> <*file2*> ...

uncompress [-cfv] <*file1*> <*file2*> ...

compress reduces the size of a file and renames the file by adding a .Z extension. As much of the original file characteristics (modification time, access time, file flags, file mode, user ID, and group ID) are retained as permissions allow. If compression would not reduce a file's size, the file is ignored.

uncompress restores a file reduced by compress to its original form, and renames the file by removing the `.Z` extension.

`-c`	Writes compressed or uncompressed output to standard output without modifying any files.
`-f`	Forces compression of a file, even when compression would not reduce its size. Additionally, forces files to be overwritten without prompting for confirmation.
`-v`	Prints the percentage reduction of each file.
`-b <bits>`	Specifies the upper bit code limit. Default is 16. Bits must be between 9 and 16. Lowering the limit results in larger, less-compressed files.

cp

`cp` — Copies files.

`cp [-R (-H | -L | -P)] [-f | -i] [-p] `*<source> <target>*

`cp [-R (-H | -L | -P)] [-f | -i] [-p] `*<source1> <source2> ... <directory>*

In its first form, `cp` copies the contents of *<source>* to *<target>*.

In its second form, `cp` copies the contents of the list enumerated by *<source1> <source2>* ... to the directory named by *<directory>*. The names of the files themselves are not changed. If `cp` detects an attempt to copy to itself, that attempt fails.

`-R` — If *<source>* is a directory, `cp` recursively copies the directory. This option also causes symbolic links to be copied, rather than indirected through. Created directories have the same mode as the corresponding source directory.

`-H` — If `-R` is specified, symbolic links on the command line are followed, but symbolic links in the tree traversal are not.

`-L` — If `-R` is specified, all symbolic links are followed.

`-R` — If `-R` is specified, no symbolic links are followed.

`-f` — Forces an existing file to be overwritten. If permissions do not allow copy to succeed, forces the existing file to be removed and a new file to be created, without prompting for confirmation. The `-i` option is ignored if the `-f` option is specified.

`-i` — Invokes an interactive mode that prompts for a confirmation before overwriting an existing file.

`-p` — Causes `cp` to retain as much of the modification time, access time, file flags, file mode, user ID, and group ID information as permissions allow.

crontab

`crontab` — Maintains crontab files for individual users.

`crontab [-u `*<user>*`] `*<file>*

`crontab [-u `*<user>*`] [-l | -r | -e]`

`crontab` is the program that installs, removes, or lists the tables the `cron` (8) executes for users. Each user can have his own `crontab`, which is stored in `/var/cron/tabs/`. The `crontab` is not edited directly.

If /var/cron/allow exists, the <user> must be listed in the file to be able to use cron. If /var/cron/allow does not exist, but /var/cron/deny exists, <user> must not be listed in this file to use this command. If neither file exists (depending on site-dependent configuration), either only the super user may use this command or all users may be able to use this command.

The first form of the command installs a crontab from <file> or standard input, if - is given instead of <file>. The second form of the command displays, removes, or edits the installed crontab.

-u <user>	Specifies the name of the user. If not specified, the user issuing the command is assumed. If crontab is being used inside an su command, -u should be used.
-l	Lists the current crontab on standard output.
-r	Removes the current crontab.
-e	Edits the current crontab using the editor specified by the environment variables VISUAL or EDITOR. On exiting the editor, the modified crontab is automatically installed.

Basic format of a crontab statement, with value ranges shown here:

```
minute hour day_of_month month day_of_week [<user>] <command>
0-59 0-23 1-31 1-12 0-7 (Sunday may be 0 or 7)
```

Fields may be separated by spaces or tabs. * may be used as the value of a field to mean all possible values for that field. A field value may be further specified by providing a single value, a comma-separated list of values, a range of values, or a comma-separated list of single values or ranges of values.

Step values may be specified by use of *<range>/<number>*. For example, 0-23/2 would be every other hour. 0-23/2 is equivalent to the value list 0, 2, 4, 6, 8, 10, 12, 14, 16, 18, 20, 22. Step values may also be specified by */<number>. For example, every other hour could also be specified by */2 in that field.

Names may also be used for the month and day_of_week fields. Names are the first three characters of the actual name. Case does not matter. Lists or ranges of names, however, may not be used.

The <user> field is specified only in a system crontab.

defaults

defaults	Accesses the Mac OS X user defaults system.

```
defaults read [ <domain name> [ <key> ] ]
defaults write <domain name> [ {'<domain rep>' | <domain name> <key>
'<value rep>'}
defaults delete [ <domain name> [ <key> ] ]
defaults { domains | find <word> | help }
```

`defaults` allows users to read, write, and delete Mac OS X user defaults from the command line. Applications use the defaults system to record user preferences and other information that must be maintained when applications aren't running, such as the default font for new documents. Because applications access the defaults system while they are running, you should not modify the results of a running application.

User defaults belong to *<domains>*, which typically correspond to individual applications. Each domain has a dictionary of keys and values to represent its defaults. Keys are always strings, but values can be complex data structures comprised of arrays, dictionaries, strings, and binary data.

Although all applications, system services, and other programs have their own domains, they also share a domain called NSGlobalDomain. If a default is not specified in the application's domain, it uses the default listed in the NSGlobalDomain instead.

`read`	Prints all of the user's defaults for every domain to standard output.
`read` *<domain name>*	Prints all of the user's defaults for the specified *<domain name>* to standard output.
`read` *<domain name> <key>*	Prints the value for the default of the *<domain name>* identified by *<key>*.
`write` *<domain name> <key>* '*<value rep>*'	Writes *<value rep>* as the value for *<key>* in *<domain name>*. *<value rep>* must be a property list, and must be enclosed in single quotes. For example:

```
defaults write MyApplication "Default Color" '(255, 0, 0)'
```

sets the default color in MyApplication to the array containing 255, 0, 0 (red, green, blue components). Note that the key is in quotes because of the space in its name.

`write` *<domain name>* '*<domain rep>*' Overwrites the defaults information in *<domain name>* with that specified in *<domain rep>*. *<domain rep>* must be a property list representation of a dictionary, and must be enclosed in single quotes. For example,

```
defaults write MyApplication '[ "Default Color" = (255, 0, 0); "Default
Font" = Helvetica; } '
```

overwrites any previous defaults for MyApplication and replaces them with the ones specified.

`delete` *<domain name>*	Deletes all default information for *<domain name>*.
`delete` *<domain name> <key>*	Deletes the default named *<key>* in *<domain name>*.
`domains`	Prints the names of all domains in the user's defaults system.
`find` *<word>*	Searches for *<word>* in the domain names, keys, and values of the user's defaults, and prints out a list of matches.
`help`	Prints a list of possible command formats.

diff

diff — Finds differences between two files.

diff [options] <from-file> <to-file>

In its simplest form, diff compares the contents of two files. A filename of - stands for text read from the standard input. As a special case, diff - - compares a copy of standard input to itself.

If <from-file> is a directory and <to-file> is not, diff compares the file in <from-file> whose filename is that of <to-file> and vice versa. The nondirectory file must not be -.

If both <from-file> and <to-file> are directories, diff compares corresponding files in both directories, in alphabetical order; the comparison is not recursive unless -r or -recursive option is specified. diff never compares the actual content of a directory as if it were a file. The file that is fully specified may not be standard input because standard input is nameless and the notion of "file with the same name" does not apply.

Because diff options begin with -, normally <from-file> and <to-file> may not begin with -. However, — as an argument itself treats the remaining arguments as filenames even if they begin with -.

Multiple single-letter options, unless they can take an argument, can be combined into a single command-line word. Long named options can be abbreviated to any unique prefix of their name.

Option	Description
-<lines>	Shows <lines> (an integer) lines of context. This option does not specify an output format by itself; it has no effect unless it is combined with -c or -u.
-q	
—brief	Reports only whether the files differ, not the details of the differences.
-c	Uses the context output format.
-C <lines>	
—context[=<lines>]	Uses the context output format, showing <lines> (an integer) lines of context, or 3 if <lines> is not given.
—changed-group-format=<format>	Uses <format> to output a line group containing differing lines from both files in if-then-else format.
-D <name>	Makes merged if-then-else format output, conditional on the preprocessor <name>.
-e	
—ed	Makes output that is valid ed script.
-x <pattern>	

`—exclude=<pattern>`	When comparing directories, ignores files and subdirectories whose base names match `<pattern>`.
`-X`	
`—exclude-from=<file>`	When comparing directories, ignores files and subdirectories whose base names match any pattern contained in `<file>`.
`-t`	
`—expand-tabs`	Expands tabs to spaces in the output, to preserve the alignment of tabs in the input files.
`-f`	Makes output that looks vaguely like an ed script but has changes in the order it appears in the file.
`-F <regexp>`	In context and unified format, for each hunk of differences, shows some of the last preceding line that matches `<regexp>`.
`—forward-ed`	Makes output that looks vaguely like an ed script but has changes in the order it appears in the file.
`-h`	This option has no effect; is present for Unix compatibility.
`—help`	Prints help information.
`—horizontal-lines=<lines>`	Does not discard the last `<lines>` lines of the common prefix and the first `<lines>` lines of the common suffix.
`-i`	
`—ignore-case`	Ignores changes in case; considers uppercase and lowercase letters equivalent.
`-I <regexp>`	Ignores changes that just insert or delete lines that match `<regexp>`.
`—ifdef=<name>`	Makes merged if-then-else format output, conditional on the preprocessor macro `<name>`.
`-w`	
`—ignore-all-space`	Ignores whitespace when comparing lines.
`-B`	
`—ignore-blank-lines`	Ignores changes that just insert or delete blank lines.
`—ignore-matching-lines=<regexp>`	Ignores changes that just insert or delete lines that match `<regexp>`.
-b	
—ignore-space-change	Ignores changes in amount of whitespace.

Option	Description
-T	
—initial-tab	Outputs a tab rather than a space before the text of a line in normal or context format. This causes the alignment of tab in the line to look normal.
-L *<label>*	
—label=*<label>*	Uses *<label>* instead of the filename in the context format and unified format headers.
—left-column	Prints only the left column of the two common lines in side-by-side format.
—line-format=*<format>*	Uses *<format>* to output all lines in if-then-else format.
-d	
—minimal	Changes the algorithm to perhaps find a smaller set of changes. This makes diff slower.
-n	
—rcs	Outputs RCS-format diffs; like -f except that each command specifies the number of lines affected.
-N	
—new-file	In the directory comparison, if a file is found in only one directory, treats it as present but empty in the other directory.
—new-group-format=*<format>*	Uses *<format>* to output a group of lines taken from just the second file in if-then-else format.
—new-line-format=*<format>*	Uses *<format>* to output a line taken from just the second file in if-then-else format.
`—old-group-format=<format>`	Uses `<format>` to output a group of lines taken from just the first file in if-then-else format.
`—old-line-format=<format>`	Uses `<format>` to output a line taken from just the first file in if-then-else format.
`-p`	
`—show-c-function`	Shows which C function each change is in.
`-l`	
`—paginate`	Passes the output through pr to paginate it.
`-r`	
`—recursive`	When comparing directories, recursively compares any subdirectories found.
-s	
—report-identical-files	Reports when two files are the same.

Option	Description
-S <*file*>	
—starting-file=<*file*>	When comparing directories, starts with the file <*file*>. This is used for resuming an aborted comparison.
—sdiff-merge-assist	Prints extra information to help sdiff. sdiff uses this option when it runs diff. This option is not intended for users to use directly.
—show-function-line=<*regexp*>	In context and unified format, for each hunk of differences, shows some of the last preceding line that matches <*regexp*>.
-y	
—side-by-side	Uses the side-by-side output format.
-H	
—speed-large-files	Uses heuristics to speed handling of large files that have numerous scattered small changes.
—suppress-common-lines	Does not print common lines in side-by-side format.
-a	
—text	Treats all files as text and compares them line-by-line, even if they do not seem to be text.
-u	Uses the unified output format.
-U <*lines*>	
—unified[=<*lines*>]	Uses the unified output format, showing <*lines*> (an integer) lines of context, or 3 if <*lines*> is not given.
`—unchanged-group-format=` `<format>`	Uses `<format>` to output a group of common lines taken from both files in if-then-else format.
`—unchanged-line-format=` `<format>`	Uses `<format>` to output a line common to both files in if-then-else format.
`-p`	
`—undirectional-new-file`	When comparing directories, if a file appears only in the second directory of the two, treats it as present but empty in the other.
`-v`	
`—version`	Outputs the version number of `diff`.
-W <columns>	
—width=<columns>	Uses an output width of <columns> in side-by-side format.

df

`df`	Displays free disk space.

`df [-ikln] [-t <type>] [<file> | <filesytem> ...]`

`-i`	Includes statistics on the number of free inodes.
`-k`	Reports number in kilobyte counts. Default is 512-byte block sizes.
`-l`	Displays statistics only about mounted file systems with the `MNT_LOCAL` flag set. If a non-local file system is given as the argument, a warning is issued and no information is displayed.
`-n`	Prints out previously obtained statistics from the file system. This option should be used if it is possible that one or more file systems are in a state such that there is a long delay before they can provide statistics.
`-t <type>`	Displays information for file systems of the specified type. More than one type may be specified in a comma-separated list of the list of file system types.

If the environment variable `BLOCKSIZE` is set, and the `-k` option is not used, the block counts are displayed according to the environment variable.

du

`du`	Displays disk usage statistics.

`du [-H | -L | -P] [-a | -s] [-ckrx] [<file> ...]`

`du` displays the file system block usage for each file argument and for each directory in the file hierarchy rooted in each directory argument. If no file is specified, the block usage of the hierarchy rooted in the current directory is displayed.

`-H`	Follows symbolic links on the command line. Symbolic links encountered during tree traversal are not followed.
`-L`	Follows all symbolic links.
`-P`	Does not follow symbolic links.
`-a`	Displays an entry for each file in the file hierarchy.
`-s`	Displays only the grand total for the specified files.
`-c`	Displays the grand total after all the arguments have been processed.

`-k`	Displays the statistics in 1024-byte blocks. Default is 512-byte blocks.
`-r`	Generates a warning message about directories that cannot be read. This is the default.
`-x`	Does not traverse file system mount points.

`du` counts the storage used by symbolic links and not the files they reference unless `-H` or `-L` is specified. If either `-H` or `-L` is specified, the storage used by a symbolic link is not counted or displayed. `-H`, `-L`, and `-P` override each other. The option specified last is the one executed.

Files with multiple hard links are counted and displayed once per `du` execution.

If the environment variable `BLOCKSIZE` is set and the `-k` option is not used, the block counts are displayed according to the environment variable.

dump

`dump` File system backup.

`dump [-0123456789cnua] [-B <records>] [-b <blocksize>] [-d <density>] [-f <file>] [-h <level>] [-s <feet>] [-T <date>] <filesystem>`

`dump [-W || -w]`

(The 4.3BSD option syntax is implemented for backward compatibility, but is not documented.)

`dump` examines files on a file system and determines which files need to be backed up. These files are copied to the given disk, tape, or other storage medium for safekeeping. A dump that is larger than the output medium is broken into multiple volumes. On most media, the size is determined by writing until an end-of-media indication is returned.

On media that cannot reliably return an end-of-media each volume is of a fixed size; the actual size is determined by the tape size and density and/or block count options. By default, the same output filename is used for each volume after prompting the operator to change media.

`-0-9`	Dump levels. A level `0`, full backup, guarantees the entire file system is copied. A level number above `0`, an incremental backup, tells dump to copy all files new or modified since the last dump of the same or lower level. The default level is `9`.
`-c`	Changes the defaults for use with a cartridge tape drive, with a density of 8000 bpi and a length of 1700 feet.
`-n`	Notifies all operators in the operator group whenever dump requires operator attention.

`-u` Updates the file `/etc/dumpdates` after a successful dump. The format of `/etc/dumpdates` is readable by people, consisting of one free format record per line: file system name, increment level, and `ctime` (3). There may be only one entry per file system at each level.

`-B <records>` The number of kilobytes per volume, rounded down to a multiple of the block size. This option overrides the calculation of the tape size.

`-b <blocksize>` The number of kilobytes per `dump` record. Because the IO system slices all requests into chunks of `MAXBSIZE` (typically 64KB), it is not possible to use a larger block size without having problems later with restore. Therefore, `dump` constrains writes to `MAXBSIZE`.

`-d <density>` Sets the tape density to `<density>`. The default is 1600 bpi.

`-f <file>` Writes the backup to `<file>`. `<file>` may be a special device file, such as a tape drive or disk drive, an ordinary file, or `-` (standard output). Multiple filenames may be given as a single argument separated by commas. Each file will be used for one `dump` volume in the order listed. If the `dump` requires more volumes than the number of names listed, the last filename will be used for all remaining volumes after prompting for media changes. If the name of the file is of the form `<host>:<file>` or `<user>@<host>`: file, `dump` writes to the named file on the remote host using `rmt`.

`-h <level>` Honors the user `nodump` flag only for dumps at or above the given `<level>`. The default honor level is 1, so that incremental backups omit such files but full backups retain them.

`-s <feet>` Attempts to calculate the amount of tape needed at a particular density. If this amount is exceeded, `dump` prompts for a new tape. It is recommended to be a bit conservative on this option. The default tape length is 2300 feet.

`-T <date>` Uses the specified date as the starting time for the `dump` instead of the time determined from looking in `/etc/dumpdates`. The format of the date is the same as that of `ctime` (3). This option is useful for automated `dump` scripts that wish to `dump` over a specified period of time. The `-T` flag is mutually exclusive from the `-u` flag.

`-W` Tells the operator what file systems need to be dumped. The information is gleaned from `/etc/dumpdates` and `/etc/fstab`. The `-W` flag causes dump to print out, for each file system in `/etc/dumpdates` the most recent `dump` date and level, and highlights of those file systems that should be dumped. If the `-W` flag is set, all other options are ignored, and `dump` exits immediately.

`-w` Is like `W`, but prints only those file systems that need to be dumped.

`dump` requires operator intervention on these conditions: end of tape, end of `dump`, tape write error, tape open error, or disk read error (if there are more than a threshold of 32). In addition to alerting all operators implied by the `-n` flag, `dump` interacts with an operator on `dump`'s control terminal at times when `dump` can no longer proceed, or if something is grossly wrong. All questions `dump` poses must be answered by typing `yes` or `no`.

Because making a `dump` involves a lot of time and effort for full `dump`s, `dump` checkpoints itself at the start of each tape volume. If writing that volume fails for some reason, `dump` will, with operator permission, restart itself from the checkpoint after the old tape has been rewound and removed, and a new tape has been mounted.

`dump` tells the operator what is going on at periodic intervals, including (usually low) estimates of the number of blocks to write, the number of tapes it will take, the time to completion, and the time to the tape change.

dumpfs

`dumpfs` Dumps file system information.

`dumpfs [`*<filesystem>*` | `*<special>*`]`

`dumpfs` prints out the super block and cylinder group information for the file system or special device specified. The listing is very long and detailed. This command is useful mostly for finding out certain file system information such as the file system block size and minimum free space percentage.

emacs

`emacs` Editor.

`emacs [`*<command command-line switches>*`] [`*<file1> <file2>*`...]`

`emacs` is a powerful editor that can actually do more than edit files. It has an extensive information system, which can be accessed in `emacs` with the key sequence <Ctrl+h i> (holding the

Control key and `h` then `i`). The information system can be navigated using the arrow keys to move around and pressing the Enter key to make a selection.

`emacs` has an interactive help facility, `<Ctrl+h>`. The information facility is one of the types of help available. A help tutorial is available with `<Ctrl+h t>`. Help Apropos `<Ctrl+h a>` helps the user find a command given its functionality. Help character `<Ctrl+h c>` describes a given character's effect.

The following are `emacs` options of general interest:

`<file>`	Edits the specified `<file>`.
`+<number>`	Moves the cursor to the line number specified by `<number>`. (Do not include a space between + and `<number>`.)
`-q`	Does not load an init file.
`-u <user>`	Loads the init file of the specified `<user>`.
`-t <file>`	Uses the specified `<file>` as the terminal instead of using stdin/stdout. This must be the first argument specified in the command line.
`-nw`	Tells `emacs` not to use its special X interface. If this option is given when invoking `emacs` in an `xterm`(1) window, the `emacs` display is done in that window. This must be the first option specified in the command line.

The following are basic `emacs` key sequences:

`Ctrl+x Ctrl+s`	Saves the file.
`Ctrl+x Ctrl+c`	Exits `emacs`.

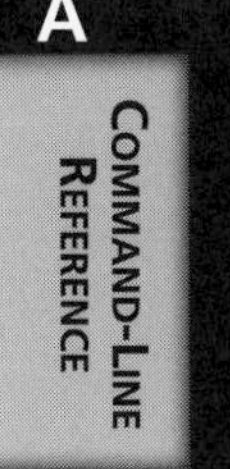

exports

`exports`	Defines remote mount points for NFS requests.

The `exports` file specifies remote mount points for NFS mount protocol per the NFS server specification.

In a `mount` entry, the first field(s) specifies the directory path(s) within a server file system that clients can mount. There are two forms of this specification. The first form is to list all `mount` points as absolute directory paths separated by whitespace. The second form is to specify the pathname of the root of the file system followed by the `-alldirs` flag. This form allows hosts to mount at any point within the file system, including regular files if the `-r` option is used in `mountd`. The pathnames should not have any symbolic links, or `.` or `..` components.

The second component of a line specifies how the file system is to be exported to the host set. The options specify whether the file system is exported read-only or read-write and how the client UID is mapped to user credentials on the server.

The third component of a line specifies the client host set. The set may be specified with three ways. The first is to list the host names separated by whitespace. Standard Internet dot addresses may be used instead. The second way is to specify a netgroup, as defined in `netgroup`. The third way is to specify an Internet subnetwork using a network and network mask.

Export options are as follows:

`-maproot=user`	Credential of the specified user is used for remote access by `root`. The credential includes all groups to which the user is a member on the local machine. The user may be specified by name or number.
`-maproot=user:group1:group2...`	Specifies the precise credential to use for remote access by `root`. The elements of the list may be names or numbers. Note that `user:` should be used to distinguish a credential containing no groups from a complete credential for the user.
`-mapall=user`	
`-mapalluser:group1:group2:...`	Specifies a mapping for all client UIDs, including `root`, using the same semantics as `-maproot`.
`-r`	Synonym for `-maproot` for backward compatibility with older export file formats.

When neither `-maproot` nor `-mapall` is specified, remote accesses by `root` result in a credential of `-2:-2`. All other users are mapped to their remote credential. If a `-maproot` option is given, remote access by `root` is mapped according to the option instead of `-2:-2`. If `-mapall` is given, the credentials of all users, including `root`, are mapped as specified.

`-kerb`	Specifies that the Kerberos authentication server should be used to authenticate and map client credentials. This option requires that the kernel be built with the `NFSKERB` option.
`-ro`	Specifies that the file system should be exported read-only.

fetchmail

`fetchmail`	Fetches mail from a POP-, IMAP-, or ETRN-capable server.

`fetchmail [options] [<mailserver>...]`

`fetchmailconf`

`fetchmail` fetches mail from remote servers and delivers it to your local machine. The retrieved mail can be read via conventional programs, such as `mail` or `elm`. `fetchmail` can be run in daemon mode to repeatedly poll one or more servers at a specified interval.

If `fetchmailconf` is available, it can be used to assist in setting up and editing your `.fetchmailrc` configuration file. `fetchmailconf` runs under the X Window System and requires `pythong` and `tk`. If `fetchmailconf` is not available, you can also use a text editor to create your `.fetchmailrc` file.

`fetchmail` can be run at the command line, but the preferred way is through the `.fetchmailrc` file in your home directory. See the `fetchmail` man page for details on setting up a `.fetchmailrc` file.

If you run `fetchmail` at the command line and also have a `.fetchmailrc` file, options specified in the command line override specifications in the `.fetchmailrc`. Each server that you specify on the command line will be queried according to the options given. If no server is specified, each poll entry of the `.fetchmailrc` is queried.

Almost all the options have a corresponding keyword that can be used to declare them in the `.fetchmailrc`. The following options rarely have to be used at the command line after you have a working `.fetchmailrc`.

-?	
—help	Displays a list of options with brief descriptions.
-V	
—version	Displays version information.
-c	
—check	Checks for messages without fetching them.
-s	
—silent	Silent mode. Suppresses progress/status and error messages. Is overridden by -verbose.
-v	
—verbose	Verbose mode. Produces diagnostic output. Overrides -silent. Doubling the option (-v -v) causes extra diagnostic information to be printed.
-d	
—daemon	Runs as a daemon once per n seconds.
-N	
—nodetach	Does not detach daemon process.
-q	
—quit	Kills daemon process.
-L	
—logfile	Specifies logfile name.
—syslog	Uses syslog(3) for most messages when running as a daemon.

`—invisible`	Does not write Received and enables host spoofing.
`—postmaster`	Specifies last resort recipient.
`—nobounce`	Redirects bounces from user to postmaster.
`-a`	
`—all`	Retrieves all messages, both read and unread. Default is to retrieve only unread messages.
`-k`	
`—keep`	Saves new messages after retrieval. Default is to delete messages from the server after they have been retrieved. This does not work with ETRN.
`-K`	
`—nokeep`	Deletes new messages after retrieval. Useful if you have specified a default of -keep in `.fetchmailrc`. Option is forced on with ETRN.
-F	
—flush	POP/IMAP only. Deletes previously retrieved messages from server. Does not work with ETRN. If your MTA hangs and fetchmail is aborted, the next time you run fetchmail, it will delete the messages that were not delivered to you. The -keep option is recommended instead.
-p <*proto*>	
—protocol <*proto*>	Specifies retrieval protocol to use when retrieving mail from the remote server. If no protocol is specified AUTO is assumed. See man page for list of protocols.
-U	
—uidl	Forces UIDL (unique ID listing) use (POP3 only). Forces client-side tracking of newness of messages.
-P	
—port	Specifies TCP/IP port for making connection. Rarely necessary, as the protocols have well-established default port numbers.
-t	
—timeout	Specifies server nonresponse timeout in seconds.
—plugin	Specifies external command to open TCP connection. Useful for using socks or a special firewall setup.
—plugout	Specifies external command to open SMTP connection.

-r <*folder*>	
—folder <*folder*>	Specifies remote folder name.
-S <*hosts*>	
—smtphost <*hosts*>	Specifies a hunt list of SMTP forwarding hosts.
-D <*domain*>	
—smptaddress <*domain*>	Sets SMTP delivery domain to use.
-Z <nnn>	
—antispam <nnn>[,<nnn> [,<nnn>...]	Sets antispam response values. A value of -1 disables this option. For the command-line option, list should be a comma-separated list.
—mda	Forces mail to be passed to an MDA directly rather than forwarded to port 25. Not recommended unless running an SMTP listener is impossible.
—lmtp	Uses LMTP (Local Mail Transfer Protocol, RFC2033) for delivery. Service port must be specified because the default port 25 will not be accepted.
—bsmtp	Appends fetched mail to a BSMTP file. File contains the SMTP commands that would normally be generated by fetchmail when passing mail to an SMTP listener daemon.
-l	
—limit	Does not fetch messages larger a specified size. Takes a maximum octet size as argument. Does not work with ETRN.
-w	
—warnings	Interval in seconds between warning mail notification.
-b	
—batchlimit	Sets batch limit for SMTP connections. Default is 0, no limit.
-B	
—fetchlimit	Sets fetch limit for number of messages accepted from a given server in a single poll. Does not work with ETRN.
-e	
—expunge	Makes deletions final after a given number of messages. Does not work with ETRN.
-u <name>	
—username <name>	Specifies user identification to be used when logging in to the mailserver. Default is login name on the client machine running fetchmail.

-A	
—preauth	Specifies preauthentication type. Possible values are password, kerberos_v5, or kerberos.
-f <pathname>	
—fetchmailrc <pathname>	Specifies an alternative run control file. Unless -version is also on, the name file must have permissions no more open than 0600 or else be /dev/null.
-i <pathname>	
—iidfile <pathname>	Specifies alternative name for the .fetchids file used to save POP3 UIDs.
-n	
—norewrite	Does not rewrite header addresses. Normally fetches rewrite headers in fetched mail so that any mail IDs local to the server are expanded to full addresses so that replies on the client are addressed correctly, rather than to the local users.
-E	
—envelope	Changes the header that fetchmail assumes will carry a copy of the mail's envelope address.
-Q	
—qvirtual	Prefix to remove from local user ID. Useful if you are using fetchmail to retrieve mail for an entire domain and your ISP is using qmail.

fg

`fg`	Foregrounds a job.

`fg [%<job>...]`

`%<job>`

`fg`

Brings the specified jobs (or, if no argument is given, the current job) to the foreground, continuing each as though it had stopped. *<job>* may be any acceptable form as described in jobs.

find

`find` Finds files.

`find [-H | -L | -P] [-Xdx] [-f <file>] <file> .... <expression>`

`find` recursively descends the directory tree of each file listing, evaluating an `<expression>` composed of primaries and operands.

Options

`-H` Causes the file information and file type returned for each symbolic link on the command line to be those of the file referenced, rather than those of the link itself. If the file does not exist, the information is for the link itself. File information of symbolic links not on the command line is that of the link itself.

`-L` Causes the file information and file type returned for each symbolic link to be those of the referenced file, rather than those of the link itself. If the referenced file does not exist, the information is for the link itself.

`-P` Causes the file information and file type returned for each symbolic link to be those of the link itself.

`-X` Permits find to be safely used with xargs. If a filename contains any delimiting characters used by xargs, an error message is displayed and the file is skipped. The delimiting characters include single quote, double quote, backslash, space, tab, and newline.

`-d` Causes a depth-first traversal of the hierarchy. In other words, directory contents are visited before the directory itself. Default is for a directory to be visited before its contents.

`-x` Excludes find from traversing directories that have a device number different from that of the file from which the descent began.

`-h` Causes the file information and file type returned for each symbolic link to be those of the referenced file, rather than those of the link itself. If the referenced file does not exist, the information returned is for the link itself.

`-f` Specifies a file hierarchy for find to traverse. File hierarchies may also be specified as operands immediately following the options listing.

Primaries (expressions)

All primaries that can take a numeric argument allow the number to be preceded by +, -, or nothing. n takes on the following meanings:

+n More than n

-n Less than n

n Exactly n

-atime n — True if the file was last accessed n days ago. Note that find itself will change the access time.

-ctime n — True if the file's status was changed n days ago.

-mtime n — True if the file was last modified n days ago.

-newer <*file*> — True if the current file has a more recent modification time than <*file*>.

-exec <*command*>; — True if <*command*> returns a zero value exit status. Optional arguments may be passed to <*command*>. The expression must be terminated by a semicolon. If {} appears anywhere in the command name or arguments, it is replaced by the current pathname.

-follow — Follows symbolic links.

-fstype — True if the file is contained in a file system specified by -fstype. Issue the command:

```
sysctl vfs
```

to determine the available types of file systems on the system. There are also two pseudo-types: local and rdonly. local matches any file system physically mounted on the system where the find is being executed; rdonly matches any mounted read-only file system.

-group <*gname*> — True if the file belongs to the specified group name. If <*gname*> is numeric and there is no such group name <*gname*>, it is treated as the group ID.

-user <*uname*> — True if file belongs to the user <*uname*>. If <*uname*> is numeric and there is no such user <*uname*>, it is treated as the user ID.

-nouser — True if the file belongs to an unknown user.

-nogroup — True if the file belongs to an unknown group.

-inum n — True if the file has inode number n.

-links n — True if the file has n links.

-ls — Always true. Prints the following file statistics: inode number, size in 512-byte blocks, file permissions, number of hard links, owner, group, size in bytes, last modification time, and filename. If the file is a symbolic link, the display of the file it is linked to is preceded by ->. The display from this ls is identical to that displayed by ls -dgils.

-ok <command>
: Same as -exec, except that confirmation from the user is requested before executing <command>.

-name <pattern>
: True if the filename contains <pattern>. Special shell pattern matching characters ([,], *, ?) may be used as part of <pattern>. A backslash (\) is used to escape those characters to explicitly search for them as part of <pattern>.

-path <pattern>
: True if the pathname contains <pattern>. Special shell pattern matching characters ([,], *, ?) may be used as part of <pattern>. A backslash (\) is used to escape those characters to explicitly search for them as part of <pattern>. Slashes (/) are treated as normal characters and do not need to be escaped.

-perm [-]<mode>
: <mode> may be either symbolic or octal (see chmod). If <mode> is symbolic, a starting value of zero is assumed, and <mode> sets or clears permissions without regard to the process's file mode creation mask. If mode is octal, only bits 0777 of the file's mode bits are used in the comparison. If <mode> is preceded by a dash (-), this evaluates to true if at least all the bits in <mode> are set in the file's mode bits. If <mode> is not preceded by a dash, this evaluates to true if the bits in <mode> match exactly the file's mode bits. If <mode> is symbolic, the first character may not be a dash.

-print0
: Always true. Prints the current pathname followed by a null character.

-print
: Always true. Prints the current pathname followed by a newline character. If none of -exec, -ls, -ok, or -print0 is specified, -print is assumed.

-prune
: Always true. Does not descend into current file once the pattern has been matched. If -d is specified, -prune has no effect.

-size n[c]
: True if the file size, rounded up, is n 512-byte blocks. If c follows n, it is true if the file size is n bytes.

`-type t`	True if the file is of the specified type. Possible file types are `W` Whiteout `b` Block special `c` Character special `d` Directory `f` Regular file `l` Symbolic link `p` FIFO `s` Socket

Operators

Primaries may be combined using the following operators (in order of decreasing precedence):

`(`*`expression`*`)`	True if the parenthesized expression evaluates to true.
`!`*`expression`*	True if the expression is false (`!` is the unary, not the operator).
`expression` `[-and]` *`expression`* *`expression expression`*	True if both expressions are true. The second expression is not evaluated if the first is false. (`-and` is the logical AND operator.)
`expression` `-or` *`expression`*	True if either expression is true. The second expression is not evaluated if the first is true. (`-or` is the logical OR operator.)

from

`from`	Prints names of those who have sent mail.
`from [-s` *`<sender>`*`] [-f` *`<file>`*`] [`*`<user>`*`]`	
`-s` *`<sender>`*	Only prints entries from addresses containing the string *`<sender>`*.
`-f` *`<file>`*	Examines *`<file>`* instead of the invoker's mailbox. If `-f` is used, *`<user>`* should not be used.
`<user>`	Examines *`<user>`*'s mailbox rather than the invoker's mailbox. Privileges are required.

fsck

`fsck`	File system consistency check and interactive repair.

`fsck [-dpfyn] [-l <maxparallel>] [-t <fstype>] [-T <fstype>:<fsoptions>] <special> | <node> ...`

`fsck` invokes file system–specific programs to check the special devices listed in the `fstab` (5) file or in the command line for consistency.

`-d`	Debugging mode. Prints the commands without executing them. Available only if `fsck` is compiled to support it.
`-p`	Preen mode.
`-f`	Forces checking of file systems, even when they are marked clean (for file systems that support this).
`-y`	Assumes yes as the answer to all operator questions.
`-n`	Assumes no as the answer to all operator questions, except CONTINUE?.
`-l <maxparallel>`	Limits the number of parallel checks to the number specified by `<maxparallel>`. By default, the limit is the number of disks, running one process per disk. If a smaller limit is given, the disks are checked in round robin, one file system at a time.
`-t <fstype>`	Invokes `fsck` only in the comma-separated list of file system types. If the list starts with no, invokes `fsck` for the file system types that are not specified in the list.
`-T <fstype>:<fsoptions>`	List of comma-separated file system specific options for the specified file system type, in the same format as `mount` (8).

fstab

`fstab`	Static information about the file systems.

The `fstab` files contains descriptive information about the various file systems. The `fstab` is only read by programs, not written by them. Each file system is described on a separate line. Fields in each line are separated by tabs or spaces. The order of records in the `fstab` is important because `fsck` (8), `mount` (8), and `umount` (8) sequentially iterate through the `fstab`.

The first field (fs_spec) describes the block special device or remote file system to be mounted. For file systems of type ffs, the special filename is the block special filename, and not the character special filename.

The second field (fs_file) describes the mount point for the file systems. For swap partitions, the field should be specified as none.

The third field (fs_vfstype) describes the type of file system. The currently supported file systems are

`adosfs`	AmigaDOS file system.
`cd9660`	ISO 9660 CD ROM.
`fdesc`	An implementation of `/dev/fd`.
`ffs`	A local file system.
`kernfs`	Various kernel statistics.
`mfs`	A local memory-based file system.
`msdos`	MSDOS FAT file system.
`nfs`	Sun Microsystems compatible Network File System.
`procfs`	A local file system of process information.
`swap`	Disk partition to be used for swapping.
`union`	A translucent file system.

The fourth field (fs_mntops) describes mount options associated with the file system. It is formatted as a comma-separated list of options. It contains at least the mount type and any additional options appropriate to the file system type.

The option `auto` can be used in the `noauto` form to cause a file system not to be automatically mounted (with `mount -a` or at system boot time).

The options `userquota` and/or `groupquota` cause the file system to be automatically processed by `quotacheck` (8) command, and user and/or group disk quotas are enabled with `quotaon` (8). By default, file system quotas are maintained in the files named quota.user and quota.group located at the root of the associated file system. The defaults may be overridden by using the appending to the quota option =<*absolute-path-to-quota-file*>.

The fifth field (fs_freq) is used by `dump` (8) to determine which file systems need to be dumped. If the field is not present or is zero, a value of zero is returned, and dump assumes that the file system does not need to be dumped.

The sixth field (fs_passno) is used by `fsck` (8) to determine the order in which file system checks should be done at reboot time. The `root` file system should be specified with a value of 1. Other file systems should have a value of 2. File systems within a drive are checked sequentially, whereas file systems on different drives are checked at the same time to use parallelism available in the hardware. If the field is not present or is zero, a value of zero is returned, and `fsck` assumes that the file system does not need to be checked.

ftp

`ftp`	File transfer program.

`ftp [-dgintv] [<hostname> [<port>]]`

The remote host with which `ftp` is to communicate can be specified on the command line. Done this way, `ftp` immediately tries to establish a connection with the remote host. Otherwise, `ftp` enters its command interpreter mode, awaits commands from the user, and displays the prompt `ftp>`.

`-d`	Enables debugging.
`-g`	Disables filename globbing.
`-i`	Turns off interactive mode when transferring multiple files.
`-n`	Does not attempt auto-login upon initial connection. If auto-login is not disabled, `ftp` checks for a `.netrc` file in the user's directory for an entry describing an account on the remote machine. If no entry is available, `ftp` prompts for the login name on the remote machine (defaults to the login name on the local machine), and if necessary, prompts for a password.
`-t`	Enables packet tracing.
`-v`	Enables verbose mode. Default if input is from a terminal. Shows all responses from the remote server as well as transfer statistics.

When `ftp` is in its command interpreter mode awaiting instructions from the user, there are many commands that the user may issue. Some of them include:

`ascii`	Sets the file transfer type to network ASCII. Although this is supposed to be the default, it is not uncommon for an `ftp` server to indicate that binary is its default.
`binary`	Sets the file transfer type to support binary image transfer.
`bye`	Terminates the `ftp` session and exits `ftp`. An end of file also terminates the session and exits.
`quit`	Same as `bye`.
`cd <remote_directory>`	Changes the current working directory on the remote host to `<remote_directory>`.
`cdup`	Changes the current working directory on the remote host to the parent directory.
`close`	Terminates the `ftp` session with the remote host and returns to the command interpreter.
`disconnect`	Same as `close`.

dir [<*remote-directory*> [<*local_file*>]]
Prints a listing of the directory on the remote machine. Most Unix systems produce an ls -l output. If <*remote_directory*> is not specified, the current directory is assumed. If <*local_file*> is not specified, or is -, the output is sent to the terminal.

ftp <*hostname*> [<*port*>]
Same as open.

open <*hostname*> [<*port*>]
Attempts to establish an ftp connection on <*hostname*> at <*port*>, if <*port*> is specified.

glob
Toggles filename expansion for mdelete, mget, and mput. If globbing is turned off, filename arguments are taken literally and not expanded.

delete <*remote_file*>
Deletes the specified <*remote_file*> on the remote machine.

mdelete <*remote_files*>
Deletes the specified <*remote_files*> on the remote machine.

get <*remote_file*> [<*local-file*>]
Downloads <*remote_file*> from the remote machine to the local machine. If <*local_file*> is not specified, the file is also saved on the local machine with the name <*remote_file*>.

recv <remote_file> [<local_file>]
Same as get.

mget <remote_files>
Downloads the specified <remote_files>.

put <local_file> [<remote_file>]
Uploads the specified <local_file> to the remote host. If <remote-_file> is not specified, the file as saved on the remote host with the name <local_file>.

send <local_file> [<remote_file>]
Same as put.

mput <local_files>
Uploads the specified <local_files>.

msend
Same as mput.

help [<command>]
Displays a message describing <command>. If <command> is not specified, a listing of known commands is displayed.

?
Same as help.

lcd <*directory*>
Changes the working directory on the local machine. If <*directory*> is not specified, the user's home directory is used.

ls [<*remote_directory*> [<*local_file*>]]
Prints a list of the files in a directory on the remote machine. If <*remote_directory*> is not specified, the current working directory is assumed. If <*local_file*> is not specified or is -, the output is printed to a terminal.

	Note that if nothing is listed, the directory might only have directories in it. Try ls `-l` or `dir` for a complete listing.
`mkdir <directory>`	Makes the specified `<directory>` on the remote machine.
`rmdir <directory>`	Removes the specified `<directory>` from the remote machine.
`passive`	Toggles passive mode. If passive mode is turned on (off by default), the `ftp` client sends a `PASV` command for data connections rather than a `PORT` command. `PASV` command requests that the remote server open a port for the data connection and return the address of that port. The remote server listens on that port and the client then sends data to it. With the `PORT` command, the client listens on a port and sends that address to the remote host, who connects back to it. Passive mode is useful when `ftp`ing through a firewall. Not all `ftp` servers are required to support passive mode.
`pwd`	Prints the current working directory on the remote host.
`verbose`	Toggles verbose mode. Default is on. In verbose mode, all responses from the `ftp` server are shown as well as transfer statistics.

ftpd

`ftpd`	Internet File Transfer Protocol server.

`ftpd [-AdDhlMSU] [-T <maxtimeout>] [-t <timeout>] [-u <mask>]`

`ftpd` is the Internet File Transfer Protocol process. It uses the TCP protocol and runs on the port specified as `ftp` in services directory of the NetInfo database.

`-A`	Permits only anonymous FTP connections. All others are refused.
`-d`	Turns on debugging. Debugging information in written to the `syslog` using `LOG_FTP`.
`-D`	Detaches and becomes a daemon. Accepts connections on the FTP port and forks child processes to handle them. This has a lower overhead than starting the service from `inetd`(8) and is useful on busy servers to reduce the load.
`-h`	Uses data ports in the high port range (usually 40000–44999) for passive connections.

-l	Each successful and failed ftp (1) session is logged to the syslog using LOG_FTP. If specified twice (-l -l), the logging of retrieve (get), store (put), append, delete, make directory, remove directory, and rename operations and their arguments also occurs.
-M	Enables multihomed mode. Instead of using ~ftp for anonymous transfers, a directory matching the fully qualified domain name of the IP address of the connected client, located in ~ftp, is used instead.
-S	Logs all anonymous transfers to /var/log/ftpd, if the file exists.
-U	Logs each concurrent ftp (1) session to the file /var/log/ftpd, making them visible to commands such as who (1).
-T *<maxtimeout>*	A client may also request a different timeout period. The maximum period may be set to *<timeout>* in seconds. Default is 2 hours.
-t *<timeout>*	Sets the inactivity timeout period to *<timeout>* seconds. Default is 15 minutes.
-u *<mask>*	Changes default umask from 027 to *<mask>*.

ftpd supports the following FTP requests, case ignored.

ABOR	Aborts previous command.
ACCT	Specifies account (ignored).
ALLO	Allocates storage (vacuously).
APPE	Appends to a file.
CDUP	Changes to the parent directory of the current working directory.
CWD	Changes current working directory.
DELE	Deletes a file.
HELP	Gives help information.
LIST	Gives list files in a directory (ls -lgA).
MKD	Makes a directory.
MDTM	Shows last modification time of file.
MODE	Specifies data transfer mode.
NLST	Gives name list of files in directory.
NOOP	Does nothing.
PASS	Specifies password.

PASV	Prepares for server-to-server transfer.
PORT	Specifies data connection port.
PWD	Prints current working directory.
QUIT	Terminates session.
REST	Restarts incomplete transfer session.
RETR	Retrieves a file.
RMD	Removes a directory.
RNFR	Specifies rename-from filename.
RNTO	Specifies rename-to filename.
SITE	Nonstandard commands (see next section).
SIZE	Returns size of file.
STAT	Returns status of server.
STOR	Stores a file.
STOU	Stores a file with a unique name.
STRU	Specifies data transfer structure.
SYST	Shows operating system type of server system.
TYPE	Specifies data transfer type.
USER	Specifies username.
XCUP	Changes to parent of current working directory (deprecated).
XCWD	Changes working directory (deprecated).
XMKD	Makes a directory (deprecated).
XPWD	Prints the current working directory (deprecated)
XRMD	Removes a directory (deprecated).

The following non-standard commands are supported by the `SITE` request:

UMASK	Changes the `umask`; for example, `SITE UMASK 002`.
IDLE	Sets the idle-timer; for example, `SITE IDLE 60`.
CHMOD	Changes the mode of a file; for example, `SITE CHMOD0 0CHMOD1 1CHMOD2`.
HELP	Gives help information.

The remaining `ftp` requests specified in Internet RFC 959 are recognized, but not implemented.

`ftpd` interprets filenames according to the globbing conventions by `csh` (1). This allows users to use the following metacharacters: `*?[]{}~`

ftpd authenticates users according to these rules:

1. Login name must be in the password database and not have a null password.

2. Login name must not appear in /etc/ftpusers.

3. User must have a standard shell returned by getusershell (3).

4. If the username appears in /etc/ftpchroot, the sessions root is changed to the user's home directory by chroot (2), as for an anonymous or ftp account. The user must still supply a password. This feature is a compromise between an anonymous account and a fully privileged account. This account should also be set up as for an anonymous account.

5. If the username is anonymous or ftp, an anonymous FTP account must be present in the password file for user ftp. The connecting user may specify any password, customarily an e-mail address.

Associated files:

/etc/ftpusers	List of unwelcome/restricted users.
/etc/ftpchroot	List of normal users who should be chrooted.
/etc/ftpwelcome	Welcome notice.

gnumake, make

gnumake	GNU make utility to maintain groups of programs.

gnumake [-f *<makefile.]* *[<option>]* ... [*<target>*] ...

For more details, see the make.info file.

In OS X /usr/bin/make is a symbolic link to /usr/bin/gnumake.

The make utility determines automatically which pieces of a large program need to be recompiled, and issues the commands to recompile them. The make utility is not limited to programs. It can be used to describe any task where some files must be updated automatically from others whenever the others change.

To prepare to use make, you must write a file called the makefile that describes the relationships among files in your program, and then states the commands for updating each file. In a program, typically the executable file is updated from object files, which are in turn made by compiling source files.

After a suitable makefile exists, each time you change source files, this simple shell command:

```
make
```

performs all necessary recompilations. The gnnumake program uses the makefile database and the last-modification times of files to decide which files need to be updated. For each of those files, it issues the commands recorded in the database.

`make` executes commands in the makefile to update one or more targets, where the target is typically a program. If `-f` is not present, make looks for the makefiles `GNUmakefile`, `makefile`, and `Makefile`, in that order. Normally, you should call your makefile either makefile or `Makefile`. Note that on Mac OS X, `makefile` and `Makefile` are identical due to the case-insensitive HFS+ file system. We recommend using `Makefile`. GNUmake is not recommended because it would not be understood by other versions of make. If makefile is `-`, the standard input is read.

`make` updates a target if it depends on prerequisite files that have been modified since the target was last modified, or if the target does not exist.

-b	
-m	The options are ignored for compatibility with other versions of make.
-C *<dir>*	Changes to directory *<dir>* before reading the makefiles or doing anything else. If multiple C options are specified, each is interpreted relative to the previous one. This is typically used with recursive invocations of make.
-d	Prints debugging information in addition to normal processing.
-e	Gives variables taken from the environment precedence over variables from makefiles.
-f *<file>*	Uses *<file>* as the makefile.
-i	Ignores all errors in commands executed to remake files.
-I <dir>	
-I<dir>	Specifies a directory <dir> to search for included makefiles. If several -I options are used to specify several directories, the directories are searched in the order specified. Unlike the arguments to other flags of make, the directories given with -I flags may come directly after the flag: I<dir> is allowed, as well as -I <dir>. This syntax is allowed for compatibility with the C preprocessor's -I flag.
-j <jobs>	Specifies the number of jobs (commands) to run simultaneously. If there is more than one -j option, the last one is effective. If the -j option is given without an argument, make does not limit the number of jobs that can run simultaneously.
-k	Continues as much as possible after an error. Although the target that failed and those that depend on it can't be made, the other dependencies of these targets can be processed all the same.

-l	
-l <*load*>	Specifies that no new jobs (commands) should be started if there are other jobs running and the load average is at least <*load*> (a floating-point number). With no argument, removes a previous load limit.
-n	Prints commands that would be executed, but does not execute them.
-o <*file*>	Does not remake the file <*file*> even if it is older than its dependencies, and does not remake anything on account of changes in <*file*>. Essentially the file is treated as very old and its rules are ignored.
-p	Prints the database (rules and variable values) that results from reading the makefiles; then executes as usual or as otherwise specified. This also prints the version information by the -v switch. To print the database without trying to remake any files, use make -p -f/dev/null.
`-q`	Question mode. Does not run any commands, or print anything. Just returns an exit status that is zero if the specified targets are already up to date, nonzero, or otherwise.
`-r`	Eliminates use of the built-in implicit rules. Also clears out the default list of suffixes for suffix rules.
`-s`	Silent operation. Does not print the commands as they are executed.
`-S`	Cancels the effect of `-k` option. This is never necessary except in a recursive make when `-k` might be inherited from the top-level make via `MAKEFLAGS`, or if you set `-k` in `MAKEFILES` in your environment.
`-t`	Touches files (marks them up-to-date without really changing them) instead of running their commands.
`-v`	Prints the version of the `make` program plus a copyright, list of authors, and notice that there is no warranty.
`-w`	Prints a message containing the working directory before and after other processing. This might be useful for tracking down errors from complicated nests of recursive make commands.
`-W <file>`	Pretends that the target has just been modified. When used with `-n`, this shows you what would happen if you were to modify the file. Without `-n`, it is almost the same as

running touch on the given file before running make, except that the modification time is changed only in the imagination of make.

grep

grep

egrep

fgrep — Prints lines matching a pattern.

grep [options] <*pattern*> <*file1*> <*file2*>...

grep [options] [-e <*pattern*> | -f <*file*>] <*file1*> <*file2*> ...

grep searches the list of files enumerated by <*file1*> <*file2*> ..., or standard input if no file is specified or if - is specified. By default, the matching lines are printed.

Two additional variants of the program are available as egrep (same as grep -E) or fgrep (same as grep -F).

-A <*num*>	Prints <*num*> lines of trailing context after matching lines.
—after-context=<*num*>	Same as -A <*num*>.
-a	Processes a binary file as if it were a text file. Equivalent to -binary-files=text option.
—text	Same as -a.
-B <*num*>	Prints <*num*> lines of leading context before matching lines.
—before-context=<*num*>	Same as -B <*num*>.
-C <*num*>	Prints <*num*> lines of output context. Default is 2.
-<*num*>	Same as -C <*num*>.
—context[=<*num*>]	Same as -C <*num*>.
-b	Prints the byte offset within the input file before each line of output.
—byte-offset	Same as -b.
—binary-files=<*type*>	Assumes a file is of type <*type*> if the first few bytes of a file contain binary data. Default <*type*> is binary, and grep normally outputs a one-line message indicating the file is binary, or nothing if there is no match. If <*type*> is without-match, it is assumed that a binary file does not match. Equivalent to -I option.

	If <*type*> is text, it processes the file as though it were a text file. Equivalent to -a option. Warning: Using this option could result in binary garbage being output to a terminal, some of which could be interpreted by the terminal as commands, resulting in unwanted side effects.
`-I`	Assumes a binary file does not match. Equivalent to `-binary-files=without-match` option.
`-c`	Prints a count of matching lines for each file. Combined with `-v`, counts nonmatching lines.
`—count`	Same as `-c`.
`-v`	Inverts matching to select non-matching lines.
`—invert-match`	Same as `-v`.
`-d <action>`	If input file is a directory, uses `<action>` to process it. If `<action>` is `read`, `grep` reads directories as if they were normal files. This is the default. If `<action>` is `skip`, it silently skips directories. If `<action>` is `recurse`, it recursively reads files under the directory. Equivalent to `-r`.
—directories=<*action*>	Same as -d <*action*>.
-r	Recursively reads files under directories. Equivalent to -d recursive option.
—recursive	Same as -r.
-f <*file*>	Reads a list of patterns from <*file*>, which contains one pattern per line. An empty file has no patterns and matches nothing.
—file=<*file*>	Same as -f <*file*>.
-e <*pattern*>	Uses <*pattern*> as the pattern. Useful for protecting patterns beginning with -.
`-regexp=<pattern>`	Same as `-e <pattern>`.
`-G`	Interprets `<pattern>` as a basic regular expression. This is the default behavior.
`—basic-regexp`	Same as above.
`-E`	Interprets `<pattern>` as an extended regular expression. Equivalent to `egrep`.
`-extended-regexp`	Same as `-E`.
`-F`	Interprets `<pattern>` as a list of fixed strings, separated by newlines, any of which are to be matched. Equivalent to `fgrep`.
—fixed-strings	Same as -F.

-H	Prints the filename for each match.
—with-filename	Same as -H.
-h	Suppresses filenames on output when multiple files are searched.
—no-filename	Same as -h.
—help	Displays a brief help message.
-i	Ignores case in <*pattern*> and input files.
—ignore-case	Same as -i.
-L	Prints a list of files that do not have matches. Stops scanning after the first match.
`-l`	Prints a list of files that contain matches.
`—mmap`	If possible, uses `mmap`(2) system call rather than the default `read`(2) system call. Sometimes `-mmap` results in better performance. However, it can cause unexpected behavior, such as core dumps, if the file shrinks while `grep` is reading it or if an I/O error occurs.
`-n`	Output includes the line number where the match occurs.
`—line-number`	Same as `-n`.
`-q`	Quiet. Suppresses normal output. Scanning stops on the first match. Also see the `-s` and `-no-messages` options.
—quiet	Same as -q.
—silent	Same as -q.
-s	Suppresses error messages about nonexistent or unreadable files.
—no-messages	Same as -s.
-V	Prints the version number of grep to standard error. Includes the version number in all bug reports.
—version	Same as -V.
-w	Selects only lines that have matches that form whole words.
—word-regexp	Same as -w.
-x	Selects only those matches that exactly match the whole line.
—line-regexp	Same as -x.
-Z	Outputs a zero byte (the ASCII NUL character) instead of the character that normally follows a filename. This option

	makes the output unambiguous, even for filenames containing unusual characters such as newlines.
—null	Same as -Z.
-y	Obsolete equivalent for -i.
-U	Has no effect on platforms other than MS-DOS and MS Windows. On those platforms, treats files as binary files to affect how CR characters are handled.
—binary	Same as -U.
-u	Has no effect on platforms other than MS-DOS and MS Windows. On those platforms, reports Unix-style byte offsets; that is, with CR characters stripped off.
—unix-byte-offsets	Same as -u.

gzip, gunzip, zcat

gzip

gunzip

zcat Compresses or expands files.

gzip [-acdfhlLnNrtvV19] [-S <*suffix*>] <*file1*> <*file2*> ...

gunzip [-acfhlLnNrtvV] [-S <*suffix*>] <*file1*> <*file2*> ...

zcat [-fhLV] <*file1*> <*file2*> ...

gzip reduces the size of a file and renames the file by adding the .gz extension. It keeps the same ownership modes, and access and modification times. If no files are specified, or if the filename - is specified, standard input is compressed to standard output. gzip compresses regular files, but ignores symbolic links.

Compressed files can be restored to their original form by using gunzip, gzip -d, or zcat.

gunzip takes a list of files from the command line, whose names end in .gz, -gz, .z, -z, _z, or .Z, and which also begin with the correct magic number, and replaces them with expanded files without the original extension. gunzip also recognizes the extensions .tgz and .taz as short versions of .tar.gz and .tar.Z, respectively. If necessary, gzip uses the .tgz extension to compress a .tar file.

zcat is equivalent to gunzip -c. It uncompresses either a list of files on the command line or from standard input and writes uncompressed data to standard output. zcat uncompresses files that have the right magic number, whether or not they end in .gz.

Compression is always formed, even if the compressed file is slightly larger than the original file.

Option	Description
`-a`	ASCII text mode. Converts end-of-lines using local conventions. Supported only on some non-Unix systems.
`—ascii`	Same as `-a`.
`-c`	Writes output to standard output and keeps the original files unchanged.
`—stdout`	Same as `-c`.
`—to-stdout`	Same as `-c`.
`-d`	Decompresses.
`—decompress`	Same as `-d`.
`—uncompress`	Same as `-d`.
`-f`	Forces compression or decompression, even if the file has multiples links or if the corresponding file already exists, or if the compressed data is read from or written to a terminal. If `-f` is not used, and `gzip` is not working in the background, the user is prompted before a file is overwritten.
`-h`	Displays a help screen and quits.
`—help`	Same as `-h`.
`-l`	Lists the following fields for each compressed file: compressed (compressed size) uncompressed (uncompressed size) ratio (compression ratio; 0.0% if unknown) `uncompressed_name` (name of uncompressed file) Uncompressed size is `-1` for files not in `gzip` format. To get an uncompressed size for such files, use `zcat <file1.Z> | wc -c` Combined with `-verbose`, it also displays method (compression method) `crc` (32-bit CRC of the uncompressed data) `date and time` (time stamp of the uncompressed file) Compression methods supported are `deflate`, `compress`, `lzh`, and `pack`. `crc` is listed as `ffffffff` when the file is not in `gzip` format.
`—list`	Same as `-l`.
`-L`	Displays the `gzip` license and quits.
`—license`	Same as -L

`-n`	When compressing, does not save the original filename and time stamp by default. (Always saves the original name if it has to be truncated.) When decompressing, it does not restore the original name (only removes `.gz`) and time stamp (only copies it from compressed file), if present. This is the default.
`—no-name`	Same as `-n`.
`-N`	When compressing, always saves the original filename and time stamp. This is the default. When decompressing, it restores the original time stamp and filename if present.
`—name`	Same as `-N`.
`-q`	Suppresses all warnings.
`—quiet`	Same as `-q`.
`-r`	Traverses the directory structure recursively. If a filename specified on the command line is a directory, `gzip/gunzip` descends into the directory and compresses/decompresses the files in that directory.
—recursive	Same as -r.
-S <*suffix*>	Uses <*suffix*> instead of .gz. Any suffix can be used, but it is recommended that suffixes other than .z or .gz be avoided to avoid confusion when transferring them to other systems. A null suffix (-S "") forces gunzip to try decompression on all listed files, regardless of suffix.
—suffix <*suffix*>	Same as -S <*suffix*>.
-t	Test. Checks the integrity of the compressed file.
—test	Same as —test.
-v	Verbose. Displays the name and percentage reduction for each file compressed or decompressed.
—verbose	Same as -v.
-V	Version. Displays the version number and compilation options and quits.
—version	Same as -V.
-<n> —fast —best	Regulates the speed of compression as specified by -<n>, where -1 (or —fast) is the fastest compression method (least compression) and -9 (or —best) is the slowest compression method (most compression). Default compression option is -6.

halt, reboot

halt

reboot — Stops the system.

Restarts the system.

halt [-nqd]

reboot [-nqd]

The halt and reboot utilities flush the system cache to disk, send all running processes a SIGTERM and subsequently a SIGKILL and, respectively, halts or restarts the system. The action is logged, including adding a shutdown record into the login accounting file.

`-n`	Does not flush the file system cache. This option probably should not be used.
`-q`	Quickly and ungracefully halts/restarts the system, and only flushes the file system cache. This option probably should not be used.
`-d`	Creates a dump before rebooting. This option is useful for debugging system dump procedures or capturing the state of a corrupted or misbehaving system.

Normally, `shutdown` (8) is used when the system needs to be halted or restarted to warn users of their impending doom.

head

`head` — Displays the first lines of a file.

`head [-n <number>] <file1> <file2> ...`

`head [-n <number>]`

`-n <number>`	Displays the first `<number>` of lines. If n is not specified, the default is 10.

id

`id` — Returns user identity.

`id [<user>]`

`id -G [-n] [<user>]`

`id -g [-nr] [<user>]`

`id -u [-nr] [<user>]`

`id -p [<user>]`

The `id` utility displays the user and group names and numeric ID of the calling process to standard output. If the real and effective IDs are different, both are displayed; otherwise, only the real ID is displayed.

If a `<user>` (login name or user ID) is specified, the user and group IDs of that user are displayed. In this case, the real and effective IDs are assumed to be the same.

`-G`	Displays the different group IDs (effective, real, and supplementary) as whitespaced numbers in no particular order.
`-g`	Displays the effective group ID as a number.
`-u`	Displays the effective user ID as a number.
`-n`	Displays the name of the user or group ID for the -G, -g, and `-u` options instead of the number. If any of the ID numbers cannot be mapped into names, the number will be displayed as usual.
`-r`	Displays the real ID for the `-g` and `-u` options instead of the effective ID.
`-p`	Displays the output in human-readable form. If the username returned by `getlogin`(2) is different from the login name referenced by the user ID, the name returned by getlogin(2) is displayed, preceded by the keyword login. The user ID as a name is displayed, preceded by the keyword uid. If the effective user ID is different from the real user ID, the real user ID is displayed as a name, preceded by the keyword euid. If the effective group ID is different from the real group ID, the real group ID is displayed as a name, preceded by the keyword `rgid`. The list of groups to which the user belongs is then displayed as names, preceded by the keyword groups. Each display is on a separate line.

ifconfig

`ifconfig` Configures network interface parameters.

`ifonfig <interface> <address_family> [<address> [<dest address>]] [<parameters>]`

`ifconfig <interface> [<protocol family>]`

`ifconfig -a [-d] [-u] [<address family>]`

`ifconfig -l [-d] [-u] [<address family>]`

`ifconfig` assigns an address to a network interface and/or configures network interface parameters. It must be used at boot time to define the network address of each network interface. It may also be used at a later time to redefine an interface's network address or other operating parameters.

Only the super user may modify the configuration of a network interface.

`-a`	Produces a full listing of all available interfaces.
`-l`	Produces a name-only listing of all available interfaces.
`-d`	Limits a listing to those interfaces that are down.
`-u`	Limits a listing to those interfaces that are up.

Available operands for `ifconfig` are

`<address>`	For the DARPA-Internet family, the address is either a hostname in the hostname database or a DARPA internet address expressed in the Internet standard "dot notation."
`<address family>`	Specifies the *`<address family>`* that effects interpretation of the remaining parameters. The address or protocol families currently supported are `inet`, `iso`, and `ns`.
`<interface>`	*`<interface>`* parameter is a string of the form *`<name physical unit>`*, such as `en0`.

The following parameters may be set with `ifconfig`:

`alias`	Establishes an additional network address for this interface. This is sometimes useful when changing network numbers, while still accepting packets for the old interface. A *`<netmask>`* should be used with this parameter. If the new *`<alias>`* address is on the same subnet as an existing address assigned to this interface, the netmask must be 255.255.255.255. If a netmask is not supplied, the command will use the one implied by the address itself. If the all ones netmask is used, the system will handle route installation. If another is used, a route to that address might have to be added by hand; for example, "`route add -host xx.xx.xx.xx -interface 127.0.0.1`", where `xx.xx.xx.xx` is the alias. In either case, the route might have to be deleted by hand when the alias is removed (`-alias` or `delete`).
`arp`	Enables the use of the Address Resolution Protocol in mapping between network level addresses and link level addresses (default). This is currently implemented for mapping between DARPA Internet addresses and 10 Mb/s ethernet addresses.

`-arp`	Disables the use of the Address Resolution Protocol.
`broadcast`	(`inet` only) Specifies the address to use to represent broadcasts to the network. The default broadcast address is the address with a host part of all 1s.
`debug`	Enables driver-dependent bugging code. This usually turns on extra console logging.
`-debug`	Disables driver-dependent debugging code.
`delete`	Removes the network address specified. This would be used if you incorrectly specified an alias or it was no longer needed.
`dest_addr`	Specifies the address of the correspondent on the other end of a point-to-point link.
`down`	Marks an interface down. When an interface is marked down, the system does not attempt to transmit messages through that interface. If possible, the interface is reset to disable reception as well. This does not automatically disable routes using the interface.
`ipdst`	Specifies an internet host to receive IP packets encapsulating NS packets bound for a remote network
`metric` *<n>*	Sets the routing metric of the interface to *<n>*, default 0. The routing metric is used by the routing protocol. Higher metrics make a route less favorable. Metrics are counted as addition hops to the destination network or host.
`netmask` *<mask>*	(`inet` and ISO) Specifies how much of the address to reserve for subdividing networks into subnetworks. The `mask` includes the network part of the local address and the subnet part, which is taken from the host field of the address. The `mask` can be specified as a single hexadecimal number beginning with 0x, as a dot-notation internet address, or as a pseudo-network name listed in the network table networks. The `mask` contains 1s for the bit positions in the 32-bit address that are to be used for the network and subnet parts, and 0s for the host part.
`nsellength` *<n>*	(ISO only) Specifies a trailing number of bytes for a received NSAP used for local identification the remaining leading part of which is taken to be the NET (Network Entity Title). The default is 1, which is conformant to US GOSIP. When an ISO address is set in an `ifconfig`, it is really the NSAP that is being specified.

`trailers`	Requests the use of a trailer link–level encapsulation when sending (default). If a network interface supports trailers, the system encapsulates outgoing messages such that the number of memory-to-memory copy operations performed by the receiver is minimized. On networks that support Address Resolution Protocol, this flag indicates that the system should request that other systems use `trailer` when sending to this host. Currently used by Internet protocols only.
`-trailers`	Disables the use of a `trailer` link–level encapsulation.
`link[0-2]`	Enables special processing of the link level of the interface.
`-link[0-2]`	Disables special processing at the link level with the specified interface.
`up`	Marks an interface up. May be used to enable an interface after `ifconfig` down has been run. It happens automatically when setting the first address on an interface. If the interface was reset when previously marked down, the hardware is reinitialized.

ipfw

`ipfw` Controlling utility for IP firewall.

```
ipfw [-q] [-p <preproc> [-D <macro>[=<value>]] [-U <macro>] <file>
ipfw [-f | -q] flush
ipfw [-q] zero [<number> ...]
ipfw delete <number> ...
ipfw [-aftN] list [<number>...]
ipfw [-ftN] show [<number>...]
ipfw [-q] add [<number>] <action> [log] <proto> from <src> to <dst>
[via <name> | <ipno>] [<options>]
```

If used as shown in the first line, a `<file>` is read line by line and applied as arguments to `ipfw`.

A preprocessor can be specified using `-p <preproc>` where `<file>` is to be piped through. Typical preprocessors include `m4` and `cpp`. Optional `-D` and `-U` macro specification can be given to pass on to the preprocessor.

Each incoming and outgoing packet is sent through the `ipfw` rules. In the case of a host acting as a gateway, packets that are forwarded by the host are processed twice: once when entering and once when leaving. Each packet can be filtered based on the following associated information:

Receive Interface (recv)	Interface over which packet was received.
Transmit Interface (xmit)	Interface over which packet would be transmitted.
Incoming (in)	Packet was just received.
Outgoing (out)	Packet would be transmitted.
Source IP Address	Sender's IP address.
Destination IP Address	Target's IP address.
Protocol	IP protocol, including but not limited to IP (`ip`), UDP (`udp`), TCP (`tcp`), or ICMP (`icmp`).
Source Port	Sender's UDP or TCP port.
Destination Port	Target's UDP or TCP port.
Connection Setup Flag (`setup`)	Packet is a request to set up a TCP connection.
Connection Established Flag (`established`)	Packet is part of an established TCP connection.
All TCP Flags (`tcpflags`)	One or more of the TCP flags: close connection (`fin`), open connection (`syn`), reset connection (`rst`), push (`psh`), acknowledgement (`ack`), urgent (`urg`).
Fragment Flag (`frag`)	Packet is a fragment of an IP packet.
IP Options (`ipoptions`)	One or more IP options: strict source route (`ssrr`), loose source route (`lsrr`)), record route (`rr`), timestamp (`ts`).
ICMP Types (`icmptypes`)	One or more of the ICMP types: echo reply (0), destination unreachable (3), source quench (4), redirect (5), echo request (8), router advertisement (9), router solicitation (10), time-to-live exceeded (11), IP header bad (12), timestamp request (13), timestamp reply (14), information request (15), information reply (16), address mask request (17), address mask reply (18).

Note that it could be dangerous to filter on source IP address or source TCP/UDP port because either or both could be spoofed.

The `ipfw` utility works by going through the rule list for each packet until a match is found. All rules have two associated counters: a packet count and a byte count. These are updated when a packet matches the rule.

Rules are ordered by line number, from 1 to 65534. Rules are tried in increasing order, with the first matching rule being the one that applies. Multiple rules may have the same number and are applied in the order they were added.

If a rule is added without a number, it is numbered 100 higher than the highest defined rule number, unless the highest rule number is 65435 or greater, in which case the new rules are given that same number.

One rule is always present: `65535 deny all from any to any.`

This rule, not to allow anything, is the default policy.

If the kernel option `IPFIREWALL_DEFAULT_TO_ACCEPT` has been enabled, the default rule is `65535 allow all from any to any.`

The preceding rule is the default rule in OS X.

`add`	Adds a rule.
`delete`	Deletes the first rule with number *<number>*, if any.
`list`	Prints out the current rule set.
`show`	Equivalent to `ipfw -a` list.
`zero`	Zeroes the counters associated with rule number *<number>*.
`flush`	Removes all rules.

The following options are available:

`-q`	Uses quiet mode when adding, flushing, or zeroing (Implies `-f`). Useful for adjusting rules by executing multiple `ipfw` commands in a script.
`-f`	Does not ask for confirmation for commands that can cause problems if misused (for example, `flush`).
`-a`	Shows counter values while listing. See also `show`.
`-t`	Shows last match timestamp while listing.
`-N`	Tries to resolve addresses and service names in output.

Available options for *<action>*:

`allow`	Allows packets that match rule. The search terminates. Aliases are `accept.q`, `pass`, and `permit`.
`deny` Alias is `drop`.	Discards packets that match rule. The search terminates.
`reject`	(Deprecated) Discards packets that match rule, and tries to send an ICMP host unreachable notice. The search terminates.
`unreach` *<code>*	Discards packets that match rule, and tries to send an ICMP unreachable notice with code *<code>*, where *<code>* is a number from 0 to 255, or one of these aliases: `net`, `host`, `protocol`, `port`, `needfrag`, `srcfail`,

net-unknown, host-unknown, isolated, net-prohib, host-prohib, tosnet, toshost, filter-prohib, host-precedence, precedence-cutoff. The search terminates.

reset — TCP packets only. Discards packets that match rule, and tries to send a TCP reset (RST) notice. The search terminates.

count — Updates counters for all packets that match rule. The search continues with the next rule.

divert *<port>* — Diverts packets that match rule to divert (4) socket bound to port *<port>*. The search terminates.

tee *<port>* — Sends a copy of packets matching rule to the divert (4) socket bound to port *<port>*. The search terminates.

fwd *<ipaddr>* [,*<port>*] — Changes to the next hop on matching packets to *<ipaddr>*, which can be a dotted quad address or hostname. If *<ipaddr>* is not directly reachable, the route as found in the local routing table for that IP address is used instead. If *<ipaddr>* is a local address, when a packet enters the system from a remote host, it is diverted to *<port>* on the local machine, keeping the local address of the socket set to the original IP address for which the packet was destined. This is intended for use with transparent proxy servers. If *<ipaddr>* is not a local address, then *<port>*, if specified, is ignored, and the rule applies only to packets leaving the system. If *<port>* is not given, the port in the packet is used instead. The kernel must have been compiled with option IPFIREWALL_FORWARD.

skipto *<number>* — Skips all subsequent rules numbered less than *<number>*. The search continues with the first rule numbered *<number>* or higher.

If a packet matches more than one divert and/or tee rule, all but the last are ignored.

If the kernel was compiled with IPFIREWALL_VERBOSE, when a packet matches a rule with the log keyword, a message is printed on the console. If the kernel was compiled with IPFIREWALL_VERBOSE_LIMIT, logging ceases after the number of packets specified by the option is received for that particular entry. Logging can then be reenabled by clearing the packet counter for that entry.

Console logging and the log limit are adjustable dynamically through the sysctl (8) interface.

Available options for <*proto*> are

`ip`	Matches all packets. The same as the alias `all`.
`tcp`	Matches only TCP packets.
`udp`	Matches only UDP packets.
`icmp`	Matches only ICMP packets.
<*number*|*name*>	Matches only packets for the specified protocol. See `/etc/protocols` for a complete list.

<*src*> and <*dst*> have the form:

<*address*/*mask*> [<*ports*>]

<*address*/*mask*> may be specified as

`ipno`	Has the form `1.2.3.4`—only this exact number matches the rule.
`ipno/bits`	Has the form `1.2.3.4/24`—in this case, all IP numbers from `1.2.3.0` to `1.2.3.255` match.
`ipno:mask`	Has the form `1.2.3.4:255.255.240.0`—in this case, all IP numbers from 1.2.0.0 to 1.2.15.255 match.

The sense of match can be inverted by preceding an address with the not modifier, causing all other addresses to match instead. This does not affect the selection of port numbers.

Rules can apply to packets when they are incoming or outgoing or both. The keyword `in` indicates that the rule should match only incoming packets. The keyword `out` indicates that the rule should match only outgoing packets.

To match packets going through a certain interface, specify the interface with `via`.

`via` <*ifX*>	Matches packets going through the interface <*ifX*>.
`via` <*if**>	Matches packets going through the interface <*if**>, where

`*` is any unit.

`via any`	Matches packets going through some interface.
`via ipno`	Matches packets going through the interface having the IP address <*ipno*>.

The keyword `via` causes the interface to always be checked. If `recv` or `xmit` is used instead, only the receive or transmit interface (respectively) is checked. By specifying both, it is possible to match packets based on both receive and transmit interfaces. For example:

```
ipfw add 100 deny ip from any to any out recv en0 xmit en1
```

The `recv` interface can be tested on either incoming or outgoing packets, whereas the `xmit` interface can be tested only on outgoing packets. So, `out` is required (and `in` is invalid) whenever `xmit` is used. Specifying `via` together with `xmit` or `recv` is invalid.

Options available for <*options*>:

`frag`	Matches if the packet is a fragment and it is not the first fragment of the datagram. `frag` may not be used in conjunction with either `tcpflags` or TCP/UDP port specifications.
`in`	Matches if the packet was on the way in.
`out`	Matches if the packet was on the way out.
`ipoptions <spec>`	Matches if the IP header contains the comma-separated list of options specified in <*spec*>. The supported IP options are `ssrr` (strict source route), `lsrr` (loose source route), `rr` (record packet route), and `ts` (timestamp). The absence of a particular option may be denoted with a `!`.
`established`	TCP packets only. Matches packets that have the `RST` or `ACK` bits set.
`setup`	TCP packets only. Matches packets that have the `SYN` bit set but no `ACK` bit.
`tcpflags <spec>`	Matches if the TCP header contains the comma-separated list of flags specified in <*spec*>. The supported TCP flags are `fin`, `syn`, `rst`, `psh`, `ack`, and `urg`. The absence of a particular flag may be denoted by a `!`. A rule that contains a `tcpflags` specification can never match a fragmented packet that has a non-zero offset.
`icmptypes <types>`	Matches if the ICMP type is in the list <*types*>. The list may be specified as any combination of ranges or individual types separated by commas.

Important points to consider when designing your rules:

Remember that you filter both packets going in and out. Most connections need packets going in both directions.

Remember to test very carefully. It is a good idea to be at the console at the time.

Don't forget the loopback interface.

jobs

`jobs`	Displays the table of current jobs.
`jobs [-l]`	
`-l`	Lists jobs in long format. This includes the job number and its associated process ID.

There are several ways to refer to a job. `%` introduces a job name. Job number 1 is `%1`. An unambiguous string of characters at the beginning of the name can be used to refer to a job; that is, the form `%<first-few-characters-of-job>`. An unambiguous string of characters in the job name can also be used to refer to a job; that is, the form `%?<text-string>` specifies a job whose name contains `<text-string>`.

Output pertaining to the current job is marked with `+`; output from a previous job, `-`. `%+`, `%`, and `%%` refers to the current job. `%-` refers to the previous job.

kill

`kill` — Sends a signal to a process or terminates a process.

`kill [-<signal>] %<job> | <pid>`

`kill -l`

`-l` — Lists the signal names.

`<signal>` — Specifies which signal to send to a process. If `<signal>` is not specified, the TERM (terminate) signal is sent. `<signal>` may be a number or name.

`%<job>` — Specifies the job that should receive a signal.

`<pid>` — Specifies the process ID which should receive a signal. The process ID can be determined by running ps.

Signal `KILL` (9) is a sure way to kill a process. Signal `HUP` is another common signal to send to a process. You may want to send a `HUP` signal to a process to get it to reread its configuration file.

last

`last` — Indicates last logins of `users` and `ttys`.

`last [-n] [-f <file>] [-h <host>] [-t <tty>] [<user1> <user2> ...]`

`last` lists the sessions of specified users, ttys, and hosts, in reverse time order. Each line of output contains the username, the `tty` from which the session was conducted, any hostname, the start and stop times for the session, and the duration of the session. If the session is still in progress or was cut short by a crash or shutdown, `last` indicates that.

`-n` — Limits the report to `n` lines.

`-f <file>` — Reads `<file>` instead of the default `/var/log/wtmp`.

`-h <host>` — Lists sessions from `<host>`. `<host>` may be a name or Internet number.

-t <*tty*> — Lists sessions on <*tty*>. <*tty*> may be given fully or abbreviated. For example, last -t p3 is equivalent to last -t ttyp3.

If multiple arguments are given, the information that applies to any of the arguments is printed. For example, last root -t console would list all sessions of root as well as all sessions on the console.

The pseudo-user reboot logs in at system reboot, so last reboot gives an indication of the mean time between reboots.

cat

cat — Concatenates and prints files.

cat [-nbsvetu] <*file1*> <*file2*> ...

cat [-nbsvetu] [-]

cat reads files in sequential command-line order and writes them to standard output. A single dash represents standard input.

-n	Numbers all output lines.
-b	Numbers all output lines, except blank lines.
-s	Squeezes multiple adjacent empty lines, causing single-spaced output.
-v	Displays nonprinting characters. Control characters print as ^X for control-X; delete (octal 0177) prints as ^?; non-ASCII characters with the high bit set are printed as M- (for meta) followed by the character for the low seven bits.
-e	Implies -v option. Displays a dollar sign ($) at the end of each line as well.
-t	Implies -v option. Displays tab characters as ^I as well.
-u	Guarantees unbuffered output.

locate

locate — Finds files.

locate <*pattern*>

Searches a database for all pathnames that match <*pattern*>. The database is rebuilt periodically and contains the names of all publicly accessible files.

Shell and globbing characters (`*`, `?`, `\`, `[`, and `]`) may be used in *<pattern>*, although they have to be escaped. Preceding a character by `\` eliminates any special meaning for it. No characters must be explicitly matched, including `/`.

As a special case, a pattern with no globbing characters (`foo`) is matched as (`*foo*`).

Useful files:

`/var/db/locate.database` Database

/usr/libexec/locate.updatedb Script to update database

ln

`ln`	Makes links.

`ln [-fhns]` *<source> <target>*

`ln [-fhns]` *<source1> <source2> <source3> ... <directory>*

In the first form, `ln` links *<source>* to *<target>*. If *<target>* is a directory, a link named *<source>* is placed in *<target>*.

In the second form, `ln` makes links to the files enumerated by *<source1> <source2. <source3>* ... in *<directory>*. The links have the same names as the sources in the list.

There are two types of links: hard links and symbolic links. The default is hard links. A hard link to a file is indistinguishable from the original directory entry. Hard links may not normally refer to directories and may not span file systems.

A symbolic link refers by name to the file to which it is linked. Symbolic links may refer to directories and may span file systems.

`-f`	Forces the link to occur by unlinking any already existing links.
`-h`	If *<target>* or *<directory>* is a symbolic link, it is not followed. This is most useful when used with `-f`, to replace a symbolic link that might point to a directory.
`-n`	Same as `-h`. Retained for compatibility with other implementations of `ln`.
`-s`	Creates a symbolic link; this is most like the idea of aliases you're already familiar with.

lpq

lpq	Displays the queue of print jobs.

lpq [-la] [-P<*printer*>] [<*job#*>...] [<*user*>...]

-P<*printer*>	Specifies <*printer*> as the printer. Otherwise, the site's default printer is used or the value of the PRINTER environment variable.
-l	Displays the queue information in long format. Includes the name of the host from which the job originated.
-a	Displays the local queues for all printers.
<*job#*>	Displays information on the specified job numbers.
<*user*>	Displays information on all jobs for the specified users.

lpr

lpr	Sends a job to the printer.

lpr [-P<*printer*>] [-#<*num*>] [-C <*class*>] [-J <*job*>] [-T <*title*>] [-U <*user*>] [-i [<*numcols*>]] [-1234<*font*>] [-w<*num*>] [-cdfglnptv] <*file1*> <*file2*> ...

lpr creates a printer job in a spooling area to be printed when facilities become available. A print job consists of a control file and one or more data files, which are copies of the specified files. lpr uses a spooling daemon, lpd, to print the files or to send the files to a remote host if the printer is on a remote host.

-c	Assumes that files contain data produced by cifplot(1).
-d	Assumes that files contain data from tex (DVI format from Stanford).
-f	Uses a filter that interprets the first character of each line as a standard FORTRAN carriage control character.
-g	Assumes that files contain standard plot data as produced by plot routines.
-l	Uses a filter that allows control characters to be printed and suppresses page breaks.
-n	Assumes that files are assumed to contain data from ditroff (device independent troff).
-p	Uses pr(1) to format the files (equivalent to print).

`-t`	Assumes that files contain data from `troff`(1).
`-v`	Assumes that files contain a raster image for devices like Benson Varian.

The following options apply to the handling of the print job:

`-P<printer>`	Forces output to a specific printer. Normally the default printer for the site is used, or the value of the environment variable `PRINTER` is used.
`-h`	Suppresses the printing of a banner page.
`-m`	Sends mail upon completion.
`-r`	Removes the file on completion of the spooling or upon completion of printing (with the `-s` option).
`-s`	Uses symbolic links. Usually files are copied to the spool directory. The `-s` option uses a symbolic link to the data files rather than copying them to the spool directory. Files sent to the printer in this manner should not be modified or removed until they are printed.

The following options apply to copies, the page display, and headers:

`-#<num>`	Prints the number of copies specified by *<num>*.
`-[1234]<font>`	Specifies a *<font>* to be mounted on font position `i`. The daemon constructs a `.railmag` file referencing the font pathname.
`-C <class>`	Specifies the job classification to be used on the banner page. Replaces the name returned by `hostname`(1) with *<class>*.
`-J <job>`	Specifies the job name to be used on the banner page. Normally, the first filename is used.
`-T <title>`	Uses *<title>* for `pr`(1) instead of the filename.
`-U <user>`	Specifies *<user>* as the name to print on the banner page. It is only honored if the real user ID is daemon, and is intended for instances in which print filters requeue jobs.
`-i [<numcols>]`	Indents the output. If *<numcols>* is specified, it prints *<numcols>* of blank spaces before each line. Otherwise, eight characters are printed.
`-w<num>`	Uses *<num>* as the page width for `pr`(1).

lprm

`lprm`	Removes print jobs from the queue.

`lprm [-P<printer>] [-] [<job#>...] [<user>...]`

`-P<printer>`	Specifies *<printer>* as the printer. Otherwise, the site's default printer is used or the value of the PRINTER environment variable.
`-`	Removes all print jobs in the queue owned by the user invoking the command. If invoked by super user, removes all print jobs from the queue.
<job#>	Removes from the queue the print job specified by *<job#>*. The *<job#>* can be determined by using `lpq`(1).
<user>	Removes jobs in the print queue owned by the specified *<user>*.

ls

`ls`	Lists files or directory contents.

`ls [-ACFLRSTWadfgilnoqrsktcux1] <file1> <file2> ...`

`ls [-ACFLRSTWadfgilnoqrsktcux1]`

`-A`	Lists all entries except for '`.`' and '`..`'. Always set for super user.
`-C`	Forces multicolumn output. Default when output is to a terminal.
`-F`	Displays a symbol, if applicable, after each file to denote the following: Slash (`/`) for a directory; asterisk (`*`) for an executable; an at sign (`@`) for a symbolic link; a percent sign (`%`) for a whiteout; an equal sign (`=`) for a socket; a vertical bar (`|`) for a FIFO.
`-L`	If the argument is a symbolic link, the file or directory the link references rather than the link itself is displayed.
`-R`	Recursively lists subdirectories.
`-S`	Sorts by size, largest file first.
`-T`	Displays complete time information, including month, day, hour, minute, second, and year.
`-W`	Displays whiteouts.

`-a`	Lists all files in the directory, including files whose names begin with a dot (`.`).
`-d`	If the argument is a directory, it is listed as a plain file, rather than listing its contents. If the argument is a symbolic link, its link information is not displayed.
`-f`	Does not sort output.
`-g`	Does nothing. Is kept for compatibility with older versions of `ls`.
`-i`	Lists the argument's serial number (`inode` number).
`-l`	Lists in long format. Displays file mode, number of links, owner name, group name, size of the file in bytes, date and time file was last modified, and the file. If displayed to a terminal, the first line of output is the total number of 512-byte blocks used by the files in the directory.
`-n`	Displays user and group ID as numbers rather than names in a long (`-l`) output.
`-o`	Includes file flags in a long (`-l`) output.
`-q`	Forces printing of non-graphic characters in filenames as character `?`. Default when output is to a terminal.
`-r`	Reverses sort order to reverse alphabetic order; smallest first or oldest first, as appropriate.
`-s`	Displays file size in 512-byte blocks, where partial units are rounded up to the next integer value. If the output is to a terminal, the first line displayed is the total number of 512-byte blocks used by files in the directory.
`-k`	Modifies the `-s` option to report sizes in kilobytes.
`-t`	Sorts by time modified (most recently modified first) before sorting in alphabetic order.
`-c`	Uses time when file status was last changed for sorting (`-t`) or printing (`-l`).
`-u`	Uses time of last access for sorting (`-t`) or printing (`-l`).
`-x`	Forces multicolumn output sorted across the page rather than down the page.
`-v`	Forces unedited printing of non-graphic characters. Default when output is not to a terminal.
`-1`	Forces output to one entry per line. Default when output is not to a terminal.

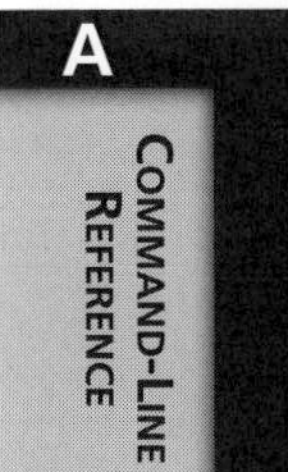

-1, -C, -l, and -x options override each other. The last option specified determines the format used.

-c and -u options override each other. The last option specified determines the file time used.

mail

mail	Sends and receives mail.

mail [-iInv] [-s <*subject*>] [-c <*cc-addr*>] [-b <*bcc-addr*>] <*to-addr*>...

mail [-iInNv] -f [<*name*>]

mail [-iInNv] [-u <*user*>]

mail

-i	Ignores tty interrupt signals. Especially useful for communication on noisy phone lines.
-I	Forces interactive mode, even when input isn't a terminal. Particularly useful for using the ~ character, which is only available in interactive mode.
-n	Ignores /etc/mail.rc upon startup.
-v	Verbose mode.
-s <*subject*>	Specifies the subject. Uses only the first argument after the flag. Be certain to use quotes for any subjects with spaces.
-c <*cc-addr*>	Sends a carbon copy to the users specified in <*cc-addr*>.
-b <*bcc-addr*>	Sends a blind copy to the users specified in <*bcc-addr*>. The list should be a comma-separated list.
-f [<*name*>]	Reads the contents of your mbox or the file specified by <*name*>. When you quit, mail writes undeleted messages back to this file.
-u <*user*>	Equivalent to -f /usr/mail/<*user*>.

Here are some of the useful options available within mail:

-<*n*>	Displays the previous message, if <*n*> is not specified; otherwise, displays the <*n*>th previous message.
?	Displays a brief summary of commands.
help	Same as ?.
^D	Sends the composed message.
!<*shell_command*>	Executes the shell command that follows.
<*return*>	

`n` `+`	Goes to the next message in sequence.
`Reply` `R`	Replies to the sender of the message. Does not reply to any other recipients of the message.
`reply` `r`	Replies to the sender and all other recipients of the message.
`respond`	Same as `reply`.
`mail <user>` `m`	Sends mail to the *<user>* specified. Takes login names and distribution group names as argument.
`delete` `d`	Takes as its argument a list of messages and marks them to be deleted. Messages marked for deletion are not available for most other commands.
`dp` `dt`	Deletes the current message and prints the next message.
`undelete` `u`	Takes a message list as its argument and unmarks the messages for deletion.
`edit` `e`	Takes as its argument a list of messages and points a text editor at each one in turn.
`inc`	Checks for any new incoming messages that have arrived since the session began and adds those to the message list.
`save` `s`	Takes as its argument a list of messages and a filename and saves the messages to the filename. Each message is appended to the file. If no message is given, saves the current message.
`write` `w`	Similar to save, except saves only the body of messages.
`unread` `U`	Takes as its argument a list of messages and marks them as not read.

`alias`	
`a`	With no arguments, prints out the list of currently defined aliases. With one argument, prints out the specified alias. With multiple arguments, creates a new alias or edits an old one.
`unalias`	Takes as its argument a list of names defined by alias commands and discards the remembered groups of users.
`exit`	
`ex`	
`x`	Exits mail without making any changes to the user's mbox, system mailbox, or the `-f` file that was being read.
`xit`	Same as `exit`.
quit	
q	Terminates the session, saving all undeleted messages in the user's mbox.

man

`man` Displays online manual pages.

`man [-achw] [-C <file>] [-M <path>] [-m <path>] [<section>] <name1> <name2> ...`

`man [-M <path>] [-m <path>] -k <keyword1> <keyword2> ...`

`-a`	Displays all the manual pages for a specified section and name combination. (Default is to display only the first page found.)
`-c`	Copies the manual page to the standard output instead of using `more`(1) for pagination.
`-h`	Displays on the SYNOPSIS lines of the requested manual pages.
`-w`	Lists the pathnames of manual pages that would be displayed for the specified section and name combination.
`-C <file>`	Uses the specified file instead of the default configuration file. This allows users to configure their own manual environment. See `man.conf`(5) for more details.

`-M <path>`	Overrides the list of standard directories where `man` searches for manual pages. The path specified must be a colon-separated list of directories. The search path may also be specified by the `MANPATH` environment variable.
`-m <path>`	Adds to the list of standard search directories. The path specified must be a colon-separated list of directories. These directories are searched before the standard list or directories specified by `-M` or `MANPATH`.
`-k <keyword>`	Displays a list of manual pages that contain the `<keyword>`.

The optional `<section>` argument restricts `man`'s search to the specified section.

mkdir

`mkdir`	Creates one or more new directories.

`mkdir [-p] [-m mode] <directory> ...`

`<directory>` is an absolute or relative pathname, including the name of the directory to create.

`-m` [mode]	Set the permissions on the directory to the given mode. See `chmod` for more information on permission modes.
`-p`	Creates "inbetween" directories if needed. For example, if you are creating the directory `/Users/jray/Images/Vacation` and the Images directory doesn't already exist, the `-p` option will automatically force its creation.

more, page

more

page	Pages through data or text files.

more [-cdflsu] [-n] [+<*linenumber*>] [+/<*pattern*>] <*file1*> <*file2*> ...

more pages through data a screenful at a time. When the user enters a carriage return at the More prompt at the bottom of the screen, one more line is displayed. When the user presses the space bar, another screenful of data is displayed. When more is invoked as page, each screenful is cleared before the next is displayed.

-c	Draws each page by beginning at the top of the screen and erasing each line just before it draws on it. This option is ignored if the screen is unable to clear to the end of a line.
-d	Prompts user with "Press space to continue, 'q' to quit." at the end of each screenful. Responds to illegal user input with "Press 'h' for instructions." instead of ringing the bell.
-f	Counts logical rather than screen lines. Long lines are not folded. Useful when trying to display lines containing non-printing characters or escape sequences.
-l	Does not treat ^L (form feed) as a page break. Where form feeds occur, more pauses after them, as if the screen were full. Particularly recommended if piping nroff output through ul.
-s	Squeezes multiple blank lines of output into one blank line of output. Useful for viewing nroff output.
-u	Suppresses underlining or standout mode, whichever the terminal is capable of displaying.
-n	Specifies the number of lines to use per screenful rather than the default.
+<*linenumber*>	Starts at <*linenumber*>.
+/<*pattern*>	Starts two lines before the line containing the regular expression pattern <*pattern*>.

Additional options for interacting with more when it pauses (i is an optional integer argument, defaulting to 1):

i<*return*>	Displays i more lines. Advances one line if i is not given.
i<*space*>	Displays i more lines. Advances another screenful if i is not given.
^D	Displays 11 more lines. If i is given, scroll size is set to i.
d	Same as ^D.
iz	Same as typing <*space*>, except that if i is given, scroll size becomes i.
is	Skips i lines and prints a screenful of lines.
if	Skips i screenfuls and prints a screenful of lines.
i^F	Same as if.
ib	Skips back i screenfuls and prints a screenful of lines.

i^B	Same as ib.
q	Exits.
Q	Exits.
=	Displays the current line number.
v	Starts the editor at the current line number, if the environment variable EDITOR is set to vi or ex. If no EDITOR is specified, vi is the default.
h	Displays the help menu.
i/*<expression>*	Searches for the i-th occurrence of the regular expression *<expression>*. If the input is a file rather than a pipe, and there are less than i occurrences, the file remains unchanged. Otherwise, the display advances to two lines before the line containing *<expression>*.
in	Searches for the i-th occurrence of the last regular expression entered.
'	(Single quote) Goes to the point where the last search was started. If no search has been done on the file, it goes back to the beginning of the file.
!*<command>*	Invokes a shell that executes *<command>*. The characters % and !, when used in the *<command>*, are replaced with the current filename and the previous shell command, respectively. If there is no current filename, % is not expanded. To escape expansion, use \% and \%, respectively.
i:n	Skips to the i-th next file given in the command line, or to the last file if i is beyond range.
i:p	Skips to the i-th previous file in the command line, or to the first file if i is beyond range. If more is in the middle of displaying a file, it goes to the beginning of the file. If more is displaying from a pipe, the bell rings.
:f	Displays current filename and line number.
:q	Exits.
:Q	Exits.
.	(Dot) Repeats the previous command.

mount

`mount`	Mounts file systems.

`mount`

`mount [-Aadfruvw] [-t <type>]`

`mount [-dfruvw] <special> | <node>`

`mount [-dfruvw] [-o <options>] [-t <type>] <special> | <node>`

`mount` invokes a file system-specific program to prepare and graft the `<special>` device or remote node (`rhost:path`) on the file system tree at the point `<node>`. If neither `<special>` nor `<node>` is specified, the appropriate information is taken from the `fstab` file.

The system maintains a list of currently mounted file systems. If no arguments are given to `mount`, this list is displayed.

`-A`	Causes `mount` to try to mount all the file systems listed in the `fstab` except those for which the `noauto` option is specified.
`-a`	Similar to `-A` flag, except that if a file system (other than the `root` file system) appears to be mounted already, `mount` does not try to mount it again. `mount` assumes that a file system is already mounted if a file system of the same type is mounted on a given `mount` point.
`-d`	Causes everything to be done except the invocation of the file system–specific program. This option is useful in conjunction with the `-v` option to determine what the `mount` command is trying to do.
`-f`	Forces the revocation of write access when trying to downgrade a file system `mount` status from read-write to read-only.
`-r`	Mounts the file system read-only (even `root` may not write to it). The same as the `rdonly` option to the `-o` option.
`-u`	Indicates that the status of an already mounted file system should be changed. Any of the options available in `-o` may be changed. The file system may be changed from read-only to read-write, or vice versa. An attempt to change from read-write to read-only fails if any files on the file system are currently open for writing unless `-f` is also specified.
`-v`	Enables verbose mode.
`-w`	Sets the file system object to read-write.

`-t <type>`	Specifies the file system type as `<type>`. Default is type `ffs`. The option can be used to indicate the actions should be performed only on the specified file system `<type>`. More than one type may be specified in a comma-separated list. The prefix `no` added to the type list may be used to specify that the actions should not take place on `<type>`. For example, mount `-a -t nonfs,mfs` indicates that all file systems should be mounted except those of type NFS and MFS. mount attempts to execute a program called `mount_XXX` where `XXX` is the specified `<type>`.
`-o`	Specifies certain options. The options are specified in a comma-separated list.

The following options are available for the `-o` option:

`async`	Specifies that all I/O to the file system should be done asynchronously. This is a dangerous flag to set, and should not be used without being prepared to re-create the file system if the system crashes.
`force`	Same as `-f`. Forces the revocation of write access when trying to downgrade a file system `mount` status from read-write to read-only.
`noatime`	Does not update `atime` on files in the system unless `mtime` or `ctime` is being changed as well. This option is useful for laptops or news servers on which the extra disk activity associated with updating the `atime` is not wanted.
`noaccesstime`	Synonym for `noatime`. Provided for compatibility with other operating systems.
`nodev`	Does not interpret character or block special devices on the file system. The option is useful for a server that has file systems containing special devices for architectures other than its own.
`noexec`	Does not allow the execution of any binaries on the mounted file system. This option is useful for a server containing binaries for an architecture other than its own.
`nosuid`	Does not allow `set-user-identifier` or `set-group-identifier` bits to take effect.
`rdonly`	Same as `-r`. Mounts the file system read-only. Even `root` may not write to it.
`sync`	Specifies that all I/O to the file system should be done asynchronously.

`update`	Same as `-u`. Indicates that the status of an already mounted file system should be changed.
`union`	Causes the namespace at the `mount` point to appear as the union of the mounted file system root and the existing directory. Lookups are done on the mounted file system first. If operations fail due to a nonexistent file, the underlying file system is accessed instead. All creates are done in the mounted file system.

Any additional options specific to a given file system type may be passed as a comma-separated list. The options are distinguished by a leading `-`. Options that take a value have the syntax `-option=value`.

mountd

`mountd`	Services remote NFS `mount` requests.

`/sbin/mountd [-dn] [<exportsfile>]`

`mountd` is the server for NFS `mount` requests from other client machines. `mountd` listens for service requests at the port indicated in the NFS server specification.

`-d`	Enables debugging mode. `mountd` does not detach from the controlling terminal and prints debugging messages to standard error.
`-n`	Does not require that clients make `mount` requests from reserved ports. Normally only `mount` requests from reserved ports are accepted. This option should be specified only if there are clients, such as PCs, that need it. The use of `-n` is strongly discouraged because it opens a wide variety of security problems.
`<exportsfile>`	Specifies an alternative location for the exports file.

mount_nfs

`mount_nfs`	Mounts NFS file systems.

`mount_nfs [-23KPTUbcdilqs] [-D <deadthresh>] [-I <readdirsize>] [-L <leaseterm>] [-R <retrycnt>] [-a <maxreadahead>] [-g <maxgroups>] [-m <realm>] [-o <options>] [-r <readsize>] [-t <timeout>] [-w <writesize>] [-x <retrans>] <rhost>:<path> <node>`

`-2`	Uses NFS Version 2 protocol.

-3	Uses NFS Version 3 protocol. Default is to try version 3 first and fall back to version 2 if the `mount` fails.
-K	Passes Kerberos authentication to the server for client-to-server user-credential mapping. This requires that the kernel be built with the `NFSKERB` option.
-P	The kernel uses a reserved port number to communicate with clients. This option is ignored and exits for compatibility with older systems.
-T	Uses TCP transport instead of UDP. This is recommended for servers that are not on the same LAN cable as the client. This is not supported by most non-BSD servers.
-U	Forces the `mount` protocol to use UDP transport, even for TCP NFS mounts. Necessary for some old BSD servers.
-b	Backgrounds the `mount`. If a `mount` fails, forks a child process that keeps trying the `mount` in the background. This option is useful for a file system that is not critical to multiuser operation.
-c	Does not do a `connect` (2) for UDP mounts. This must be used for servers that do not reply to requests from the standard NFS port number 2049. It may also be required for servers with more than one IP address, if replies come from an address other than the one specified in the `mount` request.
-d	Turns off the dynamic retransmit timeout estimator. This may be useful for UDP mounts that exhibit high retry rates; it is possible for the dynamically estimated timeout to be too short.
-i	Makes the `mount` interruptible. The file system calls that are delayed due to an unresponsive server fail with `EINTR` when a termination signal is posted for the process.
-l	Used with NQNFS and NFSV3 to specify that the `ReaddirPlus` RPC should be used. This option reduces RPC traffic for cases such as `ls -l`, but floods the attribute and name caches with preferred entries. Probably most useful for client to server network interconnects with a large bandwidth * delay product.
-q	Uses the leasing extensions to NFSV3 to maintain cache consistency. This protocol version 2 revision to Not Quite NFS (NQNFS) is only supported by this updated release of NFS code. It is not backward compatible to the version

	1 NQNFS protocol that was part of the first release of 4.4 BSD-Lite.
`-s`	Soft `mount`. File system calls `fail` after retry round trip timeout intervals.
`-D <deadthresh>`	Used with NQNFS to set the dead server threshold to *`<deadthresh>`* number of round trip timeout intervals. After *`<deadthresh>`* retransmit timeouts, cached data for the unresponsive server is assumed to still be valid. Values may be set in the range of 1–9, with 9 being an infinite dead threshold that never assumes cached data is still valid. This option is not generally recommended and is still experimental.
`-I <readdirsize>`	Sets the `readdir` read size to *`<readdirsize>`*. The value should normally be a multiple of `DIRBLKSIZ` that is <= the read size for the `mount`.
`-L <leaseterm>`	Used with NQNFS to set the lease term to *`<leaseterm>`* seconds. Only use this option for `mounts` with a large round-trip delay. Values are normally in the 10–30 seconds range.
`-R <retrycnt>`	Sets the retry count for doing the mount to *`<retrycnt>`*.
`-a <maxreadahead>`	Sets the read-ahead count to *`<maxreadahead>`*. This value may be in the 0–4 range, and determines how many blocks are read ahead when a large file is being read sequentially. A value larger than 1 is suggested for `mounts` with a large bandwidth * delay product.
`-g <maxgroups>`	Sets the maximum size of the group list for the credentials to *`<maxgroups>`*. This should be used for `mounts` on old servers that cannot handle a group list size of 16, as specified in RFC 1057. Try 8 if users in a log of groups cannot get a response from the `mount` point.
`-m <realm>`	Sets the Kerberos `real` to the string argument *`<realm>`*. Used with the `-K` option for `mounts` to other realms.
`-o <options>`	Options are specified as a comma-separated list of options. See `mount` (8) for a listing of the available options.
`-r <readsize>`	Sets the `read` data size to *`<readsize>`*. It should normally be a power of 2 >= 1024. This should be used for UDP mounts when the fragments dropped due to timeout value are getting large while actively using a `mount` point. Use `netstat` (1) `-s` to get the fragments dropped due to timeout value. See `-w` option.

-t <*timeout*> Sets the initial retransmit timeout to <*timeout*>. May be useful for fine-tuning UDP mounts over networks with high packet loss rates or an overloaded server. Try increasing the interval if `nfsstat` (1) shows high retransmit rates while the file system is active or reducing the value if there is a low retransmit rate but long response delay observed. Normally the `-d` option is also used when using this option to fine-tune the timeout interval.

-w <*writesize*> Sets the write data size to <*writesize*>. See comments regarding the `-r` option, but using the fragments dropped due to timeout value on the server rather than the client. The `-r` and `-w` options should only be used as a last resort to improve performance when mounting servers that do not support TCP `mounts`.

-x <*retrans*> Sets the retransmit timeout count for soft `mounts` to <*retrans*>.

mv

`mv` Moves files.

`mv [-fi]` <*source*> <*target*>

`mv [-fi]` <*source1*> <*source2*> <*source3*> ... <*directory*>

In the first form, `mv` renames <*source*> to the name provided by <*target*>. If <*source*> is a file, a file is renamed. Likewise, if <*source*> is a directory, a directory is renamed.

In the second form, `mv` moves the list enumerated by <*source1*> <*source2*> <*source3*> ... to the directory named by <*directory*>.

`-f` Forces an existing file to be overwritten.

`-i` Invokes an interactive mode that prompts for a confirmation before overwriting an existing file.

The last of any `-f` or `-i` options determines the behavior of `mv`.

natd

`natd` Network Address Translation Daemon.

`natd [-ldsmvu] [-dynamic] [-i` <*inport*>`] [-o` <*outport*>`] [-p` <*port*>`] [-a` <*address*>`] [-n` <*interface*>`] [-f` <*configfile*>`]`

`natd [-log] [-deny_incoming] [-log_denied] [-use_sockets] [-same_ports]`

[-verbose] [-log_facility *<facility_name>*] [-unregistered_only] [-dynamic] [-inport *<inport>*] [-outport *<outport>*] [-port *<port>*] [-alias_address *<address>*] [-interface *<interface>*] [-config *<configfile>*] [-redirect_port *<linkspec>*] [-redirect_address *<localIP>* *<publicIP>*] [-reverse] [-proxy_only] [-proxy_rule *<proxyspec>*] [-pptalias *<localIP>*]

natd provides a Network Address Translation facility for use with divert (4) sockets. It is intended for use only with NICs—if you want to do NAT on a PPP link, use the -alias switch to ppp (8).

natd normally runs in the background as a daemon. It is passed raw IP packets as they travel into and out of the machine, and will possibly change these before reinjecting them into the IP packet stream.

natd changes all packets destined for another host so that their source IP number is that of the current machine. For each packet changed in this way, an internal table entry is created to record this fact. The source port number is also changed to indicate the table entry applying to the packet. Packets that are received with a target IP of the current host are checked against this internal table. If an entry is found, it is used to determine the correct target IP number and port to place in the packet.

-l

-log — Logs various aliasing statistics and information to the file /var/log/alias.log. This file is truncated each time natd is started.

-d

-deny_incoming — Rejects packets destined for the current IP number that have no entry in the internal translation table.

-s

-use_sockets — Allocates a socket (2) to establish an FTP data or IRC DCC send connection. This option uses more system resources, but guarantees successful connections when port numbers conflict.

-m

-same_ports — Tries to keep the same port number when allocating outgoing packets. With this option, a protocol such as RPC will have a better chance of working. If it is not possible to maintain the port number, it will be silently changed as usual.

-v

-verbose — Doesn't call fork (2) or daemon (3) on startup. Instead, stays attached to the controlling terminal and displays all packet alterations to the standard output. This option should be used only for debugging.

-u

-unregistered_only — Alters only outgoing packets with an unregistered source address. According to RFC 1918, unregistered source addresses are 10.0.0.0/8, 176.16.0.0/12, and 192.168.0.0/16.

-log_denied — Logs denied incoming packets via syslog (see also log_facility).

-log_facility <facility_name> — Uses specified log facility when logging information via syslog. Facility names are as in syslog.conf (5).

-dynamic — If the -n or -interface option is used, natd monitors the routing socket for alterations to the <interface> passed. If the interface's IP number is changed, natd will dynamically alter its concept of the alias address.

-i <inport>

-inport <inport> — Reads from and writes to <inport>, treating all packets as packets coming into the machine.

-o <output>

-outport <outport> — Reads from and writes to <outport>, treating all packets as packets going out of the machine.

-p <port>

-port <port> — Reads from and writes to <port>, distinguishing packets as incoming or outgoing using the rules specified in divert. If <port> is not numeric, it is searched for in /etc/services database. If this flag is not specified, the divert port named natd is used as a default.

-a <address>

-alias_address <address> — Uses <address> as the alias address. If this option is not specified, the -n or -interface option must be used. The specified address should be the address assigned to the public network interface.

All data passing out through this address's interface is rewritten with a source address equal to <address>. All data arriving at the interface from outside is checked to see whether it matches any already-aliased outgoing connection. If it does, the packet is altered accordingly. If not, all -redirect_port and -redirect_address assignments are checked and action is taken. If no other action can be made and if -deny_incoming is not specified, the packet is delivered to the local machine and port as specified in the packet.

`-n <interface>`

`-interface <interface>` — Uses `<interface>` to determine the alias address. If there is a possibility that the IP number associated with `<interface>` might change, the `-dynamic` flag should also be used. If this option is not specified, the `-a` or `-alias_address` flag must be used. The specified `<interface>` must be the public network interface.

`-f <configfile>`

`-config <configfile>` — Reads the configuration from `<configfile>`. `<configfile>` contains a list of options, one per line in the same form as the long form of the command-line flags. For example, the line

```
alias_address 158.152.17.1
```

specifies an alias address of `158.152.17.1`. Options that don't take an argument are specified with an option of `yes` or `no` in the configuration file. For example, the line

```
-log yes
```

is synonymous with `-log`. Empty lines and lines beginning with # are ignored.

`-redirect_port <proto> <targetIP>:<targetPORT> [<aliasIP>:]<aliasPORT> [<remoteIP>[:<remotePORT>]` — Redirects incoming connections arriving to given port to another host and port. `<proto>` is either `tcp` or `udp`; `<targetIP>` is the desired target IP number; `<targetPORT>` is the desired target PORT number; `<aliasPORT>` is the requested PORT Number and `<aliasIP>` if the aliasing address. `<remoteIP>` and `<remotePORT>` can be used to specify the connection more accurately, if necessary. For example, the argument

```
tcp inside1:telnet 6666
```

means that `tcp` packets destined for port `6666` on this machine will be sent to the `telnet` port on the `inside1` machine.

`-redirect_address <localIP> <publicIP>` — Redirects traffic for public IP address to a machine on the local network. This function, known as static NAT, is normally useful if your ISP has allocated a small block of IP addresses to you, but it can be used in the case of a single address:

```
redirect_address 10.0.0.8 0.0.0.0
```

The preceding command would redirect all incoming traffic to machine `10.0.0.8`.

If several address aliases specify the same public address as follows

redirect_address 192.168.0.2 <public_addr>

redirect_address 192.168.0.3 <public_addr>

redirect_address 192.168.0.4 <public_addr>

the incoming traffic will be directed to the last translated local address (192.168.0.4), but outgoing traffic to the first two addresses still be aliased to specified public address.

`-reverse`	Reverses operation of `natd`. This can be useful in some transparent proxying situations in which outgoing traffic is redirected to the local machine and `natd` is running on the incoming interface (it usually runs on the outgoing interface).
`-proxy_only`	Forces `natd` to perform transparent proxying only. Normal address translation is not performed.
`-proxy_rule [<type> encode_ip_hdr | encode_tcp_stream] port <xxxx> server <a.b.c.d:yyyy>`	Enables transparent proxying. Packets with the given port going through this host to any other host are redirected to the given server and port. Optionally, the original target address can be encoded into the packet. Use `encode_ip_header` to put this information into the IP option field or `encode_tcp_stream` to inject the data into the beginning of the TCP stream.
`-pptpalias <localIP>`	Allows PPTP packets to go to the defined `localIP` address. PPTP is VPN or secure IP tunneling technology being developed primarily by Microsoft. For its encrypted traffic, it uses an old IP encapsulation protocol called GRE. This `natd` option will translate any traffic of this protocol to a single server to be serviced with `natd`. If you are setting up a server, don't forget to allow the TCP traffic for PPTP setup. For a client or server, you must allow GRE (protocol 47) if you have a firewall list active.

netinfo

`netinfo`	Network administrative information.

NetInfo is a hierarchical database of administrative information. The hierarchy is composed of directories. Each directory may have zero or more properties associated with it. Each property has a name and zero or more values.

Searching

Almost everything that uses NetInfo for lookups searches the local domain first. If the answer is not found in the local domain, the next domain level is searched, and so on.

Database Format

The top level of the database, the `root` directory, contains a single property called master. This property indicates which server is the master of the database; that is, which server contains the master copy of the database.

A second property can be installed in the `root` directory to limit who can connect to the domain. By default, everyone can connect to the domain. They can read anything there, but not write. If this default is undesired, the property called `trusted_networks` can be enabled. Values for it should be the network or subnet addresses that are assumed to contain trusted machines. A name may be given instead of an address. If a name is given, that name should be listed as a subdirectory of `/networks` in the same domain and resolve to the appropriate network address.

At the second level, the following directories exist:

`aliases`

`groups`

`machines`

`mounts`

`networks`

`printers`

`protocols`

`rpcs`

`services`

`users`

These directories mostly contain a single property called `name`.

The directory `machines` may contain these properties having to do with automatic host installation in addition to `name`:

`promiscuous`	If it exists, the `bootpd` (8) daemon is promiscuous. Has no value.
`assignable_ipaddr`	A range of IP addresses to be automatically assigned, specified with two values as endpoints.
`configuration_ipaddr`	Temporary IP address given to unknown machines in the process of booting.
`default_bootfile`	Default bootfile to assign to a new machine.
`net_passwd`	Optional property. Encrypted password for protecting automatic host installations.

The directory /aliases contains directories describing individual mailing addresses. The relevant properties of each directory under aliases are as follows:

name	Name of the alias.
members	List of members belonging to the alias.

The directory /groups contains directories that refer to individual system groups. The relevant properties of each directory under groups are as follows:

name	Name of the system group.
passwd	Password of the group.
gid	Associated group ID.
users	List of users belonging to the system group.

The directory /machines contains directories that refer to individual machines. The relevant properties of each directory under machines are as follows:

name	Name of the machine. This property can have multiple values if the machine name has aliases.
ip_address	IP address of the machine. This property can have multiple values if the machine has multiple IP addresses. This address must be stored in decimal-dot notation, with no leading zeroes.
en_address	Ethernet address of the machine. The address must be stored in standard six-field hex ethernet notation, with no leading zeroes.
serves	List of information about the NetInfo domain that the machine serves. Each value in the list has the format *<domain_name>*/*<domain_tag>*. The *<domain_name>* is the external domain name that the machine serves as seen by this level of the hierarchy. The *<domain_tag>* is the internal name associated with the actual process on the machine serving the domain.
bootfile	Name of the kernel that this machine will use when NetBooting.
bootparams	List of Bootparams protocol key-value pairs. For example, root=parrish:/ has the Bootparams key root and the Bootparams value parrish:/.
netgroups	List of netgroups to which the machine belongs.

The directory /mounts contains directories that refer to file systems. The relevant properties of each directory under mounts are as follows:

name	Name of the file system. For example, /dev/od0a or papazian:/.

`dir`	Name of the directory upon which the file system is mounted.
`type`	File system type of the `mount`.
`opts`	List of `mount` (8) options associated with the mounting of the file system.
`passno`	Pass number on parallel `fsck` (8).
`freq`	Dump frequency, in days.

The directory `/networks` contains directories that refer to Internet networks. The relevant properties of each directory under `networks` are as follows:

`name`	Name of the network. If the network has aliases, there may be more than one value for this property.
`address`	Network number of this address. This value must be in decimal-dot notation, with no leading zeroes.

The directory `/printers` contains directories that refer to printer entries. The relevant properties of each directory under `printers` are as follows:

name	Name of the printer. If the printer has aliases, this property will have multiple values.
lp, sd, and so on	`Printcap` (5) properties associated with the printer.

The directory `/protocols` contains directories that refer to transport protocols. The relevant properties of each directory under `protocols` are as follows:

`name`	Name of the protocol.
`number`	Associated protocol number.

The directory `/services` contains directories that refer to ARPA services. The relevant properties of each directory under `services` are as follows:

`name`	Name of the service. If the service has aliases, the property will have multiple values.
`protocol`	Name of the protocol on which the service runs. If the service runs on multiple protocols, the property will have multiple values.
`port`	Associated port number of the service.

The directory `/users` contains information that refers to users. The relevant properties of each directory under `users` are as follows:

`name`	Login name of the user.
`passwd`	Encrypted password of the user.
`uid`	User ID of the user.
`gid`	Default group ID of the user.

realname	Real name of the user.
home	Home directory of the user.
shell	Login shell of the user.

netstat

netstat — Shows network status.

netstat [-Aan] [-f <address_family>] [-M <core>] [-N <system>]

netstat [-dghirmnrs] [-f <address_family>] [-M <core>] [-N <system>]

netstat [-dn] [-I <interface>] [-M <core>] [-N <system>] [-w <wait>]

netstat [-p <protocol>] [-M <core>] [-N <system>]

netstat symbolically displays the contents of various network-related data structures. There are a number of output formats, depending on the options used for the information presented.

The first form displays a list of active sockets for each protocol.

The second form displays the contents of one of the other network data structures according to the option selected.

The third form, with a <wait> interval specified, netstat continuously displays the information regarding packet traffic on the configured network interfaces.

The fourth form, displays statistics about the named protocol.

-A	Shows the address of any protocol control blocks associated with sockets with the default display. Used for debugging.
-a	Shows the state of all sockets with the default display. Normally sockets used by server processes are not shown.
-n	Shows network addresses as numbers. Normally, netstat interprets addresses and attempts to display them symbolically. This option may be used with any of the display formats.
-f <address_family>	Limits statistics or address control block reports to those of the specified <address_family>. The following address families are recognized: inet (for AF_INET); ipx (for AF_IPX); ns (for AF_NS); iso (for AF_ISO); local (for AF_LOCAL); unix (for AF_UNIX).
-M <core>	Extracts values associated with the name list from the specified <core> instead of the default /dev/kmem.
-N <system>	Extracts the name list from the specified <system> instead of the default /bsd.

`-d`	Shows the number of dropped packets.
`-g`	Shows information relating to multicast (group address) routing. By default, shows the IP multicast virtual-interface and routing tables. If `-s` option is also specified, shows multicast routing statistics.
`-h`	Shows the state of the IMP host table (obsolete).
`-i`	Shows the state of interfaces that have been auto-configured (interfaces statically configured into a system, but not located at boot time are not shown). If the `-a` option is also specified, multicast addresses currently in use are shown for each ethernet interface and for each IP interface address. Multicast addresses are shown on separate lines following the interface address with which they are associated.
`-m`	Shows statistics recorded by the memory management routines. The network manages a private pool of memory buffers.
`-r`	Shows the routing tables. When `-s` is also specified, shows routing statistics instead.
`-s`	Shows per-protocol statistics. If this option is repeated, counters with a value of zero are suppressed.
`-I` *<interface>*	Shows information about the specified *<interface>*. Used with a *<wait>* interval.
`-w` *<wait>*	Shows network interface statistics at intervals of *<wait>* seconds.
`-p` *<protocol>*	Shows statistics about *<protocol>*, which is either a well-known name for a protocol or an alias for it. Some protocol names and aliases are listed in `/etc/protocols`. A null response typically means that there are no interesting numbers to report. The program complains if *<protocol>* is unknown, or if there is no statistics routine for it.

The routing table display indicates the available routes and their status. Each route consists of a destination host or network and a gateway to use in forwarding packets. The flags field shows a collection of information about the route stored as binary choices. The individual flags are discussed in `route` (8) and `route` (4) `man` pages. The mapping between letters and flags is as follows:

1	RTF_PROTO2	Protocol-specific routing flag 1.
2	RTF_PROTO1	Protocol specific routing flag 2.
B	RTF_BLACKHOLE	Just discards `pkts` during `ukpdates`.

C	RTF_CLONING	Generates new routes on use.
D	RTF_DYNAMIC	Created dynamically by redirect.
G	RTF_GATEWAY	Destination requires forwarding by intermediary.
H	RTF_HOST	Host entry (otherwise inet).
L	RTF_LLINFO	Valid protocol to link address translation.
M	RTF_MODIFIED	Modified dynamically by redirect.
R	RTF_REJECT	Host or net unreachable.
S	RTF_STATIC	Manually added.
U	RTF_UP	Route usable.
X	RTF_XRESOLVE	External daemon translates proto to link address.

newfs

newfs — Constructs a new file system.

newfs [-NO] [-S *<sector-size>*] [-a *<maxcontig>*] [-b *<blocksize>*] [-c *<cylinders>*] [-d *<rotdelay>*] [-e *<maxbpg>*] [-f *<frag-size>*] [-i *<bytes>*] [-k *<skew>*] [-l *<interleave>*] [-m *<free-space>*] [-n *<nrpos>*] [-o *<optimization>*] [-p *<sectors>*] [-r *<revolutions>*] [-s *<size>*] [-t *<fstype>*] [-u *<sectors>*] [-x *<sectors>*] [-z *<tracks>*] *<special>*

newfs replaces the more obtuse mkfs (8) program. Before running newfs, the disk must be labeled using disklabel. newfs builds a file system on the specified special device basing its defaults on the information in the disk label. Typically, the defaults are reasonable; however, newfs has numerous options to allow the defaults to be selectively overridden.

-N — Causes the file system parameters to be printed out without really creating the file system.

-O — Creates a 4.3BSD format file system. This option is primarily used to build root file systems that can be understood by older boot ROMs.

-a *<maxcontig>* — Specifies the maximum number of contiguous blocks that will be laid out before forcing a rotational delay (see the -d option). The default value is 8. See tunefs (8) for more details on how to set this option.

-b *<blocksize>* — Specifies the block size of the file system, in bytes.

`-c <#cylinders/group>`	Specifies the number of cylinders per cylinder group in a file system. The default is 16.
`-d <rotdelay>`	Specifies the expected time (in milliseconds) to service a transfer completion interrupt and initiate a new transfer on the same disk. The default is 0 milliseconds. See `tunefs` (8) for more details on how to set this option.
`-e <maxbpg>`	Indicates the maximum number of blocks any single file can allocate out of a cylinder group before it is forced to begin allocating blocks from another cylinder group. The default is about one quarter of the total blocks in a cylinder group. See `tunefs` (8) for more details on how to set this option.
`-f <frag-size>`	Specifies the fragment size of the file system in bytes.
`-i <number-of-bytes-per-inode>`	Specifies the density of `inodes` in the file system. The default is to create an `inode` for each 4096 bytes of data space. If fewer `inodes` are desired, a larger number should be given.
`-m <free-space-%>`	Specifies the percentage of space reserved from normal users; the minimum free space threshold. The default value used is 5%. See `tunefs` (8) for more details on how to set this option.
`-n <number-of-rotational-positions>`	Specifies the number of distinct rotational positions. The default is 1.
`-o <optimization-preference>`	Space or time. The file system can either be instructed to try to minimize the time spent allocating blocks or try to minimize the space fragmentation on the disk. If the value of `minfree` is less than 5%, the default is to optimize for time. See `tunefs` for more details on how to set this option.
`-s <size>`	Specifies the size of the file system in sectors.

The following options override the standard sizes of the disk geometry. Their default values are taken from the disk label. Changing these defaults is useful only when using `newfs` to build a file system whose raw image will eventually be used on a different type of disk than the one on which it is initially created (for example, a write-once disk). Note that changing any of these values from their defaults will make it impossible for `fsck` to find the alternate superblocks if the standard superblock is lost.

`-S <sector-size>`	Specifies the size of a sector in bytes (almost never anything but 512).

`-k` *<sector 0 skew, per track>*	Describes perturbations in the media format to compensate for a slow controller. Track skew is the offset of sector 0 on track N relative to sector 0 on track N–1 on the same cylinder.
`-l` *<hardware sector interleave>*	Describes perturbations in the media format to compensate for a slow controller. *Interleave* is a physical sector interleave on each track, specified as the denominator of the ratio:

`sectors read/sectors passed over`

Thus, an interleave of 1/1 implies contiguous layout, whereas 1/2 implies logical sector 0 is separated by one sector from logical sector 1.

`-p` *<spare sectors per track>*	Spare sectors (bad sector replacements) are physical sectors that occupy space at the end of each track. They are not counted as part of the sectors/track (`-u`) because they are not available to the file system for data allocation.
`-r` *<revolutions/minute>*	Specifies the speed of the disk in revolutions per minute.
`-z` *<#tracks/cylinder>*	Specifies the number of tracks/cylinder available for data allocation by the file system.
`-t` *<fstype>*	Sets the file system type of the file system you wish to create. `newfs` will be smart enough to run the alternative `newfs_XXX` program instead.
`-u` *<sectors/track>*	Specifies the number of sectors per track available for data collection by the file system. This does not include sectors reserved at the end of each track for bad block replacement (see the `-p` option).
`-x` *<spare sectors per cylinder>*	Spare sectors (bad sector replacements) are physical sectors that occupy space at the end of the last track in the cylinder. They are deducted from the sectors/track (`-u`) of the last track of each cylinder since they are not available to the file system for data allocation.

nfsiod

`nfsiod`	Local NFS asynchronous I/O server.

`nfsiod [-n` *<num-servers>*`]`

`nfsiod` runs on an NFS client machine to service asynchronous I/O requests to its server. It improves performance, but is not required for correct operation.

-n *<num_servers>*	Specifies the number of servers to be started. A client should run enough daemons to handle its maximum level of concurrency, typically 4 to 6.

nfsd

nfsd	Remote NFS server.

nfsd [-rut] [-n *<num-servers>*]

nfsd runs on a server machine to service NFS requests from client machines. At least one nfsd must be running for a machine to function as a server. By default, four servers for UDP transport are started.

nfsd listens for service requests at the port indicated in the NFS server specification.

-r	Registers the NFS service with portmap (8) without creating any servers. This option can be used along with -u or -t to re-register NFS if the portmap server is restarted.
-u	Serves UDP NFS clients.
-t	Serves TCP NFS clients.
-n *<num_servers>*	Specifies the number of servers to start. A server should run enough daemons to handle the maximum level of concurrency from its clients, typically 4–6.

nidump

nidump	Extracts text or flat file–format data from NetInfo.

nidump [-t] { -r *<directory>* | *<format>* } *<domain>*

nidump reads the specified NetInfo domain and dumps a portion of its contents to standard output. When a flat-file administration format is specified, nidump provides output in the syntax of the corresponding flat file. Allowed values for *<format>* are aliases, bootparams, bootptab, exports, fstab, group, hosts, networks, passwd, printcap, protocols, rpc, and services.

If -r is used, the first argument is interpreted as a NetInfo directory path, and its contents are dumped in a generic NetInfo format.

-t	Interprets the domain as a tagged name.
-r	Dumps the specified directory in raw format. Directories are delimited in curly braces. Properties within a directory are listed in the form property = value;. Parentheses introduce a comma-separated list of items. The special property

name `CHILDREN` is used to hold a directory's children, if any. Spacing and line breaks are significant only within double quotes, which may be used to protect any names with metacharacters.

niload

niload [-v] [-d | m] [-p] [-t] {-r *<directory>* | *<format>*} *<domain>*

niload loads information from standard output into the specified NetInfo *<domain>*. If *<format>* is specified, the input is interpreted according to the flat-file format *<format>*. Acceptable values for *<format>* are aliases, bootparams, bootptab, fstab, group, hosts, networks, passwd, printcap, protocols, rpc, and services.

If -r *<directory>* is specified instead of *<format>*, the input is interpreted as raw NetInfo data, as generated by nidump -r, and is loaded into *<directory>*.

niload overwrites entries in the existing directory with those contained in the input. Entries that are in the directory, but not in the input, are not deleted unless -d is specified. niload must be run as the super user on the master NetInfo server for *<domain>*, unless -p is specified.

`-v`	Verbose mode. Prints + for each entry loaded, and - for each entry deleted (flat-file-formats only).
`-d`	Deletes entries that are in the directory, but not in the input.
`-m`	Merges new values into the directory when the input contains a duplicate name.

Note: Only one of `-d` or `-m` may be specified. If neither option is specified, existing entries in the NetInfo database will remain unchanged when the input contains a duplicate name.

`-p`	Prompts for the `root` password of the given domain so that the command may be run from locations other than the master.
`-u` *`<user>`*	Authenticates as *`<user>`*. Implies `-p`.
`-P` *`<password>`*	Provides *`<password>`* on the command line. Overrides `-p`.
`-t` *`<host>/<tag>`*	Interprets the domain as a tagged domain. For example, `trotter/network` refers to the domain `network` on the machine `trotter`. The machine name can be specified as an actual name or an IP address.
`-T` *`<seconds>`*	Sets the read and write timeout to *`<seconds>`*. Default is 30 seconds.
`-r` *`<directory>`*	Loads entries in raw format, as generated by `nidump -r`. The first argument should be the path of a NetInfo directory into which the information is loaded. The specified

	directory might be renamed as a result of contents of the input, particularly if the input includes a top-level name property. If the specified directory does not exist, it is created.
<domain>	NetInfo *<domain>* that is receiving input. If the value is .for *<domain>*, it refers to the local NetInfo database.

niutil

`niutil`	NetInfo utility.

`niutil -create [opts] <domain> <path>`

`niutil -destroy [opts] <domain> <path>`

`niutil -createprop [opts] <domain> <path> <key> [<val>...]`

`niutil -appendprop [opts] <domain> <path> <key> <val>...`

`niutil -mergeprop [opts] <domain> <path> <key> <val>...`

`niutil -insertval [opts] <domain> <path> <key> <val> <index>`

`niutil -destroyprop [opts] <domain> <path> <key>`

`niutil -destroyval [opts] <domain> <path> <key> <val>`

`niutil -renameprop [opts] <domain> <path> <oldkey> <newkey>`

`niutil -read [opts] <domain> <path>`

`niutil -list [opts] <domain> <path>`

`niutil -rparent [opts] <domain>`

`niutil -resync [opts] <domain>`

`niutil -statistics [opts] <domain>`

`niutil` allows you to perform arbitrary reads and writes on the specified NetInfo *<domain>*. To perform writes, `niutil` must be run as root on the NetInfo master for the database, unless `-p`, `-P`, or `-u` is specified.

The directory specified by *<path>* is separated by / characters. A numeric ID may be used for a path in place of a string. Property names may be given in a path with an =. The default property name is name. The following examples both refer to a user with user ID 3:

`/name=users/uid=3`

`/users/uid=3/`

Options:

`-t` *<host>*/*<tag>*	Interprets the domain as a tagged domain. For example, `parrish/network` is the domain tagged `network` on machine `parrish`.

-p	Prompts for the root password or the password of <user> if combined with -u.
-u <user>	Authenticates as <user>. Implies -p.
-P <password>	Provides the root password or the password of <user> if combined with -u. Overrides -p.
-T <seconds>	Sets the read and write timeout to <seconds>. Default is 30 seconds.

Operations:

-create <domain> <path>	Creates a new directory with the specified path.
-destroy <domain> <path>	Destroys the directory with the specified path.
-createprop <domain> <path> <key> [<val>...]	Creates a new property in the directory <path>. <key> is the name of the property. 0 or more property values may be specified. If the named property already exists, it is overwritten.
-appendprop <domain> <path> <key> <val>...	Appends new values to an existing property in directory <path>. <key> is the name of the property. 0 or more property values may be specified. If the named property does not exist, it is created.
-mergeprop <domain> <path> <key> <val>...	Merges new values into an existing property in the directory <path>. <key> is the name of the property. 0 or more property values may be specified. The values are appended to the property only if they do not already exist. If the named property does not exist, it is created.
-insertval <domain> <path> <key> <val> <propindex>	Inserts a new value into an existing property in the directory <path> at position <propindex>. <key> is the name of the property. If the named property does not exist, it is created.
-destroyprop <domain> <path> <key>	Destroys the property with name <key> in the specified <path>.
-destroyval <domain> <path> <key> <val>	Destroys the specified value in the property named <key> in the specified <path>.
-renameprop <domain> <path> <oldkey> <newkey>	Renames the property with name <oldkey> in the specified <path>.
-read <domain> <path> in the specified <domain>.	Reads the properties associated with the directory <path>
-list <domain> <path>	Lists the directories in the specified <domain> and <path>. Directory IDs are listed along with directory names.

`-readprop <domain> <path> <key>`	Reads the value of the property named `<key>` in the directory `<path>` of the specified `<domain>`.
`-readval <domain> <path> <key> <index>`	Reads the value at the given index of the named property in the specified directory.
`-rparent <domain>`	Prints the current NetInfo parent of a server. The server should be explicitly given using the `-t <host>/<tag>` option.
`-resync <domain>`	Resynchronizes NetInfo. If a domain name is given, the master resynchronizes all clones. If the `-t <clone>/<tag>` option is used instead, only that clone is resynchronized. Using `-t <master>/<tag>` resynchronizes the whole domain.
`-statistics <domain>`	Prints server statistics on the specified `<domain>`.
`-domainname <domain>`	Prints the domain name of the given domain.
`<domain>`	If the value is **.**for `<domain>`, it is referring to the local NetInfo database.

nohup

`nohup` Invokes a command immune to hangups.

`nohup <utility> [<arg> ...]`

`nohup` invokes `<utility>` with its arguments and at this time sets the signal `SIGHUP` to be ignored. If the standard output is a terminal, the standard output is appended to the file `nohup.out` in the current directory. If standard error is a terminal, it is directed to the same place as the standard output.

The following variable is utilized by `nohup`:

`HOME`

If the output file `nohup.out` cannot be created in the current directory, the `nohup` utility uses the directory named by `HOME` to create the file.

passwd

`passwd` Modifies a user's password.

`passwd [-l] [-k] [-y] [<user>]`

`passwd` changes the user's local, Kerberos, or YP password. The user is first prompted for his old password. The user is prompted for a new password, and then prompted to retype the new password for verification.

The new password should be at least six characters in length. Use of a variety of lowercase letters, uppercase letters, numbers, and metacharacters.

`-l` Updates the user's local password.

`-k` Updates the Kerberos database, even if the user has a local password. After the password has been verified, `passwd` transmits the information to the Kerberos authenticating host.

`-y` Updates the YP `passwd`, even if the user has a local password. The `rpc.yppasswdd` (8) daemon should be running on the YP master server.

If no flags are specified, the following occurs:

If Kerberos is active, the user's Kerberos password is changed, even if the user has a local password.

If the password is not in the local database, an attempt to update the YP password occurs.

To change another user's Kerberos password, run `kinit` (1) followed by `passwd`. The super user is not required to supply the user's password only if the local password is being modified.

pico

`pico` A text editor.

Commands in `pico` are given as sequences using the Control key. The online help and bottom lines of instructions denote the control key with carat character: ^. Because a manual page for `pico` is not available in OS X, we have included here a copy of the available functions in `pico` from the online help:

`^G (F1)` Display this help text.

`^F` Move forward a character.

`^B` Move backward a character.

`^P` Move to the previous line.

`^N` Move to the next line.

`^A` Move to the beginning of the current line.

`^E` Move to the end of the current line.

`^V (F8)` Move forward a page of text.

`^Y (F7)` Move backward a page of text.

`^W (F6)` Search for (where is) text, neglecting case.

`^L` Refresh the display.

`^D` Delete the character at the cursor position.

`^^` Mark cursor position as beginning of selected text. Note: Setting mark when already set unselects text.

`^^` Mark cursor position as beginning of selected text. Note: Setting mark when already set unselects text.

`^K` (F9) Cut selected text (displayed in inverse characters). Note: The selected text's boundary on the cursor side ends at the left edge of the cursor. So, with selected text to the left of the cursor, the character under the cursor is not selected.

`^U` (F10) Uncut (paste) last cut text inserting it at the current cursor position.

`^I` Insert a tab at the current cursor position.

`^J` (F4) Format (justify) the current paragraph. Note: paragraphs delimited by blank lines or indentation.

`^T` (F12) Invoke the spelling checker.

`^C` (F11) Report current cursor position.

`^R` (F5) Insert an external file at the current cursor position.

`^O` (F3) Output the current buffer to a file, saving it.

`^X` (F2) Exit pico, saving buffer.

---

ping

`ping` Sends `ICMP ECHO_REQUEST` packets to network hosts.

`ping [-DdfLnqRrv] [-c` *`<count>`*`] [-I` *`<ifaddr>`*`] [-i` *`<wait>`*`] [-l` *`<preload>`*`] [-p` *`<pattern>`*`] [-s` *`<packetsize>`*`] [-T` *`<tos>`*`] [-t` *`<ttl>`*`] [-w` *`<maxwait>`*`]` *`<host>`*

`ping` uses the ICMP protocol's mandatory `ECHO_REQUEST` datagram to elicit an `ICMP ECHO_RESPONSE` from a host or gateway. `ECHO_REQUEST` datagrams (pings) have an IP and ICMP header, followed by a `struct timeval` and then an arbitrary number of pad bytes used to fill out the packet.

`-D` Sets the `Don't Fragment` bit.

`-d` Sets the `SO_DEBUG` option on the socket being used.

`-f` Flood `ping`. Outputs packets as fast as they come or one hundred times per second, whichever is more. Only `root` may use this option. This option can be very hard on a network and should be used with caution.

`-L` Disables the loopback so that the transmitting host does not see the ICMP requests. This option is for multicast pings.

`-n` Displays numeric output only. Does not make any attempt to lookup symbolic names for host addresses.

Option	Description
`-q`	Enables quiet output. Displays only the summary lines at startup time and when finished.
`-R`	Includes `RECORD_ROUTE` option in the `ECHO_REQUEST` packet and displays the route buffer on returned packets. The IP header is large enough for only nine such routes. Many hosts ignore or discard this option.
`-r`	Bypasses the normal routing tables and sends directly to a host on the attached network. If the host is not on a directly attached network, an error is returned. This option can be used to ping a local host through an interface that has no route through it.
`-v`	Enables verbose output. Lists ICMP packets received other than `ECHO_RESPONSE` packets.
`-c` *<count>*	Stops after sending and receiving *<count>* `ECHO_RESPONSE` packets.
`-I` *<ifaddr>*	Specifies the interface to transmit from on machines with more than one interface. For unicast and multicast pings.
`-i` *<wait>*	Sets the interval between sending each packet to *<wait>* seconds. Default is to wait one second. This option is incompatible with the `-f` option.
`-l` *<preload>*	Sends *<preload>* number of packets as fast as possible before falling into its normal mode of behavior. Only `root` may set a preload value.
`-p` *<pattern>*	Up to 16 pad bytes can be specified to fill out a packet that is sent. This is useful for diagnosing data-dependent problems in a network. For example, `-p ff` causes the sent packet to be filled with all 1s.
`-s` *<packetsize>*	Specifies the number of data bytes to be sent. The default is 56, which translates to 64 ICMP data bytes when combined with the 8 bytes of ICMP header data. If `-D` or `-T` is specified, or `-t` for a unicast destination, a raw socket is used and the 8 bytes of header are included in *<packetsize>*.
`-T` *<tos>*	Uses the specified type of service.
`-t` *<ttl>*	Uses the specified time-to-live.
`-w` *<maxwait>*	Sets the number of seconds to wait for a response to a packet before transmitting the next one to *<maxwait>*. Default is 10.

popd

`popd`	Pops the directory stack and changes to the new top directory.

`popd [-p] [-l] [-n | -v] [+<n>]`

`popd`

Without arguments, `popd` pops the directory stack and returns to the new top directory. Elements in the directory stack are numbered from 0 starting at the top.

`-p`	Overrides the `pushdsilent` shell variable. (The `pushdsilent` shell variable can be set to prevent `popd` from printing the final directory stack.)
`-l`	Lists the output in long form.
`-v`	Prints one entry per line, preceded by its stack position.
`-n`	Wraps entries before they reach the edge of the screen.
`+<n>`	Discards the `<n>`th directory in the stack.

If both `-n` and `-v` are specified, `-v` takes precedence.

printcap

`printcap`	Printer capability database.

`printcap` is a simplified version of the `termcap` (5) database used to describe line printers. The `printcap` format is one of the formats understood by `niload`. Each `printcap` entry describes a single printer.

The default printer is normally `lp`, although the environment variable `PRINTER` may be used to override this. Each spooling utility supports an option, `-P<printer>` to allow a specific printer destination to be named.

Capabilities

Name	Type	Default	Description
`af`	`str`	`NULL`	Name of accounting file.
`br`	`num`	`none`	If `lp` is a `tty`, sets the baud rate (`ioctl` call).
`cf`	`str`	`NULL`	`cifplot` data filter.
`df`	`str`	`NULL`	Text data filter (DVI format)
`fc`	`num`	`0`	If `lp` is a `tty` clear flag bits (`sgtty.h`).

Name	Type	Default	Description
ff	str	`\f'	String to send for a form feed.
fo	bool	false	Prints a form feed when device is opened.
fs	num	0	Like fc, but sets bits.
gf	str	NULL	Graph data filter (plot format).
hl	bool	false	Prints the burst header page last.
ic	bool	false	Driver supports (nonstandard) ioctl to indent printout.
if	str	NULL	Name of text filter that does accounting.
lf	str	/dev/console	Error logging filename.
lo	str	lock	Name of lock file.
lp	str	/dev/lp	Device name to open for output.
ms	str	NULL	List of terminal modes to set or clear.
mx	num	1000	Maximum file size (in BUFSIZ blocks), 0=unlimited.
nd	str	NULL	Next directory for list of queues (unimplemented).
nf	str	NULL	ditroff data filter (device-independent troff).
of	str	NULL	Name of output filtering program.
pc	num	200	Price per foot or page in hundredths of cents.
pl	num	66	Page length in lines.
pw	num	132	Page width in characters.
px	num	0	Page width in pixels.
py	num	0	Page length in pixels.
rf	str	NULL	Filter for printing FORTRAN-style text files.
rg	str	NULL	Restricted group. Only members of group are allowed access.
rm	str	NULL	Machine name for remote printer.
rp	str	``lp''	Remote printer name argument.
rs	bool	false	Restricts remote users to those with local accounts.

Name	Type	Default	Description
`rw`	`bool`	`false`	Opens the printer device for reading and writing.
`sb`	`bool`	`false`	Short banner (one line only).
`sc`	`bool`	`false`	Suppresses multiple copies.
`sd`	`str`	`/var/spool/lpd`	Spool directory.
`sf`	`bool`	`false`	Suppresses form feeds.
`sh`	`bool`	`false`	Suppresses printing of burst page header.
`st`	`str`	`status`	Status filename.
`tf`	`str`	`NULL`	`troff` data filter (`cat phototype-setter`).
`tr`	`str`	`NULL`	Trailer string to print when queue empties.
`vf`	`str`	`NULL`	Raster image file.
`xc`	`num`	`0`	If `lp` is a tty, clears local mode bits.
`xs`	`num`	`0`	Like `xc`, but sets bits.

ps

`ps` Displays process status report.

`ps [-aCcefhjMmrSTuvwx] [-O <fmt>] [-o <fmt>] [-p <pid>] [-t <tty>] [-U <username>]`

`ps [-L]`

`-a`	Includes information about processes owned by others in addition to yours.
`-C`	Changes the way CPU percentage is calculated by using a raw CPU calculation that ignores resident time. This normally has no effect.
`-c`	Changes the command column output to contain just the executable name rather than the full command line.
`-e`	Displays the environment as well.
`-f`	Shows command-line and environment information about swapped-out processes. This is honored only if the user's user ID is 0.

-h	Repeats the header information so that there is one header per page of information.
-j	Prints information associated with the following keywords: user, pid, ppid, pgid, sess, jobc, state, tt, time, and command.
-l	Displays information associated with the following keywords: uid, pid, ppid, cpu, pri, nice, vsz, rss, wchan, state, tt, time, and command.
-M	Prints the threads corresponding with each taskll.
-m	Sorts by memory usage, rather than by process ID.
-r	Sorts by current CPU usage, rather than by process ID.
-S	Changes the way the process time is calculated by summing all exited children to their parent process.
-T	Displays information about processes attached to the device associated with standard output.
-u	Displays information associated with the following keywords: user, pid, %cpu, %mem, vsz, rss, tt, state, start, time, and command. The -u option implies the -r option.
-v	Displays information associated with the following keywords: pid, state, time, sl, re, pagein, vsz, rss, lim, tsiz, %cpu, %mem, and command. The -v option implies the -m option.
-w	Uses 132 columns to display information, instead of the default, which is your window size. If -w option is specified more than once, ps uses as many columns as necessary, regardless of your window size.
-x	Displays information about processes without controlling terminals.
-O *<fmt>*	Adds the information associated with the space or comma separated list of keywords specified, after the process ID, in the default information displayed. Keywords may be further defined with an = and a string. Keywords further specified in this manner are displayed in the header as specified rather than using the standard header.
-o *<fmt>*	Displays information associated with the space or comma-separated list of keywords specified. Keywords may be further defined with an = and a string. Keywords further specified in this manner are displayed in the header as specified rather than using the standard header.

`-p <pid>`	Displays information associated with the specified process ID `<pid>`.
`-t <tty>`	Displays information about processes attached to the specified terminal device `<tty>`.
`-U <usernam>`	Displays information about processes belonging to the specified `<username>`.
`-L`	Lists the set of available keywords.

The following is a list of the definitions of the keywords that some of the options already include. More keywords are available than are defined here.

`%cpu`	Percentage CPU usage (alias `pcpu`).
`%mem`	Percentage memory usage (alias `pmem`).
`command`	Command and arguments.
`cpu`	Short-term CPU usage factor (for scheduling).
`jobc`	Job control count.
`lim`	Memory use limit.
`nice`	Nice value (alias to `ni`).
`pagein`	`Pageins` (total page faults).
`pgid`	Process group number.
`pid`	Process ID.
`ppid`	Parent process ID.
`pri`	Scheduling priority.
`re`	Core residency time (in seconds; 127 = infinity).
`rss`	Resident set size (real memory).
`rsz`	Resident set size + (text size/text use count) (alias `rs-size`).
`sess`	Session pointer.
`sl`	Sleep time (in seconds; 127 = infinity) .
`start`	Time started.
`state`	Symbolic process state (alias `stat`).
`tsiz`	Text size (in kilobytes).
`tt`	Control terminal name (two-letter abbreviation).
`uid`	Effective user ID.
`user`	Username (from `uid`).
`vsz`	Size of process in virtual memory in kilobytes (alias `vsize`).
`wchan`	Wait channel (as a symbolic name).

pushd

`pushd` Pushes a directory onto the directory stack.

`pushd [-p] [-l] [-n | -v] [<dir> | +<n>]`

`pushd`

Without arguments, `pushd` exchanges the top two elements of the directory stack. If `pushdtohome` is set, `pushd` without arguments does `pushd ~`, like `cd`.

`-p`	Overrides the `pushdsilent` shell variable. (The `pushdsilent` shell variable can be set to prevent `pushd` from printing the final directory stack.)
`-l`	Lists the output in long form.
`-v`	Prints one entry per line, preceded by their stack positions.
`-n`	Wraps entries before they reach the edge of the screen.
`<dir>`	Pushes the current directory into the stack and changes to the specified `<dir>`.
`+<n>`	Rotates the `<n>`th directory to the top of the stack and changes to that directory.

If both `-n` or `-v` are specified, `-v` takes precedence.

pwd

`pwd` Prints current working directory

`pwd [-L|P]`

`-L`	Prints the logical path of the current working directory, as defined by the shell in the environment variable `PWD`.
`-P`	Default. Prints the physical path to the current working directory, with symbolic links resolved.

restore

`restore` Incremental file system restore.

`restore -i -b <blocksize> -f <file> -s <filenumber>`

(The 4.3BSD option syntax is implemented for backward compatibility, but is not documented.)

`restore` restores files from backup media created with the `dump` command.

A full backup of a file system may be restored and subsequent incremental backups layered on top of it. Single files and directory subtrees may be restored from full or partial backups.

`-i`	Interactive. After reading in the directory information from the media, restore invokes an interactive interface that allows you to browse through the `dump` files directory hierarchy and select individual files to be extracted. See the listing of interactive commands that follows.
`-b` *<blocksize>*	Specifies the block size, the number of kilobytes per `dump` record. If the option is not specified, it tries to determine the media block size dynamically.
`-f` *<file>*	Reads the backup from *<file>*. *<file>* may be a special device, such as a tape drive or disk drive, an ordinary file, or `-` (standard input). If *<file>* is of the form *<host>*:*<file>* or *<user>*@*<host>*:*<file>*, restore reads from the named file on the remote host using `rmt` (8).
`-s` *<filenumber>*	Skips to *<filenumber>* when there are multiple files on the same tape. File numbering starts at 1.

Interactive commands:

`add` *<file>*	Adds the specified file or directory to the list of files to be extracted. If the argument is a directory, it and all its descendants are added to the list. Files that are on the extraction list are prepended with a ``*'' when they are listed by `ls`.
`delete` *<file>*	Deletes the current file or directory and its descendants from the list of files to be extracted.
`extract`	Extracts all files on the extraction list from the `dump`.
`cd` *<directory>*	Changes to the specified directory.
`ls` *<directory>*	Lists the current or specified directory.
`pwd`	Prints the full pathname of the current working directory.
`help`	Lists the available commands.
`quit`	Ends the session, even if there are files listed for extraction.

rm

`rm` Removes directory entries.

`rm [-f | -i] [-dPRrW] <file1> <file2> ...`

`-f` Forces the removal of files without prompting the user for confirmation. If the file does not exist, no error diagnostic is displayed. The `-f` option overrides any previous `-i` options.

`-i` Invokes an interactive mode that prompts for confirmation before removing a file. The `-i` option overrides any previous `-f` options.

`-d` Attempts to remove directories as well as other types of files.

`-P` Overwrites regular files before deleting them. Files are overwritten three times before being deleted: first with byte pattern 0xff, and then 0x00, and then 0xff.

`-R` Attempts to recursively remove files. Implies `-d` option.

`-r` Same as `-R`.

`-W` Attempts to undelete files. This option can only be used to recover files covered by whiteouts.

`rm` removes symbolic links, but not the files referenced by the links.

Also, it is an error to attempt to remove the files "`.`" and "`..`".

rmdir

`rmdir` Removes directories.

`rmdir [-p] <directory1> <directory2> ...`

`rmdir` removes each *<directory>* argument specified, provided it is empty. Arguments are processed in the order listed on the command line. To remove a parent directory and subdirectories of the parent directory, the subdirectories must be listed first.

`-p` Attempts to remove the specified directory and its parent directories, if they are empty.

scp

`scp`	Secure remote copy.

`scp [-pqrvC46] [-S <program>] [-P <port>] [-c <cipher>] [-i <identity_file>] [-o <option>] [[<user>@]<host1>:]<file1> [...] [[<user>@]<host2>:]<file2>`

`-p`	Preserves modification times, access times, and modes from the original file.
`-q`	Disables the progress meter.
`-r`	Recursively copies entire directories.
`-v`	Verbose mode. Causes `scp` and `ssh` to print debugging messages.
`-C`	Enables compression. Passes the flag to `ssh`(1) to enable compression.
`-4`	Forces `scp` to use IPv4 addresses only.
`-6`	Forces `scp` to use IPv6 addresses only.
`-S <program>`	Specifies *`<program>`* to use for the encrypted connection. Program must understand `ssh`(1) options.
`-P <port>`	Specifies the port to connect to on the remote the host.
`-c <cipher>`	Selects the cipher to use for encrypting the data transfer. Option is passed directly to `ssh`(1).
`-i <identity_file>`	Specifies the file from which the identity (private key) for RSA authentication is read.
`-o <option>`	Passes specified option to `ssh`(1).

sed

`sed`	Stream editor.

`sed [-an] <command> [<file> ...]`

`sed [-an] [-e <command>] [-f <command_file>] [<file>]`

`sed` reads one or more text files, or standard input if no file is specified, makes editing changes according to a single command specified by *`<command>`* or by using the `-e` or `-f` options. The input is then written to standard output. All commands are applied to the input in the order they are specified, regardless of their origin.

`-a`	By default, the files listed as parameters for the `w` functions are created or truncated before any processing begins. This option causes `sed` to delay opening each file until a command containing the related `w` function is applied to a line of input.
`-n`	By default, each line of input is echoed to the standard output after all the commands have been applied to it. This option suppresses the default output behavior.
`-e` <*command*>	Appends editing commands specified by the <*command*> argument to the list of commands.
`-f` <*command_file*>	Appends editing commands found in the file <*command_file*> to the list of commands. The editing commands should be listed one per line.

The form of a `sed` command is as follows:

`[address[,address]]function[arguments]`

Whitespace may be inserted before the first address and the function portions of the command.

Normally, `sed` cyclically copies a line of input, not including its terminating newline character into a pattern space (unless there is something left after the `D` function), applies all the commands with addresses that select that pattern space, copies the resulting pattern space to the standard output (except if `-n` is used), appends a newline, and deletes the pattern space.

Some of the functions use a hold space to save all or part of the pattern space for subsequent retrieval.

Addresses

An address is not required, but if specified, must be a number that counts input lines cumulatively across input files, a `$` that addresses the last line of input, or a context address that consists of a regular expression preceded and followed by a delimiter.

A command line with no addresses selects every pattern space.

A command line with two addresses selects the inclusive range from the first pattern space that matches the first address through the next pattern space that matches the second. If the second address is a number less than or equal to the line number first selected, only that line is selected. Starting at the first line of the selected range, `sed` starts looking again for the first address.

Editing commands can be applied to nonselected pattern spaces by use of `!`, the negation function.

Regular Expressions

`sed` regular expressions are basic regular expressions (see `regex` (3)) with these additions:

1. In context addresses, any character other than \ or the newline character may be used to delimit a regular expression by prefixing the first use of that delimiter with \. Also, putting \

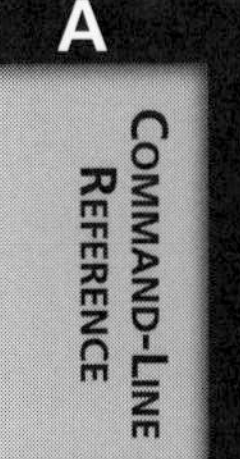

before the delimiting character causes the character to be treated literally, which does not terminate the regular expression. For example, in the context address `\xabc\xdefx`, the second `x` stands for itself, so that the regular expression is `abcxdef`.

2. The escape sequence `\n` matches a newline character embedded in the pattern space. A literal newline character must not be used in the regular expression of a context address or in the substitute command.

One special feature of `sed` regular expressions is that they can default to the last regular expression used. If a regular expression is empty (just the delimiter characters are specified), the last regular expression encountered is used instead. The last regular expression is defined as the last regular expression used as part of an address or substitute command, and at run time, not compile time. For example, the command `/abc/s//XXX/` substitutes `XXX` for the pattern `abc`.

Functions

In the following list of commands, the maximum number of permissible addresses for each command is indicated by `[0addr]`, `[1addr]`, or `[2addr]`, representing zero, one, or two addresses.

The argument *<text>* consists of one or more lines. To embed a newline in the text, precede it with a `\`. Other backslashes in text are deleted and the following character taken literally.

The `r` and `w` functions take an optional *<file>* parameter, which should be separated from the function letter by white space. Each file given as an argument to sed is created (or its contents truncated) before any input processing begins.

The `b`, `r`, `s`, `t`, `w`, `y`, `!`, and `:` functions all accept additional arguments. The following synopses indicate which arguments have to be separated from the function letters by whitespace.

Two of the functions take a function list. This is a list of `sed` functions separated by newlines, as follows:

```
{ function
  function
  . . .
  }
```

The { can be preceded by whitespace and can be followed by whitespace. The function can be preceded by whitespace. The terminating } must be preceded by a newline or optional white space.

The following lists the functions:

Maximum Number of Addresses	Command	Description
[2addr] }	{*<function_list>*	Executions *<function-list>* | only when the pattern space is selected.

Maximum Number of Addresses	Command	Description
[1addr]	a\	
<text>		Writes *<text>* to standard output immediately before each attempt to read a line of output, whether by executing the N function or beginning a new cycle.
[2addr]	b *<label>*	Branches to the : function with the specified label. If the label is not specified, it branches to the end of the script.
[2addr]	c\	
<text>		Change. Deletes the pattern space. With zero or one address or at the end of a two-address range, *<text>* is written to standard output.
[2addr]	d	Deletes the pattern space and starts the next cycle.
[2addr]	D	Deletes the initial segment of the pattern space through the first newline character and starts the next cycle.
[2addr]	g	Replaces the contents of the pattern space with the contents of the hold space.
[2addr]	G	Appends a newline character followed by the contents of the hold space to the pattern space.
[2addr]	h	Replaces the contents of the hold space with the contents of the pattern space.
[2addr]	H	Appends a newline character followed by the contents of the pattern space.
[1addr]	i\	
<text>		Insert. Writes *<text>* to the standard output.

Maximum Number of Addresses	Command	Description
`[2addr]`	`l`	Writes the pattern space to the standard output in a visually unambiguous form. The form is as follows:
Backslash		`\\`
Alert		`\a`
Form-feed		`\f`
Newline		`\n`
Carriage return		`\r`
Tab		`\t`
Vertical tab		`\v`
		Nonprinting characters are written as three-digit octal numbers with a preceding backslash for each byte in the character (most significant byte first).
		Long lines are folded, with the point of folding indicated by displaying a backslash followed by a newline. The end of each line is marked with a $.
`[2addr]`	`n`	Writes the pattern space to the standard output if the default output has not been suppressed, and replaces the pattern space with the next line of input.
`[2addr]`	`N`	Appends the next line of input to the pattern space, using an embedded newline character to separate the appended material from the original contents. (The current line number changes.)
`[2addr]`	`p`	Writes the pattern space to standard output.
`[2addr]`	`P`	Writes the pattern space, up to the first newline character, to the standard output.
`[1addr]`	`q`	Branches to the end of the script and quits without starting a new cycle.

Maximum Number of Addresses	Command	Description
[1addr]	r *<file>*	Copies the contents of *<file>* to the standard output immediately before the next attempt to read a line of input. If *<file>* cannot be read for any reason, it is silently ignored and no error condition is set.
[2addr]	t *<label>*	Test. Branches to the : function bearing the *<label>* if any substitutions have been made since the most recent reading of an input line or execution of a t function. If no label is specified, branches to the end of the script.
[2addr]	w *<file>*	Appends the pattern space to the *<file>*.
[2addr]	x	Exchanges the contents of the pattern and hold spaces.
[2addr]	!*<function>* !*<function_list>*	Applies the *<function>* or *<function_list>* only to the lines that are not selected by the address(es).
[0addr]	:*<label>*	This function does nothing. It bears a *<label>* to which the b and t commands may branch.
[1addr]	=	Writes the line number to the standard output followed by a newline character.
[0addr]		Empty lines are ignored.
[0addr]	#	# and the remainder of the line are ignored (treated as a comment), with the single exception that if the first two characters in the file are #n, the default output is suppressed. This is the same as specifying the -n option in the command line.

Maximum Number of Addresses	Command	Description
[2addr]	`y/<string1>/<string2>`	Replaces all occurrences of the characters in `<string1>` in the pattern space with the corresponding characters from `<string2>`. Any character other than a backslash or newline can be used instead of a slash to delimit the strings. Within `<string1>` and `<string2>`, a backslash followed by any character other than a newline is that literal character, and a backslash followed by an `n` is replaced by a newline character.
[2addr]	`s/<regular expression>/<replacement>/<flags>`	Substitutes the replacement string for the first instance of the regular expression in the pattern space. Any character other than the backslash or newline can be used instead of a slash to delimit the regular expression. Within the regular expression and the replacement, the regular expression delimiter itself can be used as a literal character if it is preceded by a backslash. An ampersand appearing in the replacement is replaced by the string matching the regular expression. The special meaning of the `&` in this context can be suppressed by preceding it with a backslash. The string `\#` where `#` is a digit is replaced by the text matched by the corresponding back reference expression (see `re_format` (7)).

A line can be split by substituting a newline character into it. To specify a newline character in the replacement string, precede it with a backslash.

The value of `<flags>` in the substitute function is zero or more of the following:

`0 ... 9` Makes the substitution only for the nth occurrence of the regular expression in the pattern space.

`g` Makes the substitution for all nonoverlapping matches of the regular expression, not just the first one.

`p` Writes the pattern space to standard output if a replacement was made. If the replacement string is identical to that which it replaces, it is still considered to have been a replacement.

`w <file>` Appends the pattern space to `<file>` if a replacment was made. If the replacement string is identical to that which it replaces, it is still considered to have been a replacement.

showmount

showmount	Shows remote NFS mounts on host.
showmount [-ade3] [<host>]	
-a	Lists all mount points in the form <host>:<dirpath>. -
d	Lists directory paths of mount points instead of host.
-e	Shows the export list of <host>.
-3	Uses mount protocol version 3, compatible with NFS version 3. shutdown
`shutdown`	Closes down the system at a given time.

`shutdown [-] [-fhkrn] <time> [<warning_message>]`

`shutdown` provides an automatic way for the super user to nicely notify users of an impending shutdown.

`-f`	shutdown arranges for file systems to not be checked upon reboot.
`-h`	Halts the system at the specified *<time>* when shutdown executes `halt` (8).
`-k`	Kicks everybody off. The `-k` option does not actually halt the system, but does leave the system multiuser with logins disabled for all users except the super user.
`-r`	Shuts the system down and executes reboot (8) at the specified *<time>*.
`-n`	Prevents normal `sync` (2) before stopping.
<time>	The time when the system is to be brought down. *<time>* can be a word, such as now for immediate shutdown, or a future time in one of two formats: *<+number>* or *<yymmddhhmm>*, where the year, month, and day may be defaulted to the current system values. The first form brings the system down in *<number>* minutes and the second at the absolute time specified.
<warning_message>	Any other arguments comprise the warning message that is broadcast to users currently logged on the system.
`-`	Reads the warning message from standard input.

Starting at ten hours before shutdown, the system displays the shutdown warning message. Warning messages are displayed at regular intervals, with the messages being displayed more frequently as impending shutdown approaches. Five minutes before shutdown, or immediately, if shutdown is in less than five minutes, logins are disabled by creating an `/etc/nologin` and copying the warning message there. The file is removed just before shutdown occurs.

At shutdown time, a message is written in the system log, with the time of shutdown, who initiated shutdown, and the reason.

ssh-agent

`ssh-agent`	Authentication agent.
`ssh-agent` *<command> <args>* `...`	
`ssh-agent [-c	-s]`	
`ssh-agent -k`	
`-c`	Generates C-shell commands on stdout. Default if `SHELL` looks like it is a csh-style shell.
`-s`	Generates Bourne shell commands on stdout. Default if `SHELL` does not look like it is a csh-style shell.

`-k` Kills the current agent (given by the `SSH_AGENT_PID` environment variable).

`<command>` When given, is executed as a subprocess of the agent. When the command dies, so does the agent.

`ssh-agent` holds private keys used for public key authentication (RSA, DSA). `ssh-agent` starts at the beginning of an X session or a login session, and all other programs or windows are started as clients of the `ssh-agent` program. Through the use of environment variables, the agent can be located and automatically used for authentication when logging in to other machines using `ssh`(1).

ssh-keygen

`ssh-keygen` Generates authentication keys.

```
ssh-keygen [-dq] [-b <bits>] [-N <new_passphrase>] [-C <comment>] [-f
<output_keyfile>]
ssh-keygen -p [-P <old_passphrase>] [-N <new_passphrase>] [-f
<keyfile>]
ssh-keygen -x [-f <input_keyfile>]
ssh-keygen -X [-f <input_keyfile>]
ssh-keygen -y [-f <input_keyfile>]
ssh-keygen -c [-P <passphrase>] [-C <comment>] [-f <keyfile>]
ssh-keygen -l [-f <input_keyfile>]
ssh-keygen
```

`-d` Creates a DSA key for SSH2 protocol.

`-q` Quiet mode. Used by `/etc/rc` when creating a new key.

`-b <bits>` Specifies number of bits in the key to create. Minimum is 512. Default is 1024. Key sizes greater than that are considered to improve security little but make things slower.

`-N <new_passphrase>` Specifies a new passphrase.

`-C <comment>` Specifies a comment.

`-f <keyfile>` Specifies the filename of the key file.

`-p` Changes the passphrase of the private key. Asks for the filename of the private key, the old passphrase, and a new passphrase.

`-P <old_passphrase>` Specifies the old passphrase.

`-x` Reads a private `OpenSSH` keyfile and outputs an SSH2-compatible keyfile to standard output.

`-X`	Reads an unencrypted SSH-compatible private (or public) key file and prints an `OpenSSH` compatible private or public key to standard output.
`-y`	Reads a private `OpenSSH` DSA format file and prints an `OpenSSH` DSA public key to standard out.
`-c`	Requests changing the comment in the public and private key files. Asks for the file containing the private keys, the passphrase, and the new comment.
`-l`	Shows the fingerprint of the specified public or private key file.

sort

`sort` Sorts lines of text.

`sort [-cmus] [-t <separator>] [-o <output_file>] [-bdfiMnr]] [+<POS1> [-<POS2>]] [-k <POS1> [,<POS2>]] [<file> ...]`

`sort` sorts, merges, or compares all the lines from the given files, or the standard input if no files are given. A name of `-` means standard input. By default, `sort` writes the results to standard output.

`sort` has three modes of operation: sort (default), checking for sortedness, and merge. These options affect the mode of operation:

`-c`	Checks whether given files are already sorted. If they are not all sorted, prints an error message and exits with a status of 1.
`-m`	Merges the given files by sorting them as a group. Each input file should already be sorted. It always works to sort rather than merge. merge is an option because it is faster when it is set up properly.

If any key fields are specified, `sort` compares each pair of fields, in the order specified on the command line, according to associated ordering options, until a difference is found or no fields are left.

If any global options (`Mbdfinr`) are given, but no key fields are specified, `sort` compares lines according to global options.

If all keys compare equal, or if no ordering options were specified at all, `sort` compares lines byte-by-byte in machine collating sequence. The `-s` option disables the last resort comparison, producing a stable report.

The following options affect the ordering of the output lines. They may be specified globally or as part of a specific key field.

`-b`	Ignores leading blanks when finding sort keys in each line.
`-d`	Sorts in dictionary order; ignores all characters except letters, digits, and blanks.
`-f`	Folds lowercase characters into the equivalent uppercase characters.
`-i`	Ignores characters outside the ASCII range 040–0176 (inclusive).
`-M`	Compares as months. The first three nonblank characters are folded into lowercase and sorted `jan < feb < ... < dec`. Invalid names compare low to valid names. Option implies `-b`.
`-n`	Compares by arithmetic value an initial numeric string consisting of any amount of whitespace, an optional `-` sign, and zero or more digits. Option implies `-b`.
`-r`	Reverses the result of the comparison so that lines of greater value appear earlier rather than later in the sort.

Other available options:

`-o` *<output_file>*	Writes to the specified *<output_file>* instead of to standard output. If *<output_file>* is one of the input files, sort writes to a temporary file before writing to the *<output_file>*.
`-t` *<separator>*	Uses character *<separator>* as the field separator when finding the sort keys in each line. By default, fields are separated by the empty string between a non-whitespace character and a whitespace character.
`-u`	For default case or `-m` option, outputs the first of a sequence of lines that compare equal. For `-c` option, checks that no pair of consecutive lines compare equal.
`+`*<POS1>* `[-`*<POS2>*`]`	Specifies a field within each line to use as a sorting key. The field consists of the portion of the line starting with *<POS1>* and up to but not including *<POS2>*, or to the end of the line, if *<POS2>* is not specified. The fields and character positions are numbered starting with 0.
`-k` *<POS1>*`[,`*<POS2>*`]`	Alternative syntax for specifying sorting keys. The fields and character positions are numbered starting with 1.
`-s`	Disables the last resort comparison.

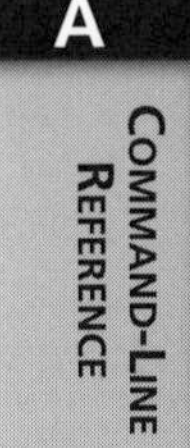

A position has the form `f.c`, where `f` is the number of the field to use, and `c` is the number of the first character from the beginning of the field (for *+POS*) or from the end of the previous field (*-POS*). The `.c` part of a position may be omitted, in which case it is taken to be the first character in the field. If the `-b` option has been given, the `.c` part of a field specification is counted from the first nonblank character of the field (for *+POS*) or from the first nonblank character following the previous field (*-POS*).

A *+POS* or *-POS* argument may also have any of the option letters `Mbdfinr` appended to it, in which case the global ordering options are not used for that particular field. The `-b` option may be independently attached to either or both of the *+POS* and *-POS* parts of a field specification, and if it is inherited from the global options, it will be attached to both. If a `-n` or `-M` option is used, thus implying a `-b` option, the `-b` option is taken to apply to both *+POS* and *-POS* parts of a key specification. Keys may span multiple fields.

strings

`strings` Finds the printable strings in an object or binary file.

`strings [-] [-a] [-o] [-`*<number>*`] [`*<file>*` ...]`

`strings` looks for ASCII strings in binary files or standard input. `strings` is useful for identifying random object files and many other things. A string is any sequence of four (the default) or more printing characters ending with a newline or a `null`. Unless the `-` flag is given, strings looks in all sections of the object files except the (`_TEXT`, `_text`) section. If no files are specified, standard input is read.

`-`	Looks for strings in all bytes of the files (the default for non-object files).
`-a`	Looks for strings in all sections of the object file (including the (`_TEXT`, `_text`) section).
`-o`	Writes each string preceded by its byte offset from the start of the file.
`-`*<number>*	The decimal *<number>* is used as the minimum string length rather than the default of 4.

su

`su` Switches user identity.

`su`

`su [-Kflm] [`*<login>*` [`*<shell_arguments>*`]]`

`-K`	Does not attempt to use Kerberos authentication for the user.
`-f`	Prevents the reading of `.cshrc` if the invoked shell is csh.
`-l`	Simulates a full login. Environment is discarded except for `HOME`, `SHELL`, `PATH`, `TERM`, and `USER`. `HOME` and `SHELL` are

set to the target login's default. USER is set to the target login, unless the target login has a UID of 0, in which case it is unmodified. PATH is set to /bin:/usr/bin. TERM is imported from your current environment. The invoked shell is the target login's. su changes directory to the target login's home directory.

-m	Leaves the environment unmodified. The invoked shell is your login shell and no directory changes are made. As a security precaution, if the target user's shell is a non-standard shell, and the caller's real UID is nonzero, su fails.

If su is executed by root, no password is requested, and a shell with the appropriate user ID is executed. No additional Kerberos tickets are obtained.

The -l and -m options are mutually exclusive. The last one listed is the one executed.

Only users in the wheel group (normally GID 0) can su to root. By default, unless reset by a startup file, the super user prompt is set to # as a reminder of its power.

tail

tail	Displays the last part of a file.

tail [-f | -F | -r] [-b *<number>* | -c *<number>* | -n *<number>*] *<file>*

tail [-f | -F | -r] [-b *<number>* | -c *<number>* | -n *<number>*]

-f	Waits for and displays additional data that *<file>* receives, rather than stopping at the end of the file.
-F	Similar to -f, except that every five seconds, tail checks whether *<file>* has been shortened or moved. If so, tail closes the current file, opens the filename given, displays its entire contents, and waits for more data. This option is especially useful for monitoring log files that undergo rotation.
-r	Displays the file in reverse order, by line. The default is to display the entire file in reverse. This option also modifies the -b, -c, and -n options to specify the number of units to display, rather than the number of units to display from the beginning or end of the input.
-b *<number>*	Specifies location in number of 512-byte blocks.
-c *<number>*	Specifies location in number of bytes.
-n *<number>*	Specifies location in number of lines.

If *<number>* begins with +, it refers to the number of units from the beginning of the input. If *<number>* begins with -, it refers to the number of units from the end of the input.

tar

`tar`	Creates, extracts, or appends to tape archives.

`tar [-] <c | t | x | r | u> [fbemopvwzZhHLPX014578] [<archive>] [<blocksize>] [-C <directory>] [-s <replstr>] <file1> <file2> ...`

`tar` saves files to and restores files from a single file. Although that single file may have originally been intended to be magnetic tape, magnetic tape is not required.

One of the following flags is required:

`-c`	Creates a new archive or overwrites an existing one.
`-t`	Lists the contents of an archive. If any files are listed on the command line, only those files are listed.
`-x`	Extracts files from an archive. If any files are listed on the command line, only those files are extracted. If more than one copy of a file exists in an archive, earlier copies are overwritten by later copies.
`-r`	Appends the specified files to an archive. This only works on media on which an end-of-file mark can be overwritten.
`-u`	Alias to `-r`.

In addition to the required flags, any of these options may be used:

`-f <archive>`	Filename where the archive is stored. Default is `/dev/rmt8`.
`-b <blocksize>`	Sets the blocksize to be used in the archive. Any multiple of 512 between 10240 and 32256 may be used.
`-e`	Stops after the first error.
`-m`	Does not preserve modification time.
`-o`	Does not create directories.
`-p`	Preserves user ID, group ID, file mode, and access and modification times.
`-v`	Verbose mode.
`-w`	Interactively renames files.
`-z`	Compresses the archive using `gzip`.
`-Z`	Compresses the archive using `compress`.
`-h`	Follows symbolic links as if they were normal files or directories.
`-H`	Follows symbolic links given on the command line only.
`-L`	Follows all symbolic links.
`-P`	Does not follow any symbolic links.

-X	Does not cross mount points in the file system.
[-014578]	Selects a backup device, /dev/rmtN.
-C *<directory>*	Sets the working directory for the files. When extracting, files are extracted into the specified directory. When creating, specified files are matched from the directory.
-s *<replstr>*	Modifies the file or archive member names specified by the pattern or file operands according to the substitution expression *<replstr>*, using the syntax of ed(1) in this format: /old/new/[gp] old is the old expression. new is the new expression. The optional trailing g applies the substitution globally. That is, it continues to apply the substitution. The first unsuccessful substitution stops the g option. The optional trailing p causes the final result of a successful substitution to be written to standard error in this format: *<original pathname>* >> *<new pathname>* Multiple -s *<replstr>* options can be specified. They are applied in the order listed.

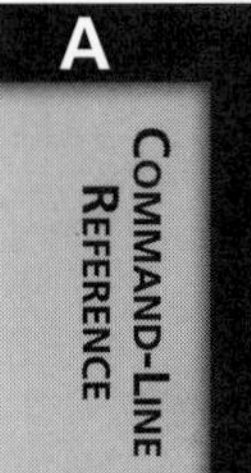

top

top — Displays system usage statistics.

top [-u] [-w] [-k] [-s *<interval>*] [-e | -d | -a] [-l *<samples>*] [*<number>*]

top

-u	Sorts by CPU usage and displays usage starting with the highest usage.
-w	Generates additional columns of output data. The additional columns include VPRVT and the delta information for #PRTS, RSHRD, RSIZE, and VSIZE.
-k	Causes top to traverse and report the memory object map for pid 0 (kernel task). This option is optional; it is expensive to traverse the object maps because the kernel task may have a large number of entries.
-s *<interval>*	Samples processes at the specified *<interval>*. Default is one-second intervals.

`-e`	Switches to event counting mode where counts reported are absolute counters. Options `-w` and `-k` are ignored.
`-d`	Switches to an event counting mode in which counts are reported as deltas relative to the previous sample. Options `-w` and `-k` are ignored.
`-a`	Switches to an event counting mode where counts are reported as cumulative counters relative to when top was launched. Options `-w` and `-k` are ignored.
`-l` *`<samples>`*	Switches from default screen mode to a logging mode suitable for saving the output to a file. If *`<samples>`* is specified, top samples the number of samples specified before exiting. The default is 1.
`<number>`	Limits the number of processes displayed to *`<number>`*.

Typing `q` causes top to exit immediately.

Columns displayed in default data mode:

`PID`	Unix process ID.
`COMMAND`	Unix command name.
`%CPU`	Percentage of CPU used (kernel and user).
`TIME`	Absolute CPU consumption (`min:secs.hundredths`).
`#TH`	Number of threads.
`#PRTS(delta)`	Number of mach ports.
`#MERG`	Number of memory regions.
`VPRVT(-w only)`	Private address space currently allocated.
`RPRVT(delta)`	Resident shared memory (as represented by the resident page count of each shared memory object).
`RSHRD(delta)`	Total resident memory. (Real pages that this process currently has associated with it. Some may be shared by other processes.)
`VSIZE(delta)`	Total address space currently allocated (including shared).

Columns displayed in event counting modes:

`PID`	Unix process ID.
`COMMAND`	Unix command name.
`%CPU`	Percentage of CPU used (kernel and user).
`TIME`	Absolute CPU consumption (`min:secs.hundredths`).
`FAULTS`	Number of page faults.
`PAGEINS`	Number of requests for pages from a pager.
`COW_FAULTS`	Number of faults that caused a page to be copied.
`MSGS_SENT`	Number of mach messages sent by the process.

MSGS_RCVD	Number of mach messages received by the process.
BSDSYSCALL	Number of BSD system calls made by the process.
MACHSYSCALL	Number of MACH system calls made by the process.
CSWITCH	Number of context switches to this process.

traceroute

traceroute	Prints the route packets take to a network host.

traceroute [-d] [-D] [-g *<gateway_addr>*] [-l] [-m *<max_tt>*] [-n] [-p *<port>*] [-q *<nqueries>*] [-r] [-s *<src_addr>*] [-t *<tos>*] [-v] [-w *<wait-time>*] *<host>* [*<packetsize>*]

traceroute uses the IP protocol time-to-live field and attempts to elicit an ICMP TIME_EXCEEDED response from each gateway along the path to the same host.

The only mandatory parameter is *<host>*>—the destination host or IP number. The default probe datagram length is 38 bytes, but this can be increased by specifying a packet size (in bytes) after the destination host name.

-d	Turns on socket-level debugging.
-D	Dumps the packet data to standard error before transmitting it.
-g *<gateway_addr>*	Adds *<gateway_addr>* to the list of addresses in the IP Loose Source Record Route (LSRR) option. If no gateways are specified, the LSRR option is omitted.
-l	Displays the ttl value of the returned packet. This is useful for checking asymmetric routing.
-m *<max_ttl>*	Sets the maximum time-to-live (maximum number of hops) used in outgoing probe packets. The default is 30 hops. The same default is used for TCP connections.
-n	Prints hop addresses numerically rather than symbolically and numerically (saves a nameserver address-to-name lookup for each gateway found on the path).
-p *<port>*	Sets the base UDP port number used in probes to *<port>*. Default is 33434. traceroute hopes that nothing is listening on UDP *<base>* to *<base+nohops+1>* at the destination host, so that an ICMP PORT_UNREACHABLE message will be returned to terminate the route tracing. If something is listening on a port in the default range, this option can be used to pick an unused port range.
-q *<nqueries>*	Sets the number of probes per ttl to *<nqueries>*. Default is three probes.

Option	Description
`-r`	Bypasses the normal routing tables and sends directly to a host on an attached network. If the host is not on a directly attached network, an error is returned. This option can be used to ping a local host through an interface that has no route through it.
`-s` *<src_addr>*	Uses the following IP address (which must be given as an IP number, not a host name) as the source address in outgoing probe packets. On hosts with more than one IP address, this option can be used to force the source address to be something other than the IP address of the interface that the probe packet is sent on. If the IP address is not one of this machine's interfaces, an error is returned and nothing is sent.
`-t` *<tos>*	Sets the type-of-service in probe packets to *<tos>*. Default is 0. Value must be a decimal integer in the range 0 to 255. This option can be used to see whether different types-of-service result in different paths. Not all values of TOS are legal or meaningful. See the IP spec for definitions. Useful values are probably `-t 16` (low delay) and `-t 8` (high throughput).
`-v`	Sets to verbose output. Lists ICMP packets received other than `TIME_EXCEEDED` and `UNREACHABLE` packets.
`-w` *<waittime>*	Sets the time to wait for a response to a probe to *<waittime>* seconds. Default is three seconds.

tunefs

`tunefs` Tunes up an existing file system.

`tunefs [-A] [-a` *<maxcontig>*`] [-d` *<rotdelay>*`] [-e` *<maxbpg>*`] [-m` *<minfree>*`] [-o` *<optimize_preference>*`] [`*<special>* `|` *<filesystem>*`]`

`tunefs` is designed to change the dynamic parameters of a file system that affect the layout policies. The parameters which are to be changed are indicated by the flags given here:

Option	Description
`-A`	The file system has several backups of the superblock. Specifying this option will cause all backups to be modified as well as the primary super-block. This is potentially dangerous—use it with caution.
`-a` *<maxcontig>*	Specifies the maximum number of contiguous blocks that will be laid out before forcing a rotational delay (see `-d`). The default value is 1 because most device drivers require

	an interrupt per disk transfer. Device drivers that can chain several buffers together in a single transfer should set this to the maximum chain length.
`-d <rotdelay>`	Specifies the expected time (in milliseconds) to service a transfer completion interrupt and initiate a new transfer on the same disk. It is used to decide how much rotational spacing to place between successive blocks in a file.
`-e <maxbpg>`	Indicates the maximum number of blocks any single file can allocate out of a cylinder group before it is forced to begin allocating blocks from another cylinder group. Typically, this value is set to about one quarter of the total blocks in a cylinder group. The intent is to prevent any single file from using up all the blocks in a single cylinder group, thus degrading access times for all files subsequently allocated in that cylinder group. The effect of this limit is to cause big files to do long seeks more frequently than if they were allowed to allocate all the blocks in a cylinder group before seeking elsewhere. For file systems with exclusively large files, this parameter should be set higher.
`-m <minfree>`	Specifies the percentage of space held back from normal users; the minimum free space threshold. The default value used is 10%. This value can be set to zero, but up to a factor of three in throughput will be lost over the performance obtained at a 10% threshold. Note that if the value is raised above the current usage level, users will be unable to allocate files until enough files have been deleted to get under the higher threshold.
`-o <optimize-preference>`	The file system can either try to minimize the time spent allocating blocks, or it can attempt to minimize the space fragmentation on the disk. If the value of minfree (see above) is less than 10%, the file system should optimize for space to avoid running out of full-sized blocks. For values of minfree greater than or equal to 10%, fragmentation is unlikely to be problematical, and the file system can be optimized for time.
`-p`	This option shows a summary of what the current tuneable settings are on the selected file system. More detailed information can be obtained in the `dumpfs`(8) manual page.

umount

`umount`	Unmounts file systems.

`umount [-fv] <special> | <node>`

`umount -a [-fv] [-h <host>] [-t ufs | lfs | <external_type>]`

`-f`	Forcibly unmounts the file system. Active special devices continue to work, but all other files return errors if further accesses are attempted. The root file system cannot be forcibly unmounted.
`-v`	Enables verbose mode.
`-a`	All the file systems described in `fstab` (5) are unmounted.
`-h <host>`	Unmounts only file systems mounted from `<host>`. This options implies the `-a` option, and unless specified with the `-t` option, only unmounts NFS file systems.
`-t ufs | lfs | <external_type>`	Unmounts file systems of the specified type. More than one type may be specified in a comma-separated list. The list of file system types can be prefixed by `no` to specify file system types that should not be unmounted.

uptime

`uptime`	Shows how long the system has been running.

`uptime`

`uptime` displays the current time, the length of time the system has been up, the number of users, and the load average of the system over the last 1, 5, and 15 minutes.

uuencode

uuencode

uudecode	Encodes a binary file.

Decodes a binary file.

uuencode [<*file*>] <*name*>

uudecode [<*file*> ...]

uuencode and uudecode are used to transmit binary files over transmission mediums that only support simple ASCII data.

uuencode reads <*file*> (or by default the standard input) and writes an encoded version to the standard output. The encoding uses only printing ASCII characters and includes the mode of the file and the operand <*name*> for use by uudecode.

uudecode transforms uuencoded files (or by default the standard input) into the original form. The resulting file is named <*name*> and has the mode of the original file except that setuid and execute bits are not retained. uudecode ignores any leading and trailing lines.

vi, ex, view

vi	
ex	
view	Screen-oriented text editor.

Line-oriented screen editor.

Read-only version of vi.

vi [-eFlRrSv] [-c <*cmd*>] [-t <*tag*>] [-w <*size*>] [<*file1*> <*file2*> ...]

ex [-eFlRrSsv] [-c <*cmd*>] [-t <*tag*>] [-w <*size*>] [<*file1*> <*file2*> ...]

view [-eFlRrSv] [-c <*cmd*>] [-t <*tag*>] [-w <*size*>] [<*file1*> <*file2*> ...]

vi is a screen-oriented text editor; ex is a line-oriented editor. vi and ex are different interfaces to the same program. view is equivalent to vi -R, the read-only option to vi.

The following options are available:

-e	Starts to edit in ex mode.
-F	Doesn't copy the entire file when first starting to edit. Default is to make a copy in case someone else modifies the file during your edit session.
-l	Starts editing with the lisp and showmatch options set.
-R	Starts editing in read-only mode.
-r	Recovers the specified file. If no file is specified, it lists the files that could be recovered. If no recoverable files with the specified name exist, vi starts editing as if the option has not been issued.
-S	Runs with secure edit option set, which disallows all access to external programs.
-s	Enters batch mode. Applicable only to ex. It is useful for running ex scripts.
-v	Starts editing in vi mode.

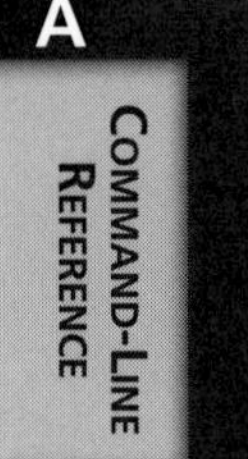

-c *<cmd>*	Executes *<cmd>* immediately after starting the edit session. It is especially useful for initial positioning in the file, but is not limited to positioning commands.
-t *<tag>*	Starts editing at the specified *<tag>*.
-w *<size>*	Sets the initial window size to *<size>* lines.

vi has two modes: command mode and input mode. Command mode is the initial and normal mode. Completion of the input mode returns the user to command mode. Pressing the *<ESC>* key ends a partial command.

Input mode is required to input some types of edits. Input mode is terminated by pressing *<ESC>*. Upon termination of input mode, the user is returned to command mode.

Some commands for moving around in a file:

h	Moves the cursor one character to the left.
l	Moves the cursor one character to the right.
j	Moves the cursor one line down.
k	Moves the cursor one line up.
<arrow keys>	The arrow keys often also function properly.
*<num>*G	Moves the cursor to the line number specified by *<num>*. If *<num>* is not specified, the cursor moves to the last line of the file.

Some commands for inputting text (input mode):

i	Inserts text before the cursor.
a	Appends new text after the cursor.
A	Appends new text at the end of the line where the cursor is.
o	Opens a new line below the line where the cursor is and allows the user to start entering text on the new line.
O	Opens a new line above the line where the cursor is, and allows the user to start entering text on that new line.

Some commands for copying text:

yy	Copies the line the cursor is on.
p	Appends the copied line after the line the cursor is on.

Some commands for deleting text:

dd	Deletes the line the cursor is on.
*<num>*dd	Deletes *<num>* lines, starting with the line the cursor is on.
dw	Deletes the word the cursor is on.
x	Deletes the character the cursor is on.

Some other useful text manipulation:

r<*x*>	Replaces the character the cursor is on with <*x*>.
J	Joins the line the cursor is on with the line below it.

Some commands for pattern searching:

/<*pattern*>	Searches forward in the file for <*pattern*>, starting with the location of the cursor.
?<*pattern*>	Searches backwards in the file for <*pattern*>, starting with the location of the cursor.
n	Repeats the last / or ? pattern search.
N	Repeats the last / or ? pattern search in reverse.

Some commands to write the file:

:w<*return*>	Writes the file back to the filename originally specified when vi was started.
:w <*filename*><*return*>	Writes the file to the filename specified by <*filename*>.

Some commands to quit editing and exit vi:

:q<*return*>	Exits vi. Refuses to quit if there are any unsaved modifications, or if the file is read-only.
:q!	Exits vi, even if there are any unsaved modifications.
ZZ	Exits vi, saving changes.

W

`w`	Displays who the present users are and what they are doing

`w [-hin] [-M <core>] [-N <system>] [<user>]`

`w` displays a summary of the current activity on the system, including what each user is doing. The first line displays the current time of day, how long the system has been running, the number of users logged in to the system, and the load averages. The load average numbers give the number of jobs in the run queue average over 1, 5, and 15 minutes.

The output fields are the user's login name, the name of the terminal where the user is logged on, the host from which the user is logged in, the time the user logged in, the time since the user last typed anything, and the name and arguments of the current process.

`-h`	Suppresses the heading.
`-i`	Sorts output by idle time.
`-n`	Shows network addresses as numbers. Normally `w` interprets addresses and attempts to display them symbolically.

-M *<core>*	Extracts values associated with the name list from the specified core instead of the default /dev/kmem.
-N *<system>*	Extracts the name list from the specified system instead of the default /netbsd.
<user>	If specified, restricts output to *<user>*.

wget

wget — Downloads files and Web pages via HTTP or FTP.

w [-options] [URL]

wget is the fastest and easiest way to download files from a URL directly to your system. Given a properly formatted http:// or ftp:// URL, wget will download and retrieve an individual file, or multiple levels of files from the given location.

-r	Recursively retrieves files from the given URL.
-l *<#>*	When recursively retrieving, limits the depth of the download to a given number (for example, -l 5 retrieves five layers of links deep within a Web site).
-k	Converts Web page links from absolute to relative during the download process.
-m	Mirrors the URL locally.
-A *<extension list>*	Retrieves only files with the listed extensions.
-R *<extension list>*	Does not retrieve files with the listed extensions.
-D *<domain list>*	Retrieves files from only the listed domains.
-L	Follows relative links only.
-H	Follows links to remote hosts.
-I *<directory list>*	Retrieves files from the listed directories.
-X *<directory list>*	Excludes files from the listed directories.
-nh	Does not perform DNS hostname lookups.
-np	Only descends into a directory heirarchy. Does not ascend to the parent directory.

whatis

`whatis`	Displays the manual page header summary information for a command.

`whatis [-M <path>] [-m <path>] <command1> <command2> ...`

`-M <path>`	Overrides the list of standard directories where whatis searches for its database, named `whatis.db`. The path specified must be a colon-separated list of directories. The search path may also be specified by the `MANPATH` environment variable.
`-m <path>`	Adds to the list of standard search directories. The path specified must be a colon-separated list of directories. These directories are searched before the standard list or directories specified by `-M` or `MANPATH`.

which

`which`	Locates a command and displays its path or alias.

`which <name1> <name2> ...`

`which` displays the location of the specified commands, and displays which files would have been executed had the names been given as commands. Both aliases and paths are taken from the user's `.cshrc` file.

who

`who`	Displays who is logged in.

`who [-mTuH] [<file>]`

`who am i`

`who` displays a list of all users currently logged on, showing for each user the login name, tty name, the date and time of login, and hostname, if not local.

`-m`	Only prints information about the current terminal (POSIX way of saying "Who am I?").
`-T`	Prints a character after the username indicating the state of the terminal line: + if the terminal is writable; - if it is not writable; ? if a bad line is encountered.
`-u`	Prints the idle time for each user.

`-H`	Writes column headings above the regular output.
`am i`	Returns the invoker's real username.
`<file>`	Gathers information from the specified `<file>`, rather than the default `/var/run/utmp`. An alternative `<file>` is usually `/var/log/wtmp`. The `wtmp` file contains a record of every login, logout, crash, shutdown and date change since `wtmp` was truncated or created. If `/var/log/wtmp` is being used as the file, the username may be empty or one of these special characters: `|`, }, ~. Logouts produce an output line without any username.

whoami

`whoami`	Displays the effective user ID.

`whoami`

`whoami` has been made obsolete by the `id` (1) utility, and is equivalent to `id -un`. The command `id -p` is suggested for normal interactive use.

`whoami` displays your effective user ID as a name.

Administration Reference

This appendix contains a number of useful modifications that you might want to make to your OS X environment. These suggestions range in urgency from "If you don't do this, you're in danger of a typo trashing your whole machine," to "We think this is a relatively cool enhancement that you'll probably like." We've listed these in what we feel is the order of importance for each to be implemented.

Fix `rm` so that it always runs in interactive mode

As `root`, edit `/etc/csh.login` or `/usr/share/init/tcsh/login` and add a line like the following:

```
alias rm rm -i
```

You could add it to your home directory `.cshrc` file or, following Apple's odd convention for providing shell preferences, to the `login.mine` or `aliases.mine` file in `~/Library/init/tcsh/` instead. But if the line is put in either of these locations, it will apply only to you as a user, rather than to every user of your system.

After this modification is made, `rm` will prompt for confirmation before removing any files. If you want remove many files without being prompted for confirmation, escape the `rm` with the shell escape `\` and add the `-f` (force) flag for good measure. That is, issue the command as `\rm -f <files>`, instead of `rm <files>`.

Turn on access to the `root` account

Refer to Chapter 11, "Additional System Components," for instructions how to do this in one of several different ways. You'll need the `root` user enabled, or you'll have to continually jump through some annoying validation hoops to perform a number of tasks in this book. We recommend that you use the `root` account only in very limited circumstances. But the use of the `sudo` command for all `root`-requiring work, as being promoted in many Internet OS X forums, provides just one more avenue for error and frustration.

We've provided copious cautions regarding the best use of `root` throughout the book, and we do want you to understand that that account has amazing power over the system. Use it carefully, but don't be afraid of it.

Add directories to the system's path

Add the current directory, `./`, to your `$path` shell variable. This will allow you to execute commands that are located in your current directory without typing `./` in front of the command name.

If you want to make this change for all users on your system, edit /usr/share/init/tcsh/login. Change the section of code that says

```
set path = (                                                    \
                ~/bin                                           \
                /usr/local/bin /usr/bin /bin                    \
                /usr/local/sbin /usr/sbin /sbin                 \
           )
```

so that it says

```
set path = (                                                    \
                ~/bin                                           \
                /usr/local/bin /usr/bin /bin                    \
                /usr/local/sbin /usr/sbin /sbin ./              \
           )
```

While you're at it, you might want to add another directory. It doesn't have any executables in it now, but we'll be adding applications to it in Chapter 17, "Troubleshooting Software Installations, and Compiling and Debugging Manually." Extend the path further to

```
set path = (                                                    \
                ~/bin                                           \
                /usr/local/bin /usr/bin /bin                    \
                /usr/local/sbin /usr/sbin /sbin                 \
                /usr/local/netpbm/bin ./
           )
```

Whenever you extend the path, always make sure that the current directory, ./, is the last thing in the path.

If you prefer to make these changes for your own account only, add the following to your home directory .cshrc file (or ~/Library/init/tcsh/tcsh.mine):

```
set path = ($path ./)
```

Or, to add the netpbm directory as well, add the following:

```
set path = ($path /usr/local/netpbm/bin ./)
```

Tweak your user environment so that the shell prints additional information at the prompt

With a few changes, your shell can print the name of the current command number at the prompt. This would initially appear to be a convenience/appearance-only tweak, but it turns out to be very useful both for command history purposes and for keeping track of where you're doing what.

Add the following code to your `.cshrc` file (or `~/Library/init/tcsh/tcsh.mine`):

```
set cdcmd=''
set cdcmd='echo -n "^[]0;$cwd^G"'

set norm_suf='\!''> '
set root_suf='\!''# '
if ( ($SHELL == /bin/csh) || ($SHELL =~ *tcsh)) then
        alias _normal   'set prompt="$HOST $cwd:t $norm_suf"'
        alias _root     'set prompt="%S$HOST%s $cwd:t $root_suf"'
        if ( `whoami` =~ *root* ) then
            alias prmpt_s _root
        else
            alias prmpt_s _normal
        endif
endif


if ($term == xterm) then
        alias win_s 'eval "$cdcmd"'
        alias cd 'chdir \!*;prmpt_s;win_s'
else
        alias win_s 'echo $cwd'
        alias cd 'chdir \!*;prmpt_s'
endif
prmpt_s;win_s
```

This code snippet is provided on the Mac OS X Unleashed Web site for your convenience.

Remember to turn back to this code and look at it more carefully after you have read through Chapter 18, “Advanced Unix Shell Use: Configuration and Programming (Shell Scripting).” It's not the most elegant shell script, but it should give you some ideas on how you can configure your environment to adjust itself to varying circumstances automatically.

Turn off coredumps

Unix has a friendly feature that when a program crashes, Unix tries its best to keep a record of what was going on with the system and program at the time of its demise. For a normal user, especially one who isn't a programmer, this isn't a particularly useful feature, so it's usually best to disable it.

Add the following line to `/usr/share/init/tcsh/login` or, preferably, your home directory `.cshrc` or `~/Library/init/tcsh/tcsh.mine`:

```
limit coredumpsize 0
```

If you're ever programming and decide that you need coredumps temporarily, you can issue the command `unlimit coredumpsize` to turn on coredumps for the duration of the shell.

Automate updating the locate database

The `locate` feature is a great way to find files on your system. To initialize the `locate` database, you must first run the command:

```
/usr/libexec/locate.updatedb
```

Unfortunately, your system is likely to grow and expand more frequently than you can remember to update the `locate` database. To automate the process, use the `/etc/daily` or `/etc/weekly` scripts to automate the process. Simply add the update line to the end of either of these script files (depending on whether you want daily or weekly updates), and the `locate` command will automatically be kept informed of the latest files on your system.

Hardwire critical services

Although the Mac OS X interface makes it simple to start and stop services, it also opens up the possibility for users to inadvertently shut down critical services by clicking in the wrong place. To hardwire important services, you can remove their dependency on the `/etc/hostconfig` file, which is usually checked while the computer is booting.

For example, the script that starts the SSH daemon (`/System/Library/StartupItems/SSH/SSH`) first checks to see whether `SSHSERVER:=-YES-` is included in the `/etc/hostconfig` file before it starts. A user, thinking that he's affecting only his account, could easily shut down SSH service by stopping Remote Access within the Sharing System Preference panel.

To make sure that the service always starts at boot time, remove the enclosing shell script condition. In the case of the SSH script, this consists of these lines:

```
if [ "${SSHSERVER:=-NO-}" = "-YES-" ]; then
        <startup script goes here>
fi
```

Removing the starting `if` condition, and the ending `fi` statement will cause the service to start no matter what.

Changes such as this are recommended only for machines that are being used as servers. Even though administrative users can still control the processes, they won't be able to inadvertently alter the boot-up configuration without manually editing the startup files.

Disable Graphical Login

If you operate Mac OS X in a public setting, be sure to use the Login System Preference Panel to force login using username and password. By default, Mac OS X 10.1 will display a login screen with an icon representing each user account. While this is an attractive display, it removes 50% of the protection from the system. Rather than having to guess a username and password, a potential attacker only needs the password. If you only use the operating system within a closed environment, there is no need to take this precaution. Add indexing codes here.

Limit access appropriately

As a final note, we'd like to again stress the necessity to limit access to only those individuals who need it. Although most of the changes listed in this appendix are for any user, the administrator must make the decisions as to who or what has access to the computer. We highly recommend exploring TCP Wrappers, the Mac OS X firewall system, and exploiting configuration files such as `/etc/sudoers` and `/etc/ftpusers`.

Keeping track of how your system is being used will be the toughest part of running a Mac OS X multi-user system. As we've repeated throughout the book: "Less is more." The fewer services you run, the better. The less access you give to the outside world, the better. Follow this rule, and you'll have no problem maintaining a secure and stable Mac OS X installation.

INDEX

Symbols

A

E

G

J

K

L

O

P

T

U

V